THE SUPPLEMENT TO
THE TWELFTH MENTAL
MEASUREMENTS YEARBOOK

EARLIER PUBLICATIONS IN THIS SERIES

THE SUPPLEMENT TO THE TWELFTH MENTAL MEASUREMENTS YEARBOOK

JANE CLOSE CONOLEY and JAMES C. IMPARA

Editors

LINDA L. MURPHY

Managing Editor

The Buros Institute of Mental Measurements
The University of Nebraska-Lincoln
Lincoln, Nebraska

1996
Distributed by The University of Nebraska Press

Note to Users

TABLE OF CONTENTS

INTRODUCTION

This volume, *The Supplement to the Twelfth Mental Measurements Yearbook (12MMY-S),* is fourth in our *Supplement* series. Feedback from readers suggests the *Supplements* are accomplishing their intended purpose of making evaluative information on key psychological and educational tests available in a timely manner.

The *12MMY-S* contains reviews of tests newly revised since the publication of the *Twelfth Mental Measurements Yearbook (12MMY).* These same reviews will also comprise about a third of the *Thirteenth MMY* (projected publication in early 1998). The *12MMY-S* is a bridge between the *Twelfth* and *Thirteenth Yearbooks* and is useful to professionals whose work and scholarship demand rapid access to critical test reviews written by distinguished measurement experts. The increased numbers of new and revised tests being published makes essential our efforts to publish descriptions and reviews in a timely manner.

The Buros Institute of Mental Measurements serves the psychological and educational measurement communities. Our frequent publication schedule is consistent with the proud tradition of our founder, Oscar K. Buros, continuing innovative attempts to improve the quality of testing products made available to consumers. These reviews are also available electronically through SilverPlatter™, available in many academic libraries.

THE SUPPLEMENT TO THE TWELFTH MENTAL MEASUREMENTS YEARBOOK

The *12MMY-S* contains reviews of tests that are new or significantly revised since the publica-
tion of the *Twelfth MMY* in 1995. We have included reviews of tests that were available before our production deadline of December 1, 1996. These reviews plus reviews of additional new or revised tests since 1995 will appear in the *Thirteenth MMY.* Reviews, descriptions, and references associated with older tests can be located in other Buros publications such as previous *MMYs* and *Tests in Print IV.*

The contents of the *12MMY-S* include: (*a*) a bibliography of 105 commercially available tests, new or revised, published as separates for use with English-speaking subjects; (*b*) 206 critical test reviews by well-qualified professional people who were selected by the editors on the basis of their expertise in measurement and, often, the content of the test being reviewed; (*c*) a test title index with appropriate cross references; (*d*) a classified subject index; (*e*) a publishers directory and index, including addresses and test listings by publisher; (*f*) a name index including the names of all authors of tests, reviews, or references; (*g*) an index of acronyms for easy reference when a test acronym, not the full title, is known; and (*h*) a score index to refer readers to tests featuring particular kinds of scores that are of interest to them.

A list of the names and affiliations of all reviewers contributing to the *12MMY-S* is also included. This *Supplement* also includes bibliographies of references for specific tests related to the construction, validity, or use of these tests in various settings. Reviewer's references are included in the *12MMY-S* as well as cross references to previous reviews and reference lists.

The volume is organized like an encyclopedia, with tests being ordered alphabetically by title.

If the title of a test is known, the reader can locate the test immediately without having to consult the Index of Titles.

The page headings reflect the encyclopedic organization. The page heading of the left-hand page cites the number and title of the first test listed on that page, and the page heading of the right-hand page cites the number and title of the last test listed on that page. All numbers presented in the various indexes are test numbers, not page numbers. Page numbers are important only for the Table of Contents and are indicated at the bottom of each page.

INDEXES

As mentioned earlier, the *12MMY-S* includes six indexes invaluable as aids to effective use: (*a*) Index of Titles, (*b*) Index of Acronyms, (*c*) Classified Subject Index, (*d*) Publishers Directory and Index, (*e*) Index of Names, and (*f*) Score Index. Additional comment on these indexes is presented below.

Index of Titles. Because the organization of the *12MMY-S* is encyclopedic in nature, with the tests ordered alphabetically by title throughout the volume, the test title index does not have to be consulted to find a test for which the title is known. However, the title index has some features that make it useful beyond its function as a complete title listing. It includes cross-reference information useful for tests with superseded or alternative titles or tests commonly (and sometimes inaccurately) known by multiple titles. It is important to keep in mind that the numbers in this index, like those for all *TIP* and *MMY* indexes, are test numbers and not page numbers.

Index of Acronyms. Some tests seem to be better known by their acronyms than by their full titles. The Index of Acronyms can help in these instances; it refers the reader to the full title of the test and to the relevant descriptive information and reviews.

Classified Subject Index. The Classified Subject Index classifies all tests listed in the *12MMY-S* into 17 major categories: Achievement, Behavior Assessment, Developmental, Education, English, Foreign Languages, Intelligence and Scholastic Aptitude, Mathematics, Miscellaneous, Multi-Aptitude, Neuropsychological, Personality, Reading, Sensory-Motor, Social Studies, Speech and Hearing, and Vocations. Each test entry includes test title, population for which the test is intended, and test number. The Classified Subject Index is of great help to readers who seek a listing of tests in given subject areas. The Classified Subject Index represents a starting point for readers who know their area of interest but do not know how to further focus that interest in order to identify the best test(s) for their particular purposes.

Publishers Directory and Index. The Publishers Directory and Index includes the names and addresses of the publishers of all tests included in the *12MMY-S* plus a listing of test numbers for each individual publisher. This index can be particularly useful in obtaining addresses for specimen sets or catalogs after the test reviews have been read and evaluated. It can also be useful when a reader knows the publisher of a certain test but is uncertain about the test title, or when a reader is interested in the range of tests published by a given publisher.

Index of Names. The Index of Names provides a comprehensive list of names, indicating authorship of a test, test review, or reference.

Score Index. The Score Index is an index to all scores generated by the tests in the *12MMY-S*. Test titles are sometimes misleading or ambiguous, and test content may be difficult to define with precision. But test scores represent operational definitions of the variables the test author is trying to measure, and as such they often define test purpose and content more adequately than other descriptive information. A search for a particular test is most often a search for a test that measures some specific variables. Test scores and their associated labels can often be the best definitions of the variables of interest. It is, in fact, a detailed subject index based on the most critical operational features of any test—the scores and their associated labels.

HOW TO USE THIS SUPPLEMENT

A reference work like the *12MMY-S* can be of far greater benefit to a reader if a little time is taken to become familiar with what it has to offer and how one might use it most effectively to obtain the information wanted. The first step in this process is to read the Introduction to the *12MMY-S* in its entirety. The second step is to become familiar with the six indexes and particularly with the instructions preceding each index listing. The third step is to make actual use of the book by looking up needed information. This third step is simple if one keeps in mind the following possibilities:

1. If you know the title of the test, use the alphabetical page headings to go directly to the test entry.

2. If you do not know, cannot find, or are unsure of the title of a test, consult the Index of Titles for possible variants of the title or consult the appropriate subject area of the Classified Subject Index for other possible leads or for similar or related tests in the same area. (Other uses for both of these indexes were described earlier.)

3. If you know the author of a test but not the title or publisher, consult the Index of Names and look up the author's titles until you find the test you want.

4. If you know the test publisher but not the title or author, consult the Publishers Directory and Index and look up the publisher's titles until you find the test you want.

5. If you are looking for a test that yields a particular kind of score, but have no knowledge of which test that might be, look up the score in the Score Index and locate the test or tests that include the score variable of interest.

6. Once you have found the test or tests you are looking for, read the descriptive entries for these tests carefully so that you can take advantage of the information provided. A description of the information provided in these test entries will be presented later in this section.

7. Read the test reviews carefully and analytically, as described earlier in this Introduction. The information and evaluation contained in these reviews are meant to assist test consumers in making well-informed decisions about the choice and applications of tests.

8. Once you have read the descriptive information, you may want to order a specimen set for a particular test so that you can examine it firsthand. The Publishers Directory and Index has the address information needed to obtain specimen sets or catalogs.

Making Effective Use of the Test Entries. The test entries include extensive information. For each test, descriptive information is presented in the following order:

a) TITLE. Test titles are printed in boldface type. Secondary or series titles are set off from main titles by a colon.

b) PURPOSE. For each test we have included a brief, clear statement describing the purpose of the test. Often these statements are quotations from the test manual.

c) POPULATION. This is a description of the groups for which the test is intended. The grade, chronological age, semester range, or employment category is usually given. "Grades 1.5–2.5, 2–3, 4–12, 13–17" means that there are four test booklets: a booklet for the middle of first grade through the middle of the second grade, a booklet for the beginning of the second grade through the end of third grade, a booklet for grades 4 through 12 inclusive, and a booklet for undergraduate and graduate students in colleges and universities.

d) PUBLICATION DATE. The inclusive range of publication dates for the various forms, accessories, and editions of a test is reported.

e) ACRONYM. When a test is often referred to by an acronym, the acronym is given in the test entry immediately following the publication date.

f) SCORES. The number of part scores is presented along with their titles or descriptions of what they are intended to represent or measure.

g) ADMINISTRATION. Individual or group administration is indicated. A test is considered a group test unless it may be administered *only* individually.

h) FORMS, PARTS, AND LEVELS. All available forms, parts, and levels are listed.

i) MANUAL. Notation is made if no manual is available. All other manual information is included under Price Data.

j) RESTRICTED DISTRIBUTION. This is noted only for tests that are put on a special market by the publisher. Educational and psychological restrictions are not noted (unless a special training course is required for use).

k) PRICE DATA. Price information is reported for test packages (usually 20 to 35 tests), answer sheets, all other accessories, and specimen sets. The statement "$17.50 per 35 tests" means that all accessories are included unless otherwise indicated by the reporting of separate prices for accessories. The statement also means 35 tests of one level, one edition, or one part unless stated otherwise. Because test prices can change very quickly, the year that the listed test prices were obtained is also given. Foreign currency is assigned the appropriate symbol. When prices are given in foreign dollars, a qualifying symbol is added (e.g., A$16.50 refers to 16 dollars and 50 cents in Australian currency). Along with cost, the publication date and number of pages on which print occurs is reported for manuals and technical reports (e.g., '95, 102 pages). All types of machine-scorable answer sheets available for use with a specific test are also reported in the descriptive entry. Scoring and reporting services provided by publishers are reported along with information on costs. In a few cases, special computerized scoring and interpretation services are given in separate entries immediately following the test.

l) FOREIGN LANGUAGE AND OTHER SPECIAL EDITIONS. This section concerns foreign language editions published by the same publisher who sells the English edition. It also indicates special editions (e.g., Braille, large type) available from the same or a different publisher.

m) TIME. The number of minutes of actual working time allowed examinees and the approximate length of time needed for administering a test are reported whenever obtainable. The latter figure is always enclosed in parentheses. Thus, "50(60) minutes" indicates that the examinees are allowed 50 minutes of working time and that a total of 60 minutes is needed to administer the test. A time of "40–50 minutes" indicates an untimed test that takes approximately 45 minutes to administer, or—in a few instances—a test so timed that working time and administration time are very difficult to disentangle. When the time necessary to administer a test is not reported or suggested in the test materials but has been obtained through correspondence with the test publisher or author, the time is enclosed in brackets.

n) COMMENTS. Some entries contain special notations, such as: "for research use only"; "revision of the ABC Test"; "tests administered monthly at centers throughout the United States"; "subtests available as separates"; and "verbal creativity." A statement such as "verbal creativity" is intended to further describe what the test claims to measure. Some of the test entries include

factual statements that imply criticism of the test, such as "1990 test identical with test copyrighted 1980."

o) AUTHOR. For most tests, all authors are reported. In the case of tests that appear in a new form each year, only authors of the most recent forms are listed. Names are reported exactly as printed on test booklets. Names of editors generally are not reported.

p) PUBLISHER. The name of the publisher or distributor is reported for each test. Foreign publishers are identified by listing the country in brackets immediately following the name of the publisher. The Publishers Directory and Index must be consulted for a publisher's address.

q) FOREIGN ADAPTATIONS. Revisions and adaptations of tests for foreign use are listed in a separate paragraph following the original edition.

r) SUBLISTINGS. Levels, editions, subtests, or parts of a test available in separate booklets are sometimes presented as sublistings with titles set in small capitals. Sub-sublistings are indented and titles are set in italic type.

s) CROSS REFERENCES. For tests that have been listed previously in a Buros Institute publication, a test entry includes—if relevant—a final paragraph containing a cross reference to the reviews, excerpts, and references for that test in those volumes. Cross reference "T4:467" refers to test 467 in *Tests in Print IV*, "9:1023" refers to test 1023 in *The Ninth Mental Measurements Yearbook*, "T3:144" refers to test 144 in *Tests in Print III*, "7:637" refers to test 637 in *The Seventh Mental Measurements Yearbook*, "P:262" refers to test 262 in *Personality Tests and Reviews I*, "2:1427" refers to test 1427 in *The 1940 Yearbook*, and "1:1110" refers to test 1110 in *The 1938 Yearbook*. Test numbers not preceded by a colon refer to tests in this *Supplement*; for example, "See 45" refers to test 45 in this volume. In the case of batteries and programs, the paragraph also includes cross references—from the battery to the separately listed subtests and vice versa—to entries in this volume and to entries and reviews in earlier editions of *TIP* and the *MMY*.

If a reader finds something in a test description that is not understood, the descriptive material presented above can be referred to again and can often help to clarify the matter.

ACKNOWLEDGEMENTS

The publication of any book requires the efforts of many people. Some of those people responsible for this book, who deserve special attention, are Linda Murphy, Gary Anderson, Jane Gustafson, Janice Nelsen, Rosemary Sieck, Barbara S. Plake, a long list of reviewers, a dedicated group of graduate students, and our various advisory committees. More specifically, Linda Murphy, our Managing Editor made certain we stayed the course even when other activities looked like they might stand in the way of production. She did so with only mild and tactful prodding, not an easy task with such distractible editors as us.

Gary Anderson, editorial assistant, smiled and worked with good cheer in spite of our vagueness and uneven scheduling impositions. Similarly, Rosemary Sieck, our data entry specialist did a magnificent job of ensuring accurately typed reviews. Jane Gustafson's marketing efforts make the enterprise viable, and Janice Nelsen's wonderful attitude and overall helpfulness is part of the glue that holds the entire Institute together. Barbara S. Plake, the Director of the Institute, provided vision, leadership, and support for this book and for the many other efforts of the Institute.

These people in particular, our colleagues, along with those who are recognized below, work very hard at making the *Yearbooks* and the *Supplements* look good. Although our names are listed as the editors, the success of the Institute is really because of their efforts.

In addition to our colleagues in the Institute, we would be remiss if we did not extend our thanks to the many reviewers who have prepared reviews for this book. They take time from their busy schedules to share their expertise by providing thoughtful and insightful test reviews. This way of "giving something back to the profession" deserves not only our thanks, but the thanks of all those who find the reviews useful. Without them, the *Yearbooks* and the *Supplements* would not be possible.

The Buros Institute of Mental Measurements is part of the Department of Educational Psychology of the University of Nebraska—Lincoln. Many of the students in the department and from other departments in the university have contributed to the publication of this volume. We express our appreciation to these graduate research assistants who helped with the publication of the *12MMY-S*: Ted Carter, Elisabeth Emmer, George Gonzalez, Jessica Jonson, Gary Loya, Annie Mitchell, Heidi Paa, Robert Spies, and Suthakaran Veerasamy.

We also rely on the advice and suggestions from our National and Departmental Advisory Committees. These individuals give of their time and expertise on many issues that influence the way we operate. The current members of the National Advisory Committee are: Gary Melton, Anthony Nitko, Charles Peterson, Lawrence Rudner, and Frank Schmidt. Our Departmental Advisory Committee members (in addition to the Buros professional staff) are: Deborah Bandalos, Terry Gutkin, Ellen McWhirter, and Gregg Schraw.

SUMMARY

The *MMY* series is a valuable resource for people interested in studying or using testing. Once the process of using the series is understood, a reader can gain rapid access to a wealth of information. Our hope is that with the publication of the *12MMY-S*, test authors and publishers will consider carefully the comments made by the reviewers and continue to refine and perfect their assessment products.

James C. Impara
Jane Close Conoley
December 1996

Tests and Reviews

[1]
AAMR Adaptive Behavior Scale—School, Second Edition.

Purpose: "Used to assess adaptive behavior."

Population: Ages 3–21.

Publication Dates: 1981–1993.

Acronym: ABS-S:2.

Scores, 21: 16 domain scores (9 part one domain scores: Independent Functioning, Physical Development, Economic Activity, Language Development, Numbers and Time, Prevocational/Vocational Activity, Self-Direction, Responsibility, Socialization; 7 part two domain scores: Social Behavior, Conformity, Trustworthiness, Stereotyped and Hyperactive Behavior, Self-Abusive Behavior, Social Engagement, Disturbing Interpersonal Behavior), 5 factor scores (Personal Self-Sufficiency, Community Self-Sufficiency, Personal-Social Responsibility, Social Adjustment, Personal Adjustment).

Administration: Individual.

Price Data, 1994: $89 per complete kit including examiner's manual ('93, 118 pages), 25 examination booklets, and 25 profile/summary forms; $39 per 25 examination booklets; $18 per 25 profile/summary forms; $35 per examiner's manual; software scoring and report system available ($79 for Apple or IBM, $89 for Macintosh).

Time: Administration time not reported.

Comments: Previously called AAMD Adaptive Behavior Scale.

Authors: Nadine Lambert, Kazuo Nihira, and Henry Leland.

Publisher: PRO-ED, Inc.

Cross References: See T4:2 (42 references); for a review of an earlier edition by Stephen N. Elliot, see 9:3 (9 references); see also T3:6 (55 references); for reviews of an earlier edition by Morton Bortner and C. H. Ammons and R. B. Ammons, see 8:493 (25 references); see also

T2:1092 (3 references); for reviews of an earlier edition by Lovick C. Miller and Melvyn I. Semmel, see 7:37 (9 references).

TEST REFERENCES

1. Lovett, D. L., & Harris, M. B. (1987). Identification of important community living skills for adults with mental retardation. *Rehabilitation Counseling Bulletin, 31,* 34–41.

2. Perry, A., & Factor, D. C. (1989). Psychometric validity and clinical usefulness of the Vineland Adaptive Behavior Scales and the AAMD Adaptive Behavior Scale for an autistic sample. *Journal of Autism and Developmental Disorders, 19*(1), 41-55.

3. Henderson, D., & Vandenberg, B. (1992). Factors influencing adjustment in the families of autistic children. *Psychological Reports, 71,* 167–171.

4. Rousey, A., Best, S., & Blacher, J. (1992). Mothers' and fathers' perceptions of stress and coping with children who have severe disabilities. *American Journal on Mental Retardation, 97,* 99-109.

5. Cheramie, G. M. (1994). The AAMD Adaptive Behavior Scale—School Edition, Part Two: Test-retest reliability and parent-teacher agreement in a behavior disordered sample. *Perceptual and Motor Skills, 79,* 275-283.

6. Macmillan, D. L., Siperstein, G. N., & Gresham, F. M. (1996). A challenge to the viability of mild mental retardation as a diagnostic category. *Exceptional Children, 62,* 356–371.

Review of the AAMR Adaptive Behavior Scale—School, Second Edition by ROBERT G. HARRINGTON, Professor of Educational Psychology and Research, University of Kansas, Lawrence, KS:

The primary use of the Adaptive Behavior Scale—School, Second Edition (ABS-S:2) is to assess the adaptive functioning of school-age children who may be mentally retarded; however, it also has been utilized to evaluate adaptive behavior characteristics of autistic children (Perry & Factor, 1989) and to identify behavior-disordered children (Cheramie & Edwards, 1990). Heber (1961) has defined adaptive behavior as the manner in which individuals cope with the natural and social demands of their environment, and more recently, Grossman (1983) has elaborated on this basic definition to include standards of maturation, learning, personal independence, and/or social responsibility in reference to age peers and cultural group. Adaptive behavior in combination with significantly below average intellectual functioning continues to play a major role in identifying individuals with mental delays as exemplified in the *1992 Diagnosis, Classification, and System of Supports* (American Association on Mental Retardation, 1992).

The ABS-S:2 is the 1993 revision of the 1975 and 1981 AAMD Adaptive Behavior Scales. Part 1 of the scale focuses on personal independence behaviors grouped into nine domains. Part 2 deals with social behaviors grouped into seven domains. The ABS-S:2 can be completed by professionals with direct information about the target child or can be administered in interview fashion by a third party. In this latter case, good interviewing skills are a prerequisite. The ABS-S:2 is relatively easy for the experienced professional to administer, score, and interpret. The instrument comes complete with a comprehensive, easy-to-follow examination booklet and a separate profile summary form. The ABS-S:2 renders a combination of 16 domain scores with a standard score mean of 10 and standard deviation of 3 and three factor scores on Part 1 and two factor scores on Part 2 with standard score means of 100 and standard deviations of 15. In total, the ABS-S:2 yields five types of scores including raw scores, percentiles, domain standard scores, factor standard scores, and age equivalents. Norms are provided for a normal sample and for a sample of children with mental retardation. Unlike the previous edition of the test there are no separate norms for individuals who are trainable mentally retarded. Although interest scores can be compared using a regression procedure, the clinician is cautioned to never compare domain and factor scores because domain scores are contained in the factor scores.

The scale was normed using a stratified random sampling procedure on 2,074 persons with mental retardation and 1,254 persons without mental retardation from a national U.S. sample. Items were selected for inclusion on the ABS-S:2 based upon careful review of items from previous versions of the test and based upon their interrater reliability and ability to discriminate groups varying with respect to adaptive behavior levels. Because the ABS-S:2 contains relatively few item changes from previous versions, earlier studies of item reliability are relied upon heavily by the authors to support the item reliability of the current test (Bensberg & Irons, 1986; Brulle & Hoernicke, 1984; Givens, 1980; Givens & Ward, 1982; Lambert & Windmiller, 1981; Mayfield, Forman, & Nagel, 1984).

In an internal consistency study of the standardization samples the factor scores were found to be the most reliable, yielding coefficients in excess of .90 in most instances for both standardization groups. The standard errors of measurement for the ABS-S:2 scores were uniformly low reflecting a high degree of scale reliability. In one test-retest reliability study of 25 male and 20 female employees in a sheltered workshop, results supported the stability of the test with correlations generally in the .90 range and above (Nihira, Leland, & Lambert, 1993), but in a second test-retest study in which high school teachers completed protocols on 45 students with emotional disturbances in grades 9 through 11, three of the subtests received coefficients in the .70 range and most were at least in the .80 range. A reliability coefficient of at least .80 is considered minimal and thus this second study is somewhat disappointing leading one to question whether the reduced test reliability might be attributed to the sample of children with emotional disturbances under study. In an interscorer reliability study two trained professionals tabulated the raw scores for each domain and factor for 15 completed protocols. Partial correlations were in the high .90 range demonstrating excellent interscorer agreement for simply calculating standard scores from raw scores. Unfortunately, however, no interscorer agreements are reported for interviewers deriving raw scores for individual items, which of course is the more subjective scoring task. The unanswered question of whether two independent interviewers would agree on how to score a response to individual items on the test is a serious omission to the examiner's manual.

The validity of the ABS-S:2 is based heavily upon previous research on earlier versions of the scale (Cheramie & Edwards, 1990; Lambert & Windmiller, 1981) and some recent research into its content, criterion-related, and construct validity. Content validity of Part 1, the Adaptive Behavior Scale, was established through a critical review of domains and items in other existing behavior rating scales, through item analyses to determine which items discriminated between groups of individuals judged to be functioning at different adaptive behavior levels, and by the degree to which correlations showed each item measured adaptive behavior independent of intelligence. Part 2, The Maladaptive Behavior Scale, was developed based upon descriptions of types of behavior considered unacceptable or beyond the tolerance threshold of those with daily contact with individuals with mental retardation. Median item discrimination coefficients that were generated for the domains and factors as a result of item analysis using the point-biserial correlation technique were, on the average, substantially above the .20 minimum recommended by Garrett (1965) for discriminating power or item validity at all ages assessed by the scale. In several small sample studies of the criterion-related validity of the ABS-S:2 with the Vineland Adaptive Behavior Scale (Sparrow, Balla, & Cichetti, 1984; Nihira, Leland, & Lambert, 1993), and the ABS-S:2 with the short form of the Adaptive Behavior Inventory (ABI; Brown & Leigh, 1986) results showed that Part 1, the Adaptive Behavior Scale, correlated moderately well with these other adaptive behavior scales, but Part 2, the Maladaptive Scale, correlated poorly with these measures of adaptive behavior. This finding is to be expected and provides support for the criterion-related validity of the ABS-S:2.

Because adaptive behavior is an age-related construct the test developers tested whether scores increased with age for samples of 3- to 17-year-olds with and without mental retardation, and a sample of adults with developmental disabilities. Mean raw scores rose steadily with the normal subjects, were less pronounced with the subjects with mental retardation, and the increases were almost nonexistent for the adults with developmental disabilities. Correlation coefficients between raw scores and age confirmed these results. This progression of scores for the three groups sampled provides support for the age-related nature of adaptive behavior. A review of an intercorrelation matrix for the ABS-S:2 domains and factors from Part 1 and Part 2 of the scale shows moderate to strong correlations for those domains and factors contained in Part 1 and those

in Part 2, but as expected, little correlation between domains and factors on Part 1 and Part 2. This finding supports the contention that the domains and factors on the two separate parts of the scale are related. To evaluate the relationship between the ABS-S:2 and mental ability tests several studies were conducted and reported in the examiner's manual comparing the ABS-S:2 with the Stanford-Binet Intelligence Scale (Terman & Merrill, 1972); the Leiter International Performance Scale (Levine, 1982), the Slosson Intelligence Test (Slosson, 1971), the Wechsler Adult Intelligence Scale—Revised (WAIS-R; Wechsler, 1981), the Wechsler Intelligence Scale for Children—Revised (WISC-R; Wechsler, 1974), the Peabody Picture Vocabulary Test—Revised (PPVT-R; Dunn & Dunn, 1981), and the General Mental Ability Quotient of the Detroit Tests of Learning Aptitude—3 (DTLA-3; Hammill, 1992). Results showed moderate positive correlations between domain and factor scores on Part 1 and these measures of mental ability, but nonsignificant positive correlations and even negative correlations between the domain and factor scores on Part 2 and the mental ability tests. These results are as expected and provide support for the construct validity of the scale.

Visual analyses of descriptive differences in mean raw scores among adults with mental retardation, young people with mental retardation, and young people without mental retardation are presented in tabular form as evidence of the discriminative validity of the ABS-S:2, but the authors present no statistical tests to better make their case. The authors concede the ABS-S:2 has less discriminative validity at the younger age levels due to the fact that both normal children and children with mental retardation are developing new skills in adaptive behavior. A LISREL VII analysis was conducted as a confirmatory factor analysis of the factor structure of the ABS-S:2 of students with mental retardation. Standardized path coefficients depicting the factor loadings associated with each component were fairly large and positive showing support for the factorial validity of the ABS-S:2. Finally, as a test of the ecological validity of the scale 50 teachers and 50 teacher aides completed ABS-S:2 protocols on 50 students with emotional disabilities. Correlations between these two groups are in the .50 to .90 range showing a good relationship between the observations of respondents and demonstrating that respondents report similar behavior patterns across environments.

In summary, there are still some outstanding questions left unanswered about the reliability and validity of the ABS-S:2. Some of the reliability coefficients are below the desirable .90 level needed for making critical diagnostic decisions about the adaptive functioning status of children. Furthermore, there is some evidence that Part 1 of the scale is probably inappropriate for children with physical disabilities, sensory impairments, emotional disabilities, and for very young children. In particular, there is evidence that in evaluating the adaptive behavior levels of deaf-blind children, the language development items (Domain IV) of the ABS-S:2 should be modified to allow credit to be given for alternative methods of communication, such as sign language, Braille, and finger spelling as has been suggested previously (Suess, Cotten, & Sisson, 1983). Otherwise these children will be penalized and scores will represent an underestimate of their true adaptive behaviors in the Language Development domain.

In future research the test developers must show evidence for the interscorer reliability of test items. Furthermore, they should demonstrate statistically the discriminative validity of the scale. More independent research using larger sample sizes should be conducted on the validity of the instrument. It is clear the test developers are overrelying upon research from the two previous versions of the test to bolster their position for the reliability and validity of the current scale.

Previous versions of the ABS have been among the most widely used measures (Allen-Meares & Lane, 1983; Cantrell, 1982; Coulter & Morrow, 1978). When compared to other available measures of adaptive behavior such as the Scales of Independent Behavior (SIB; Bruininks, Woodcock, Weatherman, & Hill, 1984) and the Vineland Adaptive Behavior Scales (VABS; Sparrow, Balla, & Cicchetti, 1984), it is clear that the ABS-S:2 does make a contribution to the area of adaptive behavior assessment. It is a very comprehensive scale that covers not only adaptive behaviors but maladaptive behaviors as well. However, it is unclear what role the Maladaptive Behavior Scale should play in the identification of children

with mental retardation or emotional disturbances. It has considerable item coverage. It is easy to score and administer. It is adapted for use by teachers in public school classrooms and can be computer scored. Unfortunately, no interpretive case studies are provided in the Examiner's Manual. When deciding among the various available adaptive behavior scales it is probably best for the examiner to ask the following important questions: Does the adaptive behavior scale cover areas that I am interested in assessing? Does the adaptive behavior scale have a sufficient floor given the age level and adaptive behavior level of the client I am assessing? Can the assessment results be translated into useful intervention plans? The answers to these questions will vary with the referred individual, and for this reason no general recommendation can be made for any adaptive behavior scale. The ABS-S:2 is, however, a major improvement over the previous version of the scale given that it has addressed many of the criticisms mentioned by Sattler (1988) and should be given serious consideration whenever the adaptive behavior of a school-age subject must be evaluated for possible mental retardation or whenever independent functioning skills need to be assessed as a part of a multifaceted assessment.

REVIEWER'S REFERENCES

Heber, R. (1961). A manual on terminology and classification on mental retardation (2nd ed.). *Monograph Supplement to the American Journal of Mental Deficiency* (now Retardation).

Garrett, H. (1965). *Testing for teachers* (2nd ed.). New York: American Book Company.

Slosson, R. L. (1971). Slosson Intelligence Test. East Aurora, NY: Slosson Educational Publications.

Terman, L. M., & Merrill, M. A. (1972). Stanford-Binet Intelligence Scale, 1972 Norms Edition. Boston: Houghton-Mifflin.

Wechsler, D. (1974). Wechsler Intelligence Scale for Children—Revised. San Antonio: The Psychological Corporation.

Coulter, W. A., & Morrow, H. W. (1978). Requiring adaptive behavior measurement. *Exceptional Children, 45,* 133–135.

Givens, T. (1980). Scorer reliability on the AAMD Adaptive Behavior Scale—Public School Version Part One. *Psychology in the Schools, 17,* 335–338.

Dunn, L. M., & Dunn, L. M. (1981). Peabody Picture Vocabulary Test—Revised. Circle Pines, MN: American Guidance Service.

Lambert, N. M., & Windmiller, M. (1981). AAMD Adaptive Behavior Scale—School Edition. Monterey, CA: Publishers Test Service.

Wechsler, D. (1981). Wechsler Adult Intelligence Scale—Revised. San Antonio: The Psychological Corporation.

Cantrell, J. K. (1982). Assessing adaptive behavior: Current practices. *Education and Training of the Mentally Retarded, 17,* 147–149.

Givens, T., & Ward, L. C. (1982). Stability of the AAMD Adaptive Behavior Scale—Public School Version. *Psychology in the Schools, 19,* 166–169.

Levine, M. N. (1982). Leiter International Performance Scale. Los Angeles: Western Psychological Services.

Allen-Meares, P., & Lane, B. A. (1983). Assessing the adaptive behavior of children and youths. *Social Work, 28,* 297–301.

Grossman, H. J. (Ed.). (1983). *Classification in mental retardation.* Washington, DC: American Association on Mental Deficiency (now Retardation).

Suess, J. F., Cotten, P. D., & Sisson, G. F. P., Jr. (1983). The American Association on Mental Deficiency—Adaptive Behavior Scale: Allowing credit for alternative means of communication. *American Annals of the Deaf, 128,* 390–393.

Bruininks, R. H., Woodcock, R. W., Weatherman, R. F., & Hill, B. K. (1984). Scales of Independent Behavior (SIB). Chicago, IL: The Riverside Publishing Co.

Brulle, A. R., & Hoernicke, F. A. (1984). A brief report on the reliability of the public school version of the AAMD Adaptive Behavior Scale. *Mental Retardation and Learning Disability Bulletin, 122*, 115–118.

Mayfield, K. L., Forman, S. G., & Nagel, R. J. (1984). Reliability of the AAMD Adaptive Behavior Scale—Public School Version. *Journal of School Psychology, 22*, 53–61.

Sparrow, S. S., Balla, D. A., & Cicchetti, D. V. (1984). Vineland Adaptive Behavior Scales. Circle Pines, MN: American Guidance Service.

Bensberg, G. J., & Irons, T. (1986). A comparison of the AAMD Adaptive Behavior Scale and the Vineland Adaptive Behavior Scale within a sample of persons classified as moderately and severely mentally retarded. *Education and Training of the Mentally Retarded, 21*, 220–229.

Brown, L., & Leigh, J. E. (1986). Adaptive Behavior Inventory. Austin, TX: PRO-ED, Inc.

Sattler, J. M. (1989). *Assessment of children*. San Diego, CA: Sattler Publishing Co.

Perry, A., & Factor, D. C. (1989). Psychometric validity and clinical usefulness of the Vineland Adaptive Behavior Scales and the AAMD Adaptive Scales for an autistic sample. *Journal of Autism and Developmental Disorders, 19*, 42–55.

Cheramie, G. M., & Edwards, R. P. (1990). The AAMD ABS-SE Part Two: Criterion-related validity in a behavior-disordered sample. *Psychology in the Schools, 27*, 186–195.

American Association on Mental Retardation. (1992). *Mental retardation: Definition, classification, and systems of support* (9th ed.). Washington, DC: American Association on Mental Retardation.

Hammill, D. D. (1992). Detroit Tests of Learning Aptitude—Third Edition. Austin, TX: PRO-ED, Inc.

Nihira, K., Leland, H., & Lambert, N. (1993). Adaptive Behavior Scale—Residential and Community: Second Edition. Austin, TX: PRO-ED, Inc.

Review of the AAMR Adaptive Behavior Scale—School: Second Edition by TERRY A. STINNETT, Associate Professor, Department of Applied Behavioral Studies in Education, Oklahoma State University, Stillwater, OK:

The AAMR Adaptive Behavior Scale—School: Second Edition (ABS-S:2) is the most recent revision of the 1975 AAMD Adaptive Behavior Scale, Public School Version (ABS-PSV). The ABS-PSV was first revised in 1981 and the scale was renamed the AAMD Adaptive Behavior Scale, School Edition (ABS-SE). The ABS-SE was a notable improvement over the first version of the scale (Elliott, 1985) and the ABS-S:2 revision has improved the scale further.

The authors of the ABS-S:2 define the adaptive behavior construct as the individual's typical performance in coping with environmental demands. The scale is designed to measure school-age children's personal and community independence and adaptive qualities that are associated with personal and social performance and adjustment. Those qualities are reflected by the specific domains and factors included on the instrument. The authors propose the scale to be useful for determining an individual's strengths and weaknesses in specific adaptive behavior domains and factors, for identifying students who are significantly below their peers in adaptive functioning,

for documenting an individual's progress and assessing the effects of intervention programs, and for research. The ABS-S:2 likely will be used to diagnose persons with developmental disabilities in conjunction with individually administered intelligence measures.

The ABS-S:2 is appropriate for use with individuals through 21 years of age. Adaptive behavior ratings can be obtained first person when the rater has personal knowledge of the individual being rated or through a third party informant interview. The third party informant should be a person who knows the individual well. If the informant does not have information to give answers to all items, then additional or alternate informants must be obtained. However, information from several individuals should not be combined into a single rating.

The ABS-S:2 has been logically divided by its authors into two parts. Part 1 contains nine behavior domains with 18 subdomains intended to measure personal independence and personal responsibility in daily living. Part 2 contains seven domains that pertain to behaviors that relate to personality and behavior disorders. The Part 1 domains include Independent Functioning (24 items), Physical Development (6 items), Economic Activity (6 items), Language Development (10 items), Numbers and Time (3 items), Prevocational/Vocational Activity (3 items), Self-Direction (5 items), Responsibility (3 items), and Socialization (7 items with one supplemental item for females). The Part 2 domains include Social Behavior (7 items), Conformity (6 items), Trustworthiness (6 items), Stereotyped and Hyperactive Behavior (5 items), Self-Abusive Behavior (3 items), Social Engagement (4 items), and Disturbing Interpersonal Behavior (6 items with one supplemental item).

Part 1 items are presented in two different formats. One format presents a number of separate component behaviors ordered by difficulty level within each item for the overall adaptive skill that is being assessed (e.g., table manners). The rater picks a single option from the list of behaviors for the item that represents the highest level of the task the person can usually achieve. Because the options within the items are ranked and assigned point values by difficulty level, higher point values indicate performance of higher adaptive level. These items can have different maximum point values based on the number of options within each item. For example, an item with three options could have a maximum of 3 points, whereas an item with six options could have 6 points value. Other Part 1 items are formatted so that the rater indicates by circling "yes" or "no" whether the person can accomplish tasks. Socially acceptable behaviors are give 1 point and inappropriate behaviors are given zero points. These different item types are scattered throughout Part 1 so users should be vigilant to ensure the protocol is correctly completed. The different item formats could especially be a problem if a first party rater completes the protocol instead of having an experienced user of the scale collect the data through interview.

Part 2 items are of a third type. The rater responds to a 3-point Likert that typifies the frequency the individual performs certain behaviors (i.e., "N" never, "O" occasionally, and "F" frequently). There is also space on the protocol for raters to write in additional behaviors that are not included in the item; hence, Part 2 can reflect idiosyncrasies of the person being rated.

The ABS-S:2 raw scores are the total number of points obtained on the scale's items within the specific domains. A positive feature of the scale is that there are Mental Retardation Norms or Non-Mental Retardation norms available for users to select at their discretion. However, the authors do not provide suggestions to help users determine which norm set to use. Raw scores can be converted to standard scores ($M = 10$, $SD = 3$), percentile rank scores, and age equivalent scores for all nine Part 1 domains. Similarly, standard scores and percentile rank scores can also be derived for the seven Part 2 domains. Age equivalents are not available for the Part 2 domains. The authors report performance on the Part 2 domains is not age related, that is the raw scores for these domains did not increase or decrease with age sufficiently to calculate age equivalent scores. Rating labels are available for all domains (e.g., Very Superior to Very Poor). Finally, three factor scores can be calculated from Part 1 items: Personal Self-Sufficiency, Community Self-Sufficiency, and Personal-Social Responsibility. Part 2 items can yield two factor scores: Social Adjustment and Personal Adjustment. Part 1 factor scores can be converted to standard scores ($M = 100$, $SD = 15$), percentile ranks, and age equivalent scores. Part 2 factors render similar scores except for age equivalents. Users are advised to transfer raw scores from the examination booklet to a separate Profile/Summary form. The Profile/Summary form contains a workspace for computing the factor scores, a comments/recommendations section, and a profile page for graphic presentation of the individual's adaptive functioning. The Profile/Summary form is well designed and should facilitate the interpretive process. An ABS-S:2 Software Scoring and Report System is also available (Bryant, Lynn, and Pearson, 1993) in Apple II, Macintosh, and IBM PC and compatible formats.

NORMATIVE SAMPLES AND STANDARDIZATION. The ABS-S:2 has an improved standardization sample from earlier versions of the scale. There are separate norms for people with mental retardation ($N = 2,074$) and for those without mental retardation ($N = 1,254$). Both samples include a more diverse geographic representation than earlier versions of the scale (40 states for the MR sample and 44 for the Non-MR sample). The authors indicate that in some instances they were able to compare the sample demographics to the nation as a whole and the manual has tables that contain the percentage of demographic characteristics in the school-aged population versus the sample for comparative purposes. However, no description of the source of the population estimates is presented for users. Nevertheless, the samples are of good size and diversity to be suited for most applications and are certainly improved over earlier versions of the scale.

The ABS-S:2 reports percentages of students in the Mental Retardation sample group by IQ score (e.g., 12% [IQ<20], 48% [20–49], and 40% [50–70]). However, the IQ ranges reported in the MR sample do not include people with mental retardation who have intellectual functioning from 71 to 75 even though the intellectual functioning criterion in the 1992 AAMR definition of Mental Retardation specifies the upper limit IQ cutoff at 75. Gresham, MacMillan, and Siperstein (1995) note that shifting the IQ criterion from 70 and below to 75 and below could result in twice as many people being eligible for the diagnosis of mental retardation (using the IQ criterion alone). "There are more cases falling in the range of 71 to 75 (2.80%) than in the entire range associated with mild mental retardation, which is IQs ranging from 55 to 70 (2.51%)" (Gresham et al., 1995, p. 5). This could make use of the MR norms problematic for those individuals with IQs in the range of 71 to 75. Because the MR norms are collapsed across all of the reported IQ ranges and those persons with IQs from 71 to 75 were omitted, estimates of adaptive behavior for these individuals could be lower than if they had been included in the norms. Although users of the instrument should not view this as a serious problem with the norms, it is an instance of the scale not being consistent with the new AAMR definition of mental retardation (American Association on Mental Retardation, 1992).

RELIABILITY. Internal consistency estimates (alpha coefficients) are reported separately by age and averaged for all ages for all domains and factors for both the Mental Retardation and the Non-Mental Retardation samples. Homogeneity among items within each domain and factor for both norm groups is excellent. The coefficient alphas are higher for the Mental Retardation sample. Alphas (averaged across ages using z-transformation) ranged from .98 (Independent Functioning domain, Personal Self-Sufficiency factor, and Community Self-Sufficiency factor) to .82 (Prevocational/Vocational Activity domain). The majority of the averaged coefficients were in the range of .90 (17 of 21 alphas ≥.90) and at the specific age groups most alphas were also in the .90s. The lowest internal consistency estimates were for the Prevocational/Vocational Activity domain (5-year-, 8-year-, and 9-year-olds, .80) and the Self-Abusive Behavior domain (19-year- and 21-year-olds, .80).

For the Non-Mental Retardation group the averaged alphas ranged from .97 (Social Behavior domain) to .82 (Prevocational/Vocational Activity domain) [9 of 21 alphas ≥.90]. At specific age groups, all coefficients equalled or exceeded .80, except for 5-year-olds (.79, Prevocational/Vocational Activity domain), 6-year-old (.79, Responsibility domain), 7-year-olds (.79, Economic Activity domain), and 13-year-olds (.79, Economic Activity domain).

Standard Errors of Measurement, derived from the internal consistency reliability estimates, are presented for all domains and factors for each age group and averaged across the ages. The SEMs are available for both sets of norms.

Test-retest reliability data are reported from two studies; both used a 2-week time interval between the ratings. In Study 1, supervisors of individuals employed in a sheltered workshop setting rated the individuals with the Adaptive Behavior Scales—Residential and Community: Second Edition (ABS-RC:2). The ABS-S:2 is a shortened version of the ABS-RC:2. The items that comprise the ABS-S:2 were extracted from the ABS-RC:2 to calculate the ABS-S:2 estimates. However, the individuals who were rated were older than individuals who might be assessed with the ABS-S:2 (i.e., the median age of those who were rated in the study was 42 years). The stability coefficients were corrected to remove error variance associated with internal consistency and corrected and uncorrected estimates are presented. Uncorrected estimates ranged from .98 (Economic Activity domain, Community Self-Sufficiency factor) to .82 (Stereotyped and Hyperactive Behavior domain, Personal Adjustment factor), whereas corrected estimates ranged from .99 (Independent Functioning, Trustworthiness, Self-Abusive Behavior, Social Engagement domains) to .85 (Personal Adjustment factor). Although these estimates are of sufficient magnitude to demonstrate temporal stability (in the short term), a study of the scale using a greater interval between test and retest is needed before users can be confident the test has long-term stability. Also, it would be helpful if such a study was based on individuals of the appropriate age for the ABS-S:2.

In Study 2, Florida high school teachers rated 9th through 11th grade students who were receiving services for emotional disturbance. Uncorrected estimates ranged from .89 (Self-Abusive Behavior domain) to .42 (Economic Activity domain). Corrected estimates ranged from .98 (Social Behavior domain) to .72 (Personal Self-Sufficiency factor). The reliabilities for the Independent Functioning domain, the Personal Self-Sufficiency factor, and the Community Self-Sufficiency factor were inadequate with this sample of students (.75, .72, and .78 respectively). Also the estimates for the Socialization domain, Social Engagement domain, and the Personal Adjustment factor were marginal (.80., .80, and .81).

The authors also have included interscorer reliability estimates. Two professionals trained in the use of the scale scored the same 15 completed ABS-S:2 protocols. There was a high degree of agreement between the scorers; rs ranged from .95 to .99 across the domains and factors of the scale.

Because the ABS-S:2 is likely to be administered to several parties as part of an adaptive behavior assessment, interrater reliability becomes critical for the scale. A study of interrater reliability is included in the validity section of the manual and referred to as ecological validity. Fifty students with emotional disturbance who were attending school in Florida were rated with the ABS-S:2. The students' teacher and the teacher's aide completed the scale. There was a high degree of agreement between the teachers and aides. Part 1 domain/factor rs ranged from .49 to .92 and Part 2 domain/factor rs ranged from .53 to .88. The scale has excellent interrater reliability.

VALIDITY. The ABS-S:2 contains relatively few item changes and the authors suggest validity studies of earlier versions of the scale might be of interest. Reports of these studies are in an appendix in the ABS-S:2 manual. The ABS items have been analyzed over time with different groups known to vary in their level of adaptive functioning and have been demonstrated to have discriminative power (e.g., Cheramie & Edwards, 1990; Gully & Hosch, 1979). As the scale was developed, items were retained based on interrater reliability and discriminative power with various groups in different settings.

ITEM CHARACTERISTICS. For this revision (ABS-S:2) an item analysis was conducted by computing item-total correlations (point-biserial correlations of each item with domain and factor scores at each age group). The authors selected .30 as their standard for acceptable item validity. Tables in the manual contain the *median* item to domain/factor score correlations for both the MR and the Non-MR samples. Although it is not completely clear, it appears that these correlations are the median of all item correlations within a domain or factor. Unfortunately, the individual item-total correlations are not presented, which makes evalu-

ation of individual items impossible. Because medians are reported in the tables, one-half of the individual item correlations would have fallen below each of the reported table values (and one-half also would have fallen above the reported coefficient). This suggests that some items (e.g., those with correlations below the medians in the range of .30) would have marginal item validity. Adding to the confusion in this section of the manual, the authors state the developmentally disabled sample served as subjects for the analysis; however, correlation tables are presented for both samples. One analysis was based on ABS-S:2 ratings of the developmentally disabled individuals who represent the MR norms. Although not reported in the manual, a communication with the scale's publisher confirmed the same procedure was also applied to the ratings of the individuals who represented the Non-MR norms (see Tables 6.3 and 6.4 in the ABS-S:2 manual). In spite of these problems, the median item point-biserial correlations reported for domains and factors for the MR norms demonstrate the ABS-S:2 items (on average) are related to and account for variance in the domain and factor scores. The item-total correlations with the Non-MR sample were lower and thus do not predict the domain/factor scores as well for this group. The authors declare these results provide evidence of item validity, but sagacious users likely will find these data unclear.

CRITERION-RELATED VALIDITY. Reports of three studies of the criterion-related validity for the ABS-S:2 are in the manual. In Study 1, individuals in the standardization sample ($n = 63$) of the ABS-RC:2 were also administered the Vineland Adaptive Behavior Scales (VABS; Sparrow, Balla, & Cicchetti, 1984). The appropriate items for the ABS-S:2 were extracted from the ABS-RC:2. Part 1 domain and factor scores of the ABS-S:2 were correlated with the VABS: rs ranged from .71 (Physical Development domain) to .31 (Socialization domain). The correlation between the ABS-S:2 Pre-Vocational/Vocational Activity domain and the VABS was not significant, nor was the correlation between the Self-Direction domain and the VABS. The Part 2 domain and factor scores were not significantly related to the VABS, except for the Self-Abusive Behavior Domain ($r = -.30$).

In Study 2 the relationship of the ABS-S:2 with the Adaptive Behavior Inventory was examined (ABI: Brown & Leigh, 1986). Thirty students with mental retardation from a central Florida school district were evaluated with both scales. Correlations for the Part 1 domains/factors ranged from .67 (Community Self-Sufficiency factor) to .37 (Responsibility domain) with the ABI. No Part 2 domains/factors were significantly related to the ABI.

Study 3 examined the relationship of the ABS-S:2 with the VABS. Twenty-nine students from the standardization sample of the ABS-S:2 were also administered the VABS. Correlations for the Part 1 domains/factors ranged from .65 (Language Development domain) to .37 (Responsibility domain) with the VABS. The Economic Activity domain and the Prevocational/Vocational domain were not significantly related to the VABS nor were any of the Part 2 domains/factors.

The correlations were generally in the moderate range between the Part 1 domains/factors and criterion measures across the three reported studies and provide evidence of the scale's criterion-related validity. This suggests that the ABS-S:2, the VABS, and the ABI to a degree all measure adaptive behavior, but also that each scale is measuring something unique from the others. Users should not consider each of the instruments to reflect similar aspects of the adaptive behavior construct. It is not clear in the manual exactly what scores were used for the criterion measures, but it appears that only the total scores were used. Stronger support for the scale's criterion-related validity might have been evident if the ABS-S:2 domain and factor scores had been correlated with the VABS domain scores in addition to the VABS Adaptive Behavior Composite score and likewise with the ABI subtest scores. The Part 2 domain/factor scores do not appear to reflect adaptive behavior and the authors contend that these items represent maladaptive behaviors. The items obviously describe maladaptive behaviors, but the authors do not provide any empirical evidence other than the high internal consistency estimates and the high intercorrelations among the Part 2 domain/factors.

CONSTRUCT VALIDITY. Construct validity for the ABS-S:2 was assessed by examining the relationship of the domains/factors with age, the scale's relation with a variety of mental ability tests, the pattern of intercorrelation among the scale's domains/factors, and through confirmatory factor analysis.

Raw scores of three groups were examined to determine whether they were age related: (a) students without mental retardation aged 3 to 17 years; (b) students with mental retardation aged 3 to 17 years; and (c) adults with developmental disabilities. As expected, age was related to adaptive behavior functioning for the students without mental retardation (rs ranged from .22 to .56). Examination of the Part 1 raw score means for this group generally revealed a pattern of higher scores associated with increasing age. Adaptive behavior was less related to age for the other two groups; rs for the adult group ranged from -.04 to .10 and for the group of students with mental retardation rs ranged from .10 to .23. The maladaptive behavior domains and factors generally were not related to age for any of the groups (most rs were nonsignificant or negligible).

The authors also presented the domain/factor intercorrelations for the Mental Retardation sample and the Non-Mental Retardation sample. The Part 1 domains/factors are intercorrelated as are the Part 2 domains/factors for both groups. Furthermore, the Part 1 scores are inversely related to the Part 2 scores as would be predicted because Part 1 and Part 2 are supposed to measure constructs that are somewhat opposing (i.e., adaptive vs. maladaptive behaviors). These data could be analyzed further with exploratory factor analysis, but this type of analysis was not conducted. Because the test's authors present an interpretive model for examining strengths and weaknesses across the domains and factors of the ABS-S:2, data from exploratory factor analyses could also be used to examine the specific variance (subtest specificity) for domains and factors. It would be helpful if users had estimates of each domain's unique variance before interpreting domains as separate adaptive behavior strengths and weaknesses. Until those data are available users should be cautious about interpreting relative adaptive behavior strengths and weaknesses on the ABS-S:2.

A confirmatory factor analysis of the ABS-S:2 is presented in the manual but is not described in sufficient detail to be critically evaluated. The data seem to fit well the 5-factor model proposed by the authors. However, the factor-loading coefficients (standardized path coefficients) associated with each component of the factors are blanked (not displayed, see Table 6.20) except for the factor on which they loaded. To exacerbate this problem, no cutoff criterion is reported in the manual. Users have no way of determining whether the components loaded on other factors in addition to the one that was reported.

A series of studies reported in the manual examined the relationship of the ABS-S:2 with mental ability tests. The Part 1 domains/factors were found to be moderately related to the Wechsler Adult Intelligence Scale—Revised (WAIS-R; Wechsler, 1981) (rs ranged from .27 to .73), the Slosson Intelligence Test (SIT; Slosson, 1971) (rs ranged from .41 to .67), the Stanford-Binet Intelligence Scale (S-B; Terman & Merrill, 1972) (rs ranged from .47 to .71), the Leiter International Performance Scale (LIPS; Levine, 1982) (rs ranged from .35 to .71), the Wechsler Intelligence Scale for Children—Revised (WISC-R; Wechsler, 1974) (rs ranged from .28 to .61), the Peabody Picture Vocabulary Test—Revised (PPVT-R; Dunn & Dunn, 1981) (rs ranged from .37 to .58), and the Detroit Tests of Learning Aptitude—3 (DTLA-3; Hammill, 1992) (rs ranged from .38 to .72 with the Responsibility domain not significant). The majority of the correlations between the mental ability tests and the Part 2 domains/factors were not significant or negligible with the exception of the Social Engagement domain and the DTLA-3 ($r = -.33$).

SUMMARY. The ABS-S:2 is a timely revision of an important instrument and it has been improved from earlier forms. Based on careful review of the scale, I recommend it for use with some reservations. The scale has an excellent standardization sample and should be appropriate for use with a wide variety of individuals. The scale's psychometric qualities are good. However, further validity research is needed, especially construct validity. There is also a need for subtest specificity estimates to guide users of the scale in making empirically based interpretations regarding relative strengths and weaknesses. In sum, the ABS-S:2 is recommended for use. It has been and remains one of the best available scales for assessment of adaptive behavior.

REVIEWER'S REFERENCES

Slosson, R. L. (1971). Slosson Intelligence Test. East Aurora, NY: Slosson Educational Publications.
Terman, L. M., & Merrill, M. A. (1972). Stanford-Binet Intelligence Scale, 1972 Norms Edition. Boston, MA: Houghton-Mifflin.
Wechsler, D. (1974). Wechsler Intelligence Scale for Children—Revised. San Antonio, TX: The Psychological Corporation.
Gully, K. J., & Hosch, H. M. (1979). Adaptive Behavior Scale: Development as a diagnostic tool via discriminant analysis. American Journal of Mental Deficiency, 83, 518–523.
Dunn, L., & Dunn, L. (1981). Peabody Picture Vocabulary Test—Revised. Circle Pines, MN: American Guidance Service.
Wechsler, D. (1981). Wechsler Adult Intelligence Scale—Revised. San Antonio, TX: The Psychological Corporation.
Levine, M. N. (1982). Leiter International Performance Scale. Los Angeles, CA: Western Psychological Services.
Sparrow, S., Balla, D., & Cicchetti, C. (1984). Vineland Adaptive Behavior Scales. Circle Pines, MN: American Guidance Service.
Elliott, S. N. (1985). [Review of the AAMD Adaptive Behavior Scale]. In J. V. Mitchell, Jr. (Ed.), The ninth mental measurements yearbook (pp. 2–5). Lincoln, NE: Buros Institute of Mental Measurements.
Brown, L., & Leigh, J. (1986). Adaptive Behavior Inventory. Austin, TX: PRO-ED, Inc.
Cheramie, G. M., & Edwards, R. P. (1990). The AAMD ABS-SE Part Two: Criterion-related validity in a behavior-disordered sample. Psychology in the Schools, 27, 186–195.
American Association on Mental Retardation. (1992). Mental Retardation: Definition, classification, and systems of supports (9th ed.). Washington, DC: Author.
Hammill, D. (1992). Detroit Tests of Learning Aptitude—Third Edition. Austin, TX: PRO-ED, Inc.
Bryant, B. R., Lynn, G., & Pearson, N. (1993). ABS-S:2 Software Scoring and Report System. Austin, TX: PRO-ED, Inc.
Gresham, F. M., MacMillan, D. L., & Siperstein, G. N. (1995). Critical analysis of the 1992 AAMR definition: Implications for school psychology. School Psychology Quarterly, 10, 1–19.

[2]
ACCUPLACER: Computerized Placement Tests.

Purpose: Designed to assist colleges in determining student entry skills in reading, writing, mathematics, and levels of English proficiency; scores aid in the appropriate placement of students into entry level courses.

Population: Entry level students in 2-year and 4-year institutions.

Publication Dates: 1985–1993.

Acronym: CPTs.

Administration: Individual.

Price Data, 1995: Annual licensing fee and per student fee, cost available from publisher.

Time: Untimed.

Comments: Administered on computer adaptively.

Author: The College Board.

Publisher: The College Board.

    a) READING COMPREHENSION.

    Comments: Each student is administered a fixed number of items which are selected adaptively depending on student responses to prior items.

    Price Data: $1 per test.

    b) WRITING.

    Scores: Total score only.

    Comments: Each student is administered a fixed number of items which are adaptively delivered.

    Price Data: $1 per test.

    c) ARITHMETIC.

    Scores: Total score only.

Comments: Each student is administered a fixed number of items which are adaptively delivered.
Price Data: $1 per test.
d) ELEMENTARY ALGEBRA.
Scores: Total score only.
Comments: Each student is administered a fixed number of items which are adaptively delivered.
Price Data: $1 per test.
e) COLLEGE LEVEL MATHEMATICS.
Comments: Each student is administered a fixed number of items covering the areas of Intermediate Algebra, College Algebra and Precalculus.
Price Data: $2 per test.
f) LEVELS OF ENGLISH PROFICIENCY.
Scores: 3 modules: Language Usage, Sentence Meaning, Reading Skills.
Comments: Designed to identify the English proficiency levels of students; each student takes a fixed number of items; the 3 tests are administered separately.
Price Data: $2 per test.

Review of the ACCUPLACER: Computerized Placement Tests by MARTIN A. FISCHER, Program Director, Program in Communication Disorders, Department of Human Services, Western Carolina University, Cullowhee, NC:

SUMMARY. The ACCUPLACER is a computer program designed to facilitate the evaluation and placement of college students into appropriate courses. The ACCUPLACER is composed of four sections: Computerized Placement Tests (CPTs), Computerized Placement Advising and Management Software (CPAMS), Placement Validation and Retention Service (PVRS), and School to College Placement Articulation Software Service (PASS).

COMPUTERIZED PLACEMENT TESTS. The CPTs are made up of six test areas and several supplemental skills tests. Each test is designed to evaluate a student's ability in a specific academic area. Test areas include: Reading Comprehension, Sentence Skills, Arithmetic, Elementary Algebra, College-Level Mathematics, and Levels of English Proficiency. Supplementary Skill tests include: Arithmetic and Elementary Algebra. All of the tests consist primarily of multiple-choice questions with some open-ended questions.

Each test is designed to evaluate a specific ability as follows:

Reading Comprehension (RC) is made up of 17 questions. The questions contain either a passage followed by a question based on its content, or two sentences in which the examinee answers a question about the relationship between them.

Sentence Skills (SS) contains 17 questions of two types. "Sentence correction" questions require that the examinee demonstrate an understanding of sentence structure by choosing the most appropriate word or phrase to substitute for the underlined portion of a given sentence. "Construction shift" questions require that a sentence be rewritten according to specifications while retaining essentially the same meaning as the original.

Arithmetic Test includes 16 questions drawn from three broad categories including: operations with whole numbers and fractions, operations with decimals and percents, and applications and problem solving.

Elementary Algebra Test includes 12 questions drawn from three categories including: operations with integers and rationales; operations with algebraic expressions; and solutions of equations, inequalities, and word problems.

College-Level Mathematics Test (CLM) is an optional test that consists of 35 to 40 questions from six general categories including: algebraic operations, solution of equations and inequalities, coordinate geometry, applications and other algebra topics, functions, and trigonometry.

Levels of English Proficiency Test (LOEP) is designed to assess the English skills of students who have learned English as a second language or who are native English speakers with limited proficiency. The major use of the test is in determining the appropriate placement of students into English as a second language and developmental courses at the time of college entry. Tests include 20 questions each evaluating reading skills, sentence meaning, and language use.

COMPUTERIZED PLACEMENT ADVISING AND MANAGEMENT SOFTWARE. The CPAMS is a computer system for evaluating information obtained from the CPTs and recommending student placement into courses best suited for them. It is also designed to track student progress and maintain records. "The system is designed primarily for incoming students" (p. 2-1). CPAMS features individual student and roster reporting options. Reports available include course assignment listings, test scores, and data based on variables specified by the operator. These variables specify which data are to be included in the reports. The system is designed to run as a standalone or networked using IBM or compatible microcomputers.

THE PLACEMENT VALIDATION AND RETENTION SERVICE. The PVRS is offered by the College Board to users of the ACCUPLACER system. The purpose of the service is to help colleges use the CPT results more effectively in placing incoming students into the appropriate courses. The PVRS provides analysis of data supplied by the college to determine the relationship between student's placement test scores and their grades in college courses.

RELIABILITY AND VALIDITY. Overall reliability and validity appeared to be quite good. Three reliability indices were used including: standard errors of measurement conditional on score level (CSEM), test-retest reliability (based on 2-week to 2-month intervals), and a measure of the consistency of placement decisions. Simulations conducted on 1,800 hypothetical examinees resulted in CSEMs with a high degree of score accuracy for the CPTs as well as high reliability coefficients ranging from .86 to .92. Test-retest reliability resulted in correlation coefficients ranging from .76 to .96. Reliability of classification estimated for selected CPTs ranged from .91 to .96. Throughout the CPTs, significant steps were made to minimize item bias including analysis for cultural and linguistic bias. Both content and predictive validity were evaluated and appeared to be adequate.

EVALUATION. The ACCUPLACER manual is comprehensive and contains an excellent set of instructions for both installation and operation of the CPTs. Also in the manual is a series of background readings that include an introduction to CPTs, guides for implementing the CPT, and information on validating the CPT results.

The manual suggested that no computing skills or knowledge of CPTs are required for installation or administration. This proved to be the case. The program was easily installed in less than 10 minutes from four floppy disks onto an IBM-compatible (DOS) computer (it can also be installed onto a network). Once installed, the in-

structions for customizing the CPTs were clear and comprehensive. Similarly, the on-screen (menu driven) instructions for students taking the CPTs were unambiguous.

The CPTs were easy to customize by following the on-screen help commands. Each testing session began with a series of questions about the student's academic and linguistic background. From these questions, using the Seamless Serial Testing feature, the CPTs automatically adjusted to the level to the examinee. Subsequent questions were automatically selected based on performance as the test proceeded. The order of CPT presentation was easily preset by the examiner and the sequence was simple to modify. On-screen directions allowed the examinee to complete each test in approximately 15 minutes (the tests are untimed). Each answer needed to be confirmed before the next question was presented. This made it easy to change errors or impulsive responses. Following completion of the CPTs, test results were compiled on several reports for analysis. The reports were comprehensive and could be combined with information such as major field of study, advisors, and placement rules to generate course assignments. Data were easily transferred to floppy disks that could be sent to the College Board's Placement Validation and Retention service for further analysis.

CONCLUSION. The ACCUPLACER appears to be an excellent system for providing CPT evaluation and placement of students in appropriate courses. The system is easy to install and operate and is extremely flexible. Results appeared reliable and can be evaluated and reported in a variety of ways. Subsequent reports can be generated and sent to the Placement Validation and Retention Service for in-depth analysis.

Review of the ACCUPLACER: Computerized Placement Tests by STEVEN V. OWEN, Professor of Educational Psychology, University of Connecticut, Storrs, CT:

The ACCUPLACER is a test management and reporting system developed jointly by the College Entrance Examination Board and Educational Testing Service. The ACCUPLACER has four main parts, only one of which—Computerized Placement Tests (CPTs)—is reviewed here.

CPTs are to be used for assessing basic skills to assist in course placement decisions for college students. The skills covered by the CPTs include arithmetic, basic algebra, college-level mathematics, sentence skills, and reading comprehension. More recent versions of the ACCUPLACER also include a computerized test termed "Levels of English Proficiency," or LOEP. LOEP is meant for students whose native language is something other than English, or whose native English is substandard.

Item pools were developed and refined based on analyses from item response theory. Using between 12,000 and 30,000 students to collect calibration data for each test, ETS employed a 3-parameter IRT model to develop item difficulty and discrimination estimates. The Rasch difficulty estimates are used by the computer to create the adaptive testing routine.

Before computerized testing begins, the student responds to several biographical questions, such as years of English and mathematics in high school, whether or not English is the first language, and how many years since the last mathematics course. Each of the CPTs is adaptive, which means that different students will answer different questions based on their answers on previous questions. At the beginning of any CPT, an item is selected randomly from an item set of moderate difficulty. The student's response to the initial test item sets in motion the adaptive process. Generally speaking, an incorrect answer will bring up an easier item; a correct response delivers a more difficult question. The software is constrained by content, however. New items are chosen in order to maintain content validity for each test. In mathematics, the starting options are more varied. Here the test administrator may choose a beginning test (e.g., arithmetic or basic algebra), or the student may choose, or the computer will select a starting point based on the student's earlier responses to background questions. The adaptive testing situation makes for an extremely efficient assessment; although tests are untimed, student typically spend only 15 or 20 minutes per test.

There are additional advantages to a computerized operation. The tests are self-instructional and little proctor assistance is needed. If the tests are loaded on a network, multiple test takers can be served simultaneously, each taking different tests at different speeds. Finally, CPTs provide almost immediate feedback to students. At the conclusion of testing, personalized score reports can be printed. Scores may also be aggregated across students, stored in a computer file, and summarized and printed in various ways for college personnel.

The ACCUPLACER's Technical Data Supplement (College Entrance Examination Board, 1993) gives summaries of psychometric information for the CPTs. Instead of reporting overall (and misleading) standard errors of measurement, ETS reports estimated standard errors for each possible score within each test. Two-week stability estimates (for very small samples) range from .73 to .96. Reliability estimates of cut-scores across the various tests range from .91 to .96.

The Technical Data Supplement also reports content and predictive validity evidence for the CPTs. The content validation process involved panels of experts who offered advice about item content and wording. Tables of specifications were used to assure representative sampling of item within domains. For predictive validity, 50 colleges were recruited over a 2-year period. For each CPT, teacher-awarded grades from relevant courses were regressed against CPT scores. (For example, English composition grades were correlated with Sentence Skills scores.) Median validity coefficients (uncorrected for restriction of range) were fairly low for language arts CPTs: Reading Comprehension, .18; Sentence Skills, .15 to .20. Without explanation, no validity coefficients are reported for Writing. The various mathematics CPTs fared generally better, with median coefficients between .19 and .49. For the LOEP measure, correlations with various English-as-a-second-language courses ranged from .09 to .48.

Norm tables are complete and easy to follow. Instructions for installation on a computer or computer network are simple as well. The summary score reports, for individual students and for administrative aggregates, are easy to arrange and to read. Working through the computer menus is not much challenge, even for computer novices. The CPTs run very quickly. I tested the programs on an ancient IBM 386 computer and on a Pentium-133 without discernible differences in program speed.

Loading the maximum number of tests onto a computer hard drive does not require mountains of memory.

What could be better about the ACCUPLACER's CPTs? Several things. Although a newer version is available, the earlier version 4.0 was the one made available for review. The ACCUPLACER is DOS-based, which is out of step with an increasingly Windows-based computer universe. Computer literate students accustomed to a point-and-click operation may be puzzled by having to use arrow keys to move through menus. And the screen graphics are poorly done. I tested the program with various monitor resolutions, but nothing would make the print inviting. Clunky looking words will probably not depress CPT scores, but they give the impression of dated software and are irritating while reading. But even with their technological backwardness, the ACCUPLACER's CPTs have much to recommend them.

REVIEWER'S REFERENCE

College Entrance Examination Board. (1993). *ACCUPLACER Computerized Placement Tests technical data supplement.* Princeton, NJ: Author.

[3]
Adult Attention Deficit Disorder Behavior Rating Scale.

Purpose: Designed to "identify behavior that will support a diagnosis of Attention Deficit Disorder (ADD)."
Population: Ages 16 and above.
Publication Date: 1993.
Acronym: AADDBRS.
Scores, 10: Inattention, Impulsivity, Hyperactivity, Anger Control, Academics, Anxiety, Confidence, Aggressiveness, Resistance, Social.
Administration: Individual.
Price Data, 1993: $35 per complete kit including manual (23 pages), 25 rating sheets, and 25 profile sheets; $9.50 per 25 replacement forms (rating sheets and profile sheets).
Time: (15–30) minutes.
Comments: An extension of the Attention Deficit Disorder Behavior Rating Scale (T4:226).
Authors: Ned Owens and Betty White Owens.
Publisher: Ned Owens M.Ed. Inc.

Review of the Adult Attention Deficit Disorder Behavior Rating Scale by ROBERT J. MILLER, Associate Professor of Special Education, Mankato State University, Mankato, MN:

The Adult Attention Deficit Disorder Behavior Rating Scale (AADDBRS) "was designed, specifically, to identify behavior that will support a diagnosis of Attention Deficit Disorder (ADD)" (manual, p. 2). The instrument was "not meant to be a diagnostic instrument and should not be used as such" (manual, p. 2). This instrument is suggested as a screening device to gather information for a medical diagnosis of Attention Deficit Disorder and the manual authors suggest it is to be used in conjunction with test results from the Wechsler Adult Intelligence Scale (WAIS) and the Bender Visual Motor Gestalt Test.

The adult instrument consists of 50 items related to the behavior of the subject with 5 items in each of 10 factors. These 10 factors are suggested by the authors as important for diagnosing ADD. The factors are divided into organic factors including Inattention, Impulsivity, and Hyperactivity; and, environmental factors including Anger Control, Academics, Anxiety, Confidence, Aggressiveness, Resistance, and Social. The organic factors are considered primary to the diagnosis of Attention Deficit Disorder. The environmental (secondary) factors are "precipitated" by the organic factors.

Each of the 50 items on the Scale is gender neutral and consists of a simple statement or phrase of two to eight words. Instructions for the adult completing the Scale are to rate each of the 50 behaviors with the use of a Likert-type scale ranging from a rating of 1 = *You have not exhibited this behavior as a child or an adult*; 2 = *You have exhibited this behavior as a child or an adult to a slight degree*; 3 = *You have exhibited this behavior as a child or an adult to a considerable degree*; 4 = *You have exhibited this behavior as a child or adult to a large degree*; and, 5 = *You have exhibited this behavior as a child or an adult to a very large degree.* The Adult Attention Deficit Disorder Behavior Rating Scale uses the same format as the previously published Child Scale and the same Scale Profile sheet is used for both scales. The Adult Scale is to be completed by the examinee. It is also recommended that other people who are familiar with the adult complete the Scale. The AADDBRS is untimed and simple to administer. The administration time of the scale is suggested to be from 15 minutes to 30 minutes.

Cumulative raw scores from the completed AADDBRS are to be transferred and charted for each factor on the Adult Attention Deficit Disorder Behavior Rating Scale Profile with cumulative raw score in each factor of 1—7 rated as "normal," 8—16 identified as "at risk," and 17—25 identified as "very high risk." The authors suggest that adults scoring 8 or more points on the Inattention and Impulsivity factors meet the behavior criteria for Attention Deficit Disorder without Hyperactivity and should be referred to their medical doctor for the possibility of medical intervention. According to the test Profile, adults scoring 8 or more on Inattention, Impulsivity, and Hyperactivity factors meet the criteria for Attention Deficit Disorder with Hyperactivity and should be referred to their medical doctor for the possibility of medical intervention. There is no discussion in the manual of the rationale for the score of 8 or higher as representative of ADD or ADHD. No empirical justification for a score of 8 or more as significant to a diagnosis of ADD or ADHD is provided in the manual.

Additional information provided regarding the Adult Attention Deficit Disorders Behavior Rating Scale is woefully inadequate. Information on a single study of 50 adults who had been diagnosed and treated for ADD was included in the manual as supportive documentation. The age range of the subjects was 16 to 55 and a profile of the "average" scores of the 50 adults on each of the 10 factors is included in the manual. Additionally, average IQ scores for this group and average WAIS subtests scores are provided for the group of 50 adults.

No demographic information is included regarding the gender, socioeconomic status, or distribution of ages of the sample of this study. No information was included regarding minority group representation or whether the sample was gathered from rural, urban, or suburban locations. No information was provided regarding subjects not currently identified as ADD who might have completed the Scale. This lack of the ability to compare the results of a profile to some sort of larger norm group including adults without ADD limits the usefulness of the instrument and brings into question the raw score of "eight or more" as a meaningful construct in gathering information for the diagnosis of ADD or ADHD. Presenting a chart of mean scores of 50 adult subjects is of

limited value and any broad generalizations based on this single study of adults would be inappropriate. Finally, no information is included in the manual regarding either the reliability or the validity of the AADDBRS for adults or children.

The manual contains a comparison of the 50 adults' scores using the Adult Scale to scores of 50 children using the Child Scale. In their comparison of the test results of these groups, the authors chart the "average child" and "average adult" score on the AADDBRS Profile. They also compare the mean scores of adults on the WAIS, with children on the Wechsler Intelligence Scale for Children (WISC-R) as well as providing mean subtest scores for the adult sample on the WAIS and the children's sample on the WISC-R. The authors include no information concerning the 50 children used as a comparison group. The authors appear to be attempting to convince the examiner that "average" scores of adults and "average" scores for children change little on the AADDBRS and on subtests of intelligence tests over time. The comparison of these groups given the amount of information furnished in the manual is inappropriate.

According to the test manual authors, each adult completing the test "should be told to be sure to include his childhood behaviors as well as his adult behavior" (manual, p. 18). I am concerned about the wisdom and value of these instructions. The rationale for using both childhood remembrances and current behavior is flawed. Childhood behavior may, or may not, have much relevance to the current behavior of that adult. As a child, I may perceive myself as: "Fail to complete assigned tasks" (Item 1) to a "very large degree" and scoring myself as "5." However, I may be confident that I no longer exhibit this behavior as an adult. How will I rate myself? Under the current directions of the Scale, I must rate myself a "5" because I demonstrated that behavior as a child. As a result of this rating of my behavior my Scale score may be inappropriately inflated. My initial score of "5" on Item 1 and four additional scores of "1" on the total of five foils places my raw score at "9" even if I do not believe I have any concerns regarding my behavior as an adult. I would not recommend the use of the Adult Attention Deficit Disorders Behavior Rating Scale as a screening device for ADD or ADHD.

Review of the Adult Attention Deficit Disorder Behavior Rating Scale by JAMES C. REED, Chief Psychologist, St. Luke's Hospital, New Bedford, MA:

The Adult Attention Deficit Disorder Behavior Rating Scale is based on a previous scale that was developed for children. In fact, the same profile sheet is used for both scales. The scale consists of 50 items, and the person taking the test rates each item on a scale from 1 to 5: 1. "you have not exhibited this behavior as a child or an adult" ... 5. "you have exhibited this behavior as a child or an adult to a very large degree." The columns are summed and the scores are referred to a normative table. For each of the 10 factors a score between 8 and 16 indicates that the person is at risk for the behavior, and a score between 17 and 25 places the person at very high risk. The authors report that the adult scale had been administered to 50 adults who have been diagnosed as having attention deficit disorder and as having been treated with success. The age range was from 16 to 55.

In the manual the directions on page 18 for the administration of the adult scale refer to page 11 for the diagnosis of attention deficit disorder. Page 11, however, is in the section of the manual that pertains to children. Consequently, the inference can be made that one uses the same interpretive procedures for the adults as one does for the children. In the children's section it is stated, "The first three behaviors, Inattention, Impulsivity, and Hyperactivity, are required for a diagnosis of Attention Deficit Disorder with Hyperactivity. These behaviors are classified on the profile sheet as Primary/Organic behaviors, because they are organically, or neurologicallly caused" (p. 2). The manual authors also state the disorder is a chemical disorder and neurological weaknesses need to be explored. For adults the implication is strongly present, if not directly stated, that the Wechsler Adult Intelligence Scale (WAIS), should be used to explore the neurological basis.

In considering this scale for use, there are several factors to be reviewed. From a positive standpoint, it might be said that the scale has face (perhaps a better word would be "faith") validity. The 50 items represent behaviors that most would consider, in one form or another, to be indicative of an ADD. However, these behaviors could also be indicative of a number of other behavioral and/or psychiatric problems, and nowhere in the manual do the authors present any information concerning the uniqueness of these behaviors to attention deficit disorder. In other words, there are no objective indications of validity. The sample of 50 adults is not specified with respect to any defining characteristic. It is impossible for the reader to know how the diagnosis was made of attention deficit disorder for these adults. It is also unknown, or at least not given, as to the population from which they were drawn.

Another limitation of the scale is that there is no information presented about the independence of the 10 factors. No reliability coefficients are reported, no correlation coefficients between the factors are given, and no evidence is presented to show these factors will differentiate ADD persons from other behaviorally disordered groups.

The authors stated that ADD is a chemical disorder, but the basis for this statement or evidence in support of it is not presented. They recommend the use of the WAIS to detect subtle neurological disorders. It is highly questionable whether the WAIS is a suitable instrument for detecting subtle neurological disorders, and the available literature suggests that it is not. Furthermore, the pattern analysis recommended by the authors is not explicit and it fails to consider the low reliability of the WAIS subtests. For example, in the manual, the authors indicate the score on the Information subtest for ADD persons is often relatively lower than that of Comprehension and Similarities because "the person can not sit still or pay attention long enough to acquire the information" (p. 19). What constitutes relative lowness is not stated. Other equally undefined pattern interpretations for the WAIS are also given.

In summary, the scale consists of 50 items that many observers would agree are characteristic of ADD to some extent or another. However, the psychometric limitations of the scale are compelling. There are no reliability or validity coefficients. The adult population on which the test was developed is not defined. Validating data for the risk and the high risk categories are not presented. The test appears to be lacking in psychometric characteristics that specialists in test construction deem important. At present the scale might be regarded as an exploratory instrument, for it is only recently, as the authors point out, that the concept of an attention deficit disorder among adults has come into existence.

[4]
Alcohol Clinical Index.

Purpose: "To identify alcohol problems among patients."
Population: Adults at-risk for alcohol problems.
Publication Date: 1987.
Administration: Individual.
Price Data, 1990: $9.75 per user's booklet (31 pages); $9.95 per 50 questionnaires (specify test).
Time: Administration time not reported.
Authors: Harvey A. Skinner and Stephen Holt.
Publisher: Addiction Research Foundation [Canada].

a) CLINICAL SIGNS.
Scores, 6: Hand, Head, Abdomen, Body, Locomotor Function, Total.
b) MEDICAL HISTORY.
c) ALCOHOL USE.
d) RISK FACTORS.
Scores, 2: Early Indicators, Risk Factors.

Review of the Alcohol Clinical Index by STEVEN I. PFEIFFER, Professor, Graduate School of Education, Kent State University, Kent, OH:

The Alcohol Clinical Index (ACI) was designed as a brief and economic screening instrument for use by physicians and allied health care professionals to identify alcohol use problems among patients in primary care settings. The ACI consists of two components: a 17-item clinical signs checklist (CSC) and a 13-item Medical History Questionnaire (MHQ).

The test authors, Drs. Skinner and Holt, advocate administering laboratory tests (e.g., serum gamma-glutamyl-transferase and mean corpuscular volume) and brief alcohol questionnaires (e.g., CAGE questionnaire, Alcohol Dependence Scale) to corroborate a positive finding on the ACI.

The ACI was derived from a comprehensive set of 108 clinical indicators of alcohol abuse (Skinner, Holt, Sheu, & Israel, 1986; also test manual). It is recommended that the 17 clinical signs should be elicited by a physician or nurse as part of a physical examination (illustrative items: "rhinophyma-varying degrees of epithelial thickening, dilation of sebaceous follicles and bluish-red discoloration of the distal portion of the nose"; "gynecomastia-male only, glandular and fatty tissue enlargement of both breasts").

The 13 Medical History items can either be self-completed by the patient or administered by the physician or nurse. Illustrative items include: "Do you often wake up with headache?" and "Do you find it hard to remember recent events?"

The manual reports the diagnostic rule that if either clinical signs or Medical History is greater than or equal to four then there is a "high likelihood of alcohol abuse or dependence" (p. 6). The manual recommends, however, as mentioned above, corroboration using laboratory tests and alcohol questionnaires. Although a decision rule is provided, the manual offers no evidence to support the diagnostic sensitivity, specificity, or predictive power of the ACI.

Similarly, the manual includes no information to suggest that any estimates of reliability or validity were obtained. Also, it is uncertain what type, if any, of pilot testing or validation was undertaken, and basic information on the sample used for test development is sorely missing. There are no norms in the manual, and one has no idea if the test or test items are biased across different racial, ethnic, or geographic regional groups.

A study by Skinner and Holt, along with two coinvestigators, reports a higher predictive power for the ACI than with laboratory tests in distinguishing an outpatient group with alcohol problems from social drinkers (Skinner, Holt et al., 1986). This same investigation provides the data that led to the diagnostic rule reported in the test manual (88%–90% accuracy was achieved by the decision rule of clinical signs or medical history of four or more).

However, a recently published validity study with lower socioeconomic alcohol-dependent men obtained overall predictive values for the ACI not nearly as favorable as those reported by the test authors. For example, The Clinical Signs Checklist yielded 70% accuracy regardless of cutoff point (ranging from 1 through 5). The Medical History questionnaire generated somewhat better outcomes, with an overall accuracy of 84% (Alterman, Gelfund, & Sweeney, 1992).

The ACI is a brief, economical, and easy-to-administer screening instrument to identify primary care patients with alcohol problems. The authors appropriately recognized the need for future investigators to evaluate the diagnostic sensitivity and specificity of the index (Skinner, Holt et al., 1986). Research is also needed to evaluate sources of measurement error and estimates of reliability, content and construct validity, and possible test and item bias (e.g., one item on the clinical signs checklist inquires about tattoos). Until these much needed reliability, validation, and norming steps are undertaken, the ACI should be restricted to use as a research tool and not in individual clinical decision making.

REVIEWER'S REFERENCES

Skinner, H. A., Holt, S., Sheu, W. J., & Israel, M. (1986). Clinical versus laboratory detection of alcohol abuse: The Alcohol Clinical Index. *British Medical Journal, 292,* 1703–1708.

Alterman, A. I., Gelfund, L. A., & Sweeney, K. K. (1992). The Alcohol Clinical Index in lower socioeconomic alcohol-dependent men. *Alcoholism: Clinical and Experimental Research, 16,* 960–963.

Review of the Alcohol Clinical Index by WIL-LIAM I. SAUSER, JR., Professor and Executive Director for Outreach, College of Business, Auburn University, Auburn, AL:

The Alcohol Clinical Index consists of 13 objective medical history questions that can be answered "yes" or "no," plus 17 observable clinical signs that could be recognized easily by trained health care professionals. According to the manual, it is intended for use as a low-cost screening device, administered by primary care physicians or nurses, "to identify patients who drink excessively but who do not consider themselves 'alcoholics.' The basic strategy is to intervene with brief counseling before the patient has developed major symptoms of alcohol dependence" (p. 2).

In the manual, the test developers cite epidemiological evidence from the U.S.A. and Canada indicating that roughly 5% of North American adults are alcoholics, 20% are problem drinkers, 60% are social drinkers, and 15% abstain from consuming alcohol. There are a number of clinical assessment devices available to identify alcoholics (Ingram, Sauser, & Owens, 1989); a purpose of the Alcohol Clinical Index, however, is to distinguish between social drinkers and problem drinkers, the latter group being defined in the manual as those individuals who "do *not* show major symptoms of alcohol dependence ... [but] drink at levels that have increased health risk and ... may have accrued some consequences related to drinking in the recent past" (p. 1).

It is these problem drinkers who the test developers view as a rich target audience for early detection and intervention programs. They argue that such early detection and intervention might curb the incidence of alcohol-related problems, which have staggering economic and social-psychological costs. Skinner, Holt, and Israel (1981) note that in the United States "alcohol-related problems cost nearly $43 billion in 1975 as a result of lost production, motor vehicle accidents, crime, social problems, and demands for health care services. Indeed, over 12% of the total expenditure on health care for adults ... was for alcohol-related medical service" (p. 1142).

The Alcohol Clinical Index is very simple and straightforward. Literate patients could complete the medical history in a matter of minutes; illiterate or visually impaired patients would have no difficulty responding to the questions administered orally. Similarly, a medical professional could easily detect the presence or absence of the clinical signs during the course of a routine physical examination. The Alcohol Clinical Index, when administered alongside other simple questionnaires recommended by the test developers (and included within the manual), appears to be effective for use as a screening device for identifying problem drinkers.

Despite its simplicity, the Alcohol Clinical Index is built upon significant scientific research. The authors cite 11 of their published research articles (readily available in most medical libraries) substantiating the effective use of the Alcohol Clinical Index in the manner they recommend. Most impressive is a study of 131 outpatients with alcohol problems, 131 social drinkers, and 52 patients from family practice (Skinner, Holt, Sheu, & Israel, 1986), which found "a probability of alcohol abuse exceeding 0.90 ... if four or more clinical signs or four or more medical history items from the index were present" (p. 1703). This study serves as the basis for the diagnostic rule given in the manual, "If Clinical Signs ≥4 or Medical History ≥4 then there is a high likelihood of alcohol abuse or dependence. Investigate further using the laboratory tests and alcohol questionnaires" (p. 6).

One warning is in order: personnel specialists and human resource managers must recognize that the Alcohol Clinical index is a medical examination that leads to medical diagnosis and intervention. It should *not* be used as a routine employment screening device lest the potential employing organization run afoul of the Americans with Disabilities Act (Veres & Sims, 1995).

In summary, the Alcohol Clinical Index is a short, easily administered medical screening device that may be used by primary care physicians and nurses to detect problem drinkers, who may be further examined and targeted for early intervention programs. Although presented in a simple, easy-to-understand manual, the Alcohol Clinical Index is the product of rigorous scientific study.

REVIEWER'S REFERENCES
Skinner, H. A., Holt, S., & Israel, Y. (1981). Early identification of alcohol abuse: I. Critical issues and psychosocial indicators for a composite index. *Canadian Medical Association Journal, 124*, 1141–1152.

Skinner, H. A., Holt, S., Sheu, W. J., & Israel, Y. (1986). Clinical versus laboratory detection of alcohol abuse: The Alcohol Clinical Index. *British Medical Journal, 292*, 1703–1708.

Ingram, J. J., Sauser, W. I., Jr., & Owens, C. A. (1989). Assessment: Determination of client needs and progress. In D. R. Self (Ed.), *Alcoholism treatment marketing: Beyond TV ads and speeches* (pp. 207–223). New York: Haworth.

Veres, J. G., III, & Sims, R. R. (Eds.). (1995). *Human resource management and the Americans with Disabilities Act*. Westport, CT: Quorum.

[5]
Aprenda: La Prueba De Logros en Español.

Purpose: Designed as a "norm-referenced achievement test for Spanish-speaking students."

Publication Date: 1990–1991.

Administration: Group.

Price Data, 1996: $23 each examination kit (Primary 1-Intermediate 3) including test booklet and directions for administering ('90, 47 pages), practice test and directions, and hand-scorable answer folder (Preprimer-$22); $15 for 25 practice tests and directions; $109 for machine-scorable test booklets and $74.50 for hand-scorable test booklets (Preprimer through Primary 3); $74.50 for reusable test booklets and $17 for hand- and machine-scorable answer folders (Intermediate 1-3); $30.50 per norms booklet; $23.50 per index of instructional objectives; $41.50 per technical data report; $56 per multilevel norms booklet ('91, 173 pages); price data for scoring services available from publisher.

Foreign Language Edition: Test booklets written in Spanish.

Author: The Psychological Corporation.

Publisher: The Psychological Corporation.

a) PREPRIMER (NIVEL PREPRIMARIO).
Population: Grades K.5–1.5.
Scores, 7: Sounds and Letters, Word Reading, Sentence Reading, Total Reading, Listening to Words and Stories, Mathematics, Total.
Time: (145) minutes.

b) PRIMARY 1 (PRIMER NIVEL PRIMARIO).
Population: Grades 1.5–2.5.
Scores, 11: Word Reading, Reading Comprehension, Total Reading, Language, Spelling, Listening, Concepts of Numbers, Mathematics Computation, Mathematics Applications, Total Mathematics, Total.
Time: (235) minutes.

c) PRIMARY 2 (SEGUNDO NIVEL PRIMARIO).
Population: Grades 2.5–3.5.
Scores, 11: Reading Vocabulary, Reading Comprehension, Total Reading, Language, Spelling, Listening, Concepts of Numbers, Mathematics Computations, Mathematics Applications, Total Mathematics, Total.
Time: (230) minutes.

d) PRIMARY 3 (TERCER NIVEL PRIMARIO).
Population: Grades 3.5–4.5.
Scores, 14: Reading Vocabulary, Reading Comprehension, Total Reading, Language Mechanics, Language Expression, Total Language, Study Skills, Spelling, Listening, Concepts of Number, Mathematics Computation, Mathematics Applications, Total Mathematics, Total.
Time: (275) minutes.

e) INTERMEDIATE 1 (PRIMER NIVEL INTERMEDIO).
Population: Grades 4.5–5.5.
Scores, 14: Reading Vocabulary, Reading Comprehension, Total Reading, Language Mechanics, Language Expression, Total Language, Study Skills, Spelling, Listening, Concepts of Numbers, Mathematics Computation, Mathematics Applications, Total Mathematics, Total.
Time: (285) minutes.

f) INTERMEDIATE 2 (SEGUNDO NIVEL INTERMEDIO).
Population: Grades 5.5–6.5.
Scores: Same as *e* above.
Time: Same as *e* above.

g) INTERMEDIATE 3 (TERCER NIVEL INTERMEDIO).
Population: Grades 6.5–8.9.
Scores: Same as *e* above.
Time: Same as *e* above.

Review of the Aprenda: La Prueba de Logros en Español by MARIA MEDINA-DIAZ, Assistant Professor of Educational Measurement and Evaluation, School of Education, University of Puerto Rico, Rio Piedras, PR:

Aprenda: La Prueba de Logros en Español "was developed to respond to concerns about the assessment of academic achievement of Spanish-speaking students" (p. 9) in the United States who "lack the English-language skills required for demonstrating their achievement on English-language tests" (p. 9). It is a norm-referenced test designed to measure achievement of those students from Kindergarten through grade 8 whose primary language of instruction is Spanish and "to provide information upon which decisions for improving instruction can be made" (p. 9).

Aprenda items reflect mostly the content measured by the Stanford Achievement Test Series, Eighth Edition and cover additional objectives related with the domain and usage of the Spanish language. The test items comprising Mathematics Computation, which are independent of language, are the same items that are in corresponding levels of the Stanford Battery ("Cálculos matemáticos"). No information is provided in the technical manual regarding who participated in writing the items and how the test specifications were prepared.

The tryout items were reviewed by Spanish-speaking content experts and editors, measurement specialists, and teachers of bilingual education programs. An advisory panel of eight bilingual educators reviewed the tryout items to detect item bias (i.e., gender, ethnic/class, and regional caused by language differences among Hispanic populations) and stereotypes. In addition, statistical procedures for detecting item bias by gender groups were applied and items exhibiting large differences were flagged for possible exclusion from the pool of tryout items. No information on the criterion used to flag items, nor on the number of items flagged and excluded was supplied in the technical report.

The authors advise that the items were checked for readability and vocabulary by comparing the items with Spanish-language instructional materials. No detailed procedures and statistical indexes related to the readability levels of the test were reported in the technical manual. Despite the authors' efforts, I think there are regional differences among Spanish-speaking people for some of the vocabulary words on the test. For example, the following words have different meanings among Spanish-speaking students: "mecate," "maceta," "sonajas," "cuadras," "pelotas," "soccer," "armijo," "pastel," "puré," calcetín," "chamarra," "pila," "lumbre," "calificaciones," "cuadernos," "tinaja," "revista," "pegadura," and "cubeta." The semantic structure of the stem, the content, and vocabulary

included in the test items are most consistent with Mexican-American population usage in the United States.

In addition, a careful examination of the pictures and activities of the children show stereotyped messages. For example, in the Preprimer test most of the girls are wearing ribbons and in some items are the passive figures. Also, the usage of Hispanic-origin names gives the misleading impression that all Spanish-speaking children have names such as "Lupita," "Pepe," and "Lola."

NORMS. The samples for the spring and fall 1989 standardization and normalization procedures were selected to represent the national Spanish-speaking school population in terms of region of the United States and country of origin based on the 1980s U.S. Census data. Districts with bilingual programs were selected from 15 states around the country. "Approximately 7000 students from 94 school districts participated in the spring standardization, with another 1800 students" in grades 1 through 6 in the "equating levels program and 1000 in the equating to the Stanford" (p. 23) test. Approximately 3,000 students participated in the fall standardization. Sufficient details about how the sample was selected are not provided in the technical manual. No data of the sample characteristics by school grade levels were reported.

VALIDITY. The specific procedures for developing the test blueprint and the tryout items are not detailed in the technical manual. Evidence in support of content validity can be found by comparing the test content and the Aprenda's Index of Instructional Objectives (IIO), which includes specific item-by-item objectives and p-values (difficulty indexes) calculated with the national sample of students. Each instructional objective is represented by 1 through 18 items across the different subtests. The items that measure the same clusters of skills (or content cluster) were grouped together for analyzing the student's performance in comparison with the norms. Common content objectives across test levels include: (a) Number Concepts (whole numbers and fractions), (b) Number Calculations (whole numbers), (c) Mathematical Applications (problem solving, geometry/measurement), and (d) Listening (vocabulary and listening comprehension). The same content objectives are found in the three intermediate test levels. A good addition are the subtests of Study Skills and Thinking Skills in Primary 3 and Intermediate tests. The Thinking Skills are embedded throughout the battery and an individual's score is reported.

In order to use the test data meaningfully, the authors recommend users compare local curriculum objectives with the behavior called for in the test items and what is included in the IIO. According to the authors "Aprenda uses the same stringent criteria as those established for the Stanford series and assesses important instructional objectives at each grade [level] from Kindergarten to Grade 8" (p. 9). There is no additional information, however, about the match of the test to frequently used textbooks or any attempt to link the test to various state-level objectives.

Subtest and total scores increase from fall to spring of the same school years supporting the authors' claim that the Aprenda is sensitive to developmental instructional sequences. However, this claim should be taken cautiously because the mean p-values in some instances (particularly in the intermediate levels) for the subtests and the total battery in the spring administration for the previous grade level were greater than in the fall administration of the next grade level. Overall, there is a very small increment in the mean difficulty values (p-values) across grade levels suggesting the test items are a bit easier for the students from one grade level to another. The p-values for content clusters provide useful information about the item-objectives difficulty levels with the national sample.

RELIABILITY. Kuder-Richardson 20 reliability coefficients, mean, standard deviations, and standard errors of measurement for fall and spring standardization samples (i.e., national school and Spanish-speaking school populations) for each test, subtests, and grade level are presented in tables. The reliability coefficients for all grades for the subtests ranged from .661 to .966 with the national sample and ranged from .695 to .961 with the Spanish-speaking sample. For the basic battery for every grade level and group, the reliability estimates exceeded .95. Kuder-Richardson 21 reliability coefficients were also calculated for the cluster content of each subtest. A great variation is found in these estimates across content cluster and grade levels. Alternate-form reliability coefficients

were not reported. Correlations between subtests ranged from .43 to .86. These reliability-related estimates are quite acceptable for a test battery of this kind.

TEST ADMINISTRATION. For each test level, there is a booklet entitled *Directions for Administering* that includes two versions: students' directions in Spanish and directions for the administrator in English (English/Spanish); and students' directions in Spanish and directions for the administrator in Spanish (Spanish/Spanish). This booklet also contains a brief description of the subtests and the test materials. Test administration should be divided in several sittings and the total time allocated to each one is reported. The total testing time suggested is 75 minutes. The administration of a complete battery can take 2 or 3 days.

Students in kindergarten through grade 3 take the test in machine-scorable booklets. Separate answer sheets are used by students in grades 4 through 8. A Practice test is included to be administered to all students a week before the test.

In the Preprimer ("Nivel Primario") and Primary 1 ("Primer Nivel Primario") tests, the instructions and test items are read to the students. Guidelines for the time for pausing between each item are not provided. The inclusion of a Listening subtest at all levels is a distinct feature of the battery, but the administration procedures raise some concern. Although the teacher's familiar voice may be comforting to the students, the threat to standardization could be substantial across various teachers. Two additional concerns are the length of the tests (Preprimer, 195 items; Primary 1, 265 items; Primary 2, 284 items; Primary 3, 355 items; Intermediate levels, 357 items) and the number of items of the same type (18 items in some cases) that the student should answer related to each objective. This may affect students' fatigue, motivation, and anxiety for answering the tests, particularly in kindergarten and first grade.

TEST REPORTING. Aprenda can be hand scored or machine scored. Individual test results are reported using raw scores and norm-referenced scores (i.e., percentile ranks, stanines, grade equivalents, and scaled scores). Procedures for converting raw scores to scaled scores, and scaled scores to obtain percentile ranks, stanines, and grade equivalents are well explained in the Multilevel Norms Booklet. Norms tables are included by reference group (National School Population or Spanish-speaking School Population), grade (K—8), and time of the year (spring or fall).

Individual and class reports also provide raw scores in the content cluster of the subtests in the battery. This may be helpful in identifying students' strengths and weaknesses in specific objectives within a content area. For individual students, the raw score on a particular content cluster is converted to a stanine and then to a performance category (Below average, Average, and Above average). This provides a comparison with the performance of the national sample of the students at the same grade level and time of year. The percent of students in each of the performance categories can be determined for groups of students.

SUMMARY. Most of the criticisms of the Aprenda test battery result of the absence of specific and essential information about its construction and support for validity. Fine differences in vocabulary and instructional experiences among these students are not quite captured in this instrument or any other achievement test yet designed. Deficiencies can be reduced, however, by further revisions. As an achievement battery, its reliability and difficulty indexes are quite acceptable. The individual and class reports provide useful information for instructional purposes. The potential user must check the purposes, objectives, and content carefully to be assured of a match between the test and the contexts in which it is used.

Review of the Aprenda: La Prueba de Logros en Español by SALVADOR HECTOR OCHOA, Assistant Professor of Educational Psychology, Texas A&M University, College Station, TX:

The Aprenda: La Prueba de Logros en español is designed to assess the achievement of students who receive instruction in Spanish. The Aprenda was designed to closely correlate with the content of the Stanford Achievement Test Series. Although the Aprenda is not a direct translation of the Stanford Achievement Test Series, it was designed to equate to the Stanford Achievement Test Series, Eighth Edition "in order to maintain the capability for tracking growth when students exit a bilingual program" (p. 26 of technical manual).

The Aprenda standardization sample and its description have limitations. First, the test publishers conducted a fall and spring standardization procedure. The sample for the spring standardization consisted of 7,000 students; and the Fall standardization was made up of 3,000 pupils. No reason is given in the technical manual as to why the size of the standardization samples differed so significantly.

Second, the technical manual author states that "94 school districts ... participated in the Spring standardization sample" (p. 23), but Appendix 6 lists only 49 school districts. Appendix 6, however, does list an additional 45 school districts that were included in the fall standardization sample. It appears that there is a clerical error on page 23 of the manual.

Third, the test publisher reports that both standardization samples represented "the national Spanish-speaking school population in terms of region of the United States and country of origin" (p. 23). Data provided on Table 3 of the technical manual, however, indicate that this is not the case. On Table 3, the test publishers report the West geographical region has 30% of the total U.S. Spanish-speaking school enrollment. The percentages of students in the spring and fall standardization samples from the West geographical region of the United States, however, were 68% and 82%, respectively. The Northeast, Midwest, and South regions were not adequately represented. Similarly, on Table 3, the test publishers report that Cubans constitute 6% of the total U.S. Spanish-speaking school enrollment. The percentage of students in both standardization samples whose country of origin is Cuba was zero. Fourth, no information is provided in the manual concerning the gender, age, grade level, and socioeconomic status characteristics of the sample. Thus, one is unable to discern if a sufficient number of students were included across all age and grade levels.

With respect to the sample used to equate the Aprenda with the Stanford, the manual author reports it consisted of 1,000 students who were "identified by their school districts as being equally proficient in English and in Spanish" (p. 26). The manual does not contain, however, necessary information with respect to gender, age, grade level, socioeconomic status, country of origin, and geographical region. Moreover, the test publishers fail to provide the criteria school districts used to identify students who were balanced bilinguals in English and Spanish. This is especially critical given that it is difficult to find students who are truly balanced bilingual students across reading, writing, listening, and speaking. All four of these domains influence achievement.

With respect to reliability, the manual contains information only about internal consistency. The Kuder-Richardson Formula 20 coefficients reported for the total battery across all grade levels on all seven levels of the Aprenda are in the mid to high .90s. This is quite good. An overwhelming majority of the cluster scores across all grade levels on all seven levels of the Aprenda are above .80 and are more than acceptable. The manual, however, did not include any information pertaining to test-retest reliability.

The manual does contain a discussion of the three major types of validity. With respect to content validity, the national norms booklet author states, "the Aprenda was constructed to match those objectives of the Stanford Achievement Test Series that are appropriate for students receiving most of their instruction in Spanish" (p. 11). Five thousand items were field tested with 8,500 bilingual school children who were from the United States, Mexico, and Puerto Rico. Only items that had a biserial correlation coefficient of .35 or greater and a mid-range level of difficulty were included in the final form. Criterion-related validity was demonstrated by showing progression "[across] differing points in the instructional sequence" (i.e., from Fall to Spring) (p. 36). Construct validity was demonstrated by correlating corresponding subtests at adjacent levels (i.e., Nivel Preprimario/Preprimer with Primer Nivel Primario/Primary 1; Primer Nivel Primario/Primary 1 with Segundo Nivel Primario/Primary 2; etc.).

With respect to test administration, the Aprenda has a separate test administration booklet for all seven battery levels. This booklet provides sufficient information pertaining to test administration. The Spanish instructions that are read to students are succinct, clear, and grammatically correct. The layout of test items in the test booklets is appropriate. Moreover, the national norms booklet provides sufficient information on how to use the tables of norms.

With respect to item bias, the manual contains a list of personnel who served as the minority advisory panel. This panel reviewed items for possible gender, regional, and ethnic/class bias.

The Aprenda test helps to address the need for measures to assess the academic achievement of pupils with limited English proficiency in the United States. One primary strength of the Aprenda is that it uses the Stanford Achievement Test, English Edition as its model for test content. Moreover, it is not a translation of the Stanford Achievement Test. This is an important advantage of the Aprenda because translating English tests into Spanish can be problematic given that psychometric properties and item-difficulty levels can change in these situations. Many commercial instruments in Spanish are mere translations of English instruments. The primary limitation of the Aprenda is its standardization sample. The test publisher's efforts to obtain a nationally representative sample of Spanish-speaking school students in the United States is commendable given that many instruments in Spanish are not normed on students with limited English proficiency. The standardization sample of the Aprenda, however, does not reflect the Spanish-speaking school-age population of the United States. Examiners should proceed with caution when using the Aprenda with Spanish-speaking students from different geographical regions and different countries of origin than those represented in the norm population.

[6]
ASIST: A Structured Addictions Assessment Interview for Selecting Treatment.

Purpose: To assess alcohol and drug use for the purpose of selecting treatment.
Population: Adults.
Publication Dates: 1984-1990.
Acronym: ASIST.
Scores: 12 sections: Identifying Information, Basic Information, Alcohol Use, Psychoactive Drug Use, Health Screening, Other Life Areas, Previous Treatment, Client Preference for Treatment, Treatment Assessment Summary, Treatment Plan, Actual Referrals, Assessment Worker's Observation.
Administration: Individual.
Price Data, 1994: $25 per 10 questionnaires; $35 per Assessment Handbook ('90, 200 pages).
Foreign Language Edition: Questionnaire available in French.

Time: Administration time not reported.
Author: Addiction Research Foundation.
Publisher: Addiction Research Foundation [Canada].

Review of the ASIST: A Structured Addictions Assessment for Selecting Treatment by WESLEY E. SIME, Professor, University of Nebraska-Lincoln, Lincoln, NE:

The ASIST is a structured interview designed to aid therapists and administrators in determining the severity of need and the best treatment intervention for individuals who exhibit alcohol and/or drug abuse symptoms. The ASIST is more than an instrument, rather it includes a very comprehensive manual that could serve as a procedures model for developing a new program for establishing a community-based referral system.

The instrument itself assesses four different categories that include alcohol use, drug use, physical and emotional health, and "other life" areas. Other life areas include accommodation, family issues, social issues, education/training, work, financial, leisure, and legal concerns. Each of these four areas contains a standard sequence of inquiry that includes questions about "what concerns do you have," "do you feel that you need help" in order to control this area, "what behavioral disturbances do you experience," "how important now is help to you," and finally "what is the severity of the rating" as viewed by the therapist (p. 23). It also includes a determination of all previous treatment, specifically defining which was most helpful. A treatment assessment form elicits the client's preference for treatment compared with the assessment worker's preference for treatment followed by the agreed upon treatment plan (usually a compromise).

The treatment plan contains an assessment of the problem, the goals to be accomplished, the recommended interventions, a specific section for client responsibility and therapist or assessment worker responsibility, and finally, case manager responsibilities. In comparison to other similar instruments, the last three items (listed above) seem to be the most salient elements in structuring a viable treatment plan.

The physical health screening questions include a variety of medical disorders of which two (rheumatic fever and tuberculosis) seem to be irrelevant to substance abuse and others such as the pulmonary disorders related to smoking and/or infectious diseases and the neurological disorders related to long-term substance abuse are notably absent. Certainly this part of the instrument could be more useful if it included a more comprehensive and relevant list of medical disorders related to substance abuse.

The procedural manual for this instrument includes a thorough description of intake assessment references in the community, treatment guidelines, case management, a clinical procedural policy regarding crisis emergencies, withdrawal, and security issues. It also provides an interesting and useful procedure for developing a community resource directory.

The appendix includes three articles on substance use, all of which were published by the Addiction Research Foundation 10–15 years ago, making them somewhat outdated.

My major concern about this instrument is its general utility for others in the field. Unfortunately, the instrument is regionally and nationally specific. The manual is prepared in accordance with statutes from the province of Ontario and the Ministry of Health for Canada. The Ontario Health Insurance Program (OHIP) requirements punctuate the entire document and specific terms such as "are useful only in Canada" appear frequently. The spelling of terms (e.g., centre) is generic to the King's English and terms such as HMRI (Health Ministries Regional District Codes) and HSC (homes for special care) in the Ministries of Health and Victorian Order of Nurses are applicable only for current Canadian and/or Ontario users. Standards for blood alcohol content (.08) at the legal limit may not be uniform across other provinces or in some U.S. states where the legal limit is .10. In addition, the limit for percent of alcohol in beer in Ontario is known to be 5% whereas many of the U.S. beers are 3.2%. Finally, there is reference to Canadian laws on patient records.

Demographic questions specify two alternative language response options (French and English only). For more universal usage, Spanish language options should be included. It is unfortunate that the authors did not take the time to prepare a separate version of the workbook and the instrument, which would be applicable to other populations beyond those in Ontario or Canada.

A more serious issue of attending to detail is noted in two sections of the ASIST where typographical errors have apparently persisted throughout the past 10 to 12 years of usage (this instrument came out in 1984 and was edited again in 1989). The word aggressive is misspelled in Section 3.12, and the term "now" was misspelled as "know" in Section 5.6 under physical health. [Editor's note: Both of these errors have been corrected in the most recent printing of the revised version.]

I am very concerned that no data are reported regarding the functional utility of this instrument after 10–12 years of usage. In the ASIST, client recommendations are found on a risk-o-graph (p. 8), which defines the amount of drinks per day against body weight for males and females. There is a criterion line for three different levels of risk, but these have not been defined nor data provided supporting the validity of such criteria. It should also be noted that there are no measures of reliability regarding the instrument and no assessment of the instrument's predictive or construct validity to make appropriate referrals of treatment outcome based on those referrals.

This instrument is hand scored with no extra provision for machine scoring. There is no description of how the instrument was formulated and how it has been revised over the years. Although the validity remains essentially undetermined and there is no way of assessing the advantage of this instrument over other available options in the area of substance abuse, it is, however, a very practical tool for identifying the severity of symptoms for clients. It should be noted that the instrument is designed for case managers and administrators who need a relatively simple and nonclinical device for assessing need for therapy. By using this instrument to make client needs assessments, it would appear that trained and experienced clerical workers could function as well as mental health counselors.

Review of the ASIST: A Structured Addictions Assessment Interview for Selecting Treatment by NICHOLAS A. VACC, Professor and Chairperson, and GERALD A. JUHNKE, Assistant Professor of Counseling and Educational Development, School of Education, The University of North Carolina at Greensboro, Greensboro, NC:

A Structured Addictions Assessment Interview for Selecting Treatment (ASIST) was designed to structure the assessment and referral process for alcohol- and drug-abusing clients and to propose a treatment selection. The ASIST is a structured interview, which includes recommendations at specific points in the interview for possibly administering the Alcohol Dependence Scale (ADS; T4:145) and the Drug Abuse Screening Test (DAST; see the Drug Use Questionnaire, Test 34 this volume), respectively. Also available is an Assessment Handbook, which is equivalent to a technical manual, that includes procedures for addictions assessment/referral services including ASIST.

The interview format provides data relating to 12 areas: Identifying Information (e.g., client name, address), Basic Information (e.g., date of birth, referral source), Alcohol Use (e.g., family drinking history, personal drinking history), Psychoactive Drug Use (e.g., drug types and amounts used), Health Screening (e.g., medical history), Other Life Areas (e.g., relationship, employment, or legal problems), Previous Treatment, Client Preference for Treatment (e.g., client-identified goals), Treatment Assessment Summary, Treatment Plan, Actual Referrals, and Assessment Workers' Observation Form. The same format is used for both males and females. No indication is given within the ASIST or the Assessment Handbook concerning the average completion time for the interview.

The ADS and DAST are independent instruments and are recommended as an element of the ASIST assessment and referral process; these instruments are not included in the ASIST booklet. However, the Assessment Handbook provides both scoring and interpretation guidelines for the use of the ADS and DAST. The instruments appear integral to the ASIST interview process, and they are also available from the agency, Addiction Research Foundation, which produced the Assessment Handbook and the ASIST.

The ADS has 25 questions presented in a multiple-choice self-report format (Personal communication, Linda Omerea, May 17, 1996). Although the purpose of the ADS is not clearly indicated within the Assessment Handbook or the ASIST, it seems to reflect the respondent's alcohol use. The Handbook includes an ADS scoring key and interpretation guide. The ADS score is determined by first matching the client's responses to the respective item scores indicated in the ADS scoring key, and then summing the matching scores to provide an ADS score, which is interpreted using the ADS interpretation guide. This guide is broken into four quartiles and provides a suggested interpretation of alcohol dependence (i.e., low, moderate, substantial, severe) and general clinical guidelines (e.g., "Abstinence is probably the only reasonable treatment goal" [p.H.3.8]).

The DAST is a 20-question screening instrument presented in a dichotomous, yes-no, self-report format. Although the purpose for the administration of the DAST is not specifically stated within the Assessment Handbook of the ASIST, directions given to the client suggest that the instrument will reflect the client's current involvement with drugs other than alcohol. The Handbook contains a sample of the DAST, a scoring scheme, and a DAST scoring table that reports drug-abuse severity ranging from 0 for "None Reported" to 20 for "Severe Level." The score is obtained by summing the number of client scores that correspond with the scoring scheme.

The Assessment Handbook indicates that formal validity studies regarding the ASIST interview procedure have been conducted only on the ADS and DAST, but information regarding these studies is not provided. However, Skinner and Allen (1982) and Ross, Gavin, and Skinner (1990) reported validity and reliability data for the ADS, and Skinner (1983) and Saltstone, Halliwell, and Hayslip (1994) presented validity and reliability estimates for the DAST. Validity estimates range between .06 and .86 for the ADS and the Alcohol-Related Measures items (Horn, Wanberg, & Foster, 1974), and were found to be .69 (Skinner & Allen, 1992) and .79 (Ross, Gavin, & Skinner, 1990) for the ADS and the Michigan Alcoholism Screening Inventory (MAST). Validity estimates range from -.38 to .55 for the DAST and a variety of relevant indices (Skinner, 1983), and a correlation of .41 was found for the DAST and the MAST (Saltstone, Halliwell, & Hayslip, 1994). Reliability estimates for the DAST and ADS are high with both being above .90. Subjects initially used for the development of the DAST (i.e., 223 subjects [Skinner, 1983]) and the ADS (i.e., 225 subjects [Skinner & Allen, 1982]) were volunteers who sought help at the Clinical Institute of the Addiction Research Foundation in Toronto, Canada. The subjects were overwhelmingly male (72% and 80%, respectively); no indications were noted as to ethnic or racial distributions.

The Assessment Handbook was designed for the Canadian Ministry of Health Addictions Services, and a substantial amount of the information and forms included were intended to match the services requirement format of the Canadian Ministry of Health Information Services, thus having limited utility outside such governmental agencies. In general, some sections of the handbook are elementary and limited in usefulness to all but the least experienced addictions professionals. The Assessment Handbook includes suggestions regarding topics such as client cancellations, no-shows, subpoenas, and evening appointments. Yet, omitted in the Assessment Handbook are important topics such as information about the age range and needed reading competencies of clients completing the DAST and ADS.

The authors have attempted to create a broad-spectrum alcohol and other drug-intake procedure to accommodate the assessment of all clients. However, the proposed clinical guidelines are very general and too nonspecific to be of substantial value to most addiction professionals. Also, the print quality of the ASIST is lower than expected for a commercial instrument. Despite these many limitations, the ASIST has some qualities that make it a useful instrument. First, it provides a thorough intake format that requires the joint identification of specific client goals. Second, basic life needs related to health, food, shelter, and social interactions are identified. Third, the treatment assessment summary provides the addictions professional and the client with an "urgency rating." Based upon the client's self-report, this rating indicates the most pressing issues facing the client. Thus, counselor and client can rank order the immediacy of presenting concerns. Fourth, the ASIST provides the client and counselor with a list of identified goals and their corresponding responsibilities. The DAST and ADS appear to hold clinical merit as brief initial assessment tools to provide a measure of alcohol and drug misuse.

In summary, the ASIST interview has some merit, particularly because it addresses a population for which comprehensive instruments are needed. However, it is impossible to judge adequately the potential value of the instrument because of the lack of sufficient information. This instrument could best be classified as being in the research or developmental stage. As an "in-house" procedure to aid an agency in the assessment and referral process for alcohol- and drug-abusing clients, the ASIST offers some promise. Yet, much needs to be done before it reaches the criterion of *The Standards for Educational and Psychological Testing* (American Educational Research Association, American Psychological Association, & National Council on Measurement in Education, 1985).

REVIEWER'S REFERENCES

Horn, J. L., Wanberg, K. W., & Foster, F. M. (1974). The Alcohol Use Inventory. Denver, CO: Center for Alcohol Abuse Research and Evaluation.

Skinner, H. A. (1983). The Drug Abuse Screening Test. *Addictive Behaviors, 7,* 363-371.

Skinner, H. A., & Allen, B. A. (1982). Alcohol dependence syndrome: Measurement and validation. *Journal of Abnormal Psychology, 91,* 199-209.

American Educational Research Association, American Psychological Association, & National Council on Measurement in Education. (1985). *Standards for educational and psychological testing.* Washington, DC: American Psychological Association, Inc.

Ross, H. E., Gavin, D. R., & Skinner, H. A. (1990). Diagnostic validity of the MAST and the Alcohol Dependence Scale in the assessment of DSM-III alcohol disorders. *Journal of Studies on Alcohol, 51,* 506-513.

Saltstone, R., Halliwell, S., & Hayslip, M. A. (1994). A multivariate evaluation of the Michigan Alcoholism Screening Test and the Drug Abuse Screening Test in a female offender population. *Addictive Behaviors, 19,* 455-462.

[7]
Assessment of Chemical Health Inventory.

Purpose: "Designed to evaluate the nature and extent of adolescent and adult chemical use and associated problems."

Population: Adolescents, adults.

Publication Dates: 1988–1992.

Acronym: ACHI.

Scores: 9 factors (Chemical Involvement, Alienation, Family Estrangement, Personal Consequence, Depression, Family Support, Social Impact, Self Regard, Family Chemical Use) yielding Total score.

Administration: Individual.

Price Data, 1993: $179.95 per starter set including microcomputer disk containing 25 administrations and user manual ('92, 119 pages); $9 per 10 response forms; $5.75 (sold in multiples of 50) per microcomputer disk to administer and score ACHI; $29.95 per manual.

Time: (15–25) minutes.

Comments: Requires 4th grade reading level; may be taken and scored on computer (or administered on paper); mail-in service available.

Authors: Daniel Krotz, Richard Kominowski, Barbara Berntson, and James W. Sipe.

Publisher: RENOVEX Corporation.

Review of the Assessment of Chemical Health Inventory by PHILIP ASH, Director, Ash, Blackstone and Cates, Blacksburg, VA:

The Assessment of Chemical Health Inventory is a 128-item self-administered computer-based instrument intended to assist chemical dependency counselors in evaluating the nature and extent of adolescent and adult substance (alcohol and other drugs) abuse. Both an adolescent form and an adult form are available; both come on disk for computer administration and in a paper-and-pencil machine-scannable version that must be entered into a computer for scoring and analysis. Most of the items in the two versions are identical; a few reflect adolescent/adult differences (e.g., among the biodata items, the adolescent version asks "With whom do you live?" whereas the adult version asks for level of educational attainment).

The first six items inquire as to biographical data (e.g., age, ethnicity, religion, sex, and living arrangements or educational level). The remaining 122 items are cast in a Likert-type five-choice response format (*Strongly Agree* to *Strongly Disagree*), scored in ascending or descending order so that the highest weight is assigned to the most negative or pathological response, yielding higher scores for the more serious abusers. In obtaining composite (factor or subtest) scores, however, each item is differentially weighted, and the factor scores are also differentially weighted to obtain the overall assessment score (user manual, p. 4). The source or method of arriving at these differential weights is not described. The resultant factor scores and the ACHI Assessment Score are transformed to standard scores, which are presented in the Assessment Report.

The computer-generated Assessment Report yields means and standard deviations for the standard scores for 11 measures: ACHI Assessment Score [total], Berntson Social Desirability Scale, and nine "factor" scores including Use Involvement, Personal Consequences, Family Estrangement, Alienation, Social Impact, Family Chemical Use, Self Regard/Abuse, Depression, and Family Support, as well as a Validity Check, a list of Critical Life Items if any of a particular subset of items is responded to in a significantly deviant fashion, a discussion ("ASSESSMENT SCORE") of the meaning of the respondent's ACHI Assessment Score, and a RECOMMENDATION as to further work with the respondent.

According to information received from Dr. James W. Sipe, one of the main authors of the instrument and a member of the staff of RENOVEX, which distributes the inventory, the ACHI is no longer advertised nor included in any catalog, and the company that developed the software is no longer in business. RENOVEX sells copies of administration materials to previous and current users, but apparently no new customers are added.

The main and probably only source of information about the Inventory is contained in the user manual. A computer-based search of the psychological and social sciences literature (January 1974—September 1995) failed to reveal a single reference to the ACHI, or to a book or paper authored by any of the named authors of the Inventory, or even to any reference in which any of them were cited.

For purposes of administration, use, and interpretation, the main parts of the manual include a summary "Characteristics of ACHI" (p. 1); "ACHI: Abstract and Review" (pp. 2–7), outlining general measurement principles with limited reference to any characteristics of the ACHI itself; "ACHI: The Development Stages" (pp. 8–11); "Validation Protocols," describing four "validation" projects (pp. 13–15); "Research and Design" (pp. 16–41); and six sections dealing with actual application: "ACHI Installation," "Administrative Guidelines," "ACHI Tutorial," a sample Assessment Report, "Clinical Interpretation," and "Clinical Applications" (pp. 42–88). The first four sections were apparently written by Dr. Sipe. The "Research and Design" chapter was written by Barbara and Bruce Berntson and Bryan Davis. No authorship is given for the applications sections or chapters.

Overall, the manual is not very well written, including misspellings (e.g., "expirimental" is repeatedly used; "randon" for "random"; "compromising" for "comprising"), and apparent typographical or clerical errors. More importantly, however, there are significant inconsistencies both within the sections authored by Dr. Sipes and by Dr. Berntson et al., and among the differently authored sections.

ITEM SOURCES. We are told (Validation Project 1, p. 13) that "Subject matter experts from Minnesota identified 508 questions assumed to have value in distinguishing among chemical use,

abuse, and dependency" *or that* "this study was designed to identify ...items, taken from four existing questionnaires consisting of 255 items" (Research and Design, p. 16). Validation Project I involved the administration of the 508 items to two adolescent samples ($N = 416$), on the basis of which 255 items were selected to have "good construct validity" (p. 13) "through face validation" (p. 9) decided upon by the participating substance abuse counselors.

FACTOR ANALYSES. At least two factor analyses are reported. The first, based upon the 255 items selected by face validity analysis of the original pool of 508 items, yielded (principal components analysis with varimax rotation) 30 (or 29, depending upon who wrote the sections) composites. This was apparently followed by a principal components with varimax rotation of 100 items (how selected?). It should be noted, however, the output of "merely a numerical technique with no direct clinical or substantive significance" (p. 20) was "scrutinized from a clinical perspective in an attempt to achieve composite indices that, while being empirically verified, were also meaningful and of clinical usefulness" (p. 20)! These procedures "culminated in ten composites" (p. 20). However, detailed data are provided for only eight (pp. 22–26), and only nine are included in the assessment report printout.

ITEM DISTRIBUTION. The final instrument contains 128 items on the paper-and-pencil forms, as indicated in the summary sheet. It should be noted, however, that in the Research and Design (R&D) chapter the ACHI is referred to as "a 100 item questionnaire" (p. 16). The item content (of only eight) of the nine "factors," of the Berntson Social Desirability Scale, and of the Critical Life Items, are given in the R&D chapter. Analysis of the list found that at least *26* item numbers did not occur in any of the lists (although some may belong in Factor 7 [Self Regard/Abuse], for which item data were missing). About 80 items were each included in only one of the lists, and about 19 items were each included in two lists. The list for Factor 3 (Family Estrangement) was obviously in error, with the array "8, 23, 26, 27, 30, 21, 23, 27 ...." Item 6, a biodata item (adult/Educational Level; adolescent/Family Living Arrangement) was also included in the group of items for Factor 2 (Personal Consequences). To add to the confusion, the factor numbers given with the factor definitions (pp. 40–41) are different from the factor numbers assigned to the "Composite Characteristics" table (Table II, pp. 22–26).

NORMS. The summary (p. 1) indicates case numbers for the samples used: adults/150 nonclinical, 100 clinical; adolescents/1,288 nonclinical, 688 clinical. All the adults came from one (Minneapolis) sample, and the summary agrees with the text. However, the numbers for adolescents came from three samples. Adding the sample numbers for adolescents in these three studies (no study involved both adults and adolescents) yields totals discrepant with those given in the summary: 1,088 nonclinical, 619 clinical. Where the higher numbers in the summary came from is not explained. Furthermore, the user manual contains no norms tables of any sort.

RELIABILITY. The reliabilities reported in the summary are coefficient alpha internal consistency estimates (.74–.94), and based upon data from Validation Research Project II—Salt Lake City (pp. 13–14), which involved administration of a prior 255-item questionnaire to 981 adolescents (851 control and 130 expirimental [sic]). Alpha coefficients were also reported (Table II, pp. 22–26) for eight of the nine factors for a combined sample derived from Validation Project II (Salt Lake City) plus Validation Project III (Detroit, or Michigan). These factor alphas were in about the same range as reported in the summary.

No coefficient alpha data were presented for the adult sample. Furthermore, no other reliability measures (test-retest, alternate forms) are reported in the user manual.

VALIDITY. At least four approaches to validation are claimed in the manual.

The first is "concurrent validity" based on a correlation between a score (ACHI Assessment Score?) and "staff assessment" (p. 1), with $r = .82$. This is mentioned in one line on the summary (p. 1), but not referred to or elaborated upon anywhere else in the manual.

The second is "face validity," apparently based upon the item selection and reduction from 508 to 255 items in Validation Project I (p. 13).

The third is discriminant analysis, done on 29 (p. 14) or 30 (p. 18) "composites," in which percent of correct identification as between clinical

and nonclinical samples yielded "hit" rates usually above 90% in Validation Projects II, III, and IV. Discriminant function analysis, however, is a suboptimal approach to validation. As Tatsuoka and Tiedeman (1954) point out, discriminant function analysis may be used to (a) identify group differences, (b) study and understand such differences, and (c) classify people. There is nothing in the technique that implies prediction, such as a statement that a person with this score will, if untreated, exhibit substance abuse behavior. Rulon (1951) presents a satirical fable about classifying a hexagon as a square or a circle. For most psychological testing purposes, regression equations against appropriate criteria provide a more effective technique (Anastasi, 1988, p. 191). Other substance abuse scales have reported criterion-related validities based upon number of different substances used, frequency of use, incidence of hospitalization or legal offenses while "under the influence," and similar measures. What the summary describes as "concurrent validity" (p. 1) would probably qualify as a criterion-based approach, but no information on the claim cited is available.

The fourth approach to validity claimed by the authors is by way of canonical correlations. Typically, in canonical correlation a correlation matrix of predictors (e.g., test scores) is correlated with a matrix of quantified criteria (observed or rated behaviors) for a defined sample of subjects. The manual authors nowhere describe the input to the canonical correlations reported for Validation Projects III and IV (pp. 14–15), and no mention is made of canonical correlation in the summary. It is this reviewer's understanding, however, that the two correlation matrices used were (a) the correlation matrix among the item responses for the clinical sample and (b) the item intercorrelation matrix for the nonclinical sample. Unlike in its usual application, therefore, the two matrices each consisted of the same variables, but based upon different human samples. The very high (above .90) resulting canonical correlations would therefore be expected, and would not reflect any aspect of the *validity* of the instrument. In fact, it seems to be a methodologically inappropriate use of canonical correlation.

In short, evidence supporting the validity of the ACHI for assessing substance abuse seems to be thin to negligible. The manual contains a Level of Care guide (pp. 82–82), based primarily upon the ACHI Assessment Score, providing "rules of thumb" (p. 82) that range from in-patient candidacy; through out-patient candidacy; to education, counseling, and contracting, but without any explicit data showing why the recommendations move by standard deviations above and below the mean.

In summary, since its inception as a 508-item experimental inventory much effort seems to have been expended in collecting and analyzing sample data on abusers and nonabusers. However, the user manual is poorly organized, carelessly written, and afflicted with many internal inconsistencies. The data supporting reliability and validity concerns are, at best, weak. As noted above, although the summary provides number of cases for norms, no tables of norms are presented in the manual. Self-administration of the ACHI by computer is not difficult, although a couple of glitches were noted in the program as this reviewer took it. The format of the printed assessment report is not easy to follow and far from optimum in design. In this reviewer's opinion current users should take the time to evaluate the instrument again, and possibly consider other inventories such as the Personal Experience Inventory (PEI; T4:1971) (Winters & Henly, 1989), the Chemical Dependency Assessment Survey (Oetting, Beauvais, Edwards, & Waters, 1984), and the Drug Use Screening Inventory (Tarter, 1990).

REVIEWER'S REFERENCES

Rulon, P. J. (1951). The stanine and the separile: A fable. *Personnel Psychology, 4*, 99–114.

Tatsuoka, M. M., & Tiedeman, D. V. (1954). Discriminant analysis. *Review of Educational Research, 24*, 402–420.

Oetting, E., Beauvais, F., Edwards, R., & Waters, M. (1984). The Drug and Alcohol Assessment System. Fort Collins, CO: Rocky Mountain Behavioral Sciences Institute.

Anastasi, A. (1988). *Psychological testing* (6th ed.). New York: Macmillan Publishers.

Winters, K. C., & Henly, G. A. (1989). Personal Experience Inventory. Los Angeles: Western Psychological Services.

Tarter, R. (1990). Evaluation and treatment of adolescent drug abuse: A decision-tree method. *American Journal of Drug and Alcohol Abuse, 16*, 1–46.

Review of the Assessment of Chemical Health Inventory by BETSY WATERMAN, Assistant Professor, Counseling and Psychological Services Department, State University of New York at Oswego, Oswego, NY:

The Assessment of Chemical Health Inventory (ACHI) was developed to assess chemical misuse among adolescents and adults. This instrument is designed to be self-administered and is an attempt to provide a more objective look at chemical use than many other current measures provide. The 128 test items were developed from within a Disease Model theoretical orientation and reflect the criterion outlined in the *DSM-III-R*. It appears there are two forms, one for adolescents and one for adults, although this is not clearly stated in the manual. The authors indicate that approximately 20 minutes is required for administration. Reading level is reported to be at the fourth grade level. Use with special populations (e.g., poor or nonreaders) is discussed briefly and the authors indicate the items can be read aloud to those who cannot read adequately.

Administration procedures are outlined in the manual, including standardized verbal instructions. The inventory can be administered on a computer or by having the individual fill in the appropriate circles on a response form. There are opportunities for practice trials to familiarize the respondent with the computerized format. The manual also includes instruction for using the software program. Testing administration is generally straightforward and requires individuals to respond to a statement, such as, "I use drugs or alcohol to change the way I feel" (p. 35), by selecting from among five choices (*Strongly Disagree, Disagree, No Opinion, Agree,* or *Strongly Agree*). The computer format allows for immediate scoring. The printed profile presents client identifying information, demographic data, and validity checks including "paired opposites" (p. 52) items and the Berntson Social Desirability Scale.

ACHI scores range from 1.00 to 9.00. They are presented on a graph and compared with the means of chemically dependent individuals. "Levels of care" (e.g., inpatient treatment) are suggested in the manual as they relate to the score earned. Scores between 1.00 and 5.07 are considered to be typical ranges of substance use and scores above 6.08 indicate possible need for treatment. Nine factor scores are presented in a profile (Chemical Involvement, Alienation, Family Estrangement, Personal Consequences, Depression, Family Support, Social Impact, Self-Regard, and Family Chemical Use) and compared to the means of nonclinical groups. Critical items (e.g., suicidal ideation) that may require immediate attention are also identified on the printout.

The ACHI was constructed and validated in four separate phases and in four locations: Minnesota, Salt Lake City, Detroit, and Minneapolis, respectively. During Phase I, 508 original items were identified by experts in the chemical dependency field. Subjects ranged in age between 14 and 20 years and were in outpatient (N = 116) or inpatient (N = 300) treatment programs. Of the original 508 items, 255 were identified by the authors as having good "construct" validity, although it appears they are actually referring to face validity in this case.

In Phases II to IV, validity studies were conducted in which the ACHI was used to distinguish between users and nonusers of chemical substances. A total of 981 adolescents between the ages of 13 and 18 provided the sample in Phase II. It was not clear how gender and racial groups were reflected in experimental and control samples. Three hundred and ten adolescents, aged 13 to 18, served as the sample in Phase III with equal numbers of white and black subjects reflected in the pool. Two hundred and fifty adults participated in Phase IV. It should be noted that the control sample in this final phase included 150 individuals attending a community college. No age range or mean was given for this group of individuals. This sample may not be very different in age than the upper end of the previous adolescent group samples. The ACHI was reported as able to classify correctly 94% to 99% of nonusers and 74% to 88% of those who were chemically dependent.

Data from both Salt Lake City and Michigan were combined and analyzed, and, according to the authors, resulted in 10 composites or factors. Only 8 were reported in the validation study itself: Chemical Use Involvement, Social Impact, Personal Consequence, Family Chemical Use, Family Estrangement, Depression, Alienation, and Family Support. A ninth factor is reported elsewhere in the manual as Self Regard/Abuse. Cronbach alphas and standardized item alphas for the ACHI ranged between .74 and .94 across items within factors. There was no information about test-retest reliability in the manual.

The ACHI is an instrument designed to identify individuals who are chemically dependent. It is easy to administer and can be taken on a computer allowing for quick scoring and interpretation. Although the instrument appears to have an adequate ability to discriminate substance users from nonusers, a number of annoying problems exist. The manual is difficult to use and appears to have been constructed in a fragmented way. Information regarding the norming samples was extremely hard to follow and terms such as face validity and construct validity appear incorrectly used. The manual is not integrated into a coherent format, omits key pieces of information (such as the years when the validation studies were completed), and includes conflicting pieces of information. Numbers do not add up and clear explanations regarding missing data are not included. Although not conceptually problematic, numerous misspellings and typographical errors are distracting.

The computer-assisted feature is appealing but the software is outdated. The software included with the instrument was available on a 5.25-inch floppy disk that will run only on older IBM or compatible PCs. Most 486 and Pentium computers cannot use the current disk included in the package. The directions assume that the computer boots up on a floppy drive, which is not consistent with most modern computers and, overall, instructions were not easily generalizable to different computer setups. The authors would be encouraged to include both size disks (3.5-inch and 5.25-inch) with the test manual and it would be useful to have Windows, DOS, and Macintosh versions available.

In spite of the annoying problems related to this instrument the instrument appears to have been reasonably well constructed. Although norming information is confusing, it does seem that the instrument is effective in discriminating between users and nonusers a majority of the time. Problems related to "faking good" exist with this instrument as they do with other measures of this type, and it is unlikely that the ACHI has overcome this difficult problem. Overall, this instrument appears to have value in identifying those who are chemically dependent as well as determining possible family, social, or emotional factors that may be negatively impacting upon the individual. Revising the manual, integrating and extending the norming information, and updating the computer software would enhance this instrument's utility.

[8]
Auditory Continuous Performance Test.

Purpose: "Designed to help ... identify children who have auditory attention disorders ... Also yields information that will help diagnose children as having Attention Deficit/Hyperactivity Disorder."

Population: Ages 6–0 to 11–11.

Publication Date: 1994.

Acronym: ACPT.

Scores, 4: Inattention Errors, Impulsivity Errors, Total Error Score, Vigilance Decrement.

Administration: Individual.

Price Data, 1995: $75 per complete kit including examiner's manual (52 pages), test audiocassette, and 12 record forms; $11 per 12 record forms; $32 per examiner's manual; $40 per 1 test audiocassette.

Time: (15) minutes.

Author: Robert W. Keith.

Publisher: The Psychological Corporation.

Review of the Auditory Continuous Performance Test by NADEEN L. KAUFMAN, Professor of Clinical Psychology, California School of Professional Psychology, San Diego, CA and ALAN S. KAUFMAN, Senior Research Scientist, Psychological Assessment Resources, Inc. (PAR), Odessa, FL:

The Auditory Continuous Performance Test (ACPT) is an individually administered, continuous performance test, given by audiocassette, that is normed for children ages 6 years 0 months to 11 years 11 months. It is an auditory vigilance task that was developed to measure children's auditory skills "to help you determine if an attention problem is one of the underlying factors contributing to a child's learning problems" (examiner's manual, p. 1). The ACPT was intended to measure auditory attention, as distinct from auditory processing skills, which the author claims can be measured with his 1986 test, SCAN: A Screening Test for Auditory Processing Disorders (T4:2336). The author indicates in the Introduction that differential diagnosis between auditory attentional problems and auditory processing deficiencies is important, and can be conducted by comparing test results on the ACPT and SCAN; he does not, however, offer guidelines for making such a comparison or provide joint data on the two tests.

In addition to identifying children with auditory attention disorders, the "ACPT also yields information that will help diagnose children as having Attention Deficit/Hyperactivity Disorder (ADHD)" (examiner's manual, p. 1). Indeed, the use of the ACPT for ADHD assessment is so pervasive throughout the brief manual that even the two possible scores a child can obtain on the ACPT (Pass or Fail) are defined in terms of ADHD. For example, "Fail" is defined as follows: "The score obtained is most similar to the scores of children in the standardization sample who were identified as having ADHD" (examiner's manual, p. 7). In fact, that statement makes no sense at all because the standardization sample is subsequently defined as "children between the ages of 6 and 11 years who had not been diagnosed as having ADHD" (examiner's manual, p. 27). Such carelessness is common in this manual, which begins with a misspelled Foreword ("Forward").

Additional purposes of the ACPT are for verifying "a clinician's or teacher's observations of poor attending behaviors," measuring "the effects of behavioral modification programs," and "the effects of stimulant medication" for children diagnosed as having ADHD, and as a research tool for differentiating "children who have learning disabilities or language disorders from children who have central auditory processing disorders" (examiner's manual, pp. 1–2). None of these purposes are addressed in the section on validity. Whereas parent's ratings of attention are compared to ACPT scores, no ratings by teachers or clinicians are provided. Similarly, an ADHD sample was tested on the ACPT, but no data are presented on the effects of behavior modification programs or stimulant medication. And no data are offered on the ACPT scores of children with known learning problems or with any exceptionality other than ADHD. In general, the author shows little awareness of the burgeoning research on ADHD or understanding of the prevalence of the comorbidities that exist within the ADHD population.

The ACPT requires the child to listen to an audiocassette tape of a man who speaks rapidly and in a monotone, but with a pleasant voice and good articulation. The man says a 96-word list of 20 common monosyllables (e.g., room, drop, else, five); he then repeats, without pausing, the same 96-word list an additional five times. The six trials take about 11 minutes; an extra 4 minutes are needed for set-up and a brief warm-up exercise for an estimated total testing time of 15 minutes. The child is listening for a single target word (dog) that appears 20 times per 96-word trial, and responds to each target word by raising his or her thumb. Children can make either errors of Inattention (not giving a "thumbs up" to dog) or Impulsivity (giving a "thumbs up" to a wrong word). The Total Error Score equals the sum of these two types of errors, and this score is converted to Pass or Fail based on a norms-based criterion score that ranges from 38 errors required to fail at age 6 years to only 16 errors at ages 10–11. Examiners also compute a Vigilance Decrement Score for each child, which equals the number of correct "dog" responses on Trial 1 minus the number of correct "dog" responses on Trial 6. Unusual Vigilance Decrement Scores are appropriately determined from distributions of such scores; those decrements that occur less than 10% of the time in the normal population are considered unusual.

Although administration of the ACPT is easy, scoring is not. The voice on the tape speaks so rapidly that the *examiner* must be quite vigilant to note each correct or incorrect "thumbs up" on the record form. The notations must be made with extreme rapidity to ensure that the examiner does not miss an incorrect "thumbs up" that follows closely on the heels of a correct response. The examiner's task is made more difficult by an unnecessarily small 5.5 x 8.5-inch record form with small print and small boxes for recording check marks. The objectivity of scoring that is possible with computerized continuous performance tests as the Gordon Diagnostic System (T4:1051), Conner's Rating Scales (T4:636), Test of Variables of Attention (TOVA; Test 99, this volume), or Intermediate Visual and Auditory Continuous Performance Test (IVA, Sandford & Turner, 1994) is just not feasible with an audiocassette administration; neither is the recording of more subtle aspects of the response such as response latency.

The standardization sample, though small (N = 510) is very well stratified by age (85 for each year of age between 6 and 11), gender, race/ethnicity, geographic region, and parent education level. The main concern about the standardization is a change that was made *after* standardization. The word "dark," though included among the list of stimulus words during standardization, was de-

leted from the audiocassette tape when it was revealed that too many normal children confused "dog" with "dark." (No other words sound even remotely like "dog.") Elimination of items based on standardization data is common practice and usually of no particular concern. In this instance, however, the stimulus is like one long 11-minute item. It would seem to make quite a difference whether this long list of words does or does not include a distractor word that is very similar to the target word. One might speculate that elimination of all of the "dark" stimuli would have affected the number of errors of inattention or impulsivity that the children in the norms group made to the other stimuli. The elimination of such an obviously similar-sounding word also raises other questions that are not addressed in the manual: Why were normal children's difficulties with "dark" not noticed during the three pilot studies that preceded standardization? Did the author initially intend to measure auditory processing or discrimination, as well as attention, when the test was originally designed?

Reliability data are meager and unimpressive. The author correctly does not report measures of internal consistency on this one-item test, but the appropriate type of reliability—test-retest—is offered only for 46 7-year-olds (r = .67) and 40 9-year-olds (r = .74). How does one determine the stability for children of other ages? How does one have confidence in test results that suggest inadequate reliability? Why are correlations reported between error scores on the test and retest, when the only scores reported are Pass and Fail? Why are no stability data presented for these categorical scores?

The one construct validity study was quite good, as the author offers data for 220 children diagnosed with ADHD, who were tested off medication, versus data for a sample of 220 normal individuals who were matched on the basis of age, race, and gender. Presumably the latter group was taken from the normative sample, but this was not stated. The mean Total Error Scores for the ADHD sample were significantly higher than the mean scores for normal children, and the mean Vigilance Decrement Scores were significantly higher for ADHD children for each age except 11. However, the author does not indicate whether the differences in Total Error Scores were significant for each age or for the total sample, or whether an appropriate correction was made for multiple comparisons in either analysis. A discriminant analysis was also conducted with these samples, and the resultant hit rates of 68% to 76% (median = 69%) are not particularly impressive. The values are inflated to some extent by the experimental design; the author investigated three different criterion scores and only reported data for the one that produced the best discrimination. Also, no mention is made whether or not the percents obtained for each age were significantly better than chance.

The one concurrent validity study used a curious choice of criterion: the six-item Attention Scale on the Devereux Scales of Mental Disorders. The Devereux is not frequently used for ADHD populations, whereas other checklists, such as Conners' or Achenbach's behavior rating scales, are commonly used in ADHD research and include reliable attentional scales.

Overall, the ACPT has the advantage of measuring auditory attention, in contrast to the numerous available measures of visual attention. The ACPT has better norms than most computerized continuous performance tests, but the norms for the ACPT are compromised by a substantial change from the standardization to the final version of the test (deleting the word "dark," which closely resembled the target word "dog"). Scoring is subjective because of the human error that is introduced by the audiocassette format, and this format also cannot take advantage of computer technology, which permits recording of response latencies. Reliability data for the ACPT are largely lacking, and the data that are presented indicate inadequate stability of the error scores. A good construct validation study of ADHD children was conducted, but the analyses were not reported in sufficient detail to permit full evaluation of the construct validity.

For examiners who wish to evaluate children's attention, the various computerized continuous performance tests such as the Gordon, TOVA, Conners, and IVA are to be preferred to the ACPT. If auditory attention is an important aspect of the assessment, then examiners are encouraged to use the IVA (which alternates auditory with visual stimuli and gives separate scores and comparisons for each) instead of the ACPT.

REVIEWER'S REFERENCE

Sanford, J. A., & Turner, A. (1994). Intermediate Visual and Auditory Continuous Performance Test. Richmond, VA: Braintrain.

Review of the Auditory Continuous Performance Test by JOSEPH G. LAW, JR., Associate Professor of Behavioral Studies and Educational Technology, University of South Alabama, Mobile, AL:

The Auditory Continuous Performance Test (ACPT) was developed in order to provide a standardized tool for assessing auditory attention problems. The author's hope was to improve differentiation of children with auditory figure-ground problems from those with Attention Deficit/Hyperactivity Disorder (ADHD). The ACPT consists of tape-recorded stimuli that are presented to the child. In each of the six test presentations 20 monosyllabic words such as *drop* and *low* are repeated and reorganized so that the total items in each presentation is 96. Embedded within these words is the target word, *dog*. The child is asked to raise his or her thumb whenever the target word is presented. A trial word list using the same stimuli is administered up to three times in order to verify the child correctly understands the instructions prior to actual testing.

The manual contains specific examples and directions for administration of both the trial and test word lists. One-page folded record forms, an audio cassette, and the examiner's manual are provided in the test kit. The ACPT is quite easy to administer and to score. Impulsivity and Inattention errors are summed to make an error score that is then placed on the first page of the record form. The criterion scores for the child's age group is obtained from a table on the front page of the record form. The child's success is noted by circling either the words *Pass* or *Fail* on the cover.

The format of the record form enables easy recording of demographic information, the child's correct responses and errors, as well as analysis of inattention and impulsivity errors. There is adequate room to make behavioral observations, record the results of prior hearing tests, and keep diagnostic records about prior assessment for ADHD.

The 46-page manual contains 16 pages of information on the design, development, and technical characteristics of the test as well as information on the sample. There were three pilot studies using a total of 48 children in the early development of the ACPT and the standardization group consisted of 510 children aged 6 to 11 years. None had been diagnosed with ADHD. These children were tested at 72 sites and the racial and ethnic proportions of the sample regarding whites, African-Americans, Hispanics and others was roughly equivalent to that of the 1990 census. There were six age levels from 6 years 0 months to 11 years 11 months and 85 children in each of the six age ranges.

To establish cutoff scores, 220 of the children in the standardization sample were compared to a like number who were diagnosed as having ADHD. These children were matched on the basis of gender, race, and age. Those who were taking stimulant medication were tested when not on medicine. A signal detection model was used in a discriminant analysis to determine the number of hits, misses, correct rejections, and false alarms. The ACPT accurately discriminated between children with and without ADHD about 70% of the time for all ages combined. The rate at which the ACPT incorrectly placed ADHD children in the pass category ranged from 18% to 29%. The overall rate at which the normal students were mislabeled as having ADHD was 2% to 8%.

Validity studies are reported in the manual. For 528 children tested, correlations between the Attention scale of the child form of the Devereux Scales of Mental Disorders and the ACPT averaged .41, indicating a moderately strong relationship between the two instruments. In another study, Keith and Engineer (1991) studied 20 children diagnosed with ADHD and found the ACPT to be very sensitive to the effects of stimulant medication.

A test-retest reliability study of 86 children is reported. The between-test interval averaged 5.9 days. Test retest reliability for 46 children aged 7 to 7 years 11 months was .67 and for children ranging from 9 years to 9 years 11 months was .74. Unfortunately, such data for children older than 10 years of age were not included.

This is a promising new test of auditory attention. It has better documentation of reliability and validity in the manual than the Auditory Discrimination and Attention Test (Carey, 1995) and considerably more test items. Test-retest reliability seems adequate for the ages tested. Norms and technical data reported in the manual are adequate.

The ACPT is a short, easily administered test with good psychometric properties. The upper age limit of 11 years 11 months limits its use to a certain extent. How well it correlates with visual continuous performance tests in the assessment of ADHD is an empirical question much in need of research. Although it promises to be an excellent research and clinical instrument, more research on its validity is needed before routine use for diagnosis or assessment of treatment effectiveness in clinical populations.

REVIEWER'S REFERENCES

Keith, R. W., & Engineer, P. (1991). Effects of methylphenidate on the auditory processing abilities of children with attention deficit-hyperactivity disorder. *Journal of Learning Disabilities, 24*(10), 630–636.

Carey, K. T. (1995). [Review of the Auditory Discrimination and Attention Test.] In J. C. Conoley & J. C. Impara (Eds.), *The twelfth mental measurements yearbook* (p. 40). Lincoln, NE: Buros Institute of Mental Measurements.

[9]
Beck Anxiety Inventory [1993 Edition].

Purpose: "Measures the severity of anxiety in adults and adolescents."

Population: Adults and adolescents.

Publication Dates: 1987–1993.

Acronym: BAI.

Scores: Total score only.

Administration: Group or individual.

Price Data, 1994: $46 per complete kit including 25 record forms and manual ('93, 23 pages); $25.50 per 25 record forms; $22.50 per manual.

Foreign Language Edition: Also available in Spanish.

Time: (5–10) minutes.

Authors: Aaron T. Beck and Robert A. Steer.

Publisher: The Psychological Corporation.

Cross References: See T4:267 (2 references).

TEST REFERENCES

1. Livneh, H. (1988). Assessing outcome criteria in rehabilitation: A multicomponent approach. *Rehabilitation Counseling Bulletin, 32,* 72–94.

2. Sokol, L., Beck, A. T., Greenberg, R. L., Wright, F. D., & Berchick, R. J. (1989). Cognitive therapy of panic disorder: A nonpharmacological alternative. *The Journal of Nervous and Mental Disease, 177,* 711–716.

3. Middleton, H. C. (1990). An enhanced hypotensive response to clonidine can still be found in panic patients despite psychological treatment. *Journal of Anxiety Disorders, 4,* 213–219.

4. Middleton, H. C. (1990). Cardiovascular dystonia in recovered panic patients. *Journal of Affective Disorders, 19,* 229–236.

5. Beck, A. T., & Steer, R. A. (1991). Relationship between the Beck Anxiety Inventory and the Hamilton Anxiety Rating Scale with anxious outpatients. *Journal of Anxiety Disorders, 5,* 213–223.

6. Dyck, M. J. (1991). Positive and negative attitudes mediating suicide ideation. *Suicide and Life-Threatening Behavior, 21,* 360–373.

7. Clark, D. B., Leslie, M. I., & Jacob, R. G. (1992). Balance complaints and panic disorder: A clinical study of panic symptoms in members of a self-help group for balance disorders. *Journal of Anxiety Disorders, 6,* 47-53.

8. Fydrich, T., Dowdall, D., & Chambless, D. L. (1992). Reliability and validity of the Beck Anxiety Inventory. *Journal of Anxiety Disorders, 6,* 55-61.

9. Otto, M. W., Pollack, M. H., Sachs, G. S., & Rosenbaum, J. F. (1992). Hypochondriacal concerns, anxiety, sensitivity, and panic disorder. *Journal of Anxiety Disorders, 6,* 93-104.

10. Öst, L. G., Hellström, K., & Kåver, A. (1992). One versus five sessions of exposure in the treatment of injection phobia. *Behavior Therapy, 23,* 263–282.

11. Borden, J. W., Lowenbraun, P. B., Wolff, P. L., & Jones, A. (1993). Self-focused attention in panic disorder. *Cognitive Therapy and Research, 17*, 413-425.

12. Gidycz, C. A., Coble, C. N., Latham, L., & Layman, M. J. (1993). Sexual assault experience in adulthood and prior victimization experiences. *Psychology of Women Quarterly, 17*, 151-168.

13. Jacob, R. G., Woody, S. R., Clark, D. B., Lilienfeld, S. O., Hirsch, B. E., Kucera, G. D., Furman, J. M., & Durrant, J. D. (1993). Discomfort with space and motion: A possible marker for vestibular dysfunction assessed by the Situational Characteristics Questionnaire. *Journal of Psychopathology and Behavioral Assessment, 15*, 299-324.

14. Jolly, J. B. (1993). A multi-method test of the cognitive content-specificity hypothesis in young adolescents. *Journal of Anxiety Disorders, 7*, 223-233.

15. Jolly, J. B., Aruffo, J. F., Wherry, J. N., & Livingston, R. (1993). The utility of the Beck Anxiety Inventory with inpatient adolescents. *Journal of Anxiety Disorders, 7*, 95-106.

16. Osman, A., Barrios, F. X., Aukes, D., Osman, J. R., & Markway, K. (1993). The Beck Anxiety Inventory: Psychometric properties in a community population. *Journal of Psychopathology and Behavioral Assessment, 15*, 287-297.

17. Steer, R. A., Ranieri, W. F., Beck, A. T., & Clark, D. A. (1993). Further evidence for the validity of the Beck Anxiety Inventory with psychiatric outpatients. *Journal of Anxiety Disorders, 7*, 195-205.

18. Beck, J. G., & Zebb, B. J. (1994). Behavioral assessment and treatment of panic disorder: Current status, future directions. *Behavior Therapy, 25*, 581-611.

19. Borden, J. W. (1994). Panic disorder and suicidality: Prevalence and risk factors. *Journal of Anxiety Disorders, 8*, 217-225.

20. Brown, H. D., Kosslyn, J. M., Breiter, H. C., Baer, L., & Jenike, M. A. (1994). Can patients with obsessive-compulsive disorder discriminate between percepts and mental images? A signal detection analysis. *Journal of Abnormal Psychology, 103*, 445-454.

21. Burgess, E., & Haaga, D. A. F. (1994). The Positive Automatic Thoughts Questionnaire (ATQ-P) and the Automatic Thoughts Questionnaire—Revised (ATQ-RP): Equivalent measures of positive thinking? *Cognitive Therapy and Research, 18*, 15-23.

22. Clark, D. A., Beck, A. T., & Beck, J. S. (1994). Symptom differences in major depression, dysthymia, panic disorder, and generalized anxiety disorder. *American Journal of Psychiatry, 151*, 205-209.

23. Clark, D. A., Steer, R. A., & Beck, A. T. (1994). Common and specific dimensions of self-reported anxiety and depression: Implications for the cognitive and tripartite models. *Journal of Abnormal Psychology, 103*, 645-654.

24. Clark, D. M., Salkovskis, P. M., Hackmann, A., Middleton, H., Anastasiades, P., & Gelder, M. (1994). A comparison of cognitive therapy, applied relaxation and imipramine in the treatment of panic disorder. *British Journal of Psychiatry, 164*, 759-769.

25. Cox, B. J., Direnfeld, D. M., Swinson, R. P., & Norton, G. R. (1994). Suicidal ideation and suicide attempts in panic disorder and social phobia. *American Journal of Psychiatry, 151*, 882-887.

26. Durham, R. C., Murphy, T., Allan, T., Richard, K., Treliving, L. R., & Fenton, G. W. (1994). Cognitive therapy, analytic psychotherapy and anxiety management training for generalized anxiety disorder. *British Journal of Psychiatry, 165*, 315-323.

27. Goldstein, A. J., & Feske, U. (1994). Eye movement desensitization and reprocessing for panic disorder: A case series. *Journal of Anxiety Disorders, 8*, 351-362.

28. Joiner, T. E., Jr. (1994). Contagious depression: Existence, specificity to depressed symptoms, and the role of reassurance seeking. *Journal of Personality and Social Psychology, 67*, 287-296.

29. Jolly, J. B., Dyck, M. J., Kramer, T. A., & Wherry, J. N. (1994). Integration of positive and negative affectivity and cognitive content-specificity: Improved discrimination of anxious and depressive symptoms. *Journal of Abnormal Psychology, 103*, 544-552.

30. Jolly, J. B., & Dykman, R. A. (1994). Using self-report data to differentiate anxious and depressive symptoms in adolescents: Cognitive content specificity and global distress? *Cognitive Therapy and Research, 18*, 25-37.

31. Jolly, J. B., & Kramer, T. A. (1994). The hierarchical arrangement of internalizing cognitions. *Cognitive Therapy and Research, 18*, 1-14.

32. Kaspi, S. P., Otto, M. W., Pollack, M. H., Eppinger, S., & Rosenbaum, J. F. (1994). Premenstrual exacerbation of symptoms in women with panic disorder. *Journal of Anxiety Disorders, 8*, 131-138.

33. Khawaja, N. G., Oei, T. P. S., & Baglioni, A. J. (1994). Modification of the catastrophic cognitions questionnaire (CCQ-M) for normals and patients: Exploratory and LISREL analyses. *Journal of Psychopathology and Behavioral Assessment, 16*, 325-342.

34. Lecci, L., Karoly, P., Briggs, C., & Kuhn, K. (1994). Specificity and generality of motivational components in depression: A personal projects analysis. *Journal of Abnormal Psychology, 103*, 404-408.

35. McDermut, W., & Haaga, D. A. F. (1994). Cognitive balance and specificity in anxiety and depression. *Cognitive Therapy and Research, 18*, 333-352.

36. Rifai, A. H., George, C. J., Stack, J. A., Mann, J. J., & Reynolds, C. F. (1994). Hopelessness in suicide attempters after acute treatment of major depression in late life. *American Journal of Psychiatry, 151*, 1687-1690.

37. Sobell, L. C., Toneatto, T., & Sobell, M. (1994). Behavioral assessment and treatment planning for alcohol, tobacco, and other drug problems: Current status with an emphasis on clinical applications. *Behavior Therapy, 25*, 533-580.

38. Solomon, A., & Haaga, P. A. F. (1994). Positive and negative aspects of sociotropy and autonomy. *Journal of Psychopathology and Behavioral Assessment, 16*, 243-252.

39. Steer, R. A., Clark, D. A., & Ranieri, W. F. (1994). Symptom dimensions of the SCL-90-R: A test of the tripartite model of anxiety and depression. *Journal of Personality Assessment, 62*, 525-536.

40. Stein, M. B., Asmundson, G. J. G., Ireland, D., & Walker, J. R. (1994). Panic disorder in patients attending a clinic for vestibular disorders. *American Journal of Psychiatry, 151*, 1697-1700.

41. Alford, B. A., & Gerrity, D. M. (1995). The specificity of sociotropy-autonomy personality dimensions to depression vs. anxiety. *Journal of Clinical Psychology, 51*, 190-195.

42. Alford, B. A., Lester, J. M., Patel, R. J., Buchanan, J. P., & Giunta, L. C. (1995). Hopelessness predicts future depressive symptoms: A prospective analysis of cognitive vulnerability and cognitive content specificity. *Journal of Clinical Psychology, 51*, 331-339.

43. Carter, A. S., Grigorenko, E. L., & Pauls, D. L. (1995). A Russian adaptation of the Child Behavior Checklist: Psychometric properties and associations with child and maternal affective symptomatology and family functioning. *Journal of Abnormal Child Psychology, 23*, 661-684.

44. Dugas, M. J., Letarte, H., Rheaume, J., Freeston, M. H., & Ladouceur, R. (1995). Worry and problem solving: Evidence of a specific relationship. *Cognitive Therapy and Research, 19*, 109-120.

45. Freeston, M. H., Ladouceur, R., Provencher, M., & Blais, F. (1995). Strategies used with intrusive thoughts: Context, appraisal, mood, and efficacy. *Journal of Anxiety Disorders, 9*, 201-215.

46. Gidcyz, C. A., Hanson, K., & Layman, M. J. (1995). A prospective analysis of the relationships among sexual assault experiences. *Psychology of Women Quarterly, 19*, 5-29.

47. Gillis, M. M., Haaga, D. A. F., & Ford, G. T. (1995). Normative values for the Beck Anxiety Inventory, Fear Questionnaire, Penn State Worry Questionnaire, and Social Phobia and Anxiety Inventory. *Psychological Assessment, 7*, 450-455.

48. Haaga, D. A. F., Fine, J. A., Terrill, D. R., Stewart, B. L., & Beck, A. J. (1995). Social problem-solving deficits, dependency, and depressive symptoms. *Cognitive Therapy and Research, 19*, 147-158.

49. Joiner, T. E. (1995). The price of soliciting and receiving negative feedback: Self-verification theory as a vulnerability to depression theory. *Journal of Abnormal Psychology, 104*, 364-372.

50. Kumar, G., & Steer, R. A. (1995). Psychosocial correlates of suicidal ideation in adolescent psychiatric inpatients. *Suicide and Life-Threatening Behavior, 25*, 339-346.

51. Neron, S., Lacroix, D., & Chaput, Y. (1995). Group vs. Individual cognitive behaviour therapy in panic disorder: An open clinical trial with a six month follow-up. *Canadian Journal of Behavioural Science, 27*, 379-392.

52. Pawluk, L. K., Hurwitz, T. D., Schluter, J. L., Ullevig, C., & Mahowald, M. W. (1995). Psychiatric morbidity in narcoleptics on chronic high dose methylphenidate therapy. *The Journal of Nervous and Mental Disease, 183*, 45-48.

53. Reynolds, W. M., & Kobak, K. A. (1995). Reliability and validity of the Hamilton Depression Inventory: A paper-and-pencil version of the Hamilton Depression Rating Scale clinical interview. *Psychological Assessment, 7*, 472-483.

54. Riley, W. T., McCormick, M. G. F., Simon, E. M., Stack, K., Pushkin, Y., Overstreet, M. M., Carmona, J. J., & Magakian, C. (1995). Effects of alprazolam doses on the induction and habituation processes during behavioral panic induction treatment. *Journal of Anxiety Disorders, 9*, 217-227.

55. Romach, M., Busto, U., Somer, G., Kaplan, H. L., & Sellers, E. (1995). Clinical aspects of chronic use of alprazolam and lorazepan. *American Journal of Psychiatry, 152*, 1161-1167.

56. Steer, R. A., Beck, A. T., & Beck, J. S. (1995). Sex effect sizes of the Beck Anxiety Inventory for psychiatric outpatients matched by age and principal disorders. *Assessment, 2*, 31-38.

57. Steer, R. A., Clark, D. A., Beck, A. T., & Ranieri, W. F. (1995). Common and specific dimensions of self-reported anxiety and depression: A replication. *Journal of Abnormal Psychology, 104*, 542-545.

58. Steer, R. A., Kumar, G., Ranieri, W. F., & Beck, A. T. (1995). Use of the Beck Anxiety Inventory with adolescent psychiatric outpatients. *Psychological Reports, 76*, 459-465.

59. Stein, M. B., Kirk, P., Prabhu, V., Grott, M., & Terepa, M. (1995). Mixed anxiety-depression in a primary-care clinic. *Journal of Affective Disorders, 34*, 79-84.

60. Watson, D., Weber, K., Assenheimer, J. S., Clark, L. A., Strauss, M. E., & McCormick, R. A. (1995). Testing a tripartite model: I. Evaluating convergent and discriminant validity of Anxiety and Depression Symptom Scales. *Journal of Abnormal Psychology, 104*, 3-14.

61. Horowitz, M., Sonneborn, D., Sugahara, C., & Maercker, A. (1996). Self-regard: A new measure. *American Journal of Psychiatry, 153*, 382-385.

62. Jacob, R. G., Furman, J. M., Durrant, J. D., & Turner, S. M. (1996). Panic, agoraphobia, and vestibular dysfunction. *American Journal of Psychiatry, 153*, 503-512.

63. Stein, M. B., Baird, A., & Walker, J. R. (1996). Social phobia in adults with stuttering. *American Journal of Psychiatry, 153*, 278-280.

64. Taylor, S., Koch, W. J., Woody, S., & McLean, P. (1996). Anxiety sensitivity and depression: How are they related? *Journal of Abnormal Psychology, 105*, 474-479.

65. Trappler, B., & Friedman, S. (1996). Posttraumatic stress disorder in survivors of the Brooklyn Bridge shooting. *American Journal of Psychiatry, 153,* 705–707.

Review of the Beck Anxiety Inventory by E. THOMAS DOWD, Professor of Psychology, Kent State University, Kent, OH:

Aaron T. Beck, M.D., and his associates have designed well-constructed and widely-used tests for years, with the twin virtues of simplicity and brevity. The Beck Anxiety Inventory (BAI) is no exception. At 21 items, it is certainly short and easy to understand as well. Each of the 21 items represents an anxiety symptom that is rated for severity on a 4-point Likert scale (0–3), ranging from *Not at all* to *Severely; I could barely stand it.* The scoring is easy, as the points for each item are simply added to form the total score.

The test kit I received contained a brief manual, several answer sheets for the BAI as well as for the BDI and the BHS, and a complete computer-scoring package. Although not stated as such, I suspect that the instrument can be ordered without the computer scoring package.

The manual, which is quite short, appears to have been written for a clinician rather than a researcher. The guidelines for administration and scoring are quite adequate, as are the data on reliability and validity. But the description of the scale development is inadequate, as it refers the reader to the original Beck, Epstein, Brown, and Steer (1988) article. In addition, the descriptions of other studies on the instrument are unacceptably brief.

The BAI was originally developed from a sample of 810 outpatients of mixed diagnostic categories (predominantly mood and anxiety disorders). Two successive factor analyses on different samples then reduced the number of items to 21, with a minimum item-total correlation of .30. The original development appears to have been very well done and is described in detail in Beck et al. (1988).

The reliability and validity data are thorough and informative but are based only on three studies: Beck et al. (1988), Fydrich, Dowdall, and Chambless (1990), and Dent and Salkovskis (1986). Of these, the first used a mixed diagnostic group, the second used patients diagnosed with *DSM-III-R* anxiety disorders, and the third used a nonclinical sample. The manual authors quite appropriately caution the reader the instrument was developed on a psychiatric population and should be interpreted cautiously with nonclinical individuals. The normative data tables are very thorough and informative, including means, standard deviations, coefficient alpha reliabilities, and corrected item-total correlations for five anxiety diagnostic groups with the highest representation in the sample. This apparently unpublished clinical sample consists of 393 outpatients who were seen at the Center for Cognitive Therapy in Philadelphia between January 1985 and August 1989.

Internal consistency reliability coefficients are uniformly excellent, ranging between .85 and .94. Test-retest reliability data from Beck et al. (1988) showed a coefficient of .75 over one week. The validity data are quite comprehensive, including content, concurrent, construct, discriminant, and factorial validity. In general, the data show excellent validity, even regarding the difficult problem of untangling anxiety and depression. Especially interesting to this reviewer were the factorial validity data. One factor analysis (Beck et al., 1988) found two factors ($r = .56$, $p < .001$) that seemed to reflect somatic and cognitive/affective aspects of anxiety, respectively. A cluster analysis on the clinical sample showed four clusters that are labeled Neurophysiological, Subjective, Panic, and Autonomic. The separate clusters showed acceptable reliability, considering the small number of items in each, and discriminant function analyses found some significant differences among the clusters.

Two demographic variables, gender and age, appear to be significantly related to anxiety. Women were found to be more anxious than men and younger people were found to be more anxious than older people. Because of this, the authors caution users to adjust scores somewhat on interpretation, though how much is a little vague.

As I mentioned earlier, a computer-scoring package came with the BAI, including large and small disks and a very detailed instruction manual. According to the manual, this package provides three modes of test administration and interpretive profiles for the Beck Depression Inventory (BDI; Test 10, this volume), The Beck Hopelessness Scale (BHS; T4:269), the Beck Anxiety Inventory (BAI; Test 9, this volume), and the Beck Scale for Suicide Ideation (BSSI; T4:270) separately and together. The profile includes clinical group references and a history of the patient's scores on previous administrations, in addition to data on that test. However, the package I received (as indicated in the manual and the README file) included only the separate profile reports and the BDI, BAI, and BHS. A note at the end of the manual suggested that some of this material would not be available until December 1992, so apparently I received an older version of the computer-scoring package. [Editor's note: A 1994 version of the computer-scoring package is now available and produces integrative narrative reports.] Scoring of each test is not free once the package has been purchased. Credits must be purchased for the Use Counter (included) that is installed between the computer and the printer.

In summary, the Beck Anxiety Inventory is another of the useful instruments designed by Beck and his colleagues. There are only a few deficits. First, the manual is too brief to give as much information as many users might like (though the computer scoring manual is very comprehensive). Second, there have been too few studies conducted on the BAI, with the result that it rests on an uncomfortably small data base. This is particularly apparent for the gender and age differences. The clusters of anxiety disorders identified thus far appear to be especially promising and further research should be conducted here. Clinicians, however, will find this a very useful test, especially when combined with the other Beck instruments into a comprehensive computer-scored interpretive profile.

REVIEWER'S REFERENCES

Dent, H. R., & Salkovskis, P. M. (1986). Clinical measures of depression, anxiety and obsessionality in nonclinical populations. *Behavioral Research and Therapy, 24*, 689–691.

Beck, A. T., Epstein, N., Brown, G., & Steer, R. A. (1988). An inventory for measuring clinical anxiety: Psychometric properties. *Journal of Consulting and Clinical Psychology, 56*, 893–897.

Fydrich, T., Dowdall, D., & Chambless, D. L. (1990, March). *Aspects of reliability and validity for the Beck Anxiety Inventory.* Paper presented at the National Conference on Phobias and Related Anxiety Disorders, Bethesda, MD.

Review of the Beck Anxiety Inventory by NIELS G. WALLER, Associate Professor of Psychology, University of California, Davis, CA:

While describing the development of the Beck Anxiety Inventory, Beck et al. (Beck, Epstein, Brown, & Steer, 1988) note that a number of studies have reported correlations greater than .50 between widely used anxiety and depression scales. Similar findings have been reported by others (Lovibond & Lovibond, 1995), and formal reviews of this topic (Clark & Watson, 1991; Dobson,

1985) conclude that anxiety and depression scales frequently correlate between .40 and .70. No one expects these scales to be uncorrelated because of the high comorbidity rates of anxiety and mood disorders (Maser & Cloninger, 1990). Yet many researchers (Riskind, Beck, Brown, & Steer, 1987) feel uncomfortable when measures of conceptually distinct constructs correlate as highly as .50.

The Beck Anxiety Inventory (BAI; Beck & Steer, 1990; Beck, Epstein, Brown, & Steer, 1988) is a brief self-report scale that was designed "to measure symptoms of anxiety which are minimally shared with those of depression" (Beck & Steer, 1990, p. 1). The 21 symptoms on the BAI were selected from three existing measures: (a) The Anxiety Check List (Beck, Steer, & Brown, 1985), (b) the PDR Check List (Beck, 1978), and (c) the Situational Anxiety Check List (Beck, 1982). The item pools of these scales were combined and winnowed using Jackson's (1970) method of scale construction. After eliminating identical or highly similar items, Beck and his colleagues used factor analysis to cull items for the final scale. Scales that are developed by this method often have high reliabilities, and coefficient alpha (Cortina, 1993) for the BAI is typically in the mid-.90s (Beck, Epstein, Brown, & Steer, 1988; Jolly, Aruffo, Wherry, & Livingston, 1993; Kumar, Steer, & Beck, 1993).

The BAI items are measured on a 4-point Likert scale that ranges from *Not at all* (0 points) to *Severely; I could barely stand it* (3). The instructions for the test ask subjects to "indicate how much you have been bothered by each symptom during the PAST WEEK, INCLUDING TODAY, by placing an X in the corresponding space in the column next to each symptom" (manual, p. 4). Notice these instructions focus on a 2-week time frame; and consequently, the BAI should measure state anxiety better than trait anxiety. Beck et al. (1988) report a 1-week test-retest correlation of .75 for the BAI, whereas Creamer, Foran, and Bell (1995) report a 7-week correlation of .62.

The factor structure of the BAI has been investigated in clinical (Beck, et al., 1988; Hewitt & Norton, 1993; Kumar et al., 1993) and nonclinical (Creamer et al., 1995) samples. Many studies have found two correlated dimensions (*r* = approximately .55) that have been interpreted as measuring somatic (example markers: *Feelings of choking,*

Shaky) and subjective (example markers: *Fear of the worst happening, Fear of losing control*) symptoms of anxiety. A similar structure emerged in a recent factor analysis of data from the computer-administered BAI (Steer, Rissmiller, Ranieri, & Beck, 1993).

The underlying structure of the BAI has also been investigated with cluster analysis. The BAI manual authors report that a centroid cluster analysis of clinical data uncovered four symptom clusters representing (a) neurophysiological, (b) subjective, (c) panic, and (d) autonomic symptoms of anxiety. Interestingly, a similar structure was uncovered in a recent factor analysis of the scale (Osman, Barrios, Aukes, Osman, & Markway, 1993). Regarding the cluster solution, Beck and Steer (1990) have suggested the cluster subscales "may assist the examiner in making a differential diagnosis" (p. 6) and that "profile analyses of BAI subscales appear promising" (p. 18). In my opinion, neither of these statements is supported by the data. The BAI subscales are highly correlated; consequently, subscale profiles will almost certainly be unreliable for most test takers. For example, from data reported in Table 5 of the BAI manual, it is easy to calculate the reliabilities for the cluster-subscale difference scores. For some of these scores the reliabilities are as low as .50. In other words, it is difficult to obtain reliable profiles when scales are composed of only four or five items.

Because of the goals of the BAI authors, it is appropriate to ask how strongly the BAI correlates with popular depression scales, such as The Beck Depression Inventory (BDI; Beck & Steer, 1993; Test 10, this volume). In clinical samples, correlations between the BAI and BDI have ranged from .48 to .71 (Beck et al., 1988; Fydrich, Dowdall, & Chambless, 1992; Hewitt & Norton, 1993; Steer, Ranieri, Beck, & Clark, 1993). A Bayesian (Iversen, 1984, p. 41–44) posterior estimate for these data suggests that $r = .587$ with a 95% probability that the population correlation lies between .545 and .626. In nonclinical samples (Creamer et al., 1995; Dent & Salkovskis, 1986), correlations between the BAI and BDI have ranged from .50 to .63. The Bayesian estimate of r for these data is .591 with a 95% probability that the population correlation lies between .548 and .631.

In conclusion, it appears that Beck was not successful in developing an anxiety scale with high discriminant validity. Nevertheless, he did develop a highly reliable scale that can be administered in 5 to 10 minutes. Thus, the BAI appears to be a useful addition to the growing number of clinical anxiety measures.

REVIEWER'S REFERENCES

Jackson, D. N. (1970). A sequential system for personality scale development. In C. D. Spielberger (Ed.), *Current topics in clinical and community psychology* (vol. 2, pp. 61–96). New York: Academic Press.

Beck, A. T. (1978). *PDR Check List*. Philadelphia: University of Pennsylvania, Center for Cognitive Therapy.

Beck, A. T. (1982). *Situational Anxiety Check List (SAC)*. Philadelphia: University of Pennsylvania, Center for Cognitive Therapy.

Iversen, G. R. (1984). *Bayesian statistical inference*. Beverly Hills, CA: Sage.

Beck, A. T., Steer, R. A., & Brown, G. (1985). *Beck Anxiety Check List*. Unpublished manuscript, University of Pennsylvania.

Dobson, K. S. (1985). The relationship between anxiety and depression. *Clinical Psychology Review, 5*, 307–324.

Dent, H. R., & Salkovskis, P. M. (1986). Clinical measures of depression, anxiety, and obsessionality in non-clinical populations. *Behaviour Research and Therapy, 24*, 689–691.

Riskind, J. H., Beck, A. T., Brown, G., & Steer, R. A. (1987). Taking the measure of anxiety and depression: Validity of reconstructed Hamilton scales. *Journal of Nervous and Mental Disease, 175*, 475–479.

Beck, A. T., Epstein, N., Brown, G., & Steer, R. A. (1988). An inventory for measuring clinical anxiety: Psychometric properties. *Journal of Consulting & Clinical Psychology, 56*, 893–897.

Beck, A. T., & Steer, R. A. (1990). *Manual for the Beck Anxiety Inventory*. San Antonio, TX: The Psychological Corporation.

Maser, J. D., & Cloninger, C. R. (Eds.). (1990). *Comorbidity of mood and anxiety disorders*. Washington, DC: American Psychiatric Press.

Clark, L. A., & Watson, D. (1991). Theoretical and empirical issues in differentiating depression from anxiety. In J. Becker, & A. Kleinman (Eds.), *Psychosocial aspects of depression*. Hillsdale, NJ: Erlbaum.

Frydrich, T., Dowdall, D., & Chambless, D. L. (1992). Reliability and validity of the Beck Anxiety Inventory. *Journal of Anxiety Disorders, 6*, 55–61.

Beck, A. T., & Steer, R. A. (1993). *Beck Depression Inventory, manual*. San Antonio, TX: The Psychological Corporation.

Cortina, J. M. (1993). What is coefficient alpha? An examination of theory and applications. *Journal of Applied Psychology, 78*, 98–104.

Hewitt, P. L., & Norton, G. R. (1993). The Beck Anxiety Inventory: A psychometric analysis. *Psychological Assessment, 5*, 408–412.

Jolly, J. B., Aruffo, J. F., Wherry, J. N., & Livingston, R. (1993). The utility of the Beck Anxiety Inventory with inpatient adolescents. *Journal of Anxiety Disorders, 7*, 95–106.

Kumar, G., Steer, R. A., & Beck, A. T. (1993). Factor structure of the Beck Anxiety Inventory with adolescent psychiatric inpatients. *Anxiety, Stress, and Coping, 6*, 125–131.

Osman, A., Barrios, F. X., Aukes, D., Osman, J. R., & Markway, K. (1993). The Beck Anxiety Inventory: Psychometric properties in a community population. *Journal of Psychopathology and Behavioral Assessment, 15*, 287–297.

Steer, R. A., Rissmiller, D. J., Ranieri, W. F., & Beck, A. T. (1993). Structure of the computer-assisted Beck Anxiety Inventory with psychiatric inpatients. *Journal of Personality Assessment, 60*, 532–542.

Steer, R. A., Ranieri, W. F., Beck, A. T., & Clark, D. A. (1993). Further evidence for the validity of the Beck Anxiety Inventory with psychiatric outpatients. *Journal of Anxiety Disorders, 7*, 195–205.

Creamer, M., Foran, J., & Bell, R. (1995). The Beck Anxiety Inventory in a non-clinical sample. *Behavior Research and Therapy, 33*, 477–485.

Gillis, M. M., Haaga, D. A. F., & Ford, G. T. (1995). Normative values for the Beck Anxiety Inventory, Fear Questionnaire, Penn State Worry Questionnaire, and Social Phobia and Anxiety Inventory. *Psychological Assessment, 7*, 450–455.

Lovibond, P. F., & Lovibond, S. H. (1995). The structure of negative emotional states: Comparison of the Depression Anxiety Stress Scales (DASS) with the Beck Depression and Anxiety Inventories. *Behaviour and Therapy Research, 33*, 335–343.

[10]

Beck Depression Inventory [1993 Revised].

Purpose: "Designed to assess the severity of depression in adolescents and adults."

Population: Adolescents and adults.

Publication Dates: 1961–1993.

Acronym: BDI.

Scores: Total score only; item score ranges.
Administration: Group or individual.
Price Data, 1994: $46 per complete kit including 25 record forms and manual ('93, 24 pages); $25.50 per 25 record forms; $22.50 per manual.
Foreign Language Edition: Also available in Spanish.
Time: (5–15) minutes.
Authors: Aaron T. Beck and Robert A. Steer.
Publisher: The Psychological Corporation.
Cross References: See T4:268 (660 references); for reviews by Collie W. Conoley and Norman D. Sundberg of a previous edition, see 11:31 (286 references).

TEST REFERENCES

1. Phil, B. M. (1983). Depression and hostility in selfmutilation. *Suicide and Life-Threatening Behavior, 13,* 71– 84.

2. Wallace, J. E., Becker, J., Coppel, D. B., & Cox, G. B. (1983). Anticonformity aspects of depression in mild depressive states. *Journal of Personality, 51,* 640–652.

3. Gilbert, M. J., & Cervantes, R. C. (1986). Patterns and practices of alcohol use among Mexican Americans: A comprehensive review. *Hispanic Journal of Behavioral Sciences, 8,* 1–60.

4. Smith, K., & Crawford, S. (1986). Suicidal behavior among "normal" high school students. *Suicide and Life-Threatening Behavior, 16,* 313–325.

5. Dunn, S. E., Putallaz, M., Sheppard, B. H., & Lindstrom, R. (1987). Social support adjustment in gifted adolescents. *Journal of Educational Psychology, 79,* 467–473.

6. Merkel, W. T., & Wiener, R. L. (1987). A reconsideration of the Willoughby Personality Schedule with psychiatric inpatients. *Journal of Behavior Therapy and Experimental Psychiatry, 18,* 13–18.

7. Prezant, D. W., & Neimeyer, R. A. (1988). Cognitive predictors of depression and suicide ideation. *Suicide and Life-Threatening Behavior, 18,* 259–264.

8. Strauman, T. J., & Higgins, E. T. (1988). Selfdiscrepancies as predictor of vulnerability to distinct syndromes of chronic emotional distress. *Journal of Personality, 56,* 685–707.

9. Arena, J. G., Goldberg, S. J., Saul, D. L., & Hobbs, S. H. (1989). Temporal stability of psychophysiological response profiles: Analysis of individual response stereotypy and stimulus response specificity. *Behavior Therapy, 20,* 609–618.

10. Barlow, D. H., Craske, M. G., Cerny, J. A., & Klasko, J. S. (1989). Behavioral treatment of panic disorder. *Behavior Therapy, 20,* 261–282.

11. Blanchard, E. B., Kolb, L. C., Taylor, A. E., & Wittrock, D. A. (1989). Cardiac response to relevant stimuli as an adjunct in diagnosing post-traumatic stress disorder: Replication and extension. *Behavior Therapy, 20,* 535–543.

12. Blanchard, E. B., McCoy, G. C., Berger, M., Musso, A., Pallmeyer, T. P., Gerardi, J., Gerardi, M. A., & Pangburn, L. (1989). A controlled comparison of thermal biofeedback and relaxation training in the treatment of essential hypertension IV: Prediction of short-term clinical outcome. *Behavior Therapy, 20,* 405–415.

13. Chibnall, J. T., & Tait, R. C. (1989). The Psychosomatic Symptom Checklist revisited: Reliability and validity in a chronic pain population. *Journal of Behavioral Medicine, 12,* 297-307.

14. Clark, L. A., Watson, D., & Leeka, J. (1989). Diurnal variation in the positive affects. *Motivation and Emotion, 13,* 205–234.

15. Cooper, N. A., & Clum, G. A. (1989). Imaginal flooding as a supplementary treatment for PTSD in combat veterans: A controlled study. *Behavior Therapy, 20,* 381–391.

16. Craighead, L. W., & Blum, M. D. (1989). Supervised exercise in behavioral treatment for moderate obesity. *Behavior Therapy, 20,* 49–59.

17. Earls, C. M., & David, H. (1989). A psychosocial study of male prostitution. *Archives of Sexual Behavior, 18,* 401-419.

18. Fantuzzo, J. W., Dimeff, L. A., & Fox, S. L. (1989). Reciprocal peer tutoring: A multimodal assessment of effectiveness with college students. *Teaching of Psychology, 16,* 133-135.

19. Feehan, M., & Marsh, N. (1989). The reduction of bruxism using contingent EMG audible biofeedback: A case study. *Journal of Behavior Therapy and Experimental Psychiatry, 20,* 179–183.

20. Freedman, M., & Oscar-Berman, M. (1989). Spatial and visual learning deficits in Alzheimer's and Parkinson's disease. *Brain and Cognition, 11,* 114-126.

21. Gannen, L., & Pardie, L. (1989). The importance of chronicity and controllability of stress in the context of stress-illness relationships. *Journal of Behavioral Medicine, 12,* 357-372.

22. Joffe, R. T., & Regan, J. J. (1989). Personality and response to tricyclic antidepressants in depressed patients. *The Journal of Nervous and Mental Disease, 177,* 745-749.

23. Johnson, C., Tobin, D., & Enright, A. (1989). Prevalence and clinical characteristics of borderline patients in an eatingdisordered population. *The Journal of Clinical Psychiatry, 50,* 9–15.

24. Keane, T. M., Fairbank, J. A., Caddell, J. M., & Zimering, R. T. (1989). Implosive (flooding) therapy reduces symptoms of PTSD in Vietnam combat veterans. *Behavior Therapy, 20,* 245– 260.

25. Kennedy, S. H., Craven, J. L., & Roin, G. M. (1989). Major depression in renal dialysis patients: An open trial of antidepressant therapy. *The Journal of Clinical Psychiatry, 50,* 60–63.

26. King, A. C., Taylor, C. B., Haskell, W. L., & DeBusk, R. F. (1989). Influence of regular aerobic exercise on psychological health: A randomized, controlled trial of healthy middle-aged adults. *Health Psychology, 8,* 305–324.

27. LaKey, B. (1989). Personal and environmental antecedents of perceived social support developed at college. *American Journal of Community Psychology, 17,* 503-519.

28. Lahmeyer, H. W., Reynolds, C. F., III, Kupfer, D. J., & King, R. (1989). Biologic markers in borderline personality disorder: A review. *The Journal of Clinical Psychiatry, 50,* 217–225.

29. Louks, J., Hayne, C., & Smith, J. (1989). Replicated factor structure of the Beck Depression Inventory. *The Journal of Nervous and Mental Disease, 177,* 473-479.

30. Lynch, P. M., & Zamble, E. (1989). A controlled behavioral treatment study of Irritable Bowel Syndrome. *Behavior Therapy, 20,* 509–523.

31. Marmar, C. R., Gaston, L., Gallagher, D., & Thompson, L. W. (1989). Alliance and outcome in late-life depression. *The Journal of Nervous and Mental Disease, 177,* 464-472.

32. Marsh, K. L., & Weary, G. (1989). Depression and attributional complexity. *Personality and Social Psychology Bulletin, 15,* 325–336.

33. McNamee, G., O'Sullivan, G., Lelliott, P., & Marks, I. (1989). Telephone-guided treatment for housebound agoraphobics with panic disorder: Exposure vs. relaxation. *Behavior Therapy, 20,* 491–497.

34. Miller, I. W., Norman, W. H., Keitner, G. I., Bishop, S. B., & Dow, M. G. (1989). Cognitive-behavioral treatment of depressed inpatients. *Behavior Therapy, 20,* 25–47.

35. Niederche, G., & Yoder, C. (1899). Metamemory perceptions in depressions of young and older adults. *The Journal of Nervous and Mental Disease, 177,* 4-14.

36. Otto, M. W., Dougher, M. J., & Yeo, R. A. (1989). Depression, pain, and hemispheric activation. *The Journal of Nervous and Mental Disease, 177,* 210-218.

37. Sachs, G. S., Gelenberg, A. J., Bellinghausen, B., Wojcik, J., Falk, W. E., Farhadi, A. M., & Jenike, M. (1989). Ergoloid mesylates and ECT. *The Journal of Clinical Psychiatry, 50,* 87–90.

38. Schmidt, U., & Marks, I. M. (1989). Exposure plus prevention of bingeing vs. exposure plus prevention of vomiting in bulimia nervosa: A crossover study. *The Journal of Nervous and Mental Disease, 177,* 259-266.

39. Slavin, L. A., & Compas, B. E. (1989). The problem of confounding social support and depressive symptoms: A brief report on a college sample. *American Journal of Community Psychology, 17,* 57-66.

40. Sohlberg, S., Norring, C., Holmgren, S., & Rosmark, B. (1989). Impulsivity and long-term prognosis of psychiatric patients with anorexia nervosa/bulimia nervosa. *The Journal of Nervous and Mental Disease, 177,* 249-258.

41. Sokol, L., Beck, A. T., Greenberg, R. L., Wright, F. D., & Berchick, R. J. (1989). Cognitive therapy of panic disorder: A nonpharmacological alternative. *The Journal of Nervous and Mental Disease, 177,* 711-716.

42. Stiffman, A. R. (1989). Suicide attempts in runaway youths. *Suicide and Life-Threatening Behavior, 19,* 147–159.

43. Stravynski, A., Lesage, A., Marcouiller, M., & Elie, R. (1989). A test of the therapeutic mechanism in social skills training with avoidant personality disorder. *The Journal of Nervous and Mental Disease, 177,* 739-744.

44. Tschann, J. M., Johnston, J. R., & Wallerstein, J. S. (1989). Resources, stressors, and attachment as predictors of adult adjustment after divorce: A longitudinal study. *Journal of Marriage and the Family, 51,* 1033-1046.

45. Vitaliano, P. D., Maiuro, R. D., Russo, J., & Mitchell, E. S. (1989). Medical student distress: A longitudinal study. *The Journal of Nervous and Mental Disease, 177,* 70-76.

46. Wilson, A., Passik, S. D., Faude, J., Abrams, J., & Gordon, E. (1989). A hierarchical model of opiate addiction: Failures of self-regulation as a central aspect of substance abuse. *The Journal of Nervous and Mental Disease, 177,* 390-399.

47. Zemore, R., & Veikle, G. (1989). Cognitive styles and proneness to depressive symptoms in university women. *Personality and Social Psychology Bulletin, 15,* 426–438.

48. Agras, W. S., Taylor, C. B., Feldman, D. E., Losch, M., & Burnett, K. F. (1990). Developing computer-assisted therapy for the treatment of obesity. *Behavior Therapy, 21,* 99–109.

49. Anderson, I. M., Parry-Billings, M., Newsholme, E. A., Poortmans, J. R., & Cowen, P. J. (1990). Decreased plasma tryptophan concentration in major depression: Relationship to melancholia and weight loss. *Journal of Affective Disorders, 20,* 185-191.

50. Baer, L., Jenike, M. A., Ricciardi, J. N., II, Holland, A. D., Seymour, R. J., Minichiello, W. E., & Buttolph, M. L. (1990). Standardized assessment of personality disorders in obsessive-compulsive disorder. *Archives of General Psychiatry, 47,* 826-830.

51. Beitman, B. D., Kushner, M., Lamberti, J. W., & Mukerji, V. (1990). Panic disorder without fear in patients with angiographically normal coronary arteries. *The Journal of Nervous and Mental Disease, 178,* 307-312.

52. Bless, H., Bohner, G., Schwarz, N., & Strack, F. (1990). Mood and persuasion: A cognitive response analysis. *Personality and Social Psychology Bulletin, 16,* 331-345.

53. Breslau, N. (1990). Does brain dysfunction increase children's vulnerability to environmental stress? *Archives of General Psychiatry, 47,* 15–20.

54. Brown, T. A., & Cash, T. F. (1990). The phenomenon of nonclinical panic: Parameters of panic, fear, and avoidance. *Journal of Anxiety Disorders, 4,* 15-29.

55. Bulik, C. M., Carpenter, L. L., Kupfer, D. J., & Frank, E. (1990). Features associated with suicide attempts in recurrent major depression. *Journal of Affective Disorders, 18,* 29-33.

56. Christehnsen, A. J., Smith, T. W., Turner, C. W., Holman, J. M., Jr., & Gregory, M. C. (1990). Type of hemodialysis and preference for behavioral involvement: Interactive effects on adherence in end-stage renal disease. *Health Psychology, 9,* 225-236.

57. Christensen, L., & Burrows, R. (1990). Dietary treatment of depression. *Behavior Therapy, 21,* 183–193.

58. Clark, D. C., Sommerfeldt, L., Schwarz, M., Hedeker, D., & Watel, L. (1990). Physical recklessness in adolescence: Trait or byproduct of depressive/suicidal states? *The Journal of Nervous and Mental Disease, 178,* 423-433.

59. Craighead, W. E. (1990). There's a place for us: All of us. *Behavior Therapy, 21,* 3–23.

60. Deutscher, S., & Cimbolic, P. (1990). Cognitive processes and their relationship to endogenous and reactive components of depression. *The Journal of Nervous and Mental Disease, 178,* 351-359.

61. Devins, G. M., Mandin, H., Hons, R. B., Burgess, E. D., Klassen, J., Taub, K., Schorr, S., Letourneau, P. K., & Buckle, S. (1990). Illness, intrusiveness, and quality of life in end-stage renal disease: Comparison and stability across treatment modalities. *Health Psychology, 9,* 117-142.

62. Devins, G. M., Mann, J., Mandin, H., Paul, L. C., Hons, R. B., Burgess, E. D., Taub, K., Schorr, S., Letourneau, P. K., & Buckle, S. (1990). Psychosocial predictors of survival in end-stage renal disease. *The Journal of Nervous and Mental Disease, 178,* 127-133.

63. Dykstra, S. P., & Dollinger, S. J. (1990). Model competence, depression, and the illusion of control. *Bulletin of the Psychonomic Society, 28,* 235–238.

64. Egeland, B., Kalkoske, M., Gottesman, N., & Erickson, M. F. (1990). Preschool behavior problems: Stability and factors accounting for change. *Journal of Child Psychology and Psychiatry and Allied Disciplines, 31,* 891-909.

65. Ellis, H. C., Seibert, P. S., & Herbert, B. J. (1990). Mood state effects on thought listening. *Bulletin of the Psychonomic Society, 28,* 147–150.

66. Freedman, M. (1990). Object alternation and orbitofrontal system dysfunction in Alzheimer's and Parkinson's disease. *Brain and Cognition, 14,* 134-143.

67. Ganzini, L., McFarland, B. H., & Cutler, D. (1990). Prevalence of mental disorders after catastrophic financial loss. *The Journal of Nervous and Mental Disease, 178,* 680-685.

68. Garvey, M., DeRubeis, R. J., Hollon, S. D., Evans, M. D., & Tuason, V. B. (1990). Does 24-h urinary MHPG predict treatment response to antidepressants? II. Association between imipramine response and low MHPG. *Journal of Affective Disorders, 20,* 181-184.

69. Gelenberg, A. J., Wojcik, J. D., Falk, W. E., Baldessarini, R. J., Zeisel, S. H., Schoenfeld, D., & Mok, G. S. (1990). Tyrosine for depression: A double-blind trial. *Journal of Affective Disorders, 19,* 125-132.

70. Hartley, L., Lebovits, A. H., Paddison, P. L., & Strain, J. J. (1990). Issues in the identification of premenstrual syndromes. *The Journal of Nervous and Mental Disease, 178,* 228-234.

71. Heimberg, R. G., Hope, D. A., Dodge, C. S., & Becker, R. E. (1990). DSM-III-R subtypes of social phobia: Comparison of generalized social phobics and public speaking phobics. *The Journal of Nervous and Mental Disease, 178,* 172-179.

72. Ingram, R. E., Atkinson, J. H., Slater, M. A., Saccuzzo, D. P., & Garfin, S. R. (1990). Negative and positive cognition in depressed and nondepressed chronic-pain patients. *Health Psychology, 9,* 300-314.

73. Jackson, J. L., Calhoun, K. S., Amick, A. E., Maddever, H. M., & Habif, V. L. (1990). Young adult women who report childhood intrafamilial sexual abuse: Subsequent adjustment. *Archives of Sexual Behavior, 19,* 211-221.

74. Kleinman, P. H., Miller, A. B., Millman, R. B., Woody, G. E., Todd, T., Kemp, J., & Lipton, D. S. (1990). Psychopathology among cocaine abusers entering treatment. *The Journal of Nervous and Mental Disease, 178,* 442-447.

75. Lerner, M. S., & Clum, G. A. (1990). Treatment of suicide indicators: A problem-solving approach. *Behavior Therapy, 21,* 403–411.

76. Lewinsohn, P. M., Clarke, G. N., Hops, H., & Andrews, J. (1990). Cognitive-behavioral treatment for depressed adolescents. *Behavior Therapy, 21,* 385–401.

77. Littlefield, C. H., Rodin, G. M., Murray, M. A., & Craven, J. L. (1990). Influence of functional impairment and social support on depressive symptoms in persons with diabetes. *Health Psychology, 9,* 737-749.

78. Lowe, C. F., & Chadwick, P. D. J. (1990). Verbal control of delusions. *Behavior Therapy, 21,* 461–79.

79. Mattick, R. P., Andrews, G., Hadzi-Pavlovic, D., & Christensen, H. (1990). Treatment of panic and agoraphobia: An intergrative review. *The Journal of Nervous and Mental Disease, 178,* 567-576.

80. Mavissakalian, M. R., Jones, B., & Olson, S. (1990). Absence of placebo response in obsessive-compulsive disorder. *The Journal of Nervous and Mental Disease, 178,* 268-270.

81. McCullough, J. D., Braith, J. A., Chapman, R. C., Kasnetz, M. D., Carr, K. F., Cones, J. H., Fielo, J., & Roberts, W. C. (1990). Comparison of dysthymic major and nonmajor depressives. *The Journal of Nervous and Mental Disease, 178,* 596-597.

82. McCullough, J. P., Braith, J. A., Chapman, R. C., Kasnetz, M. D., Carr, K. F., Cones, J. H., Fielo, J., Shoemaker, O. S., & Roberts, W. C. (1990). Comparison of early and late onset dysthymia. *The Journal of Nervous and Mental Disease, 178,* 577-581.

83. McNally, R. J., Cassidy, K. L., & Calamari, J. E. (1990). Taijin-kyofu-sho in a Black American woman: Behavioral treatment of a "culture-bound" anxiety disorder. *Journal of Anxiety Disorders, 4,* 83-87.

84. Meneese, W. B., & Yutrzenka, B. A. (1990). Correlates of suicidal ideation among rural adolescents. *Suicide and Life Threatening Behavior, 20,* 206–212.

85. Middleton, H. C. (1990). An enhanced hypotensive response to clonidine can still be found in panic patients despite psychological treatment. *Journal of Anxiety Disorders, 4,* 213-219.

86. Middleton, H. C. (1990). Cardiovascular dystonia in recovered panic patients. *Journal of Affective Disorders, 19,* 229-236.

87. Moos, R. H. (1990). Depressed outpatients' life contexts, amount of treatment, and treatment outcome. *The Journal of Nervous and Mental Disease, 178,* 105-112.

88. Neimeyer, R. A., & Feixas, G. (1990). The role of homework and skill acquisition in the outcome of group cognitive therapy for depression. *Behavior Therapy, 21,* 281–292.

89. Nelson, G. M., & Beach, S. R. H. (1990). Sequential interaction in depression: Effects of depressive behavior on spousal aggression. *Behavior Therapy, 21,* 167–182.

90. Nutt, D. J., Glue, P., Lawson, C., & Wilson, S. (1990). Flumazenil provocation of panic attacks. *Archives of General Psychiatry, 47,* 917-925.

91. O'Leary, K. D., Riso, L. P., & Beach, S. R. H. (1990). Attributions about the marital discord/depression link and therapy outcome. *Behavior Therapy, 21,* 413–422.

92. Pennebaker, J. W., Czajka, J. A., Cropanzano, R., Richards, B. C., Brumbelow, S., Ferrara, K., Thompson, R., & Thyssen, T. (1990). Levels of thinking. *Personality and Social Psychology Bulletin, 16,* 743-757.

93. Pollard, C. A., Detrick, P., Flynn, T., & Frank, M. (1990). Panic attacks and related disorders in alcohol-dependent, depressed, and nonclinical samples. *The Journal of Nervous and Mental Disease, 178,* 180-185.

94. Rabbit, P., & Alison, V. (1990). "Lost and Found": Some logical and methodological limitations of self-report questionnaires as tools to study cognitive ageing. *British Journal of Psychology, 81,* 1-16.

95. Renneberg, B., Goldstein, A. J., Phillips, D., & Chambless, D. L. (1990). Intensive behavioral group treatment of avoidant personality disorder. *Behavior Therapy, 21,* 363–377.

96. Roy-Byrne, P. P., Cowley, D. S., Greenblatt, D. J., Shader, R. I., & Hommer, D. (1990). Reduced benzodiazepine sensitivity in panic disorder. *Archives of General Psychiatry, 47,* 534–538.

97. Self, C. A., & Rogers, R. W. (1990). Coping with threats to health: Effects of persuasive appeals on depressed, normal, and antisocial personalities. *Journal of Behavioral Medicine, 13,* 343-357.

98. Sheehan, D. Y., Raj, A. B., Harnett-Sheehan, K., Soto, J., & Lewis, C. P. (1990). Adinazolam sustained release formulation in the treatment of generalized anxiety disorder. *Journal of Anxiety Disorders, 4,* 239-246.

99. Smith, T. W., Peck, J. R., & Ward, J. R. (1990). Helplessness and depression in rheumatoid arthritis. *Health Psychology, 9,* 377-389.

100. Starkstein, S. E., Preziosi, T. J., Bolduc, P. L., & Robinson, R. G. (1990). Depression in Parkinson's disease. *The Journal of Nervous and Mental Disease, 178,* 27-31.

101. Steketee, G. (1990). Personality traits and disorders in obsessive-compulsiveness. *Journal of Anxiety Disorders, 4,* 351-364.

102. Stinson, D., & Thompson, C. (1990). Clinical experience with phototherapy. *Journal of Affective Disorders, 18,* 129-135.

103. Tang, C. S., & Critelli, J. W. (1990). Depression and judgment of control: Impact of a contingency on accuracy. *Journal of Personality, 58,* 717–727.

104. van den Burg, W., Bouhuys, A. L., van den Hoofdakker, R. H., & Beersma, D. G. M. (1990). Sleep deprivation in bright and dim light: Antidepressant effects on major depressive disorder. *Journal of Affective Disorders, 19,* 109-117.

105. Vitaliano, P. P., Maiuro, R. D., Russo, J., Katon, W., DeWolfe, D., & Hall, G. (1990). Coping profiles associated with psychiatric, physical health, work, and family problems. *Health Psychology, 9,* 348-376.

106. Webster-Stratton, C., & Hammond, M. (1990). Predictors of treatment outcome in parent training for families with conduct problem children. *Behavior Therapy, 21,* 319–337.

107. Weddington, W. W., Brown, B. S., Haertzen, C. A., Cone, E. J., Dax, E. M., Herring, R. I., & Michaelson, B. S. (1990). Changes in mood, craving, and sleep during short-term abstinence reported by male cocaine addicts. *Archives of General Psychiatry, 47,* 861-868.

108. Whitaker, A., Johnson, J., Shaffer, D., Rapoport, J. L., Kalikow, K., Walsh, B. T., Davies, M., Braimen, S., & Dolinsky, A. (1990). Uncommon troubles in young people: Prevalence estimates of selected psychiatric disorders in nonreferred adolescent population. *Archives of General Psychiatry, 47,* 487–496.

109. Williams, K. E., & Chambless, D. L. (1990). The relationship between therapist characteristics and outcome of in vivo exposure treatment for agoraphobia. *Behavior Therapy, 21,* 111–116.

110. Williamson, D. A., Prather, R. C., McKenzie, S. J., & Blown, D. C. (1990). Behavioral assessment procedures can differentiate bulimia nervosa, compulsive overeater, obese, and normal subjects. *Behavioral Assessment, 12,* 239-252.

111. Barkley, R. A., Fischer, M., Edelbrock, C., & Smallish, L. (1991). The adolescent outcome of hyperactive children diagnosed by research criteria: III. Mother-child interactions, family conflicts and maternal psychopathology. *Journal of Child Psychology and Psychiatry and Allied Disciplines, 32,* 233-255.

112. Baum, J. G., Clark, H. B., & Sandler, J. (1991). Preventing relapse in obesity through posttreatment maintenance systems: Comparing the relative efficacy of two levels of therapist support. *Journal of Behavioral Medicine, 14,* 287-302.

113. Becker, J. V., Kaplan, M. S., Tenke, C. E., & Tartaglini, A. (1991). The incidence of depressive symptomatology in juvenile sex offenders with a history of abuse. *Child Abuse & Neglect, 15,* 531-536.

114. Beckham, J. C., Keefe, F. J., Caldwell, D. S., & Roodman, A. A. (1991). Pain coping strategies in rheumatoid arthritis: Relationships to pain, disability, depression and daily hassles. *Behavior Therapy, 22,* 113–124.

115. Boggiano, A. K., & Barrett, M. (1991). Gender differences in depression in college students. *Sex Roles, 25,* 595-605.

116. Boggiano, A. K., Barrett, M., Silvern, L., & Gallo, S. (1991). Predicting emotional concomitants of learned helplessness: The role of motivational orientation. *Sex Roles, 25,* 577-593.

117. Boyce, P., Hickie, I., & Parker, G. (1991). Parents, partners or personality? Risk factors for post-natal depression. *Journal of Affective Disorders, 21,* 245-255.

118. Burnette, M. M., Koehn, K. A., Kenyon-Jump, R., Hutton, K., & Stark, C. (1991). Control of genital herpes recurrences using progressive muscle relaxation. *Behavior Therapy, 22,* 237–247.

119. Catanzaro, S. J. (1991). Adjustment, depression, and minimal goal setting: The moderating effect of performance feedback. *Journal of Personality, 59,* 243–261.

120. Corrigan, P. W. (1991). Social skills training in adult psychiatric populations: A meta-analysis. *Journal of Behavior Therapy and Experimental Psychiatry, 22,* 203–210.

121. Cox, B. J., Endler, N. S. & Swinson, R. P. (1991). Clinical and nonclinical panic attacks: An empirical test of a panic-anxiety continuum. *Journal of Anxiety Disorders, 5,* 21-34.

122. Craske, M. G., Brown, T. A., & Barlow, D. H. (1991). Behavioral treatment of panic disorder: A two-year follow-up. *Behavior Therapy, 22,* 289–304.

123. Cutler, S. E., & Nolen-Hoeksema, S. (1991). Accounting for sex differences in depression through female victimization: Childhood sexual abuse. *Sex Roles, 24,* 425-438.

124. Denham, S. A., Zahn-Waxler, C., Cummings, E. M., & Iannotti, R. J. (1991). Social competence in young children's peer relations: Patterns of development and change. *Child Psychiatry and Human Development, 22,* 29-44.

125. Dyck, M. J. (1991). Positive and negative attitudes mediating suicide ideation. *Suicide and Life-Threatening Behavior, 21,* 360–373.

126. Edwards, M. C., Finney, J. W., & Bonner, M. (1991). Matching treatment with recurrent abdominal pain symptoms: An evaluation of dietary fiber and relaxation treatments. *Behavior Therapy, 22,* 257–267.

127. Fairburn, C. G., Jones, R., Peveler, R. C., Carr, S. J., Solomon, R. A., O'Connor, M. E., Burton, J., & Hope, R. A. (1991). Three psychological treatments for bulimia nervosa. *Archives of General Psychiatry, 48,* 463-469.

128. Field, T., Morrow, C., Healy, B., Foster, T., Adlestein, D., & Goldstein, S. (1991). Mothers with zero Beck Depression scores act more "depressed" with their infants. *Development and Psychopathology, 3,* 253-262.

129. Gabardi, L., & Rosén, L. A. (1991). Differences between college students from divorced and intact families. *Journal of Divorce & Remarriage, 15*(3/4), 175-191.

130. Gelernter, C. S., Uhde, T. W., Cimbolic, P., Arnkoff, D. B., ViHone, B. H., Tancer, M. E., & Bartko, J. J. (1991). Cognitive-behavioral and pharmacological treatments of social phobia. *Archives of General Psychiatry, 48,* 938-945.

131. Günther, V., & Kryspin-Exner, I. (1991). Ergopsychometry in depressive patients. *Journal of Affective Disorders, 23,* 81-92.

132. Harris, E. S. (1991). Adolescent bereavement following the death of a parent: An exploratory study. *Child Psychiatry and Human Development, 21,* 267-281.

133. Haviland, M. G., Hendryx, M. S., Cummings, M. A., Shaw, D. G., & MacMumary, J. P. (1991). Multidimensionality and state dependency of alexithymia in recently sober alcoholics. *The Journal of Nervous and Mental Disease, 179,* 284-290.

134. Hayne, C. H., & Louks, J. L. (1991). Dysphoria in male alcoholics with a history of hallucinations. *The Journal of Nervous and Mental Disease, 179,* 415-419.

135. Jarrett, R. B., Giles, D. Z., Gullion, C. M., & Rush, A. J. (1991). Does learned resourcefulness predict response to cognitive therapy in depressed outpatients? *Journal of Affective Disorders, 23,* 223-229.

136. Kerns, R. D., Haythronthwaite, J., Rosenberg, R., Southwick, S., Giller, E. L., & Jacob, M. C. (1991). The Pain Behavior Checklist (PBCL): Factor structure and psychometric properties. *Journal of Behavioral Medicine, 14,* 155-167.

137. Kuch, K., Cox, B. J., Woszczyna, C. B., Swinson, R. P., & Shulman, I. (1991). Chronic pain in panic disorder. *Journal of Behavior Therapy and Experimental Psychiatry, 22,* 255–259.

138. Levitt, A. J., Joffe, R. T., & MacDonald, C. (1991). Life course of depressive illness and characteristics of current episode in patients with double depression. *The Journal of Nervous and Mental Disease, 179,* 678-682.

139. Loranger, A. W., Lenzenweger, M. F., Gartner, A. F., Susman, V. L., Herzig, J., Zammit, G. K., Gartner, J. D., Abrams, R. C., & Young, R. C. (1991). Trait-state artifacts and the diagnosis of personality disorders. *Archives of General Psychiatry, 48,* 720-728.

140. Lucas, J. A., Telch, M. J., & Bigler, E. D. (1991). Memory functioning in panic disorder: A neuropsychological perspective. *Journal of Anxiety Disorders, 5,* 1-20.

141. Maes, M., Bosmans, E., Suy, E., Vandervorst, C., Dejonckheere, C., & Raus, J. (1991). Antiphospholipid, antinuclear, Epstein-Barr and cytomegalovirus antibodies, and soluble interleukin-2 receptors in depressive patients. *Journal of Affective Disorders, 21,* 133-140.

142. Magnusson, A., & Kristbjarnarson, H. (1991). Treatment of seasonal affective disorder with high-intensity light. *Journal of Affective Disorders, 21,* 141-147.

143. Mark, M. M., Sinclair, R. C., & Wellens, T. R. (1991). The effect of completing the Beck Depression Inventory on self-reported mood state: Contrast and assimilation. *Personality and Social Psychology Bulletin, 17,* 457-465.

144. McCullough, J. D. (1991). Psychotherapy for dysthymia: A naturalistic study of ten patients. *The Journal of Nervous and Mental Disease, 179,* 734-740.

145. McGorry, P. D., Chanen, A., McCarthy, E., Van Riel, R., McKenzie, D., & Singh, B. S. (1991). Posttraumatic stress disorder following recent-onset psychosis: An unrecognized postpsychotic syndrome. *The Journal of Nervous and Mental Disease, 179,* 253-258.

146. Meesters, Y., Lambers, P. A., Jansen, J. H. C., Bouhuys, A. L., Beersma, D. G. M., & van den Hoofdakker, R. H. (1991). Can winter depression be prevented by light treatment? *Journal of Affective Disorders, 23,* 75-79.

147. Morrow, K. B. (1991). Attributions of female adolescent incest victims regarding their molestation. *Child Abuse & Neglect, 15,* 477-483.

148. Morse, C. A., Dennerstein, L., Farrell, E., & Varnavides, R. (1991). A comparison of hormone therapy, coping skills training, and relaxation for the relief of premenstrual syndrome. *Journal of Behavioral Medicine, 14,* 469-489.

149. Nelson, L. J., & Hekmat, H. (1991). Promoting healthy nutritional habits by paradigmatic behavior therapy. *Journal of Behavior Therapy and Experimental Psychiatry, 22,* 291–298.

150. Nirenberg, T. D., Wincze, J. P., Bansal, S., Liepman, M. R., Engle-Friedman, M., & Begin, A. (1991). Volunteer bias in a study of male alcoholics sexual behavior. *Archives of Sexual Behavior, 20,* 371-379.

151. O'Hara, M. W., Schlechte, J. A., Lewis, D. A., & Wright, E. J. (1991). Prospective study of postpartum blues. *Archives of General Psychiatry, 48,* 801-806.

152. Öst, L. G., Salkovskis, P. M., & Hellström, K. (1991). Onesession therapist-directed exposure vs. self-exposure in the treatment of spider phobia. *Behavior Therapy, 22,* 407–422.

153. Perry, S., Fishman, B., Jacobsberg, L., Young, J., & Frances, A. (1991). Effectiveness of psychoeducational interventions in reducing emotional distress after human immunodeficiency virus antibody testing. *Archives of General Psychiatry, 48,* 143-147.

154. Peselow, E. D., Corwin, J., Fiere, R. R., Rotrosen, J., & Cooper, T. B. (1991). Disappearance of memory deficits in outpatient depressives responding to imipramine. *Journal of Affective Disorders, 21,* 173-183.

155. Piper, W. E., Azim, H. F. A., Joyce, A. S., & McCallum, M. (1991). Transference interpretations, therapeutic alliance, and outcome in short-term individual psychotherapy. *Archives of General Psychiatry, 48,* 946-953.

156. Piper, W. E., Azim, H. F. A., Joyce, A. S., McCallum, M., Nixon, G. W. H., & Segal, P. S. (1991). Quality of object relations versus interpersonal functioning as predictors of therapeutic alliance and psychotherapy outcome. *The Journal of Nervous and Mental Disease, 179,* 432-438.

157. Reiter, S. R., Otto, M. W., Pollack, M. H., & Rosenbaum, J. F. (1991). Major depression in panic disorder patients with comorbid social phobia. *Journal of Affective Disorders, 22,* 171-177.

158. Rubin, K. H., Both, L., Zahn-Waxler, C., Cummings, E. M., & Wilkinson, M. (1991). Dyadic play behaviors of children of well and depressed mothers. *Development and Psychopathology, 3,* 243-251.

159. Sagar, H. J., Sullivan, E. V., Cooper, J. A., & Jordan, N. (1991). Normal release from proactive interference in untreated patients with Parkinson's disease. *Neuropsychologia, 29,* 1033–1044.

160. Schneider, M. S., Friend, R., Whitaker, P., & Wadhwa, N. K. (1991). Fluid noncompliance and symptomatology in end-stage renal disease: Cognitive and emotional variables. *Health Psychology, 10,* 209-215.

161. Simonds, J. F., McMahon, T., & Armstrong, D. (1991). Young suicide attempters compared with a control group: Psychological, affective, and attitudinal variables. *Suicide and Life-Threatening Behavior, 21,* 134–151.

162. Smith, S. S., Joe, G. W., & Simpson, D. D. (1991). Parental influences on inhalant use by children. *Hispanic Journal of Behavioral Sciences, 13,* 267-275.

163. Souza, F. G. M., Mauder, A. J., Foggo, M., Dick, H., Shearing, C. H., & Goodwin, G. M. (1991). The effects of lithium discontinuation and the non-effect of oral inositol upon thyroid hormones and cortisol in patients with bipolar affective disorder. *Journal of Affective Disorders, 22,* 165-170.

164. Spring, B., Wurtman, J., Gleason, R., Wurtman, R., & Kessler, K. (1991). Weight gain and withdrawal symptoms after smoking cessation: A preventive intervention using d-finfluramine. *Health Psychology, 10,* 216-223.

165. Stanton, A. L., Burker, E. J., & Kershaw, D. (1991). Effects of resercher follow-up of distressed subjects: Tradeoff between validity and ethical responsibility? *Ethics & Behavior, 1,* 105–112.

166. Stein, M. B., & Uhde, T. W. (1991). Endocrine, cardiovascular, and behavioral effects of intravenous protirelin in patients with panic disorder. *Archives of General Psychiatry, 48,* 148-156.

167. Steketee, G., Quay, S., & White, K. (1991). Religion and guilt in OCD patients. *Journal of Anxiety Disorders, 5,* 359-367.

168. Sternberger, L. G., & Burns, G. L. (1991). Obsessive compulsive disorder: Symptoms and diagnosis in a college sample. *Behavior Therapy, 22,* 569–576.

169. Stotland, S., & Zuroff, D. C. (1991). Relations between multiple measures of dieting self-efficacy and weight change in a behavioral weight control program. *Behavior Therapy, 22*, 47–59.

170. Strain, E. C., Stitzer, M. L., & Bigelow, G. E. (1991). Early treatment time course of depressive symptoms in opiate addicts. *The Journal of Nervous and Mental Disease, 179*, 215-221.

171. Taylor, S., & Rachman, S. J. (1991). Fear of sadness. *Journal of Anxiety Disorders, 5*, 375-381.

172. Teti, D. M., & Gelfand, D. M. (1991). Behavioral competence among mothers of infants in the first year: The mediational role of maternal self-efficacy. *Child Development, 62*, 918–929.

173. Thase, M. E., Bowler, K., & Harden, T. (1991). Cognitive behavior therapy of endogenous depression: Part 2: Preliminary findings in 16 unmedicated patients. *Behavior Therapy, 22*, 469–477.

174. Thase, M. E., Simons, A. D., Cahalane, J. F., & McGeary, J. (1991). Cognitive behavior therapy of endogenous depression: Part 1: An outpatient clinical replication series. *Behavior Therapy, 22*, 457–467.

175. Thase, M. E., & Wright, J. H. (1991). Cognitive behavior therapy manual for depressed inpatients: A treatment protocol outline. *Behavior Therapy, 22*, 579–595.

176. Townsley, R. M., Beach, S. R. H., Fincham, F. D., & O'Leary, K. D. (1991). Cognitive specificity for marital discord and depression: What types of cognition influence discord? *Behavior Therapy, 22*, 519–530.

177. Vallejo, J., Gasto, C., Catalan, R., Bulbena, A., & Menchon, J. M. (1991). Predictors of antidepressant treatment outcome in melancholia: Psychosocial, clinical and biological indicators. *Journal of Affective Disorders, 21*, 151-162.

178. Van Ameringen, M., Mancini, C., Styan, G., & Donison, D. (1991). Relationship of social phobia with other psychiatric illness. *Journal of Affective Disorders, 21*, 93-99.

179. Wagner, W. G. (1991). Depression in mothers of sexually abused vs. mothers of nonabused children. *Child Abuse & Neglect, 15*, 99-104.

180. Warner, P., Bancroft, J., Dixson, A., & Hampson, M. (1991). The relationship between perimenstrual depressive mood and depressive illness. *Journal of Affective Disorders, 23*, 9-23.

181. Webster-Stratton, C., & Spitzer, A. (1991). Development, reliability, and validity of the Daily Telephone Discipline Interview. *Behavioral Assessment, 13*, 221-239.

182. Welch, G. W., & Ellis, P. M. (1991). FACTOREP: A new tool to explore the dimensions of depression. *Journal of Affective Disorders, 21*, 101-108.

183. Whipple, E. E., & Webster-Stratton, C. (1991). The role of parental stress in physically abusive families. *Child Abuse & Neglect, 15*, 279-291.

184. Whitley, B. E., Jr., Michael, S. T., & Tremont, G. (1991). Testing for sex differences in the relationship between attributional style and depression. *Sex Roles, 24*, 753-758.

185. Wilson, K. G., Sandler, L. S., Asmundson, G. J. G., Larsen, D. K., & Ediger, J. M. (1991). Effects of instructional set on self-reports of panic attacks. *Journal of Anxiety Disorders, 5*, 43-63.

186. Agostinelli, G., Sherman, S. J., Presson, C. C., & Chassin, L. (1992). Self-protection and self-enhancement biases in estimates of population prevalence. *Personality and Social Psychology Bulletin, 18*, 631-642.

187. Arndt, I. O., Dorozynsky, L., Woody, G. E., McLellan, A. T., & O'Brien, C. P. (1992). Desipramine treatment of cocaine dependence in methadone-maintained patients. *Archives of General Psychiatry, 49*, 888-893.

188. Asle, H., & Torgersen, S. (1992). Mental health locus of control in first-degree relatives of agoraphobic and depressed inpatients. *Psychological Reports, 71*, 579-586.

189. Bagby, R. M., Cox, B. J., Schuller, D. R., Levitt, A. J., Swinson, R. P., & Joffe, R. T. (1992). Diagnostic specificity of the dependent and self-critical personality dimensions in major depression. *Journal of Affective Disorders, 26*, 59-64.

190. Barber, J. P., & DeRubeis, R. J. (1992). The ways of responding: A scale to assess compensatory skills taught in cognitive therapy. *Behavioral Assessment, 14*, 93-115.

191. Barkley, R. A., Anastopoulos, A. D., Goevremont, D. C., & Fletcher, K. E. (1992). Adolescents with attention deficit hyperactivity: Mother-adolescent interactions, family beliefs and conflicts and maternal psychopathology. *Journal of Abnormal Child Psychology, 20*, 263-288.

192. Barlow, D. H., Rapee, R. M., & Brown, T. A. (1992). Behavioral treatment of generalized anxiety disorder. *Behavior Therapy, 23*, 551–570.

193. Beach, S. R. H., & O'Leary, K. D. (1992). Treating depression in the context of marital discord: Outcome and predictors of response of marital therapy versus cognitive therapy. *Behavior Therapy, 23*, 507–528.

194. Beer, J., & Beer, J. (1992). Burnout and stress, depression, and self-esteem of teachers. *Psychological Reports, 71*, 1331-1336.

195. Beer, J., & Beer, J. (1992). Depression, self-esteem, suicide ideation, and GPAs of high school students at risk. *Psychological Reports, 71*, 899-902.

196. Benson, L. T., & Deeter, T. E. (1992). Moderators of the relation between stress and depression in adolescents. *The School Counselor, 39*, 189–194.

197. Berenbaum, H. (1992). Posed facial expressions of emotion in schizophrenia and depression. *Psychological Medicine, 22*, 929-937.

198. Bernstein, G. A., & Garfinkel, B. D. (1992). The Visual Analogue Scale for Anxiety—Revised: Psychometric properties. *Journal of Anxiety Disorders, 6*, 223-239.

199. Boyacioglu, G., & Karanci, A. N. (1992). The relationship of employment status, social support, and life events with depressive symptomotology among married Turkish women. *International Journal of Psychology, 27*, 61–71.

200. Brand, E., & Clingempeel, W. G. (1992). Group behavioral therapy with depressed geriatric inpatients: An assessment of incremental efficacy. *Behavior Therapy, 23*, 475–482.

201. Brewerton, T. D., Mueller, E. A., Lesem, M. D., Brandt, H. A., Quearry, B., George, D. T., Murphy, D. L., & Jimerson, D. C. (1992). Neuroendocrine response to M-chlorophenylpiperazine and L-tryptophan in bulimia. *Archives of General Psychiatry, 49*, 852-861.

202. Brown, T. A., & Deagle, E. A. (1992). Structured interview assessment of nonclinical panic. *Behavior Therapy, 23*, 75–85.

203. Brubeck, D., & Beer, J. (1992). Depression, self-esteem, suicide ideation, death anxiety, and GPA in high school students of divorced and nondivorced parents. *Psychological Reports, 71*, 755-763.

204. Carroll, K. M., & Rounsaville, B. J. (1992). Contrast of treatment-seeking and untreated cocaine abusers. *Archives of General Psychiatry, 49*, 464-471.

205. Chambless, D. L., Renneberg, B., Goldstein, A., & Graceley, E. J. (1992). MCMI-diagnosed personality disorders among agoraphobic outpatients: Prevalence and relationship to severity and treatment outcome. *Journal of Anxiety Disorders, 6*, 193-211.

206. Chan, D. W. (1992). Coping with depressed mood among Chinese medical students in Hong Kong. *Journal of Affective Disorders, 24*, 109-116.

207. Clark, D. B., Leslie, M. I., & Jacob, R. G. (1992). Balance complaints and panic disorder: A clinical study of panic symptoms in members of a self-help group for balance disorders. *Journal of Anxiety Disorders, 6*, 47-53.

208. Clarke, G. N., Lewinsohn, P. M., Hops, H., & Seeley, J. R. (1992). A self-and parent-report measure of adolescent depression: The Child Behavior Checklist Depression Scale (CBCL-D). *Behavioral Assessment, 14*, 443-463.

209. Clarke, G., Hops, H., Lewinsohn, P. M., Andrews, J., Seeley, J. R., & Williams, J. (1992). Cognitive-behavioral group treatment of adolescent depression: Prediction of outcome. *Behavior Therapy, 23*, 341–354.

210. Cole, P. M., Barrett, K. C., & Zahn-Waxler, C. (1992). Emotion displays in two-year-olds during mishaps. *Child Development, 63*, 314–324.

211. da Roza Davis, J. M., Sharpley, A. L., Solomon, R. A., & Cowen, P. J. (1992). Sleep and 5-HT$_2$ receptor sensitivity in recovered depressed patients. *Journal of Affective Disorders, 24*, 177-182.

212. Diamond, R., White, R. F., Myers, R. H., Mastromauro, C., Koroshetz, W. J., Butters, N., Rothstein, D. M., Moss, M. B., & Vasterling, J. (1992). Evidence of presymptomatic cognitive decline in Huntington's disease. *Journal of Clinical and Experimental Neuropsychology, 14*, 961-975.

213. Evans, M. D., Hollon, S. D., DeRubeis, R. J., Piasecki, J. M., Grove, W. M., Garvey, M. J., Tugson, V. B. (1992). Differential relapse following cognitive therapy and pharmacotherapy for depression. *Archives of General Psychiatry, 49*, 802-808.

214. Fahy, T. J., O'Rourke, D., Brophy, J., Schazmann, W., & Sciascia, S. (1992). The Galway study of panic disorder I: Clomipramine and lofepramine in DSM-III-R panic disorder: A placebo controlled trial. *Journal of Affective Disorders, 25*, 63-76.

215. Florin, I., Nostadt, A., Reck, C., Franzen, U., & Jenkins, M. (1992). Expressed emotion in depressed patients and their partners. *Family Process, 31*, 163-172.

216. Fydrich, T., Dowdall, D., & Chambless, D. L. (1992). Reliability and validity of the Beck Anxiety Inventory. *Journal of Anxiety Disorders, 6*, 55-61.

217. Garske, G. G., & Thomas, K. R. (1992). Self-reported selfesteem and depression: Indexes of psychosocial adjustment following severe traumatic brain injury. *Rehabilitation Counselor Bulletin, 36*, 44–52.

218. Geisser, M. E., Robinson, M. E., & Pickren, W. E. (1992). Differences in cognitive coping strategies among painsensitive and pain-tolerant individuals on the cold-pressor test. *Behavior Therapy, 23*, 31–41.

219. Goldstein, M. J. (1992). Commentary on "expressed emotion in depressed patients and their partners." *Family Process, 31*, 172-174.

220. Hatch, J. P., Moore, P. J., Bocherding, S., Cyr-Provost, M., Boutros, N. N., & Seleshi, E. (1992). Electromyographic and affective responses of episodic tension-type headache patients and headache-free controls during stressful task performance. *Journal of Behavioral Medicine, 15*, 89-112.

221. Hay, D. F., Zahn-Waxler, C., Cummings, E. M., & Iannotti, R. J. (1992). Young children's view about conflict with peers: A comparison of the daughters and sons of depressed and well women. *Journal of Child Psychology and Psychiatry and Allied Disciplines, 33*, 669-683.

222. Hibbard, M. R., Gordon, W. A., Stein, P. N., Grober, S., & Sliwinski, M. (1992). Awareness of disability in patients following stroke. *Rehabilitation Psychology, 37*, 103–119.

223. Hollon, S. D., DeRubeis, R. J., Evans, M. D., Wiemer, M. J., Garvey, M. J., Grove, W. M., & Tuason, V. B. (1992). Cognitive therapy and pharmacotherapy for depression: Singly and in combination. *Archives of General Psychiatry, 49*, 774-781.

224. Hops, H., & Seeley, J. R. (1992). Parent participation in studies of family interaction: Methodological and substantive considerations. *Behavioral Assessment, 14*, 229-243.

225. Hutchinson, R. L., Tess, D. E., Gleckman, A. D., & Spence, W. C. (1992). Psychosocial characteristics of institutionalized adolescents: Resilient or at risk? *Adolescence, 27*, 339-356.

226. Jack, D. C., & Dill, D. (1992). The silencing the self scale: Schemas of intimacy associated with depression in women. *Psychology of Women Quarterly, 16*, 97-106.

227. Kerr, J., & Beer, J. (1992). Specific and diversive curiosity and depression in junior high school students of divorced and nondivorced parents. *Psychological Reports, 71*, 227-231.

228. Kettlewell, P. W., Mizes, J. S., & Wasylyshyn, N. A. (1992). A cognitive-behavioral group treatment of bulimia. *Behavior Therapy, 23,* 657–670.

229. Laberge, B., Gauthier, J., Cotè, G., Plamondon, J., & Cormier, H. J. (1992). The treatment of coexisting panic and depression: A review of the literature. *Journal of Anxiety Disorders, 6,* 169-180.

230. Lam, R. W., Buchanan, A., Mador, J. A., Corral, M. R., & Remick, R. A. (1992). The effects of ultraviolet-A wavelengths in light therapy for seasonal depression. *Journal of Affective Disorders, 24,* 237-244.

231. Leadbeater, B. J., & Linares, O. (1992). Depressive symptoms in Black and Puerto Rican adolescent mothers in the first 3 years postpartum. *Development and Psychopathology, 4,* 451-468.

232. Lee, S., Chow, C. C., Shek, C. C., Wing, Y. K., & Chen, C-N. (1992). Folate concentration in Chinese psychiatric outpatients on long-term lithium treatment. *Journal of Affective Disorders, 24,* 265-270.

233. Lester, D., & Anderson, D. (1992). Depression and suicidal ideation in African-American and Hispanic American high school students. *Psychological Reports, 71,* 618.

234. Loas, G., Salinas, E., Guelfi, J. D., & Samuel-Lajeunesse, B. (1992). Physical anhedonia in major depressive disorder. *Journal of Affective Disorders, 25,* 139-146.

235. MacKinnon-Lewis, C., Lamb, M. E., Arbuckle, B., Baradaran, L. P., & Volling, B. L. (1992). The relationship between biased maternal and filial attributions and the aggressiveness of their interactions. *Development and Psychopathology, 4,* 403-415.

236. McKnight, D. L., Nelson-Gray, R. O., & Barnhill, J. (1992). Dexamethasone suppression test and response to cognitive therapy and antidepressant medication. *Behavior Therapy, 23,* 99–111.

237. Miller, S., & Watson, B. C. (1992). The relationship between communication attitude, anxiety, and depression in stutterers and nonstutterers. *Journal of Speech and Hearing Research, 35,* 789–798.

238. Mintz, J., Mintz, L. I., Arruda, M. J., & Hwang, S. S. (1992). Treatments of depression and the functional capacity to work. *Archives of General Psychiatry, 49,* 761-768.

239. Moes, D., Koegel, R. L., Schreibman, L., & Loos, L. M. (1992). Stress profiles for mothers and fathers of children with autism. *Psychological Reports, 71,* 1272-1274.

240. Moran, P. B., & Eckenrode, J. (1992). Protective personality characteristics among adolescent victims of maltreatment. *Child Abuse & Neglect, 16,* 743-754.

241. Mulhern, R. K., Fairclough, D. L., Smith, B., & Douglas, S. M. (1992). Maternal depression, assessment methods, and physical symptoms affect estimates of depressive symptomatology among children with cancer. *Journal of Pediatric Psychology, 17,* 313–326.

242. Öst, L. G., Hellström, K., & Kåver, A. (1992). One versus five sessions of exposure in the treatment of injection phobia. *Behavior Therapy, 23,* 263–282.

243. Otto, M. W., Pollack, M. H., Sachs, G. S., & Rosenbaum, J. F. (1992). Hypochondriacal concerns, anxiety, sensitivity, and panic disorder. *Journal of Anxiety Disorders, 6,* 93-104.

244. Perry, S., Fishman, B., Jacobsberg, L., & Francis, A. (1992). Relationships over 1 year between lymphacyte subsets and psychosocial variables among adults with infection of Human Immunodeficiency Virus. *Archives of General Psychiatry, 49,* 396-401.

245. Philips, H. C., Fensta, H. N., & Samson, D. (1992). An effective treatment for urinary incoordination. *Journal of Behavioral Medicine, 15,* 45-63.

246. Politano, P. M., Stapleton, L. A., & Correll, J. A. (1992). Differences between children of depressed and non-depressed mothers: Locus of control, anxiety and self esteem: A research note. *Journal of Child Psychology and Psychiatry and Allied Disciplines, 33,* 451-455.

247. Pop, V. J., Komproe, I. H., & van Son, M. J. (1992). Characteristics of the Edinburgh Post Natal Depression Scale in the Netherlands. *Journal of Affective Disorders, 26,* 105-110.

248. Renneberg, B., Chambless, D. L., & Gracely, E. J. (1992). Prevalence of SCID-diagnosed personality disorders in agoraphobia outpatients. *Journal of Anxiety Disorders, 6,* 111-118.

249. Riggs, D. S., Hiss, H., & Foa, E. B. (1992). Marital distress and the treatment of obsessive compulsive disorder. *Behavior Therapy, 23,* 585–597.

250. Rousey, A., Best, S., & Blacher, J. (1992). Mothers' and fathers' perceptions of stress and coping with children who have severe disabilities. *American Journal on Mental Retardation, 97,* 99-109.

251. Rubin, R. T., Heist, E. K., McGeoy, S. S., Hanada, K., & Lesser, I. M. (1992). Neuroendocrine aspects of primary endogenous depression. *Archives of General Psychiatry, 49,* 558-567.

252. Sanchez-Bernardos, M. L., & Sanz, J. (1992). Effects of the discrepancy between self-concepts on emotional adjustment. *Journal of Research in Personality, 26,* 303-318.

253. Sandler, L. S., Wilson, K. G., Asmundson, G. J. G., Larsen, D. K., & Ediger, J. M. (1992). Cardiovascular reactivity in nonclinical subjects with infrequent panic attacks. *Journal of Anxiety Disorders, 6,* 27-39.

254. Shek, D. T. L. (1992). Meaning in life and psychological well-being: An empircial study using the Chinese version of the purpose in life questionnaire. *The Journal of Genetic Psychology, 153,* 185-200.

255. Siblerud, R. L. (1992). A comparison of mental health of multiple sclerosis patients with silver/mercury dental fillings and those with fillings removed. *Psychological Reports, 70,* 1139-1151.

256. Startup, M., Rees, A., & Barkham, M. (1992). Components of major depression examined via the Beck Depression Inventory. *Journal of Affective Disorders, 26,* 251-260.

257. Stein, M. B., Tanar, M. E., & Uhde, T. W. (1992). Heart rate and plasma norepinephrine responsivity to orthostatic challenge in anxiety disorders: Comparison of patients with panic disorder and social phobia and normal control subjects. *Archives of General Psychiatry, 49,* 311-317.

258. Stein, P. N., Gordon, W. A., Hibbard, M. R., & Sliwinski, M. J. (1992). An examination of depression in the spouses of stroke patients. *Rehabilitation Psychology, 37,* 121-130.

259. Stuart, S., Simons, A. D., Thase, M. E., & Pilkonis, P. (1992). Are personality assessments valid in acute major depression? *Journal of Affective Disorders, 24,* 281-290.

260. Sung, H., Lubin, B., & Yi, J. (1992). Reliability and validity of the Korean Youth Depression Adjective Check List (Y-DACL). *Adolescence, 27,* 527-533.

261. Thornton, B., & Leo, R. (1992). Gender typing, importance of multiple roles, and mental health consequences for women. *Sex Roles, 27,* 307-317.

262. Wetzel, R. D., Murphy, G. E., Carney, R. M., Whitworth, P., & Knesevich, M. A. (1992). Prescribing therapy for depression: The role of learned resourcefulness, a failure to replicate. *Psychological Reports, 70,* 803-807.

263. Whatley, S. L., & Clopton, J. R. (1992). Social support and suicidal ideation in college students. *Psychological Reports, 71,* 1123-1128.

264. Wierson, M., & Forehand, R. (1992). Family stressors and adolescent functioning: A consideration of models for early and middle adolescents. *Behavior Therapy, 23,* 671–688.

265. Yeaworth, R. C., McNamee, M. J., & Pozehl, B. (1992). The Adolescent Life Change Event Scale: Its development and use. *Adolescence, 27,* 783-802.

266. Zakowski, S. G., McAllister, C. G., Deal, M., & Baum, A. (1992). Stress, reactivity, and immune function in healthy men. *Health Psychology, 11,* 223–232.

267. Zamble, E. (1992). Behavior and adaptation in long-term prison inmates. *Criminal Justice and Behavior, 19,* 409–425.

268. Ackerman, M. D., D'Attilio, J. P., Antoni, M. H., Rhamy, R. K., Weinstein, D., & Politano, V. A. (1993). Patient-reported erectile dysfunction: A cross-validation study. *Archives of Sexual Behavior, 22,* 603-618.

269. Addington, D., Addington, J., & Maticka-Tyndale, E. (1993). Rating depression in schizophrenia: A comparison of a self-report and an observer report scale. *The Journal of Nervous and Mental Disease, 181,* 561-565.

270. Ahles, T. A. (1993). Cancer pain: Research from multidimensional and illness representation models. *Motivation and Emotion, 17,* 225–243.

271. Albright, J. S., Alloy, L. B., Barch, D., & Dykman, B. M. (1993). Social comparison by dysphoric and nondysphoric college students: The grass isn't always greener on the other side. *Cognitive Therapy and Research, 17,* 485-509.

272. Alden, J. D., & Harrison, D. W. (1993). An initial investigation of bright light and depression: A neuropsychological perspective. *Bulletin of the Psychonomic Society, 31,* 621–623.

273. Allen, H. I., Liddle, P. F., & Frith, C. D. (1993). Negative features, retrieval processes and verbal fluency in schizophrenia. *British Journal of Psychiatry, 163,* 769-775.

274. Andrew, B., Hawton, K., Fagg, J., & Westbrook, D. (1993). Do psychosocial factors influence outcome in severely depressed female psychiatric inpatients? *British Journal of Psychiatry, 163,* 747-754.

275. Baron, P., & Campbell, T. L. (1993). Gender differences in the expression of depressive symptoms in middle adolescents: An extension of earlier findings. *Adolescence, 28,* 903-911.

276. Beck, A. T., Steer, R. A., Beck, J. S., & Newman, C. F. (1993). Hopelessness, depression, suicidal ideation, and clinical diagnosis of depression. *Suicide and Life-Threatening Behavior, 23,* 139-145.

277. Beck, A. T., Steer, R. A., & Brown, G. (1993). Dysfunctional attitudes and suicidal ideation in psychiatric outpatients. *Suicide and Life-Threatening Behavior, 23,* 11-20.

278. Birchwood, M., Mason, R., MacMillan, F., & Healy, J. (1993). Depression, demoralization and control over psychotic illness: A comparison of depressed and non-depressed patients with a chronic psychosis. *Psychological Medicine, 23,* 387-395.

279. Brent, D. A., Perper, J. A., Moritz, G., Liotus, L., Schweers, J., Roth, C., Balach, L., & Allman, C. (1993). Psychiatric impact of the loss of an adolescent sibling to suicide. *Journal of Affective Disorders, 28,* 249-256.

280. Brewer, B. W. (1993). Self-identity and specific vulnerability to depressed mood. *Journal of Personality, 61,* 343–364.

281. Byrne, B. M., & Baron, P. (1993). The Beck Depression Inventory: Testing and cross-validating a hierarchical factor structure for nonclinical adolescents. *Measurement and Evaluation in Counseling and Development, 26,* 164-178.

282. Carro, M. G., Grant, K. E., Gotlib, I. H., & Compas, B. E. (1993). Postpartum depression and child development: An investigation of mothers and fathers as sources of risk and resilience. *Development and Psychopathology, 5,* 567-579.

283. Carroll, K. M., Power, M. D., Bryant, K., & Rounsaville, B. J. (1993). One-year follow-up status of treatment-seeking cocaine abusers: Psychopathology and dependence severity as predictors of outcome. *The Journal of Nervous and Mental Disease, 181,* 71-79.

284. Channon, S., Baker, J. E., & Robertson, M. M. (1993). Working memory in clinical depression: An experimental study. *Psychological Medicine, 23,* 87-91.

285. Channon, S., Jones, M., & Stephenson, S. (1993). Cognitive strategies and hypothesis testing during discrimination learning in Parkinson's disease. *Neuropsychologia, 31,* 75-82.

286. Christensen, L., Bourgeois, A., & Cockroft, R. (1993). Electroencephalographic concomitants of a caffeine-induced panic reaction. *The Journal of Nervous and Mental Disease, 181,* 327-330.

287. Connelly, B., Johnston, D., Brown, J. D. R., Mackay, S., & Blackstock, E. G. (1993). The prevalence of depression in a high school population. *Adolescence, 28,* 149-158.

288. Conway, M., Grannopoulos, C., Csank, P., & Mendelson, M. (1993). Dysphoria and specificity in self-focused attention. *Personality and Social Psychology Bulletin, 19,* 265-268.

289. Cooper, J. A., & Sagar, H. J. (1993). Incidental and intentional recall in Parkinson's disease: An account based on diminished attentional resources. *Journal of Clinical and Experimental Neuropsychology, 15,* 713-731.

290. Cooper, J. A., Sagar, H. J., & Sullivan, E. V. (1993). Short-term memory and temporal ordering in early Parkinson's disease: Effects of disease chronicity and medication. *Neuropsychologia, 31,* 933-949.

291. Corcoran, R., & Thompson, P. (1993). Epilepsy and poor memory: Who complains and what do they mean? *British Journal of Clinical Psychology, 32,* 199-208.

292. Dahlquist, L. M., Czyewski, D. I., Copeland, K. G., Jones, C. L., Taub, E., & Vaughan, J. K. (1993). Parents of children newly diagnosed with cancer: Anxiety, coping, and marital distress. *Journal of Pediatric Psychology, 18,* 365–376.

293. David, A. S. (1993). Spatial and selective attention in the cerebral hemispheres in depression, mania, and schizophrenia. *Brain and Cognition, 23,* 166-180.

294. de Man, A. F., Leduc, C. P., & Labrèche-Gauthier, L. (1993). Correlations of suicidal ideation in French-Canadian adolescents: Personal variables, stress, and social support. *Adolescence, 28,* 819-830.

295. de Man, A. F., Leduc, C. D., & Labrèche-Gauthier, L. (1993). A French-Canadian scale for suicide ideation for use with adolescents. *Canadian Journal of Behavioural Science, 25,* 126-134.

296. deBears, E., Lange, A., Blonk, R. W. B., Koele, P., van Balkom, A. J. L. M., & van Dyck, R. (1993). Goal attainment scaling: An idiosyncratic method to assess treatment effectiveness in agoraphobia. *Journal of Psychopathology and Behavioral Assessment, 15,* 357–373.

297. Derry, P. A., Chovaz, C. J., McClachlan, R. S., & Cummings, A. (1993). Learned resourcefulness and psychosocial adjustment following temporal lobectomy in epilepsy. *Journal of Social and Clinical Psychology, 12,* 454–470.

298. Dorman, A., O'Connor, A., Hardiman, E., Freyne, A., & O'Neil, H. (1993). Psychiatric morbidity in sentenced HIV-positive prisoners. *British Journal of Psychiatry, 163,* 802-805.

299. Dunn, G., Sham, P., & Hand, D. (1993). Statistics and the nature of depression. *Psychological Medicine, 23,* 871-889.

300. Dura, J. R. (1993). Educational intervention for a Huntington's disease caregiver. *Psychological Reports, 72,* 1099-1105.

301. Fairburn, C. G., Jones, R., Peveler, R. C., Hope, R. A., & O'Connor, M. (1993). Psychotherapy and bulimia nervosa: Longer-term effects of interpersonal psychotherapy, behavior therapy, and cognitive behavior therapy. *Archives of General Psychiatry, 50,* 419-428.

302. Fals-Stewart, W., Marks, A. P., & Schafer, J. (1993). A comparison of behavioral group therapy and individual behavior therapy in treating obsessive-compulsive disorder. *The Journal of Nervous and Mental Disease, 181,* 189-193.

303. Fitzgerald, H. E., Sullivan, L. A., Ham, H. P., Zucker, R. A., Bruckel, S., Schneider, A. M., & Noll, R. B. (1993). Predictors of behavior problems in three-year-old sons of alcoholics: Early evidence for the onset of risk. *Child Development, 64,* 110-123.

304. Flick, S. N., Roy-Byrne, P. P., Cowley, D. S., Shores, M. M., & Dunner, D. L. (1993). DSM-III-R personality disorders in a mood and anxiety disorders clinic: Prevalence, comorbidity, and clinical correlates. *Journal of Affective Disorders, 27,* 71-79.

305. Ford, J. G., Lawson, J., & Hook, M. (1993). Further development of the public-private congruence technique. *Psychological Reports, 73,* 872-874.

306. Fremouw, W., Callahan, T., & Kashden, J. (1993). Adolescent suicidal risk: Psychological, problem solving, and environmental factors. *Suicide and Life-Threatening Behavior, 23,* 46-62.

307. Gidycz, C. A., Coble, C. N., Latham, L., & Layman, M. J. (1993). Sexual assault experience in adulthood and prior victimization experiences. *Psychology of Women Quarterly, 17,* 151-168.

308. Gillis, J. S. (1993). Effects of life stress and dysphoria on complex judgements. *Psychological Reports, 72,* 1355-1363.

309. Gonman, J., Leifer, M., & Grossman, G. (1993). Nonorganic failure to thrive: Maternal history and current maternal functioning. *Journal of Clinical Child Psychology, 22,* 327-336.

310. Goodman, S. H., Brogan, D., Lynch, M. E., & Fielding, B. (1993). Social and emotional competence in children of depressed mothers. *Child Development, 64,* 516-531.

311. Gould, R. A., Clum, G. A., & Shapiro, D. (1993). The use of bibliotherapy in the treatment of panic: A preliminary investigation. *Behavior Therapy, 24,* 241–252.

312. Grubb, H. J., Sellers, M. I., & Waligroski, K. (1993). Factors related to depression and eating disorders: Self-esteem, body image, and attractiveness. *Psychological Reports, 72,* 1003-1010.

313. Hagopian, L. P., & Slifer, K. J. (1993). Treatment of separation anxiety disorder with graduated exposure and reinforcement targeting school attendance: A controlled case study. *Journal of Anxiety Disorders, 7,* 271-280.

314. Haller, D. L., Knisely, J. S., Dawson, K. S., & Schnoll, S. H. (1993). Perinatal substance abusers: Psychological and social characteristics. *The Journal of Nervous and Mental Disease, 181,* 509-513.

315. Haslam, N., & Beck, A. T. (1993). Categorization of major depression in an outpatient sample. *The Journal of Nervous and Mental Disease, 181,* 725-731.

316. Hortacsu, N., Cesur, S., & Oral, A. (1993). Relationship between depression and attachment styles in parent- and institution-reared Turkish children. *The Journal of Genetic Psychology, 154,* 329-337.

317. Huzel, L. L., Delaney, S. M., & Stein, M. B. (1993). Lymphocyte A B-adrenergic receptors in panic disorder: Findings with a highly selective ligand and relationship to clinical parameters. *Journal of Anxiety Disorders, 7,* 349-357.

318. Jackson, H. J., & Pica, S. (1993). An investigation into the internal structure of DSM-III antisocial personality disorder. *Psychological Reports, 72,* 355-367.

319. Jacob, R. G., Woody, S. R., Clark, D. B., Lilienfeld, S. O., Hirsch, B. E., Kucera, G. D., Furman, J. M., & Durrant, J. D. (1993). Discomfort with space and motion: A possible marker for vestibular dysfunction assessed by the Situational Characteristics Questionnaire. *Journal of Psychopathology and Behavioral Assessment, 15,* 299–324.

320. Jacobs, G. D., Benson, H., & Friedman, R. (1993). Home-based central nervous system assessment of a multifactor behavioral intervention for chronic sleep-onset insomnia. *Behavior Therapy, 24,* 159–174.

321. Jacobs, K. W., & Boze, M. M. (1993). Correlations among scales of the Beck Depression Inventory and the Profile of Mood States. *Psychological Reports, 73,* 431-434.

322. Jacobson, S. W., Jacobson, J. L., Sokol, R. J., Martier, S. S., & Ager, J. W. (1993). Prenatal alcohol exposure and infant information processing ability. *Child Development, 64,* 1706-1721.

323. James, L. D., Thorn, B. E., & Williams, D. A. (1993). Goal specification in cognitive-behavioral therapy for chronic headache pain. *Behavior Therapy, 24,* 305–320.

324. Jolly, J. B. (1993). A multi-method test of the cognitive content-specificity hypothesis in young adolescents. *Journal of Anxiety Disorders, 7,* 223-233.

325. Kenardy, J., & Dei, T. P. S. (1993). Phobic anxiety in panic disorder: Cognition, heart rate, and subjective anxiety. *Journal of Anxiety Disorders, 7,* 359-371.

326. King, A. C., Taylor, C. B., & Haskell, W. L. (1993). Effects of differing intensities and formats of 12 months of exercise training on psychological outcomes in older adults. *Health Psychology, 12,* 292–300.

327. Kirkham, M. A. (1993). Two-year follow-up of skills training with mothers of children with disabilities. *American Journal on Mental Retardation, 97,* 509-520.

328. Lakey, B., Baltman, S., & Bentley, K. (1993). Dysphoria and vulnerability to subsequent life events. *Journal of Research in Personality, 27,* 138-153.

329. Lapp, W. M., & Collins, R. L. (1993). Relative/proportional scoring of the Ways of Coping Checklist: Is it advantageous or artifactual? *Multivariate Behavioral Research, 28,* 483– 512.

330. Lester, D. (1993). Depression, suicidal preoccupation and scores on the Rokeach Value Survey: A correction. *Psychological Reports, 73,* 1202.

331. Lester, D. (1993). Functional and dysfunctional impulsivity and depression and suicidal ideation in a subclinical population. *The Journal of General Psychology, 120,* 187-188.

332. Lester, D., & Schaeffler, J. (1993). Self-defeating personality, depression, and suicidal ideation in adolescents. *Psychological Reports, 73,* 113-114.

333. Linden, W., Chambers, L., Maurice, J., & Lenz, J. W. (1993). Sex differences in social support, self-deception, hostility and ambulatory cardiovascular activity. *Health Psychology, 12,* 376-380.

334. Lubin, B., Whitlock, R. V., Schemmel, D. R., & Swearingin, S. E. (1993). Evaluation of a brief measure of depressive mood for use in a university counseling center. *Psychological Reports, 72,* 379-385.

335. Maddock, R. J., Gietzen, D. W., & Goodman, T. A. (1993). Decreased lymphocyte beta-adrenoreceptor function correlates with less agoraphobia and better outcome in panic disorder. *Journal of Affective Disorders, 29,* 27-32.

336. Marcel, B. B., Samson, J., Cole, J. O., & Schatzberg, A. F. (1993). Discrimination of facial emotion in depressed patients with visual-perceptual disturbances. *The Journal of Nervous and Mental Disease, 181,* 583-584.

337. McCormick, R. A. (1993). Disinhibition and negative affectivity in substance abusers with and without a gambling problem. *Addictive Behaviors, 18,* 331-336.

338. McGreal, R., & Joseph, S. (1993). The Depression-Happiness Scale. *Psychological Reports, 73,* 1279-1282.

339. Meesters, Y., Jansen, J. H. C., Beersma, D. G. M., Bouhuys, A. L., van den Hoofdakker, R. H. (1993). Early light treatment can prevent an emerging winter depression from developing into a full-blown depression. *Journal of Affective Disorders, 29,* 41-47.

340. Meesters, Y., Jansen, J. H. C., Lambers, P. A., Bouhuys, A. L., Beersma, D. G. M., & van den Hoofdakker, R. H. (1993). Morning and evening light treatment of seasonal affective disorder: Response, relapse, and prediction. *Journal of Affective Disorders, 28,* 165-177.

341. Miller, D. A. F., McCluskey-Fawcett, K., & Irving, L. M. (1993). Correlates of bulimia nervosa: Early family mealtime experiences. *Adolescence, 28,* 621-635.

342. Mindell, J. A., & Durand, V. M. (1993). Treatment of childhood sleep disorders: Generalization across disorders and effects on family members. *Journal of Pediatric Psychology, 18,* 731–750.

343. Moore, R. G., & Blackburn, I. (1993). Sociotropy, autonomy and personal memories in depression. *British Journal of Clinical Psychology, 32,* 460-462.

344. Morrissette, D. L., Skinner, M. H., Hoffman, B. B., Levine, R. E., & Davidson, J. M. (1993). Effects of antihypertensive drug atenolol and nifedipine on sexual function in older men: A placebo-controlled, crossover study. *Archives of Sexual Behavior, 22,* 99-109.

345. Morano, C. D., Cisler, R. A., & Lemerond, J. (1993). Risk factors for adolescent suicidal behavior: Loss, insufficient familial support, and hopelessness. *Adolescence, 28,* 851-865.

346. Nixon, C. D., & Singer, G. H. S. (1993). Group cognitive-behavioral treatment for excessive parental self-blame and guilt. *American Journal on Mental Retardation, 97,* 665-672.

347. Nofzinger, E. A., Thase, M. E., Reynolds, C. F., III, Frank, E., Jennings, R., Garamoni, G. L., Fasiczka, A. L., & Kupfer, D. J. (1993). Sexual function in depressed men. *Archives of General Psychiatry, 50,* 24-30.

348. Ollendick, T. H., Lease, C. A., & Cooper, C. (1993). Separation anxiety in young adults: A preliminary examination. *Journal of Anxiety Disorders, 7,* 293-305.

349. Page, S., & Bennesch, S. (1993). Gender and reporting differences in measures of depression. *Canadian Journal of Behavioural Science, 25,* 579-589.

350. Park, C. L., & Cohen, L. H. (1993). Religious and nonreligious coping with the death of a friend. *Cognitive Therapy and Research, 17,* 561-577.

351. Persons, J. B., Burns, D. D., Perloff, J. M., & Miranda, J. (1993). Relationships between symptoms of depression and anxiety and dysfunctional beliefs about achievement and attachment. *Journal of Abnormal Psychology, 102,* 518-524.

352. Pibernik-Okanovil, M., Roglic, G., Prasek, M., & Metelko, Z. (1993). War-induced prolonged stress and metabolic control in type 2 diabetic patients. *Psychological Medicine, 23,* 645-651.

353. Pincus, T., Pearce, S., McClelland, A., & Turner-Stokes, L. (1993). Self-referential selective memory in pain patients. *British Journal of Clinical Psychology, 32,* 365-374.

354. Pinto, A., & Francis, G. (1993). Cognitive correlates of depressive symptoms in hospitalized adolescents. *Adolescence, 28,* 661-672.

355. Poulakis, Z., & Wertheim, E. H. (1993). Relationships among dysfunctional cognitions, depressive symptoms, and bulimic tendencies. *Cognitive Therapy and Research, 17,* 549-559.

356. Prince, J. D., & Berenbaum, H. (1993). Alexithymia and hedonic capacity. *Journal of Research in Personality, 27,* 15-22.

357. Raj, B. A., Corvea, M. H., & Dagon, E. M. (1993). The clinical characteristics of panic disorder in the elderly: A retrospective study. *Journal of Clinical Psychiatry, 54,* 150-155.

358. Rierdan, J., & Koff, E. (1993). Developmental variables in relation to depressive symptoms in adolescent girls. *Development and Psychopathology, 5,* 485-496.

359. Rokke, P. D. (1993). Social context and perceived task difficulty as mediators of depressive self-evaluation. *Motivation and Emotion, 17,* 23-40.

360. Rosenblatt, A., & Attkisson, C. C. (1993). Assessing outcomes for sufferers of severe mental disorder: A conceptual framework and review. *Evaluation and Program Planning, 16,* 347-363.

361. Rosenfarb, I. S., Burker, E. J., Morris, S. A., & Cush, D. T. (1993). Effects of changing contingencies on the behavior of depressed and nondepressed individuals. *Journal of Abnormal Psychology, 102,* 642-646.

362. Roy, A. (1993). Features associated with suicide attempts in depression: A partial replication. *Journal of Affective Disorders, 27,* 35-38.

363. Rude, S. S., & Burnham, B. L. (1993). Do interpersonal and achievement vulnerabilities interact with congruent events to predict depression? Comparison of DEQ, SAS, DAS, and combined scales. *Cognitive Therapy and Research, 17,* 531-548.

364. Rugle, L., & Melamed, L. (1993). Neuropsychological assessment of attention problems in pathological gamblers. *The Journal of Nervous and Mental Disease, 181,* 107-112.

365. Saddler, C. D., & Sacks, L. A. (1993). Multidimensional perfectionism and academic procrastination: Relationships with depression in university students. *Psychological Reports, 73,* 863-871.

366. Sanders, M. R., Patel, R. K., LeGrice, B., & Shepherd, R. W. (1993). Children with persistent feeding difficulties: An observational analysis of the feeding interactions of problem and non-problem eaters. *Health Psychology, 12,* 64-73.

367. Schmidt, P. J., Grover, G. N., & Rubinow, D. R. (1993). Alprazolam in the treatment of premenstrual syndrome. *Archives of General Psychiatry, 50,* 467-473.

368. Schotte, C., Maes, M., Beuten, T., Vandenbossche, B., & Cosyns, P. (1993). A videotape as introduction for cognitive behavioral therapy with depressed inpatients. *Psychological Reports, 72,* 440-442.

369. Schultz, G., & Melzack, R. (1993). Visual hallucinations and mental state: A study of 14 Charles Bonnet Syndrome hallucinators. *The Journal of Nervous and Mental Disease, 181,* 639-643.

370. Senra, C., & Polaino, A. (1993). Concordance between clinical and self-report depression scales during the acute phase and after treatment. *Journal of Affective Disorders, 27,* 13-20.

371. Shagle, S. C., & Barber, B. K. (1993). Effects of family, marital, and parent-child conflict on adolescent selfderogation and suicidal ideation. *Journal of Marriage and the Family, 55,* 964-974.

372. Shaw, D. S., & Vondra, J. I. (1993). Chronic family adversity and infant attachment security. *Journal of Child Psychology and Psychiatry and Allied Disciplines, 34,* 1205-1215.

373. Silverman, R. J., & Peterson, C. (1993). Explanatory style of schizophrenic and depressed outpatients. *Cognitive Therapy and Research, 17,* 457-470.

374. Simons, A. D., Angell, K. L., Monroe, J. M., & Thase, M. E. (1993). Cognition and life stress in depression: Cognitive factors and the definition, rating, and generation of negative life events. *Journal of Abnormal Psychology, 102,* 584-591.

375. Smith, J. E., Waldorf, V. A., & McNamara, C. L. (1993). Use of implosive therapy scenes to assess the fears of women with bulimia in two response modes. *Behavior Therapy, 24,* 601-618.

376. Soloff, P. H., Cornelius, J., George, A., Nathan, S., Perel, J. M., & Ulrich, R. F. (1993). Efficacy of phenelzine and haloperidol in borderline personality disorder. *Archives of General Psychiatry, 50,* 377-385.

377. Spangler, D. L., Simons, A. D., Monroe, S. M., & Thase, M. (1993). Evaluating the hopelessness model of depression: Diathesis-stress and symptoms components. *Journal of Abnormal Psychology, 102,* 592-600.

378. Spencer, M. B., Cole, S. P., DuPree, D., Glymph, A., & Pierre, P. (1993). Self-efficacy among urban African American early adolescents: Exploring issues of risk, vulnerability, and resilience. *Development and Psychopathology, 5,* 719-739.

379. Spoov, J., Suominen, J. Y., Lahdelma, R. L., Katile, H., Kymäläinen, O., Isometsa, E., Liukko, H., & Aurinen, J. (1993). Do reversed depressive symptoms occur together as a syndrome? *Journal of Affective Disorders, 27,* 131-134.

380. Steer, R. A., Ranieri, W. F., Beck, A. T., & Clark, D. A. (1993). Further evidence for the validity of the Beck Anxiety Inventory with psychiatric outpatients. *Journal of Anxiety Disorders, 7,* 195-205.

381. Steiger, H., Leung, F., Thibaudeau, J., & Houle, L. (1993). Prognostic utility of subcomponents of the borderline personality construct in bulimia nervosa. *British Journal of Clinical Psychology, 32,* 187-197.

382. Stein, M. B., Enns, M. W., & Kryger, M. H. (1993). Sleep in nondepressed patients with panic disorder: II. Polysomnographic assessment of sleep architecture and sleep continuity. *Journal of Affective Disorders, 28,* 1-6.

383. Stevens-Ratchford, R. G. (1993). The effect of life review reminiscence activities on depression and self-esteem in older adults. *The American Journal of Occupational Therapy, 47,* 413-420.

384. Telch, C. F., & Agras, W. S. (1993). The effects of a very low calorie diet on binge eating. *Behavior Therapy, 24,* 177-193.

385. VanAmeringen, M., Mancini, C., & Streiner, D. L. (1993). Fluoxetine efficacy in social phobia. *Journal of Clinical Psychiatry, 54,* 27-32.

386. VanHasselt, V. B., Null, J. A., Kempton, T., & Bukstein, O. E. (1993). Social skills and depression in adolescent substance abusers. *Addictive Behaviors, 18,* 9-18.

387. Waterman, J., & Lusk, R. (1993). Psychological testing in evaluation of child sexual abuse. *Child Abuse & Neglect, 17,* 145-159.

388. Whitley, B. E., Jr., & Gridley, B. E. (1993). Sex role orientation, self-esteem, and depression: A latent variable analysis. *Personality and Social Psychology Bulletin, 19,* 363-369.

389. Wiederman, M. W., & Allgeier, E. R. (1993). The measurement of sexual-esteem: Investigation of Snell and Papini's (1989) Sexuality Scale. *Journal of Research in Personality, 27,* 88-102.

390. Wilson, T. D., & Kraft, D. (1993). Why do I love thee?: Effects of repeated introspections about a dating relationship on attitudes toward the relationship. *Personality and Social Psychology Bulletin, 19,* 409-418.

391. Zane, G., & Williams, S. L. (1993). Performance-related anxiety in agoraphobia: Treatment procedures and cognitive mechanisms of change. *Behavior Therapy, 24,* 625-643.

392. Addeo, R. R., Greene, A. F., & Geisser, M. E. (1994). Construct validity of the Robson Self-Esteem Questionnaire in a college sample. *Educational and Psychological Measurement, 54,* 439-446.

393. Agras, W. S., Rossiter, E. M., Arnow, B., Telch, C. F., Raeburn, S. D., Bruce, B., & Koran, L. M. (1994). One-year follow-up of psychosocial and pharmacologic treatments for bulimia nervosa. *The Journal of Clinical Psychiatry, 55,* 179-183.

394. Agras, W. S., Telch, C. F., Arnow, B., Eldredge, K., Wilfley, D. E., Raeburn, S. D., Henderson, J., & Marnell, M. (1994). Weight loss, cognitive-behavioral, and desipramine treatments in binge eating disorder: An additive design. *Behavior Therapy, 25,* 225-238.

395. Alden, L. E., Bieling, P. J., & Wallace, S. T. (1994). Perfectionism in an interpersonal context: A self-regulation analysis of dysphoria and social anxiety. *Cognitive Therapy and Research, 18,* 297-316.

396. Alfano, M. S., Joiner, T. E., & Perry, M. (1994). Attributional style: A mediator of the shyness-depression relationship. *Journal of Research in Personality, 28,* 287-300.

397. Alford, B. A., & Correia, C. J. (1994). Cognitive therapy of schizophrenia: Theory and empirical status. *Behavior Therapy, 25,* 17-33.

398. Allen-Burge, R., Storandt, M., Kincherf, D. A., & Rubin, E. H. (1994). Sex differences in the sensitivity of two self-report depression scales in older depressed inpatients. *Psychology and Aging, 9,* 443-445.

399. Arndt, I. O., McLellan, T., Dorozynsky, L., Woody, G. E., & O'Brien, C. P. (1994). Desipramine treatment for cocaine dependence: Role of antisocial personality disorder. *The Journal of Nervous and Mental Disease, 182,* 151-156.

400. Asmundson, G. J. G., & Stein, M. B. (1994). Selective processing of social threat in patients with generalized social phobia: Evaluation using a dot-probe paradigm. *Journal of Anxiety Disorders, 8,* 107-117.

401. Atkinson, S. D. (1994). Grieving and loss in parents with a schizophrenic child. *American Journal of Psychiatry, 151,* 1137-1139.

402. Atlas, G., & Morier, D. (1994). The sorority rush process: Self-selection, acceptance criteria, and the effect of rejection. *Journal of College Student Development, 35,* 346-353.

403. Basoglu, M., Marks, I. M., Kilic, C., Swinson, R. P., Noshirvani, H., Kuch, K., & O'Sullivan, G. (1994). Relationship of panic, anticipatory anxiety, agoraphobia, and global improvement in panic disorder with agoraphobia treated with alprazolam and exposure. *British Journal of Psychiatry, 164,* 647-652.

404. Basoglu, M., Paker, M., Paker, O., Ozmen, E., Marks, I., Incesu, C., Sahin, D., & Sarimurat, N. (1994). Psychological effects of torture: A comparison of tortured with nontortured political activists in Turkey. *American Journal of Psychiatry, 151,* 76-81.

405. Bazin, N., Perruchet, P., DeBonis, M., & Feline, A. (1994). The dissociation of explicit and implicit memory in depressed patients. *Psychological Medicine, 24,* 239-245.

406. Beach, S. R. H., Whisman, M. A., & O'Leary, K. D. (1994). Marital therapy for depression: Theoretical foundation, current status, and future directions. *Behavior Therapy, 25,* 345–371.

407. Beck, J. G., & Zebb, B. J. (1994). Behavioral assessment and treatment of panic disorder: Current status, future directions. *Behavior Therapy, 25,* 581–611.

408. Benkelfat, C., Ellenbogen, M. A., Dean, P., Palmour, R. M., & Young, S. N. (1994). Mood-lowering effect of tryptophan depletion: Enhanced susceptibility of young men at genetic risk for major affective disorders. *Archives of General Psychiatry, 51,* 687-697.

409. Berman, W. H., Heiss, G. E., & Sperling, M. B. (1994). Measuring continued attachment to parents: The Continued Attachment Scale—Parent Version. *Psychological Reports, 75,* 171-182.

410. Blood, G. W., Blood, I. M., Bennett, S., Simpson, K. C., & Susman, E. J. (1994). Subjective anxiety measurements and cortisol responses in adults who stutter. *Journal of Speech and Hearing, 37,* 760–768.

411. Boone, D. E. (1994). Validity of the MMPI-2 depression content scale with psychiatric inpatients. *Psychological Reports, 74,* 159-162.

412. Borden, J. W. (1994). Panic disorder and suicidality: Prevalence and risk factors. *Journal of Anxiety Disorders, 8,* 217-225.

413. Bromberger, J. T., Wisner, K. L., & Hanusa, B. H. (1994). Marital support and remission of treated depression: A prospective pilot study of mothers of infants and toddlers. *The Journal of Nervous and Mental Disease, 182,* 40-44.

414. Brown, H. D., Kosslyn, J. M., Breiter, H. C., Baer, L., & Jenike, M. A. (1994). Can patients with obsessive-compulsive disorder discriminate between percepts and mental images? A signal detection analysis. *Journal of Abnormal Psychology, 103,* 445-454.

415. Bruch, M. A., & Heimberg, R. G. (1994). Differences in perceptions of parental and personal characteristics between generalized and nongeneralized social phobics. *Journal of Anxiety Disorders, 8,* 155-168.

416. Burgess, E., & Haaga, D. A. F. (1994). The Positive Automatic Thoughts Questionnaire (ATQ-P) and the Automatic Thoughts Questionnaire—Revised (ATQ-RP): Equivalent measures of positive thinking? *Cognitive Therapy and Research, 18,* 15-23.

417. Burgess, M., Marks, I. M., & Gill, M. (1994). Postal self-exposure treatment of recurrent nightmares. *British Journal of Psychiatry, 165,* 388-391.

418. Burns, D. D., Rude, S., Simons, A. D., Bates, M. A., & Thase, M. E. (1994). Does learning resourcefulness predict the response to cognitive behavioral therapy for depression? *Cognitive Therapy and Research, 18,* 277-291.

419. Burns, D. D., Sayers, S. L., & Moras, K. (1994). Intimate relationships and depression: Is there a causal connection? *Journal of Consulting and Clinical Psychology, 62,* 1033-1043.

420. Calamari, J. E., Faber, S. D., Hitsman, B. L., & Poppe, C. J. (1994). Treatment of obsessive compulsive disorder in the elderly: A review and case example. *Journal of Behavior Therapy and Experimental Psychiatry, 25,* 95–104.

421. Carmichael, M. S., Warburton, V. L., Dixen, J., & Davidson, J. M. (1994). Relationships among cardiovascular, muscular, and oxytocin responses during human sexual activity. *Archives of Sexual Behavior, 23,* 59-79.

422. Carroll, K. M., Rounsaville, B. J., Gordon, L. T., Nich, C., Jatlow, P., Bisighini, R. M., & Gawin, F. H. (1994). Psychotherapy and pharmacotherapy for ambulatory cocaine abusers. *Archives of General Psychiatry, 51,* 177-187.

423. Chadwick, P. D. J., Lowe, C. F., Horne, P. J., & Higson, P. J. (1994). Modifying delusions: The role of empirical testing. *Behavior Therapy, 25,* 35–49.

424. Cheng, W. C., Shuckers, P. L., Hauser, G., Burch, J., Emmett, J. G., Walker, B., Law, E., Wakefield, D., Boyle, J., Lee, M., & Thyer, B. A. (1994). Psychosocial needs of family caregivers of terminally ill patients. *Psychological Reports, 75,* 1243-1248.

425. Chouinard, G., Saxena, B. M., Nair, N. P. V., Kutcher, S. P., Bakish, D., Bradwejn, J., Kennedy, S. H., Sharma, V., Remick, R. A., Kukha-Mohamad, J. A., Belanger, M. C., Snaith, J., Beauclair, L., Pohlmann, H., & D'Souza, J. (1994). A Canadian multicentre placebo-controlled study of a fixed dose of brofaromine, a reversible selective MOA-A inhibitor, in the treatment of major depression. *Journal of Affective Disorders, 32,* 105-114.

426. Christensen, A. J., Wiebe, J. S., Smith, T. W., & Turner, C. W. (1994). Predictors of survival among hemodialysis patients: Effect of perceived family support. *Health Psychology, 13,* 521-525.

427. Christenson, G. A., Faber, R. J., deZwaan, M., Raymond, N. C., Specker, S. M., Ekern, M. D., Mackenzie, T. B., Crosby, R. D., Crow, S. J., Eckert, E. D., Mussell, M. P., & Mitchell, J. E. (1994). Compulsive buying: Descriptive characteristics and psychiatric comorbidity. *The Journal of Clinical Psychiatry, 55,* 5–11.

428. Clark, D. A., Beck, A. T., & Beck, J. S. (1994). Symptom differences in major depression, dysthymia, panic disorder, and generalized anxiety disorder. *American Journal of Psychiatry, 151,* 205-209.

429. Clark, D. A., & Steer, R. A. (1994). Use of nonsomatic symptoms to differentiate clinically depressed and nondepressed hospitalized patients with chronic medical illnesses. *Psychological Reports, 75,* 1089-1090.

430. Clark, D. A., Steer, R. A., & Beck, A. T. (1994). Common and specific dimensions of self-reported anxiety and depression: Implications for the cognitive and tripartite models. *Journal of Abnormal Psychology, 103,* 645-654.

431. Clark, M. E. (1994). Interpretive limitations of the MMPI-2 anger and cynicism content scales. *Journal of Personality Assessment, 63,* 89-96.

432. Cloitre, M., Shear, M. K., Cancienne, J., & Zeitlin, S. B. (1994). Implicit and explicit memory for catastrophic associations to bodily sensation words in panic disorder. *Cognitive Therapy and Research, 18,* 225-240.

433. Cohan, C. L., & Bradbury, T. N. (1994). Assessing responses to recurring problems in marriage: Evaluation of the Marital Coping Inventory. *Psychological Assessment, 6,* 191-200.

434. Cohen, D. S., Friedrich, W. N., Jaworski, T. M., Copeland, D., & Pendergrass, T. (1994). Pediatric cancer: Predicting sibling adjustment. *Journal of Clinical Psychology, 50,* 303-319.

435. Cowen, P. J., Power, A. C., Ware, C. J., & Anderson, I. M. (1994). 5-HT$_{1A}$ receptor sensitivity in major depression: A neuroendocrine study with buspirone. *British Journal of Psychiatry, 164,* 372-379.

436. Cox, B. J., Direnfeld, D. M., Swinson, R. P., & Norton, G. R. (1994). Suicidal ideation and suicide attempts in panic disorder and social phobia. *American Journal of Psychiatry, 151,* 882-887.

437. Craig, A. R., Hancock, K. M., & Dickson, H. G. (1994). Spinal cord injury: A search for determinants of depression two years after the event. *British Journal of Clinical Psychology, 33,* 221-230.

438. Crews, W. D., Jr., & Harrison, D. W. (1994). Cerebral asymmetry in facial affect perception by women: Neuropsychological effects of depressed mood. *Perceptual and Motor Skills, 79,* 1667-1679.

439. Crews, W. D., Jr., & Harrison, D. W. (1994). Functional assymetry in the motor performance of women: Neuropsychological effects of depression. *Perceptual and Motor Skills, 78,* 1315-1322.

440. Crittenden, P. M., Claussen, A. H., & Sugarman, D. B. (1994). Physical and psychological maltreatment in middle childhood and adolescence. *Development and Psychopathology, 6,* 145-164.

441. Crocker, J., Luhtanen, R., Blaine, B., & Broadnax, S. (1994). Collective self-esteem and psychological well-being among White, Black, and Asian college students. *Personality and Social Psychology Bulletin, 20,* 503-513.

442. Cross, S. E., & Markus, H. R. (1994). Self-schemas, possible selves, and competent performance. *Journal of Educational Psychology, 86,* 423-438.

443. Damos, D. L., & Parker, E. S. (1994). High false alarm rates on a vigilance task may indicate recreational drug use. *Journal of Clinical and Experimental Neuropsychology, 16,* 713-722.

444. de Man, A. F., & Leduc, C. P. (1994). Validity and reliability of a self-report suicide ideation scale for use with adolescents. *Social Behavior and Personality, 22,* 261-266.

445. DeLuca, J., Barbieri-Berger, S., & Johnson, S. K. (1994). The nature of memory impairments in multiple sclerosis: Acquisition versus retrieval. *Journal of Clinical and Experimental Neuropsychology, 16,* 183-189.

446. DeSimone, A., Murray, P., & Lester, D. (1994). Alcohol use, self-esteem, depression, and suicidality in high school students. *Adolescence, 29,* 939-942.

447. Dumas, J. E., & Serketich, W. J. (1994). Maternal depressive symptomatology and child maladjustment: A comparison of three process models. *Behavior Therapy, 25,* 161–181.

448. Durham, R. C., Murphy, T., Allan, T., Richard, K., Treliving, L. R., & Fenton, G. W. (1994). Cognitive therapy, analytic psychotherapy and anxiety management training for generalized anxiety disorder. *British Journal of Psychiatry, 165,* 315-323.

449. Ehlers, A., Hofmann, S. G., Herda, C. A., & Roth, W. T. (1994). Clinical characteristics of driving phobia. *Journal of Anxiety Disorders, 8,* 323-339.

450. Engel, N. A., Rodrigue, J. R., & Geffken, G. R. (1994). Parent-child agreement on ratings of anxiety in children. *Psychological Reports, 75,* 1251-1260.

451. Fagerström, R. (1994). Correlation between depression and vision in aged patients before and after cataract operations. *Psychological Reports, 75,* 115-125.

452. Fallon, B. A., & Nields, J. A. (1994). Lyme disease: A neuropsychiatric illness. *American Journal of Psychiatry, 151,* 1571-1583.

453. Fava, M., Bless, E., Otto, M. W., Pava, J. A., & Rosenbaum, J. F. (1994). Dysfunctional attitudes in major depression: Changes with pharmacotherapy. *The Journal of Nervous and Mental Disease, 182,* 45-49.

454. Fear, C. F., Littlejohns, C. S., Rouse, E., & McQuail, P. (1994). Propofol anaesthesia in electroconvulsive therapy. *British Journal of Psychiatry, 165,* 506-509.

455. Fichter, M. M., Quadflieg, N., & Rief, W. (1994). Course of multi-impulsive bulimia. *Psychological Medicine, 24,* 591-604.

456. Fimm, B., Bartl, G., Zimmerman, P., & Wallesch, C. (1994). Different mechanisms underlie shifting set on external and internal cues in Parkinson's disease. *Brain and Cognition, 25,* 287-304.

457. Flannery, R. B., Jr., Perry, J. C., Penk, W. E., & Flannery, G. J. (1994). Validating Antonovsky's sense of coherence scale. *Journal of Clinical Psychology, 50,* 575-577.

458. Fox, K. M., & Gilbert, B. O. (1994). The interpersonal and psychological functioning of women who experienced childhood physical abuse, incest, and parental alcoholism. *Child Abuse & Neglect, 18,* 849-858.

459. Frueh, B. C., Mirabella, R. F., Chobot, K., & Fossey, M. D. (1994). Chronicity of symptoms in combat veterans with PTSD treated by the VA mental health system. *Psychological Reports, 75,* 843-848.

460. Fuller, K. H., Waters, W. F., & Scott, O. (1994). An investigation of slow-wave sleep processes in chronic PTSD patients. *Journal of Anxiety Disorders, 8,* 227-236.

461. Gallagher-Thompson, D., & Steffen, A. M. (1994). Comparative effects of cognitive-behavioral and brief psychodynamic psychotherapists for depressed family categories. *Journal of Consulting and Clinical Psychology, 62,* 543-549.

462. Garety, P. A., Kuipers, L., Fowler, D., Chamberlain, F., & Dunn, G. (1994). Cognitive behavioural therapy for drugresistant psychosis. *British Journal of Medical Psychology, 67,* 259-271.

463. Garvey, M. J., Hollon, S. D., & DeRubeis, R. J. (1994). Do depressed patients with higher pretreatment stress levels respond better to cognitive therapy than imipramine? *Journal of Affective Disorders, 32,* 45-50.

464. George, M. S., Kellner, C. H., Bernstein, H., & Goust, J. M. (1994). A magnetic resonance imaging investigation into mood disorders in multiple sclerosis: A pilot study. *The Journal of Nervous and Mental Disease, 182,* 410-412.

465. Gilbert, P., Pehl, J., & Allan, S. (1994). The phenomenology of shame and guilt: An empirical investigation. *British Journal of Medical Psychology, 67,* 23–36.

466. Glover, H., Ohlde, C., Silver, S., Packard, P., Goodnick, P., & Hamlin, C. L. (1994). Vulnerability scale: A preliminary report of psychometric properties. *Psychological Reports, 75,* 1651-1668.

467. Goldstein, A. J., & Feske, U. (1994). Eye movement desensitization and reprocessing for panic disorder: A case series. *Journal of Anxiety Disorders, 8,* 351-362.

468. Goodale, T. S., & Stoner, S. B. (1994). Sexual abuse as a correlate of women's alcohol abuse. *Psychological Reports, 75,* 1496-1498.

469. Gournay, K., & Brooking, J. (1994). Community psychiatric nurses in primary health care. *British Journal of Psychiatry, 165,* 231-238.

470. Greene, B., & Blanchard, E. B. (1994). Cognitive therapy for irritable bowel syndrome. *Journal of Consulting and Clinical Psychology, 62,* 576-582.

471. Greif, G. L., & Hegar, R. L. (1994). Parents who abduct: A qualitative study with implications for practice. *Family Relations, 43,* 283-288.

472. Gruen, R. J., Gwadz, M., & Morrobel, D. (1994). Support, criticism, emotion and depressive symptoms: Gender differences in the stress-depression relationship. *Journal of Social and Personal Relationships, 11,* 619-624.

473. Gruen, R. J., Schuldberg, D., Nelson, E. A., Epstein, L., Weiss, L., & Quinlan, D. M. (1994). Network orientation and depressive symptomatology: Development of the Network Utilization Scale. *Journal of Social and Clinical Psychology, 13,* 352–365.

474. Hardy, G. E., & Barkham, M. (1994). The relationship between interpersonal attachment styles and work difficulties. *Human Relations, 47,* 263–281.

475. Harnish, M. J., Beatty, W. W., Nixon, S. J., & Parsons, O. A. (1994). Performance by normal subjects on the Shipley Institute of Living Scale. *Journal of Clinical Psychology, 50,* 881-888.

476. Haslam, N., & Beck, A. T. (1994). Subtyping major depression: A taxometric analysis. *Journal of Abnormal Psychology, 103,* 686-692.

477. Hayward, P., Ahmad, T., & Wardle, J. (1994). Into the dangerous world: An in vivo study of information processing in agoraphobics. *British Journal of Clinical Psychology, 33,* 307-315.

478. Hegel, M. T., Ravaris, C. L., & Ahles, T. A. (1994). Combined cognitive-behavioral and time-limited alprazolam treatment of panic disorder. *Behavior Therapy, 25,* 183–195.

479. Henriques, J. B., Glowacki, J. M., & Davidson, R. J. (1994). Reward fails to alter response bias in depression. *Journal of Abnormal Psychology, 103,* 460-466.

480. Heppner, P. P., Kivlighan, D. M., Good, G. E., Roehlke, H. J., Hills, H. I., & Ashby, J. S. (1994). Presenting problems of university counseling center clients: A snapshot and multivariate classification scheme. *Journal of Counseling Psychology, 41,* 315-324.

481. Hermas, S. L., & Lester, D. (1994). Physical symptoms of stress, depression, and suicidal ideation in high school students. *Adolescence, 29,* 639-641.

482. Hertel, P. T., & Milan, S. (1994). Depressive deficits in recognition: Dissociation of recollection and familiarity. *Journal of Abnormal Psychology, 103,* 736-742.

483. Hetherington, M. M., & Burnett, L. (1994). Ageing and the pursuit of slimness: Dietary restraint and weight satisfaction in elderly women. *British Journal of Clinical Psychology, 33,* 391-400.

484. Hewitt, P. L., Flett, G. L., & Weber, C. (1994). Dimensions of perfectionism and suicide ideation. *Cognitive Therapy and Research, 18,* 439-460.

485. Hill, C. R., & Safran, J. D. (1994). Assessing interpersonal schemas: Anticipated responses of significant others. *Journal of Social and Clinical Psychology, 13,* 366–379.

486. Hiss, H., Foa, E. B., & Kozak, M. J. (1994). Relapse prevention program for treatment of obsessive-compulsive disorder. *Journal of Consulting and Clinical Psychology, 62,* 801-808.

487. Hjelle, L. A., & Bernard, M. (1994). Private self-consciousness and the retest reliability of self-reports. *Journal of Research in Personality, 28,* 52-67.

488. Holroyd, S., Rabins, P. V., Finkelstein, D., & Lavrisha, M. (1994). Visual hallucinations in patients from an ophthalmology clinic and medical clinic population. *The Journal of Nervous and Mental Disease, 182,* 273-276.

489. Ingram, R. E., Bernet, C. Z., & McLaughlin, S. C. (1994). Attentional allocation in individuals at risk for depression. *Cognitive Therapy and Research, 18,* 317-332.

490. Ingram, R. E., Partridge, S., Scott, W., & Bernet, C. Z. (1994). Schema specificity in subclinical syndrome depression: Distinctions between automatically versus effortfully encoded state and trait depressive information. *Cognitive Therapy and Research, 18,* 195-209.

491. Ivanoff, A., Jang, S. J., Smyth, N. J., & Linehan, M. M. (1994). Fewer reasons for staying alive when you are thinking of killing yourself: The Brief Reasons for Living Inventory. *Journal of Psychopathology and Behavioral Assessment, 16,* 1-13.

492. Ivarsson, T., Lidberg, A., & Gillberg, C. (1994). The Birleson Depression Self-Rating Scale (DSRS). Clinical evaluation in an adolescent inpatient population. *Journal of Affective Disorders, 32,* 115-125.

493. Joiner, T. E., Jr. (1994). Contagious depression: Existence, specificity to depressed symptoms, and the role of reassurance seeking. *Journal of Personality and Social Psychology, 67,* 287-296.

494. Joiner, T. E., Schmidt, K. L., & Metalsky, G. I. (1994). Low-end specificity of the Beck Depression Inventory. *Cognitive Therapy and Research, 18,* 55-68.

495. Jolly, J. B., & Kramer, T. A. (1994). The hierarchical arrangement of internalizing cognitions. *Cognitive Therapy and Research, 18,* 1-14.

496. Joseph, S. (1994). Subscales of the Automatic Thoughts Questionnaire. *The Journal of Genetic Psychology, 155,* 367-368.

497. Kaspi, S. P., Otto, M. W., Pollack, M. H., Eppinger, S., & Rosenbaum, J. F. (1994). Premenstrual exacerbation of symptoms in women with panic disorder. *Journal of Anxiety Disorders, 8,* 131-138.

498. Kazdin, A. E., & Mazurick, J. L. (1994). Dropping out of child psychotherapy: Distinguishing early and late dropouts over the course of treatment. *Journal of Consulting and Clinical Psychology, 62,* 1069-1074.

499. Keenan, K., & Shaw, D. S. (1994). The development of aggression in toddlers: A study of low-income families. *Journal of Abnormal Child Psychology, 22,* 53-77.

500. Kinderman, P. (1994). Attentional bias, persecutory delusions and the self-concept. *British Journal of Medical Psychology, 67,* 53–66.

501. Kirkby, R. J. (1994). Changes in premenstrual symptoms and irrational thinking following cognitive-behavioral coping skills training. *Journal of Consulting and Clinical Psychology, 62,* 1026-1032.

502. Kirkpatrick, B., Buchanan, R. W., Breier, A., & Carpenter, W. T. (1994). Depressive symptoms and the deficit syndrome of schizophrenia. *The Journal of Nervous and Mental Disease, 182,* 452-455.

503. Koenig, L. J., Isaacs, A. M., & Schwartz, J. A. J. (1994). Sex differences in adolescent depression and loneliness: Why are boys lonelier if girls are more depressed? *Journal of Research in Personality, 28,* 27-43.

504. Kogan, E. S., Kabacoff, R. I., Hersen, M., & VanHasselt, V. B. (1994). Clinical cutoffs for the Beck Depression Inventory and the geriatric depression scale with older adult psychiatric outpatients. *Journal of Psychopathology and Behavioral Assessment, 16,* 233–242.

505. Kopelman, M. D., Christensen, H., Puffett, A., & Stanhope, N. (1994). The great escape: A neuropsychological study of psychogenic amnesia. *Neuropsychologia, 32,* 675–691.

506. Kopelman, M. D., Green, R. E. A., Guinan, E. M., Lewis, P. D. R., & Stanhope, N. (1994). The case of the amnesic intelligence officer. *Psychological Medicine, 24,* 1037-1045.

507. Kranzler, H. R., Burleson, J. A., Del Boca, F. K., Babor, T. F., Korner, P., Brown, J., & Bohn, M. J. (1994). Buspirone treatment of anxious alcoholics: A placebo-controlled trial. *Archives of General Psychiatry, 51,* 720-731.

508. Kranzler, H. R., Kadden, R. M., Babor, T. F., & Rounsaville, B. J. (1994). Longitudinal, expert, all data procedure for psychiatric diagnosis in patients with psychoactive substance use disorders. *The Journal of Nervous and Mental Disease, 182,* 277-283.

509. Kring, A. M., Smith, D. A., & Neale, J. M. (1994). Individual differences in dispositional expressiveness: Development and validation of the Emotional Expressive Scale. *Journal of Personality and Social Psychology, 66,* 934-949.

510. Kuyken, W., & Brewin, C. R. (1994). Stress and coping in depressed women. *Cognitive Therapy and Research, 18,* 403-412.

511. Lakey, B., & Dickinson, L. G. (1994). Antecedents of perceived support: Is perceived family environment generalized to new social relationships? *Cognitive Therapy and Research, 18,* 39-53.

512. Law, W. A., Martin, A., Mapou, R. L., Roller, T. L., Salazar, A. M., Temoshok, L. R., & Rundell, J. R. (1994). Working memory in individuals with HIV infection. *Journal of Clinical and Experimental Neuropsychology, 16,* 173-182.

513. Leadbeater, B. J., & Bishop, S. J. (1994). Predictors of behavioral problems in preschool children of inner-city African-American and Puerto Rican adolescent mothers. *Child Development, 65,* 638–648.

514. Lecci, L., Karoly, P., Briggs, C., & Kuhn, K. (1994). Specificity and generality of motivational components in depression: A personal projects analysis. *Journal of Abnormal Psychology, 103,* 404-408.

515. Leddy, M. H., Lambert, M. J., & Ogles, B. M. (1994). Psychological consequences of athletic injury among highlevel competitors. *Research Quarterly for Exercise and Sport, 65,* 347–354.

516. Lee, D. Y., & Uhlemann, M. R. (1994). Development of an instrument to assess clinicans' recognition memory using a videotaped stimulus interview. *Journal of Clinical Psychology, 50,* 802-809.

517. Lenzenweger, M. F., & Korfine, L. (1994). Perceptual aberrations, schizotypy, and the Wisconsin Card Sorting Test. *Schizophrenia Bulletin, 20,* 345–357.

518. Lester, D. (1994). Depression and suicidal preoccupation in high school and college students. *Psychological Reports, 75,* 984.

519. Lightsey, O. R., Jr. (1994). "Thinking positive" as a stress buffer: The role of positive automatic cognitions in depression and happiness. *Journal of Counseling Psychology, 41,* 325-334.

520. Lightsey, O. R., Jr. (1994). Positive automatic cognitions as moderators of the negative life event-dysphoria relationship. *Cognitive Therapy and Research, 18,* 353-365.

521. Lubin, B., & Whitlock, R. V. (1994). Development of a critical item scale for the Depression Adjective Check Lists. *Journal of Clinical Psychology, 50,* 841-846.

522. Lyness, S. A., Eaton, E. M., & Schneider, L. S. (1994). Cognitive performance in older and middle-aged depressed outpatients and controls. Journal of Gerontology: *Psychological Sciences, 49*(Pt.1), 129-136.

523. Lyon, H. M., Kaney, S., & Bentall, R. P. (1994). The defensive function of persecutory delusions: Evidence from attribution tasks. *British Journal of Psychiatry, 164,* 637-646.

524. MacGillivray, R. G., & Baron, P. (1994). The influence of cognitive processing style on cognitive distortion in clinical depression. *Social Behavior and Personality, 22,* 145-156.

525. MacLeod, A. K., & Tarbuck, A. F. (1994). Explaining why negative events will happen to oneself: Parasuicides are pessimistic because they can't see any reason not to be. *British Journal of Clinical Psychology, 33,* 317-326.

526. Malla, A. K., & Norman, R. M. G. (1994). Prodromal symptoms in schizophrenia. *British Journal of Psychiatry, 164,* 487-493.

527. Matson, N. (1994). Coping, caring and stress: A study of stroke carers and carers of older confused people. *British Journal of Clinical Psychology, 33,* 333-344.

528. McClennan, H., Joseph, S., & Lewis, C. A. (1994). Causal attributions for marital violence and emotional response by women seeking refuge. *Psychological Reports, 75,* 272-274.

529. McCullough, J. D., McCune, K. J., Kaye, A. L., Braith, J. A., Friend, R., Roberts, W. C., Belyea-Caldwell, S., Norris, S. L. W., & Hampton, C. (1994). Comparison of community dysthymia sample at screening with a matched group of nondepressed community controls. *The Journal of Nervous and Mental Disease, 182,* 402-407.

530. McCullough, J. D., McCune, K. J., Kaye, A. L., Braith, J. A., Friend, R., Roberts, W. C., Belyea-Caldwell, S., Norris, S. L. W., & Hampton, C. (1994). One-year prospective replication study of an untreated sample of community dysthymia subjects. *The Journal of Nervous and Mental Disease, 182,* 396-401.

531. McDermut, W., & Haaga, D. A. F. (1994). Cognitive balance and specificity in anxiety and depression. *Cognitive Therapy and Research, 18,* 333-352.

532. McFarland, C., & Miller, D. T. (1994). The framing of relative performance feedback: Seeing the glass as half empty or half full. *Journal of Personality and Social Psychology, 66,* 1061-1073.

533. McKean, K. J. (1994). Using multiple risk factors to assess the behavioral, cognitive, and affective effects of learned helplessness. *The Journal of Psychology, 128,* 177-183.

534. Molock, S. D., Kimbrough, R., Lacy, M. B., McClure, K. P., & Williams, S. (1994). Suicidal behavior among African American college students: A preliminary study. *The Journal of Black Psychology, 20,* 234-251.

535. Moore, R. G., & Blackburn, I-M. (1994). The relationship of sociotropy and autonomy to symptoms, cognition, and personality in depressed patients. *Journal of Affective Disorders, 32,* 239-245.

536. Morin, C. M., Stone, J., McDonald, K., & Jones, S. (1994). Psychological management of insomnia: A clinical replication series with 100 patients. *Behavior Therapy, 25,* 291–309.

537. Munford, M. B. (1994). Relationship of gender, self-esteem, social class, and racial identity to depression in Blacks. *The Journal of Black Psychology, 20,* 157-174.

538. Naidoo, P., & Pillay, Y. G. (1994). Correlations among general stress, family environment, psychological distress, and pain experience. *Perceptual and Motor Skills, 78,* 1291-1296.

539. Napholz, L. (1994). Sex role orientation and psychological well-being among working Black women. *The Journal of Black Psychology, 20,* 469-482.

540. Nelson, L. D., Cicchetti, D., Satz, S. M., & Mitrushina, M. (1994). Emotional sequelae of stroke: A longitudinal perspective. *Journal of Clinical and Experimental Neuropsychology, 16,* 796-806.

541. Ness, R., Handelsman, L., Aronson, M. J., Hershkowitz, A., & Kanof, P. D. (1994). The acute effects of a rapid medical detoxification upon dysphoria and other psychopathology experienced by heroin abusers. *The Journal of Nervous and Mental Disease, 182,* 353-359.

542. Nolan, R., & Willson, V. L. (1994). Gender and depression in an undergraduate population. *Psychological Reports, 75,* 1327-1330.

543. O'Connor, B. P., & Vallerand, R. J. (1994). Motivation, self-determination, and person-environment fit as predictors of psychological adjustment among nursing home residents. *Psychology and Aging, 9,* 189-194.

544. Okasha, A., Bishry, A., Khalil, A. H., Darwish, T. A., Sief el Dawla, A., & Shohdy, A. (1994). Panic disorder: An overlapping or independent entity? *British Journal of Psychiatry, 164,* 818-825.

545. Olmsted, M. P., Kaplan, A. S., & Rockert, W. (1994). Rate and prediction of relapse in bulimia nervosa. *American Journal of Psychiatry, 151,* 738-743.

546. Organista, K. C., Muñoz, R. F., & González, G. (1994). Cognitive behavioral therapy for depression in low-income and minority medical outpatients: Description of a program and exploratory analyses. *Cognitive Therapy and Research, 18,* 241-259.

547. Orloff, L. M., Battle, M. A., Baer, L., Ivanjack, L., Pettit, A. R., Buttolph, M. L., & Jenike, M. A. (1994). Long-term follow-up of 85 patients with obsessive-compulsive disorder. *American Journal of Psychiatry, 151,* 441-442.

548. Palosaari, U., & Aro, H. (1994). Effect of timing of parental divorce on the vulnerability of children to depression in young adulthood. *Adolescence, 29,* 681-690.

549. Patrick, M., Hobson, R. P., Castle, D., Howard, R., & Maughan, B. (1994). Personality disorder and the mental representation of early social experience. *Development and Psychopathology, 6,* 375-388.

550. Peterson, C., & Ulrey, L. M. (1994). Can explanatory style be scored from TAT protocols? *Personality and Social Psychology Bulletin, 20,* 102-106.

551. Pianta, R. C., & Egeland, B. (1994). Predictors of instability in children's mental test performance at 24, 48, and 96 months. *Intelligence, 18,* 145-163.

552. Pianta, R. C., & Egeland, B. (1994). Relation between depressive symptoms and stressful life events in a sample of disadvantaged mothers. *Journal of Consulting and Clinical Psychology, 62,* 1229-1234.

553. Power, M. J., Katz, R., McGuffin, P., Duggan, C. F., Lam, D., & Beck, A. T. (1994). The Dysfunctional Attitude Scale (DAS). A comparison of Forms A and B and proposals for a new subscaled version. *Journal of Research in Personality, 28,* 263-276.

554. Preasser, K. J., Rice, K. G., & Ashby, J. S. (1994). The role of self-esteem in mediating the perfectionism-depression connection. *Journal of College Student Development, 35,* 88-93.

555. Prodromidis, M., Abrams, S., Field, T., Scafidi, F., & Rahdert, E. (1994). Psychosocial stressors among depressed adolescent mothers. *Adolescence, 29,* 331-343.

556. Rathus, J. H., Reber, A. S., Manza, L., & Kushner, M. (1994). Implicit and explicit learning: Differential effects of affective states. *Perceptual and Motor Skills, 79,* 163-184.

557. Ravindran, A. V., Welburn, K., & Copeland, J. R. M. (1994). Semi-structured depression scale sensitive to change with treatment for use in the elderly. *British Journal of Psychiatry, 164,* 522-527.

558. Reed, M. K. (1994). Social skills training to reduce depression in adolescents. *Adolescence, 29,* 293-302.

559. Richards, M. H., & Duckett, E. (1994). The relationship of maternal employment to early adolescent daily experience with and without parents. *Child Development, 65,* 225-236.

560. Richman, H., & Nelson-Gray, R. (1994). Nonclinical panicker personality: Profile and discriminative ability. *Journal of Anxiety Disorders, 8,* 33-47.

561. Rifai, A. H., George, C. J., Stack, J. A., Mann, J. J., & Reynolds, C. F. (1994). Hopelessness in suicide attempters after acute treatment of major depression in late life. *American Journal of Psychiatry, 151,* 1687-1690.

562. Robbins, P. R., & Tanck, R. H. (1994). Depressed mood and early memories: Some negative findings. *Psychological Reports, 75,* 465-466.

563. Roemer, L., & Borkovec, T. D. (1994). Effects of suppressing thoughts about emotional material. *Journal of Abnormal Psychology, 103,* 467-474.

564. Roesler, T. A. (1994). Reactions to disclosure of childhood sexual abuse: The effect of adult symptoms. *The Journal of Nervous and Mental Disease, 182,* 618-624.

565. Roesler, T. A., & McKenzie, N. (1994). Effects of childhood trauma on psychological functioning in adults sexually abused as children. *The Journal of Nervous and Mental Disease, 182,* 145-150.

566. Rohde, P., Lewinsohn, P. M., & Seeley, J. R. (1994). Responses of depressed adolescents to cognitive-behavioral treatment: Do differences in initial severity clarify the comparison of treatments? *Journal of Consulting and Clinical Psychology, 62,* 851-854.

567. Romney, D. M. (1994). Cross-validating a causal model relating attributional style, self-esteem, and depression: An heuristic study. *Psychological Reports, 74,* 203-207.

568. Rose, D. T., Abramson, L. Y., Hodulik, C. J., Halberstadt, L., & Leff, G. (1994). Heterogeneity of cognitive style among depressed inpatients. *Journal of Abnormal Psychology, 103,* 419-429.

569. Rosen, R. C., Kostis, J. B., Jekelis, A., & Taska, L. S. (1994). Sexual sequelae of antihypertensive drugs: Treatment effects on self-report and physiological measures in middle-aged male hypertensives. *Archives of Sexual Behavior, 23,* 135-152.

570. Rosenfarb, I. S., Becker, J., & Khan, A. (1994). Perceptions of parental and peer attachments by women with mood disorders. *Journal of Abnormal Psychology, 103,* 637-644.

571. Rosenfarb, I. S., Becker, J., Khan, A., & Mintz, J. (1994). Dependency, self-criticism, and perceptions of socialization experiences. *Journal of Abnormal Psychology, 103,* 669-675.

572. Russo, J. (1994). Thurstone's scaling model applied to the assessment of self-reported depressive severity. *Psychological Assessment, 6,* 159-171.

573. Salamero, M., Marcos, T., Gutiérrez, F., Rebull, E. (1994). Factorial study of the BDI in pregnant women. *Psychological Medicine, 24,* 1031-1035.

574. Santor, D. A., Ramsay, J. O., & Zuroff, D. C. (1994). Nonparametric item analyses of the Beck Depression Inventory: Evaluating gender item bias and response option weights. *Psychological Assessment, 6,* 255-270.

575. Santor, D. A., & Zuroff, D. C. (1994). Depressive symptoms: Effects of negative affectivity and failing to accept the past. *Journal of Personality Assessment, 63,* 294-312.

576. Sanz, J., & Avia, M. D. (1994). Cognitive specificity in social anxiety and depression: Self-statements, self-focused attention, and dysfunctional attitudes. *Journal of Social and Clinical Psychology, 13*, 105–137.

577. Schaaf, K. K., & McCanne, T. R. (1994). Childhood abuse, body image disturbance, and eating disorders. *Child Abuse & Neglect, 18*, 607-615.

578. Scheier, M. F., Carver, C. S., & Bridges, M. W. (1994). Distinguishing optimism from neuroticism (and trait anxiety, self-mastery, and self-esteem): A reevaluation of the Life Orientation Test. *Journal of Personality and Social Psychology, 67*, 1063-1078.

579. Schill, T., & Sharp, M. (1994). Self-defeating personality, depression, and pleasure from activities. *Psychological Reports, 74*, 680-682.

580. Schwartz, L., Slater, M. A., & Birchler, G. R. (1994). Interpersonal stress and pain behaviors in patients with chronic pain. *Journal of Consulting and Clinical Psychology, 62*, 861-864.

581. Shapiro, D. A., Barkham, M., Rees, A., Hardy, G. E., Reynolds, S., & Startup, M. (1994). Effects of treatment duration and severity of depression on the effectiveness of cognitive-behavioral and psychodynamic-interpersonal psychotherapy. *Journal of Consulting and Clinical Psychology, 62*, 522-534.

582. Shaw, D. S., Vondra, J. I., Hommerding, K. D., Keenan, K., & Dunn, M. (1994). Chronic family adversity and early child behavior problems: A longitudinal study of low income families. *Journal of Child Psychology and Psychiatry and Allied Disciplines, 35*, 1109-1122.

583. Shear, M. K., Pilkonis, P. A., Cloitre, M., & Leon, A. C. (1994). Cognitive behavioral treatment compared with nonprescriptive treatment of panic disorders. *Archives of General Psychiatry, 51*, 395-401.

584. Siblerud, R. L., Motl, J., & Kienholz, E. (1994). Psychometric evidence that mercury from silver dental fillings may be an etiological factor in depression, excessive anger, and anxiety. *Psychological Reports, 74*, 67-80.

585. Smith, T. W., Christensen, A. J., Peck, J. R., & Ward, J. R. (1994). Cognitive distortion, helplessness, and depressed mood in rheumatoid arthritis: A four-year longitudinal analysis. *Health Psychology, 13*, 213-217.

586. Smyth, N. J., Ivanoff, A., & Jang, S. J. (1994). Changes in psychological maladaptation among inmate parasuicides. *Criminal Justice and Behavior, 21*, 357–365.

587. Sobell, L. C., Toneatto, T., & Sobell, M. (1994). Behavioral assessment and treatment planning for alcohol, tobacco, and other drug problems: Current status with an emphasis on clinical applications. *Behavior Therapy, 25*, 533–580.

588. Soloff, P. H., Liss, J. A., Kelly, T., Cornelius, J., & Ulrich, R. (1994). Risk factors for suicidal behavior in borderline personality disorder. *American Journal of Psychiatry, 151*, 1316-1323.

589. Solomon, A., & Haaga, P. A. F. (1994). Positive and negative aspects of sociotropy and autonomy. *Journal of Psychopathology and Behavioral Assessment, 16*, 243–252.

590. Spicer, K. B., Brown, G. G., & Gorell, J. M. (1994). Lexical decision in Parkinson disease: Lack of evidence for generalized bradyphrenia. *Journal of Clinical and Experimental Neuropsychology, 16*, 457-471.

591. Spiegel, D. A., Bruce, T. J., Gregg, S. F., & Nuzzarello, A. (1994). Does cognitive behavior therapy assist slow-taper alprazolam discontinuation in panic disorder? *American Journal of Psychiatry, 151*, 876-881.

592. Steer, R. A., Clark, D. A., & Ranieri, W. F. (1994). Symptom dimensions of the SCL-90-R: A test of the tripartite model of anxiety and depression. *Journal of Personality Assessment, 62*, 525-536.

593. Stein, M. B., Asmundson, G. J. G., Ireland, D., & Walker, J. R. (1994). Panic disorder in patients attending a clinic for vestibular disorders. *American Journal of Psychiatry, 151*, 1697-1700.

594. Stephens, G. C., Prentice-Dunn, S., & Spruill, J. C. (1994). Public self-awareness and success-failure feedback as disinhibitors of restrained eating. *Basic and Applied Social Psychology, 15*, 509-521.

595. Stiles, W. B., & Shapiro, D. A. (1994). Disabuse of the drug metaphor: Psychotherapy process-outcome correlations. *Journal of Consulting and Clinical Psychology, 62*, 942-948.

596. Strong, J., Ashton, R., & Stewart, A. (1994). Chronic low back pain: Toward an integrated psychosocial assessment model. *Journal of Consulting and Clinical Psychology, 62*, 1058-1063.

597. Sunderland, T., Cohen, R. M., Molchan, S., Lawlor, B. A., Mellow, A. M., Newhouse, P. A., Tariot, D. N., Mueller, E. A., & Murphy, D. L. (1994). High-dose selegiline in treatment-resistant older depressive patients. *Archives of General Psychiatry, 51*, 607-615.

598. Sutker, P. B., Uddo, M., Brailey, K., Vasterling, J. J., & Errera, P. (1994). Psychopathology in war-zone deployed and nondeployed Operation Desert Stonm troops assigned graves registration duties. *Journal of Abnormal Psychology, 103*, 383-390.

599. Tan, J. C. H., & Stoppard, J. M. (1994). Gender and reactions to dysphoric individuals. *Cognitive Therapy and Research, 18*, 211-224.

600. Thase, M. E., Reynolds, C. F., Frank, E., Jennings, J. R., Nofzinger, E., Fasiczka, A. L., Garamoni, G., & Kupfer, D. J. (1994). Polysomnographic studies of unmedicated depressed men before and after cognitive behavioral therapy. *American Journal of Psychiatry, 151*, 1615-1622.

601. Thase, M. E., Reynolds, C. F., Frank, E., Simmons, A. D., McGeary, J., Fasiceka, A. L., Garamoni, G. G., Jennings, R., & Kupfer, D. J. (1994). Do depressed men and women respond similarly to cognitive behavior therapy. *American Journal of Psychiatry, 151*, 500-505.

602. Tomarken, A. J., & Davidson, R. J. (1994). Frontal brain activation in repressors and nonrepressors. *Journal of Abnormal Psychology, 103*, 339-349.

603. Tremblay, P. F., & King, P. R. (1994). State and trait anxiety, coping styles, and depression among psychiatric inpatients. *Canadian Journal of Behavioural Science, 26*, 505–519.

604. Troop, N. A., Holbrey, A., Trowler, R., & Treasure, J. L. (1994). Ways of coping in women with eating disorders. *The Journal of Nervous and Mental Disease, 182*, 535–540.

605. Upmanyu, V. V., & Upmanyu, S. (1994). Depression in relation to sex role identity and hopelessness among male and female Indian adolescents. *The Journal of Social Psychology, 134*, 551-552.

606. Vaughan, K., Armstrong, M. S., Gold, R., O'Connor, N., Jenneke, W., & Tarrier, N. (1994). A trial of eye movement desensitization compared to image habituation training and applied muscle relaxation in post-traumatic stress disorder. *Journal of Behavior Therapy and Experimental Psychiatry, 25*, 283–291.

607. Vera, M. N., Vila, J., & Godovy, J. F. (1994). Cardiovascular effects of traffic noise: The role of negative self-statements. *Psychological Medicine, 24*, 817-827.

608. Wall, J. E., & Holden, E. W. (1994). Aggressive, assertive, and submissive behaviors in disadvantaged, inner-city preschool children. *Journal of Clinical Child Psychology, 23*, 382-390.

609. Wallston, K. A., Stein, M. J., & Smith, C. A. (1994). Form C of the MHLC Scales: A condition-specific measure of locus of control. *Journal of Personality Assessment, 63*, 534-553.

610. Weary, G., & Edwards, J. A. (1994). Individual differences in causal uncertainty. *Journal of Personality and Social Psychology, 67*, 308-318.

611. Webber, E. M. (1994). Psychological characteristics of binging and nonbinging obese women. *The Journal of Psychology, 128*, 339-351.

612. Webster-Stratton, C. (1994). Advancing videotape parent training: A comparison study. *Journal of Consulting and Clinical Psychology, 62*, 583-593.

613. Wegner, D. M., & Zanakos, S. (1994). Chronic thought suppression. *Journal of Personality, 62*, 615–640.

614. Westefeld, J. S., & Liddell, D. L. (1994). The Beck Depression Inventory and its relationship to college student suicide. *Journal of College Student Development, 35*, 145-147.

615. Wind, T. W., & Silvern, L. (1994). Parenting and family stress as mediators of the long-term effects of child abuse. *Child Abuse & Neglect, 18*, 439-453.

616. Wong, J. L., & Whitaker, D. J. (1994). The stability and prediction of depressive mood states in college students. *Journal of Clinical Psychology, 50*, 715-722.

617. Yee, C. M., & Miller, G. A. (1994). A dual-task analysis of resource allocation in dysthymia and anhedonia. *Journal of Abnormal Psychology, 103*, 625-636.

618. Young, A. H., Sharpley, A. L., Campling, G. M., Hockney, R. A., & Cowen, P. J. (1994). Effects of hydrocortisone on brain 5-HT function and sleep. *Journal of Affective Disorders, 32*, 139-146.

619. Zuroff, D. C. (1994). Depressive personality styles and the five-factor model of personality. *Journal of Personality Assessment, 63*, 453-472.

620. Agras, W. S., Telch, C. F., Arnow, B., Eldredge, K., Detzer, M. J., Henderson, J., & Marnell, M. (1995). Does interpersonal therapy help patients with binge eating disorder who fail to respond to cognitive-behavioral therapy? *Journal of Consulting and Clinical Psychology, 63*, 356-360.

621. Akillas, E., & Efran, J. S. (1995). Symptom prescription and reframing: Should they be combined? *Cognitive Therapy and Research, 19*, 263–279.

622. Albright, J. S., & Henderson, M. C. (1995). How real is depressive realism? A question of scales and standards. *Cognitive Therapy and Research, 19*, 589–609.

623. Alford, B. A., & Gerrity, D. M. (1995). The specificity of sociotropy-autonomy personality dimensions to depression vs. anxiety. *Journal of Clinical Psychology, 51*, 190-195.

624. Alford, B. A., Lester, J. M., Patel, R. J., Buchanan, J. P., & Giunta, L. C. (1995). Hopelessness predicts future depressive symptoms: A prospective analysis of cognitive vulnerability and cognitive content specifity. *Journal of Clinical Psychology, 51*, 331-339.

625. Arnold, E. H., & O'Leary, S. G. (1995). The effect of child negative affect on maternal discipline behavior. *Journal of Abnormal Child Psychology, 23*, 585–595.

626. Baer, L., Rauch, S. L., Ballantine, T., Martuza, R., Cosgrove, R., Cassem, E., Girionas, I., Manzo, P. A., Dimino, C., & Jenike, M. A. (1995). Cingulotomy for intractable obsessive-compulsive disorder: Prospective long-term followup of 18 patients. *Archives of General Psychiatry, 52*, 384– 392.

627. Baker, J. D., Williamson, D. A., & Syloe, C. (1995). Body image disturbance, memory bias, and body dysphoria: Effects of negative mood induction. *Behavior Therapy, 26*, 747–759.

628. Ball, S. A., Carroll, K. M., Babor, T. F., & Rounsaville, B. J. (1995). Subtypes of cocaine abusers: Support for a Type A-Type B distinction. *Journal of Consulting and Clinical Psychology, 63*, 115-124.

629. Baran, S. A., Weltzin, T. E., & Kaye, W. H. (1995). Low discharge weight and outcome in anxorexia nervosa. *American Journal of Psychiatry, 152*, 1070-1072.

630. Barber, J. P., Luborsky, L., Crits-Christoph, P., & Diguer, L. (1995). A comparison of core conflictual relationship themes before psychotherapy and during early sessions. *Journal of Consulting and Clinical Psychology, 63*, 145-148.

631. Bartelstone, J. H., & Trull, T. J. (1995). Personality, life events, and depression. *Journal of Personality Assessment, 64*, 279-294.

632. Basoglu, M., & Parker, M. (1995). Severity of trauma as predictor of long-term psychological status in survivors of torture. *Journal of Anxiety Disorders, 9*, 339–350.

633. Basoglu, M., Marks, M., Sengun, S., & Marks, I. M. (1995). The distinctiveness of phobias: A discriminant analysis of fears. *Journal of Anxiety Disorders, 9*, 89-101.

634. Bauserman, S. A. K., Arias, I., & Craighead, W. E. (1995). Marital attributions in spouses of depressed patients. *Journal of Psychopathology and Behavioral Assessment, 17*, 231–249.

635. Beatty, S., & Hewitt, J. (1995). Affective reactions to failure as a function of effort and depression. *Perceptual and Motor Skills, 80*, 33-34.

636. Bentall, R. D., Kaney, S., & Bowen-Jones, K. (1995). Persecutory delusions and recall of threat-related, depression-related, and neutral words. *Cognitive Therapy and Research, 19*, 445–457.

637. Betz, N. E., Wohlegmuth, E., Serling, D., Harshbarger, J., & Klein, K. (1995). Evaluation of a measure of self-esteem based on the concept of unconditional positive regard. *Journal of Counseling and Development, 74*, 76–83.

638. Blanchard, E. B., Hickling, E. J., Taylor, A. E., & Loos, W. (1995). Psychiatric morbidity associated with motor vehicle accidents. *The Journal of Nervous and Mental Disease, 183*, 495–504.

639. Blatt, S. J., Quinlan, D. M., Pilkonis, P. A., & Shea, M. T. (1995). Impact of perfectionism and need for approval on the brief treatment of depression: The National Institute of Mental Health Treatment of Depression Collaborative Research Program revisited. *Journal of Consulting and Clinical Psychology, 63*, 125-132.

640. Blatt, S. J., Zohar, A. H., Quinlin, D. M., Zuroff, D. C., & Mongrain, M. (1995). Subscales within the dependency factor of the Depressive Experiences Questionnaire. *Journal of Personality Assessment, 64*, 319-339.

641. Bouhuys, A. L., Bloem, G. M., & Groothuis, T. G. G. (1995). Induction of depressed and elated mood by music influences the perception of facial emotional expressions in healthy subjects. *Journal of Affective Disorders, 33*, 215-226.

642. Brackney, B. E., & Karabenick, S. A. (1995). Psychology and academic performance: The role of motivation and learning strategies. *Journal of Counseling Psychology, 42*, 456–465.

643. Bradley, B. P., Mogg, K., Millar, N., & White, J. (1995). Selective processing of negative information: Effects of clinical anxiety, concurrent depression, and awareness. *Journal of Abnormal Psychology, 104*, 532–536.

644. Brown, C., Schulberg, H. C., & Madonia, M. J. (1995). Assessing depression in primary care practice with the Beck Depression Inventory and the Hamilton Rating Scale for Depression. *Psychological Assessment, 7*, 59-65.

645. Brown, E. J., Heimberg, R. G., & Juster, H. R. (1995). Social phobia subtype and avoidant personality disorder: Effect on severity of social phobia, impairment, and outcome of cognitive behavioral treatment. *Behavior Therapy, 26*, 467–486.

646. Brown, G. P., Hammen, C. J., Craske, M. G., & Wickens, T. D. (1995). Dimensions of dysfunctional attitudes as vulnerabilities to depressive symptoms. *Journal of Abnormal Psychology, 104*, 431–435.

647. Bunce, S. C., Larsen, R. J., & Peterson, C. (1995). Life after trauma: Personality and daily experiences of traumatized people. *Journal of Personality, 63*, 165–188.

648. Burch, J. W. (1995). Typicality range deficit in schizophrenics' recognition of emotion in faces. *Journal of Clinical Psychology, 51*, 140-152.

649. Carroll, K. M., Nich, C., & Rounsaville, B. J. (1995). Differential symptom reduction in depressed cocaine abusers treated with psychotherapy and pharmacotherapy. *The Journal of Nervous and Mental Disease, 183*, 251–259.

650. Carter, A. S., Grigorenko, E. L., & Pauls, D. L. (1995). A Russian adaptation of the Child Behavior Checklist: Psychometric properties and associations with child and maternal affective symptomatology and family functioning. *Journal of Abnormal Child Psychology, 23*, 661–684.

651. Carter, M. M., Hollon, S. D., Carson, R., & Shelton, R. C. (1995). Effects of a safe person on induced distress following a biological challenge in panic disorder with agoraphobia. *Journal of Abnormal Psychology, 104*, 156-163.

652. Cash, T. F., & Szymanski, M. L. (1995). The development and validation of the Body-Image Ideals Questionnaire. *Journal of Personality Assessment, 64*, 466–477.

653. Castonguay, L. G., Hayes, A. M., Goldfried, M. R., & DeRubeis, R. J. (1995). The focus of therapist interventions in cognitive therapy for depression. *Cognitive Therapy and Research, 19*, 485–503.

654. Chambless, D. L., & Williams, K. E. (1995). A preliminary study of African Americans with agoraphobia: Symptom severity and outcome of treatment with in vivo exposure. *Behavior Therapy, 26*, 501–515.

655. Chochinou, H. M., Wilson, K. G., Enns, M., & Mowchun, N., Lander, S., Levitt, M., & Clinch, J. J. (1995). Desire for death in the terminally ill. *American Journal of Psychiatry, 152*, 1185–1191.

656. Christensen, A. P., & Oei, T. P. S. (1995). The efficacy of cognitive behaviour therapy in treating premenstrual dysphoric changes. *Journal of Affective Disorders, 33*, 57-63.

657. Christensen, A. P., & Oei, T. P. S. (1995). Correlates of premenstrual dysphoria in help-seeking women. *Journal of Affective Disorders, 33*, 47-55.

658. Christensen, L., & Duncan, K. (1995). Distinguishing depressed from nondepressed individuals using energy and psychosocial variables. *Journal of Consulting and Clinical Psychology, 63*, 495–498.

659. Conway, K. (1995). Miscarriage experience and the role of support systems: A pilot study. *British Journal of Medical Psychology, 68*, 259–267.

660. Cournoyer, R. J., & Mahalik, J. R. (1995). Cross-sectional study of gender role conflict examining college-aged and middle-aged men. *Journal of Counseling Psychology, 42*, 11-19.

661. Crowson, J. J., & Cromwell, R. L. (1995). Depressed and normal individuals differ both in selection and in perceived tonal quality of positive-negative messages. *Journal of Abnormal Psychology, 104*, 305-311.

662. Dalack, G. W., Glassman, A. H., Rivelli, S., Covey, L., & Stetner, F. (1995). Mood, major depression, and fluoxetine response in cigarette smokers. *American Journal of Psychiatry, 152*, 398-403.

663. Dalgleish, T., Cameron, C. M., Power, M. J., & Bond, A. (1995). The use of an emotional priming paradigm with clinically anxious subjects. *Cognitive Therapy and Research, 19*, 69-89.

664. Davies, F., Morman, R. M. G., Cortese, L., & Malla, A. K. (1995). The relationship between types of anxiety and depression. *The Journal of Nervous and Mental Disease, 183*, 31-35.

665. De Beurs, E., van Balkom, A. J. L. M., Lange, A., Koele, P., & van Dyck, R. (1995). Treatment of panic disorder with agoraphobia: Comparison of fluvoxamine, placebo, and psychological panic management combined with exposure and of exposure in vivo alone. *American Journal of Psychiatry, 152*, 683-691.

666. DeMan, A. F., & Leduc, C. P. (1995). Suicidal ideation in high school students: Depression and other correlates. *Journal of Clinical Psychology, 51*, 173-181.

667. Dobson, K. S., & Pusch, D. (1995). A test of the depressive realism hypothesis in clinically depressed subjects. *Cognitive Therapy and Research, 19*, 179–194.

668. Dugas, M. J., Letarte, H., Rheaume, J., Freeston, M. H., & Ladouceur, R. (1995). Worry and problem solving: Evidence of a specific relationship. *Cognitive Therapy and Research, 19*, 109-120.

669. Dumas, J. E., & Wekerle, C. (1995). Maternal reports of child behavior problems and personal distress as predictors of dysfunctional parenting. *Development and Psychopathology, 7*, 465–479.

670. Eckhardt, M. J., Stapleton, J. M., Rawlings, R. R., Davis, E. Z., & Grodin, D. M. (1995). Neuropsychological functioning in detoxified alcoholics between 18 and 35 years of age. *American Journal of Psychiatry, 152*, 53-59.

671. Ehlers, A. (1995). A 1-year prospective study of panic attacks: Clinical course and factors associated with maintenance. *Journal of Abnormal Psychology, 104*, 164-172.

672. Ehlers, A., & Breuer, P. (1995). Selective attention to physical threat in subjects with panic attacks and specific phobias. *Journal of Anxiety Disorders, 9*, 11-31.

673. Eitel, P., Hatchett, L., Friend, R., Griffin, K. W., & Wadhwa, N. K. (1995). Burden of self-care in seriously ill patients: Impact on adjustment. *Health Psychology, 14*, 457– 463.

674. Ethier, L. C., Lacharité, C., & Couture, G. (1995). Childhood adversity, parental stress, and depression of negligent mothers. *Child Abuse & Neglect, 19*, 619–632.

675. Everson, S. A., Matthews, K. A., Guzick, D. S., Wing, R. R., & Kuller, L. H. (1995). Effects of surgical menopause on psychological characteristics and lipid levels: The healthy women study. *Health Psychology, 14*, 435–443.

676. Feske, U., & Chambless, D. L. (1995). Cognitive behavioral versus exposure only treatment for social phobia: A metaanalysis. *Behavior Therapy, 26*, 695–720.

677. Field, T., Fox, N. A., Pickens, J., & Nawrocki, T. (1995). Relative right frontal EEG activation in 3- to 6-month-old infants of depressed mothers. *Developmental Psychology, 31*, 358-363.

678. Field, T., Pickens, J., Fox, N. A., Nawrocki, T., & Gonzalez, J. (1995). Vagal tone in infants of depressed mothers. *Development and Psychopathology, 7*, 227-231.

679. Flett, G. L., Vredenburg, K., & Krames, L. (1995). The stability of depressive symptoms in college students: An empirical demonstration of regression to the mean. *Journal of Psychopathology and Behavioral Assessment, 17*, 403–415.

680. Foa, E. B., Riggs, D. S., & Gershuny, B. S. (1995). Arousal, numbing, and intrusion: Symptom structure of PTSD following assault. *American Journal of Psychiatry, 152*, 116-120.

681. Frasure-Smith, N., Lespérance, F., & Talajic, M. (1995). The impact of negative emotions on prognosis following myocardial infarction: Is it more than depression? *Health Psychology, 14*, 388–398.

682. Freeston, M. H., Ladouceur, R., Provencher, M., & Blais, F. (1995). Strategies used with intrusive thoughts: Context, appraisal, mood, and efficacy. *Journal of Anxiety Disorders, 9*, 201-215.

683. Gershuny, B. S., & Sher, K. J. (1995). Compulsive checking and anxiety in a nonclinical sample: Differences in cognition, behavior, personality and affect. *Journal of Psychopathology and Behavioral Assessment, 17*, 19–38.

684. Gidcyz, C. A., Hanson, K., & Layman, M. J. (1995). A prospective analysis of the relationships among sexual assault experiences. *Psychology of Women Quarterly, 19*, 5-29.

685. Ginter, G. G. (1995). Differential diagnosis in older adults: Dementia, depression, and delirium. *Journal of Counseling and Development, 73*, 346-351.

686. Goldsmith, D. F., & Rogoff, B. (1995). Sensitivity and teaching of dysphoric and nondysphoric women in structured versus unstructured situations. *Developmental Psychology, 31*, 388-394.

687. Godding, P. R., McAnulty, R. D., Wittrock, D. A., Britt, D. M., & Khansur, T. (1995). Predictors of depression among male cancer patients. *The Journal of Nervous and Mental Disease, 183*, 95-98.

688. Goldman, L., & Haaga, D. A. F. (1995). Depression and the experience and expression of anger in marital and other relationship. *The Journal of Nervous and Mental Disease, 183*, 505–509.

689. Golombok, S., Cook, R., Bish, A., & Murray, C. (1995). Families created by the new reproductive technologies: Quality of parenting and social and emotional development of the children. *Child Development, 66*, 285-298.

690. Grant, G. M., Salcedo, V., Hynan, L. S., Frisch, M. B., & Poster, K. (1995). Effectiveness of quality of life therapy for depression. *Psychological Reports, 76*, 1203–1208.

691. Grant, J. R., & Cash, T. F. (1995). Cognitive-behavioral body image therapy: Comparative efficacy of group and modest contact treatment. *Behavior Therapy, 26,* 69–84.

692. Green, M. W., & Rogers, P. J. (1995). Impaired cognitive functioning during spontaneous dieting. *Psychological Medicine, 25,* 1003–1010.

693. Griffin, K. W., Friend, R., & Wadhwa, N. K. (1995). Measuring disease severity in patients with end-stage renal disease: Validity of the Craven et al. ESRD Severity Index. *Psychological Medicine, 25,* 189-193.

694. Haaga, D. A. F., Ahrens, A. H., Schulman, P., Seligman, M. E. P., DuRubeis, R. J., & Minarik, M. L. (1995). Metatraits and cognitive assessment: Application to attributional style and depressive symptoms. *Cognitive Therapy and Research, 19,* 121-142.

695. Haaga, D. A. F., Fine, J. A., Terrill, D. R., Stewart, B. L., & Beck, A. J. (1995). Social problem-solving deficits, dependency, and depressive symptoms. *Cognitive Therapy and Research, 19,* 147–158.

696. Halberstadt, A. G., Cassidy, J., Stifter, C. A., Parke, R. D., & Fox, N. A. (1995). Self-expressiveness within the family context: Psychometric support for a new measure. *Psychological Assessment, 7,* 93-103.

697. Hammen, C. L., Burge, D., Daley, S. E., Davila, J., Paley, B., & Rudolph, K. D. (1995). Interpersonal attachment cognitions and prediction of symptomatic responses to interpersonal stress. *Journal of Abnormal Psychology, 104,* 436–443.

698. Hedlund, S., & Rude, S. S. (1995). Evidence of latent depressive schemas in formerly depressed individuals. *Journal of Abnormal Psychology, 104,* 517–525.

699. Hobfoll, S. E., Ritter, C., Lavin, J., Hulsizer, M. R., & Cameron, R. P. (1995). Depression prevalence and incidence among inner-city pregnant and postpartum women. *Journal of Consulting and Clinical Psychology, 63,* 445-453.

700. Hodges, J. R., & Patterson, K. (1995). Is semantic memory consistently impaired early in the course of Alzheimer's disease? Neuroanatomical and diagnostic implications. *Neuropsychologia, 33,* 441–459.

701. Hoffart, A. (1995). Psychoanalytical personality types and agoraphobia. *The Journal of Nervous and Mental Disease, 183,* 139-144.

702. Hofmann, S. G., Newman, M. G., Ehlers, A., & Roth, W. T. (5). Psychophysiological differences between subgroups of social phobia. *Journal of Abnormal Psychology, 104,* 224-231.

703. Ingram, R. E., Fidaleo, R. A., Friedberg, R., Shenk, J. L., & Bernet, C. Z. (1995). Content and mode of information processing in major depressive disorder. *Cognitive Therapy and Research, 19,* 281–293.

704. Ito, L. M., DeAraudjo, L. A., Hemsley, D. R., & Marks, I. M. (1995). Beliefs and resistance in obsessive-compulsive disorder: Observations from a controlled study. *Journal of Anxiety Disorders, 9,* 269–281.

705. Jackman, L. P., Williamson, D. A., Netemeyer, R. G., & Anderson, D. A. (1995). Do weight-preoccupied women misinterpret ambiguous stimuli related to body size? *Cognitive Therapy and Research, 19,* 341–355.

706. Johnson, J. G. (1995). Event-specific attributions and daily life events as predictors of depression symptom change. *Journal of Psychopathology and Behavioral Assessment, 17,* 39– 49.

707. Johnson, J. G., Williams, J. B. W., Rabkin, J. G., Goetz, R. R., & Remien, R. H. (1995). Axis I psychiatric symptoms associated with HIV infection and personality disorder. *American Journal of Psychiatry, 152,* 551-554.

708. Johnson, W. G., Schlundt, D. G., Barclay, D. R., Carr-Nangle, R. E., & Engler, L. B. (1995). A naturalistic functional analysis of binge eating. *Behavior Therapy, 26,* 101–108.

709. Joiner, T. E. (1995). The price of soliciting and receiving negative feedback: Self-verification theory as a vulnerability to depression theory. *Journal of Abnormal Psychology, 104,* 364-372.

710. Kagan, N. I., Kagan, (K). H., & Watson, M. G. (1995). Stress reduction in the workplace: The effectiveness of psychoeducational programs. *Journal of Counseling Psychology, 42,* 71-78.

711. Kalichman, S. C., Sikkema, K. J., & Somlai, A. (1995). Assessing persons with human immunodeficiency virus (HIV) infection using the Beck Depression Inventory: Disease processes and other potential confounds. *Journal of Personality Assessment, 64,* 86-100.

712. Kashubeck, S., & Christensen, S. A. (1995). Parental alcohol use, family relationship quality, self-esteem, and depression in college students. *Journal of College Student Development, 36,* 431–443.

713. Kelly, A. E., & Achter, J. A. (1995). Self-concealment and attitudes toward counseling in university students. *Journal of Counseling Psychology, 42,* 40-46.

714. Kok, R. M., Heeren, T. J., Hooijer, C., Dinkgreve, M. A. H. M., & Rooijmans, H. G. M. (1995). The prevalence of depression in elderly medical inpatients. *Journal of Affective Disorders, 23,* 77-82.

715. Kranzler, H. R., Burleson, J. A., Korner, P., Del Boca, F. K., Bohn, M. J., Brown, J., & Liebowitz, N. (1995). Placebo-controlled trial of fluoxetine as an adjunct to relapse prevention in alcoholics. *American Journal of Psychiatry, 152,* 391-397.

716. Kroeger, D. W. (1995). Self-esteem, stress, and depression among graduate students. *Psychological Reports, 76,* 345-346.

717. Kubany, E. S., Abueg, F. R., Owens, J. A., Brennan, J. M., Kaplan, A. S., & Watson, S. B. (1995). Initial examination of a multidimensional model of trauma-related guilt: Applications to combat veterans and battered women. *Journal of Psychopathology and Behavioral Assessment, 17,* 353–376.

718. Kuch, K., Cox, B. J., & Direnfeld, D. M. (1995). A brief self-rating scale for PTSD after road vehicle accident. *Journal of Anxiety Disorders, 9,* 503–514.

719. Kumar, G., & Steer, R. A. (1995). Psychosocial correlates of suicidal ideation in adolescent psychiatric inpatients. *Suicide and Life-Threatening Behavior, 25,* 339–346.

720. Kuyken, W., & Dalgleish, T. (1995). Autobiographical memory and depression. *British Journal of Clinical Psychology, 34,* 89-92.

721. Lam, R. W., Gorman, C. P., Michalon, M., Steiner, M., Levitt, A. J., Corral, M. R., Watson, G. D., Morehouse, R. L., Tam, W., & Joffe, R. T. (1995). Multicenter, placebo-controlled study of fluoxetine in seasonal affective disorder. *American Journal of Psychiatry, 152,* 1765–1770.

722. Law, W. A., Mapou, R. L., Roller, T. L., Martin, A., Nannis, E. D., & Temoshok, L. R. (1995). Reaction time slowing in HIV-1-infected individuals: Role of the preparatory interval. *Journal of Clinical and Experimental Neuropsychology, 17,* 122-133.

723. Lehmicke, N., & Hicks, R. A. (1995). Relationships of response-set differences on Beck Depression Inventory scores of undergraduate students. *Psychological Reports, 76,* 15-21.

724. Lester, D., & Akande, A. (1995). Depression in Nigerian and American students. *Psychological Reports, 76,* 906.

725. Lester, D., & Akande, A. (1995). Gender and depression in undergraduates: A comment. *Psychological Reports, 76,* 22.

726. Loss, N., Beck, S. J., & Wallace, A. (1995). Distressed and nondistressed third- and sixth-grade children's self-reports of life events and impact and concordance with mothers. *Journal of Abnormal Child Psychology, 23,* 397-409.

727. Lundy, A., Gottheil, E., Serota, R. D., Weinstein, S. P., & Sterling, R. C. (1995). Gender differences and similarities in African-American crack cocaine abusers. *The Journal of Nervous and Mental Disease, 183,* 260–266.

728. Macdiarmid, J. I., & Hetherington, M. M. (1995). Mood modulation by food: An explortion of affect and cravings in "chocolate addicts." *British Journal of Clinical Psychology, 34,* 129-138.

729. MacLeod, A. K., & Cropley, M. L. (1995). Depressive future-thinking: The role of valence and specificity. *Cognitive Therapy and Research, 19,* 35-50.

730. Malone, K. M., Haas, G. L., Sweeney, J. A., & Mann, J. J. (1995). Major depression and the risk of attempted suicide. *Journal of Affective Disorders, 34,* 173-185.

731. Mancini, C., Van Ameringen, M., & Macmillan, H. (1995). Relationship of childhood sexual and physical abuse to anxiety disorders. *The Journal of Nervous and Mental Disease, 183,* 309–314.

732. Manne, S. L., Lesanics, D., Meyers, P., Wollner, N., Steinherz, P., & Redd, W. (1995). Predictors of depressive symptomatology among parents of newly diagnosed children with cancer. *Journal of Pediatric Psychology, 20,* 491–510.

733. Markowitz, J. C., Klerman, G. L., Clougherty, K. F., Spielman, L. A., Jacobsberg, L. B., Fishman, B., Frances, A. J., Kocsis, J. H., & Perry, S. W. (1995). Individual psychotherapies for depressed HIV-positive patients. *American Journal of Psychiatry, 152,* 1504–1509.

734. Mavissakalian, M. R., Hamann, M. S., Haidar, S. A., & De Groot, C. M. (1995). Correlates of DSM-III personality disorder in generalized anxiety disorder. *Journal of Anxiety Disorders, 9,* 103-115.

735. McClain, L., & Abramson, L. Y. (1995). Self-schemas, stress, and depressed mood in college students. *Cognitive Therapy and Research, 19,* 419–432.

736. McKnight, J. D., & Glass, D. C. (1995). Perceptions of control, burnout, and depressive symptomatology: A replication and extension. *Journal of Consulting and Clinical Psychology, 63,* 490-494.

737. Mendelberg, H. E. (1995). Inpatient treatment of mood disorders. *Psychological Reports, 76,* 819–824.

738. Meszaros, A., Engelsmann, F., Meterissian, G., & Kusalic, M. (1995). Computerized assessment of depression and suicidal ideation. *The Journal of Nervous and Mental Disease, 183,* 487–488.

739. Mghir, R., Freed, W., Raskin, A., & Katon, W. (1995). Depression and posttraumatic stress disorder among a community sample of adolescent and young adult Afghan refugees. *The Journal of Nervous and Mental Disease, 183,* 24-30.

740. Mogg, K., Bradley, B. P., & Williams, R. (1995). Attentional bias in anxiety and depression: The role of awareness. *British Journal of Clinical Psychology, 34,* 17-36.

741. Moilanen, D. L. (1995). Validity of Beck's cognitive theory of depression with nonreferred adolescents. *Journal of Counseling and Development, 73,* 438–442.

742. Morris, S. J., & Kanfer, F. H. (1995). Self-evaluation, self-description, and self-standards in subclinical depression. *Journal of Psychopathology and Behavioral Assessment, 17,* 261–282.

743. Nezu, C., Nezu, A. M., Rothenberg, J. L., Dellicarpini, L., & Groag, I. (1995). Depression in adults with mild mental retardation: Are cognitive variables involved? *Cognitive Therapy and Research, 19,* 227–239.

744. Noor, N. M. (1995). Work and family roles in relation to women's well-being: A longitudinal study. *British Journal of Social Psychology, 34,* 87–106.

745. Nurmi, J., Onatsu, T., & Haavisto, T. (1995). Underachievers' cognitive and behavioral strategies: Self-handicapping at school. *Contemporary Educational Psychology, 20,* 188-200.

746. Oei, T. P. S., & Free, M. L. (1995). Do cognitive behaviour therapies validate cognitive models of mood disorders? A review of the empirical evidence. *International Journal of Psychology, 30,* 145–180.

747. Ogles, B. M., Lambert, M. J., & Sawyer, J. D. (1995). Clinical significance of the National Institute of Mental Health Treatment of Depression Collaborative Research Program Data. *Journal of Consulting and Clinical Psychology, 63,* 321-326.

748. Oldman, A., Walsh, A., Salkovskis, P., Fairburn, C. G., & Cower, P. J. (1995). Biochemical and behavioural effects of acute tryptophan depletion in abstinent bulimic subjects: A pilot study. *Psychological Medicine, 25,* 995–1001.

749. Pace, T. M., & Trapp, M. D. C. (1995). A psychometric comparison of the Beck Depression Inventory and the Inventory for Diagnosing Depression in a college population. *Assessment, 2,* 167-172.

750. Park, S., Holzman, P. S., & Lenzenweger, M. F. (1995). Individual differences in spatial working memory in relation to schizotypy. *Journal of Abnormal Psychology, 104,* 355-363.

751. Parra, E. B., Arkowitz, H., Hannah, M. T., & Vasquez, A. M. (1995). Coping strategies and emotional reactions to separation and divorce in Anglo, Chicana, and Mexicana women. *Journal of Divorce & Remarriage, 23,* 117–129.

752. Parry, B. L., Cover, H., Mostofi, N., Leveau, B., Sependa, P. A., Resnick, A., & Gillin, J. C. (1995). Early versus late partial sleep deprivation in patients with premenstrual dysphoric disorder and normal comparison subjects. *American Journal of Psychiatry, 152,* 404-412.

753. Pawluk, L. K., Hurwitz, T. D., Schluter, J. L., Ullevig, C., & Mahowald, M. W. (1995). Psychiatric morbidity in narcoleptics on chronic high dose methylphenidate therapy. *The Journal of Nervous and Mental Disease, 183,* 45-48.

754. Paykel, E. S., Ramana, R., Cooper, Z., Hayhurst, H., Kerr, J., & Barocka, A. (1995). Residual symptoms after partial remission: An important outcome in depression. *Psychological Medicine, 25,* 1171–1180.

755. Perry, W., McDougall, A., & Viglione, D. (1995). A five-year follow-up on the temporal stability of the ego impairment index. *Journal of Personality Assessment, 64,* 112-118.

756. Peterson, C., & De Avila, M. E. (1995). Optimistic explanatory style and the perception of health problems. *Journal of Clinical Psychology, 51,* 128-132.

757. Philpot, V. D., Holliman, W. B., & Madonna, S. (1995). Selfstatements, locus of control, and depression in predicitng self-esteem. *Psychological Reports, 76,* 1007–1010.

758. Pincus, T., Pearce, S., McClelland, A., & Isenberg, D. (1995). Endorsement and memory bias of self-referential pain stimuli in depressed pain patients. *British Journal of Clinical Psychology, 34,* 267-277.

759. Power, M. J., Duggan, C. F., Lee, A. S., & Murray, R. M. (1995). Dysfunctional attitudes in depressed and recovered depressed patients and their first-degree relatives. *Psychological Medicine, 25,* 87-93.

760. Ramana, R., Paykel, E. S., Cooper, Z., Hayhurst, H., Saxty, M., & Surtees, P. G. (1995). Remission and relapse in major depression: A two-year prospective follow-up study. *Psychological Medicine, 25,* 1161–1170.

761. Rauch, S. L., Savage, C. R., Alpert, N. M., Miguel, E. C., Baer, L., Brieter, H. C., Fischman, A. J., Manzo, P. A., Moretti, C., & Jenike, M. A. (1995). A positron emission tomographic study of simple phobic symptom provocation. *Archives of General Psychiatry, 52,* 20–28.

762. Reynolds, W. M., & Kobak, K. A. (1995). Reliability and validity of the Hamilton Depression Inventory: A paper-andpencil version of the Hamilton Depression Rating Scale clinical interview. *Psychological Assessment, 7,* 472–483.

763. Ricciardi, J. N., & McNally, R. J. (1995). Depressed mood is related to obsessions, but not to compulsions, in obsessive-compulsive disorder. *Journal of Anxiety Disorders, 9,* 249-256.

764. Richards, A., French, C. C., & Dowd, R. (1995). Hemisphere asymmetry and the processing of emotional words in anxiety. *Neuropsychologia, 33,* 835–841.

765. Robins, C. J., Hayes, A. M., Block, P., Kramer, R. J., & Villena, M. (1995). Interpersonal and achievement concerns and the depressive vulnerability and symptom specificity hypotheses: A prospective study. *Cognitive Therapy and Research, 19,* 1-20.

766. Rogers, J. H., Widiger, T. A., & Krupp, A. (1995). Aspects of depression associated with borderline personality disorder. *American Journal of Psychiatry, 152,* 268-270.

767. Rudd, M. D., Joiner, T. E., Jr., & Rajab, M. H. (1995). Help negation after acute suicidal crisis. *Journal of Consulting and Clinical Psychology, 63,* 499-503.

768. Rudd, M. D., & Rajab, M. H. (1995). Specificity of the Beck Depression Inventory and the confounding role of comorbid disorders in a clinical sample. *Cognitive Therapy and Research, 19,* 51-68.

769. Rude, S. S., & Burnham, B. L. (1995). Connectedness and neediness: Factors of the DEQ and SAS dependency scales. *Cognitive Therapy and Research, 19,* 323-340.

770. Sachdev, P., & Hay, P. (1995). Does neurosurgery for obsessive-compulsive disorder produce personality change? *The Journal of Nervous and Mental Disease, 183,* 408–413.

771. Sanders, B., & Becker-Lausen, E. (1995). The measurement of psychological maltreatment: Early data on the Child Abuse & Trauma Scale. *Child Abuse & Neglect, 19,* 315–323.

772. Santor, D. A., Zuroff, D. C., Ramsay, J. Q., Cervantes, P., & Palacios, J. (1995). Examining scale discriminability in the BDI and CES-D as a function of depressive severity. *Psychological Assessment, 7,* 131-139.

773. Satel, S. L., Krystal, J. H., Delgado, P. L., Kosten, T. R., & Charney, D. S. (1995). Tryptophan depletion and attenuation of cue-induced craving for cocaine. *American Journal of Psychiatry, 152,* 778-783.

774. Savournin, R., Evans, C., Hirst, J. F., & Watson, J. P. (1995). The elusive factor structure of the Inventory of Interpersonal Problems. *British Journal of Medical Psychology, 68,* 353–369.

775. Schmidt, N. B., & Harrington, P. (1995). Cognitive-behavioral treatment of body dysmorphic disorder: A case report. *Journal of Behavior Therapy and Experimental Psychiatry, 26,* 161–167.

776. Schneider, B., & Varghese, R. K. (1995). Scores on the SF-36 Scales and the Beck Depression Inventory in assessing mental health among patients on hemodialysis. *Psychological Reports, 76,* 719–722.

777. Schumaker, J. F., Warren, W. G., Carr, S. C., Schreiber, G. S., & Jackson, C. C. (1995). Dissociation and depression in eating disorders. *Social Behavior and Personality, 23,* 53-58.

778. Segal, Z. V., Gemar, M., Truchon, C., Guirguis, M., & Horowitz, L. M. (1995). A priming methodology for studying self-representation in major depressive disorder. *Journal of Abnormal Psychology, 104,* 205-213.

779. Seiner, S. H., & Gelfand, D. M. (1995). Effects of mothers' simulated withdrawl and depressed affect on mother-toddler interactions. *Child Development, 66,* 1519–1528.

780. Senra, C. (1995). Measures of treatment outcome of depression: An effect size comparison. *Psychological Reports, 76,* 187-192.

781. Sequin, M., Lesage, A., & Kiely, M. C. (1995). Parental bereavement after suicide and accident: A comparative study. *Suicide and Life-Threatening Behavior, 25,* 489–498.

782. Shapiro, D. A., Rees, A., Barkham, M., Hardy, G., Reynolds, S., & Startup, M. (1995). Effects of treatment duration and severity of depression on the maintenance of gains after cognitive-behavioral and psychodynamic-interpersonal psychotherapy. *Journal of Consulting and Clinical Psychology, 63,* 378-387.

783. Shaw, D. S., & Vondra, J. I. (1995). Infant attachment security and maternal predictors of early behavior problems: A longitudinal study of low-income families. *Journal of Abnormal Child Psychology, 23,* 335-357.

784. Shean, G. D., & Heefner, A. S. (1995). Depression, interpersonal style, and communication skills. *The Journal of Nervous and Mental Disease, 183,* 485–487.

785. Siegrist, M. (1995). Inner speech as a cognitive process mediating self-consciousness and inhibiting self-deception. *Psychological Reports, 76,* 259-265.

786. Simons, A. D., Gordon, J. S., Monroe, S. M., & Thase, M. E. (1995). Toward an integration of psychologic, social, and biologic factors in depression: Effects on outcome and course of cognitive therapy. *Journal of Consulting and Clinical Psychology, 63,* 369-377.

787. Smith, W. P., Comptn, W. C., & West, W. B. (1995). Meditation as an adjunct to a happiness enhancement program. *Journal of Clinical Psychology, 51,* 269-273.

788. Solomon, S., Greenberg, J., Psyzczynski, T., & Pryzbylinski, J. (1995). The effects of mortality salience on personallyrelevant persuasive appeals. *Social Behavior and Personality, 23,* 177–190.

789. Spencer, T., Wilens, T., Biederman, J., Faraone, S. V., Ablon, S., & Lapey, K. (1995). A double-blind, crossover comparison of methylphenidate and placebo in adults with childhood-onset attention deficit hyperactivity disorder. *Archives of General Psychiatry, 52,* 434–443.

790. Steer, R. A., Clark, D. A., Beck, A. T., & Ranieri, W. F. (1995). Common and specific dimensions of self-reported anxiety and depression: A replication. *Journal of Abnormal Psychology, 104,* 542–545.

791. Steer, R. A., Kumar, G., Ranieri, W. F., & Beck, A. T. (1995). Use of the Beck Anxiety Inventory with adolescent psychiatric outpatients. *Psychological Reports, 76,* 459–465.

792. Stein, M. B., Kirk, P., Prabhu, V., Grott, M., & Terepa, M. (1995). Mixed anxiety-depression in a primary-care clinic. *Journal of Affective Disorders, 34,* 79-84.

793. Stiles, W. B., & Shapiro, D. A. (1995). Verbal exchange structure of brief psychodynamic-interpersonal and cognitive-behavioral psychotherapy. *Journal of Consulting and Clinical Psychology, 63,* 15-27.

794. Stiles, W. B., Shapiro, D. A., Harper, H., & Morrison, L. A. (1995). Therapist contributions to psychotherapeutic assimilation: An alternative to the drug metaphor. *British Journal of Medical Psychology, 68,* 1–13.

795. Streichenwein, S. M., & Thornby, J. I. (1995). A long-term double-blind, placebo-controlled crossover trial of the efficacy of fluoxetine for trichotillomania. *American Journal of Psychiatry, 152,* 1192–1196.

796. Sullivan, M. J. L., Bishop, S. R., & Pivik, J. (1995). The Pain Catastrophizing Scale: Development and validation. *Psychological Assessment, 7,* 524–532.

797. Sutker, P. B., Davis, J. M., Uddo, M., & Ditta, S. R. (1995). Assessment of psychological distress in Persian Gulf troops: Ethnicity and gender comparisons. *Journal of Personality Assessment, 64,* 415-427.

798. Sutker, P. B., Davis, J. M., Uddo, M., & Ditta, S. R. (1995). War zone stress, personal resources, and PTSD in Persian Gulf War returnees. *Journal of Abnormal Psychology, 104,* 444–452.

799. Swanson, S. C., Templer, D. I., Thomas-Dobson, S., Cannon, W. G., Streiner, D. L., Reynolds, R. M., & Miller, H. R. (1995). Development of a three-scale MMPI: The MMPI-TRI. *Journal of Clinical Psychology, 51,* 361-374.

800. Teasdale, J. D., Taylor, M. J., Cooper, Z., Hayhurst, H., & Paykel, E. S. (1995). Depressive thinking: Shifts in construct accessibility or in schematic mental models? *Journal of Abnormal Psychology, 104,* 500–507.

801. Teti, D. M., Gelfand, D. M., Messinger, D. S., & Isabella, R. (1995). Maternal depression and the quality of early attachment: An examination of infants, preschoolers, and their mothers. *Developmental Psychology, 31,* 364-376.

802. Thomas, A. M., Forehand, R., & Neighbors, B. (1995). Change in maternal depressive mood: Unique contributions to adolescent functioning over time. *Adolescence, 30,* 41–52.

803. Tivis, L. J., & Parsons, O. A. (1995). An investigation of verbal spatial functioning in chronic alcoholics. *Assessment, 2,* 285–292.

804. Tran, G. Q., & Chambless, D. L. (1995). Psychopathology of social phobia: Effects of subtype and of avoidant personality disorder. *Journal of Anxiety Disorders, 9,* 489–501.

805. Trief, P. M., Carnrike, C. L. M., Jr., & Drudge, O. (1995). Chronic pain and depression: Is social support relevant. *Psychological Reports, 76*, 227-236.

806. Trull, T. J. (1995). Borderline personality disorder features in nonclinical young adults: I. Identification and validation. *Psychological Assessment, 7*, 33-41.

807. Tucker, D. D., & Schlundt, D. G. (1995). Selective information processing and schematic content related to eating behavior. *Journal of Psychopathology and Behavioral Assessment, 17*, 1–17.

808. Varnado, P. J., Williamson, D. A., & Netemeyer, R. (1995). Confirmatory factor analysis of eating disorder symptoms in college women. *Journal of Psychopathology and Behavioral Assessment, 17*, 69–79.

809. Viglione, D. J., Lovette, G. J., & Gottlieb, R. (1995). Depressive Experiences Questionnaire: An empirical exploration of the underlying theory. *Journal of Personality Assessment, 65*, 91–99.

810. Vlaeyen, J. W. S., Haazen, I. W. C. J., Schuerman, J. A., Kole-Snijders, A. M. J., & van Eek, H. (1995). Behavioural rehabilitation of chronic low back pain: Comparison of an operant treatment, an operant-cognitive treatment and an operant-respondent treatment. *British Journal of Clinical Psychology, 34*, 95-118.

811. Vrana, S. R., Roodman, A. & Beckham, J. C. (1995). Selective processing of trauma-relevant words in posttraumatic stress disorder. *Journal of Anxiety Disorders, 9*, 515–530.

812. Wallace, J., & Pfohl, B. (1995). Age-related differences in the symptomatic expression of major depression. *The Journal of Nervous and Mental Disease, 183*, 99-102.

813. Watson, D., Weber, K., Assenheimer, J. S., Clark, L. A., Strauss, M. E., & McCormick, R. A. (1995). Testing a tripartite model: I. Evaluating convergent and discriminant validity of Anxiety and Depression Symptom Scales. *Journal of Abnormal Psychology, 104*, 3-14.

814. Weekes, J. R., Morison, S. J., Millson, W. A., & Fettig, D. M. (1995). A comparison of native, metis, and caucasian offender profiles on the MCMI. *Canadian Journal of Behavioural Science, 27*, 187–1908.

815. Weizman, A., Burgin, R., Harel, Y., Karp, L., & Gavish, M. (1995). Platelet peripheral-type benzodiazepine receptor in major depression. *Journal of Affective Disorders, 33*, 257-261.

816. Wells, P. A., Willmoth, T., & Russell, R. J. H. (1995). Does fortune favour the bald? Psychological correlates of hair loss in males. *British Journal of Psychology, 86*, 337–344.

817. Whisman, M. A., Miller, I. W., Norman, W. H., & Keitner, G. I. (1995). Hopelessness, depression in depressed inpatients: Symptomatology, patient characteristics, and outcome. *Cognitive Therapy and Research, 19*, 377–398.

818. Woody, G. E., McLellan, A. T., Luborsky, L., & O'Brien, C. P. (1995). Psychotherapy in community methadone programs: A validation study. *American Journal of Psychiatry, 152*, 1302–1308.

819. Worling, J. R. (1995). Adolescent sibling-incest offenders: Differences in family and individual functioning when compared to adolescent nonsibling sex offenders. *Child Abuse & Neglect, 19*, 633–643.

820. Yager, J., Rorty, M., & Rossotto, E. (1995). Coping styles differ between recovered and nonrecovered women with bulimia nervosa, but not between recovered women and non-eating disordered control subjects. *The Journal of Nervous and Mental Disease, 183*, 86-94.

821. Yang, B., & Clum, G. A. (1995). Measures of life stress and social support specific to an Asian student population. *Journal of Psychopathology and Behavioral Assessment, 17*, 51– 67.

822. Yin, Z., Zapata, J. T., & Katims, D. S. (1995). Risk factors for substance use among Mexican–American school–age youth. *Hispanic Journal of Behavior Sciences, 17*, 61–76.

823. Zeitlin, S. B., & Polivy, J. (1995). Coprophagia as a manifestation of obsessive-compulsive disorder: A case report. *Journal of Behavior Therapy and Experimental Psychiatry, 26*, 57–63.

824. Zettle, R. D., & Herring, E. L. (1995). Treatment utility of the sociotropy/autonomy distinction: Implications for cognitive therapy. *Journal of Clinical Psychology, 51*, 280-289.

825. Baker, M., Milich, R., & Manolis, M. B. (1996). Peer interactions of dysphoric adolescents. *Journal of Abnormal Child Psychology, 24*, 241–255.

826. Breitbart, W., Rosenfeld, B. D., & Passik, S. D. (1996). Interest in physician-assisted suicide among ambulatory HIV infected patients. *American Journal of Psychiatry, 153*, 238– 242.

827. Channon, S. (1996). Executive dysfunction in depression: The Wisconsin Card Sorting Test. *Journal of Affective Disorders, 39*, 107–114.

828. Cheung, E. C. (1996). Cultural differences in optimism, pessimism, and coping: Predictors of subsequent adjustment in Asian American and Caucasian American college students. *Journal of Counseling Psychology, 43*, 113–123.

829. Clark, M. E. (1996). MMPI-2 negative treatment indicators content and content component scales: Clinical correlates and outcome prediction for men with chronic pain. *Psychological Assessment, 8*, 32–38.

830. Coleman, M. J., Levy, D. L., Lenzenweger, M. F., & Holzman, P. S. (1996). Thought disorder, perceptual aberrations, and schizotypy. *Journal of Abnormal Psychology, 105*, 469–473.

831. Corbitt, E. M., Malone, K. M., Haas, G. L., & Mann, J. J. (1996). Suicidal behavior in patients with major depression and comorbid personality disorders. *Journal of Affective Disorders, 39*, 61–72.

832. Dahlquist, L. M., Czyzewski, D. I., & Jones, C. L. (1996). Parents of children with cancer: A longitudinal study of emotional distress, coping style, and marital adjustment two and twenty months after diagnosis. *Journal of Pediatric Psychology, 21*, 541–554.

833. Davis, J. M., Adams, H. E., Uddo, M., Vasterling, J. J., & Sutker, P. B. (1996). Physiological arousal and attention in veterans with posttraumatic stress disorder. *Journal of Psychopathology and Behavioral Assessment, 18*, 1–20.

834. Deffenbacher, J. L., Oetting, E. R., Thwaites, G. A., Lynch, R. S., Baker, D. A., Stark, R. S., Tacker, S., & ElswerthCox, L. (1996). State-trait anger theory and the utility of the Trait Anger Scale. *Journal of Counseling Psychology, 43*, 131–148.

835. Delahanty, D. L., Dougall, A. L., Schmitz, J. B., Hawken, L., Trakowski, J. H., Jenkins, F. J., & Baum, A. (1996). Time course of natural killer cell activity and lymphocyte proliferation in response to two acute stressors in healthy men. *Health Psychology, 15*, 48–55.

836. Dimitrov, M., Grafman, J., & Hollnagel, C. (1996). The effects of frontal lobe damage on everyday problem solving. *Cortex, 32*, 357–366.

837. Fastenau, P. S., Denburg, N. L., & Abeles, N. (1996). Age differences in retrieval: Further support for the resourcereduction hypothesis. *Psychology and Aging, 11*, 140–146.

838. Foa, E. B., Franklin, M. E., Perry, K. J., & Herbert, J. D. (1996). Cognitive biases in generalized social phobia. *Journal of Abnormal Psychology, 105*, 433–439.

839. Giesler, R. B., Josephs, R. A., & Swann, W. B., Jr. (1996). Self-verification in clinical depression: The desire for negative evaluation. *Journal of Abnormal Psychology, 105*, 358–368.

840. Gould, R. A., Ball, S., Kaspi, S. P., Otto, M. W., Pollack, M. H., Shekhar, A., & Fava, M. (1996). Prevalence and correlates of anger attacks: A two site study. *Journal of Affective Disorders, 39*, 31–38.

841. Greene, J. D. W., Baddeley, A. D., & Hodges, J. R. (1996). Analysis of the episodic memory deficit in early Alzheimer's disease: Evidence from the Doors and People Test. *Neuropsychologia, 34*, 537–551.

842. Hewitt, P. L., Flett, G. L., & Ediger, E. (1996). Perfectionism and depression: Longitudinal assessment of a specific vulnerability hypothesis. *Journal of Abnormal Psychology, 105*, 276–280.

843. Horowitz, M., Sonneborn, D., Sugahara, C., & Maercker, A. (1996). Self-regard: A new measure. *American Journal of Psychiatry, 153*, 382–385.

844. Jacob, R. G., Furman, J. M., Durrant, J. D., & Turner, S. M. (1996). Panic, agoraphobia, and vestibular dysfunction. *American Journal of Psychiatry, 153*, 503–512.

845. Johnson, S. K., DeLuca, J., & Natelson, B. H. (1996). Depression in fatiguing illness: Comparing patients with chronic fatigue syndrome, multiple sclerosis and depression. *Journal of Affective Disorders, 39*, 21–30.

846. Jolly, J. B., Dyck, M. J., Kramer, T. A., & Wherry, J. N. (1994). Integration of positive and negative affectivity and cognitive content-specificity: Improved discrimination of anxious and depressive symptoms. *Journal of Abnormal Psychology, 103*, 544-552.

847. Kelly, V. A., & Myers, J. E. (1996). Parental alcoholism and coping: A comparison of female children of alcoholics with female children of nonalcoholics. *Journal of Counseling and Development, 74*, 501–504.

848. Kinderman, P., & Bentall, R. P. (1996). Self-discrepancies and persecutory delusions: Evidence for a model of paranoid ideation. *Journal of Abnormal Psychology, 105*, 106–113.

849. Kissane, D. W., Bloch, S., Dowe, D. L., Snyder, R. D., Onghena, P., McKenzie, D. P., & Wallace, C. S. (1996). The Melbourne Family Grief Study, I: Perceptions of family functioning in bereavement. *American Journal of Psychiatry, 153*, 650–658.

850. Kissane, D. W., Bloch, S., Onghena, P., McKenzie, D. P., Snyder, R. D., & Dowe, D. L. (1996). The Melbourne Family Grief Study, II: Psychosocial morbidity and grief in bereaved families. *American Journal of Psychiatry, 153*, 659–666.

851. Koivisto, M., Portin, R., & Rinne, J. O. (1996). Perceptual priming in Alzheimer's and Parkinson's diseases. *Neuropsychologia, 34*, 449–457.

852. Kopper, B. A., & Epperson, D. L. (1996). The experience and expression of anger: Relationships with gender, gender role socialization, depression, and mental health functioning. *Journal of Counseling Psychology, 43*, 158–165.

853. Maes, M., Smith, R., Christophe, A., Cosyns, P., Desnyder, R., & meltzer, H. (1996). Fatty acid composition in major depression: Decreased omega 3 fractions in cholesteryl esters and increased C20: 4 omega 6/C20: 5 omega 3 ratio in cholesteryl esters and phospholipids. *Journal of Affective Disorders, 38*, 35–46.

854. McNally, R. J., Amir, N., & Lipke, H. J. (1996). Subliminal processing of threat cues in posttraumatic stress disorder. *Journal of Anxiety Disorders, 10*, 115–128.

855. Monroe, S. M., Roberts, J. E., Kupfer, D. J., & Frank, E. (1996). Life stress and treatment course of recurrent depression: II. Postrecovery associations with attrition, symptom course, and recurrence over 3 years. *Journal of Abnormal Psychology, 105*, 313–328.

856. Nunn, K. P., Lewin, T. J., Walton, J. M., & Carr, V. J. (1996). The construction and characteristics of an instrument to measure personal hopefulness. *Psychological Medicine, 26*, 531–545.

857. Power, M. J., Comeron, C. M., & Dalgleish, T. (1996). Emotional priming in clinically depressed subjects. *Journal of Affective Disorders, 38*, 1–11.

858. Radcliffe, J., Bennett, D., Kazak, A. E., Foley, B., & Phillips, P. C. (1996). Adjustment in childhood brain tumor survival: Child, mother, and teacher report. *Journal of Pediatric Psychology, 21*, 529–539.

859. Richards, A., French, C. C., & Randall, F. (1996). Anxiety and the use of strategies in the performance of sentencepicture verification task. *Journal of Abnormal Psychology, 105*, 132–136.

860. Rush, A. J., Gullion, C. M., Basco, M. R., Jarrett, R. B., & Trivedi, M. H. (1996). The Inventory of Depressive Symptomatology (IDS): Psychometric properties. *Psychological Medicine, 26*, 477–486.

861. Smith, D. W., & Frueh, B. C. (1996). Compensation seeking, comorbidity, and apparent exaggeration of PTSD symptoms among Vietnam combat veterans. *Psychological Assessment, 8*, 3–6.

862. Spalletta, G., Troisi, A., Saracco, M., Ciani, N., & Pasini, A. (1996). Symptom profile, Axis II comorbidity and suicidal behavior in young males with DSM–III–R depressive illnesses. *Journal of Affective Disorders, 39*, 141–148.

863. Stein, M. B., Baird, A., & Walker, J. R. (1996). Social phobia in adults with stuttering. *American Journal of Psychiatry, 153*, 278–280.

864. Stout, J. C., Salmon, D. P., Butters, N., Taylor, M., Peavy, G., Heindel, W. C., Delis, D. C., Ryan, L., Atkinson, J. H., Chandler, J. L., Grant, I., & The HNRC Group. (1995). Decline in working memory associated with HIV infection. *Psychological Medicine, 25*, 1221–1232.

865. Taylor, S., Koch, W. J., Woody, S., & McLean, P. (1996). Anxiety sensitivity and depression: How are they related? *Journal of Abnormal Psychology, 105*, 474–479.

866. Terry, D. J., Mayocchi, L., & Hynes, G. J. (1996). Depressive symptomatology in new mothers: A stress and coping perspective. *Journal of Abnormal Psychology, 105*, 220–231.

867. Trappler, B., & Friedman, S. (1996). Posttraumatic stress disorder in survivors of the Brooklyn Bridge shooting. *American Journal of Psychiatry, 153*, 705–707.

868. Van Ameringen, M., Mancini, C., & Wilson, C. (1996). Buspirone augmentation of selective serotonin reuptake inhibitors (SSRIs) in social phobia. *Journal of Affective Disorders, 39*, 115–121.

869. Waldstein, S. R., Polefrone, J. M., Fazzari, T. V., Manuck, S. B., Jennings, J. R., Ryan, C. M., Muldoon, M. F., & Shapiro, A. P. (1996). Hypertension and neuropsychological performance in men: Interactive effects of age. *Health Psychology, 15*, 102–109.

870. Watkins, P. C., Vache, K., Verney, S. P., Muller, S., & Mathews, A. (1996). Unconscious mood-congruent memory bias in depression. *Journal of Abnormal Psychology, 105*, 34–41.

Review of the Beck Depression Inventory [1993 Revised] by JANET F. CARLSON, Associate Professor of Counseling and Psychological Services, State University of New York—College at Oswego, Oswego, NY:

The Beck Depression Inventory (BDI) is a well-known and widely used self-report inventory that taps overall severity of depression in adolescents and adults. The original BDI was developed by Beck and his associates in 1961 (Beck, Ward, Mendelson, Mock, & Erbaugh, 1961) and revised in 1971, at which time it was introduced at the Center for Cognitive Therapy (CCT) of the University of Pennsylvania Medical School where a large portion of research bearing on the BDI has been conducted. The current edition consists of 21 symptoms and attitudes, which the subject rates on a 4-point scale of severity. Test takers are asked to rate the items for the past week, including the day on which the test is taken. The items cover cognitive, affective, somatic, and vegetative dimensions of depression, although the inventory itself was developed atheoretically. Collectively, the items correspond reasonably well to the symptoms of depression listed in the *Diagnostic and Statistical Manual of Mental Disorders* (4th ed.) (*DSM-IV*, American Psychiatric Association, 1994).

APPLICATIONS. The use of the BDI has expanded well beyond its original intended application with psychiatric populations. In addition to its continued use among this population, it is accepted and commonly used by clinicians as a screening instrument among normal populations. The test authors are careful to avoid endorsing the use of the BDI for purposes other than those for which it was developed, and simply acknowledge that many practitioners have found the inventory useful in these other contexts. The test authors indicate the vast amount of research and attending literature has supported the use of the BDI in myriad applications, from research, to screening, to assessment of therapeutic outcomes. Despite the extensive body of research bearing on numerous aspects of the BDI, the test manual itself contains only "an overview of the published information on the revision" despite noting that "specific characteristics of the revised BDI have not previously been described in detail" (p. 1).

ADMINISTRATION, SCORING, AND INTERPRETATION. The BDI may be administered individually or in group format, in written or oral form. Instructions to the test taker were modified slightly from the previous edition, as the current version directs test takers to described themselves or their feelings over the past week, including the present day. Thus, the 1993 edition taps more trait aspects of depression whereas the earlier version appears to have measured state aspects of depression. The test manual authors indicate that total administration time is no more than 15 minutes, irrespective of the mode of administration. A total score is obtained by simply summing the ratings given by the test taker on all items. Interpretation is based on the total score, which may range from 0 to 63. Among depressed patients, scores in the 0–9 range denote "Minimal" depression, 10–16 suggest "Mild" depression, 17–29 are considered "Moderate", and scores in the 30–63 range indicate "Severe" levels of depression. Within the normal population, total scores above 15 may be indicative of possible depression, although further assessment would be essential in order to confirm the presence of depression. Computer software is available from The Psychological Corporation, which offers the Beck Computer Scoring program (Beck & Steer, 1992). The program scores and interprets the BDI, as well as the several other instruments developed by Beck.

The test authors note that in addition to the total score, responses to individual items should be considered in an effort to understand and extract clinically meaningful data. In particular, the clinical relevance of Item 2, which the authors term the pessimism/hopelessness item, and Item 9, the suicide ideation item, is noted. Because the severity of depression, as assessed by the BDI, is independent of symptom types, the test authors suggest that overall patterns of responses be considered in order to ascertain whether the individual patient demonstrates symptoms that are more cognitive, more somatic, more vegetative, or more affective. Elucidating the nature of the most prominent symptoms may have important treatment implications.

TECHNICAL ASPECTS. The section of the test manual that covers psychometric characteristics presents information from six normative-outpatient samples used by the CCT to establish reliability estimates and provide evidence of scale validation. The total normative sample consisted of 944 outpatients with mixed diagnoses (n = 248), single episodes of major depression (n = 113), recurrent episodes of major depression (n = 168), Dysthymic disorder (n = 99), alcoholism (n = 105), or heroine addiction (n = 211). Gender and race distributions of the six normative samples are presented in the test manual, as are means, standard deviations, percentages of item endorsement, and item-total correlations.

Alpha reliability coefficients across the six samples ranged from .79 to .90. Item-total correlations ranged from .07 to .68, with most values being in the .30 or better range. The authors cite several studies related to the stability of BDI scores over time, using patient and nonpatient groups. It appears that nonpsychiatric samples demonstrate somewhat more stable BDI scores (in the .60 to .90 range) than patient samples (in the .48 to .86 range). These results are not unexpected, given that depressed individuals who are undergoing treatment are expected to improve.

Validation evidence for the BDI is provided in the test manual under the headings of content, discriminant, construct, and concurrent validity. The test authors report on two studies that compared the content of the revised BDI to *DSM-III* criteria for affective disorders and found that two-thirds of the criteria were addressed by the BDI

items. The authors note that the lack of items related to the omitted criteria was intentional, and provide an appropriate rationale for not including items that reflected these criteria. The test authors cite several studies bearing on the ability of the BDI to differentiate psychiatric patients from normals, patients with Dysthymic Disorder from those with Major Depressive Disorder, and patients with Generalized Anxiety Disorders from those with Major Depressive Disorder. Based on research findings, the test authors extracted two subscales that can be calculated by summing the ratings for appropriate items. Items 1 through 13 comprise the cognitive-affective subscale, and Items 14 through 21 comprise the somatic-performance subscale. A score greater than 10 on the cognitive-affective subscale indicates moderate depression. Correlation coefficients between the BDI and the Beck Hopelessness Scale and the Hamilton Rating Scale for Depression ranged from .38 to .76 and from .40 to .87, respectively, across the six normative-outpatient samples. Among patients with mixed depressive disorders, correlation coefficients between the BDI and the Symptom Checklist-90-Revised and the Minnesota Multiphasic Personality Inventory-Depression scale were .76 and .61, respectively.

Factor analyses with clinical and nonclinical samples have been conducted. Some of the findings are presented briefly in the test manual. The test authors note the number of factors extracted varied with the characteristics of the samples used, and with the method of extraction employed. Brown, Schulberg, and Madonia (1995) indicate that the many factor analyses of the BDI have found anywhere from three to seven factors and note that "[s]tudies using latent structure analysis suggest that the BDI represents one general syndrome of depression that subsumes three highly inter-correlated factors ... reflect[ing] negative attitudes toward self, performance impairment, and somatic disturbance, as originally described by Beck and Lester" (p. 59). Compared to other measures of depression, the BDI appears to tap more of the cognitive or cognitive-affective components of depression than other instruments such as the Hamilton Rating Scale for Depression (T4:2261) and the Zung Self-Rating Scale (e.g., Brown, Schulberg, & Madonia, 1995; Lambert, Hatch, Kingston, & Edwards, 1986; Santor, Zuroff, Ramsay, Cervantes, & Palacios, 1995).

Because so much additional information concerning the psychometric properties of the BDI is contained in the literature and is not contained in the test manual, potential users would be well advised to consult the literature for further information. Prior reviews of the earlier editions of the BDI have indicated the importance of doing so as well. One previous reviewer (Conoley, 1992) summarized the findings of a reference that the reviewer found particularly useful, in that it presents a review and meta-analysis of the reliability and validity literature for the BDI (Beck, Steer, & Garbin, 1988). Readers are referred to these sources for elaboration.

CRITIQUE. In general, the information referenced in the test manual and elsewhere is favorable and supportive of the BDI as far as its use with the intended population and, perhaps, others (Brown, Schulberg, & Madonia, 1995; Conoley, 1992; Santor, Zuroff, Ramsay, Cervantes, & Palacios, 1995; Stehouwer, 1985; Sundberg, 1992). The BDI has been widely used over at least the last 25 years, and has been recognized for its solid contributions to the measurement of depression. Potential users must be prepared, however, to ferret out some information beyond that presented in the test manual that may affect their choice of instruments. In particular, test users should bear in mind that the BDI is not intended to be a diagnostic instrument. Thus, in clinical applications, it is best regarded as a screening instrument for depression or as an indicator of the extent of depression, and should not serve as the sole means by which depression is assessed.

The availability of software to score and interpret the BDI makes its use as a screening and/or research instrument quite practical and it seems likely that the BDI will continue to enjoy widespread applications in these venues. In situations where the ratings given to somatic or performance items could be attributable to another cause (e.g., a medical condition where fatigue is a symptom or side effect of treatment), the use of the cognitive-affective subscale may be particularly helpful, although further evidence of the validity and reliability of the subscale is needed. Similarly, validity and reliability evidence to establish the probity of various modifications to administration noted in the test manual would be useful additions.

All items on the BDI contribute to the total score (i.e., there are no filler items) and items clearly are aimed at assessing aspects of depression. The four response options presented for each item are numbered from 0 to 3, in order of increasing severity, and scoring blanks are presented on each side of the test form. These characteristics make administration, scoring, and interpretation straightforward and, for many users, probably contribute to the appeal of this instrument. But these traits make faking rather easy as well. In cases where test takers might be motivated to deceive (e.g., competency to stand trial, custody hearings, involuntary commitment procedures, social desirability), the test user is advised to use additional or less transparent means of assessment.

SUMMARY. The BDI has made, and is likely to continue making, a noteworthy contribution to the assessment of depression. The expansion of its use beyond that originally intended by the test authors is likely attributable to its obvious strengths. Working in its favor are the facts that it is a simple measure that is easily and rapidly administered, encompasses the majority of symptoms associated with depression, has been well researched, can be scored and interpreted via computer software, and can be considerably less expensive than other screening or research tools that require individual administration.

REVIEWER'S REFERENCES

Beck, A. T., Ward, C. H., Mendelson, M., Mock, J., & Erbaugh, J. (1961). An inventory for measuring depression. *Archives of General Psychiatry, 4*, 561–571.

Stehouwer, R. S. (1985). [Review of Beck Depression Inventory]. In D. J. Keyser & R. C. Sweetland (Eds.), *Test critiques* (Vol. II) (pp. 83–87). Kansas City, MO: Test Corporation of America/Westport Publishers.

Lambert, M. J., Hatch, D. R., Kingston, M. D., & Edwards, B. C. (1986). Zung, Beck, and Hamilton rating scales as measures of treatment outcome: A meta-analytic comparison. *Journal of Consulting and Clinical Psychology, 54*, 54–59.

Beck, A. T., Steer, R. A., & Garbin, M. G. (1988). Psychometric properties of the Beck Depression Inventory: Twenty-five years of evaluation. *Clinical Psychology Review, 8*, 77–100.

Beck, A. T., & Steer, R. A. (1992). *Beck computer scoring*. San Antonio, TX: The Psychological Corporation.

Conoley, C. W. (1992). [Review of the Beck Depression Inventory (Revised Edition)]. In J. J. Kramer & J. C. Conoley (Eds.), *The eleventh mental measurements yearbook* (pp. 78–79). Lincoln, NE: The Buros Institute of Mental Measurements.

Sundberg, N. D. (1992). [Review of the Beck Depression Inventory (Revised Edition)]. In J. J. Kramer & J. C. Conoley (Eds.), *The eleventh mental measurements yearbook* (pp. 79–81). Lincoln, NE: The Buros Institute of Mental Measurements.

American Psychiatric Association. (1994). *Diagnostic and statistical manual of mental disorders* (4th ed.). Washington, DC: Author.

Brown, C., Schulberg, H. C., & Madonia, M. J. (1995). Assessing depression in primary care practice with the Beck Depression Inventory and the Hamilton Rating Scale for Depression. *Psychological Assessment, 7*, 59–65.

Santor, D. A., Zuroff, D. C., Ramsay, J. O., Cervantes, P., & Palacios, J. (1995). Examining scale discriminability in the BDI and CES-D as a function of depressive severity. *Psychological Assessment, 7*, 131–139.

Review of the Beck Depression Inventory by NIELS G. WALLER, *Associate Professor of Psychology, University of California, Davis, CA:*

The Beck Depression Inventory (BDI) is a brief self-report measure of depressive symptoms in adolescents and adults. It has been a clinical mainstay for more than 35 years (Beck, Ward, Mendelson, Mock, & Erbaugh, 1961) and, not surprisingly, the BDI has spawned a rich and extensive research literature. To date, the BDI—in one form or another—has been used in over 3,000 studies. Most of these have used a 21-item long form (Beck, Ward, Mendelson, Mock, & Erbaugh, 1961), although authorized (Beck & Beck, 1972) and unauthorized short forms have also been used. A new edition of the BDI, called the BDI-II (Beck, Steer, & Brown, 1996) is scheduled for release in 1996. At the time of this writing the BDI-II was not available; thus my review focuses on the BDI, although I also discuss some promised features of the BDI-II.

The BDI can be administered via paper and pencil, a computer, or orally in approximately 5–15 minutes. In other words, in less time than it takes to drink a cup of coffee, a clinician or researcher can gather information on 21 signs of depression severity: (1) Sadness, (2) Pessimism, (3) Sense of Failure, (4) Dissatisfaction, (5) Guilt, (6) Punishment, (7) Self-dislike, (8) Self-accusations, (9) Suicidal ideas, (10) Crying, (11) Irritability, (12) Social withdrawal, (13) Indecisiveness, (14) Body Image Change, (15) Work difficulty, (16) Insomnia, (17) Fatigability, (18) Loss of Appetite, (19) Weight Loss, (20) Somatic Preoccupation, and (21) Loss of Libido. These symptoms were not selected to reflect any particular theory of depression. The items of the BDI-II, on the other hand, are tailored to the current criteria of depression as outlined in the *Diagnostic and Statistical Manual of Mental Disorders, Fourth Edition* (*DSM-IV*).

BDI items comprise four self-descriptive statements. For example, Item 10—which measures Crying—reads as follows: "(0) *I don't cry any more than usual;* (1) *I cry more now than I used to;* (2) I cry all the time now; (3) I used to be able to cry, but now I can't cry even though I want to*" (p. 1, BDI Questionnaire). Notice that each statement is preceded by a scoring weight. The weights range from 0 to 3; consequently BDI total scores range from 0 to 63. The scoring weights were rationally derived such that higher weights signify greater symptom severity in clinical populations. For some items, as discussed below, the scoring weights are not appropriate for nonclinical samples. All items

are face valid (transparent) and scored in the same direction. Thus, BDI scores can be easily distorted with respect to faking (Beck & Beamesderfer, 1974; Dahlstrom, Brooks, & Peterson, 1990; Lees-Haley, 1989); obviously, the scale should be administered only to cooperative examinees with no motivation to malinger.

The BDI was originally designed to measure the severity of depressive symptoms in clinical samples. Nevertheless, it is frequently used as a screening instrument in nonclinical samples (Barrera & Garrison-Jones, 1988) even though the manual author warns "there is considerable debate concerning the use of the BDI for screening" (p. 2). Santor, Ramsay, and Zuroff (1994) have recently shown why the BDI can perform nonoptimally in nonclinical populations. Using a nonparametric item response model (Ramsay, 1991), these authors compared the BDI item-scoring weights in clinical and nonclinical samples. They found the estimated and original (rationally derived) weights were similar in their clinical sample but that "differences implied by the a priori weights may not be warranted for some options in the nonpatient college sample" (p. 266). For example, regarding Item 10, their analyses indicated that "*at any level of depression,* it is more likely that an individual [from a nonclinical sample] will choose Option 3 than Option 2" (p. 259, italics added).

The aforementioned scoring problems *may* be alleviated in the BDI-II. The product bulletin notes that "Dr. Beck ... used Item Response Theory (IRT) to examine how well the four response options are differentiated from each other, and how well the set of response options measures the underlying dimension (latent trait) of self-reported depression. Based on these analyses ... several response options were reworded and subsequently tested on a large clinical sample (N = 500)." By relying on IRT while revising the BDI, Beck and his colleagues have set a new standard for clinical test revision. I hope Beck or other researchers will publish IRT item parameter estimates (Reise & Waller, 1990) for the BDI and BDI-II so that these scales can be administered by a computerized adaptive test (Waller & Reise, 1989).

The BDI manual contains a weak and inadequate summary of the scale's properties. Rather than reviewing the psychometric characteristics of the BDI in sufficient detail, the manual directs readers elsewhere for more comprehensive reviews (e.g., Beck, Steer, & Garbin, 1988). Much of the manual is a presentation of BDI summary statistics—such as item means, standard deviations, endorsement percents, and item-total correlations—for six normative outpatient samples: (a) mixed diagnostic; (b) major depression, single episode; (c) major depression, recurrent episode; (d) dysthymic disorder; (e) alcoholism; and (f) heroin addiction. Data from nonclinical samples are conspicuously absent. For the clinical samples, the BDI reliabilities are uniformly high (mean coefficient alpha = .86). The product bulletin promises that the BDI-II is even more reliable.

The weakest parts of the manual are the sections on test validity. Five types of validity are discussed: (a) content, (b) discriminant, (c) construct, (d) concurrent, and (e) factorial. The content and organization of these sections leaves much to be desired. Consider, for example, that under the heading: Discriminant Validity, we find evidence that the BDI *discriminates* psychiatric patients from normal controls. This is surely a desiderata, but it does not speak to the discriminant validity of the instrument. As Campbell and Fiske (1959) remind us, tests are invalidated when they yield high correlations with other tests purporting to measure *different* things. In other words, they are invalidated when they fail to *discriminate* between conceptually distinct constructs—such as depression and anxiety (Clark & Watson, 1991). I hope a future manual will report correlations between the BDI and scales that are not designed to measure depression, such as the Beck Anxiety Inventory (Beck & Steer, 1990; Test 9, this volume).

Our review materials also included a copy of the Beck Computer Scoring Program (BCS, version 1). This stand-alone product can be used to (a) administer, (b) score, and (c) interpret the BDI and several other Beck scales (The Beck Hopelessness Scale [T4:269], the Beck Anxiety Inventory [Test 9, this volume], and The Beck Scale for Suicidal Ideation [T4:270]). Overall, the program passed a very rigorous test: I was able to load the program, take the BDI, and generate an interpreted report without opening the manual. Noteworthy features of the BCS include (a) the ability to return to previously administered items and (b) the ability to display the test instructions during any point of the scale administration. I found the interpretive summaries to be both useful and conservative, though they err on the side of redundancy. For example, a sample report for Jane Doe concludes that: "Ms Doe expresses higher levels of hopelessness and anxiety than depression. Viewed together, the moderate hopelessness, severe anxiety, and mild depression indicate that she views the future with considerable hopelessness and anxiety but is not very depressed by this view." Scores on the computer-administered BDI are comparable to those from the paper-and-pencil version (Steer, Rissmiller, Ranieri, & Beck, 1994).

As a clinician trained in psychometric theory, I am skeptical of 5-minute assessment scales. Nevertheless, as a Minnesota-trained dust-bowl empiricist, I also listen to the data. In the case of the BDI, the data speak loud and clearly. The BDI is an excellent measure of depressive symptoms when it is used *in clinical samples with cooperative subjects.* The BDI-II promises to be a useful screening measure in nonclinical samples. In situations where subjects may be motivated to malinger, other scales with validity checks, such as the Minnesota Multiphasic Personality Inventory—2 (MMPI-2) (Butcher, Dahlstom, Graham, Tellegen, & Kaemmer, 1989; T4:1645) should provide more trustworthy data.

REVIEWER'S REFERENCES

Campbell, D. T., & Fiske, D. W. (1959). Convergent and discriminant validation by the multitrait-multimethod matrix. *Psychological Bulletin, 56,* 81–105.

Beck, A. T., Ward, C. H., Mendelson, M., Mock, J., & Erbaugh, J. (1961). An inventory for measuring depression. *Archives of General Psychiatry, 4,* 561–571.

Beck, A. T., & Beck, R. W. (1972). Screening depressed patients in a family practice. *Postgraduate Medicine, 52*(6), 81–85.

Beck, A. T., & Beamesderfer, A. (1974). Assessment of depression: The depression inventory. In P. Pichot (Ed.), *Modern problems in pharmacopsychiatry* (pp. 151–169). Basel, Switzerland: Karger.

Barrera, M., & Garrison-Jones, C. V. (1988). Properties of the Beck Depression Inventory as a screening instrument for adolescent depression *Journal of Abnormal Child Psychology, 16(3),* 263–273.

Beck, A. T., Steer, R. A., & Garbin, M. G. (1988). Psychometric properties of the Beck Depression Inventory: Twenty-five years of evaluation. *Clinical Psychology Review, 8,* 77–100.

Butcher, J. N., Dahlstrom, W. G., Graham, J. R., Tellegen, A., & Kaemmer, B. (1989). *Minnesota Multiphasic Personality Inventory—2 (MMPI-2): Manual for administration and scoring.* Minneapolis: University of Minnesota Press.

Lees-Haley, P. R. (1989). Malingering traumatic mental disorder on the Beck Depression inventory: Cancerphobia and toxic exposure. *Psychological Reports, 65,* 623–626.

Waller, N. G., & Rise, S. (1989). Computerized adaptive personality assessment: An illustration with the Absorption scale. *Journal of Personality and Social Psychology, 57,* 1051–1058.

Beck, A. T., & Steer, R. A. (1990). *Manual for the Beck Anxiety Inventory.* San Antonio, TX: The Psychological Corporation.

Dahlstrom, W. G., Brooks, J. D., & Peterson, C. D. (1990). The Beck Depression Inventory: Item order and the impact of response sets. *Journal of Personality Assessment, 55,* 224–233.

Reise, S. P., & Waller, N. G. (1990). Fitting the two-parameter model to personality data. *Applied Psychological Measurement, 14,* 45–58.

Clark, L. A., & Watson, D. (1991). Tripartite model of anxiety and depression: Psychometric evidence and taxonomic implications. *Journal of Abnormal Psychology, 100,* 316–336.

Ramsay, J. O. (1991). Kernel smoothing approaches to nonparametric item characteristic curve estimation. *Psychometrika, 56,* 611–630.

Santor, D. A., Ramsay, J. O., & Zuroff, D. C. (1994). Nonparametric item analyses of the Beck Depression Inventory; Evaluating gender item bias and response option weights. *Psychological Assessment, 6,* 255–270.

Beck, A. T., Steer, R. A., & Brown, G. (1996). Beck Depression Inventory II. San Antonio, TX: Harcourt Brace & Company, The Psychological Corporation.

[11]

Career Attitudes and Strategies Inventory: An Inventory for Understanding Adult Careers.

Purpose: "Developed to assess some common attitudes, feelings, experiences, and obstacles that influence the careers of employed and unemployed adults."
Population: Adults seeking vocational counseling.
Publication Dates: 1992–1994.
Acronym: CASI.
Scores: 9 scales: Job Satisfaction, Work Involvement, Skill Development, Dominant Style, Career Worries, Interpersonal Abuse, Family Commitment, Risk-Taking Style, Geographical Barriers.
Administration: Individual.
Price Data, 1996: $68 per kit including manual ('94, 53 pages), 25 inventory booklets, 25 handscorable answer sheets, and 25 interpretive summary booklets.
Time: (35) minutes.
Comments: Also includes Career Obstacles Checklist designed to assess "personal problems that may influence an individual's job situation."
Authors: John L. Holland and Gary D. Gottfredson.
Publisher: Psychological Assessment Resources, Inc.

Review of the Career Attitudes and Strategies Inventory: An Inventory for Understanding Adult Careers by MICHAEL B. BROWN, Assistant Professor of Psychology, East Carolina University, Greenville, NC:

The Career Attitudes and Strategies Inventory (CASI) is a relatively brief, self-scoring assessment of adult career attitudes and behaviors. It is intended to provide an assessment of job stability, and it is suggested that the profile of scores provides a status report on the positive and negative aspects of clients' career adjustment. The nine scales of the CASI measure areas related to career adaptation. Examples of scales include Job Satisfaction, Work Involvement, Family Commitment, and Geographical Barriers. Following in the tradition of John Holland's Self-Directed Search (Test 84, this volume) the inventory is meant to be completed and scored by the client. Clients use a questionnaire containing 130 items, indicating their self-rating on a separate self-scoring answer sheet. The answer sheet also contains a separate career obstacle checklist listing 21 potential career obstacles. Clients follow the directions on the answer sheet to obtain raw scores, transferring the raw score to a profile sheet in the four-page Interpretive Summary. The Interpretive Summary also includes brief interpretive statements for each scale.

MATERIALS. The materials are attractively done. The four-page test booklet is well designed and easy to read. The separate one-page answer sheet is a two-part carbonless form that is used for self-scoring. The answer sheet requires the client to indicate an answer of True, Mostly True, Mostly False, or False for each item on the inventory. The two true responses are both designated by an upper case letter "T," with a darker colored T to be circled for True and the lighter colored T circled for Mostly True. A similar system using an upper case letter "F" is used to indicate False or Mostly False. This answer system, combined with the compact layout of the answer sheet, may prove confusing for some clients. Professionals who use the CASI must ensure clients understand the directions for answering and are able to maintain their place as they complete the survey. The manual authors state the client must be able to do "simple math" to self-score the inventory. Again, some clients may need more guidance to follow the directions for scoring. The four-page Interpretive Summary has a profile on which to plot scores, and three interpretive statements for each scale. Each interpretation corresponds to one of three ranges of raw score distribution. The interpretive summaries are clearly written but very brief. These interpretations may require more detailed explanation and integration by the professional, particularly for clients with less education and verbal sophistication.

MANUAL. The manual is very brief (only 45 pages) but clearly written and organized. Practical applications of the CASI and scoring procedures are concisely described. Interpretive information includes a description of each scale along with 14 case profiles. The illustrative profiles are helpful and include persons with a range of ages and occupations, although occupations that require more education and training seem to predominate. The major limitation of the illustrative profiles is the brevity of case material and corresponding interpretations. There is a section on becoming a competent user of the inventory that is well done, and there is a short "test" to help the user assess understanding of the basic concepts of the CASI. The major concern about this section is that it implies the inventory has greater psychometric sophistication than is warranted by the technical characteristics of the instrument.

TECHNICAL CHARACTERISTICS. There are significant limitations in the technical characteristics of the CASI that must be considered when using this inventory. The current version of the CASI is the third version in the development of the inventory and was derived from item analyses of previous versions. The normative sample consists of 747 persons ranging in age from 17 to 77 years of age. Women are overrepresented in the norm group (64% women, 36% men), although the manual authors point out there appears to be little substantive difference in the scores of men and women. The majority of the group is composed of persons with some education beyond high school (only 10% of the sample had 12 or fewer years of education). It is difficult to ascertain the actual ethnic identification of the group, as over one-third of the group were not asked to provide an ethnic identification. There is no indication of the geographical or socioeconomic status of the sample. Normative data for career obstacles are considered "approximate" (p. 36) as identical instructions were not given to each group used in the norming process.

Internal consistency reliability coefficients for the CASI scales ranged from .76 to .92, which is adequate for this type of inventory. Test-retest reliability was assessed using a small group of working adults. The average interval was 13 days, and test-retest reliabilities ranged from .66–.94.

Validity is inferred through a number of means. One of the difficulties in assessing the validity of the CASI is that different versions were used at different points during its development to assess validity. Caution is suggested in interpretation of validity because both the norm group and the CASI itself appear to have undergone substantial changes from the first to the third version. Validity is addressed through correlation of the CASI and the Hoppock Job Satisfaction Blank, a two-item indicator of general happiness, career search activities, and measures of vocational identity and personality type. The CASI and the Hoppock Job Satisfaction Blank have a correlation of .86, whereas the CASI and the measure of general happiness have a correlation of .71. Construct validity is inferred through an examination of the intercorrelations between various CASI scales, which are said to "appear predictable from the scale titles" (p. 28). As an example, the Job Satisfaction Scale is negatively correlated with the Career Worries and Interpersonal Abuse Scales.

OVERALL EVALUATION. The CASI has serious drawbacks presented by the lack of adequate norms and limitations in the determination of its validity. The structure and appearance of the materials give it a look of psychometric sophistication that exceeds its present technical state. This is of particular importance when used with client self-scoring and interpretation, when there is the danger the client would consider the results to be more exact than warranted. I recommend that its use by a client be preceded by a discussion of the limitations of the instrument and the meaning of its scale scores. The CASI may be most useful to the career counselor or vocational psychologist when used as a checklist to obtain a client's self-rating in a number of areas that are relevant to career adjustment. As such it can be used to rapidly "screen" for client opinions and attitudes and generate information for discussion between client and counselor. I would certainly find it useful as a pre-interview survey, a device to generate discussion, or to identify potentially problematic areas that would benefit from further exploration. It should be used in an ipsative rather than normative fashion until better psychometric data are produced. When detailed information in specific domains of the client's career attitudes or strategies is necessary, additional inventories (such as the Adult Career Concerns Inventory [12:18] or the Salience Inventory [T4:2321]) should be considered.

Review of the Career Attitudes and Strategies Inventory: An Inventory for Understanding Adult Careers by RICHARD T. KINNIER, Associate Professor, Counseling Psychology Program, Arizona State University, Tempe, AZ:

The Career Attitudes and Strategies Inventory (CASI) was designed "to assess some common attitudes, feelings, experiences, and obstacles that influence the careers" of adults (manual, p. 1). The CASI consists of 130 items in nine scales related to the test taker's career. They are: Job Satisfaction, Work Involvement, Skill Development (motivation to improve one's work performance), Dominant Style (leader versus follower), Career Worries, Interpersonal Abuse (experienced at work), Family Commitment (as it relates to career commitment), Risk-Taking Style (willingness to take or experience risk), and Geographic Barriers (extent to which one is motivated to stay in or move to a geographical location). A separate item asks test takers to check (from a list) any career obstacles they are currently experiencing. According to the authors, the test should be used to supplement (not supplant) other career-relevant information such as the client's abilities and interests. The results should be used in counseling to stimulate further career-related thinking and exploration by the client.

Each of the 130 items is answered on a 4-point scale consisting of the categories, "False," "Mostly False," "Mostly True," and "True" as they relate to the test taker. The items are clearly written. The test booklet and answer sheet are clearly presented and easy to use. All responses fit on one side of the answer sheet. The instructions are clear. According to the authors, the test takes about 35 minutes to complete.

The CASI is self-administered and can be self-scored. The directions for scoring are clear and easy to follow. To score, individuals remove the top layer of the answer sheet. On the revealed bottom sheet, responses are numbered. Those numbers are simply summed for each scale. Raw scores are then entered and plotted on a profile sheet. Raw score plots are clearly displayed for each scale and raw scores are easily transformed to *T*-scores listed at the bottom of the profile sheet.

The authors describe the test as "self interpreted" but they also state that "most clients will also require or want help with the interpretation of the profiles from a counselor" (p. 3). I would recommend the test be used only in conjunction with counseling. Although the interpretation of each scale seems fairly straightforward, the implications of the scores for a person's career development and choice are more complex and best addressed in counseling.

The interpretive guide for the scales consists of verbal descriptions of three levels (the top 25%, the middle 50%, and the bottom 25% of the

norms). The verbal descriptions are clearly written. One slight annoyance is that the profile sheet is on the back page of the interpretive guide, which does not allow the test taker to look at both simultaneously. Having a separate page for the profile sheet would be preferable, in my opinion. The authors provide 14 illustrative profiles with brief descriptions of the test takers. Having a few illustrative cases seems useful for practice in interpretation but all 14 do not seem needed. The sections in the manual on "Becoming a Competent User" and "Some Practical Applications" are brief and helpful guides for counselors who may consider using the CASI. Overall, the manual is well organized and well written. Also, its brevity makes for easy reading and quick familiarity with the test.

TEST DEVELOPMENT. The CASI was developed by two highly respected theoreticians in the area of career counseling and testing. The development of their test followed a typical path of tests of this type. First, items were constructed on the basis of theoretical criteria and common sense. Several people contributed potential items. Next, items were deleted or refined on the basis of factor and item analyses. In the manual, the authors refer to the analyses but the actual data from those analyses are not in the manual. The current version of the CASI is the third version of refined items.

NORMS. The standardization sample consisted of 747 adults. About 64% are women and 34% are men (a few did not report their sex). The mean age was 38 (*SD* = 11 years). The ethnic makeup of the sample is predominantly European American (i.e., 79%). They are a highly educated sample (about 90% went beyond high school, over 50% graduated from college, and over 25% obtained a postgraduate degree). The authors claim the sample is heterogeneous in age and education but in comparison with national norms, this sample seems slightly more female, more European American, and more educated. Also, although there is a wide range of occupations represented in the sample, "a few occupations were overrepresented" (p. 33), according to the authors. Apparently there was an overrepresentation of career counselors. The authors claim they reduced the influence of overrepresentation by "reconstituting" the sample, presumably by removing subjects so that "no more than 30 individuals from a single occupation were included in the final normative groups" (p. 33). Unfortunately, 30 is still a large number in terms of proportionality. However, in spite of the slight bias of the sample on the basis of sex, education, ethnicity, and occupation, I think the sample is still a reasonable norm group for this type of test and its intended use.

The authors report they combined samples from the second and third versions of the test to create their final norm group. This procedure can be problematic if some items were changed or deleted between Versions 2 and 3, which apparently did happen. However, for practical purposes this may not be significant because the authors recommend broad-band interpretation anyway. In my opinion, the broad-band interpretation guide is a strength of the measure.

RELIABILITY. Reliability was evaluated by internal consistency and test-retest correlational analyses. Cronbach alphas were computed on each of the scales for several samples. According to the authors, "alphas for version 3 are based on samples of 564 to 596 persons" (p. 29). It is not clear to what the range of 564 to 596 refers, perhaps it reflects differential completion of the scales. The authors should clarify that. Alpha coefficients ranged from .76 to .92. Alphas on another sample of about 40 "working adults" ranged from .77 to .95. A test-retest correlational analysis was also computed on that sample (range of time period = 6 to 21 days). The coefficients ranged from .66 to .94. Overall, the scales seem to be internally consistent and fairly stable over a short period of time. I would characterize the evidence of reliability as fairly good in comparison with other similar kinds of measures.

VALIDITY. Validity was evaluated mainly by correlational analyses. Scales were correlated with each other and with other relevant variables. The authors claim the correlations are generally supportive of both convergent and discriminant validity. I would concur the results are generally supportive. But I would hasten to add that this measure is still in an early stage of development and refinement. Certainly more independent research is needed to establish real confidence in its validity. Also, at this time validity has been more clearly demonstrated in some scales than in others. For example, the scale Job Satisfaction correlates

highly with Hoppock's Job Satisfaction Blank (r = .84) and correlates negatively with the scale Career Worries (r = -.21) as would be predicted. There seems to be good evidence that both Job Satisfaction and Career Worries are valid scales.

In contrast, although the scale Interpersonal Abuse correlates negatively with Job Satisfaction (r = -.41) as would be expected, it also correlates negatively with measures of Extraversion, Agreeableness, and Emotional Stability; and it correlates positively with Family Commitment. Of course, conclusions about causation must be speculative but the pattern does raise the question: To what extent is the scale a measure of actual abuse from others or more a reflection of psychological instability, dislike of work, or antisociability of the individual. I am also troubled by the fact that so many different kinds of unpleasant social encounters (i.e., sexual harassment; prejudice on the basis of race, sex, or other condition or preference; power abuses; and unfriendliness or meanness of fellow employees) are categorized under Interpersonal Abuse. One score on Interpersonal Abuse may be too general to be practically informative as to what is actually going on at work.

The scales that I think have the most compelling face validity and empirical support at this time are: Job Satisfaction, Skill Development, Dominant Style, Career Worries, Risk-taking Style, and Career Obstacles.

CONCLUSION. The CASI is a self-administered and self-scored measure of perceptions individuals have about their careers. The test consists of 130 items and takes approximately 35 minutes to take. The test booklet and answer sheet are clearly presented, the booklet and manual are easy to read, and the test is easy to take and to score. Although the interpretation of the nine scale scores is fairly straightforward, the implications of the scores for a person's career development and choice are more complex and best addressed in the context of counseling. The norms are adequate given the way the scores are supposed to be interpreted (i.e., broad bands). The scales are fairly reliable. Tests of validity (mainly convergent and discriminant correlations) are generally encouraging.

At this early stage of development, some scales seem more valid and useful than others.

Future research might address this. In the meantime, the CASI can serve as a useful supplement to the conventional self-assessment interventions for career counseling. It is a unique measure in that, unlike most other career-related tests, it assesses perceptions the test-taker has about his or her current job and career.

[12]

Career Development Inventory [Consulting Psychologists Press, Inc.]

Purpose: "Measures several affective and cognitive aspects of the earlier stages of career development."
Population: Grades 8–12, college.
Publication Dates: 1979–1984.
Acronym: CDI.
Scores, 8: Career Planning, Career Exploration, Decision Making, World-of-Work Information, Knowledge of Preferred Occupational Group, Career Development Attitudes, Career Development Knowledge and Skills, Total.
Administration: Group.
Levels, 2: School Form, College and University Form.
Price Data, 1993: $30 per sampler set including user's manual ('81, 27 pages) and supplement ('84, 20 pages), test booklet, and prepaid answer sheets for both high school and college and university inventories; $23 per 25 reusable high school test booklets; $48 per 10 prepaid high school answer sheets; $45 per 25 reusable college and university test booklets; $48 per 10 prepaid college and university answer sheets; $19 per user's manual; $22 per technical manual ('84, 47 pages); $35 per complete manual set.
Time: (55–65) minutes.
Authors: Donald E. Super, Albert S. Thompson, Richard H. Lindeman, Jean P. Jordaan, and Roger A. Myers.
Publisher: Consulting Psychologists Press, Inc.
Cross References: See T4:391 (20 references); for a review by James W. Pinkney, see 9:195 (4 references).

TEST REFERENCES

1. Blustein, D. L. (1987). Decision-making styles and vocational maturity: An alternative perspective. *Journal of Vocational Behavior, 30*, 61–71.
2. Blustein, D. L. (1987). Social cognitive orientations and career development: A theoretical and empirical analysis. *Journal of Vocational Behavior, 31*, 63–80.
3. Nevill, D., & Super, D. E. (1988). Career maturity and commitment to work in university students. *Journal of Vocational Behavior, 32*, 139–151.
4. King, S. (1990). Background and family variables in a causal model of career maturity: Comparing hearing and hearing-impaired adolescents. *Career Development Quarterly, 38*, 240–260.
5. Orstein, S., & Isabella, L. (1990). Age vs. stage models of career attitudes of women: A partial replication and extension. *Journal of Vocational Behavior, 36*, 1–19.
6. Biller, E. F., & Horn, E. E. (1991). A career guidance model for adolescents with learning disabilities. *The School Counselor, 38*, 279–286.
7. Luzzo, D. A. (1992). Ethnic group and social class differences in college students' career development. *Career Development Quarterly, 41*, 161–173.
8. Luzzo, D. A. (1993). Reliability and validity testing of the Career Decision-Making Self-Efficacy Scale. *Measurement and Evaluation in Counseling and Development, 26*, 137–143.
9. Gussin, E. A., Kelly, K. R., & Feldhusen, J. F. (1993). Sex differences in the career development of gifted youth. *The School Counselor, 41*, 90–95.
10. Hess, W. D., & Winston, R. B., Jr. (1995). Developmental task achievement and students' intentions to participate in developmental activities. *Journal of College Student Development, 36*, 314–321.
11. Luzzo, D. A. (1995). Gender differences in college students' career maturity and perceived barriers in career development. *Journal of Counseling and Development, 73*, 319–322.
12. Luzzo, D. A. (1995). The relative contributions of self-efficacy and locus of control to the prediction of career maturity. *Journal of College Student Development, 36*, 61–66.
13. Jackson, G. C., & Healy, C. C. (1996). Career development profiles and interventions for underrepresented college students. *The Career Development Quarterly, 44*, 258–269.
14. Ohler, D. L., Levinson, E. M., & Barker, W. F. (1996). Career maturity in college students with learning disabilities. *The Career Development Quarterly, 44*, 278–288.
15. Savickas, M. L., & Hartung, P. J. (1996). The Career Development Inventory in review: Psychometric and research findings. *Journal of Career Assessment, 4*, 171–188.
16. Smallman, E., & Sowa, C. J. (1996). Career maturity levels of male intercollegiate varsity athletes. *The Career Development Quarterly, 44*, 270–277.

Review of the Career Development Inventory by DONNA L. SUNDRE, Associate Assessment Specialist/Associate Professor of Psychology, James Madison University, Harrisonburg, VA:

GENERAL INFORMATION. The Career Development Inventory (CDI) represents an assessment outcome of more that 40 years of research on adolescent career decision-making readiness, development, and maturity. According to the User's Manual, the CDI is designed to measure "career development and vocational or career maturity" (p. 1). In its present form, the authors contend the instrument can be used for "individual counseling, group assessment, and program evaluation and planning" (p. 3). Two forms are available intended for different audiences. The School Form is designed for students in grades 8–12, and the College and University Form is designed for higher education use. The latter form was modified to fit a college context and to address occupations more common to college students.

Both forms of the CDI produce eight scales: Career Planning (CP); Career Exploration (CE); Decision Making (DM); World of Work Information (WW); Knowledge of Preferred Occupation (PO), a cognitive scale; Career Development Attitudes (CDA), a conative scale that combines CP and CE; Career Development Knowledge and Skills (CDK), a cognitive scale that combines DM and WW; and Career Orientation Total (COT), the combination of CP, CE, DM, and WW. The instrument is divided into two parts: Part I—Career Orientation; and Part II—Knowledge of Preferred Occupation. When using the School Form, the Preferred Occupation (PO) scale is considered useful only for grade 11–12 students given the advanced terms, ideas, and maturity expected to be a part of development of occupations and choice.

PRACTICAL EVALUATION. Test booklets for both forms are reusable and durable. Administration of the instruments is straightforward, and the manual contains excellent directions and guidance. Hand scoring is not recommended for a variety of reasons: Reports use standard scale scores rather than raw scores; the CE scale score is calculated using differential item weights; and the Knowledge of Preferred Occupation (PO) scale requires a different key for each of the 20 occupational groups. Hand scoring may not be an option for this instrument.

The User's Manual Volume I, published in 1981, contains development information related to both forms and statistical and measurement findings related to the School Form; it is exceptionally well written and organized. Great care has been taken in its development and presentation. An extensive reference section and appendix including norming tables, scale statistics, and factor analysis results are also provided. The manual will be very useful to many counselors; this reviewer was particularly impressed with Chapter III: Uses of CDI Results. Users will find cogent advice for planning meaningful activities to engage individual clients, organizing guidance programs, and designing evaluation and research. Regarding uses of the instruments with individuals, the individual item responses for the career planning and career exploration scales would be very useful for working with individuals. The score reporting program provides group item response patterns; however, the individual responses are not available. The Supplement to the User's Manual (1982) contains eight sections and an appendix. Most of this information describes minor variations and supplementation for the College and University (CU) Form compared to the School (S) Form. A presentation of case studies was a thoughtful addition. The section on norms, reliability, and validity included in this manual pertains solely to the CU Form.

Subsequent to the publication of the User's Manual (1981) and the Supplement (1982) the scoring service and computer-generated reports appear to have been revised in 1986 in two important ways. First a graphic percentile rank profile is now displayed. It is nice to have such a straightforward result presentation; however, there is some danger in overreliance on normative data with this type of data. For example, the authors cite research indicating that many senior students are not well prepared for the transition to work or to college and know very little about their preferred occupations. Average scores on many of these scales should be cause for concern and counseling rather than calm. The second improvement in the score report is the addition of a local norms column alongside the national norms. This is an important improvement.

There is also a somewhat more recently published (1984) Technical Manual that contains greater detail on the development of the instrument and its earlier forms as well as additional reliability and validity studies, uses of the CDI, and a more extensive reference section.

NORMS. The authors of the User's Manual are forthright in indicating that the norms are not representative of the target population. As mentioned earlier, the 1986 revisions to the computerized score reports have augmented the earlier reports with a local norm option, a fine addition. The School Form is intended for grades 8–12. The answer sheets also provide scoring for grades 7, 8, and junior college, yet the norming samples do not include representatives of these groups. It is unclear how norms for these groups were generated, and for junior college students using the School Form, the appropriateness of some of the items is also in question.

The College and University (CU) norms are based on a small (N = 1,345), underrepresentative sample of students spanning first year through seniors. A total of 13 institutions participated in the norming, and, of these, two had to be eliminated because the grade level of the participants was not specified. Due to the small overall number of subjects and overrepresentation of a single institution, graduate students were not included in the standardization sample. The authors note that the sample is not representative. In addition, the local norm option on the score report mentioned earlier will be beneficial.

RELIABILITY. The School Form User Manual (1981) contains internal consistency and standard errors of measurement (*SEM*) indicators of reliability for grades 9–12 for total groups and by gender. In general, these reliabilities are sufficient; however, two scales, Decision Making (DM) and Preferred Occupation (PO) are problematic, particularly for females. The authors mentioned the discrepancy but did not address it. The authors also indicate the reliability for the PO scale improves in the 11th and 12th grades when compared to reliabilities observed for the 9th and 10th grades. However, I did not find this conclusion borne out by the coefficients; for females grades 9–12 the Cronbach alpha coefficients were .53, .53, .67, and .57 respectively; the coefficients for males grades 9–12 were .61, .55, .64, and .71. The *SEM*s, of course, correspond with the reliabilities, and are considerably larger for DM and PO than the other scales. The manual contains useful guidance to users on interpretation and application of *SEM*s, and the final chapter has realistic caveats concerning use of particular scale scores with individuals. The technical manual contains 3-week test-retest reliabilities for the School Form from two high school samples; the overall reliabilities for three scales—Decision Making (.70 at School L and .69 at School T), World of Work (.67 and .68), and Preferred Occupation (.61 and .63)—appeared fairly unstable. All other scales were adequate.

In the Supplement to the User Manual (1982) the authors address the CU Form regarding internal consistency via Cronbach's alpha and *SEM*s. The alphas, in general, appear adequate; however, the presentation of alphas by class level for the cognitive subscales (DM, WW, and PO) is not reported due to lack of variability, which constricted the interitem correlations, and according to the authors, rendered the alphas inappropriate. Although all the raw score means and standard deviations are not presented, the example provided suggests a very significant reduction in variability. The alphas reported for these scales for the total group and by gender are considerably lower than the other scales. Further, the *SEM*s reported for all three of these scales are in double digits, indicating low reliabilities. Because a primary purpose of using the instrument is for work with individuals, these findings are troubling. The authors' contention that the alphas were rendered inappropriate due to lack of variance seems to beg the question of the appropriateness of the instrument's

design and item development. An assumption is made that career maturity is developmental in nature; one would also assume there will be variation on this maturity and that if grade level norms are desired and appropriate, there will be sufficient variance with which to estimate this maturation. This is not the case for these subscales, at least not with this item pool. Upon review of the means and standard deviations reported for the entire group in Table 1, there is some evidence for the presence of a ceiling effect for the DM and WW scales. Although the authors cite Anastasi (1982) to support the inappropriateness of reporting alphas when the variance is restricted, my interpretation differs; at no time does Anastasi suggest that the alphas are rendered inappropriate. She clearly indicates that, "For tests designed to cover a wide range of age or ability, the test manual should report separate reliability coefficients for relatively homogenous subgroups within the standardization sample" (Anastasi, 1988, p. 132). If the score reports provide normative differences by college year, and they do, it follows that the alphas should also be reported and considered appropriate. In the Technical Manual the authors reported 2-week test-retest reliabilities for the College Form; again, the cognitive scales appeared fairly unreliable over a very brief period of time with the following coefficients reported: Decision Making, .65; World of Work, .43, and Preferred Occupation, .62. Clearly, caution should be advised regarding use of these scales, particularly with individuals.

VALIDITY. Validity is without question the essential attribute of any measure. The authors present evidence for content and construct validity and suggest that criterion validity will be addressed in subsequent work. The item content for both forms of the instrument is derived from past research and explication of Super's model for career maturity. The current forms of the instruments were generated from preliminary forms.

The construct validity was investigated through testing for theoretically expected subgroup performance (sex, grade, and academic program) differences and factor analysis. Separate hypotheses are advanced for the two forms and will be discussed separately.

For the School Form, construct validity was explored through observation of predicted subgroup differences by year of school, sex, academic program, and factor structure. The general absence of sex differences was considered consistent with expectations, although in the 11th and 12th grades females begin to outperform males on the cognitive scales. The authors suggest this result would be expected. The general pattern in the School Form of somewhat increasing total and scale scores over grades is consistent with theory. In fairness, the research shows almost as great career development differences within grades as between. A more appropriate and rigorous assessment of the model would incorporate repeated measures of scales over an extended period of time. This is precisely the design the authors describe as in progress in the final chapter of the User's Manual; however, the Technical Manual published in 1984 indicated that this study is still underway. Differences observed by curricular program also appear to make sense, although the observed differences are generally small.

For the College Form, construct validity was reviewed using the same general techniques as for the School Form: year in college, sex, and major field differences. Observed increases in scale scores by years in college were largely not evident and certainly not compelling. The differences observed over the 4-year period amount to approximately one half a standard deviation or less, and sometimes the direction of change is not discernible. In contrast to the School Form, at the college level, the existence of sex differences on the cognitive scales, with girls outperforming boys, was taken to be evidence of construct validity; however, the observed differences are *considerably* smaller than one *SEM*. Major field differences were, for some scales, quite large, and these results were considered consistent with expectations.

Reports of a series of discriminant analyses using linear combinations of the five scales, and canonical correlation analyses using the conative and cognitive sets of scales, conducted for both forms of the instrument are included in the Technical Manual. Although significant findings are apparent, because the scales will not be used or reported as linear combinations or sets, these results are not helpful to users. The use of more powerful statistical techniques and subsequent significant findings does not render the generally meager scale score differences observed and reported in the earlier manuals of more practical significance. The theoretical grounds for these analyses and logic supporting the expectations are not well explicated in the Technical Manual, and the interpretations of the results were unconvincing, particularly for the College Form.

Of more interest and practical utility is the presentation of correlations of CDI scales with other recognized assessment instruments. These results demonstrated consistent positive correlations between the cognitive subscales and measures of academic abilities such as the Differential Aptitude Battery and the Iowa Tests of Educational Development as well as some moderate correlations of the conative subscales with attitudinal measures from other career maturity scales such as the Salience Inventory (SI) from the Work Importance Study. It was also reassuring to see that socioeconomic status did not impact the CDI scales for either form of the instrument. The results of the analyses supported the two-factor structure upon which the instrument was designed.

The factor analysis results are consistent with those predicted. Across both forms of the instrument, the predicted two-factor structure consistently emerges. The first factor has all of the cognitive scales (DM, WW, and PO) loading on it, and the second factor, conative in nature, is defined by the two attitudinal scales (CE and CP). This factor structure appears to be quite stable across sex and over years in school. A minor qualm regarding the report of factor analysis as evidence of construct validity will be mentioned here. This reviewer considers factor structures and their stability as indicators of content validity rather than construct validity; the issue of construct validity addresses the issue of factor score meaning, not composition.

A final consideration regarding the factor structure is that if there are only two underlying dimensions consistently identified, why use five subtests? Obviously, the authors have attempted to design the scales around Super's model; however, given the low reliabilities for the cognitive subscales, it would seem prudent to use the more reliable and discernible factors to assess hypothesized career maturity. Interestingly, the Technical Manual contains study results using profile types based upon the composite scales (CDA, attitudinal and CDK, knowledge and skills) indicating such applications have promise.

SUMMARY EVALUATION. The essential question in construct validity is whether or not the inferences we wish to make about career development and maturity on the basis of these scores are warranted. The same issue is central to selection of an instrument. At this stage of development for the CDI, the standardization sample is not adequate for either form of the instrument, the reliability of several scales is quite questionable in regard to item homogeneity as well as stability over fairly brief periods of time, and the validity of inferences counselors would like to make regarding individuals has not been well established. Clearly, the collection of validity evidence is a cumulative and ongoing process, and users of the instrument will contribute to the establishment of better norms and validity evidence than are currently provided by the publisher.

REVIEWER'S REFERENCES

Anastasi, A. (1982). *Psychological testing* (5th ed.). New York: Macmillan Publishing Company.
Anastasi, A. (1988). *Psychological testing* (6th ed.). New York: Macmillan Publishing Company.

[13]

Career Interest Inventory.

Purpose: "Designed to assist students in making decisions concerning their educational and vocational plans."
Publication Dates: 1989–1991.
Administration: Group.
Price Data, 1994: $11.50 per examination kit including Level 1 machine-scorable answer document, Level 2 hand-scorable booklet, directions for administering, and student profile; $32.50 per counselor's manual ('91, 120 pages); $11.50 per 25 Exploring Interests: An Introduction to the Career Interest Inventory; $4.50 per directions for administering ('90, 29 pages); $1.62 scoring charge per Level 1 answer document; $.59 for first copy and $.17 per each additional copy of individual report; $.56 for first copy and $.05 per each additional copy of counselor's report (by Teacher/Counselor or School); $.53 for first copy and $.18 per each additional copy of student record label; $.42 for first copy and $.10 per each additional copy of occupational interest report (by School); $.27 for first copy and $15.58 per set of career planning summary (by Teacher/Counselor); $.20 for first copy and $15.58 per set of career planning summary (by School); $.15 for first copy and $13.35 per set of career planning summary (by District); $70 (not refundable)

plus $.28 per pupil for student data tape; $.35 per pupil for student data diskette; $12.50 for first 1,000 and $3.20 per each additional 1,000 for return of test booklets; $6.39 for first 1,000 plus $1.74 per each additional 1,000 for return of answer documents; $10.47 for first 1,000 plus $3.20 per each additional 1,000 for return of mixed documents.
Time: (30–40) minutes.
Author: The Psychological Corporation.
Publisher: The Psychological Corporation.

a) LEVEL 1.
Population: Grades 7–9.
Scores, 47: 15 Occupational Interests (Social Science, Clerical Services, Health Services, Agriculture, Customer Services, Fine Arts, Mathematics and Science, Building Trades, Educational Services, Legal Services, Transportation, Sales, Management, Benchwork, Machine Operation), 16 High School Subject Interests (Speech or Drama, Metal Shop or Woodworking, Mathematics, Auto Repair, Science, Cooking or Sewing, Art or Music, Farming or Livestock Care, Newspaper Writing, Typing or Office Machines, Social Studies, Health Care, Creative Writing, Computers, English or Literature, Bookkeeping or Office Practices), 16 High School Activity Interests (Mathematics Club, Farming Club, Speech or Debate Team, School Library Aide, School Play, Automobile Club, Science Fair, Teacher's Aide, Student Government, Office Helper or Assistant, School Literary Magazine, School Officer, Photography Club, Business Club, School Newspaper, Computer Club).
Price Data: $37.50 per 25 hand-scorable booklets; $37.50 per 25 Type 1 machine-scorable answer documents; $37.50 per 25 Type 2 machine-scorable answer documents.

b) LEVEL 2.
Population: Grades 10–12 and adults.
Scores, 35: 15 Occupational Interests (same as Level 1), 20 Post-High School Course Interests (Marketing or Sales, Computer Programming, Electronics or Electrical Trades, Plumbing or Welding, Automotive Repair, Carpentry or Home Building, Word Processing or Typing, Haircutting or Styling, Bookkeeping or Office Practices, Cooking or Sewing, Music or Art, Farming or Livestock Care, Mathematics or Science, English or Foreign Language, Business Law or Management, Creative Writing, Speech or Drama, Photography, Health Care, Newspaper Writing).
Price Data: $40.50 per 25 hand-scorable booklets; $40.50 per 25 Type 1 machine-scorable answer documents; $40.50 per 25 Type 2 machine-scorable answer documents.

Review of the Career Interest Inventory by WILLIAM D. SCHAFER, Associate Professor of Measurement, Statistics, and Evaluation, University of Maryland, College Park, MD:

The Career Interest Inventory (CII) was designed to assess interest in activities linked to 15 occupational groups representative of the spectrum of career fields described in the U.S. Department of Labor's (1977, 1986) *Dictionary of Occupational Titles* (DOT). It is available in two levels. Level 1, recommended for students in grades 7–9, contains 120 work activity statements, 16 school subject areas (course-taking activities), and 16 extracurricular school activities (152 items). Level 2, recommended for students in grades 10–12 and adults, contains 150 work activity statements and 20 school subject areas (170 items). Examinees are to respond to a 5-point scale indicating the degree to which they would like or dislike doing the activity. It may be administered to groups; although it is not timed, examinees are expected to complete the CII in about 40 minutes, including administrative time, which is consistent with the time structure of most schools. It may be hand scored by the examinees, also in groups, or machine scored. The materials used depend on the type of scoring. The CII may be used in conjunction with the Differential Aptitude Tests (DAT; 12:118) with a combined report produced if machine scoring is elected.

The manual for administering the CII, with modifications for either format, is clear. It contains the statements to be read in black type and explanatory material with activity directions in red. It gives directions for examinees to score their own responses if hand scoring is used. Also available are a folder to be used to help students think about career choice issues, including work values, in preparation for the CII; a workbook for use in career exploration; and a counselor's manual that contains test-development and technical information and presents useful recommendations for interpretation and use in practice.

Scoring the CII is straightforward. Responses to the 8 (Level 1) or 10 (Level 2) job activity statements are summed separately within each of the occupational groups to yield 15 scores that range from 8 to 40 (Level 1) or 10 to 50 (Level 2). A consistency index is used to assess the degree

that responses are differentiated within each occupational group, but few suggestions appear in the counselor's manual about its use. Subject area and school activity (Level 1 only) scores are not combined but are keyed to the occupational groups.

The occupational groups were designed to represent similar work activities and educational needs within each group as well as to span combinations of activities dealing with data (intangibles), people (or animals), or things (inanimate tangibles) and the nine primary occupational categories as described by the DOT. They are keyed to the U.S. Department of Labor's (1979) *Guide for Occupational Exploration* (GOE) interest areas.

Examinees are also asked to indicate their educational plans after high school from among four choices (none, vocational/technical, college or university, or military) or undecided. Appropriateness of these plans, based on expert judgment, is related to each of the 15 occupational groups. Although helpful, this information seems particularly prone to misuse and the cautions in the counselor's manual about overinterpreting it should be emphasized.

The CII was developed using a nationally representative sample of participants who completed developmental versions that oversampled items in each occupational group. Each item was written to summarize a DOT description of an occupation and was reviewed for vocabulary level (fifth grade at most) and absence of bias or stereotyping. The final scales were constructed based on item-scale correlations for males, females, and the total group, and on breadth of occupational group representation. Internal consistency reliability coefficients (alphas) of the scales range from .82 to .94 for Level 1 and from .87 to .94 for Level 2. These are certainly adequate. Overestimation that would be expected when the same sample is used to select items and to estimate alphas is not severe in this case because each coefficient was estimated with over 34,000 participants. Yet, the fact that a consistency index is calculated for each scale implies the interests each represents may not be as homogeneous as the alpha coefficients suggest. No data on stability are available.

Correlations among the 15 scales ranged from .00 to .84 for Level 1. The largest correlation was between Building Trades and Machine Operation, which becomes .93 when corrected for attenuation. For Level 2, the correlations ranged from .01 to .86, the largest, again for Building Trades and Machine Operation, becomes .92 after correction. Other notably large correlations were between Machine Operation and Transportation (.80 for Level 1, .82 for Level 2), Building Trades and Transportation (.77 for Level 1, .79 for Level 2), Management and Sales (.76 for Level 1, .70 for Level 2), Benchwork and Building Trades (.69 for Level 1, .75 for Level 2), Benchwork and Transportation (.62 for Level 1, .71 for Level 2), Clerical Services and Management (.70 for both levels), Clerical Services and Educational Services (.70 for Level 1, .69 for Level 2), and Customer Services and Educational Services (.70 for level 1, .68 for Level 2). The absence of any negative correlations is more indicative of some of the difficulties in assessing interests than a criticism of the CII.

Principal components factor analysis and varimax rotation were applied to each level item-by-item correlation matrix. At Level 1, an 8-factor solution was judged best, with all but 2 factors having high loadings with items from two or fewer scales. The 2 factors that had strong loadings with more than two scales' items were called Working with Hands or Things and Helping People. At Level 2, the best solution was for 10 factors, 7 of which with high loadings with items from two or fewer scales. The other 3 were called Working with Hands or Things, Helping People, and Business. These results seem consistent with the large interscale correlations noted earlier between Benchwork, Building Trades, Machine Operation, and Transportation (Working with Hands or Things) and between Clerical Services, Customer Services, and Educational Services (Helping People). Perhaps these scales do not represent interests that are as distinct from each other as those of the other scales.

Other than internal structure, validity evidence is available through correlations with judgmentally matched scales of the Ohio Vocational Interest Survey Second Edition (OVIS II). Correlations were generally strong with the exception of the CII Health Services scale, which correlated .10 with the OVIS II Medical Services scale and .08 with the OVIS II Health Services scale. Correlations with other inventories should be stud-

ied in future research as should predictive validity of the CII for such outcomes as effectiveness of career exploration, career choice, and career satisfaction.

In practice, the 15 occupational group interest results are interpreted as raw scores and compared with each other. It is claimed the occupational group scales are directly comparable because they are raw scores, and that because both males and females were included in the representative population they are sex fair. Each of these claims deserves consideration.

Although interests across the 15 occupational groups may actually differ in the general population, it seems reasonable to compare observed occupational group differences to evaluate whether the CII raw scores should be compared with each other. This may be done by estimating Cohen's (1988) effect size index, $d = |M1 - M2|/s$. According to Cohen, a large effect size is $d = .80$, approximately the difference between "college graduates and persons with a 50–50 chance of passing an academic high school curriculum" (p. 27).

Means, standard deviations, and ns are available in the manual for each grade level from 7 though 12 on each of the 15 occupational group scales. The difference between the highest and lowest means produces effect size estimates that range from .92 to 1.03. For each grade, Fine Arts ranks among the top three occupational group scale means and Machine Operation is lowest. Other popular (high mean) occupational scales are Educational Services, Legal Services, Mathematics/Science, Management, and Health Services, whereas other comparatively unpopular occupational scales are Transportation, Building Trades, and Benchwork.

Means, standard deviations, and ns are also available by sex at each grade level. The largest effect size estimate between sexes at each grade level is for Machine Operation, with the larger means for males. Also favoring males, in approximate decreasing effect-size order are Building Trades, Transportation, Benchwork, Mathematics/Science, Sales, and Agriculture. Scales favoring females are, in approximate decreasing effect-size order, Educational Services, Customer Services, Clerical Services, Social Science, Health Services, Legal Services, Fine Arts, and Management. Interestingly, the least popular occupational groups overall are those with the largest effect-size differences favoring males.

In the light of these effect sizes, claims of sex fairness and raw score comparability may be questionable. Of course, comparisons based on some form of scaled scores by grade within sex and occupational group may also lead to questionable interpretations. Perhaps several approaches (e.g., raw scores and scaled scores overall and within subpopulations) should be considered as a way to enhance meaningful career exploration in actual use, but no convenient way to facilitate that beyond the information discussed above is provided in the manual.

The CII is an attractive and easy-to-use tool for career exploration. The link with the DAT is a helpful feature. However, the evidence supporting its validity is both sparse and mixed and the information it provides to counselors and examinees may be oversimplified for use in career exploration, which is a very complex process.

REVIEWER'S REFERENCES

United States Department of Labor. (1977). *Dictionary of occupational titles* (4th ed.). Washington, DC: Government Printing Office.

United States Department of Labor. (1979). *Guide for occupational exploration* (4th ed.). Washington, DC: Government Printing Office.

United States Department of Labor. (1986). *Dictionary of occupational titles* (4th ed. Supplement). Washington, DC: Government Printing Office.

Cohen, J. (1988). *Statistical power analysis for the behavioral sciences* (2nd ed.). Hillsdale, NJ: Lawrence Erlbaum Associates.

Review of the Career Interest Inventory by SHELDON ZEDECK, *Chair and Professor of Psychology, Department of Psychology, University of California, Berkeley, CA:*

The Career Interest Inventory (CII) is designed to be a career-guidance instrument that assists students in making decisions concerning their educational and work plans. It is designed to provide information that links interests to occupations that are described in the *Dictionary of Occupational Titles* (4th ed.) (United States Department of Labor, 1977) as well as designed to provide information concerning students' interests in a variety of school activities and/or subjects.

There are 120 job activity and 32 high school subject and activity statements on Level 1 (designed for grades 7–9) and 150 job activity and 20 post-high school course statements on Level 2 (designed for grades 10–12 and adults) of the CII. Examples of statements are "take a course in government and economics," "research new ways to drill for oil," and "run a printing press."

The items are clear and nonbiased. The 5-point response scale ranges from "1" or "dislike the activity a great deal" to "5" or "like the activity very much."

For purposes of interpreting the results and for guidance, the user is referred to a number of ancillary materials such as the Counselor's Manual for Interpreting the Career Interest Inventory, the Guide to Careers Student Workbook, and the Exploring Interests: An Introduction to the Career Interest Inventory. Students are encouraged to work through the latter booklet prior to completing the CII: this booklet gets the student thinking about careers, values, likes, and dislikes, either by open-ended questions or checklists to which the student responds. The "Directions for Administering" the CII are quite exhaustive and easy to follow. The directions lay out a script for administering and scoring the inventory.

Results from the CII are used to counsel students about educational and occupational alternatives; by measuring students' interests in 15 occupational groups, the test provides insight into careers described in other sources such as the *Guide for Occupational Exploration* (United States Department of Labor, 1979) and the *Occupational Outlook Handbook* (United States Department of Labor, 1990). In addition, if students' abilities are also assessed, such as by the Differential Aptitude Tests (12:118), information about students' interests can be linked to abilities and aptitudes. The CII Score Report provides profiles and graphic results for the occupational groups, subject areas, and school activities; the student is also presented with a narrative that highlights his or her interests, likes, and dislikes. An available option is to obtain a group report that summarizes the results for, as an example, a class or school.

The Counselor's Manual for Interpreting the Career Interest Inventory is quite detailed, informative, and easy to understand. Information is presented on the history of interest measurement, how to score the instrument, how to interpret the results—raw scores and profiles, and how to use the results for career exploration and planning. Valuable sections of the manual address the way in which the CII can be used with students at risk of dropping out of school as well as those who are disadvantaged or handicapped.

In addition to providing a student's raw score for an occupational group, a useful scoring feature is a consistency index. This index is used to differentiate identical raw scores between those that reflect indifference (i.e., responding to some likes and some dislikes for the items in an occupational group), and those that indicate being undecided (i.e., responding with a midpoint value to most, if not all, of the statements within the occupational group).

The manual also contains sections on the development of the instrument as well as on reliability and validity. The sample of approximately 100,000 that participated in the initial stages of development are representative of the population in terms of geographic region, socioeconomic status, urban classification, and ethnicity. Items were retained on the inventory if they met item-scale correlation criteria. The primary criterion was that the scale should be homogeneous (the coefficient alphas for the scales are all in the .80s or .90s). The argument for content validity is made on the basis of the instrument's representation of the world of work. Statements were written to cover activities in the *Dictionary of Occupational Titles* (United States Department of Labor, 1977) or interests in the *Guide for Occupational Exploration* (United States Department of Labor, 1979). Factor analytic results are presented to support the claim that there is homogeneity of items within an occupational group and that the groups are relatively independent of each other. In addition, evidence is presented for the correlation between the CII and the Ohio Vocational Interest Survey, a measure also based, in part, on the *Dictionary of Occupational Titles* (United States Department of Labor, 1977).

What is most obviously missing, however, is any empirical evidence of a link between test results and satisfaction or performance in any occupational group or subject. Without such information, the utility of the instrument is diminished. Furthermore, no information is offered on the instrument's comparison to more popular interest inventories such as the Strong Interest Inventory (12:374).

In conclusion, the first edition of the CII requires further data collection. In addition, due to its linkage to several occupational sources, such as the *Dictionary of Occupational Titles* (U.S. Department of Labor, 1977), the items used on the instrument should be monitored for appropriateness, relevance, and timeliness. The CII will require modification when the *Dictionary* is revised.

REVIEWER'S REFERENCES

United States Department of Labor. (1979). *Guide for occupational exploration* (4th ed.). Washington, DC: Government Printing Office.
United States Department of Labor. (1977). *Dictionary of occupational titles* (4th ed.). Washington, DC: Government Printing Office.
United States Department of Labor. (1990). *Occupational outlook handbook* (1990–91 edition). Washington, DC: Government Printing Office.

[14]
Career Values Card Sort.

Purpose: Defines factors that affect career satisfaction, the intensity of feelings about these factors, determines areas of value conflict and congruence, helps make career decisions.
Population: Adults.
Publication Dates: 1993–1994.
Scores: No scores.
Administration: Group or individual.
Price Data, 1994: $8 per complete kit including manual ('93, 19 pages) and set of cards; $4 per set of cards; $5 per manual.
Time: (20–30) minutes.
Comments: Self-administered.
Authors: Richard L. Knowdell.
Publisher: Career Research & Testing, Inc.

Review of the Career Values Card Sort by ESTHER E. DIAMOND, Educational and Psychological Consultant, Evanston, IL:

The Career Values Card Sort Planning Kit by Richard L. Knowdell is designed to help adults define those factors likely to affect their satisfaction in the career they eventually will choose. A 19-page manual contains the rationale for the kit and the directions for a series of activities to help the individual obtain a picture of his or her career value pattern, including areas of conflict and how they might be resolved.

An overview introduces the question of what one wants in a career—values such as where to live and work, what kind of work is appealing, what kind of coworkers would be kindred spirits, working conditions desired, comfortable level of responsibility, salary level, and so on. The basic factors of a value are described as something prized, that is chosen from several alternatives, and that one is willing to support or act on. Clarification of career values is described as a task "drawing deeply from the well of experiences in both work and personal life" (p. 2).

The Card Sort activity involves sorting 41 work values into five groups denoting the individual's intensity of feeling about them: *Always Valued, Often Valued, Sometimes Valued, Seldom Valued,* and *Never Valued.* The definitions of the values themselves, according to a note in the manual (p. 4), first appeared in *PATH: A Career Workbook for Liberal Arts Students,* by Howard E. Figler, copyright 1979, and adapted by permission of the publisher, Carroll Press.

A sample summary sheet of prioritized values illustrates the interrelationship among the 41 values and their importance to the individual's tentative career decision. Prioritized values are then related to a Career Values Worksheet on which the prioritized work values are listed next to statements about their applicability to the career decision, perceived areas of conflict, and means by which the conflicts might be resolved. Finally, any changes in plans resulting from learning on the Values Card Sort are noted.

For greater depth in considering career values and the role they play in shaping one's future, five supplementary activities are suggested. The results can be shared and discussed with a counselor, a group facilitator, a classmate, or a friend.

Recalling past events in the Memory Scan brings to mind events in which *Always Valued* factors were exercised very freely. At the same time, situations where there has been little or no support for exercising *Always Valued* factors will come to mind. Analyzing one's role in the development of both kinds of situations is explored and value conflicts and their effects on decision-making patterns are examined.

The activity Growing Person/Changing Values emphasizes the fact that as one grows, circumstances change and, inevitably, values change accordingly. To anticipate these changes, the respondent considers three stages of life—10 years earlier, the present, and 10 years from now. What key incidents brought about changes in values in the last 10 years? What circumstances (for example, graduation, marriage, parenting, divorce, job or career change, and so on) might bring about even more changes in the next 10 years? The respondent is asked, also, to consider the psychological gains and losses experienced as a result— "the people, places, things, and organizations left behind" and "the new people, places, things, and organizations added" (p. 16).

The New Career/Life Landscapes activity asks the reader to consider how his or her career and life might differ if all the *Always Valued* factors were realized. Would one's sense of self be affected? What changes would there be in one's relationships and in one's job duties and working conditions? And how would allocations of time to work and to personal life change? This activity seems rather static and forced. It does not challenge the imagination as the earlier two activities do. It does not add insights or further the understanding of the very important way in which career values can impact all of one's life.

The fourth activity asks the individual how in charge they feel of building thier *Alway Valued* factors into their life and career. They are to copy their prioritized *Always Valued* and rate from *1 - not at all* to *5 - completely* how in charge they feel of building the factor into their career.

The fifth activity, Career Values Diary, helps the individual trace how closely day-to-day activities accommodate those values listed as *Always Valued.* Conflicts are more easily detected and ways to resolve them determined. Even here, only one suggestion hints at the importance of integrating all the information involved in sorting, reexamining, and revising one's *Always Valued* list. That suggestion involves keeping a free-flowing narrative of feelings about careers considered and processing it periodically to note factors that bring one joys and sadness, hope and frustration—factors that cannot always be easily separated. The diary, however, should help the individual integrate all the complex bits of information identified in the earlier card sort activities into a realistic, manageable career plan in which values play their appropriate role.

The Career Values Card Sort Planning Kit is clearly not a test. It is a workbook, but one that is very uneven in style and audience level. The word level and the diction range from condescendingly elementary to highly sophisticated and possibly beyond the reading and comprehension level of the average adult. (Remember that the definitions of the 41 values originated in a career workbook for liberal arts students, whose reading level can be assumed to have been higher than that of the average adult.) A number of the exercises are extremely mechanical and repetitious of earlier exercises, without consistently integrating what has been learned up to that point to create a more comprehensive picture of the individual's "career self" (p. 4).

Beyond the brief statement in the manual about the origin of the 41 career values definitions, no information is given about how the instrument was developed, the population on whom it has been tried out, reliability, content and construct validity, freedom from bias, and results of item analysis. There are no scores.

In a telephone conversation with the author, Richard Knowdell, he stated that he had no technical information, that the kit is mainly "a learning tool" that has face validity and has been used with thousands of clients. He is not planning to produce any further material about its development and use.

The test user looking for a career values instrument of established worth had better look elsewhere. A number of career guidance tests deal with values, but in a more complete context, and they provide technical information to support much of their claim about the utility of their instrument. The Career Values Card Sort Planning Kit might be useful as a purely exploratory "learning tool," with exercises that one could choose or reject to build a unique "career-self" profile, but there is no empirical evidence of its actual usefulness in planning for a satisfying career.

Review of the Career Values Card Sort by RICHARD T. KINNIER, Associate Professor, Counseling Psychology Program, Arizona State University, Tempe, AZ:

The Career Values Card Sort was designed to help individuals identify or clarify their career-related values. It consists of 41 cutout cards. Each card is approximately 3 inches by 2 inches. Value labels (e.g., "INDEPENDENCE," "SECURITY," "FAST PACE") are printed on each card in bold, capitalized letters. Under each value label is a brief definition of the value. For example, under the label of "SECURITY" are the words, "Be assured of keeping my job and a reasonable financial reward." The author does not report how that particular value list was constructed (which is a problem that I will discuss later). Nevertheless, the number of values (41) seems manageable, the list seems representative of the career values found in other career value assessments, and the definitions are clearly written.

In addition to the 41 value-labeled cards, 5 same-sized cutout cards labeled, "ALWAYS VALUED," "OFTEN VALUED," "SOMETIMES VALUED," "SELDOM VALUED," and "NEVER VALUED" are included. These are to be used as column headings. I think that it would be preferable to have the category cards look different from the 41 value-label cards (perhaps be bigger and a different color for easier sorting).

Individuals using the Card Sort are instructed to "deal your cards into the appropriate column" (manual, p. 3). Individuals are further instructed to: "Lay your cards out so that you can see all your choices in one glance. Move quickly, follow your feelings" and "your ALWAYS VALUED column should have no more than eight cards in it" (manual, p. 3).

After the cards are laid out, individuals are instructed to rank order the values and to transcribe them onto a summary sheet of prioritized values in order to have a more permanent record of their rankings. A summary sheet sample and a blank summary sheet are included in the manual. The basic self-administration and the transcription of the sortings are fairly straightforward and clearly described procedures.

There is no scoring system other than the transcription of rank-ordered value labels onto a summary sheet. Beyond that the author provides several additional exercises or activities for the user. These activities are similar to the values clarification or self-assessment exercises found in numerous career-development workbooks or textbooks published during the past two decades. They include activities such as considering one's values in light of an imminent career decision. For another activity the author suggests that participants keep logs of their work activities for a week at a time and then consider how their highest values are accommodated. In another the author asks participants to complete the sentence, "As a result of my learnings on the Values Card I plan to …" (manual, p. 4). Worksheet samples and blank worksheets for completing some of the exercises are found inside the manual.

Some individuals may find some of the activities helpful. However, I found a few of the activities to be less than inspiring or engaging. For example, I found some of the instructions for the Career Values Diary activity to be tedious and I thought the Career Values Worksheet sample was somewhat unclear. Unfortunately, in my opinion, the practice of overstocking career development manuals and assessments with superficially developed exercises is commonplace. In these kinds of manuals or assessments I would rather see a shorter list of critically and popularly acclaimed activities or at least some guidance from the author(s) about which activities are most highly recommended.

TEST DEVELOPMENT AND NORMS. The author provides no information on how the Card Sort was developed. A list of four "Objectives" is found on page 3 and a brief overview of career values is presented on page 1. The overview is basically a brief reference to the criteria of a clarified value (from the values clarification literature). There are no norms for this assessment device.

RELIABILITY AND VALIDITY. No formal procedures were used (and/or reported in the manual) on how the list was constructed. In my opinion, the list does have good face validity but a more formal validation procedure is needed.

No reliability studies were reported in the manual. The most appropriate type of reliability probably would be test-retest. Evidence that individuals' sortings are fairly stable over a short period of time would be a good indication that the Card Sort was reliable and would provide some support for the validity of that particular list of values.

CONCLUSION. The Career Values Card Sort is a self-administered card sort designed to help individuals identify or clarify their career-related values. It consists of 41 values, each printed and defined on separate cards. The cards are nicely formatted and the directions for how to sort the cards and transcribe the values are clear.

I think that the exercise of sorting and thinking about the implications of the rankings can be an effective intervention for helping individuals with their career decision making. I was less impressed with the quality and clarity of some of the supplemental activities. I would encourage the author to be more selective in his recommendation of activities.

The Card Sort has good face validity but more psychometric work is needed. Specifically, the list of values should be more formally validated. One way to do this would be to construct the list

from established measures (e.g., the Rokeach Value Survey [12:334]) and then to have expert judges refine the list. Additionally, a test-retest study could provide us with an indication of the Card Sort's temporal reliability.

In the meantime, the Card Sort appears to be a useful device. For most people the assessment would probably be an enjoyable and helpful experience.

[15]
CAT/5 Listening and Speaking Checklist.

Purpose: "Designed to help the teacher in evaluating two important aspects of the reading/language arts domain: listening and speaking."
Population: Grades K–12.
Publication Date: 1993.
Scores: Overall Rating Index.
Administration: Group.
Levels, 3: Grades K–3, 4–8, 9–12.
Price Data, 1994: $16.95 per review kit including sample copy of each of the 3 levels, teacher's guide (28 pages), and class summary folder; $21 per classroom package including 30 checklists, teacher's guide, and class summary folder; $9.55 per teacher's guide; $1.65 per class summary folder.
Time: Administration time not reported.
Comments: Student self-evaluation forms, a checklist assessment plan, and a letter to parents are also available.
Authors: CTB Macmillan/McGraw-Hill.
Publisher: CTB Macmillan/McGraw-Hill.

Review of the CAT/5 Listening and Speaking Checklist by GERALD S. HANNA, Professor of Educational Psychology and Assessment, Kansas State University, Manhattan, KS:

The CAT/5 Listening and Speaking Checklist is an informal oral language measure for grades K through 12. It was designed to help teachers to (a) determine if additional evaluation is needed, (b) monitor instruction and help in planning lessons, and (c) facilitate reporting to parents. This reviewer agrees with the developers of the checklist that listening and speaking outcomes are often underevaluated and that the above goals are important.

Each level of the checklist contains a useful list of listening and speaking outcomes common to curricula at its level. The checklist also provides for customization by means of adding local outcomes and omitting outcomes that do not reflect local curricula. Examination of the varied outcomes listed would seem a helpful way for teachers to avoid overlooking important skills.

Table 1 of the teacher's guide provides a contrast of formal and informal evaluation methods. Several of the contrasts seem questionable. One is the contention that formal evaluation is designed for comparative measurement whereas informal evaluation is designed for diagnostic measurement and classroom instruction. This contrast does not hold up under scrutiny. Criterion-referenced (i.e., noncomparative) interpretations are frequently appropriate for formally secured assessment data and for informally gathered information. Moreover, normreferenced instruments are often designed and used to enhance classroom instruction.

Perhaps the most worrisome contrast is the contention that the quality of formal evaluation is judged by validity and reliability whereas the quality of informal evaluation is judged by effect on instruction. Is not some degree of consistency of data an absolute prerequisite to utility for any purpose, including diagnosis and instruction? And is effect upon instruction not a fundamental validity consideration?

Yet the CAT/5 Listening and Speaking Checklist is offered without validity information, as though being an informal instrument rendered issues of score utility irrelevant. Along these lines, the teacher's guide does not adequately report the rationale or procedures of instrument development. This falls short of prevailing professional standards as, for example, detailed in *Standards for Educational and Psychological Testing* (AERA, APA, & NCME, 1985).

The overall rating index and the cut points are reported to be based on a field trial "in classrooms across the country in Grades K through 12" (p. 10). Unfortunately the number of classrooms, their locations, and the qualifications of their teachers are not reported.

Teachers are wisely advised in the teacher's guide to observe students on multiple occasions because "a single observation is a far less reliable indicator of true performance than are repeated observations of the same behavior" (p. 10). Thus, reliability is correctly recognized as an important attribute of assessments.

Nonetheless, the teacher's guide provides no information concerning the reliability of the scores

or the errors of measurement. The professional standards reflected in the *Standards for Educational and Psychological Testing* (AERA, APA, & NCME, 1985) state very clearly that "for each total score, subscore, or combination of scores that is reported, estimates of relevant reliabilities and standard errors of measurement should be provided in adequate detail to enable the test user to judge whether scores are sufficiently accurate for the intended use of the test" (p. 20). Without some indication of the consistency of scores produced by a typical teacher who would use the instrument, reliance on the scores is not justified.

Ratings of 3 are to be given for "maximal ability of mastery," whereas a rating of 2 represents only minimal or rudimentary ability. One wonders how consistent the meaning of these numbers would be from teacher to teacher. In rating such skills as "demonstrates appropriate telephone skills," interrater consistency would be enhanced at each level if it were clear just which skills were deemed appropriate. Would teachers in a given school agree? Similarly in rating such listening skills as "applies understanding to new situations," what basis of judgment is to be used in rating adequacy of application to various situations? It seems likely that teachers would differ greatly in the standards they apply to such ratings. If so, how meaningful would reports to parents be? It is unfortunate that there are no data concerning these reliability issues.

Because interpretations are made in a (rather unusual) criterion-referenced manner, the meaning of the interpretations requires a clear description of the content domains to which they are referenced. In this reviewer's judgment, the domains are not adequately described to render criterion-referenced interpretations meaningful.

In summary, the CAT/5 Listening and Speaking Checklist provides a highly flexible list of outcomes that teachers may rate with unknown reliability to make criterion-referenced interpretations of student achievement in inadequately described content domains. The overall lack of attention to reporting the instrument's technical quality makes it impossible for this reviewer to recommend it for purposes other than research.

REVIEWER'S REFERENCE

American Educational Research Association, American Psychological Association, & National Council on Measurement in Education. (1985). *Standards for educational and psychological testing.* Washington, DC: American Psychological Association, Inc.

Review of the CAT/5 Listening and Speaking Checklist by RICHARD M. WOLF, Professor of Psychology and Education, Teachers College, Columbia University, New York, NY:

The CAT/5 Listening and Speaking Checklist was developed to assist teachers in appraising their students' performance in listening and speaking. It can be used for informal assessment of student performance or in a more formal way such as judging the quality of an oral presentation. Three levels of the instrument are available: (a) kindergarten through grade 3, (b) grades 4 through 8, and (c) grades 9–12. The levels differ in the amount of complexity that is to be appraised. A teacher's guide is provided to acquaint the user with the importance of appraising these unquestionably important educational outcomes. Some discussion is provided as to what constitutes listening and speaking to assist the teacher on not only the importance of these two areas, but also some idea of what they are. The actual instrument is intended to be used with one student at a time. That is, the teacher is to focus on a target student and render the needed appraisals. The teacher may use each section, listening and speaking, separately. Suggestions are provided for teachers on how to complete the checklist.

The actual items comprising the checklist seem fairly reasonable although no evidence is provided to justify them. Unfortunately, the instrument is not a checklist but a series of rating scales that call for ratings from 1 (minimal or rudimentary ability) to 3 (maximal ability or mastery). Unfortunately, these are neither defined further nor are examples given as to what constitutes each level. This is left to the teacher to decide. A procedure is presented for aggregating the ratings and for determining whether the overall rating represents further evaluation/instruction suggested, basic, proficient, or advanced proficiency. No justification for the index needed to achieve a particular level is provided. This is unfortunate. Presumably, some analysis of speaking and listening was carried out to establish content validity, but this is not mentioned. No evidence is provided about the reliability of the scores produced by the instrument.

Of the two sections of the instrument, the listening section is the most problematic. It presumes that the teacher will ask the student a series of questions to determine whether he or she has correctly comprehended orally presented material. The basis for this statement is the presence of such items as "recalls events and details," "describes story characters," and "predicts outcomes from story." The implication is that this section of the instrument will be administered in an individual testing session. Whether teachers will be able to do so during regular class sessions is problematic.

The speaking section is not without problems either. Although the speaking behavior section of the instrument seems reasonable, the section on participation is questionable. Items such as "takes turns," "listens to others," and "is considerate of others' ideas and feelings" are questionable for inclusion in an instrument designed to measure speaking proficiency.

In summary, this instrument is intended for teachers to use in an informal or formal way to assess the listening and speaking performance of students. Although it is called a checklist, it is actually a series of rating scales with ill-defined scale points and an unjustified way of determining an overall index of speaking or listening proficiency. No evidence is supplied to support either the validity or reliability of the scores. Despite this, teachers may find some parts of the instrument useful in appraising student performance in these critical areas. However, caution should be exercised in making inferences about student proficiency on the basis of the numerical values obtained. There is no basis provided for that. Also, each teacher will need to decide what constitutes each level of each rating scale.

[16]
Child Development Inventory.

Purpose: "Designed to provide systematic ways of obtaining in-depth developmental information from parents."

Population: Ages 1–3 to 6–3.

Publication Dates: 1968–1992.

Acronym: CDI.

Scores, 9: Social, Self Help, Gross Motor, Fine Motor, Expressive Language, Language Comprehension, Letters, Numbers, General Development.

Administration: Individual.

Price Data, 1993: $55 per complete set including 10 test booklets, 25 answer sheets, 25 CDI profiles, and manual ('92, 44 pages) with scoring template; $13 per 10 test booklets; $9 per 25 answer sheets; $9 per 25 CDI profiles; $25 per manual with scoring template; $27 per specimen set.

Time: [30–50] minutes.

Comments: Formerly called the Minnesota Child Development Inventory.

Author: Harold Ireton.

Publisher: Behavior Science Systems, Inc.

Cross References: See T4:436 (14 references); for a review of an earlier edition by Jane A. Rysberg, see 9:712; see also T3:1492 (6 references); for a review by William L. Goodwin, see 8:220 (3 references).

Review of the Child Development Inventory by JEAN POWELL KIRNAN, Associate Professor of Psychology, and DIANA CRESPO, Research Assistant, Trenton State College, Trenton, NJ:

The Child Development Inventory (CDI) was developed in 1992 as a replacement for the Minnesota Child Development Inventory (MCDI). The purpose of the inventory has remained the same: the involvement of the parent(s) in the collection of information for the purpose of identifying and assessing children for developmental problems. The need for parental involvement is obvious in that they provide a unique perspective of the child in environments and situations not observable to teachers and other professionals. Additionally, the involvement of the parent(s) at the assessment stage eases the way for involvement in later stages should remediation be warranted.

The CDI differs from the MCDI in several ways: (a) the addition of items to increase comprehensiveness of the inventory; (b) deletion of poor items; (c) update and improvement of the normative sample; and (d) modification of the dimensions that are measured. Specifically, the Situation Comprehension and Personal-Social scales were dropped. Three scales (Letters, Numbers, and Social) were added, as well as 30 problem items related to health and growth. Thus, the CDI provides a user with eight scale scores (Social, Self-Help, Gross Motor, Fine Motor, Expressive Language, Language Comprehension, Letters, and Numbers), a General Development score, and a checklist of problems. Additionally, the MCDI covered ages 1 to 6 years whereas the CDI covers ages 15 months to 6 years.

The items for the CDI trace their development back to the MCDI. Approximately 2,000 statements were developed through a survey of the literature and psychological tests for preschool-age children. These were then reduced to 673 on the basis of whether the statement: (a) described developmental skills in children; (b) was observable by parents; (c) was descriptive and clear; and (d) was potentially age discriminating.

These 673 items were then further reduced on the basis of their age discriminating power. Age discrimination was determined by analyzing the responses of a group of white children ($N = 887$ for the MCDI and $N = 568$ for CDI). Items that showed an increasing percentage passing with increasing age were selected. These data were also used to determine the age level of the items. Age level was defined as the age at which at least 75% of the parents had answered "Yes."

The CDI yields separate scores on eight scales along with a measure of general development. The author states the scales were not derived through factor analysis. It is unclear exactly how the scales were determined. At a minimum, the use of a panel of subject matter experts (SMEs), consisting of educators, child development professionals, and parents, would support the integrity of the scales. Most of the items appear face valid; however, there are some troubling issues. For example, two of the items in the Social scale refer to playing a game with rules. This might be perceived as a social or a cognitive skill. Additionally, several of the scales have very few items in the higher age groups. From age 4 to age 6 and 1/2, there are only three additional items in the Social scale. Again the development of the items and scales without the input of several experts leaves the instrument open to criticism.

A major criticism of the MCDI still characteristic of the CDI is the normative sample. The normative sample for the CDI consists of 568 primarily white children from a working-class neighborhood in Minneapolis-Saint Paul. The lack of geographical, socioeconomic, and ethnic diversity is disturbing. Additionally, no date is given as to the year when data were collected.

The author recognizes the restrictive nature of the sample but suggests the behaviors measured are descriptive of most children in the country. Again, the opinion of objective SMEs would strengthen this claim. The development of local norms is suggested for any user who is working with children who differ substantially from the normative group. However, the determination of "substantial differences" is left to the reader.

Completion of the CDI requires that the parent possess a good command of the English language (a 7th to 8th grade reading level). Should there be difficulty in understanding the items or otherwise completing the form, the author suggests the use of the Child Development Review (CDR), which is an interview alternative to the CDI. Such advice should not be given without providing data on the comparability of the two instruments, the CDI and the CDR.

The Child Development Inventory is administered in a reusable booklet with a separate optically scannable answer sheet. Background information about the child and family is requested on the answer sheet.

There are 300 items on the test; however, there are 320 available spaces on the answer sheet. The instruction booklet explains that the test was trimmed, yet, the answer sheet was not. The questions themselves are divided into different categories dealing with various abilities. Despite this division, the items within each category are not ordered chronologically. For example, a question about jumping over objects with two feet might be followed by an item assessing the ability to sit without being aided.

The respondent answers according to whether the child partakes in the activity. Respondents answer either "Yes" or "No" to the items. The author instructs the test-taker to respond "No" if the child does not engage in the activity, has just begun to engage in the activity, or only engages in the activity sometimes. A "Yes" response should be indicated when the child currently demonstrates the activity or used to engage in the activity.

Some of the questions are vague. For example, one item questions if the child directs other children. It is unclear if this is intended in a helpful manner or in a negative, directive fashion. Interpretation by the reader could leave various respondents with a different understanding of the item. The result would be that the test-takers are answering different questions.

There is a potential problem for leniency in responses. The respondents, normally parents, may be hesitant to admit to difficulties faced by their child. The use of a wider response range than the dichotomous "yes/no" might allow for a perception of greater flexibility in responding. A 3-point or 5-point scale ranging from "rarely" to "frequently" might increase response accuracy. Finally, a social desirability scale could be added to identify "suspicious" forms.

The administration is approximately 40 minutes. However, this does not include the scoring. The scoring of the test takes about 25 minutes and is accomplished by placing a template, which is provided, over the scantron sheet. The score for each section is simply the number of "Yes" responses for that section. The General Development score is derived by adding the "Yes" responses to select items representing each of the separate scales.

The score for each of the eight scales is then plotted on a separate CDI profile sheet. A line signifying the child's age is drawn. This is accomplished after completing an age calculation described in the manual. The chronological age line serves as a high point. Those areas that exceed this line are the situations in which the child excels. Using a table in the manual, the examiner then marks the age levels that are 25% and 30% below the child's chronological age. These age guides provide a lower boundary for the norm. It allows the person interpreting the results to be easily aware of the problem areas for the child. Those scales that dip below the 30% line (known as delay scores) should be of concern to the test taker.

The test author states that often children age 4 or older achieve a delay score due to the fact that so few items exist in some of the scales at these age levels. In these cases, one is directed to look to other evidence to support or refute this finding. This shortcoming suggests that certain scales are not valid for these upper age groups.

Interpretation of the problem items is nonsystematic at best. This scale is not scored and appears on the profile in a format for the user to "mark" those problems identified by the respondent. Frequency with which these problems were endorsed by the normative group is presented by sex and age in Table 6 in the manual. However, the utility of these data is questionable. The author reports that the frequency of problems cited for 5-year-olds is relatively low, probably due to the fact that parents of this age group were given the option of responding to this section of the questionnaire. Additionally, one problem was endorsed by more than 50% of the respondents. The author suggests that this may not be a problem but a "challenge" to parents. Why, then, is it still included? Could there be other statements that may not necessarily indicate problem areas? Again, the inclusion of a panel of experts would help resolve some of these issues.

The author notes the MCDI used separate male and female norms for scoring; however, the CDI uses combined norms. The problem with this attempt to achieve simplicity is that the gender differences still exist. The difference between this test and the former is that now the administrator has to keep in mind that the differences are there. In the user's manual, gender differences are listed by item within scales for 32 items. It is unclear how the user is to take these differences into account when interpreting the scores.

The reliability of the CDI was demonstrated using Cronbach's coefficient alpha measure of internal consistency. Coefficients were calculated for the separate scales at each age level and demonstrate a wide range from .33 to .96. Within each scale, the lower coefficients tend to appear in the higher age groups reflective of the previously noted problem of few additional items in these ages. This problem raises the question of the validity of these measures for the older ages. No measures of test-retest reliability are presented.

The validity of the CDI was assessed in a variety of ways. Measures of developmental traits may be analyzed for their relationship with age. According to theory, scores on the trait should increase with age; thus, a positive relationship should exist whereby the mean score increases for each scale as age increases. The author presents data that partially supports the developmental nature of the scales.

A study of 132 kindergarten students demonstrated a relationship between CDI scores and scores on math and reading skills tests. Although some of these correlations were nonsignificant, the Expressive Language, Language Comprehension, Letters, Numbers, and General Development scales all showed significant correlations with both skills tests in the range of .31 to .69.

Intercorrelations are also presented. The high correlations between scales in some age groups suggest that the scales are not measuring unique developmental factors. For example, in the lowest age group (2 to 2 and 1/2 years old), the Number scale correlates .82 and .84 with Expressive Language and Language Comprehension, respectively, Again, the lack of factor analysis in scale development and the small number of items in the lower age group raise questions about the validity of the CDI Number scale in young children.

Too many issues are left to the user to decide: accuracy of parental responses, interpretation of gender differences, interpretation of the problem items, validity of the scales at different ages, and the usefulness of the normative sample. Additionally, the lack of objective decision making via statistical means or by use of a panel of judges in the item writing, item selection, and scale development raises issues regarding the comprehensiveness of the scales. Norms are nonrepresentative and reliability and validity statistics support the weaknesses in higher age groups for some scales and lower age groups for others. The availability of other instruments (such as the Battelle Developmental Inventory [T4:263; reviewed by Harrington, 1985]) with greater reliability and validity, representative norms, and clearer interpretation of results, leave these reviewers unable to recommend the CDI.

REVIEWERS' REFERENCE
Harrington, R. G. (1985). [Review of the Battelle Developmental Inventory.] In D. J. Keyser & R. C. Sweetland (Eds.), *Test critiques*, (vol. 2). Kansas City, MO: Test Corporation of America.

Review of the Child Development Inventory by STEPHANIE STEIN, *Associate Professor of Psychology, Central Washington University, Ellensburg, WA:*

The Child Development Inventory (CDI) is a questionnaire intended to identify developmental concerns in children ages "15 months to six years of age and for older children who are judged to be functioning in the one to six-year range" (manual, p. 2). The questionnaire consists of 270 developmental items and 30 problem items that address parental concerns about the hearing, vision, health, behavior, and emotional development of their child. The parent responds to each developmental item by marking a YES or NO and by marking a YES next to any relevant problem item. The author suggests the questionnaire requires a seventh to eighth grade reading level.

The CDI is a 1992 revision of the Minnesota Child Development Inventory (MCDI). According to the author, the changes in the newly revised inventory include (a) a revision of items to make them more comprehensive and to "eliminate poor items" (p. 2), and (b) more contemporary norms. The author also states that the CDI is "simpler and easier to use" (p. 2), although he does not explain what makes it so. In addition, the scales of the CDI have been reformulated from the MCDI, eliminating the scale Situation Comprehension and restructuring the Comprehension-Conceptual scale into three scales called Language Comprehension, Letters, and Numbers. Finally, the CDI has 30 problem items, which do not make up a scale and are not normed but are intended to "complement the results from the inventory scales" (p. 3). The manual for the CDI is well written and sufficiently detailed in the description of the items within each scale and the scoring procedures. Several case examples are given to help the examiner understand how to interpret the results.

The author explains that the items for the MCDI were selected from 2,000 initial items developed through reviews of the literature and relevant tests as well as generated by the author to fill in "gaps in the literature" (p. 2). After reducing the item pool to 673 statements, the "age discriminating power of these items was then determined on an item validation sample of 887 white children" (p. 2) who were roughly equal between the sexes and ranged in age from 1 month to 6 and a half years. An age level was assigned to each item, indicating "the age at which at least 75 percent of parents answered YES to the statement" (p. 2). Unfortunately, the author does not explain how the new CDI items were developed, only that they "included most of the MCDI items" (p. 2). A review of the items by age grouping indicates there are relatively few items at the older ages (above 5 years). Finally, in developing the nine inventory scales, the author made the questionable decision to forgo factor analysis. Consequently, the moderate to high scale intercorrelations suggest the individual scales may not necessarily be measuring distinctly different skills.

The reliability data presented for the CDI consist of Cronbach's alpha internal consistency correlations for each scale by age grouping. The coefficients range from a weak .33 in the Gross Motor scale for ages 5-0 to 5-5 to a high of .96 in the Expressive Language scale for ages 2-0 to 2-5.

The mean coefficients for the various scales range from about .67 in Gross Motor to about .84 in Language Comprehension and across scales within age group from .58 for the 5-0- to 5-5-year-olds to about .85 for ages 12–17 months. Although the manual author states that "this is an acceptable set of scale reliabilities" (p. 38), the inventory does not appear to be sufficiently reliable at the older ages (5 years and above), with the exception of the Letters scale. In addition, the author would be advised to either completely eliminate the Gross Motor scale for children above the age of 4—5 years or to increase or revise the items to make a more reliable measure at the older ages. It would also be helpful to collect reliability data on both test-retest reliability to determine the stability of this measure and interjudge reliability of ratings by both parents.

The information in the manual supporting the validity of the CDI is provided by three sources. First, the author claims that the age-scaling of the inventory adequately differentiates "younger children from more developed, more skilled older children" (p. 36). He further states that, "among the norm group children, low scores for age are relatively infrequent, especially for the General Development Scale" (p. 37). In addition, two validity studies are briefly described. In one, the CDI scores for 132 beginning kindergarten students were compared to their group-administered reading and math scores on a first grade pretest. The reading scores correlated moderately (.56 to .69) with the Letter, Number, and General Development scales. In the second study, CDI results were obtained on 26 children (ranging from 2 to 6 years) enrolled in an early intervention program in Saint Paul. Seventy-three percent of the children ($n = 19$) "had CDI Profiles that were delayed in one or more areas" (p. 38). Although these studies provide a good start in establishing the validity of the CDI, further validity evidence should be provided before the test user can use the inventory with confidence, knowing that it measures what it is supposed to measure.

The test user might surmise that the dropping of the word "Minnesota" from the title of the CDI means that the norms are more nationally representative than the MCDI. This conclusion would be incorrect. The norm group for the CDI consists entirely of 568 children from South Saint

Paul, Minnesota, most of them white (95%) and apparently middle class (the only CDI data given is parent education level which averages around 13.4). The geographically, racially, and culturally narrow norm group is perhaps the biggest weakness of this instrument. In addition, there are only 19 children in the norm group ages 6-0 to 6-2, making the norms very questionable for the older children.

Overall, the CDI appears to be a useful rough screening device for identifying possible developmental problems in young children. However, it does not have adequate reliability, validity, or norm-group representativeness to be used in the actual *diagnosis* of developmental delays or *placement decisions*. The reliability coefficients and norms suggest that this instrument is more appropriate for assessing developmental concerns in children below the age of 5-5 years than in older children.

[17]

Children's Apperception Test [1991 Revision].

Purpose: A projective "method of investigating personality by studying the dynamic meaningfulness of the individual differences in perception of standard stimuli."
Population: Ages 3–10.
Publication Dates: 1949–1992.
Acronym: C.A.T.
Scores: No scores.
Administration: Individual.
Editions, 3: Animal, Human, Supplement, plus Short Form.
Price Data, 1993: $85 per C.A.T.—A, C.A.T.—S, C.A.T.—H, manual ('91, 24 pages), 30 recording and analysis blanks, and 10 copies of Haworth's Schedule of Adaptive Mechanisms in C.A.T. Responses; $23.50 per C.A.T.—A or C.A.T.—H; $27.50 per C.A.T.—S; $9.30 per 25 recording and analysis blanks (short form); $9.30 per 30 Haworth's Schedules.
Time: (15–20) minutes.
Authors: Leopold Bellak and Sonya Sorel Bellak.
Publisher: C.P.S., Inc.
Cross References: See T4:444 (4 references); for reviews by Clifford V. Hatt and Marcia B. Shaffer of an earlier edition, see 9:219 (1 reference); see also T3:396 (1 reference), T2:1451 (23 references), and P:419 (18 references); for reviews by Bernard L. Murstein and Robert D. Wirt, see 6:206 (19 references); for reviews by Douglas T. Keeny and Albert I. Rabin, see 5:126 (15 references); for reviews by John E. Bell and L. Joseph Stone and excerpted reviews by M. M., Genn, Herbert Herman, Robert R. Holt, Laurance F. Shaffer, and Adolf G. Woltmann, see 4:103 (2 references).

TEST REFERENCES
1. Cramer, P. (1987). The development of defense mechanisms. *Journal of Personality, 55*, 597–614.
2. McNeil, T. F., & Kaij, L. (1987). Swedish high-risk study: Sample characteristics at age 6. *Schizophrenia Bulletin, 13*, 373–381.
3. Jarvelin, M. R., Moilanen, I., Vikevainen-Tervonen, L., & Huttunen, N. (1990). Life changes and protective capacities in enuretic and non-enuretic children. *Journal of Child Psychology and Psychiatry and Allied Disciplines, 31*, 763-774.

Review of the Children's Apperception Test [1991 Revision] by HOWARD M. KNOFF, Professor of School Psychology, Department of Psychological Foundations, University of South Florida, Tampa, FL:

The Children's Apperception Test (CAT) is a projective personality assessment instrument, consisting of 10 pictures showing different animals engaged in various "human," relationship-oriented interactions. The CAT was designed to elicit and provide insight into how children from ages 3 to 10 perceive, interpret, respond to, and resolve different developmental problems from a psychodynamic and/or psychosexual perspective. Extending Henry Murray's theoretical orientation and work with the Thematic Apperception Test with adults, and based on the untested (at least from a contemporary perspective) assumption that animals are children's preferred identification figures, the authors selected the pictures and themes for the 10 cards based on their own experience and their belief that the clinical success of the instrument was all the validation necessary for these choices. The authors state that the CAT can be clinically useful to any psychologically trained professional in "determining what dynamic and structural factors might be related to a child's behavior and problems in a group, in school or kindergarten, or at home" (manual, p. 2), and they suggest, without empirical support, that the instrument is culture-fair and also can be used in child development research or as a therapeutic play technique. Besides the 10 pictures, the CAT comes with a manual, separate interpretive protocols, and an additional manual with 10 additional puzzle-like cards that constitute a "supplement" to the CAT.

TEST ADMINISTRATION AND SCORING. Introduced as a game rather than a test in order to develop rapport, the CAT is administered by presenting the child with the stimulus cards, one at a time and in a specified order, asking him or her to tell a story about the picture by including (a) what is going on in the picture, (b) what the animals are doing, (c) what happened before in the story, and

(d) what will happen later. Prompting (but not suggesting responses to) the child is encouraged if necessary. Clinicians record all of the child's responses verbatim, and they can go over selected (or all of the) stories after the administration to probe for elaboration on specific points. Critically, with no other structured directions noted in the manual, the CAT uses, at most, a quasi-structured administration process that is too dependent on the clinician for an objective and unbiased assessment of the child—even prior to interpretation. That is, without a standardized post-test inquiry, the potential that a clinician could self-select specific conflict areas for elaboration, based on the background or referral reasons of a case, and bias both these additional responses and the interpretation of the instrument, is likely. Moreover, many of the assumptions inherent in the suggested administration directions are untested or, at least, no research is cited by the authors to validate their recommended procedures.

Assuming that children's interpretation of the CAT cards "must be a function of continually present psychological forces which at that moment manifest themselves in relation to the given stimulus material" (manual, p. 4), the 10 cards presumably address the following issues: feeding problems, oral problems, sibling rivalry, attitudes toward parents, relationships to parents as (sexual) couples, jealousy toward same-gender parent figures, fantasies about aggression, acceptance by the adult world, fear or loneliness at night, and toileting behavior and parents' response to it. Relative to interpretation, it is recommended that the child's responses to the "latent content" of the cards be analyzed, across and within the cards, using a structured CAT protocol that considers 10 variables: (a) the Main Theme, (b) the Main Hero, (c) the Main Needs and Drives of the Hero, (d) the child's Conception of the Environment, (e) how the child sees and reacts to the figures in the cards, (f) Significant Conflicts described, (g) the Nature of the Child's Main Anxieties, (h) the child's Main Defenses, (i) the Adequacy of Superego as Manifested by "Punishment" for "Crime," and (j) the Integration of the Child's Ego. Significantly, although these variables are described in the manual, the empirical basis for the descriptions and their validity, through independent research, are not. Further, although four CAT case studies are pro-

vided, they demonstrate nothing relative to the psychometric integrity of the instrument other than its subjective, potentially biased nature.

In addition to the primary CAT test materials, scoring protocol, and interpretive guidelines, the authors' manual suggests the possible use of (a) a short form of the CAT, (b) an alternative interpretive approach analyzing 12 ego functions from an "ego psychological" perspective, (c) another interpretive approach focusing on defense mechanisms and the psychoanalytic process of identification, and (d) the CAT-Supplement. All of this discussion, and the accompanying protocols or materials, are consistent with other parts of the manual in the absence of an empirical foundation, a dependence on an untested psychodynamic perspective, and a belief that "a projective test does not need validation and the establishment of norms" (manual, p. 17). Moreover, as noted above, the CAT-Supplement has different stimulus materials and its own manual, which describes its purpose, administration and scoring, and interpretation. The Supplement is, in essence, a separate instrument; it has all of the same assumptions and weaknesses of the CAT itself, it does not add to the clinical utility of the CAT, and its inclusion in the CAT materials is confusing and questionable.

PSYCHOMETRIC PROPERTIES. Although the authors allude to the development of norms for the CAT along with issues of reliability and validity, no psychometric data for the instrument are reported in the manual. The authors, however, do cite references to some work that has addressed this area, but much of this research is largely nonempirical and case-study-oriented, of questionable methodological and technical integrity, and lacking in convergent and discriminant validity with most clinical populations (e.g., Knoff, 1993; Knoff, Batsche, & Carlyon, 1993). As noted above, the authors state that the CAT, along with other projective tests, need not demonstrate such properties because "the individual case can stand by itself" (p. 17). This statement is indefensible and, in the end, leaves the CAT largely untested, putting any clinical interpretations or decisions derived from it in doubt. The psychometric integrity of the CAT must be established. However, the question still remains as to whether this projective instrument, given its underlying psychological orientation and assumptions, can ever be sensitive and efficacious enough to be useful as a clinical assessment or intervention tool.

OTHER CONCERNS. A number of critical issues already have been addressed; however, some additional critique is warranted and described below:

1. As noted earlier, a number of forms related to interpretation are presented in the manual. Although some of these forms lack explicit instructions and guidelines, the presence of these many forms is confusing both from a theoretical and a practical use perspective. A single systematic and objective scoring and interpretive approach to the CAT is greatly needed if the instrument is to demonstrate any clinical utility. The next edition of the manual should present this approach and exclude other superfluous or unvalidated forms or approaches.

2. In the section of the manual that describes "typical" themes of responses to each of the CAT cards, no information is provided to indicate how "typical" was determined. That is, no empirical, normative, or even developmental data were presented to validate the assertions. Once again, the subjective nature of this instrument's development, scoring, and interpretation is apparent, and concerns about its clinical use are reinforced.

3. The lack of an objective scoring approach and norms for this instrument means that a number of potential developmental and demographic differences across the 3- through 10-year-old age span cannot be tested. For example, differences across age, gender, socioeconomic status, expressive language output, race, and others need to be assessed so that any differences that arise can be integrated into scoring and interpretative procedures. In the manual, the authors note that "statements made about the CAT are thus far based on approximately 200 records of children between the ages of three and ten inclusive" (p. 17). However, they fail to elaborate on this assertion, providing no data, documentation, or critical analysis. The CAT remains largely untested, despite the large number of articles published on its use.

4. Finally, the CAT was first published in 1949, and the manual reviewed was the eighth revised edition. This manual's bibliography, however, is largely outdated. Indeed, many of the 83 references included are from 1960 or earlier. Future editions of this manual should completely update the current CAT, and should present a critical review of the research such that the psychometric integrity of the instrument and its clinical utility can be fairly appraised.

CONCLUSIONS. The authors' claim that there is no need to validate or norm projective instruments such as the CAT represents the strongest rationale to dismiss this test as a viable personality assessment measure. Indeed, the absence of empirical data supporting its use renders the CAT a research tool at best, and certainly not an instrument that should contribute to clinical diagnosis or intervention development. A great deal of test development and research demonstrating the CAT's reliability and validity is needed before this instrument can even approach the claims made by the authors. Despite its following, the CAT should not be available to clinicians in its present form. The CAT is an historical anachronism. It is now outdated in the context of contemporary personality assessment with children.

REVIEWER'S REFERENCES

Knoff, H. M. (1993). The utility of Human Figure Drawings in personality and intellectual assessment: Why ask why? *School Psychology Quarterly, 8,* 191–196.

Knoff, H. M., Batsche, G. M., & Carlyon, W. (1993). Projective techniques and their utility in child psychotherapy. In T. R. Kratochwill & R. J. Morris (Eds.), *Handbook of psychotherapy with children and adolescents* (pp. 9–37). Hillsdale, NJ: Lawrence Erlbaum Associates.

Review of the Children's Apperception Test [1991 Revision] by ROBERT C. REINEHR, Professor of Psychology, Southwestern University, Georgetown, TX:

The Children's Apperception Test (CAT) was designed in 1949 as a projective technique for use with children ages 3–10 years. It is a direct descendant of the Thematic Apperception Test (T4:2824) and is presented as a method of studying "the dynamic meaningfulness of the individual differences in perception of standard stimuli" (manual, p. 1).

The CAT consists of 10 pictures, each occupying an entire 8.5 by 11-inch card. Each picture is a line drawing depicting animals in various activities, chosen to suggest the most important life situations of children. The choice of these situations is frankly psychoanalytic: Orality, identification with parental and sibling figures, and primal scene fears are all listed as target situations. One picture depicts a mature dog spanking a puppy in a room where a toilet is the only other prominent feature.

The Supplement to the Children's Apperception Test (CAT-S) is a further collection of 10 pictures intended to elicit material concerning problems that are more specific to a given child: concerns with physical disability, for example, or about the mother's pregnancy. These pictures are also line drawings, although smaller than the pictures in the CAT, each page containing three or four pictures. They are printed on heavy cardboard and each may be popped out for individual presentation. The pop-outs are irregular in shape, although all are rounded in a manner resembling the bubbles used for dialogue in comic strips.

Separate manuals are provided for the CAT and the CAT-S. The CAT manual contains descriptions of and typical responses to the pictures, a section suggesting variables to be considered when interpreting the responses to the pictures, a recording and analysis blank, and a checklist (the Haworth Schedule of Adaptive Mechanisms) to be used as an aid in interpretation. There is also some discussion of the use of a shorter method of interpretation, some examples of responses taken from sample records, and a brief discussion of a "research aspect," in which is stated the authors' belief that a projective test does not need validation and the establishment of norms to the extent required by other tests. It is their opinion that the individual case can stand by itself and that normative information, although useful for special situations, is not necessary.

The manual for the CAT-S contains a description of and typical responses to each of the pictures, some discussion of the possible use of normative information, and the partial results of two small studies of thematic frequency. For the basic principles of interpretation, the reader is referred to the CAT manual.

Neither manual meets the standards recommended in the American Psychological Association *Standards* (American Educational Research Association, American Psychological Association, & National Council on Measurement in Education, 1985). There is no information regarding internal consistency, retest reliability, or interscorer reliability. There is no validity information of any kind. Clinical speculation and the unsupported opinion of the test interpreter are the basis for the evaluation of CAT stories.

Whatever the value of the argument that projective techniques should not be subject to the same standards as other tests, it is certainly necessary that test developers provide at least some evidence that different interpreters of the test data will draw the same or similar conclusions and that these conclusions will be of the sort that may be verified outside the testing situation. The CAT and CAT-S manuals do not address these issues in any way.

Although some reviewers have argued that the long history of usage by clinicians suggests that the CAT can serve as a valuable clinical tool in the hands of a skilled examiner, there is no evidence to this effect. There is, in fact, no objective evidence to suggest that the responses to these pictures can be interpreted in a manner that is useful in any scientific sense. The CAT is at best an aid to a system of clinical inference that is itself highly suspect. The use of the technique as a method of developing a personality description is entirely unjustified by any scientific standard.

REVIEWER'S REFERENCE

American Educational Research Association, American Psychological Association, & National Council on Measurement in Education. (1985). *Standards for educational and psychological testing.* Washington, DC: American Psychological Association, Inc.

[18]
Children's Category Test.

Purpose: "Designed to assess non-verbal learning and memory, concept formation, and problem-solving abilities."

Population: Ages 5-0 to 16-11.

Publication Date: 1993.

Acronym: CCT.

Scores, 6: Subtest I, Subtest II, Subtest III, Subtest IV, Subtest V, Total.

Administration: Individual.

Levels, 2: Level 1 (Ages 5 to 8), Level 2 (Ages 9 to 16).

Price Data, 1994: $280 per complete kit including manual (72 pages), 25 Level 1 record forms, 25 Level 2 record forms, stimulus booklet, and color response cards (1 for each level); $17.50 per 25 record forms; $35 per manual; $120 per Level 1 stimulus booklet; $95 per Level 2 stimulus booklet; $9 per 2 response cards.

Time: (15–20) minutes.

Author: Thomas Boll.

Publisher: The Psychological Corporation.

Review of the Children's Category Test by MARK D. SHRIVER, Assistant Professor, University of Nebraska Medical Center, Omaha, NE:

The Children's Category Test (CCT) is an adaptation of the Category Test, which is a part of the Halstead-Reitan Neuropsychological Test Battery. The CCT was "designed to assess non-verbal learning and memory, concept formation, and problem-solving abilities" (p. 1). "In addition, the CCT directly assesses the cognitive processes required for successful academic achievement by measuring the child's ability to learn, to solve problems, and to develop, test, and modify hypotheses" (p. 1). Also, "the task itself is a learning experience rather than a demonstration of acquired skills, ability, or knowledge. Second, the test does not require a verbal or a motor response and it does not have a strict time limit" (p. 1). The appropriateness of an author's purposes or stated applications for a test is dependent upon the supporting reliability and validity evidence provided. This review will discuss the CCT's reliability and validity given the test's stated purposes.

There are two levels to the CCT. Level 1 is for children 5.0 to 8.11 years old and Level 2 is for children and adolescents 9.0 to 16.11 years old. Specific directions for standardized administration of the CCT are provided in chapter 3 and are easy to read and follow. Administration of the CCT takes approximately 15–20 minutes and examiners are strongly encouraged not to take longer than 25 minutes (p. 5). The manual states that examiners should adhere carefully to standardized administration and verbal directions as "Changes in the phrasing or presentation of a test item or other deviations from standard subtest directions could reduce the validity of test results" (p. 10). However, it is noted on page 8 of the manual that the examiner should attempt to attain the child's best performance and "If the child appears confused or does not understand the task, repeat and elaborate upon the instructions but do not reveal the underlying principle of the subtest…. You may also ask the child to carefully study each picture, to describe the stimulus, to recall how pictures change, and to think of the possible reason for a correct response." The manual does not include a discussion of how this type of support from the examiner or differences in administration from standard directions between examiners may affect individual student performance and affect the reliability and validity of the resultant scores.

It should be noted that page 14 of the manual, in the section describing the directions for Level 1, shows a picture of the Level 2 materials (Figure 3.1). In addition, the test author claims in at least two places in the manual (p. 1 and p. 48) that the test "requires neither a verbal response nor a motor response"; however, obviously one or the other is required if the examiner is to determine the examinee's response.

User qualifications are provided on page 2 of the manual and state that, "Although a trained technician can administer and score the CCT under supervision, responsibility for interpreting the results must lie with those who have appropriate graduate or professional training and experience in neuropsychological assessment." According to the Acknowledgments in the manual, it appears that part of the reason for developing the CCT was to increase its use in schools (p. iii). The user qualifications for this test, however, may disqualify many school psychologists who do not have supervised training in neuropsychological assessment.

The CCT record forms are easy to complete. Scoring consists primarily of counting and summing the number of errors across the subtests for each level. A standard score (T score) with a mean of 50 and standard deviation of 10 is computed based on the total number of errors across all the level subtests. A 90% and 95% confidence interval and percentile rank for the standard score are also provided in the manual.

TEST DEVELOPMENT. It is not clear from the manual how the CCT was developed from the Category Test. It does appear that the CCT was 1 of 12 shortened versions initially generated from the Category Test and subsequently examined for their respective degree of correlation with the Category Test. The CCT (1 of the 12) apparently met criteria for having higher correlations with the original measure than the other shortened tests. Level 2 of the CCT "was chosen based on its number of items and the distribution of those items across the 6 subtests of the original Category Test" (p. 27). Level 1 "contains the same number of items (80) distributed across the same number of subtests (5) as the Reitan-Indiana Neuropsychological Test Battery for Young Children" (p. 27). The manual refers the test user to Reeder and Boll (1992) for more detailed information. The manual would be more user-friendly, however, if it provided more detailed information for the potential test user. For example, how were items chosen to be included on each of the 12 shortened tests? Was there a cut-off for correlations between the shortened tests and original test to determine if the tests may be measuring the same construct? What were the correlations that were found between the shortened tests and the original test? In addition, no information is provided in the manual describing if the test has been analyzed for differential validity across groups (e.g., ethnic, cultural, gender).

STANDARDIZATION. A stratified random sampling plan was used to ensure appropriate representation of children across age, gender, race/ethnicity, parent education, and geographic region. For the entire standardization sample (n = 920), these goals were generally met in comparison with 1988 U.S. Census data. The norming sample is reported to be representative of the educational mainstream. Special education students being served in mainstream classrooms were not excluded so that 7% of the sample consists of children identified as learning disabled, speech/language impaired, emotionally disturbed, or physically impaired and 5.2% of the sample were in gifted and talented programs. Although representation of the children across demographic variables looks good, there are only 70 or 80 children at each one-year age level, which limits comparisons of an individual child with the norm group at each year of age. Also, it should be noted that only English-speaking children are included in the norms, and it is unclear if there are children with *severe* motor deficits or language disorders in the standardization sample, a population with which the manual indicates this test may be particularly useful (pp. 1 and 48).

RELIABILITY. Level 1 and Level 2 were each divided into equivalent halves and Spearman-Brown correlations were computed to evaluate internal consistency. Internal consistency correlations averaged .88 for Level 1 across one-year age levels (range = .86–.91) and averaged .86 for Level 2 (range = .81–.89) across the one-year age levels (p. 33). These reliabilities are good, but suggest that additional assessment information be used when making decisions about an individual.

Standard errors of measurement are provided in the manual and for Level 1 average 3.46 with a range or 3.00 to 3.74 across the one-year age levels, and for Level 2 average 3.74 with a range of 3.32 to 4.36 across the one-year age levels (p. 33). These *SEM*s comprise approximately a 2/3 standard deviation around the standard score, and computed confidence intervals at 95% comprise greater than a standard deviation around the standard score (range = 5 to 8 points across all ages) (p. 62). These are higher than desired for using this test to make decisions about individuals.

Test-retest reliabilities across 10 to 42 days were only computed at ages 8, 12, and 16 years with about 30–40 children at each age (p. 35). Reliabilities are moderate averaging .75 (p. 35). Given that this test is purported to assess actual learning within the subtests, it would be expected that error scores decrease with additional administrations of the test, and they did. However, the learning that takes place during and between administrations of the CCT also decreases reliability or stability of the test over time. The author states that a lack of changes in error scores over time is "an indicator of abnormality in most instances" (p. 49). This "abnormality" apparently is perceived to lie within the child. Evidence for this statement is not provided in the manual, however. In other words, it is unclear if changes or lack of changes in errors on the CCT are reflective of neurological impairments or ineffective teaching or both.

VALIDITY. Correlations are presented between the CCT and the Vocabulary subtest of the Wechsler Intelligence Scale for Children—Revised (WISC-R) (N = 920); the Performance, Verbal, and Full Scale scores of the Wechsler Intelligence Scale for Children—Third Edition (WISC-III) for 26 children with Attention Deficit Hyperactivity Disorder; and the California Verbal Learning Test—Children's Version (CVLT-C), a neuropsychological measure that assesses verbal learning and memory (N = 920). Low negative correlations (some statistically significant) were found in comparison with the WISC-R Vocabulary subtest and the CVLT-C, suggesting that the CCT is measuring something different from these tests. These correlations do not provide evidence, however, of what the CCT is purported to measure. Low positive correlations (.22, .14, and .27) were found in comparison with the Full Scale, Verbal, and Performance scores of the WISC-III

(p. 39). In addition, evidence is presented that children make fewer errors on the CCT as they mature (p. 41).

The criterion-related evidence presented includes significant correlations for the current Level 1 (.881) and Level 2 (.716) total scores with the original CCT total scores for the two levels (p. 42) for 110 children referred for a neuropsychological evaluation. The manual states that these correlations suggest that the current CCT and the original CCT are "parallel forms" (p. 42); however, approximately 25% of the variance for Level 1 and approximately 50% of the variance for Level 2 are not explained by the correlation between the current and original CCT. The manual also indicates that there are consistent significant differences between the performance of children with neurological impairments and normal children on the CCT; however, the studies cited to support this statement are from 1977 and earlier, so it is difficult to determine if the manual is referring to the current CCT or the original CCT (p. 43). Evidence for one version of the test is not necessarily evidence for the other version.

Predictive validity evidence is presented for 313 children and reveals low to moderate correlations with group-administered academic achievement test scores for reading (overall correlation = -.28) and math (overall correlation = -.34) (p. 44) and for teacher assigned grades for math (-.20), spelling, (-.38), and reading (-.20) (p. 45). The correlations for predictive validity are lower than those for widely used intelligence tests and suggest that if prediction of academic performance is the primary reason for an evaluation then review of past academic performance (i.e., grades) and administration of an intelligence test (e.g., WISC-III) are still most appropriate.

SUMMARY. The reliability and validity evidence presented in the manual does not support the intended stated purposes and applications of this test. This test is meant to serve as a measure of a student's ability to learn, and it was developed to facilitate more wide-spread use in the schools. However, this measure should only be administered by someone as part of a comprehensive neuropsychological battery and interpreted by a individual with training in neuropsychology. In addition, it is unclear if the learning context of this instrument represents or correlates significantly with the typical classroom context in which students learn. Minimal evidence is provided regarding the construct validity of this instrument. It still appears that if an examiner wants to assess how a child learns in the classroom, then the examiner should observe the child performing with the academic curriculum in the classroom. Short of this, the examiner may observe the child performing in the academic curriculum in a clinical context, or conduct a direct skills assessment with content similar to the child's actual curriculum (Shapiro, 1996). Additional research is needed to determine what information the CCT provides over and above such a complete psychoeducational evaluation.

REVIEWER'S REFERENCES

Reeder, K. P., & Boll, T. J. (1992). A shortened intermediate version of the Halstead Category Test. *Archives of Clinical Neuropsychology, 7,* 53–62.

Shapiro, E. S. (1996). *Academic skills problems: Direct assessment and intervention* (2nd ed.). New York: The Guilford Press.

Review of the Children's Category Test by NICHOLAS A. VACC, *Professor of Counseling and Educational Development, School of Education, The University of North Carolina at Greensboro, Greensboro, NC:*

The Children's Category Test (CCT) was designed as a measure of nonverbal learning ability for children between the ages of 5.0 to 16.11. The author intended that the CCT would (a) assess diversified groups of individuals for whom many existing psychometric procedures may not be usable and (b) offer the option of being administered to individuals with limited verbal ability and restricted motor activity. The CCT, which is individually administered, is designed to assess nonverbal learning and memory, concept formation, and problem-solving abilities. The author reports that the CCT provides information on a child's ability to change problem-solving strategies, to develop alternate solutions, and to profit from previous experience. An attribute of the CCT is its lack of reliance on expressive language skills, thus increasing the utility of the instrument for diverse groups of individuals. The author purports that a primary value of the CCT is that it assesses the "learning experience" (p. 1) as opposed to being a measure of acquired skills, ability, or knowledge. The underlying assumption is that the CCT assesses cognitive processes required for successful achievement, by measuring a child's ability to learn and solve problems. The instrument is intended not to be affected by learning disorders, verbal or motor deficits, neurological deficits, or emotional handicaps. In essence, the instrument is attempting to provide information on a child's cognitive ability to learn.

The CCT was derived through a series of assessment transformations that began with the Halstead-Reitan Neuropsychological Test Battery (T4:1119), which employed the Category Test. The Category Test was modified and named the Short Category Test (T4:2455), with its primary distinction being the absence of the equipment required for assessment in the Category Test and a corresponding reduction in the amount of time to administer the instrument. The primary purpose of the tests remained the same: to assess an individual's ability to solve problems that require abstract concept formation based on the presentation of geometric shapes and configurations. The CCT was developed as a children's form of the Short Category Test, which was recommended as an assessment instrument for use with individuals aged 15 years through adulthood.

The author states that "a trained technician can administer and score the CCT under supervision" (p. 2). He recommends, however, that assessment professionals who are involved in education or neuropsychological assessment and who have an educational background at the graduate level would be best suited for administering the test and interpreting the results. The test contains two parts: Level 1 for children between the ages of 5.0 years to 8.11 years, and Level 2 for children between the ages of 9.0 years to 16.11 years. Level 1 contains 80 items and Level 2 has 83 items. The CCT follows the same theoretical tradition as the Category Test with stimuli presented following several established principal ideas. The test materials comprise four components: a reusable Level 1 test booklet, a reusable Level 2 test booklet, a manual, and separate record forms for each level. All materials provided are attractive, user friendly, and nicely developed. The manual is particularly helpful in providing (a) a contextual backdrop for the CCT; (b) a clear presentation for administration and scoring procedures; (c) standardization, reliability, and validity data; and (d) a section on clinical applications and interpretations. The test

booklets for Levels 1 and 2 are functional and easy to use, and they correspond well with the record form, which is clearly formatted. The front-page information provides a general overall description of the child to be assessed, including behavioral observations and summary score information that is parallel to the structure of the test booklet.

The CCT requires approximately 20 minutes to administer. However, the author advises test administrators to complete a level of the CCT within 25 minutes; longer intervals could impact performance negatively because concepts are learned and each of the subtests are accumulative. Test administrators need the manual, the Level 1 or Level 2 stimulus book, the Level 1 or Level 2 record form, and either the color response card for Level 1 or the number response card for Level 2. The author advises establishing rapport with the examinee, and provides specific suggestions for prompting and providing general statements such as "That was a hard one, but let's try the next one now" (p. 9) or "I think you can do it" (p. 9). Although the CCT is designed to be administered in a standard format, such prompting varies the conditions and may have an effect on test performance depending on the skill of the test administrator.

Standardization of the CCT was developed using children based on the March 1988 U.S. Bureau of Census report, with consideration given to the variables of age, gender, race, ethnicity, geographic region, and parent-education level. The total sample of 920 children ranged in age from 5 to 16 years. Approximately 7% were children who had been identified as having a learning disability. The proportion of males and females was approximately 50%. Race and ethnicity backgrounds included African Americans, Hispanic, Caucasian, and a small group classified as Others, which included Asian Americans and Native Americans. Parents' level of education was subdivided as follows: less than high-school education, high-school education (which was the predominant group), 13 to 15 years of education, and 16+ years of education. The number of children from each geographic region (i.e., northeast, north central, south, and west) was in accordance with the proportions living in each area as specified in the Census data. Based on the characteristics of the standardization sample, standard scores were developed with the distribution of raw scores for each age converted to a scale with a mean of 50 and a standard deviation of 10.

Reliability was estimated using the Spearman-Brown formula, with estimates ranging from .87 to .91 for Level 1 and from .81 to .89 for Level 2. The standard error of measurement varied by age from 3.00 to 3.74 for Level 1 and from 3.32 to 4.36 for Level 2. Test-retest stability was reported for testing over a period of time of 10 to 42 days with a subsample of 106 children; retest coefficients by age groups varied from .70 to .79.

Validity of the CCT was examined by construct and criterion-related validity. Construct validity information was obtained by investigating the relationship between the CCT and the Wechsler Intelligence Scale for Children—Revised (WISC-R) Vocabulary Subtest, the Wechsler Intelligence Scale for Children—Third Edition (WISC-III), and the California Verbal Learning Test—Children's Version (CVLT-C). Correlations between the CCT and the WISC-III ranged from .14 to .27. Correlations between the CCT and the CVLT-C ranged from .15 to -.27 for a subsample of 320 children for Level 1 and from -.10 to -.37 for a subsample of 600 children for Level 2.

Criterion-related validity evidence is also presented in the manual comparing the CCT and the Category Test, which yielded correlations of .02 to .88 for Level 1 and from .28 to .72 for Level 2. The degree of relationship between these two tests is rather dispersed. The relationship for full-scale scores for Levels 1 and 2 (i.e., .88 and .72, respectively), however, is convincing. The author also presents comparisons between the CCT and achievement test scores and school grades. In each situation, negative correlations existed ranging between -.08 and -.59, based on age-group analyses. Generally speaking, there is a negative correlation between achievement and performance on the CCT, and positive correlations between the CCT and the Category Test. However, in using the Category Test as a criterion, the authors have viewed prediction in a broad sense.

Within the manual section on clinical applications and interpretations, the author points out that the CCT is unique in that it can offer a measure of a child's learning capacity that is independent of previously acquired knowledge and skill, thus tending to be more a measure of verbal ability

that includes receptive or expressive aspects of learning. Accordingly, the CCT is purported to be able to provide a new dimension in evaluating a child's potential that could be viewed as independent of (a) the educational environment of the child and (b) effects due to extreme emotional pathology. In the same regard, the CCT is an assessment tool that is recommended for use with children with neurological injury or deterioration. The assumption underlying the CCT's use is that the CCT requires neither verbal nor motor responses and does not have a strict time limit. Although it is well known that more traditional achievement and ability tests are good predictors of a child's achievement in school, the CCT provides an alternate source of information concerning the child's capacity to learn. Again, the intent of the CCT is to go beyond evidence of knowledge acquisition by testing learning and other types of cognitive processes that are viewed as important in functioning. Accordingly, performance on the CCT is an index of a child's ability to learn (i.e., to benefit from trial and error experiences and to sort out elements in a given specified situation).

In summary, if assessment is viewed as a comprehensive process of gathering information about a child across developmental areas with strengths rather than deficits being emphasized, then the CCT adds another dimension to the assessment process. I believe the CCT would be helpful in obtaining a multidimensional, integrated understanding of a child's learning. I recommend its use as part of a battery of instruments when doing a comprehensive assessment of a child.

[19]
Children's Personality Questionnaire, 1985 Edition.

Purpose: Designed to measure personality traits to predict and evaluate the course of personal, social, and academic development.
Population: Ages 8–12.
Publication Dates: 1959–1985.
Acronym: CPQ.
Scores, 14 to 18: 14 primary factors [Cool vs. Warm (A), Concrete Thinking vs. Abstract Thinking (B), Affected by Feelings vs. Emotionally Stable (C), Phlegmatic vs. Excitable (D), Obedient vs. Dominant (E), Sober vs. Enthusiastic (F), Expedient vs. Conscientious (G), Shy vs. Bold (H), Tough-Minded vs. Tender-Minded (I),

Vigorous vs. Guarded (J), Forthright vs. Shrewd (N), Self-Assured vs. Apprehensive (O), Undisciplined Self-Conflict vs. Controlled (Q3), Relaxed vs. Tense (Q4)]; 4 optional secondary factors (Extraversion, Anxiety, Tough Poise, Independence).

Administration: Group.

Forms, 4: A, B, C, D.

Price Data, 1994: $29.25 per handscoring introductory kit including test booklet (Form A) and technical handbook with scoring keys ('85, 79 pages); $14 per technical handbook; $18 per 25 reusable test booklets (Form A or B); $24.25 per 25 reusable test booklets (Form C or D); $10.75 per 50 answer sheets; $15 per 50 answer-profile sheets; $10.75 per 50 profile sheets; $13.50 per scoring key (separate scoring keys required for Forms A/C and B/D); $20.25 per 25 machine-scorable answer sheets; $23.75 per computer interpretation introductory kit including test booklet (Form A), technical handbook, and machine-scorable answer sheet; $20 or less per computer interpretation.

Foreign Language Editions: German and Spanish editions available (Forms A and B, 1963); South African edition available from Human Sciences Research Council in Pretoria, South Africa.

Time: (30–60) minutes per form.

Comments: Test booklet is entitled "What You Do and What You Think."

Authors: Rutherford B. Porter and Raymond B. Cattell.

Publisher: Institute for Personality and Ability Testing, Inc.

Cross References: See T4:454 (9 references); for reviews by Steven Klee and Howard M. Knoff, see 9:222 (11 references); see also T3:1129 (60 references); for a review by Harrison G. Gough, see 8:520 (46 references); see also P:38 (14 references); for reviews by Anne Anastasi, Wilbur L. Layton, and Robert D. Wirt of the 1963 edition, see 6:122 (2 references).

TEST REFERENCES

1. Marjoribanks, K. (1992). Ability and personality correlates of children's attitudes and aspirations. *Psychological Reports, 71,* 847-850.

2. Waterman, J., & Lusk, R. (1993). Psychological testing in evaluation of child sexual abuse. *Child Abuse & Neglect, 17,* 145-159.

3. Kurian, M., Verdi, M. P., Caterino, L. C., & Kulhavy, R. W. (1994). Relating scales on the Children's Personality Questionnaire to training time and belt rank in ATA taekwondo. *Perceptual and Motor Skills, 79,* 904-906.

Review of the Children's Personality Questionnaire, Second Edition by ROSA A. HAGIN, Professor Emeritus, Fordham University—Lincoln Center, New York, NY:

The Children's Personality Questionnaire (CPQ) was designed as a psychometric measure of personality traits in children, ages 8 through 12 years. The publication date of the test is 1975, although the *Children's Personality Questionnaire* *Handbook* on which much of this review is based, was revised in 1985 to incorporate information from previous editions, norm tables, and additional references.

According to the handbook (1985), the CPQ's theoretical basis lies in the work of Cattell (1957), whose research identified objectively determined source traits believed to comprise personality structure and to be of potential importance in clinical, educational, and counseling practice. The test's authors believe these traits remain relatively consistent throughout the lifespan and, therefore, can be recognized and measured in comparable tests at other ages. In the Institute for Personality and Ability Testing series adjoining the CPQ are the Early School Personality Questionnaire (ESPQ; T4:843) for ages 6–8, the High School Personality Questionnaire (HSPQ; T4:1159) for adolescents, and the Sixteen Personality Factor Questionnaire (16PF; 12:354) for adults.

Suggested users of the CPQ include (a) schools and camps to screen out for individual attention and guidance children who need help with emotional conflicts and behavior disorders, (b) school and occupational counselors to raise the accuracy of estimates of scholastic promise, (c) clinicians whose work requires a diagnostic instrument dealing with basic personality concepts, and (d) school psychologists to keep developmental records of emotional maturity of students. The test authors emphasize the comprehensive and unitary nature of the CPQ. Unlike what they call special-purpose tests that deal with only single dimensions of personality, the CPQ is said to address the major dimensions factor-analytically demonstrable in research on personality by R. B. Cattell and colleagues.

Four forms of the test are available; each form consists of two parts, containing a total of 140 forced-choice items. The authors suggest that each form should be given in two sittings, not longer than 50 minutes. Authors state that the items are expressed in language within the reading vocabulary of an average child of 8 years, but the items may be read aloud and words may be explained if necessary. It is generally recommended that more than one form of the test be used and that interpretation be made on the composite score for each factor. Norms are available for girls, boys, and for mixed gender groups. Raw scores can be transformed into n-stens (a normalized standard-ten scale) and percentiles. Directions for computation of s-stens (standard deviation stens) for special purposes are also included. Stencils are provided for hand scoring. Computerized scoring with a brief computerized interpretive report is also available.

The CPQ measures a set of 14 factorially independent dimensions of personality (or source traits) identified by letters, technical names (e.g., threctia/parmia or sizothymia/affectothymia), and popular descriptions (e.g., shy/adventurous, reserved/ warmhearted). Four secondary order factors can be calculated from equations utilizing combinations of the sten scores for the primary factors: Extraversion, Anxiety, Tough Poise, and Independence.

Although the theoretical foundations of the CPQ are well explained in the handbook, data concerning the technical characteristics of the test are incomplete for the applications the authors have proposed. These inadequacies are apparent in the description of normative samples, as well as in evidence for reliability and validity.

The sections of the handbook dealing with test design and construction describe principles for "good" test construction, but fail to show how these principles were applied in the design of the CPQ. For example, although authors of Appendix D acknowledged the need for sampling based on a stratification of age, gender, socioeconomic, and geographic factors, no data are provided on the composition of the normative sample except the size of the sample for each set of norms and the total number of answer sheets analyzed (15,000). Given that the age range of the test extends from latency into early adolescence, the omission of age distributions is a particularly serious omission.

Although the handbook authors clearly state the four forms of the test are equivalent, the equivalence coefficients in Table 5 raise questions about this statement. With Forms A and B, coefficients (even with Spearman-Brown corrections) range as low as .37 and with Forms C and D as low as .33. Considering the importance placed on the interpretation of single factors, test-retest data also raise questions. Most test-retest coefficients for single forms range between .50 and .70, and some are as low as .37. When two forms are combined, as suggested in the handbook, coeffi-

cients range from .46 to .87, but are generally on the order of .62 to .79. These coefficients imply the need to ask a child to read and reply to 240 items, as much as 200 minutes of testing time, to obtain marginally reliable responses.

The handbook's discussions of validity data rest heavily on the construct validity implicit in the hypothesized structure of personality based on Cattell's factor analyses. Although Table 6 of the handbook contains CPQ Direct Validity Coefficients, no explanation of it is provided. Also absent is information on the selection of items and systematic evidence of their relationship to the factor used to describe them. The section of the handbook describing criterion relationships useful in educational, clinical, and social psychology presents some more sophisticated evidence of what the authors call concrete validity. However, this evidence consists of individual studies scattered through the literature of the years 1960–1970, rather than any recent systematic studies with the normative samples.

To summarize, the CPQ is a personality measure with familiar theoretical foundations in the psychometric study of personality structure. However, its handbook does not contain sufficient information about its technical characteristics to justify its use in decision making in school, counseling, or clinical settings. Information is needed about the characteristics of the standardization sample and the methods for selection of items. Improved reliability is needed if the 14 factors are to be used as individual measures of traits. Finally, systematic longitudinal research is necessary to determine the stability of the factors across ages, an assumption that has been made both within the CPQ and in relation to adjoining tests of the IPAT series, the ESPQ and HSPQ.

REVIEWER'S REFERENCE

Cattell, R. B. (1957). *Personality and motivation structure and measurement.* New York: World Book Company.

Review of the Children's Personality Questionnaire, 1985 Edition by TERRY A. STINNETT, Associate Professor of Applied Behavioral Studies in Education, Oklahoma State University, Stillwater, OK:

The Children's Personality Questionnaire (CPQ) is a self-report inventory intended to measure unitary personality traits in children between the ages of 8 and 12 years. The CPQ is one in a series of tests that includes the Early School Personality Questionnaire (ESPQ; T4:843), the High School Personality Questionnaire (HSPQ; T4:1159), and the Sixteen Personality Factor Questionnaire (16 PF; 12:354). The CPQ overlaps by one year with the HSPQ (age 12) and with the ESPQ (age 8) at the upper and lower ends of its age range. However, the authors offer no suggestions to guide users for selecting one test over another at the overlapping ages in the CPQ manual. Nonetheless, because all of these tests measure the same personality factors that are purported to be consistent across the lifespan, the authors suggest they can be used to make developmental comparisons for children across a wide age range. There is also a reference in the 1985 handbook, that was apparently also in earlier versions of the CPQ materials, to the Pre-School Personality Questionnaire (PSPQ). To date this instrument has not been published, but the reference to it in the current manual remains. This illustrates a major criticism of the current CPQ; the manual is shamefully outdated and in need of revision. For example, perusing the reference lists and bibliographic supplements in the manual reveals the most recent citations are from 1977! The only change from the 1975 edition to the current version appears to be that the manual and the norms have been compiled into one document. In all previous versions the norm tables for the CPQ were published separately from the handbook (manual); in this revision the norms are contained in the manual. The CPQ handbook desperately needs revision and updating. A very brief PsychLit search covering the time period from 1974 to 1996 yielded 25 articles in which the researchers used the CPQ. An updated manual is needed badly and should summarize a current literature review related to the test.

The authors of the CPQ state five purposes for the instrument: (a) for screening the personality functioning of those children suspected to have emotional and behavioral disorders who might need individual attention and guidance, (b) to provide personality data useful for predicting scholastic achievement and creativity for school and occupational purposes; (c) for delineating basic personality traits in children who might be referred for clinical practice to provide developmental data that reflect response to treatment, etc.; (d) for measurement of personality and emotional development associated with the child's educational experience; and (e) to provide an objective basis for discussing and comparing the personality functioning of children with parents and teachers. There is a well-written interpretive section in the manual (Chapter 9: Criterion Relations useful in Educational, Clinical, and Social Psychology) that can be used to guide users in interpretation of CPQ scores in relation to the test's stated purposes. But like most other aspects of the manual, the material is clearly dated and in need of substantial revision. Such a revision should also include applications in school psychology.

The CPQ was designed to measure 14 primary dimensions or "source traits" that reflect Cattell's conceptualization of personality. These personality traits are labeled with the letters of the alphabet, have technical names, and also are presented with more understandable clinical descriptions for use in communicating with laypersons. Four broad second-order personality factors can also be derived by combining various scores from the primary traits in specified ways. The test has four equivalent forms (A, B, C, and D), which are divided into two sections each (e.g., A_1 and A_2 comprise Form A, B_1 and B_2 comprise Form B, etc.). Each section contains 70 items; thus, each form has a total of 140 items. Users should find the administration and scoring procedures straightforward. However, children with low intellectual ability or poor reading skills will likely have difficulty completing the protocols unassisted. Raw scores from the CPQ can be converted to "n-stens," "s-stens," and percentile rank scores. Users may wonder why the revised CPQ does not use a more common standard score transformation. Interpretation might be made easier for users if the T-score (mean = 50, standard deviation = 10) or the typical deviation score metric (mean = 100, standard deviation = 15) were adopted in place of the sten. There are separate standard score tables provided for gender (boys, girls, and combined) by form (A, B, C, D, A + B, C + D, and A + B + C + D). The equivalent forms and section format of the CPQ allow test users the flexibility of administering the questionnaire in short sessions if needed. The authors also suggest that the parallel forms can allow users to administer different versions of the questionnaire immediately without worrying about retest effects in the same form were used repeatedly. They recommend that at least two complete forms (or all four forms) be administered for the most precise assessment of personality. As would be expected, the combined forms have higher test-retest reliabilities than any single form in isolation. Use of combined forms, however, will significantly increase the time needed for administration of the CPQ.

Reliability estimates are presented based on the 1975 edition of the CPQ. Test-retest reliabilities of the 14 factors, based on a 1-week interval, ranged from .46 to .87 (median $r = .71$) for combined Forms A + B and from .62 to .84 (median $r = .765$) for Forms C + D. Test-retest reliabilities for all four forms combined are not presented in the manual. In general, the test-retest reliabilities of the CPQ are too low for users to have much confidence in the test's temporal stability. Internal consistency reliabilities are not reported for single forms of the test, but combined forms yielded KR_{21} coefficients ranging from .32 to .79 (median = .71) for Forms A + B, .26 to .71 (median = .625) for Forms C + D, and .49 to .86 (median = .80) for Forms A + B + C + D. Clearly some of the factors are not homogeneous.

The authors also report correlations of the 14 factors between Forms A + B and C + D as estimates of alternate-form reliability. They did not present the other possible form comparisons. The rs (after Spearman-Brown correction) ranged from .37 to .75 (median = .615) for Forms A + B and from .33 to .72 (median = .545) for Forms C + D. These equivalence coefficients are quite low considering the forms are supposed to be parallel. As a result, users should not consider results derived from one form to the next as directly comparable.

A number of other serious problems that confront potential users of the CPQ need to be addressed. The standardization sample is not described in sufficient detail for objective evaluation. In Appendix D in the handbook the authors reported the sample reflected children from four geographic regions, three ethnic groups, three levels of socioeconomic status, and two levels of community size, but the exact sampling design demographics are not reported. The Ns that comprise the separate norm tables are simply included as notes under each table. The current handbook is also unclear as to when these data were collected.

The test's development is not adequately described and the handbook does not contain detailed information regarding the CPQ's validity. In terms of construct validity, this is a glaring omission, especially for a test that has been derived through factor analyses. Because fundamental psychometric information is omitted from the manual, a thorough technical evaluation of the scale is impossible. As a result, the scale cannot be recommended for use. The CPQ needs to be completely revised or it should be retired.

[20]
Children's Role Inventory.

Purpose: "A measure assessing the roles played by children in their alcoholic families."
Population: Adult children of alcoholics.
Publication Date: 1988.
Acronym: CRI.
Scores: 4 role categories: Hero, Mascot, Lost Child, Scapegoat.
Administration: Group.
Manual: No manual.
Price Data: Available from publisher.
Time: Administration time not reported.
Authors: Ann E. Potter and Dale E. Williams.
Publisher: Dale E. Williams (the author)

TEST REFERENCE

1. Williams, D. E., & Potter, A. E. (1994). Factor structure and factorial replication of the Children's Roles Inventory. *Educational and Psychological Measurement, 54,* 417-427.

Review of the Children's Role Inventory by STEPHEN N. AXFORD, Psychologist, Pueblo School District No. Sixty, Pueblo, CO, and University of Phoenix, Southern Colorado Campus, Colorado Springs, CO:

The Children's Role Inventory (CRI), as described by its authors, is a "measure assessing the roles played by children in their alcoholic families" (p. 71). In fact, the instrument, contrary to what its name may convey, is apparently designed to be used with adult children of alcoholics rather than juveniles. This assumption is based on the fact that all subjects used in the validation of the instrument were self-reported adult children of alcoholics. The CRI specifically is designed to measure self-esteem and use of social support. The authors suggest that the CRI may have utility in "isolating those [adult] children who may be at risk for developing esteem and alcohol-related problems" (p. 77).

The group-administered CRI comprises 60 items employing a 5-point Likert scale. Materials include: a research article (Potter & Williams, 1991) describing the construction and validation of the instrument; the scale or protocol sheet used by the examinee to rate items (e.g., "When I was a child, I ... was an achiever"); and a scoring key with items arranged in four categories: Hero, Mascot, Lost Child, and Scapegoat. Administration instructions are limited to a brief statement on the single-page scale, simply stating, "Circle the number that best fits how each word or phrase describes how you were or how you acted in the family in which you were raised."

Although no technical manual currently exists for the CRI, the authors, in personal correspondence with the Buros Institute, indicated that development of such a manual is a goal of theirs. Nevertheless, normative scores are not provided. Also absent, outside the limited information provided in the research article, are instructions for interpreting data. Of course, this places limitations on the CRI for clinical use at the present time.

Three studies are reported by the authors, related to the development and validation of the CRI. In general, the authors were diligent and appropriately cautious in terms of attention to issues related to theoretical conceptualization, research design and methodology, and interpretation of results. The authors are off to a good start in developing and validating the CRI.

The first of the studies focused on item development and selection. The authors employed children of alcoholics to generate items. Subjects were 140 self-declared adult children of alcoholics participating in a support group, Adult Children of Alcoholics (ACA). Five psychologists specializing in alcohol addiction reviewed the 100 items generated and employed a rating system for assigning items with "best" fit to categories. Eighty-two items were selected for the first version of the CRI. Adequate levels of internal consistency (Cronbach's alpha ranged from .89 to .95) were observed.

The second study focused on cross-validating the internal consistency and construct validity of the first study. Subjects included 142 ACA members, 28 men and 114 women. Ranging from .90 to .95, internal consistency was observed to be within quite acceptable limits. However, given that all subjects were members of a support group, although "data were collected anonymously and within a 2-week time span," there does seem to be the potential of cohort contamination of results. In any case, through item analysis/item deletion, employing a rank-ordering system using corrected item-total correlation, 15 items for each subscale or category were retained.

The third study was conducted to: "(1) obtain convergent and discriminant validity evidence for the CRI and (2) compare the responses of self-identified adult children of alcoholics with a control sample" (p. 71). One-hundred-thirty-eight ACA subjects (27 men, 111 women) were employed. As acknowledged by the authors, these subjects were not screened and thus there was the possibility that subjects may have participated in the previous two studies. All ACA subjects chosen for participation "scored above the recommended cut off indicative of parental drinking problems on the Children of Alcoholics Screening Test" (pp. 73–74). A comparison sample of 105 adult subjects (24 men, 81 women) denying parental alcoholism and scoring below the recommended cutoff on the Children of Alcoholics Screening Test was employed. For both the clinical and comparison samples, "CRI subscales were differentially predictive of self-esteem as well as size of and satisfaction with one's social support network" (p. 70). Also, reliability results were replicated for both samples. Internal consistency for both samples was observed to be adequate (with correlations ranging from .89 to .92).

The authors acknowledge several limitations related to their research: In completing the inventory, subjects were required to recall childhood memories; the clinical samples were all solicited from the ACA support group (thus, it is uncertain as to whether the obtained results can be generalized to the larger population of children of alcoholics); and subjects were not screened for prior participation, which may have contaminated results for the second and third studies. In addition, all subjects were recruited from a limited geographic region (Omaha/Council Bluffs metro area, and Lincoln, NE). Ethnicity is not addressed. Nevertheless, the authors appear to have conducted their research carefully. The results from the studies reported are encouraging and warrant continued research using the CRI.

In summary, the initial research in developing and validating the CRI is encouraging. However, as the authors seem to acknowledge, additional research is needed before interpretive results can be generalized beyond the clinical sample (i.e., ACA support group members) used in the study, in terms of differential diagnosis and preventative care. Thus, it is not recommended that the CRI be used as a primary method, within a clinical context, for gathering diagnostic information regarding children of alcoholics. The CRI may be useful, however, as an adjunct or supplementary measure when working with children of alcoholics. However, the CRI does seem to possess ample technical merits to be used in research. Also, with additional validation and standardization, the CRI has potential to be used as an important clinical tool.

REVIEWER'S REFERENCE

Potter, A. E., & Williams, D. E. (1991). Development of a measure examining children's roles in alcoholic families. *Journal of Studies on Alcohol, 52,* 70–77.

Review of the Children's Role Inventory by KATHLEEN D. PAGET, *Division Director, The Center for Child and Family Studies, College of Social Work, University of South Carolina, Columbia, SC:*

The Children's Role Inventory (CRI) is an adult self-report scale designed to measure the roles played by children in their families. Comprising 60 adjectives, the measure requires respondents to rate themselves retrospectively on a Likert scale from 0 ("Strongly disagree or very unlike me") to 4 ("Strongly agree or very like me"). The scale is based on the popular conceptualization that children growing up in families affected by alcoholism assume "roles or defensive behavior patterns in response to the parental alcoholism and the imbalanced family system" (Potter & Williams, p. 70). The four roles that form the foundation for the measure were described more than 10 years ago as the Hero, Mascot, Lost Child, and Scapegoat (Black, 1981; Wegscheider, 1981). According to the test developers, "all children of alcoholics are thought to assume one or more of these roles" (Potter & Williams, p. 70).

The genesis of the scale suggests that it was developed as a tool for research purposes rather than as an instrument to be marketed for use by practitioners. No manual accompanies the scale; instead, supporting documentation results from three studies conducted by the test developers and published in the same article (Potter & Williams, 1991). In the first study, items were generated and responded to by adult children of alcoholics, and their responses were used to refine the measure. The second study incorporated a refined measure to cross-validate internal consistency findings. The third study resulted in convergent and discriminant validity evidence through a comparison of self-identified adult children of alcoholics with a comparison sample. In reporting the results of these studies, the test developers used scoring procedures that compiled items into the four categories, but they did not detail how specific numerical ratings were incorporated into the final scores. Thus, in contrast to many measures marketed for practical use and supported by extensive supporting documentation, the CRI is in the very early stages of development, a reality that results in more questions than answers about its practical use. In addition to the basics of scoring, questions arise about administration, norming, and interpretation when the measure's accompanying materials are perused.

Administration procedures appear to be very easy, and the time period to complete the items is very short, possibly as short as 5 minutes. The procedures are based on certain assumptions, however, that leave the user unguided about some important aspects of the measure. Instructions are as follows: "The following words or phrases describe behaviors and characteristics of children. Circle the number that best fits how each word or phrase describes how you were or how you acted in the family in which you were raised." The lack of a more circumscribed frame of reference leaves respondents struggling to define their own temporal and relational context: Some will focus on their memories as young children whereas others will reflect more on their adolescence; some will emphasize interactions with an adult family member and others will think more often of sibling interactions. In addition, the assumption that people grow up in one family ignores the increasing number of adults who, as children, experienced multiple-family situations as a result of foster care and divorce. Moreover, although the directions ask for how the respondent "acted in the family," some respondents will extend the context to include situations outside the family. Despite the range of contexts that respondents may create for themselves when completing the items, this information is not known because the directions do not request it. In short, the vagueness of the measure's directions combine with the general scope of the trait-based adjectives to cry out for more situational specificity to the items. Information on the consistency of results across time and respondents would help temper these concerns, but at the present time, test-retest and interrater reliability coefficients are missing from the materials that accompany the measure.

Specific information about the measure's validity also is missing. Before results from the CRI can be interpreted to support the four roles that it purports to measure, more work must be done to collect construct validity information. The inter-item and inter-subscale reliability coefficients provided by the test developers are a necessary but not sufficient prerequisite to empirically derived construct validity. This is especially true because the sample used to generate items comprised individuals ("adult children of alcoholics") who had begun counseling and may have been exposed to information regarding the four roles. A factor analysis based on a priori questioning of the original clustering of items is needed. Through the use of a comparison sample and a discriminant analysis, the test developers are beginning to address the important issue that some individuals who do not grow up in families characterized by alcoholism may exhibit behavioral patterns similar to those who do. Also, in studying convergent and predictive validity, they have begun to address possible gender differences in response patterns on the CRI. Missing from published information, however, is the consideration of possible racial/ethnic differences in response patterns on the CRI. In describing the four samples used across the three published studies, no mention is made of the racial composition of the samples. Given the diversity of the American population, such information is sorely needed.

Although increased psychometric documentation has been collected and recorded over time by the developers of the CRI, the instrument is not ready for application and public use. If the developers wish for it to be, then continued refinement of the measure is needed with respect to administration, scoring, validation, and interpretation prior to the preparation and printing of a manual.

REVIEWER'S REFERENCES
Wegscheider, S. (1981). *Another chance: Hope and health for the alcoholic family.* Palo Alto, CA: Science and Behavior Books, Inc.
Black, C. (1981). *It will never happen to me.* Denver, CO: MAC Publishing.
Potter, A. E., & Williams, D. E. (1991). Development of a measure examining children's roles in alcoholic families. *Journal of Studies on Alcohol, 52,* 70–77.

[21]
Chinese Speaking Test, 1995 Edition.

Purpose: "To evaluate the level of oral proficiency in Chinese attained by American and other English-speaking learners of Chinese."
Population: Adults.
Publication Dates: 1988–1994.
Acronym: CST.
Scores: Total score only.
Administration: Individual or group.
Forms, 3: A, B, C.
Price Data, 1995: $60 per examinee for full length test; $45 per examinee for short form.
Time: (45) minutes full length; (25) minutes short form.
Comments: Examinee responses recorded on test tape scored by publisher; short form is first 25 minutes of full length test.
Author: Staff of the Division of Foreign Language Education and Testing.
Publisher: Center for Applied Linguistics.

Review of the Chinese Speaking Test, 1995 Edition by JAMES DEAN BROWN, Professor, and TE-FANG HUA, Ph.D. Candidate, University of Hawaii at Manoa, Honolulu, HI:

This review focuses on the 1989 version of the Chinese Speaking Test (CST). A newer version of the CST is in preparation, but parts of that version are still in draft form. The 1989 CST includes one Examinee Handbook, four Examinee Test Booklets, a master tape, and one Official Test Manual.

The Examinee Handbook contains the test's purpose, its timing (45 minutes), how to register and prepare, what to expect at the test, how the CST looks, and how scoring logistics work. In general, the Examinee Handbook is straightforward, clear, and complete, though more information about the scoring scale would help examinees.

Each of the four Examinee Test Booklets contains seven parts or subtests including personal conversation, giving directions, detailed description, picture sequences, topical discourse, and situations. Only the first subtest (which is not scored) has taped prompts in Chinese; all others have written and taped directions in English. Examinees are required to perform all speaking tasks in Chinese, but need not understand much spoken

Chinese, which the authors say is justified because the CST is designed to measure only speaking ability. This approach has two drawbacks: first, spoken discourse seldom occurs in a vacuum without listening; and second, directions in English are appropriate only for learners of Chinese who also speak English (thus excluding large numbers of other learners of Chinese).

The Official Test Manual contains: (a) *general information* (test format, test content, appropriate uses for the test, and laudably, a brief argument for local validation and standard setting); (b) *preparation procedures* (registering, collecting fees, maintaining test security, reporting scores, getting test materials, checking them, distributing Examinee Handbooks, and securing a test site); (c) *setup procedures*; (d) *procedures for language laboratory administrations*; (e) *procedures for individual administrations*; and (f) *technical information*. The first five sections provide ample information for proctors to set up and administer the CST effectively, and commendably, all directions that proctors must read to students are clearly blocked out and easy to identify.

The remainder of this review will focus on the Technical Information section (which includes discussions of the development process, level of difficulty, speededness issues, reliability, standard error of measurement, and validity). The authors begin this section by saying that the CST is a semidirect test of oral proficiency based on the American Council on the Teaching of Foreign Languages/Interagency Language Roundtable (ACTFL/ILR) standards. They then refer the reader to an earlier explanation of the CST adaptation of the ACTFL/ILR guidelines, which included paragraph-length descriptions in combinations of English and pinyin of the Chinese abilities of examinees at novice, novice-high, intermediate-low, intermediate-mid, intermediate-high, advanced, advanced high, and superior levels. These descriptions are adequate for test users to understand what the CST levels mean, but not to understand how points are assigned for each level. In any case, readers are told that the tests must be sent to the publisher for scoring.

The authors next explain how the CST was developed. First, a preliminary version was piloted in 1984 and 1985 using 27 students of Chinese at five institutions. Then, the four final CST forms were developed, and "a formal study of the reliabil-

ity and validity of these forms was carried out in Spring, 1986" (manual, p. 19) using 32 students, who were selected from a group of *volunteers* "so as to provide a wide and ... rectangular distribution of proficiency levels" (Clark & Li, 1986, p. 3). The sample sizes and selection methods raise serious questions about the generalizability of this study.

The authors then refer readers to Clark and Li (1986) for descriptive characteristics of the sample, raw data, and "more in-depth statistical analyses" (manual, p. 20). Readers must refer to this document (not included in the testing materials) to understand that only two raters were used to score all 32 examinees. Unfortunately, results based on just two raters may be idiosyncratic to them, and other raters might produce quite different results.

The authors next point out that the CST is not appropriate for examinees who are at novice-low, novice-mid, or novice-high levels on the ACTFL scale. Because the largest number of students of Chinese in U.S. universities fall into these levels, the applicability of the test is seriously limited.

Reliability is discussed in terms of both interrater reliability, which ranged from .89 to .96 for the four forms, and parallel forms reliability, which ranged from .90 to .99. The authors apparently overlooked the need to establish equivalent means and variances before making claims that the "four forms of the CST are parallel." To the authors' credit, they do discuss the standard error of measurement, but in terms of it being .25 on the 0—5 ILR scale (the first mention of this 0—5 scale). Indeed, there is no indication of what an examinee's score might look like. Will it be a verbal descriptor like "intermediate-high"? Or is it a number? The manual authors do not say.

In addition, no descriptive statistics are presented, no information about norms, and no description of how numerical scores are related to the scale descriptors. Elsewhere (Clark & Li, 1986), we deduced that the seven categories in the scale descriptors were converted to an 8-point 4—11 scale (with the 11th point assigned to examinees above the high-superior level).

Validity is discussed from four perspectives. First, construct validity is discussed briefly, then sidestepped with the comment that "a great deal has been written elsewhere about the construct validity of the OPI [oral proficiency interview], and no attempt is made to review this evidence here" (manual, p. 23). Second, the content validity of the CST is defended in terms of the systematic way in which the types of contents in the six subtests were developed and arranged. Insofar as test users find those particular contents representative of what they want to test, the CST is probably content valid. Third, the authors address the issue of face validity by asking the examinees if the questions "adequately probed their maximum level of speaking ability" (manual, p. 24) (*Yes* = 70%, *No* = 30%). Fourth, criterion-related validity is defended on the basis of correlations between the CST and live oral proficiency interviews, coefficients that ranged from .86 to .98 for various combinations of raters and forms, indicating that, insofar as the live interviews are valid, the CST probably is too.

To summarize, we found most of the information in the Examinee Handbook and Official Test Manual to be adequate for examinees and proctors to successfully negotiate the test administration (as long as those examinees speak English). However, the Technical Information section is much weaker: (a) the scale and its relationship to scoring are never adequately explained; (b) the small sample sizes and selection procedures limit generalizability; (c) the lack of descriptive statistics makes it difficult to interpret all statistics; (d) the inability to assess the abilities of novice-low, novice-mid, and novice-high students (the levels of most students in U.S. universities) severely limits the CST's usefulness; (e) claims for four parallel forms overlook the need for equivalent means and variances; and (f) the validity arguments are convincing only under certain fairly prescribed circumstances. Perhaps most problematic, throughout the CST documentation, references are made to other documents (e.g., Clark & Li, 1986) for information that should have been provided in the testing materials themselves.

REVIEWER'S REFERENCE

Clark, J. L. D., & Li, Y. C. (1986). *Development, validation, and dissemination of a proficiency-based test of speaking ability in Chinese and an associated assessment model for other less commonly taught languages.* Washington, DC: Center for Applied Linguistics.

Review of the Chinese Speaking Test, 1995 Edition by ANTONY JOHN KUNNAN, Assistant Professor of Education, Division of Educational Foundations and Interdivisional Studies, California State University, Los Angeles, CA:

The purpose of the Chinese Speaking Test (CST) is "to evaluate the level of oral proficiency in Chinese attained by American and other English-speaking learners of Chinese" (manual, p. 1). The CST is intended for students at proficiency levels from Intermediate to Superior following the guidelines developed by the American Council on the Teaching of Foreign Languages (ACTFL). The uses of the test could include, among others, admission to, placement within, or exemption from a Chinese study program; application for scholarship or appointment; competency testing upon exit from a Chinese program; or certification of Chinese language proficiency for occupational purposes (manual, p. 3).

FEATURES. The CST is a semidirect test, which means the test is administered via an audio-taped recording and a test booklet that contains written materials, maps, and pictures, and the test taker's responses are recorded on another audiotape and then rated. It can be administered individually or to a large group in a language laboratory in two forms: The long form lasts 45 minutes and consists of four types of questions designed to elicit speech samples of about 20 minutes duration; the short form lasts about 25 minutes and elicits speech samples of about 15 minutes duration. In Part 1 of the test, the respondent takes part in a personal conversation through several questions about his or her family and education; in Part 2 the test taker is instructed to answer and ask questions, describe a place or activity, give directions, and narrate a story based on a series of pictures; in Part 3 the test taker is instructed to talk about five different topics (two in the short form); and in Part 4 (only in the long form) the test taker is instructed to carry out a specific task based on real life situations.

The recorded speech samples are scored by specially trained raters. The score report contains the test taker's oral proficiency rating, generally based on the ACTFL proficiency guidelines and scale, ranging from Novice to Superior.

TEST DEVELOPMENT. The test manual contains the procedures adopted for the development of the CST, such as the administration of the preliminary version of the four different forms to two groups of students of Chinese, and the minor modifications made to the overall format and content. The test was revised in 1994 to include more contextualized clues. However, it is unclear how the authors arrived at the four parts to the test; whether they based their decisions on content validity, whether they followed the Oral Proficiency Interview (OPI) format, or whether they had corroboration from any statistical procedures. With regard to level of difficulty, the manual authors state the long form of the test is most appropriate for learners between the levels of Intermediate-High and Superior and the short form for learners between the levels of Novice-High to Intermediate-High on the ACTFL scale. In terms of speededness, responses to questionnaires collected from validation studies indicated that adequate time is allotted for most test takers to respond to each question.

VALIDITY. Three types of validity evidence were gathered: content validity, criterion-related validity, and construct validity. Evidence for content validity was found in the tasks: Test takers are asked to speak in Chinese, they are not required to decode Chinese, and the tasks closely parallel the OPI format. In a validation study, test takers were asked to indicate on a questionnaire if the questions in each of the tests (the OPI and the CST) adequately probed their maximum level of speaking ability: for the CST, 70% said "yes" and 30% said "no"; for the OPI, 74% said "yes" and 26% said "no," thus providing evidence of the content validity of the CST as a surrogate OPI.

Evidence for criterion-related validity of the 1988 version of the test was offered through correlations obtained from ratings of test performance by two raters who provided independent ratings of the four forms of the CST with the OPI; these correlations ranged from .92 to .98. In a further study, correlations were obtained from ratings by one rater who rated test performance of a test taker on the CST and another rater on the OPI; these slightly lower correlations ranged from .86 to .93. For these two sets of studies, sample sizes were 15 or 16 subjects. No direct correlational study has yet been reported for the revised test.

With regard to construct validation, no separate study of the CST is reported. Instead, the manual authors note that evidence from the content validation and criterion validation studies is sufficient to support the construct validation of the test as a measure of speaking proficiency. In addition, the reader is directed to construct validation studies of the OPI reported in journals.

Despite this excellent case for test validation, a major concern still exists: Why does the test use different tasks? This question should be asked as it is left unclear whether the test developers believe the oral discourse expected is going to be significantly different in each of the tasks. For example, is the oral discourse of giving directions different from giving detailed descriptions or is oral topical discourse different from oral discourse in a specific situation? The manual authors do not provide any discussion on this matter. One empirical method that could be used to establish the basis for the four tasks is to conduct an exploratory factor analysis of test performance data and to interpret the factors (see Kunnan, 1992; Bachman, Davidson, Ryan, & Choi, 1995).

RELIABILITY. Interrater reliability information was collected for the four parallel forms: The reliabilities were uniformly high ranging from .89 to .97. Parallel form reliability information was also collected: For Forms A and B the reliabilities were .95 and .99 for two raters and .90 for different raters; and for Forms C and D the reliabilities were .95 and .93 for two raters and .91 for different raters. Both these studies indicate that the test yields consistent results and trained raters are able to use the scoring guidelines consistently. In addition to these classical interrater reliability studies, a generalizability study with facets such as age, gender, native language, a decision-study with varying numbers of raters, and a many-facet Rasch measurement (examining relative severity of different raters and relative difficulty of different tasks) would have enhanced the technical strengths of the test (see Bachman, Lynch, & Mason, 1995; Lumley & McNamara, 1995).

SUMMARY. The CST is a reasonably efficient alternative to a direct test. Its validity and reliability are somewhat well established, although the sample sizes are small. Support from additional studies will enhance the confidence with which the test can be used.

REVIEWER'S REFERENCES

Kunnan, A. J. (1992). An investigation of a criterion-referenced test using G-theory, and factor and cluster analyses. *Language Testing, 9*, 30–49.

Bachman, L. F., Davidson, F., Ryan, K., & Choi, I-C. (1995). *An investigation into the comparability of two tests of English as a foreign language.* Cambridge: Cambridge University Press.

Bachman, L. F., Lynch, B. K., & Mason, M. (1995). Investigating variability in tasks and rater judgements in a performance test of foreign language speaking. *Language Testing, 12,* 238–257.

Lumley, T., & McNamara, T. F. (1995). Rater characteristics and rater bias: Implications for training. *Language Testing, 12,* 54–71.

[22]
Christensen Dietary Distress Inventory.

Purpose: Designed to provide an objective assessment of the probability of diet contributing to emotional distress.
Population: Ages 18 and above.
Publication Date: 1990.
Acronym: CDDI.
Scores: Total score only.
Administration: Group.
Price Data: Available from publisher.
Time: (10–15) minutes.
Comments: Self-report inventory.
Author: Larry Christensen.
Publisher: Pro-Health Publications.
Cross References: See T4:460 (1 reference).

TEST REFERENCE

1. Christensen, L., & Burrows, R. (1990). Dietary treatment of depression. *Behavior Therapy, 21,* 183–193.

Review of the Christensen Dietary Distress Inventory by RICHARD F. FARMER, Assistant Professor of Psychology, Idaho State University, Pocatello, ID:

The Christensen Dietary Distress Inventory (CDDI) is a 34-item self-report questionnaire designed to diagnose persons whose emotional distress is partially or completely due to the intake of specific dietary substances, namely refined sucrose and caffeine. The development of this inventory was premised on the notion that persons who experience "a dietary induced emotional distress exhibit responses which differentiate them from individuals whose emotional distress arises from sources other than diet" (manual, p. 1).

The 34 items of the CDDI assess a variety of physical symptoms and psychological complaints. Directions for the CDDI ask the respondent to read each inventory item and to determine if the item is applicable to him or her. If the item is not applicable, the respondent is instructed to go on to the next item. If the item is applicable, the respondent is asked to choose one of four or five response options that seems most accurate or applicable. The CDDI is designed for persons 18 years or older, can be administered to individuals or groups, and takes about 10 minutes to complete. The manual cautions against the use of this measure with bipolar patients and persons on psycho-

tropic medication because elevated CDDI scores may be due to these conditions rather than diet.

Items were selected for inclusion in the CDDI based on their ability to discriminate dietary responders (i.e., those whose mood disturbance decreased following dietary intervention and returned with reinstatement of pretreatment dietary intake pattern) from dietary nonresponders (i.e., those whose mood disturbance was not modified by dietary intervention). Item response options are weighted -1, 0, 1, or 2 in accordance with their ability to discriminate these two groups (see Christensen, Krietsch, & White, 1989). A total score for the measure (range: -2 to 39) is derived from the sum of the weighted values of the items endorsed. A scoring template is available to assist in scoring.

There are no normative data provided for this measure based on the rationale that the CDDI "is designed to be used for diagnostic purposes as opposed to measuring psychological constructs" (manual, p. 3). Rather, a list of potential cutoff scores is provided along with associated sensitivity and specificity indices. The test user is instructed to use the cutoff score that best meets the needs of the user (e.g., detect actual cases or minimize false classifications). The manual recommends, however, that test users select a cutoff score that maximizes the correct classification of true positives at the cost of also selecting some false positives. The manual does not contain any information on how these sensitivity and specificity values were derived other than to refer the test user to a previously published article where these values were first reported (Christensen et al., 1989). Reference to this report reveals that sensitivity and specificity indices were based on a small sample (*n* = 16 total; 7 dietary responders and 9 nonresponders) recruited from newspaper advertisements. The use of a small, unrepresentative normative sample in conjunction with an absence of data on the estimated true prevalence rate of dietary-induced emotional distress in the population suggests that these sensitivity and specificity indices should be employed with extreme caution.

Test-retest reliability data are presented for two samples (*n*s = 51 and 22) for whom the retest interval was 10 and 8.4 days, respectively. The manual reports a test-retest reliability value of .87 for both samples, presumably based on the CDDI summary scores. Absent is a mention of the degree of diagnostic concordance across testing occasions, which would appear to be a more appropriate index of this measure's reliability as it is presented as a diagnostic instrument.

The manual cites one report supportive of the measure's validity (Christensen et al., 1989), where CDDI scores were compared with the subjects' classification as dietary responders or nonresponders. The manual states that a "relationship of 0.48 [was found] between these two variables" (manual, p. 7), without further indicating who the subjects were, how they were selected, how many there were, or what method was employed for arriving at the validity coefficient. The manual goes on to provide group means on the CDDI (without standard deviations) for dietary responders ($M = 17.3$) and nonresponders ($M = 13.1$) as further indication of the measure's validity. The mean of the nonresponder sample (13.1), however, is virtually the same value as the suggested cutoff (13.0) for discriminating between persons whose emotional distress is due to diet versus some other cause. This is particularly disconcerting given that the manual instructs the test user to inform respondents who exceed a selected cutoff score that "their mood disturbance is in all probability due in part or totally to their consumption of refined sucrose and/or caffeine" (manual, p. 9). Other validity-related research by the author (Christensen & Burrows, 1991) published after the publication of the CDDI manual indicates that CDDI means for dietary responders ($n = 41$, $M = 20.2$, $SD = 4.9$) were greater than those of psychology clinic outpatients ($n = 39$, $M = 12.6$, $SD = 4.8$) and college students enrolled in an introductory psychology course ($n = 144$, $M = 10.0$, $SD = 4.3$). Although such data are encouraging, it does cast some doubt on the CDDI's differential diagnostic abilities when used in accordance with instructions provided in the manual, as the mean for the emotionally distressed outpatient group in the 1991 study (12.6) is almost the same as the suggested cutoff (13.0) for diagnosing dietary-induced mood distress.

In summary, the CDDI is presented as a diagnostic and research tool for the identification of persons whose emotional distress may be the result of dietary factors, specifically the intake of refined sucrose and caffeine. Limited psychometric data presented in the test manual appear incon-

clusive as to the CDDI's ability to accomplish its stated goal. Additional cross-validation research on the sensitivity and specificity indices with larger and more representative normative samples is urgently needed, as is additional work on the discriminative ability of the CDDI item set. Conceptual concerns related to the formatting of CDDI items warrant further consideration, such as asking respondents to speculate about the origins of their physiological symptoms and psychological complaints, as do almost half of the CDDI items. Can respondents perform such a task accurately? A related problematic aspect of this measure is that many "deviant" response options (i.e., those that contribute to a diagnosis of dietary-influenced emotional distress) indicate the respondent's uncertainty about the origin of a particular symptom or complaint. Furthermore, response options within a set at times seem poorly differentiated (e.g., "every other day" versus "several times a week") despite differential weighting. Given the present limitations of this measure, users should exercise extreme caution when making diagnostic inferences related to the cause of a given examinee's emotional distress based on CDDI scores.

REVIEWER'S REFERENCES

Christensen, L., Krietsch, K., & White, B. (1989). Development, cross-validation, and assessment of reliability of the Christensen Dietary Distress Inventory. *Canadian Journal of Behavioural Science, 21*, 1–15.

Christensen, L., & Burrows, R. (1991). Criterion validity of the Christensen Dietary Distress Inventory. *Canadian Journal of Behavioural Science, 23*, 245–247.

Review of the Christensen Dietary Distress Inventory by SANDRA D. HAYNES, Assistant Professor of Human Services, Metropolitan State College of Denver, Denver, CO:

The Christensen Dietary Distress Inventory (CDDI) is designed to assess the effects of dietary habits on psychological well-being. The inventory was developed to investigate the proposition that persons with emotional distress may experience hypoglycemic-type symptoms which aggrandize mood symptoms. If such difficulties could be identified, the author reasoned, these individuals might enjoy relief of some psychological symptoms, specifically improvement in mood, by relieving hypoglycemic symptoms via changes in diet. Research using the CDDI supported the hypothesis that persons with mood symptoms may experience hypoglycemic symptoms and further research led to the refinement of the instrument to include the ability to discriminate between those individuals who might benefit from dietary refinements from those who might not.

As it currently stands, the test can be used for adults 18 years of age or older. The instrument can be administered individually or in groups and can be completed in approximately 10 minutes. Scoring is likewise quick and easy, accomplished with a single scoring template. The resulting total score is a composite of the assigned weights for the selected responses; weights are given on the scoring template. Confusion, however, may exist for individuals taking the test. There are five possible responses for each item. Each response represents different physiological states and individuals may experience several of the states listed. Although examinees are instructed to select the single, most accurate response, selection may be difficult and confusing. This may be especially true for assessment of persons with eating disorders for whom bodily states are often denied or undetected. Thus, although items were developed in this way to discriminate between "dietary responders" versus "dietary non-responders" (i.e., those whose mood symptoms improve with changes in diet versus those whose mood symptoms do not improve), the test might not be useful with eating-disordered populations for whom concurrent mood disorders are frequent. Interpretation of the test results are likewise not clear cut. The stated purpose of the CDDI is primarily diagnostic and thus scores are not compared to a normative sample. Instead a cutoff score is used. The author, however, does not provide a specific comparison score to be used but rather leaves this decision to the individual user. The selected cutoff score is based on the percentage of false positives and false negatives the user is willing to tolerate. Suggestions for cutoff score selection are offered and a table is provided in the manual listing scores along with their calculated sensitivity and specificity. Scoring is nonetheless relatively ambiguous and the user must make assiduous effort to communicate the rationale used in selecting the cutoff score used to all persons concerned with the test results.

Subjects selected for test construction research and reliability and validity assessment were small in number and little effort was made to include comparisons between different *DSM-IV*

(*DSM-III-R* at the time of test publication) diagnosis. Regardless, reliability of the CDDI was assessed via test-retest (interval of 10 days or less) reliability measures and was found to be relatively high (approximately .87). Appropriate to the test's stated use, criterion-related validity was evaluated and was deemed adequate (.48). Content validity appears satisfactory as the method of test construction seems well construed and in line with the current literature in the area related to hypoglycemia and to mood disorders. The research was sound, outside of the noted small sample size, based on an extensive literature review and empirical testing.

It is clear that much data is needed relative to distinguishing between the influence of dietary habits on *DSM-IV* diagnostic categories. The only attempt at differentiation listed in the test manual was for bipolar mood disorder. The author reported that such subjects tended to test as dietary responders but did not, in fact, respond positively when put on a control diet. Such an omission of research is, however, understandable given that this is one of the only attempts to date to quantify the influence of diet on psychological disorders and serves to underscore the necessity of further research in this important area. At the same time, the user must remain cognizant of the fact that the test was designed for use with depressed individuals and that use outside this realm may not be appropriate. It is recommended that test manual revisions include such a statement.

The most disquieting aspect of this instrument is the recommendation of a diet at the end of the test manual. Although the recommendations are reasonable in quelling the symptoms of hypoglycemia, the diet is limited in scope and could amplify other psychological symptoms when used with certain populations (e.g., persons with eating disorders who regularly attempt diets and fail or who already engage in dietary restriction in a detrimental fashion). This points to the need for a user qualification statement in the test manual, a item that is lacking in the current publication of the manual.

The premise of the CDDI is timely given the increased interest in physiological influences on psychological states and in more "natural" remedies for psychological difficulties. This instrument, however, appears limited in application especially among persons with eating disorders and concurrent mood disorders. More research is needed to identify the effect of dietary habits on *DSM-IV* diagnoses other than mood disorders. Nonetheless, the efforts of the author of the CDDI warrant applause.

[23]

The Classroom Communication Skills Inventory: A Listening and Speaking Checklist.

Purpose: Evaluates "oral communication skills that have been determined to be important for listening and speaking in the school setting and are essential for classroom learning."

Population: Students.

Publication Date: 1993.

Acronym: CCSI.

Scores: 10 ratings: Basic Speech and Hearing Processes (Auditory Perception, Speech), Classroom Communication (Attention, Class Participation), Language Content and Structure (Vocabulary, Grammar, Organization of Language), Interpersonal Classroom Communication (Using Language for a Variety of Purposes, Conversing Effectively, Using Appropriate Nonverbal Communication Skills).

Administration: Individual.

Price Data, 1993: $25 per teacher manual (51 pages) and 25 record forms.

Time: (10–15) minutes.

Author: The Psychological Corporation.

Publisher: The Psychological Corporation.

Review of The Classroom Communication Skills Inventory: A Listening and Speaking Checklist by LINDA CROCKER, *Professor of Foundations of Education, University of Florida, Gainesville, FL:*

The Classroom Communication Skills Inventory (CCSI) is a checklist of listening and speaking skills and behaviors, designed for use by a classroom teacher. The behaviors and skills domains sampled by items on this checklist are intended to allow the administrator to draw inferences about the examinee's abilities to be an active listener and participant in normal classroom instructional settings, to identify areas of strengths and weaknesses in these classroom communication skills, and to suggest underlying reasons for identified weaknesses.

The authors describe the source of items for this checklist as a variety of disciplines such as education, speech-language pathology, psychology,

linguistics, and developmental psycholinguistics. No particular theoretical posture has been assumed in development or selection of the items included on the checklist, and no individual authors are named for this instrument.

Although the 52-item checklist is simple and straightforward to use and requires no special training for administration, the administrator must be familiar with the examinee's behavior in the natural classroom setting over a reasonable time period in order to render the types of judgments required by a number of items (e.g., "The student learns vocabulary taught in class lessons and uses the words appropriately in class assignments" or "The student converses with the teacher in one-on-one situations"). In addition, many of the items require the administrator to make subjective judgments about the examinee's performance that have an implied normative basis. For example, an administrator would need to be familiar with behavior of many students at a given grade level in order to judge whether "The student talks neither too much nor too little in class," "The student has an adequate vocabulary size," or "The student's voice is appropriate for age and gender." All items in the Basic Speech and Hearing Process are rated using a 3-point scale: "The behavior has not been observed," "The student appears to exhibit normal behavior," or "The student appears to exhibit below-normal behavior." For other subscales, the scale is expanded to 4 points to include scores for average and above average ability. Obviously, individual classroom teachers may employ substantially different standards in rating examinees on such items. This could result in students with similar levels of performance receiving different scores due to the rater's perspective and base of experience.

A positive feature of the teacher's administration manual is the generous use of examples of classroom strategies to assist students when deficiencies are detected. However, there are no other guidelines for score interpretation. The manual authors suggest that the score for each item on the checklist be interpreted individually.

The information on the sample used to estimate means, standard deviations, reliability coefficients, and standard errors of measurement is sparse. Sample sizes range from 254 for grade 3 to 467 for grade 9. The manual states that the "CCSI was administered in Fall 1992 to a random sample of students in grades 1 through 12 across the nation" (p. 34). This suggests that the authors of the manual have taken some license with the technical definition of "random sample" because it seems highly unlikely that a true random sample could have been drawn from all of the nation's school children for this test administration.

Coefficient alpha reliability coefficients are reported for each subtest and grade-level. It was surprising to note that in most instances, the shortest subtests displayed the highest reliability although according to test theory, we would predict that the longer subtests should be more reliable. In general these coefficients ranged from the mid .70s to the low .80s for sample sizes from 254 to 467 at different grades. Test retest reliability was estimated for a larger sample ($n = 1,586$) ranging from .28–.88, with a median of .82. These coefficients, however, may be inflated due to the apparent use of a more heterogeneous sample created by combining subjects across multiple grade levels.

Evidence of the construct validity of the scores is limited to the patterns of intercorrelations among the subtest and cluster scores and to results of factor analysis. This analysis also appears to have been applied to a combined sample over multiple grade levels ($n = 4,805$). These results generally provide evidence of the structural integrity of the scoring scheme; however, there is no evidence of relationship of CCSI scores to an external criterion, such as school achievement.

In summary, the primary strengths of the CCSI lie in its ease of use and the inclusion of instructional strategies to implement when an examinee's ratings for an item or set of items indicate a problem in communication skills. Weaknesses include subjectivity in scoring, limited validity evidence, a discrepancy between the types of reliability coefficients reported and the scoring guidelines, and lack of scoring guides to facilitate teachers' normative judgments. Use of this information for decision making about individual student placement or selection for special programs cannot be supported based on the psychometric data presented to date. The CCSI items, however, may provide classroom teachers with a more detailed and extensive breakdown of behaviors and skills involved in assessing student communication skills than they would think to observe informally.

Review of The Classroom Communication Skills Inventory: A Listening and Speaking Checklist by

DOLORES KLUPPEL VETTER, Professor, Department of Communicative Disorders, University of Wisconsin-Madison, Madison, WI:

The Classroom Communication Skills Inventory (CCSI) identifies a number of behaviors that are exemplars of communicative competence and classroom etiquette. The major value of the inventory is that it is a fairly exhaustive list of the skills and abilities required for good communication. In addition, it can be useful in organizing the observations of the classroom teacher. Should the teacher follow the advice in the CCSI teacher's manual and prepare an inventory for each student in the class, the resulting perspective would allow the teacher to plan activities or to arrange seating that should facilitate communication.

The content of the CCSI encompasses four broad categories: Basic Speech and Hearing Processes, Classroom Communication, Language Content and Structure, and Interpersonal Classroom Communication Skills. The CCSI uses the same scales and items for students in grades 1 through 12. There are 3 to 11 items on each scale (i.e., a total of 42 items) and guidelines are provided regarding typical expectations. Teachers, however, are encouraged to use the expectations they have developed from prior experience. They may make their actual ratings from direct observations or from their recall of students' behaviors.

The items on two of the scales, Auditory Reception and Speech, are scored as normal, below normal (referral), or not observed. A plus sign is assigned for normal performance, a minus for below normal, and 0 is assigned when a behavior is not observed. Items on the remaining scales are scored using 4 points (above expectation = 3, average = 2, below expectation = 1, or not observed = 0). When performance is rated below expectation on Auditory Reception, Speech, and Attention, the manual encourages the classroom teacher to refer the student(s) for evaluation by an appropriate specialist (e.g., speech/language pathologist, physician, or special educator).

The means, standard deviations, and standard errors of measurement are provided for random samples of students by grades (approximately 4,800 distributed from grade 1 through grade 12). These statistics require a measurement scale that is at least interval in nature (Reckase, 1984). However, the scaling used for the inventory is ordinal. Therefore, the descriptive statistics provided are not interpretable. The CCSI teacher's manual contains additional statistics that were calculated to provide evidence for internal consistency (coefficient alpha), test-retest reliability (Pearson r), and construct validity (principle-factors factor analysis with an oblique rotation). Again, however, many of these statistics require (arguably) an interval or ratio measurement scale. So, these statistics also are of little value in characterizing test performance.

Another problem becomes apparent if the teacher ignores these measurement problems and attempts a comparison of a student's scores to the descriptive statistics. The CCSI teacher's manual does not contain sufficient information for the user to determine how scores were transformed when the descriptive statistics were calculated. For example, the mean given for the scale Speech, derived from 375 grade 1 students, is 9.25. There is no information about how numbers were assigned to the plus and minus ratings of behaviors nor how to treat ratings of 0 (not observed). Therefore, the CCSI teacher's manual does not provide sufficient guidance to the teacher for making comparisons between a student's ratings and those of the reference group.

When the descriptive statistics in the CCSI teacher's manual are compared across grades, the means and standard deviations for the scales change little in magnitude (e.g., grade 1 Vocabulary mean is 7.22 with a SD of 2.03 whereas the grade 12 Vocabulary mean is 7.58 with a SD of 2.24). This would indicate that the development (or the acquisition) of vocabulary normally expected throughout elementary and secondary school is not reflected in scores derived from the use of the CCSI. Therefore, it is not clear how to follow the recommendation in the CCSI teacher's manual that the inventory be used to monitor performance changes over time.

Given the nature of the measurement scales and the consequent erroneous descriptive statistics as well as the erroneous evidence for reliability and validity, it is not possible for the data gathered through the use of the CCSI to be used to determine the "students' strengths and weaknesses, as well as to identify possible underlying reasons for those weaknesses" (manual, p. 5). Its only value is as a list of skills and abilities related to good

communication around which a classroom teacher can organize observations of students.

REVIEWER'S REFERENCE
Reckase, M. D. (1984). Scaling techniques. In G. Goldstein & M. Hersen (Eds.), *Handbook of psychological assessment* (pp. 38–53). New York: Pergamon Press.

[24]
Coaching Process Questionnaire.

Purpose: "Provides managers with an assessment of their coaching ability."
Population: Managers and employees.
Publication Date: 1992.
Acronym: CPQ.
Administration: Group.
Time: Administration time not reported.
Comments: Self-scored instrument.
Author: McBer & Company.
Publisher: McBer & Company.
 a) PARTICIPANT VERSION.
 Population: Managers.
 Scores, 5: Diagnostic Skills, Coaching Techniques, Coaching Qualities, Coaching Model, Overall CPQ score.
 Price Data, 1993: $60 per complete kit including 10 questionnaires, and 10 profiles and interpretive notes.
 b) EMPLOYEE VERSION.
 Population: Employees.
 Scores, 5: Diagnostic Skills, Coaching Techniques, Coaching Qualities, Coaching Model, Overall Employee score.
 Price Data: $25 per 10 questionnaires.

Review of the Coaching Process Questionnaire by PATRICIA A. BACHELOR, Professor of Psychology, California State University at Long Beach, Long Beach, CA:

The Coaching Process Questionnaire (CPQ) is designed as a self-administered and self-scored assessment of a manager's coaching ability. Coaching, in this context, is the two-way conversation between employees and managers designed to improve employee performance and commitment. The four elements of the coaching process, as defined by this instrument, are (a) Diagnostic Skills, (b) Coaching Qualities, (c) Coaching Techniques, and (d) Coaching Model. Diagnostic Skills assess the manager's ability to prepare for a coaching session. Coaching Techniques assess the manager's ability to communicate in a meaningful way. Coaching Qualities are personal attitudes and beliefs supportive to the coaching process. The

Coaching Model is the ability to structure the coaching session so that developmental opportunities will be understood and pursued.

The CPQ has two versions—an Employee Version and a Manager Version. The Employee Version comprises 40 items designed to assess the four aforementioned dimensions of the manager's coaching skills, behaviors, and techniques. Each statement is answered on a 5-point Likert-type scale evaluating the degree to which the employee perceives that his/her manager demonstrates the specific coaching behavior. The Manager Version consists of 40 statements that are designed to assess a manager's coaching performance and employee development. The manager responds on a 5-point Likert-type scale evaluating the degree to which he or she demonstrates a particular coaching behavior. All of the items on the Manager form of the CPQ are parallel to those on the Employee Version. For example, Question 14 on each form involves rewards for results. That is, the employee responds to the statement "My manager rewards me for achieving desired results," whereas the manager is asked to respond to "I reward employees for achieving desired results."

The employee test booklet also provides instructions for scoring the ratings on four dimensions. Each dimension, labeled only as A, B, C, and D, consists of the sum of scores on each of the 10 indicated items. These dimension scores are not explained further. The manager uses the profile and Interpretive Notes Booklet to score his or her CPQ, compare scores with other managers, and interpret feedback about the manager's coaching behavior. Areas of strength and weakness in coaching are, thereby, identified. A Coaching Process Profile is obtained by plotting, on a tear-out grid, the manager's scores on each of the four coaching dimensions as well as the Overall (total) score. This visual presentation of the manager's assessment can be compared to the preprinted 50th percentile of "more than 400 managers in a variety of industries" (p. 3, profile). No more details are provided about this norm group. The Employee average and total scores can also be plotted on this chart to provide contrasts in perceptions. Discrepancies of more than 20 points are indicative of weakness on that dimension. No additional interpretive information is provided in the materials that accompany the test booklets. The remaining pages in the manual describe the four dimensions of the coaching profile. The language is clear but written at a low level that at times seemed condescending. Most managers would certainly possess expertise that surpassed the treatment presented in the CPQ manual.

Unfortunately, a technical manual does not exist for this test. Thus, there is no mention of test development and/or modification, estimates of reliability coefficients, validity studies, or standardization and/or norm groups. Without such information about the psychometric properties of the CPQ, test users would be unable to evaluate if the test is appropriate for a specific application or interpret performances with any confidence. Nor can test consumers assess claims of accuracy or dependability of test scores for specific purposes. These qualities are essential for competent and legitimate test use. Without some type of evaluation regarding the stability, consistency, and accuracy of test scores for appropriate purposes, test users would be unable to defend their use of this test. Test examiners are ethically bound to select, administer, and interpret test scores in keeping with the test developer's standards for appropriate use of the test. The test authors are encouraged to read and promptly prepare a technical manual in conformance with the *Standards for Educational and Psychological Testing* (AERA, APA, & NCME, 1985). Thus, the present form of the Coaching Process Questionnaire can, at best, be considered in the development/research phase and its use limited only to stimulating a discussion of the coaching process among employees and their managers.

REVIEWER'S REFERENCE

American Educational Research Association, American Psychological Association, & National Council on Measurement in Education. (1985). *Standards for educational and psychological testing.* Washington, DC: American Psychological Association, Inc.

Review of the Coaching Process Questionnaire by GENEVA D. HAERTEL, Senior Research Associate, EREAPA Associates, Livermore, CA:

The Coaching Process Questionnaire (CPQ) provides managers with an assessment of their skills, techniques, and behaviors in coaching employees. There are two versions of the questionnaire: the Participant Version and the Employee Version. The Participant Version, taken by the manager, provides a self-assessment of the manager's strengths and weaknesses in coaching employees during performance reviews and employee development activities. The Employee Version, taken by a subordinate(s) of the manager, provides feedback on the manager's coaching skills, techniques, and behaviors. Both versions of the questionnaire provide scores on four elements: Diagnostic Skills, Coaching Techniques, Coaching Qualities, Coaching Model, and an overall CPQ score. In order to identify managers' strengths and weaknesses, their scores on the four coaching elements can be compared with those of a norming sample of over 400 managers and employees from a variety of industries. In addition, the results of the manager's self-assessment can be compared with his or her own employees' scores. A substantial difference of 20 or more points between the manager's score on a coaching element and his or her employees' average score on the same element signifies a weakness in the manager's use of that coaching element. (This interpretation assumes that the employees rate the manager less favorably than the manager rates him or herself.)

There are 40 items presented in the Participant Version of the CPQ. Each of the items describes a coaching behavior. When answering each item, the manager or participant is directed to recall their experiences with employees in coaching sessions. The participant rates the degree to which he or she typically demonstrates each coaching behavior on a 5-point rating scale; a rating of "1" is designated "to a small degree" and "5" is designated "to a large degree." Scores are calculated for each of the four coaching process elements: (1) Diagnostic Skills, (2) Coaching Techniques, (3) Coaching Qualities, (4) Coaching Model, and the total CPQ. Each element comprises 10 items, which are intermixed with items from the other elements. The test-taking instructions are concise and clearly written.

Like the Participant Version, the Employee Version of the CPQ has 40 items representing the four coaching process elements. An employee rates the degree to which his or her manager demonstrates each coaching behavior. The content of these 40 items matches that used in the Participant Version. However, items in the Participant Version are written in the first person, whereas in the Employee Version the employee is rating "my employer." The 40 items are rated on the same 5-point rating scale used in the Partici-

pant Version. Scores on the four elements can be calculated using a form on the back cover of the test booklet. The test-taking instructions are well written.

The CPQ Profile and Interpretive Notes, which is 11 pages in length, is the manual that accompanies the questionnaire. It states the purpose of the questionnaire and defines commonly used terms. A step-by-step scoring process is presented so that a manager can compare his or her own coaching scores with the norming population. In addition, a manager can plot his or her employees' average scores on each of the four elements and compare them with his or her own scores.

The questionnaire's conceptual framework is addressed in the manual. Each of the coaching elements is described using figures, a table, and lists of skills and attributes involved in coaching. The coaching process is depicted in a seven-step flowchart accompanied by one-to-five sentence descriptions of each step. An interesting feature of the manual is a page of commonly asked questions about the CPQ and the coaching process itself. Each question is followed by a one- or two-paragraph answer. Although the answers provide helpful direction, some lack the level of specificity needed to be truly useful. The final entry in the manual is the coaching process profile on which the manager plots his or her raw scores and the employees' average scores and converts them to percentiles based upon the norming population. Overall, the manual is clearly written, appropriate examples of coaching skills are provided, and coaching qualities are described in explicit terms. However, the manual fails to provide any information on the questionnaire's reliability or validity and little information is provided on the questionnaire's norming population.

The lack of psychometric information on the CPQ is problematic. Upon request the questionnaire publisher provided a page of information containing reliability and validity information on several instruments supported by their company. Based on the supplementary statistical information, the norming group for the CPQ was composed of 214 participants (managers) and 576 subordinates or employees. No further breakdown of characteristics of the norming group was provided. In order for consumers of the CPQ to determine the appropriateness of the questionnaire for their circumstances, more information must be provided on the norming group. It would be helpful if the following characteristics of the norming group were reported: types of industries on which the norms were developed, the managers' years of experience, ages of managers and employees, and numbers of males and females. The supplementary statistical information also provided a range of reliability estimates for the participant version (.68–.78) and for the employee version (.81–.87). Unfortunately, the type of reliability estimate calculated was not specified. Although the magnitude of the reliability estimates is satisfactory, consumers need to know whether these are test-retest or internal consistency estimates.

No validity information was presented on the questionnaire as a measure of a manager's coaching skill. However, inspection of the questionnaire reveals its face validity. Its content is focused on behaviors employed in the coaching process—such as communication and diagnostic skills. The instrument has some content validity. The questionnaire developers have presented a model of the coaching process and developed items rating each of the four elements of the model. However, the origin of the coaching model was not described, nor were there citations of empirical studies providing information about the use and characteristics of the model and the CPQ. There was no definitive statement of the universe of coaching content to be covered, nor were the processes used to generate the 40 items specified. The questionnaire's construct and criterion validity were not addressed.

In summary, the Coaching Process Questionnaire provides industry with a measure of a manager's coaching skills. The CPQ is easy to administer and score and is face valid. The questionnaire provides useful information comparing a manager's self-assessment of coaching performance with (a) a norming group of over 200 managers, and (b) employees' assessments of the manager's coaching ability. A profile of the manager's performance on the four coaching elements and overall coaching performance is available. Although the two versions of the questionnaire are clearly written, the profile and interpretive notes need to be further developed. This attractive instrument would be enhanced by providing data on the origin and

use of the coaching model and questionnaire. In addition, psychometric information about the questionnaire's norming group, reliability, and content, criterion, and construct validity must be provided. As it stands, the CPQ can be used to provide insights to managers about their own performance, as a starting point for managers' professional development activities, and for research purposes, but its psychometric characteristics have not been sufficiently documented to make it a viable instrument for the high stakes decision making required in personnel evaluation.

[25]
College Adjustment Scales.

Purpose: Identifies developmental and psychological problems experienced by college students.
Population: College and university students.
Publication Date: 1991.
Acronym: CAS.
Scores, 9: Anxiety, Depression, Suicidal Ideation, Substance Abuse, Self-Esteem Problems, Interpersonal Problems, Family Problems, Academic Problems, Career Problems.
Administration: Individual or group.
Price Data, 1996: $69 per complete kit including manual (25 pages), 25 reusable item booklets, and 25 answer sheets; $25 per 25 reusable item booklets; $25 per 25 answer sheets; $28 per manual.
Time: (15–20) minutes.
Authors: William D. Anton and James R. Reed.
Publisher: Psychological Assessment Resources, Inc.
Cross References: See T4:544 (1 reference).

TEST REFERENCES
1. Street, S., Kromrey, J. D., Reed, J., & Anton, W. (1993). A phenomenological perspective of problems experienced by high school seniors. *The High School Journal, 76,* 129–138.
2. Tloczynski, J. (1994). A preliminary study of opening-up meditation, college adjustment, and self-actualization. *Psychological Reports, 75,* 449–450.
3. Turner, P. R., Valtierra, M., Talken, T. R., Miller, V. I., & DeAnda, J. R. (1996). Effect of session length on treatment outcome for college students in brief therapy. *Journal of Counseling Psychology, 43,* 228–232.

Review of the College Adjustment Scales by WILLIAM E. MARTIN, JR., *Professor of Educational Psychology, Northern Arizona University, Flagstaff, AZ:*

According to Anton and Reed, the College Adjustment Scales (CAS) were developed "to provide a rapid method of screening college counseling clients for common developmental and psychological problems" (manual, p. 1). The CAS is a 108-item self-report measure with the following nine scales (12 items per scale): Anxiety, Depression, Suicidal Ideation, Substance Abuse, Self-Esteem Problems, Interpersonal Problems, Family Problems, Academic Problems, and Career Problems. Test takers are asked to respond to each item, based on its accuracy, using a 4-point scale ranging from *Not At All True* to *Very True*. The entire process for completing, scoring, and profiling the CAS is estimated by the test authors to take a maximum of 24 minutes.

DEVELOPMENT OF THE SCALES. The initial CAS scales were derived from problems encountered in the college population. Specifically, approximately 2,000 students presenting at a college counseling center for services completed an intake problems checklist. Based on their responses, two principal components factor analyses were conducted resulting in a 9-factor and a 7-factor solution. Information for which solution was retained was not provided.

The derived factors, along with additional adjustment problem areas, were used in a survey of assessment needs completed by 73 professionals from nine counseling centers. The survey findings of professionals, paired with the analyses of problems associated with students seeking services, resulted in the nine scales of the CAS. Next, a literature review was conducted to identify behavioral expressions for each of the scales. This resulted in an item pool of 181 items. These items were subsequently reviewed for bias by an expert panel; 14 items, which were determined to be biased, were rewritten. The internal consistency of items for each scale was derived from a study of 224 college students enrolled at four universities located in the Southeastern United States. Items were retained in the item pool based on three criteria (see manual) resulting in a final pool of 108 items. Final internal consistency reliability coefficients for the nine scales ranged from .80 to .92 with an average of .86.

VALIDITY OF THE SCALES. The reported test validity is based upon one group differences study and four convergent and discriminant validity studies that were conducted at several universities throughout the United States. In the first study, CAS scores were compared between a group receiving university counseling services and students not receiving services. The recipient group evidenced significantly higher scores on the CAS when compared to the nonrecipient group with Anxiety and Suicidal Ideation reflecting the most characteristic dimensions of the recipient group.

Independent samples from 33 university counseling centers were used to measure the convergent and discriminant validity of the CAS. The CAS subscales were correlated with subscales of several frequently used standardized tests measuring psychological constructs including anxiety, depression, hopelessness, personality, interpersonal problems, substance abuse, self-esteem, family adaptability, and career development. The procedure design was primarily multitrait-monomethod (self-report instruments). The findings reflected high correlations among scales measuring similar constructs (convergent validity) and low correlations among dissimilar constructs (discriminant validity). For example, the NEO Personality Inventory (NEO-PI) Neurotocism scales were correlated with the CAS subscales in three studies. On two similar subscales across the studies, correlations were high moderate or high. The correlations for Anxiety were .80, .71, and .80 and for Depression they were .64, .69, and .74. For dissimilar measures, low correlations, as illustrated by comparisons of the Openness subscale on the NEO-PI and all of the CAS subscales, were obtained throughout the three studies.

ADMINISTRATION, SCORING, AND INTERPRETATION. Standardized instructions for administration are provided in the CAS manual. The test-taking materials include a four-page item booklet written at a fifth grade reading level. Additionally, there is an answer sheet printed on carbonless white paper with the CAS Profile sheet on the reverse side that lists raw scores, percentiles, and T scores.

Ninety percent of the normative sample ($N = 1,146$) consisted of college and university students aged 17–30. The students were reasonably equally proportioned from first year through seniors. However, only 2% of the total sample were graduate students. The sample reflected national college enrollment proportions according to gender and ethnicity. The majority (54%) of the sample were raised in the Southeast compared to other regions of the United States: Northeast (13%), Midwest (10%), West (13%), and outside the United States (5%). Information was not available for the remainder of the sample.

Percentile scores and normalized T scores derived for each scale from the raw score frequency distributions of the standardization sample are used for interpretation of the results. As the authors found weak associations among gender and ethnic group and the CAS scores, no normative data are provided based on these variables. The authors suggest that when a student scores at or above a T score of 60 on any scale, further evaluation, and possibly intervention, are warranted in the area of adjustment difficulty. In addition to normative comparisons, brief descriptive guidelines are provided for interpretation of each scale. Three case illustrations are presented in the manual.

SUMMARY. The CAS is a useful screening tool for college and university counseling professionals to identify possible adjustment difficulties among students. It must be emphasized, however, that it is a screening tool. With only 12 items per major adjustment difficulty (e.g., suicidal ideation, career problems), there is room for diagnostic errors.

The methodology to develop the scales was reasonably sound and there is evidence for the validity of the scales. However, more validity studies are needed, especially concurrent validity studies related to profile interpretations examining the relationship between the CAS and other major psychological disturbance assessment instruments (e.g., Minnesota Multiphasic Personality Inventory—2 [MMPI–2; T4:1645]; and Millon Clinical Multiaxial Inventory [MCMI–III]). Additionally, both the descriptive guidelines for each scale and the number of case illustrations could be expanded.

Normative data are not available for students from various ethnic groups. Given specific reported college adjustment difficulties related to ethnocultural factors (Negy & Woods, 1992; Solberg, Ritsma, Davis, Tata, & Jolly, 1994), it may be valuable to generate percentile scores and T scores by ethnic group.

REVIEWER'S REFERENCES

Negy, C. R., & Woods, D. J. (1992). Mexican Americans' performance on the Psychological Screening Inventory as a function of acculturation level. *Journal of Clinical Psychology, 48*, 315–319.

Solberg, V. S., Ritsma, S., Davis, B. J., Tata, S. P., & Jolly, A. (1994). Asian-American students' severity of problems and willingness to seek help from university counseling centers: Role of previous counseling experience, gender, and ethnicity. *Journal of Counseling Psychology, 41*, 275–279.

Review of the College Adjustment Scales by EDWARD R. STARR, Assistant Professor of Counseling Psychology, State University of New York at Buffalo, Buffalo, NY:

The College Adjustment Scales (CAS) is a 108-item inventory designed as a quick and economical screening device for clinicians providing counseling services to college and university students. The authors attempt to provide clinicians with data regarding the most common developmental and psychological problems in this population. The inventory comprises nine subscales: Anxiety, Depression, Suicidal Ideation, Substance Abuse, Self-Esteem Problems, Interpersonal Problems, Family Problems, Academic Problems, and Career Problems. Subscales reflect many of the problems most frequently raised by college and university students, thus increasing its clinical relevance and utility. Notably absent among the subscales, though, is one related specifically to eating disorders.

The manual contains a brief and general introduction to the CAS and discusses the test materials, their use, administration, and scoring. The materials themselves are convenient, economical, and straightforward, requiring of respondents only a fifth grade reading level and a pen or pencil. The four-page item booklet is reusable, with responses recorded by students on a separate answer sheet. Raw data can be hand scored and plotted into a profile in less than 5 minutes. The profile form provides percentile scores, relative to the standardization sample, and T-score conversions. The CAS can be administered and scored by individuals without formal training in psychology. Training in its use and interpretation, however, requires graduate level training in an appropriate subdiscipline in psychology.

STANDARDIZATION. The CAS was standardized on 1,146 college and university students, ages 17 to 65 (although less than 10% of the sample is older than 30 years) from throughout the U.S. The sample is well represented with respect to geographic region and gender. However, with regard to race, although the sample closely reflected racial patterns in college enrollment nationally, due to the extraordinarily low college enrollments of certain minorities in the U.S. (e.g., Pacific Islanders and Native Americans) some oversampling of minority groups may have been more appropriate. Normative data for each subscale are provided in the manual.

RELIABILITY. Only measures of internal consistency are reported in the CAS manual. Reliability coefficients range between .80 and .92, with a mean of .86. Reliability estimates based on alternative forms of the CAS or test-retest procedures are not available.

VALIDITY. Five validation studies of the CAS are reported in the manual. The first study compared the standardization sample to 198 students reporting current involvement in counseling for personal, academic, or career concerns. Significant differences on the subscales were obtained using multivariate ANOVA and discriminant function analysis. The remaining four studies compared specific CAS subscale results, using moderately sized samples of college students either requesting or receiving services from a college or university counseling center, to a variety of other well-established measures of the relevant constructs (e.g., the State-Trait Anxiety Inventory, Beck Depression Inventory, Beck Hopelessness Scale, NEO-Personality Inventory, Michigan Alcoholism Screening Test, Drug Abuse Screening Test, Multidimensional Self-Esteem Inventory, Family Adaptability and Cohesion Evaluation Scales III, Career Decision Scale, and the Self-Expression Inventory). Results in each study, based on correlational analysis, are consistent with predictions, with subscales having sufficient discriminant and predictive validity.

SUMMARY. There is a clear need for screening devices for this population and very little attention has been given to the development of reliable and valid instruments. In spite of some of its limitations, the CAS is certainly a solid step in the right direction. Further research should help establish its utility.

Until further data can be generated regarding its use in cross-cultural contexts, the CAS should probably be used with some caution. Although the manual authors state the available research and normative data indicate the CAS is unbiased with respect to gender and ethnic group membership, the data provided are not particularly compelling. The CAS assumes concept equivalence in cross-cultural contexts, which may cause some problems in interpreting the meaning of results. For example, the construct self-esteem, as reflected in the CAS is one that is limited to Euro-American notions of self that give primacy to the individual, without concern for a more collective sense of identity as is typical, for instance, of Native American communities.

Given the CAS was developed and standardized exclusively on a college population, its use in other clinical settings cannot be recommended. Although it is not intended for use as a diagnostic aid, the CAS may be most effectively used adjunctively as part of a battery of assessment measures to rule out potential comorbidity.

The authors aptly note that because only about 10% of the standardization sample were over age 30, the CAS should be used cautiously with older students. When using the CAS to screen for eating disorders, one should analyze results at the item level to obtain specific data. This should be augmented with other methods of evaluation. Given the incidence, prevalence, and significance of eating disorders, particularly among women college students, a separate subscale would have been justified.

A major strength of the CAS is that it was developed for use in either individual or group settings. With the current proliferation of prevention programs, personal development workshops, and training groups open to the general student population on most campuses, it may be particularly well suited for use in identifying at-risk students attending these group experiences for counseling referrals. Overall, the CAS is a promising screening device in an area of indicated need. Its real utility awaits further research and clinical application.

[26]
College Outcome Measures Program.

Purpose: To help "colleges define and assess general education outcomes of college."
Population: College students.
Publication Dates: 1976–1991.
Acronym: COMP.
Administration: Group.
Restricted Distribution: Distribution restricted to colleges.
Price Data, 1993: $50 per complete package including specimen copies of all tests, support materials package, and technical materials package including report ('92, 180 pages); $15 per specimen copies of all instruments (1 each); $20 per support materials package including college assessment planning book, COMPguide 1 (directions) ('91, 31 pages), COMPguide 2 (support) ('91, 60 pages), guide for matching COMP outcomes to pro-

gram outcomes, good practices in general education, increasing student competence and persistence, and relevant articles; $15 per 1982–1992 technical report ('92, 180 pages); $15 per Appendices A–E; $10 per 1976–1981 technical report ('82, 96 pages); $4 per increasing student competence and persistence.

Comments: "Developed to assist in program evaluation"; 6 tests available as separates.

Authors: American College Testing Program, Aubrey Forrest (1976–1981 technical manual), and Joe M. Steele (1982–1991 technical manual).

Publisher: American College Testing Program.

a) THE OBJECTIVE TEST.

Scores, 7: Process Areas (Communicating, Solving Problems, Clarifying Values), Content Areas (Functioning within Social Institutions, Using Science and Technology, Using the Arts), Total.

Price Data: $7.50–$19 per student (depending on number tested per year).

Time: (150–160) minutes.

b) THE COMPOSITE EXAMINATION.

Scores, 9: Process Areas (Communicating, Solving Problems, Clarifying Values), Content Areas (Functioning within Social Institutions, Using Science and Technology, Using the Arts), Performance Areas (Writing, Speaking), Total.

Price Data: $11–$25 per student (depending on number tested per year).

Time: (390–400) minutes.

c) SPEAKING SKILLS ASSESSMENT.

Scores, 4: Audience, Discourse, Delivery, Total.

Price Data: $3–$6 per student (depending on number tested per year).

Time: (15–20) minutes.

d) WRITING SKILLS ASSESSMENT.

Scores, 4: Audience, Organization, Language, Total.

Price Data: Same as *c* above.

Time: (80–90) minutes.

e) ASSESSMENT OF REASONING AND COMMUNICATING.

Scores, 4: Reasoning, Writing, Speaking, Total.

Price Data: Same as *a* above.

Time: (120–130) minutes.

f) THE ACTIVITY INVENTORY.

Scores, 7: Same as *a* above.

Price Data: $2–$5 per student (depending on number tested per year).

Time: (90–100) minutes.

Cross References: See T4:587 (1 reference).

Review of the College Outcome Measures Program by ROBERT D. BROWN, Carl A. Happold Distinguished Professor Emeritus of Educational Psychology, University of Nebraska-Lincoln, Lincoln, NE:

The purpose of the College Outcome Measurements Program (COMP) instruments is to measure and evaluate the knowledge and skills: (a) that undergraduate college students are expected to acquire through their general education programs, and (b) that are important to function effectively in adult society. The complete program includes an objective test that focuses on six areas: Communicating, Solving Problems, Clarifying Values (which are considered process areas), and Functioning with Social Institutions, Using Science Technology, and Using the Arts (which are considered as content areas); performance assessments of Writing and Speaking; and an Activity Inventory that assesses student involvement in out-of-class activities related to the same six areas. Because these assessments overlap and because institutions may have different purposes and needs, it is possible for institutions to select measures most appropriate for their intents. Test content focuses on assessing students' ability to apply knowledge rather than on what factual knowledge they have acquired within specific traditional content domains. The objective test is scored only by ACT but the performance assessments can be scored by local faculty or by ACT. Guidelines are available for faculty training in scoring. An institution can add items to the package. ACT scores the Objective Test and provides information for each institution's faculty to score the Writing and Speaking assessments.

It is essential to note that the COMP program is designed for use in making judgments about the quality of general education programs rather than about the performance of individual students. Scores can be made available by the institution for feedback to individual students, but ACT does not recommend use of the scores by the institution to make academic judgments or recommendations about individual students. This distinction is important for evaluating the psychometric attributes of the COMP instruments. Costs will vary depending upon the tests selected and the student sample size. If institutions provide the ACT scores of the tested students, ACT will provide various analyses of results using the students' ACT scores as one factor.

COMP is unique in several ways. It includes an Objective Test, which employs a multiple-choice format, but unlike most such formats, each item includes two correct answers and two incorrect answers for which there is a penalty for guessing correction. It also includes a Composite Examination covering the same content as the Objective Test, but with the inclusion of writing and speaking samples. Both the Composite and the Objective Test give allegiance to the authentic test movement by including simulation activities based on "realistic stimulus materials drawn from contemporary adult society" (Comp. Guide 1, p. 6). These include materials from magazine articles, television, music, art prints, and short stories.

The COMP program has two Guides: Guide 1 describes the instruments and provides suggestions for planning to use the COMP (e.g., sampling issues), implementing COMP use, and utilizing COMP results. Guide 2 provides normative tables for freshmen and sophomores, and suggestions and examples of procedures for recruiting students and interpreting results. Both Guides provide helpful information for institutional personnel responsible for selecting and using the COMP program. The guides include little technical psychometric information. Information regarding the psychometric properties of the COMP tests are included in the COMP Technical Report 1982–1991: Clarifying and Assessing General Education Outcomes of College, ACT, 1992 and its supplements. The Technical Report and its supplements could serve as a model for its comprehensiveness concerning test development, reliability information and issues, and validity information and issues. On the other hand, the entire package of reports and supplements could be substantially improved. Much of the information is most accessible to those familiar with sophisticated measurement terminology. This reviewer wonders about the usefulness of this presentation for faculty and administrators making decisions about selecting the COMP tests and using them at their institution. A succinct and straightforward summary of this information in one of the Guides and an index and/or outline of what can be found in the technical reports would be beneficial.

RELIABILITY. As the Technical Report notes, Cronbach alpha reliability estimates for the Objective Test (Total score of .84, for six subtests it ranged from .63 to .68) and for the Composite Examination (Total score = .87, subtests .62 to .76)

are not high enough to justify interpretation and decision making about individual students. As the COMP tests are intended for use in making decisions about the performance of groups of students rather than individual student performance, the most relevant reliability information is about group means. Reported reliability coefficients of the group means for the six subtests of the Objective Tests range from .97 to .98 with an average standard error of .80. The standard error of the mean for the six subtests ranged from .29 to .36. These data suggest the Objective Tests are sufficiently reliable for assessment of group differences and changes over time for purposes of program evaluation. The same pattern holds for the Speaking, Writing, and Reasoning tests. They are more than adequately reliable for making judgments about group performance, but not about individual students. Critical for use of these instruments is the extent of interrater agreement because of the subjective nature of the tasks and scoring. Apparently scoring guidelines are adequate. Reported interrater reliabilities are in the .90s.

Intercorrelations for the subtests of the Composite Examination are reported to be in the mid .50s and .60s, for the Objective Test they are in the mid .40s to mid .50s. This leaves about 75% of the variance unexplained, which suggests the subtests are sufficiently independent to warrant assessment of different subtest outcomes for different student groups (e.g., students in one program compared to another). As might be expected, the Speaking and Writing measures are moderately correlated with each other but sufficiently independent to use in program evaluation to determine if some student groups write well but do not speak well or vice versa. The Activity Inventory has a reported total score Cronbach alpha reliability estimate of .94 with the subscales reported at .75 to .88. Subscales are moderately correlated with each other but appear to be measuring independent activity patterns.

VALIDITY. It is particularly important to note and comment on two aspects of validity: (a) traditional psychometric evidence provided by longitudinal and criteria studies, and (b) validity as determined by its use by a specific institution. The Technical Report provides substantial indications of the traditional psychometric evidence for validity. These include indications of improved scores from first year of college to senior year, differential improvement by curriculum emphasis, and significant correlations and multiple regression coefficients between COMP scores and ratings by job supervisors in a variety of professions. It is noteworthy that subscales of the Activity Inventory add significantly to the multiple regressions equations used for predicting job supervisor ratings, thus supporting those who suggest that student involvement is an important educational goal.

The Report also candidly confronts issues that must be considered whenever outcome assessments are used to evaluate programs. Among these issues are questions like: Does initial skill level affect subsequent measured growth? Are the instruments sufficiently sensitive to determine whether or not changes in program or curriculum make a difference in scores? Are there differential outcomes for student subgroups such as age, gender, and ethnicity? What impact does student motivation play in the validity of the results? How much should students be expected to improve? The studies highlighted and summarized in the Report, for the most part, support the validity of the COMP instruments, but each institution must confront these questions, the provided evidence, and their relevance for its particular context.

Validity of a test depends upon its use; this is particularly relevant for the COMP. Administrators with any integrity will not want to rely on external experts alone for judgments regarding the appropriateness of the COMP test domains and test content to assess what they believe the outcomes should be for their students. Different institutions have different requirements and expectations for their students. The COMP test designers are highly cognizant of this issue and throughout the manual and other materials, test users are continually advised to have faculty, students, and relevant administrators review carefully the appropriateness of the test content for their specific institution and its purposes. Much value could accrue to the institution by engaging in the process of thinking through its goals, describing expected student outcomes, and determining the appropriateness of the fit of the COMP tests to the institution's goals.

Another unique validity issue arises because the COMP is intended to provide information for use in assessing accomplishment of institutional goals rather than for assessing individual students. High motivation of students to perform well on the tests is not automatic. Not all students would customarily be expected to take the battery and often there would be no sanctions for an individual student doing poorly. The test manual includes a special section devoted to brainstorming different ways to motivate students to do well such as paying them and notes psychometric ways to determine if certain students perform below expectations. This is an important, but sticky issue; one not easily resolved. If seniors perform better than they did as first year students, test users want to be able to say it is because they have learned new knowledge and developed new skills, not that they sloughed off on the test when they were first year students. If the seniors, on the other hand, do less well than expected, test users want to be sure that it is an accurate indicator of student knowledge and skills and not because they did not take the test seriously.

NORMS. Hundreds of postsecondary institutions have given the COMP to thousands of students. Norm groups are provided for 2-year and 4-year institutions by grade level. Most of the 4-year groups are fairly wide-ranging with public state universities included with small private colleges. Most institutions will likely find these norms helpful as a broad gauge basis for comparison with the performance of their own students, but many will wish they had purer peer comparison groups. One possible different format would be to have norms based on student performance on the ACT College Entrance Examination (Enhanced ACT Assessment, 12:139).

SUMMARY COMMENT. The College Outcome Measures Program represents a worthy response to increasing calls for higher education to be accountable for student learning in general education and to provide concrete evidence of student writing and speaking skills. Postsecondary institutions, for the most part, have been slow, if not resistant, to be responsive to these calls. Faculty and campus administrators have traditionally relied on accreditation studies as evidence of program quality, unlike their K–12 counterparts who for decades have reported standardized achievement test scores of their students (e.g., California Achievement Test, Iowa Test of Basic Skills) to their boards, parents, and to the larger community. As a minimum, the COMP provides postsecondary institutions with a start toward an authentic and reliable assessment of whether or not students are achieving the outcomes the institutions describe in their college bulletins and mission statements. Some campuses will profit by having key administrators and faculty read the COMP guides and reports, think about the issues, and design their own assessment program. Other campuses may decide to use parts of the COMP to test their students and evaluate their programs. Still others may participate fully in ongoing, longitudinal evaluation of their general education programs through use of the full complement of the COMP instruments and the accompanying services.

All campuses should at least examine the COMP for its relevance to their programs. Key faculty and administrators should discuss carefully the potential value of an assessment program like the COMP. They need to consider the relevance of important validity issues (e.g., relevance of content to college's goals, student motivation) to their campus. Vital to this discussion is the potential use of the information garnered. Is it going to be used solely for validation of student accomplishments as they pertain to the institution's goal or is the information going to be used for making decisions about how to improve programs? It is also important that each institution weigh the relative merits and cost of designing its own procedures and instruments versus using the available, ready-made COMP package or parts of the package. The college or university cannot help but benefit from involving a broad spectrum of persons (faculty, administrators, alumnae, students, employers) in considering these choices. Given the unique validity issues, it is essential that a person with professional competence in measurement issues be a consultant to this process.

ACT has contributed a significant service to higher education by providing the COMP as a starting place for campus discussions and by providing assessment instruments that can serve as a useful core evaluation tool to many institutions.

Review of the College Outcome Measures Program by CLEBORNE D. MADDUX, Professor of Special Education and Educational Technology, University of Nevada, Reno, NV:

The American College Testing Program (ACT) developed the College Outcome Measures Program (COMP) in 1976, and it has been controversial ever since. The manual states that the purpose of the materials is to help colleges evaluate their general education program by providing a commercial, nationally standardized set of measures of the cognitive outcomes of general education in order to demonstrate to the public that general education successfully prepares students to function well in adult society.

Predictably, some faculty and others rebelled at the idea that the state of the art of standardized assessment was sufficiently advanced for a norm-referenced device or set of devices to provide a more valid and useful assessment of cognitive effects than could be obtained through a less formal and more highly individualized evaluation tailored to specific institutions. Nevertheless, by 1988, more than 450 institutions had administered one or more of the early COMP instruments. The manual states that as of 1991, this number had risen to over 500 institutions that have used one or more of the assessment instruments, and 1,500 that have used some of the other materials produced by ACT. A printed supplementary leaflet (one of many) states that about 600 institutions have administered the assessment instruments.

COMP instruments are intended to measure cognitive outcomes organized around three process areas and three content areas. Processes include Communicating, Solving Problems, and Clarifying Values, and the content areas are Functioning Within Social Institutions, Using Science and Technology, and Using the Arts. The manual recommends selecting a random sample of students and offering whatever material rewards for participation the institution can provide.

The literature that accompanies the COMP material is poorly organized, often redundant, confusing, and sometimes outdated or contradictory. The booklet that appears to be the main COMP manual is pretentious and sometimes downright silly. For example, it begins as follows:

> Many metaphors are implied by the name DIRECTIONS. One metaphor related to DIRECTIONS is that of a physical fitness regimen to keep the body in top shape. (American College Testing Program, 1991, p. 1)

Such pseudointellectual posturing is unwelcome to the bewildered reader who opens the manual in the hope of finding a clear statement of purpose, a description of materials, and directions for administration. It is not until page 3 that the manual finally includes a paragraph stating the purpose of the COMP. Such convoluted writing is typical of the COMP documentation and is found throughout the voluminous printed material that includes bound volumes; slick, commercially printed brochures; and an array of photocopied inserts and sheets produced with a personal computer and printer. One possible explanation for the lack of organization of the printed material is that it has obviously been written by many different individuals over a long period of time.

THE COMPOSITE EXAMINATION. The Composite Examination is the main instrument, making use of 15 group-administered simulation activities, requiring 4 and one-half hours for administration, and yielding six subtest scores corresponding to the three processes and contents outlined above, as well as a score for Writing, a score for Speaking, and a Total score. A confusing aspect of the various documentation supplied with the COMP materials is that the Writing and Speaking Assessment instruments are sometimes referred to as separate instruments, yet are treated as subtests of the Composite Examination.

The format of the examination requires short written responses, longer expository written responses, audiotaped oral responses, and multiple-choice responses. For three of the items, students view a supplied videotape with short vignettes ranging in length from 2 to 4 minutes. Three items require listening to a supplied audiotape with short segments from 2 to 5 minutes in length. Scoring involves using standardized rating scales by a team of five faculty members, requiring 60 minutes per student to complete the task. Training materials for faculty are provided as well as an offer of a service to rescore for assessment of interrater reliability.

Validity data are aimed at convincing the reader that those skills measured by the examination are important to adults, and that they can be improved through instruction. Studies are cited that provide some moderate evidence for these contentions. Test-retest reliability studies (14–16-week intervals) were conducted at several different institutions and produced coefficients that ranged from .66 to .88. These are incorrectly referred to as "large" (Ns ranged from 29 to 41).

THE OBJECTIVE TEST. The Objective test is a greatly abbreviated version of the Composite Examination requiring 2 and one-half hours for administration. Scoring has also been greatly simplified and relies totally on a multiple-choice, machine-scorable format. The same 15 simulation activities are employed as those used in the Composite Examination. The test yields three scores for Process, three for Content, and a total score, as does the Composite Examination. However, there are no writing and speaking scores.

Scores are equated raw scores and percentiles, and normative data are available for a variety of subpopulations including college freshmen, sophomores, and seniors; freshmen and sophomores enrolled at 2-year institutions; and those at 4-year institutions. There are also separate norms for college seniors at institutions with mean ACT scores both above and below 21.4.

The main validity information consists of correlation coefficients reflecting the relationship to scores on the Composite Examination. These range from .64 to .88. All but two, calculated separately for freshmen, seniors, and total group, were .73 or higher. Although these are referred to as "high" by the COMP documentation, it should be noted that the correlation of .64 for seniors taking both the Composite Examination and the Objective Test reflects only about 41% of shared variance. Although the two instruments are clearly related, such correlations should not be referred to as more than "low" to "moderate," particularly because none of the 21 reported coefficients exceeded .88, and the majority fell in the .70s or lower. Internal reliability was estimated with Cronbach's alpha and range from .66 to .84, with six of the seven indices in the .60–.68 range.

WRITING SKILLS ASSESSMENT, SPEAKING SKILLS ASSESSMENT, AND ASSESSMENT OF REASONING AND COMMUNICATING. Although the Writing Skills Assessment and Speaking Skills Assessment are subtests of the Composite Examination, they are each bound and priced separately. The Assessment of Reasoning and Communicating is a rescoring of these instruments and is treated in one section of the technical reports together with the Writing Skills Assessment and the Speaking Skills Assessment.

For the Writing Skills Assessment, students are asked to write a letter or a memo after listening to a taped commentary on family closeness, a taped radio broadcast on the topic of nuclear waste disposal, and a recording of selections of music. The letters or memos are to respond to specific questions or topics related to the presentation. Scoring is done by a committee of faculty members who rate each writing sample on a 5-point scale with regard to Audience, Organization, Language, and Total.

For the Speaking Skills Assessment, students are presented with three activities and told that they are to prepare to give a 3-minute oral response at a time and place to be announced. They are told that they may read anything that they think will be helpful, but are not to discuss the topics with anyone. Brief note cards are permitted, but extensive notes are not allowed. They are then presented with a paragraph about community response to pornography, instructions to persuade a friend to eat fewer sweet foods, and a color art reproduction and instructions to prepare a talk about this painting. Faculty read and rate responses in one of five categories reflecting quality with regard to Audience, Discourse, Delivery, and Total.

The Assessment of Reasoning and Communicating instrument makes use of the Writing Skills Assessment and Speaking Skills Assessment and scores the results on a 5-point scale for several categories within each of the following areas: social, scientific, and artistic reasoning in speaking and writing tasks.

With regard to validity, the manual states that faculty experts in communication were consulted to help decide on important writing and speaking outcomes to be measured. In addition, six studies conducted between 1976 and 1981 are summarized. These studies were designed to show that the outcomes measures are important in the work world and included volunteers, bank employees, business/criminal justice management personnel, practice teachers, and student nurses. In addition, a search of the literature in various journals was conducted to gather information on status indices and prestige hierarchies. A number of interrater reliability studies are presented. For Speaking, the average coefficient was .92, for Writ-

ing, .94, and for Reasoning Skills, .99. Internal consistency (Cronbach's alpha) studies are listed producing coefficients of .89 to .92 for Speaking, .78 to .79 for Writing, .74 to .75 for Reasoning, and .88 to .90 for Total Score.

THE ACTIVITY INVENTORY. The Activity Inventory consists of 54 multiple-choice questions designed to measure student involvement in various out-of-class activities. Students are presented with an activity and are asked to mark A, B, C, D, or E, with A indicating the highest level of participation and E the lowest. The inventory yields a total score and six subscores corresponding to the three areas and three processes.

Validity information consists of studies designed to demonstrate that the activities included are those that distinguish students with varying levels of education and that are common to adults who are judged to be functioning well in society. Internal consistencies (Cronbach's alpha) reported included .94 for total and the statement that all others were .75 or higher.

SUMMARY. The College Outcome Measures Program (COMP) is a highly ambitious project with extensive materials and documentation. A complete analysis of these materials is far beyond the scope of this brief review.

The usefulness of these materials hinges on the question of whether or not an institution might be better served by a more qualitative and individualized approach to the evaluation of its general education program. However, if a commercial, standardized approach is decided upon, the COMP could be useful.

The manual and other documentation for the COMP are poorly organized and poorly written, and should be improved. Discussions concerning reliability, validity, and norming are spread throughout the literature and the materials; these discussions need to be consolidated into one up-to-date volume. Although reliability and validity appear to be as good as could be expected for such an ambitious and varied instrument, claims reflecting value judgments about the technical characteristics need to be toned down considerably.

Although the instruments are not as well conceived or executed as claimed in the documentation, they have nevertheless undergone extensive development over a period of years. For institutions desiring a norm-referenced approach to evaluating general education programs, the COMP may be of interest.

[27]
Collegiate Assessment of Academic Proficiency.

Purpose: Designed to assess general education skills typically attained by the end of the first two years of college.

Population: Students in the first 2 years of college.

Publication Dates: 1989–1992.

Acronym: CAAP.

Administration: Group.

Restricted Distribution: Available to institutions signing a participation agreement and paying a participation fee.

Price Data, 1993: $175 per year institutional participation fee; test module prices (including scoring and reporting) available from publisher.

Time: 40(50) minutes per test.

Author: American College Testing.

Publisher: American College Testing.

a) WRITING SKILLS.

Publication Date: 1990.

Scores, 3: Usage/Mechanics, Rhetorical Skills, Total.

b) MATHEMATICS.

Publication Date: 1989.

Scores, 2: Algebra, Total.

c) READING.

Publication Date: 1989.

Scores, 3: Arts/Literature, Social Studies/Sciences, Total.

d) CRITICAL THINKING.

Publication Date: 1989.

Scores: Total score only.

e) SCIENCE REASONING.

Publication Date: 1989.

Scores: Total score only.

f) WRITING (ESSAY).

Publication Date: 1990.

Scores: Total score only.

Comments: Total of 3 individual essays.

Cross References: See T4:589 (1 reference).

TEST REFERENCES

1. Pascarella, E., Bohr, L., Nora, A., Desler, M., & Zusman, B. (1994). Impacts of on-campus and off-campus work on first year cognitive outcome. *Journal of College Student Development, 35,* 364-370.

2. Bohr, L., Pascarella, E. T., Nora, A., & Terenzini, P. T. (1995). Do Black students learn more at historically Black or predominantly White colleges? *Journal of College Student Development, 36,* 75-85.

3. Springer, L., Terenzini, P. T., Pascarella, E. T., & Nora, A. (1995). Influences on college students' orientations toward learning for self-understanding. *Journal of College Student Development, 36,* 5-18.

Review of the Collegiate Assessment of Academic Proficiency by STEVEN V. OWEN, Professor of Educational Psychology, University of Connecticut, Storrs, CT:

Fueled partly be accountability pressures, interest in collegiate institutional assessment surged in the 1980s. The American College Testing Program (ACT) responded by building, over a 5-year period, the Collegiate Assessment of Academic Proficiency (CAAP). The result is a collection of short tests that are meant to assess general educational skills developed over the first 2 years of college. ACT claims that scores from these tests might serve a wide variety of aims:

Evaluating program effectiveness in particular skill areas. Here, the focus is on whether the institution is meeting certain educational goals. Scores may thus be used to examine pre-to-post change, or to gauge achievement against existing standards or other institutions.

Giving diagnostic advice about individual students. Scores might indicate, for example, the need for remedial work, or readiness for more advanced coursework.

Using individual student scores as screening devices. Here, scores might signal that a student is not eligible for an upper division course, is ready for the junior year, or (with other evidence) does not qualify to graduate.

These are all high stakes decisions, and ACT warns that using CAAP scores for most of these purposes should be justified by local research.

Six tests comprise the CAAP:

Science Reasoning (45 items covering eight passages), aiming at data representation, understanding research summaries, and reconciling conflicting ideas.

Mathematics (35 items; no passages), which covers algebra, coordinate geometry, trigonometry, and calculus. The test items are meant to reflect mathematical reasoning instead of formula memorization. In addition to a total score, a separate algebra score is reported.

Reading (36 items over four passages), focusing on reading comprehension of implicit meaning and drawing conclusions from written discourse. Passages are drawn from prose, humanities, social studies, and natural sciences. Complementing the total score are two subscores for arts/literature and for social/natural sciences.

Writing Skills (72 items across seven passages). Here, the intent is to measure broad areas of diction, mechanics, and rhetorical skill. After a total score, there are subscores in usage/mechanics and rhetorical skill.

Essay Writing (two short prompts ask respondents to take a position about a proposed policy change). The Technical handbook includes the claim that respondents must "explain … why the position taken is the better (or best) alternative" (p. 18). However, nothing in the prompts themselves states that elaboration of reasons counts heavily in the holistic scoring rubric.

Critical Thinking (32 items over three passages), which revolves around argument: analyzing, evaluating, and extending the argument.

The CAAP tests put a premium on speed. Each has a 40-minute time limit, and the proportion of students not able to finish the tests range from .05 to .24. Efficiency in testing is usually a virtue, but the time limits may extract a penalty for the proficient but more reflective student.

PSYCHOMETRIC EVIDENCE FOR CAAP. For content validation and item construction, "nationally known" specialist panels gave advice about topics and their proportions within tests. ACT then recruited college faculty as item writers; over several iterations, a final item pool was assembled for pilot testing. Item analyses helped to narrow the item pool by tossing out items that were too easy or difficult, or that had weak part-whole correlations. The resulting item difficulties (averaging around .60, with Mathematics lower at around .38) will come close to maximizing the spread of scores. This objective is time tested for norm-referenced applications, but the CAAP orientation seems mainly criterion referenced. One wonders why ACT did not use construction standards (e.g., masters vs. nonmasters) more suited to its criterion-referenced claims.

Reliability evidence is given as KR-20 coefficients and standard errors of measurement. KR-20 estimates are satisfactory, ranging from .78 (Mathematics) to .93 (Writing Skills). (These were calculated by averaging separate coefficients for various subgroups reported in the CAAP Technical Handbook.) No reliability estimates are given for various subscores within tests. Neither are there interrater reliabilities reported for the scores of the Essay Writing test. And although there are parallel forms of the CAAP, no equivalence reliability estimates are reported. Stability estimates are available (over 2-year intervals) but ACT reports none of these.

Standard errors, chronically underused by practitioners, are so large as to create serious doubt about the use of CAAP scores to make decisions about individual students. As an example, consider the Mathematics standard error reported for one subgroup: 2.47 (CAAP Technical Handbook, p. 31; this is at odds with the figure of 1.96 in the CAAP User's Guide, p. 24). Developing a .95 confidence interval around an average raw Mathematics score of 15.2 gives a band of 10.3 to 20.1. If we wish to translate the bandwidth to comparable percentile ranks, we are stuck. In its norm tables (User's Guide, Appendix D), ACT gives only translations from scale scores to percentile ranks; raw score equivalents are omitted. Assuming a normal distribution of scores, we can nevertheless estimate percentile ranks from raw scores. Plain talk summary: The 95% confidence band places this person's math score somewhere between the 18th and the 82nd percentile rank. This band does not give much confidence about developing useful cutpoints (e.g., for eligibility for an advanced course). ACT's only acknowledgement about how fragile individual decisions can be comes in the discussion of the use of change scores (e.g., pre to post) (User's Guide, p. 31). This is a wise caution, because the feeble reliabilities of the CAAP change scores range from .31 to .40.

ACT provides an assortment of criterion-related validity coefficients for the various CAAP tests. Coefficients from predicting same-year GPA are modest, ranging from .34 to .38. Predicting next-year GPAs deliver predictably lower correlations, between .23 and .35.

Construct validity evidence takes a different guise. CAAP scores are said to represent "the academic skills and knowledge acquired by students during the first two years of college" (CAAP Technical Handbook, p. 44). One way of examining this is by assessing change in CAAP scores from the beginning of the freshman year to the end of the sophomore year. ACT's evidence is very slim. One gets the hint that growth in skills is small from the item analysis data: Test difficulties are not very different for freshmen and sophomores.

Using both longitudinal and cross-sectional data, ACT reports gain scores over a 2-year period (but does not say whether the gains are in raw or scaled scores). Assuming raw scores, effect sizes are not very impressive: .07 to .21 standard deviation improvement in CAAP scores over 2 years. CAAP scores, whatever they measure, are durable.

WHAT I THINK. There are two obvious hypotheses about why CAAP scores do not change much. One is that the colleges involved in the validity studies did not impart the skills measured by CAAP. Certainly college faculty would argue against this interpretation.

A second hypothesis is that the construct CAAP taps is general aptitude, which is not easily manipulable in a 2-year period. The CAAP Technical Handbook shows test intercorrelations ranging from .46 to .75 (Science and Essay Writing data were unavailable and not printed in the Handbook). For each of the two parallel forms of the CAAP, I ran the intercorrelations through a principal factor analysis; this is crudely analogous to a second-order factoring. For both forms of the CAAP, a single factor emerged, explaining 98% and 99% of the test covariation. Each test loaded in the .80s except for Mathematics, which was around .60. An internal consistency estimate for each factor was .86. Except to improve the internal consistency, I suspect that the addition of Science and Essay Writing to the factor procedure would not change the results much. What shall we call the single, strong factor? Charles Spearman would have suggested "g," and perhaps that is still a useful term. Unfortunately, g is not what ACT had in mind in constructing CAAP.

In summary, institutions should consider carefully whether the CAAP tests will deliver results that are useful in planning, program evaluation, policy development, design of interventions, and diagnosis of student progress. Institutions that already have some proxy for g (e.g., SAT or ACT scores) should ask whether another assessment will give additional useful advice. For ACT's part, they should expand what seem now like draft versions of the CAAP Technical Handbook and the CAAP User's Guide. At the very least, they should develop a convincing argument with, for instance, a multitrait, multimethod approach, that CAAP measures something more malleable than general aptitude.

Review of the Collegiate Assessment of Academic Performance by JEFFREY K. SMITH, Professor of Educational Psychology and Associate Dean, Graduate School of Education, Rutgers University, New Brunswick, NJ:

The Collegiate Assessment of Academic Performance is a set of six tests designed to provide colleges with indicators of the academic performance of their students for purposes of program evaluation and assessment of individual students. The skills measured are argued to be general educational foundation skills necessary for success in the final 2 years of an undergraduate curriculum. The tests measure Reading, Mathematics, Science Reasoning, Critical Thinking, and Writing (both through multiple-choice and essay formats). All tests employ a four-choice multiple-choice format except for the essay-based Writing test.

The Reading test consists of four passages of roughly 900 words each with nine items relating to each passage. One passage is fiction; the remaining three are drawn from the humanities, social sciences, and natural sciences. All passages are taken from published material. The Critical Thinking test contains pairs of essays presenting different points of view on various topics. Questions are based on comparisons of the arguments made by the two essays. The Mathematics test ranges from pre-algebra to introductory calculus. There is a mix of story items and solutions of equations. The Writing Skills test consists of a series of passages with underlined segments that have possible editing changes made for them. A "no change" option is included for each item. The Science Reasoning test contains passages and diagrams from biology, chemistry, physics, and the physical sciences. A series of questions is related to each of the passages. The Writing essay test consists of two 20-minute prompts consisting of a brief paragraph. The Writing test is scored holistically on a 6-point scale.

The CAAP appears to be a well-conceptualized and executed effort to measure many of the academic skills related to the type of learning that occurs in college. A review of the CAAP indicates clearly that the tests are at an appropriate level and provide strong coverage of the six areas measured. The development of the measures was based on research conducted by ACT and items were written by college faculty in the various disciplines.

Norms are available based on testing from approximately 75,000 students at colleges and universities using the CAAP. There are norms for first and second year students from public and private schools, and from 2- and 4-year institutions. ACT provides scoring services and a variety of score reports.

Extensive reliability information is provided on the CAAP, but there is only modest information concerning validity, especially for an assessment program that is well-established. Reliabilities (KR20) for the multiple-choice measures range from .76 to .95. The KR20 reliabilities are quite satisfactory for reporting group results, but are only consistently strong enough for individual level scores for the Writing Skills multiple-choice test. No test-retest or parallel form reliability information is provided. A section reporting completion rates for the measures indicates that the measure suffer from speededness. A study of 2,000 examinees found that between 5% and 16% did not complete the last five items of the tests they were taking. Although the manual argues that these reflect high completion rates, it is difficult to agree with this conclusion based on the data (e.g., in Reading, up to 20% did not reach the last 5 items of a 36-item measure).

The validity section of the technical manual is quite brief, and the data provided are not particularly encouraging. There is no information with regard to content validity except the suggestion that each institution should conduct its own content validity assessment. Although it is true that test users should judge a test for their specific purposes, this does not mean that a study of the opinions of college faculty and administrators with regard to the appropriateness of the CAAP would not be useful in helping others decide whether to use the measures. A major concern regarding content validity of the CAAP relates to the coverage of the CAAP to what is taught in college. If college disciplines can be organized into the humanities, the social sciences, and the natural sciences (including Mathematics), it would seem that the natural sciences and the humanities are well covered in the CAAP, but the social sciences are not. There are skills measures that are certainly important to the social sciences, but the work and tools of the social scientist (hypothesis generation and testing, interpretation of statistical data, the search for alternative explanations of findings, etc.) are fundamentally absent from the assessment.

A series of studies from 58 institutions regarding the relationship between CAAP scores and college grades is summarized in the technical manual. Concurrent correlations between CAAP scores and GPAs are modest (median correlations ranging from .34 to .38), and predictive correlations between second year CAAP scores and third year (GPA were even more modest (ranging between .23 and .32). (No correlations are provided for the Writing essay or the Science Reasoning test.) In a second series of studies, CAAP scores for students entering their first year of college were compared to scores of these students when they completed their second year. Gains ranged from .6 scale points to 2.3 scale points. These translate to gains of roughly .15 to .50 standard deviations. This seems to be very little growth over the course of 2 years.

The validity data do not argue strongly for the utility of the CAAP, but these results need to be put in context. First, although the correlations reported in these studies are modest, it should be kept in mind that college grade-point averages are notoriously unreliable. Second, the small gains found over time may reflect the general nature of the measures as opposed to the frequently very specific nature of college courses. Third, motivation to perform well on the part of examinees may be clouding the picture. This is a topic mentioned frequently in the materials provided with the tests.

To summarize, the CAAP presents users with a solid, traditionally conceived, set of measures of skills related to college learning. The level of difficulty is appropriate, norms are provided for comparison purposes, and scoring and reporting services are available. Reliability is solid for group comparisons, but generally not adequate for individual decisions without supporting information. Validity information is problematic, but not unusually so for a measure of this type. The CAAP provides a potentially useful alternative to locally developed measures for evaluation of college programs and as a component of a program for student placement and assessment.

[28]
Communication and Symbolic Behavior Scales.

Purpose: "A standardized method of examining communicative and symbolic behaviors of children."
Population: 9 months to 6 years.

Publication Date: 1993.

Acronym: CSBS.

Scores, 7: Communicative Functions, Gestural Communicative Means, Vocal Communicative Means, Verbal Communicative Means, Reciprocity, Social-Affective Signaling, Symbolic Behavior.

Administration: Individual.

Price Data: Available from publisher.

Time: (60–70) minutes.

Comments: Assessments videotaped for analysis.

Authors: Amy M. Wetherby and Barry M. Prizant.

Publisher: The Riverside Publishing Company.

TEST REFERENCES

1. Crais, E. R., & Roberts, J. E. (1991). Decision making in assessment and early intervention planning. *Language, Speech, and Hearing Services in Schools, 22,* 19–30.
2. Warren, S. F., & Abbeduto, L. (1992). The relation of communication and language development to mental retardation. *American Journal on Mental Retardation, 97,* 125-130.
3. Warren, S. F., Yoder, P. J., Gazdag, G. E., Kim, K., & Jones, H. A. (1993). Facilitating prelinguistic communication skills in young children with developmental delay. *Journal of Speech and Hearing Research, 36,* 83–97.

Review of the Communication and Symbolic Behavior Scales by STEVEN H. LONG, Assistant Professor of Communication Sciences, Case Western Reserve University, Cleveland, OH:

The Communication and Symbolic Behavior Scales (CSBS) is intended for the assessment of children up to 6 years of age whose functional communication age is between 8 months and 2 years. It uses a structured interaction with a child to gather information about communicative, social-affective, and symbolic abilities.

TEST MATERIALS. The CSBS includes a kit of toys and books that are used to tempt children into communicative interactions or to engage them in various types of symbolic play. A few items are edible or disposable and must be replaced after each administration of the test. Many items can be mouthed and will require sterilization.

A manual contains the procedures for administering, scoring, and interpreting the CSBS. These procedures are further illustrated on two instructional videotapes that accompany the test. Responses from a child are coded on a set of 10 score sheets. In addition, two forms are provided for the caregiver, one to describe the child prior to the assessment and the other to rate representativeness of behavior afterwards.

Because the CSBS evaluates many behaviors that must be judged visually, the examination session must be videotaped. Furthermore, it is important that the camera be properly positioned in order to capture the behaviors of interest, should they occur. If videorecording problems occur, nearly all assessment information would be lost.

TEST ADMINISTRATION. The interaction with the child is carefully organized so that materials are presented in sequence and a fixed amount of time is allowed to observe the child's play with or use of those materials. The CSBS puts the examiner in the role of introducing materials and giving direction to the child's caregiver. The behavioral sample is taken, for the most part, from the child's interaction with the caregiver rather than with the examiner. The interaction begins with a warm-up of 10–15 minutes. For the next 10–20 minutes, the child is encouraged to communicate by offering a series of alluring toys (balloons, bubbles), simple dyadic games (peek-a-boo), and mild frustrations (toys in a sealed plastic bag). This is followed by book sharing for 5 minutes, symbolic play with representational toys for 10 minutes, probes of the child's comprehension for 5 minutes, and probes of the child's play with construction toys (blocks, rings, cups) for 5 minutes. From the videotape, the form and function of all child communicative behaviors is noted on the scoring sheets, which list possible categories. Similarly, the child's social/affective signaling (e.g., shifts in gaze) is noted as well as the symbolic behavior evident during the play sequences and the conversation probes. These behaviors are then summed, weighted, and scored according to guidelines provided in the manual.

PSYCHOMETRIC ADEQUACY. The content validity of the CSBS is based on the view that language emerges as the result of interacting social, affective, cognitive, and linguistic factors. Thus, it is logical to assess behaviors in all of these domains in order to form a profile that might highlight one or more areas of development that are incommensurate with the others. Evidence for the construct validity of the CSBS appears in the age-related increases in scores shown by children in the standardization group on nearly all of the instrument's 22 scales. Adequate predictive validity is claimed on the basis of discriminant analyses of CSBS scores. These analyses show that the instrument classified children into normal, pervasive developmental disorder, and speech-language impaired groups with accuracy ranging from 60% to 98%.

Statistical analysis of reliability is quite thorough. Six of the CSBS's seven scales showed high internal consistency. Repeated administrations of the instrument to 66 children showed that scores did not differ on retesting when it occurred after an interval of less than 2 months but that differences emerged with intervals longer than that. Interexaminer reliability was .83 or better in pairwise comparison of three different raters.

The standardization group for CSBS consisted of 282 child scores distributed from 8 to 24 months. The manual authors refer to 282 "children" but the discussion makes it clear that there were actually only 216 individuals tested, of whom 66 were retested and their second scores added to the standardization sample. The authors justify adding the second scores to the norms because "they increase the relevance of the norms to their intended use and reduce the error that would be associated with estimates of developmental improvement based on different children at different ages" (p. 64). Roughly half of the 282 normative scores placed the children at a "prelinguistic" stage, the other half at a "linguistic" stage that subsumed individuals at early one-word, late one-word, and multiword levels of development. A weighting procedure was used to adjust the norms for the slight differences in the monthly distribution of the sample. Other weightings were used to adjust for gender, race, and Spanish origin so that the final norms are more in line with characteristics of the national population. The result of these weightings was to create equal representation (5.92%) at all monthly intervals except the first two. The weighted percentage of girls in the standardization sample was 48.7%; the weighted percentage of African American children, 12.1%; and the weighted percentage of children of Spanish origin, 9.4%.

Norms are reported in a series of tables, each table corresponding to one of the six CSBS scales or to a composite of several scales. The norms are expressed both as standard scores and percentile ranks, broken down (a) monthly from 8 to 24 months, and (b) by language stage. The standard error of measurement is reported for each table.

SUMMARY. The CSBS uses a structured interaction to examine early symbolic and communicative behavior in children with a functional communication age between 8 months and 2 years.

The entire interaction with the child is scripted to take between 45 and 60 minutes. Scoring is accomplished through careful review of the child's videotaped behavior and categorization of all communicative, social-affective, and symbolic acts. In the design of the instrument and in its standardization, considerable thought was given to matters of reliability and validity and the CSBS can make strong claims in those areas.

Those who would consider using the CSBS must be aware of three conditions. First, the instrument requires the involvement of the child's caretaker to complete questionnaires before and after the interaction and to participate along with the child in the interaction itself. Second, the interaction must be videotaped. Third, the procedure is lengthy. The authors do not offer an estimate of how long it will take most examiners to administer, tally, and interpret the CSBS (they do suggest 90 minutes to code). Assuming, however, that it will take at least 2 minutes to review and code every minute of videotape, then administration and coding will require 2.25 to 3 hours. Tallying the 10 worksheets may take another hour and lookup of norms an additional 15 minutes. Thus, the procedure may demand from 3.5 to 4.25 hours to complete.

Review of the Communication and Symbolic Behavior Scales by DOLORES KLUPPEL VETTER, Professor of Communicative Disorders, University of Wisconsin—Madison, Madison, WI:

The Communication and Symbolic Behavior Scales (CSBS) was designed to identify children who have or who are at risk for developing a communicative disorder. In addition, data from it may be used to establish a profile of communicative, social-affective, and symbolic functioning that will allow the monitoring of children's behavioral changes over time. It is designed for children who have a functional communication age between 8 and 24 months and whose chronological age is between 9 months and 6 years.

The CSBS uses action-based toys, books, and play materials appropriate for very young children. The evaluator, the child, and the child's caregiver are present during the assessment. Behaviors of the child are sampled during activities (i.e., communicative temptations) that range in the degree of structure provided. The activities are designed with the purpose of optimizing the occurrence of spontaneous communicative and play behaviors. Minimal interaction or direction is provided by the evaluator and the child's caregiver is requested to interact spontaneously and not to direct the child's activities. The evaluation session generally takes about one hour. It is videotaped and is scored at a later time. Finally, information is also requested from the caregiver through the use of a questionnaire and a form on which the caregiver provides ratings of the child's behaviors during the assessment. The Caregiver Questionnaire may be completed in advance, or at the time of the evaluation, and the Caregiver Perception Form is completed immediately following the evaluation.

In the CSBS manual the authors state that a trained examiner is able to score the videotape in about one hour. This may be an optimistic time estimate; the evaluation session will yield a videotape of approximately one hour's length and the behaviors that are scored involve judgments and decisions. Training for an examiner, however, will require a substantial investment of time and energy prior to the use of the CSBS. Although the administration of the procedure should be straightforward for any professional proficient in assessing developmentally young children, learning how to score the various communicative and symbolic behaviors likely will require practice. For example, while viewing the videotape, the examiner must first identify that a single communicative act has occurred by answering three questions affirmatively (i.e., Was the act a gesture, vocalization, or verbalization? Was the act directed toward the adult? Did the act serve a communicative function?). When a communicative act has been identified, it is then rated for one of three communicative functions (i.e., behavior regulation, social interaction, or joint attention), or the examiner determines that the communicative function is unclear. Each of these decisions may initially necessitate a replaying of the videotape and a rereading of the definitions before a decision can be reached regarding a single communicative act.

Information and examples are provided in the CSBS manual to assist the examiner in learning to score behaviors on the videotape. In addition, the authors prepared two videotapes that were used to train examiners for the scoring of the behaviors of the normative sample; these are provided with the CSBS to make the sampling procedures and the scoring criteria explicit.

The information obtained from the CSBS results in 18 scales that represent observed communicative behaviors (e.g., conventional use of gestures, inventory of different words) and four scales that reflect aspects of symbolic behavior (e.g., constructive play). The authors then devised seven cluster scores that reflect the child's abilities in broader domains (e.g., a cluster score for communicative functions was constructed from the individual scales of behavior regulation, social interaction, and joint attention) and that have the advantage of being more reliable than individual scales. Finally, there is a communication composite score that was constructed of the 18 communicative behavior scales. Tables are provided in the CSBS manual from which standard score equivalents for cluster and composite scores (at 1-month age intervals) may be determined; tables with percentile ranks are also given. The CSBS manual contains a detailed tutorial on the interpretation of the various types of scores, and confidence intervals are provided for the appropriate interpretation of the cluster and composite scores. The authors stress the desirability of comparing the scaled values of the scores within and among children through the use of the CSBS Profile.

The depth and extent of the information provided relevant to the standardization of the CSBS is impressive. Detailed demographic information (i.e., age, linguistic state, gender, and ethnic status) is presented for the standardization sample of 242 children. Descriptive statistics for the individual scales, and the cluster and communication composite scores are also contained in the CSBS manual. Reliability is addressed through the evaluation of (a) internal consistency of the cluster and composite scores by age and language stage of the children, (b) test-retest stability of the individual scales at two time intervals, (c) interrater reliability of the individual scales among three pairs of raters, and (d) the standard errors of measurement for cluster scores and the communication composite score. As might be expected there was some variability among the reliability estimates, but taking everything together, the CSBS yields very adequate reliability. Persuasive evidence also was presented for content, ecological, criterion-related, and construct validity. When a discriminant function analysis was applied to three groups of children (i.e., the standardization sample, a group with pervasive developmental disorders, and one with speech-language impairments), 98% of the standardization sample, 85% of the children with pervasive developmental disorders, and 60% of children with speech-language impairments were accurately classified.

In summary, the CSBS provides a procedure for evaluating early communicative and symbolic behaviors in children. The rationale for the scales is well developed and the standardization information is extensive. Examiners will have to use the video training tapes and engage in substantial practice in order to achieve reliable and valid administration, scoring, and interpretation of the information acquired through the use of the CSBS. The information obtained from a child should provide results that will facilitate comparisons with the standardization sample, that will track development within the child, and that will provide directions for intervention when necessary.

[29]
Composite International Diagnostic Interview.

Purpose: "For use in epidemiological studies of mental disorders."
Population: Adults.
Publication Date: 1993.
Acronym: CIDI.
Scores, 18: Demographics, Tobacco Use Disorder, Somatoform Disorders, Panic Disorder, Generalized Anxiety, Phobic Disorders, Major Depressive Episode and Dysthymia, Manic Episode, Schizophrenic and Schizophreniform Disorders, Eating Disorders, Alcohol Abuse and Dependence, Obsessive Compulsive Disorder, Drug Abuse and Dependence, Organic Brain Syndrome, Psychosexual Dysfunctions, Comments by the Respondent and the Interviewer, Interviewer Observations, Interviewer Rating.
Administration: Individual.
Price Data: Available from publisher.
Time: (75–95) minutes.
Author: World Health Organization.
Publisher: American Psychiatric Press, Inc.

TEST REFERENCES
1. Rogler, L. H. (1993). Culturally sensitizing psychiatric diagnosis: A framework for research. *The Journal of Nervous and Mental Disease, 181*, 401-408.
2. Asherson, P., Walsh, C., Williams, J., Sargeant, M., Taylor, C., Clements, A., Gill, M., Owen, M., & McGuffin, P. (1994). Imprinting and anticipation: Are they relevant to genetic studies or schizophrenia? *British Journal of Psychiatry, 164*, 619-624.
3. Eaton, W. W., Kessler, R. C., Wittchen, H. U., & Magee, W. J. (1994). Panic and panic disorder in the United States. *American Journal of Psychiatry, 151*, 413-420.
4. Le, F., Mitchell, P., Vivero, C., Waters, B., Donald, J., Selbie, L. A., Shine, J., & Schofield, P. (1994). Exclusion of close linkage of bipolar disorder to the Gs-alpha subunit gene in nine Australian pedigrees. *Journal of Affective Disorders, 32*, 187-195.
5. Sobell, L. C., Toneatto, T., & Sobell, M. (1994). Behavioral assessment and treatment planning for alcohol, tobacco, and other drug problems: Current status with an emphasis on clinical applications. *Behavior Therapy, 25*, 533–580.
6. Dettling, M., Heinz, A., DuFeu, P., Rommelspacher, H., Graf, K.-L., & Schmidt, L. G. (1995). Dopaminergic responsivity in alcoholism: Trait, state, or residual marker? *American Journal of Psychiatry, 152*, 1317-1321.
7. Garfinkel, P. E., Lin, E., Goering, P., Spegg, C., Goldbloom, D. S., Kennedy, S., Kaplan, A. S., & Woodside, B. (1995). Bulimia nervosa in a Canadian community sample: Prevalence and comparison of subgroups. *American Journal of Psychiatry, 152*, 1052-1058.
8. Gureje, O., Aderibigbe, Y. A., & Obikoya, O. (1995). Three syndromes in schizophrenia: Validity in young patients with recent onset of illness. *Psychological Medicine, 25*, 715– 725.
9. Kessler, R. C., Foster, C. L., Saunders, W. B., & Stang, P. E. (1995). Social consequences of psychiatric disorders, I. Educational attainment. *American Journal of Psychiatry, 152*, 1026-1032.
10. Peters, L., & Andrews, G. (1995). Procedural validity of the computerized version of the Composite International Diagnostic Interview (CIDI—Auto) in the anxiety disorders. *Psychological Medicine, 25*, 1269–1280.
11. Sartorius, N., Ustun, T. B., Korten, A., Cooper, J. E., & van Drimmelen, J. (1995). Progress toward achieving a common language in psychiatry, II: Results from the international field trials of the ICO—10 Diagnostic Criteria for Research for Mental and Behavioral Disorders. *American Journal of Psychiatry, 152*, 1427–1437.
12. Nelson, C. B., Little, R. J. A., Heath, A. C., & Kessler, R. C. (1996). Patterns of DSM-III-R alcohol dependence symptom progression in a general population survey. *Psychological Medicine, 26*, 449–460.
13. Parikh, S. V., Wasylenki, D., Goering, P., & Wong, J. (1996). Mood disorders: Rural/urban differences in prevalence, health care utilization, and disability in Ontario. *Journal of Affective Disorders, 38*, 57–65.
14. Schuckit, M. A., Tipp, J. E., Anthenelli, R. M., Bucholz, K. K., Hesselbrock, V. M., & Nurnberger, J. I. (1996). Anorexia nervosa and bulimia nervosa in alcohol-dependent men and women and their relatives. *American Journal of Psychiatry, 153*, 74–82.
15. Thompson, L. L., Riggs, P. D., Mikulich, S. K., & Crowley, T. J. (1996). Contribution of ADHD symptoms to substance problems and delinquency in conduct-disordered adolescents. *Journal of Abnormal Child Psychology, 24*, 325–347.
16. Tiemens, B. G., Ormel, J., & Simon, G. E. (1996). Occurrence, recognition, and outcome of psychological disorders in primary care. *American Journal of Psychiatry, 153*, 636–644.
17. Williams, L. M. (1996). Cognitive inhibition and schizophrenic symptom subgroups. *Schizophrenia Bulletin, 22*, 139–151.

Review of the Composite International Diagnostic Interview by MARY MATHAI CHITTOORAN, UC Foundation Assistant Professor of School Psychology and Special Education, The University of Tennessee at Chattanooga, Chattanooga, TN:

The Composite International Diagnostic Interview (CIDI), Version 1.1 is a comprehensive, standardized, and structured interview for the assessment of mental disorders in adults. Appropriate for use in a variety of cultures with respondents of diverse educational backgrounds, the core version of the CIDI is currently available in 16 languages. Although the CIDI was designed to be used in epidemiological studies of mental disorders, it is finding increased acceptance in clinical and research circles.

The CIDI had its inception in 1980, when questions from the National Institute of Mental Health Diagnostic Interview Schedule (NIMH-

DIS) and the ninth edition of the Present State Examination (PSE-9) were combined to form a draft version. Since then, items have been modified, added, and structured to correspond to the criteria for mental disorders outlined in two major diagnostic systems—the *International Classification of Diseases* (*ICD-10*) and the American Psychiatric Association's *Diagnostic and Statistical Manual—Third Edition, Revised* (*DSM-III-R*). According to the authors of the manual, feasibility and cross-cultural acceptability were established in field trials conducted in sites around the world and the CIDI was determined to have "excellent interrater reliability (kappa >.90 in almost all diagnostic categories) and good test-retest reliability" (p. 10). Subsequent field trials confirmed previous findings and suggested a high degree of diagnostic concordance between CIDI and clinical *ICD-10* and *DSM-III-R* diagnoses.

Test materials consist of a Researcher's Manual, an Interviewer's Manual, a 105-page Interview protocol, a Computer Manual, and an IBM-compatible computer diskette that includes data cleaning and entry programs as well as scoring programs for both *ICD-10* and *DSM-III-R* diagnoses. A computer-administered version of the CIDI, the CIDI-Auto, is also available and an abbreviated version, the CIDI-Quick, is under development.

The CIDI may be administered by both clinicians and nonclinicians and all interviewers undergo rigorous training sessions offered by a CIDI training center. Interview questions are standardized and are designed to elicit descriptive information about the frequency, severity, onset, and recency of symptoms. The interviewer is responsible for gathering the information, coding it appropriately, and submitting it to the editor for data cleaning, computer entry, and scoring. A positive diagnosis is made when (a) *all* criteria for a disorder are met *AND* when (b) all *positive* criteria—as distinguished from exclusionary criteria—for that disorder are met.

COMMENTARY. The CIDI has a number of excellent features. It is the result of a large-scale collaborative project that was developed over a 13-year period, with an impressive number of field trials in international settings. Content validity appears to be adequate as interview questions were constructed upon the recommendations of an international panel of experts who also judged its cross-cultural acceptability. Interrater reliability ranges from good to excellent. Test materials are sturdy, attractive, and of good quality. The CIDI offers a highly structured format with explicit directions to interviewers, which combined with the training program (arguably one of the CIDI's greatest strengths), adds to ease of administration and minimizes a significant source of potential error. Additionally, computer-generated diagnoses may obviate concerns about human error in data entry and scoring.

The CIDI is subject to the limitations of all interviews in that its results are dependent on the skills of the interviewer but this may be especially problematic if the interviewer is a nonclinician. Respondents may display behaviors that escape the nonclinician but that could be critical to an accurate diagnosis, and decision-making, particularly with borderline cases, is often heavily influenced by clinical experience. Similarly, the generation of computer diagnoses, although advantageous in many ways (Wittchen, 1993), disregards the value of human experience in decision making.

Although the CIDI does address the use of self-descriptive phrases such as "excessive," "sickly," or "a lot of trouble," other phrases like "worried a lot" are left vague and undefined. Also of concern is the fact that the interviewer is asked to comment on respondent behaviors such as the existence of neologisms, and to determine whether the respondent is "essentially normal, a little abnormal, or very abnormal" (p. 86). These are tasks that may well be beyond the capabilities of a nonclinician and although the authors recognize the need for special training in this area, there are no formal guidelines available. There is also the danger, inherent in all interviews, that questions in sensitive areas (e.g., those dealing with sexuality or drug use) may be refused or not answered truthfully. The accuracy of the CIDI's computer diagnoses cannot be evaluated in the absence of critical materials such as the computer manual and the computer programs, which were repeatedly requested from, but not provided by, the publisher.

Although the authors of the CIDI manual address the cultural acceptability of certain items, there are still a number of questions that may pose problems in certain cultures, for example, items in which a nonnative speaker of English is asked to repeat a Western colloquialism, "No if's and's or but's" (pp. 77–78) or to remember three objects, among them a penny. Respondents in foreign countries may not recognize drugs by their formal names and so may provide inaccurate information about drug use. Yet another item uses a cutoff of 140 pounds for men and 125 pounds for women as one of the preliminary criteria in determining the existence of an eating disorder; although this weight might be significant in the Western world, a slight build is the norm in many countries. The inclusion of such items is puzzling, given that the CIDI is specifically intended to be used with a cross-cultural population.

One of the greatest drawbacks of the CIDI is the lack of technical information offered to potential users. The Researcher's manual contains vague descriptions about the composition of samples used in field studies and only very sketchy information about the outcome of such studies. Limited data about the CIDI's reliability and validity are provided and the vagueness of terms such as "almost all diagnostic categories" and "good" reliability is misleading. Further, because the diagnostic utility of some of these mental disorders is still open to question, the validity of tests based on these classifications may be correspondingly poor. Additional information is also needed about criterion-related validity and the congruence between English-language versions and other versions. The advent of *DSM-IV* in 1994 also renders sections of the CIDI obsolete, at least until further revisions are undertaken.

An independent review of 53 studies abstracted in PSYCLIT (e.g., Wittchen, 1994) indicated that the CIDI is used most often to diagnose depression and alcohol and drug-related disorders, and that test-retest and interrater reliability range from moderate to good. A limited number of studies (e.g., Lyketsos, Aritzi, & Lyketsos, 1994) provide support for the inclusion of the CIDI in clinical decision making.

The CIDI, Version 1.1 is an ambitious attempt to develop a structured interview with cross-cultural acceptability that can be used for the diagnosis of mental disorders in adults. It is suggested that the CIDI be used primarily as a measure for epidemiological research, and that its use in clinical settings be limited, at least until the authors are able to provide additional technical information as well as support for its use in clinical settings. The

CIDI's sister measure, the Schedules for Clinical Assessment in Neuropsychiatry, also developed by the WHO, may serve as an alternative measure in clinical settings (Janca, Ustun, & Sartorious, 1994). The CIDI may also be profitably used in a comprehensive battery that includes a complete history, norm-referenced measures of social-emotional functioning, behavioral observations, and clinical decision making.

REVIEWER'S REFERENCES

Wittchen, H. U. (1993). Computer scoring of CIDI diagnoses: Special Issue: The WHO Composite Diagnostic Interview. *International Journal of Methods in Psychiatric Research, 3*(2), 101–107.

Janca, A., Ustun, T. B., & Sartorious, N. (1994). New versions of World Health Organization instruments for the assessment of mental disorders. *Acta Psychiatrica Scandinavica, 90*(2), 73–83.

Lyketsos, C. G., Aritzi, S., & Lyketsos, G. C. (1994). Effectiveness of office-based psychiatric practice using a structured diagnostic interview to guide treatment. *Journal of Nervous and Mental Disease, 182*(12), 720–723.

Wittchen, H. U. (1994). Reliability and validity studies of the WHO-Composite International Diagnostic Interview (CIDI): A critical review. *Journal of Psychiatric Research, 28*(1), 57–84.

Review of the Composite International Diagnostic Interview by JANICE G. WILLIAMS, Associate Professor of Psychology, Clemson University, Clemson, SC:

The Composite International Diagnostic Interview (CIDI) is a comprehensive structured interview for making psychiatric diagnoses consistent with the *Diagnostic and Statistical Manual—Third Edition, Revised (DSM-III-R)* and the *International Classification of Disease (ICD-10)*. The instrument was developed from other structured interviews, including the Diagnostic Interview Schedule, the Present State Examination, and a structured interview based on the *ICD-10* diagnostic criteria. The CIDI is intended for epidemiological research on psychiatric diagnoses, but the manual author indicates that it can be used for other clinical and research purposes, as well. The instrument can be administered by trained interviewers with no other clinical background. Training for administering the interview is a 5-day process.

Development of the CIDI was a joint project of the World Health Organization and the National Institutes for Health. A unique feature of the CIDI is its availability in 16 languages. Development included field trials to examine reliability and validity of the instrument in different countries. The CIDI has undergone a number or revisions that have addressed its comprehensiveness, its length, and its adequacy of measurement of substance abuse and dependence. Additionally, the CIDI should be undergoing current revision to incorporate changes from *DSM-III-R* to *DSM-IV*.

RELIABILITY AND VALIDITY. References cited in the CIDI indicate adequate reliabilities for most CIDI sections. Both test-retest and interrater reliabilities have been examined. A lack of test-retest reliability has been noted for CIDI time-related items, such as age at onset of symptoms. This lack of reliability might be expected, as interviews are based solely on patient recall. However, these items have been revised since those findings.

The CIDI was constructed for content validity. Items are based on the diagnostic criteria for the *DSM-III-R* and the *ICD-10*. A major shortcoming of the CIDI Researcher's Manual is failure to provide a summary of the available information on reliability and validity. References to published works are provided, but many of the journals in which they are published will not be found in the typical library. Psychometric properties of the scales are difficult to determine because of the frequency with which the sections have been revised. Currently, a new version of the CIDI should be in preparation in response to the publication of *DSM-IV*.

The most appropriate use of the CIDI is for research. Certainly the instrument would be valuable for epidemiological research on mental disorders, as well as for research on correlates of such diagnoses. Development of the instrument in 16 languages makes it a potentially pivotal instrument for advancing cross-cultural research on mental disorders. As more information is accumulated on the reliability and validity of the CIDI in the diverse languages, it may become a standard measure for study of cross-cultural issues in psychiatric diagnosis.

Currently, the CIDI should be used with some caution. At best, the CIDI can be only as useful as the classification systems on which it is based. As controversies, criticisms, and revisions of these systems continue, the same issues and arguments will apply to the CIDI. One limitation of the CIDI is its reliance on patient self-report. Although the manual states that the CIDI could be used for clinical diagnosis, it seems inappropriate to base diagnosis on an interview by an individual without a clinical background. However, the CIDI would serve as a useful adjunct to other sources of diagnostic information.

SUMMARY. The CIDI is a comprehensive interview for making diagnoses based on the *DSM-III-R* and *ICD-10*. Reliability and validity appear adequate for research purposes, although the manual does not provide enough information about psychometric properties of the scales. The CIDI has been developed in 16 languages, making it a potentially useful instrument for cross-cultural research on mental disorders.

[30]
Comprehensive Adult Student Assessment System.

Purpose: Used for "assessing adult basic skills within a functional context" to "place learnees into appropriate instructional levels, diagnose learners' needs, monitor progress, and certify mastery of functional basic skills."
Population: Adults.
Publication Dates: 1980–1993.
Acronym: CASAS.
Administration: Group.
Restricted Distribution: Agency training is required before tests can be provided.
Price Data: Available from publisher.
Time: (60) minutes per test.
Comments: The CASAS system "currently offers more than 80 standardized assessment instruments including multiple choice, written response, and performance-based assessment ... has the capacity to customize assessment to measure specific competencies and learner outcomes."
Author: CASAS.
Publisher: CASAS.

   a) APPRAISAL TESTS.
     1) *Life Skills Appraisal.*
     Scores: 2 tests: Reading, Math.
     2) *ESL Appraisal (English as a Second Language).*
     Scores: 4 tests: Reading, Listening, Writing, Oral.
     Comments: Places students into a Level A, B, or C pretest of the CASAS Listening Series.
     3) *GAIN Appraisal (Greater Avenues for Independence).*
     Scores: 3 tests: Reading, Math, Listening.
     4) *ECS Appraisal (Employability Competency System).*
     Scores: 2 tests: Reading, Math.
     Comments: Places students into Levels A, B, or C of the CASAS Basic Skills for Employability pretests.
     5) *Workplace Appraisal.*
     Scores: 2 tests: Reading, Reading/Math.

Comments: Not a pre-employment test; designed to be used at worksite to provide an initial assessment of workers' functional reading skills of materials encountered at the worksite.

6) *IRCA Pre-Enrollment Appraisal.*

Scores: 4 tests: Reading, Listening, Writing, Oral.

Comments: "Designed for use with the amnesty population, it may also be used with non-amnesty ESL students."

b) CASAS TESTS FOR MONITORING PROGRESS.

Comments: All tests serve as pre/post-tests.

1) *Life Skills Survey Achievement Tests.*

(*a*) Reading.

Levels: 4 levels (A, B, C, D), each with 2 forms.

(*b*) Math.

Levels: 4 levels (A, B, C, D), each with 2 forms.

(*c*) Listening Comprehension (for ESL students).

Levels: 3 levels (A, B, C), each with 2 forms.

2) *Basic Skills for Employability Tests.*

(*a*) Reading.

Levels: 3 levels (A, B, C), each with 2 forms.

(*b*) Math.

Levels: 3 levels (A, B, C), each with 2 forms.

(*c*) Listening Comprehension (for ESL students).

Levels: 3 levels (A, B, C), each with 2 forms.

c) CASAS TESTS FOR SPECIAL POPULATIONS.

Population: Developmentally disabled students.

Levels: 3 levels (AA, AAA, AAAA), each with 2 forms.

Comments: Pretests and corresponding posttests are available.

d) CASAS CERTIFICATION TESTS.

Comments: "Designed to determine if a student is ready to move to a higher level of instruction or to be certified as completing a program of instruction."

1) *Life Skills Certification (Exit) Tests.*

Scores: 1 test: Reading/Math.

Levels: 3 levels (A, B, C), each with 1 form.

2) *Employability Certification (Exit) Tests.*

Scores: 2 tests: Reading, Math.

Levels: 2 levels (B, C), each with 1 form for each test.

3) *GAIN Certification (Exit) Tests.*

Scores: 3 tests: Basic Skills Certification Reading/Math, ESL Certification Listening/Reading, ESL Certification Applied Performance Test.

Comments: Available only to California County Welfare Departments for use with GAIN participants.

e) CASAS TEST FOR WRITING ASSESSMENT.

Purpose: "Measures a student's functional writing skill abilities within a life skills context."

Comments: Pretest and posttest are available.

f) OCCUPATION SPECIFIC TESTS.

Purpose: "Assess whether a person is ready to enter an occupational training program."

Scores: 5 areas: Auto Mechanic, Clerical, Food Service, Health Occupations Level B, Health Occupations Level C.

g) CASAS SECONDARY DIPLOMA TESTS.

Scores: 8 areas: Math, Economics, American Government, United States History, English/Language Arts, World History, Biological Science, Physical Science.

Comments: Tests are available for pretesting and posttesting.

TEST REFERENCES

1. Frager, A. M. (1991). Adult literacy assessment: Existing tools and promising developments. *Journal of Reading, 35,* 256-259.
2. Askov, E. N. (1993). Approaches to assessment in workplace literacy programs: Meeting the needs of all the clients. *Journal of Reading, 36,* 550-554.

Review of the Comprehensive Adult Student Assessment System by RALPH O. MUELLER, Associate Professor of Educational Research, and PATRICIA K. FREITAG, Assistant Professor of Educational Research, Department of Educational Leadership, Graduate School of Education and Human Development, The George Washington University, Washington, DC:

OVERVIEW. The Comprehensive Adult Student Assessment System (CASAS) is an integrated, hierarchical array of more than 80 instruments that measure adult "basic skills in a functional context" (technical manual, p. 4). The instruments can be customized from a large item bank to be closely aligned with life skills, employability, high school completion, or English-as-a-Second-Language (ESL) curricula for adult learners. According to the authors, each assessment instrument requires about 60 minutes to be administered. The primary purpose of the instruments is to provide for "learner-centered curriculum management, assessment, and evaluation" (technical manual, p. 2). Intended applications of the instruments include (a) diagnostic placement of adult learners in appropriate program levels (although it is not clear whether or not this diagnostic function is restricted to just CASAS-based curricula); (b) progress and monitoring assessment of learners; (c) outcome measures and competency certification of adult learners in life skills, employability, or ESL training programs; and (d) reporting mechanisms for data at the local, state, and federal levels.

The major strengths of the CASAS system are (a) the explicit links from diagnostic program placement to instruction and ultimately to assessment of learner outcomes for CASAS-based adult learning programs (however, the assessment manuals are somewhat vague concerning the relationships between these three components for other adult curricula) and (b) the breadth of competency areas and assessment functions covered by CASAS (e.g., the availability of instruments for use in adult ESL and linked, multilevel assessments for use in adult special needs programs). A weakness of the CASAS system seems to be that instruments designed to measure different competencies in different learner groups are based on a number of overlapping items, making the distinction between and the selection of appropriate instruments for use in non-CASAS based programs difficult.

DOCUMENTATION. Each assessment includes supporting documentation consisting of the CASAS technical manual, test administration directions, and scoring packets. This review is based on these documents; additional materials pertinent to specific instruments, program curriculum, and student assessment are available from the publisher upon request.

The technical manual contains an overview of the adult student assessment system and is written clearly to meet the needs of program managers and instructors. The Rasch model of Item Response Theory is reviewed extensively, perhaps at the expense of detailed validity and reliability information, which is reported toward the end of the manual.

In the Test Administration Directions and the Scoring Packet, the reader finds clearly written guidelines for test administration and form-specific scoring keys. Item codes include: content area, competency area, competency outcome, and specific task format that allow for curriculum alignment, group or individual progress charts, and competency certification. Scoring keys are easy to follow and score scale conversion charts indicate,

according to the authors, (a) "accurate" score ranges and (b) the relationship between instrument levels within each competency area. Instruments in each area are constructed in hierarchical levels with overlapping items. However, the documentation lacks specifications for instrument construction or models for customizing tests to be aligned with an existing curriculum.

The authors suggest a pre-post test design for instructors to "provide standardized information about learning gains" (Test Administration Directions, p. 3). The post-test described in the Test Administration Directions is used to monitor instruction with a "certification test" recommended to "confirm the learner's skill level" (Test Administration Directions, p. 3). The time period between assessments is not specified, but one must assume the items for the certification test would be similar but not identical to those used for instruction and achievement testing.

The items include appropriate diagrams, charts, graphs, tables, reading passages, and oral components to the relevant functional contexts. However, the machine-scored answer sheets and selected response formats seem to limit the performance aspect of the tests. Clearly, reading comprehension, mathematical skills, listening comprehension, writing, speaking, and problem solving are important indicators of adult life skills and employability. The ability to think critically, problem solve, and appropriately apply these skills in complex situations may be underrepresented by CASAS items. Although the documented item bank is extensive, the number of content areas and competencies covered by CASAS, with multiple instruments at each level in each content area, places a tremendous demand on item development and field testing.

VALIDITY AND RELIABILITY. "The CASAS Item Bank provides statistically reliable and externally validated test items for the construction of instruments that measure basic skills in a functional context for youth and adults" (technical manual, p. 7). To justify this claim, two sections of the technical manual are devoted to evidence of the validity and reliability of CASAS tests. From the manual it is not clear whether or not the data in these sections were obtained from the calibration sample that is characterized broadly by the following statistics (p. 23); age range: 16–85 with 40% in the 21–30 group; ethnicity: 54% Hispanic, 18% Asian, 12% Chinese, 9% White, 4% Black; and gender: 50% female. Information on the sampling procedures used and the SES, learning abilities, and residency of participants that might be relevant to assess the "appropriate use of test instruments for specific populations" (p. 1) is not provided in the supplied manuals. Thus, although relevant data might be available in unpublished CASAS reports, these could not be reviewed.

VALIDITY. It seems that great care was taken during item-bank development to ensure the content validity of CASAS tests. With regard to the construct-related validity, the manual authors claim that "adult life skills problem-solving is the unobservable trait or ability assumed to underlie performance" (technical manual, p. 37). Unfortunately, no supporting empirical evidence is presented, constituting a violation of Standards 1.8 through 1.10 in *Standards for Educational and Psychological Testing* (American Educational Research Association, American Psychological Association, & National Council on Measurement in Education, 1985, p. 15). Similarly, contrary to Standards 1.11 through 1.13 (p. 16) specific evidence of the criterion-related validity is not provided to substantiate that, indeed, "[t]he instructional level indicated by a CASAS test depicts the learner's probability of success in accomplishing a given learning activity and related competency" (technical manual, p. 38). This is significant for adult learners in non-CASAS adult basic education. Gain scores estimated by CASAS instruments for adult learners in other education programs will likely have lower reliability than those reported in the test manuals.

Other validity evidence consists of data on three key CASAS claims that in 1993 were evaluated and supported by the Program Effectiveness Panel of the U.S. Department of Education. The claims are that "learners within educational programs that have adopted the key elements [of CASAS] (1) demonstrate significant learning gains, (2) demonstrate increased hours of participation, and (3) achieve increased goal attainment compared to programs that have not adopted the key elements" (technical manual, p. 32). The manual contains statistical analyses from various state and national studies, based on samples ranging in size from $n = 32$ to $n = 1,326$. No detailed information

on the validation samples is provided in the manual, which constitutes a violation of the *Standards* (Standard 1.5, p. 14). Although the reported data seem supportive of the above claims, note again that conclusions are based on analyses of gain scores that are known to have lower reliabilities than their raw score counterparts.

RELIABILITY. Internal consistency coefficients and IRT-based standard errors of estimate for tests from the anchor series (Forms 71 through 77) are reported in the reliability subsection of the manual (evidence of equivalence and stability reliability is not provided). KR-20 reliability coefficients for CASAS Forms 71, 72, and 74 through 77 are mostly above .80. The internal consistency data are presented separately for subgroups of students speaking various native languages ($n = 31$, Form 76, Laotian; to $n = 385$, Form 74, Spanish) as well as across the subgroups ($n = 199$, Form 77 to $n = 1,000$, Form 71). Further, IRT-based standard errors of estimate are reported for CASAS Reading Forms 74 through 77. However, it is not clear whether the calibration or some other sample was used to obtain the results nor how "local agency personnel" (technical manual, p. 1) unfamiliar with IRT are to interpret them (in partial violation of Standards 2.1 through 2.3; *Standards*, p. 20).

SUMMARY. The Comprehensive Adult Student Assessment System (CASAS) offers diagnostic, achievement, and competency tests in many content areas related to adult basic skills and employability. The broad array of instruments available are reliable indicators of learner achievement in CASAS-based adult learning programs. It is possible for these instruments to be customized to meet the assessment needs in other adult education programs as well. Empirical evidence to support construct and criterion-related validity claims would strengthen the interpretation of score data as well as promote the general use of these instruments across adult basic education programs. Similarly, a more complete description of the calibration and validation samples would improve the assessment documentation. In our opinion, more thorough descriptions of study samples, clear specifications for instrument construction, and analysis of data from field tested "performance measures" are needed. These additions would facilitate the general use of this extensive system for adult learner assessment and strengthen the program links among placement, instruction, and assessment.

REVIEWER'S REFERENCE

American Educational Research Association, American Psychological Association, & National Council on Measurement in Education. (1985). *Standards for educational and psychological testing.* Washington, DC: American Psychological Association, Inc.

Review of the Comprehensive Adult Student Assessment System by WILLIAM D. SCHAFER, Associate Professor of Measurement, Statistics, and Evaluation, University of Maryland at College Park, College Park, MD:

The Comprehensive Adult Student Assessment System (CASAS) consists of several series of tests that can be used to measure fundamental skills adults need to function productively in society. They are appropriate for both native speakers of English and English-as-a-Second-Language examinees. Taken together, over 80 tests using several item formats (selected-response, extended response, and performance assessment) are included in CASAS. Machine scoring and reporting are available and computer versions exist for some of the series of tests.

CASAS is designed to be used as part of an agency's educational program and is targeted to adults functioning at the high school level and below. The tests measure skills included in series of specific curricula that are part of an instructional package that also includes instructional materials and competency descriptions. Training in the use of CASAS is available in three phases: initial implementation, technical assistance, and ongoing program development. Agencies must engage in training as a precondition to using the CASAS tests.

The tests assess skills that are tied to the U.S. Department of Labor's Secretary's Commission on Achieving Necessary Skills (SCANS) competencies. Tests in a given series are equated. Results are scaled to a mean of 200 and range from 150 to 250 on a latent ability scale estimated using the Rasch (one-parameter logistic) model. As a point of reference, students scoring at least 225 are viewed as able to study a high school curriculum and perhaps transition to post-secondary programs.

The CASAS tests are designed to be used to place students into programs, to monitor progress, and to certify program completion. Special tests exist for developmentally disabled students. An attractive feature of CASAS is that each test measures skills in realistic contexts. An adult examinee should be motivated by the test itself to perform well both on the test and in an educational program articulated with it because the items present situations that are commonly encountered in daily living.

Since its inception in 1980, CASAS has become quite popular, having been implemented in 49 states. Data are presented in the technical manual indicating that students who participate in a CASAS program show increased learning, persistence, and goal attainment on CASAS tests. Although these are modest criteria because they extend to neither external measures nor outcomes following program completion, they are important elements in reports agencies must prepare to document effectiveness to funding sources.

Initial item bank development and calibration for the anchor series of life skills tests, which are the foundation of the instruments CASAS uses, was performed with adult basic education, English-as-a-Second-Language, and high school completion populations. The sample was predominantly Hispanic (54%), between the ages of 21 and 30 (40%), and about evenly split between men and women. No data on geographic representation or urbanicity are reported in the technical manual. The item calibration sample sizes ranged from 203 to 1,258 over pairs of forms at each of three levels of difficulty. The items were written by field-based practitioners following training and screening and were pretested in classroom contexts. New item development, item calibration, and equating of test forms is ongoing and involves data generated at sites currently using the CASAS program.

The numbers of items on the six anchor life skills tests range from 31 to 44 and their alpha coefficients range from .81 to .89. Reported in another table are alpha coefficients for language and ethnic subpopulations, which also appear adequate. Some minor numerical discrepancies between these two tables in the technical manual should be resolved. The standard errors of the two intermediate and the two advanced tests are reported by score level and range from just over 10 scaled-score units at the extremes to under 4 near the centers of the test-score ranges. The use of item-response-curve methods and reporting of standard errors by test scores are attractive technical features of CASAS. Unfortunately, similar information about the other content areas and test forms is not included in the technical manual.

Evidence from several sources is presented to support the validity of the CASAS life skills tests. The studies mentioned earlier showing that students who have studied the CASAS competencies perform at higher levels on these tests provide construct-related validity evidence, as do factor analyses that support their unidimensionality and data on parameter invariance that support the application of the Rasch model as appropriate. Use of competencies within a taxonomy of life skills in the areas of basic skills in reading and math, listening comprehension, and life-skill problem solving, judged appropriate and translated into items by adult educators, constitutes content-related evidence. Criterion-related evidence is presented showing that students with increasing CASAS test scores have increasing probabilities of passing GED subtests and that students with increasing degrees of retardation have decreasing mean achievement on the CASAS scale.

Although items were subjected to review by experts for sources of bias, no statistical analyses of differential item or test functioning are presented. Also, other than in the life-skills area, the technical adequacy of the CASAS tests is not documented in the technical manual, nor are procedures used to scale the other series described.

CASAS should be judged as a system, including curriculum and instructional support materials, and not just as a series of tests. Indeed, the tests are neither designed nor used as stand-alone instruments. Ongoing work is being used to improve CASAS and the methods used for the life-skills tests, for which scoring is dichotomous, seem appropriate and well informed by research. Unfortunately, there was no documentation to judge the methods used with extended-response and performance-assessment items, for which scoring is polytomous. It is hoped that, over time, more evidence will become available with which to evaluate the full range of tests in the system.

[31]
Comprehensive Scales of Student Abilities: Quantifying Academic Skills and School-Related Behavior Through the Use of Teacher Judgments.

Purpose: To provide "a quick teacher rating scale of student ability."
Population: Ages 6–0 to 17–0.

Publication Date: 1994.
Acronym: CSSA.
Scores, 9: Verbal Thinking, Speech, Reading, Writing, Handwriting, Mathematics, General Facts, Basic Motor Generalizations, Social Behavior.
Administration: Individual.
Price Data, 1994: $64 per complete kit including 100 profile/record forms and manual (52 pages); $39 per 100 profile/record forms; $27 per manual.
Time: (5–10) minutes.
Authors: Donald D. Hammill and Wayne P. Hresko.
Publisher: PRO-ED, Inc.

Review of the Comprehensive Scales of Student Abilities: Quantifying Academic Skills and School-Related Behavior Through the Use of Teacher Judgments by JENNIFER J. FAGER, Assistant Professor, Education and Professional Development, Western Michigan University, Kalamazoo, MI:

DESCRIPTIVE INFORMATION. The Comprehensive Scales of Student Abilities (CSSA) is designed, according to the authors, to address the needs teachers have for a "quick teacher rating scale of student ability that satisfies the psychometric criteria usually applied to norm-referenced, standardized measures" (p. 2). Thus, the instrument developers created an instrument for the purpose of identifying strengths and weaknesses for intervention, determining specific needs prior to referral for evaluation or services, measuring student abilities for research purposes, aiding in prereferral screening of large groups of students, documenting educational progress, and providing evidence of the need for referral (p. 3).

The CSSA is composed of 68 items that are grouped into nine scales designed after review of "several taxonomies of mental abilities" (p. 2). These scales include: Verbal Thinking, Speech, Reading, Writing, Handwriting, Mathematics, General Facts, Basic Motor Generalizations, and Social Behavior. Descriptions of each scale's intended measurements and the interpretation of low and high scores for each scale are defined in the examiner's manual. Each scale includes between four and eleven 9-point Likert-type items that use a rating system where *poor* is the lowest level and *good* is at the top of the continuum.

The intended population for whom the instrument is designed includes students in the United States between the ages of 6 and 17 in grades 1 through 11. The authors acknowledge that students with cultural differences such as non-English speaking or conditions such as recent family trauma might receive low scores by teachers using the instrument. It is suggested in the examiner's manual that there is a place for this information provided on the Profile/Record Form.

Teachers are to be the only raters in the process, which should take approximately 10 minutes as suggested by the instrument developers. When completing the CSSA, teachers are to respond to all of the 68 items, which will provide an overall picture of the student in relation to his or her peers. When this reviewer examined each of the 68 items it was noted that nearly half appear inappropriate for students at all levels. For example, one statement addresses the student's ability to read fluently. Some first graders of average ability may not have learned to decode words let alone read fluently. In addition, current secondary school structures also interfere with teachers' ability to complete each item with appropriate knowledge. The General Facts Scale purports to measure "knowledge of science, social studies, and everyday facts that are usually taught in a school's general curriculum" (p. 15). A high school biology teacher may have difficulty responding to the statement that addresses social studies knowledge. Teachers in self-contained classrooms would be far better equipped to respond accurately to all 68 items.

Although teachers are to be the sole raters, they can, however, solicit the assistance of others to help score and interpret the results. Many teachers are unfamiliar or uncomfortable with the measurement practices that are necessary to interpret scores and convey results to parents and other interested parties (Plake, Impara, & Fager, 1993). If a teacher is going to use the CSSA for the purposes outlined, that teacher should understand the usefulness of the information as well as the potential misuses of such data. The CSSA is to be administered on a student-by-student basis only when a need has been identified. The teachers using the CSSA should be familiar with the instrument and able to rate a student compared to typical performance of the student's peers. Results are reported in terms of raw scores, scale standard scores, and percentile ranks to allow for comparisons to be made with other instruments measuring student ability. The authors suggest the results be treated as a hypothesis that needs to be investigated further rather than as a final analysis of the child's abilities.

SAMPLING AND NORMING PROCEDURES. The instrument developers attended carefully to appropriate norming procedures. Census data from the U.S. 1990 Census were used as criteria to stratify the norm group. The CSSA was normed on a sample representing students across the country and stratified by geographical region, gender, race, residence, and ethnicity.

RELIABILITY AND VALIDITY. Reliability issues are thoroughly addressed in the examiner's manual. The instrument developers used sound theoretical bases when determining reasonable levels of internal consistency. The coefficient alphas for each of the nine scales and for the overall instrument are all over .90 and the *SEM* is small. Interrater reliability issues are also considered and meet statistical standards for instruments designed for individual student decision-making procedures. This reviewer is concerned with the reliability of a few of the scales due to the small number of items included in those scales. The "General Facts" Scale includes six items that are to measure the student's "knowledge of science, social studies, and everyday facts that are usually taught in a school's general curriculum" (p. 15). One would be hard pressed to summarize the general curriculum of a school into six statements. Besides the low number of items addressing broad constructs, the issue of reliability as it relates to individual teachers is of concern. The procedures to ensure that the instrument is administered are useful in increasing its reliability; however, if a teacher does not possess the knowledge of a student on each item and has to guess, reliability is reduced.

Appropriate attention was given to issues of validity. Content, criterion, and construct validity were examined and meet standards set in the measurement field. The constructs that serve as the foundation for the nine scales come from an examination of the literature on developmentally appropriate levels of ability for children ages 6 years through 17 years 11 months. Concerns of this reviewer are in the content of the items and how they parallel the curriculum practices of school districts. A student may receive a low score on the mathematics scale because he or she has not been introduced to the math concepts necessary to demonstrate the ability being assessed.

Beyond the concerns and cautions expressed earlier in this review it should be noted that the overall CSSA is constructed in a usable fashion. Unfortunately, many issues related to appropriateness of items for all levels, teachers' abilities to accurately report and use the results, and low numbers of items used to measure broad constructs could interfere with the use of this instrument. The authors suggested that teachers expressed a need for this type of instrument. If it is used as a stand-alone document, decisions regarding a student's placement could be inaccurately made. Although the reliability and validity data are impressive, it should be noted that all items may not apply to all students being evaluated. Students could benefit from the results as long as it is used as intended by the instrument developers. If not, it may be used as a device for labeling students without providing supportive evidence or the assistance necessary to overcome the deficiencies identified.

REVIEWER'S REFERENCE

Plake, B. S., Impara, J. C., & Fager, J. J. (1993). Assessment competencies of teachers: A national survey. *Educational Measurement: Issues and Practice, 12*(4), 10–12.

Review of the Comprehensive Scales of Student Abilities: Quantifying Academic Skills and School-Related Behavior Through the Use of Teacher Judgments by BLAINE R. WORTHEN, Professor, and XITAO FAN, Assistant Professor, Department of Psychology, Utah State University, Logan, UT:

The Comprehensive Scales of Student Abilities (CSSA) is an individually administered and norm-referenced rating instrument consisting of "objective rating scales ... designed to help quantify teacher judgments about student competencies in a variety of abilities manifested in academic settings" (examiner's manual, p. 1). Teachers using the CSSA rate each student's abilities in nine school-related areas: Verbal Thinking, Speech, Reading, Writing, Handwriting, Mathematics, General Facts, Basic Motor Generalizations, and Social Behaviors. The CSSA is intended for obtaining teachers' ratings of students of 6 to 17 years of age (grades 1 through 11).

The purposes of the CSSA are: (a) to identify strengths and weaknesses for intervention; (b) to determine specific needs prior to referral for evaluation or services; (c) to serve as a measurement device in research studies; (d) to be used as a tool in the prereferral screening of large groups of students; (e) to assist in documenting educational progress; and (f) to be used as evidence of the need for referral. The CSSA is intended to serve as a quick rating instrument of student abilities that satisfies psychometric criteria typically required of norm-referenced, standardized measures, so that the potential of such teacher perceptions can be fully tapped for the six purposes listed above.

TEST CONTENT AND ADMINISTRATION. The CSSA includes an examiner's manual and individual Profile/Record Form. Each form is used to record a teacher's ratings of a student on a total of 68 items intended, collectively, to cover the nine areas noted above. The number of items for each of the nine scales ranges from 4 to 11. As specified in the manual, the raters should be classroom teachers who have intimate knowledge about the student(s) to be rated. Each individual item is rated on a 9-point Likert-type rating scale ranging from *Poor* to *Good*, with the mid-point (5) indicating *Average*.

Nine scale scores are generated for each student; the instrument does not have a total score. The nine scales are standardized with means of 100 and standard deviation of 15. The raw score on a scale is the simple arithmetic sum of the scores of the items for that particular scale, and such raw scores can easily be transformed to both standard and percentile scores using the tables provided in the examiner's manual. The Profile/Record Form layout is such that it is easy to score items and to add item scores into scale scores.

The administration of the instrument appears to be reasonably straightforward and efficient; the examiner's manual states that a teacher can rate each student on all 68 items in about 10 minutes. The front page of the Profile/Record Form provides a section for a summary of the results in transformed scores (standard scores and percentile ranking), and another section for a Diagnostic Profile, which provides a visual display of a student's standing in the nine areas assessed. In general, the Profile/Record Form is well designed, making the administration of the instrument easy and clear.

Some items seem likely to trouble the thoughtful rater. For example, Item 36 gives "physical strength" as its descriptor, but adds "(can compete with other children in sports and play)" as further descriptive information intended to provide clarity for the rater. The rater who recognizes that flexibility, speed, and skill have more to do with success in most sports than does strength, per se, is left to wonder whether to rate Johnny's *strength* (as in weight lifting or shot put) or *competitive* success in sports (which may have more to do with agility). Other items are vague (#29), contain editorial errors (#33 and #34), or raise questions as to what basis the teacher has for rating (e.g., Item 56, intended to rate the student's "ability to think without words").

TECHNICAL CONSIDERATIONS. The rationale for developing the CSSA appears to be sound. The examiner's manual provides adequate information about instrument scoring and interpretation on the scale scores. The authors' cautionary notes concerning the correct interpretation of CSSA scores are especially appropriate for CSSA users with little or no training in educational and psychological measurement. Users are reminded about (a) noncomparability of raw scores from different scales, (b) difficulties in interpreting percentile scores, (c) the limitations and tentativeness of CSSA scores, and (d) the inability to infer causation or diagnosis from CSSA scores. Indeed, the presentation of information in the examiner's manual is relevant, accurate, well documented, and possesses a degree of clarity and completeness not seen in most test manuals. Technical issues are explained clearly in terms likely to be understood by most users.

NORMS. Normed on a sample of nearly 2,500 students from 33 states, the normative process seems to be well established for students. The characteristics of the normative sample relative to race/ethnicity, gender, urban-rural residence, and geographical region are reasonably representative of those characteristics in the intended population, as reflected in U.S. Census Bureau data. The raters, however, may be less representative of teachers at large, because (a) bias due to volunteerism may exist (370 of the 4,000 contacted volunteered to rate students in the norming process), and (b) an unspecified number of undescribed "professional colleagues" of the CSSA authors rated students "in their geographic area" (p. 19), yielding ratings of 521 students in the normative sample whose scores

may be suspect because they apparently were generated by those lacking the intimate and extensive knowledge of the students necessary to provide valid ratings.

RELIABILITY. Three types of reliability estimates are provided: test-retest, interrater reliability, and internal consistency (Cronbach's coefficient alpha), with the accompanying standard error of measurement (*SEM*) estimates for each scale.

The internal consistency estimates are impressively high, ranging from .88 to .99 for different age groups on different scales. This degree of consistency among CSSA items appears to be sufficient to warrant their use in making decisions about students.

Test-retest reliability estimates, with intervals from 14 to 21 days between administration, are also very high, ranging from .86 to .95. These reliability estimates, however, were derived on a much smaller sample (75 subjects from 7 to 17 years old) from only one private school. This sampling limitation reduces the generalizability of such reliability estimates.

Interrater reliability estimates for the CSSA are also extremely high for such a rating scale, ranging from .92 to .97. Due to the subjective nature of rating, interrater reliability is an important type of reliability estimate for the CSSA. Unfortunately, the interrater reliability estimates are by far the least trustworthy of all reliability estimates provided for the CSSA. This is so because the sample on which interrater reliability was estimated only consisted of 25 students *with learning disabilities*, ages 13–15, drawn from one private school in Texas. This severely limits any claims about the generalizability of interrater reliability estimates for the general student population.

The manual advises users to average the three types of reliability estimates (internal consistency, test-retest, and interrater) to obtain an overall estimate of the CSSA's reliability. The logic underlying this advice is flawed, however. As Anastasi (1988, pp. 126–127) has explained, the three types of reliability estimates relate to three different error sources, each independent of the other two. As such, they should not be averaged. Instead, to obtain an estimate for true score variance (reliability), which is stable over time (test-retest), consistent over items (internal consistency), and free from interscorer difference (interrater), these three sources of error should be additive, rather than being averaged.

VALIDITY. Three types of validity evidence are presented in the examiner's manual: content-related validation, criterion-related validation, and construct validation. The authors correctly point out that (a) validity is related to test use and test score interpretation, not to the test itself; and (b) as a process of evidence accumulation, validity is not dichotomous (i.e., it is not a matter of being valid or invalid, but rather, it is a matter of degree).

Several types of evidence related to content validation are presented: (a) previous empirical evidence about the relationship between teacher rating and other types of assessment results (e.g., standardized tests); (b) the use of an established taxonomy to guide the development of scale categories; and (c) use of accepted item selection procedures in decisions about item inclusion. Of the three types of evidence presented, the first two are both relevant and appear to be adequate. The authors should be commended for the extensive research related to the first type of evidence. However, the careful and accurate coverage typical of the examiner's manual is lacking in this section, as evidenced by an erroneous reference to the National Council on Measurement in Education (NCME) as the "National Council for Mathematics Education" (p. 27).

A greater concern is the reported use of the "point-biserial correlation technique" (p. 31) to obtain the item discrimination coefficients (correlation of each item score with the total raw score for the scale) when, in fact the items are not dichotomously scored. Our assumption that these are actually mislabeled Pearson product-moment correlations is supported by their magnitude; of 117 median item discrimination coefficients reported, 64 range between .90 and .96, 48 fall between .80 and .89, and the remaining 3 are .75, .76, and .76. It would be difficult to obtain such high correlations with the attenuation the point-biserial imposes on one variable (being dichotomous). Further, inclusion of items with such high item discrimination coefficients violates the test authors' selection criterion that "the magnitude of the coefficients had to be between .30 and .80" (manual, p. 31); 112 of the 117 coefficients fall

above the suggested cutoff of .80. Discrimination indices of such magnitudes are not only rather rare (at least in our experience), but also perplexing. Statistically, if an item correlates .95 with a scale, the item and the scale are essentially providing the same information. Then why use the scale, because using only the item essentially provides the same information much more efficiently?

Criterion-related validity evidence is very important for a rating scale such as the CSSA because subjective ratings of students' abilities in areas such as Reading, Mathematics, or Verbal Thinking are more indirect than administering established ability tests in these areas. Thus, the validity of CSSA ratings must be established by demonstrating that this indirect mode of assessment is closely related to the more direct, traditional modes of assessing student abilities in these areas. And here the evidence presented in the examiner's manual is not convincing. Although the CSSA scale scores were correlated with subtest scores on five existing instruments, the relatively small sample sizes (ranging from 31 to 72) were drawn from the same one-school sample of *learning disabled* students cited earlier as inadequate for establishing the CSSA's interrater reliability. Claiming that results obtained with such a special sample provide any evidence of the CSSA's criterion-related validity with the general student population is simply untenable. Moreover, some of the intercorrelations of CSSA scales with the subtests in the criterion measures do little to strengthen the claims of criterion-related validity. For example, the mathematics subtest of the Diagnostic Achievement Test for Adolescents correlates nearly as well with the CSSA Writing scale (.60) as with the CSSA Math scale (.67). The Test of Adolescent Language "Speaking" subtest is equally correlated with the CSSA Speech scale (.44) and Reading scale (.43), and its Writing subtest correlates less with CSSA's Writing scale (.70) than with CSSA's Math (.83) and Reading (.90) scales.

Several types of construct validity evidence are presented: exploratory factor analysis results, intercorrelations of CSSA scales, correlations of CSSA scales with intelligence tests, and comparison of CSSA scale scores across several groups classified with varying forms of exceptionality. Overall, the construct validation process is well conceived but, unfortunately, the actual data presented do not provide a convincing case for the construct validity of the CSSA's scales.

First, the factor analysis results are equivocal. It is unclear how items are classified into different scales because nine items are placed in scales on which they have equal or lower factor loadings than they do on other scales. For example, Item 56 loads .79 on the General Facts Scale but only .68 on the Math Scale in which it is placed. Item 46 is placed on the Handwriting Scale with a loading of .70, but loaded higher on four other factors (.75, .76, .80, and .92). Apparently some other rationale for placing items on scales occasionally overrode the factor analysis.

Second, the intercorrelations among the nine CSSA scales are so high (.54–.95, with nearly half above .80) as to cast doubt on the claim that the nine scales are measuring *different* constructs. The CSSA manual indicates that the relationship among all nine scales was unexpected, hypothesizing that this overlap may be attributable to teachers' ratings of student abilities being global and holistic. To test this, the present authors conducted a factor analysis (principal component as the factor extraction method) using the intercorrelation matrix presented in the manual. Even applying liberally the accepted criteria for extracting factors, only one factor emerged, and it accounts for 82% of the total variance. Such a potent general factor suggests that the nine scales are measuring something *in common* rather than measuring *different* constructs.

A third source of proffered validity evidence is the relationship between CSSA scales and those of the Wechsler Intelligence Scale for Children—Revised (WISC-R). Again, the evidence appears to be weak. For example, the CSSA Verbal Thinking and Reading scales have lower correlations with the WISC-R Verbal Scale (.32 and .33) than does the CSSA Math Scale (.51), whereas the opposite would be expected. This sample was restricted to students classified by Texas as having learning disabilities, thus further limiting the usefulness of these data.

A final well-conceived effort to establish construct validity is determining whether or not the instrument can successfully differentiate between or among groups of students who have already been identified (by some other means) as possessing different levels of the specific school-related abilities tapped by the CSSA. But for this purpose, only students with various types of *learning disabilities* or other types of impairment were used. Comparisons that also included students with normal and high abilities would be much more meaningful. In the absence of such comparisons, the mean scores of students with *learning disabilities* appear to be too high (most within one standard deviation of the mean) to warrant their being identified as students with serious problems. If the CSSA cannot reliably identify students already classified as *learning disabled*, it is unclear how low a student's ability must be before it is flagged by the CSSA.

SUMMARY. The CSSA has a clear rationale for its development and application. The administration, scoring, and interpretation aspects of the instrument are clearly explained and easy to implement. The norming procedures appear to have been appropriately carried out in a psychometrically sound fashion. Internal consistency reliability data are adequate, test-retest reliability estimates are equivocal, and interrater reliability data are unconvincing. The "Achilles' heel" of the CSSA, however, is its weak evidence of validity. Although some aspects of content validity evidence appear to be reasonable, the evidence of criterion-related and construct validity is unconvincing.

In spite of these shortcomings, the CSSA may be useful for "low-stakes" assessment situations, such as for exploratory research and initial rough screening of students. The shortcomings of the CSSA, especially those related to validity, should be addressed; if its inadequacies are corrected, the CSSA should prove to be useful in the various situations envisioned by its authors, who have noted that, "Further data gathered from varied samples of students throughout the country would add significantly to assumptions pertaining to the test's usefulness" (examiner's manual, p. 37). Until that happens, however, the CSSA must be considered as purely an experimental measure.

REVIEWER'S REFERENCE

Anastasi, A. (1988). *Psychological testing* (6th ed.). New York: Macmillan.

[32]

Developmental Challenge Profile: Learning from Job Experiences.

Purpose: "Designed to encourage managers and executives to think about their jobs from a developmental perspective."

Population: Managers.

Publication Date: 1993.

Scores: 16 developmental components: Transitions (Unfamiliar Responsibilities, Proving Yourself), Creating Change (Developing New Directions, Inherited Problems, Reduction Decisions, Problems with Employees), High Level of Responsibility (High Stakes, Managing Business Diversity, Job Overload, Handling External Pressure), Non-authority Relationships (Influencing Without Authority), Obstacles (Adverse Business Conditions, Lack of Top Management Support, Lack of Personal Support, Difficult Boss), Support (Supportive Boss).

Administration: Individual or group.

Price Data, 1993: $20 per profile.

Time: Administration time not reported.

Comments: Used in conjunction with BENCHMARKS (12:50) which assesses managerial strengths and weaknesses.

Authors: Patricia J. Ohlott, Cynthia D. McCauley, and Marian N. Ruderman.

Publisher: Center for Creative Leadership.

TEST REFERENCES

1. McCauley, C. D., Ruderman, M. N., Ohlott, P. J., & Morrow, J. E. (1994). Assessing the developmental components of managerial jobs. *Journal of Applied Psychology, 79,* 544-560.

2. Ohlott, P. J., Ruderman, M. N., & McCauley, C. D. (1994). Gender differences in managers' developmental job experiences. *Academy of Management Journal, 37,* 46–67.

Review of the Developmental Challenge Profile: Learning from Job Experiences by JEAN POWELL KIRNAN, Associate Professor of Psychology, and KRISTEN WOJCIK, Research Assistant, Trenton State College, Trenton, NJ:

The Developmental Challenge Profile (DCP) is a self-development tool aimed at helping managers identify learning and challenging opportunities in their *current* jobs. Thus, the emphasis is on the current job only and not previous positions. Developed by the Center for Creative Leadership (CCL), the DCP is based on the hypothesis that hands-on experiences and challenges provide one of the best methods to learn managerial and organizational skills necessary for effective leadership.

This hypothesis suggests that unlike classroom or assessment center type training, experiential learning has the benefit of a high level of motivation, and immediate and meaningful feedback of one's actions. However, as with any learning experience, the degree to which individual development occurs is dependent not only on the opportunity to learn, but on the capability of the individuals to learn from the situation, their career history, their motivation to learn, and even their personality.

The instrument may be used alone (for individual development and/or as an assessment of organizational opportunities/challenges) or in conjunction with BENCHMARKS (12:50) a CCL product designed to identify managerial practices in "need of attention." A developmental training program is available from the CCL for those human resource professionals interested in using these instruments.

The DCP measures 16 job developmental components grouped into six broad categories: Transitions (changes in job content, status, or location), Creating Change (working in ambiguity to introduce new concepts/operations or revise existing ones), High Levels of Responsibility (increased impact of decisions), Non-Authority Relationships (ability to build relationships with people not under their authority), Obstacles (reduce discomfort from people and business related problems), and Support from immediate boss (receive advice, feedback, recognition, and new opportunities).

The development of both the DCP and BENCHMARKS can be traced back to two studies involving the use of in-depth interviews with successful executives. The initial study consisted of a sample of 86 predominantly male executives, whereas the second study utilized a sample of 76 female executives. The primary topic of discussion in the interview was the identification of critical events that led to lasting change in the way these executives manage and what was learned from these critical experiences.

Teams of researchers worked individually and then in groups to identify themes in the qualitative data. This content analysis resulted in the 16 event types measured by the DCP. The initial generation of types was based on the first sample. The female sample was used to supplement these findings by providing additional items for those developmental components found to be more specific to women. More information on the gender similarities and differences in developmental components might be of interest to some users.

During the in-depth interviews, respondents were also asked to indicate what was learned from these events. This information is used in the DCP report as a method of suggesting what a respondent might learn from their current job.

Both empirical and theoretical criteria were used in the development of the 16 components. Factor analysis, item-total correlations, and a confirmatory analysis with a new sample of managers supported these 16 factors.

The Developmental Challenge Profile is a paper-and-pencil test consisting of three sections. Section I of the reusable questionnaire booklet requests the test taker's name, the date he/she started in the position, and background information on the job. Section II comprises 113 items that represent the 16 individual job components. Section III asks for the respondent's indication of his/her growth while in that position and the job's challenge level.

All responses are recorded on a separate one-page optically scannable answer sheet. Six response options are provided for the respondent to indicate the degree to which each item is characteristic of the job or manager: *not at all descriptive, slightly descriptive, moderately descriptive, quite descriptive, extremely descriptive,* and *cannot answer.*

The items in the profile cover challenges and concerns of the position, the organization, or the individual interspersed among each other. For example, an item like "The business is competitive" might be followed by "You must manage a diverse workforce." It might be less confusing for the respondent if the items were grouped together for clearer meaning.

The Developmental Challenge Profile may be administered on an individual basis or in a group setting (e.g., training programs). The instructions are simple and straightforward. About 20 to 30 minutes are needed to complete the questionnaire. Although not specifically stated in the manual, it would appear the answer sheets are mailed to the publisher for scoring, as a sample score report is provided in the manual.

In the score report, results for each job component are presented as a number ranging from 1 (not descriptive of the job) to 5 (extremely descriptive of the job). These figures are reached by averaging the responses from items on the test that correspond with each job component. There is a corresponding bar chart ranging from low to high for the "relative score." This is the respondent's score relative to that of other managers. For example, if a respondent scored low in the "Job Overload" component, it means that the manager

has less job overload relative to other managers. A separate numerical and relative score is provided for each of the 16 developmental components. No score is reported for a component if an insufficient number of questions were answered.

Also included in the score report are skills that interviewed managers who scored high on the same components learned from experience in their jobs. First, the highest rated components of the respondent are listed, then the skills from other managers. These are well detailed and organized; however, it is unclear which skills match with which component. Several steps are presented to help the individual understand his/her score report. These include discussing goals, scores, and the developmental opportunities in the position.

A norm group for the DCP is used so managers taking the test can compare their scores to a relevant sample. Updated periodically, the sample's last update was in December 1992. The current norm group consists of 1,049 managers of which 68% were male, 26% were female, and 6% did not indicate their sex. In terms of ethnic background, 85% of the norm group were Caucasian, 3% were Black, 2% Hispanic, 1% Asian, 1% American Indian, 1% some other race, and 7% did not respond. The mean age for the sample was 41.59 years.

The reliability of the DCP is reported utilizing both test-retest and internal measures of consistency. Test-retest reliabilities for the 16 components are good ranging from about .78 to .93. Careful readers will note some discrepancies between coefficients in the tables and those reported in the text. The differences are, however, slight. Alpha measures of internal consistency ranged from .52 to .80. The small number of items in some of the components may contribute to these low internal estimates. The publishers have added items in the hope of increasing the coefficients.

By the very nature of what it purports to measure, developmental opportunities in the current job, the DCP is difficult to validate. The publishers have conducted a series of studies where they have compared the DCP with aspects of on-the-job learning and characteristics of the jobs themselves hypothesized to provide different developmental challenges.

The 16 components of the DCP were compared to two measures of learning and development: (a) management responses to a 5-point scale of a global question of how much their current job was contributing to growth as a manager; and (b) an index of learning derived from managers' ratings of the degree to which they are learning 33 different lessons on their current jobs. In the first comparison, 7 of the 16 components were positively correlated, 3 were negatively correlated, and 6 showed no relationship with the overall measure of growth. In the comparison to the learning index, 13 components were positively correlated, 1 was negative, and 2 showed no relationship. It was the less attractive components of Adverse Business Conditions, Lack of Top Management Support, Lack of Personal Support, and Difficult Boss that showed either no relationship or a negative relationship with one or both of the learning measures. For example, individuals identifying a Difficult Boss on the DCP reported less development and learning on the job than those who did not have a difficult boss.

The publishers point out that although these components do not show a relationship with the overall measures, early studies with Benchmarks had tied them to the learning of specific skills. Additionally, they hypothesized that negative experiences may not be realized for their learning value while one is currently experiencing them. It would be interesting to test this hypothesis by reassessing the degree of learning after the negative experience has passed. A later study of stressful aspects of the work situation showed a relationship between these components and harmful stress. These findings support the perceived negative aspects of these four components and call for their continued research as contributors to managerial growth.

The second group of validation studies describes the relationships between the 16 components with job characteristics presumed to be related to these components. For example, individuals reporting a transition of "first time working with top executives" (p. 18) had higher scores on the transition components of Unfamiliar Responsibilities and Proving Yourself than did individuals not experiencing this transition. Further analyses are presented for job characteristics such as organizational level, primary job mission, line versus staff position, and domestic versus foreign operations with similar findings.

The research findings presented would appear to provide support that individuals reporting learning on the job score higher on the job components than those not reporting learning. Additionally, scores on the components tend to increase and decrease with job characteristics in a theoretically expected manner. A study of the DCP in use with Benchmarks would be helpful. A measurement of the individual's weaknesses could be made initially utilizing Benchmarks along with a measure of the job's challenge areas with the DCP. After a specified amount of time on the job, a follow-up administration of Benchmarks could determine if change had occurred in the areas identified by the DCP.

The usefulness of the DCP alone is questionable. What can be gained by knowing the challenges a job offers for development without knowing if the individual needs development in these areas? Additionally, one must ask the question of whether the DCP is comprehensive in its coverage of job components. Are the 16 components equally essential for all jobs and are all essential components included in the DCP? What if one needs development in areas not identified by the DCP?

Improvement to internal consistency is needed and is being pursued by the publishers. Further investigation of the negative components, continuing validation studies of the instrument in-use, and additional information on females and ethnic minorities is recommended with increasing use and larger databases of respondents. The DCP most likely will prove useful to those individuals already involved with BENCHMARKS as it is a natural extension of this measure and program. Its utility as a stand-alone instrument is questionable.

Review of the Developmental Challenge Profile: Learning from Job Experiences by EUGENE P. SHEEHAN, Associate Professor of Psychology, University of Northern Colorado, Greeley, CO:

The premises underlying the Developmental Challenge Profile: Learning from Job Experiences (DCP) are that employees learn from job experiences and that these experiences are most likely to induce learning when the employee is faced with challenging job situations. The purpose of the DCP is to examine components of managerial jobs that enable and foster learning for the job incumbent. To accomplish this, the profile measures opportunities for learning, referred to as the developmental components of jobs.

The DCP was developed from critical incident interviews with 86 executives in which they identified events or episodes that resulted in lasting change in their approach to management. These interviews generated 16 developmental components of jobs clustered into six broad categories (Transitions, Creating Change, High Levels of Responsibility, Non-Authority Relationships, Obstacles, and Support). This clustering is uneven as the number of components in each category varies from one (Support) to four (Creating Change, High Levels of Responsibility, and Obstacles). The profile uses 113 items to assess the 16 developmental components. Respondents indicate on a 5-point scale the degree to which each item is indicative of the job they currently hold. Item distribution across the 16 developmental components varies between 2 and 11.

Managers who complete the DCP receive a summary report that describes the job components. They also receive information on how their scores on each component compare with the scores of other managers in the norm group, along with information on how to interpret their scores. The authors of the DCP suggest three uses for the profile. First, the profile can provide managers with information regarding learning opportunities available in their jobs. Second, it can provide organizations with a profile of the types of development opportunities available throughout the organization and the jobs that contain these opportunities. Third, the profile can be used in combination with BENCHMARKS (12:50), an instrument also developed at the Center for Creative Leadership and designed to assess the strengths and weaknesses of managers. The combination of the two instruments should permit managers to identify whether the opportunities for development in their jobs are compatible with their strengths and weaknesses and their own personal developmental goals. Of course, the identification of learning opportunities does not mean that managers will avail themselves of such opportunities.

The DCP manual contains extensive psychometric data. Procedures used to develop and refine both individual items and the 16 developmental components are appropriate and grounded in psychometric theory. Internal consistencies of the developmental components are generally acceptable, although some give cause for concern. Eleven of the 16 alphas are .70 or higher, whereas 5 are below .67. The lowest alpha (.52) was obtained on the Proving Yourself component. Short-term test-retest reliabilities are good, ranging from .78 to .93, with the majority greater than .80.

Developmental component intercorrelations are presented, and they range from -.44 (Difficulties with Boss and Supportive Boss) to .55 (Problems with Employees and Inherited Problems). Interpretation of such a large correlation matrix (120 correlations) is difficult—data from a factor analysis would have been useful.

The validity evidence for the DCP is most impressive. The authors summarize several studies that provide validity support for the DCP. For example, most of the developmental components have statistically significant correlations with perceptions of on-the-job learning. Additionally, the developmental components behaved in different but predictable ways when compared with measures of work experience or when tested on different groups of managers.

The job components and the individual items demonstrate good face validity as indicators of a job's potential to serve as a learning experience for the employee. For example, one would assume that managers learn when they take on unfamiliar responsibilities or when they encounter and deal with adverse business conditions.

The profile was developed and validated using a sample of 692. Subsamples were used in some of the validation studies. Norms were developed using a sample of 1,049. Inadequate data are provided on these groups. Although age, sex, race, and years of managerial experience are useful descriptors, they are also rather broad. It would also be useful to know more about the type of industry and managerial responsibilities of the individuals around whom the DCP is based. This is especially pertinent in the case of the norm group, about which little descriptive data are provided.

The DCP is attractively designed with clear and easily followed instructions. The manual and trainer's guide is comprehensive, containing in-depth descriptions of the job components, information on development of the profile, psychometric data, a sample DCP summary report with discussion cases and suggestions for helping managers interpret their report, and research references.

Overall, the DCP is an interesting instrument designed to assess the opportunities for development in managerial positions. The profile has an impressive developmental background and solid psychometric support. The combination of the items and the summary report should cause managers to reflect on the learning opportunities available in their position. The psychometric data argue for the validity of the instrument and suggest that the profile will serve its intended purpose.

[33]
Diagnostic Achievement Test for Adolescents, Second Edition.

Purpose: To provide "examiners with an estimate of students' listening and speaking skills and their knowledge of information commonly taught in schools."
Population: Ages 12–0 to 18–11.
Publication Dates: 1986–1993.
Acronym: DATA-2.
Scores, 22: 13 subtest scores (Receptive Vocabulary, Receptive Grammar, Expressive Grammar, Expressive Vocabulary, Word Identification, Reading Comprehension, Spelling, Writing Composition, Math Calculation, Math Problem Solving, Science, Social Studies, Reference Skills) and 9 composite scores (Listening, Speaking, Reading, Writing, Math, Spoken Language, Written Language, Achievement Screener, Total Achievement).
Administration: Individual.
Price Data, 1994: $104 per complete kit including examiner's manual ('93, 73 pages), 25 student response forms, 25 profile/examiner record forms, and a student booklet; $29 per examiner's manual; $18 per 25 student response forms; $39 per 25 profile/examiner record forms; $22 per student booklet; $89 per Macintosh PRO-SCORE; $79 per IBM PRO-SCORE.
Time: (60—120) minutes.
Authors: Phyllis L. Newcomer and Brian R. Bryant.
Publisher: PRO-ED, Inc.
Cross References: For reviews of an earlier edition by Randy W. Kamphaus and James E. Ysseldyke, see 10:92.

TEST REFERENCE
1. Vallicorsa, A. L., & Garriss, E. (1990). Story composition skills of middle-grade students with learning disabilities. *Exceptional Children, 57,* 48-54.

Review of the Diagnostic Achievement Test for Adolescents, Second Edition by JERRILYN V. ANDREWS, Assistant for Assessment and Data Collection, Office of School Administration, Montgomery County Public Schools, Rockville, MD:

The Diagnostic Achievement Test for Adolescents, Second Edition (DATA—2) includes all nine subtests that were part of the first edition of the DATA as well as four new ones: Receptive Vocabulary, Receptive Grammar, Expressive Grammar, and Expressive Vocabulary. The addition of the four subtests is accompanied by the addition of four new composite scores: Listening, Speaking, Spoken Language, and Written Language, added to the original five in DATA. DATA—2 offers considerably broader coverage of skills of interest at the secondary school level than other individually administered achievement tests. With an estimated testing time of only 1 to 2 hours, the DATA—2 provides a wide range of information for a minimal time investment. Like the first edition, the DATA—2 materials are easy to manage, the examiner instructions are clear, and the test itself is easy to administer and score. DATA—2, like the earlier edition, offers raw scores, percentiles, and standard scores for subtests and composites.

Unfortunately, many of the weaknesses found in the original DATA have been carried forward to the second edition. The psychometric properties of the test still do not seem to have been rigorously investigated.

From the manual, it appears the original DATA items and subtests are unaltered and the norms for them are still based on the original, Phase 1, norming sample (1985–86). A second norming group, referred to as Phase 2 (1990–91), was used for the new subtests. It is not clear from the manual whether the Phase 2 norming sample was given the entire DATA—2 or given only the new subtests. Further, it appears that the norms for the new subtests and their associated composite scores are based only on the Phase 2 sample. The manual authors state that the combined Phase 1 and 2 samples include 2,085 students from 19 states; Phase 1 alone contained 1,035 students from 15 states. From that information, it is impossible to tell how many states are represented in Phase 2. The initial list from which both samples were generated was the PRO-ED customer file so it is possible that some students are in both samples. The description of these samples and how they have been used is not adequate.

The authors assert the combined norming sample is a good demographic match to the national school-aged population. The only percentage distributions included in the manual are race (white, black, other), ethnicity (African American,

American Indian, Asian, Hispanic, other), gender, region, age, and residence (rural, urban). These demographic variables have not been cross-tabulated; the user cannot tell, for example, how the percentage of African American males compares to the percent in the school-aged population. Comparing the race and the ethnicity data, it appears the racial category "white" is the summation of the ethnic categories "Hispanic" and "other" and that the racial category "other" is the summation of the ethnic categories "American Indian" and "Asian." The lack of any SES data comparing the norm group to the national population remains a major weakness. Although the test has norms for students through age 18, only 90 18-year-olds are included in the combined norming sample.

The discussion of test reliability in the examiner's manual is brief. The manual does contain coefficient alphas calculated for each of the subtests and for the composite scores; these were based on a random sample of 50 protocols from each age, 12 through 18 years. The coefficients calculated individually for each age for each of the subtests and composites were averaged over all ages; these average alphas all exceed .8, which is commendable. Standard errors of measurement are also presented and appear reasonable. There is no mention, however, of test-retest reliability. The original DATA manual contained some information on test-retest reliability but the results were rather weak. Although the DATA—2 manual contains much of the original psychometric information from the DATA, the test-retest reliability data are no longer included in the manual, and no new data on this have been added.

With the exception of content validity, the validity data are rather weak. Predictive validity has not been examined. Concurrent validity of the DATA—2 was assessed by administering it and the Wide Range Achievement Test—Revised (WRAT—R) to a total of 30 students from Austin, Texas. The ages of the students and dates of testing are not reported. All other data reported regarding concurrent validity are from the original publication of the DATA and do not include the new subtests. Exact correlations are reported only when they are significant. Potential test users should be provided with all correlations. (For a detailed discussion of the weaknesses found in the validation of the DATA, the reader is referred to the reviews by Kamphaus and by Ysseldyke in 10:92.)

The authors provide some very appropriate cautions on interpreting DATA—2 scores. They are to be particularly commended for strongly emphasizing that low scores on the DATA—2 do not mean a student has a learning disability. In their words "Low scores merely mean that a student has had difficulty with the contents of this test" (p. 36). Because individually administered achievement tests are used most often with students who are not experiencing academic success, these warnings are important.

In summary, the DATA—2 has some very strong points compared to other individually administered achievement tests. Most notable are its broad coverage of academic skills taught at the secondary level, the inclusion of subtests assessing listening and speaking skills, reasonable test administration time, and straightforward directions for administration and scoring. Its psychometric properties, however, are not adequately documented. Potential users who plan to use test norms would be well advised to use great caution or administer a test with stronger psychological underpinnings.

Review of the Diagnostic Achievement Test for Adolescents, Second Edition by GERALD E. DeMAURO, Director, Bureau of Assessment, New Jersey State Department of Education, Trenton, NJ:

The Diagnostic Achievement Test for Adolescents, Second Edition (DATA—2) is designed to provide an evaluation of students' listening and speaking skills and knowledge of acquired information. The stated purposes of the DATA—2 are to: Identify students in need of instructional intervention, identify individuals' strengths and weaknesses, document student progress in response to intervention, and serve as a research tool (manual, p. 6).

The DATA—2 is individually administered and takes between 1 and 2 hours to complete, depending upon individual student requirements. Basal and ceiling response patterns for all subtests except Writing Composition and Reference Skills are recommended.

The DATA—2 consists of 10 core and 3 optional subtests, some of which can be combined to yield an additional nine composite scores. The subtests range from having a single essay (Writing

Composition) or 30 short questions (Expressive Grammar) to 45 questions (Word Identification, Math Calculation, Math Problem Solving, Spelling, Science, Social Studies, and Reference Skills). Science, Social Studies, and Reference Skills are optional. Composite scores are Listening (Receptive Vocabulary and Receptive Grammar), Speaking (Expressive Grammar and Expressive Vocabulary), Reading (Word Identification and Reading Comprehension), Writing (Spelling and Writing Composition), Math (Math Calculation and Math Problem Solving), Spoken Language (Listening and Speaking), Written Language (Reading and Writing), Achievement Screener (Word Identification, Math Calculation, and Spelling), and Total Achievement (the 10 required subtests). All DATA—2 items are short answers, with the exception of Writing Composition, and all subtests except Spelling, Writing Composition, Math Calculation, and Math Problem Solving require oral responses.

DEVELOPMENT. The development of the original instrument (DATA) was based on a literature related to a taxonomy of content areas, spoken language, textbook reviews, subject matter vocabulary, spelling software, and a variety of curricular materials.

The original item pool was field tested in 1984 and 1985 among junior and senior high school students in West Virginia. Items were selected that had point biserial values of .3 or higher and reasonable p-values (.15 to .85).

The revised test, DATA—2, was field tested on 150 junior and senior high school students in Austin, Texas, using the same item discrimination and difficulty analyses. Median point biserial values indicate better discrimination among older students and generally high values for all subtests but Receptive Grammar where the median values for 12- and 13-year-olds were less than .30. Receptive Grammar (range = .33 to .44), Expressive Vocabulary (range = .15 to .40), Reading Comprehension (range = .38 to .43), and Social Studies (range = .11 to .49) had the lowest median item p-values across age groups.

STANDARDIZATION. The DATA—2 was standardized using 2,085 students in 19 states in two phases. The samples were chosen from PRO-ED customer files. Phase I occurred in 1985 and 1986 and Phase 2 occurred in 1990 and 1991.

Subtest scores are scaled to have a mean of 10 and a standard deviation of 3. Composite scores are scaled to have a mean of 100 and standard deviation of 15. These composite distributions are given for the numbers of subtests combined rather than for specific subtests. The varying correlations between the subtests would be an important factor for interpreting the standard scores for these composites. Scores for age groups in each half year from 12-0 to 18-11 are represented in the subtests normative tables derived from raw score means and standard deviations and then smoothed for each of the 13 subtests.

RELIABILITY. Cronbach's alpha is used to estimate internal consistency of the subtests of seven age groups, 12 to 18 years. The coefficients range from .76 to .98. Receptive Grammar (.84) has the lowest average coefficient across age groups, and Spelling and Writing Composition (.97) has the highest, using r to z transformations for averaging. Writing Composition uses an analytic method to generate scores on an essay.

CONCURRENT VALIDITY. Scores from the earlier form of DATA—2 were correlated with the Stanford Diagnostic Reading Test ($n = 33$), the Stanford Diagnostic Mathematics Test ($n = 38$), the Iowa Test of Basic Skills ($n = 67$), and the Iowa Test of Educational Development ($n = 96$). There is some evidence of convergence with related measures (e.g., Iowa Test of Basic Skills Spelling correlates well with DATA Spelling, .66).

The DATA—2 concurrent validity is estimated through the correlations of subtest scores with scores of 30 students on the Wide Range Achievement Test—Revised (Jastak & Wilkinson, 1984). Of 66 possible disattenuated correlations, 50 exceeded .35.

CONSTRUCT VALIDITY. DATA scores for 67 students are correlated with scores on the Short Form Test of Academic Aptitude (Sullivan, Clark, & Tiegs, 1974). The coefficients range from .31 (Written Composition) to .58 (Reading Comprehension) for subtests.

Age-standardized DATA scores from 40 students are correlated to scores from the Scholastic Aptitude Scale (Bryant & Newcomer, 1991), the Detroit Tests of Learning Aptitude—3 (Hammill, 1991), and the Test of Nonverbal Intelligence—2 (Brown, Sherbenou, & Johnsen, 1990). The correlations are disattenuated to correct for unreliability. Of 660 correlations, 370 exceed .35.

The authors report results supporting the DATA—2 as an achievement measure in its general correlation to age, high interrelationships among subtests (based on 100 subjects randomly sampled from the normative sample), and relationship to aptitude measures.

DATA—2 scores are also lower for students with learning disabilities, as would be expected of an achievement measure. The authors claim that high item-to-test correlations are evidence of construct validity, although this naturally would depend on the inferences that would be supported by the total test scores.

CONCLUSION. The DATA—2 is an interesting instrument in its attention to individual administration as well as its attention to computation, mechanical, and analytical skills. Clearly, there is a place for an instrument with this focus.

The test would benefit from expansion of the samples on which the validity investigations are based, as well as careful delineation of the inferences permitted by the scores. This is the central validity issue.

Although the convergent properties are well documented, evidence to support the discriminative properties of the subtests would help the interpretation of scores and the rationale for combining some scores with others to yield composites. For example, although Expressive Grammar and Expressive Vocabulary combine to form the Speaking composite, Expressive Vocabulary actually has higher correlations with Receptive Vocabulary, Receptive Grammar, and Reading Comprehension. Attention to these relationships may well recommend different weighting or combining strategies.

Finally, the focus and administrative procedures of this instrument have much to offer. Perhaps item banking strategies would improve its usefulness as a tool that could be used repeatedly. Further work is encouraged.

REVIEWER'S REFERENCES

Sullivan, E. T., Clark, W. W., & Tiegs, E. W. (1974). Short Form Test of Academic Aptitude. Monterey, CA: CTB/McGraw-Hill.

Jastak, S., & Wilkinson, G. S. (1984). Wide Range Achievement Test (revised edition). Wilmington, DE: Jastak Associates.

Brown, L., Sherbenou, R. J., & Johnsen, S. K. (1990). Test of Non-verbal Intelligence: A Language-free Measure of Cognitive Ability (2nd edition). Austin, TX: PRO-ED, Inc.

Bryant, B. R., & Newcomer, P. (1991). Scholastic Aptitude Scale. Boca Raton, FL: Psycho-Educational Services.

Hammill, D. D. (1991). Detroit Tests of Learning Aptitude (3rd edition). Austin, TX: PRO-ED, Inc.

[34]
Drug Use Questionnaire.

Purpose: To assess "potential involvement with drugs."
Population: Clients of addiction treatment.
Publication Date: 1982.
Acronym: DAST-20.
Scores: Total score only.
Administration: Group.
Price Data: Available from publisher.
Foreign Language Edition: Available in French.
Time: (5–10) minutes.
Comments: Self-report inventory; manual is entitled "Directory of Client Outcome Measures for Addiction Treatment Programs"; previously entitled Drug Abuse Screening Test.
Author: Harvey A. Skinner.
Publisher: Addiction Research Foundation [Canada].

Review of the Drug Use Questionnaire by PHILIP ASH, Director, Ash, Blackstone and Cates, Blacksburg, VA:

The Drug Use Questionnaire (DAST-20) is a 20-item yes-no response, single score inventory derived from an earlier 28-item version, the Drug Abuse Screening Test (Skinner, 1982). It should be noted, however, that although the individual copies of the inventory use the title "Drug Use Questionnaire (DAST-20)," in the manual this 20-item inventory is entitled "Drug Abuse Screening Test (DAST)," and nowhere in the nine pages of the manual is the title "Drug Use Questionnaire" used or referred to. A briefer (10-item) version is also said to have been developed, as well as an adolescent version in which the word "work" has been replaced by "school," but no reports have been published on the psychometric properties of these scales.

Modeled after the Michigan Alcoholism Screening Test (MAST; Selzer, 1971), the DAST (and/or DAST-20) is intended to help in evaluating the seriousness of an individual's drug involvement, both for client assessment and in treatment evaluation research. Focusing on features of drug dependence such as inability to stop using drugs, withdrawal symptoms, and "other consequences relating to the use or abuse of prescribed, over-the-counter and illicit drugs" (p. 82), it asks respondents to indicate "whether they have experienced each drug-related problem in the past 12 months" (p. 82).

The manual consists mostly of summaries of research previously reported for the original 28-

item DAST. It should be noted, however, the *Directory of Client Outcome Measures for Addictions Treatment Programs*, in which the manual for the DAST occupies a mere nine pages, contains a rich collection of information about a large number of substance (including alcohol) abuse measures as well as measures in other life areas. The *Directory* is well-worth perusing for its own value.

Reliability and validity data are based primarily upon studies of the original 28-item DAST, but Skinner's (1982) original report also studies the 20-item subset, and found that the two versions were "almost perfectly" (p. 83) correlated ($r = .99$).

Internal consistency estimates for both versions were high. Cronbach alpha estimates for the 28-item DAST were .92 for a sample including both alcohol and drug users, and .95 for the 20-item DAST. For a subsample of drug abusers, alpha = .86 for each version. The number of cases involved is not reported. In another study (Skinner & Goldberg, 1986), for a sample of 105 narcotics users, alpha = .74. No test-retest reliability estimates are reported.

No validity data are presented for the DAST-20 as such. For the original 28-item DAST, correlations of total score with frequency of use of specific drugs varied as follows: cannabis ($r = .55$), barbiturates ($r = .47$), amphetamines ($r = .36$), opiates other than heroin ($r = .35$). In a sample of narcotics users, DAST scores were related to the number of drugs currently used ($r = .29$), cannabis use ($r = .55$), and similar issues ($r = .30$ to .38). Correlations between .74 and .75 were found between DAST scores and DSM-II diagnosis of lifetime and current drug abuse/dependence (Gavin, Ross, & Skinner, 1989). Skinner (1982) found only modest correlations between response bias measures and DAST scores. Scores on the DAST were also found to be correlated positively with measures of impulsive and reckless behaviors ($r = .42$) and deviant attitudes ($r = .54$).

The only "norms" offered include the "average DAST [28-item] score" (p. 86) for four groups: clients with (a) alcohol problems (4.5); (b) drug and alcohol problems (15.2); (c) drug problems only (17.8); and (d) narcotics users seeking treatment (12.8). In none of the reported studies were control (nondrug-user) groups employed.

Two factor analyses yielded disparate results. One principal components analysis (Skinner, 1982)

based upon a sample including both alcohol and drug abusers yielded a "strong" single underlying drug abuse factor. The second study (Skinner & Goldberg, 1986), based upon a sample of narcotics users, yielded five dimensions (factors): drug dependence, social problems, medical problems, polydrug abuse, and previous treatment.

In summary, as a quick and dirty screen of young to middle-aged adults seeking treatment for substance abuse, the Drug Use Questionnaire (DAST-20) may serve a useful purpose in identifying at least the two extremes of minimal users (whose major problem may not be substance abuse) and very heavy users. However, one must retain a measure of skepticism with respect to the stability of data such as validity coefficients when the number of items in the scale to which they are applied has been reduced by almost a third under the scale upon which they were calculated. Even the authors state that it is only highly likely the longer scale statistics apply to the DAST-20. Also, nowhere is the rationale or related data for the deletion of 8 items of the original version given. Finally, the name change from DRUG ABUSE SCREENING TEST to DRUG USE QUESTIONNAIRE on the forms given to examinees is confusing. At the minimum, an independent manual for the 20-item DRUG USE QUESTIONNAIRE would seem to be required to meet the standards for good psychometric practice. Also, validity data and norms specific to the DAST-20 are needed.

For much more comprehensive assessment of *how* and *why* a client appears for substance abuse treatment, much more detailed and sophisticated instruments may be found, such as the Personal Experience Inventory (PEI; T4:1971; Winters and Henly, 1989), the Personal Experience Inventory for Adults (PEI-A; Test 69, this volume; Winters, 1994), the American Drug and Alcohol Survey (Oetting, Beauvais, & Edwards, 1989), and the Drug Use Screening Inventory (Tarter, 1990).

REVIEWER'S REFERENCES

Selzer, M. L. (1971). The Michigan Alcoholism Screening Test: The quest for a new diagnostic instrument. *American Journal of Psychiatry, 127*, 1653–1658.

Skinner, H. A. (1982). The American Drug Abuse Screening Test. *Addictive Behaviors, 7*, 383–371.

Skinner, H. A., & Goldberg, A. E. (1988). Evidence for a drug dependence syndrome among narcotic users. *British Journal of Addiction, 81*, 479–484.

Gavin, D. R., Ross, H. E., & Skinner, H. A. (1989). Diagnostic validity of the Drug Abuse Screening Test in assessment of DSM-III drug disorders. *British Journal of Addiction, 84*, 301–307.

Oetting, E., Beauvais, F., & (1989). The Drug and Alcohol Survey. Fort Collins, CO: Rocky Mountain Behavioral Sciences Institute.

Winters, K. C., & Henly, G. A. (1989). Personal Experience Inventory. Los Angeles: Western Psychological Services.

Tarter, R. E. (1990). Evaluation and treatment of adolescent substance abuse: A decision tree method. *American Journal of Drug and Alcohol Abuse, 16,* 1–46.

Winters, K. C. (1995). Personal Experience Inventory for Adults. Los Angeles: Western Psychological Services.

Review of the Drug Use Questionnaire by JEFFREY S. RAIN, Assistant Professor and Chairman, Industrial/Organizational Psychology Program, School of Psychology, Florida Tech, Melbourne, FL:

The Drug Use Questionnaire (entitled Drug Abuse Screening Test [DAST-20] in the manual) is a 5-minute self-report instrument purported to measure the "seriousness of drug involvement for both clinical case findings during assessment and use in treatment evaluation research" (p. 82). Items cover symptoms of drug dependence and consequences of drug use. Respondents indicate if they agree or disagree with each statement by circling "yes" or "no." The Michigan Alcoholism Screening Test (MAST; Selzer, 1971) formed the basis of the 28-item original DAST, the predecessor of the DAST-20. An adolescent version, a 10-item brief version, and a French version were developed also; however, no data were presented on which they could be reviewed. The DAST-20 is presented as one of the measures in the *Directory of Client Outcome Measures for Addictions Treatment Programs.*

Potential users of self-report measures in general, including the DAST-20, should first take into consideration those conditions under which overall validity is likely to be enhanced. Specific to alcohol and drug self-report measures, the availability of corroborating indices of drug use, the establishment of rapport with the client, the motivation of the client not to distort responses, and the length of time between current use of drugs and the assessment session each could function to reduce the usefulness of the data collected. These factors should still be considered even though research studies, in general, suggest that self-report measures can provide reliable and valid data.

Specific to the self-report issues, responses to some of the items may be dependent on the circumstances under which the DAST-20 is given and may cause a negative reaction by the client. Clients may be voluntary inpatients, court mandated participants, or individuals in crisis. Wording indicating the client's use is "abuse" (Item #3) or asking them to determine certain outcomes as being caused "because of your use of drugs" (Item #11) may provoke a reaction by the client. Clients may not be prepared to describe themselves as having "abused" drugs prior to treatment. Likewise, they may be unwilling to acknowledge the impact of their drug use/abuse on family or work before or during therapy. It should be noted that response bias analyses indicated low to moderate potential bias, though significance levels and sample sizes were not presented.

The reliability and validity data presented for the DAST-20 suggest it has the foundation to be a worthwhile screening or tracking instrument. Most of the concerns raised in reviewing the DAST-20's technical information might be answered if the *Directory of Client Outcome Measures for Addictions Treatment Programs* provided more space and thus more detailed information could have been presented. A test manual following the *Standards for Educational and Psychological Testing* (AERA, APA, & NCME, 1985) should be developed.

Reliability statistics presented were based on an earlier 28-item version of the DAST-20. Internal consistency reliabilities from the 28-item version were .86 or higher, which is very good. The only study reported that used the 20-item version yielded a coefficient alpha of .74, a substantial drop in reliability. The reliability decrease could be explained by the fact that reliability tends to decrease as the number of test items decrease. Extending this relationship, the adequacy of the reliability of the 10-item "brief" DAST must also be questioned.

Further, the level of reliability could be inflated by the number of "no" responses; the average score from the original sample was approximately 9.2, leaving half the items as "no." If "no" responses are interpreted as "not applicable" then the reliability may be in large part based on nonapplicability of an item. Disaggregating reliability by sample population would be instructive. The average score for individuals with only drug problems was 17.8 and may provide a better evaluation of reliability of the whole test.

As with the reliability examples above, validity findings raised further questions. The data suggested the 28-item version possessed elements of criterion-related and construct validity. Data for the DAST-20 were less specific; more of the data were based on the 28-item version. As with the reliability data, reporting significance levels and sample sizes would be helpful. Analyses where sufficient detail was presented indicate that the DAST is able to differentiate between individuals with alcohol only, drug and alcohol, and drug only problems.

A potential strong point of the DAST-20 may be its ability to measure change across time. The time frame may be varied from 6 months, 12 months, to 24 months. Used in this manner, it may provide a quick drug use symptoms and consequences screen on a case-by-case basis. In particular, test-retest reliabilities should be conducted to support this application.

Administration and scoring of the DAST-20 is very simple and straightforward. It is also very inexpensive. Comparison to norms and sample disaggregations was limited to data from three studies totaling 829 subjects.

In short, the DAST-20 has a good beginning and the association with its developmental underpinnings (i.e., MAST). However, more psychometric detail must be presented and additional studies conducted to increase its normative base before more definitive conclusions are drawn. Publication in the *Directory of Client Outcome Measures for Addictions Treatment Programs* may have limited the space to address some of the above issues with available validation studies. Depending on the veracity of the responses required, the DAST-20 should be used in conjunction with other indices and by experienced staff/professionals.

REVIEWER'S REFERENCES

Selzer, M. L. (1971). The Michigan Alcoholism Screening Test: The quest for a new diagnostic instrument. *American Journal of Psychiatry, 127,* 1653–1658.

American Educational Research Association, American Psychological Association, & National Council on Measurement in Education. (1985). *Standards for educational and psychological testing.* Washington, DC: American Psychological Association, Inc.

[35]
Early Language Milestone Scale, Second Edition.

Purpose: To assess speech and language development during infancy and early childhood.
Population: Birth to 36 months.
Publication Dates: 1983–1993.
Acronym: ELM Scale—2.
Scores, 4: Auditory Expressive, Auditory Receptive, Visual, Global Language.
Administration: Individual.
Price Data, 1994: $89 per complete kit including manual ('93, 95 pages), object kit, and 100 records; $29 per manual; $29 per 100 record forms; $34 per object kit.

Time: (1–10) minutes.
Author: James Coplan.
Publisher: PRO-ED, Inc.
Cross References: For a review of an earlier edition by Ruth M. Noyce, see 10:99 (2 references).

Review of the Early Language Milestone Scale, Second Edition by PHILIP BACKLUND, Associate Dean and Professor of Speech Communication, Communication Department, Central Washington University, Ellensburg, WA, and SHERWYN MORREALE, Chair, Center for Excellence in Oral Communication, University of Colorado at Colorado Springs, CO:

The original purpose of the Early Language Milestone (ELM) Scale was to serve as a screening test capable of detecting language-delayed children as early and as rapidly as possible. The scale was developed as a tool for assessing language development from birth to 36 months of age and intelligibility of speech from 18 to 48 months of age. It is not meant to substitute for formal diagnostic assessment of the language-delayed child, but identifies and quantifies language delay in very young children so that these children may receive definitive care as promptly as possible.

The 43-item scale is divided into three categories of skills: Auditory Expressive, Auditory Receptive, and Visual. Each category contains age-related benchmark skills that a child at a particular age normally would be expected to demonstrate. For example, in Auditory Expressive, one behavior called for is the child's ability to express two-word sentences, a behavior normally expected of children aged 20–24 months. Each item can be elicited through one (or more) of three different ways: parental history, direct testing, or incidental observation. Some item responses are obtained only on the basis of history or incidental observation as there would be no reliable method to induce direct response from a very young child. High stimulus items, such as orienting to a bell, are measured only through direct testing. The cutoff point for passing the scale is the age by which 90% of children in the population would be expected to demonstrate the behaviors. Therefore, the ELM Scale-2 identifies the lowest 10% of children with respect to speech and language development. Administration of the scale can be accomplished in 1 to 10 minutes depending on the response of the child and the number of items that need to be administered.

The first edition of this scale was published with a scoring method that required the examiner to determine the child's basal level only by administering items at or slightly below the child's chronological age. The basal score is calculated at the point where the child has three demonstrated appropriate responses on consecutive items. The first edition added a single forced-choice question related to unclear speech, as unclear speech is the most obvious sign of language disability.

The second edition of the scale made minor modifications to the items in the scale to improve accuracy, but the major change was the addition of instructions on how to determine an "optional point" score. The rationale for this change was, in part, due to the utility of describing a child's language in more detail than simply *pass* or *fail*. The author suggests that if the child is at risk developmentally, if the caretaker has specific concerns about the child's language development, or if detailed information is needed to determine eligibility for remedial service, to monitor progress, or for use in research, then a point score is useful. The point score is determined by first calculating the basal score, and then determining the child's ceiling level (three successive failures on consecutive items) in each skill category. Point scores can be converted to percentile values, standard score equivalents, or chronological age equivalents. High-risk children are more appropriately assessed using the point-scoring method. Failing the ELM Scale-2 by the pass/fail method automatically shifts the child from low-risk to high-risk; in such instances, the examiner is encouraged to seek more data.

The manual that comes with the scale is well developed. It includes a brief section on language development, extensive instructions on administering the test including numerous examples of patterns of item scoring at different age levels, and explicit instructions on using item prompts and determining response to prompt. The instructions for use are very clear. The scale can be administered by examiners with varying degrees of knowledge of early language development. The manual also includes an interesting and informative history of the development of the scale together with information on validation and reliability. The appendices include a number of clinical examples that illustrate the use of the scale and conversion scales to determine percentile scores, standard score equivalents, and age equivalents.

The instrument and manual are accompanied by scoring sheets and the necessary items for administering the scale, including a cup, bell, spoon, crayon, and block.

Normative data were originally obtained on the first edition of the scale using 191 pediatric patients from birth to 3 years of age and subsequently validated on several groups of developmentally delayed children. An item related to the intelligibility of speech was added in 1987 using data gathered from a sample of 235 low-risk children based on parental report (Coplan & Gleason, 1988). The point-scoring method was developed during the late 1980s with mean score and percentile distributions published in 1990 (Coplan & Gleason, 1990). The manual includes a description of a series of validation studies that compared ratings on the ELM Scale-2 with similar instruments. These studies support the ELM Scale-2 as a valid and discriminating measure of linguistic development. Reliability studies are also reported using test-retest and interobserver studies. Reported results range from .93 to .99 for interobserver reliability and .74 to .94 for test-retest reliability. The final part of this section of the manual describes the ELM Scale-2 as it fits into the broader conceptual framework of screening and infant developmental testing. This information is useful in understanding how the results are to be interpreted.

The ELM Scale-2 is a unique instrument. It facilitates routine developmental screening of very young children and permits early detection of potential problems. The addition of the point-scoring method increases the instrument's usefulness. The pass/fail method of scoring is most effectively used with low-risk subjects. High-risk, delayed, or research populations are more effectively assessed using the point-scoring method. Based on comparisons with similar instruments, the ELM Scale-2 has been shown to be equivalent to or more discriminating than similar instruments. This instrument fills a need for a discriminating, dependable, screening device that can be used routinely by a range of trained administrators without excessive demands on time or administration.

REVIEWER'S REFERENCES

Coplan, J., & Gleason, J. R. (1988). Unclear speech: Recognition and significance of unintelligible speech in preschool children. *Pediatrics, 82,* 447–452.

Coplan, J., & Gleason, J. R. (1990). Quantifying language development from birth to 3 years using the Early Language Milestone Scale. *Pediatrics, 86,* 963–971.

Review of the Early Language Milestone Scale, Second Edition by BETSY WATERMAN, Assistant Professor, Counseling and Psychological Services Department, State University of New York at Oswego, Oswego, NY:

The Early Language Milestone Scale, Second Edition (ELM Scale—2), was designed to screen for language or speech delays as early as possible in a child's development. It measures language development in infants from birth to 36 months of age and speech development in children from 1 1/2 to 4 years of age. The author suggests that this instrument can be used as part of "well-child care" (p. v), as a screening tool for large groups of children, as a means of identifying children at risk for speech and language delays, and as a research tool. A discussion with the author indicates this measure has been primarily used as a screening tool when working with low or high risk children in medical settings. It takes approximately 1 to 10 minutes to administer the scale.

The ELM Scale—2 has 43 items that are divided into three sections: Auditory Expressive (AE), Auditory Receptive (AR), and Visual (V). The author also identifies seven item clusters: Babbling, Orients to bell, One-step commands, Gesture games, Single words, name and use of objects, and Intelligibility, consisting of from 2 to 4 items each. Items are elicited by direct testing (T), caretaker report (history or H), or direct observation (O). Scoring can be done in either of two ways: a Pass/Fail method or in a point-scoring system. The latter system has been added in the new edition of the ELM Scale. The pass/fail method is intended primarily for screening. The child must pass all three divisions (Auditory Expressive, Auditory Receptive, and Visual) and must not fail any critical items, those items that 90% of children have attained, in order to pass the ELM Scale—2 as a whole.

The point-scoring method is designed for use with children at higher risk for language delays, for obtaining more precise information about the child's abilities, and for use in research. In this method, the child generally receives one point for every item or part of an item that is passed. Raw scores are determined for each division and for the test as a whole and these can be converted to percentiles, standard scores, or age equivalents. The scoring system is based on a hierarchy of skills within clusters

and the passing of an item in the cluster results in the passing of all lower items. Likewise, the failure of an item results in a failure of all higher items.

During the initial construction of the ELM, 57 items were administered to 191 typical children between the ages of 0 and 36 months. Eighty percent of this population were white and 20% were nonwhite. When possible, items were tested by all three methods, parent report, direct observation, and direct testing. When data obtained by the different methods of testing were discrepant from each other, the parent report was used. A logistic model was used to generate curves that were ultimately converted to bar graphs. Intelligibility questions were added in 1987 and normed on 235 low-risk children.

Validation studies of the original version of the ELM were conducted with over 1,500 children and with both high- and low-risk populations. Sensitivity, the proportion of the sample population correctly identified as speech/language delayed when compared with other measures of language, ranged between 83% and 100%. Specificity, the proportion of the sample population correctly identified as typical learners, was reported between 68% and 100% for all populations. Positive Predictive Values, the proportion of subjects identified by the ELM as delayed learners who then showed delays at the time of formal diagnostic testing, were reported between 67% and 95%. Negative Predictive Values, the proportion of children passing the screening test who were actually typical learners, ranged between 95% and 100%. The Bayley Scales of Infant Development (BSID), Stanford-Binet Intelligence Scale (SBIS), Peabody Picture Vocabulary Test—Revised (PPVT—R), Receptive-Expressive Emergent Language Test (REEL), Preschool Language Scale (PLS), Leiter International Performance Scale, Sequenced Inventory of Communication Development (SICD), and Illinois Test of Psycholinguistic Abilities (ITPA) were used as concurrent measures of language abilities in the young subjects in various studies.

The ELM Scale—2 point-scoring system was validated on a sample of 50 low-risk subjects. Concurrent validity, at 30 months of age, with the PPVT—R, and, at 36 months with the SBIS and ITPA ranged from .51 to .66. A test-retest correlation coefficient of .28 was reported between testing at 9 and 18 months.

One hundred subjects (57 male and 43 female) were used as the sample for reliability studies. Seventy-three White, 18 Black, 5 Hispanic, and 4 other or of unknown racial or ethnic background were included. Children at three age levels were included: 0—12 months (*n* = 49), 12–24 months (*n* = 25), and 24–36 months (*n* = 26). Interobserver reliability was reported at 98% and test-retest reliability (mean interval of 7.4 days) at 96% for the pass/fail method. Interobserver coefficients ranging from .93 to .99 and test-retest reliability ranging from .77 to .94 were reported for the point-scoring method.

The ELM Scale—2 is a quick and easy-to-administer instrument designed to identify young children (between 0 and 36 months) who may be at risk for language or speech impairment. The point-scoring system that has been added appears to enhance the sensitivity of the measure. Validation studies appear adequate although a few mild concerns exist. Although the author indicates that the instrument can be used with children over 36 months of age, no validation or reliability studies have been conducted with this age group. Information about the number of subjects across racial, ethnic, gender, and age variables in the validity samples is also not consistently reported in the manual. As with other instruments that rely heavily on the reporting of parents, findings may be affected by a desire to create a particular image of their child (good or bad) or by inaccurate memory of behaviors. The manual is quite comprehensive and generally "reader friendly" with many examples available to aid the examiner in administration and scoring. Terms such as Sensitivity and Specificity, however, were presented before their definitions, making the validation section somewhat confusing to interpret. The scoring form was not easy to follow with item numbers placed inconsistently in front of, or at the end of, the bar graph. Problems, however, are minor and this instrument appears to be an excellent one for what it is intended—the screening of children for at-risk language and speech development. It appears to be particularly useful with the youngest population of children (0 to 12 months) when compared with other similar instruments.

[36]
Ekwall/Shanker Reading Inventory—Third Edition.
Purpose: "Designed to assess the full range of students' reading abilities."

Population: Grades 1–9.
Publication Dates: 1979–1993.
Acronym: ESRI.
Administration: Individual.
Price Data: Available from publisher.
Authors: Eldon E. Ekwall and James L. Shanker.
Publisher: Allyn and Bacon.

a) GRADED WORD LIST.
Purpose: "To obtain a quick estimate of the student's independent, instructional, and frustration reading levels."
Acronym: GWL.
Scores, 3: Independent Reading Level, Instructional Reading Level, Frustration Level.
Time: (5–10) minutes

b) ORAL AND SILENT READING.
Purpose: To obtain an assessment of the student's independent, instructional, and frustration reading levels in oral and silent reading.
Scores, 3: 3 scores (Independent Reading Level, Instructional Reading Level, Frustration Level) in each of two areas (Oral, Silent Reading).
Time: (10–30) minutes.

c) LISTENING COMPREHENSION.
Purpose: "To obtain the level at which a student can understand material when it is read to him or her."
Score: Listening Comprehension Level.
Time: (5–10) minutes.

d) THE BASIC SIGHT WORDS AND PHRASES TEST.
Purpose: To determine basic sight words and basic sight word phrases that can be recognized and pronounced instantly by the student.
Scores, 2: Basic Sight Words, Basic Sight Phrases.
Time: (5–12) minutes.

e) LETTER KNOWLEDGE.
Purpose: "To determine if the student can associate the letter symbols with the letter names."
Scores, 2: Letters (Auditory), Letters (Visual).
Time: Administration time not reported.

f) PHONICS.
Purpose: "To determine if the student has mastered letter-sound (phonics)."
Scores, 9: Initial Consonants, Initial Blends and Digraphs, Ending Sounds, Vowels, Phonograms, Blending, Substitution, Vowel Pronunciation, Application in Context.
Time: Administration time not reported.

g) STRUCTURAL ANALYSIS.
Purpose: "To determine if the student can use structural analysis skills to aid in decoding unknown words."
Scores, 10: Hearing Word Parts, Inflectional Endings, Prefixes, Suffixes, Compound Words, Affixes,

Syllabication, Application in Context (Part I, Part II, Total).

Time: Administration time not reported.

h) KNOWLEDGE OF CONTRACTIONS TEST.

Purpose: "To determine if the student has knowledge of contractions."

Scores, 3: Number of Words Pronounced, Number of Words Known, Total.

Time: Administration time not reported.

i) EL PASO PHONICS SURVEY.

Purpose: "To determine if the student has the ability to pronounce and blend 90 phonic elements."

Scores, 4: Initial Consonant Sounds; Ending Consonant; Initial Consonant Clusters; Vowels, Vowel Teams, and Special Letter Combinations.

Time: Administration time not reported.

j) QUICK SURVEY WORD LIST.

Purpose: "To determine quickly if the student has mastered phonics and structural analysis."

Score: Comments.

Time: Administration time not reported.

k) READING INTEREST SURVEY.

Purpose: "To assess the student's attitude toward reading and school, areas of reading interest, reading experiences, and conditions affecting reading in the home."

Score: Comments.

Time: Administration time not reported.

Cross References: See T4:872 (3 references); for reviews by Lynn S. Fuchs and Mary Beth Marr of an earlier edition, see 9:380.

TEST REFERENCES

1. Miller, S. D., & Yochum, N. (1991). Asking students about the nature of their reading difficulties. *Journal of Reading Behavior, 23,* 465-485.
2. McCabe, P. P., Margolis, H., & Mackie, B. (1991). The consistency of reading disabled students' instructional levels as determined by the Metropolitan Achievement Test and the Ekwall Informal Reading Inventory. *Reading Research and Instruction, 30*(3), 53-62.

Review of the Ekwall/Shanker Reading Inventory—Third Edition by KORESSA KUTSICK MALCOLM, School Psychologist, Augusta County Public Schools, Fishersville, VA:

The third edition of the Ekwall/Shanker Reading Inventory provides materials and procedures for a very comprehensive assessment of a student's reading skills. The purpose of each of the tests is well defined. Examiners may choose to administer all, or selected, tests from the inventory. Skills that can be evaluated by this instrument include letter identification, various levels of phonetic skills, structural analysis skills, sight word recognition, silent and oral reading levels, reading comprehension, and listening comprehension. A reading interest inventory is also provided that enables examiners to obtain information from subjects regarding their attitudes about reading and learning. Alternate forms of the tests are available, which would allow for the retesting of students in order to monitor their skill progressions with interventions.

The authors provide detailed information regarding the procedures followed to develop this test. They cite some research that guided the test's development and likely used their extensive experiences in various reading clinics as further development support. This experience has enabled the authors to create a set of tests that should address most diagnosticians' needs in their reading assessment endeavors.

Straightforward lists of particular tests and related materials are provided to help potential examiners plan for the assessment of a student. The authors provide clear instructions on the preparation of materials. Advice about caring for frequently used materials is also provided.

Scoring procedures given for the various tests are rather typical of informal reading inventories. Various codes are used to mark errors and difficulties a student exhibits while reading particular passages or word lists. Although detailed instructions for the use of these codes are provided, a good bit of practice would be needed for an examiner to become fluent in their use.

All of the reading materials needed to administer the Ekwall/Shanker Inventory are provided in the manual. Other materials, such as tape recorders and stop watches, are to be supplied by examiners. Most of the reading materials seem appropriate in terms of type size for various reading levels. Some of the materials did appear to be visually cluttered. This might be an issue for individuals who are poor readers. More spacing and better page placement might enhance the appearance of the provided reading materials.

Unlike most informal reading inventories, the authors of this edition of the Ekwall/Shanker Reading Inventory attempt to address statistical properties of their instrument. Some minimal information is provided regarding the reliability of the instrument. One study involving interscorer reliability was reported which had moderately high correlations. Additional research into the reliability and validity of this inventory, as with most informal reading inventories, is greatly needed.

In summary, the Ekwall/Shanker Reading Inventory was found to be one of the more comprehensive, and potentially useful, instruments of its kind. Additional research into the reliability and validity of the tests that comprise this instrument would strengthen its application of placing students into reader categories. As it is presented, this inventory provides users with techniques that elicit comprehensive information regarding an individual's reading skills, such information could guide instructional programs to remediate any identified skill weaknesses.

Review of the Ekwall/Shanker Reading Inventory—Third Edition by BLAINE R. WORTHEN, Professor of Psychology, Utah State University, Logan, UT, and RICHARD R. SUDWEEKS, Associate Professor of Instructional Science, Brigham Young University, Provo, UT:

The Ekwall/Shanker Reading Inventory (ESRI) is an informal reading inventory (Johnson, Kress, & Pikulski, 1987) consisting of 11 tests for use by classroom teachers, reading specialists, and school psychologists in assessing students' reading abilities. One advantage of such inventories is that the student is expected to perform an authentic task: to read to someone else and interpret meaning in context. Another advantage is the opportunity provided to observe directly a student's performance on a varied range of reading tasks in a one-on-one setting. One disadvantage is that the results are dependent upon the examiner's ability to accurately observe, code, and rate the examinee's performance.

TEST CONTENT AND ADMINISTRATION. The core of the ESRI is a series of graded passages, ordered in terms of readability, with a series of comprehension questions accompanying each passage. The student is given a passage and asked to read orally while the teacher or examiner observes the student's performance and records any errors (omissions, insertions, substitutions, mispronunciations, or repetitions). The examiner then asks a series of prescribed questions to assess the student's comprehension. In a similar fashion, other graded passages are used to assess students'

abilities to read silently. The results of both tasks are interpreted by describing the level of passages that the student can read without outside help (the independent level), the level at which they can succeed only with help from the teacher (the instructional level), and the level at which the material becomes too difficult for the student to read (the frustration level). Hence, the results are interpreted descriptively rather than normatively. The listening comprehension level is determined by reading a different set of passages to the student and determining the highest level of passage the student can listen to and successfully answer 70% of the comprehension questions.

The ESRI includes four sets of graded passages. Each set consists of nine passages ordered in difficulty from preprimer through ninth grade levels. Sets A and C are designated for assessing students' abilities to read orally. Sets B and D are designated for assessing their abilities to read silently. The corresponding passages in all four sets are intended to be equivalent in terms of readability and the difficulty of the comprehension questions.

The ESRI also includes a graded word list consisting of 10 words at each level of difficulty from preprimer through ninth grade level. The manual authors advocate using this list to determine an appropriate entry point for a student to start the oral and silent reading passages. They include an important warning that this test by itself is an inadequate measure of a student's reading ability.

The battery also includes eight optional tests for use in diagnosing specific strengths and weaknesses of individual students. Tests 4–9 assess knowledge of sight words and phrases, decoding skills, and phonics skills. Test 10 may be used as a pretest to determine which, if any, of these optional diagnostic tests need to be administered. Test 11 is designed to assess students' reading interests.

INTERPRETATION AND USE. In general, the test manual is well done. It contains helpful directions for administering the various tests plus scoring sheets for recording students' responses. The manual authors identify the various kinds of errors to assess and provide procedures for coding and counting them. Helpful guidelines for interpreting and counting repetitions and meaningful substitutions are included; for example, pauses and self-corrected errors should not be counted.

The table on the scoring sheet for each oral passage is especially helpful. However, the manual authors acknowledge that interpretations are not as algorithmic as these tables imply and that teacher judgment is needed to classify borderline performances. Users must prepare their own flash cards for the Basic Sight Words and Phrases Test. They also must duplicate sufficient copies of the scoring sheets and may choose to use stopwatches and/or tape recorders. Otherwise, all necessary materials are included in the test manual.

Some of the prescribed comprehension questions are erroneously worded or mistyped (e.g., Question 1 in Set 4D and Question 1 in Set 5B). These errors are confusing and misleading.

TECHNICAL CONSIDERATIONS. The Harris-Jacobsen Readability Formula (Harris & Sipay, 1981) was used to establish the readability level for most of the passages. The two main variables in this formula are the number of "hard words" in the passage and the average sentence length. The authors report that both of these variables were adjusted in the passages to obtain the desired level of readability for each grade level. Because readability estimates are not reported for any of the passages, the skeptical user must either personally compute the readability of the various passages or accept the authors' judgment that the passages within each set are appropriately scaled and that corresponding passages across sets are equivalent.

The most serious weakness of the ESRI is the absence of empirical evidence of validity. Another serious weakness is the narrow definition of comprehension represented by the questions posed to the students. Comprehension is more than the ability to answer questions. Asking students to retell or summarize what they have read would provide a more insightful view of how they constructed and organized meaning. It would also provide a more direct assessment of the student's ability to comprehend the meaning of the passage as a whole.

Except at the preprimer level, each graded passage is accompanied by 10 comprehension questions. Generally, one question corresponds to each sentence in the passage. In all passages above the second grade level, the question set includes one about vocabulary and one intended to assess students' abilities to draw defensible inferences. The other 8 are factual questions designed to assess

literal recognition or recall. No attempt is made to assess students' understanding of the main idea, and the inferences that are tested are very simple.

Unless the correct answers to the questions are dependent upon having read the passage, there is no assurance that the questions assess comprehension rather than background knowledge. Inspection of the passages at Levels 4 and 5 led us to conclude that at least 3 of the 10 questions for each passage were not passage dependent. Many vocabulary questions (e.g., "What is a herd?" [Set 5A] and "What does the word 'survive' mean?" [Set 4C]) are not passage dependent.

The only reliability estimates reported are the results of one "preliminary study" involving 40 students from grades 1 through 9. Half of the students received the A and B forms first, and then received the C and D forms several days later. The other half received the same forms in the reverse sequence. The reported reliability coefficients were .82 for the oral forms (A and C) and .79 for the silent forms (B and D).

Because one examiner administered all four forms to students in grades 1 through 4, and another examiner administered the forms to students in grades 5 through 9, the authors claim that the reported correlation coefficients are measures of "intrascorer reliability." However, this claim overlooks the fact that differences between the raters are confounded with differences in the forms. Informal reading inventories are dependent upon the observational skills and judgment of the examiners; thus, the question of intrascorer consistency is important, but interscorer consistency also needs to be investigated. A well-designed generalizability study that isolated that main effects due to differences in passages, examiners, and testing occasions and the interactions among these error sources would be much more informative (Shavelson & Webb, 1991). Given the complete lack of validity data and the tentative nature of the reported reliability coefficients, the reliability and validity of the ESRI are not yet established.

SUMMARY. The Ekwall/Shanker Reading Inventory is neither a substantial improvement over the previous editions produced by Ekwall nor over other commercially published informal reading inventories. If a teacher is willing to accept the narrow definition of comprehension represented by the prescribed questions, then this inventory may be useful for obtaining an "informal" assessment of a student's reading level as a basis for making placement and grouping decisions. But we question its use by anyone interested in obtaining a comprehensive diagnosis of a student's reading strengths and weaknesses.

REVIEWER'S REFERENCES

Harris, A. A., & Sipay, E. R. (1981). *How to increase reading ability: A guide to developmental and remedial methods* (7th ed.). New York: David McKay.
Johnson, M. S., Kress, R. A., & Pikulski, J. J. (1987). *Informal reading inventories* (2nd ed.). Newark, DE: International Reading Association.
Shavelson, R. J., & Webb, N. M. (1991). *Generalizability theory: A primer.* Newbury Park, CA: Sage.

[37]
ETS Tests of Applied Literacy Skills.

Purpose: To measure adult literacy.
Population: Adults.
Publication Date: 1991.
Scores, 3: Total score for each of 3 subtests: Quantitative Literacy, Document Literacy, Prose Literacy.
Administration: Group.
Forms, 2: Forms A and B for each test.
Price Data: Available from publisher.
Time: 6(20) minutes for the battery; 2(20) minutes of any one subtest.
Authors: Educational Testing Service, Irwin J. Kirsch (manual), Anne Jungeblut (manual), and Anne Campbell (manual), with contributions from Norman E. Freeberg, Robert J. Mislevy, Donald A. Rock, and Kentaro Yamamoto.
Publisher: Simon & Schuster, Higher Education Group.

Review of the ETS Tests of Applied Literacy Skills by ROGER A. RICHARDS, Adjunct Professor of Communication, Bunker Hill Community College, Boston, MA, and Consultant, Massachusetts Department of Education, Malden, MA:

The ETS Tests of Applied Literacy Skills are presented as "refinements of the instruments used in several large-scale assessments of adult literacy" (manual, p. 1-1)—namely, those of the National Assessment of Education Progress, the Workplace Literacy Assessment project sponsored by the U.S. Department of Labor, and the National Adult Literacy Survey of the National Center for Education Statistics.

Unlike its antecedents, which "were designed to estimate accurately and reliably group distributions of literacy skills," the present tests are "designed to estimate the proficiency levels of individuals" (p. 1-1). A number of specific uses are clearly spelled out:

to assist program providers and staff in estimating the literacy proficiencies of individuals applying for or receiving services; to assist in placing individuals into appropriate existing programs; and to provide a means for assessing learner progress over time. (manual, p. 1-1)

A defining characteristic of the tests is that they combine the competency-based approach and the profile approach to the measurement of literacy. The former represents a departure from school-based content to include "a range of materials more like those that adults typically encounter at home, at work, or while traveling or shopping within their community" (p. 1-4), as emphasized by the word *Applied* in the title. (There is, by the way, no reason why the tests could not be used in a school or college setting to lend a practical tone where it is often badly needed.) The profile approach replaces a single literacy score with scores for "three distinct and important aspects of literacy—prose, document, and quantitative" (p. 1-6), as reflected in the designation of the instrument as *Tests* rather than *Test*.

There are two forms of each of the three tests: Prose Literacy, Document Literacy, and Quantitative Literacy. Each form consists of two 20-minute sections—both of which must be completed—each including 9 to 13 tasks. The Prose forms contain 24 items each; the Document forms, 26; and the Quantitative forms, 23. Although no information is given on the percentage of examinees who actually complete the tests, the time allowances seem generous. The examiner is not required to give all three tests to any given client, but may select the most appropriate.

The tests are a series of simulation tasks, well selected in terms of the structure of stimulus material, the content and/or context represented, and the nature of response required. The stimulus materials are all "real-life" sources such as actual newspaper and magazine articles, voting instructions, maps, tables of data, a routine application, and advertisements, among others. The content of these sources draws on six "adult contexts" (p. 2-1): home and family, health and safety, community and citizenship, consumer economics, work, and leisure and recreation. The response required varies from underlining sentences or graphic elements in text, to writing out answers in provided spaces, to filling out forms.

There are no multiple-choice questions; all are open-ended. Despite this fact, the scoring has straightforward guidelines that can be easily followed by nonprofessional staff members. High interscorer agreement is reported. The standards for acceptable answers are quite liberal; frequently the examinee is required to give only two or three points of five or six covered by the material. In several cases, the scoring instructions even accept an answer if it is underlined in its text instead of being written on the answer page. Clearly the intention is to give credit for what individuals can do, rather than to trip them up on technicalities.

The test content is likely to be interesting and nonintimidating to most examinees. It offers good variety and a quick pace. Because most sources require only two or three tasks to be performed, examinees are not likely to become bogged down on a single passage they find boring or difficult. The format and typography are attractive and clear, making the tests easily accessible to a wide range of examinees.

The directions for administering the test are a model of standardized procedure and of clarity. A well-written, easily understood script appropriate to the population likely to be tested is provided for the test administrator.

There is a marked contrast between the testing materials and parts of the documentation. The manual shifts from lucid exposition for the nontechnical reader to discussion of esoteric statistical theory. There is a shortage of the kinds of information that many test users have come to expect of a publisher. Some of the information is there, but hidden in out-of-the-way places. Useful data are buried in two paragraphs of a section entitled "Assembling the Test Forms," where we're told that:

> traditional item statistics … produced, including the percentage responding correctly to the item, an estimate of how well each task related to the set of tasks in its block, as well as estimates of the internal consistency or reliability of each block. (p. 2-5)

Most of these statistics are not shared with the reader. The examiner whose own literacy skills are well developed will perhaps be startled to learn the average difficulty of the subtests: .65 and .67 for the two Prose forms, .76 and .73 for the

Document forms, and .53 for both forms of Quantitative. Equivalent-forms reliability is estimated at approximately .90 for all tests.

The manual leaves some fundamental questions unanswered. For example, are the tests suitable for the full range of adult clients? We are told that the Tests of Applied Literacy Skills have been linked to the young adult literacy scales of previous tests (p. 5-3). That being the case, are the results meaningful when used with older adults? For that matter, to what population is an individual's performance on these tests being compared? A table entitled "Demographic Characteristics of Respondents Receiving New Tasks and NAEP Tests" (p. 2-4) gives minimal statistics by gender, race/ethnicity, and level of education, but provides no breakdown on the ages of the participants nor other information that would help users to know the kind of population to which their clients are being compared.

The meaning of the scores is obscure. Score conversion tables are provided for each form of each test. Converted scores range variously from 170 to 400 and 160 to 390 for Prose Forms A and B, respectively; 130 to 370 and 120 to 390 for Document Forms A and B, respectively; and 160 to 410 for both Quantitative forms (pp. 3-8 to 3-10). But what does a score of 310, for example, mean? Does it correspond to a particular percentile? We assume that the scoring system is based upon a given mean and given standard deviation. But what are these values? We know only that in the linking process cited above, means and standard deviations for the young adult literacy items were in the range of 282–292 and standard deviations just under 48 (p. 5-3). Are we to infer that the mean of the converted scores is approximately 290 and the standard deviation approximately 48? The tables do not lend themselves to this interpretation. On the Quantitative tests, for example, only 14 of the 156 scores presented on the conversion table would equal or exceed 1 *S.D.* above the mean, whereas 34 scores would fall under 1 *S.D.* below the mean.

The conversion tables are confusing in other ways. To obtain a converted score, we sum the number of right answers on the two sections of the test. On Quantitative Form A, a converted score of 300 corresponds to the following combinations of scores for Sections 1 and 2, respectively: 11+2,

10+3, 9+4, 9+5, 8+6, 8+7, 7+7, 7+8, 6+8, 5+9, 4+9, 3+10, 1+11.   Not understanding how raw scores ranging from 12 to 15 can all receive the same converted score, most test users will regard all this as so much statistical sleight-of-hand. A lengthy section entitled "Interpreting the Scores" contains an excellent account of the mental operations required to perform different kinds of tasks and of the variables that determine the ease or difficulty of any given task, but as an elucidation of the scores for the layperson, it falls short.

No guidance is provided, either, on what range of scores might indicate that an individual does or does not need to enter a literacy program. There are no suggestions concerning what kinds of scores might qualify clients for jobs of various levels and types. And no guidance is given to help users determine what level of improvement in scores following participation in a literacy program is significant. Users are apparently on their own to develop local standards as they gain experience with the tests. Initially, however, they may well be at a loss to know what the performance of their clients means relative to any benchmark or criterion.

The evidence of the tests' validity is limited. The most persuasive form of validity is their obvious face validity. The correlations among the literacy scales range from .59 to .62, thereby supporting the authors' contention that the scores yielded by the test do, in fact, measure different sets of skills. A report of efforts "to minimize construct irrelevant variance" by comparing performance of Whites, Blacks, and Hispanics indicates that the efforts were successful. The manual does not deal with other forms of validity. For example, there are no studies that compare scores on the test with performance on jobs that require various levels of literacy.

The manual displays a kind of split personality, as though it was written by two different people with very different orientations and purposes. Much of it will be of little help to practitioners who do not have a solid background in psychometrics. Few, for example, are likely to be enlightened by such explanations as "a Bayesian posterior distribution of proficiency was calculated using a diffuse prior, taking into account only performance on items they had reached" (p. 5-3). Although such passages are no doubt of interest to the specialist, one wishes that more of the manual

had been devoted to the needs of the nonspecialist. Perhaps the manual could be separated into a user's guide and a psychometric monograph.

The ETS Tests of Applied Literacy Skills appear to be a welcome addition to the tools available for measuring adult literacy in a variety of settings. They are adaptable to needs of individual clients, well constructed, easy to administer, objective to score, and of practical interest to the population for which they were designed. Their use of a profile differentiates among different kinds of literacy needed in the workplace. We look forward to the accumulation and publication of additional information that will permit users to gain a fuller understanding of the data the tests yield.

Review of the ETS Tests of Applied Literacy Skills by HERBERT C. RUDMAN, Emeritus Professor of Measurement and Quantitative Methods, Michigan State University, East Lansing, MI:

The ETS Tests of Applied Literacy Skills are a well-crafted set of tests designed to assess the quality of adult literacy along three dimensions: *Prose* (editorials, news stories, poems and the like); *Document interpretation* (job applications, payroll forms, transportation schedules, maps, tables, indexes, etc.); and *Quantitative knowledge and applications* (balancing a checkbook, figuring an appropriate amount for a tip, completing an order form, deducing the amount of interest from a loan advertisement).

These tests have their roots in several large-scale assessments of adult literacy: the young adult literacy survey published in 1986 by the National Assessment of Educational Progress (NAEP); the National Adult Literacy Survey conducted by the National Center for Educational Statistics for the U.S. Department of Education and the U.S. Department of Labor (1988); and by further investigations by the authors of the present ETS Tests of Applied Literacy Skills (TALS).

The TALS represents one end point on a content continuum that reflects daily situations faced by adults. At the other end of the continuum we would find content normally taught in schools (spelling, vocabulary, reading comprehension, mathematics, English grammar and punctuation, etc.). The authors of the TALS point out that the concept of literacy varies across historical time periods, social settings, levels of technology, and characteristics of adult populations. Just as some would argue that there is no single *g* factor of intelligence so do the studies underlying the TALS suggest that literacy is not a single-factor concept.

TEST CONTENT. The Administration and Scoring Manual that accompanies the ETS Tests of Applied Literacy Skills (TALS) presents an excellent rationale for the content used in Forms A and B of each of the three sets of literacy skills assessed and sets the basis for content and construct validity. The TALS consists of three test booklets. One test assesses Document Literacy, another Prose Literacy, and the third booklet measures Quantitative Literacy. The fundamental principle underlying the measurement of these three types of literacy is that demonstrated performance on any given task (test item) reflects the interactions among the *structure* of the stimulus materials used (e.g., narrative, graph, map, checkbook, and the like), the *context* from which these stimulus materials have been drawn (the workplace, home, the community), and the *nature of the task* or the mental processes that the individual is asked to perform. These interactions in varying forms affect the difficulty of a task and place it on a scale of difficulty in relation to other tasks.

The contexts of the adult tasks sampled for inclusion in the TALS are identified as: (a) home and family, (b) health and safety, (c) community and citizenship, (d) consumer economics, (e) the workplace, and (f) leisure and recreation.

Each of the three test booklets is organized into two sections. The authors caution those administering the tests to adhere strictly to a 20-minute testing period for each section so that all test-takers begin and end each section together. Both sections are to be completed in one sitting. Test administrators are instructed to constantly monitor the tests during these two 20-minute sessions to ensure that all students are working in the same section. If users do not adhere to these time limits, proper interpretation of test results cannot be made.

TECHNICAL ASPECTS. The Tests of Applied Literacy Skills reflect the long history of standardized test development within the Educational Testing Service. Its target populations are clearly defined, samples from these populations are clearly defined, samples from these populations are carefully drawn, and stimulus materials are well matched to the types of literacy measured. As with other ETS standardized tests, field testing included a sensitivity review of symbols, words, and phrases to avoid sexist, racist, or other potentially offensive language.

Item (task) analysis utilized a spiraled matrix sampling procedure that put samples of content from each of the three scales (Prose, Document, and Quantitative Literacy) into six booklets. A random sample was drawn from various adult populations in which the two final forms of the ETS Tests of Applied Literacy Skills could be used. These populations represented "adult basic education, community college, employment service/unemployment insurance, job training, and correctional institution programs" (p. 2-3). The field test was conducted in 30 states across the country and included 106 sites. The field test design that was followed called for testing new tasks written for TALS, as well as tasks previously used in National Assessment of Educational Progress (NAEP) studies. The new tasks were tested on 3,105 adults and the NAEP tasks were tested on 1,421 adults. All told, 4,526 adults were tested.

Up to this point, the tests were constructed in much the same way that standardized tests have been normally developed by test authors and publishers. The scoring of the TALS, however, was a more complex task. Given the nature of the test, scoring was not based on only the correct response, but on three categories: a clearly correct response, an incorrect response, and no response (blank). An answer was identified as a Category 1 if it was clearly correct, a Category 2 if it was incorrect, and a Category 0 if no response was given. The last two categories were used to differentiate between an incorrect response and a nonresponse. Scoring tables were constructed so that a raw score could only be a Category 1 (correct response). The authors assumed that a nonresponse did not necessarily mean that the test taker simply did not know the correct response. Elaborate scoring guides were framed on the basis of approximately 500 responses for each item. The authors warn of overinterpretation if the scoring guides are not carefully followed.

After considerable training within the ETS staff, the raw score results were entered into data files and traditional item statistics were used. These included percent correct (P-value) for each task, estimates of internal consistency (coefficient alpha), and the number of tasks by scale and form. Item statistics for Forms A and B are quite similar. The Prose scale mean difficulty of Form A is .65 and of Form B is .67; both forms have an equal number of items or tasks. The Document scale yields mean P-values of .76 for Form A and .73 for Form B; both forms contain 26 tasks. The Quantitative scale is the most difficult of the three scales with mean difficulty values of .53 for both Forms A and B. Estimated reliability indices for both forms range from a high of .92 to a low of .88.

SUMMARY. The authors of the ETS Tests of Applied Literacy Skills are to be commended for the care taken in the construction of these tests. The administration and scoring manual that accompanies the TALS is a comprehensive document and, on the whole, clearly written and detailed. It offers the reader a clear rationale for the content used and the standardization procedures followed. However, the elaborate and complex scoring guides contained in the manual raise doubt about the value of such guides for interpretation of the test results by users of the TALS.

The scoring of these tests introduces an element of subjectivity among the judges who will determine in which category a response will fall. In addition, judgements must be made by those scoring the test about the test takers' (a) level of knowledge, and (b) his or her proficiency in applying a set of literacy skills to selected materials that come from a variety of contexts. The Administration and Scoring Manual contains numerous tables to aid scorers and users in making these judgements but the tables may, instead, confuse rather than aid.

It is clear to this reviewer that the weakest link in the ETS Tests of Applied Literacy Skills lies not in the tests themselves, but in the scoring and interpretation portion of the Administration and Scoring Manual. Its explanation of scoring procedures to be followed, although detailed, is not helpful for interpreting and using the results. In fact, it adds an element of confusion not seen in other parts of the manual. The problems likely to be encountered by users of the TALS are not uncommon for performance assessment measures. The notion that multiple-choice tests do not yield information from a study of distractors chosen has

increased the use of the analytic and interpretive activities noted in the Administration and Scoring Manual of TALS. If the scoring of the tasks used in the ETS Tests of Literacy Skills have only one correct answer, and if the contents of the stimulus materials are similar to that used in some standardized tests employing multiple-choice formats, and if traditional statistics are used to describe test results, why make scoring and interpretation so complex? If future revisions of the TALS are contemplated, and they should be, some mechanism for interpreting the performance of test takers other than that presently used should be contemplated.

REVIEWER'S REFERENCES

Kirsch, I. S., & Jungeblut, A. (1986). *Literacy: Profiles of America's young adults* (NAEP Report No. 16-PL-02). Princeton, NJ: Educational Testing Service.

U.S. Department of Education, & U.S. Department of Labor. (1988). *The bottom line: Basic skills in the workplace.* Washington, DC: Office of Public Information, Employment and Training Administration.

[38]
Functional Fitness Assessment for Adults over 60 Years.

Purpose: Designed to "assess the functional fitness of adults over 60 years of age."
Population: Adults over age 60.
Publication Date: 1990.
Scores, 7: Body Composition (Body Weight, Standing Height Measurement), Flexibility, Agility/Dynamic Balance, Coordination, Strength, Endurance.
Administration: Group.
Price Data, 1993: $7.50 per manual (24 pages).
Time: Administration time not reported.
Authors: Wayne H. Osness, Marlene Adrian, Bruce Clark, Werner Hoeger, Diane Rabb, and Robert Wiswell.
Publisher: American Alliance for Health, Physical Education, Recreation and Dance.

Review of the Functional Fitness Assessment for Adults Over 60 Years by MATTHEW E. LAMBERT, Research Psychologist, Neurology Research and Education Center, St. Mary Hospital, Lubbock, TX:

The Functional Fitness Assessment for Adults Over 60 Years is a field test designed to assess the functional fitness of adults over 60 years old and developed by a committee of the American Alliance for Health, Physical Education, Recreation and Dance. Items for the assessment were drawn to meet the goals of being able to determine the functional capacity of older adults, establish age- and sex-related norms, publish test procedures and normative data, establish training for professionals completing such assessment, and then disseminate the test for professional use. A three-phase process was used to develop the battery with the first phase focusing on the needs for testing elderly populations. The second phase seeks to establish reliability and validity and the third phase emphasizes dissemination of the test and its results. Several parameters were selected for inclusion in the test: Body Composition, Flexibility, Agility/Dynamic Balance, Coordination, Strength/Endurance, and Endurance. The Body Composition parameter is calculated via the Ponderal Index using the subparameters—body weight and standing height.

The test manual provides detailed instructions for setting up and administering the test items utilizing simple, readily available equipment. Drawings are provided in the manual to help guide equipment setup. Administration of the test items is quite simple and can be easily completed by average elderly individuals. Warm-up activities are suggested prior to administering test items.

The Flexibility parameter is scored by the number of inches reached in each trial, whereas the Agility/Dynamic Balance, Coordination, and Endurance parameters are scored in terms of the time required to complete test trials. The Strength/Endurance parameter is scored for the number of repetitions completed in a 30-second interval. Average score ranges for each parameter are provided in the manual.

The manual includes 16 references related to the test's philosophical and scientific underpinnings. Nevertheless, no data are provided in the manual related to the assessment's reliability or validity. Because of the assessment's nature and nouveau status, adequate reliability and validity data are not fully available. Specific aspects of reliability and validity are available in the professional literature, however. For example, Shaulis, Golding, and Tandy (1994) examined test-retest reliability across three multiple practice sessions over a two-week interval for both men and women. Reliability correlations ranged from .89 to .99 for men and .71 to .98 for women across the five assessment parameters. Similarly, Bravo, Gauthier, Roy, Tessier, Gaulin, Dubois, and Peloquin (1994) assessed reliability and validity for elderly women. Again, test-retest reliability coefficients ranged from .54 to .94 for the five assessment parameters.

Validity analysis for the cardiorespiratory endurance item was conducted by comparing the performances of exercisers and nonexerciser controls. As expected, exercisers performed significantly better than nonexerciser controls, casting support for the validity of the measure. Another analysis utilized factor analyses to develop a composite battery score and the test-retest correlation coefficient was estimated at .81 and was found to have a -.64 correlation with a measure of maximal work capacity. Other reliability and validity data can be found by further review of the literature.

The Functional Fitness Assessment for Adults Over 60 Years offers a unique method for assessing fitness in the ever-growing elderly population. Although many assessment instruments focus on pathological functioning, the fitness assessment emphasizes normal physical functioning. By implication, however, pathological performances can be understood in relation to normal abilities. The only drawback to the assessment at this time is that limited reliability and validity data are available. From a review of the literature, the assessment seems to be still in the second developmental stage, namely development of reliability and validity data. Now needed is a comprehensive reliability and validation study that assesses large groups of elderly men and women from various cultural, social, and economic backgrounds. Obtaining normative data should be a priority so as to advance the assessment to its third developmental phase. Until such data are available, the Functional Fitness Assessment for Adults Over 60 Years remains a research instrument.

REVIEWER'S REFERENCES

Bravo, G., Gauthier, P., Roy, P. M., Tessier, D., Gaulin, P., Dubois, M. F., & Peloquin, L. (1994). The Functional Fitness Assessment Battery: Reliability and validity data for elderly women. *Journal of Aging and Physical Activity, 2,* 67–79

Shaulis, D., Golding, L. A., & Tandy, R. D. (1994). Reliability of the AAHPERD Functional Fitness Assessment across multiple practice sessions in older men and women. *Journal of Aging and Physical Activity, 2,* 273–279.

Review of the Functional Fitness Assessment for Adults Over 60 Years by CECIL R. REYNOLDS, Professor of Educational Psychology & Professor of Neuroscience, Texas A&M University, College Station, TX:

The functional fitness assessment was designed as a field test to assess the functional fitness of adults over 60 years of age and was developed by a committee appointed by the Council on Aging and Adult Development. The manual for the functional fitness assessment clearly designates that it is a test and refers to it as such throughout the manual. A commonsense rationale demonstrating the need for such a test is presented adequately but without references to any literature. A number of cautions therein are also provided related to risk factors (health related) associated with physical activity when evaluating functional fitness of the elderly. The test was designed purposely to allow its administration by "semiskilled professionals" (p. 2) or paraprofessionals without the use of costly laboratory equipment. The manual makes a number of claims as to the usefulness of the functional fitness assessment but these are completely without substantiation in the manual and references in the text of the manual to supportive scientific literature are nil. If the authors did not claim the functional fitness assessment to be a test, it would not be regarded as such by most familiar with the concept of measurement.

The test consists of six distinct sets of items yielding some eight scores. Interpretation of the scores provided is neither reviewed nor substantiated in the manual. The only scores provided are raw scores and no means, standard deviations, or other parameters of the raw score distributions are noted in the manual.

The discussion of reliability and validity from the test manual is, in its entirety, stated on page v. The manual states that the "items are reliable and, in some cases, statistically valid for persons of this age" (p. v). The methods by which such reliability and validity were established are not discussed in the manual. The user is simply presented with claims of reliability and validity with no treatment whatsoever of traditional concepts of reliability and validity as related to the use of measurement devices. The intended interpretations of the test are stated in broad, sweeping terms, once again without any attempt to produce quantitative evidence to support the interpretations so designated.

There is no description of the samples used in pilot testing or in the derivation of any items. The sample size is not discussed and a discussion of error in the measurement process is not presented at any point in the manual. The manual does give the examiner some choice of particular items and instructs the examiner to only administer those items that will yield valid results. This is an appropriate admonition and given the validity data in the manual, certainly argues that no items from the functional fitness assessment should be administered to anyone for any purpose other than to investigate the reliability and validity of this so-called test.

From a psychometric standpoint, the functional fitness assessment is inadequate. There is no recognition of the basic concepts of measurement, not even at the most fundamental levels of reliability, validity, and norming. There is no consideration of potential ethnic or gender bias at any point in the manual. Standard equipment is not provided for the assessment and a considerable amount of equipment is in fact necessary. Examiners are allowed to generate their own materials assuring that administration of the items will not approximate like conditions across examiners. The functional fitness assessment has nothing to recommend it at this stage of development and is likely to result in inappropriate interpretations and potentially harmful recommendations regarding activities for adults over 60 years. Examiners are cautioned strongly not to rely upon information taken from the functional fitness assessment in determining the physical fitness of adults or in making recommendations regarding their activities.

[39]
Hogan Personality Inventory [Revised].

Purpose: Measure of normal personality designed for use in personnel selection, individualized assessment, and career-related decision making.

Population: College students and adults.

Publication Dates: 1985–1995.

Acronym: HPI.

Scores: 7 primary scale scores (Intellectance, Adjustment, Ambition, Sociability, Likeability, Prudence, School Success), 6 occupational scale scores (Service Orientation, Stress Tolerance, Reliability, Clerical Potential, Sales Potential, Managerial Potential), and Validity scale score.

Administration: Group.

Price Data, 1997: $2 per 5 reusable test booklets; $12.50 per 25 answer sheets; $40 per technical manual ('95, 126 pages); $40 per specimen set including manual, sample report, reusable test booklet, and answer sheet; scoring services producing interpretive and/or graphic reports available from publisher ($30 per interpretive Personality Report; $15 per graphic; $15 per data file; $.50 per faculty research; $10 per interpretive report for Occupational Scale and Clerical, Sales, or Managerial Scales; $5 per graphic).

Time: (15–20) minutes.
Authors: Robert Hogan and Joyce Hogan (manual).
Publisher: Hogan Assessment Systems.
Cross References: See T4:1169 (7 references); for reviews of an earlier edition by James J. Hennessy and Rolf A. Peterson, see 10:140.
[Note: These reviews are based on materials received prior to the 1995 Second Edition manual—Ed.]

TEST REFERENCES

1. Hogan, J., & Hogan, R. (1989). How to measure employee reliability. *Journal of Applied Psychology, 74,* 273-279.
2. Mount, M. K., Barrick, M. R., & Strauss, J. P. (1994). Validity of observer ratings of the big five personality factors. *Journal of Applied Psychology, 79,* 272-280.

Review of the Hogan Personality Inventory (Revised) by STEPHEN N. AXFORD, Psychologist, Security Family Treatment Center, Colorado Springs, CO, and University of Phoenix, Southern Colorado Campus, Colorado Springs, CO:

As described by its authors, the Hogan Personality Inventory (HPI) "is a measure of normal personality ... primarily for use in personnel selection, individualized assessment, and career-related decision making" (p. 1, HPI manual). This seems to be an accurate description of the instrument. Examination of the HPI and its manual clearly indicates purpose and design focused on practical use within organizations.

The HPI resembles other objective personality measures such as the Minnesota Multiphasic Personality Inventory—2 (MMPI–2; T4:1645), Millon Clinical Multiaxial Inventory III (MCMI–III), and Personality Assessment Inventory (PAI; 12:290), except that it is intentionally much less clinically oriented. Instead, the HPI caters to business and administrative needs, as reflected in the language and style of writing found in the HPI manual, particularly as related to test results. Also, HPI test items, compared to items from more clinically oriented personality measures, are likely to be more palatable to examinees, as such sensitive issues as sexuality and drug use are omitted. Furthermore, business professionals are likely to find the information provided by the HPI, focusing on "social outcomes" rather than psychopathology, to be more familiar and useful than that provided by perhaps better known objective measures of personality.

Despite its intended use as a measure of "normal personality," the HPI may, nevertheless, also have clinical utility, as seems to be acknowledged by the authors. For example, the School Success scale significantly and positively correlates with the MMPI–2 Pd factor (Psychopathic Deviate). In addition, the HPI Adjustment scale, according to the authors, is sensitive to "neuroticism or negative affectivity" (p. 40, HPI manual). According to the authors, regarding the Adjustment scale, individuals "with scores below the 10th percentile may be candidates for professional assistance" (p. 40). This seems to suggest that the HPI could be used as a screening instrument for mental health referral (i.e., employee assistance programs, private providers). However, additional research (i.e., discriminative validity) would be needed before extending the HPI for this use.

The HPI materials are well written and professional looking. The manual and Interpretive Report (computer generated, not unlike those for the MMPI–2, MCMI–III, and PAI) are very "user friendly" and avoid jargon that might be confusing to individuals with limited background in psychometrics and clinical theory. However, the individual well versed in psychometrics will likely find the attention given by the authors to test construction and validation to be quite adequate. The authors also succinctly but adequately address theoretical and historical issues related to personality assessment in general, underlying constructs, application, and test construction.

The HPI provides seven primary scale scores, six occupational scale scores, and a validity scale score (similar to the MMPI F validity scale) "designed to detect careless or random responding" (p. 12, HPI manual). A positive impression management response set index, the Virtuous HIC (similar to that reported for the PAI) is also provided for the HPI.

Intellectance, Adjustment, Ambition, Sociability, Likeability, Prudence, and School Success comprise the primary scale scores. Although case studies and predictive validity research studies are reviewed by the authors, an essentially ecological or systems approach for interpretation and application of these scales seems advocated by the authors. In other words, the authors seem to emphasize the need for task analysis of specific vocations and careers (job analysis) within particular settings, as this may relate to the HPI personality scales. As noted by the authors, interpretation of scale scores is situation dependent; "sometimes high scores are desirable, sometimes low scores are desirable—

depending on the decision context" (p. 39, HPI manual). The authors also seem to advocate that organizations employ the HPI in their own predictive validation research, which then could be used for selection purposes. To be commended, the authors provide helpful information for conducting such research.

The six Occupational Scales, a useful, innovative, and unique component of the HPI, are designed and validated to predict outcomes "related to the performance requirements that are common to many jobs" (p. 63, HPI manual). These scales include: Service Orientation, Stress Tolerance, Reliability, Clerical Potential, Sales Potential, and Managerial Potential.

Extensive validation research is reported by the authors. The authors specifically address three areas of evidence: correlations with other validated tests, correlations with peer ratings, and correlations with measures of organizational performance. Scales from the following tests were correlated with HPI Scales: Armed Services Vocational Aptitude Battery, PSI Basic Skills Tests for Business, Myers-Briggs Type Indicator, Self-Directed Search, Inventory of Personal Motives, Interpersonal Adjective Scales, Big-Five Factor Markers, Minnesota Multiphasic Personality Inventory–2, and PROFILE.

In general, the validation studies yielded correlations of adequate magnitude and in the direction predicted, supporting the validity of the HPI. In addition, regarding the primary scales, internal consistency reliabilities (Cronbach's coefficient alpha) range between .70 (Likeability) and .89 (Adjustment), employing an N of 960. An average alpha of .80 is reported. With an average of .71, test-retest reliabilities for the primary scales range from .57 (Likeability) to .79 (School Success).

The HPI manual also contains detailed and clear information regarding administration and scoring. Included are instructions on the use of a computer on-line testing service, Keyed Data Entry (available scoring software), optical scanning for personal computer scoring, and mail-in or FAX scoring. Correlations between HPI alternative forms (On-Line, Verbal; Ns of 30 and 34, respectively) scales range from .80 to .92. Instructions for administering the HPI to disabled individuals are also provided.

In summary, the Hogan Personality Inventory appears to be a theoretically sound, carefully conceptualized, and well-validated instrument offering practical utility for organizations. It should appeal particularly to business professionals such as managers or those involved in personnel selection, organizational research, career counseling, and training. Within this context, it has advantages over more traditional objective measures of personality such as the MMPI–2, PAI, and MCMI–III.

Review of the Hogan Personality Inventory (Revised) by STEVEN G. LoBELLO, Associate Professor of Psychology, Auburn University at Montgomery, Montgomery, AL:

The Hogan Personality Inventory (HPI) is a self-report instrument consisting of 206 true-false items that make up seven orthogonal personality scales derived through factor analysis: Adjustment, Ambition, Sociability, Likeability, Prudence, Intellectance, and School Success. Each scale is composed of smaller groups of related items termed Homogeneous Item Composites (HICs). The HICs are recombined to form six occupational scales: Service Orientation, Stress Tolerance, Reliability, Clerical Potential, Sales Potential, and Managerial Potential. The HPI manual authors indicate that item responses give a sample of a person's usual style of self-presentation. Responses to the HPI and other objective inventories are likened to being interviewed. The information revealed in an interview or in responding to personality inventory questions is meant to communicate something about the image usually presented to others.

The HPI can be administered to individuals 16 years of age or older and takes about 20 minutes to complete. Reading level analysis indicates that items require about a fourth grade reading level. Over 11,000 (Ed. note: 30,000 in 1995 manual) people were tested for norm development and the sample fairly represents men and women, as well as people of different racial groups.

The two-sided answer sheet can be optically scanned, or the data may be entered into a personal computer for scoring with appropriate software. Hogan Assessment Systems also provides for scoring by mail or fax, but there are no hand-scoring keys available. In career assessment or personnel selection, the HPI may be administered along with an occupational interest inventory. The Adjustment factor may operate as a screen for individuals with psychiatric problems, who then may be referred for additional assessment. The focus of the HPI, however, is decidedly on the adaptive, positive aspects of personality.

Test-retest reliabilities for the seven personality scales were determined by testing 150 university students with at least a 4-week interval between administrations. These reliability coefficients range from .86 (Adjustment, School Success) to .74 (Prudence) according to one table, though the values reported in the text are different (and lower). Internal consistency for the personality scales, as determined by Cronbach's alpha, range from .89 (Adjustment) to .71 (Likeability). Alpha values for the HICs are generally moderate to strong, though a few are rather low, indicating a lack of homogeneity among content-similar items.

A detailed chapter on Validity documents the relationship between the HPI and other psychological tests such as the Minnesota Multiphasic Personality—2 (MMPI-2), the Myers-Briggs Type Indicator, and the Self-Directed Search. HPI scores were also correlated with peer ratings, which show robust relationships with the personality scales.

Each personality scale is also the subject of a small section describing the results of studies related to their construct validity. For example, a study of service dispatchers is cited, which showed that the Prudence scale correlates -.40 with hours absent and -.24 with error rates.

The discussion of the occupational scales includes a table referencing numerous validation studies that can be found in the literature for three of the scales. The reported coefficients range from moderate to low, though most are in the predicted directions. Even a modest correlation can improve predictability, which may be important if the cost of errors is high. A similar table summarizing validation research on the personality scales would be helpful to anyone wishing to investigate the construct validity of these scales in greater depth.

The manual is generally user friendly, and includes norms, clear directions for administration, interpretive guidelines, and an example of a computer-generated report. Unfortunately, the sample report follows a scale-by-scale approach to interpretation and apparently does not identify some interesting patterns discussed in the manual that require the consideration of multiple scores.

The discussion in the manual strikes me as lacking focus as the authors explain how the test was developed along the lines of socioanalytic theory, how it was modeled on the California Psychological Inventory, and how it relates to the Five-Factor Model of personality. In other parts of the manual, the authors make some ambiguous statements such as: "the HPI is uniquely designed to forecast performance in real world settings" (p. 63). Do they mean to imply that other personality inventories do not strive to accomplish this? Or do they mean the HPI has more research documenting its validity than some other inventories?

In summary, the Hogan Personality Inventory is a valid and reliable test of adaptive and positive personality characteristics that is recommended for use as part of a battery in vocational and personnel selection settings. It may appeal to individuals in these nonclinical settings who want a time-efficient measure of personality, though the absence of hand-scoring keys may be troublesome to those who do not have ready access to computers or fax machines.

[40]
House-Tree-Person and Draw-A-Person as Measures of Abuse in Children: A Quantitative Scoring System.

Purpose: "Developed to assess personality/emotional characteristics of sexually abused children."
Population: Ages 7–12.
Publication Date: 1994.
Acronym: H-T-P/D-A-P.
Scores, 4: Preoccupation with Sexually Relevant Concepts, Aggression and Hostility, Withdrawal and Guarded Accessibility, Alertness for Danger/Suspiciousness and Lack of Trust.
Administration: Individual.
Price Data, 1996: $49 per complete kit including manual (140 pages) and 10 scoring booklets; $29 per 25 scoring booklets; $42 per manual.
Time: Administration time not reported.
Comments: A projective drawing instrument; for related instruments see The Draw-A-Person, Draw A Person: A Quantitative Scoring System, Draw-A-Person Quality Scale, and Draw A Person: Screening Procedure for Emotional Disturbance (T4:813–816).
Author: Valerie Van Hutton.
Publisher: Psychological Assessment Resources, Inc.

TEST REFERENCE
1. Riordan, R. J., & Verdel, A. C. (1991). Evidence of sexual abuse in children's art products. *The School Counselor, 39*, 116–121.

Review of the House-Tree-Person and Draw-A-Person as Measures of Abuse in Children: A Quantitative Scoring System by E. THOMAS DOWD, Professor of Psychology, Kent State University, Kent, OH:

I am not sure if projective tests projectively assess the client variables they purport to measure or the hopes and wishes of their developers. Over the years, they have been quite controversial, with strong supporters on one hand and strong detractors on the other.

The controversy appears to be one of reliability and validity, perhaps more so the latter than the former. The author of this test acknowledges the controversy, without discussing it in any detail, and to her credit has attempted to resolve the controversy by developing a quantitative scoring system for this historic test to assess the potential for sexual abuse in children. Both by developing the quantitative system and by narrowing the focus of investigation, she has advanced the outlook for the continued use of projective tests.

The book is essentially a detailed description of the scoring system used in analyzing children's drawings. It assesses four constructs: Preoccupation with Sexually Relevant Concepts (SRC); Aggression and Hostility (AH); Withdrawal and Guarded Accessibility (WGA); and Alertness for Danger, Suspiciousness, and Lack of Trust (ADST). The rationale for the selection of these constructs has a certain face validity, though it is not explained other than by reference citations. Each of the four areas in turn is divided into additional categories of analysis including Behavioral, General, House, Tree, and Person, which in turn each have specific items for which to look (e.g., elongated feet, omission of arms, door very small). These are summarized in the appendix, along with literature citations from which each was drawn and presumably supported. The majority of the book is taken up with descriptions of each item, with illustrative examples of many. Chapters on interpretation, mostly consisting of two case examples, future directions for research, and normative data, including reliability and validity, complete the book.

Many of the individual items possess a certain face validity. For example, emphasis on bedroom and presence of genitals may suggest sexual abuse, whereas a clenched fist and oversized figure may indicate hostility. But what is one to do with the statement that *both* the drawing of a less mature *and* a more mature figure than the actual child may be taken as a sign of sexual abuse? Likewise, what is the rationale for the item that a door on the side of a building may indicate withdrawal or that a "Picasso" eye (one only) or an emphasis on the outline of eyes may indicate alertness for danger? There may be reasonable explanations in the projective literature but it is not obvious what they are. This is not just churlishness on my part but a question of ultimate validity.

The author compared three samples on the test: a normal sample of 145 children from public school and summer day camp settings, 20 sexually abused children who had documented histories of such by social service agencies, and 20 emotionally disturbed but nonabused children from a special education school. Concerning the normal sample, the author assures the reader that, "There was a high probability or certainty that these children were neither physically or sexually abused nor suffering from an emotional disturbance" (p. 102). No data are presented in support of this assertion, however.

The scoring system appears to have been carefully developed. Items that were confusing to raters or were scored with less that 80% agreement were dropped or reworded. Then, additional ratings on new drawings were conducted and further changes made. Perhaps as a result, the author reports mostly good interrater reliability for the scoring system: .96 for SRC, .97 for AH, .95 for WGA, and .70 for ADST.

Validity, which is entirely discriminant, is documented by the ability of the scoring system to differentiate the three groups. Two methods were used: a two-way ANOVA with group and gender as factors, and an examination of the accuracy of the classification of subjects into groups. Both methods demonstrated that the SRC was able to discriminate between the normal and sexually abused children with a high degree of predictive power. The emotionally disturbed children, especially females, tended to resemble normals. The classification rates for AH and WGA were only slightly better than the base rate, whereas the ADST was unable to differentiate significantly the abused from nonabused children at all. But the validity of the categories and items behind the scale remains undocumented and thus adequate validity can be said to be lacking.

It appears that the specifically constructed SRC scale can be of some assistance in discriminating those children who have been sexually abused from those who have not, though some emotionally disturbed males may resemble the sexually abused. The other scales were of minimal or no use, however. Perhaps the SRC scale can be of use in identifying children who have been abused and have difficulty talking about it. But there does not seem to be much point to administering the complete scale, at least for the purposes of identifying sexual abuse in children.

The author is to be commended in attempting to apply rigorous measurement standards to the fuzzy world of projective tests. In doing so, she has contributed to their increased respectability. But the question of ultimate validity remains.

Review of the House-Tree-Person and Draw-A-Person as Measures of Abuse in Children: A Quantitative Scoring System by HOWARD M. KNOFF, Professor of School Psychology, Department of Psychological Foundations, University of South Florida, Tampa, FL:

The House-Tree-Person and Draw-A-Person as Measures of Abuse in Children: A Quantitative Scoring System is a recent book that, with a supplemental scoring protocol, adapts the traditional House-Tree-Person (HTP) projective drawing technique, pairs it with the Draw-A-Person (DAP) projective drawing technique, and introduces a quantitative scoring system that is designed "for use with children in screening for possible child sexual abuse" (p. 1). Although Van Hutton suggests her scoring system focuses on other more general personality/emotional characteristics that are present in children and adults, this claim is unsubstantiated in that Van Hutton's scoring system was normed only with children between the ages of 7 and 12 years of age. Thus, this review will limit itself to the norming sample described and the resulting psychometric properties of the quantitative system.

As noted, the introduction and other parts of this book suggest that this HTP/DAP scoring system is intended to be used as a supplemental screening tool to help identify victims of sexual abuse and that this system is preliminary and in need of additional research. However, other parts of this book read as if this tool is ready for clinical use and that its psychometric properties and norming processes are sound. For example, the author states that "(t)he present work is designed to provide the diagnostician with an objective, quantifiable scoring system that has a well-grounded theoretical and research base" (p. 2). Unfortunately, neither of these assertions is true. This scale makes numerous, faulty assumptions as to the theoretical and research base that forms the foundation of this system, and there are many significant shortcomings in the system's norming process, its normative data, and in its psychometric properties. In the end, and at most, this system should be used only in research that is geared toward improving and validating the system *itself*. It should *not* be used in research attempting to concurrently validate other abuse-related tools, nor any research focusing on assessment or intervention with abused children. Further, the system definitely is not ready for any clinical use. And, given the validity and utility of projective assessment approaches in general (e.g., Gresham, 1993; Knoff, 1993; Knoff, Batsche, & Carlyon, 1993), perhaps there is little reason to pursue any continued work with this system at all.

Below, the development, the administration, scoring and interpretation, the norming, and the psychometric properties of the HTP/DAP system will be described and critiqued. Although attempting to describe the information and procedures as presented in the book, the critique will draw on related research as well as the principles and practices of sound test development.

UNDERLYING RATIONALE FOR THE DEVELOPMENT OF THE SCORING SYSTEM. According to the author, the HTP/DAP scoring system is based on (a) the premise that, because quantitative scoring systems with projective tests already exist, other systems "are both possible and useful" (p. 10); (b) projective drawing research that focuses specifically on abused children; and (c) other research that has identified other emotional characteristics that may be indicative of child abuse. To expand, the author discusses (chapter 2) the historical use of drawing tests and reviews the few quantitative scoring methods that have previously been developed with projective drawing approaches. Although demonstrating that quantitative scoring systems are possible, the author fails to note that none of these systems have been independently validated, that they are infrequently used, and that they have not focused on specific clinical populations (Knoff, Batsche, & Carlyon, 1993). Thus, there is no evidence that these scoring systems, or any future systems, are useful. The author then describes four studies, each over 10 years old, involving projective assessments with abused children. Significantly, the author does not provide a critical review of the subjects, geographic locations, or methods used in these studies, nor does she critique these studies such that the generalizability of their results can be established. Moreover, although acknowledging the poor technical adequacy of past projective drawing research, the author does not go far enough, failing to cite, for example, analyses (e.g., Knoff, Batsche, & Carlyon, 1993) that show that projective drawing research is largely nonempirical and case study oriented, of questionable methodological and technical integrity, and lacking in convergent and discriminant validity with most clinical populations. In the end, this HTP/DAP system is based primarily on general and specific (relative to abused children) projective assessment studies that cannot be clinically or psychometrically defended.

Finally, this system is based on four characteristics that "may be indicative of child abuse" (p. 99) chosen by the author from a sampling of studies completed with children of abuse. Without describing, critiquing, or validating these characteristics, the author uses these studies to create her system's four interpretive scales: the Preoccupation with Sexually Relevant Concepts (SRC); Aggression and Hostility (AH); Withdrawal and Guarded Accessibility (WGA); and Alertness for Danger, Suspiciousness, and Lack of Trust (ADST) scales. She then organizes numerous projective drawing indicators into these four scales without describing why they were chosen or the criteria used to "load" them onto a specific scale. Although Appendix A in the book provides citations meant to support why the various projective indicators are organized onto each scale, most of these citations involve studies that either are not data-based or have questionable research methodologies (Knoff, Batsche, & Carlyon, 1993).

Ultimately, the final HTP/DAP system presented involves a scoring process whereby House-Tree-Person and Draw-A-Person drawings are qualitatively analyzed across 90 projective indicators that are based on a child's comments and behaviors during the drawing process or on the presence of details in the house, tree, person, or combined drawings, respectively. The indicators are organized onto the four interpretive scales (31 on the Preoccupation with Sexually Relevant Concepts, 28 on the Aggression and Hostility, 21 on the Withdrawal and Guarded Accessibility, and 10 on the Alertness for Danger, Suspiciousness, and Lack of Trust scale), and the total number of indicators on each scale is converted to a percentile score based on the normative sample described. This scoring approach is based on the presence of isolated indicators (rather than clinical behaviors that are empirically correlated with abused children and situations), and it assumes that these indicators have equal impact or weighting relative to predicting abuse and that a total score of indicators has construct, discriminant, and/or convergent validity—psychometric characteristics not demonstrated by the system at this time.

ADMINISTRATION, SCORING, AND INTERPRETATION. Administration directions for this system consist of giving children two blank, unlined pieces of 8.5 x 11-inch paper and a #2 pencil, and asking them to draw a picture of a house, a tree, and a person on the first sheet of paper (the HTP) and a picture of another person on the second sheet of paper. Reportedly, the second human figure drawing is requested to insure that enough details are available for proper interpretation. The examiner then scores the system using the eight-page scoring booklet and the book that provides 59 pages of case study drawings that are supposed to exemplify the qualitative descriptions of the 90 projective indicators. An indicator is scored when it appears in either the HTP or DAP drawing. That is, an indicator need not be present in both drawings. The raw score for each of the four scales represents the total number of indicators present in the drawings. Raw scores then are converted to percentile ranks with normal scores at or below the 84th percentile, borderline scores (indicating a possibility of sexual abuse) between the 84th and 94th percentile, and significant scores (indicating a high probability of sexual abuse) at or above the 95th percentile. Experienced clinicians reportedly were able to score protocols in approximately 4 minutes after practice and training.

By way of critique, the request for a house, tree, and person drawing on one sheet of paper is unusual and different from the typical HTP administration that uses separate pieces of paper. Although the projective drawing interpretive research is already suspect, this creates additional questions as to whether prior projective interpretations from separate HTPs can be generalized to a conjoint HTP. Relative to scoring, the author notes that the clarity and accuracy of the scoring instructions were validated by asking a master's-level clinical psychologist and counselor to independently score 30 children's drawings. Although the interrater agreements for these clinicians were acceptable, the validation of scoring criteria based on only two individuals is highly questionable. Finally, beyond the interpretation problems already noted, the failure to document or demonstrate the discriminant validity for each of the projective indicators calls the entire system into question.

THE NORMING OF THE HTP/DAP SYSTEM. The HTP/DAP system was normed using 145 children (73 males and 72 females), ages 7 through 12, drawn from public school and summer day camp settings in two unnamed metropolitan cities (chapter 5). Critically, other than gender, demographic information relative to ethnicity, socioeconomic status, and other important variables was not included. This sample was contrasted with two additional samples, one with 20 individuals who were sexually abused and another with 20 additional individuals who were emotionally disturbed but nonabused. With the interpretation of this system dependent on the norms developed, the fact that this sample is extremely small, nonrandom, unstratified, and geographically limited is of major concern (even the author noted that "comparisons with this sample should be made with caution"; p. 73). In fact, these sampling weaknesses far outweigh the statistical analyses used to generate the norms reported, rendering these norms and their use meaningless. Further, the two contrasting samples have the same limitations making any suggestion of this system's convergent and/or discriminant validity inappropriate.

Beyond these concerns, the author reported the analyses contrasting the normative sample with the two other samples resulted in significant main effects for the SRC, the AH, and the WGA scales, but not the ADST scale. She then designated the ADST scale a "research scale" (p. 103), but this designation is not found in the Scoring Booklet to prompt clinicians who either miss this brief passage in the book or do not read the book at all.

PSYCHOMETRIC PROPERTIES. Relative to the reliability of the HTP/DAP system, only interrater reliability is considered; other types of reliability, such as test-retest and internal reliability, are not reported. Critically, although the author reports interrater reliability correlations above .90 for SRC, AH, and WGA scales and .70 for the ADST scale, these ratings are based on only two clinicians, a doctoral-level child psychologist with 20 years of experience and a master's-level counselor with 5 years experience, who each scored 41 protocols from the normal, emotionally disturbed, and the sexually abused groups noted above. Clearly, additional research establishing the reliability of this system is needed given the dependence on only two clinicians for its interrater reliability and the absence of other types of reliability data.

Relative to validity, neither construct validity nor concurrent validity were addressed in the book. Significantly, construct validation is especially needed to confirm the four scales of the HTP/DAP system that were selected from the literature by the author. As noted above, one discriminant validity study was reported involving the normative sample and the samples of emotionally disturbed and sexually abused children. Although sample discriminations occurred on the SRC and AH scales and the system's cutoff scores were determined to best discriminate abused versus nonabused children, the limited sample sizes involved in this study (i.e., a clinical sample of only 20 abused children) and the lack of descriptive information about the samples preclude any conclusion that discriminant validity was demonstrated.

CONCLUSIONS. The author correctly states that "conclusions about the likelihood of sexual abuse should never be made based on the results of any one instrument ... Hence, data should be gathered from additional sources, such as clinical interviews, medical examinations, and reports from parents and teachers" (p. 75). Indeed, given the conceptual, empirical, psychometric, and other weaknesses inherent to this system, one must question whether it provides any additional information beyond what can be gathered through these other sources. In summary and because of these weaknesses, it is apparent that the publication of this system was premature. Although significant improvements are needed relative to the system's norms, validity, and reliability, the question still remains as to whether this, or any other, projective instrument—with or without a quantitative scoring approach—can ever be sensitive and efficacious enough to be useful as a diagnostic tool in an area as complex as child abuse.

REVIEWER'S REFERENCES

Gresham, F. M. (1993). "What's wrong with this picture?": Response to Motta et al.'s review of Human Figure Drawings. *School Psychology Quarterly, 8*, 182–188.

Knoff, H. M. (1993). The utility of Human Figure Drawings in personality and intellectual assessment: Why ask why? *School Psychology Quarterly, 8*, 191–196.

Knoff, H. M., Batsche, G. M., & Carlyon, W. (1993). Projective techniques and their utility in child psychotherapy. In T. R. Kratochwill & R. J. Morris (Eds.), *Handbook of psychotherapy with children and adolescents* (pp. 9–37). Hillsdale, NJ: Lawrence Erlbaum Associates.

[41]
IDEA Reading and Writing Proficiency Test.

Purpose: To provide "comprehensive assessment for the initial identification and redesignation of Limited English Proficient (LEP) students."
Population: Grades 2–12.
Publication Dates: 1992–1993.
Acronym: IPT R & W.
Scores, 8: Reading (Vocabulary, Vocabulary in Context, Reading for Understanding, Reading for Life Skills, Language Usage), Writing (Conventions, Write a Story, Write Your Own Story).
Administration: Group.
Levels, 3: Grades 2–3, Grades 4–6, Grades 7–12.
Price Data: Available from publisher.
Foreign Language Editions: English and Spanish versions available for each level.
Time: (70–115) minutes.
Comments: Used in conjunction with the IPT Oral Language Proficiency Test.
Authors: Beverly A. Amori, Enrique F. Dalton, and Phyllis L. Tighe.
Publisher: Ballard & Tighe.

Review of the IDEA Reading and Writing Proficiency Test by JAMES DEAN BROWN, Professor, Department of ESL, University of Hawaii at Manoa, Honolulu, HI:

The IDEA Reading and Writing Proficiency Test (IPT R&W) provides "comprehensive assessment for initial identification and redesignation of Limited English Proficient (LEP) students" (examiner's manual, p. 3). These tests only claim to measure reading and writing skills. They are meant to be administered in conjunction with the IDEA Oral Language Proficiency Test.

The IPT R&W contains test booklets, answer sheets, scoring templates, examiner's manuals, and technical manuals covering Level 1 (grades 2–3), Level 2 (4–6) and Level 3 (7–12). Color-coded by level to help avoid confusion, the three levels all have the same general look and organization.

The test booklets have adequate directions and appropriately large type-face and format for the age levels involved. The multiple-choice answer sheets are the machine-scorable kind, but scoring templates are also provided for hand scoring. The picture and prose prompts in the writing subtests are clear and appropriate for the age levels being tested.

The examiner's manuals (one for each level) contain sections on: the background of the test developers, the history and development of the tests, description of the test, administering the reading test, administering the writing test, scoring the reading test, rating the writing samples, scoring the writing test, summary rules for testing, and implications for instruction. The authors also furnish a number of useful appendices: item specifications, definitions of the three student designations (non-English, limited English, and competent English), diagnostic reading profiles, directions for hand scoring the reading subtests, sample writing responses, and explanations of the standardized scores along with equivalency tables.

Throughout the examiner's manuals, those instructions that proctors should read aloud to examinees are clearly indicated in contrasting blue print. The guidelines for rating the open-ended parts of the writing subtests include rubrics, abundant examples, and guidelines for rater training. These descriptions are somewhat complex so raters must study them well in advance.

Two technical manuals are available, one for Levels 1 and 2 combined, and another for Level 3. Each of these provides sections on: information about the test designers, the test rationale and test development steps, normative information, and advice on interpreting standard scores.

In more detail, the authors explain that the test specifications were based partly on California's

Curriculum Frameworks for English and Language Arts "reflecting a nationwide trend toward a holistic approach to language learning" (technical manual, pp. 1–2), and partly on a survey of textbooks and achievement tests done by the authors.

The multiple-choice subtests (Reading and Writing Conventions) are discussed separately from the open-ended writing sample subtests in the technical manuals. The Level 1A and 2A multiple-choice Reading and Writing Conventions subtests were administered in 23 schools to 1,406 students in grades 2 and 3 (for Level 1) and grades 4 to 6 (for Level 2), and the Levels 3A and 3B tests were administered in 18 schools to 869 students in grades 7 to 12. The primary languages of 89% of the Levels 1 and 2 sample were English or Spanish; 84% of the Level 3 sample listed those two languages as primary. The authors provide abundant and clear information about the students' ages, genders, grades, ethnicities, district language designations, and teacher opinions of students' abilities.

The authors begin their statistical presentation with the percent correct and standard deviations for each of the items. Strangely, no discrimination index or item-total correlations are supplied to help readers understand the degree to which items discriminated between high and low achievers. Descriptive statistics and Cronbach alpha reliabilities are also reported. The alphas for the total Reading scores are .95, .91, .90, and .96 for the 1A, 2A, 3A, and 3B tests, respectively. The alphas for the various multiple-choice subtests are lower, ranging from .54 to .86, which makes sense because these subtests are considerably shorter. Smaller sample test-retest and alternative-forms reliabilities show similar patterns. The authors' discussion of reliability would have been much enhanced if they had provided an explanation of how the standard error of measurement can be used in decision making.

The authors defend content validity in tables of item specifications that list the competencies or concepts being tested in each subtest and the corresponding item numbers. In a few cases, competencies are tested by only one item. Nonetheless, these item specifications are exemplary because they openly display the content of the tests so that readers can judge for themselves if the tests are valid for their purposes.

The authors argue for construct validity by examining the intercorrelations among the subtests and similarities in subtest-total correlations, as well as by comparing the mean scores of different grade levels and types of students (as determined by amount of English language instruction). This latter discussion is fairly persuasive, but would be even more convincing if the statistical significance of the reported mean differences had been explored so that readers would know the probability that the observed differences occurred by chance alone.

The authors also explore criterion-related (concurrent) validity by examining the correlations of reading test percentile scores with the California Test of Basic Skills percentile scores at each grade level. These coefficients averaged .76 for the 1A and 2A tests, and .53 for the 3A and 3B tests. Then, the correlations with teachers' opinions are shown to range from .28 to .63.

Laudably, the authors also provide considerable advice on establishing cut scores for the non-English, limited English, and competent English reading designations.

The authors administered the Level 1A and 2A open-ended writing sample subtests in three schools to 143 students in grades 2 and 3 and grades 4 to 6. The 3A and 3B tests were administered in 13 schools to 117 students in grades 7 to 12. The primary language of 96.5% of the Levels 1 and 2 samples was English or Spanish; in the Level 3 sample, the percentage was 78.2%. Again, the demographic information is clear and complete.

The authors estimate the reliability of the writing subtests by examining interrater correlations (.90 to .98) and exact agreement between raters (79% to 86%). They explore criterion-related validity through examination of correlations between the writing subtest scores and three criterion measures: (1) teacher opinions of students' academic and writing abilities, (b) students' Writing Conventions subtest scores, and (c) norm-referenced language scores. These correlations are not very convincing; they range from .59 to .77 for Levels 1 and 2, and from .26 to .52 for Level 3. However, once again, advice is provided to help in establishing responsible cut points.

In sum, the IPT R&W tests are clearly organized, color coded, and appropriately formatted. These tests have clear administration procedures and provide considerable guidance for setting standards. The technical manual is reasonably comprehensive, but would be even more complete if it included some discussion of item discrimination and more explanation of the standard error of measurement. In addition, norms based on groups of non-natives other than Spanish speakers would have made the tests more useful in places where those other language backgrounds are prevalent. These last negative comments are simply meant to suggest ways that the IPT R&W tests could be enhanced. As they are, these tests provide a useful set of tools for making decisions about the reading and writing levels of Limited English Proficient students, especially if used in conjunction with the IDEA Oral Language Proficiency Test and other information about the students.

Review of the IDEA Reading and Writing Proficiency Test by ALAN GARFINKEL, Professor of Spanish and Education, Purdue University, West Lafayette, IN:

Federal legislation on bilingual education directs that federal funding be directed toward a process called transition. That process allows students who speak various languages to make a transition to the use of English after a start in their home language. The complexity of that process becomes clear when one considers that not all children enter schools in this country at the same level of development and that not all children are equally capable of listening, speaking, reading, and writing either their home language or English. When a student enters the mainstream of the proficient user of English, how is a school district to assess English proficiency in order to maximize student success at that point? The authors of the IDEA Reading and Writing Proficiency Test (IPT R&W) have carefully and conscientiously created a set of instruments that will make an important contribution to that assessment.

The IPT R&W is a standardized, group-administered set of tests of reading and writing in English for students at varying levels of English proficiency. The Reading subtest consists of sets of items in Vocabulary, Vocabulary in Context, Reading for Understanding, Reading for Life Skills, and Language usage. The Writing unit includes a segment on Conventions (such as punctuation),

describing a set of pictures of a set of sequential events, and writing one's own story based on a picture. I was particularly impressed with the Life Skills segments because they seem to me to be challenging enough to generate a measurement without being inappropriate for the age in question.

Instructions in the administrator's manuals at each level are clear and detailed. In fact, they include a script for test administrators to use. The manuals also contain assistance in holistically grading the writing samples the test generates. Criteria for identifying stages of writing proficiency ranging from "non-expressive" to "competent" are provided along with samples of student writing. The rating of "competent" is particularly useful in the context of mainstreaming because it indicates with examples there may still be things to teach and learn.

Technical manuals for tests are complete and most helpful. Technical terms in testing and measurement are clearly explained. The data supplied about the norming populations are ample. Included is information on the age, gender, grade level, and ethnicity as well as teacher opinions and expectations. A sound theoretical and practical background is cited and reliability ratings for the reading subtest are, for the most part, exceptionally high. Validity is discussed from several points of view and very well supported.

Using the IPT R&W test is likely to yield valuable information that school administrators can use in combination with other factors to make enlightened decisions on mainstreaming children of varying English proficiencies.

[42]
Individual Style Survey.

Purpose: "Intended to be an educational tool for self and interpersonal development."
Publication Dates: 1989–1990.
Administration: Group.
Price Data: Available from publisher.
Time: (60–90) minutes.
Comments: Self-administered, self-scored survey.
Author: Norman Amundson.
Publisher: Psychometrics Canada Ltd. [Canada].
　a) INDIVIDUAL STYLE SURVEY.
　Population: Adults.
　Publication Date: 1989.
　Acronym: ISS.
　Scores, 14: 8 categories of behavior (Forceful, Assertive, Outgoing, Spontaneous, Empathetic, Pa-

tient, Reserved, Analytical) yielding 4 styles (Dominant, Influencing, Harmonious, Cautious) that combine to form 2 summary scores (People/Task Orientation, Introspective/Interactive Stance).

b) MY PERSONAL STYLE.

Population: Ages 10–18.

Publication Date: 1990.

Acronym: MPS.

Scores, 14: 8 categories (Carefree, Outgoing, Straight Forward, Forceful, Precise, Reserved, Patient, Sensitive) yielding 4 styles (Influencing, Strong Willed, Cautious, Peaceful) that combine to form 2 summary scores (People/Task Orientation, Expressive/Thoughtful Stance).

Comments: Simplified version of the Individual Style Survey for use with young people.

Review of the Individual Style Survey by JEF-FREY A. ATLAS, Deputy Chief Psychologist and Associate Clinical Professor, Bronx Children's Psychiatric Center, Albert Einstein College of Medicine, Bronx, NY:

The Individual Style Survey, in its adult version, is introduced "to provide a structured activity for self and interpersonal development" (p. 1). The secondary-school youth version, like the adult booklet containing a self form as well as three others to give to friends, family, or work or teacher contacts, is introduced "to provide a way for you to find out more about yourself and others" (p. 1). These stated purposes appear to meld the aims of assessment and intervention, individually and in groups, but the Individual Style Survey (ISS) is compromised by weaknesses in construct validity and consequent real-world application.

The "Leader's Guide," in what functions as a test manual, cites foundations for the study of individual style as diverse as Jung and Adler to more current counseling and industrial psychology researchers. The theory of the behavioral descriptors draws from the earlier authors and is pictorialized in a circle bisected by people/task-oriented and thoughtful/expressive axes, evoking an image of quadrants of individual style recalling Timothy Leary's typology of personality. The implementation of the survey instrument and recommended applications draws more from the ethos of industrial psychology and counseling.

Unlike other, more straightforward career-interest inventories for adults or youth, such as the Strong-Campbell or Career Decision Making Sys-

tem, there are no norms for the ISS to compare individuals' self-descriptors to responses of groups in selected occupations or to comparative descriptive information by schooling. The construct, then, of "individual style" as characterized by self- or other-ascribed characteristics of, for example, "Influencing" (the quadrant comprising "Spontaneous" and "Outgoing") has face validity but poor construct validity. There are no data comparing responses to other descriptive data sources or behavioral outcomes, or indeed taking into account the linguistic issue of category naming, which would suggest some variety of factor analysis to discover if the different descriptors could meaningfully be added in equal ways to produce summary scores. The summary scores, given weak empirical grounding, thus carry the oracular aura of an astrology reading (e.g., those scoring high in Influencing can learn that "When your influencing style is used appropriately, it can be a powerful means of moving people to action through persuasion rather than coercion. You are energetic and inspiring and confidently express your opinions. You also have a twinkle in your eye and a good sense of humor" [test booklet, p. 16]).

A question is why such an instrument should emerge now, and in this structure, given that self-assessment (updated here to individual style) has been a documented aspect of human existence since antiquity (e.g., Augustine's *Confessions*). The ISS presumes that self-descriptions are easily accessible to consciousness or may be captured by comparing them to others' observations (recalling the "I" and "me" dialectic of G. H. Mead). The notion that such aspects of personhood can be absorbed by scores on categories such as Influencing or Cautious carries a danger (or purpose?) of reification of human qualities into commodity-like items that may be combined or altered to "fit the market" (p. 17). Indeed, in the applications section of the Leader's Guide, a Board of Directors Scenario entails possible people versus task group responses given a mandated 30% reduction in labor force due to falling oil prices (e.g., one class of group responses was "lay off employees according to seniority" [p. 17]). The ISS in this way appears topical (i.e., responsive to such events as 1970s–1980s shifts in oil prices) and yet dated, dependent upon shifts in (Western) economic crises and associated changes in corporate structures and strategies.

For a person who "under uses influencing style," the Leader's Guide suggests "allow time for a response to new ideas, give advance warning of meetings" (p. 16). The ISS is less an assessment instrument than an intervention program awaiting validation (e.g., in industrial-corporate settings). Practitioners in such settings may find the ISS a useful experimental or programmatic technique to try in joint aims of facilitating worker productivity and satisfaction, as long as the projected change in styles is not overly depended upon to cover over real organizational or micropolitical problems. (Exploitative work relations are unlikely to be "harmonized" through the ISS or any other measures). In a similar vein, the ISS offers some thoughtful general approaches in self-assessment and counseling, such as with a person who overuses the cautious style ("validate the close inspection of details, but show … action planning" [p. 16]) or who underuses the cautious style ("share the 'dream,' but slow down the process" [p. 16]). Counseling psychologists and their clients may find such leads effective but should know that changes in individual style, in or out of the workplace, are unlikely to go beneath the superficial unless change is predicated upon structural changes in the individual's lifespace or the individual's psychological means of apprehending and changing experience.

Review of the Individual Style Survey by WIL-LIAM I. SAUSER, JR., Professor and Executive Director for Outreach, College of Business, Auburn University, Auburn, AL:

The Individual Style Survey (ISS) is a very simple instrument intended, according to the manual, "to be an educational tool for self and interpersonal development. Through using the survey it is possible to acquire increased understanding of self and others. This information is an important aspect of competence development … and for team building" (p. 1). The instrument clearly is intended for use within a group training or individual counseling context. An alternate form of the ISS, employing language more appropriate for adolescents, is marketed as My Personal Style (MPS).

The author indicates that the ISS arose from the tradition of personality "type" theory espoused by such writers as Jung, Kretschmer, Adler, and Leary. This reviewer noted a striking similarity of the ISS dimensions to the four types espoused by Geier (1977) in his Personal Profile System (T4:1982). The author cites Geier's instrument, as well as Anderson's (1987) Personal Style Indicator (T4:1992), as other "systems of analysis" flowing from the personality "type" tradition. Although not cited by the author, the Myers-Briggs Type Indicator (MBTI; T4:1702) is a well-known (and better constructed, researched, and documented than the ISS; see Wiggins, 1989) example of instruments of this nature.

The ISS consists of eight words accompanied by one-sentence definitions; for example, "Spontaneous: I am instinctive and act on my impulses" (p. 4). The test-taker is directed to "Read the descriptors and then choose two descriptors most like you, continuing through the list to the two descriptors least like you" (p. 3). The rank orders of the descriptors then become scores, which are summed in various ways to produce the four "style" and two "summary" scores. One new twist with this instrument is that the test-taker is instructed, after completing the "self" form, to "give the 'others' form to three different people of your choice and ask for their honest opinions" (p. 1). Once these additional data are collected, they are melded into the scoring process as well.

The ISS is interesting and engaging, and could—in the hands of a capable trainer or counselor—be used to develop limited insight into certain characteristics and behaviors of the test-taker. The instrument itself provides some interpretive material relating to effective use, overuse, and underuse of each style. Further interpretive material is found in the manual, which draws connections between ISS styles and various styles of learning, information processing, and communicating. Unfortunately, neither the instrument nor the manual provides any definitive guidance for determining whether a certain style is being used effectively or ineffectively. The manual states, "The extent to which people are over or under using a style is a matter for individual reflection and assessment" (p. 3).

Stone (1992) rightly categorizes instruments of this ilk as "parlor games," citing their general lack of validity evidence. (Stone excepts the MBTI from this group because validation data have been presented for it.) This reviewer must agree: The author presents no shred of evidence of validity for the ISS and MPS. Furthermore, none of the standard psychometric concerns—norms, reliability evidence, test bias, reporting test results—are even mentioned in the manual. Clearly the ISS and MPS are totally inappropriate to serve as bases for decisions affecting the test-taker. Human resource professionals are warned not to use the ISS as a basis for any personnel management decisions, because it has not been demonstrated to be psychometrically sound.

The "type" approach to personality theory has some merit and enjoys considerable intuitive appeal. Although the MBTI would likely be a better choice, trainers and counselors seeking to illustrate the "type" approach might—with appropriate professional caution—use the ISS within the context of an educational module. However, given the instrument's obvious fakability, the lack of scientific rigor employed in its development, and the absence of any data documenting its psychometric quality, the Individual Style Survey should not be considered a professionally developed test, nor should it be used as a basis for any decisions regarding the test-taker. This reviewer joins Stone (1992), Wiggins (1989), and others in calling for more scientific rigor on the part of authors developing instruments from the perspective of personality "type" theory.

REVIEWER'S REFERENCES

Geier, J. G. (1977). Personal Profile System. Minneapolis: Performax Systems International.

Anderson, T. D. (1987). Personal Style Indicator. Vancouver: Consulting Resources Group.

Wiggins, J. S. (1989). [Review of the Myers-Briggs Type Indicator.] In J. C. Conoley & J. J. Kramer (Eds.), The tenth mental measurements yearbook (pp. 537–538). Lincoln, NE: The Buros Institute of Mental Measurements.

Stone, G. L. (1992). [Review of the Personal Style Assessment.] In J. J. Kramer & J. C. Conoley (Eds.), The eleventh mental measurements yearbook (pp. 287–288). Lincoln, NE: The Buros Institute of Mental Measurements.

[43]
Informal Reading Comprehension Placement Test [Revised].

Purpose: "Assesses the instructional and independent comprehension levels of students from pre-readiness (grade 1) through level twelve plus (grade 12)."

Population: Grades 1–8 for typical learners and grades 8–12 remedially; adult education students.

Publication Dates: 1983–1994.

Scores, 3: Word Comprehension, Passage Comprehension, Total Comprehension.

Administration: Individual.

Price Data, 1994: $49.95 per test.

Time: (35–50) minutes for the battery; (15–20) minutes for Part 1; (20–30) minutes for Part 2.

Comments: Automatically administered, scored, and managed; for use with adults, the placements are correlated with Tests of Adult Basic Education (T4:2812); test administered in two parts; Apple II or IBM microcomputer necessary for administration.

Authors: Ann Edson and Eunice Insel.

Publisher: Educational Activities, Inc.

Cross References: For reviews by Gloria A. Galvin and Claudia R. Wright, see 11:178.

Review of the Informal Reading Comprehension Placement Test [Revised] by DIANE J. SAWYER, Professor of Education, Middle Tennessee State University, Murfreesboro, TN:

The stated major objective of this inventory is to yield findings for use in prescribing a developmental, corrective, or remedial reading program for individuals (manual, p. 2). It is the opinion of this reviewer that the stated major objective cannot be achieved. This inventory was specifically designed to yield an estimate of an individual's instructional reading comprehension levels based upon a criterion level performance of 75% accuracy on word meaning tasks and questions related to content in brief passages. It is not possible to *prescribe* a reading program based upon such limited and global information. Further, it is doubtful that the scores obtained by means of this inventory have practical value for selecting material for independent reading or for instruction. At best, this inventory may be useful for screening individuals, in the intermediate grades and above, to estimate the level of other diagnostic tests or tasks to use in identifying the range of reading comprehension strategies and competencies an individual possesses. What to teach, or what must be learned about comprehending text, is not identified or defined by the grade level of difficulty assigned to words or passages.

The Word Comprehension subtest (Part I) consists of eight items per grade level (Levels 1 through 13 inclusive). Each item is presented in an analogic form (e.g., *jump* is to *up* as *sit* is to _____). The reader selects the best answer from the two options provided. The authors provide no information regarding the source of vocabulary included or the basis upon which words were assigned to a specific level of difficulty. The analogic format requires, in many instances, fairly sophisticated reasoning to arrive at the appropriate answer. This subtest does go beyond knowledge of individual word meanings and may be appropriately considered a measure of comprehension applied at the word level. There is much diagnostic *potential* for such a test but this would require a fairly large number of items at each level to tap the various word level comprehension strategies students at that level might be expected to apply. Further, an item analysis option would be needed to permit the teacher to identify individual competence with each of the types of strategies. In its current form, the Word Comprehension subtest can only provide an estimate of word knowledge with no opportunity to identify where or why reasoning about meaning breaks down.

The Passage Comprehension subtest (Part II) consists of graded passages (grades 1–13) ranging in length from about 40 words to about 250 words. Each passage is followed by four questions. Typically, one question involves a vocabulary item, one addresses main idea, one assesses recall of detail, and one taps inferential reasoning. No information is provided by the authors regarding the source of these passages or how the grade levels of difficulty were assigned. The upper level passages (11–13) contain quite sophisticated topic-specific vocabulary. Poor performance on these passages may not accurately reflect how students will perform in typical texts or recreational material written for the grade level. No item analysis is provided to permit examination of possible patterns of errors associate with the comprehension questions.

The Informal Reading Comprehension Placement Test may be useful in estimating a student's ability to cope with grade level texts (grades 4–12). The computer software format may be especially helpful to classroom teachers (grades 4–6) and remedial teachers (assisting students in grades 4–12) in dealing with new entrants during the school year. However, the format does not seem well suited to situations such as adult literacy classes, where estimates of individual achievement levels for a large number of students must be obtained quickly. Group-administered tests are better suited to the item constraints associated with instruction in these settings. Further, among students in grades 1–3, much more relevant information regarding overall reading ability can be gained by listening to the student read aloud. At these levels, poor comprehension is frequently associated with restricted levels of word recognition or limited word attack strategies. This test can provide no further information relative to these abilities. Similarly, teachers of older students who obtain unusually poor scores on this test should consider word recognition and word analysis competencies as a possible interfering factor.

Potential users of the Informal Reading Comprehension Placement Test should be aware that the authors offer no evidence regarding validity or reliability. It is noted that "the test was validated by over 3,000 students over ten years in the Baldwin, New York public schools" (manual, p. 4). However, no description of the school system, the student population, or the validation study is provided. It appears that determination of the effectiveness of this test in accomplishing the purpose and objective for which it was developed is left entirely to the user. Potential users should carefully consider the significant limitations of this test as it is currently presented.

Review of the Informal Reading Comprehension Placement Test [Revised] by GABRIELLE STUTMAN, Consulting Psychologist, Cognitive Habilitation Services, New York City, NY:

This test attempts a brief, sequential, and reliable computerized evaluation of reading comprehension placement level for students in grades 1–12, as well as for remedial secondary, adult, and special education. The Word Comprehension Test (WCT) (Part 1) Analogies contains 96 items using an analogy format to facilitate the assessment of both word meanings and thinking skills. Each of the 12 sets of eight words is vocabulary controlled using EDL and Dolch Word Lists. The Passage Comprehension Test (PCT) (Part 2) contains 12 graded reading passages that are controlled for vocabulary and sentence length using Spache, Frye, and Dale Chall readability formulas. Four comprehension questions follow each passage to test detail, main idea, inference, and vocabulary from the context. Results are automatically scored to provide the teacher with three levels of reading functioning: an Independent Level (WCT = 99%, PCT ≥90%), an Instructional Level (WCT ≥90%, PCT ≥75%), and a Frustration Level (WCT <90%,

PCT <51%). The latter is to be avoided in order to maximize student motivation and achievement. In addition, a Total Instructional level is also calculated as a composite of the WCT and PCT. These measures are intended to provide classroom, content area, resource teachers, and curriculum specialists with rapid student placement while minimizing teacher time. The student's record is maintained over time so that progress can be recorded. The teacher may access individual student's scores, or scores for the entire class, either on screen or hard copy. Both individual and class files are easily deleted.

The program is easy to operate for students who are able to follow written instructions such as, "Please type your first name and then press RE-TURN." Less (computer) literate students will require the aid of a teacher to begin. The test may begin at any level that the teacher wishes. Sample items are given to insure appropriate entry points, progress from level to level is smooth, and the assessment is automatically ended at the point where the student is unable to perform at 75%–80% accuracy. The publishers state that the test was validated by over 3,000 students over 10 years in the Baldwin, New York public schools. This is a very respectable sample size; however, no demographics of this sample are given, and so the user has no way of knowing the age/grade, gender, and/or English language proficiency distribution, or whether adults or remedial readers were included in the sample at all. In addition, no reliability or validity coefficients of any kind are provided. Several sections of the test have rather long runs (three in a row) of same-letter-correct choices. In a test that demands 75% competence on as few as four questions to proceed to the next level, validity may be seriously compromised by response bias. When this reviewer took the test from the beginning with a response bias of "B," she achieved reading readiness in the area of Word Comprehension. Indeed, the labels of "readiness" and "pre-readiness" at the bottom end of the assessment range are misnomers. Readiness to read is not the same thing as reading ability. Reading readiness correlates with the capacity to segregate phonemes from morphemes and/or to discriminate and recognize complex visual patterns. Pre-readiness is incompetence at making such auditory and visual discriminations. These very important aspects of developmental reading ability are not assessed, and for that reason the lowest levels would be more appropriately labeled "Nonreader" and "Beginning Reader." For beginning readers, the structure of the test response matrix may cause difficulties. The student must respond on a keyboard by pressing either an "A," "B," or "C" to indicate their choice of correct answer. Therefore, when reading the typewriter keyboard from left to right, the student must ignore irrelevant letters and deal with a letter sequence that presents itself as "A, C, B." For this reason variables of attention and confusion may interfere with the validity of the reading assessment. Changing the response alternatives to "1," "2," and "3" may enhance validity as well as ease of use. Finally, in the comprehension selection on Wild Turkeys, the word "presently" is misused to mean "currently." Usage errors such as this have no place in an educational assessment instrument. In all, although the idea of a computerized reading assessment is a very good one, much work is still to be done if this instrument is to pass muster.

[44]

The Instructional Environment System—II: A System to Identify a Student's Instructional Needs (Second Edition).

Purpose: "Designed to assist education professionals in a systematic analysis of a target student's instructional environment, which includes both school and home contexts."

Population: Grades K–12.

Publication Dates: 1987–1993.

Acronym: TIES-II.

Scores: 12 Instructional Environment Components (Instructional Match, Teacher Expectations, Classroom Environment, Instructional Presentation, Cognitive Emphasis, Motivational Strategies, Relevant Practice, Informed Feedback, Academic Engaged Time, Adaptive Instruction, Progress Evaluation, Student Understanding), 5 Home Support for Learning Components (Expectations and Attributions, Discipline Orientation, Home Affective Environment, Parent Participation, Structure for Learning).

Administration: Individual.

Forms, 4: Instructional Needs Checklist, Parent Interview Record, Home Support for Learning Form, Instructional Environment Form.

Price Data, 1994: $47.50 per TIES-II Program Kit including 15 copies of each of the 4 forms and manual ('93, 199 pages); $19.50 per replacement forms set including 15 copies of each of the 4 forms.

Time: Administration time not reported.

Comments: Observational and interview data from teachers, parents, and students is gathered by an education professional; can be used in regular classrooms, homes, special education, and in different content areas.

Authors: James Ysseldyke and Sandra Christenson.

Publisher: Sopris West, Inc.

Cross References: For reviews by Kenneth W. Howell and by William T. McKee and Joseph C. Witt of an earlier form, see 10:149.

Review of The Instructional Environment System—II: A System to Identify a Student's Instructional Needs (Second Edition) by MICHAEL J. FURLONG, Associate Professor, and JENNIFER A. ROSENBLATT, Doctoral Candidate, University of California, Santa Barbara, CA:

TIES-II is an extension and revision of the TIES (Ysseldyke & Christenson, 1987), which was developed to address a gap in traditional special education assessment procedures and models. Existing taxonomies of children's learning needs have typically focused on intra-child variables as critical in understanding the etiology and remediation of learning problems. The original TIES expanded assessment interest beyond the child to include conditions in the classroom environment that facilitate learning. TIES-II extends this ecological perspective to include various facilitative conditions in the child's home.

CONTENT. The authors of TIES-II extensively reviewed effective-instruction literature to identify teacher behaviors and classroom conditions found to be associated with positive learning outcomes. As such, they have not developed a formal test, but a procedure with which educators can systematically organize their own perceptions of the quality of the classroom instructional environment.

The classroom content of the TIES-II consists of 12 "components" organized into four instructional environment domains: *Planning Instruction* (#1 Instructional Match and #2 Teacher Expectations), *Managing Instruction* (#3 Classroom Environment), *Delivering Instruction* (#4 Instructional Presentation, #5 Cognitive Emphasis, #6 Motivational Strategies, #7 Relevant Practice, and #8 Informed Feedback), and *Monitoring/Evaluating Instruction* (#9 Academic Engaged Time, #10 Adaptive Instruction, #11 Progress Evaluation, and #12 Student Understanding). The fact that Managing Instruction has only one component (#3) leads one to wonder why it is not just referred to as classroom environment. This organization represents the authors' conceptualization of the essential components of effective classroom instruction. These 12 components are identical to those included in the original TIES but in the manual the authors have updated the discussion about empirical research identifying these components as important classroom environment characteristics.

Given the second author's interest in the role that families play in the educational process, soon after the publication of TIES, Christenson and Ysseldyke (1989) began to integrate home environment factors into their ecological model of student achievement. A primary innovation of TIES-II is the inclusion of five new components (#13 to #17) examining the types of support for student learning found within the home environment itself. These five new components assess (#13) Expectations and Attributions, (#14) Discipline Orientation, (#15) Home Affective Environment, (#16) Parent Participation, and (#17) Structure for Learning. The academic and ecological focus of the TIES-II and the integration of home factors into the assessment process should be well received by teachers and parents because it addresses issues that have high relevance to a child's educational program.

TEST MATERIALS/RESOURCES. TIES-II uses six forms, four of which are used for data gathering and observations (Instructional Needs Checklist, completed by teachers; Instructional Planning Form, Direct Observation Form, and Parent Interview Record, completed by parent or guardian) and two forms for recording and organizing summary perceptions/ratings of the 17 components mentioned above (Instructional Environment Form [components #1 to #12]; and Home Support for Learning Form [components #13 to #17]).

TIES-II is intended to be used by a team of educators working collaboratively in a consultative relationship. Observation and evaluation forms can be completed by one educator, but it is clear that a more comprehensive understanding of a child's learning environment will be obtained when multiple informants are used, notably the classroom teacher and parents. The authors have a respectful tone throughout the manual with disclaimers designed to encourage parents and teachers not to be defensive about identifying conditions in the home or school that do not appear to support the child's learning. It is particularly important to seek the input of the classroom teacher because the content of the TIES-II relates directly to the use of instructional strategies and the organization he or she brings to the classroom. Thus, there is the obvious potential for misuse of TIES-II to place blame or responsibility, at least implicitly, on the teacher for any instructional component deficits that are found. Although the authors go to great lengths in the detailed manual to discourage the use of TIES-II for evaluating teacher performance, its proper use will be increased greatly if the teacher is part of the assessment team. Inasmuch as TIES-II is not a standardized test, one of its potential strengths is to encourage communication about a child's learning environment among the classroom teacher, support personnel, administrators, and parents. This obviously cannot happen unless all parties are equal partners in the assessment process.

ADMINISTRATION/SCORING. The forms intended for use by educators are well arranged and should help facilitate thinking about ways to enhance a child's learning environment; but the ratings are completely subjective. The authors offer no data showing that different raters using TIES-II and rating the same environment would produce similar outcomes. Without such information, it is impossible to know if users of TIES-II produce biased ratings that reflect their own instructional orientation and beliefs.

Consistent with the authors' theoretic orientation, some of TIES-II response scales on the Parent Interview Record form are worded behaviorally; for example, the response category "Yes" is defined as meaning that the referent behavior occurs 80% of the time (4 to 5 days per week). However, these response anchors are not repeated on each page of the record sheets and this response format is not used throughout the parent form. In other sections of the parent form, they are asked to check if conditions related to items describing a variety of home conditions and child behaviors are "fairly typical" (i.e., "happens often") of their child. These changes in response format are likely to cause confusion among some parents. In addition, although the form is called the "Parent Interview

Record" it is structured much like any traditional parent self-report checklist. It is likely that this form will be given to parents to complete on their own. Given the heavy verbal loading of the form, this 98-item instrument has decreased utility for parents with limited English literacy skills. Similarly, the lack of translated versions of the Parent Interview Record further restricts its potential use. In addition, the core of the Parent Interview Record is a list of 56 items describing learning-related conditions in the home. The manner in which responses to these items are to be organized, however, is not provided. There is no psychometric analysis to verify the content or construct validity of these items. Although TIES-II was not developed as a norm-based checklist type of instrument, this does not eliminate the responsibility of the authors to demonstrate that items included in the parent form meet minimal standards of validity and reliability. Another concern is that the items included in this portion of the parent form are wordy with multiple elements (e.g., "My child is encouraged to work hard in school, to put forth a lot of effort, and to try again"). How some items are to be interpreted is ambiguous. For example, what does it mean if a parent indicates that they do not reward their child for "good grades"? Parent responses to the aforementioned items and other TIES-II items can have multiple meanings, thus appropriate use will require at least some direct contact with the caregiver to ensure that the meanings of their responses are understood. One final point, the items are sometimes worded in the first person, "I stay informed about by child's progress," whereas other items are worded more generally, "My child has opportunities to solve problems at home." Some items are just unnecessarily vague, for example, "My child's schoolwork is viewed on a weekly basis." The authors offer no information about how these wording variations affect responses or interpretation of the instrument.

SUMMARY. The authors have done a commendable job of organizing literature about factors associated with high levels of student academic performance. This is actually a unique resource for educators because it provides them with citations to empirical research that identifies conditions in the classroom and at home that enhance student learning. As such, it offers a useful tool as part of a comprehensive assessment (see Christenson & Ysseldyke, 1989, for an example of how to use the TIES procedures as part of the instructional planning process.) This organization of a very important body of research is well worth obtaining.

Notwithstanding the potential usefulness of TIES-II, users need to be mindful of several issues. Firstly, it has demonstrated content validity because the 17 components are carefully derived from research findings. However, the presentation of information about the components was constructed by the authors and represents their own, unverified interpretation and organization of what this research says. They did not, for example, ask experts to verify that the descriptions of their components are valid and appropriate. Secondly, the authors claim a strong link to intervention, but no specific instructional suggestions are generated by the TIES-II—this level of instructional planning is left entirely to the assessment team. If one is looking to the TIES-II to offer suggestions about specific instructional activities, they will likely be disappointed. Users are told that they need to have a strong knowledge base about academic instruction and remediation before they can make optimal use of the TIES-II. However, the TIES-II does not offer specific suggestions for obtaining this knowledge. Thirdly, there is no evidence that use of this system is associated with any of a variety of positive educational outcomes, such as prevention of student placement in special education classes or enhanced academic performance. For that matter, there is no evidence to suggest that as a result of using the TIES-II, any teacher or parent actually changed their behavior to create conditions in the classroom or at home that are favorable to enhanced learning. There is a weak link between the TIES-II consultation process and procedures or skill training options that would encourage teachers and/or parents to engage in the behaviors needed to bring about improved classroom or home learning conditions consistent with the 17 TIES-II learning components. Finally, even nearly 10 years after the publication of the original TIES, the TIES-II assessment procedures have not been independently validated by other researchers, nor has it been used extensively in research studies. Until TIES-II receives additional independent reviews demonstrating that it is validated for its stated uses

and purposes across diverse populations, it will not fulfill its objective of encouraging functional, ecologically focused assessments of youths' learning needs.

REVIEWERS' REFERENCES

Ysseldyke, J. E., & Christenson, S. L. (1987). The Instructional Environment Scale (TIES). Austin, TX: PRO-ED, Inc.

Christenson, S. L., & Ysseldyke, J. E. (1989). Assessing student performance: An important change is needed. *Journal of School Psychology, 27*, 409–425.

Thurlow, M. L., Ysseldyke, J. E., Wotruba, J. W., & Algozzine, B. (1993). Instruction in special education classrooms under varying student-teacher ratios. *Elementary School Journal, 93*, 305–320.

Review of The Instructional Environment System—II: A System to Identify a Student's Instructional Needs (Second Edition) by JERRY TINDAL, Associate Professor, Behavioral Research and Teaching, University of Oregon, Eugene, OR:

This instrument is designed to identify a student's instructional needs by using an observational rating scale and interview forms of teachers, students, and parents. The authors consider the five data-gathering tools to be the Observation Record, Student Interview Record, Teacher Interview Record, Parent Interview Record, and Instructional Needs Checklist. The intervention planning forms include the Instructional Environment Form, the Home Support for Learning Form, and the Intervention Planning Form.

The Instructional Environment System—II (TIES-II) has four data-gathering tools described in the manual: (a) an Observation Record that includes a focus on such issues as planning, management, delivery, and monitoring; (b) Student Interview Record, which addresses understanding of assignments, teacher expectations, and use of strategies for work completion; (c) Teacher Interview Record, which focuses on expectations, planning, instructional placement, assignments, and overall success; and (d) Intervention Planning Form.

The test also includes four additional forms that are completed with directions provided in a manual: (a) Parent Interview Record, (b) Instructional Needs Checklist, (c) Home Support for Learning Form, and (d) Instructional Environment Form.

In the Parent Interview, ratings are made on a 4-point scale regarding parents' perception of the child's proficiency-understanding in the basic skill areas, the child's difficulty areas, anecdotal observations, and specific observations that reflect self-statements of the parent.

The Instructional Needs Checklist includes directions for the teacher to note student strengths and weaknesses; description of concerns; checklists of instructional needs reflecting classroom characteristics, instructional plans, management of instructional needs, implementation of these needs, and evaluation of the needs; reflections on student responses to tasks; and checklists of instructional factors to get the student more engaged as well as use of instructional tasks and materials and modifications.

The Home Support for Learning Form reflects judgments on the part of the observer for five components; expectations and attributions, discipline orientation, home affective environment, parent participation, and structure for learning. An extensive comments section is provided for notes to be written on "ways the parents would like to assist their child's learning at home" and "other concerns" (p. 3).

The Instructional Environment Form provides a structure for documenting the referring concerns and contexts and then to pinpoint statements on 12 instructional components:

1. Instructional match (dealing with student's needs and goals).

2. Teacher expectations (to determine if they are both realistic and high).

3. Classroom environment (management techniques, time use, and climate).

4. Instructional presentation (lesson development, clarity of directions, and checking for understanding).

5. Cognitive emphasis (emphasizing thinking skills and learning strategies).

6. Motivational strategies (strategies to heighten student interest).

7. Relevant practice (opportunity to practice with appropriate and relevant materials).

8. Informed feedback (emphasizing immediate and specific information on performance that is corrective).

9. Academic engaged time (both involvement and maintenance).

10. Adaptive instruction (accommodations specific to the student's needs).

11. Progress evaluation (emphasizing direct and frequent measurement of progress).

12. Student understanding (of what is to be done and how it is to be done).

In all of these areas, the person completing the evaluation provides a rating of agreement-disagreement (on a 4-point scale) for each of two dimensions: (a) presence and (b) importance. In the manual appendix, extensive information is presented on each of these components, providing positive statements that reflect details of each construct (component).

The manual provides extensive documentation on information relevant to understanding many issues of instructional environments in five chapters that provide a rationale, methodology, integration of findings, technical considerations, and empirical basis for understanding. The rationale presents a well-written summary of research on effective teaching, and includes many of the major works to appear in the educational literature in the past 20 years. In the second chapter a very extensive review of empirical research and references is included. Chapter 3 provides directions to integrate the information from both the data-gathering tools and intervention planning forms. The perspective is holistic with an emphasis on making global, integrative judgments. Furthermore, the intervention planning process is oriented toward collaborative problem solving and a consultation-based program. In the fourth chapter, technical data are presented that include the sources for selecting items on the checklists and empirical support in the form of the following reliability and validity information: (a) The content sampling plan is well documented and easy to follow; (b) interrater reliability coefficients are high for all 12 components; (c) validity coefficients between ratings on the 12 components and achievement measures are low-moderate; (d) several studies that reflect percentage of students with mild disabilities at various rating values; (e) comparisons of ratings for students with mild disabilities in special and general education; (f) gender differences in the ratings; and (g) differences in ratings among students with different disability categories.

In the last chapter of the manual, correlates of academic achievement are reviewed, providing extensive literature that dates back to the late 1970s and extends forward to more recent publications. This literature is presented for each of the 12 components.

In summary, TIES-II is a very extensive data-collection tool that represents a considerable and extensive literature base appearing in the professional educational literature for the past 20 years. All components of the instrument (records and forms) are well described and formatted in a manner that is clear and easy to use. Documentation is extensive. TIES-II also is a very comprehensive instrument for understanding the classroom ecology, making it a potentially difficult one to use for novice practitioners.

[45]
Integrated Assessment System.

Purpose: "A series of performance tasks that can be used independently or in combination with a norm-referenced achievement test to offer a comprehensive view of student achievement."
Population: Grades 1–9.
Publication Dates: 1990–1992.
Acronym: IAS.
Subtests: 3.
Administration: Group.
Authors: Roger Farr and Beverly Farr (Language Arts and Spanish only).
Publisher: The Psychological Corporation.

a) IAS-LANGUAGE ARTS.
Population: Grades 1–8.
Scores, 3: Response to Reading, Management of Content, Command of Language.
Price Data, 1994: $104 per complete grade 1 package including 25 each of three student booklets and directions for administering; $182 per complete grades 2–8 package including three sets of guided-writing-activity black line masters, directions for administering, three packages of 25 response forms, and response form directions; $18 per grade 1 examination kit including student booklet, directions for administering, and one passage specific scoring rubric; $22.50 per grades 2–8 examination kit including reading passage, guided-writing-activity black line master, response form, response form directions, directions for administering, and one passage-specific scoring rubric; $26 per grade 1 activity package including 25 of one student booklet and directions for administering; $65 per grades 2–8 activity package and directions for administering; $65 per grades 2–8 activity package including 25 of one reading passage and directions for administering; $5.50 per grades 2–8 response form package; $7 per grades 1–8 directions for administering; $15.50 per grades 1–8 scoring guides; $24 per grade 1 reading passage only; $59 per grades 2–8 reading passage only; $12.50 per grades 2–8 guided-writing-activity black line masters; $35.50 per technical report ('91, 53 pages); $210.50 per scoring workshop kit including videotape, trainer's manual, 25 overhead transparencies, and masters of model papers and training papers; $130 per portfolio starter kit including classroom storage box, 25 student portfolios, and teacher's manual; $42 per student portfolio folders; $42 per teacher's manual; $63.50 per introductory videotape and viewer's guide; $4.16 per basic scoring service; $6.24 per 25 student demographic sheets.
Time: (120–240) minutes.

1) *IAS—Language Arts, Spanish Edition.*
Scores: Same as *a* above.
Price Data: $17.50 per grade 1 examination kit including student booklet, directions for administering, and a passage specific scoring rubric; $21.50 per grades 2–8 examination kit including reading passage, guided-writing-activity black line master, one response form, response form directions, directions for administering, and passage specific scoring rubric; $25 per grade 1 activity package including 25 copies of one student booklet and one directions for administering; $62.50 per grades 2–8 activity package including 25 copies of one reading passage, one directions for administering, and one guided-writing-activity black line master; $5.50 per grades 2–8 response form package including 25 response forms and response form directions; $1 per response form directions; $7 per grades 1–8 directions for administering; $15 per grades 1–8 scoring guides; $23 per 25 grade 1 reading passage; $57 per 25 grades 2–8 reading passage; $12 per grades 2–8 guided-writing-activity black line masters; $4.16 per basic scoring service; $6.24 per student demographic sheet.

b) IAS-MATHEMATICS
Population: Grades 1–9.
Scores, 4: Reasoning, Conceptual Knowledge, Communication Procedures.
Price Data: $17.50 per examination kit including student booklet, directions for administering, and scoring rubric; $27 per activity package including 25 student booklets and directions for administering; $7.50 per directions for administering; $16 per scoring guides; $120 per scoring training kit including binder and overhead transparencies; $9.31 per basic scoring holistic and analytic; $6.24 per 25 student demographic sheet.
Time: (80–90) minutes.

c) IAS-SCIENCE.
Population: Grades 1–8.
Scores, 4: Experimenting, Collecting Data, Drawing Conclusions, Communicating.

Price Data: $17.50 per examination kit including student booklet, directions for administering, and scoring rubric; $25 per activity package including 25 student booklets and one directions for administering; $7 per directions for administering; $16 per scoring guides; $30 per manipulative materials; $120 per scoring workshop kit including trainer's manual; $5.15 per basic scoring service; $6.25 per 25 student demographic sheet.

Time: (80–90) minutes.

Review of the Integrated Assessment System by GABRIEL M. DELLA-PIANA, Director of Evaluation, El Paso Collaborative for Academic Excellence, University of Texas at El Paso, El Paso, TX:

The Integrated Assessment System (IAS) is a series of performance tasks in three subject matter areas. This review focuses on Language Arts Assessment because this subtest has the greatest amount of documentation.

The purpose of the IAS-Language Arts is "to measure how well students are developing as readers and writers at the time of testing so that effective instruction can be planned" (technical report, p. 27). Elsewhere in the technical report (p. 10) two other purposes are stated: (a) to help students understand their own literacy growth and performance to guide their development as readers and writers; (b) to help administrators and other decision makers to understand how students are developing literacy skills needed to be effective citizens. The purpose of this review is to determine what we can about how well the test achieves its purposes.

Reading/Writing prompts were selected to tap the kinds of writing students are typically taught at each grade level based on a "survey ... of the leading language arts instructional programs" (technical report, p. 16). Similarly, thinking skills tapped by the prompts were to be "representative of thinking students are asked to do at [each] grade level" (p. 18). Neither of these selection processes was described in sufficient detail to judge the claims made. Though the grade level selections seem appropriate in general, this rigid classification prevents seeing that all kinds of writing are possible in some form at all grade levels. For example, the kind of "if-then" thinking that can be done in kindergarten in talking about simple experiments or narratives is really the beginning of essay writing. But essay writing is first listed in the grade 4

writing products. Thus, it would be well to guide teachers to see developmental progressions of skills that are a part of different kinds of writing as stretching over the entire range of grades (1 to 8) encompassed in the assessment, rather than fixed at one grade level.

A general scoring rubric for writing was created with three dimensions. Response to Reading (addressing reading comprehension) includes amount of information from the passage used in the writing, the accuracy of the information, and the selection or relevance of the information to the task. This reviewer found the scoring guide for Response to Reading to be generally inconsistent with the writing prompts and other instructions to the writer. For example, for the passage on The Sinking of the Titanic, the student is asked to "use the facts in the passage to write a story [the directions for administering reads, in error, "write a good essay," p. 8] from the point of view of someone who might have been on the ship when it sank" (Reading Passage, p. 3). Then, in the directions for administering this passage, the teacher directs the student to that prompt in the reading passage, and adds that "it is important that the details they use in their writing should accurately reflect what they have read" (directions for administering, p. 8). In the scoring guide, the scorer is asked to consider: "How much information from the passage does the student bring to the writing?" (p. 5). But the prompt and directions do not emphasize "how much information" is used. Again, in opposition to the prompt and directions, the scoring rubric for this passage gives a "2" (out of a possible 4 points) to a response that presents a minimal amount of information and a "4" (highest score) to one that presents "a substantial amount of information" (p. 6). Because one of the purposes of the assessment is for students to understand their own literacy growth, this scoring in opposition to directions for the writing is likely to be confusing and lacking in credibility for both student and teacher. A case in point is one "model paper" for a score of 2 on this dimension (scoring guide, p. 28). The paper was a narrative of a young couple with most of the narrative describing their getting ready for the trip on the Titanic, the waving to the family, a proposal to get married on the ship, the enjoyment of four days, and then the disaster.

Some detail from the reading passage was used up to this point. More detail from the passage came in at that stage. The point is that the narrative met the criteria for the writing prompt and the additional directions during the administration of the task and did it in a way that one knew enough about the characters to have the disaster hit home. The scoring guides for the other two dimensions (management of content or organization and development of the writing and command of language or such matters as sentence structure, word choice, and mechanics) seem more appropriate to this reviewer.

A Scoring Workshop Kit (technical manual, p. 28) is available with a trainer's manual, videotape, and other supportive material (though the scoring guide does not reference it in "materials needed," p. 3). With a 6-hour training session, evidence is reported that trained scorers obtain a reasonably high agreement with "expected scores" for the training papers. Over 70% of the judgments were in exact agreement with "expected scores" and fewer than 2% differed by more than one point. In addition, independent scorers in about 25% of the cases differed by one point or more. This would make a big difference for a student who may be rated "minimal" (2) rather than "adequate" (3), or "adequate" rather than "excellent" (4). There are procedures for resolving differences, but no study is reported for focusing on what happens in these cases. The appropriateness of the level of scoring reliability for use for individual feedback to students seems questionable.

There is no apparent guidance for the test user (student, teacher, administrator, or "other decision makers") in the scoring guide or technical report with respect to making inferences from the test information and considering implications for instruction, student development, or policy level issues. Because the purposes of the test listed above focus on these test uses, the present level of development of supportive guides for interpretation and use are severely limited.

If the teacher decides not to use the "optional" Guided Writing Activity (with its specific guide to prewriting, drafting, and revising) the teacher simply takes students through those steps, presumably in whatever way she or he chooses to follow. This introduces considerable variation in administration procedures. Directions suggest to the teacher administering the test, that "you should function as a 'coach'. That is you should motivate, guide, prod, and encourage students to produce their best work without actually doing the work for them. The amount of prompting you provide can range from very little to quite a bit depending upon the needs and abilities of your students" (directions for administering, pp. 4–5). Given the ambiguity and planned variation in directions for administration, and the lack of any suggested training for administration of the test in any of the documents listed as "needed" on page 3 of the directions for administering, there will be considerable variability in test administration procedures. This lack of standardization of procedures for administration will likely play havoc with interpretation of student performance and with making sense of whatever lines of validity evidence is gathered for inferences to be made from test performance. Thus, though some validity evidence is presented, it is not considered here because of the lack of test standardization making interpretation of any findings lacking in credibility.

In spite of the limitations in standardization of procedures, the reading passages and writing tasks appear to be useful for providing in-class practice in integrated reading and writing and could provide interpretable scores if teachers agreed upon standard procedures for administration that are consistent with the scoring guides.

The IAS-Science Assessment and IAS-Mathematics Assessment both contain a useful set of performance tasks. Both are problem-solving process and problem generating in form with an attempt to get at "real-world" (p. 15) contexts. Scoring is holistic and analytic and can be performed by the user or by the publisher. Holistic and analytic scoring are generic rather than task specific. Although the tasks appear useful for instruction and assessment, the lack of a technical report on selection of items, reliability, validity, and guides for interpretation and use make it premature to evaluate these subtests.

Review of the Integrated Assessment System by BIKKAR S. RANDHAWA, *Professor of Educational Psychology, University of Saskatchewan, Saskatoon, Canada:*

The Integrated Assessment System (IAS) was designed to assess student performance in

Language Arts, Mathematics, and Science through a series of performance tasks. As the performance tasks in three areas are independent and also the available validation and technical information for each area varies, each assessment area is reviewed in a distinct section.

IAS—LANGUAGE ARTS PERFORMANCE ASSESSMENT. The Language Arts Performance Assessment (LAPA) series of instruments is based on a sound rationale. Changes in language arts curricula and instruction, an integration of literacy skills, a focus on constructing meaning, an emphasis on problem solving and critical thinking skills, use of collaboration and cooperative learning in classrooms, and contemporary assessment approaches that advocate performance tasks are important considerations in the development of these Language Arts Assessment tools. In my view, this system is integrated within the language arts assessment domain because reading and writing are not considered as isolated areas for instruction and assessment but rather they are viewed as an integrated whole. Proficiency in one is necessary for proficiency in the other. This is where these tools distinguish from the others in the market.

The LAPA includes for each grade (2 to 8) three booklets of reading passages. The passage in the booklet is preceded by the reading/writing prompt in a colored box. Each prompt is intended to integrate reading and writing and to engage the student in problem solving and critical thinking. For each passage for a grade there is a separate manual of directions for administering, with a specific section for each prompt. The option is available for teachers to allow a variable number of class periods for each passage. Also, consistent with a teacher's instructional approach and preference, allowance is made for permitting students to collaborate and cooperate in working on the preliminary stages of the writing activity. The final draft, however, is expected to be written and revised by each student individually. For the final draft, materials in the LAPA include a response form for each passage. An optional guided writing activity form is available for teachers to use. This focused activity guide for each prompt provides structure for the writing activity. It directs students to review the pertinent and important details about the passage, to organize the required writing,

to prepare a draft of the writing required by the prompt, and to critique and rewrite a final draft. There is a separate scoring guide for each passage in the set. Scoring guides consist of an introduction to the scoring guide, six sections, and three appendices. Distinctive and prompt-specific parts of these guides are Sections 3–5 and Appendix A.

Section 1 of the scoring guides describes the type of scoring, purportedly a combination of the elements of holistic, analytic, and primary trait assessment methods. It also provides the definition of terms, the general scoring rubric, and factors to consider in assigning a score for each dimension to be scored, that is, Response to Reading, Management of Content, and Command of Language.

Section 2 deals with general procedures for scoring. It includes: following the scoring system, working with a partner, checking reliability, resolving differences, handling unexpected responses, and avoiding extraneous factors in scoring. Section 3 provides specific procedures for scoring a specific prompt. In this section, the general scoring rubric is modified to reflect the specific prompt in three dimensions to be scored.

Section 4 contains two model papers for each score point (1 to 4) for a specific prompt. Section 5 includes a sample paper to be scored by the teacher for practice and self-determination of scoring accuracy. Teachers are encouraged to use the model papers for additional practice, if deemed necessary. Each model paper is scored on only one dimension so that a teacher may use that paper to score for the other two dimensions for practice.

Section 6 is general and basically applies to three prompts for each grade. It reflects the philosophy of the assessment system and distinguishes between process and product evaluation. This section also deals with the limitations, from the authors' perspective, of the LAPA and makes useful suggestions to the users for augmenting this assessment with standardized normative tests if other purposes are intended.

The technical report for the LAPA provides extensive technical data. This includes opinions of students and teachers in the tryout samples, convergent and discriminant validity correlational tables for each prompt involving two scorers, interdimensional correlations by prompt, percentage of agreement between scorers for field test data for each prompt, interrater reliability estimates by dimension and prompt, and other descriptive statistics. However, there are several redundancies in these reported statistics as well as inappropriately derived results. For example, interdimensional correlations by prompt in Table 12 are redundant with statistics in Tables 4 to 11. Statistics in Table 12, furthermore, are slightly inflated because the data for the two scorers, I assume, are combined for calculating these statistics. On the other hand, Table 14 provides interrater reliability estimates by dimension and prompt using both Pearson and Spearman correlation procedures. It is not clear why this was done. How one is to decide which of these is appropriate for score interpretation is not explicitly stated. There are many discrepancies in the number of interrater scores for each response to a prompt reported in Tables 13 and 14.

A more serious difficulty in the reported convergent and discriminant validity evidence, Tables 4 to 11, is that for scoring a response to a prompt Scorer 1 and Scorer 2 are not two specific individuals who scored all the responses to a prompt. Multiple scorers were used and different sets of each response were scored by different pairs of scorers. Hence, the reported scores are thereby confounded and the contaminated variables might produce spuriously higher values than expected.

It is useful to have the interrater reliability evidence. However, it should be noted that it, too, is affected by the confounding of the scorer variable, as described above. For the purposes of a classroom teacher who may not have the luxury of a second reader for the student responses nor time for herself to reread the papers, this evidence serves as an assurance that scoring is reasonably robust provided instructions are strictly followed and that the teacher has undergone the type of training that the scorers of the field test responses had taken.

In summary, this set of materials is exemplary in providing classroom teachers an introduction to performance assessment in language arts. The philosophy behind the development of these materials is well articulated and the limitations of this assessment are clearly stated. The user has the responsibility to ascertain whether one short reading prompt is sufficient to provide durable evidence on the overall language ability as well as on the three components of language acquisition in the time required for the administration of each prompt. For other purposes, standardized instruments must not be ruled out as irrelevant or inappropriate.

IAS—SCIENCE PERFORMANCE ASSESSMENT. The Science Performance Assessment (SPA) system is parallel to the LAPA in that each student booklet, directions for administering, and scoring guide have the same basic structure and are based on the same philosophical orientation. At each grade level, I assume, there are two sets or forms of materials. I assumed this to be the case because there is no overall grid that orients the user to the numeric codes on each booklet, for example, 911 and 912, 921 and 922, etc. I have not quite determined the significance of the "9" in the numeric code.

For each assessment task in the SPA, one per form per grade, there are five scores available. The holistic score has a range of 0 to 6. Each of the four analytic scores, experimenting, collecting data, drawing conclusions, and communicating, has a range of 1 to 4. The scoring guide provides rubrics for each score in the holistic and analytic system. However, there is only one illustration for each holistic score, which is supposedly based on a hypothetical student response. I do not think that these responses are actual responses selected for illustration. These are transcriptions or made-up responses to demonstrate expectations for each holistic score point. Following each holistic score illustration, there is a score for that illustration for each analytic component. Only excerpts from the specific scoring rubric are provided for each analytic score assigned for the response in this illustration. Perhaps, that is sufficient for experienced scorers who have used this kind of performance assessment either in the classroom context or as a scorer in a large-scale assessment. It is not appropriate for inexperienced teachers who may only receive initial training in scoring. Such teachers need more illustrations and some unscored samples to develop consistency in scoring. The unscored samples should be followed by expert-assigned scores. Such a procedure was used in the Language Arts Assessment.

There is no evidence available for this specific performance assessment set for me to conclude that two or more independent raters would be consistent in scoring responses to these tasks. In essence, there is no technical evidence to support the use, interpretation, and consequences of these assessments. Therefore, these materials, at best, could be considered supplemental instructional materials and not assessment instruments per se in the strictest sense. Validity evidence should be available before these sets are marketed as assessment materials in science.

I do not undervalue the importance of writing in any subject. Further, I appreciate the development of critical thinking and scientific attitude. These highly valued cognitive abilities and attitudes cannot exist without a sufficiently rich knowledge base (Okagaki & Sternberg, 1990). Process approaches are important but these instructional schemes must not take hostage the content of the domain. We cannot think in vacuum. Thinking must be developed in conjunction with the development of scientific content. Everything in science cannot be learned through experimentation. Reading in science involving scientific content, that is, facts, principles, and rules and the way scientists have gone about establishing those, is also critical. It appears to me that there has to be a balance. In correcting for rote learning in science in the past, a completely process and experimental approach may lead to ignorant experimentation. The experimental approach is only one of the ways that science is learned. Hence, scientific performance is more than the evidence a teacher can get by using these materials.

Teachers planning to use these materials may like to determine the authenticity of the tasks for their specific group of students in the specific community context. The relevance, everyday use, and familiarity of the tasks to their specific students are important considerations. Such evidence should be the responsibility of providers of assessment materials. In the absence of that evidence, users bear that responsibility.

IAS—MATHEMATICS PERFORMANCE ASSESSMENT. The integrated assessment system also includes the Mathematics Performance Assessment (MPA). As stated in the SPA, these assessment materials also are parallel to and use the format and description for rubrics in the LAPA. For grades 1–9, there appear to be multigrade student task booklets, directions for administering, and scoring guides. The lowest level materials are for grades 1–3; the next set for grades 2–4; and so

on. There are two forms of materials for each grade range. Again, no explicit description is found to indicate that this is indeed the intended use. It was my initial inference from the numerical codes used and subsequently I confirmed this with the publisher.

Each task booklet consists of just one task, as is the case with the LAPA and SPA booklets. The format of the various booklets in this series is not the same, which is in contrast to the SPA booklets. The only change from booklet to booklet in the SPA was the specific reference to the task here and there. Therefore, the MPA booklets are not monotonous and boring. Students can be expected to be more interested and motivated if more than one task is used for assessment. However, the holistic scoring rubrics for the various levels are the same for all three domains of assessment regardless of the grade level, which in itself is rather interesting and curious. Should one not expect variability in expectations of the overall performance? Was it for convenience and expediency?

The rubrics for the analytic scoring of the four components, Reasoning, Conceptual Knowledge, Communication, and Procedures, provide for the same range of scores (1–4) as for the LAPA and SPA. However, the specific descriptions pertain to the mathematical content. These descriptions are used for scoring all the responses, grades 1–9. Teachers are expected to allow for developmental differences in scoring student responses.

The scoring guides for these materials are deficient in that they do not provide exemplars and guidance for teachers to score consistently. There are no specific illustrations of various types of student responses that are assigned different scores. There is no opportunity for teachers to assess their consistency, except if they happen to have a willing colleague. Such an expectation is not realistic considering the present structure of heavy demands of in-school and extracurricular duties on teachers. I understand that training materials for scorers are available for the school systems. In spite of that, it is important that assessment tasks are scored consistently and that consistency verification opportunities are available for teachers in the scoring guide for each performance task.

In the scoring guide for the Booklet 789, Form 2 on the task Color Spectrum, the typical student responses on page 18 that are supposedly illustrative of no serious major flaws for holistic scoring purposes are in fact indications of misreading of the chart. For each specific question asked, some holistic analysis is provided but there is no overall paper-wise assignment of various points. How the teachers are to synthesize these componential analyses for the holistic score to be assigned is not clear.

These materials, like the SPA, do not have accompanying validity evidence. Also, the content validity of just one task per booklet, even though the assessment may extend over two class periods and writing is encouraged in these tasks, may be questionable. Even if a task is expected to be and designed to be content valid and provides for the assessment in a teaching-like environment, no validity evidence is available. In conclusion, these tasks are interesting exercises that teachers may use in conjunction with their own assessment in mathematics and with their knowledge of the students from their daily experience with them. For diagnostic and prescriptive instructional purposes, teachers ought to seek out other available assessment instruments that have the required validity evidence for commercially available materials, as required in the *Standards for Educational and Psychological Testing* (AERA, APA, & NCME, 1985).

CONCLUSION. The title of this set of instruments is misleading. It gives the impression that assessment in Language Arts, Mathematics, and Science is integrated. From my view, integrated assessment means that it is linked or connected. This is not the case. There is no evidence to support interconnectedness or linking of the three areas. The only defensible claim is that assessment in Language Arts is integrated in the sense that reading and writing are assessed together using a common prompt or task. I have not seen any explicit statement regarding the integrated assessment in either Mathematics or Science.

Another impression one gets is that the tasks used in the three areas are authentic. I like to distinguish between performance assessment and authentic assessment. Performance assessment provides the student or the examinee an opportunity to show his or her competence on a job-related or applied situation. Authentic assessment, on the other hand, is more complex. It not only presents to the student peformance tasks but also ensures

that tasks have clear relationship to the curriculum, instruction, and as much as possible to real-life situations a student has encountered. Tasks used in these assessments are performance tasks that assess application of knowledge and problem solving but not job-related or real-life tasks. In the Language Arts area of these measures, there is evidence on the appropriateness of the tasks for curriculum and instruction. However, many tasks are not those that students experience in their daily lives or those that have relevance for job situations.

For the Mathematics and Science assessment instruments there are no technical data. Guidance to teachers on scoring, even though scoring guides are provided, is not clear and unambiguous. It seems to me that the guides do not have actual student responses as examples of various score points that are consistent with the rubrics. Teachers are basically left to fend for themselves in terms of scoring consistency. However, an expensive scoring service from the publisher is available, but it seems to defeat the purpose of these assessments. Teachers do not gain valuable insight of student strengths and weaknesses if scoring is done by professional scorers.

Language Arts Assessment is based on technically sound evidence and is, therefore, recommended as a good source of integrated language arts performance assessment. There is a need of validity evidence for both the Mathematics and Science assessments before they are recommended for use. At present, these tasks could be used as an adjunct to a teacher's own assessment attempts for instructional decisions.

REVIEWER'S REFERENCES

American Educational Research Association, American Psychological Association, & National Council on Measurement in Education. (1985). *Standards for educational and psychological testing*. Washington, DC: American Psychological Association, Inc.

Okagaki, L., & Sternberg, R. J. (1990). Teaching thinking skills: We're getting the context wrong. *Contributions to Human Development, 21*, 63–78.

[46]
INteraction CHecklist for Augmentative Communication, Revised Edition.

Purpose: Designed to assess features of interaction between augmentative system users and their partners.

Population: Augmentative system users.

Publication Dates: 1984–1991.

Acronym: INCH.

Scores, 13: Strategies (Initiation, Facilitation, Regulation, Termination); Modes (Linguistic, Paralinguistic,

Kinesic, Proxemic, Chronemic); Contexts (Familiar-Trained, Familiar-Untrained, Unfamiliar-Trained, Unfamiliar-Untrained).

Administration: Individual.

Price Data, 1993: $31 per complete kit including manual ('91, 74 pages) and 15 checklists; $8 per 15 checklists.

Time: Administration time not reported.

Comments: Behavior checklist.

Authors: Susan Oakander Bolton and Sallie E. Dashiell.

Publisher: Imaginart Communication Products.

TEST REFERENCE

1. Sutton, A. E., & Gallagher, T. M. (1993). Verb class distinctions and AAC language-encoding limitations. *Journal of Speech and Hearing Research, 36*, 1216–1226.

Review of the INteraction CHecklist for Augmentative Communication, Revised Edition by ANTHONY J. NITKO, Professor of Educational Measurement and Chairperson, Department of Psychology in Education, University of Pittsburgh, Pittsburgh, PA:

The INteraction CHecklist for Augmentative Communication (INCH), Revised Edition is a clinical checklist for assessing social communication skills of persons unable to use oral speech effectively and who must use an augmentative and alternative communication (AAC) aid. The INCH does not assess general linguistic competencies or technical skills in using an AAC aid. Instead, it focuses on whether a person is able to use an AAC aid to communicate with others in typical social settings such as the home, school, work, and community.

The INCH is a list of 32 communication behaviors (called strategies) organized into four communication scales: Initiation (6 strategies), Facilitation (13 strategies), Regulation (9 strategies), and Termination (4 strategies). Assessment consists of rating a person's use of each of the 32 strategies in each of five communication modes: Linguistic (verbal language), Paralinguistic (nonverbal vocalizations, inflections), Kinesic (facial expression, body movements, gestures), Proxemic (physical positioning, distance), and Chronemic (timing, rate). A person's usage of each strategy is rated as *present* (effective without prompting), *emerging* (needs prompting, inconsistent), *absent* (or not observed), or *not applicable.*

The ratings are summarized for each of the 32 strategies and for each of the four communication scales. A strategy that receives a majority of "present" ratings across all the appropriate modalities is labeled a *strength*. Otherwise, it is a *weakness*. Each of the four communication scales re-

ceives a numerical score obtained by counting the number of strategies that were identified as "strengths." The number of "presents" also result in a score.

The INCH ratings may be completed by communication specialists and/or paraprofessionals who observe the person directly or by an interviewer who discusses the person being rated with one or more informants (family members, educators, caregivers, employers, etc.).

Once the checklist is completed, the specific strategies identified as weak are targeted for training. The manual authors describe how to translate each weakness into a statement of a specific and measurable learning target. They also describe how to prioritize learning targets in the intervention learning sequence. Examples of intervention learning activities are provided.

TECHNICAL DATA. The INCH manual contains no empirical data to support the scientific validity of using the results for diagnosis and prescription. Descriptions of how the specific strategies were developed or selected are not given. Data supporting the listed strategies as the most critical to rate are missing. Normative data on the typical INCH performance of persons with different types and degrees of disabilities, and using different types of AAC aids, would be helpful when interpreting a person's results. The amount of confidence we should have in the INCH results could be better understood if we had data supporting stability and interrater reliabilities.

SUMMARY. The use of the INCH should probably be restricted to highly skilled social communication specialists. Even so, the INCH is best seen as an informal assessment tool rather than as a scientifically grounded instrument. At this time the manual contains no data to support the argument that INCH results may be validly used for diagnosing social communication weaknesses among persons needing to use AAC aids.

Review of the INteraction CHecklist for Augmentative Communication, Revised Edition by KENNETH G. SHIPLEY, Professor and Chair of Communicative Sciences and Disorders, California State University, Fresno, Fresno, CA:

The INteraction CHecklist for Augmentative Communication (INCH) is not a test per se but, as the authors describe it, an observational tool or checklist to assess different types of interactive behavior pertinent to helping develop nonoral communication. In their words, "the authors developed the Checklist to help clinicians describe the critical features of interaction necessary for successful communication between augmentative system users and their partners" (manual, p. 3).

The one-piece scoring sheet, which folds out, contains three different sections: (a) the cover sheet containing identifying information and an assessment of entry skills; (b) the recording sheet for scoring augmentative or alternative communication system skills by four communication strategies (Initiation, Facilitation, Regulation, and Termination) across five communication modes (Linguistic, Paralinguistic, Kinesic, Proxemic, and Chronemic); and the worksheet to summarize results and begin planning intervention strategies.

Several fundamental concepts are important in understanding the INCH, its scoresheet, and what the checklist is attempting to do. A fundamental premise of the instrument is viewing communication modes within the following categories: Linguistic, or verbal language skills; Paralinguistic, such as nonverbal vocalizations or inflection; Kinesic, such as facial expression, body movement, or gestures; Proxemic, such a physical positioning and distance; and Chronemic, or timing and rate.

These five communication modes are then evaluated across four types of communication, which are termed strategies: Initiation, such as responding to greetings or introducing self; Facilitation, such as use of eye contact or seeking help; Regulation, such as giving feedback or expanding on a message; and Terminating, such as a social farewell or indicating completion of a conversation.

A total of 32 different topics are addressed within these four areas of Initiation, Facilitation, Regulation, and Termination. As appropriate to a client, each of the 32 different topics is assessed as being *present, emerging, absent,* or *not applicable.* The effect of this scoring methodology is viewing the four communication strategies (e.g., Initiation) across five communication modes (e.g., Linguistic) by one of four response patterns (e.g., present). For example, Kinesic Initiation might be present, but Linguistic Initiation absent. The scoring sheet also allows space for clinicians to describe behaviors seen, and make a general estimate of strengths and weaknesses within each of the 32 topic areas.

The accompanying manual is subdivided into five chapters and a selected references section. The five chapters are Introduction, Components, Administration, Application and Use, and Intervention. There are relatively good descriptions of the different terminology used and definitions of the conceptual framework used found in the manual. One real strength within the manual is a number of figures to illustrate key concepts. These are highly useful for individuals without extensive experience with augmentative and alternative communication clients or methods. Chapters 4 and 5 address a number of areas pertaining to intervention, such as developing appropriate goals and procedures. Although some of the suggestions are potentially helpful, users are cautioned that some of the procedures are rather simplistic or cursory—additional training and knowledge beyond that found in the manual is advisable.

A limitation throughout the manual is the absence of appropriate literature underpinning some of the suggestions and approaches. For example, there are 16 items listed in the selected references section of the manual. However, only five of these are even cited in the text—three of these citations are listed to substantiate one thought, and one of the five citations is a dictionary. There is an absence of solid backing offered for some of the suggestions and underpinnings of the model used.

There is another point that merits consideration. Throughout the manual, the authors note that the INCH is a checklist or a tool—not a test. It is not a test per se, but it is used for assessment purposes and users do make important clinical decisions from information attained. Also, the manual authors offer a number of suggestions for interpreting results and developing treatment strategies. However, there are no data or discussions about any type of validity or reliability. There is a presumption of face validity, as well as content validity on many items contained on the checklist, but validity is not really addressed in any form. Similarly, reliability is simply not addressed. This restricts the confidence one can place in obtained results.

In summary, the INCH provides a model for looking at the needs of patients who would benefit from alternative or augmentative communication. Many of the items are highly appropriate to such an assessment. The scoring sheet is relatively easy to use, and it provides useful reference (by page number) to specific items in the manual for further clarification. As the authors have commented, the checklist should be used in combination with other materials and assessment procedures. Some of the intervention strategies and suggestions may be helpful for some clinicians. However, care should be taken not to overrely on the tool due to the fundamental validity and reliability questions that are not addressed. The user could also be more confident in the instrument if there were more thorough, appropriately cited discussions of the fundamental underpinnings of the checklist and some of the suggestions offered for intervention.

[47]
Inventory of Drinking Situations.

Purpose: "Designed to assess situations in which a client drank heavily over the past year."
Population: Ages 18 to 75.
Publication Date: 1987.
Acronym: IDS.
Scores, 8: Personal Status (Unpleasant Emotions, Physical Discomfort, Pleasant Emotions, Testing Personal Control, Urges and Temptations), Situations Involving Other People (Conflict with Others, Social Pressure to Drink, Pleasant Times with Others).
Administration: Group.
Forms, 2: IDS-100, IDS-42 (Brief Version).
Price Data, 1993: $25 per specimen set including user's guide (53 pages), 25 questionnaires, 25 answer sheets, 25 profiles; $13.50 per user's guide; $12.75 per 25 IDS-42 (Brief Version) questionnaires, 25 answer sheets, and 25 profile sheets; $14.75 per 25 IDS-100 questionnaires, 25 answer sheets, and 25 profile sheets; $140 per computer software program (50 uses); $450 per computer software program (200 uses).
Foreign Language Edition: Both forms available in French.
Time: (20–25) minutes.
Comments: IDS-42 (Brief Version) is for research use only.
Authors: Helen M. Annis, J. Martin Graham, and Christine S. Davis.
Publisher: Addiction Research Foundation [Canada].
Cross References: See T4:1265 (2 references).

TEST REFERENCES

1. Cannon, D. S., Rubin, A., Keefe, C. K., Black, J. L., Leeka, J. K., & Phillips, L. A. (1992). Affective correlates of alcohol and cocaine use. *Addictive Behaviors, 17,* 517-524.
2. Sobell, L. C., Toneatto, T., & Sobell, M. (1994). Behavioral assessment and treatment planning for alcohol, tobacco, and other drug problems: Current status with an emphasis on clinical applications. *Behavior Therapy, 25,* 533–580.
3. Sobell, M. B., Sobell, L. C., & Gavin, D. R. (1995). Portraying alcohol treatment outcomes: Different yardsticks of success. *Behavior Therapy, 26,* 643–669.

Review of the Inventory of Drinking Situations by MERITH COSDEN, Professor, Department of Education, University of California, Santa Barbara, CA:

The Inventory of Drinking Situations (IDS) is a self-report instrument designed to identify situations in which respondents drank heavily over the past year. The need for this instrument stems from the literature on relapse for clients in treatment for substance abuse. This literature indicates that certain types of situations are more likely to trigger heavy drinking than others, and that these situational "triggers" vary across individuals. The IDS can be used to understand specific drinking problems and to delineate situations under which an individual is more likely to relapse.

The IDS has 100 items that describe eight situations in which drinking is likely to occur. These situations were adapted from a taxonomy of potential relapse determinants developed by Marlatt and Gordon (1985). Five situations are defined by personal states: Unpleasant Emotions, Physical Discomfort, Pleasant Emotions, Testing Personal Control, and Urges and Temptations. The other three are social situations: Conflict with Others, Social Pressure to Drink, and Pleasant Times with Others. In developing the scale the authors considered items from extant substance abuse assessment scales as well as creating their own items based on their work with clients who were alcohol dependent. Items were reviewed by clinicians in the field and pilot tested on men in an inpatient employee assistance program.

The IDS is self-administered, and comes in paper-and-pencil and computerized formats. In either format it takes approximately 20 minutes to complete. It can be administered individually or in group settings. Correlations between paper-and-pencil and computerized versions (with a 2-week interval) of the IDS are reported for 27 clients and range from .75 to .91 across subscales. The manual notes that the IDS should not be used with individuals who are under the influence of alcohol or who are experiencing alcohol withdrawal. One concern of the reviewer is that both administration formats require the client to read and respond independently. Self-administration may be contraindicated if the client is illiterate, or if heavy drinking has impaired the client's cognitive abilities. Administration of the IDS through interview format should be considered.

Each item is rated on a 1–4 scale, as respondents indicate the frequency with which they have engaged in heavy drinking over the past year in that situation as *never, rarely, frequently,* or *almost always.* Six of the scales contain 10 items, and two of the scales, Unpleasant Emotions and Conflict with Others, contain 20 items. The manual explains all scoring procedures. Subscale scores are obtained by adding the scores for items on each subscale. Problem Index scores are derived by dividing each subscale score by the maximum possible score for that subscale and multiplying by 100. A form for graphing Problem Index scores is provided.

Scores can be interpreted in several ways. Problem Index scores, which range from 0–100, provide a general assessment of the severity of one's drinking. The manual suggests that subscale scores of 67–100 reflect a history of heavy drinking and define situations that may be risky for the client in terms of relapse. The Client Profile, consisting of the eight subscale Problem Index scores, can be used to determine patterns of drinking problems, such as whether a client drinks more in the company of others, alone, or under positive or negative affective states. Finally, a client's raw scores can be compared to the standardized scores for the normative sample.

The normative sample was originally composed of 247 clients who had received treatment for alcohol problems in a Canadian clinic. As this sample was primarily male (81.8%), an additional 96 women from the same clinic were subsequently included, resulting in a total sample of 193 males and 130 females. Education level, substance abuse history, and marital status for clients in the sample are provided in the manual, but ethnicity is not noted. Differences in subscale scores were found for men and women and as a function of age. The manual presents subscale scores by gender and three age groupings, which differ slightly for men and women. For men, the age groupings are under 36, 36–55, and over 55, and for women the groupings were under 36, 36–45, and over 45. Differences in the age groupings for men and women reflect differences in subscale score patterns by gender, as well as differences in the distribution of male and female clients in the sample by age.

The manual provides internal consistency data on each of the eight subscales. Alpha levels range from .87 to .96, reflecting high internal consistency for each subscale, whereas item-total correlations within each of the subscales was somewhat lower (.39 to .82). As noted below, there are questions raised in the literature as to whether the scale represents eight or fewer distinct situations. Other types of reliability, including interrater reliability, are not discussed in the manual.

Studies of the factor structure of the IDS do not fully support the original eight-factor structure. Initially, factors were rationally derived, based on Marlatt and Gordon's (1985) taxonomy of relapse situations. A principal components analysis was conducted separately on each of the eight subscales using scores obtained from the normative sample. Six of the eight subscales were unifactorial; the subscale labeled Conflict with Others had four factorial components, whereas Pleasant Times consisted of two factors. The nature of these subfactors was not further examined. In a subsequent study (Cannon, Leeka, Patterson, & Baker, 1990) a principal components analysis was conducted on all items based on responses by 336 male inpatients in an Alcohol Dependence Treatment Program. Three components were identified in this manner, contributing to 43% of the test variance: Negative Findings, Positive Findings, and Conflict with Others. Cannon et al. report that the authors of the IDS (Annis and her associates) were able to replicate their findings with data from the normative sample when they followed the same statistical procedures. The validity of these three subscales in relation to the validity of the original eight subscales requires further study.

The manual reports on the content validity and concurrent validity of the IDS. Content validity was evaluated by asking raters to place test items into the eight categories; they were able to do so with a high degree (92%–99%) of interrater agreement. External validity has been assessed through correlations between other measures of substance abuse, levels of drinking, and IDS subscale scores. Differences in subtest scores for heavy, moderate, and light drinkers have been noted. Integral to the significance of the IDS, however, is its ability to predict relapse situations; that is, are the situations in which clients report higher levels of drinking more likely to be those in which they experience a relapse? Studies of the predictive validity of the IDS are not available.

In addition to the original IDS, there is a computerized version for the IBM. Questions are displayed on the computer screen, and clients are asked to press the number on the keyboard that most accurately describes their behavior over the past year. The program scores the IDS, displays Problem Index scores on a bar graph, and provides a list of specific situations under which the client noted heavy drinking *frequently* or *almost always.*

A shortened form of the IDS, with 42 items, was developed as a research tool. Based on the principal components analysis of the original subscales, test items with the highest item-subscale correlations were selected for the short form. Four items were selected to represent each of the six unifactorial subscales; 18 additional items were selected to represent the two multifactorial subtests, Conflict with Others and Pleasant Times with Others; 18 additional items were selected. Internal reliability of the subscales is in the .80–.92 range, whereas correlations between the long and short form subscales range from .93 to .98. Subsequent studies (Isenhart, 1993) identified a five-factor structure for the short form of the IDS, with the five scales highly correlated with one higher-order dimension.

Although the scale specifically addresses use of alcohol, many people seeking treatment for substance abuse problems are both drug and alcohol users. Several investigators (e.g., Cannon, Rubin, Keefe, Black, Leeka, & Phillips, 1992) have used the IDS to study differences between alcohol and drug users. In doing so, Cannon et al. changed the wording of the stem in the IDS from "drank heavily" to "drank or used drugs heavily." Use of the instrument in this manner requires further psychometric study.

The IDS can provide valuable information for treatment planning for clients with drinking problems. Its strengths include its ease of administration, clinical relevance, and concurrent validity with regard to differentiating clients with moderate and heavy drinking problems. There is a need for research on the predictive validity of the instrument. Application of the IDS to populations in which both drugs and alcohol are concerns also warrants further study.

REVIEWER'S REFERENCES

Marlatt, G. A., & Gordon, J. R. (1985). *Relapse prevention: Maintenance strategies in the treatment of addictive behaviors.* New York: Guilford.

Cannon, D. S., Leeka, J. K., Patterson, E. T., & Baker, T. B. (1990). Principal components analysis of the Inventory of Drinking Situations: Empirical categories of drinking by alcoholics. *Addictive Behaviors, 15,* 265–269.

Cannon, D. S., Rubin, A., Keefe, C. K., Black, J. L., Leeka, J. K., & Phillips, L. A. (1992). Affective correlates of alcohol and cocaine use. *Addictive Behaviors, 17,* 517–524.

Isenhart, C. E. (1993). Psychometric evaluation of a short form of the Inventory of Drinking Situations. *Journal of Studies on Alcohol, 54,* 345–349.

Review of the Inventory of Drinking Situations by KEVIN L. MORELAND, Professor of Psychology and Chair, Fordham University, Bronx, NY:

The Inventory of Drinking Situations (IDS-100) is a 100-item questionnaire that assesses situations in which an alcohol rehabilitation client drank heavily *almost always, frequently, rarely,* or *never* during the past year. It was developed as a situation-specific measure of drinking that could be used to identify an individual client's high-risk situations for alcoholic relapse (User's Guide, p. 1). A 42-item short form of the IDS (IDS-42) is also available. The IDS-100 is recommended for clinical purposes whereas the IDS-42 may be preferable for research applications where time is at a premium. A computer-administered version of the IDS is available that shows promising congruence with the paper-and-pencil version used to develop the instrument.

The classification of drinking situations embodied in the IDS was based on the extensive efforts of Marlatt and his colleagues to determine what causes alcoholic relapse (e.g., Marlatt & Gordon, 1985). Eight expert judgment-based subscales are divided among two superordinate classes also based on expert judgment: Personal States and Situations Involving Other People. Most of the former are not "situations" in the way that term is ordinarily used to characterize the extrapersonal environment. Rather, they are subjective states such as Unpleasant Emotions (e.g., "When I was lonely"), Physical Discomfort (e.g., "When I had a headache"), Pleasant Emotions (e.g., "When I was enjoying myself"), and Testing Personal Control (e.g., "When I started to think I wasn't really hooked on alcohol"). The fourth Personal State, Urges and Temptations, includes a few subjective states (i.e., Urges like "When I remembered how good it [liquor] tasted") and a number of extrapersonal situations (i.e., Temptations like "When I passed by a bar"). Situations Involving Other People comprises subscales tapping Conflict With Others (e.g., "When someone criticized me"), Social Pressure to Drink (e.g., "When my boss offered me a drink"), and Pleasant Times with Others (e.g., "When I wanted to celebrate with a friend").

ITEM DEVELOPMENT. Suggestions for item content were drawn from a number of sources including other inventories, clinicians, persons recovering from alcoholism, and clients being treated for alcohol problems. "A draft of the resulting questionnaire was sent to five clinicians who had extensive experience working with alcoholics to solicit comments on item clarity and on item coverage .... Similar feedback was also solicited in a pilot testing ... on alcoholics" (User's Guide, p. 2). Formal psychometric considerations did not influence the final composition of the IDS-100. All of the subscales except Unpleasant Emotions and Conflict With Others comprise 10 items, the latter each comprise 20 items.

Despite the authors' extensive efforts to write good items, some potential problems are apparent. Some items are so general that they seem only to summarize the content of the remainder of the subscale (e.g., the Social Pressure to Drink item "When I was offered a drink and felt awkward about refusing"). Other items are so specific that the situations may be irrelevant to substantial numbers of persons with alcohol problems (e.g., "When my boss offered me a drink"). Still other items appear to tap more than one construct (e.g., the Unpleasant Emotions item, "When I was troubled and I wanted to think more clearly"). That item might better exemplify the category if it ended at "troubled." Interestingly and importantly, these potentially problematic items tended not to clear the psychometric hurdles necessary for inclusion in the IDS-42.

Items for the IDS-42 were selected by examining unrotated principal components within each of the eight IDS-100 subscales. Only Conflict with Others (4) and Pleasant Times (2) yielded more than one principal component with an eigenvalue greater than one. Items for the IDS-42 are those with the highest item-component correlations unless two items were judged too similar in content, in which case one was replaced by the next highest correlating item. The IDS-42 comprises four items for each of the unifactorial subscales and three items for each component of the multifactorial subscales. Correlations between the IDS-42 subscales and their IDS-100 counterparts ranged from .93 to .98.

NORMS. Normative data for the IDS-100 are based on 323 "individuals with a wide variety of alcohol-related problems who were assessed on admission" (User's Guide, p. 8). Multivariate analyses of this sample led the authors to provide separate T-score conversions by sex or age for every subscale except Physical Discomfort. This seems ill-advised. The total normative sample is small. Subdividing it yields some tiny subsamples (e.g., 30 men over age 55). Although it is common to study demographic variables, I believe that IDS users would be better served by studies of psychological variables (e.g., sex role identity rather than gender). Perhaps Conflict With Others *is* a curvilinear function of age, younger people tending toward more interpersonal conflict in general and the interpersonal conflicts so often generated by alcoholism eventually being somewhat offset by the mellowing of middle age. The ability to assess these hypotheses is obscured by the use of different norms for different age groups. I suggest that users calculate a single set of norms from the data available in Appendix B of the User's Guide (pp. 33–41).

For interpretive purposes the authors emphasize a "Problem Index" score, which is simply the percentage of the maximum possible score. Although these scores are, no doubt, easier to discuss with clients than are T scores, no other justification is provided for their use. I recommend that they be used only to illustrate inferences that have been properly drawn from norm-referenced scores.

Psychometric Properties.

RELIABILITY. The eight IDS-100 subscales are very internally consistent. Cronbach alphas ranged from .87 (Urges and Temptations) to .96 (Unpleasant Emotions) in a very carefully described sample "of 247 clients who had voluntarily sought treatment ... [and] their major substance of abuse was ... alcohol" (User's Guide, p. 2). Not surprisingly, the IDS-42 subscales are slightly less reliable than their IDS-100 parents, with alphas ranging from .80 (physical Discomfort and Urges and Temptations) to .92 (Conflict with Others). The User's Guide provided no data concerning the stability of either form of the IDS.

VALIDITY. The issue of content coverage was dealt with in the section on item selection. Additionally, three undescribed raters were asked to sort the IDS-100 items into the eight subscales. Interrater agreement ranged from 92% to 99%.

The test authors presented evidence that all the IDS-100 scales are positively related to drinking behavior as indexed by variables such as scores on the Alcohol Dependence Scale (Skinner & Horn, 1984). However, as the authors noted, "research is needed ... to establish its relation to relapse episodes, and to document ... its utility as a treatment planning tool" (User's Guide, p. 9).

Intercorrelations among subscales were not provided in the User's Guide, but item-level factor loadings for the IDS-42 were. Details of the factor analytic method are not provided, although it was obviously exploratory and employed an oblique rotation; the sample is presumably the same one used to assess other psychometric properties of the IDS.

The factor structure did not completely conform to the a priori structure. Items from Unpleasant Emotions and Conflict With Others merged into one factor as did Pleasant Times With Others and Social Pressure to Drink. Two new dimensions emerged composed mainly of items from Conflict With Others: Social Problems at Work and Problems With Intimacy. The first order factors composed two second order factors that reflected positive (e.g., Pleasant Emotions) and negative (e.g., Physical Discomfort) motivations to drink rather than the two superordinate a priori classes of Personal States and Situations Involving Other People.

SUMMARY. The authors of the IDS are clearly sophisticated clinicians and psychometricians. The IDS appears to be the best instrument of its kind. On the other hand, the User's Guide includes some interpretive advice that is, at best, hard to defend (e.g., emphasis on the Problem Index scores) and omits some critical information (e.g., intercorrelations among the scales). I hope the authors will soon update the decade-old User's Guide both to respond to critics and to inform users about new research that will improve the use of an already useful tool.

REVIEWER'S REFERENCES

Skinner, H. A., & Horn, J. L. (1984). *Alcohol Dependence Scale (ADS): User's guide.* Toronto: Addiction Research Foundation of Ontario.

Marlatt, G. A., & Gordon, J. R. (1985). *Relapse prevention: Maintenance strategies in the treatment of addictive behaviors.* New York: Guilford.

[48]
Job Search Inventory.

Purpose: "To help the job applicant choose realistic occupations for a job search based on a consideration of background and interests."
Population: Job applicants.
Publication Date: 1985.

Acronym: JSI.
Scores, 5: 4 ratings (Interest, Leisure, Training, Work) and Total for each work activity.
Administration: Group.
Price Data: Available from publisher.
Time: (20–60) minutes.
Comments: "For use with the occupational classification structure of the Guide for Occupational Exploration."
Author: New York State Employment Service.
Publisher: U.S. Department of Labor.

Review of the Job Search Inventory by RALPH O. MUELLER, Associate Professor of Educational Research, Department of Educational Leadership, Graduate School of Education and Human Development, The George Washington University, Washington, DC:

The Job Search Inventory (JSI) is an 81-item self-scoring instrument designed to aid job applicants in choosing employment according to their interest, leisure activities, prior training, and work experiences. It must be used in conjunction with information from the fourth edition of the *Guide for Occupational Exploration* (published by the same authors) to match obtained JSI scores to one of 66 work groups in the Guide. Two forms of the JSI are available, one designed to be used directly with the Guide, the other accompanied with an information sheet summarizing the identified work groups; according to the authors, each form should take about 50 minutes to complete.

Materials accompanying the JSI consist of a self-scoring form and an instruction sheet for administrators of the instrument. The strength of the instrument and the scoring forms is that they are both written clearly and, indeed, are self-explanatory to the job applicant. A major weakness, however, is that the information provided to administrators is insufficient. For example, no rationale is given for the incorporated items (except that they are supposed to be "typical of the occupations within a specific Work Group and unique to that Work Group" [Instruction Sheet]). Most serious, no evidence of the validity and reliability of the JSI is available. This is in clear violation of numerous standards set forth in the *Standards for Educational and Psychological Testing* (American Educational Research Association, American Psychological Association, & National Council on Measurement in Education, 1985) and should concern the potential user in search of a valid and reliable instrument to assist job applicants.

The test authors claim that completion and interpretation of JSI results "foster a more informed exploration of the occupational options of the applicant" and that it "will help insure a more realistic interpretation of the applicant's relative strengths and weaknesses in relation to occupational requirements and employment opportunities in the local labor market." In this reviewer's opinion, although possibly true for individual cases, empirical evidence should be provided before the potential user trusts this overall claim and confidently selects the JSI for a give population of job applicants.

REVIEWER'S REFERENCE

American Educational Research Association, American Psychological Association, & National Council on Measurement in Education. (1985). *Standards for educational and psychological testing.* Washington, DC: American Psychological Association, Inc.

Review of the Job Search Inventory by SHELDON ZEDECK, Chair and Professor of Psychology, Department of Psychology, University of California, Berkeley, CA:

The Job Search Inventory (JSI) is a self-assessment instrument designed to help a job applicant choose occupations for a job search based on a consideration of the applicant's background and interests. It consists of 81 short task-based statements or job titles such as "carry luggage in a hotel or airport," "settle insurance claims," or "work as a lawyer." The respondent indicates (essentially "yes" or "no") whether he or she (1) would be *interested* in doing this kind of work; (2) has ever done this in his or her *leisure* time; (3) has ever had *training* in the activity; and (4) has ever had *work experience* like the one in the activity. An accompanying document entitled Instructions for Administering and Using the Job Search Inventory informs the user that the 81 items are keyed to 66 Work Groups that compose the *Guide for Occupational Exploration* (this "guide" was not submitted for review by the test publisher nor was it available in this reviewer's library). According to the "Instructions" the "Guide" contains all the defined occupations that are described in the *Dictionary of Occupational Titles* (4th ed.). The JSI enables the applicant to use the Guide to compare his or her personal background factors to general occupational requirements and to select specific occupations for a job search.

After responding to the statements, the applicant self-scores how many of the four questions were responded to in the positive for each statement. Because each statement is keyed to a "work group," the code of which is provided to the applicant, it is feasible to identify the five highest scoring "work groups." The applicant then reads about the five "work groups" in the "Guide" and selects one for a more specific occupational search.

No psychometric evidence is presented for the instrument. We are not told how the items were chosen, how the items were keyed to the "work groups," and why there is any expected relationship between the results of tallying responses and subsequent job performance or satisfaction. There are no norms, reliability, or validity data.

In summary, there is no way to judge whether the instrument is worth the time to take. There is no prerequisite that there be discussion of the results with any professional; this situation could leave some applicants in a state of greater confusion or uncertainty than prior to taking the inventory. If one wants to find out about potential careers, they are more likely to get better information by taking the Strong Interest Inventory (12:374).

[49]

Joliet 3-Minute Speech and Language Screen (Revised).

Purpose: To "identify children with age-appropriate phonological, grammatical, and semantic structures."
Population: Grades K, 2, 5.
Publication Dates: 1983–1992.
Scores, 5: Receptive Vocabulary, Grammar (Evoked Sentences), Phonology, Voice, Fluency.
Administration: Individual.
Levels, 3: Grades K, 2, 5.
Price Data, 1994: $55 per complete kit including manual ('92, 39 pages), vocabulary plates, record-keeping manual (15 pages), 2 scoring forms, and record-keeping disk in binder.
Time: (2–5) minutes.
Authors: Mary C. Kinzler and Constance Cowing Johnson.
Publisher: The Psychological Corporation.
Cross References: For a review of the original edition by Robert E. Owens, Jr., see 9:555 (1 reference).

Review of the Joliet 3-Minute Speech and Language Screen (Revised) by MARTIN A. FISCHER,

Associate Professor, Department of Human Services, Western Carolina University, Cullowhee, NC:

The Joliet 3-Minute Speech and Language Screen (Revised) is reported to have grown "out of the authors' need to quickly and accurately identify children with age-appropriate phonological, grammatical, and semantic structures" (manual, p. 3). The screen is specifically designed for individual administration to large groups of school-age children (kindergarten, second grade, and fifth grade). It is further designed to allow for complete administration in approximately 3 minutes.

The authors suggest the areas of speech and language used in this screen (receptive vocabulary, expressive syntax, and phonology) are sufficient to reflect accurately the child's language development. Assessment techniques used include a recognition vocabulary task, for Receptive Vocabulary, and an evoked imitation task, for Expressive Syntax, Phonology, Voice, and Fluency.

Specifically, Receptive Vocabulary is assessed by presenting 24 plates (8 at each grade level), with each plate containing a picture of the target vocabulary item and three foils. A vocabulary word is presented verbally along with each plate with the instructions to "point to the one I'm saying" or "point to _____." The child's response is noted on an "Individual Screen" (IS) form as correct or incorrect. The number of errors is then compared with cutoff scores listed on the IS form for grades kindergarten, second, and fifth.

Expressive Syntax is assessed through an evoked imitation task containing 10 sentences. The sentences are read from the IS form, and errors are marked. The number of errors is then compared to individual cutoff scores for each of the three grades. Areas of expressive syntax evaluated include certain auxiliary verbs, tag questions, interrogative reversals, pronouns, articles, and copular forms.

Phonology is assessed at the same time as expressive syntax by judging phonological errors that occur during the evoked sentence task. Phonemes that are to be evaluated are printed on the IS form and are circled if incorrect.

In addition to Receptive Vocabulary, Expressive Syntax, and Phonology, the authors provide a place on the IS form to record subjective judgments regarding Voice and Fluency. Guidelines are given for evaluation of each area with suggestions for follow-up evaluations and/or referral. The Joliet contains two reproducible scoring forms (an Individual Screen, and a Class Record) and a computerized record keeping program formatted for an Apple IIe computer.

STANDARDIZATION. Standardization of the screen was conducted using 2,587 children from three ethnic backgrounds, three socioeconomic classes, and three grades (kindergarten, second, and fifth). Cutoff scores were obtained from 586 children randomly selected from the above sample population.

A test of validity using the Cochran Q test (Meyers & Grossen, 1974) suggested the Grammar portion of the Joliet correlates strongly with the Carrow Elicited Language Inventory (CELI) (Carrow, 1974) at all age levels (.05 level of significance). The vocabulary portion of the Joliet correlated strongly with the Peabody Picture Vocabulary Test (PPVT) (Dunn, 1965) at grades kindergarten and 2 but tended to be more sensitive in identifying borderline high-risk vocabulary cases at grade 5. Test-retest reliability was strong with no significant differences being observed in results obtained from two test administrations 4 weeks apart.

EVALUATION. The overall structure and format of the Joliet appears to be clear and unambiguous. Each of the 24 plates used for the recognition vocabulary task contains four black-and-white illustrations, one representing the target vocabulary word and three representing foils. All drawings appear to be appropriate, nonbiased, and discriminable at the specified grade levels. Likewise, the 10 sentences used to evaluate expressive syntax and phonology contain clear and unambiguous examples of the various syntactic and phonological structures. Test administration and scoring procedures were simple and should be familiar to individuals who have administered the PPVT and the CELI, respectively.

Several concerns must be addressed regarding the Joliet. The most significant concern is related to the basic assumptions of the authors. Specifically, the authors claim the areas of receptive vocabulary, expressive syntax, and phonology are able to sample and reflect accurately the child's language development. Although there can be no doubt that all three of these areas are of primary importance to the development of appropriate language ability, it is possible that a significant number of individuals will exhibit speech and language problems in areas not addressed by the screen. I am referring in particular to children who present with pragmatic and/or language comprehension problems. Specifically, children who exhibit inappropriate discourse/narrative ability (including the ability to follow commands or answer questions) may exhibit age-appropriate recognition vocabulary and syntactic skill and, thus, not be referred for additional testing following administration of the Joliet. Although I feel this limitation is significant, it should not be taken as a fatal criticism of the Joliet but rather as a suggestion for future revisions.

A second concern is related to the choice of the PPVT as a measure of concurrent validity. The PPVT was replaced by a revised version (PPVT-R) (Dunn, 1982) in 1982. As such, the PPVT-R should have been used as a measure of concurrent validity rather than the PPVT.

A third concern, although minor, is related to the Apple IIe format chosen for the computerized record keeping program. Although it can be argued that many public schools still use Apple II computers, the trend is rapidly moving toward Macintosh or DOS/Windows based machines. As such it would be helpful to include a program that can be used across platforms.

In summary, the Joliet appears to be a well-organized, easily administered screening tool. It can, in fact, be administered in 3 minutes and is quickly and unambiguously scored. It seems to be very effective in screening school-age children with deficits in syntax, recognition vocabulary, and/or phonology. Limitations include minimal coverage of pragmatics and language comprehension, use of an unrevised test for concurrent validity, and the inclusion of computer software that may soon become outdated.

REVIEWER'S REFERENCES

Carrow, E. (1974). Carrow Elicited Language Inventory. Chicago: Riverside Publishing Co.

Dunn, L. M. (1965). Peabody Picture Vocabulary Test. Circle Pines, MN: American Guidance Service, Inc.

Meyers, L. S., & Grossen, N. E. (1974). *Behavioral research: Theory, procedure and design*. San Francisco: W. H. Freeman.

Dunn, L. M. (1982). Peabody Picture Vocabulary Test—Revised. Circle Pines, MN: American Guidance Service, Inc.

Review of the Joliet 3-Minute Speech and Language Screen (Revised) by MALCOLM R. McNEIL, Chair, Communication Science & Disorders, University of Pittsburgh, Pittsburgh, PA and THOMAS F. CAMPBELL, Director, Audiology and Speech Pathology, Children's Hospital, Communication Science & Disorders, University of Pittsburgh, Pittsburgh, PA:

The stated purpose of the Joliet 3-Minute Speech and Language Screen is to "identify children with age-appropriate phonological, grammatical, and semantic structures" (p. 3). It is designed to be administered individually by "a certified speech-language pathologist or a carefully trained paraprofessional" (p. 4). Neither procedures for training nor criteria for establishing competence for the paraprofessional were presented other than the directions for administration and scoring provided in the manual. The examination is, as the name of the test implies, designed as a screening tool. Children who fail to meet preestablished criteria for performance "qualify for a complete speech and language evaluation" (p. 4).

CONSTRUCT VALIDITY. It is stated that the areas of "receptive vocabulary," "expressive syntax," and "phonology" provide the most accurate representation of the child's speech and language development. Although unjustified beyond this assumption, these three areas of language provide the structure for the test. Voice and fluency are also observed and scored during the administration of the grammar section.

Although there is a substantive body of literature available that debates various elicitation procedures for the evaluation of language, no theoretical motivation or clinical justification is given for the assessment of grammar through sentence repetition. The validity of this assumption is in need of support.

Criteria for failure on the Receptive Vocabulary, Grammar, Phonology, Voice, and Fluency sections of the examination are clearly stated, but are without justification. As the purpose of the screening examination is to detect children who require additional assessment, a calculation of the false positive, false negative, true positive, and true negative assignments of children is essential. These data are not reported although the authors do report the number of children from each grade level who passed and failed the examination on both the Vocabulary and Grammar sections of the test.

The criteria for failing the Phonology section of the exam is a single error of any type, even for the 5-year-old subjects. Studies on speech-sound normalization (Shriberg, Gruber, & Kwiatkowski, 1994) clearly indicate that a number of consonant sounds are not completely mastered until 6 years of age. More than 50% of the target sounds used in the screening procedure fall into the Shriberg et al. late-8 speech sound normalization group. Based on the criteria for failure, an unacceptably high probability of false positive identifications could result.

CONTENT VALIDITY. The content and procedural design of the test was constrained by the maximum administration time of 3 minutes. Within this context, Receptive Vocabulary is assessed with eight different words for kindergarten, second, and fifth grade levels. These words and the appropriate foils were selected from those that met the criteria for universality. The authors also state the words were subjected to item analysis and found to be discriminating; however, these analyses were not presented. Although the test was designed and constrained by the administration time, it is not a timed test. The authors state that the "usual" time is approximately 3 minutes.

Ten sentences reflecting the most frequently erred syntactic and morphologic structures in the authors' own therapy programs were selected for assessment and elicited from sentence repetition. These included exemplars of auxiliary verbs, tag questions, interrogative reversals, pronouns, articles, and copular forms. It is from these sentences that the phonologic evaluation is done. Although no theoretical justification or specific methods of phonological analysis of these connected speech samples were provided, the authors stated that the sentences were "loaded with phonemic content for assessing the child's acquisition of speech sounds" (p. 3).

The vocabulary words are elicited with black-and-white, hand-drawn pictured stimuli, four pictures per plate. The pictures are well drawn and appear to be discriminable and identifiable based on their sizes, shapes, and clarity of detail.

Fluency is evaluated during the administration of the Grammar section of the examination. The authors suggest that a sample of spontaneous speech may be required if there is a question concerning the adequacy of the child's fluency observed during the Grammar section of the examination. No guidance or criteria for the elicitation or adequacy of this spontaneous sample is provided.

It is recommended that the Voice sample be audiotape recorded and judged by consensus; however, there is no indication of the number of listeners that are necessary to judge the sample. It is recommended that a history be taken from the caregiver/parent with queries about chronicity of any observed voice problem.

Using the Cochran Q Test, differences in performance on the Vocabulary section of the 3-Minute Speech and Language Screen between boys and girls; blacks and whites; Hispanic-others and white; blacks and Hispanic-others; high-mid and mid socioeconomic groups; high-mid and low socioeconomic groups; and mid and low socioeconomic groups were all significant. Differences in performance on the Grammar section between boys and girls; blacks and whites; blacks and Hispanic-others; and mid and low socioeconomic groups were nonsignificantly different. Although these differences between groups were found for the Grammar section of the examination, no differences in cutoff scores were developed.

CONCURRENT VALIDITY. Of the 2,587 children administered the examination, 586 were randomly selected to establish cutoff scores and for other concurrent validation studies. The manual authors do not indicate clearly whether these 586 children were selected because they were speech or language impaired; however, they do indicate these children "were mainstreamed for the greater part of the day" (p. 21), suggesting that they, or a portion of them may not have been impaired. These children were administered both the Joliet 3-Minute Speech and Language Screen along with the Peabody Picture Vocabulary Test (Dunn, 1965) and the Carrow Elicited Language Inventory (Carrow, 1974). The time between administrations was not specified. Significant group differences between the tests were reported using the Cochran Q statistic. The observed difference in vocabulary performance between the Joliet 3-Minute Speech and Language Screen and the Peabody Picture Vocabulary Test was significant ($p<.05$) for the fifth grade group. There were no significant differences in performance on the Grammar section of the Joliet 3-Minute Speech and

Language Screen and the Carrow Elicited Language Inventory at any of the three grade levels. Correlation coefficients between the Joliet 3-Minute Speech and Language Screen and the other two measures were not reported, making direct assessment of the test's concurrent validity extremely difficult.

STANDARDIZATION. The Joliet 3-Minute Speech and Language Screen (Revised) was administered to 2,587 children from three ethnic backgrounds (black, white, and Hispanic-other), three occupation-determined socioeconomic classes (high-mid, mid, and low), and three academic grade levels (kindergarten, second, and fifth). No mention is given as to whether the proportions for each of these stratification variables matched the demographics of the general population. Using the preestablished cutoff criteria for the Vocabulary and Grammar sections of the test, it was determined that between 10.1% and 12.8% of the 2,587 children failed the examination. No specification is given as to which children failed. That is, it is unknown how many, if any, of the identified children were later found to have been accurately or inaccurately classified. Given the known prevalence and incidence of specific language and speech disorders in these populations of children (Campbell, Dollaghan, & Felsenfeld, 1995), it appears that the number identified is too high, thus suggesting inordinately high false-positive identifications.

ADMINISTRATION. The details provided in the manual for administering the test in terms of the physical environment and patient instructions for each part of the test appear to be sufficient for replicating performance (however, see reliability below). All stimuli are administered for all tasks. Repetition of the stimulus is allowed for only one stimulus in the section.

SCORING. Plus/minus scoring is used for the Receptive Vocabulary section. Cutoff scores (threshold for failure) for the Receptive Vocabulary section were set at five or more errors for all children (kindergarten, second grade, and fifth grade). As different stimuli are used for each group, the consistent criterion across groups may be appropriate.

A 2-point equal-appearing interval scale is used to evaluate the Grammar section. One point is given for omitted, substituted, unintelligible words, word additions, word transpositions, and added contractions that do not occur in the sentence. Two points are scored if a contraction is omitted. (It should be noted that the authors state in one place [p. 8] that the examiner should score 1 point if the student does not repeat an existing contraction, but in another [p. 8] that omitted contractions are scored 2 points.) Appropriately, dialectal (e.g., omitted possessive markers or copulas or substituted *be* for *have been*) differences are not scored as errors.

Phonology is scored by counting the number of omissions, substitutions, or distortions of the targeted sounds. Errors on each phoneme and each error type are scored equally. Criteria for failure is one or more sounds in error at any age level.

Abnormal fluency or "flow of speech" is, according to the authors, characterized by pauses, hesitations, interjections, prolongations, and repetitions that are obtained from a spontaneous speech sample. It is suggested that the child be rescreened if the child shows phrase or whole word repetitions, superfluous interjections, hesitation phenomena (e.g., false starts, silent pauses), or if the parent/caregiver is unconcerned with the disfluencies in the child's speech. The child should be referred for a full fluency evaluation if the child demonstrates part-word and one-syllable repetitions, prolonged sounds that occur more frequently than those considered to occur in normally disfluent children, or if the overall sample, regardless of the number disfluencies, could not be misperceived as fluent speech. Specific criteria eliciting an adequate speech sample or for judging any of these suggested observations or for determining pass/fail criteria are not given.

The voice sample is evaluated subjectively with observations directed to abnormal laryngeal tone (observing hoarseness, harshness, breathiness, pitch, loudness and flexibility pitch, and loudness). Hypernasality and hyponasality are also to be observed. Specific criteria for eliciting the speech sample or for judging "abnormal" voice in any specific parameter are not given.

RELIABILITY. *Test-Retest*: One hundred and thirteen children were retested with the 3-Minute Joliet Speech and Language Screen (Revised) 4 weeks following an initial administration. The authors report that "No significant differences were found between any of the tests at any of the grade levels" (p. 27). Only data for the Vocabulary and Grammar portions of the test are reported. These data are reported as Q Values and thus do not inform the reader about individual subject's performance between the two test administrations. It is known that as a group there were no significant differences between the children's performance on the two administrations; however, the range and standard deviation of the group's performance are not known. For example, it is not known how many children would have passed or failed the test based on the cutoff scores on either administration. It is also not known how many children changed classification from the first to the second administration. These critical omissions in the reporting of the reliability of the instrument seriously jeopardize the utility of the test.

Given the underspecified and complex perceptual judgments required on several portions of the examination (e.g., Voice and Fluency), other forms of reliability such as intra- and interjudge reliabilities are critical to have established. However, neither of these forms of reliability were reported. In addition, measures of internal consistency are not reported.

STRENGTHS AND WEAKNESSES. The strengths of the test appear to be in the test's ease and time of administration with clearly pictured stimuli used to elicit responses. Any strengths of the 3-Minute Joliet Speech and Language Screen (Revised) are, however, severely constrained by the lack of psychometric information regarding the test. The general construct validity of the test is greatly underspecified. Test procedures for eliciting the sentence repetition for the assessment of grammar, and speech samples for the assessment of fluency and voice, are poorly justified and underspecified. The derivation of the specific criteria for failure on any portion of the test is unjustified. Inter- and intrajudge reliabilities are not reported. Most importantly, the validity of the test's accurate (true positive and true negative) and inaccurate (false positive and false negative) detection of children with and without speech and language disorders has not been determined.

SUMMARY. The 3-Minute Joliet Speech and Language Screen is designed to meet an important need in the rapid identification of children K–5 that should be given formal speech and lan-

guage evaluations. Its discriminant validity is, however, unproven. Therefore, I believe the test cannot be used for the purpose for which it was designed.

REVIEWERS' REFERENCES

Dunn, L. M. (1965). Peabody Picture Vocabulary Test. Circle Pines, MN: American Guidance Service, Inc.

Carrow, E. (1974). Carrow Elicited Language Inventory. Chicago, IL: Riverside Publishing Co.

Shriberg, L. D., Gruber, F. A., & Kwiatkowski, J. (1994). Developmental phonological disorders III: Long-term speech-sound normalization. *Journal of Speech and Hearing Research, 37*, 1151–1177.

Campbell, T. F., Dollaghan, C., & Felsenfeld, S. (1995). Disorders of language, phonology, fluency, and voice: Indicators for referral. In C. Bluestone, S. Stool, & M. Kenna (Eds.), *Pediatric Otolaryngology*, Vol. 2 (3rd ed.) (pp. 1595–1606). Philadelphia: W. B. Saunders.

[50]
Kaufman Functional Academic Skills Test.

Purpose: "Measure of an adolescent's or adult's ability to demonstrate competence in reading and mathematics as applied to daily life situations."

Population: Ages 15–85 and over.

Publication Date: 1994.

Acronym: K-FAST.

Scores, 3: Arithmetic Subtest, Reading Subtest, Functional Academic Skills Composite.

Administration: Individual.

Price Data, 1994: $89.95 per complete kit including manual (110 pages), test easel, and 25 record forms; $74.95 per test easel; $19.95 per 25 record forms; $26.95 per manual.

Time: (15–25) minutes.

Comments: Examinees may respond in any language.

Authors: Alan S. Kaufman and Nadeen L. Kaufman.

Publisher: American Guidance Service.

TEST REFERENCE

1. Chen, T.-H., Kaufman, A. S., & Kaufman, J. C. (1994). Examining the interaction of age x race pretaining BlackWhite differences at ages 15 to 93 on six Horn abilities assessed by K-FAST, K-SNAP and CAIT subtests. *Perceptual and Motor Skills, 79*, 1683–1690.

Review of the Kaufman Functional Academic Skills Test by STEVEN R. SHAW, School Psychologist, The School District of Greenville County, Greenville, SC:

The Kaufman Functional Academic Skills Test (K-FAST) measures aspects of adaptive behavior involving the application of academically acquired learning to the problems of daily living. The K-FAST is useful for examinees aged 15 to 85. The K-FAST is a supplement to traditional norm-referenced academic tests and adaptive behavior measures. Although most academic tests assess skills needed to perform in school, the K-FAST assesses reading and arithmetic skills required for daily living in society. Unlike most adaptive behavior scales, the K-FAST does not use respondents or interviews with the examinee. The K-FAST requires examinees to demonstrate skills in an individual testing situation on the K-FAST. The manual reports that the K-FAST may be used in residential settings or prisons to determine the degree of self-care an examinee can manage, for making personnel decisions, and to aid in vocational counseling.

The K-FAST consists of an Arithmetic and a Reading Subtest. There are 25 items in the Arithmetic Subtest and 29 items in the Reading Subtest. Topics in the Reading Subtest include: simple directions, signs, pictorial rebuses, labels, newspapers and magazine articles, advertisements, abbreviations, and catalog information. Unlike many reading tests, the K-FAST Reading Subtest does not emphasize pronunciation. The Arithmetic Subtest includes topics such as: counting, adding and subtracting the value of coins, grocery shopping, cooking, reading maps, understanding graphs and charts, telling time and understanding time concepts, earning money and budgeting, banking, taking trips by car or taxi, and purchasing a variety of items. The subtest scores can be combined to form a Functional Academic Skill Composite. This composite score represents overall functional academic skill development.

ADMINISTRATION AND SCORING. The K-FAST is easy and quick to administer. Items are not timed. Typical time to complete an administration of the K-FAST is 15 to 25 minutes. Yet, the manual reports that some individuals may take up to 50 minutes to complete the test. A variety of personnel may administer the K-FAST. There is no special training involved. However, examiners must be thoroughly familiar with standardized test administration, discontinuation rules, and item content. The easel format is convenient for administration. The individual test records are large and easy to follow. Tables for converting raw scores to standard scores, standard score confidence intervals, percentile ranks, and descriptive categories are straightforward. The manual contains a table presenting standard score differences between Arithmetic and Reading Subtests required for statistical significance. The manual supplies no information on base rates of standard score differences. The K-FAST is quick to administer and convenient to score. Any professional with training and experience administering and scoring standardized tests will have minimal problems with the K-FAST.

NORMATIVE DATA. The K-FAST was constructed as part of a 28-subtest battery of approximately 1,850 items. After the tryout phase, the battery was divided into the K-FAST, the Kaufman Adolescent and Adult Intelligence Test (KAIT; 12:204), the Kaufman Brief Intelligence Test (K-BIT; 12:205), and the Kaufman Short Neuropsychological Assessment Procedure (K-SNAP). The national standardization of the K-FAST involved over 2,600 participants from 27 states. The norm sample consisted of 1,424 participants. The norm samples were small for the 65–69 ($N = 81$), 70–74 ($N = 93$), and 75–85+ ($N = 103$) age groups. The sample is reasonably representative of the general U.S. population for gender, ethnic group status, and education. However, the norm sample is not representative for geographic region. The Northeast and West are underrepresented and the North Central and South are overrepresented. Data were not collected from the populous states of New Jersey, Florida, Hawaii, Arizona, South Carolina, and Virginia. For most tests, geographic representation is not a significant problem. However, Arizona and Florida are two states with large, active senior populations. As a result, it is possible that the norms for ages over 65 may not be representative of the U.S. population. Despite these minor shortcomings, the K-FAST has well-developed normative data.

RELIABILITY. The manual reports data on internal consistency and stability. Internal consistency reliability was estimated using split-half reliability corrected with the Spearman-Brown formula. The mean internal consistency reliability estimate for the Arithmetic Subtests was .88 (range .83–.94). The mean internal consistency reliability estimate for the Reading Subtest was .90. Reliability coefficients ranged from .86 to .95. For the Functional Composite, the mean internal consistency reliability estimate was .94. Reliability coefficients ranged from .92 to .97. Standard errors of measurement for Arithmetic, Reading, and the Functional Composite are 5.1, 4.7, and 3.7, respectively.

Temporal stability of the K-FAST was determined by administering the K-FAST to 116 nonhandicapped adolescents and adults. The test-retest intervals ranged from 6 to 94 days with a mean of 33 days. Correlations between the two testings, corrected for variability, were .84 for Arithmetic, .88 for Reading, and .91 for the Composite. There was also a slight practice effect. The mean gain in scores was 1.0 standard score points for Arithmetic, 2.9 for Reading, and 2.3 for the Composite. Overall, the manual clearly demonstrates that the K-FAST is a reliable and stable test for ages 15 to 85.

VALIDITY. The manual presents a variety of data supporting the validity of the K-FAST. An exploratory factor analysis of the K-FAST along with the KAIT and K-SNAP indicates that both Reading and Arithmetic load significantly on the first unrotated factor (g). Both subtests also have significant loading on Crystallized intelligence. Arithmetic has significant loadings on Fluid intelligence for persons aged 20–54 and 70–85+. The authors note age changes in performance on the K-FAST. The highest raw scores are for persons between the ages of 30 and 50. This may be due to a developmental difference in education (i.e., 15-year-olds have not completed their education) or other confounding factors. The authors conducted concurrent validity studies with the Wechsler Intelligence Scale for Children—Revised (WISC-R), the Wechsler Adult Intelligence Scale—Revised (WAIS-R), the Stanford-Binet Intelligence Scale, Fourth Edition, the KAIT, the K-BIT, the K-SNAP, and the Peabody Picture Vocabulary Test—Revised (PPVT-R). Correlations are moderate to high with all tests of intelligence. However, the K-FAST should be considered a rough estimate of general intellectual ability. The K-FAST is not an appropriate estimate of intelligence, especially with reading- or mathematics-disabled persons. Concurrent validity studies were also conducted with persons who have reading disabilities, mental retardation, severe depression, Alzheimer's disease, and neurological impairments. Validity studies employed a heterogeneous clinical sample as well. The K-FAST discriminated well between normal and most clinical populations. However, the clinically depressed sample scored higher than the nonimpaired norm sample. In sum, the validity data of the K-FAST are extensive and well presented. Most data strongly support the validity of the K-FAST for many purposes.

SUMMARY. The K-FAST is a well-developed direct measure of the academic subdomain of adaptive behavior. The test is easy to administer and score. Results from the K-FAST can be invaluable in a variety of situations such as transition planning for low functioning high school students, vocational counseling, or determining functional skill loss after stroke. The norm sample was well selected. Save some potential problems with the geographic representativeness of the sample in states with large senior populations, the test is carefully and completely normed. For such a brief test, the K-FAST has outstanding reliability. The manual delves into great detail concerning the establishment of validity data. Validity is appropriately established for a variety of purposes.

The K-FAST is an excellent test for a small niche in assessment. Most often norm-referenced academic tests, intelligence tests, or adaptive behavior measures are adequate for meeting assessment needs. The K-FAST should be used to supplement, rather than replace, tests of these domains. Yet, tests of these domains do not often consider real life applications of the above constructs. Thus, if an assessment requires a brief estimate of functional academic skills, subsets of the construct of adaptive behavior, then the K-FAST is an outstanding assessment instrument.

Review of the Kaufman Functional Academic Skills Test by ROBERT T. WILLIAMS, Professor of Education, Colorado State University, Fort Collins, CO:

The Kaufman Functional Academic Skills Test (K-FAST) follows in the tradition of many other American Guidance Services assessments. That is, it is brief, it uses the ceiling/discontinue format to be applicable with a wide range of examinees; it has explicit and clear directions for administration and scoring; it uses an easel format for task stimulus; it has a clear, legible, efficient-to-use test record; and it has an excellent manual with readable tables and extensive references.

The purpose of the K-FAST is a "measure of an adolescent's or adult's ability to demonstrate competence in reading and mathematics as applied to daily life situations" (manual, p. 1). It contains 25 arithmetic items in 11 categories and 29 reading items in 9 categories. The authors suggest that the

K-FAST is to serve as a supplement, not a substitute, for popular tests of intelligence, achievement, or adaptive behavior.

The K-FAST purports to measure fluid-crystallized intelligence. From the manual, page 4, "Crystallized intelligence includes problem-solving tasks that are dependent on previously learned skills. Fluid intelligence encompasses tasks that involve novel problem-solving skills—the kind that are not acquired in formal or informal learning situations. Fluid problem solving relies heavily on flexibility, analytic ability, and adaptability. ... K-FAST Arithmetic was strongly associated with both the Fluid and Crystallized factors for most age groups." And on page 5, "the Reading Subtest measures abilities acquired from previous learning situations and through acculturation" [Crystallized].

The K-FAST was developed at the same time as the Kaufman Brief Intelligence Test (K-BIT, Kaufman & Kaufman, 1990; 12:205), the Kaufman Adolescent and Adult Intelligence Test (KAIT, Kaufman & Kaufman, 1993; 12:204), and the Kaufman Short Neurological Assessment Procedure (K-SNAP, Kaufman & Kaufman, 1994). Consultants searched adaptive inventories for topics and items. The consultants are identified without reference to their qualifications. The KAIT, K-BIT, K-SNAP, and K-FAST evolved from a national tryout of 28 subtests and about 1,850 items. Six group-administered forms and one individually administered form, including a total of 148 functional reading and 67 functional arithmetic items, were used.

The sample sizes (tryout $N = 1,140$ and standardization $N = 2,600$) are appropriate. The proportionality of age, ethnic group, geographic region in the United States, and socioeconomic level (years in school completed by individual or by parents, if still in school) of the tryout and standardization sample is excellent, falling within 5 percentage points of the U.S. population on almost all categories. There is an underrepresentation of subjects for the Northeast and an overrepresentation from the South.

Reliability is estimated for split-half (by age range), test-retest ($N = 116$; $r = .87$ to $.91$), and interrelation of subtests. Authors use "error bands" based upon Standard Error of Measurement to "make it easier to interpret the test and help examiners avoid test abuse" (p. 49).

Content validity is documented by discussing consultants' examination of adaptive inventories and the selection of concepts and items. This procedure seems appropriate. However, the credibility of the consultants is never established. The K-FAST emerged as one of the products of an ambitious effort to develop the various assessment devices named above. The mention of Fluid/Crystallized intelligence is interesting. Although references are given, there is not enough conceptual or practical information about this construct offered for the reader to understand or evaluate the application of the construct. This reviewer would have appreciated a matrix that summarized each test item by skill category and as Fluid, Crystallized, or both. Without more discussion, this construct is lacking.

Clinical validity was evaluated by comparing clinical subjects to control subjects. There is a good effort to compare clinical samples with matched controls. Differences were significant in favor of controls except for the clinically depressed population. This is a valuable model. Grouping the total clinical sample gives a large population ($N = 137$) but the weakness of these individual studies is the small sample size ($N < 35$).

Construct validity is discussed through establishing reading and mathematics tasks applied to daily situations. Probably anyone who reads, uses, or reviews the K-FAST will identify "reading and mathematics items applied to everyday life" that are not included in the assessment. In Mathematics, the authors purport to assess survival arithmetic, numerical reasoning, computational skills, and mathematical concepts. They use 25 items for one topic. In Reading, the authors purport to assess reading survival skills, recognition and comprehension of signs and written material, and practical, nonschool tasks. They use 29 items to assess nine skills. This reviewer conducted an informal content analysis and found some mathematics and reading skills to have as few as 1 item, some to have 2 items, and some to have as many as 8 items. This reviewer feels that topic coverage has been overstated and that some skills have too few items to adequately assess abilities.

Criterion-related validity is discussed with studies and analyses conducted during K-FAST development and standardization. Age changes on the K-FAST and correlates with comprehensive intelligence tests are reported to support validity. The authors caution not to interpret the K-FAST as an intelligence test. They go on to say it "can provide a good estimate of intelligence where other test scores are unavailable" (p. 9). This is an unfortunate comment. Users may not try to get other assessments or may see the K-FAST as the same as a multifaceted assessment of intellectual ability.

The K-FAST is a user-friendly, readable, brief assessment of daily life situations in reading and mathematics, which is to be a supplement to other assessment. Claims of categories of assessment do not hold. There are too few items to accurately evaluate the several categories offered by the authors. The uses and applications made in the manual sound as if they had been written by the marketing department: Everybody can use this! A sensitive, intuitive, informed teacher, tutor, or counselor could develop an informal assessment of daily life situations that could be as useful for academic, personal, or job training planning. The Comprehensive Adult Student Assessment System (CASAS, 1992; Test 30, this volume) is an adult-oriented functional assessment system that measures a broad range of adult literacy skills with application in real life situations. The CASAS measures reading, writing, math, and problem-solving skills (using separate tests for each area) in the domains of consumer resources, occupational knowledge, community resources, and health. The CASAS spans a range of abilities from nonreaders to adults at the GED or high school level. The separate surveys are untimed (and may take as long as 60 minutes each) and may be administered individually or in groups. For functional and/or work place literacy or academic or career planning, this reviewer would favor the CASAS.

REVIEWER'S REFERENCES

Kaufman, A. S., & Kaufman, N. L. (1990). Kaufman Brief Intelligence Test (K-BIT). Circle Pines, MN: American Guidance Service.
CASAS. (1992). Comprehensive Adult Student Assessment System. San Diego, CA: Foundation for Educational Achievement, Inc.
Kaufman, A. S., & Kaufman, N. L. (1993). Kaufman Adolescent and Adult Intelligence Test (KAIT). Circle Pines, MN: American Guidance Service.
Kaufman, A. S., & Kaufman, N. L. (1994). Kaufman Short Neuropsychological Assessment Procedure (K-SNAP). Circle Pines, MN: American Guidance Service.

[51]
Language Arts Assessment Portfolio.

Purpose: To "analyze and evaluate student achievement in all areas of the language arts: reading, writing, listening, and speaking."
Population: Grades 1–6.
Publication Date: 1992.

Acronym: LAAP.
Administration: Individual.
Levels: 3 levels.
Price Data, 1993: $99.95 per complete LAAP kit Level 1, 2 or 3; $23.95 per 30 portfolio folders; $23.95 per 30 evaluation booklets; $79 per LAAP training video.
Time: Administration time not reported.
Comments: Assessment done with students' own language arts materials.
Author: Bjorn Karlsen.
Publisher: American Guidance Service, Inc.

a) LEVEL I.
Population: Grade 1.
Scores: 15–24 language arts skill areas: Reading Analysis (Reading Comprehension, Oral Reading, Decoding), Optional Reading Analysis (Silent Reading Problems, Oral Reading Problems), Writing Analysis [Process (Story Creation), Product (Sentence Structure, Story Content, Spelling, Mechanics)], Optional Writing Analysis (Spelling, Mechanics), Listening Analysis [Listening in Interaction (Attentiveness, Understanding), Listening to Teaching (Memory, Interpretation)], Optional Listening Analysis (Auditory Decoding, Rhymes and Rhythms, Phonetic Elements, Structural Elements), Speaking Analysis [Oral Interaction, Oral Presentation (Delivery)], Optional Speaking Analysis (Language Development).

b) LEVEL II.
Population: Grades 2–3.
Scores: 16–25 language arts skill areas: Reading Analysis (Silent Reading Comprehension, Oral Reading, Decoding), Optional Reading Analysis (Silent Reading Problems, Oral Reading Problems), Writing Analysis [Process (Story Creation, Process Awareness), Product (Story Content, Organization, Spelling, Mechanics)], Optional Writing Analysis [Spelling Error Analysis, Mechanics (Punctuation, Capitalization)], Listening Analysis [Listening in Interaction (Attentiveness, Understanding), Listening to Teaching (Memory, Interpretation)], Optional Listening Analysis (Auditory Decoding, Phonetic Elements, Structural Elements), Speaking Analysis [Oral Interaction, Oral Presentation (Delivery)], Optional Speaking Analysis (Language Development).

c) LEVEL III.
Population: Grades 4—6.
Scores: Same as *b* above except that Attentiveness is not included for Listening Analysis.
Cross References: See T4:1384 (1 reference).

Review of the Language Arts Assessment Portfolio by ANTHONY J. NITKO, Professor of Educa-

tion, Department of Psychology in Education, University of Pittsburgh, Pittsburgh, PA:

The Language Arts Assessment Portfolio (LAAP) is an informal formative assessment system in reading, writing, listening, and speaking. The materials are organized in three levels: grade 1, grades 2–3, and grades 4–6. Each level contains a Teacher's Guide, Evaluation Booklet, Students' Self-Evaluation Booklets, portfolio folders, and a storage box. A teacher assesses students using local classroom materials and activities. The LAAP provides no tasks or test items.

Each language arts area is divided into two broad areas: a main analysis and an optional analysis. The main analysis assesses students in overall basic skills. The optional analysis obtains a more detailed diagnosis for students who do poorly in the main analysis. For example, the listening main analysis is organized into two broad skill areas: Listening in Interactions and Listening to Teaching. Listening to Teaching is further divided into the broad areas of Memory and Interpretation. Interpretation, in turn, is divided into five finer-grained skills. A teacher rates each student on each skill on a 5-point scale: excellent, satisfactory, needs improvement, beginning to learn, and serious problem. The author recommends rating four times during the school year. Each student's ratings are recorded along with information about the materials used for assessment and the teacher's comments. Students (and teachers) may include examples of the work evaluated in the folder (hence the portfolio aspect).

The Teacher's Guide, like the entire LAAP, is well organized. The broad skills are nicely described. Each narrower skill is described for assessment as follows: (a) "What to look for" (defines the narrow skills), (b) "How to assess it" (how to conduct an assessment of that specific skill), and (c) "Evaluating the responses" (the key performances on which to focus when rating a student). Suggestions and comments are made about expected student performance. It would have been useful to include suggestions for how to teach or remediate students after they are assessed.

TECHNICAL REVIEW. The LAAP was field-tested over a 2-year period at several sites in 19 states. Three field tests, a telephone survey, and a focus group discussion of the materials were part of the development process. Teachers were especially trained by the LAAP developer.

It is important to note that the LAAP is an informal classroom assessment procedure. No attempt is made to standardize the materials, assessment process, assessment training, or any other assessment aspect. Thus, the LAAP should not be used for curriculum evaluation, for accountability, or for comparing students' progress from grade to grade.

Teachers need to be trained to use the LAAP system, especially in how to administer the assessment and rate students. If the LAAP is to be used in the same school by more than one teacher per grade, training on how to rate students is especially needed to assure that ratings have the same meaning across teachers. Formal studies of other portfolio assessment systems have shown very low consistency of ratings from teacher to teacher and low generalizability of a student's performance across different kinds of tasks.

SUMMARY. The LAAP is a useful informal system for organizing a teacher's ratings of students' language arts performance in reading, writing, listening, and speaking. It is designed specifically for a classroom teacher to monitor students' progress over the course of a year. To accomplish this purpose, teachers may need special inservice training in how to use the LAAP. Appropriately, the author does not recommend using the LAAP for summative student evaluation. Lest some school officials be tempted, we add that the LAAP should not be used for either student, teacher, or school accountability programs.

Review of the Language Arts Assessment Profile by RICHARD M. WOLF, Professor of Psychology and Education, Teachers College, Columbia University, New York, NY:

The Language Arts Assessment Profile (LAAP) is an amalgam of an assessment system for teachers to appraise student performance in the areas of reading, writing, listening, and speaking; a student self-evaluation form; and a record-keeping system. It is intended for use by classroom teachers to monitor student performance in each of these four language arts areas. The three levels of the system are intended for use by teachers in grade 1, grades 2–3, and grades 4–6. The Teacher's Guide for each level runs from 57 to 71 pages, depending on the level, and provides a detailed guide about the system and how to use it.

The LAAP is basically a two-pronged assessment system. For each language arts area, there is both a teacher evaluation booklet and a student evaluation booklet. Each is laid out so that as many as four assessments can be made in each area of the language arts during the school year. The items that comprise each area appear reasonable although no evidence is furnished to justify their inclusion. For teachers, ratings are supplied for each item using a five category rating code ranging from E (excellent) to P (serious problem). A sixth category for Not applicable (NA) is also provided. The Teacher's Guide provides a description of each rating code. These definitions allow considerable latitude for teachers to impose their own standards for each rating code category. The categories seem generally reasonable although the rating of S (Satisfactory) is defined as "mastery for this level of achievement" (p. 11). Equating mastery with satisfactory performance is somewhat odd.

In addition to the teacher and student evaluation booklets, the appendix of each Teacher's Guide contains from five to eight additional forms that can be used. At grades 4–6, these are: (a) student interest survey, (b) log of contents, (c) reading log, (d) writing sample cover sheet, (e) writing peer evaluation form, (f) listening log, (g) oral presentation cover sheet, and (h) speaking peer evaluation form. Although these additional items are optional, their use could result in a very cumbersome system. Even the basic system with just the teacher and student evaluation booklets requires a good deal of management. To assist in this task, the system comes with a set of individual student folders in which to keep the records.

The LAAP underwent an extensive development process. The system was developed by the author on the basis of his experience in the field and was initially field tested in 21 sites around the United States. A second field test was carried out in 31 sites. A telephone survey of potential users and a focus group discussion were also carried out. The purpose of this work, it seems, was to work out the details of the use of the system. Unfortunately, no evidence is presented regarding the results of the field tests or the other activities carried on during the development phase. No evidence regarding either the validity or the reliability of the LAAP is provided for a potential user to judge the adequacy of the system.

One major problem in the use of the LAAP involves the determination of an overall rating in each of the four language areas. It is left entirely up to the teacher to obtain an overall rating in each language area after reviewing the specific rating of the various skills. The Teacher's Guide alerts the teacher to a possible halo effect in obtaining specific ratings but little guidance is provided on how to obtain an overall rating. In fact, the overall ratings are downplayed in the Teacher's Guide and a plea is made to use the specific ratings in a diagnostic way. If this is so, why provide for an overall rating, especially because this is what might carry considerable weight with parents?

In summary, the LAAP is a system for assessing the progress of students in the four language arts areas: reading, writing, listening, and speaking. It consists of a number of rating scales in each area for both teachers and students to use. It also includes a rather elaborate record-keeping system. Although some elementary school teachers may find the LAAP a useful way to record and store information about student progress in the language arts, others may find it cumbersome. As far as a series of measuring instruments, there is no evidence provided to establish its validity and reliability. Consequently, teachers will need to decide if the items that comprise the teacher and student evaluation booklets are relevant to their instructional goals. Use of the LAAP depends heavily on the ability of an individual teacher to find a way to use the system.

[52]
Learning and Study Strategies Inventory—High School Version.

Purpose: Designed to assist high school students "in determining their study skills strategies, problems and attitudes, and learning practices."
Population: Grades 9–12.
Publication Date: 1990.
Acronym: LASSI-HS.
Scores, 10: Attitude, Motivation, Time Management, Anxiety, Concentration, Information Processing, Selecting Main Ideas, Study Aids, Self Testing, Test Strategies.
Administration: Group.

Price Data, 1994: $2.25 per self-scored form; $2.50 per computer scored form.
Time: (25–30) minutes.
Authors: Claire E. Weinstein and David R. Palmer.
Publisher: H & H Publishing Company.

TEST REFERENCES

1. Eldredge, J. L. (1990). Learning and Study Strategies Inventory—High School Version. *Journal of Reading, 34,* 146-149.
2. Walsh, J. (1993). The promise and pitfalls of integrated strategy instruction. *Journal of Learning Disabilities, 26,* 438–442.
3. Tallent-Runnels, M. K., Olivárez, A., Jr., Candler Lotvin, A. C., Walsh, S. K., Gray, A., & Irons, T. R. (1994). A comparison of learning and study strategies of gifted and average-ability junior high students. *Journal for the Education of the Gifted, 17,* 143-160.
4. Hagborg, W. J. (1995). High school student perceptions and satisfaction with group advisory. *Psychology in the Schools, 32,* 46-51.

Review of the Learning and Study Strategies Inventory—High School Version by KENNETH A. KIEWRA, Professor of Educational Psychology, University of Nebraska—Lincoln, Lincoln, NE:

The Learning and Study Strategies Inventory—High School Version (LASSI-HS) is designed to measure learning and study strategies at the secondary school level. The LASSI-HS is an offshoot of the original LASSI, published in 1987, for use at the college level. I review the LASSI-HS with respect to (a) purpose; (b) composition; (c) administration, scoring, and interpretation; (d) test characteristics; and (e) my conclusion.

PURPOSE. The LASSI-HS is intended for use as (a) a diagnostic measure to identify strategy strengths and weaknesses; (b) a counseling tool for advising students into appropriate programs; (c) a basis for planning individual prescriptions to remedy weaknesses and enrich strengths; (d) a pre-post achievement measure to determine a student's strategy growth, and (e) an evaluation tool to assess a program's or course's success. The instrument is appropriate for 9th through 12th grade students.

COMPOSITION. The LASSI-HS is a 76-item self-report instrument incorporating a 5-point rating scale with the endpoints "very much like me" and "not at all like me." The five choices appear atop each item column for easy referral. Items are both positively stated and negatively stated to encourage thoughtful responding and discourage uncharacteristic response patterns.

The LASSI-HS is divided into 10 scales with most comprising eight items. The 10 scales appear to fit within four important factors associated with learning and studying: cognitive (e.g., information processing and concentration),

metacognitive (e.g., self-testing), motivational (e.g., motivation and time management), and affective (e.g., attitudes and anxiety), but are not based on any systematic model of studying. Still, the items are, in my estimation, reflective of important and current research and theory associated with learning and studying, and represent the best collection of items I have observed among several such inventories. The LASSI-HS, for example, assesses metacognition, motivational attributions, and organization and elaboration strategies—areas often ignored in similar instruments. However, the LASSI-HS contains some omissions. It neglects to assess, for example, whether notes are recorded adequately (completely and with examples) and whether students prepare adequately for procedural tasks (e.g., solving math word problems) by practicing problem classification and problem solving.

ADMINISTRATION, SCORING, AND INTERPRETATION. The LASSI-HS is an untimed inventory administered easily to an individual, class, or school within 20–25 minutes. Although students complete the inventory without assistance, an adult examiner is required to distribute materials, read instructions, answer student questions, and collect materials.

There are two versions of the LASSI-HS: computer scored and student scored. They are identical in content, but vary in form. The computer-scored version includes a one-page Student Directions handout and the LASSI-HS computer-scored form. This form contains the items and five "bubbles" alongside each item for recording responses.

The computer-scored forms must be checked by students and examiners so that no data are lost due to omitted items or missing student information. The completed forms are sent to the publishing company, which provides individual and class scores and graphs for each of the 10 scales within one week of receipt. The relative advantages of computer scoring are the elimination of student scoring errors and the provision of class summaries. The relative disadvantages of computer scoring are the slightly higher cost of the computer-scored forms and delayed feedback.

The student-scored version is contained within a single booklet. The booklet includes directions, test pages, scoring materials, and norming tables. The instructions appear on the booklet's front cover. Two test pages are removed from the booklet prior to testing. Students mark their responses directly on the test pages. The pressure sensitive pages transfer a student's responses onto a scoring sheet below. The scoring sheet reveals a numerical response to each item and each item's scale classification.

Students record their item score within a chart organized by the 10 scales. Next, they sum item scores to determine scale scores. These are plotted on a norming chart corresponding to their grade level (9–12). The chart provides percentile scores based on national norms. The norming data are somewhat limited and restricted; they are based on about 500–800 students at each grade level from a single southwestern city.

The test booklet and the user's manual provide brief explanations of the 10 scales to aid in interpretation. The manual also provides vague implications for remediation such as "learn techniques to enhance concentration and set priorities" (p. 15). The LASSI-HS is not equipped to remediate or enrich the behaviors measured.

TEST CHARACTERISTICS. Test characteristics are described with respect to development, reliability, and validity. The LASSI-HS was developed by adapting the original Learning and Study Strategies Inventory (LASSI). It appears that only minor modifications were made. Both forms contain the identical 10 scales and contain a nearly identical number of items (77 and 76). The adaptation was carried out by a team of experts who revised LASSI items consistent with high school vocabulary and demands. The resulting item set was field tested using 750 ninth graders although the instrument is intended for students in 9th through 12th grades. How the two forms actually differ is not mentioned.

A reliability estimate for the entire instrument was not furnished. Reliability coefficients for the 10 scales ranged from .68 (Study Aids) to .82 (Anxiety and Concentration). Reliability coefficients in this range indicate that each scale was reasonably internally consistent and adequately measured a common behavior. Intercorrelations among scale scores were not reported, however, leaving unknown the degree to which the 10 scales measure unique behaviors. My own inspection of items revealed several that might be appropriate for more than one scale. The item "I am up-to-date in my class assignments" (protocol, p. 3), for example, is included in the Motivation scale but also seems consistent with the Time Management scale. Another example is the item "I make drawings or sketches to help me understand what I am studying" (protocol, p. 4). It is classified within the Study Aid scale but represents an organization strategy that seemingly fits within the Information Processing scale.

Also not reported was test-retest reliability. Therefore, nothing is known about the stability of scores. Without this information, it is unwise to administer the inventory before and after instruction and then assume that performance changes on the inventory resulted from instruction.

No validity data are reported for the LASSI-HS. Without such data it is impossible to know whether the test scores can be interpreted as measures of learning and studying behaviors as intended. The manual provides tangential and undocumented claims for the validity of the original LASSI. No data are provided, however, relating performance on either Learning and Study Strategy Inventory to academic performance or to indices of actual learning and study behaviors (e.g., analyses of lecture notes, inspection of time logs, or teacher observations).

CONCLUSION. At face value, the LASSI-HS contains scales and items that seem to tap important learning and study behaviors. The items are the best I have seen. The lack of psychometric evidence, however, makes its use risky and premature among those demanding assurance about its construction, accuracy, and usefulness.

Review of the Learning and Study Strategies Inventory—High School Version by ROBERT T. WILLIAMS, Professor of Education, Colorado State University, Fort Collins, CO:

The Learning and Study Strategies Inventory—High School Version (LASSI-HS) is a 76-item, self-report, individually or group administered assessment of high school (grades 9–12) students' use of learning and study strategies and methods. There are two formats: self-scored or computer scored. The self-scored format gives immediate results. Recording, adding, and transferring scores demands attention to detail. Computer scoring is done by the publisher. It provides class and individual reports and a computer disk (IBM compatible) of raw data.

Separate norms are given for grades 9, 10, 11, and 12. The grade 12 norms are suggested to be appropriate for first-year college students. A review of the norm tables reveals that there is little difference in raw scores (3 or less) for the 50th percentile at any grade level. In other words, there does not seem to be any difference in the way typical students in grades 9, 10, 11, or 12 respond to the items in the scales.

The 76 items are statements that assess "covert and overt thoughts and behaviors that relate to successful learning in high school *and* that can be altered through educational interventions" (manual, p. 3). The authors maintain that "these thought processes and behaviors also contribute significantly to success in college *and* can be learned or enhanced through programs and interventions in secondary educational settings" (manual, p. 3). The authors do not provide research data or references to support these propositions.

The authors suggest the LASSI-HS may be used as a diagnostic tool, a counseling tool, a basis for planning individual prescriptions for learning interventions with students, as a prepost achievement measure, and as an evaluation tool.

The inventory has 10 scales. These scales are identified and explained using words from pages 14–17 of the manual. The coefficient alpha, a measure of internal consistency reliability, is in parentheses. *Attitude*—general attitude and motivation for succeeding in school and performing the tasks related to school success (.74); *Motivation*—the degree to which students accept responsibility for performing the specific tasks related to school success (.78); *Time Management*—the degree to which students create and use schedules (.77); *Anxiety*—how tense or anxious students are when approaching academic tasks (.82); *Concentration*—ability to concentrate and direct attention to school and school-related tasks, including study activities (.82); *Information Processing*—how well students can create imaginal and verbal elaborations and organizations to foster understanding and recall (.80); *Selecting Main Ideas*—skills at selecting important information on which to concentrate for further study in either the classroom lecture or

autonomous learning situations (.71); *Study Aids*—ability to use and create study aids that support and increase meaningful learning and retention (.68); *Self Testing*—importance of self-testing and reviewing and the degree to which students use these methods (.74); *Test Strategies*—use of test-taking and test preparation strategies (.81).

The 76 items are distributed randomly within the inventory; half of the items are stated in a positive direction and half are stated in a negative direction. Students respond to the items with a 5-point Likert-type scale of *a = Not at all like me* through *e = Very much like me*. The reviewer found the scale on the Student Response Form slightly difficult to follow.

Research and development of the LASSI, from which the LASSI-HS was created, began in 1978 in the University of Texas, Austin, Cognitive Learning Strategies Project. The manual efficiently describes the several year evolution of the LASSI and the LASSI-HS through conceptual development, item pool development, pilot testing, inventory construction, and norm development.

The authors offer information about the validity of the LASSI by saying the scale scores have been compared with other assessments, that several of the scales have been validated against performance measures, and that there have been repeated tests of user validity. There is no research or reference evidence to support any of the claims. The user validity claim supported by educational practitioners in over 700 colleges and universities and the on-going evaluation at the Cognitive Learning Project is the strongest. The user is left to accept that the validity for the LASSI transfers to the LASSI-HS.

The reliability as reported by coefficient alpha is acceptable. The derivation and interpretation of the coefficient is not explained beyond the statement "The coefficient alpha is a measure of reliability" (manual, p. 13).

The norms for the LASSI-HS were developed from a sample of 2,616 students in a "mid-sized city in the southwest" (manual, p. 20) in grades 9 ($N = 857$), 10 ($N = 500$), 11 ($N = 575$), and 12 ($N = 604$) "selected to reflect a range of ethnic backgrounds, economic conditions, and academic achievement levels" (p. 20). No gender or ethnic data are given. The geographic region is limited.

In the opinion of this reviewer, the LASSI-HS has good content and construct validity and no reported concurrent validity. The norms do not appear useful because there is no meaningful difference in the performance of the grade groups and there are no gender or ethnic norms. The Inventory has intuitive value for gaining information about how to help students, for academic counseling, and for instructional planning. A guide and resource list for planning prescriptions for students would be a useful addition to the manual. This reviewer questions the usefulness of the inventory as a pre-post achievement measure or a program evaluation tool because any intervention should "teach" the students how to answer on the post-test and would not be a measure of behavior. Changes in attendance and grades could be more stable indicators for evaluation.

[53]
Learning Preference Scales.

Purpose: "Provides a measure of the preference for cooperative, competitive and individualised learning."
Publication Date: 1992.
Acronym: LPS.
Scores, 5: Cooperation, Competition, Individualism, Combined Involvement, Cooperative Involvement.
Administration: Group.
Price Data, 1993: $59.95 per complete kit including manual (54 pages) and one copy of each scale.
Time: (10–45) minutes.
Authors: Lee Owens and Jennifer Barnes.
Publisher: Australian Council for Educational Research, Ltd. [Australia].
   a) LEARNING PREFERENCE SCALES—STUDENTS.
Population: Grades 4–12.
Acronym: LPSS.
   b) LEARNING PREFERENCE SCALES—TEACHERS.
Population: Elementary and secondary teachers.
Acronym: LPST.
   c) LEARNING PREFERENCE SCALES—PARENTS.
Population: Parents of school students.
Acronym: LPSP.

TEST REFERENCE

1. Li,. A. K. F., & Adamson, G. (1995). Motivational patterns related to gifted students' learning of mathematics, science and English: An examination of gender differences. *Journal for the Education of the Gifted, 18,* 284-297.

Review of the Learning Preference Scales by TRENTON R. FERRO, *Associate Professor of Adult and Community Education, Indiana University of Pennsylvania, Indiana, PA:*

The three Learning Preference Scales—one each for Students (LPSS), Teachers (LPST), and Parents (LPSP)—are intended to provide "systematic information on the attitudes of school students, teachers or the parents of school students towards cooperative, competitive and individualised [*sic*] learning as it take place in the classroom" (p. 3). Each scale consists of a set of statements (36, 33, and 24 respectively). Each statement is followed by four spaces representing four varying reactions the person completing the scale might have toward each statement: "completely/clearly true," "sort of true" or "a bit more true than false," "sort of false" or "a bit more false than true," or "completely/clearly false." Numerical values of 4, 3, 2, and 1 are assigned to each of these responses (or, conversely, 1, 2, 3, and 4 for negatively stated items).

The statement in each Learning Preference Scale can be divided into three equal groups of 12, 11, and 8 statements, respectively. Adding together the scores for statements in each of these groups provides three subscales representing preferences for *Cooperative, Competitive,* and/or *Individualized* learning. Two composite scales can also be obtained: *Combined Involvement* is derived by adding the Cooperative and Competitive subscale scores, and *Cooperative Involvement* is obtained by subtracting the Competitive subscale score from the Cooperative subscale score. The Student scale is designed for students from grade 4 through secondary school. The scales are not recommended for use by nonreaders. Readability levels for the three instruments, based on 90% comprehension, are Year 6 for the LPSS, Year 10 for the LPST, and Year 8 (estimated) for the LPSP (roughly speaking, "year" = "grade").

The authors of the instrument present a variety of ways in which the results of each instrument might be used. Included in the recommendations are such aspects as diagnosing attitudes of students, teachers, and parents about differing learning styles and modes and toward those expressing preferences for these differing modes; planning and carrying out varying and alternative teaching/learning strategies; contributing to policy decisions; providing information for in-service training; and improving communication among students, teachers, and parents regarding matters related to learning preferences.

The manual is well designed and easy to use. In addition to providing copies of the instrument and describing their purpose and ways to use the results derived from their use, the manual provides instructions for administering and scoring the instruments and recording and reporting the results. Information is also provided on reference groups and the development of the instruments (including a discussion of versions devised for use in the United States and in England since the original development of the instruments occurred in Australia).

The three scales have been tested for reliability through several large scale administrations in New South Wales, Western Australia, the United States, and England. Using Cronbach's alpha, the coefficients ranged from .60 to .78 on all subscales of all administrations of the LPSS, from .37 to .79 on the LPST (from .62 to .79 on the Cooperative and Competitive subscales and from .37 to .60 on the Individualized), and from .46 to .85 on the LPSP (from .71 to .85 on the Cooperative and Competitive and from .46 to .65 on Individualized). Intercorrelations among the three subscales have also been calculated using Pearson r. These findings

> support the "new theory" contention that preferences of students for Cooperative and Competitive modes of learning comprise independent dimensions. This is in contrast with the earlier "old theory" argument that preferences for Cooperative and Competitive modes were negatively related and opposed in a polar relationship. .... The data on Cooperative and Individualised [sic] preferences indicates [sic] that a moderate negative relationship prevails and that this does not vary with sex or year at school. (p. 25)

A considerable number of articles, conference papers, theses, dissertations, and research projects have been devoted to these scales and their spin-offs. However, a vast majority of this research has been done by the authors themselves and by others working with them. There is still considerable room for, and need of, testing by independent researchers. Nevertheless, the scales should certainly prove useful and valuable if they are used, as suggested by the authors, for improving teaching and learning in the classroom and for helping students, teachers, and parents better understand the variety of ways people can, and prefer to, learn. The tests are not intended to be used for individual diagnoses leading to such decisions as educational placement. Such a use would be a misuse.

Review of the Learning Preference Scales by ROBERT J. MILLER, *Associate Professor of Special Education, Mankato State University, Mankato, MN:*

There are three Learning Preference Scale instruments. These include the: (a) Learning Preference Scale—Students (LPSS), (b) Learning Preference Scale—Teachers (LPST), and (c) Learning Preference Scale—Parents (LPSP). The purpose of each instrument is to provide a measure for preference of the individual completing the scale for cooperative, competitive, and individualized learning. These instruments may be used separately or in combination. The Student instrument (LPSS) contains 36 items with 12 items in each of the three subscales mixed randomly throughout the instrument. The Teacher scale (LPST) contains 33 items arranged in the same three subscales of cooperative, competitive, and individualized learning with 11 items in each subscale. The Parent scale (LPSP) contains 24 items across the three subscales.

Each instrument is largely self-administered and the instrument may be completed alone or in a group. The Student (LPSS) form takes approximately 10 to 15 minutes to complete for older students and from 25 to 45 minutes for younger students or less competent readers. Results of readability testing by the authors suggest the reading level at which these instruments could be read by the test takers with 90% comprehension was 6th grade for the LPSS (Student form), 10th grade for the LPST (Teacher form), and an estimated 8th grade for the LPSP (Parent form). The authors do not recommend the use of this instrument with students younger than 4th grade or with students after the completion of secondary school.

The test manual includes directions for administering the student instrument to a large group. It is suggested that the Teacher and Parent forms will almost always be completed on an individual basis. Directions for completing the instrument are included on the Teacher and Parent forms but not on the Student form. Directions for the Student form are designed to be provided orally and the manual provides specific directions for student participants. Each of the 36 items in the Student form (LPSS) is a simple statement of 6 to 20 words. The test taker is to read the statement, and rate their agreement or disagreement with the statement using a 4-point Likert-type scale ranging from *True, Sort of True, Sort of False, False* regarding their learning preferences. An identical Likert-type scale is used for test takers on the LPST (Teacher) and LPSP (Parent) forms of the instrument. Scoring is done manually, by a paper-and-pencil compilation. Items that are rated by the test taker as *True* of their learning preferences receive a score of 4. Items that are *Sort of True* receive a score of 3. *Sort of False* items are scored as 2, and *False* items are scored as 1. Negative items in each scale (those requiring reverse scoring) are identified in the test manual.

Interpretation of raw scores is based on percentiles with separate reference group data provided in tables in the test manual for populations of students from New South Wales (Sidney, Australia); Western Australia (Perth, Australia); Minneapolis, Minnesota (U.S.A.); and from three Midlands counties of England. Separate tables in the manual provide the quartile scores, the mean scores, and standard deviations of scores obtained by a number of smaller subgroups of these populations. Quartile scores on the LPSS are provided for each school year group by sex and on the LPST for different subject teachers, as well as for male and female teachers separately. No information is provided regarding the LPSP (Parent) form of the instrument.

The authors suggest: "By selecting an appropriate comparison group it is possible to convert a raw score for an individual into a percentile rating, indicating that the obtained score is equal to or greater than that of a certain percentage of that comparison group" (p. 13). Implied in this statement is that one would find value in comparing a subject's score to that of the comparison group. Unfortunately, the norming of this instrument is woefully inadequate and the norm sample limits the usefulness of the instrument as a diagnostic tool and also the usefulness of comparing the subject's performance to that of the comparison group. For example, information for the United States sample was collected from one senior high school, one junior high school, and two primary schools in suburban Minneapolis in 1981. This norming population was situated in "predominately white areas" (p. 12). The total United States norm sample was 1,058 school-aged children and young adults from the Minneapolis area. Although the sample has a roughly equal distribution of boys ($n = 533$) and girls ($n = 525$) and primary ($n = 486$) and secondary students ($n = 572$), the sample is from one region of the United States and the manual provides no information regarding socio-economic status of the norming sample nor adequate information regarding minority group representation. No students from rural or urban locations were included in the United States sample. It is, therefore, difficult to gauge whether the population to which the instrument is normed is reflective of any larger population.

Alpha reliabilities were provided for each of the subscales of all three forms of the Learning Preference Scales. Three tables presented alpha reliabilities for students, teachers, and parents. The coefficients for the LPSS (Student) subscales across the international field tests of the instrument ranged as follows: (a) Cooperation subscale from .64 to .75; (b) Competition subscale from .52 to .77; and (c) Individualism subscale from .60 to .75. In all cases, the lowest reliability coefficients were found in the primary grades and the highest in the secondary grades. The alpha reliabilities for the LPSS indicate marginally adequate internal consistency.

The alpha coefficients for the LPST (Teacher) subscales of the instrument ranged as follows: (a) Cooperation subscale from .62 to .76; (b) Competitive subscale from .73 to .79; and, (c) Individualism subscale from .37 to .60. The alpha coefficients for the LPSP (Parent) subscales were as follows: (a) Cooperative subscale .71 to .82; (b) Competition subscale .78 to .85; and, (c) Individualism subscale .46 to .65. Alpha reliabilities for both the Teacher and Parent forms in the area of the Individualism subscales were low whereas all other areas were adequate.

One of the most useful types of reliability evidence for this sort of instrument is consistency over time or test-retest reliability. In the manual, the authors suggest "the LPSS seems to have been demonstrated in obtaining stable results in short-term, test-retest usage" (p. 24). However, no evidence is provided in the manual to support the test-retest reliability of this instrument. No information is provided regarding the test-retest reliability of the LPST or the LPSP.

The discussion of validity of the Learning Preference Scales provided by the authors is inadequate. Neither content validity nor predictive validity are discussed in the manual. Although construct validity is implied in the authors' discussion of the development of the instruments, no systematic evidence is provided. A discussion of validity of these instruments is needed.

The Learning Preference Scales are a set of instruments that are designed to measure the test taker's preference for cooperation, competition and individualism in the learning environment. The strength of the Learning Preference Scales is the intriguing topic of the test instruments. The weaknesses are substantial. Although the authors have collected much information on students from around the world, the end result of this huge endeavor may have been less comprehensive than the authors had hoped. The Learning Preference Scales have limited usefulness as norm-referenced instruments. For example, the norm sample in the United States is inadequate and limits the use of these instruments in comparing the subject's performance to other students. Too little information regarding the reliability and validity of the instruments is presented in the manual. Very little information was included in the manual regarding the LPSP (Parent) form of the instrument. In this reviewer's opinion, the strength of this set of instruments is the LPSS (Student) form and I would suggest its use only as a criterion-referenced instrument.

[54]

Learning Skills Profile.

Purpose: To assess the gap between personal aptitudes and critical skills required by a job.
Population: Junior high to adults.
Publication Date: 1993.
Acronym: LSP.
Scores, 36: 3 scores: Personal Learning Skill, Job Skill Demand, and Learning Gap in each of 12 skill areas: Interpersonal Skills (Leadership Skill, Relationship Skill, Help Skill), Analytical Skills (Theory Skill, Quantitative Skill, Technology Skill), Information Skills (Sense-Making Skill, Information-Gathering Skill, Information Analysis Skill), Behavioral Skills (Goal Setting Skill, Action Skill, Initiative Skill).
Administration: Group.

Price Data, 1993: $85 per complete kit including 5 workbooks and profiles, and 1 set of reusable LSP cards and instructions; $65 per 5 workbooks and profiles; $32 per reusable LSP cards and instructions.
Time: Administration time not reported.
Comments: Self-scored profile.
Authors: Richard E. Boyatzis and David A. Kolb.
Publisher: McBer & Company.

Review of the Learning Skills Profile by DAVID O. HERMAN, Associate Education Officer, Office of Educational Research, New York City Board of Education, Brooklyn, NY:

Reduced to its skeleton, the Learning Skills Profile (LSP) is a set of 12 six-item rating scales. The 12 scales represent job-related skills that may be considered as either personal characteristics of a job holder or skills demanded by the job. "Working as a member of a team" (Relationship Skill) and "Finding solutions to problems" (Goal Setting Skill) are examples of the items. Most of the item statements are simply worded, although a reference to "mathematical models" may not be clear to some users.

The user rates him or herself on all 72 items, using a 7-point scale that ranges from 1 (*No skill or experience in this area*) to 7 (*A leader or creator in this area*). Then the user rerates each item for the extent to which his or her job requires the activity. Again a 7-point scale is used, this one ranging from 1 (*Not relevant to job or career*) to 7 (*A top priority activity*). Two complete sets of total scores are obtained for the 12 learning-skill scales, with one set describing the rater ("Personal Learning Skills"), and the other describing his or her job ("Job Skill Demands").

A difference between the two scores on any scale is said to reflect a "learning gap." If the Personal Learning Skill score is less than the Job Skill Demand score, the discrepancy signifies an area in which the user needs further development; if the score difference is in the other direction, it indicates an area where the user is overskilled or overqualified for the job.

The Learning Skills Profile is a highly elaborated version of this skeleton. The 72 activity statements are printed onto two separate decks of cards. The user physically sorts one deck into seven piles to describe the self, then sorts the second deck similarly to describe the job. The numerical ratings are now transcribed, statement by statement, onto a grid on a special score sheet; this is done twice, once for the self and once for the job. Total scores for the 12 skill areas are recorded separately for the self-description and the job description, and the two sets of 12 scores are plotted on a clock-like circle graph.

The user then turns to the LSP Workbook. After reading a general introduction to the LSP, the user is directed to copy once again the two complete sets of 72 item ratings for detailed consideration. Various exercises encourage the user to reflect on the accuracy of the scores, to compare one's self-assessment with feedback from others, and to make plans to rectify any "learning gaps."

I think the Learning Skills Profile offers people, especially those in supervisory and managerial positions, an opportunity to view themselves critically and constructively. The LSP materials are so minimal, however, they cannot be judged by the usual criteria for evaluating tests. No manual or technical supplement accompanied the review kit to document, for example, the internal consistency of the scales; or whether the scale intercorrelations support the circular arrangement on the LSP graphical display (this is important because sets of scales that are adjacent on the display are said to make up super-variables or so-called "skill types"); or whether ratings are distributed about the same on all 12 scales (this is important because, in the absence of norms, interpretations of profile elevation require that a given score level have about the same meaning on all scales). The LSP offers no control for social desirability or conscious deception. It may be true that such refinements are less important with a self-evaluation exercise of this kind than with other kinds of instruments used in high-stakes settings. Nevertheless, it must be said the LSP has no known measurement characteristics.

The procedures for rating the items and interpreting the results are labor-intensive and probably tedious. Careful forms design could, I believe, place the 72 items and the two rating scales efficiently on a single sheet of paper, thus avoiding much clerical drudgery. Possibly the authors have found the recommended procedures get users deeply involved in the rating process, and thus yield more accurate results than briefer, more streamlined methods—but we do not know.

In summary, the Learning Skills Profile is rather like an elaborate, highly structured interview aimed at exploring a job holder's self-reported skills and how well they fit the demands of the job, and for planning future actions in the light of the findings. I am aware of no competition.

[55]

Life Roles Inventory.

Purpose: "Designed to assess the importance of life-career values and the relative importance of five major life roles."

Population: Junior high students–adults.

Publication Date: 1985.

Acronym: LRI.

Subtests: 2 subtests.

Administration: Group.

Price Data: Available from publisher.

Foreign Language Edition: French edition ('85) available.

Authors: George W. Fitzsimmons, Donald Macnab, and Catherine Casserly.

Publisher: Psychometrics Canada Ltd. [Canada].

a) VALUES SCALE.

Scores, 20: Ability Utilization, Achievement, Advancement, Aesthetics, Altruism, Authority, Autonomy, Creativity, Economics, Life Style, Personal Development, Physical Activity, Prestige, Risk, Social Interaction, Social Relations, Variety, Working Conditions, Cultural Identity, Physical Prowess.

Time: (20–25) minutes.

b) SALIENCE INVENTORY.

Scores, 15: 5 scores (Studying, Working, Community Service, Home and Family, Leisure) in each of 3 areas (Participation, Commitment, Role Values).

Time: (25–30) minutes.

TEST REFERENCE

1. Brintnell, E. S., Madill, H. M., Montgomerie, T. C., & Stavin, L. L. (1992). Work and family issues after injury: Do female and male client perspectives differ. *Career Development Quarterly, 41,* 145-160.

Review of the Life Roles Inventory by RICH-ARD W. JOHNSON, Director of Training at Counseling & Consultation Services of the University Health Services, and Adjunct Professor of Counseling Psychology, University of Wisconsin–Madison, Madison, WI:

The Life Roles Inventory (LRI) consists of two inventories designed to measure the importance of life goals and roles for individuals living in Canada. The two inventories, the Values Scale (VS) and the Salience Inventory (SI), are very similar to the two instruments with virtually these same names developed for use within the United States (see 10:379 and 11:339). The inventories are based on research conducted by members of the Work Importance Study, an international consortium headed by Donald Super, which includes vocational psychologists from 12 countries and which was formed in 1979 to investigate the significance of major life roles in different cultural settings.

The VS consists of 100 items that measure 20 different values. Each scale has five 4-point items, three of which are common to all countries and two of which are unique to Canada. The item content includes both work and personal values. The U.S. version of the VS scale contain 21 scales, 19 of which are identical to those on the Canadian version. The two versions of the VS differ in that two of the scales on the former version (Economic Rewards and Economic Security) have been collapsed into one scale on the latter version (Economics).

The SI assesses the relative importance of life roles for individuals as described in Super's (1980) life-career rainbow model. Each of five major life roles—Study, Work, Home and Family, Leisure, and Community Service—are evaluated in terms of three aspects of importance—Participation, Commitment, and Value Expectations—to produce a total of 15 scales. The three areas of importance include measures of behavior (Participation) and affect (Commitment and Values Expectations), but not knowledge. According to the authors, Super's Career Development Inventory (Test 12, this volume) should be used to evaluate knowledge in the area of work. The 15 scales on the two versions of the SI are identical. Both instruments contain 170 four-point items with similar content; however, the exact wording of the items frequently differs.

Both parts of the LRI (the VS and SI) have been standardized on Canadian populations. Separate norms have been established for the English and French editions of the LRI. The norms are further divided in regard to sex, type of work (professional, clerical, skilled, and unskilled), and year-in-school (postsecondary students, 12th grade students, and 10th grade students). The characteristics of the normative samples are described in some detail in the technical manual; however, it is not clear to what extent the norms are representative of the Canadian population.

In general, the SI scales have produced higher coefficients of internal consistency than the VS scales, presumably because the SI contains more items per scale than the VS. Median Cronbach alpha coefficients for the French and English adult normative samples for the 20 scales on the VS were both .80, whereas the median alphas for these same samples for the 15 scales on the SI were better than .90. Similar differences were obtained with the other normative samples. Because of such high alpha coefficients for the SI, the authors indicate that they may develop a short version of the SI for use where time is limited.

As has been noted for the U.S. versions of the VS and SI, the test-retest reliabilities of the Canadian versions of these scales run somewhat low. The test-retest reliabilities over a 4- to 6-week time period for grades 10 and 12 students ranged from .53 to .83 with a median of .65 for the French version of the LRI VS. For the English version, the reliabilities ranged from .63 to .82 with a median of .69. The test-retest reliability coefficients for the SI scales for these same students were slightly higher; however, the median rs were still only .72 and .73 for the French and English versions, respectively. These reliability coefficients indicate that one's scores could change substantially upon retesting over relatively short time periods for scales on either instrument.

Both the VS and SI exhibit content validity in the sense that the items for the scales have been selected to measure different types of values and life roles suggested by vocational theory and research in a number of cultural settings. Items for the final scales were selected on the basis of item and factor analyses.

The authors have conducted several studies to demonstrate the convergent and discriminant validities of the LRI. Their research shows that the scales on the VS and SI correlate with similar scales on other instruments. In contrast, the scales do not produce high correlations with other types of vocational measures from which they should differ. For example, correlations between scores on both the VS and SI scales and scores on interest inventory scales have been relatively low.

Research indicates that the VS significantly differentiates among students enrolled in various academic programs. In a well-conducted study of postsecondary students enrolled in three different majors (rehabilitation medicine, business, and education), the authors found the VS to be more effective than the Work Values Inventory (T4:2998) the Minnesota Importance Questionnaire (T4:1641), or the Work Aspect Preference Scale (T4:2987) in differentiating among the students.

Studies cited in the technical manual show that the SI distinguishes among individuals in different settings or circumstances in expected directions. For example, occupational therapists who were leaving the field obtained lower scores on the Commitment and Participation scales for the Work role and higher scores on the scales for the Home and Family role than did occupational therapists who had recently assumed administrative or supervisory positions. Participation, Commitment, and Role Values for Studying were rated higher by professional and skilled groups than by clerical and unskilled groups in the normative samples.

Principal component analysis of the VS indicates that five components (Personal Achievement and Development, Social Orientation, Independence, Economic Conditions, and Physical Activity and Risk) account for most of the variance in the instrument. These five components are similar to those obtained in factor analyses of work values instruments with the exception of Physical Activity and Risk, which appears to be unique to the VS. The authors conclude that some of the scales on the VS could probably be combined, a project that they suggest for further research.

In summary, the LRI contributes to the field of vocational psychology by providing measures of life roles and values that are more comprehensive than those provided by other instruments. As part of an international project, the LRI can also be used productively in cross-cultural research. It needs to be strengthened in regard to test-retest reliability. Validity data are still relatively limited.

REVIEWER'S REFERENCE

Super, D. E. (1980). A life-span, life-space approach to career development. *Journal of Vocational Behavior, 16,* 282–298.

Review of the Life Roles Inventory by S. ALVIN LEUNG, Associate Professor of Educational Psychology, The Chinese University of Hong Kong, Hong Kong:

The Life Roles Inventory (LRI) consists of two separate scales, the Values Scale and the Sa-lience Inventory. The LRI is designed to assess what a person wants to get out of work and life (values), and the importance of work roles in relation to other major life roles. The LRI can be administered to junior and senior high school and college students and to adults with different vocational needs and concerns in career and vocational guidance, general counseling, and job placement counseling.

The LRI was the result of an international research collaboration known as the "Work Importance Study." Vocational psychologists from a number of European, Asian, and American countries, led by Donald Super, developed vocational assessment instruments aimed at measuring work values and life roles of individuals. This effort resulted in several national editions of an assessment instrument, and the LRI is the Canadian edition. The LRI has both an English and a French version. Normative and psychometric information for both language versions are provided in the administrative manual and the technical manual. A back-translations process was used to ensure comparability of the two language versions. Handscoring of the LRI can be done easily by following the procedure described in the administrator's manual. Computer scoring and interpretation is also available.

The Values Scale measures 20 values on a 4-point scale (1 = *of little or no importance*, 4 = *very important*). Each item is a statement about preference (e.g., use my skills and knowledge). Each value is measured by five items resulting in a total of 100 items. The values are Ability Utilization, Achievement, Advancement, Aesthetics, Altruism, Authority, Autonomy, Creativity, Economics, Life Style, Personal Development, Physical Activity, Prestige, Risk, Social Interaction, Social Relations, Variety, Working Conditions, Cultural Identity, and Physical Prowess. For each value scale, a raw scores is computed, which is then transformed into a percentile score using the normative table provided in the administrator's manual. A profile sheet is used to plot both the raw and the percentile scores.

The Salience Inventory uses a 4-point scale (1 = *never or rarely*, 4 = *always or almost always* or 1 = *little or none*, 4 = *a great deal*) to measure meaning and importance of five life activities, which are Studying, Working, Community Service, Home and Family, and Leisure Activities. It consists of three sections. The first, Participation (50 items), measures current involvement in the five life activities. The second, Commitment (50 items), measures how one feels about the five life activities. The third is Role Values Grid, consisting of 70 items about an individual's long-term expectations to fulfill 14 values in each of the five life activities. The 14 values are Ability Utilization, Achievement, Aesthetics, Altruism, Autonomy, Creativity, Economics, Life Style, Physical Activity, Prestige, Risk, Social Interaction, Variety, and Working Conditions. Both raw scores and percentile scores are plotted.

Normative information is available for adults and for post-secondary and high school students. There is evidence that the samples were drawn from diverse geographic areas within Canada, and educational and occupational levels. The LRI scores are converted to percentile scores using normative data from the group that is most appropriate for the test taker.

Information on internal consistency and test-retest reliability are available. For internal consistency of the English version of the Values Scale, the range for adults was from .67 to .88, with a median of .80. The alphas for post-secondary students ranged from .68 to .91, with a median of .83. The alpha for grade 12 students ranged from .65 to .90, with a median of .79. On the French version, the alphas ranged from .64 to .84, with a median of .80. The alphas for grade 12 students ranged from .60 to .88, with a median of .74. Test-retest correlation coefficients for the Values Scale were computed for a high school sample in a 4- to 6-weeks time interval. The median correlation for the English and French versions of the Values Scale were .69 and .65, respectively. Given that values are relatively stable constructs, one would expect a higher degree of test-retest stability. Alternate forms correlation between the English and French versions ranged between .62 and .88, with a median correlation of .74. Again, one would expect a higher correlation between the two language versions if the two forms were highly equivalent.

On the Salience Inventory, the alpha coefficient estimates of internal consistency for French- and English-speaking adult samples ranged from .84 to .95. For English-speaking post-secondary students, the range was from .83 to .95, and for

English and French high school students, the range was from .88 to .96. The 4- to 6-weeks test-retest correlation for the English version ranged from .66 to .81, with a median of .73. For the French version, the test-retest correlation ranged .68 to .81, with a median of .72. The correlation between the English and French versions of the Salience Inventory ranged from .59 to .84, with a median of .77. For the same reasons as in the case of the Values Scale, the test-retest and alternative-forms reliability is lower than expected.

Evidence on the validity of the LRI is summarized in the technical manual. For the Values Scale, a principal component factor analysis of the items using a varimax procedure yielded factors that were similar to 14 of the 20 a priori value scales, supporting the construct validity of the Values Scale. The Values Scale correlated significantly with similar scales measuring work values. Differences in work values were observed among students in education, business, and rehabilitation medicine. Using the Values Scale scores, students were correctly classified into one of the above three academic areas.

There is some evidence on the validity of the Salience Inventory. Students were asked to rate the importance of different academic, occupational, recreational, community, and family activities, and their ratings generally converged with their Salience Inventory scores. Occupational therapists who were actively practicing in their profession rated the work role as more important in the participation and Commitment subscales of the Salience Inventory, whereas those who were not actively practicing rated home and family roles as more important.

Although the amount of research evidence on the validity of the LRI is limited and additional research studies are needed, the LRI appears to be a carefully constructed instrument that has a sound conceptual foundation in Donald Super's theoretical work on career development. There are at least three advantages of using Super's theory. First, there is a large volume of research literature on Super's theory (e.g., see Savickas, 1994), and thus the validity and utility of the LRI are complemented by the research evidence supporting Super's theory. Second, in the process of interpreting the LRI, Super's theory can be used to help individuals understand the implications of the test scores.

Third, Super's conceptual framework can be used as a basis to further research the validity of the LRI.

On a cross-cultural perspective, the LRI has two strengths. First, the instrument was conceptualized through a process of international collaboration in which the cross-cultural similarities and differences in work values and life roles were considered. Second, the Canadian LRI is in English and French, and normative information was available for both versions. To further meet the needs of an increasing multicultural society, it would be desirable for the LRI to provide additional language or normative information for other major ethnic and cultural groups in Canada, such as American Indians and Asians.

A weakness of the LRI is that both the administrator's manual and technical manual do not provide specific information on how the LRI can be used in a counseling context. A number of areas related to interpretation are not described clearly. For example, how can the LRI be used to assist individuals in different counseling situations suggested to be appropriate by the authors (career, personal, and job placement)? What information should be communicated to a test taker regarding the meaning of test scores? How can the LRI be used along with other vocational assessment instruments? What interpretation strategies can be used for individuals with specific profiles, such as those who have high scores (i.e., an elevated profile) and those with low scores (i.e., a depressed profile)? Should raw scores or percentile scores be used in interpretation? Answers to the above questions would be helpful to users of the LRI.

The print quality of the LRI administrator's manual and technical manual is poor and should be improved. Many tables are very small and are hard to read (e.g., normative tables, and tables on reliability).

Overall, the LRI is a useful instrument to help individuals with diverse vocational concerns. The LRI can be used in conjunction with other career assessment instruments (e.g., interests inventory) to counsel individuals in different stages of career and life planning. However, additional research studies are needed to further examine the reliability and validity of the LRI, and to demonstrate that the LRI produces possible outcomes for students and adults in different counseling situations.

REVIEWER'S REFERENCE

Savickas, M. L. (Ed.). (1994). From vocational guidance to career counseling: Essays to honor Donald Super [Special issue]. *The Career Development Quarterly*, 43(1).

[56]
Lifestyle Assessment Questionnaire.

Purpose: Provides individuals with a measurement of their lifestyle status in various wellness categories, offers a health risk appraisal component that lists the individual's top ten risks of death, projects an achievable health age, makes suggestions for lifestyle improvement, and offers a stimulus for positive lifestyle change by providing a guide to successful implementation of that change.

Population: Adults with a minimum of 10th grade education.

Publication Dates: 1978–1991.

Scores, 16: Physical (Exercise, Nutrition, Self-Care, Vehicle Safety, Drug Usage), Social/Environmental, Emotional (Emotional Awareness and Acceptance, Emotional Management), Intellectual, Occupational, Spiritual, Actual Age, Appraised Health Age, Achievable Health Age, Top 10 Risks of Death, Lifestyle Improvement Suggestions.

Administration: Group.

Price Data, 1993: $3 per literature set including questionnaire, results folder, Behavior Change Guide, and scannable answer sheet; $.25 per scannable answer sheet; $10 per individual National Wellness Processing Center scoring; $1,995 per software program and license.

Time: (45–60) minutes.

Comments: Computer scoring or scoring by National Wellness Institute available; information on up to four wellness areas included in scoring report; individual and group reports available.

Authors: Dennis Elsenrath, Bill Hettler, and Fred Leafgren.

Publisher: National Wellness Institute.

Cross References: See T4:1461 (3 references).

TEST REFERENCES

1. Smith, B. A. (1993). Physical exercise practices of Mexican-American college students. *College Student Journal, 27*, 146-156.
2. Fedorovich, S. E., Boyle, C. R., & Hare, R. D. (1994). Wellness as a factor in the selection of resident assistants in university student housing. *Journal of College Student Development, 35*, 248-254.
3. Patten, J. A. (1994). Dietary patterns of Hispanic and White college freshman. *College Student Journal, 28*, 39-45.

Review of the Lifestyle Assessment Questionnaire by MICHAEL B. BROWN, Assistant Professor of Psychology, East Carolina University, Greenville, NC:

The Lifestyle Assessment Questionnaire (LAQ) is a tool for evaluating an adult's habits and knowledge on a number of health and wellness dimensions. The questionnaire requires the respondent to answer 227 questions about demographics, lifestyle, and health risks. An additional 43 questions allow for the respondent to request additional information on a wide variety of health-related topics. Responses are made on an optical scanning sheet, which can be scored on site through a single site software license or through a scoring and interpretation service offered through the publisher.

Computer-generated individual and group reports are available. The individual report includes a wellness report, health-risk appraisal, and resources for further information on the topics requested by the user. The wellness report is considered an assessment of the individual's lifestyle in six life areas including occupational, emotional, intellectual, physical, social, and spiritual dimensions. Percentage scores are provided for the individual, the average scores of individuals in the organization with whom the individual is taking the assessment, and the average score of the same age/sex reference group. The health-risk appraisal provides an assessment of an individual's risk of death over the next decade and provides suggestions for lifestyle improvements. Results are presented for risk of death, life expectancy, and life expectancy if suggested changes are made. A behavior change guide called Making Wellness Work For You provides a systematic guide for making a specific behavior change. The personal growth resource list provides bibliographic resources for further information on specific health and wellness topics. The management group report provides a summary of lifestyle and health-risk status of the individuals in an organization. This report is intended to serve as both an organizational wellness needs assessment and an evaluation of the organization's wellness programming.

MANUAL. The LAQ software package comes with a ring-bound user's guide that is devoted to installation and use of the software package, interpretation of results, and a description of its technical characteristics. Several pages of technical information were provided in addition to that in the manual. Sample individual and group reports are also available with the manual. There are no guidelines on qualifications of users or overall strategy for the use of the instrument.

TECHNICAL CHARACTERISTICS. There are significant limitations with both the types and

adequacy of technical data. Although the reference group includes a large sample of over 47,000 persons, descriptive data are provided only for age and sex. No data are provided for other relevant descriptors of the norm group, such as socioeconomic status or level of education. Although the reference group includes persons from 15 years of age and older, 23% of the sample were 18 years old. With the exception of those identified as college students, the method of selection and identification of the remainder of the reference group is not specified. Based upon these limitations, it is unclear how representative the reference group is or how well the group may represent persons of different ethnic and socioeconomic groups. Information on the derivation of health-risk data is also limited. Health risk is said to be based on data from the most recent U.S. Centers for Disease Control epidemiological data, although the exact year of the data is not specified. No information is provided for how life expectancy scores are computed, or how forecast life expectancy was calculated.

Reliability data are reported for test-retest reliability over 2-week periods for the wellness scale. Test-retest reliabilities of the wellness categories ranged from .57—.87, with an average coefficient of .76. Test-retest reliability for the subscales ranged from .81–.97. However, the two studies reported in the manual included only 15 and 39 subjects, which is an inadequate number of subjects from which to ascertain reliability. The internal consistency of the wellness subscales ranged from .67–.94. However, no information was provided from which to identify the size of the group used to determine internal consistency.

Content validity is said to have been established by a panel of experts, who are not identified further in the manual. Later in the manual, content validity was said to be ascertained by two experts in measurement and health promotion. Factor analysis was said to be used to determine construct validity, but no data are provided that identify the factors utilized, resulting factor structure, or factor scores. Two studies are cited that are said to establish criterion validity. The first study reports that the LAQ emotional subscales can differentiate college students who are receiving psychotherapy from those who are not. Few additional details are provided on this study. The other criterion-validity study investigated the relationship between the LAQ wellness scales and objective physiological indicators of health. No relationship was found in the college students studied, although a relationship was found between the scores taken "as a whole" and "general health." There is a section that provides research citations for a number of health risks. Another section follows listing research studies that used the LAQ. Its placement here is potentially misleading, as the research cited does not study the technical characteristics of the LAQ, but uses the LAQ only as a measurement tool for research on wellness intervention.

OVERALL EVALUATION. The Lifestyle Assessment Questionnaire has inadequate technical data to support its use as a norm-referenced measurement tool. The reference group, although large, is not sufficiently described to allow a test user to be certain that users of various socioeconomic and ethnic groups are represented in the reference group. In addition, the reference group is heavily weighted to persons of college age. Reliability studies, although encouraging, are not large enough to demonstrate reliability. Validity data are not sufficiently described in the manual, and do not illuminate the meaning or predictive power of the scales. The scale scores for the wellness portion of the inventory have only face validity. The health-risk appraisal portion may be based on adequate epidemiological data, but this is not clear from the information provided. There is no information supporting the forecast life expectancy. This could be misleading to clients and unsophisticated users. The Health Risk Appraisal may be useful, although its suggestions for reducing risk are very generic and somewhat unimaginative. For example, suggestions to reduce risk of motor vehicle accidents include "obey all rules of the road" and "don't drive while tired." The Making Wellness Work For You behavior change guide is a thorough and well-constructed device that could be very helpful to persons who are motivated to change.

Review of the Lifestyle Assessment Questionnaire by WILLIAM E. MARTIN, JR., Professor of Educational Psychology, Northern Arizona University, Flagstaff, AZ:

According to an information pamphlet provided by the National Wellness Institute, Inc., "The Lifestyle Assessment Questionnaire (LAQ) is a pow-

erful wellness tool developed in 1976 by the Board of Directors and Cofounders of The National Wellness Institute." The LAQ is intended to serve a dual purpose for assessment and education. The assessment purpose of the LAQ is to provide individuals with a measurement of their lifestyle status in the following six wellness dimensions: occupational, intellectual, spiritual, social, physical, and emotional. The measurement information generated from the LAQ provides an educational stimulus for individuals to change their lifestyles.

The LAQ is divided into four primary sections. The first of the four sections, Personal Data, comprises 12 multiple-choice questions related to age, sex, etc. The second section is the Lifestyle Inventory. The Lifestyle Inventory has 11 subsections that relate to the six wellness dimensions. However, it is not clear to me how some of the subsections would be grouped with the six wellness dimensions (i.e., self-care, vehicle safety, and drug usage and awareness). This section has 185 statements formatted with a 5-point Likert-type response ranging from *Almost never* (less than 10% of the time) to *Almost always* (90% or more of the time). The number of questions per subsection varies from 10 to 31 questions.

The third section of the LAQ is Health Risk Appraisal and consists of interlocked questions: 33 for men and 38 for women. For this section, both multiple-choice and short answer questions are used. The final section, Topics for Personal Growth, is a listing of 43 lifestyle topics. In this section, the examinee is instructed to select four lifestyle topics for which they would like to receive additional information.

The Lifestyle Inventory of the LAQ is used to generate individual reports that compare an individual's score to those of the group with which the test was taken and to group scores for all those who have taken the LAQ since 1978. The Health Risk Appraisal scores are compared to national averages for individuals of the same sex and age. Group reports are also generated to provide direction to organizations for developing wellness programs.

DEVELOPMENT OF THE SCALES. The authors state that when the LAQ was initially developed, it was reviewed by a panel of health promotion and wellness professionals to verify the validity of the instrument's content. The 11 assessment categories of the LAQ's Lifestyle Inventory were reviewed by professionals working in each of the six wellness dimensions and the Health Risk Appraisal section was developed using research data from the Carter Center at Emory University and the Center for Disease Control.

RELIABILITY AND VALIDITY. A two-page National Wellness Institute, Inc. flyer briefly described two studies that have generated test-retest reliability and internal consistency coefficients and two studies that were intended to reflect test validity of the LAQ. The first test-retest study was conducted in 1982 with 39 parents of incoming university students. For this sample, the 2-week test-retest reliability coefficients on the Lifestyle Inventory scales ranged from .57 to .87 with an "overall" coefficient of .76. The Personal Growth section yielded a .87 coefficient and a .90 test-retest reliability coefficient was reported for the Health Risk Appraisal section. A 1985 study of 15 female university students demonstrated test-retest reliability coefficients ranging from .81 to .97; however, no time interval was identified. Additionally, coefficients of internal consistency ranging from .67 to .94 were reported as part of this study. The discussion presented relative to validity studies was too brief and unclear to report with any accuracy. For example, a result of one of the studies was "there is considerable support for external validity of the physical scales." The use of the term external validity is confusing because it is a concept related to research design not measurement. It appears that the authors meant to use the term criterion-related validity.

ADMINISTRATION, SCORING, AND INTERPRETATION. Lifestyle Assessment Questionnaires are given to the individual to self-administer and can be taken in an individual or group setting. Either way, it is not necessary for a test administrator to be present. Directions are provided throughout the questionnaire and test takers respond to questions using scannable answer sheets. Completed questionnaires can be scored either by sending the materials to the National Wellness Institute Processing Center or by purchasing a software program and license. Individual and group reports (where appropriate) are generated that provide numerical information and narrative interpretation. Scores on the individual report range from 0 to 100 and represent the percent of possible points for each area. Scores and bar charts are given for wellness dimensions and subcategories. An individual's LAQ scores are compared to those of the group (when applicable) with which the test was taken and to individuals who have taken it since 1978. The individual's Health Risk Appraisal scores are compared to a national population average for individuals of the same age and sex. Additionally, the individual report presents information concerning suggestions on increasing expected years of life, health-risk appraisal forecast information, and available resources related to various health-related topics. When a group of individuals from a shared organizational setting take the LAQ as a group, a group report is generated. The report reflects group frequency and percentage scores by dimensions and subcategories.

SUMMARY. Although the LAQ has functional use appeal, is attractively packaged, and has been used since 1978, there are technical weaknesses that must be considered in using the instrument. The first concern relates to the instrument's construct validity. Established methods in test construction appear not to have been used in the development of the LAQ scales including: (a) a theoretical grounding of the construct of wellness, (b) empirically derived factors and items, and/or (c) evidence of homogeneity in relation to the construct. Do the six dimensions of the LAQ accurately represent the construct of wellness? Do the items accurately reflect the dimensions of wellness? The validity and reliability studies presented appear weak partially because they are difficult to understand due to limited information and a lack of clarity on what is presented. Additionally, there were several methodological problems reported in the studies such as using only 15 subjects for test/restest reliability estimates and establishing content validity of the LAQ "with evaluation by two experts in measurement and health promotion." Second, there have been significant changes in knowledge of wellness since 1978. There is no evidence that the authors have adapted the LAQ to evolving research and changing knowledge about wellness. Based upon the first two concerns, it is highly recommended that a thorough literature review covering the last 20 years be completed and a factor analytic study be conducted to generate a wellness construct that is empirically derived. Then, the established steps for test construction can be followed. There is no doubt that a psychometric instrument that soundly measures a construct of wellness would be beneficial in promoting healthful practices by individuals. Accurate measurement of a valid and stable construct must, however, be demonstrated for users to have confidence in the LAQ.

[57]
Loewenstein Occupational Therapy Cognitive Assessment.

Purpose: "A cognitive battery of tests for both primary assessments and ongoing evaluation in the occupational therapy treatment of brain-injured patients."
Population: Ages 6 to 12 and brain-injured adults.
Publication Date: 1990.
Acronym: LOTCA.
Scores: 21 tests in 4 areas: Orientation (Orientation for Place, Orientation for Time), Visual and Spatial Perception (Object Identification, Shapes Identification, Overlapping Figures, Object Constancy, Spatial Perception, Praxis), Visual Motor Organization (Copying Geometric Forms, Reproduction of a Two-Dimensional Model, Pegboard Construction, Colored Block Design, Plain Block Design, Reproduction of a Puzzle, Drawing a Clock), Thinking Operations (Categorization, ROC Unstructured, ROC Structured, Pictorial Sequence A, Pictorial Sequence B, Geometric Sequence).
Administration: Individual.
Price Data, 1993: $198 per complete kit including manual (56 pages), test booklet, and other materials packed in a plastic carrying case.
Time: (30–45) minutes.
Authors: Loewenstein Rehabilitation Hospital;, Malka Itzkovich (manual), Betty Elazar (manual), Sarah Averbuch (manual), Naomi Katz (principal researcher), and Levy Rahmani (advisor).
Publisher: Maddak Inc.

Review of the Loewenstein Occupational Therapy Cognitive Assessment by ELAINE CLARK, Professor of Educational Psychology, University of Utah, Salt Lake City, UT:

The Loewenstein Occupational Therapy Cognitive Assessment (LOTCA) is a battery of tests that measure cognitive skills in patients who have suffered a brain injury. The LOTCA was intended to be used by occupational therapists who need baseline data to evaluate patient abilities and disabilities and to develop and evaluate treatment

goals. Although the authors indicate that the battery was designed as a qualitative, process-oriented assessment tool, there is no information provided in the manual that would assist test users to use the LOTCA in this manner. The majority of the manual is devoted to quantifying patient responses.

The LOTCA is composed of 20 subtests that measure four areas of cognitive functioning: Orientation, Perception, Visuomotor Organization, and Thinking Operations. The rationale for including these skills and excluding others (e.g., language) is provided in the test manual. The test is intended to be concise, taking no more than 30 to 45 minutes to administer. There are no guidelines as to who might be qualified to give the test.

ADMINISTRATION AND SCORING. The instructions for administering and scoring the LOTCA are lengthy and at times confusing. Even the authors acknowledge that some of the scoring criteria and procedures are inadequate and refer examiners to an external source for further information. According to the authors, "in order to be able to administer and score the test" (manual, p. 17), referring to the Riska Object Classification (ROC) subtest, examiners need to read a 1985 book chapter by Riska and Allen. Because the chapter was not included anywhere in the battery, and the only argument for its inclusion was that it enhances the categorization operation, it is hard to imagine that anyone would bother to look for the 1985 chapter.

Unfortunately, examiners are not provided any further assistance with the scoring sheet. In fact, the scoring sheet is limited to space to mark the subtest score (this is done on a rating scale of 1 to 4, and sometimes 1 to 5) and write two or three words in the comment section. Rather than including an essentially blank sheet of paper for examiners to write in comments, the scoring sheet would best be expanded to include instructional and scoring prompts to clarify some of the confusion.

Test users will find there are a number of minor but annoying inconsistencies in the test (e.g., the scoring sheet, test manual, and test materials). There are differences in subtest titles, order of subtest administration, and the numbering of stimulus cards. Although test users are warned about the difference in card numbering, there is no explanation as to why the cards are not numbered in the order they are intended to be presented (correct numbering would have been more helpful than a footnote in the manual alerting examiners to potential problems with this). The fact the authors failed to explain these and other problems (e.g., lack of consistency in numbering subtests and failing to include information about the necessary materials for a given test) is likely to lead potential users to conclude that sufficient care was not taken with the development of the LOTCA. This is also the conclusion one would draw from careful examination of the psychometric data.

RELIABILITY AND VALIDITY. Although reliability and validity data are reported in the manual, the numbers of subjects included in these studies are either unknown or small, and the designs are poorly described. For example, the interrater reliability coefficients for the various subtests appears high (.82 to .97); however, the number of subjects is no more than 30. It is unclear from the wording, "three pairs of raters tested ten subjects" (p. 37), if this means 10 or 30 subjects were included in the analysis. Without this and other information about the raters themselves (e.g., how well they were trained to give the LOTCA) and the design of the study (e.g., how the coefficients were averaged across the six raters), it is difficult to evaluate the quality of the reported estimates. The only other interrater reliability data mentioned in the manual were based on a sample size of one, making this analysis also difficult to evaluate.

The internal consistency coefficients appear adequate for the domains of perception (.87), visuomotor organization (.95), and thinking operations (.85), and for the individual subtests. The coefficients for the subtests ranged from .40 to .80, which is adequate given the relatively short length of the subtests. As with the interrater reliability, it is unclear how many subjects were included in the analysis.

Validity was assessed using both criterion and construct methods. As with the reliability data, a small number of subjects were included in these studies. Although a correlation coefficient of .68 does not appear to be a problem, with only 20 subjects correlations can be expected to be highly unstable (a confidence band would demonstrate this point). It is unclear why so few subjects were included in this study. It is also unclear why only one domain of the battery was assessed for criterion validity, visuomotor organization, and why only one subtest of the Wechsler Adult Intelligence Scale—Revised (Block Design), was used to evaluate the domain. This raises a question of the possibility that other Wechsler scales were given to evaluate more than the one domain but the data were not favorable.

Construct validity was evaluated using a principal component factor analysis. Two groups, 96 patients and 55 controls, were used for the analysis. Although the data from the analyses support the three factors, perception, visuomotor organization, and thinking operations, a more general factor was found for the patient group. Again, the small number of subjects included in this group could be responsible for factor differences. The problem of sample size becomes particularly serious when looking at the control group data. A factor analysis with 55 subjects and 18 variables provides little meaningful data (even a group of 96 is questionable and does not meet the common standard of 10–12 subjects per variable).

Validity was also assessed by evaluating the ability of the LOTCA to differentiate between the subjects with head injuries and strokes, and between these two groups of subjects and the controls. Wilcoxon's two-sample test was used for this purpose. The results showed that all subtests except Identification of Objects differentiated the groups at a .0001 level of significance.

TEST SCORE INTERPRETATION. There are no normative data, per se; however, the data from the 55 controls and the 48 subjects with brain injuries provide comparisons. Means and standard deviations for all three groups are included in the manual. Because two sets of scores are provided for the two groups with brain injuries (one set pertaining to the first evaluation, and the other pertaining to the second evaluation), it is somewhat unclear which set is to be used for purpose of comparison. It is also unclear how useful the data will be, given the small number of subjects and the limited range of performance (3.6 to 4.0).

Data are also provided for 240 children between the ages of 6 and 12. This is the largest sample reported in the manual, although there is no indication that the LOTCA is to be used with children. From the authors' description, the purpose of including data on "normal" children was to "verify the hierarchical order of acquiring the cognitive competencies tested in the battery" (manual, p. 36). As expected, there was greater score variability for the group of "normal" children when comparing their scores to the "normal" adults; however, the degree to which the scores varied had to do with age and the skill being measured.

SUMMARY. The LOTCA has a number of problems, not the least of which pertain to the clarity of the instructions for administering and scoring the test. Some of these problems can be expected from a test that is developed out of an emergent need to evaluate large numbers of patients with brain injuries from a war, specifically the 1973 war in Israel. It is unexpected, however, to find that these and other problems were not worked out over the course of more than two decades. Although occupational therapists may find the LOTCA helpful in providing information to develop and evaluate treatment goals, users must be aware the data provided to support the reliability or the validity are limited.

Review of the Loewenstein Occupational Therapy Cognitive Assessment by STEPHEN R. HOOPER, Associate Professor of Psychiatry, University of North Carolina School of Medicine, Chapel Hill, NC:

The Loewenstein Occupational Therapy Cognitive Assessment (LOTCA) is described by the test authors "as a first attempt to offer a practical tool to the occupational therapist engaged in neurological rehabilitation" (manual, p. 4). Based upon a dynamic view of brain-behavior relationships, as well as neuropsychological and developmental theories, the LOTCA provides a set of procedures that purportedly serve as a base for a qualitative, process-oriented, and client-centered assessment for patients from age 6 years through adulthood who have sustained brain injuries. As such, the authors state the primary goals of evaluation are: to indicate what the patient's strengths and weaknesses are across the constructs of orientation, perception, visuomotor organization, thinking operations, and attention; to establish starting points for rehabilitation; to formulate specific goals; to monitor treatment effects; and to serve as a screening for further assessment. An administration time of 30 to 45 minutes is reported, with

administration over multiple sessions being acceptable. The manual is clearly written, with approximately one-half of the manual being devoted to a description of the tests, administration, and scoring procedures.

The LOTCA is divided into five major domains that include Orientation, Perception, Visuomotor Organization, Thinking Operations, and Attention; however, total domain scores are not produced from the subtests within each domain. For most of the subtests contained within each domain, an individual's performance is scored on a scale from 1 (low) to 4 (high). For three of the subtests contained within the Thinking Operations Domain, the performance is scored on a scale of 1 to 5. These numbers do not represent interval level scaling but, rather, rank order data. Interrater reliability for the subtests ranged from .82 to .97, although specific reliability coefficients for each subtest were not listed. Despite these positive findings, there are a number of significant psychometric concerns about the LOTCA.

Nearly all of the basic psychometric data generated on the LOTCA were derived from 103 adults: 20 patients with a cranio-cerebral injury, 28 with a cerebro-vascular accident, and 55 normals. In addition to the small numbers upon which to base the psychometric findings, the patient groups were poorly described, and these problems likely had an impact on the psychometric data generated. For example, if the patients in the cranio-cerebral group included open head injuries, closed head injuries, and other such injuries, it is highly likely that the differing behavioral manifestations of this heterogeneous group would interfere with obtaining accurate estimates of reliability and validity for any one group, and generalization of these findings to other patient populations is of concern. Similar difficulties are likely by including the patients diagnosed with cerebro-vascular accidents (e.g., left hemisphere stroke versus right hemisphere stroke will manifest differently on many neurobehavioral measures). Further, 55 normal adults does little to address the basic psychometric issues important to a battery of this size.

Just because the LOTCA shows differences between the two brain injured groups and the normal controls does little to address the validity of this battery. Although one would expect the normal controls to perform more proficiently than a heterogeneous brain-injured group, it is not clear what was expected from the brain injured groups on the LOTCA. Meager criterion validity data also were presented for one dimension (i.e., Visuomotor Organization), although the method whereby this was generated (i.e., mean score of the visuomotor subtests) is not mentioned as a recommended procedure for scoring the LOTCA. A factor analysis also was attempted, but this was poorly done. The subjects-to-variables ratio was quite small, likely contributing to instability in the factor structure, and the results were confounded by inclusion of multiple assessments of the same patient.

Without the benefit of solid item analysis, item placement, and adequate reliability and validity, the LOTCA was administered to 240 normal children (40 at each age level between 6 and 12 years) in order to establish its utility for child populations. The sample was randomly chosen from a large urban public elementary school. Had the authors utilized similar procedures for the development of the LOTCA, its basic psychometric foundations would have been better received. The results of these procedures revealed clear developmental trends for many of the subtests, although there also were a number of subtests that did not evidence such trends (e.g., most of the perception tests). It would seem that these procedures would set the stage for making decisions about whether specific subtests should be included or excluded in the battery.

In summary, the LOTCA has been proposed as "a first attempt" (manual, p. 4) at a tool for occupational therapists to measure selected aspects of neurocognitive functioning in a rehabilitation setting. The intended uses proposed for the LOTCA appear worthwhile, and the battery itself is nicely organized with relatively clear administration and scoring procedures. Of significant practical concern, however, is that it is not clear how this measure will compete with and/or complement psychological and neuropsychological measurement with this patient population, or how the use of this battery will conflict with and/or facilitate the work of other specialists in a rehabilitation setting.

Along with these major pragmatic questions, there are a number of basic psychometric concerns that lead to questions regarding its utility in a rehabilitation setting. Despite initial findings presented in the LOTCA manual, basic reliability and validity issues have yet to be addressed in a satisfactory manner, particularly for adults. Although the basic structure of the battery remains conceptually adequate, the factor analysis provided little in the way of psychometric support. Consequently, the primary goals of the LOTCA have not been achieved from a psychometric perspective. Although a qualitative assessment approach guides this battery, it remains woefully inadequate from a psychometric perspective in its current form, and its routine use in any setting remains tenable at best. The authors have gathered interesting developmental data on their battery, and these data may provide the basis for obtaining the necessary psychometric data to bring this test up to basic testing standards.

[58]
Marital Check-Up Kit.

Purpose: "Designed to help couples examine their relationship and to determine ways in which it can be enriched or strengthened."
Population: Married couples.
Publication Date: 1980.
Acronym: MCK.
Scores: No scores.
Administration: Group.
Price Data: Available from publisher.
Time: Administration time not reported.
Comments: Can be administered to individuals, couples, or groups.
Author: Millard J. Bienvenu.
Publisher: Millard J. Bienvenu, Northwest Publications.

Review of the Marital Check-Up Kit by FRANK BERNT, Associate Professor of Education and Health Services, St. Joseph's University, Philadelphia, PA:

The Marital Check-Up Kit (MCK) is designed to identify potential problems in a relationship before they reach a critical stage and to strengthen communication between spouses. Its aims are congruous with those of brief marital therapies and relationship enrichment programs, which are generally considered to have small but consistently positive effects (Hahlweg & Markman, 1988; Worthington et al., 1995).

No data relating to the MCK's validity or reliability, norms, or score calculation are provided; a computer literature review yielded no studies referring to either its quality or its use. It seems appropriate, therefore, to consider the MCK as simply a set of exercises that provides a structured sequence to follow for examining the strengths and weaknesses of a marital relationship. The remainder of this review focuses on the potential utility of the exercises for marital therapy without further comment on its utility as an assessment tool.

The MCK is designed for use by marital counselors. A two-page set of directions is provided with the MCK packet. Counselors using the MCK are instructed, if married, to complete the MCK with their spouses beforehand in order to "get a better feel for how couples experience the exercises and a deeper understanding of the overall procedure and the forms used" (p. 1, directions). No theoretical framework is provided.

Instructions are quite simple. Couples receive copies (one for each partner) of the MCK and generally complete the exercises at home, reporting back to the counselor at a future session. In cases where couples cannot talk calmly about their relationship, instructions dictate that the MCK be completed in the counselor's presence. Instructions also advise counselors to practice such therapeutic habits as reassurance, praise for openness and effort, asking for feedback, and availability. The checklist itself consists of six separate exercises that focus upon the following areas: perceptions of self and spouse, communication habits, major current events in the relationship, satisfaction with partner's qualities, perception of one's own strengths and weaknesses, and feelings about oneself. Exercises vary in number and format of items; the MCK includes checklists, rating scales, and sentence completion formats. For each exercise, marital partners are instructed to complete the items separately; then to exchange and review each other's answers; then to discuss responses to items and reactions to each exercise as a whole. If these steps are accomplished without a breakdown in communication, the couple is directed to continue on to the next exercise; if there is a communication breakdown, the couple is instructed to stop and resume at a later time.

Prior to beginning the exercises, participants read a brief paragraph that likens marriage to a large house with many rooms to be enjoyed and explored, for which effective marital communication is the key that unlocks the doors. The exercises are offered as a means of beginning to forge the key. This same metaphor is repeated at the end of the six exercises, followed by a paragraph that explains how couples have different reactions to the MCK and that it is hoped that the experience has been meaningful.

The MCK provides no theoretical framework as its basis; the sense one has in completing the exercise is not one that includes clear structure or purpose. The connection between stated aims of the MCK and the exercises themselves is not at all obvious. Estimates of the time needed to complete each exercise, plus a brief explanation prior to each exercise regarding its rationale and specific purpose, would provide respondents with a clearer sense at the beginning of what the exercises involved and of where they were leading.

There is no explanation regarding how the test was constructed or of how items and types of exercises were selected. There is no indication that a pilot was ever done, nor that the MCK has ever been refined in response to user feedback. Consisting mostly of 50 separate rating items and 47 sentence completion items, the exercises seem to be many trees in search of a forest. It is difficult to determine exactly what each exercise is "for" and how each contributes to the overall aims of the MCK.

In summary, the MCK needs work, and there is little tangible evidence that it does work. There are more widely used instruments that include information on test development, validity, and reliability and that address similar issues. Well-established instruments such as the Dyadic Adjustment Scale (T4:824), the Myers-Briggs Type Indicator (T4:1702), and The FIRO Awareness Scales (T4:982) are used in marital therapy to assess marital satisfaction, personality, and communication styles (see Filsinger, 1983 and Fredman & Sherman, 1987, for extensive reviews of such instruments). The recently developed ENRICH instrument (Hawley, 1994) facilitates exploration of the multiple facets of a marital relationship, clearly identifying 13 different areas for discussion.

Most of these instruments have been developed according to APA standards and have been analyzed psychometrically, so that their strengths and weaknesses are open to scrutiny. It may be the case that marital counselors use such instruments mainly for education and planning and that they are relatively unconcerned about whether such instruments are standardized (Boughner, Hayes, Bubenzer, & West, 1994). Be that as it may, the use of such tests presupposes a level of responsibility on the part of the author to conscientiously develop, pilot, and improve such instruments and on the part of the user to correctly interpret the responses that such instruments evoke. Some form of thoughtful development and evaluation of the MCK is needed to strengthen its credibility and to minimize the likelihood of its misuse. Until such time as the author of the MCK takes steps in this direction, the reader is advised to explore the use of alternatives that have explicit theoretical bases, data to support their quality, clear instructions to assure their appropriate administration, and wider use over time to suggest their utility.

REVIEWER'S REFERENCES

Filsinger, E. E. (Ed.). (1983). *Marriage and family assessment: A sourcebook for family therapy.* Beverly Hills, CA: Sage.

Fredman, N., & Sherman, R. (1987). *Handbook of measurements for marriage and family therapy.* New York: Brunner/Mazel.

Hahlweg, K., & Markman, H. J. (1988). Effectiveness of behavioral marital therapy: Empirical status of behavioral techniques in preventing and alleviating marital distress. *Journal of Consulting and Clinical Psychology, 56*(3), 440–447.

Boughner, S. R., Hayes, S. F., Bubenzer, D. L., & West, J. D. (1994). Use of standardized assessment instruments by marital and family therapists: A survey. *Journal of Marital and Family Therapy, 20*(1), 69–75.

Hawley, D. R. (1994). Couples in crisis: Using self-report instruments in marriage counseling. *Pastoral psychology, 43*(2), 93–103.

Worthington, E. L., McCullough, M. E., Shortz, J. L., Mindes, E. J., Sandage, S. J., & Chartrand, J. M. (1995). Can couples assessment and feedback improve relationships? Assessment as a brief relationship enrichment procedure. *Journal of Counseling Psychology, 42*(4), 466–475.

Review of the Marital Check-Up Kit by W. DALE BROTHERTON, Associate Professor of Counselor Education, Western Carolina University, Cullowhee, NC:

The Marital Check-Up Kit (MCK) consists of a battery of exercises to be completed by individuals who are wanting to strengthen and enrich their relationship with one another. The MCK is designed to identify potential problems, if any, in the relationship and to create opportunities for improved communication between partners. The MCK can be used in marital counseling or in a couple's enrichment group setting and can be completed at home under the guidance of a counselor or in the direct presence of the counselor in the counseling setting. The MCK seems to be appropriate with couples who are seeking to enrich an already satisfying relationship. Although the wording of the exercises suggests the MCK is for married couples, it is this author's opinion the exercises can be adapted to be used

with nonmarried couples, with sexual orientation of the couple not being a hindrance to use of the exercises.

Counselors choosing to use the MCK should be trained in professional marriage and family counseling and maintain appropriate credentials. Because individuals in the couple relationship are not always ready to acknowledge personally, to each other, or to a counselor problems in the spousal relationship, professionals should carefully assess for severity of marital problems and the couple's ability for conflict resolution before asking couples to complete the MCK at home. In an unsupervised home environment, problems may arise and escalate unnecessarily. Couples wishing to participate in a couples group should be carefully screened as to their appropriateness for group membership and informed about group process (Association for Specialists in Group Work, 1989) before being allowed to participate.

When a couple uses the MCK, participants finish each exercise independently. After completion of an exercise, the partners share with each other their answers and discuss together differences and similarities with their responses. The MCK is meant to be self-pacing, allowing the partners to move to the next exercise when they feel ready. Most of the exercises in the MCK present to the couple a series of open-ended completion statements that ask for perceptions of how partners see each other and themselves as partners in the relationship. Although there is more emphasis placed on identifying individual and couple strengths than weaknesses, the exercises allow the partners to identify problem areas that might exist in the relationship and state what each wants from the other through the relational experience.

Two exercises in the MCK ask for partners to use a rating scale as a way of clarifying and sharing perceptions about one another. One of these exercises is about marital communication and asks for the partners to assess the frequency of identified communication behaviors exhibited by the partner and the degree of comfort the person feels with the level of sharing in the relationship. The second asks for a partner to rate his or her degree of satisfaction with the partner in 22 areas. Areas include trustworthiness, listening, affection, self-confidence, parenting, religion, and companionship.

No information could be obtained from the author as to how the MCK was normed, or the extent of its use. Because of lack of standardization, the MCK would not be appropriate as an assessment tool with couples requesting counseling or as a measure to evaluate change in the couple's relationship. More widely used instruments such as the *Couple's Therapy Workbook* by Stuart and Jacobson (1987) might be more acceptable for couples in need of counseling, whereas the MCK seems best suited as a "tune up" for couples who need only minor adjustments to a relationship that is for the most part satisfying.

REVIEWER'S REFERENCES

Stuart, R. B., & Jacobson, B. (1987). *Couple's therapy workbook.* Champaign, IL: Research Press.
Association for Specialists in Group Work. (1989). *Ethical guidelines for group counselors.* Alexandria, VA: Author.

[59]
Mathematics Topic Pre-Tests.

Purpose: "Designed as coarse screening device to help teachers find the gaps in their students' prior knowledge of particular mathematics."
Population: Form 3 (junior secondary) students in New Zealand school system.
Publication Date: 1990–1996.
Scores: 3 tests: Percentages, Integers, Measurement.
Administration: Group.
Price Data, 1996: NZ$8.10 per 20 reusable pretests (specify Percentages, Integers, or Measurement); $10.80 per 20 answer sheets; $9 per worksheet masters; $9 per teacher's manual (specify Percentages ['90, 12 pages], Integers ['90, 12 pages], or Measurement ['96, 12 pages]); $27 per specimen set.
Time: (30) minutes per test.
Authors: New Zealand Council for Educational Research, Ministry of Education, and Hamilton Region Mathematics Writing Group, and Auckland College of Education.
Publisher: New Zealand Council for Educational Research [New Zealand].

Review of the Mathematics Topic Pre-Tests by GERALD E. DeMAURO, Director, Bureau of Assessment, New Jersey State Department of Education, Trenton, NJ:

The Mathematics Topic Pre-Tests are designed to identify gaps in the mathematics knowledge of students before they encounter the topic in New Zealand Form 3 (about ninth grade in the United States). Cautions are provided against using the materials for student evaluation, because they are designed primarily to inform instruction *before* the topic is introduced, as a baseline of knowledge for further instruction.

There appears to be a great deal of flexibility in the ways in which the pretests are administered, but a 3-day model of pretesting, instructional intervention, and posttesting is provided. The two pretest topics reviewed are Percentages and Integers.

DEVELOPMENT

History. Remedial mathematics materials were first developed in 1984 for junior secondary students by educators in the Waikato/Bay of Plenty Region. The New Zealand Department of Education and the New Zealand Council for Educational research then entered a collaboration with a group that became known as the Hamilton Region Mathematics Writing Group to develop materials on percentages for Form 3 students. The materials were designed to address weaknesses in New Zealand junior secondary students that were identified in the early 1980s by the International Association for the Evaluation of Educational Achievement. Development of the integers material followed. Pools of completion-type items in both areas were developed for Forms 1–4 (grades 7–10).

Percentages. The seven objectives addressed for Percentages are: converting fractions to percentages, converting decimals to percentages, converting percentages to fractions, converting percentages to decimals, interpreting percentages from bar graphs and pie charts, expressing one quantity as a percentage of another, and calculating a given percentage of a quantity. The pretest consists of 28 items, 4 for each of the objectives.

Integers. The 10 Integer objectives addressed are: location on number lines, order of relationship, addition, subtraction, multiplication, division, knowing the addition property of zero, knowing the addition property of opposite numbers, knowing the multiplication property of zero, and knowing the multiplication property of one. The pretest consists of 32 items, 4 items for each of the first six objectives and 2 items for each of the last four objectives.

Item development. Objectives for the topics were drawn from the revised mathematics syllabus for Forms 1–4. After the above objectives were identified, they were reviewed by Form 2 mathematics teachers to assure that they were compatible with the Form 2 mathematics curriculum.

Pools of completion-type items were written by graduate mathematics students. Four test forms each for Percentages (first) and for Integers were administered to Form 2 students (Percentages) and Form 3 students (both Percentages and Integers). Item analyses were made, including identification of common errors. Students were also interviewed to provide information to help develop distractors for multiple-choice questions.

Two parallel forms each of multiple-choice pretests were developed and field tested. A final pretest and parallel posttest form were then developed from surviving items in each of the subject areas, and remedial curricula were developed based on common errors. The remedial Percentages curricula were field tested in 20 secondary schools nationwide, and the Integers remedial curricula were field tested in Auckland secondary schools. The curricula were then edited to yield two trial worksheets for each objective, 14 for the seven Percentages objectives and 20 for the 10 Integers objectives.

For all of the Percentages objectives and the first six of the Integers objectives, there are four questions per objective, covering two levels of difficulty and presented either as numerical or more abstract word problems. For the final six Integer objectives, questions alternate between numeric and more abstract word problems.

ADMINISTRATION

Each pretest topic is administered over the course of 3 days. On the first day, the pretest is administered, and students mark the papers, followed by class diagnosis and work sheet assignments on the basis of the diagnosis. On the second day, the work sheet is completed. Finally, on the third day, the posttest is administered and new work is assigned.

SCORING

Points are accumulated for items according to objective, for the type of common error, and for whether the question is a word problem or a numeric problem.

TECHNICAL CONSIDERATIONS

Reliability. In traditional American terms, the teacher's manuals provided for the pretest topics do not provide much psychometric support for the types of decisions teachers might make based on the pretest results. However, the model is similar to curriculum-based assessment models more popular in the school psychology literature in the

United States. In particular, the iterative testing and identification of errors are familiar intervention elements in such models. Use of models like this depend on the inferences drawn from results by teachers. The reliability ultimately rests on the capacity of the information to consistently recommend intervention strategies, and this is best accomplished in consideration of the student's academic history and interactions with the teacher. Clearly, these instruments are not designed to make these determinations in a vacuum.

Validity. Given the original problem of poor performance in some areas of mathematics, it remains to document that the content domain is related to the weakness, and that the test items are a representative sample of that domain. Note, criticality of the sample is less important than representative sampling here, because the results are intended to advise instructional intervention. The documentation provided about how the domain was defined and sampled is an important component of test validity, and the reader could benefit from greater detail concerning the numbers of experts involved and a little more precision about the nature of their reviews.

For the purposes of construct validity documentation, it would be helpful to demonstrate that use of the materials was related to improved performance on instruments related to the Percentage and integer measures on the International Association for the Evaluation of Educational Achievement instruments.

One important element of validity that might be overlooked is the test development strategy that began with four forms each of completion-type questions and resulted in a pre- and posttest form of multiple-choice questions in each topic. The derivation of distractors, based on an analysis of the common errors from field testing, would buttress the validity of the pretest for making curricular decisions.

CONCLUSION. The Mathematics Topic Pre-Tests are an interesting approach to instructional intervention. Although much more documentation of the development and psychometric properties of the instruments might help to support their utility for the American classroom, the instruments are consistent with curriculum-based assessment models already familiar to American educators.

Review of the Mathematics Topic Pre-Tests by MICHAEL KANE, Professor of Education, University of Wisconsin, Madison, WI:

The two Mathematics Topic Pre-Tests, one on Integers and one on Percentages, are admirable in the modesty of the claims made for them in the teacher's manuals. The tests were developed for use in remedial instruction on specific topics in the mathematics curriculum. The test on Integers is designed to help students identify their strengths and weaknesses over a set of 10 objectives on integers. The test of Percentages provides feedback on 7 objectives on percentages. Each test also provides the teacher with diagnostic information on individual students and on classes.

The tests are designed as tools to be used by teachers and students in guiding instructional decisions in limited and well-defined areas of the mathematics curriculum. The test questions are clearly related to the objectives and are of high quality. The teacher's manual is short, clear, low-key, and sensible. The materials should be easy to use, and the set of materials is flexible enough to be integrated with instruction in a variety of ways.

The tests are part of a fairly comprehensive set of instructional materials including a pretest, worksheets keyed to specific pretest results, and a posttest. The packet of materials includes a copy of the pretest and a self-diagnosing answer sheet, which directs students to certain worksheets based on their pattern of errors. The manual authors suggest that students who make few errors be given alternate work or extension work, and that students with idiosyncratic error patterns be taught individually or in small groups. Students who make the common errors identified by the self-diagnosing answer sheet are to work systematically, an objective at a time, through the worksheets. The teacher's manual suggests a detailed timetable for using the materials effectively.

No information is provided on norms, reliability, or validity, and given the intended uses of the tests, this is not surprising. The emphasis is on the use of the tests within instructional modules designed for the remediation of specific weaknesses in student mastery of the topics covered. The tests are not intended for high-stakes decisions and are not proposed for use outside of the context of remedial instruction.

Within this context, the materials seem to have been very carefully developed and very well thought through. Each objective is assessed by four or more items, and therefore the diagnostic information is likely to be dependable. Each worksheet provides brief explanations, examples, and practice items. All of the materials have been designed for ease of use by classroom teachers. The overall design of the modules does reflect a very traditional approach to mathematics instruction, involving a pretest, instruction, drill and practice, and a posttest, but there is likely to be a role for this kind of focused instruction on specific skills in even the most authentic curriculum.

[60]
Minnesota Test for Differential Diagnosis of Aphasia.

Purpose: "For the evaluation of aphasic deficit resulting from brain damage in patients."
Population: Adults.
Publication Dates: 1965–1992.
Scores, 5: Auditory Disturbances, Visual and Reading Disturbances, Speech and Language Disturbances, Visuomotor and Writing Disturbances, Disturbances of Numerical Relations and Arithmetic Processes.
Administration: Individual.
Price Data, 1993: $54.95 per complete kit including monograph, manual ('65, 23 pages), 2 sets of stimulus cards, and 25 record booklets; $12.25 per 25 record booklets.
Time: (45–120) minutes.
Author: Hildred Schuell.
Publisher: American Guidance Service, Inc.
Cross References: See T4:1653 (12 references) and T3:1511 (14 references); see also T2:2080 (4 references); for reviews by David Jones and Seymour Rigrodsky, see 7:958 (7 references); see also P:172 (8 references).

TEST REFERENCES

1. Jason, G. W. (1983). Hemispheric asymmetries in motor function: I. Left-hemisphere specialization for memory but not performance. *Neuropsychologia, 21*, 35–45.
2. Hall, P. K., & Jordan, L. S. (1987). An assessment of a controlled association task to identify word-finding problems in children. *Language, Speech, and Hearing Services in Schools, 18*, 99–111.
3. Bacon, G. M., Potter, R. E., & Seikel, J. A. (1992). Auditory comprehension of "yes—no" questions by adult aphasics. *Journal of Communication Disorders, 24*, 23–29.
4. Bloom, R. L., Borod, J. C., Obler, L. K., & Gerstman, L. J. (1993). Suppression and facilitation of pragmatic performance: Effects of emotional content on discourse following right and left brain damage. *Journal of Speech and Hearing Research, 36*, 1227–1235.
5. Nicholas, L. E., & Brookshire, R. H. (1993). A system for quantifying the informativeness and efficiency of the connected speech of adults with aphasia. *Journal of Speech and Hearing Research, 36*, 338–350.
6. Brookshire, R. H., & Nicholas, L. E. (1994). Speech sample size and test-retest stability of connected speech measures for adults with aphasia. *Journal of Speech and Hearing Research, 37*, 399–407.

7. Records, N. L. (1994). A measure of the contribution of a gesture to the perception of speech in listeners with aphasia. *Journal of Speech and Hearing, 37*, 1086–1099.

8. Windsor, J., Doyle, S. S., & Siegel, G. M. (1994). Language acquisition after mutism: A longitudinal case study of autism. *Journal of Speech and Hearing Research, 37*, 96–105.

9. Nicholas, L. E., & Brookshire, R. H. (1995). Presence, completeness, and accuracy of main concepts in the connected speech of non-brain-damaged adults and adults with aphasia. *Journal of Speech and Hearing Research, 38*, 145–156.

Review of the Minnesota Test for Differential Diagnosis of Aphasia by MATTHEW E. LAMBERT, Research Psychologist, Neurology Research and Education Center, St. Mary Hospital, Lubbock, TX:

The Minnesota Test for Differential Diagnosis of Aphasia (Minnesota Test) is the second edition of the test originally published in 1965 and based upon Hildred Schuell's work at the Minneapolis Veterans Administration Hospital. Schuell passed away in 1970 and the current test revision was completed by Joyce W. Sefer and published in 1973. The interpretive manual, *Differential Diagnosis of Aphasia with the Minnesota Test* (Schuell, 1973) is a combination of Schuell's original data along with data collected by Sefer for two of the five original aphasia categories. Inaccessibility to Schuell's actual raw data and reliance on statistical measures calculated on that data by Schuell, however, were noted as limitations to Sefer's revision.

The Minnesota Test addresses Schuell's aphasic categories: (a) Simple Aphasia—reduction in available language without perceptual or sensorimotor impairment or dysarthria; (b) Aphasia with Visual Involvement—reduction in available language with impaired discrimination, recognition, and recall of learned visual symbols; (c) Mild Aphasia with Persisting Dysfluency—simple aphasia with persisting dysfluency; (d) Aphasia with Scattered Findings Compatible with Generalized Brain Damage—reduced available language with visual impairment and dysarthria; (e) Aphasia with Sensorimotor Involvement—reduction in available language with discrimination, producing, or sequencing phonemes difficulty; (f) Aphasia with Intermittent Auditory Imperception—aphasia characterized by impairment of auditory perception; and (g) Irreversible Aphasia Syndrome—virtual complete loss of functional language skills in all modalities. Although these categories underlie the basis for the test, evaluative items are divided into five sections: (a) Auditory Disturbances; (b) Visual and Reading Disturbances; (c) Speech and Language Disturbances; (d) Visuomotor and Writing Disturbances; and (e) Disturbances of Numerical

Relations and Arithmetic Processes with each section comprising 4 (Disturbances of Numerical Relations and Arithmetic Processes) to 15 (Speech and Language Disturbances) subtests. The number of items per subtest ranges from 5 to 32. The validity of Schuell's aphasia model, however, may not completely reflect current understanding of aphasic disorders.

Administration instructions are included in a separate manual and are recommended to be read while conducting the examination. Materials necessary for completing the test include two bound card decks provided with the test and materials obtained by the examiner. These other materials include a bell, cup, box with an easily opened lid, long and short pencils, spoon, clock face with movable hands, various coins, stopwatch, flashlight, and lined and unlined paper. Although these materials can be secured easily there is no standardization, which opens the possibility of error between administrators and test materials, thereby reducing reliability and validity. On the positive side, use of these materials allows the examiner to observe gross behaviors with real world objects as they relate to aphasic problems.

Test responses are recorded in a seven-page booklet with historical and observational data. Yet, the booklet is cumbersome and difficult to use. It is oriented to a landscape position when the examiner records responses and then rotated to a portrait orientation for use with patient-entered responses. Moreover, the form is crowded with minimal space to record either responses or observations. The item sequences in some subtests are not defined, as stimuli can be presented using either a horizontal or vertical scanning approach.

Administration time requires upwards of 2 hours; although, according to the interpretive manual, it can be shortened by starting each test section with a subtest expected to be completed errorlessly by the subject. Should the subject perform poorly then movement to an earlier subtest is recommended until an adequate floor is established. The remaining section is then to be completed to establish each subject's ceiling. Time savings might be substantial, but reliability and validity are again compromised by this approach. Moreover, important aspects of aphasic behavior could be missed in easier subtests skipped over.

Additionally, the lack of precise scoring criteria may lead to idiosyncratic interpretation of subject responses. This could, in turn, result in some subtests being prematurely terminated and other producing erroneously high performances by continuation beyond the appropriate termination point. The true nature of a patient's aphasic symptoms may then be obscured by this scoring artifact.

Test scoring consists of tabulating the errors for each subtest. No composite scores are produced to represent the five test sections nor are there scores calculated with direct association to the seven aphasia types postulated by Schuell. Interpretation is undertaken by comparing the number of subtest errors with the mean errors produced by the various aphasia type patients for each subtest. A qualitative interpretation is then formulated based upon the perceived pattern reflected in the subtest performance. Combinations of subtests reflecting particular language skills and abilities are described in the manual and can be used to assist interpretation. The difficulty with this approach, as noted in the following, is the poor interpretive reliability. Qualitative interpretations, although important to understanding nuances of aphasic disorders, should not be the first line of interpretation, rather supplementary to a more quantitative and reliable approach.

Reliability data for test-retest, split-half, alternate forms, and interrater activities are absent from the manual. It is assumed that reliability information is available in the references provided at the end of the manual. Yet this information should be part of the test's overall psychometric description provided in the manual. Moreover, the references cited in the manual are outdated with publication dates ranging from 1959 to a "forthcoming volume in 1973." To make this a viable instrument, a complete reliability analysis of the Minnesota Test needs to be undertaken with standardized testing procedures and interpretive guidelines.

Given the above reliability statements, the Minnesota Test's validity is uninterpretable. As noted, the manual contains comparative subtest error scores for nonaphasics and patients for each aphasia type. The percent or number of subjects in each group producing subtest errors is noted in the manual, but extrapolation of these data to specific diagnostic statements cannot be undertaken readily.

Some attempt at concurrent validity is made through tacit relationships between test performances to global neurological, health, and demographic variables being presented in the manual. Nevertheless, no relationships between Minnesota Test performances and patients suffering specific neurological diseases are presented nor is there any discussion of performance profiles associated with specific aphasic disorders such as Wernicke's and Broca's aphasias. As with the reliability issues, a full validation effort needs to be undertaken for the Minnesota Test. All forms of validity should be assessed to make this test up-to-date with current understanding of neurological diseases, cognitive rehabilitation, and specific language disorders.

Unfortunately, there is no single statement that can be made about the Minnesota Test other than it is outdated. It provides some heuristic information about aphasic disorders, but has not kept pace with advances in understanding neurological disorders, cognitive impairments associated with those disorders, and the burgeoning area of cognitive rehabilitation. More up-to-date instruments provide complete aphasia assessments with comprehensive normative data that guide reliable assessment and intervention.

REVIEWER'S REFERENCE

Schuell, H. (1973). *Differential diagnosis of aphasia with the Minnesota Test.* Minneapolis: University of Minnesota Press.

Review of the Minnesota Test for Differential Diagnosis of Aphasia by JAMES C. REED, Chief Psychologist, St. Luke's Hospital, New Bedford, MA:

The Minnesota Test for Differential Diagnosis of Aphasia (MTDDA) has a venerable history in psychological testing stemming from its development in 1948 and its publication in 1965. Schuell died in 1970, and the revised edition in 1973, the work of James J. Jenkins, Robert Shaw, and Joyce W. Sefer, represents a change in classification and syndrome nomenclature rather than a change in the test items. Aphasia is defined as a reduction of available language that crosses all language modalities, and in the present edition the categories of aphasia are given as (a) simple aphasia, a reduction of available language in all modalities without specific perceptual or sensory motor impairment; (b) aphasia with visual involvement, a reduction of available language with coexisting impairment of discrimination, recognition, and recall of learned visual symbols; (c) mild aphasia with persisting dysfluency, resembling simple aphasia, except for the accompaniment of persisting dysfluency; (d) aphasia with findings compatible with generalized brain damage, a reduction of available language, with findings that usually include both visual involvement and some degree of dysarthria; (e) aphasia with sensory motor involvement, characterized by severe reduction of language in all modalities and accompanied by difficulty in discriminating, producing, and sequencing phonemes; (e) aphasia with intermittent auditory imperception, severe impairment of auditory perception, with some functional speech usually retained or recovered early; and (f) irreversible aphasia syndrome, characterized by an almost complete loss of functional language skills in all modalities. The MTDDA has 47 tests and for each category of aphasia the disruption of language signs or the errors characterizing the category are given along with the most discriminating tests.

Throughout the monograph, reference is made to a factor analysis that was performed when the MTDDA was being developed and five dimensions were produced. As the tests are described, their loading on each of the factors is discussed. Nowhere is the factor matrix shown with the factors representing the columns and the rows representing the tests. This method of discussing the tests and the omission of the factor matrix makes it difficult to remember which test goes with which factor(s). However, the omission may be fortunate, because the factor analysis was done on 157 aphasic patients, and many factor analysts would state that a factor analysis of a correlation matrix of 47 tests based on an N of 157 is probably quite unstable and not to be taken seriously. If the factors and the aphasia categories are viewed as a classification system that facilitates verbal communication rather than structures etched in stone, then the categories as well as the factors can serve a useful purpose.

The MTDDA may fall short on meeting certain technical criteria frequently desired by test users and consumers. For example, conventional reliability coefficients were not presented in the monograph. However, for most tests the number of subjects in the various diagnostic groups was presented along with the percentage of those subjects who made errors. For example, in a table on the performance on oral reading of words (monograph, p. 49), the number of subjects with simple aphasia was given as 12 and 25% made oral reading errors. This means that three subjects made errors in oral reading and nine did not. Because of the small N such a finding is probably unreliable, but if one looks more deeply, out of a total of 75 aphasic subjects, 81% made errors in oral pronunciation. Among nonaphasic subjects ($n = 50$), only 2% or one subject made errors. If one regards errors as a pathognomonic sign, then within any category there will be a number of false negatives, but false positives will be rare. As another illustration, in copying Greek letters (one of the visual-motor and writing tests) the median number of errors for 75 aphasics was 0, the same as for the nonaphasic, but 21% of the aphasics made errors (i.e., 15 aphasic subjects made errors and 60 did not). Again 2% of the 50 nonaphasics or one nonaphasic subject made an error in copying a Greek letter. In short, when errors occur the person making the error probably belongs to the aphasic group. By viewing the tables and research results in this light, there is solid testimony for the validity of the MTDDA. Indeed, as is discussed in the monograph, the difference between aphasic and nonaphasic language is chiefly one of degree. All normals occasionally misread, miscopy, or say the wrong word but when errors accumulate they are diagnostically significant.

As with other psychological tests, obtaining valid results will require a trained examiner. The tests are arranged in order of ascending difficulty, and it is up to the examiner to encourage the patient and to provide the reassurance that brain-damaged patients frequently require in order to obtain the best possible performance. The authors suggest it is usually better to do the testing in more than one session. This may or may not be practical.

The test booklet contains a format for the convenient recording of important data. Page 1 is a summary section for the test scores. Page 2 is for noting factors pertinent to social history, medical history, and present illness. Page 3 contains tentative guidelines for clinical ratings in comprehension, speech, reading, writing, and dysarthria, along with a suggested diagnostic scale for the degree of impairment.

In summary, the MTDDA has survived the passage of time. Further research is needed to demonstrate the stability of the factors that are listed and the validity of the aphasic categories. Nevertheless, the test is useful to determine degree of impairment for a wide range of language behaviors and to assess improvement or deterioration in language behavior over repeated evaluations. The test provides for objective findings regarding disturbances in language, and differential classification can be made by analyzing patterns of errors for groups of similar tests, even though there may be a large number of false negatives for any single one of the 47 tests. Schuell and her colleagues, through this test, have made a substantial contribution to patient assessment. In the days when hospitals, health clinics, and health providers were paid to evaluate patients the test could be highly recommended. At present, with managed care and capitation, when the same health providers are paid not to see patients, the MTDDA has a questionable future.

[61]
Motivated Strategies for Learning Questionnaire.

Purpose: "To assess college students' motivational orientations and their use of different learning strategies for a college course."
Population: College students.
Publication Date: 1991.
Acronym: MSLQ.
Scores, 15: 3 Motivation Scales [Value Component (Intrinsic Goal Orientation, Extrinsic Goal Orientation, Task Value), Expectancy Component (Control of Learning Beliefs, Self-Efficacy for Learning and Performance), Affective Component (Test Anxiety)]; 2 Learning Strategies Scales [Cognitive and Metacognitive Strategies (Rehearsal, Elaboration, Organization, Critical Thinking, Metacognitive Self-Regulation), Resource Management Strategies (Time and Study Environment, Effort Regulation, Peer Learning, Help Seeking)].
Administration: Group.
Price Data: Available from publisher.
Time: (20–30) minutes.
Authors: Paul R. Pintrich, David A. F. Smith, Teresa Garcia, and Wilbert J. McKeachie.
Publisher: National Center for Research to Improve Postsecondary Teaching and Learning.

TEST REFERENCES

1. Pintrich, P. R., & DeGroot, E. V. (1990). Motivational and self-regulated learning components of classroom academic performance. *Journal of Educational Psychology, 82,* 33–40.
2. Pintrich, P. R., Smith, D. A. F., Garcia, T., & McKeachie, W. J. (1993). Reliability and predictive validity of the Motivated Strategies for Learning Questionnaire. *Educational and Psychological Measurement, 53,* 801-813.
3. Lin, Y-G., & McKeachie, W. J. (1994). Learning of concepts and definitions in different disciplines. *Perceptual and Motor Skills, 79,* 113-114.
4. Pintrich, P. R., Anderman, E. M., & Klobucar, C. (1994). Intraindividual differences in motivation and cognition in students with and without learning disabilities. *Journal of Learning Disabilities, 27,* 360–370.
5. Karabenick, S. A., & Sharma, R. (1994). Perceived teacher support of student questioning in the college classroom: Its relation to student characteristics and role in the classroom questioning process. *Journal of Educational Psychology, 86,* 90-103.

Review of the Motivated Strategies for Learning Questionnaire by JERI BENSON, Professor of Educational Psychology, College of Education, University of Georgia, Athens, GA:

DESCRIPTION OF THE SCALE. The Motivated Strategies for Learning Questionnaire (MSLQ) consists of 81 items grouped into 15 scales. In the instructions to the MSLQ, the student is asked to respond to the items given the class in which they are taking the questionnaire. Thus, MSLQ scores are "situation-specific." Furthermore, students respond to the MSLQ items using a 7-point Likert scale, where only the first and seventh points are anchored (*not at all true of me* to *very true of me*). It is desirable to have all response options anchored so the examinees have a common reference point to evaluate each item. Without anchoring each option, it is hard to know what "internal" scale each examinee is using and this "inconsistency" can lead to unreliability.

SCALE DEVELOPMENT. The authors describe the development of the scale, which began formally in 1986 (informally in 1982) as part of a research project on college student learning and teaching. Several waves of data were collected from 1986–1987 to revise and construct the 15 subscales of the MSLQ. Thus, the MSLQ subscales are empirically derived on the basis of item and factor analyses. Because exploratory factor analysis can be highly subjective (e.g., the determination of the number of factors to extract, the method of factor rotation etc.), it would have been helpful if the authors had described the criteria they used in coming up with the 15 subscales.

SCALE ADMINISTRATION, SCORING, REPORTING, AND NORMS. The administration of the MSLQ is straightforward, using student self-report. The MSLQ is scored by averaging the item responses for each subscale. Sample student feedback information is provided in the manual using 9 of the 15 subscales. For each of the 9 subscales, the authors provide a description of what the subscale measures and suggest the student's raw score be compared to the class mean, and the three quartile scores for the class. The authors do not recommend the use of norms, stating that motivation and learning strategies can vary by student groups and types of courses.

RELIABILITY AND VALIDATION SAMPLE. The psychometric data reported are based on a sample size of 380. Of the 380 college students, 24 attended a community college, the remaining were from a 4-year university. The rationale for including the 24 community college students was not given. It is likely these 24 students are not similar to the university students and may affect the psychometric data in unknown ways.

RELIABILITY. The types of psychometric data reported in the manual are means and standard deviations for each subscale, the correlation between each subscale item and final grade in the course, and internal consistency estimates (alpha coefficients) for each subscale. Internal consistency estimates ranged from .62 to .93 for the Motivational Scales and for the Learning Strategies Scales from .52 to .80. Considering the type of error inherent in internal consistency estimates (differences in item content only), the subscale reliability should be higher if results are provided for individual students. Only three of the Motivational Scales and five of the Learning Strategy Scales showed internal consistency estimates greater than .75. Therefore, the dependability of what is being measured by the MSLQ is questionable.

The subscale intercorrelations range from .00 to .70, with over half of the correlations in the range .00 to .30. Thus, empirically the 15 scales seem to be weakly related. It would have been useful for the authors to comment on this finding in terms of whether this pattern was expected based on theory.

VALIDITY. The authors report one confirmatory factor analysis (CFA) as evidence of the MSLQ's validity. The CFA was specified such that each item was allowed to associate (load) with only one factor and the factors were allowed to be correlated. The authors ran separate CFA models for the Motivation Subscales, the Learning Strategy Subscales, and then all the subscales combined. The results did not meet the criteria specified prior to model testing. The authors state, "while the

goodness of fit indices are not stellar, they are, nevertheless, quite reasonable" (p. 79). The authors suggest their findings are less than adequate due to a broad range of course and subject characteristics from the sample of 380 students. Furthermore, the authors claim the MSLQ shows a "sound structure" and one can claim "factor validity for the MSLQ scales" (p. 80).

This reviewer does not agree with the claim of "reasonable" model-data fit nor the suggestion the MSLQ shows factor validity. It is well known in the use of CFA that acceptable statistical model-data fit can rarely be established by testing a single model. The "models" frequently tested in measurement studies are rough approximations to reality. Furthermore, the theory underlying a measure is often not clearly understood (e.g., all aspects of the theoretical domain may not be known). Therefore, the scale used to measure the construct is an approximation. It might have been more reasonable to have tested "competing" theoretical models (Jöreskog, 1993). For example, a different number of factors could be evaluated, and if the 15-factor structure emerged as the best fitting of the set of models evaluated, some evidence for the "validity" of the structure is provided. Currently, there is very little support for the purported 15-factor model of the MSLQ.

Finally, given that validity is the process by which the test scores take on meaning, the authors need to develop studies that are not solely internally driven (e.g., traditional and confirmatory factor analysis) (Nunnally, 1978; Benson & Hagtvet, 1996). That is, what external criterion is used to substantiate the scores from the MSLQ? Studies are needed which use external criteria to evaluate the relationship between students who are known to be highly motivated or report a particular learning strategy and MSLQ scores.

SUMMARY. The authors clearly present the reliability data for each of the MSLQ subscales. However, the reliability data are weak and the validity data are very limited and not convincing of the factor structure. There is no discussion in the manual of the theoretical basis of the MSLQ, only references to several articles. Additional reliability and validity studies are needed to improve the subscale accuracy and to substantiate the dimensionality of the scale. Summaries of these studies should be incorporated into the manual.

REVIEWER'S REFERENCES

Nunnally, J. C. (1978). *Psychometric theory* (2nd ed.). New York: McGraw Hill.
Jöreskog, K. G. (1993). Testing structural equation models. In K. A. Bollen & J. S. Long (Eds.), *Testing structural equation models* (pp. 294–316). Newbury Park, CA: Sage.
Benson, J., & Hagtvet, K. A. (1996). The interplay between design, data analysis and theory in the measurement of coping. In M. Zeidner & N. S. Ender (Eds.), *Handbook of coping: Theory, research and applications* (pp. 83–106). New York: John Wiley & Sons.

Review of the Motivated Strategies for Learning Questionnaire by ROBERT K. GABLE, Professor of Educational Psychology, and Associate Director, Bureau of Educational Research and Service, University of Connecticut, Storrs, CT:

The self-report Motivated Strategies for Learning Questionnaire (MSLQ) is based on a comprehensive line of research carried out by the developers in the areas of motivation (31 items) and learning strategies (31 items), which includes a section on student management of different resources (19 items). The 81 items are responded to on a 7-point Likert scale with end-point anchors of *not at all true of me* and *very true of me*. No discussion is provided regarding the selection of this particular response scale.

ADMINISTRATION. The 15 MSLQ scales can be administered as an entire instrument in about 25 minutes. Subsections of the instrument can also be selected for use.

VALIDITY. The content validity of the MSLQ is supported through extensive literature on college student learning and teaching. Although summaries of the literature are not included in the test manual, several appropriate references to relevant work are cited. A more comprehensive description of the judgmental process used to create items reflecting the literature-based concepts would be appropriate.

Reference is made to several early appropriate empirical analyses that contributed information for selecting final items for the MSLQ. Given the confirmatory factor analysis (Pilotte & Gable, 1990) and item response theory (Wright & Masters, 1982) research on the use of positive/negative item stems, the inclusion of some "reversed scored" items is an empirically unsupported approach to instrument development. It is likely that the positive and negative stems access different aspects of the targeted affective constructs.

Data are presented for the final set of items based on a sample of 380 college students from a variety of majors. Construct validity evidence is offered through confirmatory factor analytic information presented separately for the motivation and the cognitive/metacognitive items. The authors spend time describing what information is obtained from a confirmatory analysis, but provide inadequate specific evaluative statements regarding their findings. The lambda estimates presented are typical for these types of items, but appear low for more items than the authors suggest. Several items have estimates less than .75, which is not ideal for scales defined by only four items (e.g., the four items defining Help Seeking have loadings of .20, .17, .90, and .79). The lack of a high level of model fit is evident through the fit statistics, many of which exceed commonly accepted values. The summary statement, "Overall, the models show sound structures, and one can reasonably claim factor validity for the MSLQ scales" (p. 80), is not highly supported by the data from this one sample. Clearly, data from more samples are needed before such construct validity claims can be advanced.

Criterion-related (predictive) validity evidence is presented in the form of item and scale-level correlations with final course grades. The Motivation scale-level correlations range from -.27 (Test Anxiety) to .41 (Self-Efficacy for Learning and Performance) with the average magnitude of the correlation, disregarding direction, being .22. Learning Strategies scale-level correlations range from -.06 to .32 with an average of .17. The authors state that these correlations "are significant, albeit moderate, demonstrating predictive validity" (p. 4). The coefficients can be statistically significant due to the large sample size, but are associated with small to medium effect sizes. The authors overstate the evidence for predictive validity and fail to discuss any of the individual coefficients in the context of the literature base.

RELIABILITY. Item analysis (i.e., means and standard deviations) are presented; item/scale correlations should have been included. These correlations would facilitate item-level contributions to the Motivation scale reliabilities, which ranged from .62 to .93 (average = .78), and the Learning Strategies scale reliabilities, which ranged from .52 to .80 (average = .71). The authors refer to these reliabilities saying they are "robust, ranging from .52 to .93" (p. 4). The word "robust" does not seem appropriate for alpha reliabilities; the authors should describe the scale reliabilities in more depth and assist the user in understanding the problems with using data from scales with low reliabilities. Although most scales are associated with adequate alpha reliability levels, users should exercise caution with interpretations of Extrinsic Goal Orientation (.62) and Cognitive and Metacognitive Strategies: Organization (.64) scale scores due to the inadequate sampling of content evident in the four-item scales with low reliabilities.

SCORE INTERPRETATION. Scoring and score interpretation are described noting that norms are not provided because "students' responses to the questions might vary as a function of different courses, so the same individual might report different levels of motivation or strategy use depending on the course" (p. 5). Students do receive their individual scores, class scale means, and quartile information. In addition, scale descriptions and ways to increase motivation levels are included.

SUMMARY. The MSLQ results from a quality line of research at the University of Michigan in the areas of teaching and learning. The present version of the MSLQ should be considered a "research edition" until additional items are added to scales with low reliabilities and additional supportive construct validity information is available. In addition, users should be provided with more interpretation in the manual regarding the referenced literature base and data presented, such as the correlations of the MSLQ scales with final course grades.

REVIEWER'S REFERENCES

Wright, B. D., & Masters, G. N. (1982). *Rating scale analysis*. Chicago: Mesa Press.

Pilotte, W. J., & Gable, R. K. (1990). The impact of positive and negative item stems on the validity of a computer anxiety scale. *Educational and Psychological Measurement, 50*, 603–610.

[62]
NOCTI Teacher Occupational Competency Test: Audio-Visual Communications Technology.

Purpose: Designed to measure the individual's occupational competency in audio-visual communications technology.
Population: Teachers and prospective teachers.
Publication Dates: 1986–1994.
Scores, 12: 9 scores for Written part (Total and 8 subscores); 3 scores for Performance part (Process, Product, Total).
Administration: Group.

Parts, 2: Written, Performance.
Price Data: Available from publisher for test materials including Written test booklet ('94, 21 pages); Performance test booklet ('94, 11 pages); examiner's copy of Performance test ('94, 33 pages); manual for administering NOCTI TOCT Performance tests ('94, 17 pages); manual for administering NOCTI TOCT Written tests ('94, 18 pages).
Time: 180(190) minutes for Written part; 360(400) minutes for Performance part.
Comments: Test administered at least twice a year at centers approved by the publisher.
Author: National Occupational Competency Testing Institute.
Publisher: National Occupational Competency Testing Institute.
Cross References: For reviews by JoEllen V. Carlson and Anne L. Harvey, see 11:262. For a review of the NOCTI program, see 8:1153 (6 references).
[Note: These reviews are based on materials available as of September 1, 1996. The publisher advises that major revisions in the NOCTI tests are in process. These will be reviewed in the future.—Ed.]

Review of the NOCTI Teacher Occupational Competency Test: Audio-Visual Communication Technology by PATRICIA A. BACHELOR, Professor of Psychology, California State University at Long Beach, Long Beach, CA:

The 1986–87 version of the NOCTI Teacher Occupational Competency Test: Audio-Visual Communications Technology (AVCT) was reviewed for the *Eleventh Mental Measurements Yearbook* (1992) by J. V. Carlson and A. L. Harvey. Both reviewers called for the test authors to prepare a technical manual to address critical psychometric issues related to this test. Particularly shocking is the conspicuous lack of a technical manual to accompany the 1994 version of this test. Thus, the questions raised by the earlier reviewers are still unanswered as are additional questions suggested by the current version of the AVCT.

The current version of the AVCT consists of two components—a Written assessment and a Performance appraisal. This is the same format as the earlier test. The objective (Written) component comprises 200 four-option multiple-choice items distributed over nine content areas of photography (30 questions), computer graphics (21 questions), video production (29 questions), equipment repair and maintenance (21 questions), audio production (22 questions), presentation technology (20 questions), graphic design (20 questions), project management (32 questions), and related miscellaneous information (5 questions). This represents an expansion of the 1986–87 version, which consisted of 180 objective items assessing eight content areas. The items are appropriate to assess knowledge of the content areas, with most items requiring recall of basic facts and skills rather than analytic reasoning. As in the earlier version of the test, no evaluation criteria were presented, hence, performance cannot be interpreted.

The Performance appraisal requires the examinee to demonstrate his or her ability to perform, in order, the following 8 (rather than 10) "jobs": still photography—operation of 35mm camera; still photography—film development; still photography—printing; editing and splicing audio tape; audio production studio-recording and mixing; video shooting and editing; presentation equipment usage and maintenance (including slide projection, overhead projection, monitor set-up and operation, and general troubleshooting); and operating computer graphics equipment to recreate four graphic visuals. These "jobs" represent a comprehensive array of tasks that a skilled audiovisual worker should be able to perform successfully. The examination booklet gives clear and step-by-step instructions as well as estimates of the completion time. However, it is left for the examinee to record his/her start and stop time. The examinee's performance is rated on a variety of dimensions of each job on process as well as product using a 5-point rating scale of *extremely skilled worker, above average worker, average worker, below average worker,* or *inept worker*. These anchors, as in the 1986–87 test version, are not further defined. To conclude the Performance evaluation, a Summary Score (the sum of "process" and "product" points), Subscores (the percent of maximum points obtained on process and product), an Overall Performance Rating (using the aforementioned 5-point scale), as well as a narrative summary paragraph are prepared by the examiner. This represents no change from the prior version.

Three guides accompany the test components—one booklet for each of the two test components and an Evaluator's Guide. Each booklet describes test administration procedures either for the Written assessment or the Performance appraisal. These manuals are clearly written and are thorough in the presentation of the details of various aspects of test administration, such as seating arrangements and verbatim instructions, but there are no criteria for appraisal or standards upon which a rating or outcome score is determined. Also, absent is any information about examiner qualifications. Given that this test is most likely used in job-related testing and/or certification programs, this seems particularly troublesome. Without any criteria for successful performance by a specified and qualified examiner, an examinee would have difficulty interpreting his or her performance rating. It seems that this is either a criterion-referenced test without a specified yardstick for performance or a norm-referenced test without a clearly identified comparison group.

It is disappointing that there is no technical manual to accompany the revised AVCT. The authors have revised the test but failed to share any information about test development and modification, estimates of reliability coefficients, validity studies, and/or standardization samples and norm groups. The complete lack of any psychometric data related to this test is especially problematic, given that two earlier reviews contained negative comments about this noticeable gap in what has otherwise been a comprehensively documented test. Key psychometric information is absent, thereby preventing a candid appraisal of the technical properties of this instrument. A test consumer expects and is entitled to receive such information in order to make an informed decision regarding appropriate test selection and use. The *Standards for Educational and Psychological Testing* (AERA, APA, & NCME, 1985) speak very clearly and emphatically about technical manuals and what is to be housed within. It is hoped that authors of future versions of the NOCTI test series will prepare and distribute such essential materials.

REVIEWER'S REFERENCES

American Educational Research Association, American Psychological Association, & National Council on Measurement in Education. (1985). *Standards for educational and psychological testing.* Washington, DC: American Psychological Association, Inc.

Carlson, J. V. (1992). [Review of the NOCTI Teacher Occupational Competency Test: Audio-Visual Communications Technology.] In J. J. Kramer & J. C. Conoley (Eds.), *The eleventh mental measurements yearbook* (pp. 612–613). Lincoln, NE: Buros Institute of Mental Measurements.

Harvey, A. L. (1992). [Review of the NOCTI Teacher Occupational Competency Test: Audio-Visual Communications Technology.] In J. J. Kramer & J. C. Conoley (Eds.), *The eleventh mental measurements yearbook* (p. 613). Lincoln, NE: Buros Institute of Mental Measurements.

Review of the NOCTI Teacher Occupational Competency Test: Audio-Visual Communications Technology by CONNIE KUBO DELLA-PIANA, Assistant Professor of Communication, University of Texas at El Paso, El Paso, TX:

The NOCTI Teacher Occupational Competency Test: Audio-Visual Communications Technology is a set of test materials designed to assess technical knowledge and evaluate technical skills. The test is meant for teachers and prospective teachers, as well as "industrial candidates" to verify and to demonstrate occupational competence. The test is composed of two parts: a Written test and a Performance evaluation. The Written test consists of 200 four-option, multiple-choice items covering nine areas: photography, 30 items; computer graphics, 21 items; video production, 29 items; equipment repair and maintenance, 21 items; audio production, 22 items; presentation technology, 20 items; graphic design, 20 items; project management, 32 items; and related miscellaneous information, 5 items. Items are clearly and completely stated. In general, options have approximately the same grammatical structure and length. Items appear to reflect the problems they were intended to represent. In general, items require test takers to recall information about a particular task or situation (a focus on knowledge) rather than requiring them to reason from a set of givens (a focus on intellectual abilities and skills).

The Performance assessment portion of the Audio-Visual Communications Technology Test is administered in small groups under close supervision of the examiner. The Performance test consists of eight tasks or jobs, some of which must be completed in order, that is, the product of one task or job becomes the material needed to complete the next task or job. The Performance test includes: still photography, still photography/film development, still photography/printing, editing and splicing audio tape, audio production studio, video shooting and editing, presentation equipment/usage and maintenance, and computer graphics equipment/re-create 4 graphics visuals. Each task or job has an estimated completion time and test takers must record starting and completion times. It is not clear why each task or job has a listed estimated completion time or if completion time is an important criterion for success on the job. The examiner rates both process- and product-related aspects of the task or job by checking a rating scale for specified processes and products. Possible rating include: *extremely skilled worker, above average worker, average worker, below average worker,* and *inept worker.* A description of the performance ratings is not available in the written materials accompanying the test. This is a serious oversight because test developers claim that the assessment was developed "to verify [the test takers'] experience and demonstrate [their] competency" (p. 6). In addition, there is no mention of the training required to administer the Performance portion of the test. The format of the Performance Evaluation Worksheet is clear and concise, minus descriptions of the rating scale. According to the instructions given to the examiner "different candidates may work on different jobs or complete them in a different order due to availability of machines and equipment" (p. 6). This poses major management challenges for the examiner because the examiner is responsible for familiarizing each candidate with the equipment set-up, operation, and connections prior to starting each job, timing each candidate, evaluating and observing the performance of each candidate on every task or job, maintaining a separate evaluation worksheet for each candidate, monitoring candidate test-taking behavior, and insuring standardized administering of each job/task and the testing procedures as a whole. For instance, if the examiner is evaluating and observing a candidate's performance in the darkroom, he or she cannot be observing those candidates who are working at other workstations in the lab or shop and vice versa. No suggestions are presented to guide the examiner in developing a plan to meet the demands of managing the testing procedures. Although each task or job is described in terms of materials, equipment, and tools needed for the test, the layout for the lab or shop and the number of workstations needed for the number of candidates is left unstated. Is one workstation per job or task sufficient? Does the layout of the lab or shop influence performance? Are different models of the same type of equipment equivalent? Do different models of equipment affect performance? After the Performance portion of the test is completed, examiners are required to transfer their ratings on the Performance Evaluation Worksheet to the General Purpose NCS Answer Sheet. It is not clear from the instructions if there are two answer sheets, one for the Written portion of the test and one for the Performance portion.

The examiner's manual for the Written portion of the test is thorough and well organized. The same cannot be said for the Performance assessment manual. Pages were not in order or upside down. Reference in the Performance assessment manual to the "Evaluator's Copy of the Performance Assessment" did not match the written material accompanying the test. An "Evaluator's Guide" was included. In an attempt to document and judge the standardization of administration, examiners are required to complete a report on group irregularities and individual irregularities.

There was no technical manual included with the test material. Lack of technical information on test development, standards for scoring and administering, reliability, validity, and score interpretation severely limit the usefulness of the Audio-Visual Communications Technology Test. The use of the interpretation of test results for certification or job-related purposes is not justified based on the lack of technical information. Without technical information, the Audio-Visual Communications Technology Test should only be used as a formative evaluation tool for instructional purposes.

[63]
NOCTI Teacher Occupational Competency Test: Auto Body Repair, Forms B and D.

Purpose: Designed to measure the individual's occupational competency in auto body repair.
Population: Teachers and prospective teachers.
Publication Dates: 1973–1994.
Scores, 14: 11 scores for Written part (Total and 10 subscores), 3 scores for Performance part (Process, Product, Total).
Parts, 2: Written, Performance.
Administration: Group.
Price Data: Price information available from publisher for test materials including Written test booklet ('87, 24 pages), Performance test booklet ('87, 3 pages), examiner's copy of Performance test ('87, 6 pages), manual for administering NOCTI TOCT Performance tests ('94, 17 pages), and manual for administering NOCTI TOCT Written tests ('94, 18 pages).
Time: 180(195) minutes for Written part; 340(360) minutes for Performance part (Form B); 305(335) minutes for Performance part (Form D).

Comments: Test administered at least twice a year at centers approved by publisher.
Author: National Occupational Competency Testing Institute.
Publisher: National Occupational Competency Testing Institute.
Cross References: See 9:777 (1 reference); for a review of the NOCTI program, see 8:1153 (6 references).
[Note: These reviews are based on materials available as of September 1, 1996. The publisher advises that major revisions of the NOCTI tests are in process. These will be reviewed in the future.—Ed.]

Review of the NOCTI Teacher Occupational Competency Test: Auto Body Repair, Forms B & D by ROBERT J. DRUMMOND, Professor of Education and Human Services, University of North Florida, Jacksonville, FL:

The Teacher Occupational Competency Test: Auto Body Repair consists of both a Written and a Performance test. The Written form consists of 190 multiple-choice questions, covering Welding (16), Filling Operations (20), Repairing Sheet Metal (30), Refinishing (38), Panel Replacement (15), Unitized Frame Body Repair (26), Front End Alignment (8), Electrical and Assessory (9), Glass Trim and Hardware (11), and Estimating, Tools, and Safety Equipment (17). The Performance test provides several jobs for the candidate to complete. These are Metal Work, Filling; Metal Work, Straightening; Oxy-Acetylene Welding; MIG Welding; Spray Painting; Estimating; Electrical Troubleshooting; and Diagnosing Structural Damage. There are three performance scores based upon the values provided by a rater, a product score, a process score, and a total score. The total points that can be achieved are 1,050.

The manuals for the examiner are very detailed as to the directions that should be followed and cover dimensions such as visitor interruptions, room conditions, seating arrangements, answering candidates questions, and reporting individual candidate irregularities. On either of the examinations, there are no discussions or guidelines for testing individuals who have handicapping conditions. No information is provided in the manuals on how the results will be reported or what the scores mean. Are there cutoff scores? If so, how were they derived? When will candidates hear the results of the testing and in what form will the scores be reported? Even if this is provided in other sources by the NOCTI, it would be good information for the candidates to have.

There is no information provided in the manuals concerning the validity and reliability of either form. Although the tests appear to have face validity, no discussion is provided on how the tasks and items were identified and selected for the two tests. How were the KSAs (knowledge, skills, and abilities) identified and selected? Were Subject Matter Experts (SMEs) used? How were the weighting of the tasks and number of items selected accomplished? How reliable are the ratings? No information is presented on the reliability of the multiple-choice form or about the item difficulty or discrimination. No criterion-referenced validity is reported for either form. The candidates on the process examination are rated on a 5-point scale from "A" *extremely skilled worker* to "E" *inept worker*. It would seem that this type of judgment would be subjective. There are no illustrations of what constitutes extremely skilled performance and what constitutes inept performance. It would be hard for one rater to rate the large number of items on the Performance examination for very many candidates because the Performance test requires both process and product ratings. How are the raters selected and trained? What is the interrater reliability? How is the reliability of the ratings monitored?

In general, the multiple-choice items could be substantially improved. Many had split stems and did not have parallel construction. The questions also would be improved if the stem stated a question rather than an incomplete statement.

SUMMARY. The tests appear to provide a comprehensive assessment of the knowledge, process, and products related to auto body repair; however, without more information and evidence on the reliability and validity of the various forms it is hard to endorse the tests without a number of reservations. The multiple-choice items need to be sharpened. The manuals need to include more information for the candidate on how the results will be reported to the candidate and what the scores mean. Also, the manual for examiners could be improved by having more detailed guidelines and illustrations of each of the five levels of performance used to differentiate among the items on process and product scales. Certification and licens-ing examinations are high stake evaluations and need to be continuously monitored, updated, and revised in order to be fair to the population they serve.

Review of the NOCTI Teacher Occupational Competency Test: Auto Body Repair, Forms B & D by DALE P. SCANNELL, Professor of Education, Indiana University, Purdue University—Indianapolis, Indianapolis, IN:

The publisher of the occupational competency tests evidently provides generic manuals for administering the Written and the Performance tests in this series. The Experienced Worker Performance Assessment Manual is 17 pages of what appears to be photocopied materials. Quality control for the production of the manual is not adequate. Printing quality is uneven and although all materials can be read, the poor quality is distracting. In the copy reviewed, the page following the table of contents is page 16, an appendix item titled "Irregularity Report." Page 1 was found printed upside down on the back of page 15, facing page 17.

The instructions for administering the Performance assessment are appropriate and comprehensive, including detailed instructions for gathering most of the materials that will be needed and for setting up the room where the exam will be administered. All of the topics one would expect to find concerning arrangements and logistics are included in the manual. Common problems that could interfere with the exam are identified and helpful directions for handling those situations are provided.

Examiners are provided with the Examiner's Copy of Performance Test, which is an expanded form of the booklet given to each examinee. The Performance test comprises nine tasks of which eight are to be completed by each examinee; Tasks 4 and 5 are options and one is to be selected. Examiners are to observe the examinees as they work on each task and rate the process and product on a 5-point scale, ranging from A = *extremely skilled worker* to E = *inept worker*. Examples of the process categories are "proper use of equipment" and "proper use of hand tools" and examples of the product categories are "contour accurate" and "general appearance" (p. 1).

In the examiner's copy, the page for each task begins with a brief description of the job to be completed (i.e., "The candidate is to fill with plastic a 9-inch square dent in a door, hood, trunk lid or fender" (p. 3). This is followed by a list of materials, tools, and equipment needed. In the next section, Directions, an acceptable sequence of steps to complete the task is provided. The last section on the page is a statement about evaluation of the candidate: "Score the candidate according to the criteria shown on the Performance Evaluation Worksheet" (p. 3). Evidently this information is the total effort to seek consistency in scoring among various examiners. There is no evidence that examiners have received training in scoring the tasks, and the definition of scale points, shown above, seems inadequate to provide confidence that consistent grading occurs.

Job #1 involves repairing a dented car part. At no place in the materials provided for this review is there an indication of where the dented object is to be obtained. On page 2 of the Experienced Worker Performance Assessment Manual there is a reference to the "Evaluator's Copy of the Performance Assessment." Is this the same as the "Examiner's Copy of the Performance Test"? If it is, which seems likely, then the examiner is never told where to obtain the parts that are to be repaired (e.g., a dented car part).

During the examination, the evaluator is to observe the work and rate the performance, recording the score in the process section of the worksheet. Later these scores are transferred to an NCS answer sheet. At the completion of a job, the product is tagged for identification and later is rated; the ratings are recorded on the answer sheet. The manual for the test indicates that the Performance test is to be administered to small groups of examinees but the maximum number is not specified. Even with relatively small groups of examinees, evaluators will be spread thin in trying to observe and judge the process of examinees. Provisions for quality control and equity in assessment across examinees are insufficient.

A major weakness for this test is the absence of technical information about the reliability and validity of the test. Although the test seems to have face validity, no information is given about the method of establishing cut scores or the relationship between performance on the test and on the job.

For the Written part of the examination, two booklets are provided, a manual for the evaluator and the written test booklet. The manual provides the type of instructions one would expect about preparations, materials needed, and directions that are to be read to examinees in guiding them through the process. Extensive suggestions are provided for seating arrangements for rooms with individual arm chairs and those with tables. This manual refers to the existence of a coordinator for the test center. However, there is no indication of the duties of the coordinator or the relationship between that person and the evaluator.

The Written test booklet contains a brief set of directions for examinees and 190 multiple-choice test items. The directions appear to be generic and indicate that the time limit for the test will be announced. The time limit was not provided for this review. The 190 items cover 10 skill areas such as welding and refinishing. The shortest subtest is nine items and longest is 38. Most item stems are incomplete statements and most of the items focus on knowledge rather than higher order skills such as application of information. Distractors for individual items frequently are not parallel so that functionally the expected chance score will be greater than 1 in 4.

As noted earlier, technical information about the tests is not available. In response to correspondence, a NOCTI representative indicated that this test is being revised and the revision is in a pilot stage. The revised test will be named Collision Repair Technology.

The NOCTI Auto Body Repair test is an extensive examination of candidate knowledge about auto repair equipment and techniques and includes performance on selected, representative repair activities. In the absence of technical information about the test and the value of the scores obtained from the tests, one choosing to use the test will be relying primarily on the face validity of the instruments. The burden placed on examiners and the apparent lack of practices that could contribute to interexaminer consistency raise major questions about the reliability of the Performance test. Inconsistencies among the various booklets and poor print quality do not instill confidence in the values to be derived from the test.

[64]

NOCTI Teacher Occupational Competency Test: Automotive Technician.

Purpose: Designed to measure the individual's occupational competency in automotive technology.
Population: Teachers and prospective teachers.

Publication Dates: 1973–1994.

Scores, 12: 9 scores for Written part (Total and 8 subscores), 3 scores for Performance part (Process, Product, Total).

Parts, 2: Written, Performance.

Administration: Group.

Price Data: Price information available from publisher for test materials including Written test booklet ('92, 27 pages), Performance test booklet ('92, 18 pages), Evaluator's guide ('92, 35 pages), manual for administering NOCTI TOCT Written tests ('94, 18 pages), and manual for administering NOCTI TOCT Performance tests ('94, 17 pages).

Time: 180(195) minutes for Written part; (300) minutes for Performance part.

Comments: Previously listed as Auto Mechanics; test administered at least twice a year at centers approved by publisher.

Author: National Occupational Competency Testing Institute.

Publisher: National Occupational Competency Testing Institute.

Cross References: See 9:778 (2 references) and T3:1595 (1 reference); for a review by Charles W. Pendleton, see 8:1133. For a review of the NOCTI program, see 8:1153 (6 references).

[Note: These reviews are based on materials available as of September 1, 1996. The publisher advises that major revisions of the NOCTI tests are in process. These will be reviewed in the future.—Ed.]

Review of the NOCTI Teacher Occupational Competency Test: Automotive Technician by DALE P. SCANNELL, Professor of Education, Indiana University, Purdue University—Indianapolis, Indianapolis, IN:

The publisher of the occupational competency tests evidently provides generic manuals for administering the written and the performance tests in this series. The Experienced Worker Performance Assessment Manual is 17 pages of what appears to be photocopied materials. Quality control for the production of the manual is not adequate. Printing quality is uneven and although all materials can be read, the poor quality is distracting. In the copy reviewed, the page following the table of contents is page 16, an appendix item titled "Irregularity Report." Page 1 was found printed upside down on the back of page 15, facing page 17.

The instructions for administering the Performance assessment are appropriate and comprehensive, including detailed instructions for gathering most of the materials that will be needed and for setting up the room where the exam will be administered. All of the topics one would expect to find concerning arrangements and logistics are included in the manual. Common problems that could interfere with the exam are identified and helpful directions for handling those situations are provided.

Examiners are provided with a copy of the Experienced Worker Evaluator's Guide, which is an expanded form of the booklet given to each examinee. A list of the 12 tasks that comprise the Performance test and materials needed for each are provided in the manual. Examiners are to observe the examinees as they work on each task and rate the process and product on a 5-point scale, ranging from *A = extremely skilled worker* to *E = inept worker*. Examples of the process categories are "grinding of valve seat" and "adjustment of valve height" and examples of the product categories are "valve spring tension" and "valve height." These ratings are marked on a worksheet during the test and are transferred to an NCS answer sheet after the end of the test.

In the examiner's copy, the page for each task begins with a brief description of the job to be completed (i.e., "Disc Brake Assembly Service and Wheel Bearing Adjustment," p. 7). This is followed by a list of materials, tools, and supplies that must be provided, and the final section lists the actions the candidate is supposed to perform. Estimated completion times are given for each task, and the maximum time to be provided for the entire test is 5 hours. At no place in the manual is there an indication of where the examiner obtains the automobiles or assemblies on which the candidates work. It seems likely that a coordinator of the test center has additional manuals but these were not provided for this review.

A major weakness for this test is the absence of technical information about the reliability and validity of the test. Although the test seems to have face validity, no information is given about the method of establishing cut scores or the relationship between performance on the test and on the job. Evidently the test is administered to a group of candidates simultaneously but the recommended or maximum number is not indicated. Given the complexity of the tasks and the number of processes and products to be rated, one might question how an examiner can ensure adequate observation to rate the process and provide equity among candidates. Another major question raised by the materials provided is what has the publisher done to ensure interexaminer consistency in grading.

For the Written part of the examination, two booklets are provided, a manual for the evaluator and the written test booklet. The manual provides the type of instructions one would expect about preparations, materials needed, and directions that are to be read to examinees in guiding them through the process. Extensive suggestions are provided for seating arrangements for rooms with individual arm chairs and those with tables.

The test booklet contains a brief set of directions for the candidates and 200 multiple-choice test items. The items are provided in eight sections ranging in number from 16 to 37. Responses are recorded on a general purpose NCS answer sheet. A large number of the items have incomplete stems, and the emphasis is on knowledge rather than on higher order accomplishments. Technical flaws are found in a sample of the items. For example, Item 180 has overlapping responses and Item 169 includes some responses that are not appropriate for the stem.

As noted earlier, this test seems to have face validity, but a major weakness is the absence of technical manuals reporting standard psychometric data. The degree of interexaminer consistency in rating performance has not been reported. Similarly, the publishers do not indicate how the passing score has been set or how success on the test relates to performance.

The NOCTI Automotive Technician test is a comprehensive examination of knowledge about and skill in performing a variety of repairs to automobiles. The Performance test has a time limit of 5 hours; the recommended time limit for a written test with 126–200 items is 3 hours. Even though the Performance and Written tests appear to be comprehensive and appropriate, one cannot judge the value of the test in the absence of technical information about reliability, interexaminer consistency in rating performance tasks, methods by which satisfactory performance is established, and relationships between performance on the test and success as an automobile technician.

Review of the NOCTI Teacher Occupational Competency Test: Automotive Technician by GEORGE C. THORNTON III, Professor, Department of Psychology, Colorado State University, Fort Collins, CO:

Quite regrettably, NOCTI continues to fail to provide adequate technical information about the psychometric properties of its tests. Despite a long string of critical reviews of other NOCTI tests in this Yearbook dating back many years, little information beyond simple means and standard deviations for small samples is provided. The potential user has no way of evaluating the adequacy of test development, reliability, or validity for intended users. Virtually none of the professional expectations for test publication codified in the *Standards for Educational and Psychological Testing* (AERA, APA, & NCME, 1985) are met. There is little basis for evaluating whether the test accomplishes any of the lofty claims.

A slick brochure proclaims NOCTI "the leader in occupational competency testing" and lists numerous benefits of skills assessment for educators, administrators, employers, trainers, and employees. The manual purports that this test assesses the knowledge and skills of teachers and prospective teachers in the area of automotive technology. No evidence is provided to support any of these claims.

The Written test, lasting 3 hours, comprises 200 multiple-choice items covering knowledge of engines, alignment and suspension, brakes, engine electrical, drive lines, fuel and emissions systems, accessories and chassis electrical, and shop management. One summary page of statistics from NOCTI covering over 50 tests provides one line of data on the automotive test, including a reliability estimate (KR 20) of .929. This ostensibly high figure must be discounted in light of the long test length: This level of internal consistency for a test of 200 items means that the average intercorrelation of the items is only about .06. In reality, the test is quite heterogeneous, despite the seemingly high reliability estimate. A much more relevant type of reliability estimate for an occupational certification test is the consistency of making the determination of "competent" or "not competent." No such data are provided.

The Performance test, lasting 5 hours, involves 12 tasks such as servicing a cylinder head, servicing a disc brake (and) assembly, and performing wheel alignment. For each task, the evaluator observes the candidate, then evaluates several dimensions of the process carried out and the product produced. For example, when evaluating the task of a fuel system pressure test, the evaluator rates the processes of connecting gauges, safety with fuel, accurate measurement, and proper use of tools, and then rates the products of familiarity with the process, power fuel pump, and manual pressure increase. In total, 56 process subtasks and 51 product attributes are evaluated. Overall process and product scores are tabulated. Unfortunately, no evidence is reported of internal consistency of these ratings and no evidence of the interrater reliability of evaluator judgments is provided.

It is standard practice in reviews like this to comment on the adequacy of the (a) theory or plan guiding test development; (b) samples used for test development, item analysis, norming, estimates of reliability, and validation; and (c) evidence provided to support the validity of the test (i.e., the various inferences that might be made from the test scores). No such information is provided in the test manual, the slim reports sent after my repeated requests to NOCTI, or any other published or unpublished reports on the test.

Writing this review posed a serious dilemma. On the one hand, the technical evidence supporting this test from NOCTI is sorely lacking. On the other hand, faced with the practical need to test the knowledge and assess the performance of automotive technicians there may be no alternatives. About all I can say on the positive side is that the items and tasks look appropriate, and there are detailed administrator's guides for both the Written and Performance tests. But, I cannot endorse the use of this test on the basis of such superficial impressions.

REVIEWER'S REFERENCE

American Educational Research Association, American Psychological Association, & National Council on Measurement in Education. (1985). *Standards for educational and psychological testing.* Washington, DC: American Psychological Association, Inc.

[65]
NOCTI Teacher Occupational Competency Test: Scientific Data Processing.

Purpose: Designed to measure the individual's occupational competency in scientific data processing.
Population: Teachers and prospective teachers.
Publication Dates: 1988–1994.

Scores, 15: 12 scores for Written part (Total and 11 subscores), 3 scores for Performance part (Process, Product, Total).
Parts, 2: Written, Performance.
Administration: Group.
Price Data: Price information available from publisher for test materials including Written test booklet ('93, 32 pages), Performance test booklet ('93, 19 pages), examiner's copy of Performance test ('93, 22 pages), manual for administering NOCTI TOCT Written tests ('94, 18 pages), and manual for administering NOCTI TOCT Performance tests ('94, 17 pages).
Time: (180) minutes for Written part; (360) minutes for Performance part.
Comments: Test administered at least twice a year at centers approved by publisher.
Author: National Occupational Competency Testing Institute.
Publisher: National Occupational Competency Testing Institute.
Cross References: For a review by William M. Bart, see 11:263. For a review of the NOCTI program, see 8:1153 (6 references).
[Note: These reviews are based on materials available as of September 1, 1996. The publisher advises that major revisions of the NOCTI tests are in process. These will be reviewed in the future.—Ed.]

Review of the NOCTI Teacher Occupational Competency Test: Scientific Data Processing by JIM C. FORTUNE, Professor of Educational Research and Evaluation, Virginia Tech, Blacksburg, VA:

INTRODUCTION AND GENERAL DESCRIPTION. The NOCTI Teacher Occupational Competency Test: Scientific Data Processing was designed to measure scientific data processing for teachers and prospective teachers of that subject. The test is a long test composed of two parts: a Written test and a Performance test. The Written test requires 3 hours for administration and the Performance test requires 6 hours for administration. The Written test is made up of a four-choice, multiple-choice examination containing 11 subtests. These include: Computer Fundamentals, Using Software Packages, Generating Documentation, Applying Numerical Analysis, Using Operating Systems, Performing Equipment Operations, Using Languages in General, Using Basic, Using Fortran, Using Pascal, and Using C. The total test involves 179 items. Subtest scores and a total score are derived from performances on the Written tests. The Performance test involves the completion of a multi-task exercise. There are four exercises of similar, if not equal, difficulty and the instructions require the examiner to assign one to each examinee. The examinee is expected to finish the assigned exercise performing all of the required tasks. Three scores are derived from the performance of the exercise: Process, Product, and Total. The tests were designed for the experienced scientific data processor.

REASON FOR THE TESTS. The tests were designed to test competency of teachers and potential teachers in scientific data processing. After having taken the Written test, it appears to me that the test examines scientific data processing competency at an experienced worker level rather than scientific data processing competency at a level required to teach the subject. Many of the multiple-choice items require memory of terms or knowledge of order of operation that are more important at a practice level than they would be in the preparation of a lesson in such. A similar observation can be made for the Performance test.

JOB ANALYSIS. None of the materials that I received described the job analysis. Review of the content suggests potential content validity and makes one believe that a job analysis was performed. I believe that the test content is valid for the practice of scientific data processing, but I question whether or not it addresses the content at a level required to teach the material. I would expect my teacher of the subject to see the big picture rather than remembering which language is called a "high level" language. None of the materials contain a table of specifications, or the relationship of item content on the test to importance of item in practice.

RELIABILITY AND VALIDITY. None of the materials that were sent me included any reliability or validity information. A telephone call to Ferris State University made contact with a friendly, helpful staff person who provided me with the existing reliability information. This information appears slim and inconclusive to me. There appeared to be no statistics for the subtests of the Written test, and the reliability for the total score on the written test was calculated on a sample of eight subjects. KR-20 and KR-21 were calculated on the total score. KR-20 was .893 and KR-21 was .851 for this very small sample. The sample group had a mean of 97.00 (I assume the number correct

out of the 167 items scored for a percent correct of 58.1%) and a standard deviation of 15.22. The reliability reported for the Performance test was coefficient alphas calculated on 17 items and a sample of nine subjects. These reliabilities were .947 for process scores and .956 for product scores. The combined score reliability was .956.

No evidence of validity was reported. A simple description of the job analysis or of the table of specification would provide the content validity that I would expect for a test of this type. It appears to me that there are areas of expected staff behaviors that are omitted from the test. I would be curious as to why editing, verification, data summary, and description were not included on the test. I would think that my teacher of data processing would emphasize editing requirements, verification requirements, and subchecks. The length of both examinations would suggest to me that fatigue may be a threat to validity of the test.

ADMINISTRATIVE EASE. Length of both tests would create difficulty in administrative control. A 3-hour Written test and a 6-hour Performance test both suggest numerous bathroom breaks, fatigue, and difficulty in administrative control. There is no administration manual specifically for the Written test. Instead, directions for the Written tests are contained in the general Written test manual and are included in the Written test booklet and in an insert sheet in this booklet. Overall, the instructions for administration are very clear with regard to most instructions, materials, and in-session security requirements. One area on the insert sheet demands a selection of language areas, which seems a little inconsistent with the scoring descriptions. The general manual describes how to distribute the answer sheets and assessment booklets. Instructions for filling out demographics on the answer sheets are given. There is no penalty for guessing so examinees are instructed to answer every question on the Written test.

The manual for the Performance test is not as clear as the manual for the Written test. This perhaps is due to the increased difficulty of the monitoring process and the assignment of an exercise to an examinee. Yet, I would rate this manual as adequate. There is also a general performance assessment manual, which appears consistent with the specific assessment manual.

SUPPORTIVE MATERIALS. The Experienced Worker Performance Assessment Manual and the Experienced Worker Written Assessment Manual are general manuals to support the administration of these tests. These general manuals are high quality, but they contain some duplication of the specific performance administration manual. Lacking from these supportive materials are information on the job analysis, validation studies, and reliability information.

REVIEWER COMMENTARY. Much of the content of the Written test appeared to be testing small details, some of which is essential for data processing. I took the test and although I did not have a scoring key, I found that many items attended to minutiae and that these items might better serve the assessment by the reduction of the length of the test. Also, I caution that many aspects of teacher competency as to the subject matter relate to the "big picture" as opposed to so much "nitty-gritty." The Performance test appears to require too large a work sample. If I were testing for job selection in data processing, I may wish a Performance test as given. But for teacher competency, I wonder what are the costs of complexity. The Performance test assesses several traits and abilities that I suspect are not included in the scoring, such as time management, focus, planning skills, organization skills, tolerance, etc. I think I would be more pleased with the tests if I could elect to use only parts of the examinations as constructed.

Review of the NOCTI Teacher Occupational Competency Test: Scientific Data Processing by MYRA N. WOMBLE, Assistant Professor of Occupational Studies, University of Georgia, Athens, GA:

DESCRIPTION OF THE SCALE. The Scientific Data Processing test is an occupational competency test intended to assess potential teachers of vocational education programs in scientific data processing at the journey-worker level. The test has both a Performance and Written component. For the Performance test, candidates are assigned one of four programming problems, each similar in complexity and involving coding, compiling, and executing a computer program. The Written test contains 159 multiple-choice questions, 40 of which pertain to four specific programming languages.

DEVELOPMENT. The test was developed in 1988 by Associated Educational Consultants, Inc. (AEC) with the intent of integrating the finished product into the National Occupational Competency Testing Institute (NOCTI) system. Information about development of the Scientific Data Processing test was not available in the assessment manuals provided, but was obtained from NOCTI. Development of the test began by identifying occupational tasks performed by journey-workers employed in scientific data processing. According to NOCTI, minor revisions were made in 1993, but no information describing the revisions was provided.

Preliminary test content was developed by AEC with assistance from a Pennsylvania Area Vocational-Technical school, largely because the scientific data processing program at the school was considered exemplary. However, criteria used to determine "exemplary" status of the school were not provided. After review and editing of several drafts, a final duty-task list was compiled and presented to a five-member Test Development Committee.

ADMINISTRATION AND SCORING. The Performance and Written assessment manuals for examiners provide adequate details about how to administer both components of the test. Candidates are allowed 6 hours to complete the Performance test and 3 hours to complete the Written test.

PERFORMANCE TEST. During the test, examiners use a Performance Evaluation Worksheet while observing each candidate's performance level in four process and four product categories. The four process and product categories evaluated are input data, use of software, operating system/languages, and programming. Each of the four process and product categories contain criteria statements and assigned maximum score values. Evaluation of both categories requires examiners to determine the candidate's skill level, and award points accordingly, using a scale ranging from A = *extremely skilled* to E = *inept worker*. Examiners also determine and report candidates' overall performance using the same range of skill levels, and provide a written overall performance evaluation. Finally, scoring of the Performance test presents a potential problem if examiners find themselves observing and evaluating several different programming languages at the same time. Making clear distinctions among five levels of performance for each criteria statement in the two performance categories, while observing performance in several different languages, may decrease examiner's ability to score objectively.

WRITTEN TEST. The Written test is divided into seven categories each containing multiple-choice questions. The first six categories include areas such as computer fundamentals and account for 139 of the questions. The seventh category includes 40 multiple-choice questions, 10 for each of four programming languages (e.g., BASIC, FORTRAN, Pascal, C). Examinees are instructed to answer all of the questions in the first six categories, then answer 20 of the questions pertaining to only two of the four programming languages.

It should be noted that although one of the performance problems allows COBOL or RPG as choices of programming languages, questions relating to COBOL and RPG are not included in the Written test. Because candidates are allowed to complete the Performance test using COBOL or RPG, these languages should also be a part of the Written test. Also, unlike the Performance test, there is no examiner's copy of the written test. Apparently all information needed by the examiner is included in the Written Assessment Manual, but this is unclear and should be addressed. Furthermore, no information is provided regarding scoring of the written test.

VALIDITY. The Test Development Committee (TDC) included practitioners and educators with backgrounds and experiences appropriately related to scientific data processing. According to AEC, the TDC thoroughly reviewed, amended, and edited the list of competencies and further validated the list through the use of an information occupational inventory of their peers to ensure its accuracy and relevancy to the defined occupational area. Next, the AEC staff developed a rating procedure (Pertinence Index) to identify the frequency and importance of each competency. TDC members participated in this procedure to further scrutinize the list of competencies. Although this phase of the validation process provided important information (e.g., tasks to add or change), AEC's analysis procedures are not described nor easily discerned from the data tables. Therefore, the criteria used to modify the test are unknown. An independent group of experts was not used to evaluate the content validity of the Scientific Data Processing test. Instead, according to AEC, the diverse composition of the TDC provided that all identified competencies were adequately covered. AEC reviewed and edited all questions and an expert in the field, serving as a third party evaluator, reviewed and provided feedback on the structure and content of the test.

RELIABILITY. Fifteen persons participated in field testing of the Scientific Data Processing test. Participants were sufficiently knowledgeable and experienced in scientific data processing. Additional revisions to the Written and Performance tests were made based on field-test results. Because field test results were not reported, knowledge gained that led to revisions is ambiguous. Nevertheless, according to AEC, revisions made dealt with uncertainties experienced by examinees whose expertise in software and hardware was not considered in development of the questions.

National norms on a battery of NOCTI tests, of which the Scientific Data Processing test is a part, suggest that these measures have internal consistency. Reliability measures based on 1995 national norms for the Written component are KR-20 .893 and KR-21 .851 ($n = 8$). Alpha reliability coefficients based on 1991 national norms for the Performance component are process .947, product .956, and combined .956 ($n = 9$). These reliability data look promising; however, the normative data are based on too few examinees to draw any firm conclusion regarding the reliability of this scale.

SUMMARY. The rational, exhaustive approach used to develop this test suggests an attempt to establish content validity. However, because content validity is typically evaluated by independent experts in the field, the TDC's involvement in developing and validating the test items causes concern. The norm sample needs to be increased, especially considering that this test is used to assess the occupational competencies of prospective teachers. Furthermore, decreasing the length of the test and the number of programming languages allowed to complete the Performance tests should improve the usefulness and administration of this test. Also, although focus on third and fourth generation languages is laudable, con-

sideration should be given to including object oriented programming (e.g., C++), a concept rapidly
becoming a central technique in application gen-
erators. In sum, additional revisions of the scale
and sufficient norming and validity data may be
necessary before general use of the scale can be
recommended.

[66]
Occupational Interests Card Sort.

Purpose: To identify and rank occupational interests.
Population: Adults.
Publication Date: 1993–1994.
Scores: Interests Summary Sheet.
Administration: Group or individual.
Price Data, 1994: $18 per complete kit including manual
(38 pages) and cards; $10 per manual; $10 per set of
cards.
Time: (20–30) minutes.
Author: Richard L. Knowdell.
Publisher: Career Research & Testing, Inc.

*Review of the Occupational Interests Card Sort
by MICHAEL B. BUNCH, Vice President, Measurement Incorporated, Durham, NC:*

The Occupational Interests Card Sort is not
a test in the strictest sense of the word, in that it
yields no scores to be compared to a norm or a fixed
criterion. Rather, it is a tool to be used in externalizing one's thoughts about work. According to the
author, the Card Sort is designed for adults making
occupational or career decisions. It is appropriate
when the user does not want to wait for tests to be
sent away for machine scoring or other off-site
manipulation of data. When used by a counselor
as a diagnostic tool, the Occupational Interests
Card Sort is an easy way to get clients to talk about
interests. Several outplacement firms use the Occupational Interests Card Sort for just this purpose.
The card sort format allows clients to make as
many changes as they wish.

The kit contains a 38-page booklet and five
perforated sheets of cards. The client tears the 113
occupation cards and 5 category cards apart and
starts the sorting process. The 38-page booklet
then guides the client through a series of exercises
designed to clarify occupational or career goals and
identify potential career paths. Some of the exercises are well designed and would likely yield very
useful information for most individuals. Other

exercises are not as clear, either in their intent or
directions. In many instances, the content skill and
vocabulary of a trained clinician are obviously necessary. For example, although the manual provides
three different ways of defining the world of work
and classifying occupations, the fields listed in the
first sample exercise do not seem to fit into any of
the three paradigms. Persons attempting to complete the exercises without assistance would be left
to ponder where these categories came from and
how they were to classify the occupations they had
sorted into the "Definitely Interested" pile. Many
of the open-ended questions and supplementary
activities (e.g., dialogue with work, question spin-
ning) were far from helpful.

Some of the exercises are quite helpful. For
example, the card sort exercise itself is quite reveal-
ing and informative. The six-page employment
review forces the client not only to think about all
past jobs but to reflect on job satisfaction, life
satisfaction, progression, patterns, and a host of
other meaningful aspects of work they might not
think of without prompting. The selection of
occupations (113 out of thousands) seems reasonably well balanced. It is quite possible that the
primary benefit of the kit would be to expose
clients to a variety of occupations not previously
considered. If the employment review also evokes
some insights, then the entire exercise may have
been well worth the effort. The effort, by the way,
is likely to be much more than the 20–30 minutes
listed above. That amount of time barely covers
tearing the cards apart and sorting them into piles.
The exercises will take another 2 to 3 hours.

This Occupational Interests Card Sort can be
quite useful if the user has access to a trained counselor. As a stand-alone tool, it is unlikely to provide
very many insights for the average job seeker or
individual interested in changing careers. However,
with some revision of the exercises after the initial
card sort, it may even be useful to this audience.

*Review of the Occupational Interests Card Sort
by DONALD THOMPSON, Dean and Professor of
Counseling and Psychology, Troy State University
Montgomery, Montgomery, AL:*

The Occupational Interests Card Sort Planning Kit (OICS) is one of four card sort career
guidance tools published by Career Research and

Testing, Inc. Because it lacks psychometric properties such as norms, reliability, and validity data, it should not be considered a test, but rather a career guidance and planning tool. The general purpose of the card sort is to identify and rank occupational interests. The administration booklet (the only printed material available) states that the objectives of the card sort are: "1) To define and cluster occupations holding high appeal for you; 2) To identify characteristics shared in common by these occupations; 3) To identify fields holding high appeal for you; 4) To clarify degree of readiness, skill and knowledges [*sic*] needed and competency-building steps for entry into highly appealing occupations; and 5) To apply learnings from the Occupational Card Sort to your career decisions" (p. 5).

The Occupational Card Sort consists of 113 cards. Each card contains a single occupational title (e.g., physicist, farmer, florist). The user is instructed to sort the cards into one of five categories: *Definitely Interested, Probably Interested, Indifferent, Probably Not Interested,* and *Definitely Not Interested.* After sorting the cards, the user responds to an Interest Summary Sheet by listing the titles that were sorted into each category, and then answers a series of 11 questions on an Occupational Interest Worksheet. The categorized occupational titles and the answers to questions on the worksheet are designed to "enable you to clarify more specifically the kinds of work that will offer you occupational satisfaction, and to assess the steps you need to take to increase your employability in the areas" (p. 6). The instructions do not make clear how the user is to do this, and clearly some counselor intervention and assistance would be absolutely necessary to accomplish this. The three test subjects who provided feedback for this review (age range from 25 to 41) found the process fairly difficult and time consuming, but thought it did help them focus on areas of high interest, prompted them to do some in-depth thinking about job requirements, and led them to search out more information on certain occupations. They found that the card sort validated some of their own beliefs about the occupational areas that held the highest degree of interest for them.

Card sorts have been used for a variety of purposes in assessing interests, values, and personality dimensions. There appears to be considerable research regarding card sort methodology; however, no studies were located that dealt directly with this particular card sort, despite the fact that it was first published in about 1980. According to the author, the current version (copyright 1995) has only minor differences in terms of the occupation titles, and the author indicated the need to update some occupational titles (e.g., key punch operator) that are outdated. A large majority of the occupational titles are white collar and at the professional/technical level. The author indicated that he used an intuitive method (rather than some empirical process) for selecting the occupational titles included in the sort.

If used as intended, this card sort could stimulate career exploration and suggest career possibilities and broad interest areas to be explored, but it should not be used as a definitive measure of interests. Also, its use should be limited to an adult population because it relies on a knowledge of job titles that would be unfamiliar to younger persons. There is considerable research that suggests card sorts should not be used as stand-alone measures of occupational interests, but rather as part of a more comprehensive exploration of career interests.

The set of materials received for this review included the manual/user guide of 38 pages (appears to be of xerographic quality with poor resolution of some figures and print characters), and the card deck. The manual includes instructions, worksheets to help the user organize responses, and supplementary materials to help the user further explore his/her interests.

Although not stated in the manual, the author indicated in a telephone conversation that the OICS is intended for use with an adult population. Because the user is sorting occupational titles, a degree of occupational knowledge is needed for individuals to determine whether they would or would not be interested in a particular occupation. It appears to take most users between 20 to 30 minutes to complete the sort process, and considerably longer if they complete the worksheets. The OICS can be administered individually or in groups.

The three undergraduate students used as test subjects for this review indicated that they found the instructions adequate, but the process was both time consuming and not particularly stimulating. The quality of the print reproduction should be upgraded, and perhaps some colorful graphics would provide a more visually stimulating presentation. Also, the test subjects indicated that the interpretation process is not as simple as suggested, and the instructions for using the data generated in a broader exploration of career interests may be inadequate for self-administration. Only about 10% of the occupational titles require less than a college education, and there are relatively few blue collar/technical occupations.

Some of the advantages of the OICS include that it is inexpensive; a safe, nonthreatening, nontest instrument; and a good starting point to explore the interests of bright, mature adults. Also, this tool provides counselors with the necessary information to ascertain the client's level of occupational knowledge. Disadvantages include: it has no empirical evidence regarding the effectiveness as a predictor of future occupational satisfaction or success; it requires a counselor's assistance to be most useful; and it should be used only with adults who have a fairly sophisticated knowledge of the world of work, and then only for initiating a general exploration of career interests.

In summary, the Occupational Interests Card Sort is a low-tech method in an increasingly high-tech world of computer-based career counseling. This tool does not seem to have the user appeal of some of the more recent computer-based multimedia approaches to career guidance. It may be somewhat boring to subjects who have marginal motivation to complete the task. However, it could be a useful tool for initiating career exploration when it is used with older, mature, motivated, and bright clients, and in conjunction with the assistance of a counselor as part of a more comprehensive career exploration and guidance process.

[67]
Parker Team Player Survey.

Purpose: "Helps individuals identify their primary team player styles."
Population: Employees.
Publication Date: 1991.
Acronym: PTPS.
Scores, 4: Contributor, Collaborator, Communicator, Challenger.
Administration: Group or individual.
Time: (15) minutes.
Comments: Self-scored.

Author: Glenn M. Parker.
Publisher: XICOM, Inc.
   a) PARKER TEAM PLAYER SURVEY.
   Price Data, 1993: $5.50 per test booklet/manual (23 pages).
   b) PTPS: STYLES OF ANOTHER PERSON.
   Price Data: $4 per test booklet/manual (12 pages).

TEST REFERENCE

1. Kirnan, J. P., & Woodruff, D. (1994). Reliability and validity estimates of the Parker Team Player Survey. *Educational and Psychological Measurement, 54,* 1030-1037.

Review of the Parker Team Player Survey by GARY J. DEAN, Associate Professor and Chairperson, Department of Adult and Community Education, Indiana University of Pennsylvania, Indiana, PA:

GENERAL COMMENTS. The purpose of the Parker Team Player Survey (PTPS) and the Parker Team Player Survey: Styles of Another Person is to assess a person's style as a team player. Four styles are identified in the two instruments: Contributor, Collaborator, Communicator, and Challenger. The PTPS consists of a 22-page booklet, which includes the survey and information on scoring and interpretation. The Styles of Another Person is a 10-page booklet consisting of a survey and a section on scoring.

Both instruments consist of 18 forced-choice items. Each item has a stem and four responses that are rated by the respondent on a scale of 1 to 4, with 4 = *most applicable to you* (*them*, on the Styles of Another Person), 3 = *second most applicable statement,* 2 = *third most applicable statement,* and 1 = *least applicable statement.* Each response to the items represents one of the four team player styles. The ranking of the responses indicates which style the respondent would consider most appropriate for the situation posed in the item.

TECHNICAL INFORMATION. No information regarding the development of the instruments is provided in either of the booklets and there is no technical manual to accompany the booklets. Calling the publisher resulted in obtaining a reprint of an article (Kirnan & Woodruff, 1994) in which several studies regarding the validity and reliability of the PTPS were reported. According to Kirnan and Woodruff, further details of the origins of the styles are presented in a book by Parker (1991).

According to Kirnan and Woodruff, two studies were conducted to establish validity and one study was conducted to establish reliability for the PTPS. The first validity study consisted of correlating self-ratings on the PTPS for 95 employees with the ratings of them by co-workers using the PTPS Styles of Another Person. The Pearson product-moment correlation coefficients for this study ranged from .18 to .46. The second validity study involved 35 college students who performed an item sort on the PTPS. The 72 responses from the survey (18 items x 4 responses each) were typed onto slips of paper and assigned by the students to one of the four styles. The results of this study were reported as the median percent correct assignment (that is, the median percent of the students whose assignment of the responses to the styles agreed with Parker's assignment for each style). The median percents ranged from 63.5 to 85.5. The range of percents for each style was considerable, however, with a low of 9% agreement to a high of 100%. The reliability study was based on college students (n = 47) and employees (n = 62) and involved the test-retest method with a 3-week interval for the college students and a 4- to 6-week interval for the employees. Correlation coefficients ranged from .43 to .75. Cronbach's alpha calculations for the same study ranged from .20 to .65.

Kirnan and Woodruff (1994) report that the moderate levels of reliability for the PTPS reflect the low number of items and Parker's assertion that many people tend to exhibit more than one style. Also, it should be noted that the results from the item-sort study would have been clearer if means and standard deviations for the percents were reported rather than median percents. If there was a negative skew for the distribution of the agreements by the students, then a median score may, in fact, present an inflated figure for the level of agreement. The moderate correlations from the comparison of self to other ratings and the range of percents in the item sorting indicate that the validity studies also appear to have mixed results. One might question the extent to which the four styles are independent concepts of one another. Also not discussed is the extent to which the four styles are related to other measures of personality such as the Myers-Briggs Type Indicator (T4:1702). The preliminary data suggested by the Kirnan and Woodruff studies indicate that the PTPS may hold some promise, but much additional work is needed to establish the validity and reliability of the instrument.

ADMINISTRATION AND SCORING. Administration of the two instruments is relatively easy. It is designed to be self-administered. The directions are clear and an example of how to respond to the items is provided. The forced-choice format may prove uncomfortable for some people (this is acknowledged in the directions). Scoring is also relatively simple: One transfers the ranking of each response for each item to a grid. The only drawback is that the order of the responses for each item is not the same. For example, the responses for Item 1 are recorded a, b, c, d, whereas the responses for Item 2 are recorded d, a, b, c. This problem aside, scoring is relatively simple and the resulting score for each column in the grid is readily assigned to one of the four team player styles. The highest score designates the person's primary team player style.

INTERPRETATION. There are four sections on interpretation in the PTPS booklet, one section for each of the following: one primary style, two primary styles, three primary styles, and a uniform pattern. The author provided a definition of each of the four team player styles in the section entitled "Understanding and Interpreting the Results if You Have One Primary Style" (p. 9). Contributors are task oriented and provide the team with technical data although they may become bogged down in detail and lose sight of the big picture. Collaborators are goal-oriented people who see the mission of the team and are flexible and open to new ideas but may not give enough attention to basic team tasks and needs of other individuals on the team. Communicators are process and people oriented and are also conflict resolvers, but sometimes lack task orientation or fail to confront others on the team when necessary. Challengers question the goals, methods, or even the ethics of the team and are valued for their openness and candor but may become self-righteous. The sections on two and three primary styles simply reflect a combination of the positive and negative attributes of each style. The section on a uniform pattern merely mentions that a person has strengths from each of the four styles but that person's impact in the team may be diffused because of the lack of a strong preference for one style.

Interpreting the Styles of Another Person is accomplished by comparing a respondent's self-ratings to the ratings given to that person by others. A grid is provided for this purpose. The grid allows the respondent to record the scores of others for each of the four styles, average those scores, and then compare the average of the others' scores to their own score for each style.

CONCLUSION. The PTPS and Styles of Another Person are easy to take and score, with the caveat that some people may find the forced-choice format difficult. The potential applications in organizations would appear to make the instrument a valuable tool. The lack of persuasive data for reliability and validity, however, limit the usefulness of the instrument at this time. Additional studies are needed, especially in the area of establishing the independence of the four styles. Provided that the instrument is used for self-exploration and growth, it may provide some useful insights.

REVIEWER'S REFERENCES

Parker, G. M. (1991). *Team players and teamwork: The new competitive business strategy*. San Francisco: Jossey-Bass.
Kirnan, J. P., & Woodruff, D. (1994). Reliability and validity estimates of the Parker Team Player Survey. *Educational and Psychological Measurement, 54*(4), 1030–1037.

Review of the Parker Team Player Survey by RICHARD B. STUART, *Professor Emeritus of Psychiatry, University of Washington, and Regional Faculty, The Fielding Institute, Seattle, WA:*

In using the Parker Team Player Survey, respondents are asked to describe their own behavior and that of members of their team using an 18-item instrument. Each item consists of a descriptor (e.g., "During team meetings he or she usually …" [p. 2] or "When necessary, this person is able to …" [p. 3]) followed by four alternatives: "provides the team with technical data or information," "keeps the team focused on our mission or goals," "makes sure everyone is involved in the discussion," and "raises questions about our goals and methods" (p. 2). Respondents are asked to rank the applicability of each alternative to the teammate being evaluated, using a 4-point scale from "least applicable statement" (p. 1) to "most applicable to them" (p. 1). Protocols are scored by entering the number assigned to response alternative on a score sheet with four columns. By totaling the columns, relative scores are obtained for the extent to which each team member is seen as displaying each of four characteristics. "Contributors" are defined as being task-oriented; "Collaborators" as goal-oriented; "Communicators" as process-oriented; and

"Challengers" as question-oriented. Space is also provided for open-ended assessments of respondent's or teammate's strengths, performance enhancing and impeding actions, and areas of needed improvement. The manual implies that teammates' rating of each target individual can be averaged. Instructions are given for displaying transparencies that convey the ratings received by each named participant.

In two manuals consisting of 12 pages and 22 pages with large type, no theory of organizational or group behavior is presented as a rationale for the selection of the four team player styles. Rather, each is described in general terms, noting that the relevant behaviors have both positive and negative implications. Accordingly, no claim can be made that these types either exhaust the range of group-member attributes or that they represent the most salient of attributes. The manuals suggest that the strengths of teams be assessed along these four lines, with indications that certain styles may be missing, overly dominant, or inflexibly utilized in the group.

In the same vein, data are not presented on the reliability or validity of members' ratings of their own and each others' characteristics. Nor are data presented on the results one might expect when using this instrument in various types of organizations. Public presentation of the scores received by each member in this essentially sociometric assessment is a technique that definitely should have been evaluated because of its potentially disruptive effects.

The low cost and easy administration of this instrument, coupled with its rather simplistic array of performance characterizations, makes its use appealing. However, its use in groups that are moderate to high in conflict is unwise unless it is administered by a highly skilled group leader who has prepared protocols for dealing with varied types of feedback and the potential for negative as well as positive impact. At best, this instrument might be used as an "ice breaker" in group-based approaches to organizational consultation to facilitate team members' thinking about their peers' performance in concrete terms, which can either be reinforced or changed. But even this use is not without its risks. If the feedback to any individual is either strongly negative or discordant with that person's self-perception, it can result in resentment and/or alienation. Those interested in assessing team effectiveness in particular, or organizational effectiveness in general, might profit from a review of other approaches (e.g., Harrison, 1987).

REVIEWER'S REFERENCE

Harrison, M. I. (1987). *Diagnosing organizations: Methods, models, and processes.* Newbury Park, CA: Sage Publications.

[68]
The Patterned Elicitation Syntax Test with Morphophonemic Analysis.

Purpose: Designed to determine "whether a child's expressive grammatical skills are age appropriate."
Population: Ages 3–0 to 7–6.
Publication Dates: 1981–1993.
Acronym: PEST.
Scores, 13: Articles, Adjectives, Auxiliaries/Modals/Copulas, Conjunctions, Negatives, Plurals, Possessives, Pronouns, Questions, Verbs, Subject/Verb Agreement, Embedded Elements, Total.
Administration: Individual.
Price Data, 1994: $51 per complete kit including manual ('93, 18 pages), stimulus picture book, and 10 data form booklets.
Time: (15–20) minutes.
Comments: Previously titled The Patterned Elicitation Syntax Test.
Authors: Edna Carter Young and Joseph J. Perachio.
Publisher: Communication Skill Builders.
Cross References: For a review by Carolyn Peluso Atkins, see 9:921.

TEST REFERENCES

1. Eiserman, W. D., Weber, C., & McCoun, M. (1992). Two alternative program models for serving speech disordered preschoolers: A second follow-up. *Journal of Communication Disorders, 25,* 77–106.
2. Plante, E., & Vance, R. (1994). Selection of preschool language tests: A database approach. *Language, Speech, and Hearing Services in Schools, 25,* 15–24.

Review of the Patterned Elicitation Syntax Test with Morphophonemic Analysis by CLINTON W. BENNETT, Professor of Communication Sciences and Disorders, James Madison University, Harrisonburg, VA:

The Patterned Elicitation Syntax Test (PEST) presents a unique deviation from most tests of expressive grammatical skills in children; it uses a delayed imitation task and two scoring methods (criterion and norm referenced). The PEST is a screening instrument of 44 grammatical structures from Standard English. Twelve specific classes of grammatical structures are evaluated: Articles; Adjectives; Auxiliaries, Modals, and Copulas; Conjunctions; Negatives; Plurals; Possessives; Pronouns; Questions; Verbs; Subject/Verb Agreement; and Embedded Elements.

The child listens to three consecutively modeled sentences with common syntactic patterns with varied vocabulary while looking at simple black-on-white line drawings. The child then repeats the three sentences, with only the third sentence being scored. However, the authors note that the child's consistency across the three sentences can be used to draw conclusions about mastery of the grammatical structure.

The PEST stimulus items are arranged in ascending order of difficulty; therefore basal and ceiling levels were established. Three-year-olds and children suspected of significant language delays begin with Item #1 and older children begin with Item #11 and are credited with Items 1 through 10. Administration of the test is terminated after the child commits six consecutive errors.

The PEST also includes an optional morphophonemic interpretation that allows for determination of whether a child's omission of morphological markers is due to lack of morphemic knowledge or a restricted phonological system. This screening tool consists of 50 words that require the production of final consonants or consonant clusters to form plurals, possessives, and verb tenses.

The PEST normative population was only 651 children between the ages of 3-0 and 7-6 from homes where Standard English was spoken. Only children "who had no identified disability that would preclude normal language development" (p. 4) were included. The number of children per 6-month age group ranged from 51–100.

Two measures of reliability are presented in the manual: Temporal reliability was assessed by testing 106 children twice within a 2-week period. The Pearson Product Moment correlation of .94 indicates that the PEST has excellent test-retest reliability. Internal consistency was measured using split-half coefficients, which ranged from .93 to .99 across the nine age groups.

Three types of test validity are presented in the manual. Item validity was assessed to determine if the PEST is developmental (i.e., are higher scores a function of age). A series of t-tests yielded an acceptable pattern of significance between age groups, indicating that this test is developmental in its structure. Content validity was evaluated by contrasting the PEST scores with results of a spontaneous language-sample analysis from 10 normal-language and 30 language-impaired children. Correlations of .86 and .88, respectively, suggest an acceptable relationship between performance on the PEST and spontaneous use of the morphological structures assessed by the PEST. Predictive validity was used to determine if PEST performance would identify children with expressive language impairment. Thirty-five children diagnosed as language impaired from results of a full battery of diagnostic language tests and experienced clinician judgments served as subjects. The PEST scores for 34 of the 35 language-impaired children fell below the recommended cutoff (10th percentile). The remaining child was between the 10th and 25th percentile. Interestingly, 33 of 35 language-impaired children also scored below two standard deviations from the mean for their age group. These findings would indicate that a cutoff of two standard deviations from the mean would still accurately identify language-impaired children and would not identify children in the low normal range as impaired (which the 10th percentile cutoff does).

Performance on the PEST is interpreted as criterion referenced (which morphological structures were and were not successfully produced) and/or age referenced (comparison of this score to that of normal-language peers).

Criterion-referenced interpretation may be useful in determining remedial targets and documenting progress. Transferring errors from the Response Sheet to the Assessment Sheet (both in each data form booklet) allows evaluation of the 44 structures scored plus 144 additional structures which are not scored.

Age-referenced scoring can be interpreted through percentile ranks or in terms of the score's deviation from the mean for the child's age. The authors seem to favor the use of percentile ranks: "The examiner should be most interested in identifying children who score in the lowest quartile, because this represents performance out of the normal range. Children who score below the 10th percentile are almost certainly candidates for therapy" (p. 12).

Application of these recommendations will result in the overidentification of children as language-impaired. The normative population for standardization of the PEST excluded any child suspected as being "disabled"; therefore, using the lowest quartile as a cutoff would identify 25% of normal children as being language impaired; similarly, with the 10th percentile as the cutoff, 10% of normal children are found to be impaired. Because the normative sample included only normals, a cutoff using the age group mean minus two standard deviations which, theoretically, would still identify 2% of "normals"—would seem to be more clinically relevant than the authors' recommendation.

Each data form booklet is complete, containing a response sheet, in-depth assessment sheet, interpretation of morphophonemic errors, and tables for interpretation of scores (age groups, means, standard deviations, and percentile ranks). The PEST manual is user friendly with pertinent information presented in an easy-to-understand manner.

LIMITATIONS. The restricted normative sample appears to be truncated so that a 10th percentile cutoff is likely to overidentify low normal children as language impaired; the delayed-imitation task may be difficult for young children (particularly the questions forms); and use of the published norms are not appropriate for speakers of nonmainstream dialect (which the authors indicated).

CONCLUSION. The PEST is a valid and reliable screening tool for children with suspected syntactic problems. It also may serve as a probe for determining therapeutic targets and progress. However, identifying children in the lowest quartile (<25th percentile) or even below the 10th percentile will overidentify children as language impaired. The PEST is best used as a criterion-referenced measure.

Review of the Patterned Elicitation Syntax Test with Morphophonemic Analysis by SHEILA R. PRATT, Assistant Professor of Communication Science & Disorders, University of Pittsburgh, Pittsburgh, PA:

The goal of the Patterned Elicitation Syntax Test (PEST) is to assess expressive syntactic and morphophonemic skills of children within a limited period of time. The authors indicated that the PEST is primarily a screening tool that can be used to determine if children need more extensive assessment of expressive language. They also indicated that it can be used as a criterion-referenced test, as a component of a speech-language and educational assessment battery, or it can be used prescriptively. That is, they believed that the structure and analysis scheme of the PEST is useful in identifying linguistic structures that are in need of remediation.

TEST DESCRIPTION. The PEST was developed for children ages 3 to 7.5 years and includes a range of common syntactic structures and a sample of final bound morphemes. The authors indicated that the test represents structures that typically occur in children's speech but little explanation was given for why specific items were selected. The test items (a total of 44) consist of phrases and sentences that are arranged in order of increasing complexity and difficulty. With some of the items, specific words and phrases are targeted within utterances whereas with others entire sentences are targeted. Each test item is associated with a plate of three pictures. The pictures depict three structurally similar utterances. When administering the PEST, an examiner produces an utterance for each picture and then asks the child also to describe all three pictures. However, only the last utterance produced by the child is scored, thereby making the procedure a delayed imitation task.

Two analysis formats are included in the PEST—one syntactic, the other morphophonemic. The syntactic portion is the primary component of the test and the morphophonemic portion is largely supplementary. In the syntactic portion the children's productions are scored for syntactic correctness in a binary plus-minus fashion. The number of correct productions are totaled and compared to age-based norms. In the morphophonemic portion of the PEST, a number of the final bound morphemes (single consonants and clusters that form verb tenses, plurals, and possessives) are sampled from all of the utterances produced (not just the third or target productions) and are analyzed for phonological correctness. These morphophonemic results are not, however, included in the calculation of the raw test score or associated with the norms or normative process. The implication is that the morphophonemic results are to be viewed descriptively. Further, when the morphophonemic analysis is used, some type of phonological assessment is required in order to determine if errors are morphological rather than

phonological in nature. This analysis needs to occur offline from an audio recording of the test session, in part, because it and the syntactic analysis are performed on two different portions of the score sheet making response recording cumbersome if done online.

The instructions in the manual for the syntactic portion of the PEST are reasonably clear. They are vague for the morphophonemic analysis, although clarified somewhat by the directions on the score sheet. The instructions for interpreting the syntactic results are acceptable but limited relative to the morphophonemic results. In addition, not all of the required information for administration and interpretation is located where expected in the manual.

VALIDITY. One major weakness of the PEST is that the delayed imitation task on which it was based has only limited empirical support and justification. The authors suggested that the delayed imitation task reduces some of the limitations of immediate imitation such as the effects of short-term memory, restricted context, and limited communicative intent. They also indicated that language behaviors produced in a delayed imitation task may be more representative of a child's spontaneous language than immediate imitation. In addition, the PEST was described as more controlled, quicker, and less labor intensive than analyzing expressive language via spontaneous language samples. Although there may be truth in these claims, particularly the claim of control and speed, the supportive evidence is not presented in the test manual. Context and communicative intent are limited with the PEST and may not be substantively greater than that provided by direct imitation tasks. In addition, memory may play an even greater role with a delayed imitation task than direct imitation in that the amount of information presented per item is greater and the time in working memory also is likely longer. Further, the influence of producing two structurally similar sentences prior to a third target utterance was not sufficiently addressed.

The authors provided three measures of validity. They assessed content validity by comparing performance on the PEST with the production of similar structures in spontaneous speech samples from a group of children with expressive language impairment and a smaller group with normal language. The correlations between performance on the PEST and spontaneous productions were reported as .88 for the language-impaired group and .86 for the normal-language group. However, the sample size ($n = 10$) for the normal-language group was insufficient to produce a stable correlation. In addition, the procedures used to collect and analyze the language samples were poorly described. These procedures may have impacted the results. It also was unclear why only the syntactic structures sampled by the PEST were evaluated in the language sample. Information relative to predictive validity would have been obtained if the syntactic results of the PEST had been compared to the overall results of the language sample. That is, was poor performance on a language sample consistent with poor performance on the PEST?

Predictive validity was assessed by administering the PEST to 35 children previously diagnosed with expressive language impairment. Using the 10th percentile as the failure criterion, the sensitivity of the PEST was measured. Thirty-four of the 35 children tested were true failures, which is reasonably high; but because the group was restricted to only language-impaired children the results were of limited usefulness. Without testing children with a range of language skills, specificity could not be determined nor was it clear whether the high degree of predictability was a function of a biased sample. The use of the PEST as a screening tool should be questioned due to the lack of adequate sensitivity and specificity data.

As an additional measure of validity the authors evaluated the developmental nature of the test. The items were arranged in order of difficulty as reflected in the performance of their normative group, which begs the question of whether the order of the items was changed after the norms were established. If such was the case, the normative data are invalid for use with the PEST. To document that the PEST was developmental in nature, the authors tested for differences between the age groups (6-month intervals) of their normative sample. They indicated that all of their comparisons were significant although the comparisons were not specified. The manual includes a table of means, standard deviations, and t-scores for each age level but the arrangement of the data in the

table suggests that all of the comparisons were made to the youngest group, which is of only limited value. In addition, for each age group the items were viewed according to percentage of correct responses to determine if the sequence of difficulty held for each age group. Although the authors said that the trend tended to hold across the groups, more formal analyses were not reported.

RELIABILITY. The reliability of the PEST was assessed with a test-retest method to measure temporal stability and a split-half procedure to measure internal consistency. Test-retest reliability was assessed with 106 children from the normative sample. The children were tested by the same examiner 2 weeks after the initial test. The resulting correlation was .94 indicating sufficiently high temporal stability. The split-half reliability was determined by correlating the scores derived from the odd items with scores from the even items for each age level. The correlations ranged from .93 to .99 with no apparent age-related differences. Therefore, the reliability of the PEST appeared to be quite acceptable.

NORMATIVE SAMPLE. The normative sample consisted of 651 children between the ages of 3.0 and 7.5 years. The number of children in each age group was not consistent. The smallest group size was 51 and the largest was 100 with the younger groups having fewer members. The normative sample comprised 324 males and 327 females. None of the children had obvious disabilities that would have interfered with normal language development although no preliminary measures were used to document normal development or normal language. The children were English speaking and came from homes in which standard American English was spoken. The children were largely from the eastern portion of the United States but the specific setting (urban vs. rural) varied. Approximately 75% of the children were from middle-class families as determined by the family breadwinner's occupation (Warner, Meeker, & Eells, 1949).

SUMMARY OF STRENGTHS. The PEST is a novel approach to assessing syntactic and morphophonemic productions and may prove to be an effective means of screening for expressive language impairment although this needs further verification. The test materials are straightforward and easy to use. The organization of the response form is structured to facilitate error analysis. In addition, instructions and norms are included on the response form, which assists with administration and interpretation. The normative sample was of sufficient size and the reliability of the test is reasonably high.

SUMMARY OF WEAKNESSES. The major weakness of the PEST is its inadequate documentation of validity. In particular, the authors did not sufficiently substantiate the validity of the delayed imitation approach upon which the test was based. Also, characterization of the performance of the PEST as a screening tool is inadequate. Further, verification of its use as a prescriptive tool is lacking as is the use of the supplementary morphophonemic component of the test. No measures of validity or reliability are supplied for the morphophonemic portion, which weakens its applicability.

REVIEWER'S REFERENCE

Warner, W. L., Meeker, M., & Eells, K. (1949). *Social class in America: A manual of procedure for the measurement of social status.* Chicago: Science Research Associates.

[69]
Personal Experience Inventory for Adults.

Purpose: Designed to yield "comprehensive information about an individual's substance abuse patterns and problems."
Population: Age 19 and older.
Publication Dates: 1995–1996.
Acronym: PEI-A.
Scores, 37: Problem Severity Scales (Personal Involvement with Drugs, Physiological Dependence, Effects of Use, Social Benefits of Use, Personal Consequences of Use, Recreational Use, Transsituational Use, Psychological Benefits of Use, Preoccupation, Loss of Control, Infrequency—1, Self-Deception, Social Desirability—1, Treatment Receptiveness), Psychosocial Scales (Negative Self-Image, Psychological Disturbance, Social Isolation, Uncontrolled, Rejecting Convention, Deviant Behavior, Absence of Goals, Spiritual Isolation, Peer Drug Use, Interpersonal Pathology, Estrangement in the Home, Infrequency—2, Social Desirability—2), Problem Screens (Suicide Risk, Work Environment Risk, Past Family Pathology, Other Impulse-Related Problems, Significant Other Drug Problem, Sexual Abuse Perpetrator, Physical Abuse Perpetrator, Physical/Sexual Abuse Victim, Need for Psychiatric Referral, Miscellaneous).
Administration: Group.
Parts, 2: Problem Severity Scales, Psychosocial Scales.
Price Data, 1996: $135 per kit including 5 prepaid mail-in answer booklets and manual ('96, 100 pages);

$18.50 or less per mail-in answer booklet; $275 or less per IBM microcomputer scoring disk (25 uses; 3.5-inch); $19.50 or less per 10 microcomputer answer booklets for use with microcomputer disk; $17.50 each for FAX scoring service.
Time: (45–60) minutes.
Comments: Untimed self-report inventory; computer scored only.
Author: Ken C. Winters.
Publisher: Western Psychological Services.

Review of the Personal Experience Inventory for Adults by MARK D. SHRIVER, Assistant Professor, University of Nebraska Medical Center, Omaha, NE:

The stated purpose of the Personal Experience Inventory for Adults (PEI-A) is to function as "a comprehensive, standardized self-report inventory to assist in problem identification, treatment referral, and individualized planning associated with addressing the abuse of alcohol and other drugs by adults" (p. 3). It is designed to yield "comprehensive information about an individual's substance abuse patterns and problems [and] …also helps to identify the psycho-social difficulties of the referred individual" (p. 3). The PEI-A is developed from, and an extension of, the PEI (1989) which is a self-report measure of drug and alcohol use for adolescents ages 12 to 18 (see *Mental Measurements Yearbook* (1992) 11:284 for reviews by Tony Toneatto and Jalie A. Tucker).

The manual states that the PEI-A "was designed primarily as a clinical descriptive tool for use by addiction professionals" and that it "is intended to supplement a comprehensive assessment process" (p. 5). Specifically, the PEI-A was developed to measure the following characteristics:

1. The presence of the psychological, physiological, and behavioral signs of alcohol and other drug abuse and dependence.

2. The nature and style of drug use (e.g., consequences, personal effects, and setting).

3. The onset, duration, and frequency of use for each of the major drug categories.

4. The characteristics of psychosocial functioning, especially factors identified as precipitating or maintaining drug involvement and expected to be relevant to treatment goals.

5. The existence of behavioral or mental problems that may accompany drug use (e.g., sexual abuse or co-addiction).

6. The sources of invalid response tendencies (e.g., "faking bad," "faking good," inattention, or random responding).

The appropriate use of any measure for its intended purposes is dependent on its sample representation, reliability, and validity. This information is reviewed respective to the PEI-A's stated purposes described above.

TEST ADMINISTRATION. The manual provides easy-to-read instructions on test administration, which will assist with increasing standardization of the administration. The manual states that the reading level of the measure is approximately sixth grade (p. 7), and the test may be read to clients with lower reading abilities. No discussion is presented, however, regarding whether this type of administration occurred during norming of the test, or how this type of administration may affect the reliability or validity of the self-report measure, as the examiner is directly involved with administration, which runs counter to one of the intended goals for test development (p. 29).

The test is scored by computer, either through a mail-in service, a FAX service, or by computer disk. The mail-in service typically requires approximately 3–5 working days to return scores (p. 75). This may be too long in some clinical settings. Interpretations of each scale are provided in the computer-generated report.

TEST DEVELOPMENT. The content of the PEI-A is largely derived from the PEI. A panel of experts is reported to have examined the items on the PEI and made changes where necessary to adapt the items to an adult population. The panel of experts was composed of "Groups of researchers and drug treatment service providers" (p. 30), but no further indication is provided in the manual about who these individuals are, where they are from, and what respective experience/expertise they have in item/test development. Item selection and scale development proceeded on a "rational basis" (p. 30). In addition to the PEI, a drug use frequency checklist adapted from adolescent and adult national survey instruments was incorporated into the drug consumption section of the PEI-A.

The initial items and scales of the PEI-A were examined with a sample of 300 drug clinic subjects (150 males, 150 females) for internal scale consistency (alpha coefficients) and interscale correlations. Correlations between Problem Severity Scales "were somewhat higher than desired for scales intended to contribute substantial unique and reliable information about the respondent, ranging from .55 to .92" (p. 33). Alpha correlations of individual scales were good, typically within the .75 to .93 range (pp. 32–33). Following examination of the correlations on this initial sample of subjects "only minor adjustments in item assignment" were made in scales (p. 33).

The content of the Problem Severity Scales is described as "multidimensional, oriented around signs and symptoms of drug abuse and dependence, and not anchored in any single theoretical model" (p. 30). Review of the items on the measure suggests that the content appears appropriate for the purposes listed above. Review of the empirical evidence for sample comparisons, reliability, and validity will help determine if items originally developed for adolescents and refined for adults based on unknown expert opinion are truly valid for adults.

The test items were not analyzed statistically for possible bias. The test was examined for differences in internal consistency across gender and race, and significant differences were not found; however, predictive validity and differential decision making across gender and race have not yet been examined. Differences in primary language of the subjects was not discussed and it is difficult to determine how language (i.e., not primarily English) might affect responses (written or oral) on the PEI-A.

SAMPLES FOR TEST VALIDATION AND NORMING. Three samples were chosen for test norming: 895 drug clinic clients from Minnesota, Illinois, Washington, California, Missouri, and Ontario, although specific numbers from each state are not provided; 410 criminal offenders, most from Minnesota; and 690 nonclinical participants, all from Minnesota. All sample subjects were volunteers. No discussion is provided in the manual regarding the possible impact on client self-report due to the sample selection process, and whether valid interpretation of the results can be made with individuals who may be tested under some type of coercion such as for court-ordered treatment. Sample demographic information is provided in the manual regarding mean age, age range, gender, minority, percent in prior treatment, marital status, employment status, and education (p. 36).

Scores from the measure are compared with the drug clinic sample in the form of T scores; however, score comparisons (T scores) are also provided at the end of the computerized report for the nonclinic sample. Given the restricted geographic sampling of the nonclinic group, it is difficult to determine if this comparison provides useful information for individuals who are not from Minnesota. It is also unclear if the nonclinic sample participated by mail as described on page 35 of the manual or through group testing as described on page 36 of the manual. Both contexts for test taking are somewhat different from the typical administration (e.g., individualized, in drug clinic) described in the manual and may limit score interpretations even further.

The drug clinic sample is described in terms of two groups: outpatient and residential treatment. Only 37.5% of the outpatient drug clinic sample is female (approximately 188). Only 36.3% of the residential drug clinic sample is female (approximately 143). Separate T scores are provided for male and female samples (p. 36). Only approximately 113 members of the outpatient drug clinic sample are of an ethnic minority status, and approximately 68 members of the residential drug clinic sample are of an ethnic minority status. Minority is not defined further (e.g., African American, Hispanic, Native American), although it is conceivable that minority status may differentially impact drug use. In addition, although the gender representation may be an accurate reflection of general population drug use, the small sample size for females limits normative comparisons. Reported drug use patterns may also differ by gender.

Information is not provided on whether the norm groups come from rural or urban settings. A rural or urban context may impact drug use (i.e., availability of drugs). Also, specific numbers are not provided relative to the geographic regions from which the drug clinic samples originate, and as indicated by the authors (p. 36), geographic region may impact reported drug use (i.e., higher cocaine use in California and Washington reported relative to Midwest states and Ontario).

In summary, caution is advised in using the PEI-A with females, minorities, and individuals

from geographic regions other than those sampled. In addition, the comparison with nonclinic population may not be useful for individuals outside of Minnesota. The test norms appear to be useful for comparing Caucasian males with possible drug use history with the drug clinic sample.

RELIABILITY. Internal consistency reliabilities are provided (coefficient alpha) for the entire sample and provided for male, female, white, and minority samples (pp. 37–41). In addition, test-retest reliabilities are presented for one week and for one month using the drug clinic sample, although there was some intervening treatment between pre- and posttest scores (pp. 42–43). Only reliabilities for the drug clinic and nonclinic samples will be discussed as these represent the primary comparative groups for examinees.

Coefficient alphas are generally good for the Problem Severity Scales (median .89 range .72 to .94) and the Psychosocial Scales (median .81 range .67 to .91). The coefficient alphas are low for the Validity Scales (median .63 range .58 to .77) (p. 37). The authors claim the validity reliability estimates compare favorably with other instruments, and this may be true; however, these values are just acceptable given the use to be made of these scores.

Median test-retest reliabilities at one week (70 individual) were as follows: Problem Severity scales .71 (.60 to .88), Psychosocial scales .66 (.55 to .87), and Validity Indices .52 (.40 to .57). One-month test-retest reliabilities were lower as expected given intervening treatment (pp. 42–43). Given that some subjects were provided intervening treatment in the one-week test-retest group also, it can reasonably be said that test-retest reliability has not been adequately examined and no conclusions can be drawn regarding temporal stability of the test. This makes it less useful pre- and post-treatment as it is difficult to determine if changes in scores are due to treatment or lack of score stability. This is in conflict with the authors' conclusions, however, that scores can be compared pre- and posttreatment (p. 43).

In summary, the internal consistency estimates of the Problem Severity Scales and the Psychosocial Scales range from good to acceptable. More research is definitely needed on the stability of the test scores (test-retest) before conclusions can be drawn regarding the test's usefulness pre- and posttreatment.

VALIDITY. One potential use of this instrument is to determine appropriate treatment options for individuals. Drug clinic subjects ($N = 251$) were classified into three referral categories: no treatment, outpatient treatment, and residential treatment based on clinical staff ratings. Mean scores on the PEI-A Problem Severity Scales were examined and expected differences in scores were found for the three groups (p. 46). Future researchers, however, may want to look at the contribution the PEI-A provides above and beyond other information used in making referral decisions. In other words, are these mean score differences useful? Also, significant differences in mean scores according to sample group membership (nonclinical, drug clinic, and criminal offender) were also found (p. 46). Again, an empirical examination as to how this information contributes as part of a comprehensive assessment would be useful.

Seven of the Problem Screens were compared with staff ratings to determine sensitivity and specificity of the screens, essentially the degree of agreement regarding the existence of problems (p. 48). For the total sample, there were significant correlations ($p<.05$) for agreement between the PEI-A and staff ratings for negative ratings (i.e., individual not identified with having problem), but not for positive ratings (i.e., individual identified as having problem) (p. 49).

The Validity Indices were found to correlated as expected with Minnesota Multiphasic Personality Inventory (MMPI) Validity scales (p. 48).

To assess the construct validity of the scale, correlations with tests purported to measure similar constructs were examined. Moderate correlations were found between the Problem Severity Basic Scales scores and the Alcohol Dependence Scale (.41–.66; p. 44; ADS; Horn, Skinner, Wanberg, & Foster, 1982). In addition, correlations are also provided for Problem Severity Scale scores and the Drug Use Frequency Checklist; however, the Drug Use Frequency Checklist is actually part of the PEI-A so the usefulness of this information for construct validity is weakened. The Psychosocial Scales of the PEI-A were found to correlate significantly with MMPI scales, suggesting the psychosocial Scales are measuring psychopathology to some extent (p. 45), but there

does not appear to be much differentiation between the PEI-A scales as all but Rejecting Convention and Spiritual Isolation correlate highly with each of the MMPI scales. Finally, information is provided that "select" PEI-A scales (p. 45) correlate significantly with a Significant Other Questionnaire. However, the Significant Other Questionnaire is also developed from PEI-A items, which again attenuates the meaningfulness of this relationship.

In summary, the validity evidence presented in the manual does not appear to address specifically the intended purposes/applications of the test noted above. The content looks good, but much more empirical research is needed on the validity of this instrument specifically related to the applications for which it is intended. Future research should address whether this instrument contributes significantly (above and beyond other information in a comprehensive assessment) to decision making involved in assessing and treating individuals with alcohol and drug use problems.

SUMMARY. The PEI-A may be most useful for examining alcohol and drug use in white males who are compared with a drug clinic sample. Results of this test are intended to tell the clinician whether an individual is similar to individuals in the drug clinic sample and to provide some information on the impact of drugs on the individual's life. Caution is urged in using the PEI-A with females and minorities given the small sample sizes. Geographic region and urban-rural differences may also impact reports of drug use and should be considered by the test user. In addition, this test may not be useful for individuals whose primary language is not English. The use of the nonclinic scores for comparisons is questionable for individuals outside Minnesota. Estimates of the internal consistency reliability of the scales and content appear good. Additional research on test-retest reliability is needed. More research on the validity of the PEI-A as part of a comprehensive assessment is needed. The PEI-A looks promising, but users are encouraged to heed the test author's statement that this test should only be used as part of comprehensive assessment.

REVIEWER'S REFERENCES
Horn, J. L., Skinner, H. A., Wanberg, K., & Foster, F. M. (1982). Alcohol Dependence Scale (ADS). Toronto: Addiction Research Foundation.

Toneatto, T. (1992). [Review of the Personal Experience Inventory.] In J. J. Kramer & J. C. Conoley (Eds.), *The eleventh mental measurements yearbook* (pp. 660–661). Lincoln, NE: Buros Institute of Mental Measurements.

Tucker, J. A. (1992). [Review of the Personal Experience Inventory.] In J. J. Kramer & J. C. Conoley (Eds.), *The eleventh mental measurements yearbook* (pp. 661–663). Lincoln, NE: Buros Institute of Mental Measurements.

Review of the Personal Experience Inventory for Adults by CLAUDIA R. WRIGHT, Professor of Educational Psychology, California State University, Long Beach, CA:

The Personal Experience Inventory for Adults (PEI-A) is a standardized self-report instrument for use by service providers in the substance abuse treatment field to assess patterns of abuse and related problems in adult clients (age 19 or older). The two-part, 270-item PEI-A is made up of 10 problem severity scales and 11 psychosocial scales, 5 validity indicators, and 10 problem screens; it parallels in content and form the two-part, 300-item Personal Experience Inventory (PEI; 11:284) developed for use with adolescents (age 18 or younger). A broad theoretical framework, influenced by Alcoholics Anonymous, social learning, and psychiatric models, underlies the development of both inventories. The manual presents a thorough treatment of test development, standardization, and validation procedures along with clear test administration and computer-scoring guidelines and useful strategies for score interpretation. The inventory is written at a sixth-grade reading level. No provisions are made for non-English-speaking test takers.

NORMING PROCEDURES. Norm tables were constructed separately for males and females in two standardization samples (clinical and nonclinical). Normative data were obtained primarily from Midwestern Whites, raising concerns about the generalizability of score interpretations to clients classified as nonwhite. Demographic information presented in the PEI-A manual indicates that 20% of the clinical sample ($n = 895$) was classified as minority. Clinic respondents attended outpatient and residential Alcoholics Anonymous-based programs at 12 sites (located in 3 midwestern and 2 western states and 1 Canadian province). No rationale was provided for site selection. A total of 690 Minnesota residents comprised the nonclinical sample; 11% were classified as minority. A sample of 410 criminal offenders (77% were male; 68% of the sample was nonwhite) was used to provide data for some validation analyses.

Caution is warranted in applying the PEI-A norms to members of nonwhite groups in either clinical or nonclinical settings. The test developer is to be commended for briefly acknowledging this limitation. Sampling that includes more regions, broader ethnic representation, and types of treatment program sites is essential.

RELIABILITY. For 1,995 respondents, median Cronbach alphas were (a) Problem Severity Scales = .89 (range: .81–.93); (b) Psychosocial Scales = .80 (range: .75–.88); and (c) three of the five Validity Indicators = .70 (range: .65–.73). When subsamples were broken out by gender, ethnicity (white or minority), and setting (nonclinical, drug clinic, or criminal offender), patterns of reliability estimates were comparable to those obtained with the total sample. One-week ($n = 58$; .42–.78, *mdn* = .69) and one-month ($n = 49$; .39–.72, *mdn* = .52) stability indexes for problem screens were lower than desired due to respondents' exposure to treatment programs during the test-retest intervals.

CONTENT VALIDATION. Common content validation procedures were followed. Researchers and treatment providers rated PEI items intended for inclusion in the PEI-A with respect to clinical relevance and importance to adult substance abuse. Based upon rater feedback, minor item modifications were made.

CRITERION-RELATED VALIDITY. Concurrent validity evidence for the PEI-A was provided by data comparisons examining the effects on scale scores of (a) treatment history for substance abuse among drug clinic clients (no sample size reported); (b) referral recommendation (no treatment, outpatient, or residential) ($N = 251$); (c) setting (nonclinical, drug clinic, or criminal offender) ($N = 1,978$); and (d) *DSM-III-R* (American Psychiatric Association, 1987) diagnosis of abuse or dependence upon alcohol or drugs ($N = 244$). The observed group differences obtained from scores on the 10 Problem Severity Scales supported the view that individuals referred to treatment settings (outpatient or residential) had greater problems with higher substance use, dependence, and related consequences of usage compared to those for whom no drug treatment was recommended. The 11 Psychosocial Scales fared less well in distinguishing among the three groups with only three scales (Negative Self-Image, Deviant Behavior, and Peer Drug Use) yielding statistically significant differences. In a separate analysis, scores obtained from a nonclinical subsample ($n = 687$) were significantly lower on each of the 21 scales (all $p < .01$) when compared with those from drug clinic ($n = 887$) and offender ($n = 404$) groups. For the *DSM-III-R* Diagnosis comparison, clients identified as dependent on alcohol or drugs had significantly higher scores on the 5 Basic Scales when compared to those classified as abusing these substances.

Although the measure is purportedly used to assist in treatment referral, no predictive validity information was presented linking referral decisions based upon standing on the PEI-A scales and outcome success.

CONSTRUCT VALIDITY. Only modest to moderate levels of construct validity evidence were presented based on correlations between PEI-A Problem Severity Basic scale scores and performance on the Alcohol Dependence Scale (ADS; Horn, Skinner, Wanberg, & Foster, 1982) and the PEI-A Drug Use Frequency Checklist. Moderate coefficients were obtained for a sample of 89 clients indicating that the 5 Basic Scale scores were somewhat related to ADS scores (.52–.63, *mdn* = .59) and Checklist scores (.41–.66; *mdn = .55)*. For a sample of 213 clinic respondents, correlations among the 11 PEI-A Psychosocial Scales and 9 Minnesota Multiphasic Personality Inventory (MMPI) Scales yielded 62 out of 99 possible coefficients ranging from .20–.69, *mdn* = .38 (all $p < .001$) indicating, for the most part, only modest levels of shared variance (4% to 48% explained, *mdn* = 14%). Moderate coefficients (above the median) were associated with PEI-A scales that deal with personal adjustment issues (e.g., Negative Self-Image, Psychological Disturbance, Social Isolation, and Absence of Goals). PEI-A scale scores dealing with personal values and environmental influences (e.g., Rejecting Convention and Spiritual Isolation) yielded negligible correlations with the MMPI. PEI-A and MMPI validity indicators also were moderately correlated.

Inspection of intercorrelations among the 10 Problem Severity Scales revealed moderate to strong coefficients posing a multicollinearity problem. It is evident from data reported in the manual that the statistical contribution of unique variance to score interpretation associated with each of the 5 Clinical Scales adds little or no unique information (r_{xy}s ranged from .04 to .09, *mdn* = .05). This outcome was consistent with that reported for the same 10 scales of the PEI. The 5 Clinical Scales were retained "because users have found these scales helpful" (manual, p. 33). The retention of redundant scales requires more detailed explanation than that provided in the manual. For future research and test development purposes, targeting items from scales that contribute unique information for provider applications and removing redundant items would strengthen this section of the inventory.

Intercorrelations among the Psychosocial Scales revealed patterns of coefficients more distinctive of a multidimensional scale (as intended) with proportions of unique variance ranging from .18 to .57 (*mdn* = .29). However, lower reliability estimates and the inability of these scales to distinguish between referral groups is of concern.

SUMMARY. The Personal Experience Inventory for Adults (PEI-A) offers a beginning point to the service provider for assessment. Most PEI-A scale scores demonstrate adequate levels of reliability and distinguish between clinical and nonclinical groups. Current norms may be too restrictive for some settings. Based upon validity evidence provided, caution is warranted in all testing with use of scores from the Clinical Scales, which are redundant with the Basic Scales and with scores from the Psychosocial Scales, which have shown only low to moderate relationships with related constructs. PEI-A computer-generated recommendations for individual clients should be considered in light of these limitations and decisions made in conjunction with other measures.

REVIEWER'S REFERENCES
Horn, J. L., Skinner, H. A., Wanberg, K., & Foster, F. M. (1982). *Alcohol Dependence Scale (ADS)*. Toronto: Addiction Research Foundation.
American Psychiatric Association. (1987). *Diagnostic and statistical manual of mental disorders* (3rd ed.). Washington, DC: Author.

[70]
Personal Values Questionnaire.

Purpose: Measures individuals' "values related to achievement, affiliation, and power."
Population: Adults.
Publication Date: 1991.
Acronym: PVQ.

Scores, 3: Achievement, Affiliation, Power.
Administration: Group.
Price Data, 1993: $60 per complete kit including 10 questionnaires and 10 profiles and interpretive notes (10 pages).
Time: Administration time not reported.
Comments: Self-scored profile.
Authors: Joni Jay Fink and Richard Mansfield (profile and interpretive notes).
Publisher: McBer and Company.

Review of the Personal Values Questionnaire by BRIAN F. BOLTON, University Professor, Rehabilitation Research and Training Center, University of Arkansas, Fayetteville, AR:

The Personal Values Questionnaire (PVQ) is a self-report inventory that measures three value orientations: Achievement, Affiliation, and Power. The PVQ consists of 36 brief statements that are rated by the respondent using a standard 6-point format. The anchors range from *not important to me* to *extremely important to me*. Completion time is 10 minutes.

A brief document titled *Profile and Interpretive Notes* accompanies the PVQ. Included are a scoring key, a graph for plotting the score profile, and seven pages of explanatory material covering these topics: Understanding Your Personal Values, Distinguishing Between Values and Motives, Comparing Your Values and Job Requirements, and How Can You Change Your Values? The interpretive material consists mostly of commonsense discussions that reflect the PVQ item content.

The Personal Values Questionnaire evolved from an unpublished instrument named the Personal Motives and Values Questionnaire developed by David C. McClelland (1988) of Harvard University. The authors claim that the PVQ measures values related to three social motives prominent in McClelland's well-known research (i.e., need for achievement [n-ach], need for affiliation [n-aff], and need for power [n-pow]). In fact, McClelland's research demonstrated that nonconscious motives assessed with projective methodology operate much differently in explaining behavior than do cognitively based value choices.

The scores calculated for the three value scales are simply averages of the 10 items that compose each of the three scales. In other words, the scale scores are interpreted with reference to the 6-point anchored-response format. The absence of normative data constitutes a serious limitation to the use of the PVQ. Also absent is any description of the development of the instrument, as well as reliability and validity information. Unbelievably, there is no published technical manual, even though the PVQ has been marketed since 1991. Staff at McBer and Company did send some unpublished psychometric data, but these were insufficient to support any applications of the PVQ.

In summary, the Personal Values Questionnaire purports to measure three value orientations that emerged from the research of Harvard psychologist David C. McClelland. The authors of the PVQ do not provide any information about the development of the instrument, nor are any published norms, reliability data, or validity information available at this time. No test or inventory should be distributed without an accompanying technical manual. It must be concluded that there is no evidence to support the use of the PVQ in organizational consulting or career counseling.

REVIEWER'S REFERENCE

McClelland, D. C. (1988). Personal Motives and Values Questionnaire. Cambridge, MA: Department of Psychology, Harvard University.

Review of the Personal Values Questionnaire by GARY J. DEAN, Associate Professor and Chairperson, Department of Adult and Community Education, Indiana University of Pennsylvania, Indiana, PA:

GENERAL COMMENTS. The purpose of the Personal Values Questionnaire (PVQ) is to measure three values based on the work of David McClelland: Achievement, Affiliation, and Power. The instrument is self-administered, scored, and interpreted. The material consists of two parts: a three-page booklet containing a 36-item questionnaire and a 10-page booklet, the *Profile and Interpretive Notes*, for scoring and interpretation.

The questionnaire is prefaced with a brief introduction and easy-to-follow instructions. The actual questionnaire consists of 36 statements, which the respondent is asked to rate based on their importance. A 6-point scale is used to rate each item with $0 = $ *Not important to me*; $1 = $ *Of little importance to me*; $2 = $ *Of some importance to me*; $3 = $ *Important to me*; $4 = $ *Very important to me*; and $5 = $ *Extremely important to me*. Respondents mark their responses directly in the questionnaire booklet.

TECHNICAL INFORMATION. No validity or reliability data were provided with the instrument. A call to the publisher yielded several articles on both the theories of David McClelland and the reliability and validity of the PVQ. Two brief handouts (which did not contain authors, dates, or other publication information) provided some psychometric data. A handout entitled *Personal Values Questionnaire (PVQ)* stated that the PVQ was derived from an instrument called the Personal Motives and Values Questionnaire developed by David McClelland in the late 1980s. No further information was provided on the origin of the PVQ. Two studies are mentioned (without citations) in the same handout which describe the reliability and validity data. Alpha coefficients for the three values (based on a sample of 147) are Achievement = .82, Affiliation = .77, and Power = .84. A validity study was also mentioned in which the PVQ was compared to the Organizational Climate Survey Questionnaire (OCSQ) and the Management Styles Questionnaire (MSQ), two other instruments published by McBer. In this study (based on samples of 121 to 123), Achievement on the PVQ showed statistically significant convergent validity with the Rewards scale from the OCSQ and showed statistically significant discriminant validity from the Conformity scale of the OCSQ and the Affiliation scale on the MSQ. Affiliation on the PVQ showed statistically significant convergent validity with the Affiliation scale on the MSQ and showed statistically significant discriminant validity from the Coercive scale of the MSQ. There were no references to the Power scale on the PVQ. It is noted in the handout that these are preliminary data and that further study is needed.

Although the reliability coefficients are respectable, the validity studies are weak. Both reliability and validity are based on studies that are inadequately reported: All of the information cited above was contained in a three-page handout. Establishing convergent validity of the PVQ with the OCSQ and MSQ does not enhance the user's confidence in the PVQ. Both Adler (1989) and Bernardin and Pynes (1989) note that the MSQ has significant psychometric inadequacies that detract from its usability. A review of the last five *Mental Measurements Yearbooks* (Eighth through the Twelfth) did not yield a review of the OCSQ

and technical data on this instrument were not available. These factors indicate that the concurrent validity of the PVQ with the MSQ and the OCSQ is questionable.

ADMINISTRATION AND SCORING. Scoring the PVQ is relatively easy. Instructions for scoring and interpreting the questionnaire are contained in the *Profile and Interpretive Notes*. Each item is assigned a point value based on the response given to that item (i.e., *Not important to me* = 0 points for that item). Each value (Achievement, Affiliation, and Power) is measured by 10 items (6 items are presumably filler items, but this is not explained in the booklet). A final score is reached by dividing the total points for the 10 items for each of the three values by 10, resulting in a score on the original scale of 0 to 5. The final score for each of the three values is plotted in a grid so that a visual comparison can be made of the three scores.

INTERPRETATION. Interpreting the results of the PVQ is contained in four sections of the *Profile and Interpretive Notes:* Understanding Your Personal Values Profile (two pages), Distinguishing between Values and Motives (one page), Comparing Your Values and Job Requirements (two pages), and How Can You Change Your Values (two pages).

Although the 36 items on the questionnaire are general and address many different life situations, the interpretation of the instrument in the booklet is entirely related to the work environment. It is emphasized that the questionnaire measures values and not motives. The differences between values and motives are described as motives being natural drives, which are unconscious and more difficult to change than values. Comparing values to job requirements is accomplished through a 2 x 2 matrix, which juxtaposes a respondent's values that are high and low in importance to job requirements that are high and low. Although not stated any place in the booklet, it is presumed that a value is high for an individual if it is rated 3.0 (important) or higher. A value is considered high in a job if it is necessary and low if it is not necessary. It is recommended to the respondent that "By discussing your thoughts with your manager, you may get an even clearer conception of your job requirements" (p. 7). Beyond this, no clear directions are given for determining if the three values are necessary or not for a job. Four scenarios are provided to illustrate different combinations of personal values and job requirements: high value-high job requirement, high value-low job requirement, low value-low job requirement, and low value-high job requirement. One of the three values is described for each scenario as an example. The booklet concludes with a section that describes conditions under which it may be necessary to change one's personal values.

CONCLUSION. The PVQ has several positive features. First, the instrument is well designed and has a professional appearance and it is easy to administer and score. Second, interpreting the instrument for personal understanding is also readily accomplished; most people will be able to understand and apply the three values to themselves. There are several factors, however, that limit the usability of the PVQ. First, the validity and reliability studies reported are weak: They are based on small samples and the attempts to establish construct validity with the MSQ and OCSQ can only be considered very preliminary data. Second, there is a lack of formal and accessible data on the development and validity/reliability of the PVQ. Third, there are no clear guidelines for applying values to a person's job. Normative data establishing the three values for different types of jobs would not only aid in interpretation but also in establishing the validity of the instrument. Fourth, there is a lack of references to theory and the development of the PVQ. The distinction between values and motives presented in the booklet is written in understandable terms but is insufficient for a full understanding of the concepts measured by the PVQ. Fifth, the publisher should provide a technical manual that would contain all of the needed information enhancing the interpretability and usefulness of the PVQ.

REVIEWER'S REFERENCES

Adler, S. (1989). [Review of the Managerial Styles Questionnaire.] In J. C. Conoley & J. J. Kramer (Eds.), *The tenth mental measurements yearbook* (pp. 461–463). Lincoln, NE: The Buros Institute of Mental Measurements.

Bernardin, H. J., & Pynes, J. E. (1989). [Review of the Managerial Style Questionnaire.] In J. C. Conoley & J. J. Kramer (Eds.), *The tenth mental measurements yearbook* (pp. 463–465). Lincoln, NE: The Buros Institute of Mental Measurements.

[71]

Personnel Reaction Blank.

Purpose: "Aids in hiring dependable, conscientious employees."

Population: Ages 15 to adult.

Publication Dates: 1972–1988.

Acronym: PRB.

Scores: Total score only.

Administration: Group.

Price Data, 1993: $21 per sampler set including manual ('72, 12 pages) and test booklet; $15 per 25 test booklets; $24 per scoring keys; $14 per manual.

Restricted Distribution: "Sold only to companies that employ personnel psychologists or retain consultants qualified to use and interpret psychological tests."

Time: (10–15) minutes.

Authors: Harrison G. Gough and Richard Arvey.

Publisher: Consulting Psychologists Press, Inc.

Review of the Personnel Reaction Blank by DONNA L. SUNDRE, Associate Assessment Specialist/Associate Professor of Psychology, James Madison University, Harrisonburg, VA:

GENERAL. The Personnel Reaction Blank (PRB) is "intended to assess what might be called the 'dependability-conscientiousness' personality factor" (p. 2), and is purported to be useful in "any setting where dependability, conscientiousness, diligence, and restraint are relevant to the quality of work" (p. 2). The intended users of the instrument are individuals making employment selection decisions for companies. Given the massive corporate losses due to blue and white collar crime, nonproductivity, and costs associated with personnel turnover, many companies need instruments to guide difficult employee selection decisions. The manual (1977) contains evidence suggesting the construct measured by the PRB is "more relevant to effective job performance in routine, non-managerial situations" (p. 2). A listing of work groups for which the PRB has provided useful information is provided; however, very little additional information concerning these applications and no information concerning what constitutes usefulness is ever mentioned. The instrument contains 90 items, of which only 42 are scored, producing a single total score.

ADMINISTRATION AND SCORING. The instrument can be administered to either groups or individuals considered literate and aged 15 and over. The manual authors indicate individuals with reading disabilities should have the items read aloud while the administrator observes to assure the respondent records the answers in the correct spaces. Administration should take no more than 15 minutes. The scoring of the instrument involves using a confidential key and manually lining up the item numbers on the key with those on the test booklet and scoring one point for each occasion in which an X occurs in an indicated column. This is a very tedious procedure, and if a large number of instruments were to be scored at one time, the likelihood of scoring error is fairly high. Scorers are cautioned to be very careful during this process and to score each test twice to assure accuracy. A stencil scoring methodology would probably provide more reliable scoring, particularly if sections of the test were scored separately and then added to form the final score, rather than having the scorer "count the correct responses in his head" (p. 4) as advised by the manual authors.

NORMS. Norms are intended to provide information regarding the performance of a defined group; however, the PRB norming group is not specified in any way other than sample size and mention of involvement of "many different cities and states" (p. 5). Several different groups are listed in a table in the appendix; however, the selection methods and participation rates of these individuals and the degree of representativeness to the intended population(s) cannot be determined on the basis of the evidence provided.

RELIABILITY. The manual contains a two-paragraph section on reliability. Two forms of reliability evidence were provided. The internal consistency of the items comprising the test was estimated using split-half reliability coefficients corrected using the Spearman-Brown procedure. The resulting reliability coefficients were quite high for delinquent samples: $r = .97$ and $.95$ for males and females respectively, but much less impressive for college samples: $r = .73$ and $.65$ for males and females respectively, and $r = .73$ for female office workers. Study of stability of PRB scores for a very small ($N = 26$) sample of medical college students over a 5-year delay resulted in a stability coefficient of $r = .56$. This is a fairly impressive coefficient given the length of delay; however, additional evidence of stability of scores over time with larger and more appropriate samples is needed. This test is not intended to assess the conscientiousness of medical doctors. Because the test is intended to be used to assist in making decisions regarding individuals, computation and reporting of the standard error of measurement

(SEM) is an important and necessary attribute. The test developer should report these estimates for potential test users. Given the great fluctuation in reliabilities for different samples, the SEMs will vary dramatically.

VALIDITY. Inadequate evidence is provided in support of the validity of the PRB. I would have liked to see a manual section that described the instrument's content validity via a discussion of the rationale behind the development and design of the instrument as well as the writing and selection of items. The authors indicate that scores resulting from administration of the instrument fall on a continuum labeled "responsibility" with low scores indicative of the "negative, asocial pole" and high scores related to the "positive, conforming end" of this continuum. This, in and of itself, requires thoughtful explication; further, the relationship between these qualities and the content of the items composing the instrument is not readily apparent. For instance, of the 90 items comprising the instrument, 30 seek information about work preferences, though only 12 are used for scoring. Of the 12 items used, it is not apparent how indifference or liking for work as a teacher and indifference and dislike for work as an accountant, life insurance salesperson, or short order cook would be indicative of greater responsibility, and thus, higher scores on the "dependability-conscientiousness" personality factor. Of the 60 personal reactions items, 30 are used for scoring. These items sometimes defy a relationship to the proposed responsibility continuum as well. For example, how an item such as "I have very sensitive eyes" discriminates asocial and conforming respondents on the responsibility continuum really needs to be explained.

Within the validity section, correlations are provided between PRB scores and ratings of work performance; the source of these ratings and the operationalization of "effectiveness or quality of work" are not provided. The correlations are fairly weak, ranging from $r = .20$ to $r = .33$. These low validity coefficients (median = .25) are defended with the observation that "dependability-conscientiousness is only one of the many factors entering into the overall criterion of job performance" (p. 7). It would seem that the appropriate validity investigation would be to correlate PRB scores with some measure of dependability and conscientious-ness, rather than a more global construct. Al-though correlations of PRB scores with about 60 personality traits as measured by standardized tests are provided in the appendix, there is no discussion of the theoretical expectations specified by the developers for these comparisons.

Considerable evidence exists that scores on this instrument can discriminate between both male and female delinquents and nondelinquents. If the user is satisfied that membership in delin-quent or nondelinquent status is an appropriate surrogate for dependability and conscientiousness, they might find this instrument useful. There are probably more efficient means of discovering mem-bership in this population. The manual also includes evidence the instrument is susceptible to faking. This is an important admission for potential users. A sample of college student examinees were requested to take the PRB twice, first honestly and then with instructions to fake responses so as to provide an ideal employment applicant. The results indicate signifi-cantly higher scores under the faking condition for both males and females. There is no question of the differential motivation of job applicants to "look good" to potential employers. Here again, the lack of information provided about the norm group(s) and conditions under which the instrument was admin-istered call into question the generalizability of the results reported, including the potential cut-scores and score classifications presented. This conclusion is supported by results reported in the appendix, Table 2, in which descriptive statistics from various samples used for norming are presented. Data pro-vided by department store applicants, the only group identified as seeking employment, were the highest means reported for both males and females.

SUMMARY. Throughout the manual, the authors provided cogent advice to users on the creation of local norms, and decision-theoretic model data analysis, such as the comparison of scores of applicants who leave or are dismissed with those whose work is deemed satisfactory. Because this is the necessary evidence of the predictive validity of inferences users are most likely to want to make, this is precisely the information potential users should be able to review in order to determine if the test can meet their needs. In addition, the *Standards for Educational and Psychological Testing*

(AERA, APA, & NCME, 1985) state explicitly that the "principal obligation of employment testing is to produce reasonable evidence for the validity of such predictions and decisions" (p. 59). If the test devel-opers and publisher cannot follow their own good advice, I have difficulty recommending use of the instrument. Although many employers legitimately concerned with employee theft have used "integrity tests," such tests have generated considerable contro-versy due to misclassification errors and intrusiveness. Some of these tests have demonstrated considerable reliability but validity has been lacking. The PRB demonstrates neither. If an employer was desirous of such an assessment, perhaps the Employee Reliabil-ity Inventory (12:137) should be considered, because it has been subjected to more current and ongoing technical and validation study.

REVIEWER'S REFERENCE

American Educational Research Association, American Psychological Associa-tion, & National Council on Measurement in Education. (1985). *Standards for educational and psychological testing.* Washington, DC: American Psychological Association, Inc.

[72]
Pharmacy College Admission Test.

Purpose: Designed to measure general academic ability and scientific knowledge needed to begin the study of "pharmacy school curriculum."
Population: Pharmacy college applicants.
Publication Dates: 1976–1994.
Acronym: PCAT.
Scores, 5: Verbal Ability, Quantitative Ability, Biology, Chemistry, Reading Comprehension.
Administration: Group.
Restricted Distribution: Distribution restricted and test administered at licensed testing centers; details may be obtained from publisher.
Price Data: Available from publisher.
Time: (210–215) minutes.
Author: The Psychological Corporation.
Publisher: The Psychological Corporation.

Review of the Pharmacy College Admission Test by MARK ALBANESE, Associate Professor, Preven-tive Medicine and Director, Office of Medical Educa-tion Research and Development, University of Wis-consin—Madison, Madison, WI:

The Pharmacy College Admission Test (PCAT) is sponsored by the American Association of Colleges of Pharmacy (AACP). The AACP is the only organization representing the interests of pharmaceutical education and educators and is composed of approximately 3,000 faculty members from 75 schools and colleges of pharmacy in the United States and Puerto Rico. The PCAT is administered three times during the year in over 100 testing centers in the United States and Canada. It is clearly a high stakes admissions test that adheres to exacting testing standards.

The PCAT contains 270 items, which are scored for number correct. Examinees are advised to guess if they have no other means to arrive at an answer. Items are developed by subject matter expert consultants and staff. Both traditional test statistics and Item Response Theory statistics are used to determine the difficulty and discriminating power of each question. Scores are reported on a scale with a median of 200 and range from approximately 100 to 300. A composite scaled score is reported that consists of an unweighted average of the five subtest scores (Verbal Ability, Quantitative Ability, Biology, Chemistry, and Reading Comprehension).

NORMING SAMPLE. The PCAT scaled scores and percentile ranks are based on a norm group of 2,637 applicants to colleges of pharmacy who took the test on the October, 1992 PCAT administration. The norming sample is clearly not a random sample by any definition of the term. Whether it is representative of the entire population of examinees who took the PCAT in 1992 or in prior years (or in years since) cannot be determined from the information provided in the technical manual.

INSTRUCTIONS. The instructions to examinees are very clear and even provide suggestions for preparing for the exam in a manner that will enhance one's chances of optimal performance. The instructions for the test administrators are very clear and extremely detailed. Common questions asked and responses are provided to help the test administrators to field questions.

RELIABILITY AND VALIDITY. Test statistics are reported for over 3,400 examinees who took the PCAT in February 1993. Scaled score means ranged from 199.2 to 208.6 on the five sections. The standard deviations ranged from 25.2 to 31.4. Internal consistency reliability (KR20) values ranged from .82 to .89 with the reliability of the composite being .96. Intercorrelations between the section scores ranged from .32 to .71.

Verbal Ability and Quantitative Ability had the smallest correlation. Verbal Ability and Reading Comprehension had the largest correlation. Although the reliabilities of the section scores are on the low side for interpreting individual examinee scores, they are probably adequate for most purposes. The composite score represents the highest fidelity score and should probably be given the most weight in any high stakes decision to be made about an examinee.

The data from the reliability study were also analyzed to determine how the influence of a prior course in biology and chemistry influenced PCAT scores. A prior course in either subject area increased scores on that specific subject area; however, there was not a great deal of collateral advantage obtained for scores in the other sections. For instance, examinees who had increasingly greater exposure to college biology had lower mean scores on the Verbal, Reading Comprehension, and Quantitative Ability sections. There are many reasons this could occur without reflecting on the validity of the test; however, these results should probably be explored further.

Analyses of scores based on linguistic background (English vs. other) showed non-English speakers had means on the Verbal Ability and Reading Comprehension test that were more than one standard deviation below the means of their English-speaking counterparts. Scores on the Biology section were also lower for non-English speakers, however, only by about one-fifth standard deviation. Gender, regional, ethnic, and other subgroup differences in performance were never addressed—leaving issues of test and item bias to be potential problems.

The technical manual also provides 16 abstracts from studies published between 1976 and 1985 (a 1990 abstract was a review article) that have investigated various aspects of the PCAT. One study reported the PCAT alone predicted 25% of the variability in pharmacy school grades. Another study found the PCAT accounted for an additional 5% variance in pharmacy school grades after a battery of other predictors were already in the regression model. Although these abstracts provide support for the predictive validity of the PCAT, a more complete description of a subset of the studies in the technical report would help prospective test users interpret the results. Also, the overwhelming majority of the studies were published over 15 years ago. Studies with more recent data would provide users with confidence that the examination retains its validity as test content, examinees, and the health care environment undergo changes.

SUMMARY. Generally, the PCAT is a well-crafted examination for which composition is in alignment with recent advances in health professions high-stakes admission testing. Test security is well-maintained and multiple forms of the exams are available. Administration conditions are clearly described and test administrator instructions are very detailed. Although the internal consistency reliabilities of the section scores are lower than would be desired, the composite score reliability of .96 is well within the desired range for such tests. Predictive validity studies have found the PCAT effectively augments all other information available in predicting performance in pharmacy school. However, the normative data provided in the technical manual is not adequately described, research on the predictive validity of the PCAT needs to be updated with more recent studies, and information on test and item bias according to gender, race, ethnic origin, geographic region, and other factors are currently inadequate. Thus, although the PCAT generally appears to be an effective examination that meets the needs for which it was developed, caution should be exercised in interpreting the norms and using it for making decisions about underrepresented groups.

Review of the Pharmacy College Admission Test by LEO M. HARVILL, Professor and Assistant Dean for Medical Education, East Tennessee State University, Johnson City, TN:

The Pharmacy College Admission Test (PCAT) is a national examination program sponsored by the American Association of Colleges of Pharmacy to provide college admission committees with comparable information about the abilities of applicants. The technical manual states that it is designed to measure achievement in areas critical to the commencement of study in pharmacy and includes not only abilities measured by most standardized admissions tests, but also scientific subject matter in chemistry and biology. It is the opinion of this reviewer that this test does accomplish what it was designed to do.

The Credentialing and Postsecondary Education Division of The Psychological Corporation is responsible for the development, administration, and monitoring of the PCAT.

The PCAT consists of five test sections. Candidates receive separate scores for each test section and a composite score. All items are multiple choice. The Verbal Ability section contains 50 questions, 25 asking for antonyms of words and 25 seeking analogy completions. The Quantitative Ability section contains 65 questions, 25 nonverbal items in the arithmetic fundamentals of problem solving, decimals, and percentages and 40 items that sample various types of problem solving, including applications of algebra and geometry. The Chemistry section consists of 60 questions that require knowledge and understanding of basic inorganic and organic chemistry. The Biology section contains 50 questions that measure examinee knowledge and understanding of principles and concepts in basic biology with emphasis on human biology. The Reading Comprehension section is made up of 45 questions that measure the ability to comprehend, analyze, understand, and interpret the contents of reading passages dealing with scientific topics. Examinees are given one-half day to respond to the 270 test questions.

Materials furnished for this review were a copy of the PCAT (1987), the PCAT Manual of Directions for Examiners (1991), the PCAT Candidate Information Booklet with Application (1991), and the PCAT Technical Manual (1993). The format for the PCAT is excellent; the items are easy to read. The PCAT Manual of Directions for Examiners is a professional document that covers all aspects of test administration. The PCAT Candidate Information Booklet is very informative and complete.

The Technical Manual provides a good overview and description of the PCAT. There is a brief, adequate description of the development of the test. There is also a section in the manual that explains the interpretation of the test results with examples of the score reports provided for the schools and the individual examinees. There is a presentation of normative data that would be useful to deans, admission officers, and faculty in pharmacy schools in making admission decisions about examinees. It is important to note that the technical manual emphasizes more than once that the PCAT is only one tool to be used with other kinds of information in making admission decisions.

Internal consistency (Kuder Richardson 20) reliability coefficients and standard errors of measurement (*SEM*) are presented for each test section score and the composite score for the February, 1993 test administration. The section reliability coefficients range from .82 to .89, whereas the composite score coefficient is .96. The manual reports that these are satisfactorily high; the reviewer would concur with that. *SEM*s are reported in raw score units in the manual. Because the sections vary in terms of the number of items, the reviewer has calculated *SEM*s as percentages of the number of items in the section. Those values range from 5.3% to 6.2% whereas the *SEM* for the composite score is 2.7% (7.29 items on a 270-item test). These *SEM*s are good values for a test that is used to make important decisions about individual examinees.

Intercorrelations among the section scores are also presented; these lend credence to the statement that each section was designed to measure different skills. Those correlations range from a low of .32 (Verbal Ability with Quantitative Ability) to a high of .71 (Verbal Ability with Reading Comprehension). Additional validity data are presented that compare PCAT scores by level of education, number of years of college biology, number of years of college chemistry, test repeater status, and linguistic background.

The final section of the Technical Manual provides an annotated bibliography of the research studies that have been published related to the validity of the PCAT as a predictor of performance in the first year of pharmacy school. The manual states that "Research has shown that the PCAT is one of the strongest predictors of first year pharmacy grade-point average and is therefore a valid tool in the admissions process" (p. 25). The reviewer concurs with this statement. The manual further states that "The Psychological Corporation and The American Association of Colleges of Pharmacy plan to conduct periodic research on the validity and use of the PCAT. In addition, independent efforts by local institutions are encouraged and supported" (p. 25). In light of this statement, it

is somewhat discouraging to note that 12 of the 15 research studies listed were published shortly after the initial development of the test (1976 to 1980); the most recent publication was dated 1990. Perhaps more recent validity studies have been published since the publication of the technical manual in 1993 but, if not, there is a need for new validity studies using the PCAT and other possible predictors of success in the first year of pharmacy school.

In summary, the PCAT is an excellent admission test that is useful in making admission decisions in pharmacy schools. All of the publications reviewed were of excellent quality. There may be a need for further validity studies that will update those published in the late 1970s.

[73]
The Play Observation Scale.

Purpose: To assess children's free play preferences.
Population: Preschool children.
Publication Date: 1989.
Acronym: POS.
Scores: 27 possible ratings: 6 Non-Play (Transition, Unoccupied, Onlooker, Aggression, Teacher Conversation, Peer Conversation); 18 Play, 6 ratings (Functional, Exploratory, Reading, Constructive, Dramatic, Games) in each of 3 areas (Solitary, Parallel, Group); 3 Affective (Positive, Negative, Neutral).
Administration: Individual.
Price Data, 1993: $8 per complete kit including manual (19 pages).
Time: (4–5) minutes per observation.
Author: Kenneth H. Rubin.
Publisher: Kenneth H. Rubin [Canada].

TEST REFERENCES
1. Rubin, K. H., Both, L., Zahn-Waxler, C., Cummings, E. M., & Wilkinson, M. (1991). Dyadic play behaviors of children of well and depressed mothers. *Development and Psychopathology, 3,* 243-251.
2. Asendorpf, J. B. (1991). Development of inhibited children's coping with unfamiliarity. *Child Development, 62,* 1460–1474.
3. Coplan, R. J., Rubin, K. H., Fox, N. A., Calkins, S. D., & Stewart, S. L. (1994). Being alone, playing alone, and acting alone: Distinguishing among reticence and passive and active solitude in young children. *Child Development, 65,* 129–137.
4. Minnett, A., Clark, K., & Wilson, G. (1994). Play behavior and communication between deaf and hard of hearing children and their hearing peers in an integrated preschool. *American Annals of the Deaf, 139,* 420-429.
5. Rubin, K. H., Coplan, R. J., Fox, N. A., & Calkins, S. D. (1995). Emotionality, emotion regulation, and preschoolers' social adaptation. *Development and Psychopathology, 7,* 49-62.
6. Fox, N. A., Rubin, K. H., Calkins, S. D., Marshall, T. R., Coplan, R. J., Porges, S. W., Long, J. L., & Stewart, S. (1995). Frontal activation asymmetry and social competence at four years of age. *Child Development, 66,* 1770–1784.

Review of The Play Observation Scale by DENISE M. DeZOLT, Coordinator of Field Experiences and Adjunct Assistant Professor, University of Rhode Island, Kingston, RI:

RATIONALE. The Play Observation Scale (POS) is an observational system designed to facilitate evaluation of young children's social, cognitive, and nonplay behaviors. Social play includes solitary, parallel, and group play, and considers the target child relative to peers in terms of proximity and attentiveness. Functional, constructive dramatic, and games-with-rules play comprise cognitive play. To select the appropriate cognitive play code, the observer is required to determine intention/purpose of the target child's activity. Nonplay activities include exploratory behavior, reading, unoccupied behavior, onlooker behavior, transition, active conversation, aggression, and rough-and-tumble behaviors. The manual contains brief descriptors with examples of each behavior and a summary page outlining the goal or intent of each codable category within the social, cognitive, and nonplay options. Though not stated specifically in the manual, the POS appears to be designed to assess the play skills of 2–6-year-olds. Little information is provided in the manual regarding the specific purpose and uses of the POS.

ADMINISTRATION AND SCORING. The observer using the POS is instructed to observe the target child for 30 seconds prior to beginning actual recording to familiarize oneself with contextual aspects related to the child's behaviors. Then the target child is observed in 10-second intervals after which the observer codes the predominant behavior in the designated column on an easy-to-use coding sheet. If there are multiple behaviors observed in any 10-second interval, the observer codes the longest lasting behavior. If there are multiple behaviors of equal length, the most mature of the social and cognitive behaviors are coded. To enhance validity of the observations, the author recommends that the child be observed for no longer than 5 minutes per session, suggesting the importance of multiple observations, perhaps in different settings. In addition to the play categories, affective categories based on the type of interactions the target child has with playmates, including positive, negative, and neutral interactions, also are coded. The manual contains brief descriptors of each category and essentially the observer must rely on her or his own judgment of the target child's affective state. Although the manual provides no specific instructions for total scoring, it appears that the predominant behaviors coded, as noted in a total score, are indicative of the target child's current level of functioning as defined by these social and cognitive categories.

TECHNICAL QUALITIES. Limited empirical support for this scale is provided in the manual. Interobserver reliability data (percent agreement from 80%–95%) are available from published materials not included in the manual. In selected publications the author and colleagues have used this scale in several studies examining age, sex, socioeconomic status, and ecological considerations in relation to children's play behaviors.

CONCLUSIONS AND RECOMMENDATIONS FOR USE. In summary, the POS may be a useful observational tool when used primarily by professionals or trained paraprofessionals with expertise in child development and play. For example, it might best be used by members of a transdisciplinary or multidisciplinary team to gather pre- and postdata on a specific child's play skills and for development of appropriate goals and objectives related to specific skill enhancement. It may also be useful in assessing pre- and postfunctioning of children participating in a play skills enhancement group. Use of the POS in isolation is not encouraged. Rather, it may contribute information as part of a more comprehensive multifaceted assessment of social functioning. Given the lack of technical data regarding reliability and validity of the POS, caution is imperative when drawing conclusions relative to normative developmental social and cognitive play status and when making recommendations. In addition, supportive reliability and validity data regarding the POS should be included in the manual when available.

Review of The Play Observation Scale by MARK H. FUGATE, Associate Professor of School Psychology, Alfred University, Alfred, NY:

The Play Observation Scale is a direct observation system for measuring a variety of play and nonplay behaviors. The scale appears to be well grounded in relevant theory regarding children and the purposes or value of play. As a result, the scale appears to be useful for a variety of assessment, intervention, and research purposes.

The current edition of the Play Observation Scale was revised in 1989. This scale was developed by Kenneth Rubin, a well-respected author and researcher in the social and cognitive aspects of child development.

Play is an important childhood activity. As children mature socially and cognitively, specific characteristics of play will reflect these changes. Rubin constructed the Play Observation Scale as an objective measure for assessing the various social and cognitive components of play for children across a broad range of developmental levels. The manual contains a brief explanation of the theory behind the scale. However, a more extensive review of the developmental aspects of play can be found easily in a number of outside sources authored by Rubin (e.g., Rubin, Fein, & Vandenberg, 1983).

In the Play Observation Scale, the quality of play is recorded across three levels: the level of social interaction, the cognitive level of play, and the affective impact of play. The three social levels of play are identified as solitary, parallel, or group play. At the cognitive level, play is coded as either functional play, constructive play, dramatic play, or games with rules. The affective qualities of play are recorded relative to their positive, neutral, or negative implications. Categories of nonplay include: exploratory behavior, reading, unoccupied behavior, onlooker behavior, transition, active conversation, and aggression. Play behaviors are coded at 15-second intervals, allowing 10 seconds for observation and 5 seconds for scoring the observed behavior.

The value of any system for direct observation lies in its ability to estimate effectively the occurrence of actual events. This practical utility is a function of the clarity and relevance of behavior definitions and the appropriateness of the method of interval recording for capturing the behaviors of interest. In this regard the utility of the Play Observation Scale is quite good. Directions for use of the definitions and coding are easy to follow. The definitions of target behaviors are clear and appropriately relevant. Similarly, the method for recording the behaviors generally appears to capture effectively the occurrence of target behaviors. However, it is important to note the recording system may at times underestimate the occurrence of some behaviors.

According to the directions for recording behaviors, in most circumstances only one behavior may be recorded per 10-second interval. If more than one behavior occurs the behavior of longest duration is to be coded. If behaviors occur for equal amounts of time, there is a hierarchical system for coding the most mature social and/or cognitive behavior. This system for recording the occurrence of behavior provides adequate estimates of sustained play or nonplay activities; however, the process may result in underestimates of short duration, but potentially important, behaviors.

Although the Play Observation Scale appears to be a useful tool with potentially broad applicability, the accompanying manual is incomplete and somewhat inadequate. On the positive side, the manual provides the observer with clear definitions of the behaviors to be coded, explicit directions for scoring behaviors, and a number of "helpful hints" for improving coding accuracy.

On the other hand, the manual is generally lacking in psychometric information, and the scoring protocol is poorly designed and presented. Discussion of the psychometric properties of the scale is limited to two sentences regarding the reliability of the measure. In this short paragraph it is reported that interobserver agreement ranges from approximately 80% to 95% and that kappas are uniformly high. Additionally, a bibliography is provided for further reference. Although the manuscripts listed in the bibliography are quite useful for substantiating the psychometric properties of the observation scale, conducting the review of this literature is laborious. It would be helpful if the author would provide a more detailed summary of the reliability and validity information in the manual.

The structure of the scoring protocol is the primary weakness of the Play Observation Scale. Essentially the observation coding sheet provides six rows in which to code the various play and nonplay activities. It appears the form can be used to record only six intervals (1 minute) of play observation. Thus, if one is to observe a child for the recommended maximum of 10 minutes, it will require 5 coding sheets. Managing this amount of paper in an observation session can be unwieldy and inefficient. The poor organization of the coding form is complicated by absence of discussion of its use in the manual.

In general, the Play Observation Scale is an instrument that can be used to measure effectively the play activity of children. Although one must look beyond the manual for psychometric information, the scale appears to have adequate validity and reliability (as estimated by measures of interobserver agreement). The Play Observation Scale will be useful to both researchers and clinicians. Researchers should find the scale valuable for evaluating the social and cognitive development of children as evidenced in their play behavior. Clinically, the scale could be useful as a mechanism for assessing the social development of children and monitoring the effectiveness of therapeutic interventions. However, users of this instrument may need to set aside some time initially to reconstruct the coding sheet to their purposes.

REVIEWER'S REFERENCE

Rubin, K. H., Fein, G. G., & Vandenberg, B. (1983). Play. In E. M. Hetherington (Ed.), *Handbook of child psychology, (vol. 4), Socialization, personality, and social development* (pp. 693–774). New York: Wiley.

[74]
Preschool and Kindergarten Behavior Scales.

Purpose: "A behavioral rating instrument for use in evaluating social skills and problem behavior patterns of preschool and kindergarten-aged children."
Population: Ages 3–6.
Publication Date: 1994.
Acronym: PKBS.
Scores, 12: Social Cooperation, Social Interaction, Social Independence, Social Skills Total, Self-Centered/Explosive, Attention Problems/Overactive, Antisocial/Aggressive, Externalizing Problems, Social Withdrawal, Anxiety/Somatic Problems, Internalizing Problems, Problem Behavior Total.
Administration: Group.
Price Data, 1996: $39 per complete kit including manual ('94, 65 pages) and 20 test forms; $17 per 20 test forms; $24 per manual; $24 per specimen set including test manual and 1 test form.
Time: (8–12) minutes.
Comments: Ratings by individual who has interacted with and known child for at least 3 months; optional additional information section.
Author: Kenneth W. Merrell.
Publisher: PRO-ED, Inc.

Review of the Preschool and Kindergarten Behavior Scales by DAVID MACPHEE, Associate Professor of Human Development and Family Studies, Colorado State University, Fort Collins, CO:

The Preschool and Kindergarten Behavior Scales (PKBS) are meant to be used as (a) a screening tool for the early detection of social-emotional problems, (b) a multiaxial battery for classifying children with behavioral problems, (c) a basis for interventions to ameliorate social skills deficits or problem behaviors, and (d) a research tool. More generally, the PKBS was developed to fill a gap for instruments that can be used with preschoolers. Federal legislation has created a need for screening and intervention services for young children, yet few tools have been devised specifically for this age group.

DEVELOPMENT. Conceptually, the PKBS draws from research on peer and adult-related social skills, and on internalizing and externalizing disorders. The initial item pool was generated from the literature on preschool children's normal and atypical behavior. The 76 items on the final PKBS include many that duplicate either the Social Skills Rating System (Gresham & Elliot, 1990; 12:362) or the Child Behavior Checklist (Achenbach, 1992; T4:433), especially the Aggressive subscale for 4-to-5-year-olds. In terms of both theory and content, then, the PKBS strongly parallels existing measures of early social behavior.

The standardization sample included 2,855 preschoolers, 312 of whom had a developmental disability. Even though recruiting was selective—through private and public preschools, and pediatric clinics—the demographics were well representative based on 1980 census data. Few demographic differences in PKBS scores were observed, although the author's analytical approach minimized the chances that any would be found. For instance, parent occupation was collapsed into four categories and then was correlated with PKBS scores.

Another difficulty with the standardization sample is ambiguity in the unit of analysis. For example, some teachers may have rated multiple children, especially for test-retest reliability. If so, stability could be due to children's reputations and rater characteristics rather than actual child behavior (Cairns & Green, 1979), and the children's ratings would not represent independent units. As well, at least 102 children were rated by multiple informants; it is not clear which raters' data were used to derive norms.

In contrast to the Child Behavior Checklist and related measures, the PKBS does not present separate standard score tables for boys and girls. This decision is notable because, as the author notes, "there is a substantial body of research suggesting that ... girls ... [have] better social skills and [exhibit] fewer problem behaviors than boys" (p. 51). Indeed, the PKBS manual presents ample evidence supporting this conclusion, especially for externalizing behaviors. Thus, it is curious that the norm-referenced tables are subdivided by age but not gender, given similar group differences for these two variables.

PSYCHOMETRIC PROPERTIES. The PKBS has high enough alpha reliabilities (alpha ≥ .90), with the exception of the two Internalizing Problems subscales, to permit use for individual decision making. Test-retest reliabilities are high for the problem behavior area scores (Externalizing = .87; Internalizing = .80) and are adequate for the three social skills subscales (.66 to .70 over 3 months). Interrater reliability was adequate when raters knew children in the same setting, but was weak when examined across contexts: Teacher and teacher aide ratings were correlated .48 for Social Skills and .59 for Problem Behaviors; teacher-parent agreement was .38 for the Social Skills Total score and .16 for the Problem Behavior Total.

Regarding validity, factor analyses of the social skills items yielded the three subscales of Cooperation, Interaction, and Independence. A separate factor analysis of the problem behaviors produced a muddled pattern, with the broad-band solution (i.e., externalizing, internalizing problems) being the most sensible. The narrow-band subscales are less defensible in terms of their factor loadings, lower reliabilities, high correlations with broad-band scores, and absence of data on clinical utility. Factoring social skills and problem behaviors as separate item sets also obscures relations between the two constructs. For instance, Social Independence contains many items related to peer popularity (e.g., "Is accepted and liked by other children" [p. 2, record form]) that appear to be mere inverses of the Antisocial/Aggressive subscale (e.g., teases, calls people names, bothers other children). Correlations between the Social Skills Problem Behavior subscales are not given, although the two total scores are correlated -.56. And though one would expect these two subscales to be related strongly to sociometric status, such evidence was not reported.

Convergent validity was demonstrated in part by comparing the PKBS to the Social Skills Rating System. The Social Skills Total scores were highly correlated ($r = .76$) as were the two Problem Behavior scores ($r = .83$). In addition, the PKBS Problem Behavior Total score was correlated with the Hyperactivity ($r = .85$) and Conduct Problems ($r = .83$) scales of the Conners Teacher Ratings. These results are not surprising given the overlap in item content, but they do raise questions about the unique niche filled by the PKBS.

UTILITY. The norms and validity data for the PKBS do not support its use for screening. Age-graded tables list raw score ranges that correspond to functional levels (e.g., the extreme 5th percentile represents significant deficits in social skills or behavior problems, and children between the 5th and 20th percentiles have moderate deficits). However, there is no technical analysis and rationale for establishing these cut points (cf. Standard 6.9; AERA, APA, & NCME, 1985). The best defense against inappropriately labeling children is to relate classification to diagnostic criteria, yet the PKBS manual describes these functional levels only in general terms: Children with average or better scores have "probably developed adequate social skills" and "tend to be well-liked" whereas those at the extreme "may be likely to exhibit social skills deficits" (p. 22). The manual notes that these cutoffs may produce some false-positive errors, yet no data are presented on sensitivity and specificity nor is there a discussion of how misclassification rates vary with the number of individuals in each category (cf. Standard 1.23; AERA, APA, & NCME, 1985).

Criterion validity has only been assessed relative to concurrent disability status. Children with a disability had significantly lower social skills scores and more problem behaviors, although developmental level was not controlled. The PKBS also discriminated between children in special education and those in regular classrooms, with 90.2% correctly classified. This validity coefficient is impressive, yet one should bear in mind that accuracy in classifying diagnosed students cannot be generalized to screening undiagnosed populations, especially with low-base rate childhood behavior problems. Further, the manual does not provide a rationale for using special education status as a criterion variable—adaptive behavior is only one part of the placement decision—nor were the diagnostic attributes of the criterion defined (cf. Standards 1.12 and 1.13; AERA, APA, & NCME, 1985). More defensible criteria might include peer sociometric status or *DSM-IV* diagnoses.

The PKBS also is recommended as a tool to guide intervention programs, and to monitor subsequent behavior changes, but no data related to this purpose have been gathered. Such information could support its construct validity, and would be theoretically useful in determining whether enhancing social skills concomitantly reduces problem behaviors.

SUMMARY. The PKBS is most similar in content and target age to the Social Skills Rating System (SSRS) and the Child Behavior Checklist (CBC). The PKBS has more peer-related items than the SSRS, but the latter has more items and scales pertinent to social skills. The CBC for young children does not assess social skills but it does have more problem-behavior items and narrow-band scales than the PKBS. All three instruments have excellent reliabilities, though the CBC's internal reliabilities are better for problem behaviors. The primary considerations favoring the SSRS and CBC, then, are their validity and better norms. The PKBS has minimal data on its utility for screening and diagnosis whereas the SSRS and especially CBC have extensive information on cut scores and concurrent validity. The PKBS manual presents no data on sensitivity and specificity, predictive validity, nor test item bias. The Preschool and Kindergarten Behavior Scales ultimately may prove useful in early screening and diagnosis, but only if additional research supports their validity for these purposes.

REVIEWER'S REFERENCES

Cairns, R. B., & Green, J. A. (1979). How to assess personality and social patterns: Observations or ratings? In R. B. Cairns (Ed.), *The analysis of social interactions: Methods, issues, and illustrations* (pp. 209–226). Hillsdale, NJ: Erlbaum.
American Educational Research Association, American Psychological Association, & National Council on Measurement in Education. (1985). *Standards for educational and psychological testing.* Washington, DC: American Psychological Association, Inc.
Gresham, F. M., & Elliot, S. N. (1990). *Social Skills Rating System: Manual.* Circle Pines, MN: American Guidance Service.
Achenbach, T. M. (1992). *Manual for the Child Behavior Checklist/2-3 and 1992 profile.* Burlington, VT: University of Vermont Department of Psychiatry.

Review of the Preschool and Kindergarten Behavior Scales by T. STEUART WATSON, Associate Professor of Educational Psychology, Mississippi State University, Starkville, MS:

PURPOSE AND RATIONALE. The Preschool and Kindergarten Behavior Scales (PKBS) was designed as (a) "a screening tool for identifying preschool and kindergarten-aged children who are at risk for developing serious behavioral, social, and emotional problems"; (b) "a part of a multi-axial assessment battery for formally identifying and classifying children with severe behavioral and emotional problems"; (c) "a tool for assessing social skills deficiencies and behavioral problems for the purpose of identifying appropriate interventions"; and (d) "a research instrument for studying the developing social-behavioral patterns of young children" (p. 1). The test is very similar in format (i.e., conceptualization and design) to the School Social Behavior Scales (Merrell, 1993; T4:2369). The rationale provided by the author for developing yet another behavior rating scale is that, despite the impetus from federal legislation that mandates services for the preschool population, there is a lack of psychometrically sound instruments specifically designed to assess and screen children in this age range.

TEST CONTENT. The PKBS consists of 76 items rated on a 4-point (0–3) Likert-type scale across two broad dimensions, Social Skills (34 items) and Problem Behavior (42 items), to reflect the author's view that children's behavioral development is best understood by these dimensions. The Social Skills dimension was designed to assess social behavior directed toward peers and adults. This dimension is divided, based on factor analysis, into three subscales: Social Cooperation (reflects "adult-related social adjustment"); Social Interaction (reflects the peer-related social behaviors of making friends); and Social Independence (reflects peer-related social behaviors that allow one to achieve independence within one's peer group). Although never explicitly stated, it seems that items were included on a factor if their loadings were .40 or higher and factors were retained if their eigenvalues exceeded 1.00. In looking at the items that comprise each of the three subscales, there does not appear to be a clear delineation between the specific social skills being measured (a point acknowledged by the author on page 4 of the manual). For example, although the Social Cooperation subscale is "more strongly connected to adult-related social adjustment" (p. 4), at least 4 of the 12 items seem to involve peer interactions (e.g., "shares toys and other belongings") and two items are more ambiguous ("shows self-control" and "uses free time in an acceptable way," p. 6). This is not a criticism of this test per se, but a demonstration of the difficulty in summarily explaining commonality between items that happen to load on the same factor.

The Problem Behavior scale was derived a bit differently than the Social Skills scale. First, a two-factor solution was specified prior to conducting the final factor analysis because previous exploratory factor analyses yielded uninterpretable results. Then, a factor analysis was conducted for each of the two factors, labeled Internalizing and Externalizing problems. Three narrow band factors and two narrow band factors emerged from the factor analyses of the Externalizing and Internalizing Scales, respectively. The three narrow band factors of the Externalizing Scale were labeled Self-Centered/Explosive, Attention Problems/Overactive, and Antisocial/Aggressive. The two narrow band factors of the Internalizing Scale were labeled Social Withdrawal and Anxiety/Somatic Problems. Despite empirical support for these two problem areas, the distinction between the two is not clear. Although there are significant correlations within items on scales that are labeled "Internalizing" or "Externalizing," there is also significant correlation, on this test and others, between items on each of the scales (e.g., McConaughy & Skiba, 1993). Thus, separation of specific behavior problems into one of these two categories seems a bit artificial, although certainly not unusual.

STANDARDIZATION. The standardization sample appears to be generally adequate as 2,855 children (1,484 males and 1,323 females) were recruited from 16 states representing the four major geographical regions of the country. The manual provides information on subjects regarding sex, age, ethnic status, and parent's occupation. Three-year-old males and females were underrepresented in the sample (n = 110, n = 89, respectively) when compared with the number of 4-, 5-, and 6-year-olds. Ethnic status of children in the sample was very consistent with 1990 U.S. Census data. For the most part, occupation of the subject's parents closely matched the percentage found in the U.S. population. However, children of unemployed parents were underrepresented and children of "operators, fabricators, and laborers" (p. 37) were overrepresented. Eleven percent of the sample were

identified as either having a developmental disability (8.4%) or being evaluated for a developmental disability or delay (2.6%), which is consistent with national figures for preschool and kindergarten children. This section of the manual could be improved by presenting stratified data instead of percentages falling within nominal categories across several different variables.

Although it is a minor point, the author concludes on page 36 of the manual that socioeconomic status has minimal effects on a child's ratings on the PKBS. This assertion is based on low Pearson product moment correlations between PKBS scores and occupational status scores that were recorded into four socioeconomic divisions (high, middle, lower, lowest). Given the ordinal nature of the socioeconomic data, a more accurate estimate of the relationship between PKBS scores and socioeconomic status would have been obtained using a Spearman rho correlation.

ADMINISTRATION AND SCORING. The test requires no special skills in terms of administration. It is completed by someone who is familiar with the child for at least 3 months preceding the rating period, most commonly parents and teachers, and is subject to the same biases as other rating scales. The protocol is designed to facilitate reduced error and ease of scoring in that the scoring key appears in a vertical, color-shaded column beside the items. Scoring is simple and straightforward in that raw scores are summed and converted to percentile ranks, standard scores, and functional levels. Standard scores, percentile ranks, and functional levels are available for the Social Skills total, Externalizing Problems, Internalizing Problems, and Problem Behavior Total scores. Only functional levels are available for each of the subscale scores. Because the functional levels for Social Skills (e.g., high functioning, average, moderate deficit, and significant deficit) and Problem Behavior (e.g., no problem, average, moderate problem, significant problem) are merely verbal descriptors that correspond to the percentile ranks, they do not provide any additional meaningful information, such as importance of the problem or distress caused by the problem.

RELIABILITY. Internal reliability, the degree to which items on a scale measure a single concept, was estimated by both coefficient alpha and Spearman-Brown split-half methods and ranged from .81 (Anxiety/Somatic Problems, using Spearman-Brown) to .97 (Externalizing Problems, using coefficient alpha). The corresponding standard error of measurement scores were low, all of which suggest that the various scales and dimensions of the PKBS have high internal reliability and low standard deviations. Test-retest reliability was estimated at 3-week and 3-month intervals. Coefficients at 3 weeks ranged from .58 (Social Skills Total) to .87 (Self-Centered/Explosive and Externalizing Problems) and at 3 months ranged from .36 (Anxiety/Somatic Problems) to .78 (Externalizing Problems and Problem Behavior Total). These test-retest coefficients suggest that the ratings on the PKBS are relatively stable over time. Two separate studies were conducted to assess interrater reliability. One compared ratings of 82 children, ages 3–5, by their preschool teachers and classroom aides and the other compared ratings of 102 children, ages 3–5, by their preschool teachers and one parent. Correlations between teachers and aides ranged from .36 (Social Independence) to .63 (Externalizing Problems), and between teachers and parents ranged from .13 (Internalizing Problems) to .57 (Social Cooperation). These correlation coefficients are weak to moderate with the Social Independence, Social Withdrawal, and Anxiety/Somatic Problems subscales and the Internalizing Problems dimension being especially susceptible to source and/or setting variance. That is, some of the scores may depend as much on who is completing the rating form as the child's actual behavior. It is not clear if source variance is a problem for this test or whether the low interrater reliability is an accurate reflection of variability in the child's behavior in the presence of different adults and in different settings.

VALIDITY. Content validity appears to be adequate as the items bear a relationship to the conceptual dimensions of the test and correlate at a minimum level (at least .30) with the appropriate subscale and scale totals. Construct validity was demonstrated by the moderate to high item-scale and item-total correlations, the moderate intercorrelations between scale scores, and the relatively robust factor structure across sex, age, and disability categories. In addition, significant group differences were found for sex, age, and disability

categories, which were consistent with expectations based on the social skills and problem behavior literature, thus providing further evidence for construct validity. Convergent/divergent validity, a form of construct validity, was investigated by correlating scores on the PKBS with scores on the Social Skills Rating System ($n = 86$), the Matson Evaluation of Social Skills with Youngsters ($n = 116$), and the Conners Teacher Rating Scale-39 ($n = 46$). In general, high correlations were found between scores measuring similar constructs and low to moderate correlations were found between scores measuring dissimilar constructs. In terms of concurrent criterion-related validity, the PKBS correctly predicted group membership for 90.18% of special education students in the standardization sample, with the Social interaction subscale being the best predictor.

MANUAL. The author is to be commended for compiling such an organized, understandable, and user-friendly manual. The purpose and rationale of the test are clearly described as is the relationship between the test content and current research in the areas of social competence and behavioral development/psychopathology. All technical terms (e.g., discriminant analysis) are explained so that even novice test consumers can gain an understanding of complex psychometric concepts. The section on "Issues in Using Behavior Rating Scales" is a thorough primer for those who are unfamiliar with the uses, limitations, and best practices in using rating scales. In addition, the author takes the refreshing position throughout most of the manual of not going beyond the presented data in touting the test or in reaching premature conclusions about the usefulness of the test.

SUMMARY AND CONCLUSIONS. Overall, the PKBS seems to be a theoretically and psychometrically sound screening instrument for children ages 3–6. There are some noticeable weaknesses in the test (e.g., stratified standardization data, interrater reliability), but none so overwhelming as to render the test useless. With respect to its stated purposes, the PKBS appears to be appropriate as a screening measure for children at risk of developing social or behavioral problems, as part of an assessment battery for identifying and classifying children with behavior problems, and as a research tool for studying behavioral and social development. It is much less useful for identifying appropriate interventions. It may assist in identifying broad classes of target behaviors, but because the focus is on topography of behavior and not on function, it does not allow identification of potentially effective interventions. The most obvious strengths of this test are its brevity and the fact that it was designed specifically for use with young children.

REVIEWER'S REFERENCES

McConaughy, S. H., & Skiba, R. J. (1993). Comorbidity of externalizing and internalizing problems. *School Psychology Review, 22,* 421–436.
Merrell, K. W. (1993). School Social Behavior Scales. Brandon, VT: Clinical Psychology Publishing Company.

[75]
Preschool Developmental Profile.

Purpose: "Designed to be used to write an individualized education program and to serve as a way of measuring a child's developmental progress."
Population: Children with handicaps who function at the 3–6 year age level.
Publication Dates: 1977–1991.
Scores, 10: Perceptual/Fine Motor, Cognition (Classification, Number, Space, Seriation, Time), Speech and Language, Social Emotional, Self-Care, Gross Motor.
Administration: Individual.
Price Data: Available from publisher.
Time: (50–60) minutes.
Comments: See Early Intervention Developmental Profile (T4:835) for younger ages.
Authors: Diane B. D'Eugenio, Martha S. Moersch, Sara L. Brown, Judith E. Drews, B. Suzanne Haskin, Eleanor Whiteside Lynch, and Sally J. Rogers.
Publisher: The University of Michigan Press.

Review of the Preschool Developmental Profile by DOREEN WARD FAIRBANK, Assistant Professor of Psychology, Director, Meredith College Autism Program, Meredith College, Raleigh, NC:

The Developmental programming for Infants and Young Children—Volumes 1–3 was published in 1977 by the University of Michigan Press as a developmental assessment instrument for children birth to 36 months. Volume 4—Preschool Assessment and Application and Volume 5—Preschool Developmental Profile are the latest volumes in this family of assessment instruments. The Preschool Developmental Profile addition is an assessment-based programming instrument that was designed to write an individualized education program and to serve as a way of measur-

ing a child's development progress. The profile provides information for planning comprehensive developmental programs for children with all types of disabilities who function between the 3- and 6-year-old age level. The profile is intended to supplement, not replace, standard psychological, social, academic, motor, and language evaluation data.

The Preschool Developmental Profile is a preschool programming assessment with 213 items that are divided into six sections intended to represent a developmental approach and order: Perceptual/Fine Motor, Cognition, Language, Social, Self-Care, and Gross Motor development. The manual authors suggest the profile items are based on current research and theory in the various areas of development. The Language section reflects semantic theory of language development; the Cognition section provides landmarks of the preoperational stage of thought, "specifically focusing on the concepts of classification, seriation, number, space, and time; the motor sections look at the continuing development of precise neuromotor control; and the social section focuses on the cultural and environmental aspects of social functioning and contains items which center on the child's developing sexuality" (p. 2).

The profile can be administered in an hour by an experienced evaluator or a multidisciplinary team (teacher or psychologist, an occupational or physical therapist, and a speech and language therapist). The evaluator, according to the manual, should begin the administration of each section of the profile at the age level she or he thinks is appropriate for the child. The manual authors further state this can be determined from observations of the child's spontaneous play, from background information, or from watching the child's play with objects that are scorable at several levels on the profile. Each profile item is scored Pass (P) if the criteria stated on that item are met or Fail (F) when the child's behavior on an item clearly does not meet the scoring criteria. When the evaluator is unable to determine if the child's behavior meets the criteria or if the relevant behaviors are in a developing or emerging stage a Pass-Fail (PF) score is used. An Omitted (0) code is used when an item is not administered due to the nature of the child's disability. The scores are then graphed on the back cover of Volume 5 to provide a visual portrayal of the child's strengths, weaknesses, and general developmental pattern in each of the six sections.

In combination, the Preschool Assessment and Application—Volume 4 and the Preschool Developmental Profile—Volume 5 consists of an assessment manual, a Preschool Developmental Profile, and a series of sample sheet pictures and cards to be used in the assessment. The assessment manual contains Preschool Assessment and Application—Volume 4, a short history of the development of the instrument, the research findings, the theoretical concepts behind the assessment, and a description for administration and scoring of each assessment item. The item-by-item specifications are sufficiently detailed and should enhance the consistency of administration. The manual also contains a section on how to use the assessment findings to develop a program of behavioral objectives. This section should prove to be a rich and useful source of information for developing an individualized education program for a child with a disability.

The Preschool Developmental Profile—Volume 5 provides a systematic method of evaluating a child's skills, selecting appropriate objectives, designing an appropriate individualized educational program, and graphing a developmental profile. The profile is designed to be administered up to four times a year for a single child. The series of sample sheet pictures and cards consists of the picture items that are necessary in the administration of certain items.

A minor limitation of the Preschool Assessment and Application—Volume 4 is that it does not provide all of the materials needed to complete the assessment. The manual contains a list of the materials needed. The materials should be assembled in advance in a small suitcase or kit.

The manual authors describe the various changes and modifications made during the development and subsequent iterations of this profile. Several research projects that were completed during a field testing and validation phase are also described. However, the manual does not contain any information on the psychometric properties of the instruments, such as interrater and test-retest reliability of the instrument or the validity of the instrument.

The specific aims of the Preschool Assessment and Application—Volume 4 and the Preschool Developmental Profile—Volume 5 are to provide the evaluator and/or multidisciplinary team with a developmental preschool programming instrument that can (a) assess a child with a disability, functioning between 3 and 6 years old; (b) appropriately design an individual educational program relevant to the child's needs; and (c) provide follow-up assessments to determine the child's development. These additional volumes, Preschool Assessment and Application—Volume 4 and the Preschool Developmental Profile—Volume 5, of the original Developmental Programming for Infants and Young Children are an important aspect in accomplishing these aims.

Review of the Preschool Developmental Profile by DAVID MacPHEE, Associate Professor of Human Development and Family Studies, Colorado State University, Fort Collins, CO:

This instrument is to be used in writing individualized educational programs (IEPs) and to monitor children's progress toward goals in the IEP. The Preschool Developmental Profile is not a standardized instrument, and should not be used for diagnosis or prediction. Instead, it is meant to supplement information from formal disciplinary evaluations. Ideally, a transdisciplinary team (see Bergen, 1994) assesses a child's strengths and weaknesses in various domains, as well as the family's needs, and then uses the Preschool Developmental Profile to gain an integrated picture of the child as well as to formulate effective interventions. The strengths of the Profile are the synthesis of information on multiple facets of development and the focus on emergent skills as a basis for programming. Many of its items are redundant, however, with preschool diagnostic tests, meaning that a child may have to endure repetitive testing.

The Profile contains 213 items unevenly distributed across six domains; for example, Self-Care has 17 items whereas Gross Motor contains 56. Some items, especially those related to social and self-care skills, can be passed by parent report. Items were selected initially if: (a) they appeared on at least two standardized tests for preschoolers, (b) developmental research indicated their importance, or (c) the authors' personal experience indicated their relevance to programming. For instance, most items on the Cognition scale are unique to the Profile, and were based on Piagetian research and the authors' work with young children. A Piagetian approach reflects the zeitgeist of 1981 but it is out of step with the contemporary emphasis on information processing approaches. This is not a trivial issue. Information processing strategies are the foundation for academic skills (Siegler, 1991), whereas the authors note that, "The items on the cognition section, [which emphasize] understanding of the physical world, do not assess the typical school readiness skills found in most preschool scales" (p. 19). Research supports Piaget's skepticism about the malleability of preoperational thinking, yet the authors do not defend the relevance of a Piagetian approach to early intervention (cf. Standard 1.6; AERA, APA, & NCME, 1985). In other domains, however, the Profile's content is current and utilitarian. For example, the Language section focuses on semantics, consonant with recent research with younger children (Fenson et al., 1994), although pragmatic skills are largely omitted.

The Preschool Developmental Profile does not have a substantial data base to bolster either its construction or psychometrics. Most items were placed in ordinal sequence, in 6-month bands, based on expected ages for comparable items on other tests and on field testing with 92 preschoolers in Missouri for the Cognition section. Scalogram analyses of the Cognition section supported the ordinal sequence for three of the five areas. The small number of children in each age band, and the emphasis on "what is pertinent and vital to a specific child [rather] than ... what [is] applicable to all children" (p. 36), are problematic for an instrument that purports to tap normative sequences of developmental skills. If items are out of sequence, basal and ceiling levels cannot be determined accurately. On a related note, each child's profile is based on "the highest item number of a sequence of passes the child earned on each of the sections" (p. 8), which is not necessarily the ceiling (i.e., failure of all items in a band). Finally, the 6-month bands include as few as 1 and as many as 15 items. Therefore, the Profile may be less discriminating or sensitive to emergent skills than other tests that include more items per age level, and the

ceiling could vary with the number of items in a band or how one defines a sequence of passes.

The Profile manual has no empirical information on reliability or validity. This omission is appropriate for instruments that are intended as curriculum guides but the Profile also is meant to estimate developmental levels and progress. Concurrent validity could have been determined, but was not, because the Slosson was administered to some preschoolers in the field trials. Sixty-eight participants in intervention programs were given the Profile on at least two occasions but no analyses were conducted of 3-month stability nor of treatment impact. Goal-attainment scaling could be used to determine whether the Profile is valid for monitoring children's developmental progress toward IEP objectives.

One section of the manual is a description of how to use the Profile to develop specific IEP objectives. This synopsis of best practice is a strength of the Preschool Developmental Profile. Users are encouraged to examine competencies underlying various items rather than to write objectives that would train a child to perform well on a single splinter skill. The authors also recommend a focus on the whole child—both strengths and weaknesses—rather than treatment for deficits. A holistic approach minimizes labeling, provides the child with some successes, and better prepares a child for school entry. In comparison to the Humanics National Child Assessment Form (11:170), the Profile's stance is more holistic and contextual. However, the Humanics Form does have more detailed treatment plans, especially learning activities and observational exercises that can be implemented by parents.

In sum, the Preschool Developmental Profile synthesizes information on preschoolers' competencies in six domains, which then provides a basis for writing treatment plans. The Profile predates mandates for family service plans and a transdisciplinary team approach, yet its holistic orientation and emphasis on collaborative programming are contemporary. Improvements could be made, however, in terms of its data base and intervention guidelines. Specifically, the ordinal arrangement of items is critical to assessing emergent skills and monitoring progress toward treatment goals, yet age placements were based on a patchwork of intuition, other tests, and field testing with small samples of children. If a primary purpose is to monitor progress toward IEP goals, then validity data on the Profile's sensitivity to intervention should be provided. Finally, the Profile would be helpful in writing behavioral objectives for IEPs but practitioners may need supplementary resources, such as the Humanics National Child Assessment Form, for more detail on intervention strategies. In its present form, the Preschool Developmental Profile is a jack of all trades but a master of none. It lacks the psychometrics to be an adequate diagnostic tool, although it is meant to identify emergent skills and developmental profiles, and it does not have sufficient detail to write in-depth curricula for preschoolers with disabilities.

REVIEWER'S REFERENCES

American Educational Research Association, American Psychological Association, & National Council on Measurement in Education. (1985). *Standards for educational and psychological testing*. Washington, DC: American Psychological Association, Inc.

Siegler, R. S. (1991). *Children's thinking* (2nd ed.). Englewood Cliffs, NJ: Prentice Hall.

Bergen, D. (1994). *Assessment methods for infants and toddlers: Transdisciplinary team approaches*. New York: Teachers College Press.

Fenson, L., Dale, P. S., Reznick, J. S., Bates, E., Thal, D. J., & Pethick, S. J. (1994). Variability in early communicative development. *Monographs of the Society for Research in Child Development, 59* (Serial No. 242).

[76]
Preschool Language Scale—3.

Purpose: "Measures young children's receptive and expressive language ability."

Population: Ages 0 to 6–11.

Publication Dates: 1969–1992.

Acronym: PLS-3.

Scores, 3: Auditory Comprehension, Expressive Communication, Total Language Score.

Administration: Individual.

Price Data, 1994: $98 per complete kit including 12 record forms, picture book, and manual ('92, 177 pages); $22 per 12 record forms (English or Spanish); $59 per picture book; $32 per English manual; $12.50 per Spanish edition manual.

Foreign Language Edition: Spanish edition available.

Time: (20–50) minutes.

Authors: Irla Lee Zimmerman, Violette G. Steiner, and Roberta Evatt Pond.

Publisher: The Psychological Corporation.

Cross References: See T4:2084 (24 references); for an excerpted review by Barton B. Proger of an earlier edition, see 8:929 (3 references); see also T2:2024 (1 reference); for a review by Joel Stark and an excerpted review by C. H. Ammons, see 7:965.

TEST REFERENCES

1. Zagar, L. L., & Locke, J. L. (1986). The psychological reality of phonetic features in children. *Language, Speech, and Hearing Services in Schools, 17*, 56–62.
2. Dale, P. S., & Henderson, V. L. (1987). An evaluation of the Test of Early Language Development as a measure of receptive and expressive language. *Language, Speech, and Hearing Services in Schools, 18*, 179–187.
3. Hargrove, P. M., Roetzel, K., & Hoodin, R. B. (1989). Modifying the prosody of a language-impaired child. *Language, Speech, and Hearing Services in Schools, 20*, 245–258.
4. Handleman, J. S., Harris, S. L., Kristoff, B., Fuentes, F., & Alessandri, M. (1991). A specialized program for preschool children with autism. *Language, Speech, and Hearing Services in Schools, 22*, 107–110.
5. Wilson, K. S., Blackmon, R. C., Hall, R. E., & Elcholtz, G. E. (1991). Methods of language assessment: A survey of California public school clinicians. *Language, Speech, and Hearing Services in Schools, 22*, 236–241.
6. Eiserman, W. D., Weber, C., & McCoun, M. (1992). Two alternative program models for serving speech disordered preschoolers: A second follow-up. *Journal of Communication Disorders, 25*, 77–106.
7. Loeb, D. F., & Allen, G. D. (1993). Preschoolers' imitation of intonation contours. *Journal of Speech and Hearing Research, 36*, 4–13.
8. Thornburg, D. G. (1993). Intergenerational literacy learning with bilingual families: A context for the analysis of social mediation of thought. *Journal of Reading Behavior, 25*, 323-352.
9. Fazio, B. B. (1994). The counting abilities of children with specific language impairment: A comparison of oral and gestural tasks. *Journal of Speech and Hearing Research, 37*, 358–368.
10. McGregor, K. K., & Leonard, L. B. (1994). Subject pronoun and article omissions in the speech of children with specific language impairment: A phonological interpretation. *Journal of Speech and Hearing Research, 37*, 171–181.
11. Nellis, L., & Gridley, B. E. (1994). Review of the Bayley Scales of Infant Development—Second Edition. *Journal of School Psychology, 32*, 201-209.
12. Owen, M. T., & Mulvihill, B. A. (1994). Benefits of a parent education and support program in the first three years. *Family Relations, 43*, 206-212.
13. Plante, E., & Vance, R. (1994). Selection of preschool language tests: A data-based approach. *Language, Speech, and Hearing Services in Schools, 25*, 15–24.
14. Rollins, P. R., Pan, B. A., Conti-Ramsden, G., & Snow, C. E. (1994). Communicative skills in children with specific language impairments: A comparison with their language-matched siblings. *Journal of Communication Disorders, 27*, 189–206.
15. Shriberg, L. D., & Kwiatkowski, J. (1994). Developmental phonological disorders I: A clinical profile. *Journal of Speech and Hearing, 37*, 1100–1126.
16. Sommers, R. K., Fragapane, L., & Schmock, K. (1994). Changes in maternal attitudes and perceptions and children's communication skills. *Perceptual and Motor Skills, 79*, 851-861.
17. Yoder, P. J., Davies, B., & Bishop, K. (1994). Adult interaction style effects on the language sampling and transcription process with children who have developmental disabilities. *American Journal on Mental Retardation, 99*, 270–282.
18. Yoder, P. J., Davies, B., Bishop, K., & Munson, L. (1994). Effect of adult continuing wh-questions on conversational participation in children with developmental disabilities. *Journal of Speech and Hearing Research, 37*, 193–204.
19. Eiserman, W. D., Weber, C., & McCan, M. (1995). Parent and professional roles in early intervention: A longitudinal comparison of the effects of two intervention configurations. *The Journal of Special Education, 29*, 20–44.
20. Guralnick, M. J., Connor, R. T., & Hammond, M. (1995). Parent perspective of peer relationships and friendships in integrated and specialized programs. *American Journal on Mental Retardation, 99*, 457–476.
21. Janzen-Wilde, M. L., Duchan, J. F., & Higginbotham, D. J. (1995). Successful use of facilitated communication with an oral child. *Journal of Speech and Hearing Research, 38*, 658–676.
22. Yoder, P. J., Spruytenberg, H., Edwards, A., & Davies, B. (1995). Effect of verbal routine contexts and expansions on gains in the mean length of utterance in children with developmental delays. *Language, Speech, and Hearing Services in Schools, 26*, 21–32.

Review of the Preschool Language Scale—3 by J. JEFFREY GRILL, Associate Professor of Special Education, Athens State College, Athens, AL:

The third edition of the Preschool Language Scale (PLS–3) is a norm-referenced instrument, for use with children between birth and 6 years–11 months. The PLS–3 includes an examiner's manual, and an easel-style picture manual containing uncluttered, full-color drawings as stimuli for specific items. A record booklet provides space for recording and scoring responses, a task analysis checklist and profile, a clinician's worksheet, and supplemental measures including an articulation screener, space for a language sample and checklist, and a family information and suggestions page. Also needed, but not included are: a sheet of cellophane, a teddy bear, a ball, a shoe box, keys on a key ring, 3 plastic spoons and cups, a child's white sock, a watch with a second hand, and a few age-appropriate toys or books.

The examiner's manual contains especially clear, concise, and thorough administration and scoring directions, supplemented with abundant examples, and instructions for modifying procedures for special populations. Score interpretation is thoroughly discussed, with particular attention to age-equivalent scores.

Each of two 48-item subscales, Auditory Comprehension (AC) and Expressive Communication (EC), includes 4 items (tasks) at each of 12 age levels. Age levels span 6 months, except the last two, which span 12 months. However, raw score conversion tables include four age levels of 3 months each for children in the first year of life.

The test focuses on four language aspects: language precursors (attention, vocal development, social communication); semantics (vocabulary, and concepts including quality, quantity, spatial, and time/sequence); structure (morphology, syntax); and integrative thinking skills. Appropriately, language precursor tasks are found among items for children below 30 months and integrative thinking skills tasks are among those for older children. Many tasks may be scored "pass" if spontaneously performed by the child at any time during testing, even if failed initially. Of 30 such items, 25 are in the EC subscale, and all are clearly identified. In contrast to this flexibility in scoring, the distribution of test items (4 per subscale per age level) is rigidly symmetrical.

The authors carefully describe development of the PLS-3, and field testing of 236 initial items with a national sample of 451 subjects. Yet they offer no data or criteria in the manual to support the selection of the final 96 items, and no explanation for using 48 items for each subscale. More items, not necessarily equally distributed over subscales or across age levels, might more accurately reflect the normal, asymmetrical, and explosive course of language development in young children.

Standard score and percentile rank equivalents for raw scores are provided in 3-month age

intervals for children from birth to 11 months, in 6-month intervals for 1- through 4-year-olds, and in 12-month intervals for 5- and 6-year-olds for the AC and EC subscales and a Total Language (TL) composite. Age equivalents for AC, EC, and total raw scores are also provided. However, linguistically superior 5- and 6-year-olds may reach a maximum raw score of 48, but attain a scaled score less than two SDs above the mean of 100 (5-year-olds) or in the average range (6-year-olds). This suggests that the test may not be appropriate for children of these ages, or that more items are needed for these age groups.

Norms are based on the performances of 1,200 children, between the ages of 2 weeks and 6 years-11 months. Although not randomly selected, the sample (stratified using the 1986 update of 1980 U.S. Census data) approximates the U.S. population for parent education level, geographic region, and race, but not for other variables. Excluded were children identified as: language-disordered; receiving language remediation; younger than 2 weeks of age; born at less than 35 weeks gestation; and those who had "difficulties at birth." About 100 children per age level participated, except for the four 3-month intervals that included about 50 children each. Although equal numbers of boys and girls participated, the authors do not indicate that this equality was maintained within each age interval.

Four types of reliability data are reported. Internal consistency, reported as coefficients alpha, ranged from .47 to .94 across age intervals and subscales. The AC and EC subscales evidenced adequate internal consistency (i.e., coefficients of at least .80) for age groups from chronological age 1–6 through 4–5, and from 1–0 through 4–11, respectively. Total Language (TL) composite coefficients were adequate for age groups above 8 months. Standard errors of measurement, reported in standard score units, varied in consonance with internal consistency coefficients. Test-retest reliability coefficients ranged from .81 to .94 for AC, EC, and TL scores in a study of about 30 subjects each at age intervals 3–0 to 3–5, 4–0 to 4–5, and 5–0 to 5–11. Interrater reliability is reported as 89% agreement between two raters rating the open-ended EC subscale items from a random sample of 80 norm-group protocols (20 each from

3-, 4-, 5-, and 6-year-old subjects). This result from only one pair of raters is not adequate evidence of interrater reliability.

Three types of validity are discussed. Scope and sequence of PLS–3 tasks are offered as support for content validity. Construct validity was investigated via discriminant analysis to determine if the PLS–3 could differentiate between language-disordered and non-language-disordered children. Analyzing the hits and misses results of the discriminant analysis, the authors report accuracy of 66%, 80%, and 70%, respectively, for groups of fewer than 60 3-, 4-, and 5-year-olds. A correlation between AC and EC subscale standard scores of .64 is also offered as construct validity evidence. Three studies of concurrent validity, relating PLS–3 to the Denver II, the PLS-Revised Edition, and the Clinical Evaluation of Language Fundamentals—Revised (CELF—R) are reported. Of 28 infants involved in the Denver II study, all (an unspecified number) who earned a "normal" rating on the Denver II, scored within 1.5 SDs of the mean on the PLS–3. Without more information, this result is meaningless. A correlational study of the PLS–R and PLS–3, involving 29 3-year-olds, yielded coefficients of .66, .86, and .88 for the AC, EC, and TL scores. This apparent support is diminished by small sample size, restricted age range, and the criterion instrument itself. The correlational study of the PLS–3 and CELF-R, involving 58 5- to 7-year-olds, yielded coefficients of .69, .75, and .82. However, the PLS–3's questionable reliability for these age groups and limited number of items undercut this support.

In summary, the PLS–3 examiner's manual is especially valuable with clear, concise, usable information on assessing young children's language. But the test is flawed. More items, more naturally distributed over the targeted age ranges, might resolve reliability and validity problems. The PLS–3 may be used best as a quick language assessment tool for 3-, 4-, and 5-year-old children, but should not be used alone to obtain a thorough language evaluation.

Review of the Preschool Language Scale—3 by JANET A. NORRIS, Associate Professor of Communication Sciences and Disorders, Louisiana State University, Baton Rouge, LA:

The Preschool Language Scale—3 (PLS-3) is the third edition of this standardized instrument designed to assess receptive and expressive language skills with infants and young children. The test comprises two standardized subscales (i.e., Auditory Comprehension and Expressive Communication), and three optional supplemental measures (i.e., Articulation Screener, Language Sample Checklist, and Family Information and Suggestion Form). The results of the two standardized subscales are combined to create the Total Language Score. The changes in the third revision include the three supplemental measures, expanded norms, tasks that target social or interactive communication skills and integrative thinking skills, more tasks covering basic concepts, simplified scoring, and removal of articulation tasks from the standardized Expressive Communication subscale, now assembled as the Articulation Screener supplemental measure.

The precursors of receptive language skills evaluated within the Auditory Comprehension subtest focus on attention abilities. These include measures of attention to objects, attention to people, and attention to language, assessed through tasks such as eliciting a head turn to localize a sound, or following the parent's gaze. At older ages, the Auditory Comprehension subscale assesses vocabulary; concepts of quantity, quality, space, and time; sentence structure (morphology and syntax); and integrative thinking skills such as making inferences. The precursors of expressive language skills evaluated within the Expressive Communication subscale include tasks that measure the progression of vocal behaviors from undifferentiated sound productions through inflected strings of syllables. At older ages, the Expressive Communication subscale measures the expressive productions of language abilities that parallel those on the receptive subscale.

The Auditory Comprehension and Expressive Communication subscales are standardized for ages 2 weeks through 6 years 11 months. The information obtained is recommended for use in identifying language disorders; determining the severity of the disorder; evaluating relative strengths, emerging skills, and weaknesses in language; and identifying areas of language in need of more extensive testing. The supplementary tests are designed to provide additional information about articulation, syntax and morphology used in spontaneous speech, and family, medical, and educational history that can be used when making diagnostic or treatment decisions. The results of the PLS–3 are to be combined with other formal and informal assessment procedures to get a more complete and accurate view of a child's speech and language abilities, and to plan therapy goals.

The test manual contains a detailed discussion of test administration and scoring, test interpretation, standardization, additional test instruments that may be used to explore specific language abilities in greater depth when conducting follow-up testing or planning intervention, and adaptations that may be made for children who are difficult to test. Unfortunately, no modifications in scoring are suggested to accommodate for language differences related to dialectical variations even though many of the items on both the receptive and expressive subscales would be biased against nonstandard dialects. Children from different racial/ethnic groups are included in the normative sample, but because dialectical differences would be scored as errors, they would simply be overrepresented in the lower range of the normal distribution. The manual is clearly written and sufficiently detailed to provide anyone knowledgeable about language and principles of assessment with enough information to administer, score, and interpret the test.

The normative sample on which the standard scores were derived was representative of most important dimensions. More than 1,900 children from 40 states stratified for age, gender, race/ethnicity, geographic region, and mother's educational level were included in the sample. The recommended number of 100 subjects per age interval (Salvia & Ysseldyke, 1988) was maintained for all but the four infant age intervals. However, the sample population was not representative of a normal range of language abilities. Children were ineligible for participation in the standardization testing if they were previously identified as language disordered, were receiving any language remediation services, were at-risk because of prematurity, had any condition such as Down's syndrome known to cause a language disorder, or who had difficulties at birth that placed them at-risk for normal language development. The population that was tested, therefore, did not represent the normal range of language abilities, but rather only a distribution of typically developing children. Because these were distributed along the normal curve, those children falling 2 standard deviations

or more below the mean actually were average in language ability. The resulting norms, therefore, do not accurately reflect the performance of children with language disorders compared to normally developing peers. This problem should result in the overidentification of children as language disordered, when in fact their development is normal.

This predicted overidentification was not, however, the outcome of a study evaluating the construct validity of the PLS–3. In this study, the performance of 85 children with language disorders was compared to 85 matched children with no identified disorders. Standard scores correctly classified all but two of the children with typically developing language as non-language-disordered using a criterion of performance within 1.5 standard deviations from the mean. This contributed to the manual author's calculations of a range from 66% to 80% correct classification of children for the three age levels tested. However, even this moderate success represented an overestimate of the test's effectiveness. Performance on the PLS–3 selected fewer than half of the children tested (i.e., 40 out of 85) who had identified language disorders. The test correctly classified only 36%, 61%, and 45%, respectively, of the groups of 3-, 4-, and 5-year-olds with language disorders. Consequently, the test cannot be confidently used for the purposes for which it was developed, including identifying children with language disorders, and determining eligibility for treatment or special services programs. This is a particularly problematic finding, because children with disorders should have performed far below the criterion level because they were not represented in the normative sample.

This finding suggests that there may be serious problems with the construction of the PLS–3. Examination of the instrument reveals that no coherent model or theory of language was used to support the development of the PLS–3. Rather, each component of language included on the test is described according to a relatively discrete sequence of skill acquisitions. The research supporting this sequence is briefly reviewed. The criteria used for item selection during test construction, and the procedures for selecting and ordering items included on the final version of the test are briefly described. This information is used to support the content validity of the test. However, this content may not reflect the abilities that are actually used by diagnostic teams to identify children with language disorders. Furthermore, no attempt was made to determine how children with language disorders would respond to test items or tasks because this population was purposely eliminated from the field testing. It would seem that in designing a test to identify children with language disorders and to delineate their strengths and weaknesses in language, it would be important to actually include the target population in the development and validation of the test items.

The standard error of measurement (*SEM*) for the subscales is fairly large, particularly at the extreme age intervals (infants and children older than 4 years). The resulting standard score confidence bands, or the range of scores within which a child's "true" score may fall is more than one standard deviation at most of the age intervals. For example, identification of a moderate language disorder (at or greater than -1.5 standard deviations from the mean) is equivalent to a percentile rank of 6 or below. At all age intervals, the normative tables show a percentile rank of 6 could place the child anywhere between the category of a severe disorder (-2 standard deviations) to average language ability (within ±1 standard deviation) because the confidence band typically ranged from approximately 2—19 in percentile rank. Consequently, the results of the test must be interpreted cautiously when making decisions about whether a child who receives a low score actually has a language disorder.

The reliability of the PLS–3 was assessed for internal test consistency and test-retest reliability. Internal consistency was measured by assessing the degree of homogeneity between items within the two subscales. For most age intervals, the reliability coefficients were .79 or above. A sample of 85 children was employed to measure test-retest reliability. The Total Language Score at all three age intervals tested met the minimum .90 criterion recommended for diagnostic decisions (Salvia & Ysseldyke, 1988). At most age intervals, the stability coefficients for the Auditory Comprehension and Expressive Communication subscales also were acceptably high.

The concurrent validity of the PLS–3 was assessed by comparing scores on the PLS–3 with the scores of three other tests of language. Correlations between performance on the PLS–3 compared to the two other standardized instruments ranged from .66 to .88. These results suggest that the PLS–3 measured similar but not identical skills. No information is provided regarding the validity of the comparison tests, and so all that can be said is that the tests are eliciting fairly similar performance results.

Test materials are well constructed and thoughtfully designed. Pictures are colorful and attractive to preschool-aged children. Children from a range of race/ethnic groups are depicted in the drawings. The record form is well organized with many features designed to maximize the accuracy and efficiency of test administration and scoring. Several methods of summarizing and analyzing test responses and derived scores are provided to assist in test interpretation.

In summary, the PLS–3 has many positive features in its test design and scoring. Considerable effort was made to create a language test that could reliably make initial decisions regarding the presence or absence of a language disorder in preschool children. However, findings of construct validity suggest that the test may not adequately discriminate between populations of children with and without language disorders, rendering this test of limited use for its stated purposes.

REVIEWER'S REFERENCE

Salvia, J., & Ysseldyke, J. E. (1988). *Assessment in special and remedial education* (4th ed.). Boston: Houghton Mifflin.

[77]
Profiles of Problem Solving.

Purpose: "An assessment of mathematical problem solving designed for children in upper primary school."
Population: Grades 4–6.
Publication Date: 1993.
Acronym: POPS.
Scores, 5: Correctness of Answer, Method Used, Accuracy, Extracting Information, Quality of Explanation.
Administration: Group.
Price Data, 1993: A$75 per manual (64 pages) and photocopiable masters.
Time: [32]40 minutes.
Authors: Kaye Stacey, Susie Groves, Sid Bourke, and Brian Doig.
Publisher: Australian Council for Educational Research Ltd. [Australia].

Review of the Profiles of Problem Solving by MARY J. McLELLAN, Assistant Professor of Educational Psychology, Northern Arizona University, Flagstaff, AZ:

The Profiles of Problem Solving (POPS) is an assessment of mathematical problem solving for upper primary level school children. It is published by the Australian Council for Educational Research and is part of the Guideposts in Mathematics. Published in 1993, this assessment of problem-solving skills provides an approach to evaluating individual students and entire classrooms. The intended users of the POPS are classroom teachers. Although there would be valuable information gained from this evaluation tool in the process of an individualized psychoeducational evaluation, the emphasis is on classroom instruction.

The POPS comes in a nicely packaged portfolio-style pamphlet, including a manual and a set of photocopy master sheets. The master sheets are the actual assessment sheets provided to the students who complete the evaluation. In addition, student profile and score sheets are also photocopy ready. The manual provides clear and concise administration directions, as well as comprehensive scoring guidelines. The POPS takes approximately 40 minutes to complete. The timing is quite precise because students are guided through the test and provided a limited amount of time (5–7 minutes) to work on each problem. The examiner ensures that all the children engaged in the task are given the same amount of time to work on each problem.

Scoring is centered around understanding the student's approach to the task. This involves five aspects of problem solving: Correctness of Answer, Method Used, Accuracy, Extracting Information, and Quality of Explanation. Students are expected to provide their responses and an explanation of how they arrived at their answer for all of the questions. Each of the six responses the child gives are scored according to these preset criteria. Explanations of scoring criteria for each of the six problems are provided in the manual. Scores are 0, 1, or 2 for most of the questions and categories. Not all of the six questions have specific criteria in each of the aspects of problem solving. Profiles are created for each student by totaling scores from each question and scoring criteria. Each student then has a profile sheet that

identifies them as falling into the category of a beginning, developing, or advanced problem solver.

The process of development of the POPS is described in the "Background Information on POPS" (p. 47) section of the manual. This section provides an impressive description of the development of the POPS and the theoretical rationale involved. A discussion of the development of assessment of mathematical problem skills and its importance to instruction left this reviewer convinced that the POPS was developed based on sound reasoning and has a useful purpose.

A limitation of the POPS is the consumable nature of the product. The authors acknowledge that the actual questions developed may not be used again due to the practice effect that would be involved. The manual does, however, provide information to users that could assist in the development of additional questions for students. The authors also point out that the POPS is designed as an assessment strategy for teachers and a research tool. There are also "suggestions for further learning" (p. 31) that provide specific strategies and methods teachers may consider when planning to improve the problem-solving skills of their students.

The number of children used in the development of this assessment tool is impressive, considering the individual involvement required from each child and the depth of analysis applied to each child's performance. The rationale provided for using the lock-step method of administration is an example of careful evaluation of the subjects' performance on this test. The authors are to be commended for careful consideration of these details.

In conclusion, the POPS is a limited scope assessment of mathematical problem-solving skills of upper primary grade students (grades 4–6). The limit of applicable subjects is offset by the depth of information available for each student who completes the POPS. A teacher has an impressive amount of information about how each student in a class approaches mathematical problem solving once the student's tests are analyzed. The authors point out that assessment typically influences the importance placed on any aspect of instruction; therefore, the assessment of problem-solving strategies specifically could direct the emphasis of instruction to problem solving, rather than rote instruction. The authors provide an excellent justification for the development of this assessment tool and the strengths and limitations of the POPS are discussed in a clear and concise fashion. As a research tool, the POPS provides a well-developed, thorough instrument that would be a valuable addition to a research protocol.

Review of the Profiles of Problem Solving by MARIA MEDINA-DIAZ, Assistant Professor of Educational Measurement and Evaluation, School of Education, University of Puerto Rico, Rio Piedras, PR:

The convenient case of materials for the Profiles of Problem Solving (POPS) includes a test manual; a test booklet (containing a sample question, the six test questions with illustrations, and a student score sheet); an Individual Profile blank card (including three levels of performance with their point scale and descriptions); and a double-sided card for completing a Group Profile and Group Strategies. These materials are prepared in a photocopy master sheet that can be copied for administering to a group of students. A good quality copy machine is needed to do the reproduction work of the test, particularly for capturing the details of the figures and pictures included in some items (i.e., Question 3—Houses).

POPS' six items (the authors called them "questions": Question 1—Medicine, Question 2—Coin Machine, Question 3—Houses, Question 4—Light Weight, Question 5—Dice, and Question 6—Ladders) were designed to assess mathematical problem-solving performance of 4th, 5th, and 6th graders in five broad categories: Correctness of the Answer, Method Used, Accuracy, Extracting Information, and Quality of Explanation. These are problems that require more than one step and strategy for finding a solution, and they cover content concerning whole number and money operations, estimation, patterns, geometry, and measurement. Information about students' problem-solving performance in seven specific strategies (identifying numerical relationships, listing possibilities, estimating, working systematically, visualizing, finding and using patterns, and generalizing) can be extracted. The intention for the POPS was "to measure those aspects of problem solving which involve general thinking skills, used in interaction with well-absorbed mathematical

knowledge on realistic tasks" (p. 48). This may be true to some extent but limitations will be noted.

To what extent the categories and skills of problem solving measured in the items represent adequately those general thinking skills is not well established. The vocabulary employed in referring and describing these skills is part of the confusion. Are these "general thinking skills" (p. 48) equivalent to "broad aspects" (p. 47) or "broad categories of problem solving" (p. 49) measured in POPS? The classification of the student performance in each of the five categories of problem solving measured should be done with caution. The authors also recognize this lack of information for describing completely the student's process of problem solving.

The content and construct validity evidence presented is not sufficient to determine the correspondence and representation in the items of the problem-solving categories proposed. The content validity evidence based on the responses of 15 teachers to a five-item questionnaire is somewhat weak for supporting the five broad categories and the seven specific strategies of problem solving measured. However, in developing POPS as described in the manual, an analysis of the mathematical content of the problems and of the problem-solving process employed by a sample of 60 students was done. Such brief information in the manual is not enough evidence for test validity. Some attention should be given to the match between the meanings of the categories of problem solving measured (e.g., Method Used and Quality of Explanation) and the specific descriptions included in the scoring-rubrics for the test questions.

Although the authors indicate the POPS' problem solving categories and process are parallel to others (e.g., Polya, 1957; Charles & Lester, 1982), there is no empirical evidence to support either a statistical or a logical correspondence among them. Neither is there information about the relationship of the POPS with other mathematics problem-solving tests. Additional evidence for the construct validity of the test is the correlation between the items and problem-solving categories. The authors report that "most scores relating to one item were highly correlated" (p. 58) with Pearson correlations ranging from .35 to .80. Correlations between total item scores were not so high (ranging from -.03 to .46); correlations between total scores in the problem-solving categories ranged from .60 to .85; and correlations of scores for the same categories on different items were between 0 and .41. Based on these results, the construct validity of the test is not so well supported. More detailed evidence, and a logical scheme between what is measured and how it is measured, are needed for sustaining claims for the POPS.

Also, no demographic information is provided about the sample of students who participated in the interview phase ($N = 60$) as well as in the test trial using the lock step method ($N = 200$). The number of students for each grade in the trial sample is not reported. Mean scores of the trial sample are reported for categories and items, categories by sex and grade, and item scores by sex and grade. The test mean score of the trial sample was 28.2 out of 53, and the highest mean scores were in the categories of extracting information (6.2 out of 8) and correctness of answer (7.8 out of 13). Typically, there was a slight increment by grade levels in the mean scores of the items (however, "accuracy" decreased from grades 5–6 and extracting information decreased from 4–5) and of all problem-solving categories. The female students obtained higher mean scores than the males for all of the five categories of problem solving, in every question of the test (except for "Dice"). According to the authors, these results were similar to others reported by Australian researchers. No further explanation and evidence about possible item bias is presented. The generalization of the results of the POPS to other populations is limited because of the sample size, the weakness of sampling procedures, and the lack of representativeness of the diversity of students in Australia. There is no basis for norms interpretations, and in fact, only limited normative data are shown.

Limited information about inter- and intrarater reliability is reported. A sample of 50 student responses was scored by five judges (three authors of the POPS and two teachers). Values of intrarater consistency greater than .95 in the whole test are mentioned but Pearson's correlation results are incomplete. Nor are the exact value of the correlations by categories of problem solving provided. The values of the intrarater coefficients are also not reported. In addition, there are no reli-

ability data regarding the different groups of test takers. Therefore, the authors' claim about high raters' consistency in using the scoring scheme has partial support. Measures of the internal consistency between the items and categories are reported; but they are not organized in a detailed fashion. More specific and organized data about all the test's reliability estimates are needed in order to appraise the quality of the test items in assessing students' problem-solving performance.

The POPS is group administered using a format labeled "lock-step" (p. 11). This means that all students are working on the same problem at the same time and move through the problem together. After each problem is read aloud by the teacher, the students are given 5 minutes to work on each of the first five problems and 7 minutes for the last one. The trial results of the lock-step format were slightly higher than of the "free" (p. 50) format of administration. According to the authors, benefits of the lock-step procedure are a reduction of reading and comprehension difficulties, encouragement of explanation by providing reminders throughout the test, and more time to write explanations.

This test was not designed to be a self-administered test but rather is one that can be designated as a "teacher-guided test"—the test-specific directions depend heavily on the teacher. The structure of the questions and the lack of clarity and precision of the students' instructions in the test stimulate this dependency. This gives to the teacher some space and flexibility to indicate to the students what to do and further, permits students to raise doubts each time a test item is read. The test manual suggests the teacher should address them in an appropriate manner. Obviously, the kind of administration procedures suggested are too distant to be standardized. Students' comments and doubts can disturb the classroom environment for the test administration.

Another issue is that a 5-minute answering period for most of the problems can limit the extent and quality of the students' answers. Why should the students not know the amount of time they can dedicate to work in each problem? Test instructions do not mention that the teacher should indicate the time allotted to answer each question but only when the time allowed for answering each test problem is finished (after 5 or 7 minutes).

The students can have (depending on the teacher) the opportunity to review and complete "a few" (p. 16) questions. How many are few? What about a student who does not have time to do all the questions and needs extra time to think and work them out? The administration time suggested is 32 minutes for testing and 40 minutes as total time. But the real time that students of different grade levels (grades 4, 5, and 6) will need to answer them appropriately should be noted. A minor point is where to write the answers. Each item includes a rectangle labeled "answer" (except in Items 4 and 5) inside which the students should write their response. In Items 4 ("Light weight") and 5 ("Dice") a drawing is requested as an answer. These rectangles guide the examinees to highlight the answer to the question.

The authors claim that a unique feature of the POPS is that the students have to explain their method of solution and in order to facilitate this the lock-step administration format is used. The test manual indicates the teacher should emphasize that the student's work should be clearly presented but that neatness and spelling will not count. Also, in some items the teacher should emphasize the need for explanations (Questions 3, 4, and 6). A main concern is what the authors mean by a written explanation, its extension and characteristics, and what they mean by "worked out the answer" (p. 15). They point out the importance of the explanation but do not provide specific information and examples about what is expected.

Six tables including the scoring rubrics for each problem are supplied. The answers are totally or partially scored in terms of the five categories of problem solving measured. Although the rubrics are adequate in describing the features of the expected answers, some additional explanation may be needed about how to use them appropriately. Another issue in the scoring procedure is that all five categories are not used in some questions. This problem is exacerbated when each rubric shows specific meanings or descriptions for the categories. An example in the manual may help to see the scoring mechanics and the use of the rubrics, particularly in cases involving a combination of different scores in the five categories.

Each of the problem-solving categories differ in the number of points assigned (13, 14, 10, 8, and 8, respectively) and also in the spread of the scores along a continuum. This is determined by the difficulty of the category. The individual's scores are recorded on the Student Score Sheet, the totals for each of the five categories calculated, and then the results transferred to the Individual Profile form. The student's total scores across the problem-solving categories are joined in order to give a visual picture of her or his position in the three levels of "development" (p. 25) in problem solving: beginning, developing, and advanced. A description of each level is included on the back of the Individual Profile. A Group profile can be constructed from each individual's profile. Also, the answers to the POPS questions can be scored according to the seven specific strategies of problem solving proposed. Due to the limited data available for each student, the authors recommend that only group data should be collected for these strategies.

SUMMARY. The POPS represents an important attempt to measure general aspects of mathematical problem-solving performance. Despite the conceptual and technical flaws mentioned, it seems more suitable for classroom use and teaching purposes than for large-scale testing. Using the results with caution, mathematics teachers can use the POPS for screening students' problem-solving approaches. Its diagnostic information is limited. A valuable asset of the POPS is a section of suggestions for instructional activities related to the specific problem-solving categories measured, and a list of references and resources. The three criteria for selecting the problems (i.e., multi-step, familiarity, and time-on-task) should be closely checked for the users of this test with particular populations of students inside and outside of Australia because of the variety of their school experiences, and of the language and context of the problems.

REVIEWER'S REFERENCES
Polya, G. (1957). *How to solve it: A new aspect of mathematical method.* Garden City, NY: Doubleday.
Charles, R., & Lester, F. (1982). *Teaching problem solving: What, why and how.* Palo Alto, CA: Dale Seymour.

[78]

Progressive Achievement Test of Listening Comprehension [Revised].

Purpose: "Intended ... to assist teachers in determining levels of development attained by their students in the basic skills of listening comprehension."
Population: Standards 1–4 and Forms 1–4 (ages 7–14) in New Zealand school system.

Publication Dates: 1971–1994.
Acronym: PAT: Listening Comprehension.
Scores: Total score only.
Administration: Group.
Levels: 8 overlapping levels labeled Parts 1–8: Primary: Parts 1–4 (Standards 1–4); Intermediate: Parts 5–6 (Forms 1–2); Secondary: Parts 7–8 (Forms 3–4).
Price Data, 1995: $1.53 per Primary, Intermediate, or Secondary test booklet; $4.05 per Primary, Intermediate, or Secondary teacher's script; $.72 per scoring key; $1.35 per 10 answer sheets; $8.10 per Intermediate audiotape; $9 per Secondary audiotape; $5.85 per teacher's manual ('94, 32 pages).
Time: (55) minutes.
Comments: 2 forms (A & B) available (Form A is used in odd-numbered years and Form B is used in even-numbered years); this test was specifically developed for use in New Zealand schools.
Authors: Neil A. Reid, Ian C. Johnston, and Warwick B. Elley.
Publisher: New Zealand Council for Educational Research [New Zealand].
Cross References: See T4:2140 (2 references) and T3:1910 (1 reference); for a review by Roger A. Richards, see 8:453 (2 references).

TEST REFERENCE

1. Chapman, J. W. (1988). Cognitive-motivational characteristics and academic achievement of learning disabled children: A longitudinal study. *Journal of Educational Psychology, 80,* 357–365.

Review of the Progressive Achievement Test of Listening Comprehension [Revised] by SHERWYN MORREALE, Chair, Center for Excellence in Oral Communication, University of Colorado at Colorado Springs, Colorado Springs, CO, and PHILIP BACKLUND, Associate Dean and Professor of Speech Communication, Communication Department, Central Washington University, Ellensburg, WA:

The introduction to this test clearly states its general purpose, to assist teachers in the New Zealand school system in assessing students' listening comprehension skills. The test is limited in that it can only be used in New Zealand, though it could be tested for use elsewhere or could act as a format for developing other tests. Five specific functions for the instrument include: identifying children with inadequate listening skills; locating areas of weakness and strength within a class; helping teachers and students recognize the importance of listening skills and the need for instruction; providing a broad estimate of reading expectancy; and providing a measure of general verbal ability. The last two applications must be considered indirect functions of this test. Adequate rationale for the instrument is grounded in the academic literature on listening. The description of the test indicates a careful process of development that has resulted in a well-structured assessment instrument. The testing materials are thorough, well organized, well written, and relatively easy to use.

Procedural instructions for administering and scoring the test are comprehensive, clarifying its use exactly. Cautions are included for the user to replicate the procedures with precision to avoid invalidating the results. Similar cautions for interpreting the test results suggest that no test score is perfectly accurate and scores only estimate students' ability. Given these cautions, ample instructions and materials for interpreting students' scores on this test are provided. Students' raw scores indicate their level of achievement on an 11-point scale, ranging from very limited ability to a very advanced degree of competency in listening comprehension. Students' raw scores can be converted to percentile rank norms that indicate how that score compares with other students of the same age and of the same class level. Excellent guidelines are outlined for reporting test results to students and parents and for using test results of listening levels in a class to redirect teaching. More cautions for using the test suggest that: Results obtained are only estimates; national norms provided are benchmarks to inform teaching, not absolute standards expected of all students; results should be used to improve instruction and measure growth; the instrument assesses skills attainment, it does not diagnose individual weaknesses; and, the results should not be used to evaluate teaching effectiveness.

The present version of the Progressive Achievement Test of Listening Comprehension (PAT: Listening Comprehension) is the result of a careful process of development, construction, revision, and item selection that began in 1969. An array of panels and review committees, teachers, advisers, and specialists in reading and language contributed to the construction and revision processes. The only shortcoming in an otherwise careful development process would be the lack of involvement of scholars with specific background in listening and speech communication.

In 1992, the present version of the instrument was tested in 76 different schools in New Zealand and then subjected to item analyses, which resulted in two equivalent forms of the tool for each of eight class levels. The development process was followed by other investigations and surveys, the results of which were used to revise the test before its standardization. For example, to more closely approximate the real-life listening experiences of students, the final version of the instrument was revised to contain less formal material, more material from radio and TV, and more peer-originated material.

The size and representativeness of the sample used to obtain nationally standardized norms for this test were both satisfactory. The test was administered to a systematically selected, representative sample of 1,000 students at each of the eight class levels. Class percentile rank norms were calculated by class and sex. Age percentile rank norms were calculated at each level in half-year age groups.

Reliability, the stability and consistency of this test, was examined using appropriate statistical methods and yielded satisfactory findings. The reliability of the relationship between two forms of the test was examined for all eight levels. Reliability coefficients for equivalent forms ranged between .77 and .84. The internal consistency of the tool was examined by calculating split-half reliability coefficients that ranged between .85 and .90. Another estimate of internal consistency, based on the difficulty level of each item, yielded coefficients ranging from .81 to .88. The mean scores of these three reliability estimates were used to calculate standard errors of measurement for both forms of the instrument at each of the eight levels. These estimates, of the extent to which the score obtained on the test would differ from a hypothetical true score, ranged from 2.6 to 3.3.

Validity, the extent to which this test measures what it intends, also was examined satisfactorily. The content validity of the test is supported by the manner in which it was planned and constructed. It is argued that the test assesses listening skills and abilities widely accepted as important by a representative group of teachers and advisers. Also the test's items were scrutinized by practicing teachers and reading and language specialists. Consensus of informed opinion is used to speak to the high content validity of the tool. The concurrent validity of the test is supported by studies that indicate the PAT: Listening Comprehension test correlates highly with tests of a similar kind developed in other countries, despite differences in emphasis and cultural background. The PAT: Listening Comprehension test correlated positively with tests of listening comprehension and scholastic abilities such as the Stanford Achievement Test ($r = .78$ and $r = .82$); and the Test of Scholastic Abilities ($r = .70$, $r = .62$, $r = .50$). Finally the construct validity of the PAT: Listening Comprehension test was investigated during various stages of its development. Those tests consistently supported the convergent-discriminant validity of the tool.

Item bias checks of the PAT: Listening Comprehension test related to gender, ethnicity, and other types of bias. Two approaches to detecting item bias took place during the trial testing phase of test development in 1992. A subjective review of the test's items was conducted by teacher/specialist panels to examine possible bias in language, subject matter, and the representation of people in ways that might be offensive or discriminatory. Any suspect passages or items were either modified or rejected. Objective statistical analysis of ethnic item bias was also conducted. The tentative final forms of the test were administered to samples of students in different parts of the country known to have significant ethnic mix. The two approaches to item bias frequently identified different items as differentiating between ethnic groups but most differences were marginal and not consistent across class levels.

The above examinations for reliability, validity, and bias were conducted with care. The results suggest that the PAT: Listening Comprehension test measures, with stability and accuracy, that which it claims to measure, doing so without any detected bias. Additionally, the presentation of these examinations in the teacher's manual is clear and easy to understand. The only recommendations that might be offered are minor. For example, longitudinal data, measuring the instrument's predictive ability, are not reported. And the examination of the instrument's construct validity began on an early version of the instrument, an instrument that underwent changes before reaching its final form. Bias analysis was performed on the items during the instrument's development. A study of ethnic bias, related to the instrument's use, also would be informative. Other than these minor concerns, this instrument is to be lauded for its careful development and thorough presentation to the user.

[79]
Revised PSB—Aptitude for Practical Nursing Examination.

Purpose: Designed as a "method of selection, placement, guidance and counseling of incoming [practical/vocational nursing] students."
Population: Applicants for admission to practical/vocational nursing schools.
Publication Dates: 1961–1990.
Scores, 8: Academic Aptitude (Verbal, Numerical, Nonverbal, Total), Spelling, Natural Sciences, Judgment in Practical Nursing Situations, Vocational Adjustment Index.
Administration: Individual or group.
Price Data, 1993: $7 per test booklet; $15 per technical manual ('90, 86 pages); $15 per specimen set including test booklet, answer sheet, and administrator's manual ('90, 4 pages); $7 per student for scoring and reporting services.
Time: (135) minutes.
Comments: Earlier edition, now known as Original PSB—Aptitude for Practical Nursing Examination, is still available.
Authors: Anna S. Evans, Phyllis G. Roumm, and George A. W. Stouffer, Jr., with technical assistance from Psychological Services Bureau, Inc.
Publisher: Psychological Services Bureau, Inc.

Review of the Revised PSB—Aptitude for Practical Nursing Examination by MARK ALBANESE, Associate Professor, Preventive Medicine and Director, Office of Medical Education Research and Development, University of Wisconsin-Madison, Madison, WI:

The PSB—Aptitude for Practical Nursing Examination (PSB-APNE) was revised in 1991. The test itself dates from 1959 and is designed to aid schools of Practical Nursing in selecting from among their applicants those with the highest likelihood of success in the program. U.S. Bureau of Labor Statistics project rapid growth in the demand for Practical Nurses, suggesting that the Revised PSB-APNE may be in even greater demand if the number of applicants to practical nursing schools increases in a like manner.

The Revised PSB-APNE reports scores derived from simply summing the number of items answered correctly on five subtests. The examination was revised in 1991 to incorporate suggestions derived from research conducted over the 30 years since its conception. The revised examination has fewer items than the older version (370 vs. 450) and two of the five subscores have been redefined, although they bear substantial similarities to the earlier version.

The technical report states that "studies indicate that better than 90% of the examinees will complete the test within the limits of the time allowed for each test" (p. 14). The authors do not support unlimited testing time because the educational program expects students to "assimilate a large body of knowledge in a rather limited length of time" (p. 15). Thus, unlimited testing time was considered "inimical to the purposes of the testing" (p. 15). This position may be difficult to sustain in the face of students with learning disabilities and mandates under the Americans With Disabilities Act.

The test itself is a relatively radical departure from the typical admissions test to a health professions school. Rather than the usual battery of science-related subtests coupled with a reading and quantitative section (and perhaps a writing sample), this examination approaches its task from a very different angle. A Spelling test in which the examinee is to select the word with the proper spelling from among a list of three different spellings of the word is used to estimate verbal fluency. This is an obvious departure from the more common verbal analogies approach and seems somewhat simplistic.

Perhaps the most innovative aspect of the examination is the Judgment and Comprehension in Practical Nursing Situations subtest. The objective of this subtest is to "measure the ability of the individual to arrive at wise decisions and to behave with discretion and discernment" (p. 19). Questions in this section pose a nursing situation such as a patient telling the "practical nurse" they have pain and would like some pain medication. The examinee is then asked to select which of four courses of action would be best. The questions in this section have a logical feel about them and the correct answers seem to have detectable features; however, it is not clear how the correct answers were decided upon. A problem with questions that ask examinees to exercise judgment is that there may not be total agreement among content experts about what constitutes the "best" answer. In the test description, it is not clear how the correct answer was determined. At the very least, a test of this type should demonstrate evidence of agreement among experts that the correct answer is indeed the "best" approach to a situation.

The Vocational Adjustment Index is another innovative component of this examination. The 90 statements that ask the examinee to agree or disagree purport to "provide insight into the examinee's characteristic life style—their feelings, attitudes and opinions" (p. 20). The questions were based upon factors listed by program administrators, supervisors, and instructors, which were "felt to be desirable and important for the practical nurse to possess during the education period and, subsequently, in the working situation" (p. 20). This process (and more information on the details of this process would be helpful) led to eight factors being identified: (a) Attitude Toward Cooperation with Others, (b) Concern for the Welfare of Others, (c) Freedom for Nervous Tendencies, (d) Attitude Toward Authority, (e) Attitude Toward Health, (f) Occupational Stability, (g) Leadership Ability, and (h) Self-reliant. The only data reported supporting the validity of the Vocational Adjustment Index is a correlation of .73 with scores on the ETSA 8A Personal Adjustment Index based on 48 examinees. Given that there were eight factors used in developing the scale, it would be very helpful to have factor analysis data that would support reporting a single overall score; however, none is reported.

NORMING DATA. The authors (in personal communication) report "tentative" norming data from a sample of 3,669 examinees who were selected to be representative of: (a) nine regions into which the United States was divided, (b) urban and rural areas, (c) differing cultural and socioeconomic settings, and (d) differing ethnic and racial composition. The norming sample from 71 nursing programs constituted approximately 6% of approximately 1,128 schools/programs of practical nursing in the United States. According to the test developers, only tentative data are provided in the norms in the technical manual in order to keep users from simply copying the exam and using

it without purchasing the materials. Judging from subsequent reports of data, the tentative norms in the technical manual have means that are substantially below that of the actual norms. Updated norms are periodically sent to user schools/programs.

The technical report provides results from a series of reliability studies conducted with random subsamples from the norming group. Test-retest reliability (stability) for a subsample of 126 with a time interval ranging from 10 to 30 days between successive testing were between .89 and .98 for the various subtests. Internal consistency reliability values ranged from .91 to .98 for a subsample of 155 examinees. Intercorrelations among the various subtests ranged from .05 to .27 for a subsample of 126 examinees. Comparisons of the random samples to the larger norming sample showed that there was over twice the percentage of the sample drawn from the 16–20-year-old age group than for the larger norming sample (41.2% vs. 19.4%), suggesting some bias may be present.

The technical report also summarizes results of a series of criterion-related validity studies. Concurrent validity coefficients between the Verbal subtest and the Arithmetic subtest (two parts of the academic aptitude score) correlated with comparable scales on School and College Ability Test .86 and .81, respectively, for 83 examinees. Scores for Academic Aptitude correlated .92 with scores from the Wechsler Adult Intelligence Scale for 48 examinees. Correlations of each of the Revised PSB-APNE scores with cumulative GPA in 11 Practical Nursing schools produced mean predictive validity coefficients ranging from .61 to .83. Correlations between the Revised PSB-APNE subtests and Licensing Examination Scores of a sample of 64 examinees (the Licensing Examination was taken 5 years after the Revised PSB-APNE was taken) ranged from .34 to .58. Correlations between the Revised PSB-APNE subscores and the graduating class rank of 29 examinees ranged from .46 to .63. The authors report a study of minority and majority examinees, which produced means that were not different by a statistically significant margin. There were also no statistically significant gender differences reported.

CRITIQUE. The Revised PSB-APNE is an updated version of a test that has seen valuable use for over 30 years. The authors have made a laudable attempt to address earlier weaknesses in the norming sample and in improving test items that were ambiguous and in some cases obsolete. The various scores derived from the examination have a great deal of common sense value about them, although some seem to be simplistic (e.g., spelling). the Judgment and Comprehension in Practical Nursing Situations and Vocational Adjustment Index are impressive attempts to include more than just cognitive abilities into the selection criteria. However, interjudge agreement for the keyed responses on the former exam and a factor analysis of data demonstrating support for the reporting of a single score for the latter exam would help improve their credibility. The internal consistency and test-retest reliability values reported for the various subtests meet or exceed most accepted thresholds for standardized tests. The relative lack of intercorrelation between the subtest scores suggest they are relatively independent of one another. The criterion-related validity data presented suggests that the examination predicts to a surprisingly high degree the school performance that it is attempting to anticipate. It even predicts licensing examination performance 5 years later to a surprisingly high degree. Studies reporting little differences in scores according to gender and minority status are also impressive strengths of the examination.

Although the examination has considerable strengths, there are some concerns. First, the directions to test administrators are relatively sparse and are not organized in a cohesive manner. A significant omission is what to do about examinees who come late. The lack of multiple forms may become or may already be a problem. If the examination is used by any school as a mechanism to exclude applicants, it becomes a high stakes examination for some students. As a consequence, security becomes an issue and the need for multiple forms and tight controls on administration become important. If schools are only using it as a mechanism for assessing readiness for portions of the curriculum and whether students should engage in remedial work prior to beginning the program, the need for multiple forms and security measures is less critical. However, even if there is no current need for security, it may be necessary in the future. Any school using the examination needs to give thought as to whether security is an issue for them and whether this examination is sufficiently secure.

The lack of data on interjudge agreement on the key for the Judgment and Comprehension Subscale and factor analysis to support the construct validity of the Vocational Adjustment Scale are weaknesses that need to be remedied.

The test and the technical bulletin have the look of an old examination (50s–70s). The technical bulletin has some typographical errors and would be more impressive if it had the appearance of being typeset, instead of being typed on a manual typewriter (on the first page the type font changed at midpage). The authors have rigorously applied classical test theory procedures to the development of the examination; however, it would give a more polished presentation if some of the more recently developed testing theory models were also incorporated, such as generalizability theory.

The credibility of the normative data presented and the research data regarding reliability and validity is compromised by the fact that the authors present only "tentative" norming data in the technical manual. Reporting norming data that are not accurate in the technical manual creates several problems. First, the illustrative normative data are substantially different from the data reported in the substudies that are described as being drawn from the normative sample. For instance, on the test-retest reliability data for 126 examinees, the mean on the Judgment and Comprehension Practical Nursing Situations was 37.60 (*SD* = 6.1). For the norming data, the median was 29.5). Because the distribution of the norming data was stated to be symmetric, the mean should be close to this value, suggesting that the sample used to obtain the reliability data was substantially different from the norm data. The technical manual states that the reliability subsamples were "a random sample of 126 examinees in the total number of examinees participating in the norming program" (p. 50), making these discrepancies raise serious questions about veracity of the studies reported in support of the reliability and validity of the examination. Results from the various other substudies also show means that are quite markedly different from one another as well as the norming data (means differing by more than 1 standard deviation), raising further questions about the reliability and validity data.

The technical manual needs to be more clear about the fact that the normative data are not related to the studies that are subsequently reported upon and in fact are quite different from the actual norms and should absolutely not be used in interpreting scores that are reported. Perhaps "sample" should be printed diagonally across the page to reinforce the footnote that indicates that the tabulated data are illustrative. The danger in having users actually use the tentative norms for interpreting scores is that the means are substantially lower than must be the case for the real norms. This would give the impression that applicants were performing at much higher levels than they actually were. Thus, an admissions officer who inadvertently misplaced current norms and turned to the technical manual for interpreting raw scores from an applicant pool could be deluded into believing the applicant pool is substantially better than it is in actual fact. This could lead the admissions committee to make decisions they would later regret.

SUMMARY. The Revised PSB-APNE appears to be a very useful instrument for appropriate placement, advisement, and for use in the establishment of realistic goals for students entering practical nursing programs. Over 30 years of research have resulted in a test that produces scores with high internal consistency and test-retest reliabilities, relatively low intercorrelations, and impressive predictive validity estimates. However, the lack of multiple forms, relatively weak security, misleading tentative norms in the technical bulletin, and inconsistent data reported across studies raise questions about its appropriate use for high stakes admissions and selection.

Review of the Revised PSB–Aptitude for Practical Nursing Examination by ANITA TESH, Assistant Professor, School of Nursing, University of North Carolina at Greensboro, Greensboro, NC:

The Academic Aptitude test (90 items; 45 minutes) contains three types of items: (a) items in which the examinee is to determine which word in a set differs most in meaning from four others, (b) arithmetic items, and (c) items on relationships among geometric forms.

The 50-item Spelling test (15 minutes) includes some words of specialized medical vocabulary, with which applicants with high aptitude but limited medical exposure might be unfamiliar (e.g., adenoid, dyspeptic).

The Natural Sciences test (90 items; 30 minutes) includes some items that are not science per se (e.g., history of physics), and some items with little direct relationship to the practice of nursing, such as knowledge about seismic waves and the relative conductivity of metals.

The Judgment test (50 items; 30 minutes) is intended to measure the ability to "use good judgment and common sense" (technical manual, p. 19), and includes items on patient care situation, study habits, interviewing, and personal characteristics.

The Vocational Adjustment Index is composed of 90 statements (15 minutes) about the nature of work, human nature, and personal characteristics, with which the examinee must either "agree" or "disagree" (no intermediate responses). Statements are intended to assess cooperativeness, concern for others, freedom from nervous tendencies, attitudes toward authority, attitudes toward health, occupational stability, leadership, and self-reliance. Although the instructions indicate that there are "probably no 'right' or 'wrong' answers" (test booklet, p. 17) many of the items have one answer that is clearly socially desirable. These items may assess examinees' acumen regarding social expectations rather than their true attitudes.

ADMINISTRATION AND SCORING. Scoring is done by the test developer. Raw and percentile scores are reported to test users and examinees. A set of specimen questions without correct answers is available to potential examinees.

Thorough directions for administering the Revised PSB-Aptitude for Practical Nursing Examination (RPSB-APNE) are provided in the administrator's manual. No special training is necessary. The technical manual directs test users to contact the publishers for special procedures when testing the handicapped. The technical manual does not recommend a minimum score to be used for program admission, but notes that some programs prefer applicants who score at or above the 25th percentile.

NORMS. Initial norms were established in 1990 with 3,669 applicants to 71 programs of practical nursing, representing 45 states, the District of Columbia, and three Canadian schools. It is not clear whether stratified random sampling or quota sampling was used to select the programs. The technical manual contains information on age, education, and sex of the norm group. The technical manual states that norms are periodically updated, but presents no information on the schedule or procedures (p. 37). Potential test users should verify that norms are current, because composition of the applicant pool has been changing over recent years.

RELIABILITY. The technical manual includes information of the standard error of measurement for each test (but not the subtests of the Academic Aptitude test) derived from the original norm group. Other information on reliability is derived from small studies with limited representativeness.

Test-retest reliability coefficients, obtained from 126 examinees with 10 to 30 days between testings, ranged from .98 for the Spelling test to .89 for the Vocational Adjustment Index. Split-half (Odd/Even) reliabilities for 155 examinees ranged from .98 for the Academic Aptitude test to .91 for the Vocational Adjustment Index. No information is given on reliabilities of the subtests of the Academic Aptitude test. Lack of such reliability data is not in accordance with a primary standard of the *Standards for Educational and Psychological Testing* (AERA, APA, & NCME, 1985, p. 20).

VALIDITY. The technical manual (p. 53) states that content validity has been endorsed by expert judgment, but no information is given on the numbers or qualifications of experts consulted. The technical manual further asserts that the test reflects content based upon courses of study and texts, and knowledge and skills necessary during the educational period, but there are items in the Natural Sciences test that seem to this reviewer to have little relationship to practical nursing education. The technical manual states that the methods of construction of the test have ensured construct validity, but no statistical evidence of this is presented.

As evidence of concurrent criterion-related validity, the technical manual cites three small studies examining correlations between components of the RPSB-APNE and other instruments. No information is given on characteristics of the samples used in these studies. Correlations of .86 between the Verbal subtest of the RPSB-APNE and the School and College Ability Test (SCAT Series II, published by Educational Testing Service), and .81 between the Arithmetic subtest and the SCAT, are reported based on a sample of 83. Based on a sample of 48, a correlation of .92 between

the Academic Aptitude Test and The Wechsler Adult Intelligence Scale is cited. A correlation of .73 between the Vocational Adjustment Index and the ESTA 8A Personal Adjustment Index, also based on a sample of 48, is reported. No evidence of concurrent validity of other components of the RPSB-APNE is presented.

As evidence of predictive validity, the technical manual cites correlations between students' scores on the RPSB-APNE and their subsequent cumulative grade-point averages in a nonrandom sample of 11 educational programs. Correlations were: .81 for the Academic Aptitude test, .63 for the Spelling test; .83 for the Natural Sciences test, .79 for the Judgment test, and .61 for the Vocational Adjustment Index. Because all data were obtained from students admitted to practical nursing programs, these correlations are likely attenuated by restriction of range. In a study in a single program (n = 29), correlations between the RPSB-APNE and graduating class rank were found to range from .46 for the Vocational Adjustment Index to .63 for the Academic Aptitude test. Information on predictive validity of the subtests of the Academic Aptitude test, required by the *Standards for Educational and Psychological Testing* (AERA, APA, & NCME, 1985, p. 14), is not provided.

In further support of predictive validity, the test manual presents data from two unorthodox studies. In one (n = 64, 1 program) licensing examination scores were correlated with scores on the RPSB-APNE obtained 5 years after graduation. Correlations ranged from .34 for the Vocational Adjustment Index to .58 for the Natural Sciences test. Another (n = 39, 1 program) examined the relationship between final grade-point average and scores on the RPSB-APNE taken at graduation. Correlations ranged from .41 for the Vocational Adjustment Index to .60 for the Natural Sciences test. Because the RPSB-APNE is intended to predict subsequent performance in an educational program, the value of this information is unclear.

The *Standards for Educational and Psychological Testing* (AERA, APA, & NCME, 1985, p. 13) state that "evidence of validity should be presented for the major types of inferences for which the use of a test is recommended." No evidence is presented regarding validity of the RPSB-APNE for guidance and counseling, two of the stated uses of the test.

OTHER CONSIDERATIONS. The technical manual states that comparative studies have revealed no evidence of racial or gender bias. Limited details of these studies are presented. The technical manual also states that the developers have attempted to minimize cultural dependency of items, but it seems likely that some cultural dependency exists in exposure to vocabulary words, items of natural science, and situations presented in the Vocational Adjustment Index and the Judgment test.

Although timed, the technical manual states that the RPSB-APNE primarily tests power rather than speed. Time allowances are stated to be adequate for examinees able to complete the test questions (p. 14).

SUMMARY. The RPSB-APNE provides information that potentially may be useful in selecting among a pool of applicants for practical nursing education programs. Only very limited information is available on the reliability and validity of the RPSB-APNE, so potential test users should carefully assess the appropriateness of the test for their programs before using it in making admission decisions. Potential test users should bear in mind that existing validity estimates for the various components of the RPSB-APNE differ dramatically, so some parts of the test may be more appropriate to use than others. Potential users should keep in mind that scores on the test may depend on exposure to certain educational or life experiences, rather than solely on aptitude. The test manual encourages test users to develop local norms to determine the relationship of test scores to success in their programs.

Potential test users should also evaluate whether the RPSB-APNE provides more useful information than alternative sources of data, such as the College Board SAT Program (T4:581), Enhanced ACT Assessment (12:139), high school GPAs, or scores on an alternative nationally normed test such as the "NLN Assessment and Evaluation Pre-Admission Examination for Practical Nursing" (National League for Nursing, 1994). Use of the RPSB-APNE for guidance and counseling, beyond possibly counseling on choice of practical nursing as a career, does not appear to be warranted.

REVIEWER'S REFERENCES

American Educational Research Association, American Psychological Association, & National Council on Measurement in Education. (1985). *Standards for Educational and Psychological Testing.* Washington, DC: American Psychological Association, Inc.

National League for Nursing (NLN). (1994). Pre-admission Examinations for Schools of Nursing. New York, NY: National League for Nursing.

[80]
The Scales for Effective Teaching.

Purpose: "To assist administrators and teachers to work together to improve teaching."
Population: Teachers.
Publication Date: 1989.
Acronym: SET.
Scores: 15 scales: Learning Outcomes, Utilization of Instructional Materials, Instructional Techniques/Strategies, Academic Learning/Engaged Time, Positive Reinforcement of Responses, Correction of Academic Responses, Classroom Discipline, Instructional Style, Instructional Efficiency, Monitoring Student Progress During Lesson, Monitoring Student Progress After Lesson, Communication, Teaming, Organizational Commitment, Professional Development.
Administration: Individual.
Price Data, 1993: $29 per complete kit including manual (42 pages) and evaluation forms.
Time: (136–168) minutes.
Comments: Utilizes both observation and interview data.
Authors: Stevan J. Kukic, Susan L. Fister, Donald P. Link, and Janet L. Freston.
Publisher: Sopris West, Inc.

Review of The Scales for Effective Teaching by FREDERICK BESSAI, Professor of Education, University of Regina, Regina, Saskatchewan, Canada:

The Scales for Effective Teaching (SET) are more of a structured means of assessing and improving individual teacher practice than a set of scales. The authors have sought not only to provide a means of developing a comprehensive picture of a teacher's professional practice, but have also provided suggestions for the improvement of practice. In general, it is an attempt to apply the current knowledge of effective classrooms and effective teaching to teacher evaluation.

The scales are to be used in a four-phase evaluation process that includes preparation for interview and observation, the collection and recording of data, a data analysis and synthesis procedure, and finally, a data interpretation phase during which the evaluator and the teacher discuss the ratings on each of the scales, identify areas of excellence, and select areas for improvements to a higher level of performance. The latter includes selecting activities to improve performance and setting a date for future evaluation. Data are collected by observation and by interviewing the teacher. Scales 1, 2, 3, and 7 require an interview as well as a period of observation. Clear instructions are given on how to conduct the interview and several sample questions are given for each scale. Rules and suggestions are also given for observation with particular attention to objective recording before any evaluation or rating is made. After data collection, the observations are matched to a set of five behavioral statements in each scale. These represent successively higher levels of performance. For example, Scale 1 on Learning Outcomes has the statement, "conducts lessons without communicating learning outcomes" (p. 28) as the lowest level (1) and the highest level (5) includes communication of learning outcomes, checking to ensure that students understand expectations, responding to their feedback, providing a rationale, and focusing them on learning outcomes. The manual is generally clear and well written but is difficult to follow in places. The five points on each of the 15 scales are identified on the teaching profile form with numbers from 5 to 1 as headers but in the body of the form they are each filled in with the letters T-E-A-C-H. This can be confusing to the user and surely serves no statistical purpose. The same letters are also used to identify the five levels of behavioral statements for each scale in the manual and the evaluation forms. The letters have no apparent relationship to the content in either case and could be omitted. The authors mention a training program for potential users but do not state where and how it can be obtained.

One of the main strengths of the SET is that it is clearly based on identifiable teacher behaviors and these are described quite extensively with sample indicators. What is needed is more research on reliability, particularly interrater reliability, and discriminant validity. Generally, the SET can be recommended for use in clinical supervision. The scales represent a positive step toward overcoming some of the subjectivity and potential omissions and biases that are perennial problems in evaluating something as complex and multifaceted as effective teaching.

Review of The Scales for Effective Teaching by **TRENTON R. FERRO**, *Associate Professor of Adult and Community Education, Indiana University of Pennsylvania, Indiana, PA:*

The Scales for Effective Teaching (SET) is an observation and interview guide intended for use by educational administrators to evaluate efficiently and effectively the quality of teachers' teaching and to provide constructive feedback for teacher improvement. Based on the effective schools literature, the SET defines teaching in 15 areas. Each area is represented by a scale that has two components: "A set of *behavioral statements* describes five levels of effectiveness for each scale, and a set of *behavioral indicators* is provided to assist the rater in determining a level of effectiveness" (p. 5). The 15 scales cover Learning Outcomes, Utilization of Instructional Materials, Instructional Techniques/Strategies, Academic Learning/Engaged Time, Positive Reinforcement of Responses, Correction of Academic Responses, Classroom Discipline, Instructional Style, Instructional Efficiency, Monitoring Student Progress During Lesson, Monitoring Student Progress After Lesson, Communication, Teaming, Organizational Commitment, and Professional Development.

Following a brief pre-observation meeting to schedule times for conducting the observation and interview and for collecting pre-observation information, the evaluator collects and records observation data for scales 1–10 and interview data for scales 1, 2, 3, 7, and 11–15. Sample indicators and sample questions are provided as guides for both processes. The evaluator then analyzes and synthesizes the collected data by applying them to the SET rating scales (included in the manual accompanying the instrument) and developing a Teaching Profile. Finally, the evaluator and teacher meet to share the analysis and synthesis (a procedure the authors call "counsel for improvement") and to set improvement goals. The entire procedure requires at least 2 to 2 1/2 hours to complete.

The instructions for the entire procedure are quite clear and helpful. The instrument is well developed, providing a focus for, and consistency in, data collection and analysis. The well-designed manual contains ample supporting material to assist the evaluator in accomplishing her or his task. However, the users must be very familiar with the rating scales so that they will be able to collect appropriate, accurate, and adequate data and will be able to use the scales effectively when analyzing the data. Some elements of the process may require even more time than the authors allow, especially by those first learning to use the SET. Those experienced in using the process and working with the instrument should be able to reduce the time needed to complete some aspects of the process. However, the full amount of time suggested should always be given to observation and the interview for data collection. As the authors emphasize, teachers and administrators must be trained in the conceptual background and use of the SET. Failure to do so will diminish greatly the potential effectiveness of the SET.

In addition to the content described above, the manual also contains the philosophical bases and belief system underlying the development and use of the SET. "The final result should be a negotiated set of professional goals for improving teaching. These goals can serve as the basis for staff development activities for teachers and administrators. This focus promotes improvement and is the focus of SET" (p. 3). This emphasis is the strength of both the instrument and the entire process. If, then, this is the SET's primary function, careful consideration needs to be given to a second claim of utility: "The authors of SET firmly believe that evaluation and supervision are not antithetical concepts, but rather believe that sound evaluation serves as the basis for supervision" (p. 3). Herein lies the major philosophical rub. Although ideal, this perspective does not square with reality. Many situations, due to politics and labor relations, are not conducive to administrators being the best person to help with staff improvement. Those who use this instrument should have a very clear understanding of *why* they are using it—what their purposes and goals are. That, in turn, will determine *how* they use it— to improve teaching or to make personnel decisions. As this reviewer has emphasized, the instrument can serve both purposes, but interpersonal and political realities would suggest that both objectives cannot be met by the same evaluator in a single situation. In this reviewer's estimation, peer evaluation would ultimately be the most helpful and productive way to work toward the improvement of teaching. Use of the instrument by administrators should be reserved for making decisions related to retention, promotion, and tenure.

On another point, the authors claim to use the "clinical supervision" (p. 2) model, which they describe as "designed to provide fair and comprehensive feedback by minimizing subjectivity in data collection and analysis" (p. 5). However, evaluation, by definition, requires making decisions and judgments. The use of well-developed scales, protocols, and other observation and interview guides leads to consistency, but evaluation, even based on extensive data collection, is still a subjective activity; the evaluator is also an instrument, especially in analyzing data and drawing conclusions from those analyses. Ultimately, the evaluator will need to make decisions and offer suggestions. That is why the choice of who will observe and provide the feedback is so important. A "subjective" decision (which, by definition, evaluation requires) based on well-collected and analyzed data is much better than an "objective" decision (which, by definition, cannot be done) based on poorly collected and analyzed data. There is a clear need to distinguish among the various steps or elements: data collection, data analysis, and making decisions based on the analysis of the data. The strength of this instrument is that it provides a framework and process for collecting and analyzing such data. However, it cannot remove from the evaluator the ultimate requirement of making judgments and decisions.

[81]

SCAN-A: A Test for Auditory Processing Disorders in Adolescents and Adults.

Purpose: Used to identify adolescents and adults who have auditory processing disorders and who may benefit from intervention.

Population: Ages 12 to adult.

Publication Dates: 1986–1994.

Acronym: SCAN-A.

Scores, 6: Filtered Words, Auditory Figure-Ground, Competing Words, Competing Sentences, Total Test, Competing Words Ear Advantage.

Administration: Individual.

Price Data, 1994: $84.50 per complete kit including manual ('94, 69 pages), test audiocassette, and 12 record forms; $11 per 12 record forms; $37 per manual; $47.50 per test audiocassette.

Time: (20–25) minutes.

Author: Robert W. Keith.

Publisher: The Psychological Corporation.

Review of the SCAN-A: A Test for Auditory Processing Disorders in Adolescents and Adults by WILLIAM R. MERZ, Sr., Professor, School Psychology Training Program, Department of Special Education, Rehabilitation, and School Psychology, School of Education, California State University, Sacramento, Sacramento, CA:

The "SCAN-A is an upward extension of the SCAN: A Screening Test for Auditory Processing Disorders" (p. 1) designed to be used to identify auditory processing difficulties in children 3 to 11 years of age. The SCAN-A, designed for individuals 12 years or older, takes 20 minutes to administer, and is intended to do three things: "(a) describe auditory processing abilities for planning vocational, educational, and remediation goals for adolescents and adults with learning disabilities and/or language disorders; (b) describe central auditory abilities, monitor recovery, and provide a framework for counseling families of individuals who have suffered a head injury or stroke, and; (c) describe functional impairment or study that effects of medical treatment of individuals with chronic central nervous system disease" (manual, p. 1).

The test is intended for use by audiologists, speech and language pathologists, and others trained to identify auditory processing disorders for further assessment. There are four subtests: Filtered Words, Auditory Figure-Ground, Competing Words, and Competing Sentences, that are referenced to a four-page description of "What Is an Auditory Processing Disorder" (p. 4). The material includes descriptions of sensitized speech tests and dichotic (involving the simultaneous presentation of different acoustic stimuli to each ear) listening tests. The SCAN-A requires special equipment: a stereo cassette player with a speed of 1 7/8 ips (4.75 cm./sec.) and four tracks along two stereo channels. The equipment must have a frequency response of +6 db, 63-8000 Hz with a signal to noise ratio of 52 dB, a Wow and flutter of .2%, and a single volume control. Those participating in the SCAN-A testing had pure tone thresholds of 20dB at HL at any of four frequencies (500, 1000, 2000, and 4000). The field tests were conducted at 21 sites in four major regions of the country. A breakdown of those participating is presented by age, gender, and race. Examiners at university clinics, in private practice, and at military facilities participated in the trials. Twenty-three trial sites were located in 11 states and Canada where 52 audiologists administered the test. One hundred twenty-five people participated in the field trial; equal numbers were included across five age groups that were collapsed across ages to develop norms. Raw score means and standard deviations across all four subtests varied slightly, so they were transformed to z-scores. The z-scores were, in turn, transformed nonlinearly to subtest scaled scores with a mean of 10 and a standard deviation of 3 and total scores with a mean of 100 and a standard deviation of 15.

Cronbach's alpha internal consistency reliability estimates ranged from .46 to .69 for subtest scores to .77 for total scores; the test-retest reliability for total test score for three age groups collected from 1 day to 5 months was .69 resulting in a standard error of measurement of 2.8. Individual subtests had differences that ranged from 1 to 7 points; therefore variation in scores was too small for meaningful correlations. Evidence for content validity was presented to demonstrate that the tasks included ware typical of procedures used to assess auditory processing skills. Discriminant analysis, contrasting the skills of these with normal auditory processing abilities with those who have central auditory processing disorders, is presented as evidence of construct-related validity. Intercorrelations among subtests are presented as evidence of construct validity and range between .004 and .507 suggesting unique and common aspects of measurement. However, with small mean differences among subtests and restricted ranges these data must be interpreted very conservatively. Studies of left and right ear advantage are offered to demonstrate the lack of significant differences between left and right ear scores in people with normal auditory processing and people with central auditory processing disorders. Concurrent evidence of validity is presented through correlations of the scores of 29 youths 12 to 18 years old on the SCAN-A and the SCAN; the correlation corrected for attenuation is .59.

Reporting and interpretation of test scores are amply covered in 16 pages of the manual. Included is interpretation of total score, subtest scores, and subtest differences. Behavioral observations and ear advantage are emphasized in this section of the manual. Implications and recommendations for remediation are quite detailed and appear to be a strong part of the manual. No test and item bias studies are presented.

Overall, the SCAN-A offers a useful addition to the diagnosis and treatment of learning disabilities among adults. Although the norm groups are small and reliability and validity studies are rudimentary, the data presented are promising. Finding contrasting groups for validity studies is quite difficult for tasks identifying individual disability; the authors do a creditable job in the studies reported in the manual. Having auditory and visual processing assessment devices is critical for adequately diagnosing learning disability. The SCAN-A is a good start as an adequate auditory processing screening device for adults.

Review of the SCAN-A: A Screening Test for Auditory Processing Disorders in Adolescents and Adults by JACLYN B. SPITZER, Chief, Audiology and Speech Pathology, Department of Veterans Affairs, West Haven, CT:

The SCAN-A is a screening tool for central auditory processing disorders (CAPD). It is a test normed for adolescents and adults, an extension of work in diagnosis of CAPD in children, using the original version of SCAN described by Keith (1986). The test provides rapid insight, administered in approximately 20 minutes, into the functional status of the central auditory pathway.

The SCAN-A may be applied to describe central auditory function of persons with CAPD or learning disabilities, or to monitor the alteration in processing over time produced by treatment or recovery from insult. A most significant use of the test is to determine the need for referral for more detailed central evaluation.

The four subtests of the SCAN-A are: Filtered Words, Auditory Figure-Ground, Competing Words, and Competing Sentences. Each of these subtests reflects an accepted approach to the evaluation of CAPD applied in the more intensive examination of processing. The intent of the Filtered Words and Figure-Ground subtests is to examine the examinee's ability to perceive signals in a background of noise or under adverse listening conditions. The Competing Words and Competing Sentences subtests are dichotic measures that

assess hemispheric specialization. The use of degraded speech and dichotic measurement has a tradition in the assessment of lesions of the central nervous system. For adult patients, the SCAN-A is an appropriate screening tool when central dysfunction is suspected or needs to be ruled out. Furthermore, in cases of known lesions, such as post-cerebral vascular accident, recovery may be monitored via serial SCAN-A measurement.

CAPD in adolescents may be manifested by learning or reading difficulties or by behavioral disruption. Thus, application of such central measures as the SCAN-A in adolescents (the majority of whom do not have central lesions) may be useful in determining rehabilitative approaches necessary to improve classroom performance or to modify the learning environment.

The SCAN-A materials consist of an examiner's manual, record forms, and audiocassette. The manual is clearly written and emphasizes the need for controlled administration using adequate quality stereo equipment and headphones to obtain valid results. The test environment should be free of distractions. Further, the requirement for symmetrical hearing within normal limits and normal middle ear function implies that hearing assessment should precede SCAN-A administration. Test administration is greatly aided by recorded instructions prior to each subtest. Scoring of the test is straightforward.

The SCAN-A reflects careful development in its normative study (Keith & Grant, 1993). Thorough standardization data are contained in the manual. The internal consistency of the total test, estimated using Cronbach's alpha, is .77, with the subtests varying from .46 (for Auditory Figure-Ground) to .69 (for Competing Words). Thus, it is preferable to use the test in its entirety rather than to rely on any subtest individually. Test-retest reliability (time intervals from 1 day to 5 months) for the total test is .69, acceptable for clinical repeated measures.

In summary, the SCAN-A is a useful screening tool that meets the requirements for speed and ease of presentation, high internal consistency, and test-retest reliability. Its application in clinical populations has indicated that it has high hit, low miss, and low false alarms rates, making the SCAN-A a test that could be appropriately applied in adolescent and adult CAPD screening.

REVIEWER'S REFERENCES

Keith, R. W. (1986). *SCAN: A Screening Test for Auditory Processing Disorders.* San Antonio, TX: The Psychological Corporation.

Keith, R. W., & Grant, G. (1993). *Standardization of SCAN-A: A Test for Auditory Processing Disorders in Adolescents and Adults.* Presentation to the American Academy of Audiology Annual Convention, Phoenix, AZ.

[82]
School Archival Records Search.

Purpose: "Designed to overlay existing school records so that they can be coded and quantified systematically."

Population: Grades 1–12.

Publication Date: 1991.

Acronym: SARS.

Scores: 11 archival variables: Demographics, Attendance, Achievement Test Information, School Failure, Disciplinary Contacts, Within-School Referrals, Certification for Special Education, Placement Out of Regular Classroom, Receiving Chapter I Services, Out-of-School Referrals, Negative Narrative Comments.

Administration: Group.

Price Data, 1993: $35 per complete kit including user's guide, technical manual (86 pages), and 50 instrument packets.

Time: Administration time not reported.

Authors: Hill M. Walker, Alice Block-Pedego, Bonnie Todis, and Herbert H. Severson.

Publisher: Sopris West, Inc.

TEST REFERENCE

1. Campbell, F. A., & Ramey, C. T. (1994). Effects of early intervention on intellectual and academic achievement: A follow-up study of children from low income families. *Child Development, 65,* 684–698.

Review of the School Archival Records Search by JOHN CRAWFORD, *Director of Planning and Evaluation, Millard Public Schools, Omaha, NE:*

The School Archival Records Search (SARS) is a system that is intended to guide school staff through a process of coding and tracking variables designed to predict future "at risk" status of students. Specifically, the SARS is described in the manual as a screening system for elementary age students to aid in the identification of those students who are at risk for developing later behavior disorders and who have elevated risk for dropping out of high school.

About two-thirds of the manual is devoted to procedures regarding application of the SARS coding system. The only "instruments" as such are summary sheets for recording the critical indicators. There is a four-page set of questions the person carrying out the records search completes; this information can then be summarized on the two-page "Student Profile Form." The manual contains coding procedures for the recording and the summarizing of the information.

The SARS system is relatively straightforward and should be easy to implement. The information required to represent the indicators would be reasonably easy to come by in most schools. The indicators include: demographic information (name, grade, teacher, as well as the reason for being evaluated), number of schools attended, days absent, achievement, (prior) in-grade retention, within-school referrals, special education status, out-of-classroom placement, Chapter 1 (Title 1) status, out-of-school referrals, discipline contacts, and "negative" narrative comments from staff. In addition, much of the system usage and validation requires an assessment of whether the student's behavior pattern is primarily "externalizing" (e.g., aggressive, hyperactive, rule-breaking) or "internalizing" (excessive shyness, withdrawn, nonparticipative, depressive). Although in several places in the manual the SARS is referred to as the last stage of screening in another set of procedures (the Systematic Screening for Behavior Disorders), this review attends to the SARS as a stand-alone system.

There is some information presented on the issue of agreement among different raters. Most of the indicators are well defined and objective in nature, and therefore, one would expect high, near-perfect agreement among different raters who were performing scans of the same student records. For example, whether the student is currently verified as special education (and has an IEP), whether the student is receiving Chapter 1 services, and the number of in-grade retentions are variables that should not vary from one coder to another. There is some subjectivity in the determination of whether narrative comments regarding the student in his or her file qualify as "negative." The manual contains three pages of description and examples of "negative" narrative comments and has a practice exercise with correct answers. The authors do report data from five raters who judged 263 narrative comments, yielding an overall mean agreement level of 85% agreement.

However, it is a significant problem that the authors have not assessed stability of these indicators over time and did not show a zero-order intercorrelation matrix. At least half of the 11 indicators have a direct or indirect connection to special education classification. The study by Shaywitz, Escobar, Shaywitz, Fletcher, and Makuch (1992) found such instability in the primary method of identifying special education students (the "discrepancy" model that relies on the achievement vs. IQ difference) that they concluded what was often labeled a special education condition was nothing other than performance on the low end of an achievement continuum. Their data showed that only about one-fourth of elementary age students *remained* special education classified (with dyslexia) over a period as short as a three-grade span. If the SARS authors intend that their system be used as an elementary grade screening tool to anticipate high school age problems such as dropping out, then there should be serious study of stability over time of the indicators. Also, an intercorrelation matrix based on a sample representative of a normative population should be presented so the user could directly examine what appears to be significant multicolinearity. Factor loadings in the technical manual allow one to infer these correlations, but the correlation matrix might make it clear that it is really unnecessary to go to the trouble of computing factor scores. For example, "current IEP" is an indicator, and so is "nonregular classroom placement"; as is "academic/behavioral referrals" and "referral out" of the home school. In addition, the factor analyses presented are somewhat difficult to interpret because individual variable loadings are broken out by sample location (Oregon and Washington), and many non-trivial differences are evident in the data (between locations).

The issue of predictive validity is related to the question of stability of indicators over time. A careful reading of the manual is required to determine that a true predictive validity study was not done. The general impression given is that the tracking of these 11 indicators in elementary school will allow school staff to accurately predict students who will likely drop out in high school. The study by Block-Pedego (1990)—also the second author of the user's manual—was actually a *retrospective* study. That is, high school dropouts were identified and then their elementary records were examined. This is very much different from applying the screening tool to a large number of elementary

age students, forming a prediction of which ones will be at risk in high school (while the students are still in elementary grades), and then following those students into high school age to determine the accuracy of the predictions. The retrospective "accuracy" rates cited for the elementary record scan for 11th/12th graders who drop out (as well as the rates for the grade 7–10 record scan) are surely higher than they would be in the kind of study described above. See Waldie and Spreen (1993) for an example of a longitudinal study that followed subjects from ages 8–12 to adulthood to analyze the relationship between learning disability and contact with police.

Still, reliability and validity issues notwithstanding, the system could provide help to school staff—as an organizing tool and in conjunction with other information—to identify youngsters potentially in need of attention. Especially if a student's profile completed once at the end (or beginning) of a year, for *several years in a row*, began to appear stable or as an increasing "at risk" function, one could have confidence in taking action. Most schools have access to computers and database programs now. Automating the system would make it even more helpful to staff.

REVIEWER'S REFERENCES

Block-Pedego, A. (1990). Early identification and prediction of students at risk for dropping out of school using the school archival records search (SARS). *Dissertation Abstracts*. Ann Arbor, MI.

Shaywitz, S. E., Escobar, M. D., Shaywitz, B. A., Fletcher, J. M., & Makuch, R. (1992). Evidence that dyslexia may represent the lower tail of a normal distribution of reading ability. *The New England Journal of Medicine, 326*(3), 145–150.

Waldie, K., & Spreen, O. (1993). The relationship between learning disabilities and persisting delinquency. *Journal of Learning Disabilities, 26*(6), 417–423.

Review of the School Archival Records Search by ROBERT FITZPATRICK, *Consulting Psychologist, Cranberry Township, PA:*

The School Archival Records Search (SARS) uses school records to aid in identifying and making decisions about elementary-age children "at serious risk for developing behavior disorders" or "at elevated risk for later school dropout" (p. 3). Behavior disorders are characterized as "externalizing (conduct problems) or internalizing (personality)" (p. 7) disorders.

The 11 "variables" were "derived after extensive pilot testing," in a research program called Systematic Screening for Behavior Disorders (SSBD). Although the manual contains essentially no rationale for the selection of the variables, they appear to be appropriate. However, it is confusing to find the variables are named and described somewhat differently in different parts of the manual. "Demographics," for example, is scored only for and frequently referred to as "Number of different schools attended."

The idea of seeking a standardized and quantifiable way of reviewing school records relevant to behavior disorders is intuitively attractive, and the association of the SARS with the SSBD research program seems a favorable sign.

Three scoring options are described in the manual. The first option is to evaluate each of the variables separately, as indicating whether the pupil is positive (at risk) or negative (not at risk) for a behavior disorder. For example, if a student scores below the 41st percentile on national norms for an achievement test, that student is scored positive for Achievement Test Information. Results for all 11 variables are then compared with "characteristic" profiles for externalizers, internalizers, dropouts, and normals. No justification is provided for the cutoffs; no doubt the authors have evidence to support the choice of the 41st percentile and other cutoffs, but they do not report that evidence in the manual.

The second scoring option is based on factor analytic identification of three factors, called DISRUPTION, NEEDS ASSISTANCE, and LOW ACHIEVEMENT. A "domain" score is derived for each factor, by determining if two or more of the variables that load most strongly on that factor are positive. The choice of two variables seems arbitrary, and is not explained in the manual.

The third scoring option involves the calculation of factor scores with mean of 0 and standard deviation of 1. The authors describe the calculations and provide examples and a self-test for the user. Unfortunately, many of the sample calculations are in error (or else the instructions are incorrect). On one (unnumbered) page in Appendix B, 14 of 30 results are inconsistent with the relevant instructions or formulas. The user is advised to distrust the numbers in the sample calculations.

Some evidence is provided to show the SARS scores succeed in identifying children who are at risk for behavior disorders, distinguishing between externalizing and internalizing types, and predict-

ing later school dropout. However, there are problems with the evidence. The manual is poorly organized and lacks many details needed to understand and evaluate the evidence. In most cases, the effects seem modest; for example, in one of the two major studies reported, only 36% of the pupils rated by teachers as externalizers were identified by the SARS as DISRUPTIVE. A pervasive problem is that much of the evidence is circular; the SARS was originally developed in part as a criterion measure for other parts of the SSBD, and the validity of the SARS is defended because it is somewhat consistent with teacher judgments obtained with those other SSBD procedures.

Interrater reliability information is provided for small samples of raters and scorers. Although the data indicate reasonable levels of reliability, they are insufficient for evaluation of the instrument. More data on more types of reliability are needed.

Norms are also limited and poorly presented. In addition, the suggestions in the manual for their use are dubious.

The SARS is a promising instrument and the authors indicate further information about it will be forthcoming. The SARS is not yet suitable for routine implementation, but independent research and cautious applications are to be encouraged.

[83]
School Effectiveness Questionnaire.

Purpose: Assesses variables that have an impact on school effectiveness.
Population: Students, teachers, parents.
Publication Date: 1993.
Scores, 11: Effective Instructional Leadership, Clear and Focused Mission, Safe and Orderly Environment, Positive School Climate, High Expectations, Frequent Assessment/Monitoring of Student Achievement, Emphasis on Basic Skills, Maximum Opportunities for Learning, Parent/Community Involvement, Strong Professional Development, Teacher Involvement in Decision Making.
Administration: Group.
Forms, 4: Level 1 Students (Elementary), Level 2 Students (High School), Teachers, Parents.
Price Data, 1994: $8 per 10 reusable questionnaires (Teacher Form); $20 per 10 reusable questionnaires (Level 1, Level 2, Parent Forms); $10.50 per manual (45 pages); $50 per 100 Type 2 machine-scorable answer sheets; $14 per examination kit including manual, one

each of all four questionnaires, and one answer document.

Time: (15–20) minutes.

Comments: Optional data analysis software available from publisher.

Authors: Lee Baldwin, Freeman Coney III, Diane Färdig, and Roberta Thomas.

Publisher: The Psychological Corporation.

Review of the School Effectiveness Questionnaire by ROBERT FITZPATRICK, Consulting Psychologist, Cranberry Township, PA:

How should we measure the effectiveness of schools? One approach is to test the product: What have the students learned? Alternatively, we can check the process, to determine if the schools are doing the right things (supposing that we know what the right things are). The School Effectiveness Questionnaire (SEQ) represents the latter approach. It is a set of questionnaires intended to measure school effectiveness across 11 dimensions. Teachers, parents, elementary students, and high school students complete separate questionnaires. The responses of teachers contribute to all 11 summary scores, of parents to 9, and of students to 7.

The questionnaires contain from 36 (elementary students) to 70 (teachers) statements to which each respondent is asked to indicate extent of agreement. Each statement requires a judgment or calls for an opinion about the way a school functions. Some of the judgments seem quite difficult. For example, parents are to indicate whether they agree that teachers are taking time and using techniques needed for effective instruction.

The SEQ was developed in a single large school district. A committee of educational administrators, along with representatives of parents and community, reviewed literature on school effectiveness, produced the listing and definition of the 11 characteristics thought to constitute school effectiveness, and formulated initial versions of the questionnaires. After a pilot test, the questionnaires were revised and administered to "nearly 30,000 students, teachers and parents" (p. 8). Later, some further changes, not specifically described in the manual, were made prior to publication for general use. It is not clear to me whether the data reported in the manual were derived from one or more of the earlier versions of the questionnaires or from the final versions.

Although the characteristics of effective schools chosen for measurement on the SEQ are intuitively reasonable, no data are reported linking scores on this set of questionnaires with other indicators of effectiveness. Further, some users might argue for the inclusion of other characteristics as important to measure on a school effectiveness scale. Scant attention is paid to these concerns in the SEQ manual.

Coefficient alpha reliabilities, all in the high 90s for teachers and parents, and in the 70s and 80s for students are reported. According to the manual authors, these data imply that "each characteristic is represented by a highly homogeneous set of statements on specific aspects of school effectiveness" (p. 16). But some of the coefficients are not as high as might be desired, and users are not told the size or source of the sample on which the coefficients are based. No other information about reliability or generalizability of the scales is provided.

Intercorrelations among the 11 characteristics are reported for 86 teachers, 151 elementary students, and 190 secondary students. No parent data are reported. The intercorrelations for teachers are relatively high, ranging from .52 to .83, whereas those for students are lower, with values from .16 to .72. The manual argues that this is good news, in that these coefficients are lower than the alphas but not too low. Some factor analytic information would be helpful. Lacking that, the pattern of results constitutes rather weak evidence for the construct validity of the questionnaires.

Inspection of items in corresponding scales for the four questionnaires suggests that the scales for different respondent groups may function somewhat differently. For example, Parent/Community Involvement may mean quite different things to teachers, parents, and students.

The manual contains no norms. The authors may have supposed that normative information is not needed, but do recommend comparing scores to identify relative strengths and weaknesses of the schools under study. This recommendation raises some difficulties in interpretation of item or scale score mean differences. For example, achieving high scores on some of the characteristics may be quite difficult whereas other characteristics of effectiveness may be approached more loosely. Differences among the scores may reflect a daunting goal as well as a school profile. Without norms, users will not be able to understand possible scale differences. Hence, it seems there is a need for norms, and they are lacking. Even with norms, it is well to exercise caution in interpreting profiles of scores, a caution not expressed in the manual.

Manual authors also recommend comparison of scale means across groups of schools within a district, across grade levels, and in a before-and-after style to evaluate programs intended to improve school functioning. No guidance is provided as to the size of difference in means that might indicate meaningful change. Once again the lack of normative data creates interpretive difficulties.

The authors are inconsistent in describing the SEQ as a means to evaluate individual schools. They both caution against such use and suggest that schools with high or low scores be identified. It seems naive to suppose that comparisons and evaluations would not be made by administrators, school boards, and the public.

The SEQ is well packaged and appealing. If a school district or school determines that its content is appropriate, it could constitute a ready-made set of instruments for measuring educational effectiveness from a process point of view. However, its validity for general use is at best unproven, norms are nonexistent, needed data and analyses are lacking, and some of the comparisons suggested in the manual are of questionable suitability. Educators are advised to be cautious about adopting the SEQ.

Review of the School Effectiveness Questionnaire by MICHAEL HARWELL, Associate Professor of Psychology in Education, University of Pittsburgh, Pittsburgh, PA:

The School Effectiveness Questionnaire (SEQ) is a new instrument used to assess variables that have an impact on school effectiveness. Parents, teachers, and students respond to 11 subscales reflecting characteristics of school effectiveness: Instructional Leadership, Clear and Focused Mission, Safe and Orderly Environment, Positive School Climate, High Expectations, Frequent Assessment and Monitoring of Student Achievement, Emphasis on Basic Skills, Maximum Opportunities for Learning, Parent/Community Involvement, Strong Professional Development, and

Teacher Involvement in Decision Making. Each of these characteristics is described in the manual and a few references are provided for interested readers. The manual authors wisely state that SEQ information should be used in conjunction with other indicators of school effectiveness, such as standardized test scores, class grades, etc. The authors go on to state that "The School Effectiveness Questionnaire is not intended to be used to judge whether any particular school is good or bad. Instead, it is simply an instrument that yields a profile of school effectiveness that emerges from the attitudes and opinions of the people surveyed" (p. 12).

After examining SEQ scores, three tasks are identified for users that should precede any programmatic interventions: (a) Investigate what there is about the school environment that produced a particular pattern of responses; (b) design programs that will address less favorable conditions and sustain positive conditions; and (c) oversee the implementation of the designed program.

On the one hand, then, the SEQ is described as a data collection instrument the purpose of which is simply to describe; on the other hand, users are told that there are tasks to be accomplished after viewing SEQ results, tasks that use the SEQ to judge whether certain characteristics of a school are good or bad. These two purposes (describe versus evaluate) are vastly different and this ambivalent structure runs throughout the manual. Despite the claims in the manual, it is hard to imagine how any instrument purporting to assess school effectiveness would not be used for comparative purposes and have a prescriptive function.

EASE OF USE. All forms of the questionnaire are administered in groups or by mail and most respondents should have little trouble following the written directions. (Directions for younger respondents, for example, students in first grade, are read aloud.) There are no time limits. Teachers will usually administer the SEQ to students. The manual contains detailed instructions on how to do so. The administration of the teacher form is fairly unstructured. The manual authors suggest using a faculty meeting or workshop setting in which to administer the SEQ, but provide no guidance on how questions about the form might be dealt with or that teachers should probably not talk with one another while filling out the questionnaire. Parents are typically mailed the questionnaire and may fill it out jointly. No advice is given on what parents should do if they have questions or on how long they have to return the form. The manual authors do touch on a few of the obvious difficulties, for example, the likelihood of a response bias in the returned questionnaires from parents, but more information about questionnaire and survey methods would be useful. There is a substantial survey research literature to draw on to offer advice to those administering the SEQ. The manual authors indicate the reading level for the Level 1 form (grades 5–8) is 5th grade and for Level 2 (grades 9–12) is 8th grade, and that the reading level for the parent form is 10th–11th grade.

CHOOSING RESPONDENTS. The size of many schools will require that some sort of sampling scheme be employed. The authors suggest consulting someone knowledgeable in this area to construct a sampling plan. No advice is offered for what constitutes too small a sample. There is also a misstatement in the manual that "In schools of small or moderate size, a survey of all students (5th through 12th grades), all teachers, and all parents would yield the most reliable, valid, and meaningful results" (p. 20). The validity and meaningfulness of the results do not depend on attempting to sample the entire population, but, rather, on the accuracy of the inferences made from the responses. If, for example, items comprising the Instructional Leadership subscale had little to do with instructional leadership, it would not matter whether the entire population was sampled or not. The manual authors correctly note the critical issue in sampling is that the sample should be representative of the school or district population. This deserves more than a simple note; it should probably be put in boldface letters two inches high.

SCORING. Teachers, parents, and students are given varying numbers of Likert-type items to respond to; grades 5–8 respond to 36 items, each with a range of 1–3 (1 = *Disagree*, 2 = *No Opinion*, 3 = *Agree*); grades 9–12 respond to 48 items each scored 1—5 (1 = *Strongly Disagree*, 5 = *Strongly Agree*); parents respond to 44 items and teachers to 70 (both scored on the same 1–5 scale as grades 9–12). According to the manual, higher scores suggest more effective schools. The manual contains advice on machine scoring of the responses and on what descriptive statistics to calculate. Software for analyses of responses is available for purchase from the publisher. The authors recommend computing both individual item summaries as well as subscale scores (one for each characteristic) using valid responses. What constitutes an invalid response is not mentioned.

NORMS. No norms are presented, presumably because schools or school districts are complex organizations that defy attempts to produce interpretable averages. This seems quite defensible. For example, the meaning of an average Instructional Leadership score would probably show great variation across schools in ways that would make normative interpretations very difficult. Put another way, an average score for Instructional Leadership in one school might imply something quite different from a similar score in another school. Norms would also promote the comparison of one school's scores with another school's, which should be avoided. However, the lack of norms places an additional burden on the scoring system, because there are no external (normative) data to guide score interpretations.

RELIABILITY. According to the manual, a committee-developed form of the SEQ was piloted using students, parents, and teachers in 10 schools, with all grade levels represented. Unfortunately, no information about the pilot study, such as the group sample sizes and relevant demographic information, is reported. Coefficient alpha reliabilities are reported for these data for each group of respondents on each subscale as well as a total score (apparently computed as the sum of the individual subscale scores). These coefficients are quite high ($\geq$ .94) for parents and teachers and noticeably lower for students ($\geq$ .77). Intercorrelations among the subscales are also reported for teachers (N = 86) and are said to be representative of the patterns observed for students; no reliability information is reported for the parent form. The description of these correlations, which generally range between .16–.83, is misleading. The authors state, "These intercorrelations indicate that the characteristics are related and can be considered facets of school effectiveness" (p. 17). Nonsense. Nonzero correlations among the subscales in no way indicates that they are facets of school effectiveness, which would require, among other things, validity evidence. Another misstatement is, "The pattern of intercorrelations is indicative of the desired relative independence of the characteristics" (p. 17). What the authors apparently mean is that the correlations suggest that the characteristics do not overlap much, although some correlations in the .70s and .80s suggests there is a good bit of overlap. There is no such thing as relative independence.

A total of 30,000 students, parents, and teachers were surveyed with the revised instrument and their responses led to the final form of the SEQ. Why such a huge sample size was used and why the reported summary statistics in the manual are not based on 30,000 is not explained. Regardless of the sample size, what is missing here is stronger evidence the subscales do or do not overlap substantially, such as might be provided with a factor analysis or item response theory approach.

VALIDITY. No validity evidence is reported in the manual, even though such evidence is badly needed. The last section of the manual is entitled "Using the Results to Improve School Effectiveness" (p. 41) and suggests that SEQ scores can guide efforts to improve school effectiveness. What empirical evidence is offered that these 11 characteristics and the chosen scoring scheme provide valid prescriptive information? The answer is none. Could such information be obtained? Of course, by studying schools that have used the SEQ to identify strengths and weaknesses (such as those associated with the sample of 30,000). As an example, suppose five schools that had used the SEQ had each found something less than a positive school climate, and then designed, implemented, and evaluated programs intended to promote a positive school climate. Asking the respondents in these studies to answer a different questionnaire that also assesses school climate and correlating the two sets of scores would provide validity evidence. Examining whether SEQ results agreed with the perceptions of one or more independent consultants hired to assess school climate would also provide validity evidence (and so on). Until validity evidence is presented, users cannot have much confidence in SEQ scores.

INTERPRETING THE RESULTS. The information and advice offered in the interpretation section is critically flawed. Users are first told, "The primary use of the School Effectiveness Questionnaire involves studying the profile of the 11 characteristic means derived from the survey" (p. 37). The authors go on to suggest that users "Look for dimensions of school effectiveness with very low (unfavorable) means. Improvement is probably needed in these areas" (p. 37). This (and similar comments) is poor advice. Because the scoring has no natural zero point and there are no norms, what would constitute an unfavorable or favorable mean? (The authors do point out the SEQ could be used for the same school over time, which would allow within-subscale, over-time comparisons.)

Most troublesome of all is the suggestion that SEQ results can be used to "Compare the characteristic means of different groups (e.g., of schools within the district or grades within a school) to see whether their perceptions of school effectiveness differ" (p. 37). It is one thing to compare different grades within a school and quite another to use the SEQ to make between-school comparisons, even if the schools are in the same district. Whatever the difficulties of assessing a single school's effectiveness, they are compounded many times over when comparing schools, and there is *nothing* in the manual to suggest the SEQ can validly and reliably be used for this task. Put another way, the authors offer no statistical or psychometric evidence that justifies the use of the SEQ to compare schools.

ADDITIONAL ISSUES. The authors fail to acknowledge what is obvious to any educator: That indicators of school effectiveness are high-stakes statistics. This failure may be responsible for the inattention given to several related issues, such as (a) How can anonymity of responses be preserved to ensure honest answers? This deserves more attention than it receives because it is easy to conceive of settings in which maintaining anonymity would be difficult. (b) Who are the results to be reported to or made available to? Are SEQ results primarily intended for administrators? (c) What motivation would students, parents, and teachers have for participating in a thoughtful way in a survey? Another issue the SEQ authors ignore is the limitation of any paper-and-pencil questionnaire assessing a high-stakes topic like school effectiveness. Clearly, the use of the SEQ should be in conjunction with information obtained from structured interviews with members of the affected groups.

The various problems with the SEQ are exacerbated by the caliber of the psychometric and statistical work reported in the manual, which is uniformly low. For example, no item analyses, either classical or based on item response theory, are reported. A list of analyses that should have been done as part of the construction of the instrument would include, but not be limited to, factor analyses to investigate the factor structure underlying the 11 subscales, item analyses that investigate possible response sets for the items, validity evidence that inferences from the subscale scores are accurate, and suggestions that users employ various statistical procedures to examine subscale means. For descriptive analyses, users would be well advised to employ now-standard robust indicators of center and spread. The suggestion that subscale means can be compared across demographic groups provides another example of questionable advice. How are these means to be compared? Descriptively, or using inferential procedures? And what of the issue of whether a sample or an entire population is represented in the data? It might be argued that prescribing appropriate statistical analyses is outside the scope of the manual. The authors do offer advice on analyzing the responses and computing and interpreting statistics such as means, standard deviations, and frequency tables, but offer no similar advice on performing inferential analyses when comparing demographic groups. At the least, it would be helpful if the authors advised users with minimal statistical training to consult someone knowledgeable in this area.

SUMMARY. Overall, the SEQ cannot be recommended to assess school effectiveness. It clearly has a prescriptive function but the authors fail to provide validity evidence. Without such evidence no inferences can be made about schools with various scores on the 11 characteristics of school effectiveness. The manual is also riddled with highly questionable advice. Perhaps the most egregious example is the suggestion that the SEQ can be used to compare schools. In the section on choosing respondents the authors advised users to consult with someone knowledgeable about sampling. The authors would also benefit from consultation from someone knowledgeable about psychometrics and statistics in the hope of upgrading the quality of this questionnaire.

[84]
The Self-Directed Search, Form E—1990 Revision.

Purpose: Provides a "complete career assessment for those with limited reading skills."

Population: Adults and older adolescents with lower education levels.

Publication Dates: 1970–1994.

Acronym: SDS-Form E.

Scores, 6: Realistic, Investigative, Artistic, Social, Enterprising, Conventional.

Administration: Group.

Price Data, 1996: $90 per complete kit including professional user's guide ('94, 101 pages), technical manual ('94, 92 pages), user's guide ('90, 7 pages), 25 assessment booklets, 25 Jobs Finders, 25 You and Your Job booklets; $20 per professional user's guide; $20 per technical manual; $49 per 25 sets of assessment booklets and Jobs Finders; $42 per 25 Educational Opportunities Finders; $27 per 25 assessment booklets; $27 per 25 Jobs Finders; $21 per 25 You and Your Job booklets.

Foreign Language Editions: Spanish and Canadian (English) editions available.

Time: (40–60) minutes.

Author: John L. Holland.

Publisher: Psychological Assessment Resources, Inc.

Cross References: See T4:2414 (23 references); for reviews of an earlier edition by M. Harry Daniels and Caroline Manuele-Adkins, see 10:330 (19 references); also for a review of an earlier edition by Robert H. Dolliver, see 9:1098 (12 references); see also T3:2134 (55 references); for a review by John O. Crites and excerpted reviews by Fred Brown, Richard Seligman, Catherine C. Cutts, Robert H. Dolliver, and Robert N. Hansen, see 8:1022 (88 references); see also T2:2211 (1 reference).

TEST REFERENCES

1. Walsh, W. B., Bingham, R. P., & Sheffey, M. A. (1986). Holland's theory and college educated working Black men and women. *Journal of Vocational Behavior, 29,* 194-200.
2. Maddux, C. D., & Cummings, R. E. (1986). Alternate form reliability of the Self-Directed Search—Form E. *Career Development Quarterly, 35,* 136-140.
3. Abler, R. M., & Sedlacek, W. E. (1987). Computer orientation by Holland type and sex. *Career Development Quarterly, 36,* 163-169.
4. Gault, F. M., & Meyers, H. H. (1987). A comparison of two career planning inventories. *Career Development Quarterly, 36,* 332-336.
5. Johnson, J. A. (1987). Influence of adolescent social crowds on the development of vocational identity. *Journal of Vocational Behavior, 31,* 182-199.
6. Pazy, A., & Zin, R. (1987). A contingency approach to consistency: A challenge to prevalent views. *Journal of Vocational Behavior, 30,* 84-101.
7. Sandler, S. B. (1987). Dislocated workers: A response. *Journal of Employment Counseling, 24,* 146-148.
8. Strahan, R. F. (1987). Measures of consistency for Holland-type codes. *Journal of Vocational Behavior, 31,* 37-44.
9. Miller, M. J. (1987). Career counseling for high school students, grades 10–12. *Journal of Employment Counseling, 24,* 173–183.

10. Vandergoot, D. (1987). Review of placement research literature: Implications for research and practice. *Rehabilitation Counseling Bulletin, 30,* 243–272.

11. Wiggins, J. D. (1987). Effective career exploration programs revisited. *Career Development Quarterly, 35,* 297-303.

12. Greenlee, S. P., Damarin, F. L., & Walsh, W. B. (1988). Congruence and differentiation among Black and White males in two non-college-degreed occupations. *Journal of Vocational Behavior, 32,* 298-306.

13. Miller, M. J., Springer, T. P., & Wells, D. (1988). Which occupational environments do black youths prefer? Extending Holland's typology. *The School Counselor, 36,* 103–106.

14. Jones, L. K., Gorman, S., & Schroeder, C. G. (1989). A comparison between the SDS and the Career Key among career undecided college students. *Career Development Quarterly, 37,* 334-344.

15. Mazen, A. M. (1989). Testing an integration of Vroom's instrumentality theory and Holland's typology on working women. *Journal of Vocational Behavior, 35,* 327-341.

16. Alvi, S. A., Khan, S. A., & Kirkwood, K. J. (1990). A comparison of various indices of differentiation for Holland's model. *Journal of Vocational Behavior, 36,* 147-152.

17. Khan, S. B., & Alvi, S. A. (1990). A study of the validity of Holland's theory in a non-Western culture. *Journal of Vocational Behavior, 36,* 132-146.

18. Matsui, T., & Tsukamoto, S-I. (1990). Relation between career self-efficacy measures based on occupational titles and Holland codes and model environments: A methodological contribution. *Journal of Vocational Behavior, 38,* 78-91.

19. McKee, L. M., & Levinson, E. M. (1990). A review of the computerized version of The Self-Directed Search. *Career Development Quarterly, 38,* 325-333.

20. Meir, E. I., Melamed, S., & Abu-Freha, A. (1990). Vocational, avocational, and skill utilization congruences and their relationship with well-being in two cultures. *Journal of Vocational Behavior, 36,* 153-165.

21. Nordvik, H. (1990). Work activity and career goals in Holland's and Schein's theories of vocational personalities and career anchors. *Journal of Vocational Behavior, 38,* 165-178.

22. Schuttenberg, E. M., O'Dell, F. L., & Kaczala, C. M. (1990). Vocational personality types and sex-role perceptions of teachers, counselors, and educational administrators. *Career Development Quarterly, 39,* 60-71.

23. Khan, S. B., & Alvi, S. A. (1991). The structure of Holland's typology: A study in a nonwestern culture. *Journal of Cross-Cultural Psychology, 22,* 283-292.

24. Gade, E. M., Hurlburt, G., & Fuqua, D. (1992). The use of the Self-Directed Search to identify American Indian high school dropouts. *The School Counselor, 39,* 311–315.

25. Humes, C. W. (1992). Career planning implications for learning disabled high school students using the MBTI and SDS-E. *The School Counselor, 39,* 362–368.

26. Jagger, L., Neukrug, E., & McAuliffe, G. (1992). Congruence between personality traits and chosen occupation as a predictor of job satisfaction for people with disabilities. *Rehabilitation Counselor Bulletin, 36,* 53–60.

27. Leung, S. A., Conoley, C. W., Scheel, M. J., & Sonnenberg, R. T. (1992). An examination of the relation between vocational identity, consistency, and differentiation. *Journal of Vocational Behavior, 40,* 95-107.

28. Meir, E. I., & Navon, M. (1992). A longitudinal examination of congruence hypotheses. *Journal of Vocational Behavior, 41,* 35-47.

29. Miller, M. J., & Knippers, J. A. (1992). Jeopardy: A career information game for school counselors. *Career Development Quarterly, 41,* 55-61.

30. Miller, M. J., Newell, N. P., Springer, T. P., & Wells, D. (1992). Accuracy of the college majors finder for three majors. *Career Development Quarterly, 40,* 334-339.

31. Tracey, T. J., & Rounds, J. (1992). Evaluating the RIASEC circumplex using high-point codes. *Journal of Vocational Behavior, 41,* 295-311.

32. Harrington, T. F., Feller, R., & O'Shea, A. J. (1993). Four methods to determine RIASEC codes for college majors and a comparison of hit rates. *Career Development Quarterly, 41,* 383-392.

33. Jones, l. K. (1993). Two career guidance instruments: Their helpfulness to students and effect on students' career exploration. *The School Counselor, 40,* 191–200.

34. Rounds, J., & Tracey, T. J. (1993). Prediger's dimensional representation of Holland's RIASEC circumplex. *Journal of Applied Psychology, 78,* 875-890.

35. Borget, M. M., & Gilroy, F. D. (1994). Interests and self-efficacy as predictors of mathematics/science-based career choice. *Psychological Reports, 75,* 753-754.

36. Brown, S. D., & Gore, P. A., Jr. (1994). An evaluation of interest congruence indices: Distribution characteristics of and measurement properties. *Journal of Vocational Behavior, 45,* 310-327.

37. Chung, Y. B., & Harman, L. W. (1994). The career interests and aspirations of gay men: How sex-role orientation is related? *Journal of Vocational Behavior, 45,* 223-239.

38. Levinson, E. M., Rafoth, B. A., & Lesnak, L. (1994). A criterion-related validity study of the OASIS-2 Interest Schedule. *Journal of Employment Counseling, 31,* 29-37.

39. Meir, E. I. (1994). Comprehensive interests measurement in counseling for congruence. *Career Development Quarterly, 42,* 314-325.

40. Strack, S. (1994). Relation Millon's basic personality styles and Holland's occupational types. *Journal of Vocational Behavior, 45,* 41-54.

41. Thompson, J. M., Flynn, R. J., & Griffith, S. A. (1994). Congruence and coherence as predictors of congruent employment outcomes. *Career Development Quarterly, 42,* 271-281.

42. Tokar, D. M., & Swanson, J. L. (1994). Evaluation of the correspondence between Holland's vocational personality typology and the five-factor model of personality. *Journal of Vocational Behavior, 46,* 89-108.

43. Eagan, A. E., & Walsh, W. B. (1995). Person-environment congruence and coping strategies. *Career Development Quarterly, 43,* 246-256.

44. Meir, E. I., Melamed, S., & Dinur, C. (1995). The benefits of congruence. *Career Development Quarterly, 43,* 257-266.

45. Tokar, D. M., & Swanson, J. L. (1995). Evaluation of the correspondence between Holland's vocational personality typology and the five-factor model of personality. *Journal of Vocational Behavior, 46,* 89-108.

46. Mahalik, J. R. (1996). Client vocational interests as predictors of client reactions to counselor intentions. *Journal of Counseling and Development, 74,* 416–421.

47. Ohler, D. L., Levinson, E. M., & Barker, W. F. (1996). Career maturity in college students with learning disabilities. *The Career Development Quarterly, 44,* 278–288.

48. Shivy, V. A. Phillips, S. D., & Koehly, L. M. (1996). Knowledge organization as a factor in career intervention outcome: A multidimensional scaling analysis. *Journal of Counseling Psychology, 43,* 178–186.

[Note—These reviews are based on 1990 materials. The reviewers did not have the 1994 user's guide and technical manual. The revision of this test will be reviewed in an upcoming MMY—Ed.]

Review of The Self-Directed Search, Form E— 1990 Revision by JOSEPH C. CIECHALSKI, Associate Professor of Counselor and Adult Education, East Carolina University, Greenville, NC:

The 1990 Revision of The Self-Directed Search (SDS) Easy Form (Form E), like the 1985 edition of Form E, was developed as an alternate form of the regular version of the SDS. Form E was specifically designed for adolescents and adults with at least a fourth-grade reading level. It is a self-administered, self-scored, and self-interpreted interest inventory based on Holland's theory of vocational choice. Holland's theory assumes that most persons can be categorized into one of six personality and environmental types: Realistic, Investigative, Artistic, Social, Enterprising, or Conventional.

The 1990 Revision of Form E contains 192 items (11 less than the 1985 edition of Form E). A total of 73 items were replaced in the 1990 edition. Replacement items were selected from a pool of 188 new items generated by three psychologists. The resulting 73 replacement items for the 1990 Revision were selected based on item analyses and on the endorsement of at least 5% of the males and females in the sample. Like the 1985 edition, the 1990 edition of the assessment booklet is divided into six sections. These sections include: Jobs You Have Thought About (up to five jobs can be listed), Activities (liked or disliked), Skills (skills you have/ want or do not have/want), Jobs (liked or disliked), and Rating Your Abilities (best to poorest). The final section is a scoring section in which a two-letter summary (rather than a three-letter) code is obtained.

The directions for self-administering Form E have been revised for added ease and better comprehension. For example, in the section on Jobs, brief definitions follow each job listed. Examinees respond to items in the assessment booklet. A separate answer sheet is not required. Therefore, errors in transferring responses to an answer sheet are eliminated.

Scoring the 1990 edition of Form E is easy. Except for the Jobs You Have Thought About section, examinees simply total all their scores and record their top two scores in the spaces provided in the assessment booklet. Although Form E is self-scored, this reviewer suggests that the counselor check the scoring to guarantee accuracy of the results.

Next, examinees refer to the newly revised Jobs Finder to discover jobs that correspond to their two-letter Holland code. This edition of the Jobs Finder lists 797 occupations according to two-letter Holland codes. Each occupation is identified by a single digit number (ED) that indicates the training or schooling needed for the job. For example, the numbers 1 and 2 identify jobs that can be performed by someone who has graduated from grade school, the number 3 identifies jobs in which a high school diploma or some high school is needed, and the number 4 identifies jobs in which high school and possibly some other training is needed. In addition, a nine-digit *Dictionary of Occupation Titles (DOT)* number following each occupation can be used to locate more information about the occupation.

In addition to the Jobs Finder, the author has revised You and Your Job and the Professional User's Guide. The 1990 edition of You and Your Job is divided into six sections: You and Your Job, The Six Types of People (explains the six personality types in easy to understand language), Finding Your Type, Types of Jobs, Finding More About the Job (suggestions for using the Job Finder and *DOT*), and Choosing a Job. Examinees must read You and Your Job in order to understand their results. Again, this reviewer believes that examinees with low reading abilities should be assisted in understanding and using their results by their counselors.

The 1990 edition of the Professional User's Guide is well written and contains information on the reliability and equivalence between the 1985 and 1990 versions of Form E. Using Cronbach's alpha, the internal consistency was essentially unchanged for both versions. All correlations for section scales were above .80 and above .95 for the summary scales. A pairwise correlation of the summary scales was calculated and the results indicated that the correlations were consistent across both versions. In addition, frequency counts of the first letter of Holland's code between both versions were calculated. The frequency of the first letter is unchanged and in 76% of the cases, the two-letter codes were the same. Therefore, the author concluded that the 1990 and 1985 versions were equivalent.

Validity of the 1990 Revision was not addressed specifically in the Professional User's Guide. In earlier editions of the SDS, information about the predictive and concurrent validity was included in the 1985 edition of the Professional Manual. At this time, a 1990 edition of the Professional Manual was not available.

The 1990 Revision of Form E reflects the author's dedication to improving on an already popular and well-established instrument. Items have been replaced along with major revisions of the Professional User's Guide and You and Your Job. A new Jobs Finder was written especially for those individuals seeking jobs requiring a high school education or less. I hope a new edition of the Professional Manual will be published soon that, like the 1985 edition, will address the validity of the instrument. Although Form E is self-scored, examinees may need assistance from their counselor. Nevertheless, Form E remains an excellent interest instrument.

Review of The Self-Directed Search, Form E— 1990 Revision by ESTHER E. DIAMOND, Educational and Psychological Consultant, Evanston, IL:

The 1990 revision of The Self-Directed Search (SDS), Form E, described as an equivalent form of the 1985 version, is intended for test-takers 16 years of age or older with at least a fourth-grade reading ability.

The development of the 1990 revision and the determination of its equivalence to the 1985 SDS is described in a helpful Professional User's Guide. Like the 1985 revision, the 1990 version is based on Holland's RIASEC typology—the theory that most persons can be categorized as one of six personality types: Realistic, Investigative, Artistic, Social, Enterprising, and Conventional. The six personality types are matched by six types of environments on the premise that people search for environments where there are others like themselves, who share their skills, abilities, and interests. The SDS scales estimate a person's resemblance to each of the six personality types by exploring his or her experiences and preferred activities.

The 1990 version of the SDS differs from the 1985 edition in the following principal ways: All section scales—Likes, Skills, Jobs—have new items; instructions are simpler and more clear; and a new version of the Jobs Finder, which lists 797 (300 more than the earlier version) has been developed. The changes represent Holland's responses to suggestions and surveys of users of the 1985 form who wanted the items to more closely reflect the types of activities and interests of the intended test-takers. They suggested, for example, that the Jobs Finder focus more exclusively on occupations at lower levels of educational preparation.

Replacement items for consideration were generated by three psychologists considered experts in Holland theory. Unanimous agreement of all three was required for adding the items to the item pool; 188 new items were generated. Possible replacement items for each of the six RIASEC scales in the 18 section scales comprising Activities, Skills, and Jobs ranged from 2 to 32. Some involved only minor rewording of existing items. No changes were proposed for the ability ratings in the Self-Estimates section.

To study the equivalency of the 1990 Revision and the 1985 Form E, an experimental Form E booklet was developed and administered to 145 individuals ranging in age from 16 to 65, with an educational level ranging from no high school education to a high school education and some technical training—similar to the target test-taker population. Sixty-five percent of the sample were females. The sample appeared to be similar to the target test-taker population.

For each item identified for possible replacement, a replacement item was selected on the basis of its correlation with the total scale as well as its mean and standard deviation. The item also had to be endorsed by at least 5% of the males and 5% of the females in the sample. Scale replacement items were found for each section; 73 items of the total of 192 were replaced, and the six original self-rating items were retained, adding an item to each summary scale. The competencies section of the test booklet, however, contains two items that appear to be outdated—one involving use of a slide rule and another involving use of a keypunch.

A number of criteria determined the equivalence of the 1985 Form E and its 1990 Revision. Internal consistency reliability coefficients (Cronbach's alpha) were essentially unchanged across the two versions. Means and standard deviations for each of the section and summary scales showed only trivial differences. Particularly important was the requirement that each scale correlate with its adjacent, alternate, and opposite scale, as depicted on the RIASEC hexagon, in a consistent way across the two forms. Still another criterion required consistency in the appearance in the first letter of the Holland code across forms. Frequency of the first letter of the code was virtually unchanged in the 1990 version. Changes in the two-letter codes occurred in approximately 34% of the cases, but in 75.9% the two letters of the code were the same across forms. (It should be noted that two-letter Holland codes are used in the 1990 revision rather than the three-letter codes in use in earlier forms.)

A number of resource materials are designed to help in the interpretation and use of the 1990 Revision of the SDS Form E. You and Your Job introduces the program briefly, explaining the purpose of the SDS, how to find out about jobs, and choosing a job. The 1990 Assessment Booklet asks the test-takers about their likes and dislikes, the skills they have or want to learn, jobs they like or think they might like, and how they rate their competencies from best to least, on a six-letter scale. They also figure out their two-letter summary code, easier to compute than the usual three-letter code. It is suggested that they then look at the Jobs Finder (JF), which now has descriptions of 797 jobs representing a wide variety of industries and occupational groups. The jobs are categorized by Holland and *Dictionary of Occupational Titles (DOT)* codes and all require a high school education or less. Educational levels required are also listed. Additional resource materials, not specifically designed for the 1990 SDS, include The Leisure Activities Finder and the *Dictionary of Holland Occupational Codes.*

Clearly, much work has been done with the 1990 Revision to respond to users' needs, criticisms, and suggestions, and the revision is fully equivalent to the 1985 Form E. Several problems persist, however. Holland still maintains that gender influences career choice and that accurate assessment of all the influences that affect career choice would promote rather than prohibit that choice. In his favor is the inclusion of an item about sewing machines as a Realistic choice in the Skills section of the Assessment Booklet, and the recognition that some individuals may never have been exposed to certain jobs or activities in the Assessment Booklet. At least they have the chance to indicate that they "might like" or "want to learn to" do a given activity or job.

Holland has been criticized for his use of raw scores rather than standard scores to determine total test scores for each personality/occupational type and the summary code in earlier versions of the SDS. The scales used to determine the total test score did not have the same number of items in each of the RIASEC areas contributing to it. In the 1990 version, however, an equal number of items contributes to each scale—32 plus 1 each for the self-rating scales, and an equal number of items for each scale contributes to the summary score.

Still another criticism is directed against the emphasis on self-administration, scoring, and interpretation of the results. However, the various resource materials mention sources of help, including counselors, so that the criticism would appear to be minimized.

In summary, the 1990 Revision of the SDS Form E has overcome many of the earlier Form E problems. Questionable items have been changed, the reading level has been dropped to fourth grade, the questions in the Assessment Booklet are uncomplicated, and the two-letter Holland code simplifies the scoring system. The resource materials should be particularly helpful and appealing to counselors as well as test-takers. Remaining criticisms, accompanied by constructive, feasible suggestions, should elicit a response from Holland for future revisions, as they have in the case of the 1990 Revision.

[85]
The Senior Apperception Technique [1985 Revision].

Purpose: A projective instrument to gather information on forms of depression, loneliness, or rage in the elderly.
Population: Ages 65 and over.
Publication Dates: 1973–1985.
Acronym: S.A.T.
Scores: No scores.
Administration: Individual.
Price Data, 1993: $19.75 per manual ('85, 12 pages) and set of picture cards.
Time: Administration time not reported.
Author: Leopold Bellak.
Publisher: C.P.S., Inc.
Cross References: See T3:2148 (2 references); for a review by K. Warner Schaie, see 8:676 (1 reference).

Review of the Senior Apperception Technique by PAUL A. ARBISI, Assessment Clinic Director, Psychology Service, Minneapolis Veterans Affairs Medical Center, Minneapolis, MN:

Henry Murray (1943) conceived the Thematic Apperception Test (T.A.T.) as a mean of divining the underlying dynamics of personality: the "needs" and "press" of an individual's life. A primary assumption underlying a projective technique such as the T.A.T. is that in the process of creating a story, the client identifies with a particular character depicted in the stimuli and the conflicts, wishes, fear, or desires attributed to the character in the story reflect those of the client (Lindzey, 1952). Within the context of apperception techniques, effort has been made to increase the degree to which the client will identify with the characters by varying the characteristics of the stimuli. The desire to increase the identification with a character in the stories by modifying the appearance of the central character was prompted by Murray himself who suggested administering at least one card of the T.A.T. showing a figure who is approximately the same age and sex as the subject (Murray, 1943). On the other hand, too great an identification with a central character may not be altogether desirable because unacceptable or unpleasant desires are projected with less anxiety if the central character is different from the subject and perhaps a more suitable source of these censurable desires or needs (Piotrowski, 1950). For better or worse, the Senior Apperception Technique (S.A.T.) is one such extension of the T.A.T. and joins the Gerontological Apperception Test (G.A.T.) and the Projective Assessment of Aging Method (P.A.A.M.) in attempting to plumb the depths of the aged-psyche by depicting the central characters as elderly and, thus, the older adult can identify with them more easily.

STIMULUS. Impressive attempts have been made to extend the T.A.T. by varying the stimuli in order to increase the projective identification of the central character (for review see Murstein, 1965). Examples include the Thompson (1949) alteration where the figures in the T.A.T. cards are depicted as African Americans to be used with African American clients, the depiction of characters as either blue collar or white collar workers to better pull for vocationally determined identifications, and finally, in the ultimate attempt to maximize identification, actual photographs of client's heads have been superimposed onto the T.A.T. cards (Murstein, 1965). The S.A.T. contains 16 cards depicting elderly individuals that "pull" for themes that are relevant to the geriatric client, based on the authors' clinical experience or their reading of the gerontological literature. The themes vary from commonly identified issues relating to somatic concerns, institutionalization, and loss of loved ones to the less frequently addressed themes of sexual feeling of the elderly toward younger individuals. The stimuli were ostensibly designed to reflect the thoughts and feelings of the elderly yet there is only minimal information in the manual regarding how these themes were chosen or how often the cards "pull" for a stated theme. By the same token, a determined effort was made to broaden the thematic content by occasionally depicting happy or pleasant scenes rather than dour or obviously unpleasant situations. In terms of other alterations to the stimuli, the cards were designed in a larger format than the T.A.T. in hopes of compensating for the failing eyesight and presbyopia found in the elderly. The authors contend that the figures are ambiguous for sex. This assertion is not at all apparent on examination of the stimuli and one wonders why it is necessary to state something that has unclear relevance and is so evidently incorrect. Perhaps the authors wish to tap the sexual bimodality of late life. If so, it would be useful to state this goal explicitly. On the whole, the stimuli are cartoonishly rendered line drawings of situations that pull for a wide range of themes. Unlike the T.A.T., there is little ambiguity or evocative richness in the depiction of situations likely to elicit themes related to aging.

TEST OR TECHNIQUE? The authors insist that the S.A.T. is not a test, but a "technique that lends itself to many different uses" (p. 345, Bellak, 1986). Moreover, according to the authors, the S.A.T. constitutes a variation of the interview question, what ails you? This sense of semantic ambiguity may save paper by eliminating the normative tables and demographic charts that ordinarily appear in test manuals, but in this case definitional ambiguity is the first step on the road to perdition and has implications for the training and credentials of those deemed qualified to use the instrument. With regard to user qualifications, it is assumed that the prior training of the user will limit the conclusions or inferences drawn from the "technique." This thinking appears to be based upon the assumption that blind squirrels never find any acorns. This premise, of course, is absurd. Thus, the authors would have us affirm the following logical construction: If the user happens to be someone who has absolutely no training in psychometric methods or unconscious processes, then the user will only be able to facilitate the communication process and make no further inferences regarding more salient themes or underlying dynamics. It follows, alternatively, that if the user is a trained psychologist or psychiatrist familiar with projective techniques and the unconscious, then the user will be able to make meaningful inferences regarding the dynamic processes of the elderly. The manual is no more specific regarding the qualifications of users and relies upon the user to limit appropriately their inference based on the users' discretion. Apparently, a reliance upon the honor system is sufficient for the authors and publishers, but the American Psychological Association embodied in *The Standards for Educational and Psychological Testing* (AERA, APA, & NCME, 1985) finds this approach to the issue to be substandard.

Perhaps, as a means of bolstering the proposition that blind squirrels never find nuts, the manual contains few guidelines and limited suggestions regarding the interpretation of each card and no hard data to support the inferences drawn from each card or the technique *in toto*. There is nothing even approximating normative data or an adequate description of the 100 elderly subjects used to develop the "technique." As suggested by the manual author, a perusal of the acknowledgments was the only way to determine the source of these subjects. By a simple count of the acknowledged individuals and their institutional association, it appears a significant number of subjects were residents of nursing homes in New York. The homogeneous nature of the sample has implications for the generalizability of the "technique." For example, a 75-year-old resident of a nursing home who, by definition, requires significant care and attention may respond quite differently than a 75-year-old who is living independently and actively consulting to a Fortune 500 company. To be fair, the manual makes no claims for statistically sophisticated validity and reliability. The data that are presented in support of the reliability and validity of the S.A.T. consist of two pilot studies cited in the manual with two further studies cited in *The T.A.T., C.A.T., and S.A.T. in Clinical Use, Fourth Edition* (Bellak, 1986). These meager studies do little to aid in establishing the validity of the "technique" and provide nothing more than intriguing possibilities for interpretation. The empirically minded clinician is troubled by the glaring lack of data supporting the use of the S.A.T. in elderly populations.

SUGGESTIONS. (a) More explicit criteria for test users should be codified in the manual. It is alarming to imagine a group of untrained individuals administering and interpreting the T.A.T. Why should it be less alarming to imagine the same scenario with the S.A.T.? (b) Despite the authors' insistence that the S.A.T. is not a test, but a "technique," more attention needs to be paid to issues of reliability and validity. W. Grant Dahlstrom (1995), on being awarded the Bruno Klopfer Distinguished Award by the Society for Personality Assessment, described his experience in the summer of 1947 upon attending a 2-week institute offered by Bruno Klopfer on the Rorschach "technique." Dahlstrom came away with the distinct impression that Klopfer had developed an internal interpretive process whereby Rorschach-related "signs" were tabulated until a certain threshold was achieved. At that point Klopfer would assign the individual to a particular category and provide an interpretation based on the rich correlate-base of that type. In essence, an empirically driven interpretive process was applied to a projective technique that allowed for full and reasonably accurate inferences. This covert process was made overt through John Exner's system and his empirically driven interpretive strategy for the Rorschach (Exner, 1993). A bit of this type of thinking would go a long way toward improving the S.A.T. Even the most rudimentary normative data would be helpful. Would, for example, the young-old respond differently than the old-old to Card 13? More fundamentally, does the S.A.T. present an improvement over the T.A.T. for elderly populations? These questions should be addressed before this technique can be recommended, until then, *caveat emptor*.

SUMMARY. The S.A.T. is one of many variants of the T.A.T. designed to improve the projective "yield" by using stimuli that depict the characters as physically similar to the elderly client. The authors insist that the S.A.T. is not a "test" but a "technique" and accordingly provide little validity or reliability data in the manual. Thus, it is difficult to evaluate the merits of the S.A.T. by any but the most obvious means. With face validity in mind, at best the S.A.T. could facilitate communication between an elderly client and an empathetic therapist. At worst, the S.A.T. represents an ageist and extraneous method of assessing the elderly that does not provide an improvement over the T.A.T., an age-irrelevant instrument with infinitely more clinical data to support it.

REVIEWER'S REFERENCES

Murray, H. A. (1943). *Thematic Apperception Test manual*. Cambridge: Harvard University Press.

Thompson, C. E. (1949). The Thompson modification of the thematic apperception test. *Rorschach Research Exchange and Journal of Projective Techniques, 13*, 469–478.

Piotrowski, Z. A. (1950). A new evaluation of the thematic apperception test. *Psychoanalytic Review, 37*, 101–127.

Lindzey, G. (1952). Thematic apperception test: Interpretive assumption and related empirical evidence. *Psychological Bulletin, 49*, 1–21.

Murstein, B. I. (1965). The stimulus. In B. I. Murstein (Ed.), *Handbook of projective techniques* (pp. 509–546). New York: Basic Books.

American Educational Research Association, American Psychological Association, & National Council on Measurement in Education. (1985). *Standards for educational and psychological testing*. Washington, DC: American Psychological Association, Inc.

Bellak, L. (1986). *The T.A.T., C.A.T., and S.A.T. in clinical use* (4th ed.). Orlando, FL: Grune & Stratton.

Exner, J. E. (1993). *The Rorschach: A comprehensive system. I: Basic applications* (3rd ed.). New York: Wiley.

Dahlstrom, W. G. (1995). Pigeons, people, and pigeon-holes. *Journal of Personality Assessment, 64*, 2–20.

Review of the Senior Apperception Technique by MICHAEL G. KAVAN, Associate Dean for Student Affairs and Associate Professor of Family Practice, Creighton University School of Medicine, Omaha, NE:

The Senior Apperception Technique (S.A.T.) is a projective "technique" originally designed to "elucidate the problems of elderly individuals" (Bellak & Bellak, 1986, p. 341). More specifically, it is an apperceptive method designed to elicit a person's "meaningfully subjective interpretation of a perception" (Bellak, 1986, p. 17). The S.A.T. consists of 16 black-and-white pictures featuring one or more elderly persons in various situations. These pictures are meant to elicit themes and psychological problems in the elderly. These themes, which were derived from the gerontological literature and the authors' personal clinical experience, concern matters such as social interaction, familial issues, loneliness, anxiety, and, of course, sex. The S.A.T. is seen by the authors as a necessary extension of the Thematic Apperception Technique (T.A.T.; Morgan & Murray, 1935) due to the necessity to assess the growing number of elderly persons in the United States. Other than summarizing additional studies using the S.A.T. no changes are noted between the 1985 revision and its predecessor.

ADMINISTRATION AND SCORING. The S.A.T. may be administered by persons from a variety of professions. Qualifications of those administering the pictures depend only on how they intend to use the technique. The clinician is instructed to hand each picture to the elderly person for viewing. Beyond this, the only specific instructions provided within the manual for the administration of the S.A.T. pictures are for Picture #16, which includes these special instructions: "Here is the picture of a sleeping person having a dream. Tell me in some detail what the dream might be about—make it a lively dream" (p. 6). Also, the following statement is recommended for occasions in which there is a lack of response: "Maybe we will come back to this one" (p. 5). One is left to assume that methods similar to instructions provided for the T.A.T. or Children's Apperception Technique (Bellak, 1986) are to be used for the remaining S.A.T. pictures as well. It is recommended that no more than 5 minutes be given per picture and that each interview last no more than

one-half hour, which would appear to be difficult if the maximum time is allowed for each picture (i.e., 5 minutes x 16 pictures = 80 minutes). Instructions are given that there is no need to administer all pictures to each person. Responses may be written or tape recorded by the administrator. No information regarding scoring is provided within the manual. The manual does contain a summary of typical themes seen in response to the various pictures. Because the S.A.T. is considered a technique as opposed to a test, the authors claim that it does nothing more than "facilitate the process of communicating one's feeling and thoughts by responding to standard stimuli rather than to standard clinical questions" (p. 9). It is recommended that if one is to make inferences about preconscious and unconscious processes, then this type of interpretation can be accomplished by methods described by Bellak (1975) for the C.A.T. and T.A.T.—information that is not included in the S.A.T. manual.

RELIABILITY AND VALIDITY. No reliability or validity data are provided within the manual. Several studies conducted with the S.A.T. are summarized and suggest: (a) The elderly did not differ substantially from a control group of students in regard to responses involving despair, death, and other negative images; (b) sex continued to be a major theme in elderly responses; (c) elderly and female responses were noted as more positive than those of younger and male subjects; (d) the S.A.T. was effective in discriminating between emotionally cognitively impaired and nonimpaired nursing home residents; and (e) affiliation was the most important content theme. A section on suggestions for future research is also included within the manual, but interestingly, does not include any recommendations to develop a scoring system or to establish reliability, validity, and/or normative data.

NORMS. No normative data are provided within the manual. Bellak (1986) indicates that normative data on a technique such as this are "hardly very useful" because the clinician is interested primarily in the responses characteristic of the "individual" (p. 39).

SUMMARY. The S.A.T. is an apperceptive technique meant to elicit concerns held by the elderly. Its construction is based on a review of the gerontological literature, the authors' personal clinical experiences, and a subjectively based method of paring down and revising the pictorial stimuli. The manual contains limited information about test construction, administration, scoring, interpretation, reliability, validity, and norms. As such, the S.A.T. comes nowhere close to being a test as defined by the *Standards for Educational and Psychological Testing* (American Educational Research Association, American Psychological Association, & National Council on Measurement in Education, 1985). Instead, it is, as the authors admit, "only a slight variation on the clinical technique of asking people to tell us what ails them" (p. 9). In light of this admission, the authors should, at least, be given credit for realizing that the S.A.T. is nothing more than a collection of pictures meant to facilitate the communication of feelings and thoughts by the elderly. As such, it should be used for this purpose only. Potential users of the S.A.T. are cautioned against using the S.A.T. in research and clinical settings beyond this limited purpose of the technique.

REVIEWER'S REFERENCES

Morgan, C. D., & Murray, H. A. (1935). A method for investigating phantasies: The Thematic Apperception Test. *Archives of Neurology and Psychiatry, 34,* 289–306.

Bellak, L. (1975). *The T.A.T., C.A.T., and S.A.T. in clinical use* (3rd ed.). Orlando, FL: Grune & Stratton.

American Educational Research Association, American Psychological Association, & National Council on Measurement in Education. (1985). *Standards for educational and psychological testing.* Washington, DC: American Psychological Association, Inc.

Bellak, L. (1986). *The T.A.T., C.A.T., and S.A.T. in clinical use* (4th ed.). Orlando, FL: Grune & Stratton.

Bellak, L., & Bellak, S. S. (1986). The S.A.T. In L. Bellak (Ed.), *The T.A.T., C.A.T., and S.A.T. in clinical use* (4th ed.; pp. 341–360). Orlando, FL: Grune & Stratton.

[86]

Situational Confidence Questionnaire.

Purpose: Designed to help clients identify high-risk drinking relapse situations.

Population: Adult alcoholics.

Publication Dates: 1987–1988.

Administration: Group.

Editions, 2: Computerized, print.

Authors: Helen M. Annis and J. Martin Graham.

Publisher: Addiction Research Foundation [Canada].

a) SITUATIONAL CONFIDENCE QUESTIONNAIRE.

Acronym: SCQ-39.

Scores, 9: Unpleasant Emotions/Frustrations, Physical Discomfort, Social Problems at Work, Social Tension, Pleasant Emotions, Positive Social Situations, Urges and Temptations, Testing Personal Control, Average.

Price Data, 1993: $14.75 per 25 questionnaires; $13.50 per user's guide ('88, 49 pages); $70 per 50 uses software edition (includes user's guide); $225 per 200 uses software edition (includes user's guide); $25 per specimen set including user's guide and 25 questionnaires.

Time: (10–15) minutes.

b) ALCOHOL CONFIDENCE QUESTIONNAIRE.

Acronym: ACQ-16.

Scores: Total score only.

Time: Administration time not reported.

Comments: Brief version of the Situational Confidence Questionnaire; test items listed in SCQ user's guide.

Cross References: See T4:2467 (1 reference).

TEST REFERENCES

1. Heather, N., Tebbutt, J., & Greeley, J. C. (1993). Alcohol cue exposure directed at a goal of moderate drinking. *Journal of Behavior Therapy and Experimental Psychiatry, 24,* 187–195.

2. Miller, K. J., McCrady, B. S., Abrams, D. B., & Labouvie, E. W. (1994). Taking an individualized approach to the assessment of self-efficacy and the prediction of alcoholic relapse. *Journal of Psychopathology and Behavioral Assessment, 16,* 111–120.

3. Sobell, L. C., Toneatto, T., & Sobell, M. (1994). Behavioral assessment and treatment planning for alcohol, tobacco, and other drug problems: Current status with an emphasis on clinical applications. *Behavior Therapy, 25,* 533–580.

4. Sobell, M. B., Sobell, L. C., & Gavin, D. R. (1995). Portraying alcohol treatment outcomes: Different yardsticks of success. *Behavior Therapy, 26,* 643–669.

Review of the Situational Confidence Questionnaire by MERITH COSDEN, Professor, Department of Education, University of California, Santa Barbara, CA:

The Situational Confidence Questionnaire (SCQ-39) is a self-report measure of self-efficacy for being able to control one's drinking. The scale is based on the premise that cognitive factors, including self-efficacy, play a role in relapse and relapse prevention. The SCQ was designed to determine self-efficacy for controlled drinking across potential drinking situations, and to assess domains in which clients with substance abuse problems are most likely to relapse.

The 39 items on the SCQ are linked to items on the revised Inventory of Drinking Situations (IDS; Test 12, this volume) by the same authors (see Cosden, this volume, for a critique). On the IDS, individuals are asked to rate the frequency with which they have engaged in heavy drinking under specific situations; on the SCQ, they are asked about their confidence in being able to resist the urge to drink heavily in these same situations.

Thus, the items and subscales used on the SCQ were derived from the items and subscales of the IDS. Initially, the IDS was composed of 100 items fit into eight subscales. Five subscales described personal states that might result in drinking (i.e., Unpleasant Emotions, Physical Discomfort, Pleasant Emotions, Testing Personal Control, and Urges and Temptations), and three subscales described social situations that could promote drinking (i.e., Conflict with Others, Social Pressure to Drink, and Pleasant Times with Others). These situations were derived from a review of literature on factors related to relapse for men with drinking problems. An early version of the SCQ had 100 items, which were matched to each of the 100 original IDS items.

The number of items on the IDS was reduced by selecting the 42 items that had the highest item-subscale correlations. These 42 items include four items in each of the six original subscales, which were found to be unifactorial, and 18 items from the original Conflict with Others and Pleasant Times with Others subscales, which were found to be multifactorial. In a subsequent confirmatory factor analysis, three items were found to be strongly related to more than one variable and dropped, resulting in the current 39 items. A second confirmatory factor analysis, based on the 39 items, resulted in a model with eight different subscales, reflecting a regrouping of items. A final, confirmatory factor analysis conducted on the new model was satisfactory, supporting the following factors: Unpleasant Emotions/Frustration, Physical Discomfort, Social Problems at Work, Social Tension, Pleasant Emotions, Positive Social Situations, Urges and Temptations, and Testing Personal Control. A series of confirmatory factor analyses conducted on the first order correlation matrix determined the best second order factor structure. Although the model for the IDS placed all subscales into two categories, the best fit for the SCQ data was a three-factor model; the first four subscales were grouped under a factor labeled Negative Affect Situations, the second two subscales were grouped under a factor called Positive Affect Situations, and the last two subscales were grouped under a factor named Urges and Testing.

The normative sample for the 42-item SCQ consisted of 424 clients in two Canadian substance abuse treatment facilities. The gender (27% female, 73% male), age (average 41 years, range from 18–76), educational history (44% completed high school), and alcohol abuse histories (average 8 years of problem drinking) were provided. Neither ethnicity nor history of abuse of other drugs were described, however.

The construct validity of the SCQ was assessed by correlating subscale scores with measures of problem drinking. In the manual, significant correlations are reported between number of drinks, number of days spent drinking, and all subscale scores. There is little differentiation between subscale scores with one exception: Only Positive Social Situations was significantly correlated with time drinking with others, indicating that clients who reported less confidence in their ability to restrain from heavy drinking in positive social situations also reported drinking more in social situations. In a study of construct validity, Miller, Ross, Emmerson, and Todt (1989) found significant differences between clients with long-term and short-term sobriety on all subscales of the SCQ except Testing Personal Control. Few studies to date have attempted to assess the predictive validity of the SCQ. Two unpublished studies by Solomon and Annis and Annis and Davis are cited in the manual. In the first study, SCQ scores obtained at intake to a substance abuse program failed to predict frequency of relapse (drinking episodes) and only weakly predicted the amount of drinking that occurred during these episodes. In the second study, the authors reported that clients tended to have a serious relapse under the two conditions (reflected in lower subscale scores) in which they rated themselves as having the least amount of control.

The SCQ can be administered as a paper-and-pencil questionnaire or electronically using an IBM computer. It can also be administered individually or in small groups. The manual includes an estimate that it takes 10–15 minutes to complete the SCQ. Clients are asked to imagine themselves in a situation and rate their confidence in their ability to abstain from heavy drinking in that situation. Heavy drinking is not objectively defined, and is left to the client's perception. A scale ranging from 0% (not at all confident) to 100% (completely confident) is presented with each item. Subscale scores are obtained by calculating the mean confidence ratings for all items in a subscale. Clinically, subscale scores can be considered alone, or as part of a client profile. The manual also has tables that can be used to translate raw scores into standard scores for comparison with the normative sample.

The SCQ has been modified across studies to fit the needs of subgroups of substance abusers. Miller et al. (1989), for example, used the SCQ to assess the needs of clients in an abstinence-oriented program. Thus, they changed the stem to ask clients about their ability to avoid drinking altogether rather than their ability to avoid drinking heavily. In addition, they modified the rating scale to present alternatives in 10-point, rather than 20-point, increments. Despite these changes, the authors report similar subscale findings to those found on the original scales. In a further derivation from the original scale, Barber, Cooper, and Heather (1991) developed a Situational Confidence Questionnaire (Heroin) to assess the needs of heroin users. They changed the stem on the original SCQ to ask respondents about their confidence in resisting the urge to use heroin, but otherwise maintained the content and format of the questions. The impact of these changes on the reliability and validity of the scale requires further evaluation.

The authors of the SCQ have also developed a shorter form of the scale, called the Alcohol Confidence Questionnaire (ACQ). The ACQ has 16 items, 2 from each of the eight subscales. The manual presents a Cronbach alpha of .95 for the ACQ, whereas scores on the ACQ showed a correlation of .99 with scores on the SCQ. These psychometric properties of the ACQ suggest that it is a promising, if untested, measure of self-efficacy.

The authors note limitations to the SCQ, including the possibility that clients may fake responses in order to appear to be progressing in treatment. A major limitation noted by this reviewer is the lack of utility of the subscale scores. In most reported studies, problem drinking is associated with lower confidence ratings across most, or all, situations (subscales). There is little support for the use of individual subscales in determining specific relapse situations. This is not surprising, as psychometrically, the subscales have not been stable across studies. The SCQ appears most effective in providing a global measure of clients' perceptions of their ability to resist heavy drinking. Future use of the scale should focus on its utility as a global correlate and predictor of self-efficacy for drinking, or in develop-

ing more stable subscales, which can be used to predict specific relapse situations.

REVIEWER'S REFERENCES

Miller, P. J., Ross, S. M., Emmerson, R. Y., & Todt, E. H. (1989). Self-efficacy in alcoholics: Clinical validation of the Situational Confidence Questionnaire. *Addictive Behaviors, 14,* 217–224.

Barber, J. G., Cooper, B. K., & Heather, N. (1991). The Situational Confidence Questionnaire (Heroin). *The International Journal of the Addictions, 26,* 565–575.

Review of the Situational Confidence Questionnaire by CECIL R. REYNOLDS, Professor of Educational Psychology & Professor of Neuroscience, Texas A&M University, College Station, TX:

The Situational Confidence Questionnaire (SCQ) was "developed as a tool for therapists to monitor the development of a client's self-efficacy in relation to drinking situations over the course of treatment" (p. 1). It is also intended to be a measure of alcohol-related self-efficacy (not defined) for researchers interested in treatment outcomes and alcohol relapse. The original conceptualization of the instrument is modeled around the work of Albert Bandura in the area of self-efficacy. The authors believe the SCQ will be useful in repeat administrations during treatment and as an indication of treatment response. The various scores provided by the SCQ were derived through a series of factor analyses including exploratory and multiple confirmatory analyses with adjustments made in various criteria for defining factors until the authors arrived at the eight subscales they prefer.

The manual presents a 10-page discussion of the psychometric properties of the SCQ that include its normative and developmental samples, reliability evidence, validity evidence, scaling, and suggestions for interpretation. The recommended uses and description of the population for which the test is intended are presented appropriately in the manual although user qualifications are neglected.

The sample used for test development and norming is not of adequate size and is not sufficiently representative to substantiate the item selection, to establish appropriate norms, and to support conclusions regarding the use of the instrument for the intended purposes. The samples were, in fact, samples of convenience and although appearing to be a large *N* (424), the age range of the sample (from 18 years to 76 years) and the presence of clear age differences in responses to the SCQ renders the samples inadequate. The test development sample and norming sample were the same. Changes in items and item selection are not discussed in the manual. It is not known if any changes in items were made based upon the responses of the sample or what item selection procedures were applied.

Items on the SCQ are rated by examinees on a 6-point scale. Reliability estimates for the subscales are provided for the entire age range. This would likely inflate the reliability of various subscales because there are clear age effects. It would be desirable for reliability coefficients to be reported separately by age level. When age effects are present and reliability coefficients in the form of Cronbach's alpha are reported across the entire age range, spurious inflation of reliability estimates occurs as item variances are increased disproportionately to total test variance. The reliability coefficients reported are incredibly high, with some subscales consisting of only three items having reliability coefficients as high as .93. Standard errors of measurement are reported in raw score format although standard scores are provided for interpretation, thus complicating considerably the application of the standard errors of measurement to the interpretation of standard score reporting of individual performance.

The authors provide a good discussion of the validity of the SCQ particularly providing evidence of concurrent validity and some limited predictive validity data. The authors overinterpret the outcome of these studies, however. When applied to prediction of alcohol use in certain situations and during treatment, no validity coefficients in excess of .24 are reported. The authors interpret Pearson correlations of this magnitude as providing strong predictions of behavior. The SCQ shows a variety of weak to moderate relationships to external variables and certainly does not possess adequate validity to substantiate interpretations of the performance of any individual patient. Although it may be useful in evaluating treatment outcomes based on large samples, clinical decisions about an individual patient clearly are not substantiated on the basis of evidence provided.

The scaling of the SCQ is inadequately described. A table of T-scores is provided and the discussion in the manual leads one to believe these are normalized T-scores. The manual refers to the percentage of individuals falling within one standard deviation of the mean when T-scores are normal yet an examination of the tables reveals the T-scores provided clearly are not normalized. This is misleading in the application and interpretation of these T-scores and needs clarification. This is largely characteristic of much of the information provided in the manual. The psychometric discussions are quite brief with particular methods mentioned but not described (with the exception of some of the factor analytic studies).

No data regarding test and item bias are provided with regard to ethnicity, gender, language, geographic region, or other factors. No item analyses for possible bias were conducted and the methods by which items were selected for inclusion for the final version of the test are not described.

Directions for administration and scoring of the SCQ are relatively straightforward and easily accomplished in the test booklets provided. This represents a plus for the SCQ. Another strength is its derivation from a clear theory for which the authors are to be lauded. From a psychometric perspective, however, the SCQ has many weaknesses, rendering it unusable except in large research projects. From a clinical perspective, it certainly should not be used in any way to make decisions about treatment compliance, intervention, or predicted outcomes for an individual patient.

[87]
The Stieglitz Informal Reading Inventory: Assessing Reading Behaviors from Emergent to Advanced Levels.

Purpose: Designed to provide educators with information about students' reading behaviors.
Population: Grades 1–9.
Publication Date: 1992.
Acronym: SIRI.
Scores, 7: Graded Words in Context (Independent, Instructional, Frustration), Graded Reading Passages (Word Recognition, Oral Comprehension, Prior Knowledge, Interest).
Administration: Individual.
Price Data: Available from publisher.
Time: (20–30) minutes.
Author: Ezra L. Stieglitz.
Publisher: Allyn and Bacon.

Review of The Stieglitz Informal Reading Inventory: Assessing Reading Behaviors from Emergent to Advanced Levels by KORESSA KUTSICK MALCOLM, School Psychologist, Augusta County Public Schools, Fisherville, VA:

The Stieglitz Informal Reading Inventory was designed to provide professionals who are involved in the diagnosis of reading skills and behaviors a more comprehensive test than has been available previously. In the manual, the author provides a summary of reading inventories research that highlights the strengths and weaknesses of these tests. The rationale for the development of the Stieglitz Inventory was to incorporate the positive attributes, and address the weaknesses of, this form of reading assessment.

The author contends the Stieglitz Inventory differs from other tests of its kind in several ways. The test incorporates the standard practice of evaluating a reader's knowledge of basic sight words as well as obtaining information regarding the informal, instructional, and frustration reading levels of students. In addition to these, Stieglitz has included materials and procedures to measure an individual's skill at reading words in context as well as those needed to assess the prereading skills of young or nonreading subjects. This second assessment strategy involves analysis of a subject's dictated story, which includes review of the student's reading of his or her own story, identifications of words in that story, and review of the subject's general awareness of oral and written communication. One very positive feature of the Stieglitz Inventory is that it allows examiners to obtain more subjective information about a student's reading history (i.e., familiarity with particular topics), which can be incorporated into the interpretation of the individual's reading performance. Another interesting feature of the Stieglitz Inventory is that it provides for the assessment of the differences between a subject's reading of narrative and expository text. This difference could be useful in determining types of reading materials that would be of most interest, or of most necessity, to subjects involved in remedial reading activities.

One of the most positive aspects of the Stieglitz Inventory is that it provides for a rather detailed analysis of a student's reading skills. Examiners may select the extent to which they want to examine an individual's reading skills based on the amount of time they have available to assess

subjects, as well as on the level of analysis needed to design instructional programs for those subjects. Comprehensive information is provided which allows extensive error analysis. The scoring codes utilized in this process may be somewhat difficult for examiners to master; however, the recommendation to tape record reading sessions should help first time users to obtain accurate analyses of subjects' readings.

Reading materials necessary to administer the Stieglitz Inventory are included in the manual. Examiners may photocopy particular sets of materials to fit their evaluation needs. Users of this test would be encouraged to obtain their own three-ringed binder to keep the materials in order, as the presented format of the manual would not hold up well with extensive wear. Lamination of the reading materials might also be necessary for this same reason. Other materials, such as carbon paper and a tape recorder or computer screen/word processing program, must be supplied by the test user.

Reading difficulties of the presented passages of the Stieglitz Inventory were obtained by two different techniques. The Spache Readability Formula was applied to the grade 1 through grade 3 passages and the Fry Readability Graph was applied to the grade 4 through grade 9 passages. The author did not provide great detail on how the passages were selected, with the exception that some were obtained from children's literature and magazines, whereas others were written specifically for this inventory. It was noted that attempts were made to find high interest materials, although again, no specific information was presented that indicated whether or not the passages would actually be of interest to intended readers.

Almost no statistical reliability or validity data were provided for this inventory. This is a common problem with reading inventories. Users of the Stieglitz Inventory are not provided information as to how well the obtained reading levels might correlate with other measures of reading (such as standardized measures found in most achievement batteries) or with actual reading performances of students in an applied setting. This does limit the application of this inventory for comparison of reading levels between students or to a norm, which is often required in the diagnosis of reading difficulties for special services eligibility.

Overall, the Stieglitz Informal Reading Inventory seems to represent good progress in the development of reading inventories. Information regarding the reliability and validity of this test should be obtained and reported before examiners could use it for identification of reading problems. If used just to analyze a particular subject's strengths and weaknesses in reading, examiners might find the Stieglitz Informal Reading Inventory to be a user-friendly instrument with good potential.

Review of The Stieglitz Informal Reading Inventory: Assessing Reading Behaviors from Emergent to Advanced Levels by STEPHANIE STEIN, Associate Professor of Psychology, Central Washington University, Ellensburg, WA:

The primary purpose of the Stieglitz Informal Reading Inventory (SIRI) is to assist educators in placing students in basal readers and diagnosing strengths and weaknesses in areas such as word recognition and comprehension. It appears the main way the SIRI differs from most published informal reading inventories (IRIs) is in its comprehensiveness.

The SIRI provides the traditional informal reading measure of graded word passages for determining students' independent, instructional, and frustration reading levels. In doing so, however, the SIRI looks at student performance on both narrative and expository passages as well as assessing passage comprehension on literal and interpretive-level questions. This inventory also assesses students' prior knowledge about and interest in the passage topic to provide further information in interpreting test results. In determining the appropriate level to begin testing in the graded word passages, the SIRI uses lists of graded words in sentences to determine how well the student identifies words in context, rather than the traditional use of words in isolation. Lists of graded words in isolation are also provided as an option to assess sight word recognition and decoding.

To obtain information on "emergent" readers (those students whose base reading level on the graded words in context is below first grade), the SIRI provides guidelines on using a dictated story assessment strategy. The students are shown a photograph, dictate a story to the examiner about the photograph, and then attempt a variety of tasks such as reading their dictated story, identifying words in isolation, and copying their story. This assessment strategy is based on the "language experience approach" (LEA), a controversial method of teaching reading to young children. For those educators who believe in the LEA, this may be a useful tool. Most examiners will probably have difficulty, however, translating the results of this measure into practical instructional information.

The entire SIRI test and manual are combined in a single wire-bound booklet with perforated pages that can be torn out if necessary and photocopied. Two sets of graded words in context, two sets of graded words in isolation, four sets of graded passages, and 10 photographs for the dictated story assessment are provided for 11 levels in reading: preprimer, primer, and 1st through 9th grade. Each word list and passage has a student copy (large print for the lower levels) and a teacher copy.

The SIRI has some notable strengths. The author provides very detailed information regarding the administration, scoring, and interpretation of the numerous tests and diagnostic procedures. Many diagnostic options are described in the manual. Case examples are provided to assist the examiner in learning about the instrument. The four sets of equivalent forms enable teachers to monitor student progress over time with less worry about practice effects. Finally, the author specifies how most of the materials were developed (through review of the literature and other IRIs, consultation with experts, and some field testing).

One of the limitations of this instrument may be its ambitiousness. It purports to measure many skills. The scoring and testing procedures appear to be more complicated than many other IRIs and might require extensive practice to master. However, the main limitation of the SIRI is similar to that of most other published IRIs—an insufficient degree of technical information on reliability, validity, and norms. As with most IRIs, there are no norms to speak of, though I see very little reason why this trend must continue. The author refers to field testing of different parts of the instrument with various numbers of students in grades 1–12 in Rhode Island and the surrounding vicinity. However, there are no data about the breakdown of students at each grade level tested or the demographics of the students.

To the author's credit, the SIRI manual contains some information addressing reliability and validity issues rather than ignoring them altogether. Some evidence of alternative forms reliability is provided in that 80% to 85.7% of the 48 students in a study were given identical placements regardless of the graded reading passage form used.

The author also attempts some arguments in favor of the validity of the SIRI. All four forms of the graded reading passages were administered to 240 students (no grade level given) and the composite results were compared to teacher estimates of students' instructional levels. A little over half of the students (56.3%) were given identical placements with both methods. Although the author states that "this comparison was significant beyond the .001 level" (p. 276), it still seems disconcerting that almost half of the comparisons resulted in *different* placements, ranging from 28.3% off by one grade level to 4.6% off by as much as three grade levels. The remainder of the validity evidence relates to practice effects and interest level. Finally, the author indicates that, on Forms A and B, "the higher-order questions were, as expected, more difficult for students to answer than lower-order questions" (p. 279) with incorrect responses on literal comprehension questions ranging from 14.3% to 21.5% and ranging from 29.4% to 32.6% on interpretive questions.

In summary, the SIRI is one of the more comprehensive informal reading inventories on the market. It is probably not as easy and convenient to use as many other similar measures but it does provide more types of reading information than most and might be particularly attractive to reading specialists who have the time and interest to learn the instrument. Although the psychometric support for the SIRI is weak in terms of reliability and validity, it is frankly better than many other informal reading inventories. However, the author should still be encouraged to provide further psychometric support for the SIRI as well as more detailed information about the demographics of the students involved in the field testing of the instrument.

[88]
Stress Indicator & Health Planner.

Purpose: "Assists people to identify their present health practices, pinpoint problem areas and plan for improved health, productivity and well-being."
Population: Adults.

Publication Dates: 1990–1993.
Acronym: SIHP.
Scores, 10: Physical Distress, Psychological Distress, Behavioral Distress, Total Distress Assessment, Interpersonal Stress Assessment, Nutritional Assessment, Health Assessment, Total Wellness Assessment, Time-Stress Assessment, Occupational Stress Assessment.
Administration: Group.
Price Data, 1993: $12 per test booklet; $12 per Professional's Guide ('93, 12 pages); $15 per Releasing Relaxation: Mind and Body audiotape.
Time: (30) minutes for Basic; (180–360) minutes for Facilitated/Advanced.
Comments: Self-administered and self-scored.
Authors: Gwen Faulkner and Terry Anderson.
Publisher: Consulting Resource Group International, Inc.

Review of the Stress Indicator & Health Planner by DENNIS C. HARPER, Professor of Pediatrics and Rehabilitation Counseling, University of Iowa Hospitals and Clinics, Iowa City, IA:

The Stress Indicator and Health Planner (SIHP) is a "Self-assessment and planning tool for managing stress, developing wellness and improving performance" (booklet cover), designed by Faulkner and Anderson. The SIHP is presented as a concise guide to review the following five aspect of human functioning: Personal Distress, Interpersonal Stress, Wellness Assessment, Timed-Stress Assessment, and Occupational Stress Assessment. The first section of the SIHP is the Stress Indicator. The authors indicate this is not a psychometric test but a self-assessment and learning tool to promote an individual's awareness of personal stress, coping style, and lifestyle habits. The second section of the SIHP is the Health Planner. The Health Planner is a series of questions providing feedback and educational information in relation to coping and problem-solving skills. Test administration is either individual or in small groups. Administration times are approximately 20 minutes for the Stress Indicator. Use of the Health Planner is an individual process and can range from half an hour to 2.5 hours depending upon how the facilitator or user wishes to structure the experience of progressing through the information in the Health Planner.

The authors indicate the development of the instrument was in response to the need in the fields of health psychology, health promotion, and corporate wellness for a brief and comprehensive self-assessment tool. From a theoretical standpoint the authors note that self-awareness of perceived stress, coping abilities, and lifestyle habits is beneficial in improving health. Health is defined from a "holistic" perspective. Active participation in health planning is reported to increase well-being.

The Stress Indicator and Health Planner profile consists of a 15-page self-administered document. It is easily read, well organized, and well presented graphically. The Professional's Guide to the Stress Indicator and Health Planner contains interpretive material, use and application, theoretical and practical understanding of the impact of stress, and description of the limitations of the Stress Indicator and Health Planner. Data are also presented in this manual on interpretation of scores, reliability and validity, and appropriate disclaimers of liability. Specific stress and wellness resources are presented.

The application of the Stress Indicator and Health Planner is as an aid to individuals who wish to gain knowledge about their stress levels and health habits. The authors suggest the material be presented by a trained professional experienced in health psychology to maximize impact. No other information is offered regarding the credentials of trainers. The authors assert the SIHP has been used by a variety of consumers and professionals in disciplines including medicine, psychology, sociology, nursing, and health science. The authors further assert that hospitals and corporations have found the SIHP useful in improving their awareness of stress and assessing harmful lifestyle habits.

After the profile is completed specific scores are compared to data presented in the profile planner. Scores are characterized in terms of Low Stress, Moderate Stress, and High Stress. Specific cautions are offered in the Professional's Guide in terms of the limitations of the materials as well as their particular interpretations. For example, transitory stress problems should be understood as potentially inflating scores, the SIHP is not intended as a substitute for competent medical/professional assessment of health. Each individual section of the SIHP consists of a series of specific questions where the respondent is requested to indicate a number from 1 through 5 reflective of the severity/frequency/intensity of the particular question. Total scores represent a weighted score

in each of the five areas. Normative data are not presented for the test's interpretive section. In fact, little information is presented describing exactly how to score and interpret the normative outcome. The authors report some brief reliability and validity information. A 1-week test-retest reliability project was attempted with 26 college students completing the SIHP. Correlation coefficients greater than +.88 on all five scales are reported. Face validity was described following a study of 152 college students completing the SIHP rating the extent that they found the scores on the SIHP to be accurate on a 5-point Likert scale. The average score for the group was 4.36. No other specific information was given on the psychometrics of scale construction or scale development.

The SIHP is, as the authors intend, a guide for examining stress and health issues. It reflects the personal bias of the two particular authors, it has some face validity, but lacks any theoretical support or empirical psychometric data. It is read easily, presented clearly, but moderately to highly priced per booklet. The utility of this instrument probably lies heavily on its face validity. The authors' assertions that the instrument assist people to identify their present health practices, pinpoint problem areas, and plan for improved health, productivity, and well-being are certainly not supported by available data.

Review of the Stress Indicator & Health Planner by BARBARA L. LACHAR, Assistant Professor of Psychiatry (Psychology), Baylor College of Medicine, Houston, TX:

The Stress Indicator and Health Planner (SIHP) is a self-assessment and planning instrument designed for individual or group administration. The authors state the SIHP is not a psychometric test, but an instrument designed to promote self-awareness of personal stress, coping style, and life style habits. Behavioral change is also a goal. However, in order to fulfill these functions, any assessment instrument must be developed and evaluated in accordance with psychometric standards.

STRESS INDICATOR. Part One, the Stress Indicator (SI) is divided into five sections: Personal Distress, Interpersonal Stress, Wellness, Time-Stress, and Occupational Stress. Individuals rate their physical symptoms, emotional symptoms, feelings, behaviors, interpersonal difficulties, and job satisfaction. These ratings are combined to produce scores on the five sections.

Users rate items on a Likert scale anchored by numbers from 1 to 5. Descriptors of percentage time (10 to 90%), and adjectives ranging from "rarely" to "almost always" are also provided. Numerical ratings are summed across the items in each section, and plotted on a scale for interpretation as "low," "moderate" or "high stress." There is no further explanation of the meaning of these levels, nor are there recommendations to accompany specific assessment results. The Professional's Guide, a 12-page booklet, contains little information relevant to administration or the interpretation of results.

The SI is defined as an evaluation of stress, but assesses physical symptoms, emotional symptoms, behavioral problems, and health behaviors. There is no clear delineation between stress and illness. For example, the Personal Distress dimension is a combination of a checklist of both somatic and psychological complaints. Many of the physical symptoms, such as shortness of breath, chest pain, and headache pain may be signs of serious illness requiring medical attention. Similarly, items concerning psychological distress such as "feelings of hopelessness or helplessness" and "thoughts of suicide as a way out" may be more diagnostic of a depressive disorder. Appropriate recommendations for medical attention are not provided in either the SIHP booklet or the Professional's Guide.

HEALTH PLANNER. Following the self-assessment, users complete Part Two, the Health Planner (HP), which consists of five parts of educational text titled: Stress Management, Effective Communication, Health Practices, Time Management, and Occupational Stress. The first section, Stress Management, fails to provide a definition of stress, but includes a brief section on irrational thinking as a source of stress. However, no directions or opportunities are provided for the user to assess thinking. There are also no instructions on how to modify irrational thoughts to produce less stress. Similar comments apply to other sections as there is no self-appraisal for Communication Techniques nor specific exercises for altering perceived communication problems. The sections on Aerobic Exercise, Relaxation, and Smoking Cessation similarly are lacking specific examples of recom-

mended exercise, guidance for how to practice relaxation, and instructions for breathing exercises.

Although there are sound recommendations that can serve to educate users, some statements in the HP appear superficial, limited, or unsubstantiated. The authors make recommendations and report global conclusions from research without support. Examples include "experts estimate 60-90% of all diseases are stress and lifestyle related" (test booklet, p. 13) and "Studies have shown that many times smokers have quit during transition times in their lives so that the required motivation and time are best known by the specific smoker" (test booklet, p. 16). These statements lack an appropriate supporting reference in either the SIHP or Professional's Guide. There are six sections titled "New Directions for Growth" containing four blank lines that appear to serve as opportunities for users to plan their behavioral changes, but these plans do not readily follow from the results of the SI assessment.

PROFESSIONAL'S GUIDE. The Professional's Guide is described as providing the theoretical background and rationale for the development of the SIHP. It is the only manual available. The guide presents a brief discussion of stress and health, but no coherent theory is offered as the basis for the SIHP. Neither is there a rationale for the selection of either the dimensions or their items. Measures of situational stressors, including stressful life events, daily hassles, safety, and financial insecurity are noticeably lacking. Even where citations are made, the appropriate reference is not always provided.

The guide authors state the SIHP has been used in a variety of settings including hospitals, businesses, and government agencies. No norms are provided and no data regarding results are offered.

Test-retest reliability for all five scales of the SIHP is estimated to be at least .88 based on a study of 26 college students retested after a 1-week interval. Additionally, the authors claim that they have established face validity by having 152 college students rate their scores on the SIHP for accuracy. Results indicate that none of the students rated their results as inaccurate. As this is the only evidence offered of reliability and validity, there is a need for studies to establish the construct validity of this tool as a measure of stress and wellness.

Suggested studies include internal consistency reliability, factor analysis, and correlations of SI dimension scores with alternative measures of stress, anxiety, depression, and wellness. Additionally, scores of individuals with different physical diagnoses such as headache, lumbar strain, and coronary artery disease could be compared with those of a control group. It is also recommended that data be analyzed to obtain correlations between scores and job performance, productivity, absences, and health care costs. Studies reporting the percentage of users who make behavioral changes resulting in measurable health improvements are also required to support the validity of this instrument.

Health and stress appraisals have the potential to contribute to individual education and behavior change. The SIHP attempts to measure a variety of dimensions relating to stress and health, in addition to motivating behavioral change. However, the SIHP lacks the documentation, careful construction, and research effort necessary to support claims of utility and to justify its cost.

[89]
Stuttering Severity Instrument for Children and Adults, Third Edition.

Purpose: "Measures stuttering severity for both children and adults."
Population: School-age children and adults.
Publication Dates: 1980–1994.
Acronym: SSI-3.
Scores, 8: Frequency, Duration, Physical Concomitants (Distracting Sounds, Facial Grimaces, Head Movements, Movements of the Extremities, Total), Total.
Administration: Individual.
Forms, 2: Reading, Nonreading.
Price Data, 1994: $64 per complete kit; $29 per 50 test record and frequency computation forms; $37 per examiner's manual ('94, 48 pages) and picture plates.
Time: Administration time not reported.
Comments: Tape recorder necessary for speech sample.
Author: Glyndon D. Riley.
Publisher: PRO-ED, Inc.
Cross References: See T4:2613 (5 references).

TEST REFERENCES

1. Pindzola, R. H., & White, D. T. (1986). A protocol for differentiating the incipient stuttering. *Language, Speech, and Hearing Services in Schools, 17*, 2–15.
2. Runyan, C. M., & Runyan, S. E. (1986). A fluency rules therapy program for young children in the public schools. *Language, Speech, and Hearing Services in Schools, 17*, 276–284.
3. Pindzola, R. H., Jenkins, M. M., & Lokken, K. J. (1989). Speaking rates of young children. *Language, Speech, and Hearing Services in Schools, 20*, 133–138.
4. Watson, B. C., Pool, K. D., Devous, M. D., Freeman, F. J., & Finitzo, T. (1992). Brain blood flow related to acoustic laryngeal reaction time in adult developmental stutterers. *Journal of Speech and Hearing Research, 35*, 555–561.
5. Ramig, P. R. (1993). High reported spontaneous stuttering recovery rates: Fact or fiction? *Language, Speech, and Hearing Services in Schools, 24*, 156–160.
6. Wolk, L., Edwards, M. L., & Conture, E. G. (1993). Coexistence of stuttering and disordered phonology in young children. *Journal of Speech and Hearing Research, 36*, 906–917.
7. Berkowitz, M., Cook, H., & Haughey, M. J. (1994). A nontraditional fluency program developed for the public school setting. *Language, Speech, and Hearing Services in Schools, 25*, 94–99.
8. Blood, G. W., Blood, I. M., Bennett, S., Simpson, K. C., & Susman, E. J. (1994). Subjective anxiety measurements and cortisol responses in adults who stutter. *Journal of Speech and Hearing, 37*, 760–768.
9. Caruso, A. J., Chodzko-Zajko, W. J., Bidinger, D. A., & Sommers, R. K. (1994). Adults who stutter: Responses to cognitive stress. *Journal of Speech and Hearing, 37*, 746–754.
10. Kelly, E. M. (1994). Speech rates and turn-taking behaviors of children who stutter and their fathers. *Journal of Speech and Hearing, 37*, 1284–1294.
11. Throneburg, R. N., & Yairi, E. (1994). Temporal dynamics of repetitions during the early stage of childhood stuttering: An acoustic study. *Journal of Speech and Hearing, 37*, 1067–1075.
12. Watson, B. C., Freeman, F. J., Devous, M. D., Chapman, S. B., Finitzo, T., & Pool, K. D. (1994). Linguistic performance and regional cerebral blood flow in persons who stutter. *Journal of Speech and Hearing, 37*, 1221–1228.
13. Zebrawski, P. M. (1994). Duration of sound prolongation and sound/syllable repetition in children who stutter: Preliminary observations. *Journal of Speech and Hearing Research, 37*, 254–263.
14. Blood, G. W. (1995). A behavioral-cognitive therapy program for adults who stutter: Computers and counseling. *Journal of Communication Disorders, 28*, 165–180.
15. Blood, G. W. (1995). POWER2: Relapse management with adolescents who stutter. *Language, Speech, and Hearing Services in Schools, 26*, 169–179.
16. Dietrich, S., Barry, S. J., & Parker, D. E. (1995). Middle latency auditory responses in males who stutter. *Journal of Speech and Hearing Research, 38*, 5–17.
17. Kelly, E. M. (1995). Parents as partners: Including mothers and father in the treatment of children who stutter. *Journal of Communication Disorders, 28*, 93–105.
18. Zebrowski, P. M. (1995). The topography of beginning stuttering. *Journal of Communication Disorders, 28*, 75–91.
19. Blood, I. M. (1996). Disruptions in auditory and temporal processing in adults who stutter. *Perceptual and Motor Skills, 82*, 272–274.
20. McCauley, R. J. (1996). Familiar strangers: Criterion referenced measures in communication disorders. *Language, Speech, and Hearing Services in Schools, 27*, 122–131.

Review of the Stuttering Severity Instrument for Children and Adults, Third Edition by RONALD B. GILLAM, Assistant Professor of Communication Sciences and Disorders, The University of Texas at Austin, Austin, TX:

The Stuttering Severity Instrument for Children and Adults, Third Edition (SSI-3) is the second revision of the Stuttering Severity Instrument (Riley, 1972; 1980). Like the two preceding versions, the purpose of the SSI-3 is to measure and quantify stuttering severity objectively. The author suggests the SSI-3 should be used to augment information from patient interviews, speech samples, and other speech and language tests in evaluating the severity of stuttering in children and adults.

When the SSI-3 is administered to children with less than a third grade reading level, examiners rate conversation samples. Black-and-white line drawings of a farm scene, a dinosaur scene, a ship yard scene, and a space scene are provided for use in eliciting speech during conversations with the examiner. A sample dialogue is provided in the manual. Examiners are also advised to obtain and analyze a sample of the child's speech at home.

Examiners analyze speech samples for frequency of stuttering, duration of stuttering events, and physical concomitants of stuttering. Frequency of stuttering is assessed by summing repetitions, audible prolongations, and silent prolongations of sounds or syllables and dividing this value by the total number of syllables contained in the speech samples. This percentage is converted to a Frequency score. Duration of stuttering is assessed by measuring the length of the three longest stuttering events. The average duration is converted to a Duration score. Physical events that accompany stuttering are assessed by qualitative judgments of the degree of noticeability/distractibility of nonspeech sounds, abnormal facial movements or tension, head movements, and movements of the extremities that accompany stuttering. Each type of physical concomitant is rated according to a 6-point Likert scale that ranges from 0 (none) to 5 (severe and painful-looking). Values for the four judgments are summed to yield a Physical Concomitants score.

When the SSI-3 is administered to children or adults who read at or above a third-grade level, examiners obtain speech samples in reading and conversation contexts. Two reading passages that vary in length between 160 and 228 syllables are provided at third-grade, fifth-grade, seventh-grade, and adult reading levels. The conversation sample is obtained while the patient and the examiner converse about familiar topics such as school, jobs, recent holidays, favorite TV shows, or current movies. Separate tables are provided for scoring stuttering frequency during speaking and reading tasks, and the Frequency score is derived by summing the two task scores. Duration and Physical Concomitants scores are derived in the same manner as described previously for nonreaders.

Frequency, Duration, and Physical Concomitants scores are summed to yield a Total Overall score that is converted into percentile and severity ratings. Conversion tables are available for preschoolers (ages 2-10 to 5-11), school-age children (ages 6-1 to 16-11), and adults (ages 17-0 and up).

Intra- and interexaminer reliability figures are based on extremely small samples, but appear to be adequate for clinical purposes. Unfortunately, measures of the stability and internal consistency of the SSI-3 are not reported. Therefore, no judgments can be made concerning the stability of the

SSI-3 across times or situations, and there is no way to estimate the standard error of measurement.

Criterion-related validity was assessed by correlating the Total Overall score to the Frequency score. Correlations are within the acceptable range. However, a better approach would have been to correlate Overall scores with percentages of stuttered syllables. Reports of construct validity are not convincing. At minimum, the author should have correlated overall scores with stuttering history, (in months), and he should have used factor analysis to support the constructs of frequency, duration, and physical concomitants as separate factors.

Unfortunately, there are numerous other difficulties with this test, many of which are related to insufficient information concerning procedures and norms. For example, examiners are encouraged to analyze samples of children's speech collected in their homes, but guidelines for collecting and selecting these samples are too vague to insure that the collected samples are similar in nature to samples that were collected for the norming group. Additionally, there are no guidelines for selecting reading passages. Readability affects reading fluency and should also affect speech fluency while reading aloud. Precise instructions about methods for assigning and selecting reading passages are needed to control for potential confounding effects related to reading fluency.

There are also problems with scoring the SSI-3. Ratio-level measures of frequency and duration are converted to ordinal-level scores, but the author does not provide information about how the "stanine intervals" (p. 15) were derived. Additionally, Likert scale values are summed to obtain a Physical Concomitants score. These procedures serve to dilute discrete measures of complex behaviors into numeric values that have little specific meaning and even less discriminating power.

Finally, there are problems with interpreting the SSI-3. Percentile and severity ratings are based on relatively small samples of stutterers from one state who span wide age ranges (72 preschoolers, 139 school-age children, and 60 adults). Unfortunately, no information is provided about the criteria for including subjects in the normative sample or the exact ages of the individuals. Additional interpretation problems are related to reliability and validity. Because stuttering is a highly variable behavior, it is surprising that the author does not provide information about test-retest reliability or internal consistency. Stability across time and conditions is a necessary prerequisite for determining whether a test actually measures what it purports to measure. It is difficult, therefore, to judge the validity of the SSI-3.

In summary, there are a number of flaws in the SSI-3 that limit its usefulness. Lack of necessary information about procedures for collecting speech samples, scoring conversions that decrease power, a small and undefined normative sample, and lack of critical reliability data interfere with the interpretability of test results. Perhaps the author says it best when he notes, "Reliance on quantifiable test scores, which are limited by their definitions of the behaviors and by their reliability, may lead to conclusions that are incomplete and incorrect" (p. 1). This test would make a poor substitute for clinical insight. At best, beginning clinicians and speech and language clinicians with relatively little experience with stutterers might use the SSI-3 as a partial means for calibrating and/or confirming clinical impressions of stuttering in conversation and/or reading contexts. This would comprise a very small part of a comprehensive stuttering evaluation.

REVIEWER'S REFERENCES

Riley, G. D. (1972). A stuttering severity instrument for children and adults. *Journal of Speech and Hearing Disorders, 37,* 314–322.

Riley, G. G. (1980). Stuttering Severity Instrument for Children and Adults (Revised). Austin, TX: PRO-ED, Inc.

Review of the Stuttering Severity Instrument for Children and Adults, Third Edition by REBECCA McCAULEY, Associate Professor, Communication Sciences, University of Vermont, Burlington, VT:

TEST STRUCTURE. The Stuttering Severity Instrument for Children and Adults (SSI-3) is designed to assess stuttering severity for clinical and research purposes among preschool children (ages 2-10 to 5-11), school-aged children (6-1 to 16-11), and adults (17-0 and older). There are two versions of the instrument—one for readers and one for nonreaders (i.e., children who read below the third grade level). Both versions require assessment of stuttering frequency, duration, and physical concomitants, that are combined to provide a single score with an associated 5-point descriptive severity level ranging from "very mild" to "very severe" (p. 11).

TEST ADMINISTRATION AND INTERPRETATION. The instrument requires at least two 200-syllable speech samples for assessment. Because children are thought to be more affected by the clinical setting, one of their samples consists of a video- or audio-taped conversation recorded at home with (usually) a parent. For older children and adults, one sample consists of a conversation with the examiner and the other, the reading of an age-appropriate passage. During the conversation in which she or he participates, the examiner is instructed to "interject questions, interruptions, and mild disagreements to simulate the pressures of normal conversation at home and elsewhere" (p. 7)—an instruction likely to introduce considerable variability in the nature of samples obtained.

Three subtest scores are calculated from the speech samples—the percentage of syllables stuttered, the mean duration of the longest three stutters, and a rating for the presence of physical concomitants in four areas: Distracting Sounds, Facial Grimaces, Head Movements, and Movements of the Extremities. Stuttering examples are given during the description of percentage of syllables stuttered calculation, but no other explicit definitions are provided, thus making the approach used in this instrument one that might be described as involving a perceptual definition of stuttering.

Although specific scoring procedures for each subtest measure are stated, the range of variables possibly affecting both the stuttering behavior itself and the possible reliability of the examiner are alarmingly numerous and include the immediacy of measurement (on-line versus from a recorded sample) and type of recording used (audio versus video).

NORMS. Norms consist of group means and standard deviations. For two of the three age groups, sample sizes were generally smaller than a desirable 100 per group (i.e., $n = 72$ for preschoolers, 139 for school-age children, and 60 for adults). The normative population is insufficiently described: The reader is told only they came from a variety of clinical and public school sources and, if older than 8 years of age, had generally received stuttering treatment. Despite the disappointing nature of these norms, however, they constitute the best available for standardized severity measures of stuttering.

Interpretation of test results consists primarily of the assignment of a percentile score and associated severity label using the norms for each group but there is no justification for the specific percentile intervals used.

RELIABILITY. The methods used to document reliability depart from those typically reported for standardized measures, probably because of the considerable difficulty reported in the research literature of obtaining acceptable levels of agreement for at least some of the measures included in this scale (Cordes & Ingham, 1994). The author notes that "a special procedure" was used "to improve reliability of stuttering measurements" (p. 15), which consisted of using stanine values for percentage and duration measures. This procedure is problematic given that test interpretation is not based on those same values. In addition, percentage of agreement was calculated by dividing the smaller score by the larger score for each judgment pair—a measure of agreement that has been termed "one of the least stringent" of such measures (Cordes & Ingham, 1994). Additional problems with the reported agreement data include a lack of clarity, from my perspective, concerning what units were used as "judgment pairs" in the calculation of agreement and a lack of information concerning agreement for live versus off-line scoring of some measures. Thus, despite a reported "intra/interexaminer reliability" averaging from 82 to 93% for experienced raters (manual, p. 16) and despite appropriate suggestions that examiners calculate and seek to improve their self-agreement as a means of improving reliability, users of this instrument should be skeptical about its overall reliability.

VALIDITY. Three types of *criterion-related evidence* for validity are presented. Two of these, however, involve correlations to highly related measures sharing the same author—one between the SSI-3 and one of its subtests, SS%, and the other (Yaruss & Conture, 1992) between an earlier version of the SSI-3, the SSI-R (Riley, 1980) and the Stuttering Prediction Instrument (Riley, 1981), a "companion instrument to the SSI-3" (manual, p. 17). As the third source of criterion-related evidence, the author unconvincingly and somewhat unclearly argues from the previously discussed reliability data.

Hypotheses studied to provide evidence of *construct validity* were "tested" on a single set of data, namely, part-whole correlation matrices for the three age groups. These hypotheses were that severity would "increase with the length of time the individual has stuttered" (p. 17) and that subtests would be "related to each other, because they are parts of the overall construct of severity" (p. 17). Unfortunately, whereas the second hypothesis was somewhat supported by low to moderate correlations between subtests, the first hypothesis was not really tested, but advanced through a restatement of the descriptive statistic values.

SUMMARY. This is a widely used measure of stuttering severity, designed to be used for individuals ages 2 and above. Methods vary depending upon client age and reading ability, but include the assessment of stuttering Frequency, Duration, and Physical Concomitants, which are combined to derive a 5-point severity rating. Norms, reliability, and validity data provided are unsatisfactory. Nonetheless, this instrument represents the only standardized measure of its kind. Consequently, clinicians should use this measure cautiously and consider the development of local norms and the assessment of their own reliability as necessary to its use in quality clinical service.

REVIEWER'S REFERENCES
Riley, G. (1980). Stuttering Severity Instrument for Children and Adults (Revised). Austin, TX: PRO-ED, Inc.
Riley, G. (1981). Stuttering Prediction Instrument. Austin, TX: PRO-ED, Inc.
Yaruss, J., & Conture, E. (1992). Relationship between mother-child speaking rates in adjacent fluent utterances. *ASHA, 34,* 210.
Cordes, A. K., & Ingham, R. J. (1994). The reliability of observational data: II. Issues in the identification and measurement of stuttering events. *Journal of Speech and Hearing Research, 37*(2), 279–294.
Lewis, K. E. (1995). Do SSI-3 scores adequately reflect observations of stuttering behaviors? *American Journal of Speech-Language Pathology, 4,* 46–59.

[90]

Substance Abuse Relapse Assessment.

Purpose: Designed to assess and monitor relapse prevention and coping skills.

Population: Adolescents and adults.

Publication Date: 1993.

Acronym: SARA.

Scores: 4 parts: Substance Abuse Behavior, Antecedents of Substance Abuse, Consequences of Substance Abuse, Responses to Slips.

Administration: Individual.

Price Data, 1996: $75 per introductory kit including 25 interview record forms, 25 each of 3 relapse prevention planning forms, and manual (31 pages) with stimulus card; $27 per 25 interview record forms; $11 per 25 relapse prevention planning forms (specify Form 1—Pretreatment, Form 2—Current, or Form 3—Relapse); $28 per manual with stimulus card.

Time: (60) minutes.

Authors: Lawrence Schonfeld, Roger Peters, and Addis Dolente.

Publisher: Psychological Assessment Resources, Inc.

Review of the Substance Abuse Relapse Assessment by MICHAEL G. KAVAN, Associate Dean for Student Affairs, Creighton University School of Medicine and Associate Professor of Family Practice, Creighton University School of Medicine, Omaha, NE:

The Substance Abuse Relapse Assessment (SARA) is a structured interview designed to assist in developing relapse prevention goals and monitoring the achievement of these goals within substance abuse treatment programs. The major aim of the SARA is to identify the antecedents and consequences of pretreatment alcohol and/or drug use and to use this information to develop individualized treatment plans. The SARA is based on, and therefore, similar to, several drinking profiles (e.g., Drinking Profile [Marlatt, 1976], Comprehensive Drinker Profile [Marlatt & Miller, 1984], Gerontology Alcohol Project Drinking Profile [Dupree, Broskowski, & Schonfeld, 1984]). It consists of a manual with stimulus card, a four-part interview record form, and three relapse prevention planning forms. The interview record form consists of questions regarding substance abuse behavior, antecedents and consequences of use, and responses to slips. The relapse prevention planning forms allow the examiner to identify the client's substance abuse behavior chain, pretreatment skills used to avoid relapse, and current relapse prevention goals.

ADMINISTRATION AND SCORING. The SARA is designed to be administered individually to adolescents and adults who have a history of substance abuse, whose ability to avoid substance abuse relapse is in question, or who are involved in substance abuse treatment programs. It may be administered by any professional with appropriate training in substance abuse assessment and intervention. It is recommended that examiners should also have experience in the use of structured interviews and in the development of individualized

treatment plans. Instructions for the interview record form are fairly clear and easy for examiners to follow. However, some clients may have difficulty keeping track of the multiple response options read to them for certain questions. For these questions, it may have been more useful to allow the examiner to show the client the various response options listed in the interview record form or present a stimulus card to the client. A stimulus card is used to identify client feelings associated with the relapse and to determine how confident the client is regarding his or her ability to avoid substance use. The examiner may request additional information throughout the interview to clarify responses or information that is contradictory.

Once the interview record form is completed, the interviewer uses this information to complete the relapse prevention planning forms, which identify behavior chain(s) (i.e., antecedents, behaviors, and consequences) associated with substance use as well as various pretreatment and proactive coping skills. Those working with the client can then use this information to discuss relapse prevention issues during treatment. It is also recommended that these forms be revised as new information is disclosed by the client during the course of treatment. No other information is provided within the manual regarding the scoring of the SARA. Administration time is approximately one hour.

RELIABILITY AND VALIDITY. No data are provided within the manual regarding reliability or validity. The manual does provide a sample case illustration for "Joe," which highlights how the various components of the SARA can be used to develop a treatment plan for a client. Limited guidelines are provided regarding how to systematically apply the information from the relapse prevention planning forms to a treatment plan. Of importance to note is that no data are provided regarding the impact of such planning on outcome.

NORMS. The SARA was "field tested" with 101 inmates (63 males and 38 females; ages 17 to 47 years) in a sheriff's office substance abuse treatment program in Tampa, Florida. Limited data are provided from this field test. Information is provided on the inmates' major problem substances, major locations of use, persons with whom the inmates have used substances most frequently, and various antecedents to use for this group. The authors indicate that this preliminary study indicated that emotional and situational events were the major precipitants of alcohol and drug use. As such, it is recommended that treatment plans be designed to address various negative emotional, interpersonal conflicts, and peer pressure through skills training, behavioral rehearsal, and practice situations. Beyond these, the manual contains no other normative information.

SUMMARY. The SARA is a structured interview designed to assist in developing relapse prevention goals and monitoring the achievement of these goals within substance abuse treatment programs. The major goal of the SARA, which is to identify the antecedents and consequences of pretreatment alcohol and/or drug use and to use this information to develop individualized treatment plans, is admirable and desirable. However, the SARA provides no data regarding its ability to accomplish this feat. Likewise, no information is provided within the manual regarding the SARA's ability to influence treatment outcomes. In fact, the only data provided within the manual relate to a field test of 101 inmates in a Florida county jail. Surely, these are not the only persons with substance abuse problems that could possibly benefit from the SARA. Additional studies with more diverse groups are certainly necessary. Another problem with the SARA is that it fails to incorporate useful relapse prevention issues such as the quality of the client's social support network, the quality of the client's primary intimate relationships (Marlatt, 1985), and self-attribution for behavior change (Annis, 1991) into the interview process. In addition, the Interview Record Form is based on recall, which is subject to a variety of biases. Until these problems are addressed, the SARA is unfortunately relegated to only a somewhat useful, structured method for obtaining information about substance use and relapse; nothing more.

REVIEWER'S REFERENCES

Marlatt, G. A. (1976). The Drinking Profile: A questionnaire for the behavioral assessment of alcoholism. In E. J. Mash & L. G. Terdal (Eds.), *Behavior therapy assessment: Diagnosis, design, and evaluation* (pp. 127–137). New York: Springer.

Dupree, L. W., Broskowski, H., & Schonfeld, L. (1984). The Gerontology Alcohol Project: A behavioral treatment program for elderly alcohol abusers. *The Gerontologist, 24,* 510–516.

Marlatt, G. A., & Miller. W. R. (1984). The Comprehensive Drinker Profile. Odessa, FL: Psychological Assessment Resources, Inc.

Marlatt, G. A. (1985). Situational determinants of relapse and skill training interventions. In G. A. Marlatt & J. R. Gordon (Eds.), *Relapse prevention: Maintenance strategies in the treatment of addictive behaviors* (pp. 77–127). New York: Guilford.

Annis, H. M. (1991). A cognitive-social learning approach to relapse: Pharmacotherapy and relapse prevention counseling. *Alcohol and Alcoholism (Supplement), 1,* 527–530.

Review of the Substance Abuse Relapse Assessment by JEFFREY S. RAIN, Assistant Professor and Chairman, Industrial/Organizational Psychology Program, School of Psychology, Florida Tech, Melbourne, FL:

The Substance Abuse Relapse Assessment (SARA) was designed to assess and monitor relapse prevention and coping skills. Setting aside debates between medical, psychodynamic, and behavioral approaches to alcohol, tobacco, and other drug (ATOD) treatment and debates over abstinence versus relapse prevention, the SARA appears to be a very comprehensive, theory-driven, practical guide for identifying relapse risk potential and assisting in treatment planning. Whereas the SARA purports to excel in these areas, except for a limited field test, it lacks research studies specific to the instrument itself.

Addressing psychometric criteria first, the SARA is a very new instrument and lacks empirical evidence of support. In fact, statistical documentation is nonexistent. The only data presented in the manual are the descriptions of the original sample of 101 inmates of a law enforcement substance abuse treatment program in Florida. Data on reliability, validity, bias, administration, and other standard criteria for psychometric quality are not presented. Evaluations of the majority of the technical aspects of the SARA are thus precluded from this review.

With the psychometric deficits stated, a number of potentially very strong positives emerge on the SARA's practical and administrative side. The Professional Manual primarily consists of a description of the SARA and its administration as well as a case illustration and sample treatment plan. Instructions are comprehensive and easy to follow. Particularly helpful is the detailed sample case illustration, which provides clarification for instances where the administrator is unclear exactly how to complete the SARA.

Another positive feature of the SARA is the ability of this instrument to provide a good foundation on which to build treatment plans. Twelve-step programs, if used, also appear to integrate well with the SARA. Additionally, the SARA recognizes the reality of multiple-substance abuse and does not limit itself to a single substance. It does have the flexibility to consider a primary ATOD focus as well as secondary ATOD foci.

Whereas the time frame of the SARA is a 30-day reporting period, the authors acknowledge the changing nature of substance abuse relapse prevention. Therefore, the SARA should be considered a dynamic instrument requiring regular updating. At a minimum it is designed to be used before, during, and after treatment. Given the frequency of updating and the detail involved, the authors' stated caution for conditions potentially precluding the completion of the SARA cannot be overstated. Depending on the situation, the SARA may require multiple sessions to complete. Some of the effort may be reduced by having portions of the updating completed by clients as "homework" (p. 6). However, it should be noted that the detail of information requested places a heavy burden on both client and practitioner. Clients may not be capable of contributing fully to the SARA or be able to complete homework assignments with sufficient detail.

From a theoretical standpoint, the SARA is very well supported by a behavior-based approach. Applying functional analysis to substance abuse identifies a chain of behaviors (i.e., antecedents, behaviors, and consequences or ABCs) that have an impact on the abuse (e.g., Cummings, Gordon, & Marlatt, 1980). The functional analysis approach is a cornerstone of behavior therapy and, therefore, may not be readily adopted by all practitioners, but has been shown to be an effective treatment approach for substance abuse (e.g., Baer, Marlatt, & McMahon, 1993).

On the whole, the theoretical foundations give the SARA clear clinical application. Wholesale endorsement of the SARA must be reserved until its individual research base is more fully established. Still, the SARA is very user friendly, though administratively demanding. Data from the SARA appear to be highly generalizable to various traditional treatment programs (e.g., 12-step programs) as well as other alcohol, tobacco, and other drug (ATOD) cases. The proof of the SARA will be in the research but the theoretical base, instructions, and case illustrations are a solid beginning.

REVIEWER'S REFERENCES

Cummings, C., Gordon, J. R., & Marlatt, G. A. (1980). Relapse: Prevention and prediction. In W. R. Miller (Ed.), *The addictive behaviors* (pp. 291–321). Oxford, UK: Pergamon Press.

Baer, J. S., Marlatt, G. A., & McMahon, R. J. (Eds.) (1993). *Addictive behaviors across life span: Prevention treatment and policy issues.* Newbury Park: Sage.

[91]

Substance Abuse Screening Test.

Purpose: "Designed to screen-out those students who are unlikely to have a substance abuse problem."
Population: Ages 13—adult.
Publication Date: 1993.
Acronym: SAST.
Scores: Total Level of Risk.
Administration: Group.
Forms, 2: Response Form, Observation Report.
Price Data, 1996: $55 per complete kit including 50 Response Forms, 50 Observation Reports, and manual (34 pages); $22 per 50 Response Forms; $14 per 50 Observation Reports; $25 per manual.
Time: (5) minutes.
Authors: Terry Hibpshman and Sue Larson.
Publisher: Slosson Educational Publications, Inc.

Review of the Substance Abuse Screening Test by MARY LOU KELLEY, Professor of Psychology, Louisiana State University, Baton Rouge, LA:

The Substance Abuse Screening Test (SAST) was developed to aid in the screening of adolescents and young adults (ages 13–30) who are and are not at risk for substance abuse. The authors explicitly state that the measure is not intended for diagnosis or labeling and thus, provide an appropriately conservative statement of purpose and test limitations. The primary test consists of a 30-item questionnaire requiring the respondent to indicate whether or not each statement is true of their feelings or behavior. Items range in content from those that explicitly ask about alcohol or drug use to those tapping perceptions of loneliness, family conflict, and general mood states, among other characteristics assumed to be associated with substance abuse risk. The authors do not distinguish between alcohol and illicit drug use/abuse as they believe abusers represent a heterogeneous sample that is not functionally differentiated by the type of substance abused. However, most of the items that specifically tapped substance abuse asked about drinking rather than drug use. The authors purport that the items represent those that differentiate abusers from nonabusers. However, statistical data supporting this conclusion were not provided in the technical manual.

The test materials also include an Observation Report form for the evaluator to record observations in response to several open-ended questions as well as to provide general comments. The authors indicate that the Observation Report allows for the personalization of the screening but that, as with the SAST, the instrument is not to be used diagnostically.

The administration, scoring, and test interpretation procedures were described succinctly and clearly. The scoring involves simply summing the number of endorsed items. Three procedures are provided to aid in score interpretation. Raw scores can be placed in one of four risk levels, converted to standardized scores with a mean of 100 and standard deviation of 15; or entered into a Bayesian table for estimating substance abuse likelihood. All interpretation procedures are relatively easy to use although it is unclear how the authors determined the cutoff levels for the classification system.

Discussions of the psychometric characteristics of the test and the technical development of the instrument were often lacking in important details. For example, the authors identified the states from which the standardization sample came and the age range; however, there was no mention of the number of subjects, SES, gender, or racial composition of the sample, nor the number of individuals included who had a substance abuse problem. In contrast, the authors did provide data on mean test scores of substance abusers, nonabusers, and a variety of comparison groups as well as means based on respondent age, race, and gender. The authors did report significant differences between groups, which supported the validity of the instrument. The authors provided data on the item-total correlation coefficients, the magnitudes of which were acceptable. The authors concluded that test-retest reliability was not applicable because test stability was not a desired feature of the instrument because an individual's score should improve with treatment. This conclusion regarding test stability is wholly inaccurate as most tests assessing clinical symptomatology are potentially sensitive to treatment effects. Overall, the psychometric properties of the instrument are impossible to interpret given the lack of information on the standardization sample as well as the limited reliability data.

The test developers do not provide information on the relationship of the test scores to other measures of substance abuse. Also, it appeared that the authors included a sample of known substance abusers in, or about to enter, treatment. It is not clear how treatment resistant or denying substance abusers would respond to the questionnaire. It would have been useful had the authors included a lie scale as a component of the instrument to assess the influence of social desirability. It appears the measure would not be very useful in detecting substance abusers who are reticent in reporting about their patterns of use.

In summary, the Substance Abuse Screening Test is a short, easily administered and scored instrument for assessing drug and alcohol use. The test is intended for screening only and is not diagnostic. The authors reported that items differentiated abusers from nonabusers. Although the test has some positive features, I cannot recommend use of the instrument as a screening measure at this point given the limited psychometric data. Specifically, additional data are needed addressing the reliability and content validity of the instrument. Furthermore, it is unclear how substance abusers not interested in treatment would score on the instrument. It is my concern that the test would lead to excessive numbers of false negatives given the direct nature of many of the items.

Review of the Substance Abuse Screening Test by MARIELA C. SHIRLEY, Assistant Professor, Department of Psychology, University of North Carolina at Wilmington, Wilmington, NC:

The Substance Abuse Screening Test (SAST) was developed as a brief measure to identify individuals "who may be at risk of substance abuse" (manual, p. 7), and to help with referral decisions (manual, p. 1). Although it is questionable whether true risk can be determined in a format other than a longitudinal design, the SAST's goal is consistent with screening tests focused on the early identification of individuals with possible substance abuse problems who require further evaluation (Connors, 1995; Miller, Westerberg, & Waldron, 1995). This test comprises two parts: (a) a 30-item self-report response form, and (b) an optional 5-item qualitative Observation Report. The SAST can be administered either individually or in a group format by staff with little training in addictions or assessment. The Observation Report should be completed by an examiner who is familiar with the individual being screened, particularly when self-report is suspect. Potential for bias in observer reporting is not addressed.

The SAST was not intended to be a diagnostic instrument; it was designed to screen out individuals who do not have substance abuse problems. However, 12 of the 30 items significantly overlap with *DSM-IV* criteria for dependence (i.e., alcohol). In adolescents, questions on withdrawal and tolerance may not be appropriate. SAST items were developed using a rational approach based on the test developers' experience and a literature review, and the test includes items that directly and indirectly assess for substance abuse (problem areas assessed include: aggression, conduct disorder/ antisociality, parental conflicts, school problems, self-esteem, alienation, affect, attention/concentration, and mild cognitive impairment). Age of onset of use and family history of substance abuse are not assessed. An initial pool of 181 items was reduced to 30 by using the following approaches: (a) a rational approach, (b) by how well items discriminated between individuals with and without substance abuse problems based on item correlation with the total test score and diagnostic type (r range .49 to .77), and (c) by elimination of items considered to be redundant (where their correlation was lower than the similar retained item). A coefficient alpha of .895 was obtained as an estimate of internal consistency reliability. Principal components factor analysis was used on the final items to determine unidimensionality (manual, p. 15), with the first principal component dominating other factors in the analysis.

The standardization sample was obtained from samples in Kentucky, New York, Nebraska, and Kansas. No information is provided in the test manual regarding how the sample was obtained, its size, or characteristics (e.g., socio-demographics, sample size by age range, percentage of substance users vs. nonsubstance users, etc.). The age range selected (13–30) is arbitrary and confounds adolescents with adults. The authors indicate that the test discriminates well: (1) between individuals who have/do not have substance use problems (manual, p. 3); and (b) between substance abusers and individuals with other types of problems (e.g., psychiatric disorders, learning problems, behavior disorders, and physical disabilities). Scores were developed based on the probability that an individual will have a problem given the score and individual demographic characteristics (manual, p. 4). However, no data on sampling information are provided despite inferences that there were no differences for gender and race or for presence/ absence of a substance use problem.

According to the authors, the SAST has strong face validity. However, whether *risk* (i.e., individuals without current substance use problems who are at risk for developing problems) for the development of a substance use disorder (risk reduction screening) vs. *need* for further assessment in individuals who already have a substance abuse problem (disease detection screening) is measured (construct validity) is open to question (Cooney, Zweben, & Fleming, 1995). Overall, the test appears to assess *deviance* (where one behavioral problem area could be substance abuse). If so, the Problem Oriented Screening Instrument for Teenagers (POSIT) is a better measure that assesses multiple behavior problem areas and discriminates between adolescents in treatment and school settings (Rahdert, 1991). Concurrent or convergent validity relative to other widely used measures in the field that screen for potential substance abuse problems (e.g., Adolescent Drinking Index [12:17], Adolescent Alcohol Involvement Scale [Mayer & Filstead, 1979] Personal Experience Screening Questionnaire [Winters, 1992], Drug Use Screening Inventory [Tarter, 1990; Tarter & Hegedus,1991], Problem Oriented Screening Instrument for Teenagers [Rahdert, 1991], Rutgers Collegiate Substance Abuse Screening Test [Bennett et al., 1993]) or a reference test (e.g., Michigan Alcoholism Screening Test [Selzer, 1971]) is not provided. Strong agreement between the total score and known history of substance abuse is claimed, yet poor documentation is provided. In an attempt to develop a test to assess *risk* the authors appear to confuse concurrent validity with predictive validity. In determining risk, predictive validity is more appropriate as the question would be "What is the likelihood that ... will develop a substance abuse problem?" Further cautions of the impact of positive screens should be provided (i.e., on employability, insurability, scholarships, etc.).

Scoring is based on categorical yes/no responses with most substance abuse items requiring endorsement if the individual "ever or usually" had these symptoms. This may not be congruent with their "current" situation. In a review of special considerations in evaluating adolescents, Miller, Westerberg, and Waldron (1995) emphasized that although 90% of adolescents experiment with substances, many mature out after age 21. Interpretation of raw scores can be done in one of three ways: (a) risk level range, (b) standardized scores, and (c) Bayesian table of the likelihood that a problem exists.

Risk level cutoffs were based on efforts at maximizing sensitivity while minimizing specificity. A total score of 1–9 or 1–11 (for ages 13–18 and over 18 respectively) is unremarkable. Borderline risk is based on a score of 10–14 or 12–17 (for ages 13–18 and over 18 respectively). Moderate risk requires a score of 15–18 or 18–20, and high risk scores are 19–30 or 21–30 (for ages 13–18 and over 18 respectively for each of these risk ranges). Data are not provided on how cutoff scores were devised and what methods were used to link these to risk levels. At least 12 items bear some direct relationship to *DSM-IV* criteria (e.g., Item 20: "Once I start drinking it is hard for me to stop"). Presumably, one could endorse 9 of the 12 items yet be considered "unremarkable."

Standard scores use a mean of 100 (*s.d.* = 15) and are based on a sample of individuals who do not have a substance abuse problem and excludes substance abusers or individuals with other disorders. Standard scores were calibrated so that higher scores indicate lower risk and lower scores indicate higher risk (manual, p. 9). Again, there is no information on the sample used to derive these standard scores.

Finally, Bayesian tables are provided to help determine the likelihood that the SAST will accurately identify individuals with known problems using population baserates (manual, p. 25). Professionals utilizing these tables need to know the baserates of the community in which they live; this is often not the case as population estimates are usually given for much larger groupings of cities or socio-demographic categories. In addition, baserates for particular sample characteristics (e.g., blacks in rural communities, certain professions, etc.) are not always available. Even if baserate information were available, it is questionable how this would be utilized in a clinical setting or in facilitating a referral for further assessment. No test-retest or interrater reliability estimates are presented.

In summary, construct validity and other psychometric properties of the SAST are questionable. Although screening for substance use problems in adolescents is important, this measure is poorly developed, poorly documented, and offers no advantage over other screening instruments. Studies are needed to further evaluate its predictive validity.

REVIEWER'S REFERENCES

Selzer, M. L. (1971). The Michigan Alcoholism Screening Test: The quest for a new diagnostic instrument. *American Journal of Psychiatry, 127,* 1653–1658.

Mayer, J., & Filstead, W. J. (1979). The Adolescent Alcohol Involvement Scale: An instrument for measuring adolescents' use and misuse of alcohol. *Journal of Studies on Alcohol, 40,* 291–300.

Tarter, R. E. (1990). Evaluation and treatment of adolescent substance abuse: A decision tree method. *American Journal of Drug and Alcohol Abuse, 16,* 1–46.

Rahdert, E. R. (Ed.). (1991). *The Adolescent Assessment/Referral System manual.* Rockville, MD: U.S. Department of Health and Human Services.

Tarter, R. E., & Hegedus, A. M. (1991). The Drug Use Screening Inventory: Its application in the evaluation and treatment of alcohol and other drug abuse. *Alcohol Health and Research World, 15,* 65–75.

Winters, K. C. (1992). Development of an adolescent alcohol and other drug abuse screening scale: Personal Experience Screening Questionnaire. *Addictive Behaviors, 17,* 479–490.

Bennett, M. E., McCrady, B. S., Frankenstein, W., Laitman, L. A., Van Horn, D. H. A., & Keller, D. S. (1993). Identifying young adult substance abusers: The Rutgers Collegiate Substance Abuse Screening Test. *Journal of Studies on Alcohol, 54,* 522–527.

Connors, G. J. (1995). Screening for alcohol problems. In J. P. Allen & M. Columbus (Eds.), *Assessing alcohol problems: A guide for clinicians and researchers* (pp. 17–29) NIAAA Treatment Handbook Series 4 (NIH Publication No. 95-3745). Rockville, MD: National Institute on Alcohol Abuse and Alcoholism.

Cooney, N. L., Zweben, A., & Fleming, M. F. (1995). Screening for alcohol problems and at-risk drinking in health care settings. In R. K. Hester & W. R. Miller (Eds.), *Handbook of alcoholism treatment approaches: Effective alternatives* (2nd ed.; pp. 45–60). Boston, MA: Allyn & Bacon.

Miller, W. R., Westerberg, V. S., & Waldron, H. B. (1995). Evaluating alcohol problems in adults and adolescents. In R. K. Hester & W. R. Miller (Eds.), *Handbook of alcoholism treatment approaches: Effective alternatives* (2nd ed.; pp. 61–88). Boston, MA: Allyn & Bacon.

[92]
Substance Use Disorder Diagnosis Schedule.

Purpose: Designed to elicit information related to the diagnosis of substance use disorders.

Population: Suspected alcohol or drug abusers.

Publication Date: 1989.

Acronym: SUDDS.

Scores: Scores for 12 substances (Alcohol, Marijuana, Cocaine, Sedatives, Tranquilizers, Stimulants, Heroin, Other Opioids, Hallucinogens, PCP, Inhalants, Other/Mixed); ratings for Stress; and a Depression Screen.

Administration: Individual.

Price Data: Available from publisher.

Time: (30–45) minutes.

Comments: Structured diagnostic interview; also available as a computer-administered interview.

Authors: Patricia Ann Harrison and Norman G. Hoffmann.

Publisher: New Standards, Inc.

TEST REFERENCES

1. Veneziano, C., & Veneziano, L. (1992). Psychological characteristics of persons convicted of driving while intoxicated. *Psychological Reports, 70,* 1123-1130.

2. Watson, D., Weber, K., Assenheimer, J. S., Clark, L. A., Strauss, M. E., & McCormick, R. A. (1995). Testing a tripartite model: I. Evaluating convergent and

discriminant validity of Anxiety and Depression Symptom Scales. *Journal of Abnormal Psychology, 104*, 3-14.

Review of the Substance Use Disorder Diagnosis Schedule by ANDRÉS BARONA, Professor of Educational Psychology and School Psychology Training Director, Arizona State University, Tempe, AZ:

The Substance Use Disorder Diagnosis Schedule (SUDDS) is a structured diagnostic interview used to obtain information about specific events and behaviors useful for corroborating *DSM-III* and *DSM-III-R* diagnoses of alcohol and/or other drug dependencies. Development of the SUDDS was based on a perceived need for a structured diagnostic interview for the specific purpose of detecting substance use disorder. The 1989 version of the SUDDS represents changes and revisions of the Diagnostic Interview Schedule (DIS; Robins, Helzer, Ratcliff, & Seyfried, 1982) and the Substance Abuse Modified Diagnostic Interview (SAMDIS; Hoffman & Harrison, 1984).

The SUDDS consists of 99 items that address general background information; exposure to life events that may lead to stress or depression; and use of coffee, tobacco, alcohol, and other drugs. A "fixed-phrasing" format is used in which the examiner first elicits affirmation (yes/no) or occurrence responses on the alcohol section without probing positive responses. A follow-up of positive responses occurs at the end of the alcohol section. This two-stage process also is used to inquire about other substance use. In instances of multiple substance use, initial administration of the SUDDS is aimed at determining if a lifetime pattern of substance-use disorder can be established. Positive responses are further queried in a second administration to determine if the behavior(s) have occurred within the past year. In most instances a trained interviewer can administer the SUDDS in approximately 30 minutes. However, a history of multiple drug use will significantly increase administration time.

Information obtained from the interview is coded onto one of two diagnostic checklists (*DSM-III; DSM-III-R*) designed to assist in determining if the respondent meets the respective *DSM* criteria for substance use disorder. Positive substance use and symptomology are coded as current (i.e., occurring within the past year) or lifetime (i.e., occurring prior to the past year). The *DSM-III-R* checklist additionally provides guidelines to classify positive responses into *DSM* symptom categories and facilitate diagnoses.

A computer-assisted version of the SUDDS also is available to facilitate ease of administration for some clients and available evidence suggests that interviewer-administered and computer-administered versions are equally effective (Davis, Hoffman, Morse, & Luehr, 1992).

ADVANTAGES. The SUDDS provides clinicians an efficient way to obtain sufficient/comprehensive information to make diagnoses regarding substance use disorder according to *DSM-III* and *DSM-III-R* criteria. Use of the more fully developed *DSM-III-R* Diagnostic checklist, which includes a listing of *DSM-III-R* psychoactive Substance Use Disorder Diagnoses Codes, allows for quick reference and diagnosis. The structured format eliciting information about numerous observable events and behaviors related to substance use permits the clinician to defend objectively the diagnosis and to verify when necessary the veracity of responses by interviews with family members and other collateral sources.

WEAKNESSES. Given its length (many of the 99 items have multiple subsections), the detailed nature of the questions, and the authors' description of the instrument, the SUDDS seems most useful as a confirmatory measure. In spite of its reported quick and easy administration, it may be limited in its usefulness as a screening instrument or with populations in which drug use has not been a priori established. Although adequate for providing useful information for diagnosing substance use disorder, the SUDDS provides limited information to help clinicians determine if other diagnoses are warranted. Similarly, behaviors useful for developing treatment regimens are not included in the interview. The fixed-phrasing format limits clinical interaction and may require additional meetings to obtain information useful in developing therapeutic interventions. In addition, although the authors clearly do not consider the SUDDS to be a psychometric instrument but rather a diagnostic aid, it is questionable whether most interviewers will use it in this manner. Finally, the SUDDS-IV, which covers the key content of the *DSM-IV*, either is already available or in final stages of development. This newer version is designed to provide "clear documentation of specific events and behaviors which can be used to support a diagnosis or demonstrate that the individual denies the occurrence of events frequently associated with abuse or dependence" (N. G. Hoffman, personal communication, February 21, 1996). Although field trials have not been completed and normative data is not yet available, it is likely that the more current SUDDS-IV will have greater clinical utility.

SUMMARY. The SUDDS is a structured fixed-format interview designed to obtain data about specific events and behaviors indicative of a *DSM-III* or *DSM-III-R* diagnosis of substance use disorder. As a clinical measure, it appears useful for corroborating and formulating specific diagnoses involving substance use disorders. The SUDDS is likely to provide clinicians with sufficient documentation to satisfy the requirements of various agencies (e.g., mental health facilities, insurance companies), as well as to defend a diagnosis made on the basis of *DSM-III* or *DSM-III-R* descriptors. Moreover, it provides an opportunity for clinicians to verify the veracity of data critical to accept or rule out a specific diagnosis.

Psychometric data involving the SUDDS are not available. Normative and additional research data involving the SUDDS and its newer version, the SUDDS-IV, would be useful in better determining the psychometric utility of the instrument. However, as an interview technique, the measure is useful in systematically collecting information related to substance use and is likely to be useful with populations where the incidence of abuse is relatively high.

REVIEWER'S REFERENCES
Robins, L. N., Helzer, J. E., Ratcliff, K. S., & Seyfried, W. (1982). Validity of the Diagnostic Interview Schedule, Version II: DSM-III diagnoses. *Psychological Medicine, 12*, 855—870.
Hoffmann, N. G., & Harrison, P. A. (1984). Substance Abuse Modified Diagnostic Interview Schedule (SAMDIS). *Psychological Documents, 14*, 10.
Davis, L. J., Jr., Hoffmann, N. G., Morse, R. M., & Luehr, J. G. (1992). Substance Use Disorder Diagnostic Schedule (SUDDS): The equivalence and validity of a computer-administered and an interview-administered format. *Alcoholism Clinical and Experimental Research, 16*(2), 250–254.

Review of the Substance Use Disorder Diagnosis Schedule by STEVEN I. PFEIFFER, Professor, Graduate School of Education, Kent State University, Kent, OH:

The Substance Use Disorder Diagnosis Schedule (SUDDS) is a structured interview for documenting the diagnosis for alcohol and other drug dependencies. The instrument was developed from an earlier version called the Substance Abuse Modified Diagnostic Interview Schedule (SAMDIS) (Hoffman & Harrison, 1984).

The interview consists of a wide range of questions within seven areas: general demographic data, psychosocial stressors, a brief screen for depression, coffee consumption and smoking habits, and alcohol and drug use. Administration time can be as brief as 30 minutes with a client with minimal alcohol use to as long as 60 minutes for a client with extensive and longstanding drug involvement.

The manual states that the SUDDS is designed to assist in the diagnosis of substance use disorders. It is not recommended as a screening device, but rather is described as an in-depth inquiry with individuals already identified as likely alcohol and drug users.

The authors are to be commended for their thoughtful attention to providing detailed and clear instructions that facilitate administration and ensure a standardized interview process. The manual also provides helpful guidelines that assist in establishing *DSM-III-R* diagnoses—a useful feature of the test.

As mentioned earlier, the manual describes the test as a revision of the SAMDIS, which was based on *DSM-III* diagnostic criteria and "other widely used criteria sets" (p. 11). However, no information is provided on the procedures followed in the development of the SUDDS, including no description of how items were selected, which "widely used (diagnostic) criteria sets" (p. 11) were used, or if a pilot phase occurred.

Face validity appears acceptable, and item coverage is extensive. Nevertheless, the manual provides no evidence that any research was conducted to determine representative content coverage or construct validity. For example, no panel of experts were invited to validate the content of the SUDDS, no inter-item correlation or factor analyses were performed, and no studies were undertaken comparing the SUDDS with other substance use instruments.

Equally surprising and disappointing is the fact that the authors provide no evidence of reliability. It is critical for a clinical tool to be sufficiently reliable for use in individual decision making; the SUDDS, unfortunately, does not furnish any information on interrater, test-retest, or internal consistency. Relatedly, no effort was made to evaluate item or test bias. This is a particularly telling weakness in that one might expect interview questions on a substance use scale potentially to be influenced by culture, gender, ethnicity, SES, and geographic region.

Although the manual offers guidelines for making a *DSM-III-R* diagnosis, there are no standardization data or norms. The test user is not provided cut scores or thresholds for making a diagnosis, apparently because the authors did not undertake any validation studies before publishing the SUDDS. It is unknown, for example, what the sensitivity or specificity of the SUDDS might be for different groups of high-risk substance using populations.

The SUDDS is a structured interview for documenting suspected alcohol and drug dependency. The test has acceptable face validity and extensive item coverage, including questions on psychosocial stressors and depressive symptoms associated with substance abuse. Unfortunately, the test falls far short in omitting information on test development, norming, reliability, and validity. The manual does not provide cut scores to aid in interpreting test results, and until these weaknesses are addressed in a revised manual, the SUDDS should only be used as a research tool or in clinical practice to help formulate hypotheses but not make differential diagnoses.

REVIEWER'S REFERENCE

Hoffman, N. G., & Harrison, P. A. (1984). Substance Abuse Modified Diagnostic Interview Schedule (SAMDIS). *Psychological Documents, 14,* 10.

[93]
Test of Academic Achievement Skills—Reading, Arithmetic, Spelling, and Listening Comprehension.

Purpose: Measures a child's reading, arithmetic, spelling, and listening comprehension skills.
Population: Ages 4–0 to 12–0.
Publication Date: 1989.
Scores, 6: Spelling, Total Reading (Letter/Word Identification, Listening Comprehension, Total), Arithmetic, Total.
Administration: Individual.
Price Data, 1990: $46.95 per complete kit including 25 test booklets, manual (74 pages), and card; $23.95 per 25 test booklets; $16.95 per manual; $8.95 per card; $17.95 per specimen set including manual and one test booklet.

Time: (15–25) minutes.
Author: Morrison F. Gardner.
Publisher: Psychological & Educational Publications, Inc.

Review of the Test of Academic Achievement Skills—Reading, Arithmetic, Spelling, and Listening Comprehension by C. DALE CARPENTER, Professor of Special Education, Western Carolina University, Cullowhee, NC:

The Test of Academic Achievement Skills—Reading, Arithmetic, Spelling, and Listening Comprehension (TAAS-RAS) is a simple academic achievement screening instrument measuring basic skills for children ages 4 to 12. It is meant to be individually administered and the directions and materials are straightforward. This is an untimed instrument.

The Spelling subtest uses a dictation format and appears to use more regular than irregular words in the way they are spelled. Reading actually consists of two subtests: Letter/Word Identification and Listening Comprehension. The first uses the standard format of requiring students to read a graded word list whereas Listening Comprehension consists of the examiner reading a short passage to the student and orally asking five–six questions about the passage. The 6–12-year-old Arithmetic subtest is a computational test. Subtests for younger children down to the age of 4 are slightly different, including some number identification, number comparison, and simple computational problems.

TECHNICAL CHARACTERISTICS. The test was standardized on 899 children ages 4 through 11. Besides being approximately equally divided between males and females, no other information is available. The only estimate of reliability provided is internal consistency calculated using the Kuder-Richardson 20 formula. Median coefficients ranged from .72 for Listening Comprehension to .93 for Reading Word Identification. Criterion-related validity is reported by showing correlations between TAAS scores and scores on such tests as the Test of Kindergarten/First Grade Readiness Skills (Test 95, this volume) and subtests of the Wide-Range Achievement Test—Revised (10:389) and the Wechsler Intelligence Scale for Children—Revised (9:1351) among others. Correlations are generally low. Higher correlation coefficients were reported when correlating TAAS scores with the Test of Auditory-Perceptual Skills (T4:2742).

To determine content validity, items on each subtest must be examined. The format of the Spelling subtest is preferred to multiple-choice tests. However, the list of words seems heavily weighted toward phonetically regular words and no explanation of the source of the word list is provided except to say that all items were submitted by teachers and went through piloting and item analysis. For the reading words used, there is also no more elaboration on source of list. Although the Listening Comprehension subtest format has an advantage of tapping comprehension not confounded by reading ability, the questions are limited. There are no main idea questions or questions requiring inferences or questions about vocabulary. Furthermore, neither of the Reading subtests measures reading comprehension, considered by many experts to be the most important component of reading. Likewise, the Arithmetic subtest does not measure mathematical reasoning. Content validity for the TAAS lacks a comprehensive approach to academic achievement.

SUMMARY. The Test of Academic Achievement Skills is at best a screening option for children aged 4 through 12. Lacking acceptable technical properties and offering nothing that other instruments do not have, there appears little reason to choose this instrument. It is much like the Wide Range Achievement Test (WRAT3; 12:414), which is more popular and based on a larger standardization sample. More comprehensive academic achievement tests such as the Wechsler Individual Achievement Test (T4:2938), Woodcock-Johnson Psycho-Educational Battery (12:415), and the Kaufman Test of Educational Achievement (T4:1348) appear to be better choices.

Review of the Test of Academic Achievement Skills—Reading, Arithmetic, Spelling, and Listening Comprehension by STEVE GRAHAM, Professor of Special Education, University of Maryland, College Park, MD:

The Test of Academic Achievement Skills—Reading, Arithmetic, Spelling, and Listening Comprehension (TAAS-RAS) is designed to assess preschool to preteen children's mastery of basic academic skills. The instrument provides professional examiners, such as psychologists, teachers, therapists, and counselors, information about a child's academic achievement, strengths, and weaknesses in reading, spelling, and arithmetic. According to the author, results from the test can be used to determine a child's readiness for school, promotion to the next grade, or need for remedial assistance.

The test is given individually and takes 30 minutes or less to administer. Reading achievement is assessed by examining the child's ability to name letters and words presented on a laminated card (Letter/Word Identification score) and answer questions about stories read aloud by the examiner (Listening Comprehension score). A child's performance on the Letter/Word Identification and Listening Comprehension scales are used to calculate a Total Reading score. Spelling is assessed by asking the child to write letters and words presented orally by the examiner. Arithmetic is measured by assessing the child's skill in naming written numbers, identifying the larger or smaller of two numbers, determining the number before or after a specific number, calculating simple oral word problems, and answering a variety of computational problems (e.g., 43 - 14 = ____).

The TAAS-RAS is easy to administer and score. A minor inconsistency between the manual and the test booklet, however, may cause some confusion concerning the administration of the easiest items in each domain to students who are 6 years old. The manual indicates that the easiest items, such as saying or writing letters, are administered to 4- and 5-year-olds, whereas the test booklet indicates that they are to be given to children 4 to 6 years of age.

Raw scores obtained for each academic domain are converted to scaled scores, percentile ranks, and age-equivalent scores. The sum of the scaled scores is used to obtain a percentile rank and an academic quotientfor the test as a whole. A median academic age is obtained by computing the average between the next to highest and next to lowest age-equivalent scores on the four subtests. The author should be commended for providing appropriate cautions in the text of the manual on the use of age-equivalent scores. Recommendations or procedures for computing confidence intervals, however, are notably absent. The standard error of measurement for each measure by age is provided in the test manual.

One significant drawback to the TAAS-RAS is that the test items do not adequately represent the knowledge, behaviors, and skills involved in reading, spelling, and arithmetic. To specify the content of these domains, preschool through sixth-grade teachers were asked to indicate what children were expected to learn in each area. Unfortunately, this approach resulted in a very narrow conceptualization of the content underlying each domain. In the area of Reading, for example, phonological awareness, word attack skills, fluency, and reading comprehension are not assessed.

Inadequate procedures were also used in norming the TAAS-RAS. The instrument was standardized on a small sample of 899 students, attending just nine schools. No information on the race, ethnicity, SES, or locale of the students in the normative sample is provided. Purposefully excluded from the normative sample were children with learning problems and other special needs. This is a curious omission, as the test is most likely to be used with children experiencing problems in school.

The author of the TAAS-RAS does not present a strong or convincing case regarding the reliability and validity of the instrument. Only one measure of reliability was established. The Kuder-Richardson 20 formula was used to estimate the internal consistency of the various subtests at ages 4 through 11. On the basis of this single measure, it does not appear that the Listening Comprehension or Arithmetic subtests are reliable enough to be used to make decisions about individual students (all but one reliability estimate was below .90). The Spelling and Word Recognition subtests, however, were reliable enough to warrant individual decision making for most children ages 7 to 11 (all but one reliability estimate was greater than or equal to .90).

Similarly, information on the validity of the instrument is quite meager. For students in the normative sample, correlations between subtests at each age level were computed, resulting in low to moderate associations—suggesting that each subtest assesses a unique aspect of academic achievement. Validity was further evaluated by examining the relationship between scores on the TAAS-RAS

and other measures of academic achievement. Performance on the TAAS-RAS was only moderately correlated to performance on the Test of Kindergarten/First Grade Readiness Skills (Test 95, this volume) and the Wide Range Achievement Test—Revised (10:389). Despite the claim by the author that the test can be used to make decisions about readiness for school or promotion to the next grade, data on the predictive validity of the test is conspicuously absent.

It should be noted that several of the stories for the Listening Comprehension subtest present scenarios that provide a poor match to the backgrounds of many school-age children. One story, for instance, involves a vacation ending with a visit with the family friend, the senator! Furthermore, all of the stories included in this subtest are stilted and uninteresting, and the comprehension questions students are asked focus exclusively on the recall of factual information (e.g., "What color is the cat?").

In summary, the TAAS-RAS should not be used to make decisions about a child's readiness for school or promotion, as there is currently no evidence on the predictive validity of the instrument. The test also provides limited information on a child's academic achievement and strengths and weaknesses, as it does not sample adequately the domains of reading, spelling, or arithmetic.

[94]
Test of Academic Performance.

Purpose: Developed to assess achievement in four curriculum areas: Mathematics, Spelling, Reading, and Writing.
Population: Grades K–12.
Publication Date: 1989.
Acronym: TOAP.
Scores, 6: Basic subtests (Mathematics, Spelling, Reading Recognition, Reading Comprehension), Optional subtests (Written Composition, Copying Rate).
Administration: Individual and group.
Price Data, 1997: $82 per complete set including examiner's manual (182 pages), 25 student response forms, 25 record forms, and package of four reading stimulus cards.
Time: 15(20) minutes for Mathematics subtest; 7.5(12.5) minutes for Spelling subtest; 7.5(12.5) minutes for Reading Recognition subtest; 20(25) minutes for Reading Comprehension subtest; 10(15) minutes for Written Composition subtest; 1(6) minutes for Copying Rate subtest.

Authors: Wayne Adams, David Sheslow, and Lynn Erb.
Publisher: The Psychological Corporation.

Review of the Test of Academic Performance by
STEVE GRAHAM, Professor of Special Education,
University of Maryland, College Park, MD:

The Test of Academic Performance (TOAP) is designed to provide an estimate of a child's academic achievement, identify above-average or below-average performance, and measure changes in performance over time. The instrument samples content in reading, writing, and mathematics from kindergarten to grade 8. The test can be administered, however, to students in grades 9 through 12, as norms are also provided for high school students. Although the authors do not specifically indicate for whom the test is designed or the particular situations where it should be applied, it is most likely to be used with children experiencing difficulty in school, especially those being tested for special education placement or receiving special education services.

The TOAP includes a battery of six subtests. The two reading subtests, Reading Recognition and Reading Comprehension, are given individually and measure, respectively, the ability to name words presented on a laminated card and answer questions about stories read silently. The other four subtests are administered either individually or in a group. The Mathematics subtest assesses the ability to answer increasingly difficult computation problems during a set period of time. The Spelling subtest measures the ability to write correctly words presented orally by the examiner. Written Composition, an optional subtest for children age 8 and above, evaluates the quality of a composition produced during a 10-minute period. Copying Rate, another optional subtest for kindergarten through grade 8, assesses the number of words the child copies in 1 minute.

It should be noted the TOAP is a power or speed test—all of the subtests involve completing tasks under timed conditions. The time requirements for the Spelling, Reading Recognition, and Reading Comprehension subtests require extra vigilance on the part of the examiner, as items on each must be completed in a specific period of time. On the Reading Comprehension subtest, for example, the child has 30 seconds to answer each comprehension question posed by the examiner.

According to the authors, a primary goal in designing the TOAP was to develop an instrument that could be administered quickly and easily. Although the first part of this goal was actualized, the second part was not. The full test takes about 45 minutes to an hour to give, and the administration time can be reduced by 12 to 15 minutes if the two optional subtests are not included. Nevertheless, examiners using the test for the first time are likely to be frustrated by the complexity of the administration rules, including ceiling criteria that change from subtest to subtest as well as time limits that vary depending upon the age of the child and the subtest under consideration.

Scoring procedures for Mathematics and Reading Comprehension are also unnecessarily complicated, as two different methods for scoring each subtest are provided. Written Composition is the most challenging subtest to score, however, requiring the examiner to count the number of words produced and rate on a 3-point scale three attributes of both form and content. Although the manual contains practice exercises for scoring six compositions, some examiners may require more practice and guidance in order to use the two rating scales reliably and validly. Furthermore, the rationale underlying the procedures for scoring the Copying Rate subtest are unclear. The examiner is directed to count the number of words copied, scoring as correct any word in which half of the letters were copied. A more precise measure would simply be to count the number of letters copied.

With the exception of the two optional subtests, raw scores are converted to scaled scores, standard scores, percentiles, and grade-equivalent scores. Confidence intervals are established for either standard scores or percentiles. Norms for both age and grade are included in the manual. The authors are to be commended for providing appropriate cautions on the interpretation of the results from the overall test and on specific types of scores.

For the two optional subtests, Written Composition and Copying Rate, raw scores are converted to an index that shows a child's standing (high, medium, or low) at a particular grade level. More traditional indices were not developed for these two subtests, because there was considerable overlap of score ranges between grade levels for students participating in the standardization process.

In constructing the TOAP, the authors indicated their goal was to construct a measure that would accurately match curricula in today's schools. At each grade level, they reportedly selected a small number of critical, instructional objectives from the broad range of possible objectives. One or more items for each of the selected objectives were then developed and field tested. Although the authors provide a detailed description on the methods used for field testing, it is not clear how instructional objectives at each grade level were selected. It is obvious, however, that the authors' goal of constructing a measure that would match today's curricula was only partially met. In the area of mathematics, for example, methods for computing various operations were emphasized, but the applications of these operations were not. Similarly, important aspects of reading such as phonological awareness, word attack skills, and fluency were not assessed.

The standardization sample was drawn from six school districts in six states, with at least one district in each major region of the United States. Approximately 300 students per grade were tested, except in grades 9 through 12 where number of students per grade averaged 99. With a few exceptions, the standardization sample was similar to national norms on sex, race, and residence. Children of Spanish origin appeared to be underrepresented in the standardization sample, whereas students from the South were overrepresented. Although mainstreamed students with disabilities were included in the testing, students in self-contained classes were not. This is an unfortunate omission, as the test is likely to be used with these students.

The authors of the TOAP do not present a strong or convincing case regarding the reliability or validity of the instrument. No reliability data were provided for the Copying Rate subtest. Test-retest reliability was established at only two grade levels for the other five tests, and neither the Mathematics or Written Composition subtests were reliable enough to be used to make decisions about individual students. Interrater reliability for scoring the Written Composition subtest was only .76. Finally, the authors erroneously used internal consistency coefficients as a measure of reliability for the four basic subtests. Internal consistency coefficients produce artificially high estimates when used with speeded tests.

Data on the validity of the instrument were limited to intercorrelations between the subtests, and correlations between grade level items in Mathematics and Spelling and corresponding performance on the complete subtest. Although the data from these analyses were consistent with the conceptual framework underlying the instrument, additional research is clearly needed.

In summary, the TOAP provides a quick, but not necessarily easy-to-administer estimate of a child's academic achievement. At the present time, the instrument appears to be best suited for experimental work. Further refinement as well as additional evidence supporting the reliability and validity of the test are needed before the TOAP can be recommended as an instrument for estimating a child's academic performance or monitoring changes in achievement.

Review of the Test of Academic Performance by CLEBORNE D. MADDUX, *Professor of Special Education and Educational Technology, University of Nevada, Reno, NV:*

The Test of Academic Performance (TOAP) is yet another attempt to provide a quick achievement test of basic academic subjects to compete with the Wide Range Achievement Test Revision 3 (WRAT3; Wilkinson, 1993; 12:414). The TOAP includes subtests in similar format to the format of the WRAT3 in Mathematics, Spelling, and Reading Recognition. Unlike the WRAT3, however, the test also includes a Reading Comprehension subtest and two supplementary subtests (Written Composition and Copying Rate). Raw scores can be converted to scaled scores, standard scores (based on age or grade), percentile ranks, and grade equivalents. Instructions for calculating confidence intervals for standard scores are included.

The manual authors suggest the test is useful only for screening. They further suggest the two reading subtests must be administered individually, and the other four may be used in a group setting.

The test manual is lengthy and can be confusing due to separate sets of instructions in Mathematics and Spelling, depending on whether the examiner chooses to administer the entire subtests or use the basal/ceiling procedures. The manual contains guidelines for deciding when to choose each procedure, but novice examiners who are likely to use the test will find them vague and ambiguous on this topic. Making the decision calls for considerable judgment and expertise on the part of the examiner. It would have been advisable for the test authors to decide when each procedure was to be used and to offer hard and fast rules based on the child's age or grade.

All answers are found in the Examiner's Record Form, a separate booklet from the Student Response Form. The former is poorly designed and visually confusing because it employs very small print and a crowded, busy format. This separation means the two forms must be kept together to allow others both to see student responses and review results. This is a disadvantage, and the two forms could be consolidated if the subtest answers were moved to the Examiner's Manual.

MATHEMATICS. There are 45 arithmetic calculation items in this subtest. The majority are mechanical addition, subtraction, multiplication, or division algorithms. No discussion of the rationale for this algorithm approach to mathematics was found in the manual.

READING RECOGNITION. The Reading Recognition subtest includes 45 words that the student is asked to read aloud until four out of five in a single row are incorrectly pronounced.

READING COMPREHENSION. The Reading Comprehension subtest consists of seven short silent reading passages of increasing difficulty. Students are given 3 minutes to read each passage and four questions are asked about each passage after it is removed from sight. Entry point is determined by performance on the Reading Recognition subtest, and ceiling rules are provided on the Examiner's Record Form.

COPYING RATE. This optional subtest consists of two sentences for the student to copy. Printing or cursive is acceptable and the number of words correctly copied is the raw score. A word is considered correctly copied if more than half the letters are correct.

WRITTEN COMPOSITION. This optional subtest consists of asking examinees above second grade to write for 10 minutes after being asked to "Explain what is best and worst about a rainy day and why" (p. 14). A subjective scoring system requires the examiner to judge both content and form as low, middle, or high. A score for length is also calculated, and the three scores are aggregated to produce one score up to 18 points.

NORMATIVE DATA. The TOAP was normed in 1984 and 1985 on 3,216 students in six school districts in six states. After gathering the sample and recording grade, age, sex, race, Spanish origin, and region, 1980 U.S. Census data were consulted and the sample was weighted "to approximate even more closely the observed percentages of the population represented by each of these demographic groups" (examiner's manual, p. 14). There was at least one school district from each of the four main geographic regions in the United States. Each school district contributed a class at each grade from kindergarten through eighth grade. Three hundred ninety-six students were in grades 9 through 12 but the authors give no information as to how these students were selected.

RELIABILITY. Test-retest reliability data are reported only for students in grades 3 and 7. Correlations between the two administrations 3 to 4 weeks apart range from .94 and .95 for grades 3 and 7 in Reading Recognition to .31 and .51 for grades 3 and 7 in Reading Comprehension. Test-retest correlations are poor, with only two of the six subtest administrations exceeding .90 at the third grade level, and only one exceeding .90 at the seventh grade level. Internal consistency of subtests are reported by age level and are unacceptably low when the short form of each subtest is administered. Internal consistencies are acceptable for complete Mathematics and Spelling subtests and for Reading Recognition, but are low for Reading Comprehension (.40 for age 5, and .75 for ages 14–18).

VALIDITY. The manual contains sketchy information related to face and content validity, stating only that all items "were either reviewed, revised, or written by teachers familiar both with the K–8 mathematics, reading, and language arts curricula and with standardized test development" (p. 81). A research study is referred to but no details or reference are provided.

Subtest intercorrelations at grades 1, 3, 5, and 7 are presented as evidence of construct validity. These vary in size but are all significant beyond the .001 level. No data or discussion of criterion-related or concurrent validity appear in the manual.

SUMMARY. The TOAP is a norm-referenced achievement test probably intended as an alternative to the WRAT3. The manual is confusing and poorly organized, and the student and examiner forms should be consolidated.

Authors of the TOAP are to be commended for attempting to measure Reading Comprehension in addition to simple word recognition skills. Internal consistency of this subtest indicates that further development is needed.

Information on reliability and validity is incomplete, but it appears that use of the short form of the various subtests is not supported.

The TOAP shows some potential, particularly with regard to utility as a screening instrument that includes a measure of Reading Comprehension. Further development is needed, however, before the TOAP can be considered a serious competitor for the WRAT3.

REVIEWER'S REFERENCE

Wilkinson, G. S. (1993). The Wide Range Achievement Test 3. Wilmington, DE: Jastak Associates/Wide Range.

[95]

Test of Kindergarten/First Grade Readiness Skills.

Purpose: "To assess a child's readiness for kindergarten or for first grade".
Population: Ages 3–6 to 7–0.
Publication Date: 1987.
Acronym: TKFGRS.
Scores, 3: Reading, Spelling, Arithmetic.
Administration: Individual.
Price Data, 1994: $37.95 per complete kit including manual (32 pages), 25 record booklets, and 8 cards; $15 per manual; $19.50 per 25 record booklets; $5.95 per 8 cards; $16 per specimen set including manual and samples.
Time: (20–25) minutes.
Author: Karen Gardner Codding.
Publisher: Psychological & Educational Publications, Inc.

Review of the Test of Kindergarten/First Grade Readiness Skills by D. JOE OLMI, Assistant Professor, School Psychology Program and Director, School Psychology Service Center, Department of Psychology, University of Southern Mississippi, Hattiesburg, MS:

The Test of Kindergarten/First Grade Readiness Skills (TKFGRS) is a norm-referenced instrument that was designed by its author to be used by instructional personnel and assessment specialists to determine a child's preacademic and academic readiness for kindergarten or first grade in reading, spelling, and arithmetic. Additionally, the instrument was designed to determine "areas of low functioning" (p. 5).

The TKFGRS was normed on 373 children from 3 to 7 years of age at 6-month intervals. Information about normative sampling procedures was absent from the technical portions of the manual. Approximately equal numbers of males and females comprised each 6-month age interval. Statements of ethnic diversity of the normative sample were made, but the manual included no demographic breakdown, other than by age and gender. It is assumed by this reviewer that the author's sample was either limited in demographics or was a sample of convenience because no other information was made available.

Each academic section has certain "domains of activities" (p. 8), for example, within the Reading section, domains include letter identification (matching either uppercase letters with lowercase letters, saying the presented letter, or completing a sequence of letters), phonetic identification, word identification, and story comprehension. Likewise, the Spelling and Arithmetic sections have specific domains of activity. The instrument offers 43 Reading items, 22 Spelling items, and 31 Arithmetic items. All items must be administered to a child, and each item is scored plus (correct) or minus (incorrect). Information in the manual indicated that all items were free from bias, although no procedures for making such determinations were suggested.

Performance on the TKFGRS results in raw scores that are converted to age equivalents, scaled scores, percentile ranks, and stanines. The scaled scores have a mean of 100 with a standard deviation of 15.

Item selection was based on content validity, item difficulty, item-to-test correlations, and criterion-related validity. The measures against which the TKFGRS was compared for validity purposes were the Wechsler Preschool and Primary Scale of Intelligence (WPPSI) Vocabulary and Arithmetic scores, the Wechsler Intelligence Scale—Revised (WISC-R) Vocabulary and Arithmetic scores, and the Test of Auditory-Perceptual Skills (TAPS) scores. The correlations were less than adequate, ranging from .14 between the Spelling section of the TKFGRS and the WPPSI Vocabulary score to .54 between the TAPS Auditory Processing score and the Reading section. The average correlation between sections and any of the validity measures was .39. The author should have attempted to establish validity of a preacademic/academic assessment device using other measures of academic ability as opposed to measures of cognitive ability and auditory perception. Normatively and psychometrically, the TKFGRS is lacking.

The TKFGRS contains a technical and administration manual, test cards for each section, and a record booklet. The administration of the TKFGRS is simple and the record booklet is user friendly. Training requirements for administration are minimal. Administration time was not indicated other than it would take longer to administer the instrument to older children than younger children. A shortcoming of the administration guidelines is that all items must be administered. Given that the sampling of academic behaviors of the TKFGRS is rather small to begin with, this would seem an unnecessary requirement which will more than likely result in frustration for younger children who are academically deficient.

In summary, this reviewer would not advise the use of the TKFGRS. At best, it is a poor screener of academic abilities for preschool and early elementary children. Many other strategies could be more functional to the instructional or assessment specialist including teacher-constructed criterion-related measures or other more sound assessment strategies. The instrument is plagued by shortcomings associated with normative sampling, item selection, and validity procedures. It was unclear to this reviewer whether the instrument is intended to be used for screening or diagnosis. In either case, the TKFGRS falls short on all accounts.

Review of the Test of Kindergarten/First Grade Readiness Skills by J. STEVEN WELSH, Director, School Psychology Program, Nicholls State University, Thibodaux, LA:

The purpose of the Test of Kindergarten/First Grade Readiness Skills (TKFGRS) is to provide educators, counselors, and psychologists a criterion measure of academic readiness of young children entering kindergarten or the first grade. The manual author states that the instrument will assist professionals in determining areas of academic deficiency or "low functioning" in children.

The manual author suggests the test may be used with children age 3.6 years old to 7.0 years old and measures academic skill development in Reading, Spelling, and Arithmetic.

The norm sample included 373 children ranging from 3 years to 7 years of age. Children were enrolled in either public or private elementary schools. None of the children in the standardization sample had learning disabilities, hearing impairments, or visual impairments. Subjects were divided by age into seven groups in 6-month increments. The sample was 53.4% male and 46.6% female. Unfortunately, the manual does not provide the reader data regarding the racial/ethnic makeup of the sample, geographic region of the sample, at what point in the academic year data were collected, and the ratio of children in public schools to private schools. Children who had not had exposure to "readiness skills" and non-English-speaking children were eliminated from the standardization group. The manual does not specifically define "exposure to readiness skills" (p. 7) or by what manner children were assessed and eliminated from the sample.

The Reading section of the TKFGRS assesses letter identification by having the child match upper and lower case letters, respond to a visually presented letter stimulus and say the correct letter, and complete a sequence of letters with the next correct letter. Stimuli of letter items are presented to the child on a 4-inch x 8-inch card. Phonetic identification is accomplished by having the child produce the sounds of six letter pairs. The examiner says the letter to the child and then asks the child to produce the sound of the letter. The manual does not indicate if the letter is identified only for the sample item or for all letters in the subtest. Word identification requires a child to read from a list of nine words. Story comprehension is a measure of listening comprehension that requires a child to answer a series of questions after the examiner has read the passage. The Spelling section requires the child to write individual letters or words from dictation. The Arithmetic section requires the child to write numbers from dictation, complete written computations, verbally respond to orally presented problems, tell time, and correctly identify numbers within a sequence of numbers.

The manual provides very limited information regarding the reliability and validity of the TKFGRS. Estimates of internal consistency using Cronbach's alpha were provided for the Reading, Spelling, and Arithmetic subtests. Coefficients for the Reading section on the instrument ranged from .87 to .93 with an overall reliability coefficient of .96. The Spelling section reliability coefficients ranged from .66 to .91, with an overall coefficient of .95. Reliability estimates for the Arithmetic section ranged from .69 to .91 with an overall section coefficient of .94. The manual does not report data regarding split-half or test-retest reliability. No data regarding a child's scores on this instrument and subsequent performance in school were included in the manual.

Content validity is addressed in the manual and is discussed in terms of how the items on the TKFGRS are analogous to the items of tests that purport to measure the same ability. The manual goes on to indicate that "within each test section, different kinds of items were used in measuring the stated behaviors" (p. 10). The manual indicated that the items that were included in the final pool had item difficulty ranges from .185 to .858 for Reading, .09 to .563 for Spelling, and .029 to .853 for Arithmetic.

Criterion-related validity was established by correlating readiness section scores to a child's performance on the Wechsler Intelligence Test for Children (WISC-R) or the Wechsler Preschool and Primary Scale of Intelligence (WPPSI) Vocabulary subtest for the TKFGRS Reading and Spelling sections. The WISC-R or WPPSI Arithmetic subtest scores were used to establish criterion validity of the TKFGRS Arithmetic section. The scores for each TKFGRS subtest were also correlated to performance on the Test of Auditory-Perceptual Skills (TAPS). Correlation coefficients were uniformly low with the WISC-R Vocabulary score and TKFGRS Reading section correlation of .33. The correlations between the WISC-R or the WPPSI with the Spelling section were .23 and .14 respectively. The correlations between the WISC-R or WPPSI with the Arithmetic section were .43 and .45. Correlations between the TAPS and the Reading, Spelling, and Arithmetic sections of the TKFGRS were .54, .43, and .52 respectively. The manual leads the reader to believe that the author considered these low correlations sufficient to establish adequate criterion-related validity. It is not clear if it was the intent of the author to establish that the TKFGRS was measuring constructs that differ from those traditionally associated with achievement measures, namely intellectual

functioning. Other technical data comparing TKFGRS and other measures of academic readiness or achievement were not reported in the manual.

The TKFGRS manual indicated that the instrument yields standard scores with a mean of 100 and a standard deviation of 15. However, these data are not provided in the tables. Scaled scores are reported in a range from 1 to 19 with an apparent mean of 10. The manual does not provide estimates of the standard error of measurement for overall scores or for the various age categories. Age equivalents, percentiles, and stanine score are reported in table form in the manual.

Considering the dearth of information provided about the standardization sample, limited technical data regarding the reliability and validity of the TKFGRS, and confusing tables, it is recommended the potential user proceed with caution if screening and school placement decisions will be made based on a child's performance on this instrument. The wisdom of dropping children without exposure to academic readiness skills from the standardization sample for an instrument designed to assess academic readiness skills is questionable. Assessment of this type is typically accomplished to identify at-risk children who may not be prepared for entering school and who might benefit from programs to help them become "ready." Head Start is an example of such a program. It would seem that including a percentage of these "non exposed children" in the standardization sample might positively improve the predictive validity of the instrument. The TKFGRS does not appear to offer a particularly robust measure of academic readiness and should not be used as a diagnostic tool. Future editions of the TKFGRS will certainly be improved if more precise technical data are presented in the manual. Additionally, the test would be further strengthened if other nonacademic factors of school readiness such as developmental and social-emotional readiness factors are included.

[96]

Test of Orientation for Rehabilitation Patients.

Purpose: Measures orientation to person and personal situation, place, time, schedule, and temporal continuity.
Population: Adult and adolescent inpatient rehabilitation patients.
Publication Date: 1993.
Acronym: TORP.
Scores, 6: Person and Personal Situation, Place, Time, Schedule, Temporal Continuity, Total Test.

Administration: Individual.
Price Data, 1993: $29.95 per 25 test booklets; $99 per complete kit including 25 test booklets, manual (100 pages), and laminated response cue cards.
Time: Administration time not reported.
Comments: "Designed to be administered and scored by a variety of rehabilitation personnel."
Authors: Jean Deitz, Clara Beeman, and Deborah Thorn.
Publisher: The Psychological Corporation.
[Note: The publisher advised in November 1996 that this test is now out of print.—Ed.]

TEST REFERENCES

1. Deitz, J. C., Tovar, V. S., Thorn, D. W., & Beeman, C. (1990). The Test of Orientation for Rehabilitation Patients: Interrater reliability. *The American Journal of Occupational Therapy, 44,* 784-790.
2. Ottenbacher, K. J., & Tomchek, S. D. (1993). Reliability analysis in therapeutic research: Practice and procedures. *The American Journal of Occupational Therapy, 47,* 10-16.

Review of the Test of Orientation for Rehabilitation Patients by JAMES K. BENISH, School Psychologist, Helena Public Schools, Adjunct Professor of Special Education, Carroll College, Helena, MT:

The Test of Orientation for Rehabilitation Patients (TORP) is an individually administered criterion-referenced test of orientation to Person and Personal Situation, Place, Time, Schedule, and Temporal Continuity. Designed for adult and adolescent patients, "it was created to assess patients who are believed to be confused or disoriented secondary to traumatic head injury, cerebrovascular accident, seizure disorder, brain tumor, or any other neurological condition resulting in such symptoms" (manual, p. 3). This measurement tool is designed to screen patients or monitor patient progress over time. The TORP contains 46 test items grouped within five domains, and each item serves as either an open-ended or auditory recognition task question. The recognition task questions are used when a patient cannot recall the answer to an open-ended question. Recognition task questions have the correct answer randomly placed within a group of three distractors, which includes an alternate distractor in the event one of the original distractors is the correct answer. The TORP was developed to "(a) aid in diagnosis; (b) facilitate management, care, and planning; (c) facilitate the evaluation of treatment effectiveness; and (d) be useful as a research measure" (manual, p. 21).

Instructions for administering the TORP are clearly described in the test manual. "Examiner Response Procedure" cards are supplied to allow for quick reference during testing. There are no time limits specified in the manual, but total test time is to be recorded on the score sheet. It is recommended that testing be completed in one session, whenever possible. A training module is included that provides detailed steps to facilitate testing continuity. Authors suggest that training is best accomplished with a partner. Scoring is accomplished by converting domain and total test raw scores to percentage points. The score sheet allows for corrected scores based on the number of items administered. There are separate daily and weekly graphs to display total test corrected scores. Patient progress can be monitored fairly easily with these graphs.

TEST DEVELOPMENT. Test items were developed through an extensive review of literature based on the premise there was a specific need to assess patients with brain injuries in an inpatient rehabilitation setting. The authors selected items for the TORP by administering them to brain-injured and non-brain-injured patients. Test items were then reviewed by an interdisciplinary group composed of researcher, educators, and clinicians. A content validity study served to determine the 46 items that were grouped into respective domains. This process was described in detail in the manual.

STANDARDIZATION SAMPLE. It was unclear how many patients were assessed during test item development. However, subject numbers were given for construct validity and interrater reliability studies. Items selected for the final version were "piloted on patients with brain injuries and patients without brain injuries" (manual, pp. 21–22). It was also unclear as to the category breakdown of individuals studied by age, gender, type of brain trauma, etc. used in the study.

RELIABILITY AND VALIDITY. Test-retest reliability was good, with intraclass correlation coefficients of .85 for the non-brain-injured and .95 for the brain-injured groups, respectively, for total scores. Intraclass correlations for domain scores ranged from .72 to a respectable .92. An interrater reliability study comparing 34 brain-injured patients with 35 non-brain-injured patients suggested excellent reliability for both domain and total test scores. The authors noted that studies of concurrent and predictive validity would add value to test research. Such studies would enhance the standardization of this criterion-referenced test.

SUMMARY. The Test of Orientation for Rehabilitation Patients (TORP) is an easily administered measure of orientation to Person and Personal Situation, Place, Time, Schedule, and Temporal Continuity. It is designed for adolescent to adult populations receiving inpatient rehabilitation services. The manual and test protocol are clearly and concisely written. Practice modules are included to help increase consistency in test administration among rehabilitation personnel. Aside from limited statistical and research data found in the manual, the TORP could prove worthwhile for rehabilitation personnel either as a screening tool to determine deficiencies due to brain injury or to monitor progress in an inpatient setting.

Review of the Test of Orientation for Rehabilitation Patients by ELAINE CLARK, Associate Professor of Educational Psychology, University of Utah, Salt Lake City, UT:

The Test of Orientation for Rehabilitation Patients (TORP) measures orientation in adolescent and adult rehabilitation patients. The TORP was designed to provide a more thorough, quantifiable, reliable, and valid assessment of orientation than other tests afford. The TORP is more comprehensive than most of its competitors. It consists of 46 items that measure five orientation domains. In addition to assessing whether the patient knows who and where they are, and what the current time-frame is (Person, Place, and Time), the TORP assess the patient's awareness of discrete events in their current schedule and the passage of time (Schedule and Temporal Continuity).

The TORP is designed to be administered by a variety of rehabilitation personnel, including speech and language pathologists, psychologists, occupational therapists, nurses, and physicians. The test authors recommend that examiners have prior experiences with rehabilitation patients and knowledge of general testing principles and specific TORP procedures. A well-designed training module is included that will help with TORP administration and scoring; however, examiners should heed the advice of experience working with rehabilitation patients. Problems can be anticipated whenever a

test not only starts with the question, "what is your first name," but gives credit for it. Examiners need to be well prepared if they intend to ask 46 questions to patients who are not only disoriented but potentially agitated. Examiners may want to make sure their rehabilitation experience is also with patients who are in the early stages of recovery from brain injury.

ADMINISTRATION AND SCORING. The test manual and test form are clearly written and will answer most of the questions that examiners will have about administering and scoring the TORP. Detailed instructions are presented in two sections—one a section that pertains to the preparation for administrating the test, and the other a section pertaining to actual test administration and scoring. General guidelines and specific examples make these manual sections very helpful. Issues regarding scheduling (e.g., what to do if the patient cannot complete the test in one sitting) and testing environment (e.g., insuring that prompts such as clocks and calendars are not in view) are some of the issues discussed. The test form also provides scoring guidelines and prompts for most of the test instructions. Because some key instructions are omitted (e.g., discontinue the test if Item #1 is failed and timing of the test), examiners will definitely need to review the manual thoroughly. In addition to administration instructions on the test form itself, laminated examiner response procedure charts are provided to help examiners make decisions about questionable patient responses (e.g., when the patient gives two answers, one that is correct and the other that is incorrect).

Test items are scored as the test is administered. A separate score sheet is provided for this purpose. Each item is scored as spontaneously correct (SC), recognition correct (RC), or incorrect (I). Like the test booklet itself, the score sheet is easy to use. In addition to providing information about individual items, the SC, RC, and I scores are calculated for each domain and the total test (percentage scores are also calculated using conversion tables included in the manual). A data sheet is also included to calculate domain corrected scores and the total test corrected scores (corrected scores take into account items that are not administered to a particular patient). Daily and weekly graphs are included for repeated test administrations.

These graphs are helpful in evaluating progress over time.

TRAINING MODULE. The training module is likely to clear up any remaining questions about giving and scoring the TORP. The module consists of filling out two case protocols and passing two competency tests. The cases provide good examples of rehabilitation patients and give the more novice interviewer a sense of what might be found in the patient's chart (e.g., history of injury, therapy evaluations, progress notes, and daily schedules). The cases also provide an opportunity to practice the administration and helpful hints for scoring. Although the multiple-choice competency tests allows examiners to receive further feedback about testing procedures and gives further information about the test itself, examiners are likely to find this exercise laborious, and for the more experienced tester, unnecessary.

RELIABILITY AND VALIDITY. Limited content and construct validity data are provided. Content validity was studied by having 11 "experts" judge the items. An index of item-objective congruence was used to study the items and Lu's (1971) coefficient of agreement was used to study the five behavioral domains. These analyses supported the inclusion of 46 of the 49 original items. Construct validity was evaluated by comparing the TORP scores of 25 rehabilitation patients with brain injuries and 25 rehabilitation patients without brain injuries. Although current thought on construct validity is that it be more broadly defined to include other types of support (e.g., concurrent and criterion validity), more support than what the authors have provided is expected. The fact that rehabilitation patients with brain injuries scored lower than those without does not provide adequate evidence that the test measures orientation. It is obviously feasible that these two groups of patients could be discriminated by a number of functions besides orientation.

Interrater and test-retest reliability data were collected. Interrater reliability was based on the test protocols of 34 subjects with brain injury and 35 without. The coefficients for the total test score were .98 and .99, respectively, for the subjects with and without brain injury. The reliability coefficients for the individual domains were similarly adequate with coefficients for the subjects with brain injury ranging from .89 to 1.00 for orientation to Place and orientation to Time, respectively. Coefficients for subjects without brain injury were also high: .94 for orientation for Person and Personal Situation, and .99 for orientation to Time, Schedule, and Temporal Continuity.

Test-retest data were collected over a 3- to 5-day period. For total test scores, subjects with brain injuries had a coefficient of .95 and for those without brain injuries, a coefficient of .85. Domain stability coefficients for the brain injury group ranged from .72 (orientation to Schedule) to .92 (orientation to Place). There was greater variability for the group without brain injury. Domain coefficients ranged from .25 (orientation to Place) to .86 (orientation for Person and Personal Situation). The magnitude of test and retest score differences for the subjects without brain injuries, however, suggests that the problem is a lack of score variability not stability.

TEST SCORE INTERPRETATION. The normative sample for the test includes 35 rehabilitation patients without brain injuries. Examinees' total and domain corrected scores are compared to the high and low scores and the percentile scores of this group of subjects. It should be noted that 90% of the standardization subjects missed five items or less, and 50% missed one or two items or less. The range of total scores for the normative sample was 1.76 to 2.00 (possible range is 1.00 to 2.00). A total test cutoff score of 1.24 is used to indicate problems with orientation (each domain has its own cutoff score). Without describing how this very small normative sample was selected and what their characteristics are (e.g., why were they in rehabilitation), it is difficult to interpret the meaning of the cutoff scores. Demographics of this sample are limited to information about their sex (16 males and 19 females), age (15 to 87), and socioeconomic background ("varied"). Such a limited sample makes it difficult to know how orientation is distributed among a "normal" population.

SUMMARY. The authors have provided a more comprehensive evaluation of orientation than most other tests on the market; however, this may be at a cost. Administering 46 two-part items to disoriented and potentially agitated patients is likely to be perceived by overburdened rehabilitation personnel as too time-consuming and discarded in favor of shorter measures of orientation. The problem of length is a very serious concern given the fact that TORP is intended to be given more than once to assess progress over time. Although the authors should be commended for their efforts in designing well-written and well-organized test materials, including a training module, they have failed to provide adequate data that would convince users that the time invested in this test is worth it. In addition to providing support for reliability, which the authors have done, support must be provided for the validity of the test and the usefulness of the test scores. A small and poorly defined normative sample will not convince the test users the authors intended to convince, that is, those with knowledge about tests and measurement. Although the authors acknowledge the need for additional data that describe the performance of rehabilitation patients without brain injuries, it would have been better to have provided such data before publishing the test.

REVIEWER'S REFERENCE

Lu, K. H. (1971). A measure of agreement among subjective judgments. *Educational and Psychological Measurement, 31,* 75–84.

[97]
Test of Phonological Awareness.

Purpose: "Measures young children's awareness of individual sounds in words."
Population: Ages 5–8.
Publication Date: 1994.
Acronym: TOPA.
Scores: Total score only.
Administration: Group.
Editions, 2: Kindergarten, Early Elementary.
Price Data, 1994: $98 per complete kit including examiner's manual (38 pages), 25 kindergarten student booklets, 25 early elementary student booklets, 25 kindergarten profile/examiner forms, and 25 early elementary profile/examiner forms; $27 per examiner's manual; $29 per 25 student booklets (specify kindergarten or early elementary); $9 per 25 profile/examiner forms (specify kindergarten or early elementary).
Time: (15–20) minutes.
Authors: Joseph K. Torgesen and Brian R. Bryant.
Publisher: PRO-ED, Inc.

TEST REFERENCES

1. Catts, H. W. (1993). The relationship between speechlanguage impairments and reading disabilities. *Journal of Speech and Hearing Research, 36,* 948–958.
2. Foster, K. C., Erickson, G. C., Foster, D. F., Brinkman, D., & Torgesen, J. K. (1994). Computer administered instruction in phonological awareness: Evaluation of the Daisy Quest program. *Journal of Research and Development in Education, 27,* 126–137.

3. Felton, R. H., & Pepper, P. P. (1995). Early identification and intervention of phonological deficits in kindergarten and early elementary children at risk for reading disability. *School Psychology Review, 24,* 405–414.

Review of the Test of Phonological Awareness by STEVEN H. LONG, Assistant Professor of Communication Sciences, Case Western Reserve University, Cleveland, OH:

The Test of Phonological Awareness (TOPA) measures young children's ability to match words with same or different phonemes in initial or final position. Its major purpose is in identifying during the early school years children who are at risk for reading difficulties.

TEST MATERIALS. The TOPA comes in two versions, one intended for administration to kindergarten (age 5–6) students and the other for early elementary (6–8) students. Both versions consist of two forms: (a) a booklet with black-and-white line drawings that the student marks in response to test stimuli; and (b) a record form used to score the responses from the booklet. The graphics style and layout of the student booklet is reminiscent of the Boehm Test of Basic Concepts—Revised (Boehm, 1986; T4:314). Procedures for administering and scoring the TOPA are given in an accompanying manual.

TEST ADMINISTRATION. The TOPA can be administered individually or to groups of children. The kindergarten version consists of two tasks, each performed with 10 items. In the first task, the examiner speaks a stimulus word, then speaks three response words. Each of the four words is pictured in the child's booklet. The child is asked to mark the response word that begins with the same sound as the stimulus word. In the second task, the examiner speaks four words. The child is asked to mark the word that has a different first sound than the other three. The only difference in the early elementary version of the TOPA is that the child is asked to identify words with same or different final sounds.

Because the TOPA is administered with live voice it is important that the examiner possess "speech that is sufficiently clear" (p. 5). According to the manual, this disqualifies individuals with articulation deficits and also ones who speak in a dialect different from that of the students. In multicultural environments, the latter requirements must be carefully noted.

The TOPA is scored simply by counting the number of items marked correctly. Normative tables can then be consulted in the manual.

PSYCHOMETRIC ADEQUACY. The TOPA is described as a measure of analytic phonological awareness; that is, it determines whether children can group or contrast words based on phonemic differences. The content validity of the test derives from the belief that such phonological awareness facilitates early reading acquisition.

Stimulus items for the TOPA were selected after an analysis of word familiarity and articulatory ease. Items were then tested with children in the targeted age range and final selections were made from items that had an average pass rate between 58% and 83%. No analysis was performed to assess possible cultural bias in the items selected. The unfamiliarity of words, such as hut, jack, and bulb to children from less mainstream backgrounds could pose a problem for test validity.

Test-retest reliability was calculated with and without an adjustment for internal consistency of response. The kindergarten version showed a test-retest correlation of .84–.94 (6-week interval); the early elementary version was .69–.77 (8-week interval). The lower coefficient of the early elementary version is attributed to the influence of reading instruction during first and second grade, which produces more rapid change in phonological awareness.

The standardization group for the kindergarten version was 857 students; for the early education version it was 3,654 students. Both groups were reasonably evenly distributed across regions of the United States, gender, and core ethnic groups. No indication is given of the language background (monolingual, bilingual) or socioeconomic status of the standardization groups.

Norms are reported in 6-month intervals for the ages 5-0 to 6-11 and yearly intervals for the ages 6-0 to 8-11. Different norms are given for 6-year-olds enrolled in kindergarten and enrolled in first grade at the time of testing. The manual notes that kindergartners in the standardization group were tested during the second half of the school year. This timing should be followed, if the norms are to be applied equitably.

SUMMARY. The TOPA examines children's abilities to differentiate the initial and final sounds of words. From this performance, it is suggested, an inference can be made about a child's readiness for reading. The test format is simple and administration should be completed rapidly in most instances. The TOPA's most apparent shortcoming is that it is at risk for bias if the dialect of the examiner does not match that of the students or if a child's cultural background does not include certain of the lexical items on the test.

REVIEWER'S REFERENCE

Boehm, A. E. (1986). Boehm Test of Basic Concepts—Revised. San Antonio, TX: The Psychological Corporation.

Review of the Test of Phonological Awareness by REBECCA McCAULEY, Associate Professor, Communication Sciences, University of Vermont, Burlington, VT:

TEST STRUCTURE. This test was designed for group assessment of children's abilities to isolate individual speech sounds in spoken words for purposes of identification, general screening, and research. The test consists of two forms: The TOPA—Kindergarten, designed for children in kindergarten, and the TOPA—Early Elementary, designed for children in grades 1 and 2. The TOPA—Kindergarten focuses on children's awareness of initial sounds, requiring children to indicate which word from a set of three words contains the same initial sound as the stimulus word (the Initial Sound-Same Subtest) and which word from a set of four words contains a different initial sound from the other three (the Initial Sound-Different Subtest). The TOPA—Early Elementary focuses on children's awareness of final sounds, requiring children to perform assessments comparable to those required by children in the TOPA—Kindergarten, except on final rather than initial sounds.

TEST ADMINISTRATION AND INTERPRETATION. The test may be given by professionals who have a background in educational assessment and whose speech is precise and matches the dialect of the children being tested. Its directions are clear and comprehensive for both forms of the test, an important achievement in light of the test's use with groups of children who are likely to be prereaders. In their discussion of test score interpretation and norms, the authors caution users about the sensitivity of the test to the time during the school year in which it is administered (because the test's norms were collected in the Spring) and about its relative insensitivity to differences among children with higher levels of phonological awareness. Test scores are reported as raw scores, percentiles, and several standard scores.

NORMS. Relatively large groups of children were used to standardize the two forms of the test; specifically, 857 children for the TOPA—Kindergarten and 3,654 for the TOPA—Early Elementary form. The resulting normative samples were nationally representative in terms of race, ethnicity, gender, and geographic location. Most subgroup sample sizes fell beyond a desirable 100 per cell. Several subgroups fell below these levels, including 5-year-olds tested using the TOPA—Kindergarten (e.g., N = 38 for African American, 23 Hispanic, 3 Native American, and 6 Oriental subgroups).

RELIABILITY. High internal consistency was found when the test results for 100 children at each age level were examined. Those data are reported both as correlation coefficients and as standard errors of measurement. Test-retest reliability was examined using a procedure recommended by Anastasi (1988), in which a standard test-retest paradigm is followed by a procedure designed to remove the error associated with internal consistency. When both forms of the test were examined in this way, a very high adjusted stability estimate of .94 was obtained for the TOPA—Kindergarten; whereas only a "high" adjusted correlation of .77 was obtained for the TOPA—Early Elementary. The authors speculate that the lower performance of the TOPA—Early Elementary may have been due to the use of a longer test-retest interval (8 weeks instead of 6) or to the greater response of the older children to their ongoing reading instruction.

VALIDITY. The content validity evidence provided by the test authors consists of a relatively detailed review of the existing literature on the emergence of phonological awareness in children and an impressive account of the test's development, which included two item tryouts preceding standardization and a final item analysis following standardization. Because the test focuses on the identification of children with possible problems rather than the measurement of phonological awareness abilities across both high and low levels of performance, items were selected with higher levels of difficulty than might usually be the case in a norm-referenced test.

Both concurrent and predictive criterion-related validity evidence are provided. Direct evidence of concurrent validity consists of moderate to high positive correlations between one or both versions of the test with the Word Analysis and Word Identification subtests of the Woodcock Reading Mastery Tests (Woodcock, 1987) and three measures of phonological awareness (i.e., a measure of sound isolation, a measure of sound segmentation, and a set of five different phonological tasks taken from a computer-adaptive test, Undersea Challenge [Foster, Erickson, Foster, & Torgesen, in press]). Predictive validity was examined only for the TOPA—Kindergarten. That evidence consists of moderate correlations between TOPA scores obtained during kindergarten and children's performance in alphabetic reading on the Word Analysis subtest of the Woodcock Reading Mastery Test and the finding that 18 of 23 children who fell in the lowest quartile on the TOPA also fell below the median in alphabetic reading skills in first grade.

Evidence of construct validity for this test begins with the careful elaboration of the construct being tested (which was provided in the description of item selection) and of other aspects of the test's development. It is further supported not only by the other evidence of validity described above, but also by three explicit arguments. First, the authors cite work by Stanovich and his colleagues (1984) and by Wagner and his colleagues (in press) in which the types of tasks used in the TOPA were shown to be closely related to a variety of other phonological awareness tasks. Second, the authors describe a training study examining the relationship between performance on the TOPA and children's response to a 12-week training in phonological awareness. Results of that study indicated that children who performed best initially on the TOPA also showed the greatest gains in training. As a third type of evidence, the authors discuss research demonstrating that children's performance on the TOPA items was unlikely to have been due to their responding to global phonological similarity, a possible confound suggested in the literature.

SUMMARY. The TOPA makes a substantial contribution to the group assessment of phonological awareness in young school-age children. For children in kindergarten through grade 3 (ages 5 to 8-11), its merit as a screening tool is attested by a strong history of test development and validation. Test-retest reliability for the TOPA—Early Elementary fell a bit below a recommended level of .80, but appears likely to have been affected by the length of test-retest interval and by ongoing training on related skills. Other evidence of reliability and validity is generally quite adequate. The provision of predictive validity evidence for the TOPA—Early Elementary version is particularly impressive given probable uses of the test.

REVIEWER'S REFERENCES

Stanovich, K. E., Cunningham, A. E., & Cramer, B. B. (1984). Assessing phonological awareness in kindergarten children: Issues of task comparability. *Journal of Experimental Child Psychology, 38*, 175–190.

Woodcock, R. (1987). Woodcock Reading Mastery Tests—Revised. Circle Pines, MN: American Guidance Service.

Anastasi, A. (1988). *Psychological testing* (6th ed.). New York: Macmillan.

Foster, K. C., Erickson, G. C., Foster, D. F., & Torgesen, J. K. (in press). *Undersea challenge*. Unpublished software, Adventure Learning Software, Orem, UT.

Wagner, R. K., Torgesen, J. K., & Rashotte, C. (in press). The development of reading-related phonological processing abilities: New evidence of bi-directional causality from a latent variable longitudinal study. *Developmental Psychology*.

[98]

Test of Understanding in College Economics, Third Edition.

Purpose: To measure college students' understanding of college economics.

Population: Introductory economics students.

Publication Dates: 1967–1991.

Acronym: TUCE III.

Scores: Total score only.

Administration: Group.

Editions, 2: Microeconomics, Macroeconomics.

Price Data: Available from publisher.

Time: (40–45) minutes per test.

Author: Phillip Saunders.

Publisher: National Council on Economic Education.

Cross References: See T2:1970 (10 references); for a review by Christine H. McGuire, see 7:902.

Review of the Test of Understanding in College Economics, Third Edition by JOSEPH C. CIECHALSKI, Associate Professor of Counselor and Adult Education, East Carolina University, Greenville, NC:

The third edition of the Test of Understanding in College Economics (TUCE III) was designed to assess a student's ability to understand and apply microeconomic and macroeconomic terms, concepts, and principles. Like its two pre-decessors, the TUCE III was developed by the American Economic Association's Standing Committee on Economic Education and the Joint Council on Economic Education. Unlike previous editions, the TUCE III consists of a single-form macroeconomics test and a single-form microeconomics test.

Both the macroeconomics and microeconomics test booklets contain 33 multiple-choice items. The last 3 items on each test deal with international economic concepts and may be omitted at the discretion of the examiner. Only 3 items on the macroeconomics test and 4 questions on the microeconomics test of the TUCE III have the same wording as the TUCE II. All of the remaining items of the TUCE III are either completely new, revised, or edited versions of the items on the TUCE II.

The TUCE III is easy to administer. Examinees are instructed to read the directions on the front of the test booklets. The directions are clear, and important points are printed in boldface type and underlined. Examiners need to inform the examinees whether they are to answer all 33 items or to skip the last three (international) items and answer 30 items. Responses to the items are made on separate answer sheets. However, answer sheets are not provided in the test package. Instead, answer sheets in use at the examiner's institution can easily be adapted for use on the TUCE III. Examiners may use different colored answer sheets or have examinees indicate the form of the test they are taking on their answer sheet.

The macroeconomics and microeconomics tests may be either hand or machine scored. Instructions for developing a hand-scoring stencil or scoring by machine are explained in the test manual. The score for each test is the total number of correct responses. Total scores may be converted to either percentiles or *T*-scores using conversion tables. Conversion tables for those who answered 30 items or all 33 items are provided in the manual. These conversion tables include pre- and posttest results for those who will administer the TUCE III before and after instruction.

The norming sample for the TUCE III consisted of 2,724 students who took the 30-item macroeconomics test and 2,726 students who took the 30-item microeconomics test at the beginning and end of the course. In addition, a norming sample consisting of those tested on all 33 items of the macroeconomics and microeconomics tests was described in the manual. This norming sample consisted of 1,324 students for the 33-item macroeconomics test and 1,426 students for the 33-item microeconomics test. Separate norming tables are provided in the manual for those taking either the 30-item or the entire 33-item test. The author of the manual points out that neither the macroeconomics test nor the microeconomics test samples are random. Unlike the previous editions, the norming group for TUCE III included students attending 2-year colleges. Thus, the TUCE III sample is larger and more representative of higher education institutions than the two previous editions.

Reliability coefficients for the microeconomics and macroeconomics tests were calculated using the Kuder-Richardson 20 formula and the results are reported in Table 5 of the test manual. For the microeconomics test, the reliability coefficients are .80 for the 30-item test and .81 for the entire 33-item test. According to the manual, these coefficients are higher than those of previous editions of TUCE for the micro forms. For the macroeconomics test, the reliability coefficients are .77 for the 30-item test and .75 for the entire 33-item test. The author claims that these results are comparable to most of the previous macroeconomics forms, but not as high as TUCE II Macro Form A. The standard error of measurement for TUCE III ranged from a low of 2.50 for the 33-item micro test to a high of 2.53 for the 33-item macro test.

Evidence of content validity is provided in Tables 1 and 2 of the test manual. Table 1 classifies each of the 33 macroeconomics items into one of six content areas and into one of three cognitive categories (Recognition and Understanding; Explicit Application; and Implicit Application items) covering basic terms, concepts, and principles and Table 2 does the same for each of the 33 microeconomics items. The purpose of the content categories is to ensure adequate coverage of the basic content of college principles courses. The purpose of the cognitive categories is to ensure that the items measure beyond simple recall and recognition. According to the manual, two-thirds of the items on both tests of TUCE III are application items.

The TUCE III reflects the Joint Council on Economic Education's commitment to provide a quality instrument to assess the principles of macroeconomics and microeconomics. It is an easy instrument to administer, score, and interpret. The test manual is comprehensive and well written. In addition, the manual describes the test's strengths and limitations in detail. Those who have used any of the previous editions of the TUCE will find the TUCE III to be even better. Those who have not are advised by this reviewer and the author of the test manual to order a specimen set and decide for themselves whether the content of their courses is congruent with the content sampled by the TUCE III.

Review of the Test of Understanding in College Economics, Third Edition by JENNIFER J. FAGER, Assistant Professor, Education and Professional Development, Western Michigan University, Kalamazoo, MI:

DESCRIPTIVE INFORMATION. The Joint Council on Economic Education published the third edition of the Test of Understanding in College Economics (TUCE III) to join three additional economics-focused tests to complete a comprehensive examination of economic understanding. Although this review does not focus on the other exams, it should be noted that the publishers are aware of the need for economic understanding at the elementary, middle, and high school levels and they have met that need by providing exams to assess this understanding.

Like previous editions of this exam, the authors of the Test of Understanding in College Economics, Third edition (TUCE III) consulted with a group of economists representing the many professions impacted by economics. These consultants provided input into the constructs represented in the TUCE III that led to its current format varying from previous editions. Changes in the format of the TUCE III represent changes in college course foci. The TUCE III has a single-form microeconomics test and a single-form macroeconomics test and each test includes questions on international economics to respond to the variations in university course content. The authors suggest that international economics is an unsettled issue in economics departments. Some departments teach the content in microeconomics and others in macroeconomics, thus the questions are represented on each test version.

The TUCE III has two primary objectives, according to the authors: (a) to serve as an instrument for measuring specific outcomes in introductory economics courses at the college level; and (b) to enable instructors to compare their students to national norms (p. 1). Each of the two tests in the TUCE III includes 33 multiple-choice questions. Each of the 33 questions on the macro test represent content from six broad categories and three cognitive categories. The same holds true for the micro test questions. The international economics test questions are at the end of each test allowing the instructor to include or eliminate them depending on the course content.

Macroeconomics questions are classified into the following categories: measuring aggregate economic performance, aggregate supply, productive capacity, and economic growth, income and expenditure approach to aggregate demand and fiscal policy, monetary approach to aggregate demand and monetary policy, policy combinations, and international economics. The micro content categories include: the basic economic problem; markets and the price mechanism; costs, revenue, profit maximization, and market structure; market failures, externalities, government intervention and regulation; and income distribution and government redistribution policies, and international economics. In addition to focusing on content, the authors prepared a cognitive structure to ensure attention was given to the application of the content constructs. Although the authors concede that students may not use mental processes to apply knowledge they have learned, they have reduced the likelihood that memorization will be the sole reason for success on the TUCE III.

The questions on both forms of the test are clear, well formulated, and relatively free from psychometric error. Administration of each test requires 45 minutes unless both tests are given during the same session—then 90 minutes should be set aside. A school's individual multiple-choice answer sheets may be used, thus reducing costs and the need to send responses away for scoring. The procedure for collecting norming data is purposefully broader than for previous TUCE editions. The authors recognized the large number of students taking economics courses at 2-year institutions and data collected from these schools were included for the first time. In all, 53 schools representing scores from 2,724 (macroeconomics) or 2,726 (microeconomics) students were used to prepare the norm tables. Test users should be satisfied with the scales available in the examiner's manual for comparison purposes.

Previous editions of the TUCE reported reliability information for tests that included micro and macro questions. Since separating the questions into two distinct tests, the authors are able to report reliability information more accurately. The K-R 20 reliability estimate for the micro test is .80 when the international economics questions are excluded and .81 for the 33-item test. Reliability coefficients for the macro test are .77 for the 30 items and .75 for the 33 items. It is likely that these reliability scores can be attributed to the low number of test items per content category. As a result, the authors note that the TUCE III is designed to be a norm-referenced test to be used to discriminate across a broad range of student ability and is not to be substituted for teacher-made tests (p. 7).

The manual that accompanies the test deserves a separate note. The authors attended to detail when creating the examiner's manual for the TUCE III. It is explicit in the directions provided and allows little room for misinterpretation or misuse of the test. Specific uses are provided at the end of the opening section. The intentions for TUCE III use include evaluation, controlled experiments, and individual student evaluation, as well as a teaching aid. Specific cautions are given for each of these uses that will prevent the economics instructor from inaccurate use of the test results.

If the TUCE III is used as it is intended, economics instructors will be provided with information useful for measuring the economic understanding of their students. It is a highly convenient instrument for evaluating students' knowledge of broad economic constructs in both micro- and macroeconomics.

[99]

Test of Variables of Attention.

Purpose: For screening, diagnostic evaluation, and monitoring treatment of children and adults with attention deficit disorder.

Population: Ages 4 and over.

Publication Dates: 1988–1993.
Acronym: T.O.V.A.
Scores: 7 variables: Errors of Omission, Errors of Commission, Response Time, Variability, Anticipatory Responses, Multiple Responses, Post-Commission Response Time.
Administration: Individual.
Price Data: Available from publisher.
Time: [11 and 22.5] minutes.
Comments: Available for Apple IIe, Macintosh, and IBM or compatible computers; formerly called the Minnesota Computer Assessment.
Authors: Lawrence M. Greenberg (test and manuals) and Tammy Rose Dupuy (manuals).
Publisher: Universal Attention Disorders, Inc.

TEST REFERENCE
1. Greenberg, L. M., & Waldman, I. D. (1993). Developmental normative data on the Test of Variables of Attention. *Journal of Child Psychology and Psychiatry and Allied Disciplines, 34,* 1019–1030.

Review of the Test of Variables of Attention by ROSA A. HAGIN, Research Professor of Psychology, and PETER DELLA BELLA, Instructor in Psychiatry, Department of Psychiatry, New York University School of Medicine, New York, NY:

The Test of Variables of Attention (T.O.V.A.) is a standardized, visual, continuous performance test designed for use in diagnosing and monitoring medication in children and adults with attention deficit disorders. This 23-minute fixed-interval computerized test is available for Macintosh and IBM/IBM-compatible computers and has modest system requirements. It requires no use of language, no right-left discrimination, nor recognition of numerals or letters. Two easily discriminated visual stimuli (a square containing a small square adjacent to the top or bottom edge of the larger square) are presented for 100 milliseconds at 2-second intervals. The stimulus within the inner square adjacent to the top edge is the designated target. The T.O.V.A. presents two 11-minute test conditions: frequent and infrequent presentation of targets. The first condition, which is an infrequent presentation of targets (target to non-target ratio of 1:3.5), is designed to measure attention; the second condition, which is a frequent presentation of targets (target to nontarget ratio of 3.5:1), is designed as a measure of impulsivity. Scores on seven variables are produced. The author defines and interprets these variables as follows:

1. Errors of omission (failures to respond to a target), which are interpreted as an indication of inattention.

2. Errors of omission (responding inappropriately to a nontarget), which are interpreted as an indication of impulsivity or disinhibition.

3. Mean correct response times, which are interpreted as measures of processing speed.

4. Standard deviations of response times, which are interpreted as measures of variability.

5. Anticipatory response (responses made before the two stimuli can be differentiated), which can be used to determine whether the subject followed the instructions.

6. Post-commission mean correct response times (mean times of correct responses immediately following a commission error), which may help to differentiate subjects with behavior disorders from subjects with attentional problems.

7. Multiple responses (more than one response per stimulus), which may be interpreted to reflect immaturity or neurological dysfunction.

The T.O.V.A. kit consists of a computer disk, microswitch/scorebox, and manuals for installation of software and interpretation of test results. Purchasers receive five free computerized test interpretations initially; thereafter, full interpretations are offered for a fee. Licensed clinical psychologists may purchase, in addition to the kit, raw data scorings for a one-page "self scoring" at the cost of $5.00 for each test administration.

Two well-designed videotapes demonstrate how the T.O.V.A. can be used by the clinician for several major purposes: to screen for Attention Deficit Hyperactivity Disorder (ADHD) in schools, to diagnose the disorder, to predict response to medication, to establish optimal dosage, and to monitor the psychopharmacotherapy over time. The test may also be used to compare responses to different doses of the same medication and, presumably, it may also be used to compare responses to different medications.

A major component of the T.O.V.A. is the challenge test, which assesses peak drug effect an hour and a half after the baseline test has been completed. According to the interpretation manual, comparisons of baseline scores (while not on medication) with those earned in the challenge test (on medication) enable the clinician to determine not only whether the subject has ADHD, but also to make some hypotheses concerning dosage. Detailed clinical instructions for dosage adjustment procedures are contained in the interpretation manual.

A psychiatrist might find that utilizing a laboratory paradigm like the challenge test to measure the effects of medication on the pertinent psychophysiologic parameters would be advantageous. Because there is a prompt dose-dependent relationship between stimulant medication and improvement of the symptoms of ADHD, treatment may involve a stepwise adjustment of dosage upwards over several visits and simultaneously reassessing the client's progress with each increase in dose. This is often accomplished through parent, teacher, and patient reports. The process is laborious and often hampered by reliance on consistent and timely completion and return of behavior rating scales. The response to scales is further beset by such threats to validity as nonblindness to treatment and fatigued raters, who may complete their ratings for the week at one moment in time. The use of a laboratory measure, such as the T.O.V.A., although it should not be used as a substitute for more global measures of clinical status, nevertheless introduces a welcome measure of objectivity into the evaluation.

On the other hand, the impression of objectivity inherent in the numerical values can also be misleading in focusing both diagnosis and treatment. Medication remains the standard and, too often, the only approach to treatment of ADHD. The knowledgeable clinician includes medication as part of a *multimodal approach* that aims at ameliorating and reversing the collateral damage of ADHD and its frequently encountered concomitants.

To his credit, T.O.V.A.'s author points out in the videotapes, manuals, and reports the need to relate the laboratory values of the T.O.V.A. to all relevant clinical information including interviews, physical examinations, psychological testing, and behavior ratings. Much less emphasis is given to treatment techniques that might be alternatives or adjuncts to medication. For example, the case studies in the interpretation manual did not deal with any related clinical information, but were confined to discussion of T.O.V.A. parameters. Of the 15 cases presented in the interpretation manual, all but 2 resulted in a trial of medication.

Individuals diagnosed with ADHD are often found to have other comorbid conditions such as learning disorders, oppositional-defiant disorder, conduct disorders, or tic disorders. They may additionally suffer from academic problems, low self-esteem, ostracism by their peers, and the psychological effects of avoidant or exasperated parents and teachers who have been compelled to set limits on their behaviors. Problems such as low self-esteem can be dealt with through individual child therapy; out-of-control behaviors can be dealt with through parent training and behavior therapy; socialization difficulties can be addressed in individual and group therapy and also through social skills training; children may often need educational intervention and close consultation between the clinician and the teacher; family therapy can be a useful adjunct to help parents and other family members adjust to the demands created by the disorder. All of these interventions need to be considered as well as medication.

Viewed in terms of the standards for psychological tests, the T.O.V.A. manuals and supporting documents raise questions about the independent use of this measure in making decisions about children and adults. The three manuals received for review appear to have been collated from unpublished papers and few actual research publications. One manual is undated, so that it is not possible to relate the manuals to each other in the development of the instrument. The proofing errors, errors in paging, and near duplication of whole paragraphs within the text do not build confidence in the data presented.

Norms for the test variables appear in two of the manuals, the T.O.V.A. Interpretation Manual and the Test of Variables of Attention Computer Program, which appears to be a technical manual for computer installation. Both of these manuals contain 1989/93 copyright dates, but the norms tables are dated 7/94. Separate norms, based on a total of 1,590 subjects are provided for males and females, ages 4 through 80 plus years grouped in 2-year intervals for ages 4–19 and 10-year intervals thereafter. The normative sample is not otherwise identified, except in the installation manual, which describes the subjects as "normal." In view of the many factors that influence scores on continuous performance tests—experience with computer games; motivation; IQ levels; effects of caffeine and nicotine; presence of psychostimulant, anticonvulsant, or antidepressant medications; comorbid conditions such as depression—this is a serious lack of information.

Nor is adequate evidence of test-retest reliability provided. An undated manual refers to test-retest results with 33 randomly selected normal children, 40 ADHD subjects, and 24 normal adults, producing no significant differences in paired *t*-tests, except for a decrease in commission errors on the first half of the test from the first to second test. No citation for this study is given, nor is more conventional evidence of reliability provided. With the recommended use of repeated challenge tests for recommending or adjusting dosage of medication, this lack of evidence of reliability is also serious.

Questions of validity are also not dealt with in a straightforward fashion. The major issue is one of content validity (i.e., whether this small sample of behavior is a valid estimate of characteristic behavior of the individual under study). The test author has broad clinical insights in work with people with attentional problems, but there is a very limited research data base and/or detailed longitudinal case studies for many of the broad generalizations and detailed interpretations of the test variables.

Finally, there is a marked commercial tone in the supporting materials provided by the publisher. For example, the publisher sent a sample mathematical calculation showing that purchasers will recoup the cost of the equipment in the first five tests and earn a net income of $255 in addition. Another memo from the publisher inquires whether the purchaser wished to be placed on the publisher's referral list. Still another advertises the publisher's computerized interpretation service that provides immediate results based on over 10,000 protocols, an amazing number in that the published norms are based on 1,500 records. Finally, a memo addressed to health care providers (HMOs) indicates that the T.O.V.A. can be administered by a nurse or specially trained technician, providing an immediately generated report for the clinician. It states that "With the report in hand, the clinician can present findings to the parent. Results are presented in a simple, easy to understand format and demonstrates [*sic*] clearly the neurological basis of ADD. This helps the clinician by increasing

parent compliance and reducing time spent with explanations and data collecting from outside sources." This kind of advertising seems contrary to ethical standards for the distribution of tests to qualified purchasers and the professional cautions recommended in the T.O.V.A.'s own manuals.

In summary, the T.O.V.A. holds promise in contributing to the diagnosis and management of individuals with attentional disorders. It draws upon the work of a child psychiatrist who shares his extensive clinical knowledge. The test equipment itself is well designed and its use is well explained in the manuals. However, existing manuals do not provide adequate information about the nature of the normative sample, the test's research foundations, and technical characteristics of reliability and validity. It is to be hoped that the author and publisher will remedy these gaps in order to insure ethical distribution and professionally responsible use of the test materials.

Review of the Test of Variables of Attention by MARGOT B. STEIN, Clinical Assistant Professor of Psychiatry, University of North Carolina School of Medicine, Chapel Hill, NC:

The Test of Variables of Attention Computer Program (T.O.V.A.), formerly called the Minnesota Computer Assessment (MCA) and authored by Lawrence M. Greenberg, is a fixed-interval, visual continuous performance test, used to assess attention deficit disorders and monitor medication treatment. It has three principal clinical uses with regard to Attention Deficit Disorders: to screen students suspected of having attention deficits and students referred for learning disability assessments; as a diagnostic tool used as part of a multifaceted, multidisciplinary assessment of children, adolescents, and adults who may have an attention deficit; and to help determine the dosage level and monitor the use of medication over time. This 22.5-minute computerized test, which is nonlanguage based and uses geometric shapes rather than alphanumeric stimuli, can be used with IBM or IBM-compatible and Macintosh computers. The test requires no right-left discrimination and is said to have negligible practice effects. The T.O.V.A. variables include *errors of omission* (interpreted as a measure of inattention), *errors of commission* (interpreted as a measure of impulsivity), *mean correct response times* (interpreted as a measure of processing and response time), *standard deviations* of response times (interpreted as a measure of variability or consistency of performance), *anticipatory responses* (used to determine whether the subject followed the instructions), *post-commission mean correct response time* (which, the authors state, may help to differentiate conduct disordered from ADD subjects), and *multiple responses* (which, the authors believe, can indicate neurological immaturity).

The installation and administration of the T.O.V.A. are straightforward and require little background knowledge on the part of the consumer. The system is easily installed on the computer using the T.O.V.A. disk (available in both 3.5-inch and 5.25-inch sizes) and microswitch/scorebox. The subject then sits before a computer screen on which flash target stimuli at fixed 2-second intervals, and presses the hand-held microswitch when he or she perceives the target stimulus. The test instrument includes a practice test of 2.25 minutes, followed by the 22.5-minute test for clients above age 5 (4- and 5-year-olds take a shorter version of the test that lasts 11 minutes). The instrument contains two different test situations. In the first two quarters of the test, the target (a colored square containing a small square near the top edge) is presented once every three and a half nontargets. These two quarters are characterized by the "infrequent" presentation of the target, the most commonly utilized form of continuous performance test, and one that generates boredom and, relatedly, errors of omission. A unique feature of the T.O.V.A. is that during the second half of the test the target is present three and a half times to every nontarget presentation. This type of presentation sets up an expectation in the subject and a rhythm that makes errors of commission more common than in the first half of the test.

Two manuals are provided with the T.O.V.A. software package that also includes a microswitch, modem, and two T.O.V.A. videos. The Installation Manual contains information necessary to install and administer the test, and the Interpretation Manual contains information about the test results, variables, interpretations, and case examples. They are detailed, well organized, and clearly written with respect to administration and scoring. The author presents a plausible rationale for the

T.O.V.A., particularly for its use in adjusting (titrating) stimulant medication dosages. However, the reference section is brief, and relies heavily on the research of the author and his collaborators. The manual has a succinct introductory review of attention deficit disorders that points out the complex etiology of attentional dysfunction, particularly when it involves hyperactivity. The author also emphasizes the importance of providing multisituational, multiobserver, and multiinstrument assessments for clients with possible attention deficits, including standardized behavior ratings completed by both parents and teachers in conjunction with the T.O.V.A., in order to arrive at a valid diagnosis. The author also reminds the consumer that appropriate interventions for attention deficits are not limited to medication, but also should include parental counseling that draws on behavior modification techniques, as well as environmental adjustments.

The T.O.V.A. is scored and interpreted either by the staff administering the test using hand calculations, or by a Certified T.O.V.A. Interpreter using the software program and microswitch. There is a charge for each computer scoring and interpretation, raw data, scores (standard deviations, standard scores, percentile scores and *T* scores), written interpretation, and graphics. An appendix contains the normative tables arranged by 15 bands. Eight of these are 2-year age bands for ages 4–5 through 18–19, six 10-year age bands (20–79), and one 80+ age band.

It should be noted, however, that a full summary of the normative data on the T.O.V.A. is not available in either manual, although these data can be found in a journal article and unpublished manuscript form (Greenberg & Waldman, 1993; Greenberg & Crosby, 1992). The manual makes brief mention of developmental normative data on 1,500 normal children and adults (ages 4–80+) on which the norms listed in the appendix are based. Male and female norms are available, but there is no mention of other variables such as race/ethnicity or socio-economic class. Greenberg also refers to research on the effects of psychostimulant medication on the T.O.V.A. performance of children with attention deficits both pre-treatment and on-medication and on varying amounts of stimulant medication.

The T.O.V.A.'s statistical properties are not presented in much detail for analysis in the manuals, although the manual does refer to high test-retest reliability for 33 randomly selected normal children, 40 ADD subjects, and 24 normal adults. With regard to sensitivity and specificity, the author cites his study of 73 youngsters with ADD with and without hyperactivity and matched (age, sex) normals, in which 85% of normal and 72% of the ADD subjects were correctly classified using a standardized score of T.O.V.A. False positives and false negatives were somewhat high (15% and 28% respectively). The author states in the T.O.V.A. Computer Program Manual that "preliminary results suggest respectable specificity for the T.O.V.A. in combination with the CPTQ-A [Conners Parent-Teacher Questionnaire]" (p. 6).

The purpose and design of the T.O.V.A. invite comparisons with another fixed-interval, visual continuous performance test, the Gordon Diagnostic System (GDS; 1986; T4:1051), which also has been computerized and standardized. The T.O.V.A. is distinguished by a number of features including the use of nonsequential geometric stimuli (rather than alphanumeric stimuli), two test conditions (target infrequent and target frequent) built into the same test, and the use of a specially designed hand-held microswitch (rather than a button on the computer) with an insignificant error of measurement (20 msec) and which minimizes muscular fatigue. The duration of the T.O.V.A. (11 and 22.5 minutes) also is longer than the GDS (8 minutes). Both instruments measure the performance of persons age 4 through adulthood. GDS norms include socioeconomic class variables using the Hollingshead Index, but not race/ethnicity variables. Unlike the GDS, Greenberg reported a significant correlation between standardized IQ scores and performance on the T.O.V.A. Unlike the GDS, the T.O.V.A. offers computerized individual scoring (standard deviations, standard scores, percentile scores, and T-scores) and interpretation (at additional cost).

In summary, the T.O.V.A. is primarily a nonlanguage-based continuous performance test designed for use in the diagnosis and treatment of children and adults in combination with standardized behavior ratings, a thorough developmental history, and other data. At this time, perhaps the most appropriate use of the T.O.V.A. is as a pre-post measure to predict pharmacotherapy outcome and to titrate dosage levels to psychostimulants. Apparently, it is also used by clinicians to screen large populations, such as schoolchildren, for ADD. However, this test probably should be used with caution for this purpose, until more inclusive normative data, including information about socioeconomic status and race/ethnicity, are available.

REVIEWER'S REFERENCES

Gordon, M. (1986). The Gordon Diagnostic System. DeWitt, NY: GSI, Inc.
Greenberg, L. M., & Crosby, R. D. (1992). *A summary of developmental normative data in the T.O.V.A.: Ages 4–80+*. Unpublished manuscript.
Greenberg, L. M., & Waldman, I. D. (1993). Developmental normative data on the Test of Variables of Attention (T.O.V.A.). *Journal of Child Psychology and Psychiatry and Allied Disciplines, 34*, 1019–1030.

[100]
Test of Visual-Motor Skills.

Purpose: To assess a child's visual-motor functioning.
Population: Ages 2–13.
Publication Date: 1986.
Acronym: TVMS.
Scores: Total score only.
Administration: Group or individual.
Price Data, 1994: $35 per 15 test booklets and manual (72 pages); $23.50 per 15 test booklets; $14.95 per manual; $15.50 per manual and sample of test designs.
Time: (3–5) minutes.
Author: Morrison F. Gardner.
Publisher: Psychological and Educational Publications, Inc.
Cross References: See T4:2791 (1 reference).

TEST REFERENCES

1. Carr, S. H. (1989). Louisiana's criteria of eligibility for occupational therapy services in the public school system. *The American Journal of Occupational Therapy, 43*, 503-506.
2. Goldstein, D. J., & Britt, T. W., Jr. (1994). Visual-motor coordination and intelligence as predictors of reading, mathematics, and written language ability. *Perceptual and Motor Skills, 78*, 819-823.

Review of the Test of Visual-Motor Skills by DEBORAH ERICKSON, *Professor of Counseling, Niagara University, Niagara University, NY:*

The Test of Visual-Motor Skills (TVMS) was designed to assess visual perception and visual motor integration skills of children from ages 2 to 13. The test requires the child to visually perceive and replicate with his or her hand, nonlanguage forms. If used in conjunction with the Test of Visual-Perceptual Skills (Non-Motor) (TVPS; T4:2798), published in 1982 by Special Child Publications, an examiner can determine if a child has the ability to perceive forms correctly or if the child has difficulty due to poor visual-motor functioning.

The TVMS consists of 26 forms, with specific characteristics that allow for measurement of various types of motor functioning. The designs are purported to be free from cultural and gender bias and the figures are common to children living in all parts of the United States and other countries. The manual is clearly written and directions for administration and scoring are adequate. There is a slight amount of judgment necessary for scoring; however, this is true with most tests of visual-motor skill that require a child to draw figures (e.g., Bender Gestalt Test; T4:291).

The test development was reported clearly in the manual. Item analysis was thorough, and the final forms were developed from a stimulus pool of 140 forms and reduced by a panel of teachers and psychologists and actual administration to students. Standardization of the test included 1,009 children considered to be normally functioning and residing in the San Francisco Bay area. The item difficulties ranged from .37 to .98, with a median value of .63. The item/total test score correlations ranged from .34 to .86 with a median value of .78. Test development would have been enhanced if the standardization procedure could have occurred in various geographic locations with more students at each age level.

Test reliability indicates a consistent test. Cronbach's coefficient alpha, reflecting internal consistency of the test for children at each age level, was from .31 to .90, with a median value of .82. Except for the .31 reliability coefficient, which occurred at the 2-0 to 2-11 age level, the scores were within the range acceptable for a reliable and consistent measurement. The SEMs ranged from .88 to 2.99 with a median value of 2.08.

Test validity, indicating that the test measures what it is supposed to measure, was evaluated through content validation, item validation, and criterion-related validation strategies. Professionals in the field of psychology and testing reviewed the items selected for the test to ascertain the degree to which the items were similar to those used in other tests of visual-motor skills (content validity). The relationship between an individual item and a criterion (item validity) was assessed by correlating the test with the Developmental Test of Visual Motor Integration Test (VMI; 12:111) and the manual states only those items correlating highly with the VMI were selected. Criterion-related validity was evaluated by correlating the total TVMS score with the scores from the Bender Visual-Motor Gestalt Test (T4:291) and the VMI. Correlation's between the Bender and the TVMS ranged from .48 to .77 with an overall correlation of .75. The correlation between the VMI and TVMS ranged from .25 to .76 with an overall correlation between the two tests of .92.

Interpretative scores for the TVMS can be obtained through standard scores, scaled scores, percentile ranks, and stanines—all corresponding to the raw scores by chronological age.

In summary, the TVMS is a well-constructed test and can be used with confidence for assessing a child's level of visual-motor functioning. If used in conjunction with the Test of Visual-Perceptual Skills (Non-Motor) (TVPS), an examiner can assess both "how a child visually perceives non-language forms (TVPS) ... and how a child translates with his or her hand what is visually perceived (TVMS)" (p. 5).

Review of the Test of Visual-Motor Skills by JANET E. SPECTOR, Assistant Professor of Education, University of Maine, Orono, ME:

The Test of Visual-Motor Skills (TVMS) assesses a student's ability to reproduce by hand a series of geometric designs. According to the test's author, the TVMS is useful in identifying students who might have "fine-motor problems of one kind or another—such as difficulty in writing letters and words with good legibility; directional confusion; slow psychomotor speed; etc." (p. 5). In addition, the measure is designed as a companion to the author's (non-motor) Test of Visual-Perceptual Skills (TVPS; Gardner, 1982; T4:2798). Gardner claims that when used together, the TVMS and the TVPS help the examiner to distinguish between poor visual-motor performance due to visual-perceptual problems and poor performance due to fine-motor difficulties. Unfortunately, the manual provides no data to support this claim.

The TVMS comprises a series of 26 designs, each of which is presented as a bold, black-lined drawing on white paper. The measure is similar in content and procedure to the Developmental Test of Visual-Motor Integration (VMI; Beery & Buktenica, 1989; 12:111). Unlike the VMI, however, each TVMS item is included on a separate page. This feature is particularly advantageous when testing young children who might be distracted by the presence of multiple stimuli. Furthermore, the use of white rather than green paper (as on the VMI) makes the test more suitable for children who have visual impairment.

Although the TVMS is easily administered, scoring is apt to be difficult for the novice examiner. For 24 of the 26 items, three scores are possible; 2 (the design is copied with precision), 1 (the design is copied with minor errors), and 0 (the design is copied incorrectly). On the one hand, the provision of partial credit is an improvement over the VMI, where slight errors result in total loss of credit. On the other hand, scoring guidelines are problematic on four counts. First, Designs 2 (horizontal line) and 4 (diagonal line) are scored only as 1 or 0, but the rationale for this exception is not discussed. Second, the number of scoring examples is insufficient for many designs. Design 1 (circle) includes at least four examples for each possible score (i.e., 0, 1, or 2), but 18 of the designs include only one example of a 2. Third, some of the guidelines are unnecessarily vague. For instance, on Design 5, a score of 2 requires that lines be of "equal length," whereas a score of 1 specifies that lines be "similar in length" (p. 24). If a line is off by 1/16 of an inch, is it considered "equal" or "similar"? Such ambiguity could easily be eliminated by providing more precise guidelines. Fourth, the size of the reproduction relative to the stimulus affects scoring on some (e.g., Design 2), but not all, designs (e.g., Design 10). It is not clear why this is the case, particularly because the only corrective feedback permitted is on Design 1, which does not require that the drawing be similar in size to the stimulus.

A major weakness of the test is its norms, a shortcoming that undermines its viability as a norm-referenced device. The manual claims that "the norms for the TVMS were derived from groups which are representative of the population of children from age 2 through 12 years, 11 months" (p. 12). However, the test was standardized in one geographic region (San Francisco Bay area), using a sample of 1,009 children from 13 schools and a hospital. No information regarding race or socioeconomic status is provided. Furthermore, the number of students sampled at the youngest ($n =$

38) and oldest ($n = 54$) age levels is small and the proportion of males and females is imbalanced at some ages.

Another problem area is reliability. According to the manual, test reliability was estimated using only one approach, internal consistency. Cronbach's alpha ranged from .31 at age 2 to .90 at age 5, with a median reliability of .82. Clearly, the test should not be used with 2-year-olds. At most other ages, the test fails to meet the recommended standard (i.e., .9) for use in high-stakes decisions regarding an individual student (Salvia & Ysseldyke, 1995). Furthermore, the manual includes no mention of test-retest reliability. In the absence of information about test stability over time, the TVMS falls short even as a screening instrument.

Interrater reliability was assessed in a sample of 217 children in grades 1, 3, and 5 and 41 kindergartners, using two raters (registered occupational therapists). Across the ages, interrater reliability ranged from .80 to .89. These estimates are lower than those reported for the most recent version of the VMI, in which examiners received from 2 to 5 hours of training. The TVMS's author does not indicate the type of training that scorers received prior to participating in his scoring study, so it is difficult to determine whether the results in the manual will generalize to other scorers, particularly those who are not occupational therapists.

Finally, the manual includes a brief discussion of "item validity," content validity, and criterion validity. What the author calls "item validity" (the correlation between each item and total test score) would be more appropriately considered as evidence of reliability (i.e., internal consistency). Other validity data generally support the claim that the test is primarily a measure of design copying skill and that it assesses a construct similar to that of the VMI. However, the author fails to show that performance on the test correlates with performance on fine-motor tasks other than design copying (e.g., handwriting, drawing) or that it is predictive of future performance. It is therefore not clear why examiners would want to identify students who do not do well on this test.

Overall, the TVMS is a quick and easily administered measure of design copying skill that might be of interest to teachers or occupational therapists who need to assess the progress of children who have difficulty with fine-motor tasks. However, given the limitations of the standardization sample and the results of reliability studies, the test should not be used at all at age 2 or for high-stakes decision making at other ages (e.g., determination of eligibility for special services). Until the author provides evidence regarding test-retest reliability and predictive validity, the test is not recommended as a screening measure.

REVIEWER'S REFERENCES
Gardner, M. F. (1982). *Test of Visual-Perceptual Skills (Non-Motor)*. San Francisco: Special Child Publications.
Beery, K. E., & Buktenica, N. A. (1989). *The Developmental Test of Visual-Motor Integration (3rd rev.)*. Cleveland: Modern Curriculum Press.
Salvia, J., & Ysseldyke, J. E. (1995). *Assessment* (6th ed.). Boston: Houghton Mifflin Company.

[101]
Test on Appraising Observations.

Purpose: Designed to test one aspect of critical thinking: judging credibility.
Population: Grade 10 to adult.
Publication Dates: 1983–1990.
Administration: Group.
Price Data: Available from publishers.
Authors: Stephen P. Norris (multiple-choice format and constructed-response format) and Ruth King (multiple-choice format).
Publisher: Faculty of Education, Memorial University of Newfoundland [Canada].
 a) MULTIPLE-CHOICE FORMAT.
 Publication Date: 1983.
 Scores: Total score only.
 Parts, 2: A, B.
 Time: (40–45) minutes.
 b) CONSTRUCTED-RESPONSE VERSION.
 Publication Date: 1986.
 Scores, 2: Answer-Choice, Justification.
 Time: (40–45) minutes.
Cross References: See T4:2806 (1 reference).

Review of the Test on Appraising Observations by MICHAEL KANE, Professor of Education, University of Wisconsin, Madison, WI:

Both forms of the Test on Appraising Observations, the multiple-choice version and the constructed-response version, have a very specific interpretation, focusing on a particular part of critical thinking, the appraisal of observation reports. The proposed interpretation is stated in the title of the test, it is suggested by the content of the test and the scoring key, and it is emphasized in the manual. The clarity and specificity of the proposed interpretation contributes to the value of the test in various contexts by making misuse and misinterpretation less likely.

NORMS. The norms data are very limited, and at best provide a very rough indication of what scores mean in a norm-referenced sense. The manual authors state the test is designed primarily for senior high school students but is useful at the junior high and college levels. Percentiles for eight relatively small convenience samples are reported in the manual. The largest group consists of 287 students in grades 10, 11, and 12, "in a wealthy neighborhood in southern Ontario," and the smallest group consists of "48 non-academic grade 10 students taking general science in a large metropolitan area in Canada's Atlantic Provinces" (p. 6). Although one would not want to base a norm-referenced interpretation on any of these samples, they do provide some indication of how different groups might be expected to perform, and therefore add to the interpretability of the scores.

VALIDITY. The section on validity in the manual is organized in terms of three kinds of evidence: criterion-related, content-related, and construct-related, with most of the space devoted to criterion evidence. However, the most convincing validity evidence is based on the close relationship between the tasks included in the test and the intended interpretation.

The authors propose to interpret the test scores in terms of the ability to appraise observations and see this ability as a psychological construct. They expand on this interpretation in the section on construct-related evidence. Based on their previous work and other sources, the authors present a fairly detailed outline of principles for judging the credibility of observations, and argue that, for purposes of the Test on Appraising Observations, good thinking be defined as thinking in accordance with these principles. The test items, which are keyed to the principles, provide a thorough sampling of the list of principles, and the manual and Norris (1992) contain evidence indicating that students who answer items correctly generally do so by using the appropriate principles. This argument is quite persuasive.

However, there are some possible counterarguments that are not addressed in the manual. In addition to concerns about generalizability, which are discussed below, response bias represents a potentially serious threat to validity. Each item is embedded in a story and includes two contradictory statements made by different characters in the story. The instructions suggest that there are three possible answers to each item: (a) that there is more reason to believe the first statement, (b) that there is more reason to believe the second statement, and (c) that there is no reason to believe either statement over the other. In fact, however, one of the two statements is always the keyed answer, and the third option is always incorrect. The test is forced-choice, but the instructions state that it is not forced-choice. Now, when two witnesses flatly contradict each other (as they do in each of the items) and there is no material evidence to support either of the two accounts, there is good reason to suspect both accounts, and therefore, a cautious student might pick the third option. The cautious student who can appraise observations effectively could thereby get a low score.

The section in the manual on validity begins with a fairly lengthy discussion of correlations between the Test on Appraising Observations and several general tests of critical thinking (e.g., Watson-Glaser) for a group of 172 students in grades 10 to 12, from a large metropolitan school district in Canada. These correlations, which are presented as criterion-related evidence, range from .20 to .62 for the multiple-choice version, and from .06 to .25 for the constructed-response version. Unfortunately, it is not clear what these results mean. The tests being used as criteria cover much more than the ability to appraise observations; and therefore, correlations with these criteria are at best marginally relevant to the validity of the specific interpretation being proposed for the Test on Appraising Observations.

RELIABILITY. The data on reliability in the manual are limited to alpha coefficients (with values between .54 and .80) for the eight norms groups mentioned earlier. No data on interrater reliability or test-retest reliability are reported.

The alpha reliabilities are hard to interpret for at least two reasons. First, the items are presented within the context of long stories. The constructed-response version includes 25 items in one story, and the multiple-choice version includes 50 items within two stories. The instructions to examinees state that, for each item, examinees can use information from previous items, but should not use information from later items. The lack of independence among the items resulting from the nesting of items within stories would tend to inflate the alpha coefficients. On the other hand, the convenience samples used to estimate the alpha coefficients would tend to be more homogeneous than the target population as a whole, and this restriction of range would tend to lower the alpha coefficients. The alpha coefficients are subject, therefore, to conflicting biases of unknown magnitude.

A more thorough analysis of the generalizability of the scores is needed. The interpretation of the scores in terms of ability to appraise observations would suggest generalization over items, over the contexts in which the observations are set, and over occasions, and for the constructed-response format, over scorers. The alpha coefficients address generalization over items, but no data are provided on the potential impact of variation over occasions, over the context of the items, or over scorers.

OVERALL EVALUATION. The Test on Appraising Observations has a very clear and focused interpretation, and the two forms of the test were systematically developed to yield scores consistent with this interpretation. The potential uses of the test discussed in the manual are generally quite reasonable. The test should prove useful for research purposes and for formative and summative evaluation of programs that include the appraisal of observations among their goals. The test could also be used for the formative evaluation of student progress. The use of group performance on particular items to diagnose specific deficiencies in reasoning for the group, as suggested in the manual, is not justified because the items have not been shown to be of equal difficulty in any sense, and it is reasonable to expect that some items may call for more subtle judgments than other items. Given the limited evidence for generalizability and the possibility of response bias, the test should not be used for high-stakes decisions.

REVIEWER'S REFERENCE

Norris, S. P. (1992). A demonstration of the use of verbal reports of thinking in multiple-choice critical thinking test design. *The Alberta Journal of Educational Research*, 38, 155–176.

Review of the Test on Appraising Observations by JEFFREY K. SMITH, Professor of Educational Psychology, Rutgers, The State University of New Jersey, New Brunswick, NJ:

The Test on Appraising Observations measures secondary school students' ability to judge correctly the credibility of reports of observations. That is, how good are the examinees in judging which of two reports of an event is more credible based on principles of judging credibility (e.g., if one person has no preconceived notion about how the observation will turn out, then that person's observation will be more credible than a person who does have such preconceived notions). The authors argue that this ability is a component of overall observation ability and that observation ability is in turn a component of critical thinking.

There are two forms of the test, one multiple choice and one constructed response. The multiple-choice format is based on two scenarios that involve individuals making statements based on observations. It allows examinees to choose from one of three options: The first statement is more credible, the second statement is more credible, or there is no reason to believe that either statement is more credible. The constructed response format uses only the first of the two scenarios, but requires the examinee to provide a justification for the response given. The constructed response format can be scored either for right answers or for valid justifications.

The Test on Appraising Observations has much to recommend it. The theoretical development of the measure appears to be sound. The technical documentation provided in the manual that accompanies the test is clear, thorough, and modest in its claims. The test is easy to administer and score. Professional literature is available that supports the use of the measure, in particular the multiple-choice form of the measure (Norris, 1992; 1990).

There are also some problems with the measure. First, the reliability and validity data reported for the measure are not particularly strong, especially with regard to the constructed response format. For the multiple-choice version, reliabilities across seven different samples range from .58 to .76; for the constructed response version the reliabilities in two studies were .54 and .80 for the right answer scoring and .71 and .74 for the justification scoring. Criterion-related validity was investigated by correlating the measure with seven established indicators of critical thinking such as the Watson-Glaser Critical Thinking Appraisal and the Cornell Critical Thinking Test. Validity coefficients ranged from .22 to .62 for the multiple-choice format, and from .06 to .25 for the constructed response format. The multiple-choice format and the constructed response format correlate at .42, suggesting substantial differences across the two formats. The data suggest that the multiple-choice version of the measure is much stronger than the constructed response format.

A second problem is that the measures purport to address only a fairly limited component of the overall concept of critical thinking ability. Most of the validity and reliability studies were conducted on high school students, but it is somewhat difficult to imagine what practical applicability there is for the instrument at the high school level except for research purposes.

Overall, the Test on Appraising Observations appears to be a useful tool for measuring a limited aspect of critical thinking. Although there are some problems with reliability, the validity for the multiple-choice version of the test seems reasonable, and validity is the key issue. One should keep in mind, however, there are a host of critical thinking measures available that are more comprehensive than what is presented here. The question for a potential user of the measure is whether this aspect of critical thinking is what is needed in a given situation.

REVIEWER'S REFERENCES
Norris, S. P. (1990). Effect of eliciting verbal reports of thinking on critical thinking test performance. *Journal of Educational Measurement, 27,* 41–58.
Norris, S. P. (1992). A demonstration of the use of verbal reports of thinking in multiple-choice critical thinking test design. *The Alberta Journal of Educational Research, 38,* 155–176.

[102]
TestWell: Health Risk Appraisal.

Purpose: "Designed to provide an awareness of how current behaviors and physical health measurements impact health risks."

Population: Adults with a minimum of 10th grade education.

Publication Date: 1992.

Scores, 5: Appraised Age, Achievable Age, Positive Lifestyle Behaviors, Top 10 Risks of Death, Suggestions for Improvement.

Administration: Group.

Manual: No manual.

Price Data, 1993: $99.95 per interactive version, single user license; $329.95 per interactive version, multiuser license; $279.95 per group/batch version; $.50 per group/batch entry questionnaire booklet; $390 per reproduction rights (educational institutions only); $395 per scanner support capability.
Time: (20) minutes.
Comments: Requires IBM or compatible computer hardware.
Author: National Wellness Institute, Inc.
Publisher: National Wellness Institute, Inc.

Review of the TestWell: Health Risk Appraisal by BARBARA L. LACHAR, Assistant Professor of Psychiatry (Psychology), Baylor College of Medicine, Houston, TX:

INTRODUCTION. National Wellness Institute's TestWell: Health Risk Appraisal is one of many health-risk appraisal instruments that have become available since the 1970s. A health-risk appraisal is an assessment that relates an individual's identifying information, physiological measurements, family medical history, and health behaviors to available mortality statistics and epidemiological data. These appraisals are designed to provide education and promote favorable health behaviors by emphasizing risk. The majority of such measures use self-report data, often a questionnaire, to assess individual risk factors. Answers to these questions are used to calculate the estimated risk of death and potential decrease in risk from national mortality statistics. Mathematical calculations produce results in terms of the risk of death per 100,000 individuals of the same age and sex. Feedback consists of a chart that displays the risk of mortality from the 10 leading causes of death and information concerning ways to reduce the risk. Appraisals have many common characteristics, but they differ according to target group and amount and type of information collected.

Health-risk appraisals have been criticized, in general, for their inability to predict mortality for any one individual although they are presumed statistically accurate for large groups. In general, their ability to actually contribute to changes in individual behavior or longevity has not been proven. Health promotion is a laudable goal, but the extent to which these interventions alter behavior or outcome is unknown. Counseling is recommended as an accompaniment to feedback of health-risk re-

sults in order to increase the likelihood of health behavior change.

DESCRIPTION. The TestWell: Health Risk Appraisal is available as a software program designed to inform users how current behaviors, family health history, and physical health measurements relate to health risks. Both an interactive individual version and a group/batch software version are available. IBM or IBM-compatible hardware, with a minimum of 640K RAM and 4 megabytes, is required as well as DOS versions of 3.3 or later. Graphics-supporting monitors and printers are also recommended, although monochrome monitors and dot matrix printers are compatible. Scoring by scanner is an option.

Assessments are completed either interactively online or by questionnaire for group/batch administration. Item content differs for males and females. There are 39 questions for males, which include 4 specific questions dealing with risk of testicular and prostate cancer. Women respond to 44 questions, 9 of which are specific to female health risks. Administration time is approximately 10 to 20 minutes. Information on specific disease states, such as a personal history of cancer, a previous myocardial infarction, autoimmune illness, or renal dysfunction are excluded. There are six questions relating to use of tobacco, two questions on use of alcohol and drinking and driving, two concerning diet, and one on exercise. Family history is limited to diabetes, breast cancer, and early mortality due to heart attack.

REPORTS. The individual report lists the actual age, appraised risk age, and achievable risk age. The appraised risk age is the age of the relevant demographic group that matches the individual's calculated health risks. Positive lifestyle behaviors or strengths are highlighted. The top 10 risks of death per 100,000 for a group with similar responses are displayed, in tabular and bar chart form, in comparison to the risks for an individual's demographic group. Next, each of the 10 risk factors is listed with specific health- or safety-promoting recommendations. An achievable risk age is calculated and presented with suggestions for attainment. The proportion of risk, for example, .39 years, that could be eliminated or "gained" is provided for each recommendation.

The program allows the maintenance of separate group files and permits data from groups to be merged, as well. The group profile report provides an analysis of specific group results and is divided into seven sections, including group demographics. The first section, the Management Summary, presents a chart of modifiable group risk behaviors with the number of individuals and percentage endorsing each risk. The second section, Group Health Age looks at the actual health age, the appraised health age, and the achievable health age for both men and women. The appraised age is defined as the age equivalent to the risk of dying for the average person in the group and the achievable age indicates the improvement that could be attained with health-promoting behavioral changes. Group demographics and health-related characteristics, such as weight, blood pressure, cholesterol, and exercise behavior are displayed according to age and sex. The data regarding men's and women's health concerns are displayed separately. The final section reports on quality of life indicators such as ratings of health status and life satisfaction. Although security is protected by required logon information, confidentiality of results could be a concern of users and may need to be addressed.

RELIABILITY AND VALIDITY. There is no technical manual describing the theory, item construction, development, validity or reliability of this instrument. Although a psychometric test may be judged by the quality of its manual, health-risk appraisals are not typical psychometric tools and many do not make these statistics available. However, no information is provided concerning the currency of the epidemiological data, the specific reference groups, nor the validity of the predictions. It is not known whether data from relevant age and ethnic groups are used to calculate the estimated health risk age.

SUMMARY. The TestWell: Health Risk Appraisal is a cost-efficient, brief health promotion tool that can be used for individual education or to aggregate group health status information for organizations. Administration may be accomplished by paper-and-pencil questionnaire or by personal computer. The program is capable of producing both individualized reports and management summaries. Results are provided in terms of a health risk age and an achievable health age as well as the chance of death per 100,000 individuals for 10 leading causes of death in the next 10 years.

STRENGTHS. This health-risk appraisal can be used by individuals of varying ages and ethnicity. The program utilizes current health information such as blood cholesterol level and blood pressure but accepts default values if these are unknown. Processing is immediate and tailored education information is provided. Health risks are rank ordered and quantified. The relative advantages of behavioral change are presented and prioritized along with quantitative measures of risk reduction.

WEAKNESSES. Accuracy of prediction of information for any one individual is unknown as are the source, timeliness, and composition of the epidemiological data. There is no way of incorporating current information on past or present disease states, nor are risks of Human Immunodeficiency Virus (HIV) included in the calculations.

The TestWell: Health Risk Appraisal shares many of the strengths and weaknesses of other health appraisal instruments. It appears to have broad appeal and applicability. Its usefulness may be to rapidly disseminate health education information and to summarize data on group health risks. These data can provide baseline information to both stimulate and evaluate the extent of behavioral change when employed as pre and post measures.

REVIEWER'S REFERENCE

Beery, W., Wagner, E. H., Graham, R. M., Karon, J. M., & Pezzullo, S. (1984). *Description, analysis and assessment of health/hazard risk appraisal programs.* Springfield, VA: National Technical Information Service.

Review of the TestWell: Health Risk Appraisal by STEVEN G. LoBELLO, Associate Professor of Psychology, Auburn University at Montgomery, Montgomery, AL:

The TestWell: Health Risk Appraisal, produced by the National Wellness Institute, is designed to give an estimate of risk of dying of the 10 leading causes of death for a given age group. The program also calculates an "appraised health age" and an "achievable age." The former is an expression in years of a person's age given their risk factors (e.g., a 35-year-old who smokes and drinks heavily may have an appraised health age of 44 years); the latter gives an estimate in years of risk if lifestyle changes are made.

The printed questionnaire consists of 44 items for women and 39 questions for men that ask about a variety of health-related issues. A separate answer sheet is used, although a copy was not available for examination. Item content deals with smoking and alcohol consumption, safe driving practices, blood pressure, dietary practices and cholesterol level, and preventive health care behaviors such as frequency of breast self-examination for women and testicle self-examination for men.

A computer program is needed to score the completed questionnaire, or the items can be answered directly on the computer. When the questionnaire is taken from the computer, the program automatically presents the appropriate questions for men and women. Another option is to process questionnaires from a number of respondents to produce a group profile of health risk. The program is easy enough to use, although the computer graphics are rather primitive. Menu options allow users to view their health risk profile and read recommendations on-screen, or print out a paper copy. With on-screen viewing users see a graph or two that may not reproduce on paper with all printers.

The manual for the Health Risk Appraisal gives general information on how to load and use the computer software. There is little documentation about how risk is evaluated or how the program was developed. An appendix contains the items that are used to calculate risk. For some diseases there are no questions on the inventory that assess individual risk. Instead, the program reports a population risk for an individual's age and sex. For example, there are no questions about sexual practices or intravenous (IV) drug use, but because HIV/AIDS is a relatively high risk for some age groups, one's personal risk is given as the population risk. Although there are statements acknowledging this program peculiarity, it is possible for people to be misled by the data. For HIV/AIDS, someone who practices safe sex and refrains from IV drug use would have a lower risk than the population base-rate, whereas someone who engages in these behaviors would be at higher risk than indicated by the program.

There are no validity or reliability data reported but there are warnings that such an assessment is not a substitute for a medical examination. In addition, it is not recommended for use in people who already have been diagnosed with can-

cer, heart disease, kidney disease, or other serious health problems. After risk has been assessed, a list of recommendations for improving chances of survival is provided. Some of the recommendations are sensible, such as those dealing with weight reduction and eating a low-fat diet. Others are inane. For individuals judged to be at risk for death by homicide, it is recommended that they "avoid arguments with people you don't know."

Another problem with the inventory is the user must be able to report systolic and diastolic blood pressure, serum cholesterol level, and low and high density lipoprotein levels. Recognizing that most people are not aware of these numbers, the program automatically enters default values. Of course, when this is done, accuracy of risk appraisal is sacrificed.

The TestWell: Health Risk Appraisal is the sort of instrument seen at health fairs and other activities designed to raise individual and community awareness of health-related issues. It does not meet the minimal standards of psychological tests and probably should not be regarded as one. Rather, it is better regarded as an information source, and not a very accurate one at that.

One danger with devices of this type is that an employer could introduce it into the workplace and gain access to employee health data under the guise of providing a "health benefit." An unscrupulous employer looking to minimize insurance costs might use this instrument to sort out high-risk from low-risk employees. (This is unlikely, but possible.) And although it does not meet the usual standards of psychological tests, it would probably be wise to control its distribution to minimize the chance of such mischief.

[103]
Vocational Interest Inventory—Revised.

Purpose: "Measures the relative strength of an individual's interest in eight occupational areas."
Population: High school juniors and seniors.
Publication Dates: 1981–1993.
Acronym: VII-R.
Scores, 8: Service, Business Contact, Organization, Technical, Outdoor, Science, General Culture, Arts and Entertainment.
Administration: Group.
Price Data, 1996: $79.50 per complete kit including manual ('93, 63 pages), 4 test reports and mail-in answer

sheets; $45 per manual; $9.80 (or less) per test report; $150 or less per microdisk (IBM; 25 uses).

Time: (20–25) minutes.

Comments: Based on Ann Roe's occupational classifications.

Author: Patricia W. Lunneborg.

Publisher: Western Psychological Services.

Cross References: For reviews by Jo-Ida Hansen and Richard W. Johnson, see 9:1339 (2 references).

TEST REFERENCES

1. Lunneborg, C. E., & Lunneborg, P. W. (1991). Who majors in psychology? *Teaching of Psychology, 18,* 144-148.

2. Tracey, T. J., & Rounds, J. (1994). An examination of the structure of Roe's eight interest fields. *Journal of Vocational Behavior, 44,* 279-296.

Review of the Vocational Interest Inventory— Revised by DAVID O. HERMAN, Associate Educational Officer, Office of Educational Research, New York City Board of Education, Brooklyn, NY:

The Vocational Interest Inventory—Revised (VII-R), a forced-choice interest inventory, is designed to help students in the upper high school grades to focus their thinking on college majors and vocations that are consonant with their interest patterns. Scores are produced on eight scales, each corresponding to a broad group of occupations.

The first 56 items present pairs of occupational titles (e.g., Police Chief, Draftsperson), and the student is to indicate the one that would interest him or her more. The second 56 items all offer a choice of two activities (e.g., Baby-sit, Talk people into voting for our schools) of which the respondent chooses the more interesting. All of the items are said to have been written at the 10th grade level, yet one must wonder if most high school students know the nature and duties of some of the jobs (e.g., "theatrical speculator" and "library page"). And surely "hand typesetter" is a vanishing occupation with little general relevance today.

The VII-R items are printed on both sides of a single scannable answer document, and students mark their responses directly on the sheet. (The print is quite small, but should be readily legible for most high school students.) The marked answer document is sent to the publisher for scoring and reporting. The inventory may also be administered on-line to a student seated at a microcomputer; in this case, the necessary scoring and reporting software is available from the publisher. Details of the scoring procedures, such as scoring keys, norms, and the algorithm for selecting interpretive statements are considered proprietary information, and are not available to users.

The computer-produced test report is extensive. It begins with a general introduction and a description of the eight scales, and presents a profile of percentile scores with a special interpretation of those at or above the 75th percentile, including a list of jobs related to the highest score or scores. These job titles are grouped separately according to whether they require only high school graduation or a bachelor's degree or greater. Following is a list of 25 college majors ranked according to the similarity of the student's profile to the mean profiles of people who graduated in those majors. Students who intend to continue their education beyond high school are likely to find this information helpful in their planning.

The two choices offered by each of the 112 items represent different scales. Early versions of the inventory were subjected to several rounds of tryout and revision between 1969 and 1978. The 1978 version is the one in use today. Items were redrafted when necessary to avoid options with extreme endorsement rates (greater than 80% or less than 20%), options that correlated higher with scales other than the one for which they were intended, and options that correlated more than .15 with sex. Thus, the forced-choice format made possible some level of control at the item level for sex bias, and the author felt that separate-sex norms for interpreting raw scores were unnecessary. Yet the strategy was only partly successful, for sex differences still remain on some of the scales; some of the reported mean scores of males and females differ by about one standard deviation.

Norms for the VII-R are based on the performance of more than 27,000 high school juniors and seniors. They were tested in 1987 in the state of Washington, as part of a statewide pre-college testing program. Although very large, the sample has this severe geographic limitation. Sample members intended to obtain more post-high school education than do typical students in the United States (i.e., all but 6% of the sample planned to get at least a 2-year college degree). Although the resulting norms *may* resemble those that would be developed from a representative national sample, the manual contains no evidence that they do. Furthermore, nearly all of the developmental work on the inventory was carried out on similar samples tested in the same state about 20 years ago; if response tendencies are different in other parts of the country, or if they have shifted appreciably over time, not only could the norms be misleading but also the controls for sex bias and for item-endorsement rates could be compromised.

The manual contains internal-consistency estimates of reliability; split-half reliability coefficients range from .40 (Technical) to .80 (Scientific). These statistics reflect not only the homogeneity of the eight scales, but also the validity of the corresponding occupational categories used in developing the inventory—in this case, categories proposed by Anne Roe in the 1950s. Thus, the alpha of the .40 may mean that the author developed the Technical scale inadequately, or that Roe's Technical group is inherently disparate, or both. Six-month retest coefficients are also available, and range from .66 (Technical) to .85 (Scientific).

Several types of validity evidence for the VII-R are reported in the manual. Collectively, the studies show, for example, that both the VII-R scale with the highest score and the entire profile have been found associated with high school students' intended college majors, and with the college majors or vocational/technical programs that they actually chose later on; and that the VII-R scales that correlated highest with scores on Holland's Vocational Preference Inventory and the Strong-Campbell Interest Inventory were generally as predicted. Factorial studies are supportive of the scale's theoretical structure—and of Roe's scheme for organizing occupations. The VII-R is clearly measuring in a domain that is relevant to its stated purpose.

SUMMARY. The Vocational Interest Inventory—Revised appears to have been competently and conscientiously assembled. The interpretive printout impresses me as thorough and helpful. A great deal of information relevant to validity is reported in the manual.

This review has mentioned a few relatively minor concerns, for example, some isolated items that may mystify high school students, and the low reliability of some scales (which is of less concern with this kind of instrument than with one used for high-stakes selection and placement). The major obstacle to recommending the VII-R for general use, however, is the homogeneous group on which it has been developed and normed—college-bound students in Washington. At the very least, national norms will be essential if the publisher wishes to see the inventory used more widely. In the meantime, other well-developed instruments such as the Vocational Preference Inventory (T4:2910) and the Strong Interest Inventory (12:374) offer very strong competition.

Review of the Vocational Interest Inventory—Revised by JOSEPH G. LAW, JR., Associate Professor of Behavioral Studies, University of South Alabama, Mobile, AL:

The Vocational Interest Inventory—Revised (VII-R) contains 112 forced-choice items and is designed to help high school students select a college major. Half of the items focus on activities and half on occupational titles. Computerized reports are available that compare the respondent's profile to Anne Roe's eight interest areas. The test items are written at the 10th grade level and the inventory is designed to be both self-administered and interpreted. The manual contains a brief introductory chapter, a chapter on interpretation, a chapter on test development and standardization, and a fourth chapter on technical issues related to reliability and validity.

The VII-R has a number of positive characteristics for the career counselor. At 112 items, it is fairly quickly administered. The one-page (front and back) computer answer sheet is easy to complete. The computer-generated report contains easy-to-read narrative and graphical feedback to the student. One unique feature is the use of same-sex norms. The manual author notes that any item with a phi coefficient greater than +.15 or -.15 with gender was rewritten or removed. Items with endorsements greater than 80% or less than 20% were removed to correct for social desirability. The manual contains numerous tables with data on the norm group as well as case studies to assist in interpretation.

The 1993 edition of the VII-R has the same 112 items as the original edition, although new norms on 27,444 high school students in Washington State were collected in 1987. Stable norms are a plus, but the limited geographical sampling is a weakness. Although 14% of the sample consists of minorities, only 2% were Black—significantly affecting the VII-R's applicability for that population of students. Most students in the norm group planned to complete at least 4 years of college. Only 2% planned to stop with a high school diploma, only 4% to attend vocational/technical school, and 6% to get a 2-year college degree. The VII-R's lack of focus on predicting occupational choice limits its usefulness for counselors who work with clients who are not college-bound.

The 1990 Strong Interest Inventory (SCII; 12:374) is a good benchmark with which to compare the VII-R's psychometric qualities. The median alpha for the SCII Basic Interest Scales was .91 for females, .92 for males, and .90 for both genders on General Occupational Themes (Worthen, 1995). Alpha coefficients ranging from .41 to .80 (median r = .65) for the eight full scales in a study of 670 high school juniors are reported in the manual. The median alpha for split-half reliability was .66. Test-retest correlations between the two instruments are more difficult to compare because of differing intervals. However, the median test-retest correlation of .87 for the SCII over a 3-year period exceeds the median correlation of .76 for the VII-R over a 6-month interval. Correlations between the Vocational Preference Inventory and the VII-R reported in the manual range from .30 to .60 and offer some support to the construct validity of the test.

Unfortunately, the limitations of the VII-R that were noted in its predecessor (Hansen, 1985) are still largely present. The VII-R is based on a limited and nonrepresentative norm group. The 10th grade reading level and emphasis on predictive validity for selecting college majors limits its usefulness with non-college-bound students. Test-retest reliability reported in the manual is limited to a 6-month interval. Its merits include ease of use and interpretation and adherence to Anne Roe's well-known typology. The VII-R's stability and validity do not compare favorably to venerable instruments such as the Strong, but may be a useful tool for college counselors who want an inventory with mixed sex norms based on high functioning students.

REVIEWER'S REFERENCES

Hansen, J. I. (1985). [Review of the Vocational Interest Inventory.] In J. V. Mitchell, Jr. (Ed.), *The ninth mental measurements yearbook* (pp. 1677–1678). Lincoln, NE: Buros Institute of Mental Measurements.

Worthen, B. R., & Sailor, P. (1995). [Review of the Strong Interest Inventory, 4th Edition.] In J. C. Conoley & J. C. Impara (Eds.), *The twelfth mental measurements yearbook* (pp. 999–1002). Lincoln, NE: Buros Institute of Mental Measurements.

Wiig Criterion Referenced Inventory of Language.

Purpose: "Designed to assist speech-language pathologists and special and regular educators in the diagnosis of children with language disorders and language delays."

Population: Grades 1–8 with Diagnosis of a Language Disorder.

Publication Date: 1990.

Acronym: Wiig CRIL.

Scores: 4 modules: Semantics, Morphology, Syntax, Pragmatics.

Administration: Individual.

Price Data, 1994: $198 per complete kit including Professional's Guide (63 pages), all 4 stimulus manuals and 10 each of all four record forms; $54.50 per module package (specify Semantics, Morphology, Syntax, or Pragmatics) including stimulus manual and 10 record forms; $30 per 20 record forms (specify Semantics, Morphology, Syntax, or Pragmatics); $25 per Professional's Guide.

Time: Untimed.

Author: Elisabeth H. Wiig.

Publisher: The Psychological Corporation.

Review of the Wiig Criterion Referenced Inventory of Language by CLINTON W. BENNETT, Professor of Communication Sciences and Disorders, James Madison University, Harrisonburg, VA:

The Wiig Criterion Referenced Inventory of Language (Wiig CRIL) is designed to complement norm-referenced assessment results of the semantic, morphemic, syntactic, and pragmatic abilities of children with impaired language. The Wiig CRIL is a series of selected probes, formatted in four expressive language modules: Semantic (8 probe sets: semantic relations and referential terms for quantitative, spatial, and temporal concepts); Morphology (19 probes; noun plurals, noun possessives, regular past tense, and noun and verb irregular forms); Syntax (18 probes: basic structures, coordinated and subordinated phrases, and subject-object relative clauses); and Pragmatics (13 probes: social interaction, joint attention, and behavior regulation speech acts). Each probe, which consists of 10 items, relates to one selected concept of oral language and a curriculum-referenced objective for English literacy. Probes require expressive language responses which, as the author noted, require language comprehension and "represent the skills expected of the student in both natural- and school-language interactions" (p. 6).

The testing format involves picture naming, sentence completion, parallel production (termed closure by some), and speech act elicitation.

The Wiig CRIL is not designed to be used as a diagnostic tool or assessment for eligibility. Rather, after a child has been identified as language impaired, probe sets would be selected based upon the child's performance on other assessment instruments. This inventory has three major purposes: (a) extension testing for baseline data for levels of success/failure in specific expressive language skills; (b) establishing intervention targets (assist in developing IEP objectives or classroom curriculum-based objectives); and (c) assessing habilitative progress using portions of the inventory as pre- and posttests.

The norm-reference extension testing is recommended when a child's performance is below normal—defined by the author as 1 or 1.5 standard deviations below the mean or below the 16th percentile for the child's age. Application of these recommendations may result in the overidentification of children as language impaired. I believe a cutoff using minus two standard deviations from the mean for age would be more clinically relevant than the author's recommendation. [Editor's note: *The Standards for Educational and Psychological Testing* (AERA, APA, & NCME, 1985) recommend setting cutscores based on local norms rather than routinely using publisher's recommendations.] Other bases for selecting specific probes are areas of weakness from standardized subtests and existing relationships between standardized tools and this inventory. Of particular use to clinicians might be the appendices in the Wiig CRIL establishing relationships between this measure and the subtests of the Clinical Evaluation of Language Fundamentals—Revised (CELF-R; T4:521) and Clinical Evaluation of Language Fundamentals—Preschool (T4:520). The manual also includes five developed appendices that relate literacy objectives to spoken language usage so that probes can be selected based upon the child's performance of curriculum objectives.

Being a criterion-referenced measure, Wiig appropriately recommended interpretation of performance: 80%–100% is mastery; 60%–80% indicates a transition stage of linguistic development in which the students need further instruction to more fully develop the concept; 30%–60% performance is the emergence stage in which the student has limited linguistic

control of the concept; and below 30% is indicative of random performance or no awareness of the concept. Using these criterion levels, the clinician can establish baselines and prioritize language habilitation goals and have reference points for therapeutic progress.

Validity and reliability are not discussed in the manual. Rationales for the linguistic concepts tested are not presented; however, the scope of the concepts assessed in the four modules appear to be sufficiently broad with the exception of pragmatics, which seems limited. The combined number of concepts addressed in the semantics, morphological, and syntactic modules is 45.

Each individual record form booklet is complete, containing the linguistic concept assessed in each probe, a response sheet for each probe, and results summaries in chart and graph forms for a 3-year period. The Wiig CRIL manual is user friendly with pertinent information presented in an easy-to-understand manner. The author presents a sound theoretical basis and the administration and scoring instructions are clear and concise. An appendix of acceptable dialectal variations of Black English, Appalachian English, Southern White Nonstandard English, General American Nonstandard, and influences of Spanish will be of use to clinicians.

The Wiig CRIL is the best available instrument of its kind. Its strength is as probes for determining therapeutic targets and documenting progress.

Review of the Wiig Criterion Referenced Inventory of Language by JUDITH R. JOHNSTON, Professor of Audiology and Speech Sciences, University of British Columbia, Vancouver, British Columbia, Canada:

The Wiig Criterion Referenced Inventory of Language (CRIL) is intended to aid speech-language pathologists and educators in their assessment of a child's language competence. It is meant for in-depth description following an initial diagnostic decision that the child's language development is below age expectations. The various CRIL modules consist of sets of pictures and questions designed to elicit specific language patterns in four domains: Morphology, Syntax, Semantics, and Pragmatics. Each language pattern/category (e.g., *Noun + Verb* or *progressive verb ending –ing*) is sampled by 10 items that are scored as a separate subtest. Evaluators can present whichever subtests are suggested by standardized test performance. The manual suggests that results can be used to document current knowledge, plan educational/intervention programs, and assess progress.

Description of a child's knowledge of specific language patterns is essential to the assessment process, and many speech language pathologists and educators would welcome elicitation probe materials for this purpose. Features of the CRIL, however, raise concerns about validity and thus limit its value. First, elicited language responses may not provide a valid picture of a child's language knowledge. Elicitation tasks often require high level, "metalinguistic" abilities, and responses are not motivated by self-generated communicative intentions. For these reasons, performance on elicitation probes can substantially underestimate the real-life language abilities of young children. In the CRIL Subordinate Clauses subtest, for example, the child is asked "Can you tell about both things [pictured events] in one sentence? Use the word 'when'" (p. 157). Normal acquisition data indicate that children who would have difficulty understanding these directions could nevertheless be using constructions with "when." Likewise, the Pragmatics module requires children to assume the speaking role for a series of pictured characters and to imagine what they might say in the illustrated situations. Children who would not yet be capable of such role playing should still be able to use language for real-life Greetings and Farewells.

Discrepancies of this sort would seem to compromise the utility of CRIL data in setting goals for educational programs. Samples of spontaneous language would provide a more valid basis for teaching. Although Language Sampling may be inefficient when evaluating specific content vocabulary, most of the CRIL syntactic and morphological patterns are easily evaluated with this technique. Data on the predictive relationships between CRIL performance and spontaneous language could identify the language levels and patterns where elicitation probes would be most valid, but the manual does not provide this information.

The CRIL also raises concerns about content validity. This "Inventory of Language" is understandably selective in its coverage, but the manual provides no discussion of why certain patterns were selected for testing, nor does it discuss the presumed nature of these patterns. For example, 7 of the 18 Syntax subtests focus on the use of conjunctions, but there are no subtests for phrasal and sentential verb complements (e.g., "John told *Joey to stop hitting him*" or "The boy learned *how to build a kite*"). Moreover, 4 of the conjunction subtests actually test the same syntactic patterns, differing only in the specific conjunctions that are required. Similar shortcomings are found in the Pragmatics module where 5 of 13 subtests focus on the same communicative purpose (i.e., to request information), and differ primarily in the specific question words that are needed. Also, there is no coverage of children's ability to construct multisentence texts such as narratives or explanations despite the large literature showing that this is an area of difficulty for school-age language-disordered children. In the Semantics module, many subtest labels imply that relational structures are being tested (e.g., "Action-Object"), when, in fact, the child need only supply single-word answers to questions such as "What is she doing." These, and other, facts about the scope and content of the CRIL appear to require considerable justification, but none is provided.

A third concern is presented by the CRIL claim that probe sets "are arranged, as closely as possible, in order of emergence in natural language or in relative order of difficulty" (p. 8). The research behind particular sequences is not referenced, however, and a number of sequence decisions seem dubious. For example, reversible full passives are listed prior to coordination of noun phrases, and noun derivatives are listed prior to subject pronouns. A more thorough search of the child language literature would have strengthened this aspect of the Inventory.

In summary, the CRIL is well intended but poorly designed. A set of elicitation tasks could be a valuable adjunct to standardized language tests in an assessment process that was oriented towards educational planning. However, such materials would need to be well motivated in scope and sequence, and to make appropriate task demands. They would focus on those aspects of language knowledge that are the most difficult to infer from samples of spontaneous speech, and on relatively advanced language patterns where metalinguistic competence is no longer at issue. The CRIL does not meet these criteria.

[105]
Wonderlic Basic Skills Test.

Purpose: "A short form measure of adult language and math skills ... designed to measure the job-readiness of teenagers and adults."

Population: Teenagers and adults.

Publication Date: 1994–1996.

Acronym: WBST.

Scores, 9: Test of Verbal Skills (Word Knowledge, Sentence Construction, Information Retrieval, Total), Test of Quantitative Skills (Explicit Problem Solving, Problem Solving, Interpretive Problem Solving, Total), Composite Score.

Subtests, 2: Test of Verbal Skills, Test of Quantitative Skills.

Administration: Group or individual.

Forms: 2 equivalent forms for each subtest: VS-1, VS-2 for Test of Verbal Skills; QS-1, QS-2 for Test of Quantitative Skills.

Price Data, 1996: $80 per 25 tests, manual ('96, 92 pages), and necessary software for either the Verbal or Quantitative subtests; $110 per composite set including 25 Verbal subtests, 25 Quantitative subtests, manual, and necessary software; price information for User's Manual for Ability-to-Benefit Testing ('96, 83 pages) available from publisher.

Time: 20 (25) minutes for each subtest.

Comments: The Verbal and Quantitative Skills subtests may be administered together or separately, and are available as separate booklets; scoring requires using IBM-compatible PC; the WBST has been approved by the U.S. Department of Education for use in qualifying postsecondary students for Title 10 Federal financial assistance and schools using the WBST for this purpose must follow special procedures and guidelines published in the User's Manual for Ability-to-Benefit Testing.

Authors: Eliot R. Long, Victor S. Artese, and Winifred L. Clonts.

Publisher: Wonderlic Personnel Test, Inc.

[Note: The following reviews are based on test materials received prior to September 1996 and do not reflect information, including updated reliability data, included in the 1996 test manuals—Ed.]

Review of the Wonderlic Basic Skills Test by THOMAS F. DONLON, Director, Test Development and Research, Thomas Edison State College, Trenton, NJ:

The Wonderlic Basic Skills Test (WBST) is a brief, multiple-choice test intended to measure the language and math skills of adults, and to be used in assessing the job-readiness of teenagers and adults. As stated in the user's manual: "Job readiness means having sufficient language and math skills to successfully handle the written and computational requirements of the job" (p. 4).

Each form of the WBST comes in two booklets, the Test of Verbal Skills and the Test of Quantitative Skills. Each test booklet is attractively designed and presents its material with a clear type face and an open, clean-looking, layout. There are 50 questions in a Verbal test, 45 in a Quantitative test, and all tests have a 20-minute time limit. The questions are in ascending order of difficulty and the subject is told this up front and is advised not to skip around, but to continue with each question in order.

Actually, each test is composed of three subtests, called GED 1, GED 2, and GED 3, presented sequentially in that order, and extensive use is made of the subscores that these yield. Generally, more test content is given to measuring at GED Level 2 than the others.

The reference to GED levels is a reference to a Department of Labor (DOL) system for describing job requirements in terms of six levels of ability, covering all ability levels through the completion of college, and on three dimensions: Reasoning, Mathematics, and Language. The WBST Verbal and Quantitative scales are obvious analogs to DOL Language and Mathematics scales, and so, for example, Computer Operator is said to require Level 3 mastery in Verbal, and a Level 2 mastery in Quantitative, in the eyes of the Department of Labor. The WBST Composite Score, which is based on all of the items, both verbal and quantitative, is offered as an estimator of the Reasoning dimension of the Department of Labor schema.

Brief DOL descriptions of the meanings of the math and verbal levels are presented. In these, typical statements are "Add and subtract two digit numbers" (Level 1, p. 26); "Add, subtract, multiply, and divide all units of measure" (Level 2, p. 26). These brief and general DOL descriptions have essentially been operationally defined as the test content of the WBST, using the judgment of consultant-experts. The WBST is thus considered to be tied to the DOL scales, and to provide a description of individuals in terms of their DOL level of attainment. The test is aimed at workers in jobs that can be described within the first three levels of the scales, spanning the skills taught in primary school and up through 10th grade. The publisher states: "The job title, the required language and math skills, and WBST test performance can all be linked through the GED scales" (p. 4).

The 95 items that an examinee confronts are really worked over: The WBST Individual Score

Report provides an opportunity for 18 scaled score results, all expressed on a scale from 0 to 500. There are Total scores on the Verbal, Quantitative, and Composite scales; there are nine GED subscale scores (three levels by three kinds of score, Verbal, Quantitative, and Composite), and there are six special additional scales, three for the Verbal test, three for the Quantitative Skills test. For each GED subscale, a score of 265 is considered to be a required minimum for succeeding at that level, whereas a score of 350 or more indicates "mastery" (p. 25). The manual states that "A score of 265 is representative of correctly responding to approximately 65% of the test content at that level" (p. 25). It also states that "Like the GED Level scores, subscale scores of 265 indicate modest success with the materials in that skill area" (p. 25).

The three scales that slice the verbal material in a different way yield scores in Word Knowledge, Sentence Construction, and Information Retrieval, and the three scales that slice the mathematical material in a different way yield scores in Explicit Problem Solving, Applied Problem Solving, and Interpretive Problem Solving. This additional scale information is intended to guide the interpretation of generally low level scores on the basic GED level scales, by providing another opportunity for the subject to demonstrate strength.

All of the scales are defined using Item Response Theory (IRT) methodology, and a part of the user's manual is devoted to a presentation concerning this methodology. The manual notes that IRT has been a fairly recent introduction in educational and psychological assessment. Because of this recency, there is as yet no widely agreed-upon set of standards for describing the operations that are carried out in the development. The descriptions of the development of the WBST scales appeared to this reviewer to fall short of the mark. Calls to appropriate persons in the Wonderlic organization were rewarded with careful, patient, and clarifying discussion, but a substantial part of what was being said could have been presented in the manual. The largest focus was on the logical basis for holding that 265 on a WBST scale constitutes "minimum competency" (p. 25) and 350 is "mastery" (p. 25) in the sense of defining the GED level meanings. Basically, this logical basis is derived from the extensive item development by Wonderlic, both from a content and an internal statistical point of view. The concepts and language

of the Department of Labor work were used to make the test. The test is not "linked" to the GED scale system in any empirical or statistical way. There is no demonstration that DOL rating scales are accurately reflected in WBST operations.

It seemed to this reviewer that the internal statistical steps could have been more fully described. Important decisions, such as the decision to restrict GED scale estimation to the subset of items that define that scale, are not mentioned in the manual. It is clear from the presentation of scale overlap in Figure 5 on page 40 that one could make cross-scale estimations, improving the Level 1 estimate by incorporating information from Level 2 and 3 items. The present practice was defended as safeguarding the interpretations of the scales, pointing to the spectre of an examinee who can succeed on GED Levels 2 and 3, and would get a handsome Level 1 estimate from these, but who cannot, in fact, do the Level 1 material. The point is not that the procedures used are in error; it is that they are insufficiently described in the manual.

A potentially useful set of median WBST scores for various occupations is being developed, enabling employers to gauge the general levels of scaled scores attained by the typical worker in a job. As noted in the manual, this can provide a practical benchmark to use in areas where the employer's experience is not sufficient.

No data concerning reliability or score precision derived from the IRT development are reported. Test-retest alternate-form correlations for Verbal were .86 (46 cases) and .79 (64 cases), and for Quantitative they were .90 (38 cases) and .84 (58 cases). In a shift from IRT, internal consistency reliabilities (Cronbach's alpha) of about .92 are reported for the two verbal and the two quantitative tests. The inflating character of speededness for these results is acknowledged, but the failure to provide any summary of the IRT information on the accuracy of the score estimates, via graphical or tabular presentation, seems an error. The score report itself does generate an IRT error statement, bracketing the observed score with a "Probable Score Range," but this guide to score interpretation comes too late to be useful in test selection.

This reviewer took the tests, but selected answers so that only every fourth item was answered correctly. This yielded a score, but the score was asterisked to a warning that the response pattern was "significantly different than expected" and that "Retesting this examinee may be appropriate." This is an excellent feature. The use of IRT and computer administration in this way is a significant advance, and the move by Wonderlic to incorporate it has to be commended.

The lack of any data on the precision of the scores is exacerbated by the large number of scales. Scales made up of 11 or 12 items will not demonstrate high levels of precision even when IRT methods are being used to generate the score. We are assured that the scale score ranges were constrained to intervals where the change in the standard error of measurement was no greater than the change in scale score. But test users are somewhat at sea in making score comparisons.

The relationship between WBST median score and grade level is used to develop a table of Grade Level Equivalent Scores for grades 6 to 12. This work draws upon a 1,404-person within-school sample, spanning grades 8 through 12, and a 4,043-person adult (over 21) group, in the workforce. Although not considered "a national sample" (p. 30), the fairly large groups were examined from a number of demographic standpoints, and considered closely similar to national samples. The comparison of the student data and the adult data indicated that youngsters presently in 8th grade scored higher than adults in the work force whose reported last grade was the 8th grade. Accordingly, the adults were considered to have an associated grade level one year prior to the year they left school, and these "shifted" (p. 32) adult results were used to smooth, extrapolate, and develop the equivalents. The processes seem judgmental and approximate. The manual states that "Grade equivalent scores are commonly required for qualifying students for training programs. They are also used for counseling students" (p. 30), but it is unclear whether these "students" are also "adults" or not. Over the years, quite a bit of measurement scar tissue had developed through debates on the merits and limits of grade equivalent scores. The development here presumably meets someone's practical needs, but it is difficult to evaluate it.

The Wonderlic Basic Skills Test seems in general to be a practical route to a set of descriptions of workforce personnel that are carefully based on a comprehensive and detailed content foundation logically related through expert judgment to the GED levels. As such, it could guide effective decisions about the subjects. The use of warning signals associated with the scores derived from response records that are internally inconsistent must be applauded. But the multiplicity of scales and the absence of summary accuracy information could lead some users to rely on results of indifferent value. IRT does not miraculously cure the likely unreliability of a score derived from 11 items. The WBST is presented as a work in progress, with the promise of additional data over time. This promise is a welcome one.

Review of the Wonderlic Basic Skills Test by GERALD S. HANNA, Professor of Educational Psychology and Assessment, Kansas State University, Manhattan, KS:

Designed to measure the job-related verbal and math skills of adults and teenagers seeking entry-level employment or entering vocational training programs, the Wonderlic Basic Skills Test (WBST) is intended for use in career counseling and applicant selection. It surveys those language and quantitative skills identified as necessary for jobs classified in the lower three levels of the six-level General Education Development (GED) scales of the U.S. Department of Labor.

The computer-generated Individual Score Report compares the examinee's scores with the skill-level requirements of the job designated on the answer sheet. In addition, it reports grade equivalent scores and the GED skill levels achieved. Also reported are percentile ranks with respect to adults at work and with respect to those employed in the job in question. Although scoring is complex, owing to its reliance on Item Response Theory (IRT), it can be done locally by means of a IBM-compatible PC and publisher-furnished diskette.

NORMATIVE DATA. In general, the reference groups used to provide the various kinds of normative data are not described in sufficient detail to allow the reader to judge the extent to which they are representative of the respective national populations of students in school and adult workers. [Editor's Note: Charts on pages 75–77 of the 1996 user's manual include age, sex, and race demographic information.]

VALIDITY. This reviewer judges the developmental history of the test, particularly, its linkage to the job and skill descriptions in the *Dictionary of Occupational Titles*, to be consistent with its purposes. In particular, the decision to focus test content on skills identified as job requirements (in contrast to curriculum taught) seems very sound and the content seems to be appropriate for the instrument's purpose. Items are well written, varied, and balanced in both content and format. Moreover, they are clearly relevant to the world of work without being job specific, gender specific, or subculture specific. Content-related validity evidence is, therefore, judged very favorably.

The user's manual commendably points out that the WBST does not assess all job-relevant attributes, only verbal and quantitative skills. Likewise, readers are warned that it does not provide detailed diagnostic information.

As is often the case with new instruments, predictive validity studies have not, to date, been reported. Because this is the kind of validity evidence that would merit the most weight in judging the utility of the test, its absence—although understandable—is unfortunate.

Confidence in the WBST would be enhanced by the presence of more construct-related validity evidence. Although grade-progression data support the instrument's validity, and a good discussion describes how item ordering minimized the impact of speededness upon scores, other kinds of construct-related evidence would be desirable. For example, this reviewer would have appreciated reports of studies concerning test wiseness, sensitivity to coaching, context dependence, and discriminant validity of subscores.

To amplify on the latter, three subscores are provided for each of verbal and math skills. This seems questionable on two grounds. First if, as the user's manual reports, each subtest measures one dominant factor, then how meaningful are subfactors? This question could have been addressed by reporting the intercorrelations among the three subscores of each major part of the WBST. Yet no evidence of the subscores' discriminant validity is offered. Second, how reliable are the subscores likely to be in view of the fact that each is assessed in an average of less than 7 minutes? This query could have been answered by reporting reliability of the subscores.

RELIABILITY. Although the WBST subtests are somewhat speeded, internal consistency coefficient alphas are reported. They hover around .92. To their credit, the authors point out the likelihood that the alphas overestimate reliability because of test speededness. There is, therefore, a great need for unbiased estimates of reliability.

Regrettably, the only other reliability data reported are for alternate forms (given with unreported time interval) for small samples that are not described in terms of demographics, means, or standard deviations. These impossible-to-interpret coefficients have a median of .85.

Internal consistency reliability estimates take into account content sampling error while ignoring other major sources of measurement error, such as (a) variation over a few days or weeks; (b) examiner errors, such as provision of incorrect time limits; and (c) scoring errors, such as those caused by incorrect data entry for local computerized scoring. Considering the inflation of the alphas to an unknown extent because of speededness and their insensitivity to several major sources of error, this reviewer concludes that the user's manual fails to report sufficient information to enable one to make an informed judgment concerning the reliability of the three major scores of the instrument. In addition, no reliability data are presented for the six subscores.

What is sorely needed are alternate-form reliability studies with an interval of, for instance, 1 to 3 weeks between administrations by different examiners. Such a study could and should report meaningful reliability for *all* scores and subscores.

On a positive note, the use of IRT enabled the standard errors of measurement to vary with score level—a desirable feature that is uncommon.

SUMMARY. The WBST is a short instrument designed to assess selected areas of achievement as they apply to the workplace. It resulted from a sophisticated developmental program. Its content is judged very favorable, but other validity data are extremely meager at this time. Its normative samples are scantily described. Finally, its reliability has not been adequately investigated. It is to be hoped that new editions of the user's manual will soon correct most of these deficits.

CONTRIBUTING TEST REVIEWERS

MARK ALBANESE, Associate Professor, Preventive Medicine and Director, Office of Medical Education Research and Development, University of Wisconsin—Madison, Madison, WI

JERRILYN V. ANDREWS, Assistant for Assessment and Data Collection, Office of School Administration, Montgomery County Public Schools, Rockville, MD

PAUL A. ARBISI, Assessment Clinic Director, Psychology Service, Minneapolis Veterans Affairs Medical Center, Minneapolis, MN

PHILIP ASH, Director, Ash, Blackstone and Cates, Blacksburg, VA

JEFFREY A. ATLAS, Deputy Chief Psychologist and Associate Clinical Professor, Bronx Children's Psychiatric Center, Albert Einstein College of Medicine, Bronx, NY

STEPHEN N. AXFORD, Psychologist, Pueblo School District No. Sixty, Pueblo, CO, and University of Phoenix, Southern Colorado Campus, Colorado Springs, CO

PATRICIA A. BACHELOR, Professor of Psychology, California State University at Long Beach, Long Beach, CA

PHILIP BACKLUND, Associate Dean and Professor of Speech Communication, Communication Department, Central Washington University, Ellensburg, WA

ANDRÉS BARONA, Professor of Educational Psychology and School Psychology Training Director, Arizona State University, Tempe, AZ

PETER DELLA BELLA, Instructor in Psychiatry, Department of Psychiatry, New York University School of Medicine, New York, NY

JAMES K. BENISH, School Psychologist, Helena Public Schools, Adjunct Professor of Special Education, Carroll College, Helena, MT

CLINTON W. BENNETT, Professor of Communication Sciences and Disorders, James Madison University, Harrisonburg, VA

JERI BENSON, Professor of Educational Psychology, College of Education, University of Georgia, Athens, GA

FRANK BERNT, Associate Professor of Education and Health Services, St. Joseph's University, Philadelphia, PA

FREDERICK BESSAI, Professor of Education, University of Regina, Regina, Saskatchewan, Canada

BRIAN F. BOLTON, University Professor, Rehabilitation Research and Training Center, University of Arkansas, Fayetteville, AR

W. DALE BROTHERTON, Associate Professor of Counselor Education, Western Carolina University, Cullowhee, NC

JAMES DEAN BROWN, Professor, Department of ESL, University of Hawaii at Manoa, Honolulu, HI

MICHAEL B. BROWN, Assistant Professor of Psychology, East Carolina University, Greenville, NC

ROBERT D. BROWN, Carl A. Happold Distinguished Professor Emeritus of Educational Psychology, University of Nebraska-Lincoln, Lincoln, NE

MICHAEL B. BUNCH, Vice President, Measurement Incorporated, Durham, NC

THOMAS F. CAMPBELL, Director, Audiology and Speech Pathology, Children's Hospital,

Communication Science & Disorders, University of Pittsburgh, Pittsburgh, PA

JANET F. CARLSON, Associate Professor of Counseling and Psychological Services, State University of New York—College at Oswego, Oswego, NY

C. DALE CARPENTER, Professor of Special Education, Western Carolina University, Cullowhee, NC

MARY MATHAI CHITTOORAN, UC Foundation Assistant Professor of School Psychology and Special Education, The University of Tennessee at Chattanooga, Chattanooga, TN

JOSEPH C. CIECHALSKI, Associate Professor of Counselor and Adult Education, East Carolina University, Greenville, NC

ELAINE CLARK, Professor of Educational Psychology, University of Utah, Salt Lake City, UT

MERITH COSDEN, Professor, Department of Education, University of California, Santa Barbara, CA

JOHN CRAWFORD, Director of Planning and Evaluation, Millard Public Schools, Omaha, NE

DIANA CRESPO, Research Assistant, Department of Psychology, Trenton State College, Trenton, NJ

LINDA CROCKER, Professor of Foundations of Education, University of Florida, Gainesville, FL

GARY J. DEAN, Associate Professor and Chairperson, Department of Adult and Community Education, Indiana University of Pennsylvania, Indiana, PA

CONNIE KUBO DELLA-PIANA, Assistant Professor of Communication, University of Texas at El Paso, El Paso, TX

GABRIEL M. DELLA-PIANA, Director of Evaluation, El Paso Collaborative for Academic Excellence, University of Texas at El Paso, El Paso, TX

GERALD E. DeMAURO, Director, Bureau of Assessment, New Jersey State Department of Education, Trenton, NJ

DENISE M. DeZOLT, Coordinator of Field Experiences and Adjunct Assistant Professor, University of Rhode Island, Kingston, RI

ESTHER E. DIAMOND, Educational and Psychological Consultant, Evanston, IL

THOMAS F. DONLON, Director, Test Development and Research, Thomas Edison State College, Trenton, NJ

E. THOMAS DOWD, Professor of Psychology, Kent State University, Kent, OH

ROBERT J. DRUMMOND, Professor of Education and Human Services, University of North Florida, Jacksonville, FL

DEBORAH ERICKSON, Professor of Counseling, Niagara University, Niagara University, NY

JENNIFER J. FAGER, Assistant Professor, Education and Professional Development, Western Michigan University, Kalamazoo, MI

DOREEN WARD FAIRBANK, Assistant Professor of Psychology, Director, Meredith College Autism Program, Meredith College, Raleigh, NC

XITAO FAN, Assistant Professor of Psychology, Utah State University, Logan, UT

RICHARD F. FARMER, Assistant Professor of Psychology, Idaho State University, Pocatello, ID

TRENTON R. FERRO, Associate Professor of Adult and Community Education, Indiana University of Pennsylvania, Indiana, PA

MARTIN A. FISCHER, Associate Professor and Program Director, Program in Communication Disorders, Department of Human Services, Western Carolina University, Cullowhee, NC

ROBERT FITZPATRICK, Consulting Psychologist, Cranberry Township, PA

JIM C. FORTUNE, Professor of Educational Research and Evaluation, Virginia Tech, Blacksburg, VA

PATRICIA K. FREITAG, Assistant Professor of Educational Research, Department of Educational Leadership, Graduate School of Education and Human Development, The George Washington University, Washington, DC

MARK H. FUGATE, Associate Professor of School Psychology, Alfred University, Alfred, NY

MICHAEL J. FURLONG, Associate Professor, Graduate School of Education, Counseling, University of California, Santa Barbara, Santa Barbara, CA

ROBERT K. GABLE, Professor of Educational Psychology, and Associate Director, Bureau of Educational Research and Service, University of Connecticut, Storrs, CT

ALAN GARFINKEL, Professor of Spanish and Education, Purdue University, West Lafayette, IN

RONALD B. GILLAM, Assistant Professor of Communication Sciences and Disorders, The University of Texas at Austin, Austin, TX

STEVE GRAHAM, Professor of Special Education, University of Maryland, College Park, MD

J. JEFFREY GRILL, Associate Professor of Special Education, Athens State College, Athens, AL

GENEVA D. HAERTEL, Senior Research Associate, EREAPA Associates, Livermore, CA

ROSA A. HAGIN, Professor Emeritus, Fordham University—Lincoln Center, New York, NY

GERALD S. HANNA, Professor of Educational Psychology and Assessment, Kansas State University, Manhattan, KS

DENNIS C. HARPER, Professor of Pediatrics and Rehabilitation Counseling, University of Iowa Hospitals and Clinics, Iowa City, IA

ROBERT G. HARRINGTON, Professor of Educational Psychology and Research, University of Kansas, Lawrence, KS

LEO M. HARVILL, Professor and Assistant Dean for Medical Education, East Tennessee State University, Johnson City, TN

MICHAEL HARWELL, Associate Professor of Psychology in Education, University of Pittsburgh, Pittsburgh, PA

SANDRA D. HAYNES, Assistant Professor of Human Services, Metropolitan State College of Denver, Denver, CO

DAVID O. HERMAN, Associate Educational Officer, Office of Educational Research, New York City Board of Education, Brooklyn, NY

STEPHEN R. HOOPER, Associate Professor of Psychiatry, University of North Carolina School of Medicine, Chapel Hill, NC

TE-FANG HUA, Ph.D. Candidate, Department of ESL, University of Hawaii at Manoa, Honolulu, HI

RICHARD W. JOHNSON, Director of Training at Counseling & Consultation Services of the University Health Services, and Adjunct Professor of Counseling Psychology, University of Wisconsin–Madison, Madison, WI

JUDITH R. JOHNSTON, Professor of Audiology and Speech Sciences, University of British Columbia, Vancouver, British Columbia, Canada

GERALD A. JUHNKE, Assistant Professor of Counseling and Educational Development, School of Education, The University of North Carolina at Greensboro, Greensboro, NC

MICHAEL KANE, Professor of Education, University of Wisconsin, Madison, WI

ALAN S. KAUFMAN, Senior Research Scientist, Psychological Assessment Resources, Inc. (PAR), Odessa, FL

NADEEN L. KAUFMAN, Professor of Clinical Psychology, California School of Professional Psychology, San Diego, CA

MICHAEL G. KAVAN, Associate Dean for Student Affairs, and Associate Professor of Family Practice, Creighton University School of Medicine, Omaha, NE

MARY LOU KELLEY, Professor of Psychology, Louisiana State University, Baton Rouge, LA

KENNETH A. KIEWRA, Professor of Educational Psychology, University of Nebraska—Lincoln, Lincoln, NE

RICHARD T. KINNIER, Associate Professor, Counseling Psychology Program, Arizona State University, Tempe, AZ

JEAN POWELL KIRNAN, Associate Professor of Psychology, Trenton State College, Trenton, NJ

HOWARD M. KNOFF, Professor of School Psychology, Department of Psychological Foundations, University of South Florida, Tampa, FL

ANTONY JOHN KUNNAN, Assistant Professor of Education, Division of Educational Foundations and Interdivisional Studies, California State University, Los Angeles, CA

BARBARA L. LACHAR, Assistant Professor of Psychiatry (Psychology), Baylor College of Medicine, Houston, TX

MATTHEW E. LAMBERT, Research Psychologist, Neurology Research and Education Center, St. Mary Hospital, Lubbock, TX

JOSEPH G. LAW, JR., Associate Professor of Behavioral Studies and Educational Technology, University of South Alabama, Mobile, AL

S. ALVIN LEUNG, Associate Professor of Educational Psychology, The Chinese University of Hong Kong, Hong Kong

STEVEN G. LoBELLO, Associate Professor of Psychology, Auburn University at Montgomery, Montgomery, AL

STEVEN H. LONG, Assistant Professor of Communication Sciences, Case Western Reserve University, Cleveland, OH

DAVID MACPHEE, Associate Professor of Human Development and Family Studies, Colorado State University, Fort Collins, CO

CLEBORNE D. MADDUX, Professor of Special Education and Educational Technology, University of Nevada, Reno, NV

KORESSA KUTSICK MALCOLM, School Psychologist, Augusta County Public Schools, Fisherville, VA

WILLIAM E. MARTIN, JR., Professor of Educational Psychology, Northern Arizona University, Flagstaff, AZ

REBECCA McCAULEY, Associate Professor, Communication Sciences, University of Vermont, Burlington, VT

MARY J. McLELLAN, Assistant Professor of Educational Psychology, Northern Arizona University, Flagstaff, AZ

MALCOLM R. McNEIL, Chair, Communication Science & Disorders, University of Pittsburgh, Pittsburgh, PA

MARIA MEDINA-DIAZ, Assistant Professor of Educational Measurement and Evaluation, School of Education, University of Puerto Rico, Rio Piedras, PR

WILLIAM R. MERZ, SR., Professor, School Psychology Training Program, Department of Special Education, Rehabilitation, and School Psychology, School of Education, California State University, Sacramento, Sacramento, CA

ROBERT J. MILLER, Associate Professor of Special Education, Mankato State University, Mankato, MN

KEVIN L. MORELAND, Professor of Psychology and Chair, Fordham University, Bronx, NY

SHERWYN MORREALE, Chair, Center for Excellence in Oral Communication, University of Colorado at Colorado Springs, Colorado Springs, CO

RALPH O. MUELLER, Associate Professor of Educational Research, Department of Educational Leadership, Graduate School of Education and Human Development, The George Washington University, Washington, DC

ANTHONY J. NITKO, Professor of Educational Measurement and Chairperson, Department of Psychology in Education, University of Pittsburgh, Pittsburgh, PA

JANET A. NORRIS, Associate Professor of Communication Sciences and Disorders, Louisiana State University, Baton Rouge, LA

SALVADOR HECTOR OCHOA, Assistant Professor of Educational Psychology, Texas A&M University, College Station, TX

D. JOE OLMI, Assistant Professor, School Psychology Program and Director, School Psychology Service Center, Department of Psychology, University of Southern Mississippi, Hattiesburg, MS

STEVEN V. OWEN, Professor of Educational Psychology, University of Connecticut, Storrs, CT

KATHLEEN D. PAGET, Division Director, The Center for Child and Family Studies, College of Social Work, University of South Carolina, Columbia, SC

STEVEN I. PFEIFFER, Professor, Graduate School of Education, Kent State University, Kent, OH

SHEILA R. PRATT, Assistant Professor of Communication Science & Disorders, University of Pittsburgh, Pittsburgh, PA

JEFFREY S. RAIN, Assistant Professor and Chairman, Industrial/Organizational Psychology Program, School of Psychology, Florida Tech, Melbourne, FL

BIKKAR S. RANDHAWA, Professor of Educational Psychology, University of Saskatchewan, Saskatoon, Canada

JAMES C. REED, Chief Psychologist, St. Luke's Hospital, New Bedford, MA

ROBERT C. REINEHR, Professor of Psychology, Southwestern University, Georgetown, TX

CECIL R. REYNOLDS, Professor of Educational Psychology & Professor of Neuroscience, Texas A&M University, College Station, TX

ROGER A. RICHARDS, Adjunct Professor of Communication, Bunker Hill Community College, Boston, MA, and Consultant, Massachusetts Department of Education, Malden, MA

JENNIFER A. ROSENBLATT, Doctoral Candidate, Graduate School of Education, University of California, Santa Barbara, Santa Barbara, CA

HERBERT C. RUDMAN, Emeritus Professor of Measurement and Quantitative Methods, Michigan State University, East Lansing, MI

WILLIAM I. SAUSER, JR., Professor and Executive Director for Outreach, College of Business, Auburn University, Auburn, AL

DIANE J. SAWYER, Professor of Education, Middle Tennessee State University, Murfreesboro, TN

DALE P. SCANNELL, Professor of Education, Indiana University, Purdue University—Indianapolis, Indianapolis, IN

WILLIAM D. SCHAFER, Associate Professor of Measurement, Statistics, and Evaluation, University of Maryland at College Park, College Park, MD

STEVEN R. SHAW, School Psychologist, The School District of Greenville County, Greenville, SC

EUGENE P. SHEEHAN, Associate Professor of Psychology, University of Northern Colorado, Greeley, CO

KENNETH G. SHIPLEY, Professor and Chair of Communicative Sciences and Disorders, California State University, Fresno, Fresno, CA

MARIELA C. SHIRLEY, Assistant Professor, Department of Psychology, University of North Carolina at Wilmington, Wilmington, NC

MARK D. SHRIVER, Assistant Professor, University of Nebraska Medical Center, Omaha, NE

WESLEY E. SIME, Professor of Health and Human Performance, University of Nebraska-Lincoln, Lincoln, NE

JEFFREY K. SMITH, Professor of Educational Psychology and Associate Dean, Graduate School of Education, Rutgers, The State University of New Jersey, New Brunswick, NJ

JANET E. SPECTOR, Assistant Professor of Education, University of Maine, Orono, ME

JACLYN B. SPITZER, Chief, Audiology and Speech Pathology, Department of Veterans Affairs, West Haven, CT

EDWARD R. STARR, Assistant Professor of Counseling Psychology, State University of New York at Buffalo, Buffalo, NY

MARGOT B. STEIN, Clinical Assistant Professor of Psychiatry, University of North Carolina School of Medicine, Chapel Hill, NC

STEPHANIE STEIN, Associate Professor of Psychology, Central Washington University, Ellensburg, WA

TERRY A. STINNETT, Associate Professor of Applied Behavioral Studies in Education, Oklahoma State University, Stillwater, OK

RICHARD B. STUART, Professor Emeritus of Psychiatry, University of Washington, and Regional Faculty, The Fielding Institute, Seattle, WA

GABRIELLE STUTMAN, Consulting Psychologist, Cognitive Habilitation Services, New York City, NY

RICHARD R. SUDWEEKS, Associate Professor of Instructional Science, Brigham Young University, Provo, UT

DONNA L. SUNDRE, Associate Assessment Specialist/Associate Professor of Psychology, James Madison University, Harrisonburg, VA

ANITA TESH, Assistant Professor, School of Nursing, University of North Carolina at Greensboro, Greensboro, NC

DONALD THOMPSON, Dean and Professor of Counseling and Psychology, Troy State University Montgomery, Montgomery, AL

GEORGE C. THORNTON, III, Professor, Department of Psychology, Colorado State University, Fort Collins, CO

JERRY TINDAL, Associate Professor, Behavioral Research and Teaching, University of Oregon, Eugene, OR

NICHOLAS A. VACC, Professor and Chairperson, Department of Counseling and Educational Development, School of Education, The University of North Carolina at Greensboro, Greensboro, NC

DOLORES KLUPPEL VETTER, Professor of Communicative Disorders, University of Wisconsin—Madison, Madison, WI

NIELS G. WALLER, Associate Professor of Psychology, University of California, Davis, CA

BETSY WATERMAN, Assistant Professor, Counseling and Psychological Services Department, State University of New York at Oswego, Oswego, NY

T. STEUART WATSON, Associate Professor of Educational Psychology, Mississippi State University, Starkville, MS

J. STEVEN WELSH, Director, School Psychology Program, Nicholls State University, Thibodaux, LA

JANICE G. WILLIAMS, Associate Professor of Psychology, Clemson University, Clemson, SC

ROBERT T. WILLIAMS, Professor of Education, Colorado State University, Fort Collins, CO

KRISTEN WOJCIK, Research Assistant, Department of Psychology, Trenton State College, Trenton, NJ

RICHARD M. WOLF, Professor of Psychology and Education, Teachers College, Columbia University, New York, NY

MYRA N. WOMBLE, Assistant Professor of Occupational Studies, University of Georgia, Athens, GA

BLAINE R. WORTHEN, Professor of Psychology, Utah State University, Logan, UT

CLAUDIA R. WRIGHT, Professor of Educational Psychology, California State University, Long Beach, CA

SHELDON ZEDECK, Chair and Professor of Psychology, Department of Psychology, University of California, Berkeley, CA

INDEX OF TITLES

This title index lists all the tests included in The Supplement to the Twelfth Mental Measurements Yearbook. *Citations are to test entry numbers, not to pages (e.g., 14 refers to Test 14 and not page 14). Test numbers along with test titles are indicated in the running heads at the top of each page, and page numbers, used only in the Table of Contents and not in the indexes, appear at the bottom of each page. Superseded titles are listed with cross references to current titles, and alternative titles are also cross referenced.*

INDEX OF ACRONYMS

This Index of Acronyms refers the reader to the appropriate test in The Supplement to the Twelfth Mental Measurements Yearbook. *In some cases tests are better known by their acronyms than by their full titles, and this index can be of substantial help to the person who knows the former but not the latter. Acronyms are only listed if the author or publisher has made substantial use of the acronym in referring to the test, or if the test is widely known by the acronym. A few acronyms are also registered trademarks (e.g., SAT); where this is known to us, only the test with the registered trademark is referenced. There is some danger in the overuse of acronyms, but this index, like all other indexes in this work, is provided to make the task of identifying a test as easy as possible. All numbers refer to test numbers, not page numbers.*

CLASSIFIED SUBJECT INDEX

The Classified Subject Index classifies all tests included in The Supplement to the Twelfth Mental Measurements Yearbook *into 17 major categories: Achievement, Behavior Assessment, Developmental, Education, English, Foreign Languages, Intelligence and Scholastic Aptitude, Mathematics, Miscellaneous, Multi-Aptitude, Neuropsychological, Personality, Reading, Sensory-Motor, Social Studies, Speech and Hearing, and Vocations. Each category appears in alphabetical order and tests are ordered alphabetically within each category. Each test entry includes test title (capitalized), population for which the test is intended (lower case), and the test entry number in* The Supplement to the Twelfth Mental Measurements Yearbook. *All numbers refer to test entry numbers, not to page numbers. Brief suggestions for the use of this index are presented in the introduction.*

ACHIEVEMENT

Aprenda: La Prueba De Logros en Español, grades K.5–1.5, 1.5–2.5, 2.5–3.5, 3.5–4.5, 4.5–5.5, 5.5–6.5, 6.5–8.9, see 5

Collegiate Assessment of Academic Proficiency, students in the first 2 years of college, see 27

Diagnostic Achievement Test for Adolescents, Second Edition, ages 12–0 to 18–11, see 33

Integrated Assessment System, grades 1–9, see 45

Kaufman Functional Academic Skills Test, ages 15–85 and over, see 50

Test of Academic Achievement Skills—Reading, Arithmetic, Spelling, and Listening Comprehension, ages 4–0 to 12–0, see 93

Test of Academic Performance, grades K–12, see 94

Wonderlic Basic Skills Test, teenagers and adults, see 105

BEHAVIOR ASSESSMENT

AAMR Adaptive Behavior Scale—School, Second Edition, ages 3–21, see 1

Adult Attention Deficit Disorder Behavior Rating Scale, ages 16 and above, see 3

Preschool and Kindergarten Behavior Scales, ages 3-6, see 74

Substance Abuse Relapse Assessment, adolescents and adults, see 90

Test of Variables of Attention, ages 4 and over, see 99

DEVELOPMENTAL

EDUCATION

ENGLISH

FOREIGN LANGUAGES

INTELLIGENCE AND SCHOLASTIC APTITUDE

MATHEMATICS

MISCELLANEOUS

MULTI-APTITUDE

NEUROPSYCHOLOGICAL

PERSONALITY

READING

SENSORY-MOTOR

SOCIAL STUDIES

SPEECH AND HEARING

VOCATIONS

PUBLISHERS DIRECTORY
AND INDEX

This directory and index gives the addresses and test entry numbers of all publishers for in-print tests represented in the Supplement to the Twelfth Mental Measurements Yearbook. *Please note that all numbers in this index refer to test entry numbers, not page numbers. Publishers are an important source of information about catalogs, specimen sets, price changes, test revisions, and many other matters.*

Addiction Research Foundation, Marketing Services, 33 Russell Street, Toronto, Ontario M5S 2S1, Canada: 4, 6, 34, 47, 86

Allyn & Bacon, Department 894, 160 Gould Street, Needham Heights, MA 02194–2310: 36, 87

American Alliance for Health, Physical Education, Recreation, and Dance, 1900 Association Drive, Reston, VA 22091: 38

American College Testing, 2201 N. Dodge Street, P.O. Box 168, Iowa City, IA 52243: 26, 27

American Guidance Service, 4201 Woodland Road, Circle Pines, MN 55014–1796: 50, 51, 60

American Psychiatric Press, Inc., 1400 K Street, N.W., Suite 1101, Washington, DC 20005: 29

Australian Council for Educational Research Ltd., 19 Prospect Hill Road, Private Bag 55, Camberwell, Victoria 3124, Australia: 53, 77

Ballard & Tighe, 480 Atlas Street, Brea, CA 92821: 41

Behavior Science Systems, Inc., P.O. Box 580274, Minneapolis, MN 55440: 16

Bienvenu, Millard J., Sr., Northwest Publications, 710 Watson Drive, Natchitoches, LA 71457: 58

Career Research and Testing, Inc., 2005 Hamilton Avenue, Suite 250, San Jose, CA 95125: 14, 66

CASAS, 8910 Clairemont Mesa Blvd., San Diego, CA 92123: 30

Center for Applied Linguistics, 1118–22nd Street, N.W., Washington, DC 20037: 21

Center for Creative Leadership, One Leadership Place, P.O. Box 26300, Greensboro, NC 27438–6300: 32

The College Board, 45 Columbus Avenue, New York, NY 10023–6992: 2

Communication Skill Builders, 555 Academic Court, San Antonio, TX 78204–2498: 68

Consulting Psychologists Press, Inc., 3803 East Bayshore Road, P.O. Box 10096, Palo Alto, CA 94303: 12, 71

Consulting Resource Group International, Inc., #386—200 West Third Street, Sumas, WA 98295–8000: 88

C.P.S., Inc., P.O. Box 83, Larchmont, NY 10538: 17, 85

CTB Macmillan/McGraw-Hill, 20 Ryan Ranch Rd., Monterey, CA 93940–5703: 15

Educational Activities, Inc., P.O. Box 392, Freeport, NY 11520: 43

Faculty of Education, Memorial University of Newfoundland, St. John's, Newfoundland A1B 3XB, Canada: 101

H & H Publishing Co., Inc., 1231 Kapp Drive, Clearwater, FL 34625: 52

Hogan Assessment Systems, P.O. Box 521176, Tulsa, OK 74152: 39

Imaginart, 307 Arizona Street, Bisbee, AZ 85603: 46

Institute for Personality and Ability Testing, Inc., Test Services Division, P.O. Box 1188, Champaign, IL 61824–1188: 19

Maddak, Inc., Industrial Road, Pequannock, NJ 07440–1993: 57

McBer and Company, 116 Huntington Avenue, Boston, MA 02116: 24, 54, 70

National Center for Research to Improve Postsecondary Teaching and Learning, 2400 School of Education Building, The University of Michigan, Ann Arbor, MI 48109–1259: 61

The National Council on Economic Education, 1140 Avenue of the Americas, New York, NY 10016: 98

National Occupational Competency Testing Institute, 500 N. Bronson Avenue, Big Rapids, MI 49307–2737: 62, 63, 64, 65

National Wellness Institute, Inc., 1045 Clark Street, Suite 210, Stevens Point, WI 54481–2962: 56, 102

New Standards, Inc., 1080 Montreal Avenue, Suite 300, St. Paul, MN 55116: 92

New Zealand Council for Educational Research, Education House West, 178–182 Willis St., Box 3237, Wellington 6000, New Zealand: 59, 78

Ned Owens M.Ed., Inc., 629 W. Centerville Road, Suite 201, Garland, TX 75041: 3

PRO-ED, Inc., 8700 Shoal Creek Blvd., Austin, TX 78757–6897: 1, 31, 33, 35, 74, 89, 97

Pro-Health Publications, P.O. Box 682, College Station, TX 77841: 22

Psychological & Educational Publications, Inc., 1477 Rollins Road, Burlingame, CA 94010–2316: 93, 95, 100

Psychological Assessment Resources, Inc., P.O. Box 998, Odessa, FL 33556–9908: 11, 25, 40, 84, 90

The Psychological Corporation, 555 Academic Court, San Antonio, TX 78204–2498: 5, 8, 9, 10, 13, 18, 23, 45, 49, 72, 76, 81, 83, 94, 96, 104

Psychological Services Bureau, Inc., P.O. Box 327, St. Thomas, PA 17252: 79

Psychometrics Canada Ltd., 3rd Floor, Students' Union Building, University of Alberta, Edmonton, Alberta T6G 2J7, Canada: 42, 55

RENOVEX Corporation, 1421 Jersey Avenue N., Minneapolis, MN 55427: 7

The Riverside Publishing Co., 8420 Bryn Mawr Avenue, Chicago, IL 60631: 28

Kenneth H. Rubin, University of Waterloo, Department of Psychology, Waterloo, Ontario N2l 3G1, Canada: 73

Simon & Schuster Higher Education Group, 200 Old Tappan Road, Tappan, NJ 07675: 37

Slosson Educational Publications, Inc., P.O. Box 280, East Aurora, NY 14052–0280: 91

Sopris West, Inc., 1140 Boston Avenue, P.O. Box 1809, Longmont, CO 80501–1809: 44, 80, 82

U.S. Department of Labor, Employment and Training Administration, 200 Constitution Avenue, N.W., Washington, DC 20210: 48

Universal Attention Disorders, Inc., 4281 Katella Avenue, #215, Los Alamitos, CA 90720: 99

The University of Michigan Press, 839 Green Street, P.O. Box 1104, Ann Arbor, MI 48106–1104: 75

Western Psychological Services, 12031 Wilshire Blvd., Los Angeles, CA 90025–1251: 69, 103

Dale E. Williams, John Carroll University, Department of Psychology, University Heights, OH 44118: 20

Wonderlic Personnel Test, Inc., 1509 N. Milwaukee Avenue, Libertyville, IL 60048–1387: 105

XICOM, Inc., Sterling Forest, Woods Road, Tuxedo, NY 10987: 67

INDEX OF NAMES

This analytical index indicates whether a citation refers to authorship of a test, a test review, or a reference for a specific test. Numbers refer to test entries, not to pages. The abbreviations and numbers following the names may be interpreted as follows: "test, 73" indicates authorship of test 73; "rev, 86" indicates authorship of a review of test 86; "ref, 45(30)" indicates authorship of reference number 30 in the "Test References" section for test 45; "ref, 13r" indicates a reference (unnumbered) in one of the "Reviewer's References" sections for test 13. Names mentioned in cross references are also indexed.

Amir, N.: ref, 10(854)
Ammons, C. H.: rev, 1, 76
Ammons, R. B.: rev, 1
Amori, B. A.: test, 41
Amundson, N.: test, 42
Anastasi, A.: rev, 19; ref, 7r, 12r, 31r, 97r
Anastasiades, P.: ref, 9(24)
Anastopoulos, A. D.: ref, 10(191)
Anderman, E. M.: ref, 61(4)
Anderson, D.: ref, 10(233)
Anderson, D. A.: ref, 10(705)
Anderson, I. M.: ref, 10(49,435)
Anderson, T.: test, 88
Anderson, T. D.: ref, 42r
Andrew, B.: ref, 10(274)
Andrews, G.: ref, 10(79), ref, 29(10)
Andrews, J.: ref, 10(76,209)
Andrews, J. V.: rev, 33
Angell, K. L.: ref, 10(374)
Annis, H. M.: test, 47, 86; ref, 90r
Anthenelli, R. M.: ref, 29(14)
Anton, W.: ref, 25(1)
Anton, W. D.: test, 25
Antoni, M. H.: ref, 10(268)
Arbisi, P. A.: rev, 85
Arbuckle, B.: ref, 10(235)
Arena, J. G.: ref, 10(9)
Arias, I.: ref, 10(634)
Aritzi, S.: ref, 29r
Arkowitz, H.: ref, 10(751)
Armstrong, D.: ref, 10(161)
Armstrong, M. S.: ref, 10(606)
Arndt, I. O.: ref, 10(187,399)
Arnkoff, D. B.: ref, 10(130)
Arnold, E. H.: ref, 10(625)
Arnow, B.: ref, 10(393,394,620)
Aro, H.: ref, 10(548)
Aronson, M. J.: ref, 10(541)
Arruda, M. J.: ref, 10(238)
Artese, V. S.: test, 105
Aruffo, J. F.: ref, 9(15), 9r
Arvey, R.: test, 71
Asendorpf, J. B.: ref, 73(2)
Ash, P.: rev, 7, 34
Ashby, J. S.: ref, 10(480,554)
Asherson, P.: ref, 29(2)
Ashton, R.: ref, 10(596)
Askov, E. N.: ref, 30(2)
Asle, H.: ref, 10(188)
Asmundson, G. J. G.: ref, 9(40), 10(185,253,400,593)
Assenheimer, J. S.: ref, 9(60), 10(813), 92(2)
Association for Specialists in Group Work: ref, 58r
Atkins, C. P.: rev, 68
Atkinson, J. H.: ref, 10(72,864)
Atkinson, S. D.: ref, 10(401)
Atlas, G.: ref, 10(402)

Atlas, J. A.: rev, 42
Attkisson, C. C.: ref, 10(360)
Auckland College of Education: test, 59
Aukes, D.: ref, 9(16), 9r
Aurinen, J.: ref, 10(379)
Averbuch, S.: test, 57
Avia, M. D.: ref, 10(576)
Axford, S. N.: rev, 20, 39
Azim, H. F. A.: ref, 10(155,156)

Babor, T. F.: ref, 10(507,508,628)
Bachelor, P. A.: rev, 24, 62
Bachman, L. F.: ref, 21r
Backlund, P.: rev, 35, 78
Bacon, G. M.: ref, 60(3)
Baddeley, A. D.: ref, 10()841
Baer, J. S.: ref, 90r
Baer, L.: ref, 9(20), 10(50,414,547,626,761)
Bagby, R. M.: ref, 10(189)
Baglioni, A. J.: ref, 9(33)
Baird, A.: ref, 9(63), 10(863)
Baker, D. A.: ref, 10(834)
Baker, J. D.: ref, 10(627)
Baker, J. E.: ref, 10(284)
Baker, M.: ref, 10(825)
Baker, T. B.: ref, 47r
Bakish, D.: ref, 10(425)
Balach, L.: ref, 10(279)
Baldessarini, R. J.: ref, 10(69)
Baldwin, L.: test, 83
Ball, S.: ref, 10(840)
Ball, S. A.: ref, 10(628)
Balla, D.: ref, 1r
Balla, D. A.: ref, 1r
Ballantine, T.: ref, 10(626)
Baltman, S.: ref, 10(328)
Bancroft, J.: ref, 10(180)
Bansal, S.: ref, 10(150)
Baradaran, L. P.: ref, 10(235)
Baran, S. A.: ref, 10(629)
Barber, B. K.: ref, 10(371)
Barber, J. G.: ref, 86r
Barber, J. P.: ref, 10(190,630)
Barbieri-Berger, S.: ref, 10(445)
Barch, D.: ref, 10(271)
Barclay, D. R.: ref, 10(708)
Barker, W. F.: ref, 12(14), 84(47)
Barkham, M.: ref, 10(256,474,581,782)
Barkley, R. A.: ref, 10(111,191)
Barlow, D. H.: ref, 10(10,122,192)
Barnes, J.: test, 53
Barnhill, J.: ref, 10(236)
Barocka, A.: ref, 10(754)
Baron, P.: ref, 10(275,281,524)
Barona, A.: rev, 92
Barrera, M.: ref, 10r

Bless, H.: ref, 10(52)
Bloch, S.: ref, 10(849,850)
Block, P.: ref, 10(765)
Block-Pedego, A.: test, 82; ref, 82r
Bloem, G. M.: ref, 10(641)
Blonk, R. W. B.: ref, 10(296)
Blood, G. W.: ref, 10(410), 89(8,14,15)
Blood, I. M.: ref, 10(410), 89(8,19)
Bloom, R. L.: ref, 60(4)
Blown, D. C.: ref, 10(110)
Blum, M. D.: ref, 10(16)
Blustein, D. L.: ref, (2), 12(1)
Bocherding, S.: ref, 10(220)
Boehm, A. E.: ref, 97r
Boggiano, A. K.: ref, 10(115,116)
Bohn, M. J.: ref, 10(507,715)
Bohner, G.: ref, 10(52)
Bohr, L.: ref, 27(1,2)
Bolduc, P. L.: ref, 10(100)
Boll, T.: test, 18
Boll, T. J.: ref, 18r
Bolton, B. F.: rev, 70
Bolton, S. O.: test, 46
Bond, A.: ref, 10(663)
Bonner, M.: ref, 10(126)
Boone, D. E.: ref, 10(411)
Borden, J. W.: ref, 9(11,19) 10(412)
Borget, M. M.: ref, 84(35)
Borkovec, T. D.: ref, 10(563)
Borod, J. C.: ref, 60(4)
Bortner, M.: rev, 1
Bosmans, E.: ref, 10(141)
Both, L.: ref, 10(158), 73(1)
Boughner, S. R.: ref, 58r
Bouhuys, A. L.: ref, 10(104,146,339,340,641)
Bourgeois, A.: ref, 10(286)
Bourke, S.: test, 77
Boutros, N. N.: ref, 10(220)
Bowen-Jones, K.: ref, 10(636)
Bowler, K.: ref, 10(173)
Boyacioglu, G.: ref, 10(199)
Boyatzis, R. E.: test, 54
Boyce, P.: ref, 10(117)
Boyle, C. R.: ref, 56(2)
Boyle, D.: ref, 10(424)
Boze, M. M.: ref, 10(321)
Brackney, B. E.: ref, 10(642)
Bradbury, T. N.: ref, 10(433)
Bradley, B. P.: ref, 10(643,740)
Bradwejn, J.: ref, 10(425)
Brailey, K.: ref, 10(598)
Braimen, S.: ref, 10(108)
Braith, J. A.: ref, 10(81,82,529,530)
Brand, E.: ref, 10(200)
Brandt, H. A.: ref, 10(201)
Bravo, G.: ref, 38r

Breier, A.: ref, 10(502)
Breitbart, W.: ref, 10(826)
Breiter, H. C.: ref, 9(20), 10(414)
Brennan, J. M.: ref, 10(717)
Brent, D. A.: ref, 10(279)
Breslau, N.: ref, 10(53)
Breuer, P.: ref, 10(672)
Brewer, B. W.: ref, 10(280)
Brewerton, T. D.: ref, 10(201)
Brewin, C. R.: ref, 10(510)
Bridges, M. W.: ref, 10(578)
Brieter, H. C.: ref, 10(761)
Briggs, C.: ref, 9(34), 10(514)
Brinkman, D.: ref, 97(2)
Brintnell, E. S.: ref, 55(1)
Britt, D. M.: ref, 10(687)
Britt, T. W., Jr.: ref, 100(2)
Broadnax, S.: ref, 10(441)
Brogan, D.: ref, 10(310)
Bromberger, J. T.: ref, 10(413)
Brooking, J.: ref, 10(469)
Brooks, J. D.: ref, 10r
Brookshire, R. H.: ref, 60(5,6,9)
Brophy, J.: ref, 10(214)
Broskowski, H.: ref, 90r
Brotherton, W. D.: rev, 58
Brown, B. S.: ref, 10(107)
Brown, C.: ref, 10(644), 10r
Brown, E. J.: ref, 10(645)
Brown, F.: rev, 84
Brown, G.: ref, 10(277), 9r, 10r
Brown, G. G.: ref, 10(590)
Brown, G. P.: ref, 10(646)
Brown, H. D.: ref, 9(20), 10(414)
Brown, J.: ref, 10(507,715)
Brown, J. D.: rev, 21, 41
Brown, J. D. R.: ref, 10(287)
Brown, L.: ref, 1r, 33r
Brown, M. B.: rev, 11, 56
Brown, R. D.: rev, 26
Brown, S. D.: ref, 84(36)
Brown, S. L.: test, 75
Brown, T. A.: ref, 10(54,122,192,202)
Brubeck, D.: ref, 10(203)
Bruce, B.: ref, 10(393)
Bruce, T. J.: ref, 10(591)
Bruch, M. A.: ref, 10(415)
Bruckel, S.: ref, 10(303)
Bruininks, R. H.: ref, 1r
Brulle, A. R.: ref, 1r
Brumbelow, S.: ref, 10(92)
Bryant, B. R.: test, 33, 97; ref, 1r, 33r
Bryant, K.: ref, 10(283)
Bubenzer, D. L.: ref, 58r
Buchanan, A.: ref, 10(230)
Buchanan, J. P.: ref, 9(42), 10(624)

Delaney, S. M.: ref, 10(317)
Delgado, P. L.: ref, 10(773)
Delis, D. C.: ref, 10(864)
Della-Piana, C. K.: rev, 62
Della-Piana, G. M.: rev, 45
Dellicarpini, L.: ref, 10(743)
DeLuca, J.: ref, 10(445,845)
DeMan, A. F.: ref, 10(666)
DeMauro, G. E.: rev, 33, 59
Denburg, N. L.: ref, 10(837)
Denham, S. A.: ref, 10(124)
Dennerstein, L.: ref, 10(148)
Dent, H. R.: ref, 9r
Derry, P. A.: ref, 10(297)
DeRubeis, R. J.: ref, 10(68,190,213,223,463,653)
DeSimone, A.: ref, 10(446)
Desler, M.: ref, 27(1)
Desnyder, R.: ref, 10(853)
Detrick, P.: ref,10(93)
Dettling, M.: ref, 29(6)
Detzer, M. J.: ref, 10(620)
D'Eugenio, D. B.: test, 75
Deutscher, S.: ref, 10(60)
Devins, G. M.: ref, 10(61,62)
Devous, M. D.: ref, 89(4,12)
DeWolfe, D.: ref, 10(105)
DeZolt, D. M.: rev, 73
deZwaan, M.: ref, 10(427)
Diamond, E. E.: rev, 14, 84
Diamond, R.: ref, 10(212)
Dick, H.: ref, 10(163)
Dickinson, L. G.: ref, 10(511)
Dickson, H. G.: ref, 10(437)
Dietrich, S.: ref, 89(16)
Dietz, J.: test, 96
Diguer, L.: ref, 10(630)
Dill, D.: ref, 10(226)
Dimeff, L. A.: ref, 10(18)
Dimino, C.: ref, 10(626)
Dimitrov, M.: ref, 10(836)
Dinkgreve, M. A. H. M.: ref, 10(714)
Dinur, C.: ref, 84(44)
Direnfeld, D. M.: ref, 9(25), 10(436,718)
Ditta, S. R.: ref, 10(797,798)
Dixen, J.: ref, 10(421)
Dixson, A.: ref, 10(180)
Dobson, K. S.: ref, 10(667); 9r
Dodge, C. S.: ref, 10(71)
Doig, B.: test, 77
Dolente, A.: test, 90
Dolinsky, A.: ref, 10(108)
Dollaghan, C.: ref, 49r
Dollinger, S. J.: ref, 10(63)
Dolliver, R. H.: rev, 84
Donald, J.: ref, 29(4)
Donison, D.: ref, 10(178)

Donlon, T. F.: rev, 105
Dorman, A.: ref, 10(298)
Dorozynsky, L.: ref, 10(187,399)
Dougall, A. L.: ref, 10(835)
Dougher, M. J.: ref, 10(36)
Douglas, S. M.: ref, 10(241)
Dow, M. G.: ref, 10(34)
Dowd, E. T.: rev, 9, 40
Dowd, R.: ref, 10(764)
Dowdall, D.: ref, 9(8), 10(216), 9r
Dowe, D. L.: ref, 10(849,850)
Doyle, S. S.: ref, 60(8)
Drews, J. E.: test, 75
Drudge, O.: ref, 10(805)
Drummond, R. J.: rev, 63
D'Souza, J.: ref, 10(425)
Dubois, M. F.: ref, 38r
Duchan, J. F.: ref, 76(21)
Duckett, E.: ref, 10(559)
DuFeu, P.: ref, 29(6)
Dugas, M. J.: ref, 9(44) 10(668)
Duggan, C. F.: ref, 10(553,759)
Dumas, J. E.: ref, 10(447,669)
Duncan, K.: ref, 10(658)
Dunn, G.: ref, 10(299,462)
Dunn, L.: ref, 1r
Dunn, L. M.: ref, 1r, 49r
Dunn, M.: ref, 10(582)
Dunn, S. E.: ref, 10(5)
Dunner, D. L.: ref, 10(304)
DuPree, D.: ref, 10(378)
Dupree, L. W.: ref, 90r
Dupuy, T. R.: test, 99
Dura, J. R.: ref, 10(300)
Durand, V. M.: ref, 10(342)
Durham, R. C.: ref, 9(26), 10(448)
Durrant, J. D.: ref, 9(13,62), 10(319,844)
DuRubeis, R. J.: ref, 10(694)
Dyck, M. J.: ref, 9(6,29), 10(125,846)
Dykman, B. M.: ref, 10(271)
Dykman, R. A.: ref, 9(30)
Dykstra, S. P.: ref, 10(63)

Eagan, A. E.: ref, 84(43)
Earls, C. M.: ref, 10(17)
Eaton, E. M.: ref, 10(522)
Eaton, W. W.: ref, 29(3)
Eckenrode, J.: ref, 10(240)
Eckert, E. D.: ref, 10(427)
Eckhardt, M. J.: ref, 10(670)
Edelbrock, C.: ref, 10(111)
Ediger, E.: ref, 10(842)
Ediger, J. M.: ref, 10(185,253)
Edson, A.: test, 43
Educational Testing Service: test, 37
Edwards, A.: ref, 76(22)

Fine, J. A.: ref, 9(48), 10(695)
Finitzo, T.: ref, 89(4,12)
Fink, J. J.: test, 70
Finkelstein, D.: ref, 10(488)
Finney, J. W.: ref, 10(126)
Fischer, M. A.: rev, 2, 49
Fischer, M.: ref, 10(111)
Fischman, A. J.: ref, 10(761)
Fishman, B.: ref, 10(153,244,733)
Fiske, D. W.: ref, 10r
Fister, S. L.: test, 80
Fitzgerald, H. E.: ref, 10(303)
Fitzpatrick, R.: rev, 82, 83
Fitzsimmons, G. W.: test, 55
Flannery, G. J.: ref, 10(457)
Flannery, R. B., Jr.: ref, 10(457)
Fleming, M. F.: ref, 91r
Fletcher, J. M.: ref, 82r
Fletcher, K. E.: ref, 10(191)
Flett, G. L.: ref, 10(484,679,842)
Flick, S. N.: ref, 10(304)
Florin, I.: ref, 10(215)
Flynn, R. J.: ref, 84(41)
Flynn, T.: ref, 10(93)
Foa, E. B.: ref, 10(249,486,680,838)
Foggo, M.: ref, 10(163)
Foley, B.: ref, 10(858)
Foran, J.: ref, 9r
Ford, G. T.: ref, 9(47), 9r
Ford, J. G.: ref, 10(305)
Forehand, R.: ref, 10(264,802)
Forman, S. G.: ref, 1r
Forrest, A.: test, 26
Fortune, J. C.: rev, 65
Fossey, M. D.: ref, 10(459)
Foster, C. L.: ref, 29(9)
Foster, D. F.: ref, 97(2), 97r
Foster, F. M.: ref, 6r, 69r
Foster, K. C.: ref, 97(2), 97r
Foster, T.: ref, 10(128)
Fowler, D.: ref, 10(462)
Fox, K. M.: ref, 10(458)
Fox, N. A.: ref, 10(677,678,696), 73(3,5,6)
Fox, S. L.: ref, 10(18)
Fragapane, L.: ref, 76(16)
Frager, A. M.: ref, 30(1)
Frances, A.: ref, 10(153)
Frances, A. J.: ref, 10(733)
Francis, A.: ref, 10(244)
Francis, G.: ref, 10(354)
Frank, E.: ref, 10(55,347,600,601,855)
Frank, M.: ref, 10(93)
Frankenstein, W.: ref, 91r
Franklin, M. E.: ref, 10(838)
Franzen, U.: ref, 10(215)
Frasure-Smith, N.: ref, 10(681)

Fredman, N.: ref, 58r
Free, M. L.: ref, 10(746)
Freeberg, N. E.: test, 37
Freed, W.: ref, 10(739)
Freedman, M.: ref, 10(20,66)
Freeman, F. J.: ref, 89(4,12)
Freeston, M. H.: ref, 9(44,45), 10(668,682)
Freitag, P. K.: rev, 30
Fremouw, W.: ref, 10(306)
French, C. C.: ref, 10(764,859)
Freston, J. L.: test, 80
Freyne, A.: ref, 10(298)
Friedberg, R.: ref, 10(703)
Friedman, R.: ref, 10(320)
Friedman, S.: ref, 9(65), 10(867)
Friedrich, W. N.: ref, 10(434)
Friend, R.: ref, 10(160,529,530,673,693)
Frisch, M. B.: ref, 10(690)
Frith, C. D.: ref, 10(273)
Frueh, B. C.: ref, 10(459,861)
Frydrich, T.: ref, 9r
Fuchs, L. S.: rev, 36
Fuentes, F.: ref, 76(4)
Fugate, M. H.: rev, 73
Fuller, K. H.: ref, 10(460)
Fuqua, D.: ref, 84(24)
Furlong, M. J.: rev, 44
Furman, J. M.: ref, 9(13,62), 10(319,844)
Fydrich, T.: ref, 9(8), 10(216)

Gabardi, L.: ref, 10(129)
Gable, R. K.: rev, 61; ref, 61r
Gade, E. M.: ref, 84(24)
Gallagher, D.: ref, 10(31)
Gallagher, T. M.: ref, 46(1)
Gallagher-Thompson, D.: ref, 10(461)
Gallo, S.: ref, 10(116)
Galvin, G. A.: rev, 43
Gannen, L.: ref, 10(21)
Ganzini, L.: ref, 10(67)
Garamoni, G.: ref, 10(600)
Garamoni, G. G.: ref, 10(601)
Garamoni, G. L.: ref, 10(347)
Garbin, M. G.: ref, 10r
Garcia, T.: test, 61; ref, 61(2)
Gardner, M. F.: test, 93, 100; ref, 100r
Garety, P. A.: ref, 10(462)
Garfin, S. R.: ref, 10(72)
Garfinkel, A.: rev, 41
Garfinkel, B. D.: ref, 10(198)
Garfinkel, P. E.: ref, 29(7)
Garrett, H.: ref, 1r
Garrison-Jones, C. V.: ref, 10r
Garriss, E.: ref, 33(1)
Garske, G. G.: ref, 10(217)
Gartner, A. F.: ref, 10(139)

Graham, J. R.: ref, 10r
Graham, R. M.: ref, 102r
Graham, S.: rev, 93, 94
Grannopoulos, C.: ref, 10(288)
Grant, G.: ref, 81r
Grant, G. M.: ref, 10(690)
Grant, I.: ref, 10(864)
Grant, J. R.: ref, 10(691)
Grant, K. E.: ref, 10(282)
Gray, A.: ref, 52(3)
Greeley, J. C.: ref, 86(1)
Green, J. A.: ref, 74r
Green, M. W.: ref, 10(692)
Green, R. E. A.: ref, 10(506)
Greenberg, J.: ref, 10(788)
Greenberg, L. M.: test, 99; ref, 99(1), 99r
Greenberg, R. L.: ref, 9(2), 10(41)
Greenblatt, D. J.: ref, 10(96)
Greene, A. F.: ref, 10(392)
Greene, B.: ref, 10(470)
Greene, J. D. W.: ref, 10(841)
Greenlee, S. P.: ref, 84(12)
Gregg, S. F.: ref, 10(591)
Gregory, M. C.: ref, 10(56)
Greif, G. L.: ref, 10(471)
Gresham, F. M.: ref, 1(6), 1r, 40r, 74r
Gridley, B. E.: ref, 10(388), 76(11)
Griffin, K. W.: ref, 10(673,693)
Griffith, S. A.: ref, 84(41)
Grigorenko, E. L.: ref, 9(43), 10(650)
Grill, J. J.: rev, 76
Groag, I.: ref, 10(743)
Grober, S.: ref, 10(222)
Grodin, D. M.: ref, 10(670)
Groothuis, T. G. G.: ref, 10(641)
Grossen, N. E.: ref, 49r
Grossman, G.: ref, 10(309)
Grossman, H. J.: ref, 1r
Grott, M.: ref, 9(59), 10(792)
Grove, W. M.: ref, 10(213,223)
Grover, G. N.: ref, 10(367)
Groves, S.: test, 77
Grubb, H. J.: ref, 10(312)
Gruber, F. A.: ref, 49r
Gruen, R. J.: ref, 10(472,473)
Guelfi, J. D.: ref, 10(234)
Guinan, E. M.: ref, 10(506)
Guirguis, M.: ref, 10(778)
Gullion, C. M.: ref, 10(135,860)
Gully, K. J.: ref, 1r
Günther, V.: ref, 10(131)
Guralnick, M. J.: ref, 76(20)
Gureje, O.: ref, 29(8)
Gussin, E. A.: ref, 12(9)
Gutiérrez, F.: ref, 10(573)
Guzick, D. S.: ref, 10(675)
Gwadz, M.: ref, 10(472)

Haaga, D. A. F.: ref, 9(21,35,38,47,48), 10(416,531, 688,694,695), 9r
Haaga, P. A. F.: ref, 10(589)
Haas, G. L.: ref, 10(730,831)
Haavisto, T.: ref, 10(745)
Haazen, I. W. C. J.: ref, 10(810)
Habif, V. L.: ref, 10(73)
Hackmann, A.: ref, 9(24)
Hadzi-Pavlovic, D.: ref, 10(79)
Haertel, G. D.: rev, 24
Haertzen, C. A.: ref, 10(107)
Hagborg, W. J.: ref, 52(4)
Hagin, R. A.: rev, 19, 99
Hagopian, L. P.: ref, 10(313)
Hagtvet, K. A.: ref, 61r
Hahlweg, K.: ref, 58r
Haidar, S. A.: ref, 10(734)
Halberstadt, A. G.: ref, 10(696)
Halberstadt, L.: ref, 10(568)
Hall, G.: ref, 10(105)
Hall, P. K.: ref, 60(2)
Hall, R. E.: ref, 76(5)
Haller, D. L.: ref, 10(314)
Halliwell, S.: ref, 6r
Ham, H. P.: ref, 10(303)
Hamann, M. S.: ref, 10(734)
Hamilton Region Mathematics Writing Group: test, 59
Hamlin, C. L.: ref, 10(466)
Hammen, C. J.: ref, 10(646,697)
Hammill, D.: ref, 1r
Hammill, D. D.: test, 31; ref, 33r
Hammond, M.: ref, 10(106), 76(20)
Hampson, M.: ref, 10()
Hampton, C.: ref, 10(529,530)
Hanada, K.: ref, 10(251)
Hancock, K. M.: ref, 10(437)
Hand, D.: ref, 10(299)
Handelsman, L.: ref, 10(541)
Handleman, J. S.: ref, 76(4)
Hanna, G. S.: rev, 15, 105
Hannah, M. T.: ref, 10(751)
Hansen, J.: rev, 103
Hansen, J. I.: ref, 103r
Hansen, R. N.: rev, 84
Hanson, K.: ref, 9(46), 10(684)
Hanusa, B. H.: ref, 10(413)
Harden, T.: ref, 10(173)
Hardiman, E.: ref, 10(298)
Hardy, G.: ref, 10(782)
Hardy, G. E.: ref, 10(474,581)
Hare, R. D.: ref, 56(2)
Harel, Y.: ref, 10(815)
Hargrove, P. M.: ref, 76(3)
Harman, L. W.: ref, 84(37)
Harnett-Sheehan, K.: ref, 10(98)
Harnish, M. J.: ref, 10(475)

Hodges, J. R.: ref, 10(700,841)
Hodulik, C. J.: ref, 10(568)
Hoeger, W.: test, 38
Hoernicke, F. A.: ref, 1r
Hoffart, A.: ref, 10(701)
Hoffman, B. B.: ref, 10(344)
Hoffmann, N. G.: test, 92; ref, 92r
Hofmann, S. G.: ref, 10(449,702)
Hogan, J.: test, 39; ref, 39(1)
Hogan, R.: test, 39; ref, 39(1)
Holbrey, A.: ref, 10(604)
Holden, E. W.: ref, 10(608)
Holland, A. D.: ref, 10(50)
Holland, J. L.: test, 11, 84
Holliman, W. B.: ref, 10(757)
Hollnagel, C.: ref, 10(836)
Hollon, S. D.: ref, 10(68,213,223,463,651)
Holman, J. M., Jr.: ref, 10(56)
Holmgren, S.: ref, 10(40)
Holroyd, S.: ref, 10(488)
Holt, R. R.: rev, 17
Holt, S.: test, 4; ref, 4r
Holzman, P. S.: ref, 10(750,830)
Hommer, D.: ref, 10(96)
Hommerding, K. D.: ref, 10(582)
Hons, R. B.: ref, 10(61,62)
Hoodin, R. B.: ref, 76(3)
Hooijer, C.: ref, 10(714)
Hook, M.: ref, 10(305)
Hooper, S. R.: rev, 57
Hope, D. A.: ref, 10(71)
Hope, R. A.: ref, 10(127,301)
Hops, H.: ref, 10(76,208,209,224)
Horn, E. E.: ref, 12(6)
Horn, J. L.: ref, 6r, 47r, 69r
Horne, P. J.: ref, 10(423)
Horowitz, L. M.: ref, 10(778)
Horowitz, M.: ref, 9(61), 10(843)
Hortacsu, N.: ref, 10(316)
Hosch, H. M.: ref, 1r
Houle, L.: ref, 10(381)
Howard, R.: ref, 10(549)
Howell, K. W.: rev, 44
Hresko, W. P.: test, 31
Hua, T.: rev, 21
Hulsizer, M. R.: ref, 10(699)
Humes, C. W.: ref, 84(25)
Hurlburt, G.: ref, 84(24)
Hurwitz, T. D.: ref, 9(52), 10(753)
Hutchinson, R. L.: ref, 10(225)
Hutton, K.: ref, 10(118)
Huttunen, N.: ref, 17(3)
Huzel, L. L.: ref, 10(317)
Hwang, S. S.: ref, 10(238)
Hynan, L. S.: ref, 10(690)

Hynes, G. J.: ref, 10(866)
Iannotti, R. J.: ref, 10(124,221)
Impara, J. C.: ref, 31r
Incesu, C.: ref, 10(404)
Ingham, R. J.: ref, 89r
Ingram, J. J.: ref, 4r
Ingram, R. E.: ref, 10(72,489,490,703)
Insel, E.: test, 43
Ireland, D.: ref, 9(40), 10(593)
Ireton, H.: test, 16
Irons, T.: ref, 1r
Irons, T. R.: ref, 52(3)
Irving, L. M.: ref, 10(341)
Isaacs, A. M.: ref, 10(503)
Isabella, L.: ref, 12(5)
Isabella, R.: ref, 10(801)
Isenberg, D.: ref, 10(758)
Isenhart, C. E.: ref, 47r
Isometsa, E.: ref, 10(379)
Israel, M.: ref, 4r
Israel, Y.: ref, 4r
Ito, L. M.: ref, 10(704)
Itzkovich, M.: test, 57
Ivanjack, L.: ref, 10(547)
Ivanoff, A.: ref, 10(491,586)
Ivarsson, T.: ref, 10(492)
Iversen, G. R.: ref, 9r

Jack, D. C.: ref, 10(226)
Jackman, L. P.: ref, 10(705)
Jackson, C. C.: ref, 10(777)
Jackson, D. N.: ref, 9r
Jackson, G. C.: ref, 12(13)
Jackson, H. J.: ref, 10(318)
Jackson, J. L.: ref, 10(73)
Jacob, M. C.: ref, 10(136)
Jacob, R. G.: ref, 9(7,13,62) 10(207,319,844)
Jacobs, G. D.: ref, 10(320)
Jacobs, K. W.: ref, 10(321)
Jacobsberg, L.: ref, 10(153,244)
Jacobsberg, L. B.: ref, 10(733)
Jacobson, J. L.: ref, 10(322)
Jacobson, S. W.: ref, 10(322)
Jagger, L.: ref, 84(26)
James, L. D.: ref, 10(323)
Janca, A.: ref, 29r
Jang, S. J.: ref, 10(491,586)
Jansen, J. H. C.: ref, 10(146,339,340)
Janzen-Wilde, M. L.: ref, 76(21)
Jarrett, R. B.: ref, 10(135,860)
Jarvelin, M. R.: ref, 17(3)
Jason, G. W.: ref, 60(2)
Jastak, S.: ref, 33r
Jatlow, P.: ref, 10(422)
Jaworski, T. M.: ref, 10(434)
Jekelis, A.: ref, 10(569)

Kerns, R. D.: ref, 10(136)
Kerr, J.: ref, 10(227,754)
Kershaw, D.: ref, 10(165)
Kessler, K.: ref, 10(164)
Kessler, R. C.: ref, 29(3,9,12)
Kettlewell, P. W.: ref, 10(228)
Khalil, A. H.: ref, 10(544)
Khan, A.: ref, 10(570,571)
Khan, S. A.: ref, 84(16)
Khan, S. B.: ref, 84(17,23)
Khansur, T.: ref, 10(687)
Khawaja, N. G.: ref, 9(33)
Kiely, M. C.: ref, 10(781)
Kienholz, E.: ref, 10(584)
Kiewra, K. A.: rev, 52
Kilic, C.: ref, 10(403)
Kim, K.: ref, 28(3)
Kimbrough, R.: ref, 10(534)
Kinderman, P.: ref, 10(500,848)
King, A. C.: ref, 10(26,326)
King, P. R.: ref, 10(603)
King, R.: test, 101; ref, 10(28)
King, S.: ref, 12(4)
Kingston, M. D.: ref, 10r
Kinnier, R. T.: rev, 11, 14
Kinscherf, D. A.: ref, 10(398)
Kinzler, M. C.: test, 49
Kirk, P.: ref, 9(59), 10(792)
Kirkby, R. J.: ref, 10(501)
Kirkham, M. A.: ref, 10(327)
Kirkpatrick, B.: ref, 10(502)
Kirkwood, K. J.: ref, 84(16)
Kirnan, J. P.: rev, 16, 32; ref, 67(1), 67r
Kirsch, I. J.: test, 37
Kirsch, I. S.: ref, 37r
Kissane, D. W.: ref, 10(849,850)
Kivlighan, D. M.: ref, 10(480)
Klasko, J. S.: ref, 10(10)
Klassen, J.: ref, 10(61)
Klee, S.: rev, 19
Klein, K.: ref, 10(637)
Kleinman, P. H.: ref, 10(74)
Klerman, G. L.: ref, 10(733)
Klobucar, C.: ref, 61(4)
Knesevich, M. A.: ref, 10(262)
Knippers, J. A.: ref, 84(29)
Knisely, J. S.: ref, 10(314)
Knoff, H. M.: rev, 17, 19, 40; ref, 17r, 40r
Knowdell, R. L.: test, 14, 66
Kobak, K. A.: ref, 9(53), 10(762)
Koch, W. J.: ref, 9(64), 10(865)
Kocsis, J. H.: ref, 10(733)
Koegel, R. L.: ref, 10(239)
Koehly, L. M.: ref, 84(48)
Koehn, K. A.: ref, 10(118)
Koele, P.: ref, 10(296,665)

Koenig, L. J.: ref, 10(503)
Koff, E.: ref, 10(358)
Kogan, E. S.: ref, 10(504)
Koivisto, M.: ref, 10(851)
Kok, R. M.: ref, 10(714)
Kolb, D. A.: test, 54
Kolb, L. C.: ref, 10(11)
Kole-Snijders, A. M. J.: ref, 10(810)
Kominowski, R.: test, 7
Komproe, I. H.: ref, 10(247)
Kopelman, M. D.: ref, 10(505,506)
Kopper, B. A.: ref, 10(852)
Koran, L. M.: ref, 10(393)
Korfine, L.: ref, 10(517)
Korner, P.: ref, 10(507,715)
Koroshetz, W. J.: ref, 10(212)
Korten, A.: ref, 29(11)
Kosslyn, J. M.: ref, 9(20), 10(414)
Kosten, T. R.: ref, 10(773)
Kostis, J. B.: ref, 10(569)
Kozak, M. J.: ref, 10(486)
Kraft, D.: ref, 10(390)
Kramer, R. J.: ref, 10(765)
Kramer, T. A.: ref, 9(29,31), 10(495,846)
Krames, L.: ref, 10(679)
Kranzler, H. R.: ref, 10(507,508,715)
Kress, R. A.: ref, 36r
Krietsch, K.: ref, 22r
Kring, A. M.: ref, 10(509)
Kristbjarnarson, H.: ref, 10(142)
Kristoff, B.: ref, 76(4)
Kroeger, D. W.: ref, 10(716)
Kromrey, J. D.: ref, 25(1)
Krotz, D.: test, 7
Krupp, A.: ref, 10(766)
Kryger, M. H.: ref, 10(382)
Kryspin-Exner, I.: ref, 10(131)
Krystal, J. H.: ref, 10(773)
Kubany, E. S.: ref, 10(717)
Kucera, G. D.: ref, 9(13), 10(319)
Kuch, K.: ref, 9(34), 10(137,403,718)
Kuhn, K.: ref, 10(514)
Kuipers, L.: ref, 10(462)
Kukha-Mohamad, J. A.: ref, 10(425)
Kukic, S. J.: test, 80
Kulhavy, R. W.: ref, 19(3)
Kuller, L. H.: ref, 10(675)
Kumar, G.: ref, 9(50,58), 10(719,791), 9r
Kunnan, A. J.: rev, 21; ref, 21r
Kupfer, D. J.: ref, 10(28,55,347,600,601,855)
Kurian, M.: ref, 19(3)
Kusalic, M.: ref, 10(738)
Kushner, M.: ref, 10(51,556)
Kutcher, S. P.: ref, 10(425)
Kuyken, W.: ref, 10(510,720)
Kwiatkowski, J.: ref, 76(15), 49r
Kymäläinen, O.: ref, 10(379)

Linden, W.: ref, 10(333)
Lindstrom, R.: ref, 10(5)
Lindzey, G.: ref, 85r
Linehan, M. M.: ref, 10(491)
Link, D. P.: test, 80
Liotus, L.: ref, 10(279)
Lipke, H. J.: ref, 10(854)
Lipton, D. S.: ref, 10(74)
Liss, J. A.: ref, 10(588)
Little, R. J. A.: ref, 29(12)
Littlefield, C. H.: ref, 10(77)
Littlejohns, C. S.: ref, 10(454)
Liukko, H.: ref, 10(379)
Livingston, R.: ref, 9(15), 9r
Livneh, H.: ref, 9(1)
Loas, G.: ref, 10(234)
LoBello, S. G.: rev, 39, 102
Locke, J. L.: ref, 76(1)
Loeb, D. F.: ref, 76(7)
Loewenstein Rehabilitation Hospital: test, 57
Lokken, K. J.: ref, 89(3)
Long, E. R.: test, 105
Long, J. L.: ref, 73(6)
Long, S. H.: rev, 28, 97
Loos, L. M.: ref, 10(239)
Loos, W.: ref, 10(638)
Loranger, A. W.: ref, 10(139)
Losch, M.: ref, 10(48)
Loss, N.: ref, 10(726)
Louks, J.: ref, 10(29)
Louks, J. L.: ref, 10(134)
Lovett, D. L.: ref, 1(1)
Lovette, G. J.: ref, 10(809)
Lovibond, P. F.: ref, 9r
Lovibond, S. H.: ref, 9r
Lowe, C. F.: ref, 10(78,423)
Lowenbraun, P. B.: ref, 9(11)
Lu, K. H.: ref, 96r
Lubin, B.: ref, 10(260,334,521)
Luborsky, L.: ref, 10(630,818)
Lucas, J. A.: ref, 10(140)
Luehr, J. G.: ref, 92r
Luhtanen, R.: ref, 10(441)
Lumley, T.: ref, 21r
Lundy, A.: ref, 10(727)
Lunneborg, C. E.: ref, 103(1)
Lunneborg, P. W.: test, 103; ref, 103(1)
Lusk, R.: ref, 10(387), 19(2)
Luzzo, D. A.: ref, 12(7,8,11,12)
Lyketsos, C. G.: ref, 29r
Lynch, B. K.: ref, 21r
Lynch, E. W.: test, 75
Lynch, M. E.: ref, 10(310)
Lynch, P. M.: ref, 10(30)
Lynch, R. S.: ref, 10(834)
Lyness, S. A.: ref, 10(522)

Lynn, G.: ref, 1r
Lyon, H. M.: ref, 10(523)

Macdiarmid, J. I.: ref, 10(728)
MacDonald, C.: ref, 10(138)
MacGillivray, R. G.: ref, 10(524)
Mackay, S.: ref, 10(287)
Mackenzie, T. B.: ref, 10(427)
Mackie, B.: ref, 36(2)
MacKinnon-Lewis, C.: ref, 10(235)
MacLeod, A. K.: ref, 10(525,729)
MacMillan, D. L.: ref, 1r
Macmillan, D. L.: ref, 1(6)
MacMillan, F.: ref, 10(278)
Macmillan, H.: ref, 10(731)
MacMumary, J. P.: ref, 10(133)
Macnab, D.: test, 55
MacPhee, D.: rev, 74 75
Maddever, H. M.: ref, 10(73)
Maddock, R. J.: ref, 10(335)
Maddux, C. D.: rev, 26, 94; ref, 84(2)
Madill, H. M.: ref, 55(1)
Madonia, M. J.: ref, 10(644), 10r
Madonna, S.: ref, 10(757)
Mador, J. A.: ref, 10(230)
Maercker, A.: ref, 9(61), 10(843)
Maes, M.: ref, 10(141,368,853)
Magakian, C.: ref, 9(54)
Magee, W. J.: ref, 29(3)
Magnusson, A.: ref, 10(142)
Mahalik, J. R.: ref, 10(660), 84(46)
Mahowald, M. W.: ref, 9(52), 10(753)
Maiuro, R. D.: ref, 10(45,105)
Makuch, R.: ref, 82r
Malcolm, K. K.: rev, 36, 87
Malla, A. K.: ref, 10(526,664)
Malone, K. M.: ref, 10(730,831)
Mancini, C.: ref, 10(178,385,731,868)
Mandin, H.: ref, 10(61,62)
Mann, J.: ref, 10(62)
Mann, J. J.: ref, 9(36), 10(561,730,831)
Manne, S. L.: ref, 10(732)
Manolis, M. B.: ref, 10(825)
Mansfield, R.: test, 70
Manuck, S. B.: ref, 10(869)
Manuele-Adkins, C.: rev, 84
Manza, L.: ref, 10(556)
Manzo, P. A.: ref, 10(626,761)
Mapou, R. L.: ref, 10(512,722)
Marcel, B. B.: ref, 10(336)
Marcos, T.: ref, 10(573)
Marcouiller, M.: ref, 10(43)
Margolis, H.: ref, 36(2)
Marjoribanks, K.: ref, 19(1)
Mark, M. M.: ref, 10(143)
Markman, H. J.: ref, 58r

Meltzer, H.: ref, 10(853)
Melzack, R.: ref, 10(369)
Menchon, J. M.: ref, 10(177)
Mendelberg, H. E.: ref, 10(737)
Mendelson, M.: ref, 10(288), 10r
Meneese, W. B.: ref, 10(84)
Merkel, W. T.: ref, 10(6)
Merrell, K. W.: test, 74; ref, 74r
Merrill, M. A.: ref, 1r
Merz, W. R., Sr.: rev, 81
Messinger, D. S.: ref, 10(801)
Meszaros, A.: ref, 10(738)
Metalsky, G. I.: ref, 10(494)
Metelko, Z.: ref, 10(352)
Meterissian, G.: ref, 10(738)
Meyers, H. H.: ref, 84(4)
Meyers, L. S.: ref, 49r
Meyers, P.: ref, 10(732)
Mghir, R.: ref, 10(739)
Michael, S. T.: ref, 10(184)
Michaelson, B. S.: ref, 10(107)
Michalon, M.: ref, 10(721)
Middleton, H.: ref, 9(24)
Middleton, H. C.: ref, 9(3,4), 10(85,86)
Miguel, E. C.: ref, 10(761)
Mikulich, S. K.: ref, 29(15)
Milan, S.: ref, 10(482)
Milich, R.: ref, 10(825)
Millar, N.: ref, 10(643)
Miller, A. B.: ref, 10(74)
Miller, D. A. F.: ref, 10(341)
Miller, D. T.: ref, 10(532)
Miller, G. A.: ref, 10(617)
Miller, H. R.: ref, 10(799)
Miller, I. W.: ref, 10(34,817)
Miller, K. J.: ref, 86(2)
Miller, L. C.: rev, 1
Miller, M. J.: ref, 84(9,13,29,30)
Miller, P. J.: ref, 86r
Miller, R. J.: rev, 3, 53
Miller, S.: ref, 10(237)
Miller, S. D.: ref, 36(1)
Miller, V. I.: ref, 25(3)
Miller, W. R.: ref, 90r, 91r
Millman, R. B.: ref, 10(74)
Millson, W. A.: ref, 10(814)
Minarik, M. L.: ref, 10(694)
Mindell, J. A.: ref, 10(342)
Mindes, E. J.: ref, 58r
Minichiello, W. E.: ref, 10(50)
Ministry of Education: test, 59
Minnett, A.: ref, 73(4)
Mintz, J.: ref, 10(238,571)
Mintz, J.: ref, 10(571)
Mintz, L. I.: ref, 10(238)
Mirabella, R. F.: ref, 10(459)

Miranda, J.: ref, 10(351)
Mislevy, R. J.: test, 37
Mitchell, E. S.: ref, 10(45)
Mitchell, J. E.: ref, 10(427)
Mitchell, P.: ref, 29(4)
Mitrushina, M.: ref, 10(540)
Mizes, J. S.: ref, 10(228)
Mock, J.: ref, 10r
Moersch, M. S.: test, 75
Moes, D.: ref, 10(239)
Mogg, K.: ref, 10(643,740)
Moilanen, D. L.: ref, 10(741)
Moilanen, I.: ref, 17(3)
Mok, G. S.: ref, 10(69)
Molchan, S.: ref, 10(597)
Molock, S. D.: ref, 10(534)
Mongrain, M.: ref, 10(640)
Monroe, J. M.: ref, 10(374)
Monroe, S. M.: ref, 10(377,786,855)
Montgomerie, T. C.: ref, 55(1)
Moore, P. J.: ref, 10(220)
Moore, R. G.: ref, 10(343,535)
Moos, R. H.: ref, 10(87)
Moran, P. B.: ref, 10(240)
Morano, C. D.: ref, 10(345)
Moras, K.: ref, 10(419)
Morehouse, R. L.: ref, 10(721)
Moreland, K. L.: rev, 47
Moretti, C.: ref, 10(761)
Morgan, C. D.: ref, 85r
Morier, D.: ref, 10(402)
Morin, C. M.: ref, 10(536)
Morison, S. J.: ref, 10(814)
Moritz, G.: ref, 10(279)
Morman, R. M. G.: ref, 10(664)
Morreale, S.: rev, 35, 78
Morris, S. A.: ref, 10(361)
Morris, S. J.: ref, 10(742)
Morrison, L. A.: ref, 10(794)
Morrissette, D. L.: ref, 10(344)
Morrobel, D.: ref, 10(472)
Morrow, C.: ref, 10(128)
Morrow, H. W.: ref, 1r
Morrow, J. E.: ref, 32(1)
Morrow, K. B.: ref, 10(147)
Morse, C. A.: ref, 10(148)
Morse, R. M.: ref, 92r
Moss, M. B.: ref, 10(212)
Mostofi, N.: ref, 10(752)
Motl, J.: ref, 10(584)
Mount, M. K.: ref, 39(2)
Mowchun, N.: ref, 10(655)
Mueller, E. A.: ref, 10(201,597)
Mueller, R. O.: rev, 30, 48
Mukerji, V.: ref, 10(51)
Muldoon, M. F.: ref, 10(869)

Oetting, E.: ref, 7r, 34r
Oetting, E. R.: ref, 10(834)
Ogles, B. M.: ref, 10(515,747)
O'Hara, M. W.: ref, 10(151)
Ohlde, C.: ref, 10(466)
Ohler, D. L.: ref, 12(14), 84(47)
Ohlott, P. J.: test, 32; ref, 32(1,2)
Okagaki, L.: ref, 45r
Okasha, A.: ref, 10(544)
Oldman, A.: ref, 10(748)
O'Leary, K. D.: ref, 10(91,176,193,406)
O'Leary, S. G.: ref, 10(625)
Olivárez, A., Jr.: ref, 52(3)
Ollendick, T. H.: ref, 10(348)
Olmi, D. J.: rev, 95
Olmsted, M. P.: ref, 10(545)
Olson, S.: ref, 10(80)
Onatsu, T.: ref, 10(745)
O'Neil, H.: ref, 10(298)
Onghena, P.: ref, 10(849,850)
Oral, A.: ref, 10(316)
Organista, K. C.: ref, 10(546)
Orloff, L. M.: ref, 10(547)
Ormel, J.: ref, 29(16)
O'Rourke, D.: ref, 10(214)
Orstein, S.: ref, 12(5)
Oscar-Berman, M.: ref, 10(20)
O'Shea, A. J.: ref, 84(32)
Osman, A.: ref, 9(16); ref, 9r
Osman, J. R.: ref, 9(16); ref, 9r
Osness, W. H.: test, 38
O'Sullivan, G.: ref, 10(33,403)
Ôst, L. G.: ref, 9(10), 10(152,242)
Ottenbacher, K. J.: ref, 96(2)
Otto, M. W.: ref, 9(9,32) 10(36,157,243,453,497,840)
Overstreet, M. M.: ref, 9(54)
Owen, M.: ref, 29(2
Owen, M. T.: ref, 76(12)
Owen, S. V.: rev, 2, 27
Owens, B. W.: test, 3
Owens, C. A.: ref, 4r
Owens, J. A.: ref, 10(717)
Owens, L.: test, 53
Owens, N.: test, 3
Owens, R. E., Jr.: rev, 49
Ozmen, E.: ref, 10(404)

Pace, T. M.: ref, 10(749)
Packard, P.: ref, 10(466)
Paddison, P. L.: ref, 10(70)
Page, S.: ref, 10(349)
Paget, K. D.: rev, 20
Paker, M.: ref, 10(404)
Paker, O.: ref, 10(404)
Palacios, J.: ref, 10(772), 10r
Paley, B.: ref, 10(697)

Pallmeyer, T. P.: ref, 10(12)
Palmer, D. R.: test, 52
Palmour, R. M.: ref, 10(408)
Palosaari, U.: ref, 10(548)
Pan, B. A.: ref, 76(14)
Pangburn, L.: ref, 10(12)
Pardie, L.: ref, 10(21)
Parikh, S. V.: ref, 29(13)
Park, C. L.: ref, 10(350)
Park, S.: ref, 10(750)
Parke, R. D.: ref, 10(696)
Parker, D. E.: ref, 89(16)
Parker, E. S.: ref, 10(443)
Parker, G.: ref, 10(117)
Parker, G. M.: test, 67; ref, 67r
Parker, M.: ref, 10(632)
Parra, E. B.: ref, 10(751)
Parry, B. L.: ref, 10(752)
Parry-Billings, M.: ref, 10(49)
Parsons, O. A.: ref, 10(475,803)
Partridge, S.: ref, 10(490)
Pascarella, E.: ref, 27(1)
Pascarella, E. T.: ref, 27(2,3)
Pasini, A.: ref, 10(862)
Passik, S. D.: ref, 10(46,826)
Patel, R. J.: ref, 9(42), 10(624)
Patel, R. K.: ref, 10(366)
Patrick, M.: ref, 10(549)
Patten, J. A.: ref, 56(3)
Patterson, E. T.: ref, 47r
Patterson, K.: ref, 10(700)
Paul, L. C.: ref, 10(62)
Pauls, D. L.: ref, 9(43), 10(650)
Pava, J. A.: ref, 10(453)
Pawluk, L. K.: ref, 9(52), 10(753)
Paykel, E. S.: ref, 10(754,760,800)
Pazy, A.: ref, 84(6)
Pearce, S.: ref, 10(353,758)
Pearson, N.: ref, 1r
Peavy, G.: ref, 10(864)
Peck, J. R.: ref, 10(99,585)
Pehl, J.: ref, 10(465)
Peloquin, L.: ref, 38r
Pendergrass, T.: ref, 10(434)
Pendleton, C. W.: rev, 64
Penk, W. E.: ref, 10(457)
Pennebaker, J. W.: ref, 10(92)
Pepper, P. P.: ref, 97(3)
Perachio, J. J.: test, 68
Perel, J. M.: ref, 10(376)
Perloff, J. M.: ref, 10(351)
Perper, J. A.: ref, 10(279)
Perruchet, P.: ref, 10(405)
Perry, A.: ref, 1(2)
Perry, J. C.: ref, 10(457)
Perry, K. J.: ref, 10(838)

Rahmani, L.: test, 57
Rain, J. S.: rev, 34, 90
Raj, A. B.: ref, 10(98)
Raj, B. A.: ref, 10(357)
Rajab, M. H.: ref, 10(767,768)
Ramana, R.: ref, 10(754,760)
Ramey, C. T.: ref, 82(1)
Ramig, P. R.: ref, 89(5)
Ramsay, J. O.: ref, 10(574), 10r
Ramsay, J. Q.: ref, 10(772)
Randall, F.: ref, 10(859)
Randhawa, B. S.: rev, 45
Ranieri, W. F.: ref, 9(17,39,57,58), 10(380,592,790,791), 9r
Rapee, R. M.: ref, 10(192)
Rapoport, J. L.: ref, 10(108)
Rashotte, C.: ref, 97r
Raskin, A.: ref, 10(739)
Ratcliff, K. S.: ref, 92r
Rathus, J. H.: ref, 10(556)
Rauch, S. L.: ref, 10(626,761)
Raus, J.: ref, 10(141)
Ravaris, C. L.: ref, 10(478)
Ravindran, A. V.: ref, 10(557)
Rawlings, R. R.: ref, 10(670)
Raymond, N. C.: ref, 10(427)
Reber, A. S.: ref, 10(556)
Rebull, E.: ref, 10(573)
Reck, C.: ref, 10(215)
Reckase, M. D.: ref, 23r
Records, N. L.: ref, 60(7)
Redd, W.: ref, 10(732)
Reed, J.: ref, 25(1)
Reed, J. C.: rev, 3, 60
Reed, J. R.: test, 25
Reed, M. K.: ref, 10(558)
Reeder, K. P.: ref, 18r
Rees, A.: ref, 10(256,581,782)
Regan, J. J.: ref, 10(22)
Reid, N. A.: test, 78
Reinehr, R. C.: rev, 17
Reise, S. P.: ref, 10r
Reiter, S. R.: ref, 10(157)
Remick, R. A.: ref, 10(230,425)
Remien, R. H.: ref, 10(707)
Renneberg, B.: ref, 10(95,205,248)
Resnick, A.: ref, 10(752)
Reynolds, C. F.: ref, 9(36), 10(561,600,601)
Reynolds, C. F., III: ref, 10(28,347)
Reynolds, C. R.: rev, 38, 86
Reynolds, R. M.: ref, 10(799)
Reynolds, S.: ref, 10(581,782)
Reynolds, W. M.: ref, 9(53), 10(762)
Reznick, J. S.: ref, 75r
Rhamy, R. K.: ref, 10(268)
Rheaume, J.: ref, 9(44), 10(668)

Ricciardi, J. N.: ref, 10(763)
Ricciardi, J. N., II: ref, 10(50)
Rice, K. G.: ref, 10(554)
Richard, K.: ref, 9(26), 10(448)
Richards, A.: ref, 10(764,859)
Richards, B. C.: ref, 10(92)
Richards, M. H.: ref, 10(559)
Richards, R. A.: rev, 37, 78
Richman, H.: ref, 10(560)
Rief, W.: ref, 10(455)
Rierdan, J.: ref, 10(358)
Rifai, A. H.: ref, 9(36), 10(561)
Riggs, D. S.: ref, 10(249,680)
Riggs, P. D.: ref, 29(15)
Rigrodsky, S.: rev, 60
Riley, G.: ref, 89r
Riley, G. D.: test, 89
Riley, W. T.: ref, 9(54)
Rinne, J. O.: ref, 10(851)
Riordan, R. J.: ref, 40(1)
Rise, S.: ref, 10r
Riskind, J. H.: ref, 9r
Riso, L. P.: ref, 10(91)
Rissmiller, D. J.: ref, 9r
Ritsma, S.: ref, 25r
Ritter, C.: ref, 10(699)
Rivelli, S.: ref, 10(662)
Robbins, P. R.: ref, 10(562)
Roberts, J. E.: ref, 10(855), 28(1)
Roberts, W. C.: ref, 10(81,82,529,530)
Robertson, M. M.: ref, 10(284)
Robins, C. J.: ref, 10(765)
Robins, L. N.: ref, 92r
Robinson, M. E.: ref, 10(218)
Robinson, R. G.: ref, 10(100)
Rock, D. A.: test, 37
Rockert, W.: ref, 10(545)
Rodin, G. M.: ref, 10(77)
Rodrigue, J. R.: ref, 10(450)
Roehlke, H. J.: ref, 10(480)
Roemer, L.: ref, 10(563)
Roesler, T. A.: ref, 10(564,565)
Roetzel, K.: ref, 76(3)
Rogers, J. H.: ref, 10(766)
Rogers, P. J.: ref, 10(692)
Rogers, R. W.: ref, 10(97)
Rogers, S. J.: test, 75
Rogler, L. H.: ref, 29(1)
Roglic, G.: ref, 10(352)
Rogoff, B.: ref, 10(686)
Rohde, P.: ref, 10(566)
Roin, G. M.: ref, 10(25)
Rokke, P. D.: ref, 10(359)
Roller, T. L.: ref, 10(512,722)
Rollins, P. R.: ref, 76(14)
Romach, M.: ref, 9(55)

Schatzberg, A. F.: ref, 10(336)
Schazmann, W.: ref, 10(214)
Scheel, M. J.: ref, 84(27)
Scheier, M. F.: ref, 10(578)
Schemmel, D. R.: ref, 10(334)
Schill, T.: ref, 10(579)
Schlechte, J. A.: ref, 10(151)
Schlundt, D. G.: ref, 10(708,807)
Schluter, J. L.: ref, 9(52), 10(753)
Schmidt, K. L.: ref, 10(494)
Schmidt, L. G.: ref, 29(6)
Schmidt, N. B.: ref, 10(775)
Schmidt, P. J.: ref, 10(367)
Schmidt, U.: ref, 10(38)
Schmitz, J. B.: ref, 10(835)
Schmock, K.: ref, 76(16)
Schneider, A. M.: ref, 10(303)
Schneider, B.: ref, 10(776)
Schneider, L. S.: ref, 10(522)
Schneider, M. S.: ref, 10(160)
Schnoll, S. H.: ref, 10(314)
Schoenfeld, D.: ref, 10(69)
Schofield, P.: ref, 29(4)
Schonfeld, L.: test, 90; ref, 90r
Schorr, S.: ref, 10(61,62)
Schotte, C.: ref, 10(368)
Schreiber, G. S.: ref, 10(777)
Schreibman, L.: ref, 10(239)
Schroeder, C. G.: ref, 84(14)
Schuckit, M. A.: ref, 29(14)
Schuell, H.: test, 60; ref, 60r
Schuerman, J. A.: ref, 10(810)
Schulberg, H. C.: ref, 10(644), 10r
Schuldberg, D.: ref, 10(473)
Schuller, D. R.: ref, 10(189)
Schulman, P.: ref, 10(694)
Schultz, G.: ref, 10(369)
Schumaker, J. F.: ref, 10(777)
Schuttenberg, E. M.: ref, 84(22)
Schwartz, J. A. J.: ref, 10(503)
Schwartz, L.: ref, 10(580)
Schwarz, M.: ref, 10(58)
Schwarz, N.: ref, 10(52)
Schweers, J.: ref, 10(279)
Sciascia, S.: ref, 10(214)
Scott, O.: ref, 10(460)
Scott, W.: ref, 10(490)
Sedlacek, W. E.: ref, 84(3)
Seeley, J. R.: ref, 10(208,209,224,566)
Segal, P. S.: ref, 10(156)
Segal, Z. V.: ref, 10(778)
Seibert, P. S.: ref, 10(65)
Seikel, J. A.: ref, 60(3)
Seiner, S. H.: ref, 10(779)
Selbie, L. A.: ref, 29(4)
Seleshi, E.: ref, 10(220)

Self, C. A.: ref, 10(97)
Seligman, M. E. P.: ref, 10(694)
Seligman, R.: rev, 84
Sellers, E.: ref, 9(55)
Sellers, M. I.: ref, 10(312)
Selzer, M. L.: ref, 34r, 91r
Semmel, M. I.: rev, 1
Sengun, S.: ref, 10(633)
Senra, C.: ref, 10(370,780)
Sependa, P. A.: ref, 10(752)
Sequin, M.: ref, 10(781)
Serketich, W. J.: ref, 10(447)
Serling, D.: ref, 10(637)
Serota, R. D.: ref, 10(727)
Severson, H. H.: test, 82
Seyfried, W.: ref, 92r
Seymour, R. J.: ref, 10(50)
Shader, R. I.: ref, 10(96)
Shaffer, D.: ref, 10(108)
Shaffer, L. F.: rev, 17
Shaffer, M. B.: rev, 17
Shagle, S. C.: ref, 10(371)
Sham, P.: ref, 10(299)
Shanker, J. L.: test, 36
Shapiro, A. P.: ref, 10(869)
Shapiro, D.: ref, 10(311)
Shapiro, D. A.: ref, 10(581,595,782,793,794)
Shapiro, E. S.: ref, 18r
Sharma, R.: ref, 61(5)
Sharma, V.: ref, 10(425)
Sharp, M.: ref, 10(579)
Sharpley, A. L.: ref, 10(211,618)
Shaulis, D.: ref, 38r
Shavelson, R. J.: ref, 36r
Shaw, D. G.: ref, 10(133)
Shaw, D. S.: ref, 10(372,499,582,783)
Shaw, S. R.: rev, 50
Shaywitz, B. A.: ref, 82r
Shaywitz, S. E.: ref, 82r
Shea, M. T.: ref, 10(639)
Shean, G. D.: ref, 10(784)
Shear, M. K.: ref, 10(432,583)
Shearing, C. H.: ref, 10(163)
Sheehan, D. Y.: ref, 10(98)
Sheehan, E. P.: rev, 32
Sheffey, M. A.: ref, 84(1)
Shek, C. C.: ref, 10(232)
Shek, D. T. L.: ref, 10(254)
Shekhar, A.: ref, 10(840)
Shelton, R. C.: ref, 10(651)
Shenk, J. L.: ref, 10(703)
Shepherd, R. W.: ref, 10(366)
Sheppard, B. H.: ref, 10(5)
Sher, K. J.: ref, 10(683)
Sherbenou, R. J.: ref, 33r
Sherman, R.: ref, 58r

SCORE INDEX

This Score Index lists all the scores, in alphabetical order, for all the tests included in the Supplement to the Twelfth Mental Measurements Yearbook. Because test scores can be regarded as operational definitions of the variable measured, sometimes the scores provide better leads to what a test actually measures than the test title or other available information. The Score Index is very detailed, and the reader should keep in mind that a given variable (or concept) of interest may be defined in several different ways. Thus the reader should look up these several possible alternative definitions before drawing final conclusions about whether tests measuring a particular variable of interest can be located in this volume. If the kind of score sought is located in a particular test or tests, the reader should then read the test descriptive information carefully to determine whether the test(s) in which the score is found is (are) consistent with reader purpose. Used wisely, the Score Index can be another useful resource in locating the right score in the right test. As usual, all numbers in the index are test numbers, not page numbers.